The Illustrated Bible Dictionary
Part One: Aaron-Golan

The Illustrated Bible Dictionary

INTER-VARSITY PRESS

Co-ordination
Derek Wood

Research
Tessa Clowney (pictures)
Caroline Masom (diagrams)

Editorial
Mary Gladstone (copy-editing and proofs)
Norman Hillyer (proofs)
Rhona Pipe (proofs)
Joanne Bramwell (copy-editing)
Sue Mills (copy-editing)
Derek Wood (copy-editing)
Marie Cross (secretarial)

Maps preparation
Min Topliss
Elisabeth Pearce

Production
Michael Sims (managing)
Joanne Battisson (assistant)

Indexing
Norman Hillyer

The Illustrated Bible Dictionary

PART 1
Aaron-Golan

Organizing Editor of *The New Bible Dictionary:*

J. D. Douglas, M.A., B.D., S.T.M., Ph.D.
Editor-at-large, *Christianity Today.*

Revision Editor:

N. Hillyer, B.D., S.Th., A.L.C.D.
Formerly Librarian, Tyndale House, Cambridge.

Consulting Editors:

F. F. Bruce, M.A., D.D., F.B.A.
Emeritus Rylands Professor of Biblical Criticism and Exegesis, University of Manchester.

J. I. Packer, M.A., D.Phil., D.D.
Professor of Systematic Theology, Regent College, Vancouver.

R. V. G. Tasker, M.A., D.D.
Formerly Professor of New Testament Exegesis, University of London.

D. J. Wiseman, O.B.E., M.A., D.Lit., F.B.A., F.S.A.
Professor of Assyriology, University of London.

Additional Consulting Editors for the revised edition:

D. Guthrie, B.D., M.Th., Ph.D.
Vice-Principal, London Bible College.

A. R. Millard, M.A., M.Phil., F.S.A.
Rankin Senior Lecturer in Hebrew and Ancient Semitic Languages, University of Liverpool.

Consulting Editor for illustrations:

D. J. Wiseman,
in association with:

A. R. Millard.

J. P. Kane, Ph.D., Dip.Ed.,
Lecturer in Hellenistic Greek, University of Manchester.

K. A. Kitchen, B.A., Ph.D.,
Reader in Egyptian and Coptic, University of Liverpool.

INTER-VARSITY PRESS

TYNDALE HOUSE PUBLISHERS

HODDER AND STOUGHTON
SYDNEY AND AUCKLAND

First published 1980

Inter-Varsity Press,
38 De Montfort Street,
Leicester LE1 7GP, England.

Published and sold in the USA
and Canada by
Tyndale House Publishers,
336 Gundersen Drive, Box 80,
Wheaton, Illinois 60187, USA.

First published in Australia
in 1980 by
Hodder & Stoughton (Australia)
Pty Limited, 2 Apollo Place,
Lane Cove, NSW 2066.

Quotations from the Bible are
from the Revised Standard Version
(copyrighted 1946 and 1952,
Second Edition 1971, by the
Division of Christian Education,
National Council of the Churches
of Christ in the USA), unless
otherwise stated.

Part One

UK ISBN 0 85110 627 7
US ISBN 0 8423 1566 7
US ISBN (set) 0 8423 7575 2
US Library of Congress Catalog
Card Number 79–92540
Australia ISBN 0 340 25919 1

Typeset by Monophoto Lasercomp
in Times New Roman by
Richard Clay (The Chaucer Press)
Limited, Bungay,
Suffolk NR35 1ED, England.

Designed by
Thumb Design Partnership Limited,
20–21 D'Arblay Street,
London W1V 3FN, England.

Cartography by
George Philip and Son Limited,
12–14 Long Acre,
London WC2E 9LP, England.

Colour reproduction by
Vauvelle (Photo-litho) Limited,
Clayton Wood Close, West Park,
Leeds LS16 6QE, England.

Printed in the USA by
R. R. Donnelley & Sons Co.,
Willard, Ohio, USA.

Contents

Preface

The Illustrated Bible Dictionary is based on the text of **The New Bible Dictionary,** first published in 1962, which has now been completely revised using the Revised Standard Version of the Bible. While a few of the original articles have been omitted as superfluous and others amalgamated for easier reference, many new articles have been added. A large number have been completely re-written. Bibliographies have been brought up-to-date, cross references revised and a comprehensive index added at the end of the last volume.

In its original form **The New Bible Dictionary** has proved itself to be a steady bestseller through two decades. It came to be regarded by many throughout the world, echoing the verdict of the late Professor William F. Albright, as 'the best one-volume Bible dictionary in the English language'. The revised text is now published in an entirely new form, in three parts, with every advantage that accrues from extensive colour illustrations, photographs, diagrams and maps.

The illustrations have been chosen, not as mere decoration, but with a view to enhancing the value of the Dictionary, by increasing its scope as a source of information. If they make the work more attractive to a wider range of readers, a further advantage has been gained.

The New Bible Dictionary is a major product of the Tyndale Fellowship for Biblical Research, which was founded in close association with the Inter-Varsity Fellowship (now the Universities and Colleges Christian Fellowship) to foster evangelical biblical scholarship. The contributors to **The Illustrated Bible Dictionary,** as to its predecessor, are not, however, drawn exclusively from the ranks of the (mainly British) Tyndale Fellowship; we are deeply indebted to academic colleagues in many parts of the world for their generous co-operation.

The aim of the editors and contributors has continued to be to produce a work of reference, written in a spirit of unqualified loyalty to Holy Scripture, which will substantially further the understanding of God's Word to mankind. That loyalty to Holy Scripture involves treating as true and trustworthy all its statements of fact, theological, physical and historical, is an assumption basic to the whole Dictionary. We do not apologize for the fact that this book reflects the credal, confessional and evangelical convictions for which the Tyndale Fellowship stands—the triunity of God, the deity, atoning death, bodily resurrection and approaching return of Jesus Christ, the divine inspiration and authority of the Bible, the supernatural life of the Christian church, and all that these articles of faith bring with them. No attempt, however, has been made to impose a rigid uniformity upon the work as a whole, or to exclude the occasional expression of different viewpoints within the bounds of this basic loyalty. Nor, of course, are our contributors bound to endorse all the opinions expressed by their colleagues, whether in the Dictionary itself or elsewhere.

The task of organizing this huge revision has fallen on the shoulders of the Rev. Norman Hillyer, whose care, application and courtesy have been instrumental in bringing to birth the text as it now appears.

All who have been involved in the revision are conscious of our continuing debt to Dr J. D. Douglas, the Organizing Editor of the original work, and to Mr Ronald Inchley, the former Publications Secretary of the Inter-Varsity Fellowship. The new Dictionary builds upon their foundation.

As Consulting Editors we are the first to recognize that a major enterprise such as this is possible only because of the enthusiastic and dedicated effort of a large team of people. We wish to record our gratitude to the staff of the Inter-Varsity Press, including those specially engaged for this project, and to the typesetters, colour reproduction specialists, cartographers and printers. Considerable assistance in the preparation of the maps was given by Dr Colin Hemer and Dr John Bimson. A fully illustrated work owes a great deal to its designer, and we are glad to acknowledge here the skilful contribution of Philip Miles and his colleagues at Thumb Design Partnership Ltd.

Our hope is that **The Illustrated Bible Dictionary** will enable many to reach a deeper understanding of the Bible and a richer appreciation of its message.

F.F.B.

D.G.

A.R.M.

J.I.P.

D.J.W.

How to use this Dictionary

The work is divided into three parts and gives the reader the simplest possible access to the most comprehensive information.

Cross references
There are two methods of cross reference:
1. An asterisk before a word indicates that further relevant information will be found in the article under that title and is equivalent to the abbreviation *q.v.*
2. References in the margin provide a list of topics which do not carry articles under their own heading, but the relevant information can be found under another heading, *e.g.*

■ ADVOCATE
See Counsellor, Part 1.

Index
A comprehensive index, containing every significant reference to each topic, is to be found at the end of Part Three. This includes locations on maps and an index to illustrations.

Abbreviations
A full list of abbreviations used in the Dictionary will be found on pages xii–xvi.

Authorship of articles
The authors and co-authors of articles are indicated by their initials at the foot of each article. A full index of contributors is to be found on pages viii–xi. The entries are listed in alphabetical order of initials, not of surnames.

Bibliographies
To assist those wishing to study subjects in greater detail, bibliographies appear at the end of most of the longer articles. These usually provide references to the recent general works on the subject and may include detailed studies or books which take up a position different from that of the contributor.

Picture acknowledgments
The source and/or holder of copyright for the illustrations is indicated by initials in brackets at the end of the picture caption. The full list of sources to which these initials refer is to be found at the end of this volume.

Bible versions
The Bible translation adopted for this Dictionary is the Revised Standard Version. In a few cases contributors have selected quotations from the King James (Authorized) Version, or, when available at the time of writing, the New International Version.

Maps
There is no map supplement in the Dictionary, but maps are to be found alongside the articles themselves for easy reference.

Names of regions, provinces, kingdoms, *etc.*, are printed in large roman capitals, *e.g.* BABYLONIA

Tribes and ethnic groups: large italic capitals, *e.g. AMORITES*

Towns and villages: lower case roman, *e.g.* Jerusalem

Geographical features such as mountains, rivers, lakes, seas, *etc.*: lower case italic, *e.g. Great Sea*

Modern place-names: as above but in brackets, *e.g.* (*Mediterranean Sea*). Absolute consistency has not been possible but, in general, where the modern name is clearly derived from the ancient (*e.g.* Creta = Crete, Italia = Italy) or where it would be pedantic to place modern names in brackets (*e.g.* Egypt, Jerusalem) brackets have been omitted. In a few other cases, where nearly all the place-names are modern, the principle has been abandoned for the sake of simplicity.

Features to be noted particularly, such as the subject of the article concerned, are underlined, *e.g.* Ashdod.

Where a site was known by two or more alternative names they are divided by an oblique stroke, *e.g.* Ezion-geber/Elath.

The word 'or' indicates uncertainty about the name or the location, as does a question mark.

Transliteration
The following systems have been adopted throughout the volume. In fairness to our contributors it should be said that some have disagreed on philological grounds with our transliteration of Hebrew words generally and of the divine name *Yahweh* in particular, but have graciously subordinated their convictions to editorial policy.

Hebrew

א = '	ד = ḏ	י = y	ס = s	ר = r
בּ = b	ה = h	כּ = k	ע = '	שׂ = ś
ב = ḇ	ו = w	כ = ḵ	פּ = p	שׁ = š
גּ = g	ז = z	ל – l	פ = p̄	תּ = t
ג = ḡ	ח = ḥ	מ = m	צ = ṣ	ת = ṯ
דּ = d	ט = ṭ	נ = n	ק = q	

Long vowels		Short vowels	Very short Vowels
(ה)◌ָ = â	◌ָ = ā	◌ַ = a	◌ֲ = ^{a}
◌ֵי = ê	◌ֵ = ē	◌ֶ = e	◌ֱ = ^{e}
◌ִי = î		◌ִ = i	◌ְ = ^{e} (if vocal)
וֹ = ô	◌ֹ = ō	◌ָ = o	◌ֳ = ^{o}
וּ = û		◌ֻ = u	

Greek

α = *a*	ι = *i*	ρ = *r*	ῥ = *rh*
β = *b*	κ = *k*	σ,ς = *s*	‘ = *h*
γ = *g*	λ = *l*	τ = *t*	γξ = *nx*
δ = *d*	μ = *m*	υ = *y*	γγ = *ng*
ε = *e*	ν = *n*	φ = *ph*	αυ = *au*
ζ = *z*	ξ = *x*	χ = *ch*	ευ = *eu*
η = *ē*	ο = *o*	ψ = *ps*	ου = *ou*
θ = *th*	π *p*	ω = *ō*	υι = *yi*

Arabic

ا = '	خ = ḫ	ش = š	غ = ġ	ن = n
ب = b	د = d	ص = ṣ	ف = f	ه = h
ت = t	ذ = ḏ	ض = ḍ	ق = ḳ	و = w
ث = t	ر = r	ط = ṭ	ك = k	ى = y
ج = ğ	ز = z	ظ = ẓ	ل = l	ة = t
ح = ḥ	س = s	ع = '	م = m	

List of Contributors

A.A.J. A. A. Jones, M.A., B.D., Ph.D., formerly Head of Department of Religious Studies, Avery Hill College, London.

A.C. R. A. Cole, B.A., B.D., M.Th., Ph.D., Federal Secretary, Church Missionary Society (Australia) and Lecturer in Old Testament Language and Literature, University of Sydney.

A.E.C. A. E. Cundall, B.A., B.D., Senior Lecturer in Old Testament Studies, London Bible College.

A.E.W. A. E. Willingale, B.A., B.D., M.Th., Romford, Essex.

A.F. A. Flavelle, B.A., B.D., Minister of Finaghy Presbyterian Church, Belfast.

A.F.W. A. F. Walls, M.A., B.Litt., Professor of Religious Studies, University of Aberdeen.

A.G. A. Gelston, M.A., Senior Lecturer in Theology, University of Durham.

A.J.M.W. A. J. M. Weddeburn, M.A., B.D., Ph.D., Lecturer in New Testament Language and Literature, University of St Andrews.

A.K.C. A. K. Cragg, M.A., D.Phil., D.D., Assistant Bishop of Wakefield and Vicar of Helme, Huddersfield.

A.R. The late A. Ross, M.A., B.D., D.D., formerly Professor of New Testament, Free Church College, Edinburgh.

A.R.M. A. R. Millard, M.A., M.Phil., F.S.A., Rankin Senior Lecturer in Hebrew and Ancient Semitic Languages, University of Liverpool.

A.S. A. Stuart, M.Sc., Dip.R.M.S., Emeritus Professor of Geology, University of Exeter.

A.S.W. A. S. Wood, B.A., Ph.D., F.R.Hist.S., Principal, Cliff College, Calver, Derbyshire.

A. van S. A. van Selms, Th.D., Emeritus Professor of Semitic Languages, University of Pretoria.

B.A.M. B. A. Milne, M.A., B.D., Ph.D., Lecturer in Biblical and Historical Theology and Christian Ethics, Spurgeon's College, London.

B.F.C.A. The late B. F. C. Atkinson, M.A., Ph.D., formerly Under-Librarian, University of Cambridge.

B.F.H. B. F. Harris, B.A., M.A., B.D., Ph.D., Associate Professor of History, Macquarie University, New South Wales.

B.L.S. B. L. Smith, B.D., Th.Schol., Classics Teacher, Sydney Grammar School; Visiting Lecturer, Moore Theological College, Sydney.

B.O.B. B. O. Banwell, B.A., M.A., formerly Lecturer in Old Testament, Rhodes University; Methodist Minister, Fort Beaufort, S. Africa.

C.D.W. C. de Wit, Docteur en philologie et histoire orientales; Conservateur honoraire Musées Royaux d'Art et Histoire, Brussels; Emeritus Professor of the University of Louvain.

C.F.P. The late C. F. Pfeiffer, B.A., B.D., Ph.D., formerly Associate Professor of Old Testament, Gordon Divinity School, Beverly Farms, Massachusetts.

C.H.D. C. H. Duncan, M.A., B.D., Ph.D., Th.D., Lecturer in Philosophy, State College of Victoria, Australia; Canon of St Paul's Cathedral, Melbourne.

C.J.D. C. J. Davey, B.Sc., M.A., Inspector of Mines, Victoria, Australia.

C.J.H. C. J. Hemer, M.A., Ph.D., formerly Lecturer in New Testament Studies, University of Manchester.

C.L.F. C. L. Feinberg, A.B., A.M., Th.B., Th.M., Ph.D., Emeritus Professor of Semitics and Old Testament and Dean of Talbot Theological Seminary, Los Angeles.

D.A.H. D. A. Hubbard, B.A., B.D., Th.M., Ph.D., D.D., L.H.D., President and Professor of Old Testament, Fuller Theological Seminary, Pasadena, California.

D.B.K. D. B. Knox, B.A., B.D., M.Th., D.Phil, A.L.C.D., Principal, Moore Theological College, Sydney; Senior Canon of St Andrew's Cathedral, Sydney.

D.F. D. Freeman, B.A., Th.B., Th.M., Ph.D., Professor, Rhode Island Junior College.

D.F.P. D. F. Payne, B.A., M.A., Senior Lecturer and Head of Department of Semitic Studies, The Queen's University, Belfast.

D.G. D. Guthrie, B.D., M.Th., Ph.D., Vice-Principal, London Bible College.

D.G.S. D. G. Stradling, Magdalen College, Oxford.

D.H.F. D. H. Field, B.A., Vice-Principal, Oak Hill College, London.

D.H.T. D. H. Tongue, M.A., formerly Lecturer in New Testament, Trinity College, Bristol.

D.H.W. D. H. Wheaton, M.A., B.D., Principal, Oak Hill College, London; Canon of St Alban's Cathedral.

D.J.A.C. D. J. A. Clines, M.A., Senior Lecturer, Department of Biblical Studies, University of Sheffield.

D.J.V.L. D. J. V. Lane, Ll.B., B.D., Overseas Director, Overseas Missionary Fellowship, Singapore.

D.J.W. D. J. Wiseman, O.B.E., M.A., D.Lit., F.B.A., F.S.A., Professor of Assyriology, University of London.

D.K.I. D. K. Innes, M.A., B.D., Rector of Alford and Loxwood, West Sussex.

D.O.S. D. O. Swann, B.A., B.D., Minister of Ashford Evangelical Congregational Church, Middlesex.

D.R. de L. D. R. de Lacey, M.A., Ph.D., Lecturer in New Testament Studies, London Bible College.

D.R.H. D. R. Hall, M.A., M.Th, Superintendent Minister of the North of Scotland Mission Circuit of the Methodist Church, Aberdeen.

D.T. D. H. Trapnell, M.A., M.D., F.R.C.P., F.R.C.R., Consultant Radiologist, Westminster Hospital, London.

D.W. D. Wenham, M.A., Ph.D., Research Fellow, Tyndale House, Cambridge.

D.W.B. D. W. Baker, A.B., M.C.S., M.Phil., Assistant Professor of Biblical Studies, Bethel College, St Paul, Minnesota.

D.W.B.R. D. W. B. Robinson, M.A., Bishop in Parramatta, New South Wales; formerly Head of New Testament Department, Divinity School, University of Sydney.

D.W.G. D. W. Gooding, M.A., Ph.D., M.R.I.A., Professor of Old Testament Greek, The Queen's University, Belfast.

E.A.J. E. A. Judge, M.A., Professor of History, Macquarie University, New South Wales.

E.E.E. E. E. Ellis, Ph.D., Research Professor of New Testament Literature, New Brunswick Theological Seminary, New Jersey.

E.J.Y. The late E. J. Young, B.A., Th.M., Ph.D., formerly Professor of Old Testament, Westminster Theological Seminary, Philadelphia.

E.M.B. E. M. Blaiklock, O.B.E., M.A., Litt.D., Emeritus Professor of Classics, University of Auckland.

E.M.B.G. E. M. B. Green, M.A., B.D., Rector of St Aldate's Church, Oxford; Canon of Coventry Cathedral. Formerly Principal, St John's College, Nottingham.

E.M.Y. E. M. Yamauchi, B.A., M.A., Ph.D., Director of Graduate Studies and Professor of History, Miami University, Oxford, Ohio.

F.C.F. F. C. Fensham, M.A., Ph.D., D.D., Professor in Semitic Languages, University of Stellenbosch.

F.D.K. F. D. Kidner, M.A., A.R.C.M., formerly Warden, Tyndale House, Cambridge.

F.F. F. Foulkes, B.A., B.D., M.A., M.Sc., Lecturer in Biblical Studies, St John's College, Auckland, and Lecturer in Biblical History and Literature, University of Auckland.

F.F.B. F. F. Bruce, M.A., D.D., F.B.A., Emeritus Rylands Professor of Biblical Criticism and Exegesis, University of Manchester.

F.H.P. F. H. Palmer, M.A., Diocesan Missioner and Priest-in-charge of Blymhill and Weston-under-Lizard, Diocese of Lichfield.

F.N.H. F. N. Hepper, F.I.Biol., B.Sc., F.L.S., Assistant Keeper, The Herbarium, Royal Botanic Gardens, Kew.

F.R.S. F. R. Steele, A.B., M.A., Ph.D., Assistant Director North America for the North Africa Mission; formerly Assistant Professor of Assyriology, University of Pennsylvania.

F.S.F. F. S. Fitzsimmonds, B.A., B.D., M.Th., Vice-Principal, Spurgeon's College, London.

G.C.D.H. G. C. D. Howley, Consulting Editor of *The Witness*.

G.G.G. G. G. Garner, B.A., B. D., Director, Australian Institute of Archaeology, Melbourne.

G.I.D. G. I. Davies, M.A., Ph.D., Lecturer in Old Testament and Intertestamental Studies, University of Cambridge.

G.I.E. Mrs G. I. Emmerson, M.A., Dip.Or.Lang., Lecturer, Department of Theology, University of Nottingham.

G.O. The late G. Ogg, M.A., B.Sc., D.D., D.Litt., formerly Minister at Anstruther Easter, Fife.

G.R.B.-M. G. R. Beasley-Murray, M.A., Ph.D., D.D., James Buchanan Harrison Professor of New Testament Interpretation, Southern Baptist Theological Seminary, Louisville, Kentucky.

G.S.C. G. S. Cansdale, B.A., B.Sc., F.L.S., Consultant Biologist.

G.S.M.W. The late G. S. M. Walker, M.A., B.D., Ph.D., formerly Lecturer in Church History, University of Leeds.

G.T.M. The late G. T. Manley, M.A., sometime Fellow, Christ's College, Cambridge.

G.W. G. Walters, B.A., B.D., Ph.D., Professor of Ministry, Gordon-Conwell Theological Seminary, South Hamilton, Massachusetts.

G.W.G. G. W. Grogan, B.D., M.Th., Principal, Bible Training Institute, Glasgow.

H.A.G.B. H. A. G. Belben, M.A., B.D., formerly Principal, Cliff College, Calver, Derbyshire.

H.D.McD. H. D. McDonald, B.A., B.D., Ph.D., D.D., formerly Vice-Principal, London Bible College.

H.G.M.W. H. G. M. Williamson, M.A., Ph.D., Assistant Lecturer in Hebrew and Aramaic, University of Cambridge.

H.L.E. H. L. Ellison, B.A., B.D., formerly Senior Tutor, Moorlands Bible College.

H.M.C. H. M. Carson, B.A., B.D., Minister of Hamilton Road Baptist Church, Bangor, Northern Ireland.

H.R. H. N. Ridderbos, D. Theol., Emeritus Professor of New Testament, Kampen Theological Seminary, The Netherlands.

I.H.M. I. H. Marshall, B.A., M.A., B.D., Ph.D., Professor of New Testament Exegesis, University of Aberdeen.

J.A.M. J. A. Motyer, M.A., B.D., Principal, Trinity College, Bristol.

J.A.T. J. A. Thompson, M.A., M.Sc., B.D., B.Ed., Ph.D., formerly Reader in Department of Middle Eastern Studies, University of Melbourne.

J.B.J. J. B. Job, M.A., B.D., Tutor in Old Testament, Cliff College, Derbyshire.

J.B.P. J. B. Payne, Ph.D., Professor of Old Testament, Covenant Theological Seminary, St Louis, Missouri.

J.B.T. J. B. Torrance, M.A., B.D., Professor of Systematic Theology, University of Aberdeen.

J.B.Tr. J. B. Taylor, M.A., Bishop of St Albans.

J.C.C. J. C. Connell, B.A., M.A., formerly Director of Studies and Lecturer in New Testament Exegesis, London Bible College.

J.C.J.W. J. C. J. Waite, B.D., Principal, South Wales Bible College.

J.C.W. J. C. Whitcomb, Jr, Th.D., Professor of Theology and Director of Postgraduate Studies, Grace Theological Seminary, Winona Lake, Indiana.

J.D.D. J. D. Douglas, M.A., B.D., S.T.M., Ph.D., Editor-at-large, *Christianity Today*.

J.D.G.D. J. D. G. Dunn, M.A., B.D., Ph.D., Lecturer in New Testament, University of Nottingham.

J.E.G. J. E. Goldingay, B.A., Lecturer in Old Testament, St John's College, Nottingham.

J.G.B. Miss J. G. Baldwin, B.A., B.D., Dean of Women, Trinity College, Bristol.

J.G.G.N. J. G. G. Norman, B.D., M.Th., Pastor of Rosyth Baptist Church, Fife.

J.G.S.S.T. J. G. S. S. Thomson, B.A., M.A., B.D., Ph.D., Minister at Wigtown, Scotland.

J.H. J. W. L. Hoad, M.A., Clinical Supervisor, Princeton, New Jersey.

J.H.H. J. H. Harrop, M.A., formerly Lecturer in Classics, Fourah Bay College, University of Sierra Leone.

J.H.P. J. H. Paterson, M.A., Professor of Geography, University of Leicester.

J.H.S. J. H. Skilton, B.A., M.A., M.Div., Ph.D., Dean of the Reformed Bible Institute of the Delaware Valley; Lecturer in New Testament, Westminster Theological Seminary, Philadelphia.

J.H.Sr. The late J. H. Stringer, M.A., B.D., formerly Tutor, London Bible College.

J.I.P. J. I. Packer, M.A., D.Phil., D.D., Professor of Systematic Theology, Regent College, Vancouver, BC.

J.J.H. J. J. Hughes, B.A., M.Div., Assistant Professor of Religious Studies, Westmont College, Santa Barbara, California.

J.L.K. The late J. L. Kelso, B.A., Th.M., M.A., Th.D., D.D., Ll.D., formerly Professor of Old Testament History and Biblical Archaeology, Pittsburgh Theological Seminary, Pennsylvania.

J.M. The late J. Murray, M.A., Th.M., formerly Professor of Systematic Theology, Westminster Theological Seminary, Philadelphia.

J.M.H. J. M. Houston, M.A., B.Sc., D.Phil., Chancellor, formerly Principal, Regent College, Vancouver, BC.

J.N.B. J. N. Birdsall, M.A., Ph.D., F.R.A.S., Reader in New Testament and Textual Criticism, University of Birmingham.

J.N.G. The late J. N. Geldenhuys, B.A., B.D., Th.M.

J.P. J. Philip, M.A., Minister of Holyrood Abbey, Edinburgh.

J.P.B. J. P. Baker, M.A., B.D., Rector of Newick, East Sussex.

J.P.K. J. P. Kane, Ph.D., Dip.Ed., Lecturer in Hellenistic Greek, University of Manchester.

J.P.U.L. J. P. U. Lilley, M.A., F.C.A., Magdalen College, Oxford.

J.R. J. Rea, M.A., Th.D., Professor of Old Testament, Melodyland School of Theology, Anaheim, California.

J.Ru. J. Ruffle, M.A., Keeper of Archaeology, Birmingham City Museum.

J.S.W. J. S. Wright, M.A., formerly Principal, Tyndale Hall, Bristol; Canon of Bristol Cathedral.

J.T. J. A. Thompson, B.A., M.Div., Th.M., Ph.D., Research Consultant, American Bible Society.

J.T.W. J. T. Whitney, M.A., L.C.P., Ph.D., Head of Religious Studies, South East Essex Sixth Form College.

J.W.C. J. W. Charley, M.A., Warden of Shrewsbury House and Rector of St Peter's, Everton, Liverpool.

J.W.D. J. W. Drane, M.A., Ph.D., Lecturer in Religious Studies, University of Stirling.

J.W.M. J. W. Meiklejohn, M.B.E., M.A., formerly Secretary of the Inter-School Christian Fellowship in Scotland.

K.A.K. K. A. Kitchen, B.A., Ph.D., Reader in Egyptian and Coptic, University of Liverpool.

K.L.McK. K. L. McKay, B.A., M.A., Reader in Classics, The Australian National University, Canberra.

L.C.A. L. C. Allen, M.A., Ph.D., Lecturer in Old Testament Language and Literature, London Bible College.

L.M. L. L. Morris, M.Sc., M.Th., Ph.D., formerly Principal, Ridley College, Melbourne; Canon of St Paul's Cathedral, Melbourne.

M.A.M. M. A. MacLeod, M.A., Director, Christian Witness to Israel.

M.B. Mrs M. Beeching, B.A., B.D., M.Ed., formerly Principal Lecturer and Head of Department of Divinity, Cheshire College of Education, Alsager.

M.G.K. M. G. Kline, Th.M., Ph.D., Professor of Old Testament, Gordon-Conwell Theological Seminary, South Hamilton, Mass.

M.H.C. M. H. Cressey, M.A., Professor of Systematic Theology and Apologetics, Westminster College, Cambridge.

M.J.S. M. J. Selman, B.A., M.A., Ph.D., Lecturer in Old Testament, Spurgeon's College, London.

M.J.S.R. M. J. S. Rudwick, M.A., Ph.D., Sc.D., Professor of History of Science, The Free University, Amsterdam.

M.R.G. M. R. Gordon, B.D., Principal, Bible Institute of South Africa, Kalk Bay, South Africa.

M.R.W.F. M. R. W. Farrer, M.A., Vicar of St Paul's Church, Cambridge.

M.T.F. M. T. Fermer, B.A., B.Sc., A.R.C.S., Rector of Old Brampton and Loundsley Green, Derbyshire.

N.H. N. Hillyer, B.D., S.Th., A.L.C.D., formerly Librarian, Tyndale House, Cambridge; Vicar of Hatherleigh, Devonshire.

N.H.R. N. H. Ridderbos, D.D., Emeritus Professor of Old Testament, The Free University, Amsterdam.

P.A.B. P. A. Blair, M.A., Rector of Barking, Essex.

P.E. P. Ellingworth, B.A., M.A., Ph.D., Translation Consultant to the United Bible Societies, London.

P.E.H. P. E. Hughes, M.A., B.D., Th.D., D.Litt., Visiting Professor at Westminster Theological Seminary, Philadelphia; Associate Rector of St John's Episcopal Church, Huntingdon Valley, Pennsylvania.

P.H.D. P. H. Davids, B.A., M.Div., Ph.D., Head of Department of Biblical Studies and Language, Trinity Episcopal School for Ministry, Ambridge, Pennsylvania.

P.W. P. Woolley, B.A., Th.M., D.D., Emeritus Professor of Church History, Westminster Theological Seminary, Philadelphia.

R.A.F. R. A. Finlayson, M.A., Emeritus Professor of Systematic Theology, Free Church College, Edinburgh.

R.A.H.G. R. A. H. Gunner, B.A., M.Th., Lecturer in Religious Studies, Brooklands Technical College, Weybridge, Surrey.

R.A.S. R. A. Stewart, M.A., B.D., M.Litt., formerly Church of Scotland Minister.

R.E.N. The late R. E. Nixon, M.A., formerly Principal, St John's College, Nottingham.

R.H.M. R. H. Mounce, B.A., B.D., Th.M., Ph.D., Professor of Religious Studies and Dean of Arts and Humanities, Western Kentucky University.

R.J.A.S. R. J. A. Sheriffs, B.A., B.D., Ph.D., formerly Lecturer in Old Testament, Rhodes University, Grahamstown, Cape Province.

R.J.B. R. J. Bauckham, M.A., Ph.D., Lecturer in the History of Christian Thought, University of Manchester.

R.J.C. The late R. J. Coates, M.A., sometime Warden, Latimer House, Oxford.

R.J.McK. R. J. McKelvey, B.A., M.Th., D.Phil., Principal, The Congregational College, Manchester.

R.J.T. R. J. Thompson, M.A., B.D., Th.M., D.Theol., Principal, New Zealand Baptist Theological College, Auckland.

R.J.W. R. J. Way, M.A., Minister of St Columba's United Reformed Church, Leeds.

R.K.H. R. K. Harrison, M.Th., Ph.D., D.D., Professor of Old Testament, Wycliffe College, University of Toronto.

R.N.C. R. N. Caswell, M.A., Ph.D., Head of Religious Education, The Academical Institution, Coleraine, Northern Ireland.

R.P.G. R. P. Gordon, M.A., Ph.D., Lecturer in Old Testament, University of Cambridge.

R.P.M. R. P. Martin, M.A., Ph.D., Professor of New Testament, Fuller Theological Seminary, Pasadena, California.

R.S.W. R. S. Wallace, M.A., B.Sc., Ph.D., Emeritus Professor, Columbia Theological Seminary, Decatur, Georgia.

R.T.B. R. T. Beckwith, M.A., Warden, Latimer House, Oxford.

R.T.F. R. T. France, M.A., B.D., Ph.D., Warden, Tyndale House, Cambridge.

R.V.G.T. The late R. V. G. Tasker, M.A., D.D., formerly Professor of New Testament Exegesis, University of London.

S.S.S. S. S. Smalley, M.A., B.D., Ph.D., Canon Residentiary and Precentor of Coventry Cathedral.

T.C.M. T. C. Mitchell, M.A., Deputy Keeper, Department of Western Asiatic Antiquities, British Museum.

T.H.J. T. H. Jones, M.A., B.D., A.M.B.I.M., Principal, Hind Leys College, Shepshed, Leicestershire.

W.G.P. W. G. Putman, B.A., B.D., Methodist Minister, High Wycombe, Bucks.

W.H.G. W. H. Gispen, D.Theol., Doctorandus Semitic Languages, Emeritus Professor of Hebrew and Old Testament, The Free University, Amsterdam.

W.J.C. W. J. Cameron, M.A., B.D., Professor of New Testament Language, Literature, Exegesis and Theology, Free Church of Scotland College, Edinburgh.

W.J.M. W. J. Martin, M.A., Th.B., Ph.D., Professor Emeritus, Regent College, Vancouver, BC; formerly Head of the Department of Hebrew and Ancient Semitic Languages, University of Liverpool.

W.O. W. Osborne, M.A., M.Phil., Lecturer in Old Testament, The Bible College of New Zealand.

W.W.W. W. W. Wessel, M.A., Ph.D., Professor of New Testament, Bethel College, St Paul, Minnesota.

Abbreviations

I. Books and Journals

AASOR
Annual of the American Schools of Oriental Research

AB
Anchor Bible

ACA
Sir Moses Finley, *Atlas of Classical Archaeology*, 1977

AfO
Archiv für Orientforschung

AJA
American Journal of Archaeology

AJBA
Australian Journal of Biblical Archaeology

AJSL
American Journal of Semitic Languages and Literatures

AJT
American Journal of Theology

ALUOS
Annual of the Leeds University Oriental Society

ANEP
J. B. Pritchard, *The Ancient Near East in Pictures*, 1954; ²1965

ANET
J. B. Pritchard, *Ancient Near Eastern Texts*, 1950; ²1965; ³1969

ANT
M. R. James, *The Apocryphal New Testament*, 1924

AOTS
D. W. Thomas (ed.), *Archaeology and Old Testament Study*, 1967

ARAB
D. D. Luckenbill, *Ancient Records of Assyria and Babylonia*, 1926

ARE
J. H. Breasted, *Ancient Records of Egypt*, 5 vols., 1906–7

Arndt
W. F. Arndt and F. W. Gingrich, *A Greek–English Lexicon of the New Testament and Other Early Christian Literature*, 1957

ARV
American Revised Version (see ASV)

AS
Anatolian Studies

ASAE
Annales du Service des Antiquités de l'Égypte

ASV
American Standard Version, 1901 (American version of RV)

ATR
Anglican Theological Review

AV
Authorized Version (*King James'*), 1611

BA
Biblical Archaeologist

BANE
G. E. Wright (ed.), *The Bible and the Ancient Near East*, 1961

BASOR
Bulletin of the American Schools of Oriental Research

BC
F. J. Foakes-Jackson and K. Lake, *The Beginnings of Christianity*, 5 vols., 1920–33

BDB
F. Brown, S. R. Driver and C. A. Briggs, *Hebrew and English Lexicon of the Old Testament*, 1906

Bib
Biblica

BibRes
Biblical Research

BIES
Bulletin of the Israel Exploration Society

BJRL
Bulletin of the John Rylands Library

BNTC
Black's New Testament Commentaries

BO
Bibliotheca Orientalis

BRD
W. M. Ramsay, *The Bearing of Recent Discovery on the Trustworthiness of the New Testament*, 1914

BS
Bibliotheca Sacra

BSOAS
Bulletin of the School of Oriental and African Studies

BTh
Biblical Theology

BZ
Biblische Zeitschrift

BZAW
Beiheft, Zeitschrift für die alttestamentliche Wissenschaft

CAH
Cambridge Ancient History, 12 vols., 1923–39; revised ed. 1970–

CB
Century Bible

CBP
W. M. Ramsay, *Cities and Bishoprics of Phrygia*, 1895–7

CBQ
Catholic Biblical Quarterly

CBSC
Cambridge Bible for Schools and Colleges

CD
Qumran Damascus Document

CDC
Cairo Geniza Documents of the Damascus Covenanters

CE
Chronique d'Égypte

CGT
Cambridge Greek Testament

CIG
Corpus Inscriptionum Graecarum

CIL
Corpus Inscriptionum Latinarum

CQ
Classical Quarterly; *Crozer Quarterly*

CRE
W. M. Ramsay, *The Church in the Roman Empire before AD 170*, 1903

CTJ
Calvin Theological Journal

DAC
J. Hastings (ed.), *Dictionary of the Apostolic Church*, 2 vols., 1915–18

DBS
Dictionnaire de la Bible, Supplément, 1928–

DCG
J. Hastings (ed.), *Dictionary of Christ and the Gospels*, 2 vols., 1906–08

DOTT
D. W. Thomas (ed.), *Documents of Old Testament Times*, 1958

EAEHL
M. Avi-Yonah (ed.), *Encyclopaedia of Archaeological Excavations in the Holy Land*, 4 vols., 1975–8

EB
Expositor's Bible

EBi
Encyclopaedia Biblica

EBr
Encyclopaedia Britannica

EBT
J. B. Bauer (ed.), *Encyclopaedia of Biblical Theology*, 3 vols., 1970

EEP
K. Lake, *The Earlier Epistles of St Paul*, 1911

EGT
W. R. Nicoll, *The Expositor's Greek Testament*[6], 1910

EIs
Encyclopaedia of Islam, 1954–

EJ
C. Roth (ed.), *Encyclopaedia Judaica*, 15 vols., 1971

EQ
Evangelical Quarterly

ERE
J. Hastings (ed.), *Encyclopaedia of Religion and Ethics*, 13 vols., 1908–26

ExpT
Expository Times

FRLANT
Forschungen zur Religion und Literatur des Alten und Neuen Testaments

FT
Faith and Thought (formerly *JTVI*)

GB
Ginsburg's Bible (New Masoretico-Critical Text of the Hebrew Bible), 1896

GNB
Good News Bible (= TEV)

GTT
J. Simons, *Geographical and Topographical Texts of the Old Testament*, 1959

HAT
Handbuch zum Alten Testament

HDB
J. Hastings (ed.), *Dictionary of the Bible*, 5 vols., 1898–1904

HES
Harvard Expedition to Samaria, 1924

HHT
J. Lightfoot, *Horae Hebraicae et Talmudicae*, 1658–64

HJ
Hibbert Journal

HJP
E. Schürer, *A History of the Jewish People in the Time of Christ*, 2 vols., E.T. 1885–1901; revised ed., M. Black, G. Vermes and F. Millar (eds.), 3 vols., 1973–

HNT
H. Lietzmann, *Handbuch zum Neuen Testament*

HSS
Harvard Semitic Series

HTKNT
Herders Theologischer Kommentar zum Neuen Testament

HTR
Harvard Theological Review

HUCA
Hebrew Union College Annual

IB
G. A. Buttrick *et al.* (eds.), *Interpreter's Bible*, 12 vols., 1952–7

IBA
D. J. Wiseman, *Illustrations from Biblical Archaeology*, 1958

ICC
International Critical Commentary

IDB
G. A. Buttrick *et al.* (eds.), *The Interpreter's Dictionary of the Bible*, 4 vols., 1962

IDBS
IDB, Supplement vol., 1976

IEJ
Israel Exploration Journal

IG
Inscriptiones Graecae

IGRR
Inscriptiones Graecae ad res Romanas pertinentes

Int
Interpretation

INT
Introduction to the New Testament

IOSCS
International Organization for Septuagint and Cognate Studies

IOT
Introduction to the Old Testament

ISBE
International Standard Bible Enclopaedia, 5 vols., [2]1930

JAOS
Journal of the American Oriental Society

JB
Jerusalem Bible, 1966

JBL
Journal of Biblical Literature

JCS
Journal of Cuneiform Studies

JEA
Journal of Egyptian Archaeology

JEH
Journal of Ecclesiastical History

JewE
I. Singer *et al.* (eds.), *Jewish Encyclopaedia*, 12 vols., 1901–06

JHS
Journal of Hellenic Studies

JJS
Journal of Jewish Studies

JNES
Journal of Near Eastern Studies

JNSL
Journal of Northwest Semitic Languages

JPOS
Journal of the Palestine Oriental Society

JQR
Jewish Quarterly Review

JRAS
Journal of the Royal Asiatic Society

JRS
Journal of Roman Studies

JSOT
Journal for the Study of the Old Testament

JSS
Journal of Semitic Studies

JTS
Journal of Theological Studies

JTVI
Journal of the Transactions of the Victoria Institute (now *FT*)

JWH
Journal of World History

KAT
Kommentar zum Alten Testament

KB
L. Köhler and W. Baumgartner, *Hebräisches und aramäisches Lexicon zum Alten Testament*[3], 1967

KEK
H. A. W. Meyer (ed.), *Kritisch-exegetischer Kommentar über das Neue Testament*

KJV
King James' Version (= AV)

LA
Liber Annus (Jerusalem)

LAE
A. Deissmann, *Light from the Ancient East*[4], 1927

LBC
Layman's Bible Commentary

LOB
Y. Aharoni, *The Land of the Bible*, 1967

LOT
S. R. Driver, *Introduction to the Literature of the Old Testament*[9], 1913

LSJ
H. G. Liddell, R. Scott and H. S. Jones, *Greek–English Lexicon*[9], 1940

MM
J. H. Moulton and G. Milligan, *The Vocabulary of the Greek Testament illustrated from the Papyri and other non-literary sources*, 1930

MNTC
Moffatt New Testament Commentary

Moffatt
J. Moffatt, *A New Translation of the Bible*[2], 1936

NASB
New American Standard Bible, 1963

NBC
F. Davidson (ed.), *The New Bible Commentary*, 1953

NBCR
D. Guthrie *et al.* (eds.), *The New Bible Commentary Revised*, 1970

NCB
New Century Bible

NClB
New Clarendon Bible

NEB
New English Bible: NT, 1961; OT, Apocrypha, 1970

Nestle
Nestle's Novum Testamentum Graece[22], 1956

NIC
New International Commentary

NIDNTT
C. Brown (ed.), *The New International Dictionary of New Testament Theology*, 3 vols., 1975–8

NIV
New International Version: NT, 1974; complete Bible, 1978

NLC
New London Commentary

NovT
Novum Testamentum

NTD
Das Neue Testament Deutsch

NTS
New Testament Studies

OCD
M. Cary *et al.* (eds.), *The Oxford Classical Dictionary*, 1949

ODCC
F. L. Cross and E. A. Livingstone (eds.), *The Oxford Dictionary of the Christian Church*[2], 1974

Or
Orientalia

OTL
Old Testament Library

OTMS
H. H. Rowley (ed.), *The Old Testament and Modern Study*, 1951

OTS
Oudtestamentische Studiën

Pauly-Wissowa
See *RE*

PEQ
Palestine Exploration Quarterly

PG
J. P. Migne, *Patrologia Graeca*

Phillips
J. B. Phillips, *The New Testament in Modern English*, 1958; revised ed. 1972

PJB
Palästina-Jahrbuch

PL
J. P. Migne, *Patrologia Latina*

POTT
D. J. Wiseman (ed.), *Peoples of Old Testament Times*, 1973

P.Oxy.
Papyrus Oxyrhynchus

PRU
Le Palais Royal d'Ugarit

PTR
Princeton Theological Review

RA
Revue d'Assyriologie

RAC
T. Klausner *et al.* (eds.), *Reallexicon für die Antike und Christentum*, 1941–

RAr
Revue d'Archéologie

RB
Revue Biblique

RE
A. F. Pauly, G. Wissowa *et al.* (eds.), *Real-Encyclopädie der klassischen Altertumwissenschaft*, 1893–

RGG
K. Galling (ed.), *Die Religion in Geschichte und Gegenwart*[3], 7 vols., 1957–65

RHR
Revue de l'Histoire des Religions

RQ
Revue de Qumran

RSV
Revised Standard Version: NT, 1946; OT, 1952; *Common Bible*, 1973

RTR
Reformed Theological Review (Australia)

RV
Revised Version: NT, 1881; OT, 1885

SB
H. L. Strack and P. Billerbeck, *Kommentar zum Neuen Testament aus Talmud und Midrasch*, 6 vols., 1926–61

SBL
Society of Biblical Literature

SBT
Studies in Biblical Theology

Schürer See *HJP*

SHERK
The New Schaff-Herzog Encyclopaedia of Religious Knowledge[2], 1949–52

SIG
W. Dittenberger (ed.), *Sylloge Inscriptionum Graecarum*, 1915–24

SJT
Scottish Journal of Theology

SP
Samaritan Pentateuch

SPEM
G. S. Duncan, *St Paul's Ephesian Ministry*, 1929

SPT
W. M. Ramsay, *St Paul the Traveller and Roman Citizen*[4], 1920

ST
Studia Theologica

Strack-Billerbeck See *SB*

TB
Babylonian Talmud

TBC
Torch Bible Commentary

TCERK
The Twentieth Century Encyclopaedia of Religious Knowledge, 1955

TDNT
G. Kittell and G. Friedrich (eds.), *Theologisches Wörterbuch zum Neuen Testament*, 1932–74; E.T. *Theological Dictionary of the New Testament*, ed. G. W. Bromiley, 10 vols., 1964–76

TDOT
G. J. Botterweck and H. Ringgren (eds.), *Theologisches Wörterbuch zum Alten Testament*, 1970– ; E.T. *Theological Dictionary of the Old Testament*, trans. by J. T. Willis, 1974–

TEV
Today's English Version[4], 1976 (= GNB)

Th
Theology

THAT
E. Jenni and C. Westermann (eds.), *Theologisches Handwörterbuch zum Alten Testament*, 2 vols., 1971–6

THB
Tyndale House Bulletin (now *TynB*)

Them
Themelios

ThL
Theologische Literaturzeitung

THNT
Theologische Handbuch zum Neuen Testament

TJ
Jerusalem Talmud

TNT
Translators' New Testament (Bible Society)

TNTC
Tyndale New Testament Commentary

TOTC
Tyndale Old Testament Commentary

TR
Theologische Rundschau

TS
Texts and Studies

TSFB
Theological Students' Fellowship Bulletin

TU
Texte und Untersuchungen zur Geschichte der altchristlichen Literatur

TWBR
A. Richardson (ed.), *A Theological Word Book of the Bible*, 1950

TynB
Tyndale Bulletin (formerly *THB*)

TZ
Theologisches Zeitung

VC
Vigiliae Christianae

VT
Vetus Testamentum

VT Supp.
Vetus Testamentum, Supplementary vol.

UF
Ugarit-Forschungen: Internationales Jahrbuch für die Altertumskunde Syrien-Palästinas

WC
Westminster Commentary

WDB
Westminster Dictionary of the Bible, 1944

Wett.
J. J. Wettstein, *Novum Testamentum Graecum*, 1751–2

Weymouth
R. F. Weymouth, *The New Testament in Modern Speech*, 1903

WH
B. F. Westcott and F. J. A. Hort, *The New Testament in Greek*, 1881

WTJ
Westminster Theological Journal

ZA
Zeitschrift für Assyriologie

ZAW
Zeitschrift für die alttestamentliche Wissenschaft

ZDMG
Zeitschrift der deutschen morgenländischen Gesellschaft

ZDPV
Zeitschrift des deutschen Palästina-Vereins

ZNW
Zeitschrift für die neutestamentliche Wissenschaft

ZPEB
M. C. Tenney (ed.), *The Zondervan Pictorial Encyclopaedia of the Bible*, 5 vols., 1975

ZTK
Zeitschrift für Theologie und Kirche

Editions are indicated by small superior figures: *LOT*[9]

II. Classical Works

ad Fam.
Cicero, *Epistulae ad Familiares*

Adv. Haer.
Irenaeus, *Adversus Haereses*

Ann.
Tacitus, *Annales*

Ant.
Josephus, *Antiquities of the Jews*

Apol.
Justin Martyr, *Apologia*
Tertullian, *Apologia*

BJ
Josephus, *Jewish Wars*

Clem. Recog.
Rufinus, *Clementine Recognitions*

Contra Pelag.
Jerome, *Contra Pelagium*

Eccles. Hist.
Sozomen, *History of the Church*

EH
Eusebius, *Ecclesiastical History*

Epig.
Martial, *Epigrammaticus Latinus*

Ep. Mor.
Seneca, *Epistulae Morales ad Lucilium*

Eus.
Eusebius

Ev. Petr.
Gospel of Peter (apocryphal)

Exc. Theod.
Clement of Alexandria, *Excerpta ex Theodoto*

Geog.
Ptolemy, *Geography*; Strabo, *Geography*

Hist.
Dio Cassius, *History*; Tacitus, *History*

Hypot.
Clement of Alexandria, *Hypotyposes*

Il.
Homer, *Iliad*

Iul.
Suetonius, *C. Julius Caesar* (*Lives of the Caesars*)

In Verr.
Cicero, *In Verrem Actio*

Jos.
Josephus

Juv.
Juvenal

Lk. Hom.
Origen, *Homily on Luke*

Magn.
Ignatius, *Magnesians*

NH
Pliny, *Natural History*

Od.
Horace, *Odes*

Onom.
Eusebius, *Onomasticon de Locis Hebraicis*

Philad.
Ignatius, *Philadelphians*

Praep. Ev.
Eusebius, *Praeparatio Evangelica*

Quaest.
Seneca, *Quaestiones Naturales*

Sat.
Juvenal, *Satires*; Persius, *Satires*

Strom.
Clement of Alexandria, *Stromateis*

Trall.
Ignatius, *Trallians*

Vesp.
Suetonius, *Vespasian* (*Lives of the Caesars*)

Vit. Mos.
Philo, *De Vita Mosis* (*Life of Moses*)

III. Biblical Books

Books of the Old Testament
Gn., Ex., Lv., Nu., Dt., Jos., Jdg., Ru., 1, 2 Sa., 1, 2 Ki., 1, 2 Ch., Ezr., Ne., Est., Jb., Ps. (Pss.), Pr., Ec., Ct., Is., Je., La., Ezk., Dn., Ho., Joel, Am., Ob., Jon., Mi., Na., Hab., Zp., Hg., Zc., Mal.

Books of the New Testament
Mt., Mk., Lk., Jn., Acts, Rom., 1, 2 Cor., Gal., Eph., Phil., Col., 1, 2 Thes., 1, 2 Tim., Tit., Phm., Heb., Jas., 1, 2 Pet., 1, 2, 3 Jn., Jude, Rev.

IV. General Abbreviations

ad loc.	*ad locum* (Lat.), at the place
Akkad.	Akkadian
Apoc.	Apocrypha(l)
Aq.	Aquila's Gk. tr. of OT, *c.* AD 140
Arab.	Arabic
Aram.	Aramaic
Assyr.	Assyrian
b.	*bar/ben* (Aram./Heb.), son of
Bab.	Babylonian
BM	British Museum
c.	*circa* (Lat.), about, approximately
ch.(chs.)	chapter(s)
cf.	*confer* (Lat.), compare
Copt.	Coptic
D	Deuteronomist
DSS	Dead Sea Scrolls
E	East, eastern; Elohist
eccl. Lat.	ecclesiastical Latin
Ecclus.	Ecclesiasticus (Apoc.)
ed. (eds.)	edited by, edition, editor(s)
Egyp.	Egyptian
Eng.	English
E.T.	English translation
et al.	*et alii* (Lat.), and others
Eth.	Ethiopic
EVV	English versions
f. (ff.)	and the following (verse(s), *etc.*)
fig.	figuratively
Ger.	German
Gk.	Greek
H	Law of Holiness
Heb.	Hebrew
ibid.	*ibidem* (Lat.), the same work
idem	*idem* (Lat.), the same author
J	Yahwist
Lat.	Latin
lit.	literally
L.L.	Late Latin
loc. cit.	*loco citato* (Lat.), in the place already quoted
LXX	Septuagint (Gk. version of OT)
Macc.	Maccabees (Apoc.)
mg.	margin
mod.	modern
MS (MSS)	manuscript(s)
MT	Massoretic text
N	North, northern
n.f.	*neue Folge* (Ger.), new series
n.s.	new series
NT	New Testament
OE	Old English
OL	Old Latin
op.cit.	*opere citato* (Lat.), in the work cited above
OT	Old Testament
P	Priestly Narrative
par.	and parallel(s)
Pent.	Pentateuch
Pesh	Peshitta
Phoen.	Phoenician
pl.	plate (illustration)
Q	*Quelle* (Ger.), source thought to be behind sayings of Jesus common to Lk. and Mk.
q.v.	*quod vide* (Lat.), which see
R.	Rabbi
Rom.	Roman
S	South, southern
Sem.	Semitic
Suppl.	supplementary volume
s.v.	*sub verbo* (Lat.), under the word
Symm.	Symmachus' Gk. tr. of OT, 2nd century AD
Syr.	Syriac
Targ.	Targum
Theod.	Theodotion's Gk. tr. of OT, 2nd century AD
TR	Textus Receptus
tr.	translated, translation
Turk.	Turkish
v. (vv.)	verse(s)
v.l.	*varia lectio* (Lat.), variant reading
vol.	volume
vss	versions
Vulg.	Vulgate
W	West, western

AARON (Heb. *'ahᵃrôn*). According to the genealogy of Ex. 6:14ff., Aaron was one of the two sons of Amram and Jochebed (the other being Moses) and third in line of descent from Levi (Levi-Kohath-Amram-Aaron); according to Ex. 7:7 he was 3 years older than Moses. Miriam, their sister, was older still, if she is Moses' unnamed 'sister' of Ex. 2:4, 7ff.

Aaron first appears in the Exodus narrative as 'Aaron the Levite' who went to meet his brother Moses on the latter's return to Egypt after the theophany at the burning bush; because of his superior eloquence he was to be Moses' spokesman to the Israelites and to Pharaoh (Ex. 4:14ff.). Throughout his career he was very much a lay figure alongside his dynamic brother; on the one occasion when he acted independently of Moses' instructions he acted wrongly (Ex. 32:1–6). In addition to being Moses' spokesman he also filled a thaumaturgic role: it was he who wielded the rod which became a serpent and swallowed up the rod-serpents of the Egyptian magicians (Ex. 7:8ff.) and which, when he stretched it out, turned the Nile into blood and then brought forth the successive plagues of frogs and gnats (Ex. 7:19; 8:5f., 16f.).

After the crossing of the Sea of Reeds Aaron was one of Moses' two supporters during the battle with the Amalekites (Ex. 17:8ff.), and ascended Mt Sinai in his company (Ex. 19:24), together with his sons, Nadab and Abihu, and seventy elders of Israel; there they had a vision of the God of Israel and shared a meal in his presence (Ex. 24:9ff.). On the next occasion, however, when Moses went up Mt Sinai attended by Joshua only (Ex. 24:12ff.), Aaron was persuaded by the people to make a visible image of the divine presence and fashioned the golden bull-calf, thus incurring Moses' severe displeasure (Ex. 32:1ff.). His formula of presentation of the bull-calf to the people, 'These are your gods, O Israel, who brought you up out of the land of Egypt!' (Ex. 32:4), provided a precedent for Jeroboam I when he installed the golden bull-calves at Bethel and Dan (1 Ki. 12:28).

In the priestly legislation of the Pentateuch Aaron is installed as high priest and his sons as priests, to minister in the wilderness tabernacle (Ex. 28:1ff.; Lv. 8:1ff.). Aaron is anointed with holy oil and is henceforth 'the anointed priest' (Lv. 4:3, *etc.*; *cf.* the oil on Aaron's beard in Ps. 133:2). He and his sons receive special vestments, but Aaron's are distinctive. The headband of his turban is inscribed 'Holy to Yahweh' (Ex. 28:36); his scapular (ephod) incorporates a breastpiece with twelve jewels (one for each tribe) and accommodation for the Urim and Thummim, the objects with which the sacred lot was cast to ascertain Yahweh's will for his people (Ex. 28:15ff.).

The outstanding day of the year for Aaron (and for each 'anointed priest' who succeeded him) was the Day of Atonement (Tishri 10), when he passed through the curtain separating the outer compartment of the sanctuary (the holy place) from the inner (the holy of holies) and presented the blood of an expiatory sacrifice in the latter for the sins of the people (Lv. 16:1ff.). On this occasion he did not wear his colourful vestments of 'glory and beauty' but a white linen robe.

Aaron's wife was Elisheba, of the tribe of Judah. Their elder sons Nadab and Abihu died in the wilderness after using 'unholy fire' for the incense-offering (Lv. 10:1ff.); from their two surviving sons, Eleazar and Ithamar, rival priestly families later traced their descent (1 Ch. 24:3).

Despite Aaron's status, Moses remained Yahweh's prophet to Israel and Israel's prevailing intercessor with Yahweh, and this excited the envy of Aaron and Miriam (Nu. 12:1ff.). Aaron himself (with Moses) attracted the envy of other Levitical families, whose leader was Korah (Nu. 16:1ff.). Their doubts about Aaron's privileges were answered by the phenomenon of *Aaron's rod.

Aaron, like Moses, was debarred from entering Canaan at the end of the wilderness wanderings; he died and was buried on Mt Hor, on the Edomite border, and his functions and vestments passed to Eleazar (Nu. 20:22ff.).

The priesthood in Israel came to be known comprehensively as 'the sons of Aaron'. The 'sons of Zadok', who served as priests in the Jerusalem Temple from its dedication under Solomon to 171 BC (apart from the hiatus of the Babylonian exile), are incorporated into the family of Aaron, among the descendants of Eleazar, in the genealogy of 1 Ch. 6:1ff. 10 years after the abolition of the Zadokite priesthood Alcimus, appointed high priest by the Seleucid authorities, was recognized by the Hasidaeans as 'a priest of the line of Aaron' (1 Macc. 7:12ff.), his genealogy being reckoned perhaps through Ithamar. Ben Sira pronounces Aaron's encomium in Ecclus. 45:6ff. The men of Qumran formed a community of 'Israel and Aaron', *i.e.* of Jewish laymen and priests (CD 1:7), the priests constituting an 'Aaronic holy of holies' (1QS 8:5f., 8f.), and looked forward to the coming of an Aaronic (priestly) Messiah alongside the (lay) 'Messiah of Israel' (1QS 9:11; CD 12:23f.; 20:1).

In NT Aaron is named as the ancestor of Elizabeth, mother of John the Baptist (Lk. 1:5), and receives incidental mention in Stephen's retrospect of the history of Israel (Acts 7:40). The writer to the Hebrews contrasts Aaron's circumscribed and hereditary priesthood with the perfect and perpetual ministry of Jesus in the heavenly sanctuary (Heb. 5:4; 7:11, *etc.*).

BIBLIOGRAPHY. R. de Vaux, *Ancient Israel*², 1965, pp. 345–401.

F.F.B.

AARON'S ROD. The rebellion of Korah and his associates (Nu. 16:1ff.) made it clear that the sacral status of the tribe of Levi, and the

Almond tree (Prunus dulcis) *in blossom. Aaron's rod was probably a cutting from such a tree.* (FNH)

The clear waters of the river Barada (ancient Abana) flowing through Damascus, claimed by Naaman to be 'better than all the waters of Israel'. (ARM)

AB
See Calendar, Part 1.

priestly status of Aaron and his descendants within that tribe, should be publicly established. Accordingly, the leader of each of the tribes had his name written on the rod or sceptre (*maṭṭeh*) belonging to his tribe—Aaron's name being written on that of the tribe of Levi—and the twelve rods were placed 'in the tent of meeting before the testimony' (*i.e.* the tables of the law contained in the ark). Next morning the rod bearing Aaron's name was found to have put forth buds, blossoms and ripe almonds—a token that he was God's chosen priest. His rod was then put back 'before the testimony' as a warning against further rebellion (Nu. 17:1–11). According to Heb. 9:4 it was kept with the 'tables of the covenant' inside the ark. It was apparently the same rod that was used to strike the rock in Kadesh (Nu. 20:7–11); *cf.* the 'rod of God' (Ex. 4:20; 17:9). F.F.B.

ABADDON. The satanic angel of the bottomless pit (Rev. 9:11) whose Greek name is given as Apollyon, 'destroyer'. In Hebrew *'ăḇaddôn* means '(place of) destruction', and in the OT it is used as a synonym of *death and Sheol. (*HELL.) J.D.D.

ABANA. One of two Syrian rivers mentioned by the leprous Naaman in 2 Ki. 5:12. Named Chrysorrhoas ('golden river') by the Greeks, it is probably identical with the modern Barada, which rises in the Anti-Lebanon mountains 29 km NW of Damascus, and then, after flowing through the city, enters a marshy lake, Bahret-el-Kibliyeh, some 29 km to the E. The fertile gardens and orchards which it waters may explain Naaman's boast. J.D.D.

ABARIM. A name for the mountains which rise from the E shore of the Dead Sea, where the edge of the *Moabite plateau is broken up by a succession of E–W wadis: literally it means 'the regions beyond', *i.e.* beyond the Dead Sea from the point of view of Judah. At the N end of the range stands Mt *Nebo, from which Moses could look across over the land of Canaan (Nu. 27:12; Dt. 32:49). According to the itinerary in Nu. 33 the Israelites' last encampment before they reached the Jordan valley was in these mountains (vv. 47–48). *Iye-abarim (vv. 44–45; *cf.* Nu. 21:11) must have lain near the S end of the Dead Sea. In accordance with modern translations, against AV which translates 'passages' (*cf.* Targ.), this name should also be read in Je. 22:20, where two other mountains which overlook Canaan are mentioned.

BIBLIOGRAPHY. G. Adam Smith, *The Historical Geography of the Holy Land*[25], 1931, pp. 380–381; *GTT*, pp. 261, 444. G.I.D.

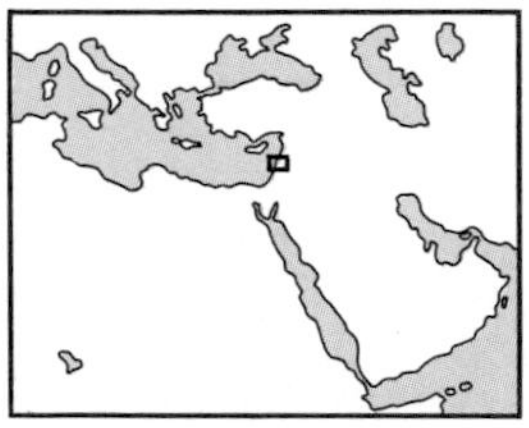

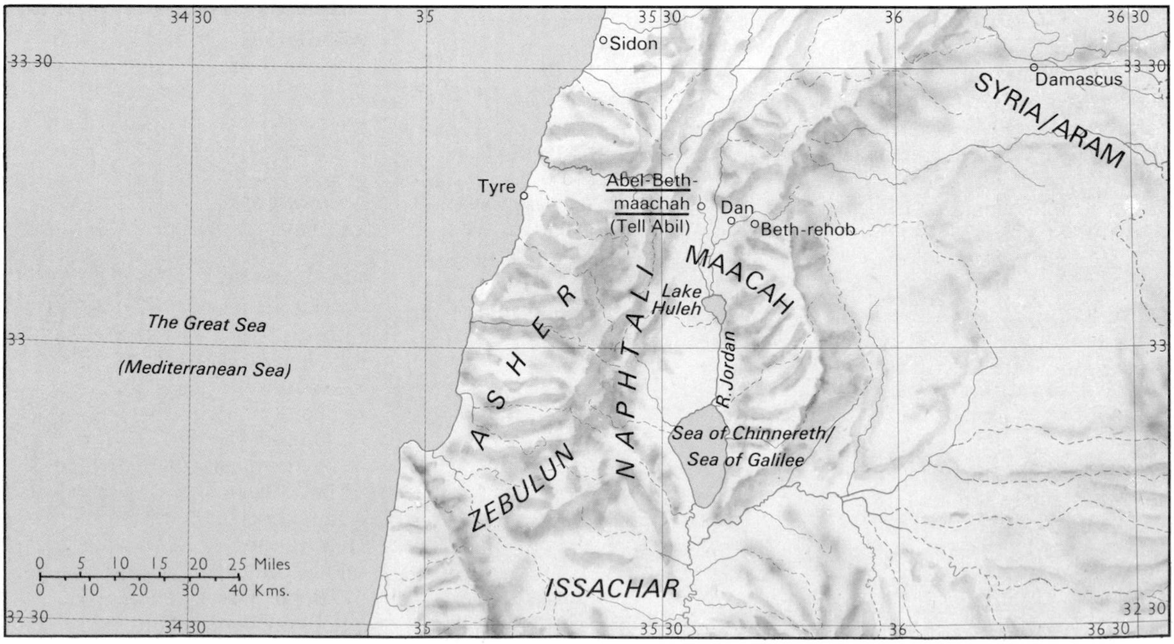

Abel of Beth-maachah, identified with Tell Abil 20 km N of Lake Huleh.

ABBA. An Aramaic word, in the emphatic state, meaning 'father'. The word passed into Hebrew, and occurs frequently in TB, where it is used by a child to its father and also as a style of address to rabbis. The term conveyed both a sense of warm intimacy and also filial respect; but in Jewish circles it has never been a form of address to the Almighty.

In the NT the word occurs 3 times, transliterated into Greek; in each instance it is a vocative, addressed to God, and the Greek equivalent is appended (Mk. 14:36; Rom. 8:15; Gal. 4:6). It appears that the double phrase was common in the Greek-speaking church, where its use may well have been liturgical. (The Lord's Prayer in its Aramaic form probably began with *'abba.*)

It appears that it was Jesus who first applied the term to God, and gave authority to his disciples to do so. Paul sees in its use a symbol of the Christian's adoption as a son of God and his possession of the Spirit.

BIBLIOGRAPHY. J. Jeremias, *The Central Message of the NT*, 1965, pp. 9–30; *idem*, *Abba*, 1966, pp. 1–67; *TDNT* 1, pp. 5ff.; 5, p. 1006; *NIDNTT* 1, pp. 614ff. D.F.P.

ABDON (Heb. *'aḇdôn*). **1.** A levitical town in Asher (Jos. 21:30, spelt *Ebron* in 19:28); Kh. 'Abdeh (Avdon), 6 km inland from *Achzib, commanding a way into the hills. **2.** Last of the minor judges; from *Pirathon (Jdg. 12:13ff.). **3.** Head of a father's house in Benjamin (1 Ch. 8:23). **4.** A Benjaminite ancestor of Saul (1 Ch. 8:30; 9:36). **5.** A member of Josiah's court (2 Ch. 34:20). J.P.U.L.

ABEDNEGO. The name given to Azariah, companion of Daniel in exile (Dn. 1:7). Made an official of a Babylonian province until deposed on refusing to bow to an image (Dn. 3:13), but restored after escaping the furnace (3:30). He is mentioned in 1 Macc. 2:59 and, by implication, in Heb. 11:33–34. The name may be an Aramaic (Chaldean?) equivalent of a Babylonian one meaning 'servant of the shining one', perhaps making word-play on the name of the Babylonian god Nabû (*NEBO). D.J.W.

ABEL. The second son of Adam and Eve, and the brother (perhaps the twin, Gn. 4:1–2) of *Cain. The name is sometimes connected with Akkadian *aplu*, Sumerian *ibila*, 'son', or Akkadian *ibilu*, 'camel', but these remain conjectures. Abel was a righteous (*dikaios*, Mt. 23:35) man and when he, as a shepherd (Gn. 4:2), brought an offering of the firstlings of his flock, God accepted it (Gn. 4:4; Heb. 11:4). He was subsequently murdered by Cain, leaving, so far as we know, no offspring. It is clear that to Christ he was a historical person (Mt. 23:35; Lk. 11:51).

BIBLIOGRAPHY. *KB*, p. 227; and *cf.* S. Landersdorfer, *Sumerisches Sprachgut im Alten Testament*, 1916, pp. 67–68. T.C.M.

ABEL. An element of certain place-names, chiefly in Transjordan. The traditional interpretation 'meadow' is not at all certain, and Baumgartner (*KB*, p. 7) prefers 'brook, watercourse', comparing Heb. *'ûḇāl, yûḇāl, yāḇāl*. 'Abel' of *MT* of 1 Sa. 6:18 (*cf.* AV) is probably a textual error, and *'eḇen* = 'stone' should be read (*cf.* LXX and modern versions). In 2 Sa. 20:18 'Abel' stands for 'Abel (of) Beth-maacah' (vv. 14–15), and in 2 Ch. 16:4 (corrupt text?) Abel-maim seems to be the same place (*cf.* 1 Ki. 15:20). The exact locations of Abel-mizraim 'beyond (or 'beside', with NEB) the Jordan' (Gn. 50:11) and Abel-keramim (Jdg. 11:33: somewhere in Ammon) are unknown, but see Skinner and Kidner on Gn. 50:11, and *LOB*, pp. 243, 371 for possible sites. G.I.D.

ABEL-MEHOLAH. A town named in conjunction with the flight of the Midianites from Gideon (Jdg. 7:22). It became part of Solomon's fifth district (1 Ki. 4:12) and was Elisha's birthplace (1 Ki. 19:16). The site is unknown, but is usually placed in the Jordan valley S of Beth-shean. D.W.B.

ABEL OF BETH-MAACHAH (Heb. *'āḇēl bêṯ ma'ᵃḵâ*, 'meadow of the house of oppression'). The town in N Naphtali in which Joab besieged Sheba, son of Bichri (2 Sa. 20:14); captured by the Syrians under Ben-hadad (*c.* 879 BC, 1 Ki. 15:20; 2 Ch. 16:4) where it is called Abel-maim. Captured by the Assyrians under Tiglath-pileser III (*c.* 733 BC, 2 Ki. 15:29). Possibly part of the Syrian state of *Maacah. It has been identified with Tell Abil 20 km N of Lake Huleh. The use of the name Abel alone in the Egyp. Execration Texts and in 2 Sa. 20:18, as well as the use of the explicative conjunction in 2 Sa. 20:14 ('Abel, *i.e.* Beth-maacah'), shows that these are two alternative names rather than one consisting of three parts. D.W.B.

ABIATHAR (Heb. *'eḇyāṯār*, 'father of excellence'). Son of Ahimelech and with him priest at Nob, he escaped alone from the massacre of his family by Saul to join David at Keilah, bringing with him an ephod (1 Sa. 22:20–22; 23:6, 9). He helped to take the ark to Jerusalem, where he was one of David's counsellors (1 Ch. 15:11; 27:34). He was sent back to Jerusalem with his son Jonathan, when David fled, to act in the king's interests against Absalom (2 Sa. 15:35ff.; 17:15). At the close of David's reign he conspired to make Adonijah king, and was expelled from office by Solomon (1 Ki. 1–2), ending Eli's line. High priest during David's reign, he seems to have been senior to Zadok (1 Ki. 2:35; *cf.* Mk. 2:26). It is uncertain whether he had a son Ahimelech or whether the two names have been transposed in 2 Sa. 8:17; 1 Ch. 24:6. In Mk. 2:26, 'when Abiathar was high priest' is better rendered 'in the passage about Abiathar', by analogy with Mk. 12:26. A.R.M.

ABIEL (Heb. *'ᵃḇî'ēl*, 'God is my father'). **1.** Saul's grandfather (1 Sa. 9:1 and 14:51). **2.** One of David's heroes (1 Ch. 11:32), called Abi-albon (2 Sa. 23:31), *albon* being a copyist's transference from the following verse. Some codices of LXX have Abiel here. R.A.H.G.

ABIEZER (Heb. *'ᵃḇî'ezer*, 'my father is help'). **1.** A clan of Manasseh (Jos. 17:2) of which Gideon was a member (Jdg. 6:11). In Gideon's time the clan was centred on Ophrah (Jdg. 6:11, 24), probably to be identified with al-Ṭayibeh N of Beth-shean. A district of Abiezer is mentioned in the Samaria Ostraca (nos. 13, 28) from *c.* 800 BC and is located SW of Shechem (see *LOB*, pp. 315–327). Iezer (Nu. 26:30) is a contraction.

ABEL-SHITTIM
See Shittim, Part 3.

ABI-ALBON
See Abiel, Part 1.

2. One of the thirty mighty men of David (2 Sa. 23:27; 1 Ch. 11:28) and a native of Anathoth, 4 km N of Jerusalem. He commanded the ninth division of David's militia in the ninth month (1 Ch. 27:12). R.P.G.

ABIGAIL (Heb. *'ᵃḇîḡayil*, 'my father is joy'(?)).

1. The wife of Nabal the Carmelite or Calebite, a wealthy boor who lived in Maon, and a contrast to her husband. She realized that his veiled insult in his refusal to give gifts to David's men, at the time of sheep-shearing, endangered the whole household, and so, on her own responsibility, she took gifts of loaves, wine, sheep, corn, raisins and figs, and waylaid David as he was planning his attack, thus preventing bloodshed. Her wisdom, beauty and dignity impressed him and he blessed God. When she told Nabal of her action he appreciated the narrowness of their escape, and from fright fell into an apoplectic fit and died—at the hand of God. David then married her and thus secured a new social position and a rich estate. With Ahinoam, the Jezreelite, she shared David's life at Gath. They were captured by the Amalekites near Ziklag and rescued (1 Sa. 30:18). She was the mother of Chileab (2 Sa. 3:3), or Daniel (1 Ch. 3:1), David's second son.

2. The wife of Ithra (2 Sa. 17:25) or Jether (1 Ch. 2:17; 1 Ki. 2:5) the Ishmaelite—terms easily confused in Hebrew—and mother of Amasa. She was a daughter of Nahash (2 Sa. 17:25) or Jesse (1 Ch. 2:13–16). Modern critics dismiss *Nahash as a scribal error. M.B.

ABIHAIL (Heb. *'ᵃḇîḥayil*, 'my father is might'). Man's and woman's name. **1.** A Levite, father of Zuriel (Nu. 3:35). **2.** The wife of Abishur (1 Ch. 2:29). **3.** A Gadite living in Bashan (1 Ch. 5:14). **4.** The mother of Rehoboam's wife Mahalath, and daughter of Eliab, David's eldest brother (2 Ch. 11:18). **5.** Father of Esther and uncle of Mordecai (Est. 2:15; 9:29). R.A.H.G.

ABIHU (Heb. *'ᵃḇîhû'*, 'my father is he' [*sc.* Yahweh]). Son of Aaron, a priest. He saw God in his glory (Ex. 24:1, 9) yet acted independently of the requirements of the ritual law and was killed by holy fire (Lv. 10:1–8). A.R.M.

ABIJAH (Heb. *'ᵃḇîyâ*, 'my father is Yahweh', or 'Yahweh is father'). A name borne by several men and women in the OT. Chief among them are the second son of Samuel (1 Sa. 8:2; 1 Ch. 6:28), a descendant of Eleazar who gave his name to the eighth of the twenty-four courses of priests (1 Ch. 24:10; *cf.* Lk. 1:5), the son of Jeroboam I (1 Ki. 14:1–18), and the son and successor of Rehoboam king of Judah (1 Ch. 3:10; 2 Ch. 11:20; 13:1). The name of the latter appears as Abijam (*'ᵃḇîyām*, 'father of sea', or 'father of west') in 1 Ki. 14:31; 15:1, 7–8. Several Heb. MSS, however, read Abijah here and this reading is supported by the LXX *Abiou.*

Abijah reigned 3 years over Judah (1 Ki. 15:2; 2 Ch. 13:2). The accounts of his reign in Kings and Chronicles stand in marked yet reconcilable contrast to each other. In the former he is censured for his adherence to the corrupt religious policy of his father (1 Ki. 15:3). The account in Chronicles (2 Ch. 13) is almost wholly concerned with a decisive victory with Yahweh's help over the numerically stronger army of Jeroboam I. Abijah's oration before the battle condemns the apostasy of the N kingdom and affirms the divine sanction attaching to the Davidic dynasty and the worship offered at the Temple at Jerusalem. J.C.J.W.

ABILENE. A region of Anti-Lebanon, attached to the city of Abila (*cf.* Heb. *'āḇēl*, 'meadow'), on the bank of the Abana (mod. Barada), some 29 km NW of Damascus (its ruins still stand round the village of Es-Suk). Abilene belonged to the Ituraean kingdom of Ptolemy Mennaeus (*c.* 85–40 BC) and his son Lysanias I (40–36 BC); it was later detached to form the tetrarchy of a younger *Lysanias, mentioned in Luke 3:1. In AD 37 it was given by the emperor Gaius to Herod Agrippa I as part of his kingdom, and in 53 by Claudius to Herod Agrippa II. *Cf.* Jos., *BJ* 2. 215, 247; *Ant.* 18. 237; 19. 275; 20. 138.

BIBLIOGRAPHY. *HJP*, 1, 1973, pp. 561–573. F.F.B.

ABIMELECH (Heb. *'ᵃḇîmeleḵ*, 'the (divine) king is my father').

1. Philistine kings of Gerar bearing this name figure in episodes involving Abraham (Gn. 20:1–18) and Isaac (Gn. 26:1–33). The similarities between the accounts have led many to suppose that they are doublets, but Abimelech may have been a cognomen of Philistine kings (*cf.* Egyptian 'Pharaoh'); there are also significant differences in the stories (and note the relevance of Gn. 20:13 for both Abraham and Isaac). Nor need the reference to the presence of Philistines in Canaan in patriarchal days be anachronistic, for 'Philistine' may mean that the Gerarites were an advance party of the Sea Peoples who later settled in Palestine; of these the Philistines were to become the dominant element. In the superscription to Ps. 34 the name Abimelech is given to Achish king of Gath.

2. A son of Gideon by a Shechemite concubine (Jdg. 8:31). With the aid of his mother's family he murdered all seventy of his brothers, with the exception of Jotham. Although he proclaimed himself 'king'—a title which his father had repudiated (Jdg. 8:23)—his territory cannot have extended beyond W Manasseh. After 3 years the Shechemites turned against their king and sided with Gaal. Abimelech responded vigorously and cruelly; he later died somewhat ingloriously while besieging Thebez. For the archaeological background to Jdg. 9, see G. E. Wright, *Shechem*, 1965, pp. 123–128.

3. A priest, the son of Abiathar (1 Ch. 18:16) according to *MT*, but perhaps a scribal error for A*h*imelech (so RSV; *cf.* 2 Sa. 8:17). R.P.G.

ABIRAM (Heb. *'ᵃḇîrām*, 'my father is exalted'). **1.** A son of Eliab, a Reubenite, who with his brother, *Dathan, and *Korah, a Levite, and others instigated a rebellion against Moses (Nu. 16). **2.** The eldest son of *Hiel of Bethel whose life was lost during the rebuilding of the fortress of Jericho *c.* 870 BC (1 Ki. 16:34; *cf.* Jos. 6:26). D.W.B.

ABISHAG (Heb. *'ᵃḇîšaḡ*; possibly, 'father has wandered'). A beautiful *Shunammite girl brought to David to nurse him in his old age. After he died, Adonijah, his eldest son, wished to marry her, but Solomon, seeing this as an attempt to gain the throne, since apparently

a king's harem were inherited by his successor (*cf.* R. de Vaux, *Ancient Israel*, 1961, p. 116), had his brother killed (1 Ki. 2:13–25).
D.W.B.

ABISHAI (Heb. *ᵃḇîšay*, 'father of gift' or 'my father is Jesse'). Son of Zeruiah and brother of Joab and Asahel (2 Sa. 2:18). 2 Sa. 23:18; 1 Ch. 11:20–21 show him to be chief of 'the three', which must mean (as the Vulgate translates) 'the second group of three', next in order to 'the three' of 2 Sa. 23:8–12. However, two Hebrew MSS and the Syriac of 2 Sa. 23:18–19 and 1 Ch. 11:20 make him the chief of 'the thirty'. He had an eventful career as a high officer in David's army.
G.W.G.

ABNER (Heb. *'aḇnēr*, but *ᵃḇînēr* in 1 Sa. 14:50). Saul's cousin and the commander-in-chief of his army (1 Sa. 14:50); one of the very few state officials mentioned in connection with Saul's reign. On Saul's death Abner secured for his remaining son Eshbaal (Ishbosheth) the allegiance of all but the Judahites (2 Sa. 2:8–10), installing him in a new capital (Mahanaim) on the E side of the Jordan. In the ensuing struggle between the house of Saul and the house of David (*cf.* 2 Sa. 3:1) Abner loyally supported his protégé until the latter insinuated that, by taking Saul's concubine, Abner was himself staking a claim to the throne. He now began to make overtures to David, promising to unite all Israel behind their rightful king. But Joab did not trust Abner and, partly to avenge the death of his brother Asahel (2 Sa. 2:18–23), murdered him in the gate of Hebron (2 Sa. 3:27).
R.P.G.

ABOMINATION. Four Hebrew words are translated thus.
1. *piggûl* is used of sacrificial flesh which has been left too long (Lv. 7:18, *etc.*). **2.** *šiqqûṣ* refers to idols ('Milcom the abomination of the Ammonites', 1 Ki. 11:5), and to customs derived from idolatry (Je. 16:18). **3.** The related word *šeqeṣ* is used in much the same way, a notable extension of meaning being its application to food prohibited for Israelites as being 'unclean' (Lv. 11:10f.). **4.** *tô'ēḇâ* is the most important word of the group. This may denote that which offends anyone's religious susceptibilities: 'every shepherd is an abomination to the Egyptians' (Gn. 46:34; so with eating with foreigners, Gn. 43:32). Or it may be used of idols (in 2 Ki. 23:13 *šiqqûṣ* is used of Ashtoreth and Chemosh and *tô'ēḇâ* of Milcom). It denotes practices derived from idolatry, as when Ahaz 'burned his son as an offering, according to the abominable practices of the nations whom the Lord drove out' (2 Ki. 16:3), and all magic and divination (Dt. 18:9–14). But the word is not confined to heathen customs. Sacrifice offered to Yahweh in the wrong spirit is 'abomination' (Pr. 15:8; Is. 1:13). So is sexual sin (Lv. 18:22). And the word attains a strongly ethical connotation when such things as 'lying lips' and 'diverse weights' are said to be an abomination to the Lord (Pr. 12:22; 20:23, *cf.* also 6:16ff., *etc.*).
L.M.

ABRAHAM. A descendant of Shem and son of Terah; husband of Sarah and, as father of Isaac, ancestor of the Hebrew nation and, through Ishmael, of other Semites (Gn. 17:5; 25:10–18). His life (Gn. 11:26–25:10; summarized in Acts 7:2–8) is taken as an example of outstanding faith in God (Heb. 11:8–12) by Jew, Christian and Muslim.

I. The name

The etymology of the name Abram (Heb. *'aḇrām*; used Gn. 11:26–17:4 and rarely elsewhere, *e.g.* 1 Ch. 1:27; Ne. 9:7) is uncertain. It probably means 'the father is exalted' and is a typical specific early W Semitic personal name form of Ab(i)ram. After the covenant of Gn. 17:5 his name is changed to Abraham (*'aḇrāhām*) and explained as 'father of a multitude' of nations. Both these name forms occur in cuneiform and Egyptian texts from the 19th century BC onwards, but not as identical persons. The latter form, possibly as popular etymology, is generally considered a dialectical variant of Abram, though a distinct new name is implied (which may incorporate an early form of Arabic *rhm* = 'multitude').

II. His career

Abraham was born in * Ur and moved with his wife Sarai, his father, brothers Nahor and Harran, and nephew Lot to Harran (Gn. 11:26–32). At the age of 75, on his father's death, Abraham moved on to Palestine (Canaan) near Bethel, to Mamre near Hebron, and to Beersheba. At each place he set up an altar and tent-shrine.

His relations with foreigners while staying near Shechem, in Egypt, Gerar and Machpelah, portray him as a respected leader of a group with whom they dealt as with an equal. He acted as acknowledged leader of a coalition which rescued his nephew Lot who had been taken from Sodom by a group of 'kings' (Gn. 14). Stress is laid on his life, not so much as a 'pilgrim', but as a 'resident-alien' (*gēr*) without a capital city. He was a wealthy man with servants (14:14) and possessions (13:2), living amicably among Canaanites (12:6), Perizzites (13:7), Philistines (21:34) and Egyptians, and negotiating with Hittites (23).

III. * Covenants

In accordance with the form of early treaty-covenants, Abraham is granted a covenant-treaty by the 'Great King' Yahweh (15:17–21) and entered into parity-treaties with contemporary powers.

(i) The land

By covenant Yahweh promised Abraham and his successors the land from the river Euphrates and SW for ever. Abraham's faith was shown both by taking steps to appropriate this divine land-grant from Beersheba (21:33) to Dan (14:14) by symbolic acts, or by taking it over as 'leader' of its multiracial inhabitants by virtue of defeating others who had once controlled it. Yet he did not set up any capital and had to purchase a place to bury his wife (Gn. 23).

(ii) The family

The same divine covenant promised and reaffirmed to him a family and nations as successors (13:16). Being childless, he first made his major-domo Eliezer of Damascus his heir (15:2). He treated his nephew like an heir, giving him a preferential share in his 'promised' land until Lot chose to move outside to Sodom (13:8–13). Then, aged 86, he had a son, Ishmael, by an Egyptian concubine, Hagar, given him by his wife. They were later expelled. Then, when Abraham was 99, the promise of family, nation and law was repeated, and Yahweh gave him his change of name and the covenant-sign of male circumcision (17). Again the covenant-promise was

ABISHALOM
See Absalom, Part 1.

ABOMINATION OF DESOLATION
See Desolating sacrilege, Part 1.

Opposite page: Genealogical table of Abraham and his family.

confirmed by another theophany at Mamre, despite Sarah's disbelief (18:1–19). A year later Isaac was born.

The great test of Abraham's faith came when Yahweh ordered him to sacrifice Isaac at Moriah. He obeyed, his hand being stayed at the moment of slaughter when a ram was provided as a substitute (22:1–14). Thereupon the covenant between Yahweh and Abraham was reaffirmed (vv. 15–20). Sarah died, aged 127, and was buried in a cave at Machpelah, the freehold of which Abraham purchased from Ephron (23). As his own death approached Abraham made Eliezer swear to obtain a wife for Isaac from his kinsfolk near Harran. Abraham's great-niece Rebekah thus became the bride of Isaac (24).

Abraham himself in his advanced age married Keturah, whose sons became the ancestors of the tribes of Dedan and Midian. After giving 'all he had' to Isaac and gifts to his other sons Abraham died, aged 175, and was buried at * Machpelah (25:1–10).

Abraham was acknowledged as one able to 'charge his children and his household after him to keep the way of the Lord by doing righteousness and justice' (18:19). He was hospitable, entertaining strangers with respect (18:2–8; 21:8).

IV. His character

Abraham openly declared his faith in God as almighty (Gn. 17:1), eternal (21:33), the most high (14:22), possessor (Lord) of heaven and earth (14:22; 24:3), and the righteous judge of nations (15:14) and of all mankind (18:25). To him Yahweh was just (18:25), wise (20:6), righteous (18:19), good (19:19) and merciful (20:6). He accepted the judgment of God upon sin (18:19; 20:11) yet interceded with him for erring Ishmael (17:20) and Lot (18:27–33). Abraham communed with God in close fellowship (18:33; 24:40; 48:15), and was granted special revelation from him in visions (15:1) and visits in human (18:1) or angelic ('messenger') form (22:11, 15). Abraham worshipped Yahweh, calling upon him by that name (13:4) and building an altar for this purpose (12:8; 13:4, 18). His clear monotheism is to be contrasted with the polytheism of his ancestors (Jos. 24:2).

Abraham's faith is perhaps best seen in his ready obedience whenever called by God. By faith he left Ur in * Mesopotamia (11:31; 15:7), an act attested by Stephen (Acts 7:2–4). Similarly he was guided to leave Harran (Gn. 12:1, 4).

He lived for 100 years in the land of Canaan, which had been promised him (Gn. 13:12; 15:18), but this was only a partial fulfilment, since he occupied just a small plot of land at Machpelah and had rights near Beersheba. The supreme trial of his faith came when he was asked to sacrifice Isaac his son, who was, humanly speaking, the only means whereby the divine promises could be fulfilled. His faith rested in a belief in God's ability, if need be, to raise his son from the dead (Gn. 22:12, 18; Heb. 11:19).

His role has been compared with a governor or ruler who, like the later kings, exercised justice under the 'Governor of all the world who will do right' (18:25). Like them he was responsible for law and order, for rescuing abducted persons, defeating the Great King's enemies, ensuring the freedom of local worship (14:20). He was able, and brave enough, to wage war against superior numbers (14:5), and was generous without seeking personal gain (13:9; 14:23).

Incidents which have been considered grave weaknesses in Abraham's character are the apparent deception of the king of Egypt and of Abimelech of Gerar by passing Sarah off as his sister to save his own life (Gn. 12:11–13; 20:2–11). Sarah was Abraham's half-sister (20:12; *cf.* 11:29). Supposed parallels with Hurrian wife-sister marriage are to be rejected. Sarah was considered faithful both to her husband and his God (Is. 51:2; Heb. 11:11; 1 Pet. 3:6), so that, while this might be an example of the way the Scriptures portray the fortunes of even the greatest heroes (*cf.* * David), it may well be questioned whether this incident is as yet fully understood.

Abraham's statement to Isaac (Gn. 22:8) has been considered deceptive in view of the task ahead. It can, however, be taken as a supreme example of faith ('*we* will come again', 22:5; *cf.* Heb. 11:17–19). This incident is moreover an early condemnation of child-sacrifice which was itself rare in the ancient Near East.

V. Theological significance

Israel was considered 'the seed of Abraham', and Yahweh's action in raising much people from one man was held to be a particularly significant fulfilment of his word (Is. 51:2; Ezk. 33:24). 'The God of Abraham' designated Yahweh throughout Scripture and was the name whereby he revealed himself to Moses (Ex. 3:15). Abraham's monotheism amid idolatry (Jos. 24:2), the way God appeared to him (Ex. 6:3), chose (Ne. 9:7), redeemed (Is. 29:22) and blessed him (Mi. 7:20), and Abraham's faith were a constant theme of exhortation and discussion (1 Macc. 2:52).

In NT times also Abraham was revered as the ancestor of Israel (Acts 13:26), of the levitical priesthood (Heb. 7:5), and of the Messiah himself (Mt. 1:1). Though the popular Jewish superstition that racial descent from Abraham brought divine blessing with it is refuted by the Baptist (Mt. 3:9) and Paul (Rom. 9:7), the unity of the Hebrews as his descendants was a picture of the unity of believers in Christ (Gal. 3:16, 29). The oath (Lk. 1:73), covenant (Acts 3:13), promise (Rom. 4:13) and blessing (Gal. 3:14) granted Abraham by God's free choice are inherited by his children by faith. Abraham's faith was a type of that which leads to justification (Rom. 4:3–12), a pre-Christ proclamation of the universal gospel (Gal. 3:8). His obedience by faith to his call from Ur to the nomadic life of a 'stranger and pilgrim' and his offering of Isaac are listed as outstanding examples of faith in action (Heb. 11:8–19; Jas. 2:21).

As a great prophet and recipient of the divine covenant Abraham plays a unique role in both Jewish (Ecclus. 44:19–21; *Bereshith Rabba*; *Pirqe Aboth* 5. 4; Jos., *Ant.* 1. 7–8) and Muslim traditions (188 refs. in Qur'an).

VI. Archaeological background

The social institutions, customs, personal and place names, and general literary and historical situations compare well with other evidence of the early 2nd millennium BC. However, though many scholars view the patriarchal narrative as substantially historical and datable, from the known occupation of named sites, to the Middle Bronze Age, *c.* 20th–19th (Albright, de Vaux), or later, 19th–17th (Rowley) or 15th–14th century BC (Gordon), a number support the theory that these narratives stem from the time of David (Emerton,

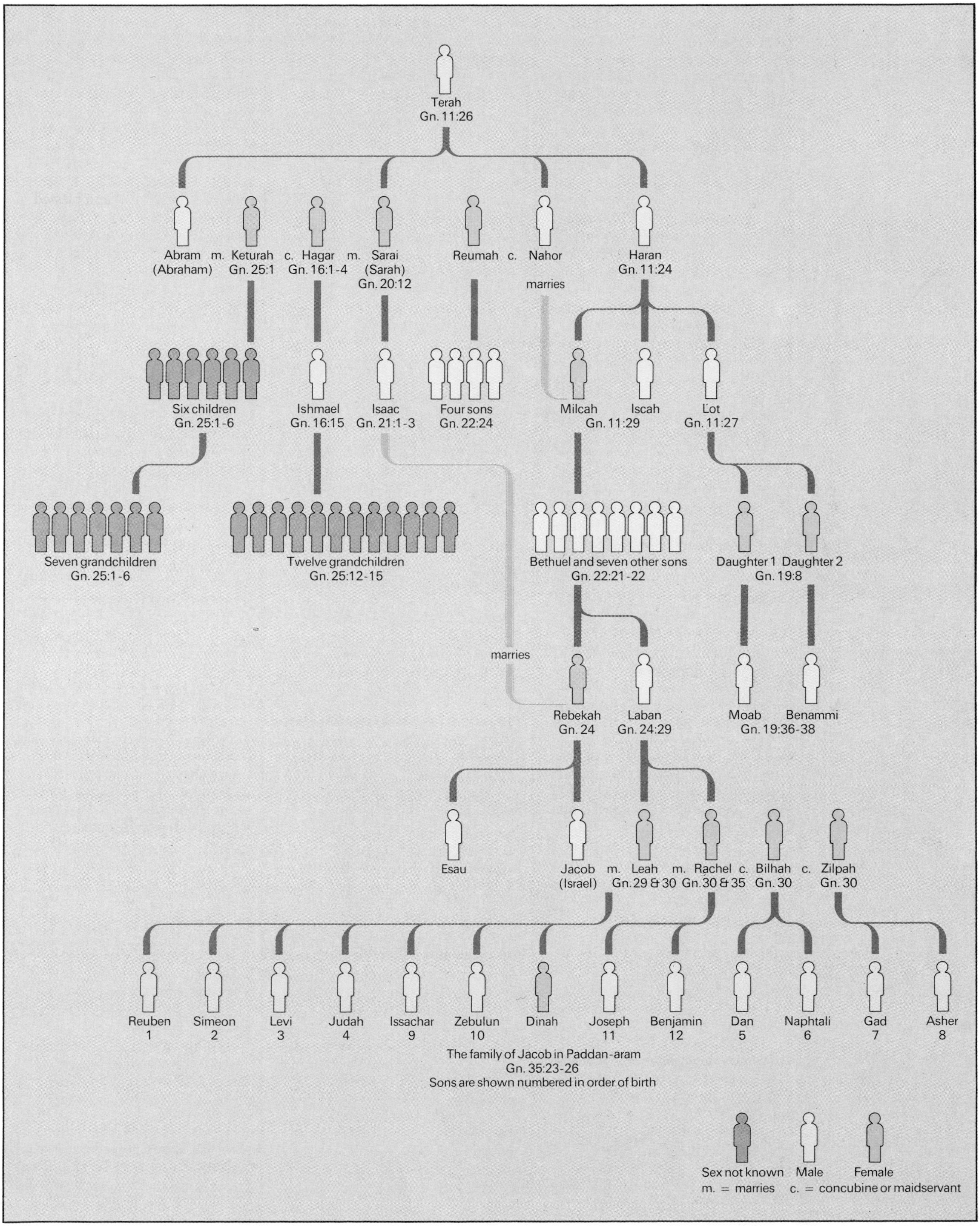
Terah
Gn. 11:26
Abram m. Keturah c. Hagar m. Sarai
(Abraham) Gn. 25:1 Gn. 16:1-4 (Sarah)
Gn. 20:12
Reumah c. Nahor
marries
Haran
Gn. 11:24
Six children
Gn. 25:1-6
Ishmael
Gn. 16:15
Isaac
Gn. 21:1-3
Four sons
Gn. 22:24
Milcah Iscah
Gn. 11:29
Lot
Gn. 11:27
Seven grandchildren
Gn. 25:1-6
Twelve grandchildren
Gn. 25:12-15
Bethuel and seven other sons
Gn. 22:21-22
Daughter 1 Daughter 2
Gn. 19:8
marries
Rebekah
Gn. 24
Laban
Gn. 24:29
Moab Benammi
Gn. 19:36-38
Esau
Jacob m. Leah m. Rachel c. Bilhah c. Zilpah
(Israel) Gn. 29 & 30 Gn. 30 & 35 Gn. 30 Gn. 30
Reuben 1
Simeon 2
Levi 3
Judah 4
Issachar 9
Zebulun 10
Dinah
Joseph 11
Benjamin 12
Dan 5
Naphtali 6
Gad 7
Asher 8
The family of Jacob in Paddan-aram
Gn. 35:23-26
Sons are shown numbered in order of birth
Sex not known Male Female
m. = marries c. = concubine or maidservant

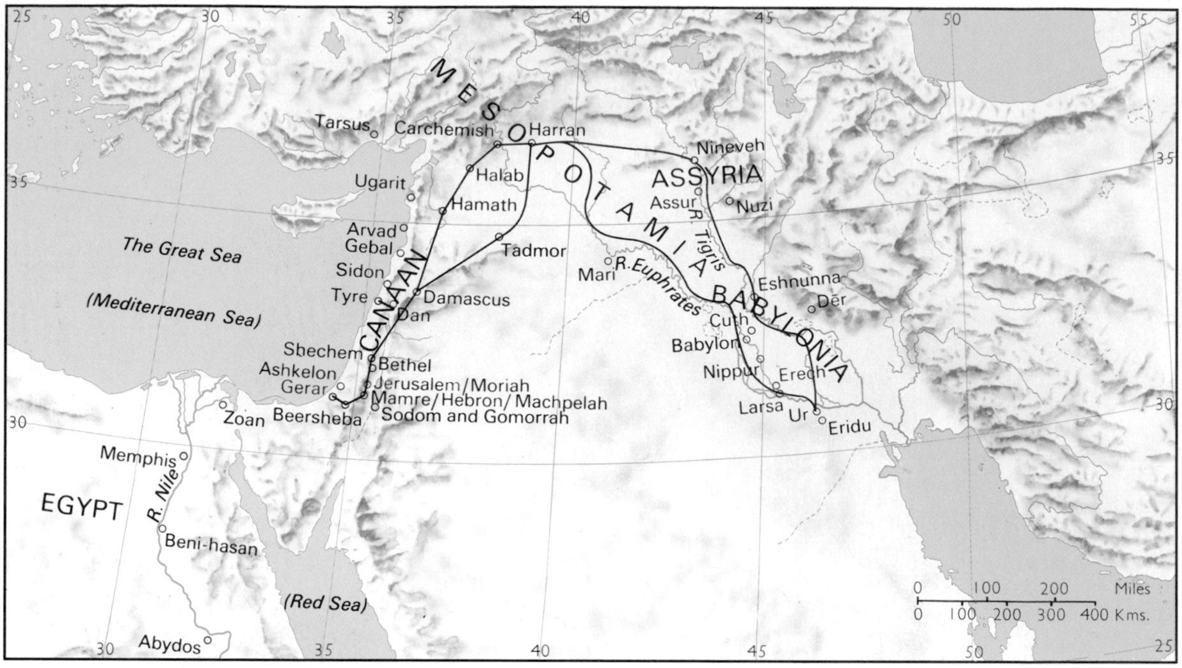

Possible routes for Abraham's journey from Ur into Canaan.

Clements), though some argue on a traditio-historical basis for a later date (Thompson, Van Seters) based on supposed anachronisms between the semi-nomadic movements, history (especially on Gn. 12) and references to Philistines, camels and certain place names (*Ur 'of the Chaldees'), all pointing to the late 1st millennium BC. For them the tradition is of later composition (Thompson, Van Seters). Most of these points can be answered individually on the basis of all available evidence (details of the *Ebla texts, *c.* 2300 BC, may provide additional data). It is to be noted that the precise details, the absence of 'saga' personification of Abraham as a tribe, and the fact that the majority of Abraham's deeds are recorded as those of an individual, are indications of early sources.

BIBLIOGRAPHY. E. A. Speiser, *Genesis*, *AB*, 1964; R. E. Clements, *Abraham and David*, 1967; D. J. Wiseman, 'Abraham' in *BS* 137, 1977, pp. 123ff., 228ff; T. L. Thompson, *Historicity of the Patriarchal Narratives*, 1974; J. A. Van Seters, *Abraham in History and Tradition*, 1975. D.J.W.

ABRAHAM'S BOSOM. A figure of speech used by Jesus in the parable of *Lazarus and Dives (Lk. 16:22–23), illustrating the 'great gulf fixed' between the bliss of paradise and the misery of Hades (*cf.* Mt. 8:11–12). The dead Lazarus is portrayed as reclining next to Abraham at the feast of the blessed, after the Jewish manner, which brought the head of one person almost into the bosom of the one who sat above him, and placed the most favoured guest in such a relation to his host (*e.g.* Jn. 13:23). To sit in Abraham's bosom, in Talmudic language, was to enter *Paradise (*cf.* 4 Macc. 13:17). Such Oriental imagery should not be regarded as evidence of Jewish belief in an interim state. J.D.D.

ABRECH. An obscure term proclaimed before Joseph as Pharaoh's chief minister (Gn. 41:43). W. Spiegelberg interpreted it as Egyp. *ib-r.k*, 'attention!', 'look out!' J. Vergote suggests *i.brk*, 'pay homage!', 'kneel!', an Egyptian imperative of a Semitic loan-word (*Joseph en Égypte*, 1959, pp. 135–141, 151). Recent discussions add nothing to these suggestions. K.A.K.

ABSALOM (Heb. *'aḇšālôm*, 'father is/of peace'). **1.** Third son of David, with a foreign mother, Maacah, daughter of Talmai, king of Geshur (2 Sa. 3:3). His personal comeliness was shared by Tamar, his sister, and was the cause of her being violated by Amnon, David's first-born son by another mother (2 Sa. 13:1–18). When Absalom learnt of this incident, he brought about the death of Amnon, thus incurring the displeasure of his father, before which he fled to Geshur (2 Sa. 13:19–39). The first part of Nathan's prophecy had come true (2 Sa. 12:10). After 3 years of exile, and a further 2 years of banishment from the court, David received his son back into favour, and was repaid by a plot against his throne (2 Sa. 15:1–15). The 'forty years' of v. 7 does not seem to square with 18:5, and the reading 'four' has been suggested. The second part of Nathan's prophecy now came true (2 Sa. 12:11a). The third part (v. 11b) was also soon fulfilled (2 Sa. 16:20–23) and there was now no turning back. There is pathos and spiritual profit in the words of David when the Levites sought to take the Ark into flight with the deposed king (2 Sa. 15:25–26). The end of Absalom is well known. With the help of Hushai (2 Sa. 15:32–37 and 17:1–16) and Joab (2 Sa. 18:1–21; see also 19:1–7) David was able to defeat him in battle. 2 Sa. 18:9–17 describes his ignominious death. The third Psalm purports to come from the period of Absalom's rebellion.

2. Rehoboam's father-in-law (2 Ch. 11:20–21; called 'Abishalom' in 1 Ki. 15:2, 10).

3. In the Apocrypha, an ambassador of Judas Maccabaeus, the father of Mattathias and Jonathan (1 Macc. 11:70; 13:11; 2 Macc. 11:17). T.H.J.

ABYSS. The Greek word *abyssos* ('bottomless [pit]', 'deep') appears 9 times in the NT. It is translated in RSV as 'abyss' (the abode of

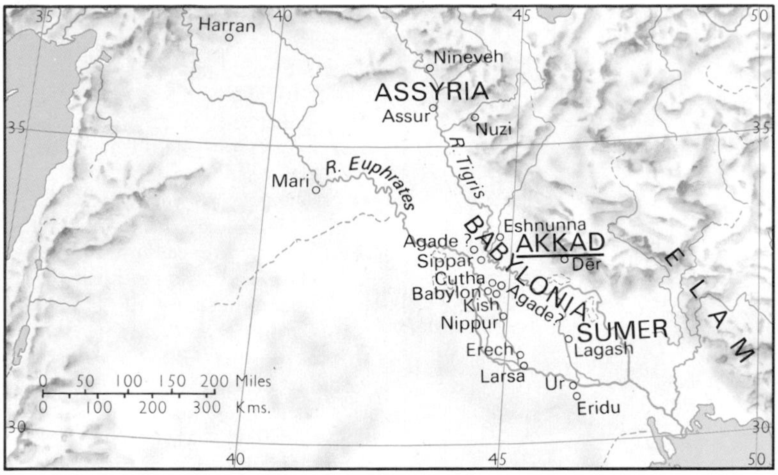

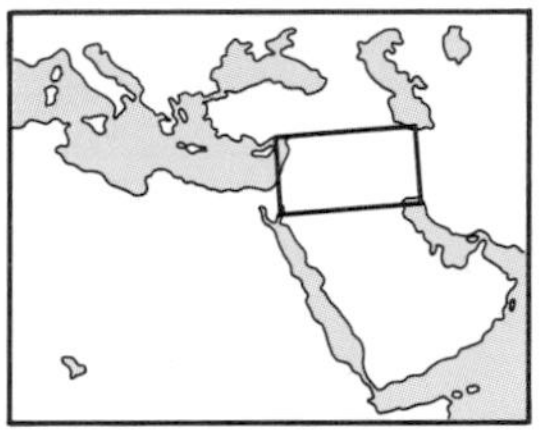

demons, Lk. 8:31; the place of the dead, Rom. 10:7) and 'bottomless pit' (the place of torment, Rev. 9:1–2, 11; 11:7; 17:8; 20:1, 3). LXX renders Heb. t^{e}*hôm*, 'deep place', as 'abyss' (Gn. 1:2, *etc.*), with reference to the primitive idea of a vast mass of water on which the world floated, or to the underworld (Ps. 71:20). (*HELL.) J.D.D.

ACCAD, AKKAD. One of the major cities, with Babylon and Erech, founded by Nimrod (Gn. 10:10). It bore the Semitic name of *Akkadu*, Sumerian *Agade*. Its precise location near Sippar or Babylon is uncertain, though some identify it with the ruins of Tell Šešubār or even Babylon itself.

Inscriptions show that an early Semitic dynasty founded by Sargon I (*c.* 2350 BC) flourished here. At this time Akkad controlled all Sumer (S Babylonia), and its armies reached Syria, Elam and S Anatolia. With the great trade and prosperity which followed the rule of Sargon and his successor Naram-Sīn the dynasty became symbolic of a 'golden age'. When Babylon later became the capital, the term 'Akkad' continued to be used to describe the whole of N Babylonia until the late Persian period in the records of the kings of *Assyria and *Babylonia.

Akkadian (Accadian) is now used as a convenient term for the Semitic Assyrian and Babylonian languages, the dialect of the famous dynasty of Agade being designated 'Old Akkadian'. D.J.W.

ACCEPTANCE. The English words 'accept', 'accepted', 'acceptable' and 'acceptance' translate a variety of Hebrew and Greek words

Bronze head from Nineveh, thought to represent Naram-Sīn of Agade. Height 36·6 cm. c. 2350 BC. (SAOB)

Top left: Akkad, the N part of Babylonia, showing two possible sites for the original city of Agade.

Sandstone stele of Naram-Sīn of Agade, from Susa, SW Persia. The victorious king stands before a stylized mountain. The horns on his headdress symbolize divine power. Height 2 m. c. 2250 BC. (MC)

Achaia: the Roman provincial name for S Greece.

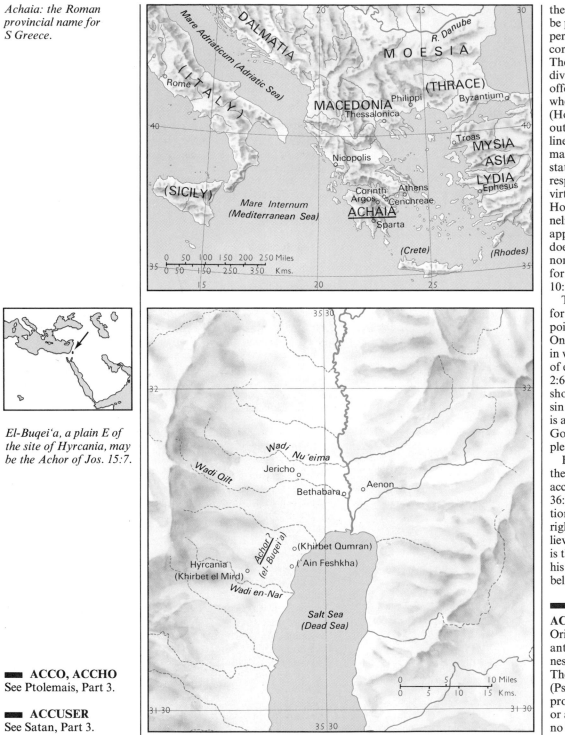

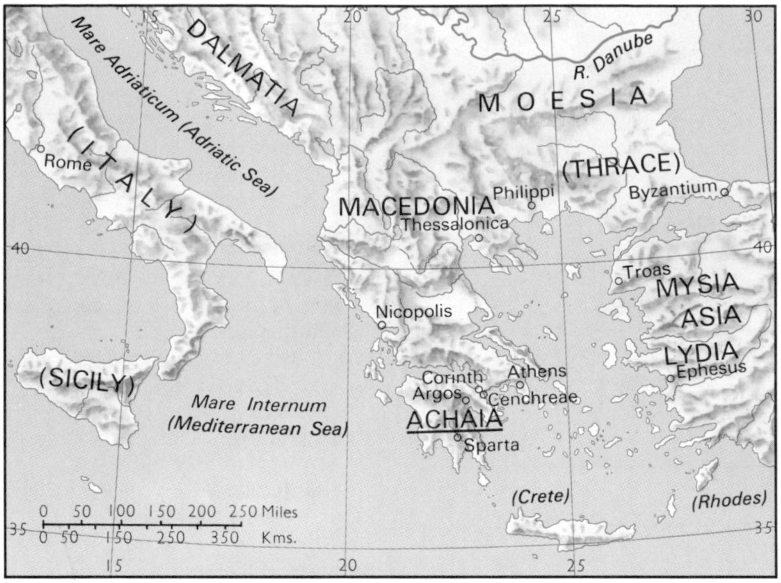

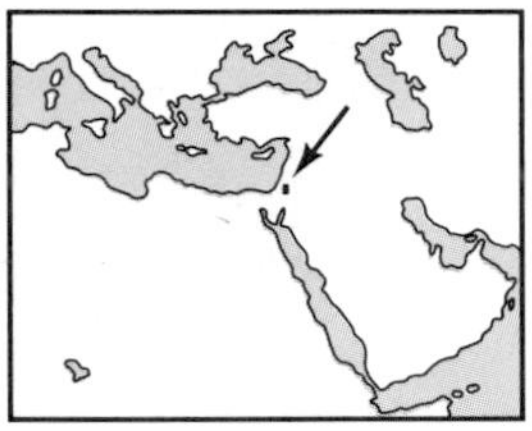

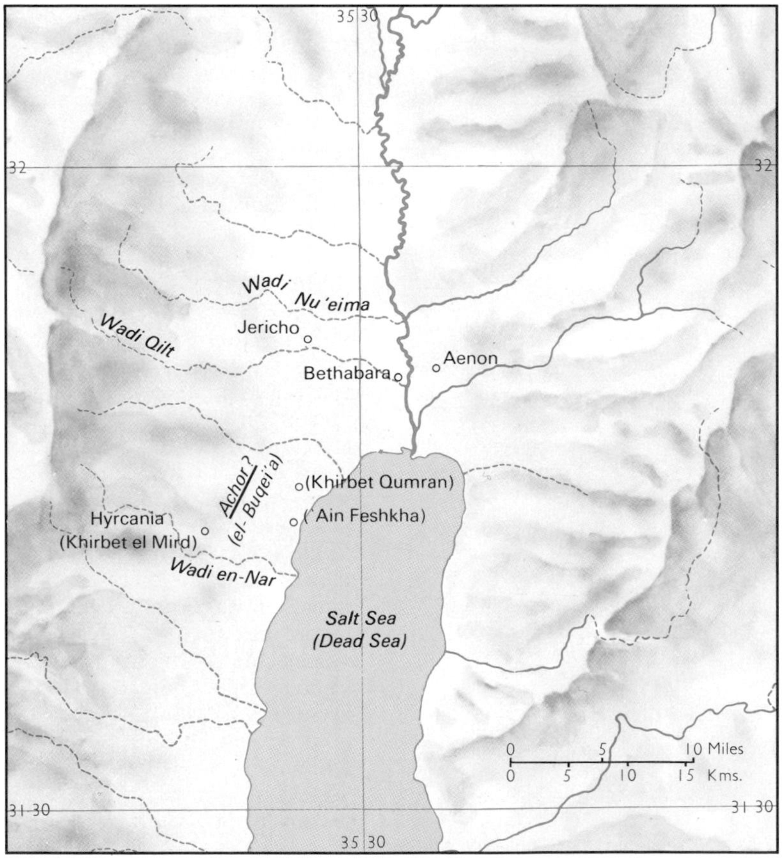

El-Buqei'a, a plain E of the site of Hyrcania, may be the Achor of Jos. 15:7.

ACCO, ACCHO
See Ptolemais, Part 3.

ACCUSER
See Satan, Part 3.

ACELDAMA
See Akeldama, Part 1.

of cognate meaning. God is normally the subject; and the object may be the worshipper's sacrifices (Ps. 119:108), his prayers (Gn. 19:21), the whole tenor of his life, and particularly his person. In contrary distinction to the pagan viewpoint, the biblical doctrine is that the prayers and sacrifices are acceptable to God because a man's person is acceptable. Thus 'the Lord had regard for Abel and his offering: but for Cain and his offering he had no regard' (Gn. 4:4–5). The acceptance of Abel's offering was a witness that Abel's person had already been accepted. Through his offerings 'he received approval as righteous, God bearing witness by accepting his gifts' (Heb. 11:4), and Cain was admonished that his offering would be accepted if his life were acceptable (Gn. 4:7).

The OT prophets inveighed against the notion, so congenial to the natural man, that God can be persuaded to accept a man's person through accepting a correctly-offered ritual worship. They constantly affirmed that the divine order was the reverse. The offerings were acceptable only when the persons were acceptable (Ho. 8:13; Mal. 1:10, 13). Throughout the Bible the teaching is underlined that God does not accept a man's person because of his social status or importance. He does not respect persons (Gal. 2:6). This is a virtue which all are to imitate. However, it was not till the Cornelius incident that the early church apprehended the truth that God does not require Jewish nationality, nor circumcision, as a prerequisite for acceptance with him (Acts 10:35).

The well-doing that God requires for acceptance must not in any point fall short of his perfections. Only those who by patience persist in well-doing may claim the reward of eternal life for their works (Rom. 2:6–7). None achieves this. All fall short of the glory of God through sin (Rom. 3:9–23). Our Lord alone is accepted. He alone has merited God's verdict: 'With thee I am well pleased.'

Ezekiel foretold that it would be the work of God to make sinners acceptable to him (Ezk. 20:40–41; 36:23–29). It is through incorporation into Christ, and the gift of his righteousness (Rom. 5:17), that believers are accepted with God. This is the work of God, who through his grace makes us 'accepted in the beloved' (Eph. 1:6, AV). D.B.K.

ACCESS. An intermediary in the Oriental court introduced suppliants and guaranteed their genuineness (*cf.* Barnabas, Acts 9:27–28). The OT portrait of God as King (Ps. 47:7) posed to NT writers the problem of the sinner's *prosagōgē* or access into his presence. He has no independent right of personal approach, and obtains introduction only through Christ (Rom. 5:2; Eph. 2:18; 3:12; 1 Pet. 3:18), whose death removes the barriers of hostility (Eph. 2:16), and enables believers to draw near with confidence to the throne of grace (Heb. 4:16). D.H.T.

ACHAIA. A small region of Greece, on the S coast of the gulf of Corinth, which twice gave its name to the whole country. In Homer the

Greeks are frequently called Achaeans. Again, in the age of the Hellenistic kings, the Achaean confederacy championed the freedom of the republics, and after its defeat by the Romans (146 BC) the name was used by them for Greece in general. The area was administered with Macedonia at first, and even after organization as a separate province (27 BC) is linked in common usage with Macedonia (Acts 19:21; Rom. 15:26; 1 Thes. 1:8). The province was in the regular senatorial allotment, and was hence governed by a proconsul (*anthypatos*, Acts 18:12), with two exceptions: from AD 15 to 44 it was under the Caesarian legate of Moesia; and from AD 67 Roman supervision was entirely suspended for several years by Nero's benevolence, and the 40 or so republics in the area enjoyed their liberty without even the appearance of permission.

The old confederacy was maintained under the Romans, with its capital at Argos, the seat of the imperial cult, but the much larger province was governed from Corinth. It is always in connection with Corinth that the name occurs in the NT, and it is uncertain whether anything more is meant (see 2 Cor. 1:1; 9:2; 11:10). We know, however, that there was a church at Cenchreae (Rom. 16:1), and there were believers at Athens (Acts 17:34). We may assume, therefore, that in referring to the household of Stephanas as the 'first converts in Achaia' (1 Cor. 16:15), Paul is applying the term to Corinth as having a primacy due to its position as the Roman capital. He is not thinking of the rest of the province.

BIBLIOGRAPHY. Pausanias 8. 16. 10–17. 4; Strabo 8; J. Keil, *CAH*, 11, pp. 556–565. E.A.J.

ACHAICUS. A Corinthian Christian (1 Cor. 16:17): on his position see *FORTUNATUS. The name suggests a slave or ex-slave of Achaia, or possibly in the service of the Mummii: it was the title of L. Mummius, creator of Roman Achaia (and destroyer of *Corinth), and was retained in his family in Paul's lifetime (*cf.* Suetonius, *Galba* 3). A.F.W.

ACHAN (Heb. *'āḵān*). A Judahite of clan Zerah, who was in the assault on Jericho and violated the sacrificial ban, stealing gold, silver and fine clothing. This was discovered when inquiry was made by lot after the failure to take Ai. Achan with his family and possessions was stoned and cremated in the Vale of *Achor (Jos. 7). Joshua, in pronouncing sentence, used the similarity of his name to the verb *'āḵar*, 'to distress'; the chronicler spells his name thus (Achar, 1 Ch. 2:7). The event is recalled in Jos. 22:20. J.P.U.L.

ACHISH. The king of Gath (called Abimelech in the title of Ps. 34) with whom David lived *incognito* when fleeing from Saul and from whom he escaped by pretending madness (1 Sa. 21:10–15). The second time David went for refuge in Gath, Achish gave him the town of *Ziklag on his border with Israel (1 Sa. 27). He appointed David as his bodyguard in a battle against Israel (1 Sa. 28:1–2), but the other Philistines would not have David fight with them (1 Sa. 29). Achish continued as king into the reign of Solomon (1 Ki. 2:39–40). D.W.B.

ACHOR (Heb. *'āḵôr*). The valley near Jericho where *Achan was executed. Jewish and Christian tradition placed it N of Jericho (Eusebius, *Onom.* 18, 84; J. T. Milik, *Discoveries in the Judaean Desert*, 1962, vol. 3, p. 262), probably in the W Nu'eima. If so, Jos. 15:7 refers to another valley, S of the Judah–Benjamin border; el-Buqei'a is likely (*GTT*, pp. 137, 139, 271; L. E. Stager, *RB* 81, 1974, pp. 94–96; Milik, Cross, *BASOR* 142, 1956, p. 17; see *SECACAH). The W Qilt has been suggested on the assumption that Jos. 7 and 15 mean the same place, but it suits neither. Is. 65:10; Ho. 2:15 are perhaps most pointed if referred to the W Nu'eima. J.P.U.L.

ACHSAH (Heb. *'aḵsâ*, 'anklet'). The daughter of Caleb who, on being married to Othniel, Caleb's nephew, as a reward for Othniel's capture of Kiriath-sepher, encouraged him to ask Caleb for extra territory and herself asked for springs of water (Jos. 15:16–17; Jdg. 1:12–15; 1 Ch. 2:49). A.E.C.

ACHSHAPH (Heb. *'aḵšāp̄*). An important Canaanite city (Jos. 11:1; 12:20), mentioned in Egyptian lists and *Papyrus Anastasi*, I (*ANET*, p. 477); near Acco, apparently E or SE. The alternatives most favoured are Tell Keisan (W. Albright, *BASOR* 83, 1941, p. 33) and Khirbet Harbaj (Tell Regev) (*LOB*, pp. 21, *etc.*). Occupied by Asher (Jos. 19:25). J.P.U.L.

ACHZIB. 1. A Canaanite harbour town assigned to Asher (Jos. 19:29) which they never occupied (Jdg. 1:31). Taken by Sennacherib in 701 BC (*ANET*, p. 287). Identified with the modern ez-Zib, 14 km N of Acco (Acre). **2.** A town of Judah (Jos. 15:44) in the Shephelah. Probably the Chezib of Gn. 38:5; conquered by Sennacherib (*cf.* Mi. 1:14); tentatively identified as the modern Tell el-Beida. D.W.B.

ACTS, BOOK OF THE. 'The Acts of the Apostles' (Gk. *praxeis apostolōn*) is the title given, since the latter years of the 2nd century AD, to the second volume of a history of Christian beginnings whose first volume we know as 'The Gospel according to Luke'.

I. Outline of contents

The book takes up the story where the Gospel (the 'first book' of Acts 1:1) ends, with the resurrection appearances of Jesus, and goes on to record his ascension, the coming of the Holy Spirit and the rise and early progress of the church of Jerusalem (1–5). Then it describes the dispersal of the Hellenistic members of that church which followed the execution of their leader Stephen, their evangelization of more distant regions as far N as Antioch, and the beginning of the Gentile mission in that city. In the course of this narrative we have also the account of Paul's conversion and Peter's evangelization of the plain of Sharon, culminating in the conversion of the first Gentile household in Caesarea. This section of Acts ends with Paul's arrival in Antioch to take part in the Gentile mission there, and Peter's departure from Jerusalem after his escape from death at the hands of Herod Agrippa I (6–12). From then on Paul's apostolic ministry is the main subject of Acts: with Barnabas he evangelizes Cyprus and S Galatia (13–14), takes part in the Council of Jerusalem (15), with Silas crosses to Europe and evangelizes Philippi, Thessalonica and Corinth (16–18), with other col-

ACHAR
See Achan, Part 1.

ACHMETHA
See Ecbatana, Part 1.

ACRE (place)
See Ptolemais, Part 3.

ACRE
See Weights and measures, Part 3.

ACTS, APOCRYPHAL
See New Testament apocrypha, Part 2.

leagues evangelizes provincial Asia from his headquarters in Ephesus (19), pays a visit to Palestine, where he is rescued from mob-violence and kept in custody for 2 years (20–26), is sent to Rome to have his case heard by the emperor at his own request, and spends 2 years there under house arrest, with complete liberty to make the gospel known to all who visit him (27–28). While the gospel was no doubt carried along all the roads which branched out from its Palestinian homeland, Acts concentrates on the road from Jerusalem to Antioch and thence to Rome.

II. Origin and purpose

The preface to the 'first book' (Lk. 1:1–4) applies equally to both parts of the work: the whole work was undertaken in order that one *Theophilus might have a consecutive and reliable account of the rise and progress of Christianity—a subject on which he already possessed a certain amount of information.

The date is not indicated precisely; Acts cannot have been written earlier than the latest event it records, Paul's spending 2 years in custody in Rome (Acts 28:30), covering probably the years 60 and 61, but how much later it was written is uncertain. If its dependence on the *Antiquities* of Josephus were established, then its date could not be earlier than AD 93, but such a dependence is improbable. We might think of a time when something had happened to stimulate special interest in Christianity among responsible members of Roman society, of whom Theophilus may be regarded as a representative. One such time was the latter part of Domitian's principate (AD 81–96), when Christianity had penetrated the imperial family. It has even been suggested that Theophilus might be a pseudonym for Domitian's cousin, Flavius Clemens. An earlier occasion may be found in the later sixties, when the moment seemed opportune to dissociate Christianity from the Jewish revolt in Palestine, or even earlier in the sixties, when the leading propagator of Christianity came to Rome as a Roman citizen to have his appeal heard by the imperial tribunal. The optimistic note on which Acts ends, with Paul proclaiming the kingdom of God in Rome without let or hindrance, might suggest a date before the outbreak of persecution in AD 64. The internal evidence for the dating of Luke is relevant here, but if it be felt that Luke, as we have it now, must be dated after AD 70, it might be considered whether the 'first book' of Acts 1:1 could not be 'Proto-Luke' (so C. S. C. Williams and others). The remitting of Paul's case to Rome would certainly make it needful for imperial officials to look more seriously into the nature of Christianity than had previously been necessary; the author of Acts may well have thought it wise to provide such people with an account of the matter.

The author, from the 2nd century onwards, has been identified (rightly, in all probability) with Luke, Paul's physician and fellow-traveller (Col. 4:14; Phm. 24; 2 Tim. 4:11). Luke was a Greek of Antioch, according to the late 2nd century anti-Marcionite prologue to his Gospel (his Antiochene origin is also implied by the 'western' reading of Acts 11:28). His presence at some of the events which he records is indicated unobtrusively by the transition from the third person to the first person plural in his narrative; the three 'we-sections' of Acts are 16:10–17; 20:5–21:18; 27:1–28:16. Apart from the periods covered by these sections, he had ample opportunity of tracing the course of events from the first, as he had access to first-hand information from people he met from time to time, not only in Antioch but also in Asia Minor and Macedonia, in Jerusalem and Caesarea, and finally in Rome. Among these informants an important place should doubtless be given to his hosts in various cities, such as Philip and his daughters in Caesarea (21:8f.) and Mnason, a foundation-member of the church in Jerusalem (21:16). He does not appear to have used Paul's Epistles as a source.

III. Historical character

The historical trustworthiness of Luke's account has been amply confirmed by archaeological discovery. While he has apologetic and theological interests, these do not detract from his detailed accuracy, although they control his selection and presentation of the facts. He sets his narrative in the framework of contemporary history; his pages are full of references to city magistrates, provincial governors, client kings and the like, and these references time after time prove to be just right for the place and time in question. With a minimum of words he conveys the true local colour of the widely differing cities mentioned in his story. And his description of Paul's voyage to Rome (27) remains to this day one of our most important documents on ancient seamanship.

IV. Apologetic emphasis

Luke is obviously concerned, in both parts of his work, to demonstrate that Christianity is not a menace to imperial law and order. He does this particularly by citing the judgments of governors, magistrates and other authorities in various parts of the empire. In the Gospel Pilate thrice pronounces Jesus not guilty of sedition (Lk. 23:4, 14, 22), and when similar charges are brought against his followers in Acts they cannot be sustained. The praetors of Philippi imprison Paul and Silas for interference with the rights of private property, but have to release them with an apology for their illegal action (16:19ff., 35ff.). The politarchs of Thessalonica, before whom Paul and his companions are accused of sedition against the emperor, are content to find citizens of that place who will guarantee the missionaries' good behaviour (17:6–9). A more significant decision is taken by Gallio, proconsul of Achaia, who dismisses the charge of propagating an illicit religion brought against Paul by the Jewish leaders of Corinth; the practical implication of his decision is that Christianity shares the protection assured by Roman law to Judaism (18:12ff.). At Ephesus, Paul enjoys the friendship of the *Asiarchs and is exonerated by the town clerk from the charge of insulting the cult of Ephesian *Artemis (19:31, 35ff.). In Judaea the governor Festus and the client king Agrippa II agree that Paul has committed no offence deserving either death or imprisonment, and that in fact he might have been liberated forthwith had he not taken the jurisdiction out of their hands by appealing to Caesar (26:32).

It might well be asked, however, why the progress of Christianity had so frequently been marked by public riots if Christians were as law-abiding as Luke maintained. His reply is that, apart from the incident at Philippi and the demonstration stirred up by the silversmiths' guild at Ephesus, the tumults which attended the proclamation of the gospel were invariably instigated by its Jewish opponents. Just as the Gospel represents the Sadducean chief priests of Jerusalem as prevailing upon Pilate to sentence Jesus to death against his better judgment, so in Acts it is Jews who are Paul's bitterest enemies in one place after another. While Acts records the steady advance of the gospel in the great Gentile centres of imperial civilization, it records at the same time its progressive rejection by the majority of the Jewish communities throughout the Empire.

V. Theological interest

On the theological side, the dominating theme of Acts is the activity of the Holy Spirit. The promise of the outpouring of the Spirit, made by the risen Christ in 1:4ff., is fulfilled for Jewish disciples in ch. 2 and for Gentile believers in ch. 10. The apostles discharge their commission in the power of the Spirit, which is manifested by supernatural signs; their converts' acceptance of the gospel is likewise attended by visible manifestations of the Spirit's power. The book might indeed be called 'The Acts of the Holy Spirit', for it is the Spirit who controls the advance of the gospel throughout; he guides the movements of the preachers, *e.g.* of Philip (8:29, 39), Peter (10:19f.), Paul and his companions (16:6ff.); he directs the church of Antioch to set Barnabas and Saul apart for the more extended service to which he himself has called them (13:2); he receives pride of place in the letter conveying the decision of the Jerusalem *Council to the Gentile churches (15:28); he speaks through prophets (11:28; 20:23; 21:4, 11) as he did in OT days (1:16; 28:25); he it is in the first instance who appoints the elders of a church to take spiritual charge of it (20:28); he is the principal witness to the truth of the gospel (5:32).

The supernatural manifestations which accompany the spread of the gospel signify not only the Spirit's activity but also the inauguration of the new age in which Jesus reigns as Lord and Messiah. The miraculous element, as we should expect, is more prominent in the earlier than in the later part of the book: 'we have a steady reduction of the emphasis on the miraculous aspect of the working of the Spirit which corresponds to the development in the Pauline Epistles' (W. L. Knox, *The Acts of the Apostles*, 1948, p. 91).

VI. Acts in the early church

Unlike most of the NT books, the two parts of Luke's history do not appear to have been primarily associated with Christian churches, whether as addressed to them or as circulating within them. Martin Dibelius may be right in thinking that the work circulated through the contemporary book trade for the benefit of the Gentile reading public for which it was intended. There may thus have been some lapse of time between the first publication of the twofold work and its more general circulation in the churches as an authoritative Christian document.

Early in the 2nd century, when the four Gospel writings were collected and circulated as a fourfold group, the two parts of Luke's history were separated from each other, to pursue their several paths. While the future of Luke was assured by reason of its incorporation with the other three Gospels, Acts proved increasingly to be such an important document that it can justly be called, in Harnack's words, the pivot-book of the NT.

The wider circulation of Acts in the churches may have had much to do, towards the end of the 1st century, with the move to collect the Pauline Epistles to form a *corpus*. If Paul tended to be forgotten in the generation following his death, Acts would certainly bring him back to Christian memory and also emphasize what an interesting and extraordinarily important man he was. But, while emphasizing the importance of Paul's role, Acts bore witness to the work of other apostles too, especially Peter.

For this last reason Marcion (*c.* AD 140) could not include Acts in his Canon, although he did include his edition of Luke as a preface to the Pauline *corpus*. Acts, while it bore eloquent witness to the apostleship of Paul, at the same time cut right across Marcion's insistence that the original apostles of Jesus had proved unfaithful to their Master's teaching. Marcion and his followers are probably the main target of Tertullian's charge of inconsistency against those heretics who confidently appeal to the exclusive apostolic authority of Paul while rejecting the one book above all others which provides independent testimony of his apostleship (*Prescription* 22f.).

To the champions of the catholic faith, on the other hand, the value of Acts now appeared greater than ever. For not only did it present irrefragable evidence of Paul's status and achievement as an apostle, but it also safeguarded the position of the other apostles and justified the inclusion of non-Pauline apostolic writings alongside the Pauline collection in the volume of Holy Writ. It was from this time that it came to be known as 'The Acts of the Apostles', or even, as the Muratorian list calls it with anti-Marcionite exaggeration, 'The Acts of *all* the Apostles'.

VII. Its abiding value

The title of Acts to occupy its traditional place between the Gospels and the Epistles is clear. On the one hand, it is the general sequel to the fourfold Gospel (as it is the proper sequel to one of the four); on the other hand, it supplies the historical background to the earlier Epistles, and attests the apostolic character of most of the writers whose names they bear.

Moreover, it remains a document of incalculable value for the beginnings of Christianity. When we consider how scanty is our knowledge of the progress of the gospel in other directions in the decades following AD 30, we may appreciate our indebtedness to Acts for the relatively detailed account which it gives of the progress of the gospel along the road from Jerusalem to Rome. The rise and progress of Christianity is a study beset with problems, but some of these problems would be even more intractable than they are if we had not the information of Acts to help us. For example, how did it come about that a movement which began in the heart of Judaism was recognized after a few decades as a distinctively Gentile religion? And how has it come about that a faith which originated in Asia has been for centuries predominantly associated, for better or worse, with European civilization? The answer is largely, though not entirely, bound up with the missionary career of Paul, apostle to the Gentiles and citizen of Rome; and of that career Luke, in Acts, is the historian. His narrative is, in fact, a source-book of the highest value for a significant phase of the history of world civilization.

BIBLIOGRAPHY. *BC*, 5 vols., 1920–33; F. F. Bruce, *The Acts of the Apostles*, 1951, and *The Book of the Acts*, 1954; C. S. C. Williams, *The Acts of the Apostles*, 1957;

ADAIAH
See Iddo, Part 2.

H. J. Cadbury, *The Book of Acts in History*, 1955; M. Dibelius, *Studies in the Acts of the Apostles*, 1956; J. Dupont, *The Sources of Acts*, 1964; A. Ehrhardt, *The Acts of the Apostles*, 1969; E. Haenchen, *The Acts of the Apostles*, 1971; W. W. Gasque, *A History of the Criticism of the Acts of the Apostles*, 1975.

F.F.B.

ADAH (Heb. *'āḏâ*, meaning uncertain). **1.** One of the wives of Lamech and mother of Jabal and Jubal (Gn. 4:19ff.). **2.** One of the wives of Esau, daughter of Elon a Hittite and mother of Eliphaz (Gn. 36:2ff.).

T.C.M.

ADAM (Heb. *'āḏām*). A town 28 km N of Jericho, near *Zarethan, controlling the Jordan fords just below the confluence of the Jabbok; modern Tell ed-Damiyeh. The blocking of the Jordan here made it possible for the Israelites to cross at Jericho (Jos. 3:10ff.).

J.P.U.L.

ADAM.

I. In the Old Testament

The first man, created (*bārā'*, Gn. 1:27) by God in his own image (*ṣelem*), on the sixth day by means of forming him (as a potter forms, *yāṣar*, Gn. 2:7) of dust from the ground (*'ᵃḏāmâ*), and uniquely breathing into his nostrils the breath of life (*nišmaṯ ḥayyîm*; see *b*, below). The result of this was that 'the man' became a living being (*nep̱eš ḥayyâ*). Sumerian and Babylonian myths of the creation of man are known, but compared with the creation story in the Bible all are crude and polytheistic.

a. Etymology

The name Adam (*'āḏām*), in addition to being a proper name, also has the connotation 'mankind', a sense in which it occurs in the OT some 500 times, so that when the noun occurs with the definite article (*hā'āḏām*) it is to be translated as the proper noun rather than as the name. The word *'adm* occurs also in Ugaritic in the sense 'mankind'. In the accounts of the *creation in Gn. 1 and 2 the article is used with *'āḏām* in all but three cases: 1:26, where 'man' in general is evidently intended; 2:5, where 'a man' (or 'no man') is clearly the most natural sense; and 2:20, the first permissible use of the proper name according to the text. The AV has projected this use back into the preceding verse (2:19) in spite of the article there, whereas RV, RSV, observing that in this occurrence, and indeed in all those (3:17, 21) without the article up to Gn. 4:25 the name is prefixed by the preposition *lᵉ-*, which might be read (*lā-* < *lᵉhā-*) to include the article without alteration to the consonantal text, prefer to assume that the Massoretes have wrongly pointed the text and that the proper name does not occur until Gn. 4:25. Though attempts have been made to determine the etymology of the name, there is no agreement, and the fact that the original language of mankind was not Hebrew renders such theories academic. It is clear, however, that the use of the word *'ᵃḏāmâ*, 'ground', in juxtaposition to the name *'āḏām* in Gn. 2:7 is intentional, a conclusion reinforced by Gn. 3:19.

b. Adam's early condition

Adam was distinguished from the animals, but this not because the epithets *nep̱eš* and *rûaḥ* were applied to him, for these terms are also used on occasion of the animals, but because he was made in God's image, given dominion over all the animals, and perhaps also because God individually breathed the breath (*nᵉšāmâ*) of life into his nostrils (*VT* 11, 1961, pp. 177–187). God made a garden for Adam in *Eden (Gn. 2:8–14) and put him in it to work it and watch over it. The word 'to work it' (*'āḇaḏ*) is that commonly used for labour (*e.g.* Ex. 20:9), so Adam was not to be idle. His food was apparently to be fruit from the trees (Gn. 2:9, 16), berries and nuts from the shrubs (*śîaḥ*, EVV plant') and cereals from the herbs (*'ēśeḇ*, Gn. 2:5). God then brought all the animals and birds to Adam for him to give them names, and presumably in the process to familiarize himself with their characteristics and potentialities (Gn. 2:19–20). It is possible that some dim reflection of this is to be found in a Sumerian literary text which describes how the god Enki set the world in order, and among other things put the animals under the control of two minor deities.

c. The Fall

God said 'It is not good that the man should be alone' (Gn. 2:18), so he made a woman (2:22), to be a help to him (*EVE). At the inducement of the serpent the woman persuaded Adam to eat from the fruit of the tree which he had been commanded by God not to touch (Gn. 3:1–7) (*FALL), and as a result he and the woman were banished from the garden (Gn. 3:23–24). It is evident that until this time Adam had had direct communion with God. When Adam and the woman recognized their nakedness they took fig leaves and sewed them together to make loin cloths (*ḥᵃgôrâ*, Gn. 3:7), evidence perhaps for the practice of such simple skills as sewing. Adam was punished by expulsion from the garden and subjection to the future lot of obtaining his livelihood in painful toil and in the sweat of his face, since the ground (*'ᵃḏāmâ*), to which he would now return at his death, was cursed and would bring forth thorn bushes and thistles. He was still to be a farmer, therefore, though his labours would be now more arduous than they had been (Gn. 3:17–19, 23). Parallels have been drawn between these episodes and the Akkadian myth of Adapa, who mistakenly refused the bread and water of life, thus losing immortality for mankind; but the connections are remote. God provided the two with leather tunics (Gn. 3:21), implying that they would now need protection from uncontrolled vegetation or cold weather.

Adam had two sons, *Cain and *Abel, but as Cain killed Abel he had another son, *Seth, to take Abel's place (Gn. 4:25) and to carry on the faithful line of descent. Adam was 130 (LXX 230) years old when Seth was born and he lived 800 (LXX 700) years after this event, making 930 years in all (Gn. 5:2–5 agreeing with LXX and Samaritan Pentateuch, the latter agreeing with *MT* in all three figures) (*GENEALOGY). In comparison, it is to be noted that the first pre-flood king, Alulim, in the Sumerian king list is given a reign of 28,800 years (a variant text gives 67,200), and his counterpart, Alōros, in Berossos' *Babylōniaka*, is credited with 36,000 years. It is to be presumed that Adam had other children than the three specifically mentioned in Genesis. The date of Adam's existence and the exact area in which he lived are at present disputed.

BIBLIOGRAPHY. *KB*³, p. 14; C. Westermann, *Biblischer Kommentar AT*, I/1, 1976; for the creation of man, see A. Heidel, *The Babylonian Genesis*², 1951, pp. 46–47, 66–72,

118–126; W. G. Lambert and A. R. Millard, *Atrahasīs. The Babylonian Story of the Flood*, 1969, pp. 8–9, 15, 54–65; S. N. Kramer, 'Sumerian Literature and the Bible', *Analecta Biblica* 12, 1959, pp. 191–192; for Enki and the world order, see *History Begins at Sumer*, 1958, pp. 145–147; for Adapa, see Heidel, *Genesis*, pp. 147–153; E. A. Speiser in *ANET*, pp. 101–103; for king list, see T. Jacobsen, *The Sumerian King List*, 1939, pp. 70–71; A. L. Oppenheim in *ANET*, p. 265. T.C.M.

II. In the New Testament

Outside the Pauline literature Adam is referred to occasionally in the Gospels: Luke sets him at the head of the genealogy of Christ (3:38), thus emphasizing the latter's kinship with all mankind (contrast Mt. 1:1f.); Jude 14 also mentions Adam as the beginning of the human race. The creation of Adam and Eve and their subsequent union are appealed to as evidence that God has willed the union of man and woman as 'one flesh' (Mt. 19:4–6; Mk. 10:6–9; RSVmg. citing Gn. 1:27; 2:24). For the Marcan tradition this means that divorce is prohibited, but Mt. 19:9 adds an exception, cases of 'unchastity'.

In the Pauline literature the union of Adam and Eve is also referred to as the basis for teaching on the relation between the sexes: Gn. 2:24 is again cited, in 1 Cor. 6:16, to show that sexual intercourse is never a trivial or ethically unimportant matter, but always a thoroughgoing union and merging of the persons of both partners, and in Eph. 5:31, where it is argued that it also refers to the union of Christ and the church. There are allusions to the order of the creation of Adam and Eve and to the divinely bestowed dignity of the former in 1 Cor. 11:7–9 to support Paul's argument for the subordination of women to men (despite vv. 11f.): men should not cover their heads, being God's 'image and glory', but women are men's 'glory' and they dishonour their heads (literally, and perhaps also figuratively, in the sense of their husbands; *cf.* vv. 3f.) by uncovering them. Similarly, 1 Tim. 2:12–14 appeals to the order of Adam and Eve's creation to support the claim that women, being subordinate, should keep silent in Christian gatherings; this inferiority is confirmed by the fact that it was Eve who was deceived and led into sin (*cf.* Ecclus. 25:24). Hence the practical teaching on the conduct of women enjoined here cannot be dismissed as simply an accommodation to the conventions of the day without also calling into question the scriptural exegesis and doctrine of creation which are held to support these practices or the logic which holds that the one follows from the other.

But the principal use of the figure of Adam in the Pauline literature is in the contrast of Adam and Christ. This may also be alluded to in the Synoptic Gospels: Mark's portrayal of Jesus' temptations (1:13) may reflect the idea that Jesus restored the state of man in Paradise—by overcoming temptation, by living with the wild beasts, by being ministered to by angels (*cf.* J. Jeremias, *TDNT* 1, p. 141). Similarly, Lk. 3:38 refers to Adam as 'the son of God', a phrase that he has already used of Jesus (1:35). This would be a positive use of the story of Adam: Christ is likened to Adam before his fall.

But for Paul there is more emphasis on the unlikeness in the midst of the likeness of Adam to Christ; this is true of both major passages in which he develops this idea, 1 Cor. 15 and Rom. 5:12–21. It would also be true of a third possible reference to this idea, in the traditional material used in Phil. 2:6–11; there is, however, no explicit reference to Adam here, nor any explicit citation of Genesis; at most one could claim only that some ideas here, *e.g.* obedience, renunciation of equality with God, imply a contrast with Adam (*cf.* R. P. Martin, *Carmen Christi*, 1967, pp. 161–164).

1 Cor. 15 refers twice to the Adam–Christ contrast: first, in vv. 21–23, Paul uses it to show that the resurrection of Jesus, which the Corinthians accept, is a pledge that 'all' will share a like destiny, just as all die (*n.b.* present tense) 'in Adam'; it is not that all died when Adam died; rather all now die like him. The phrase 'in Adam' is formed on the analogy of 'in Christ' and cannot be used to show how the latter phrase came to be formulated. Then the same contrast is picked up again in vv. 45–49: the contrast here is between the physical nature of Adam, which we all now share, and the spiritual body pledged to us at the end by virtue of Christ's resurrection. Some at Corinth, over-confident because of their spiritual gifts, needed to be reminded that they were still part of an age and a humanity dominated by death (v. 26); Paul's reply to them is that Scripture (Gn. 2:7) proves that men are physical (v. 45; it is the Adam of the end-time who is spiritual, Paul adds) and 'the spiritual does not come at first, but (rather) the physical and (only) then (subsequently) the spiritual' (v. 46; *cf. NovT* 15, 1973, pp. 301ff.); they will share in the resurrection of Christ, in a transformed, but still bodily, nature, but not while they still remain 'flesh and blood' (v. 50). The phrase 'the last Adam' (v. 45) and the interchange of 'Adam' and 'man' indicate that Paul is only too well aware that 'Adam' means 'man'.

This last point helps to explain why Paul introduces his other main reference to Adam so allusively (Rom. 5:12: 'by one man'). In the following passage he contrasts Adam who by sinning set in motion a chain-reaction of sin and its consequence, by God's decree, death, with Christ who by his obedience has inaugurated a saving process in which men receive God's gracious gift of righteousness and 'reign in life' (v. 17). V. 19 has a deterministic ring, yet note the tenses: the making righteous of many is already happening, despite the future tense, and it may be right to say that the making many sinners is still also happening; 'being made' may mean little more than 'becoming'. V. 12 makes it clear that death has not spread automatically to all men as a result of Adam's sin but rather 'because/in that all men sinned' and thus received the sentence of death in their own right; there is a solidarity of all men in sin, by means of which we share in and connive at the sinning of others, but that is not expressed by this verse. There is also a power, sin, which is more than the individual act of transgression or even the sum of the individual acts, and this is referred to in quasi-personal terms in v. 13. In vv. 13ff. Paul deals with the problem of those who did not, like Adam, have an explicit command of God to disobey; yet sin they did, as the continuing reign of death from Adam to Moses and the coming of the Law shows. Adam is 'a type of the one who was to come' and yet the development of this typology shows that it is very largely antithetical and contrasting (vv. 15–19), *i.e.* a negative use of Adam's story.

ADAMANT
See Jewels, Part 2.

ADAR
See Calendar, Part 1.

ADAR-MALEK
See Sakkuth, Part 3.

ADDAX
See Animals, Part 1.

ADONIKAM
See Adonijah, Part 1.

Moreover, whereas Adam's sin and its aftermath form an all too purely human history of man abandoned to the consequences of his own actions (*cf.* Rom. 1:24, 26, 28), the Christ side of the comparison contains a more than human element which far outweighs the negative side; hence the repeated 'much more' (5:15, 17).

There has been much discussion of the origins of the Adam–Christ idea, some seeking them in Near Eastern mythology, or, more recently and more specifically, in Gnostic speculation on the primal man. But the immediate origins should rather be sought in the variegated beliefs of contemporary Judaism and also in the teaching of Jesus: the restoration of the primal state at the end, the contrasting of Adam with various figures in Israel's history and with the Messiah (*cf.* Syr. Baruch 73f. with 56:6), and the expectation that God's 'man' (or 'the son of man') would come at the end. From these materials Paul and/or Christian tradition has fashioned the Adam–Christ typology.

Whatever views of human origins may be held, it remains true that the human race has a history and a beginning. Paul's point is then that all that history, even from the first, is marked by sin, that man is responsible for that sinful history, and that the sin of one affects others and the world around.

BIBLIOGRAPHY. C. K. Barrett, *From First Adam to Last*, 1962; M. D. Hooker, *NTS* 6, 1959–60, pp. 297–306; *NIDNTT* 1, p. 84–88; A. J. M. Wedderburn, *NTS* 19, 1972–3, pp. 339–354.

A.J.M.W.

ADAMAH (Heb. *ʼᵃḏāmāh*). A town in Naphtali (Jos. 19:36). Possibly at Qarn Hattin (Y. Aharoni, *JNES* 19, 1960, pp. 179–181, identifying it with Shemesh-adam of Egyptian sources). J.P.U.L.

ADAMI-NEKEB. A place mentioned in Jos. 19:33, on the border of Naphtali. It was apparently a pass and has been identified with the modern Kh. ed-Dâmiyeh. See *LOB*. R.A.H.G.

ADMAH. One of the Cities of the *Plain (Gn. 14:2, 8; Dt. 29:23), linked specially with *Zeboiim (Ho. 11:8). The association with Gaza (Gn. 10:19) suggests the correctness of the modern locating of the pentapolis as submerged beneath the S waters of the Dead Sea. J.A.M.

ADONI-BEZEK (Heb. *ʼᵃḏōnî-ḇezeq*, 'lord of Bezek'). Judah and Simeon, preparatory to conquering their own territory, combined to defeat 10,000 Canaanites at Bezek, probably modern Khirbet Ibziq, 21 km NE of Shechem (Jdg. 1:4–7). Their king, Adoni-bezek, not to be equated with *Adoni-zedek (Jos. 10:1–27), fled, but was recaptured and incapacitated in the contemporary customary manner. He acknowledged a certain rough justice in this, as he had inflicted similar mutilations upon seventy kings. He was brought to Jerusalem, where he died. As the Israelites were not able to hold and develop all captured cities, Jerusalem was later occupied by the Jebusites (Jdg. 1:21).

BIBLIOGRAPHY. *LOB*, p. 197.

A.E.C.

ADONIJAH (Heb. *ʼᵃḏōniyyâ*, 'my lord is Yahweh'). **1.** The fourth son of David, by his wife Haggith. After the death of the three eldest he regarded himself as the heir-presumptive. (Amnon had been murdered by his brother Absalom, who himself died in the rebellion against his father. As no mention is made of Chileab, the son of Abigail, it is assumed that he died before any question of the succession arose.) It would appear, however, that David had promised Bathsheba (1 Ki. 1:17) that her son Solomon should succeed him. It may have been knowledge of this that provoked Adonijah to make his futile attempt at gaining the crown while his father was alive. His supporters included two of his father's right-hand men, Joab the commander-in-chief of the army, and Abiathar the priest, and no doubt Adonijah hoped that they would draw the power of the army and the sanction of the priesthood. But before that hope materialized those faithful to the king, Nathan his prophet-counsellor, Zadok the priest and Benaiah the commander of the royal bodyguard, took action. While Adonijah was making a feast for his supporters, Bathsheba was instructed to approach David and remind him of his oath, and while she was yet speaking Nathan came in and reproached the king for his not having told him of his (supposed) plans for Adonijah. David confirmed his oath to Bathsheba and secured the accession of Solomon. The noise and the news of the acclamation reached Adonijah and his guests in En-rogel, and threw them into a panic. The would-be aspirant for the throne fled for sanctuary to the altar, and Solomon promised to spare his life on condition of future loyalty (1 Ki. 1). No sooner was his father dead than his former ambitions again made themselves apparent. Thus at least did Solomon interpret his request for Abishag, his father's young concubine who had nursed him in his old age. This charge of a renewed attempt on the throne was probably not without foundation in the light of oriental custom (*cf.* 2 Sa. 3:7; 16:21). The sentence of death on the ambitious and tactless Adonijah was speedily carried out (1 Ki. 2:13–25).

2. One of the Levites whom Jehoshaphat sent to teach in the cities of Judah (2 Ch. 17:8).

3. One of those who sealed the covenant (Ne. 10:16). This is the same as Adonikam (Ezr. 2:13, *etc.*). M.A.M.

ADONIRAM (Heb. *ʼᵃḏōnîrām*, 'my lord is exalted'). The official in charge of forced labour during Solomon's reign (1 Ki. 4:6; 5:14). Probably the Adoram who had the same responsibility during the reigns of David (2 Sa. 20:24) and Rehoboam (1 Ki. 12:18; 'Hadoram' in 2 Ch. 10:18). People of Israel stoned him to death as the first act of their revolt and the division of the monarchy under Jeroboam *c.* 922 BC. D.W.B.

ADONI-ZEDEK (Heb. *ʼᵃḏōnî-ṣeḏeq*, 'my lord is righteous'). An Amorite king of Jerusalem who led four other Canaanite kings against the Israelites and their allies of Gibeon. The five kings were defeated by divine intervention and hid themselves in a cave at *Makkedah. They were humbled in common oriental style, then executed by Joshua and buried in the cave (Jos. 10). The meaning of the name may be compared with Melchizedek ('my king is righteous'), king of *Salem (Gn. 14:18). There is not sufficient evidence for the existence of a god Zedek ('righteousness') to give a meaning 'my king is Zedek'. A.R.M.

ADOPTION.

I. In the Old Testament

Adoption occurs comparatively rarely in the OT. Hebrew possesses no technical term for the practice, and it makes no appearance in the laws of the OT. This situation is probably explained by the existence among the Israelites of several alternatives to the problem of infertile marriage. Polygamy and levirate * marriage lessened the need for adoption, while the principle of maintaining property within the tribe (Lv. 25:23ff.; Nu. 27:8–11; Je. 32:6ff.) allayed some of the fears of childless parents.

Adoption in the OT is considerably illuminated by comparative material from Mesopotamia and Syria. Ancient Near Eastern adoption was a legal act by which a person was brought into a new family relationship, with the full privileges and responsibilities of one who participated in that relationship by birth. Applying this description to the OT, a small number of adoptions can be identified, the majority in Gn. 12–50. A preference for adoption within the family is discernible, and it seems that the OT, in common with ancient Near Eastern texts, included adrogation and legitimation alongside adoption within a single umbrella concept, whereas Roman law made clear distinctions between these practices.

According to cuneiform legal custom, adoption would have been required for Eliezer to become Abraham's heir (Gn. 15:3) and for the sons of Hagar, Bilhah and Zilpah to participate in the inheritance of Abraham and Jacob (Gn. 16:1–4; 30:1–13; *cf.* 21:1–10). Although Eliezer's apparent removal from the inheritance is untypical (Gn. 24:36; 25:5–6), his case is paralleled by an Old Babylonian letter from Larsa (*Textes cunéiformes du Louvre* 18, 153) which indicates that a man without sons could adopt his own slave. The adoptive status of the concubines' sons is supported by Sarah's and Rachel's declarations, 'I shall be built up' (Gn. 16:2; 30:3; *cf.* RVmg.), and by Rachel's statement, 'God has . . . given *me* a son' (Gn. 30:6). Although no evidence exists for Jacob's adoption by Laban (*cf.* Gn. 31:3, 18, 30; 32:3ff.), Jacob himself probably adopted Ephraim and Manasseh. The adoption of a grandson also occurred in Ugarit (*PRU* 3, 70–71). Elsewhere in the OT, Moses (Ex. 2:10) and Esther (Est. 2:7, 15) were almost certainly adopted, probably according to non-Israelite law, though the case of Genubath (1 Ki. 11:20) is more doubtful.

An adoption formula seems to occur in Ps. 2:7 ('you are my son'; *cf.* Gn. 48:5, 'your two sons . . . are mine'). A similar phrase appears in an Elephantine adoption contract (E. G. Kraeling, *The Brooklyn Museum Aramaic Papyri*, 1953, No. 8), and a negative equivalent also occurs, chiefly in Old Babylonian texts. The OT contains no reference to adoption rites, however, since the custom of 'bearing upon the knees' (Gn. 30:3; 50:23; Jb. 3:12) is associated with birth and recognition by the head of the family.

Adoption also had a theological aspect. The nation Israel was regarded as God's son (Is. 1:2f.; Je. 3:19; Ho. 11:1), especially as his first-born (Ex. 4:22; Je. 31:9), and the Davidic king was similarly privileged, though his humanity and accountability were equally emphasized (2 Sa. 7:14; 1 Ch. 28:6f.; Ps. 89:19ff.). It was this divine choice that lay behind Paul's statement that sonship belonged to the Israelites (Rom. 9:4).

BIBLIOGRAPHY. S. I. Feigin, *JBL* 50, 1931, pp. 186–200; S. Kardimon, *JSS* 3, 1958, pp. 123–126; I. Mendelsohn, *IEJ* 9, 1959, pp. 180–183; J. van Seters, *JBL* 87, 1968, pp. 401–408. M.J.S.

II. In the New Testament

Adoption in the NT has as its background not Roman law, in which its chief aim was to continue the adoptive parent's line, but Jewish custom, which conferred the benefits of the family on the adoptee. It occurs only in Paul, and is a relationship conferred by God's act of free grace which redeems those under the law (Gal. 4:5). Its intention and result is a change of status, planned from eternity and mediated by Jesus Christ (Eph. 1:5), from slavery to sonship (Gal. 4:1ff.). The cry 'Abba! Father!' (Rom. 8:15 and Gal. 4:6; in the context of adoption) may perhaps be the traditional cry of the adopted slave. The adopted son of God possesses all family rights, including access to the Father (Rom. 8:15) and sharing with Christ in the divine inheritance (Rom. 8:17). The presence of the Spirit of God is both the instrument (Rom. 8:14) and the consequence (Gal. 4:6) of this sonship. However complete in status this adoption may be, it has yet to be finally made real in the deliverance of the creation itself from bondage (Rom. 8:21ff.).

Adoption is implicit as a relationship of grace in John's teaching about 'becoming a son' (Jn. 1:12; 1 Jn. 3:1–2), in the prodigal's acceptance into full family rights (Lk. 15:19ff.) and in Jesus' oft-repeated title of God as Father (Mt. 5:16; 6:9; Lk. 12:32).

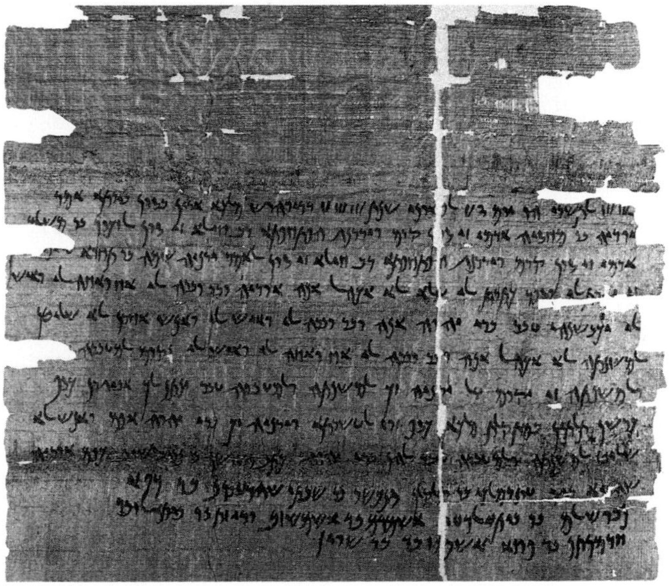

Zakkur deeds a slave Yedoniah, probably a young boy, to Uriah for adoption. 36·3 cm × 30·8 cm. 416 BC. (BrM)

BIBLIOGRAPHY. W. H. Rossell, 'New Testament Adoption—Graeco-Roman or Semitic?', *JBL* 71, 1952, pp. 233ff.; D. J. Theron, '"Adoption" in the Pauline Corpus', *EQ* 28, 1956, pp. 1ff.; F. Lyall, 'Roman Law in the Writings of Paul—Adoption', *JBL* 88, 1969, pp. 458ff. F.H.P.

ADORAIM. City of SW Judah fortified by Rehoboam (2 Ch. 11:9), identified today with the village of Dura, some 8 km SW of Hebron. It became a major Idumaean city, and as such figured in various historical events in the intertestamental period. D.F.P.

ADORAM
See Adoniram, Part 1.

ADRAMMELECH. 1. A god brought from * Sepharvaim to Samaria, where the colonists sacrificed children to him (2 Ki. 17:31). Attempts to identify the name include *'ddr mlk*, 'The king (or Molek) is powerful'. There is no need to change to read Adad-Malik.

2. One of the sons of Senna-

cherib, brother of Sharezer, who murdered their father in 681 BC (2 Ki. 19:37; Is. 37:38). This event is also recorded in the Babylonian Chronicle without naming the son (*DOTT*, pp. 70–73). A W Semitic name for one of the sons is likely, as Sennacherib's wife Naqi'a-Zakutu was of W Semitic origin; *cf.* the name *'drmlk*, king of Byblos, on a Phoen. coin of the 4th century BC.
D.J.W.

ADRAMYTTIUM. Seaport in Mysia, in Roman Asia, facing Lesbos: the site is Karatash, but the modern inland town, Edremit, preserves the name. Rendel Harris (unconvincingly) suggested a S Arabian origin for the original settlement (*Contemporary Review* 128, 1925, pp. 194ff.). Its commercial importance, once high, was declining by NT times.

An Adramyttian ship conveyed Julius and Paul from Caesarea (Acts 27:2). It was doubtless homeward bound, engaging in coastwise traffic with 'the ports along the coast of Asia', where a connection for Rome might be obtained—an expectation soon justified (vv. 5f.).

BIBLIOGRAPHY. Strabo, 13. 1. 51, 65–66; Pliny, *NH* 13. 1. 2 (for a local export); W. Leaf, *Strabo on the Troad*, 1923, pp. 318ff. A.F.W.

Old Testament Africa.

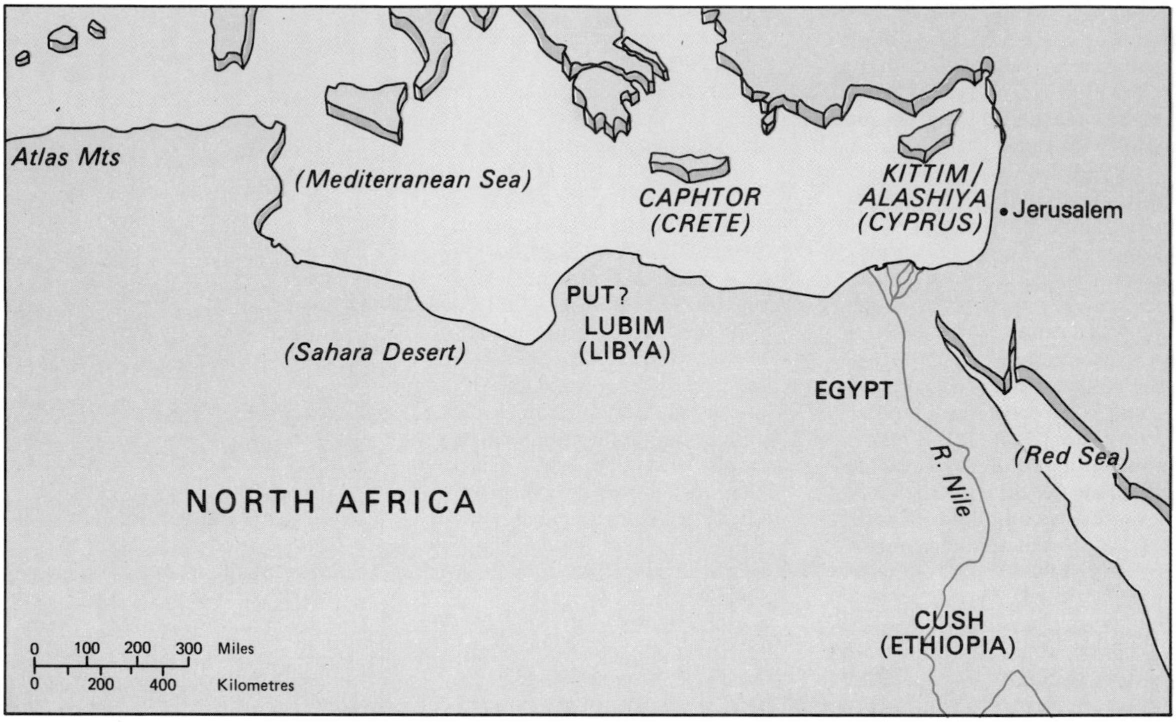

New Testament Africa.

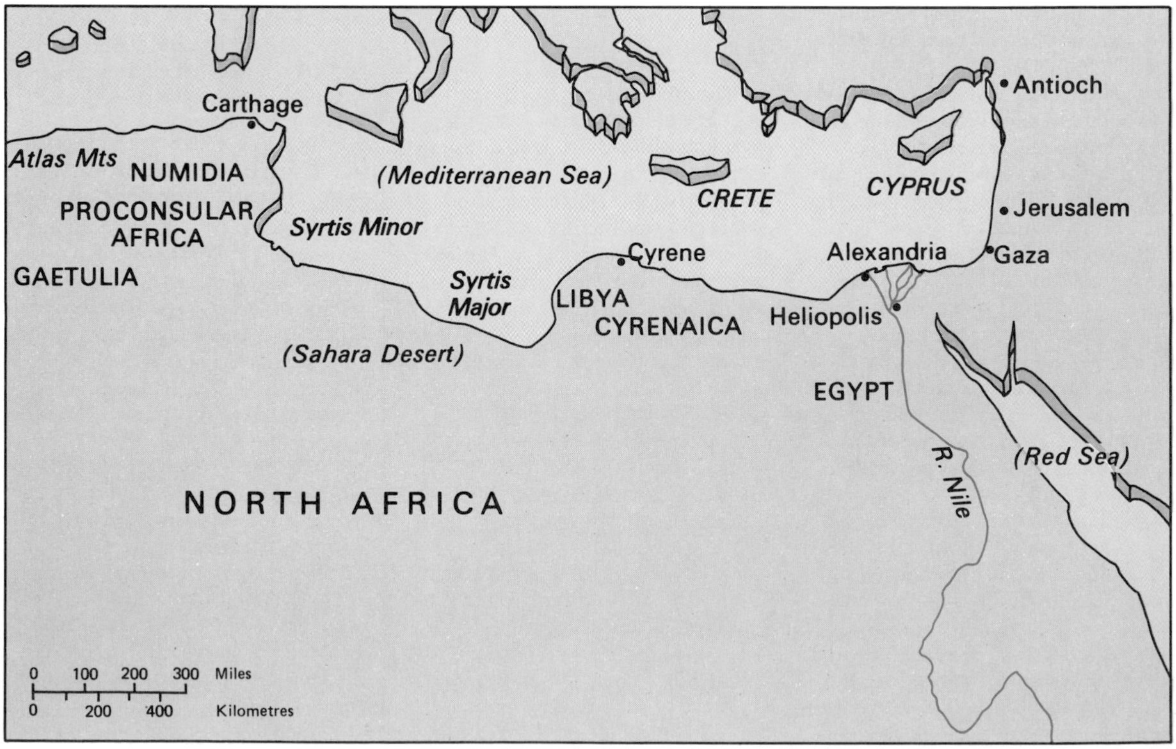

ADRIA. The 'sea of Adria' (Acts 27:27), across which the ship of the Alexandrian grain fleet, which was taking Paul to Italy, drifted in a W direction for 14 days, was the Central Mediterranean, including the Ionian Sea (*cf.* Strabo, *Geog.* 2. 5. 20; Jos. *Vita* 15; Pausanias, *Description of Greece* 5. 25. 3; Ptolemy, *Geog.* 3. 4. 1; 15. 1). It is to be distinguished from the *gulf* of Adria (*cf.* the town of Adria or Hadria N of the Po), which is known to us as the Adriatic Sea.
F.F.B.

ADULLAM. A Canaanite city in Judah (Jos. 12:15); fortified by Rehoboam (2 Ch. 11:7); mentioned by Micah (Mi. 1:15) and inhabited after the Exile (Ne. 11:30). Identified with Tell esh-Sheikh Madhkur (Ḥorvat 'Adullam), midway between Jerusalem and Lachish, the place is usually associated with the cave in which David hid when pursued by Saul (1 Sa. 22:1).
J.W.M.

ADUMMIM. A steep pass on the boundary between Judah and Benjamin (Jos. 15:7; 28:17) on the road from Jericho to Jerusalem. Traditionally the scene of the Good Samaritan story (Lk. 10:34), it is known today as Tal'at ed-Damm ('ascent of blood'), probably from the red marl of the soil, though Jerome attributed the name to the murders and robberies said to have taken place there.
J.D.D.

AENON (from Gk. *'ainōn*, 'fountain'). A place W of Jordan where John baptized (Jn. 3:23), perhaps to be identified with 'Ainun, NE of Nablus, near the headwaters of the Wadi Far'ah (hence 'there was much water there'). (*SALIM.)
F.F.B.

AFRICA

I. Early knowledge and nomenclature

The Greeks designated the continent 'Libya', but of its extent and its relation to Asia there was doubt. Herodotus (5th century BC) is already convinced of its being almost surrounded by sea, and cites (*Hist.* 4. 42) an alleged circumnavigation by a Phoenician crew in the service of Pharaoh *Neco. A translation of a Punic document, the Periplus of the Erythraean Sea, recounts a Carthaginian voyage, evidently as far as Sierra Leone, before 480 BC. The Romans applied 'Africa' to the whole continent (Pomponius Mela, 1. 4), but far more regularly to Proconsular Africa, comprising the area (roughly modern Tunisia) annexed from Carthage in 146 BC, plus the Numidian and Mauretanian domains later added. But, though the Carthaginians may have known more about the Trans-Sahara than we realize, the knowledge of Africa possessed by the ancient peoples who have left most literary remains was largely confined to the areas participating in, or accessible to, the Mediterranean civilizations, rarely penetrating the colossal barriers of the Atlas Mountains, the Sahara and the perils of the Upper Nile.

II. Africa in the Old Testament

Similarly, Israel's main concerns in Africa were naturally with her powerful neighbour, Egypt. Whether as the granary of the Patriarchs, the oppressor of the bondage or the broken reed of the period of Assyrian advance, the changing roles of Egypt could not be ignored. Despite the cruel past, a tender feeling towards Egypt remained (Dt. 23:7), which prepares us for the prophecies of Egypt's eventually sharing with Israel, in the knowledge and worship of the Lord (Is. 19—note the changing tone as the chapter proceeds). Other African peoples are mentioned from time to time (*LIBYA, *PUT), but the most frequent allusions are to Cush (*ETHIOPIA), the general designation for the lands beyond Egypt. The characteristic skin and physique of the inhabitants was remarked (Je. 13:23; Is. 45:14, and probably Is. 18:2, 7).

At some periods historical circumstances linked Egypt and Ethiopia in Hebrew eyes, and they stand together, sometimes with other African peoples, as representative nations on which God's righteous judgments will be executed (Is. 43:3; Ezk. 30:4ff.; Na. 3:9), as those who will one day recognize the true status of God's people (Is. 45:14), and as those who will ultimately receive Israel's God (Ps. 87:4, and especially Ps. 68:31). The picture of Ethiopia, symbol of the great African unknown beyond the Egyptian river, stretching out hands to God, was like a trumpet-call in the missionary revival of the 18th and 19th centuries. Even within the biblical period it had a measure of fulfilment; not only were there Jewish settlements in Africa (*cf.* Zp. 3:10) but an Ethiopian in Jewish service did more for God's prophet than true-born Israelites (Je. 38), and the high-ranking Ethiopian of Acts 8 was evidently a devout proselyte.

Despite a long tradition of perverted exegesis in some quarters, there is nothing to connect the curse of Ham (Gn. 9:25) with a permanent divinely instituted malediction on the negroid peoples; it is explicitely applied to the Canaanites.

III. Africa in the New Testament

Jesus himself received hospitality on African soil (Mt. 2:13ff.). The Jewish settlements in Egypt and Cyrene, prefigured, perhaps, in Is. 19:18f. *et alia*, were evidently a fruitful field for the early church. Simon who bore the cross was a Cyrenian, and that his relationship with Christ did not stop there may be inferred from the fact that his children were apparently well known in the primitive Christian community (Mk. 15:21). Egyptian and Cyrenian Jews were present at Pentecost (Acts 2:10); the mighty *Apollos was an Alexandrian Jew (Acts 18:24); Cyrenian converts, probably including the prophet *Lucius, shared in the epoch-making step of preaching to pure pagans at Antioch (Acts 11:20f.).

A cave at Adullam, used for shelter by fugitives. (DJW)

ADULTERY See Marriage, Part 2.

ADVERSARY See Satan, Part 3.

ADVOCATE See Counsellor, Part 1.

AFFECTIONS See Bowels, Part 1.

AGAMA
See Animals, Part 1.

AGAPE
See Love feast, Part 2.

AGATE
See Jewels, Part 2.

AGES
See Time, Part 3.

But we know nothing certain about the foundation of the Egyptian and N African churches, some of the most prominent in the world by the late 2nd century. The tradition, which cannot be traced very early, that Mark was the pioneer Evangelist of Alexandria (Eusebius, *EH* 2. 16) is itself, when applied to 1 Pet. 5:13, the only support for the theory of Peter's residence there (but *cf.* G. T. Manley, *EQ* 16, 1944, pp. 138ff.). Luke's vivid picture in Acts of the march of the gospel through the N lands of the Mediterranean may obscure for us the fact that the march through the S lands must have been quite as effective and probably almost as early. There were Christians in Africa about as soon as there were in Europe.

But Luke does not forget Africa. He shows how, by means the apostolic church never anticipated, and before the real Gentile mission began, the gospel went to the kingdom of Meroë (Acts 8:26ff.), as if in earnest of the fulfilment of the purpose of God for Africa declared in the OT.

BIBLIOGRAPHY. M. Cary and E. H. Warmington, *The Ancient Explorers*, 1929; B. H. Warmington, *The North African Provinces*, 1954; *idem, Carthage*, 1960; C. K. Meek, *Journal of African History* 1, 1960, pp. 1ff.; C. P. Groves, *The Planting of Christianity in Africa*, 1, 1948, pp. 31ff. A.F.W.

AGABUS. Derivation uncertain; possibly equals OT Hagab, Hagabah. A Jerusalem prophet whose prediction of 'a great famine' was fulfilled in the reign of Claudius (Acts 11:27–28). Suetonius, Dio Cassius, Tacitus and Eusebius mention famines at that time. At Caesarea he acted a prediction of Paul's fate at Jerusalem (Acts 21:10–11). In late traditions, one of the 'Seventy' (Lk. 10:1) and a martyr. G.W.G.

AGAG. From Balaam's use of the name (Nu. 24:7, *etc.*) it would appear to be the common title of the kings of Amalek as 'Pharaoh' was in Egypt. In particular, the name is used of the king of the Amalekites taken by Saul and, contrary to God's command, spared along with the spoil. He was slain by Samuel. Saul's disobedience was the occasion of his rejection by God (1 Sa. 15). M.A.M.

AGAGITE. An adjective applied to Haman in Est. 3:1, 10; 8:3, 5; 9:24. Josephus (*Ant.* 11. 209) makes him an Amalekite, presumably descended from *Agag, whom Saul spared (1 Sa. 15). Mordecai, who brought about Haman's fall, was, like Saul, descended from Kish (Est. 2:5; 1 Sa. 9:1). The LXX has *Bougaios* (meaning obscure) in Est. 3:1, and *Makedōn* (Macedonian) in 9:24; elsewhere it omits the adjective. J.S.W.

AGE, OLD AGE. Throughout the ancient Near East the aged were held in honour for their experience and wisdom (Jb. 12:12; 32:7). Among the Hebrews this was not simply because of the outward sign of the grey beard (hence 'aged', *zāqēn*) or of grey hair (*sbh*), but because the attainment of 'fullness of days' or 'entering into (many) days' was considered to be a sign of divine favour for fearing the Lord and keeping his commands (Lv. 19:32; Dt. 30:19–20) and thus showing dependence on the God-appointed authority (Ex. 20:12). Yet without righteousness the hoary head is no crown of glory (Pr. 16:31; *cf.* Ec. 4:13). Christ in glory is depicted as with 'white hair' (Rev. 1:14) and identified with the 'Ancient of Days' (*cf.* Dn. 7:9).

Older men were expected to lead in positions of authority and responsibility as *elders. 'The beauty of old age' is grey hair (Pr. 20:29). Age should equally be marked by wisdom (1 Ki. 12:6–8; Jb. 12:20; 15:10; 32:7). Thus failure to respect the aged is a mark of a decadent society (Is. 3:5), as of the Babylonians who 'had no compassion on old man or aged', lit. 'the one who stooped through age' (2 Ch. 36:17; but *cf.* Herodotus 2. 80). Conversely respect for age brings blessing to the community (Is. 65:20; Zc. 8:4).

The disabilities of old age are not overlooked (Ps. 71:9) and are pictured in Ec. 12:2–7 as a loss of vision, vigour and teeth, as well as increasing insomnia, anxiety and waning ambition. Abraham and Sarah were believed to be beyond the age of child-bearing (Gn. 18:11–14; *cf.* Lk. 1:18), and blindness afflicted Isaac (Gn. 27:1), Jacob (Gn. 48:10), Eli (1 Sa. 3:2; 4:15) and Ahijah (1 Ki. 14:4). Barzillai lost his sense of taste and hearing (2 Sa. 19:35), while David suffered from poor circulation, or hypothermia (1 Ki. 1:1–4). Apart from the unusual years attributed by the pre-flood *genealogies of Gn. 5 and 11, as to early Babylonian rulers, the Patriarchs attained great age (Abraham 175, Gn. 25:7; Isaac 180, Gn. 35:28; Jacob 147, Gn. 47:28; and Joseph 110, Gn. 50:22). Yet men like Moses at age 120 (Dt. 34:7), or Jehoiada at 130 (2 Ch. 24:15), were still full of vigour.

The change from maturity to 'old age' was considered as age 60 (*cf.* Lv. 27:1–8; Ps. 90:10). Thus 'at 60 one attains old age; at 70 the hoary head, at 80 special strength, at 90 bending, and at 100 (is) as though already dead' (*Pirqē Aboth* 21). This may be compared with a contemporary Babylonian view in which '60 is maturity; 70 length of days (long life); 80 old age; 90 extreme old age' (Sultan Tepe Tablet 400:45–49). D.J.W.

AGRICULTURE. The excavations of OT Jericho have demonstrated that Palestine was one of the earliest agricultural centres yet discovered. Good farming can be dated here around 7500 BC. Jericho represents irrigation culture which was common in the prehistoric period in the Jordan valley, not along the river itself but beside the streams that flowed into it. About the same time the hill country also was showing signs of agriculture, for the Natufian culture shows flint sickle-blades and hoes. Irrigation as an ancient science reached its peak and held it in Egypt and Babylonia. By Abraham's time, however, in Palestine irrigation farming was declining in importance, and even dry farming, as in the Negeb, was coming in.

Most of Palestine's farmers depended on rain. The drought of a 6 months' summer ended with the 'early rains', and as soon as the sun-baked earth could be farmed (late November or December) the seed was broadcast and ploughed under. Sometimes the land was also ploughed before seeding. The heavy winter rains gave the crops their major moisture, but the 'latter rains' of March and April were needed to bring the grain to head.

The principal grain crops were wheat and barley, the former the more valuable, but the latter had the advantage of a shorter growing season and the ability to grow on poorer soil. Various legumes, such as lentils, peas and beans, formed a secondary crop. *Vegetables added variety to the meal, with onions and garlic playing a prominent part. *Herbs, seeds and other condiments gave variety to a menu that was basically bread. Newly-sprouting wild *plants served as salads.

After the invention of the sickle, where flint teeth were set into a bone or wooden haft, the next improvement was the plough. The best tree from which to fashion a wooden plough was the oak. The poorest farmer never had a metal ploughshare (Heb. *'ēt*, as 'coulter' AV in 1 Sa. 13:20f.). By the time of David, however, iron was sufficiently plentiful, and a good-sized iron one could be used. The result was much better crops and a heavier population on the same land area.

The single-handled wooden plough had a virtue in its lightness, as the fields were often stony and the plough could be easily lifted over boulders. On level land, as in Bashan, excess rocks were gathered into piles in the fields. But on the hillsides they were built into terraces to keep the good soil from washing away and to conserve moisture. Large stones served as boundary marks of a grain field, and no fencing was used. The single-handled plough left the farmer's other hand free to use the ox-goad.

Grain crops matured first in the deep hot Jordan valley, and then the harvest season followed up the rising elevation of the land, first the coastal and Esdraelon areas, then the low hills and finally the higher mountains. The barley harvest of April and May preceded the wheat by several weeks or even a month. By that time a summer crop of millet had often been sown on other land which had been left fallow through the winter.

To harvest the crop, the grain was grasped in one hand and then cut with the sickle held in the other hand. These bundles were tied into sheaves, which in turn were loaded on to donkeys or camels to be carried to the threshing-floor. Amos mentions the use of wagons. Gleaners followed the reapers, and then animals were let into the stubble in the following order: sheep, goats and camels.

Threshing-floors were located near the village at a point where the winds would be helpful for winnowing. The floor itself was either a rock outcropping or a soil area coated with marly clay. The sheaves were scattered about a foot deep over the floor and protected at the edges by a ring of stones. The animals, which were sometimes shod for this purpose, were driven round and round until the grain was loosened. A faster method was to use a wooden sled with stones or iron fragments fastened into the under side. The grain was winnowed by tossing it into the wind with wooden shovels or fans. The

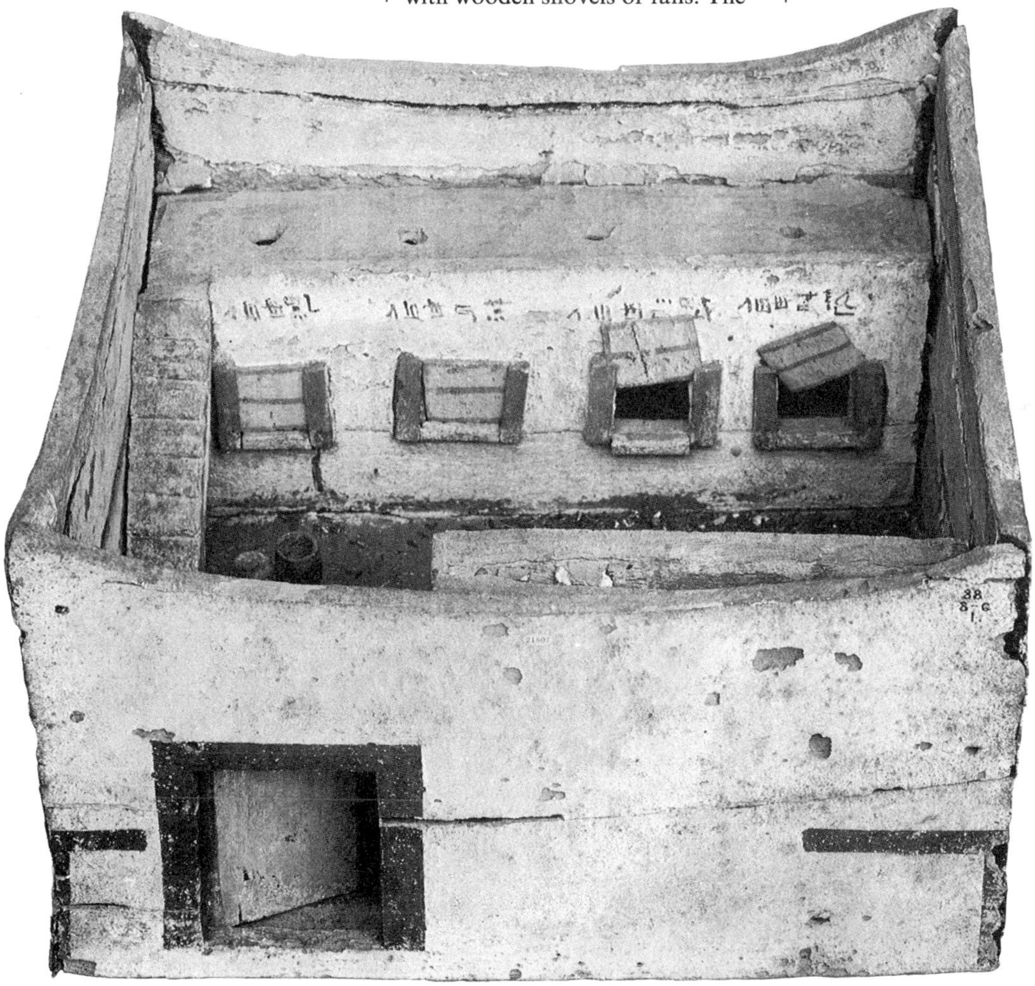

Wooden tomb-model of an Egyptian granary. Bins along two of the walls were filled through holes in their roofs reached by a staircase. The grain was emptied through sliding hatches, above which were written the types and quantities of grain. From Aswan. 6th Dynasty, c. 2250 BC. (BM)

Wooden sledge with stones fastened to the under side, used for threshing. (FNH)

A water-sweep (shaduf) *as used for irrigation. Relief from the palace of Sennacherib at Nineveh. c. 690 BC.* (BM)

AGRICULTURE OF EGYPT
See Nile, Part 2.

AGRIPPA
See Herod, Part 2.

grain might be sifted with sieves (Heb. *kᵉḇārâ* in Am. 9:9 and *nāp̄â* in Is. 30:28) to remove grit before being bagged for human use. The straw was saved as fodder for the animals. Fire in a ripening field or a threshing-floor was a major crime, as that year's food supply was lost. Samson's fox-fire episode (Jdg. 15:4–5) was a catastrophe to the Philistines. Threshing might last to the end of August or even later with bumper harvests.

The best grain lands were the benches of the Jordan valley that could be irrigated by the tributaries of the Jordan, the Philistine plain, Esdraelon (although part of it was then marshy), Bashan and Moab. But since bread was the principal food of the country, even poor bench land was often cultivated to produce grain. Narrow stair-like terraces were erected on the mountainside, and in Lebanon today they still creep up the mountains to the very snow-line. The lower hills, such as the Shephelah, gave a wider distribution to crops, adding the *vine and the *olive to the grains, making a famous trio of crops often referred to in OT. The better sections of the higher land were farmed, but much was left for grazing or forestry.

The heavy summer dews in many parts of the country supplemented the sub-soil moisture from the winter rains and made possible the cultivation of grapes, cucumbers and melons. These were far more though temporary, effort to stay valuable crops than many Bible readers realize, for Palestine has no summer rain, and most of the streams dry up. These fruits and vegetables then become an extra water ration to both man and beast. Many varieties of grapes were grown, and they were not only a valuable food item in summer but, when dried as raisins, they were also winter food. The wine made from the grape was an item of export. Grapes were usually a hillside crop, with beans and lentils grown between the vines. Is. 5:1–6 provides a picture of the vineyard.

Fruits and nuts were other means of adding variety to the menu. The olive tree and the sesame plant were principal sources of cooking oil; animal fat was very expensive. Nuts, although rich in oil, were primarily used as condiments. The pods of the carob tree were an excellent food for animals. *Flax was the only plant grown for cloth.

The farmer's major enemy was drought. The failure of any one of the three rain seasons was serious, and prolonged droughts were not uncommon, especially in certain sections of the land. The farmer was also plagued by locust invasions, plant diseases, such as the mildew, and the hot sirocco winds. War, too, was a common enemy of the farmer, for war was usually conducted at the harvest season so that the invading army could live off the land. Palestine's chief exports were wheat, olive oil and wine. These were not only shipped to other countries, but large quantities of these items were consumed by the caravans traversing the land of Palestine itself.

The levitical laws of Moses laid down certain agricultural principles, some of which have been mentioned above. These were often sound agricultural practice for soil conservation, *e.g.* fallow in the seventh year (Lv. 25), or social reasons, *e.g.* leaving the residual grain for the poor to glean (Lv. 23:22). If God's principles were not observed, the crops would not grow and famine would follow (Lv. 26:14ff.): moral and practical lessons that are still relevant and yet to be learnt throughout the world.

BIBLIOGRAPHY. D. Baly, *The Geography of the Bible*², 1974; A. Reifenberg, *The Desert and the Sown*, 1956; F. N. Hepper, *Plants in Bible Lands*, in prep.; P. J. Ucko and G. W. Dimbleby (eds.), *The Domestication and Exploitation of Plants and Animals*, 1969. J.L.K.
F.N.H.

AHAB (Heb. *'aḥ'āḇ*; Assyr. *Aḫābu*, 'the (divine) brother is father').

1. The son and successor of Omri, founder of the dynasty, who reigned as seventh king of Israel for 22 years, *c.* 874–852 BC (1 Ki. 16:28ff.). He married Jezebel, daughter of Ethbaal, king of Sidon and priest of Astarte.

I. Political history

Ahab fortified Israelite cities (1 Ki. 16:34; 22:39) and undertook extensive work at his own capital, *Samaria, as is shown also by excavation (1 Ki. 16:32). His own palace was adorned with ivory (1 Ki. 21:1; 22:39; *cf.* Am. 3:15). Throughout his reign there were frequent wars with Syria (*cf.* 1 Ki. 22:1) especially against Ben-hadad who, with his allies, besieged Samaria but was driven off (1 Ki. 20:21). Later, in battle near Aphek, Ahab heavily defeated Ben-hadad but spared his life (1 Ki. 20:26–30), perhaps in return for commercial concessions in Damascus similar to those allowed to Syrian merchants in Samaria. Economic ties were maintained with Phoenician ports through his marriage.

The Assyrian annals show that in 853 BC, at the battle of Qarqar on the Orontes, Ahab supported Ben-hadad with 2,000 chariots and 10,000 men in the successful,

Egyptian harvesting scene from the tomb of Menna. Two men with winnowing-forks heaping up heads of grain. Thebes. c. 1400 BC. (Modern copy.) (RS)

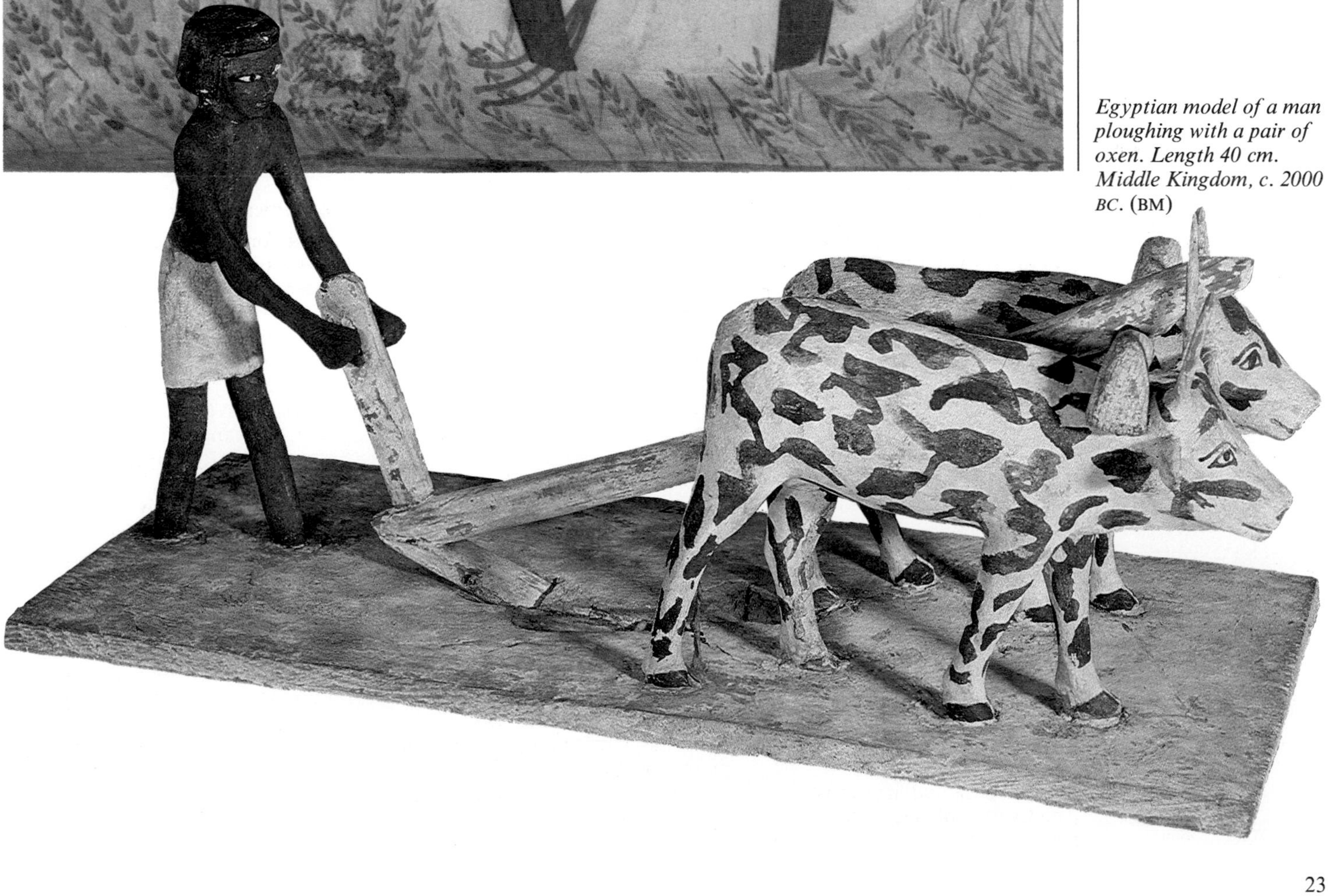

Egyptian model of a man ploughing with a pair of oxen. Length 40 cm. Middle Kingdom, c. 2000 BC. (BM)

Fragments of Phoenician-style carved ivories from Samaria. Similar ivory furniture-fittings were used in Ahab's palace. 9th cent. BC. (BM)

the advance SW by *Shalmaneser III (*cf. ANET*, pp. 278–281). This intervention was one of the first causes of the later Assyrian advances against Israel. The preoccupation with Syrian affairs enabled Moab, once Ahab's vassal, to revolt (*MOABITE STONE). Later in his reign, however, Ahab, with Jehoshaphat of Judah, once more warred against Syria (1 Ki. 22:3). Though warned by Micaiah's prophecy of the fatal outcome, Ahab entered the final battle at Ramoth-gilead, but in disguise. He was mortally wounded by a random arrow, and his body taken to Samaria for burial. His son Ahaziah succeeded to the throne (1 Ki. 22:28–40).

II. Religious affairs

Elijah was the principal prophet of the reign. Ahab was influenced by his wife Jezebel whom he allowed to build a temple dedicated to Baal (of Tyre) in Samaria with its pagan altar, *asherah* and attendants (1 Ki. 16:32). She encouraged a large group of false prophets together with the devotees of Baal (1 Ki. 18:19–20), and later instigated open opposition to Yahweh. The true prophets were slain, altars of the Lord were torn down and Elijah forced to flee for his life. One hundred prophets were, however, hidden by Obadiah, Ahab's godly minister (1 Ki. 18:3–4).

Ahab's failure to stand for the law and true justice was exemplified in the fake trial and subsequent death of Naboth, whose vineyard was annexed to the adjacent palace grounds at Jezreel (1 Ki. 21:1–16). This brought Elijah once again into open opposition; his stand was vindicated by Yahweh at the test at Carmel which routed the claims of the false prophets. Elijah prophesied the fate of Ahab, his wife and the dynasty (1 Ki. 21:20–24). The reign, marked by idolatry and the evil influence of Jezebel (1 Ki. 21:25–26), affected succeeding generations for evil, and was also condemned by Hosea (1:4) and Micah (6:16).

2. Ahab, son of Kolaiah, was one of the two false prophets denounced by Jeremiah for using the name of Yahweh. His death, by fire, at the hand of the king of Babylon was foretold by the prophet (Je. 29:21). D.J.W.

AHASUERUS (*ʾaḥašwērôš*, the Heb. equivalent of the Persian *khshayarsha*). In the Elephantine Aramaic papyri the consonants appear as *ḥsyʾrš*. The resemblance of the latter to the Greek Xerxes is reasonably close, and the Babylonian version of Xerxes' name on the Behistun inscription is close to the Hebrew as above. Xerxes I was king of Persia (485–465 BC). The name occurs in three different contexts:

1. Ezra 4:6. It is probable that in Ezr. 4:6–23 the author has deliberately introduced two later examples of opposition in the reigns of Xerxes I and his successor, Artaxerxes I. The context speaks of opposition to the building of the city walls, and not of the Temple, as

Crown prince Ahasuerus (Xerxes) standing behind the enthroned king of Persia, his father Darius I. From Persepolis, Iran. Height c. 2·50 m. 521–486 BC. (OIUC)

in 4:1–5, 24 (see J. Stafford Wright, *The Date of Ezra's Coming to Jerusalem*, 1958). An alternative but improbable theory is that the king here is Cambyses, the successor of Cyrus (529–522 BC).

2. The book of *Esther. Almost certainly Xerxes I, although the LXX reads throughout 'Artaxerxes', and some identify Ahasuerus here with Artaxerxes II (404–359 BC).

3. Dn. 9:1. The father of *Darius the Mede. J.S.W.

AHAVA. A Babylonian town and also, probably, a canal named after the town, where Ezra assembled returning exiles (Ezr. 8:15–31). The site may well be the classical Scenae (Strabo, *Geog.* 16. 1. 27), an important caravan junction not far from Babylon. D.J.A.C.

AHAZ (Heb. *'āḥaz*, 'he has grasped'). **1.** King of Judah (732–715 BC), son of Jotham. The name Ahaz is an abbreviated form of Jehoahaz. This is confirmed by an inscription of Tiglath-pileser III (*Yauhazi*, see *ANET*, p. 282). His age at the time of his accession and the length of his reign (2 Ki. 16:2; 2 Ch. 28:1) both give rise to chronological problems (*CHRONOLOGY OF THE OLD TESTAMENT).

Early in his reign, Pekah, king of Israel, and Rezin, king of Syria, tried to force him to join their anti-Assyrian alliance. Failing in this, the allies invaded Judah (2 Ki. 16:5). The Judaeans suffered heavy casualties and many were taken prisoner. The intervention of the prophet Oded secured the repatriation of the prisoners (2 Ch. 28:5–15). Isaiah sought vainly to encourage Ahaz at the height of the crisis to put his trust in Yahweh (Is. 7:1–12), but the faithless king preferred to appeal to Assyria for help. The price of Assyrian aid, besides being a heavy drain on the exchequer, was a century of vassalage for Judah. The Philistines and the Edomites took advantage of Judah's weakened condition to make hostile incursions (2 Ch. 28:17–18).

These calamities are represented as divine judgment on Ahaz for his flagrant apostasy. He 'even burned his son as an offering', encouraged corrupt worship of the high places, placed an Assyrian-type altar in the temple court, used the displaced Solomonic bronze altar for divination and closed the sanctuary (2 Ki. 16:3–4, 10–16; 2 Ch. 28:2–4, 23–25).

2. Ahaz was also the name of a son of Micah, great-grandson of King Saul (1 Ch. 8:35–36; 9:41–42). J.C.J.W.

AHAZIAH (Heb. *'ᵃḥazyâ* or *'ᵃḥazyāhû*, 'Yahweh has grasped'). **1.** Son and successor of *Ahab, king of Israel, whose religious policy he continued unchanged (1 Ki. 22:51–2 Ki. 1:18). Consequently, the main interest in his 2-year reign for the biblical narrator is his clash with *Elijah after he had sent to consult with *Baalzebub, god of Ekron. At his accession, the revolt of Moab, which the *Moabite Stone suggests may have started during the closing years of Ahab's reign, was successfully concluded (2 Ki. 1:1; 3:5). Ahaziah also faced failure in his ill-fated attempt at a maritime alliance with Jehoshaphat, king of

Alabaster vase from the ruins of the mausoleum at Halicarnassus. It was probably presented to a local ruler by Ahasuerus (Xerxes), king of Persia (485–465 BC), whose name and titles are engraved upon it in Old Persian, Babylonian cuneiform and Egyptian hieroglyphs. Height c. 29 cm. (BM)

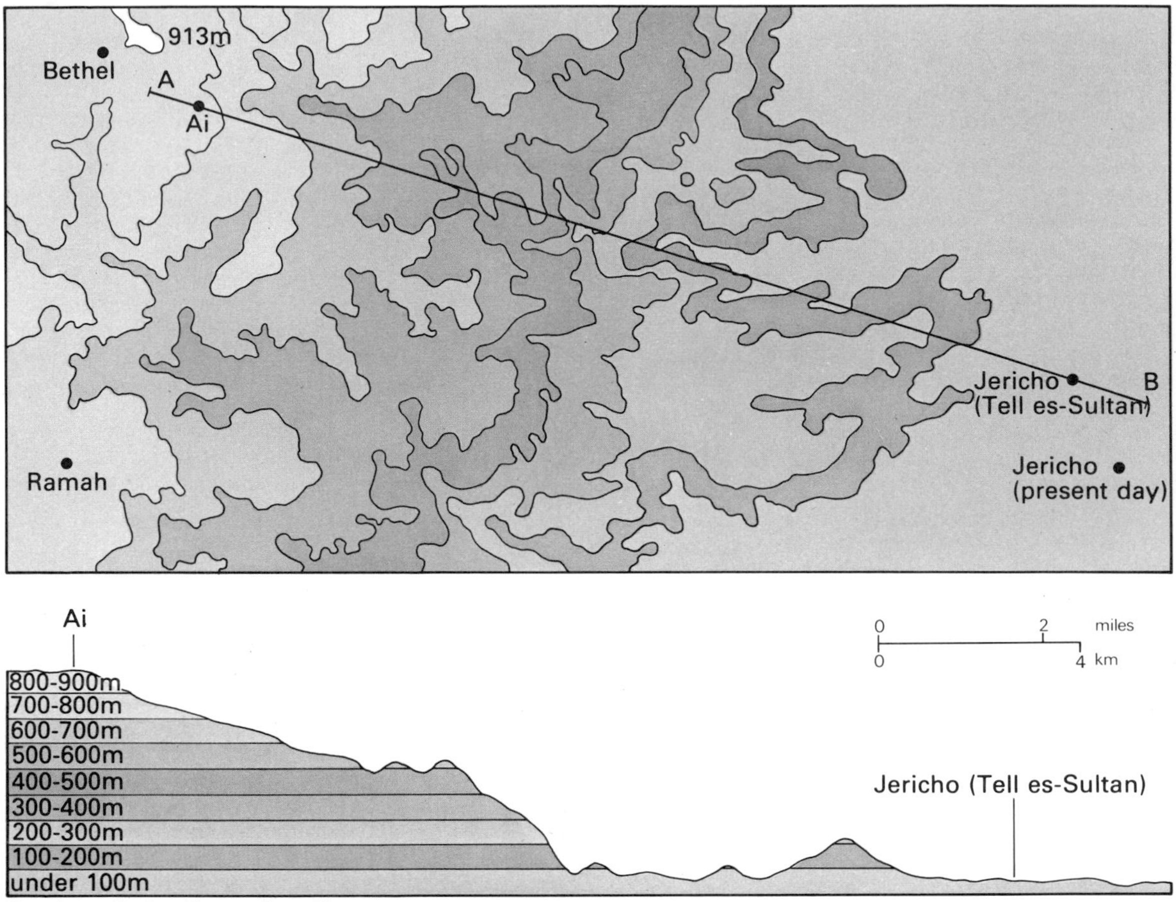

Section of plan from A to B

The situation of Ai (Et-Tell) in relation to Jericho.

Judah (2 Ch. 20:35–36; 1 Ki. 22:48–49). He died prematurely after a fall, and, having no son, was succeeded by his brother Jehoram.

2. Also called Jehoahaz (2 Ch. 21:17), a variant form of the same name: the youngest son of Jehoram, king of Judah. Complementary accounts of his accession and assassination, based on independent sources which reflect differing interests, are found in 2 Ki. 8:25–29; 9:16–29; and 2 Ch. 22:1–9. He was placed on the throne by the inhabitants of Jerusalem as the sole surviving heir. His reign of less than a year was characterized by a close association with his uncle, Jehoram, king of Israel, no doubt under the influence of his mother, *Athaliah. He was murdered during the purge of Jehu whilst visiting Jehoram, who was convalescing in Jezreel. H.G.M.W.

AHIAH
See Ahijah, Part 1.

AHIAM
See Hararite, Part 2.

AHIJAH, AHIAH. 1. A prophet from Shiloh who protested against the idolatry of Solomon. Ahijah symbolically divided his robe into 12 parts, 10 of which he gave to Jeroboam, a minor official in Solomon's government (1 Ki. 11:28ff.). Ahijah stated that the kingdom of Solomon would be divided and that 10 of the tribes would become subject to Jeroboam (1 Ki. 11:30–40). To escape the wrath of Solomon, Jeroboam fled to Egypt, where he was granted asylum by Pharaoh Shishak. After Solomon's death, Ahijah's prophecy was fulfilled when the 10 N tribes revolted from Rehoboam, Solomon's son, and Jeroboam became king of Israel (922–901 BC). Jeroboam, however, led Israel into idolatry and was also denounced by Ahijah. The prophet foretold the death of Jeroboam's son, the extinction of his house and the future captivity of Israel (1 Ki. 14:6–16).

2. In 1 Sa. 14:3, 18 Ahiah appears as the name of the great-grandson of Eli, who is elsewhere called Ahimelech, priest of Nob and father of Abiathar (1 Sa. 21:1ff.; 22:9ff.).

3. Other men bearing the name are mentioned briefly: one of Solomon's secretaries (1 Ki. 4:3); the father of Baasha (1 Ki. 15:27, 33); the son of Jerahmeel (1 Ch. 2:25, where the rendering is uncertain); the son of Ehud (1 Ch. 8:4, 7, AV respectively 'Ahoah' and 'Ahiah'); one of David's heroes (1 Ch. 11:36); a guardian of the Temple treasure (1 Ch. 26:20, where again the text is dubious); and one of Nehemiah's fellow-signatories to the covenant (Ne. 10:26, RSV 'Ahiah'). C.F.P.

AHIKAM (Heb. *'ᵃḥîqām*, 'my brother has arisen'). Son of Shaphan (probably not Shaphan the scribe, 2 Ki. 22:12), and father of *Gedaliah, whom Nebuchadrezzar appointed governor in 587 BC (2 Ki. 25:22; Je. 39:14). One of those sent by Josiah to enquire of *Huldah the prophetess (2 Ki. 22:14; 2 Ch. 34:20–22), he later saved Jeremiah from death (Je. 26:24). D.W.B.

AHIMAAZ (Heb. *'ᵃḥîma'aṣ*, 'my brother is wrath'). **1.** Father of Saul's wife, Ahinoam (1 Sa. 14:50).

2. Son of Zadok. Famed for his swift running (2 Sa. 18:27). With Jonathan, Abiathar's son, he acted as messenger from David's secret allies in Jerusalem during Absalom's rebellion (2 Sa. 15:27, 36), and escaped capture at En-rogel only by hiding in a well (2 Sa. 17:17–21). He was one of the two messengers who brought news of Absalom's defeat, though he did not report his death, either through ignorance of the fact or a natural reluctance to tell David (2 Sa. 18:19–32).

3. Solomon's commissariat officer for Naphtali, who married his daughter, Basemath (1 Ki. 4:15). Some identify with Zadok's son. J.G.G.N.

AHIMELECH (Heb. *'ᵃḥîmeleḵ*, 'brother of a king', 'my brother is king'). The name is also found on the ostraca from Samaria and an ancient Hebrew seal. **1.** Son of Ahitub, father of Abiathar, priest at Nob who gave David the showbread and Goliath's sword, for which he was killed by Saul (1 Sa. 21–22) (*AHIJAH). **2.** Son of *Abiathar, a priest under David, perhaps grandson of **1** (2 Sa. 8:17). **3.** A Hittite in David's service before he became king (1 Sa. 26:6). A.R.M.

AHIRAM. A son of Benjamin (Nu. 26:38), possibly corrupted to Ehi in Gn. 46:21 and to Aharah in 1 Ch. 8:1. J.D.D.

AHITHOPHEL (Heb. *'ᵃḥîṯōpel*, possibly 'brother of foolish talk'). A native of Giloh and David's respected counsellor (2 Sa. 16:23). When he conspired with Absalom, David prayed that his advice might be rendered useless, perhaps playing on the name (2 Sa. 15:12, 31ff.). Ahithophel suggested that Absalom should assert his authority by taking possession of his father's harem. His plan for attacking David before he could muster his forces was thwarted by the king's friend Hushai. Ahithophel, perceiving that Absalom had taken a disastrous course, went home and hanged himself lest he fall into the hands of his former lord (2 Sa. 16–17). Jehoiada and Abiathar took his place as David's counsellors (1 Ch. 28:33–34). His son, Eliam, evidently remained faithful to David, as he was one of the thirty heroes (2 Sa. 23:34). A.R.M.

AHITUB (Heb. *'ᵃḥîṭûḇ*, 'brother of good', 'my brother is good'. LXX *Achitōb* and Assyr. *Aḫuṭāb* suggest a reading Ahitob). **1.** Son of Phinehas, grandson of Eli, father of *Ahijah (1 Sa. 14:3). **2.** Father of Ahimelech, perhaps the same person as **1** (1 Sa. 22:9). **3.** A Levite, son of Amariah (1 Ch. 6:7–8), father of Meraioth and 'chief officer of the house of God' (1 Ch. 9:11). Zadok was evidently his grandson (2 Sa. 8:17; 1 Ch. 18:16; Ezr. 7:2; *cf.* 1 Ch. 9:11; Ne. 11:11). A.R.M.

AHLAB. Situated in the territory of Asher (Jdg. 1:31), it is possibly the Mehebel of Jos. 19:29. Probably to be identified with Khirbet el-Maḥālib, 8 km NE of Tyre, the Mahalib captured by *Tiglath-pileser III in 734 BC and later by *Sennacherib. See D. J. Wiseman, *Iraq* 18, 1956, p. 129. D.J.W.

AI. The name is always written with the definite article in Hebrew, *hā'ay*, the heap, ruin. The city lay E of Bethel and the altar which Abram built (Gn. 12:8) adjacent to Beth-aven (Jos. 7:2) and N of Michmash (Is. 10:28). The Israelite attack upon it, immediately following the sack of Jericho, was at first repulsed, but after Achan's sin had been punished a successful stratagem was employed. The people of Ai were killed, their king executed, and their city burned and made into 'a heap' (Heb. *tēl*; Jos. 7:1–8:29). It became an Ephraimite town (1 Ch. 7:28, 'Ayyah'), but was inhabited by the Benjaminites after the Exile (Ne. 11:31). Isaiah pictured the Assyrian armies advancing on Jerusalem by way of Ai (Is. 10:28, 'Aiath').

Modern Et-Tell (Arab. *tall*, heap, mound) about 3 km SE of Bethel (Tell Beitīn) is usually identified with Ai on topographical grounds and on the correspondence in the meanings of the ancient and modern names. Excavations in 1933–5 by Mme J. Marquet-Krause and in 1964–72 by J. A. Callaway revealed a city which prospered in the 3rd millennium BC. There was a strong city-wall and a temple containing stone bowls and ivories imported from Egypt. It was destroyed *c.* 2400 BC, perhaps by Amorite invaders. No traces of later occupation were found except for a small settlement which made use of the earlier ruins about 1200–1050 BC. Those who believe in this identification have made various attempts to explain the discrepancy between the biblical account of Joshua's conquest and the archaeological evidence. It has been suggested that the story originally referred to Bethel but was later adapted to suit Ai or even invented to explain the impressive ruin as the result of an attack by the hero Joshua. There is no evidence to support these hypotheses; indeed, it would be strange to credit a hero with failure at first. More plausible is the explanation that Ai, with its massive old walls, was used as a temporary stronghold by the surrounding population; but the account points rather to an inhabited town with its own king. While it is possible that Ai is to be located elsewhere, no completely satisfac-

AHOAH
See Ahijah, Part 1.

AHOLAH
See Oholibamah, Part 2.

AHOLIAB
See Oholiab, Part 2.

AHOLIBAH
See Oholibamah, Part 2.

Remains of an Iron Age house at Ai (probably the modern Et-Tell). The hewn stone pillars supported the roof beams. c. 1200–1050 BC. (AIA)

tory solution has yet been proposed (for the question of identification see D. Livingston, *WTJ* 33, 1970, pp. 20–44; A. F. Rainey, *WTJ* 33, pp. 175–188; D. Livingston, *WTJ* 34, 1971, pp. 39–50). The later town (Ezr. 2:28; Ne. 7:32) may be identified with some other site in the vicinity. For references to the excavation results and proposed solutions of the problem they raise, see J. A. Callaway, *EAEHL*, 1, pp. 36–52; J. M. Grintz, *Bib* 42, 1961, pp. 201–216.

Ai is also the name of a city in Moab (Je. 49:3) of unknown location. A.R.M.

AIATH
See Ai, Part 1.

AKKAD
See Accad, Part 1.

AKKADIANS
See Babylon, Part 1.

ALABASTER BOX
See Ointment, Part 2.

AIJALON, AJALON (Heb. *'ayyālôn*). **1.** A town on a hill commanding from the S the entrance to the Vale of Aijalon. The earliest traces (2000 BC) are at Tell el-Qoq'a, near Yalo. In successive phases of Israel's history it was inhabited by Danites (who could not expel the Amorites), Ephraimites and Benjaminites (Jos. 19:42; Jdg. 1:35; 1 Ch. 6:69; 8:13). A levitical town, fortified by Rehoboam to guard the NW approach to Jerusalem, it was occupied by the Philistines in the reign of Ahaz (2 Ch. 11:10; 28:18).

BIBLIOGRAPHY. D. Baly, *Geog. Companion*, 1963, pp. 92f.; *LOB*, pp. 162, 285, *etc.*

2. A town in Zebulun (Jdg. 12:12), where the judge Elon (same Heb. letters) was buried; LXX *Ailom*. Possibly Kh. el-Lōn.

BIBLIOGRAPHY. F. M. Abel, *Géographie de la Palestine*, 2, 1937, p. 241. J.P.U.L.

AKELDAMA. Acts 1:19 gives the meaning of the word (in AV Aceldama) as 'field of blood'—the Aramaic phrase being *ḥ^{a}qēl d^{e}mâ*. The ground was previously known as the Potter's Field, and this has been equated with the Potter's House (Je. 18:2) in the Hinnom Valley. Jerome placed it on the S side of this valley; and the site accepted today is there. Eusebius, however, said this ground was N of Jerusalem. The traditional site certainly can provide potter's clay; and it has long been used for burials. See J. A. Motyer in *NIDNTT* 1, pp. 93–94, for bibliography and a brief discussion of the problems. D.F.P.

AKRABBIM (Heb. *'aqrabbîm*, 'scorpions'). A mountain pass at the S end of the Dead Sea (Nu. 34:4; Jos. 15:3 ['Maaleh-acrabbim', AV]; Jdg. 1:36) between the Arabah and the hill-country of Judah, identified with the modern Naqb eṣ-ṣāfā. J.D.D.

ALALAH (Akkad., Hurrian *a-la-la-aḫ*; Egypt. *'irrḫ*). Capital of a city-state on the river Orontes in the Amq plain of N Syria from which 468 texts from Level VII (*c.* 1900–1750 BC) and IV (*c.* 1500–1470 BC) provide details which may be compared with the patriarchal period of Gn. (also *EBLA, *MARI, *UGARIT). The site of Tell Aṭšānâ (Turk. Açana) was excavated by Sir Leonard Woolley, who in 1937–9 and 1946–9 uncovered sixteen levels of occupation since *c.* 3100 BC (XVI) to *c.* 1200 (I) with early affinities with both Palestine and Mesopotamia.

The 172 texts from Yarimlim's palace (VII) were primarily contracts and ration lists. The city was controlled by a W Semitic family ruling Aleppo (Halab) whose governor Abba'el (or Abban) suppressed a revolt at Irrid near Carchemish and, *c.* 1720, gave Alalah to his brother Yarimlim (AT 1). This early covenant-treaty text, and associated agreements, describes the historical situation, stipulations, divine witnesses and curses, as is common in the later *covenant formulae. A separate document by the same scribe lists the religious obligations (AT 126). Yarimlim left the city to his son in his will (AT 6), attested by state officials, perhaps to avoid rivalry on his death (*cf.* 1 Ki. 1:17–36). However, another son, Irkabtum, succeeded and made peace with the semi-nomadic Hapiru (*HEBREW, *ABRAHAM). The city fell to the Hittite Mursilis I when he captured Aleppo (*c.* 1600 BC).

After a gap (V), Idrimi, the youngest son of a king of Aleppo, was driven into exile, as he tells in his autobiography, inscribed as a speech on his statue. After living among the Hapiru in Canaan for 7 years he received divine assurance to mount an amphibious operation to recapture Mukish. He re-entered his capital Alalah to popular acclaim, was made king and built a palace and temple with spoil taken in war (*c.* 1470 BC). This narrative has been compared with the experiences of David (1 Sa. 22:3ff.). Idrimi made treaties with neighbouring states regulating the extradition of runaway slaves (AT 3, *ANET*^{3}, p. 532). Similarly Shimei entered Philistine territory to search for his two slaves and Achish of Gath returned them on demand (1 Ki. 2:39–40). This would imply a similar type of treaty, perhaps between Solomon and Gath, following David's experience there (1 Sa. 27:5ff.). It would also throw light on the provision prohibiting the extradition of Hebrew fugitives in Dt. 23:15–16 (*IEJ* 5, 1955, pp. 65–72). Another treaty makes city elders responsible for returning fugitives (AT 2, *ANET*^{3}, pp. 531f.; Dt. 23:15–16). Alalah later came under Hittite control (Level III), as it had earlier been governed by northerners in the 20th–19th centuries BC. There is no reason

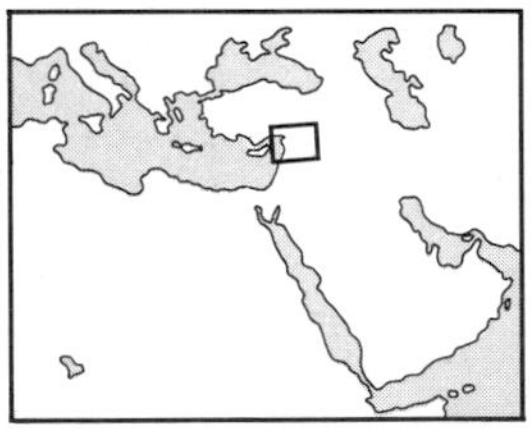

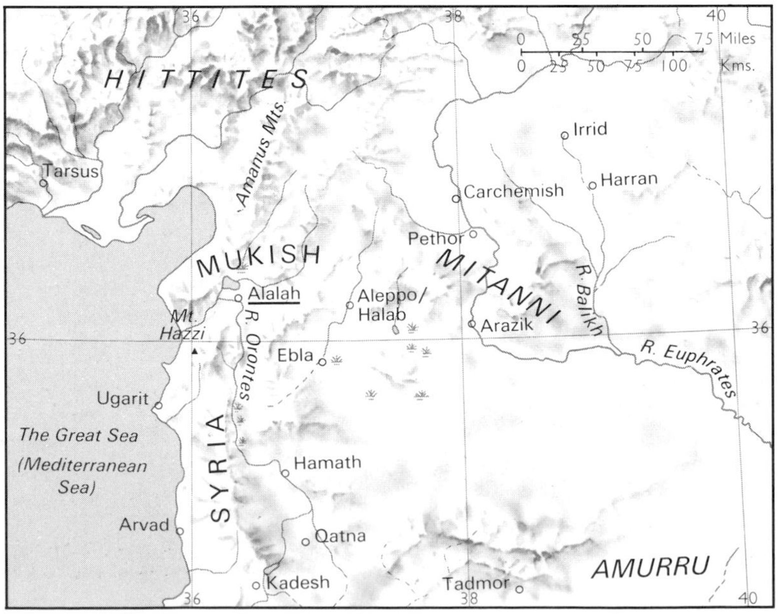

Alalah, capital of a city-state on the river Orontes.

to doubt that *Hittites might be resident in S Palestine in the days of Abraham (Gn. 23:5–7; *JTVI*, 1956, p. 124). Alalah was finally destroyed by 'Sea-peoples', perhaps those allied to the *Philistines.

The main interest in these texts for the OT lies in the comparison of customs and language with the Gn. narratives. In marriage contracts (AT 91–94), the future father-in-law was 'asked' for the bride (*cf.* Gn. 29:18), to whom betrothal gifts were made (AT 17). Some contracts state that failing a son within 7 years the husband could marry a concubine (*cf.* Gn. 29:18–21); however, if the first wife later bore a son he would be the first-born (AT 92; *cf.* Gn. 21:10).

The king held a firm control legally and economically over citizens of all classes including the élite *maryanu*-warriors (who also had religious obligations, AT 15), the freedmen and the semi-free rural retainers, among whom were listed the *hupšu* (*hop̄šî*, Dt. 15:12–18).

Some individuals were made to work off their debt by going to the palace to 'dwell in the house of the king' (AT 18–27, 32; *cf.* Ps. 23:6). Slaves were not numerous and could be received as prisoners of war or as gifts (AT 224). They were valued at *c.* 25 silver shekels and some contracts included clauses against release at a royal amnesty (AT 65). The *corvée* (*mas*) was enforced at Alalah as in later Israel (AT 246; Jos. 17:13). All this would be in the mind of Samuel at least when the Israelites asked for a similar type of kingship (1 Sa. 8).

Other customs which may illustrate biblical practices are the exchange of villages to preserve inter-state boundaries along natural and defensible features. This may be reflected in Solomon's 'gift' of 20 villages to Hiram of Tyre in return for wood and gold (1 Ki. 9:10–14; *JBL* 79, 1960, pp. 59–60). Treaty ceremonies involved the slaughter of sheep over which the participants declared: 'If ever I take back what I have given . . .', implying 'may the gods cut off my life', a similar idea to that in OT oaths (*e.g.* 1 Sa. 3:17). In some contracts clothes were given as additional payment, as also in Syria later according to 2 Ki. 5:5–27. Ahab may have attempted to justify his action in confiscating Naboth's property (1 Ki. 21:15) on the basis of the practice whereby a rebel against the king had his

Alalah tablet (no. 7). Details of a legal case heard by King Niqmepa concerning the division of property between Abba'el and his sister. The text is repeated on the envelope, which contains the seals of witnesses. 10 cm × 5 cm. (DJW)

Alalah tablet (no. 1), the deed whereby Abba'el of Aleppo gave the city of Alalah to Yarimlin. 11 cm × 6·4 cm. c. 1720 BC. (DJW)

ALDEBARAN See Stars, Part 3.

King Idrimi of Alalah enthroned. The autobiographical inscription in the form of a speech commences at his mouth. Height 1·4 m. c. 1490 BC. (BM)

property taken by the palace after the execution of an evil-doer (AT 17, *ANET*³, p. 546, no. 15). The use of *mištannu*, 'equivalent' (AT 3, *ANET*³, p. 532), in the manumission of slaves (*cf. mišneh*, Dt. 15:18) argues against Je. 16:18 as 'stigmatizing God as unreasonable and unjust' (*HUCA* 29, 1958, pp. 125f.).

The mixed Semitic and Hurrian population of the area from early times (VII) gives significant Hurrian (*HORITE) parallels to such names as Anah, Aholibamah, Alian, Ajah, Dishon, Ezer (Gn. 36), Anah and Shamgar (Jdg. 3:31), To'i (2 Sa. 8:9), Agee (2 Sa. 23:11), Eli-hepa (2 Sa. 23:32) (*JTVI* 82, 1950, p. 6).

BIBLIOGRAPHY. C. L. Woolley, *A Forgotten Kingdom*, 1953; *Alalakh*, 1955; D. J. Wiseman, *The Alalakh Tablets*, 1953 (=AT); *AOTS*, 1967, pp. 119–135; *IDBS*, 1976, pp. 16–17; Sidney Smith, *The Statue of Idrimi*, 1949; *cf. ANET*, 1969, pp. 557–558. D.J.W.

ALEXANDER. A common Hellenistic name. Its widespread adoption among Jews displeased some strict rabbis and gave rise to an amusing aetiological story that a demand by Alexander the Great for a golden statue in the Temple was countered with the proposal that all boys born that year should be called Alexander (see E. Nestle, *ExpT* 10, 1898–9, p. 527). The frequency is reflected in the NT.

1. The son of Simon of Cyrene (*RUFUS). **2.** A member of the high priestly family, unknown apart from Acts 4:6. **3.** The would-be spokesman of the Jewish interest in the Ephesian riot (Acts 19:33f.). His function was presumably to dissociate the regular Jewish community from the Christian trouble-makers: the anti-Semitism of the mob, however, allowed him no voice. **4.** A pernicious teacher of subverted morals (1 Tim. 1:20), whom Paul 'delivers to Satan' (*HYMENAEUS).

5. A bitter enemy of Paul and the gospel (2 Tim. 4:14f.), evidently (since Timothy is put on guard against him) operating in the Ephesus–Troas area. Had he been responsible for an arrest in Ephesus? He was a coppersmith (the word was then used to designate all kinds of metal-worker), though some have read the title as a proper name, 'Alexander Chalceus'. When Paul adds 'the Lord will requite him for his deeds', the tense marks this as a prediction (RSV, TEV), not a curse (AV).

Those identifying **3** and **5** (*e.g.* P. N. Harrison, *Problem of the Pastoral Epistles*, 1921, pp. 118f.) can point to the Ephesian location, the origin of the riot with the craft-guilds, and the introduction of Alexander in Acts 19:33 as if well known; but nothing there indicates the sort of opposition betokened in 2 Tim. 4:14. Little can be said for or against identifying **4** and **5**; but **3** and **4** cannot be identical, for the latter would claim to be a Christian.

A.F.W.

ALEXANDER THE GREAT. The youthful king of Macedon whose pan-hellenic expedition of 336 BC to liberate the Greeks of Asia Minor unexpectedly demolished the Persian Empire. Only the mutiny of his troops turned him back in India, and he died in 323 while planning the conquest of the W. His generals established the concert

Coin of Lysimachus, thought to represent the head of Alexander with the horn of Ammon. 297 BC. (RG)

of Hellenistic kingdoms to which the Herods performed the epilogue. Probably from necessity rather than idealism, Alexander abandoned the isolationism of the Greeks in favour of racial co-operation. Hellenism became an international norm of civilization. Hence the agonies of the Jews in the Maccabean age, and the tensions that surrounded the crucifixion. Hence also the inspiration of the cosmopolitan philosophies that chimed in with Christian ideals.

Presumably it is Alexander to whom reference is made in Dn. 8:21; 11:3.

BIBLIOGRAPHY. Arrian, *Anabasis*; Plutarch, *Life of Alexander*; C. B. Welles, *Alexander and the Hellenistic World*, 1970; R. L. Fox, *Alexander the Great*, 1973; J. R. Hamilton, *Alexander the Great*, 1973; P. Green, *Alexander of Macedon*, 1974. E.A.J.

ALEXANDRIA.

I. The city

a. Location

A great seaport on the NW coast of the Egyptian Delta, on the narrow isthmus between the sea and Lake Mareotis. It was founded in 332 BC by Alexander (the Great) of Macedon and named after himself. A small Egyptian settlement, Rakotis, was its only predecessor on the site and was absorbed into the W side of the new city; in native Egyptian parlance (exemplified by Coptic, centuries later), the name Rakotis was extended to Alexandria. The city was apparently laid out on a 'grid' plan of cross-streets and *insulae*; but as the remains of the ancient city are inextricably buried underneath its modern successor, any reconstruction of its lay-out and location of its great buildings must draw heavily on the none-too-precise literary references virtually by themselves, and hence cannot be exact. Not until the time of Ptolemy II (*c*. 285–246 BC) did Alexandria first attain to the architectural splendours so famed in later writers' accounts. Between the shore and the Pharos island stretched a connecting causeway, the 'Heptastadion' ('seven stadia', 1,300 m long); this divided the anchorage into a W harbour and an E or Great harbour, whose entrance was dominated by the Pharos lighthouse-tower. It contained also the royal harbour, and was flanked on the E by the royal palace. S of the shore-line, extending all along behind it and as far as Lake Mareotis, stretched the city.

b. Population

Right from the start, Alexandria was a thoroughly cosmopolitan city. Besides its Greek citizens and numerous poor Greek immigrants, there was a considerable Jewish community (*cf*. later, Acts 6:9; 18:24) under their own ethnarch and having their own quarter (though not restricted to it until AD 38), and quite a large native Egyptian populace, especially in the Rakotis district in the W. In Rakotis was localized the Serapeum, temple of the Egypto-Hellenistic deity Sarapis, whose cult was specially promoted by Ptolemy I, just possibly to serve as a common bond for both Greeks and Egyptians (Sir H. I. Bell).

c. The city's role

Politically, Alexandria became capital of Egypt under the *Ptolemies, Graeco-Macedonian kings of Egypt, *c*. 323–30 BC. Under the first and energetic kings of this line it became the greatest Hellenistic city of the day. Alexandria continued as Egypt's administrative capital into the Roman imperial and Byzantine epochs. Alexandria was the banking-centre of all Egypt, an active manufacturing city (cloths, glass, papyrus, *etc*.) and a thriving port. Thence were transhipped the exotic products of Arabia, India and the East, and thence in Roman times sailed the great grain-ships of Alexandria (*cf*. Acts 27:6; 28:11) to bring cheap corn for the Roman plebeians. Finally, Alexandria quickly became and long remained a brilliant seat of learning. To the reign of either Ptolemy I (323–285 BC) or Ptolemy II (285–246 BC) belongs the founding of the 'Museum', where scholars researched and taught in arts and sciences, and of the Library which eventually contained thousands of works upon many tens of thousands of papyrus rolls.

II. Judaism and Christianity

Alexandria's very large Jewish community was concentrated in the E sector, but with places of worship all over the city (Philo, *Legatio ad Gaium* 132). One famous synagogue, magnificently fitted, was so vast that flags had to be used to signal the Amen (TB *Sukkah* 51b, cited in *BC*, 1, pp. 152f.). But beyond this, Alexandria was the intellectual and literary centre of the Dispersion. It was there that the Greek OT, the Septuagint (*TEXT AND VERSIONS), was produced, and from there came such works as the Book of Wisdom (*APOCRYPHA) with its Platonic modifications of OT categories and its Greek interest in cosmology and immortality. It was the home of the voluminous *Philo, perhaps the first considerable scholar to use the biblical material as philosophic data—though 'his object is not to investigate but to harmonize' (Bigg, p. 32)—and the first major exponent of the allegorical exegesis of Scripture. Whatever the demerits of the attempted synthesis of Athens and Jerusalem by Alexandrian Jews (and some of them amount to enormities), the literary remains testify to intellectual energy, missionary concern and, despite audacious departures from traditional formation, a profound seriousness about the Scriptures.

These features had considerable indirect influence on early Greek Christianity. It is significant that the eloquent travelling preacher *Apollos, who became an important figure in the apostolic church, was an Alexandrian Jew, and 'well versed in the Scriptures' (Acts 18:24). The Epistle to the Hebrews, because of its use of terminology beloved at Alexandria, and its characteristic use of OT, has been associated, if not necessarily with him, at least with an Alexandrian background; and so, with less reason, have other NT books (*cf*. J. N. Sanders, *The Fourth Gospel in the Early Church*, 1943; S. G. F. Brandon, *The Fall of Jerusalem and the Christian Church*, 1951). Apart, however, from unreliable traditions about the agency of the Evangelist Mark (which may relate originally to the reception of his Gospel in Alexandria), the origin and early history of the Alexandrian church

ALEXANDER JANNAEUS

See Maccabees, Part 2.

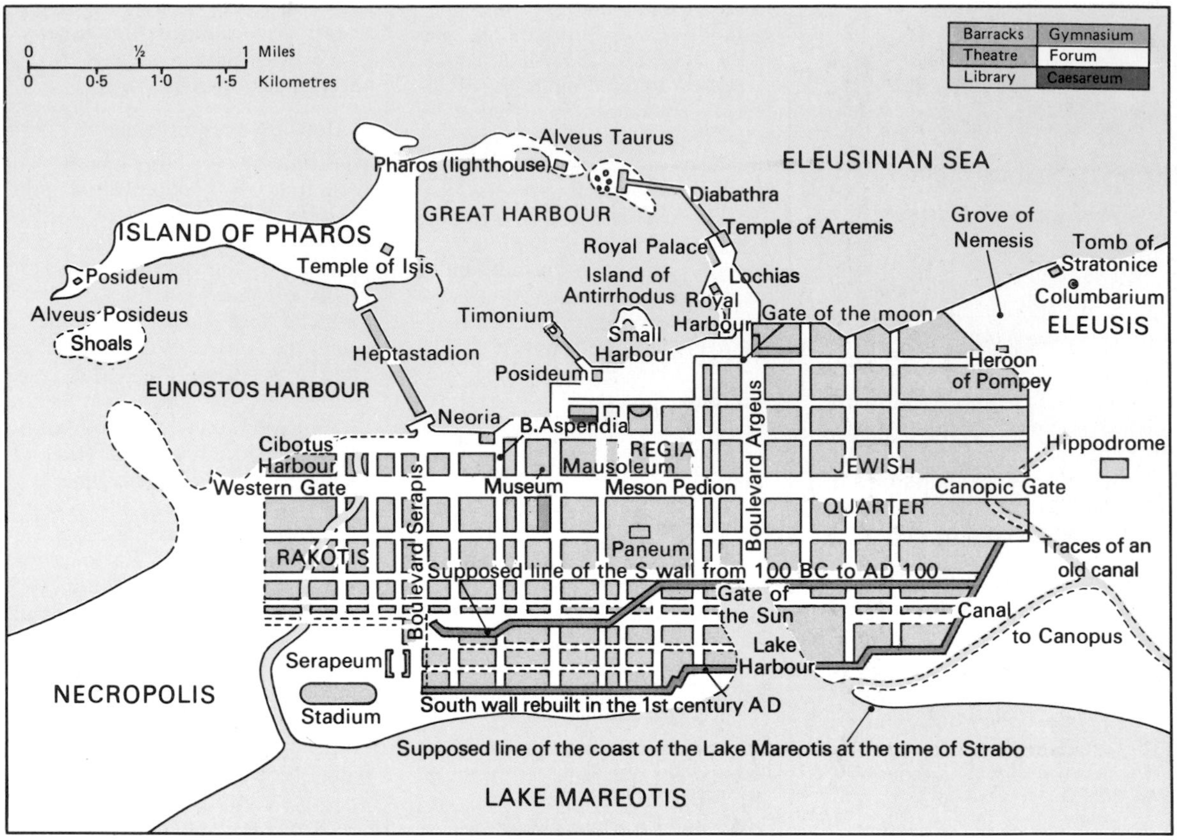

Plan of Alexandria, 100 BC to AD 100, derived mainly from literary sources, since the old city has never been excavated.

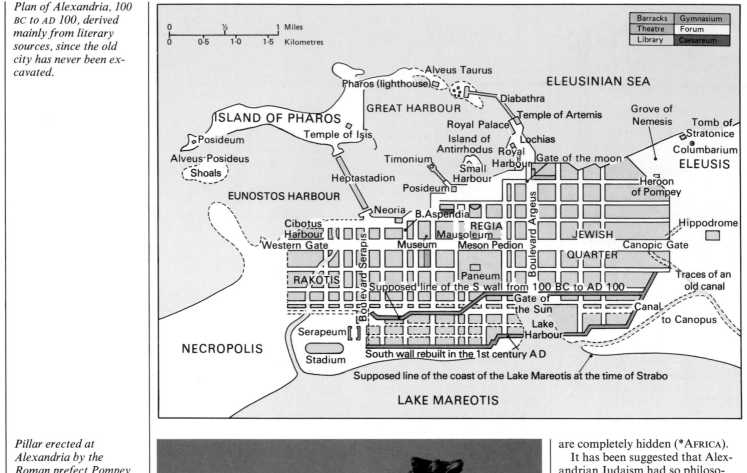

Pillar erected at Alexandria by the Roman prefect Pompey in AD 302. (RS)

are completely hidden (*AFRICA).

It has been suggested that Alexandrian Judaism had so philosophized away the Messianic hope that the earliest Christian preaching made slow headway there. There is not sufficient evidence to test this hypothesis. It is unmistakable, however, that when Alexandrian Christianity comes into full view it is patently the heir of Alexandrian Judaism. The missionary zeal, the philosophic apologetic, the allegorical exegesis, the application to biblical commentary and the passion for intellectual synthesis which sometimes leads doctrine to disaster, are common to both. Some thoroughfare, at present unlit, links Philo and Clement of Alexandria; but it is hardly too bold a conjecture that the road lies through the conversion to Christ of a substantial number of Jews or their adherents in Alexandria during the apostolic or sub-apostolic period.

BIBLIOGRAPHY. For a standard historical and cultural background for Alexandria, Ptolemaic and Byzantine, see respectively *CAH*, 7, 1928, ch. IV, sect. vii, pp. 142–148, and chs. VIII–IX, pp. 249–311, and *ibid.*, 12, 1939, ch. XIV, sect. i, pp. 476–492. Useful and compact, with reference to actual remains is E. Breccia, *Alexandrea ad Aegyptum, A Guide . . .*, 1922. A popular, readable account of the history and manner of life in ancient Alexandria is H. T. Davis, *Alexandria, the Golden City*, 2 vols., 1957. An excellent study of paganism, Judaism and the advent and triumph of Christianity in Egypt generally, and Alexandria also, is provided by Sir Harold Idris Bell, *Cults and Creeds in Graeco-Roman Egypt*, 1953. On Alexandria and Christianity, see also J. M. Creed in S. R. K. Glanville (ed.), *The Legacy of Egypt*, 1942, pp. 300–316; A. F. Shore in J. R. Harris (ed.), *The Legacy of Egypt*², 1971, pp. 390–398; C. Bigg, *The Christian Platonists of Alexandria*², 1913; J. E. L. Oulton and H. Chadwick, *Alexandrian Christianity*, 1954; L. W. Barnard, 'St Mark and Alexandria', *HTR* 57, 1964, pp. 145–150. A.F.W.

ALMIGHTY. Used of God 48 times in the OT (31 of them in Job) to translate Heb. *šaddai*, and following LXX in some verses, Gk. *pantokratōr*. Interpreted by early Jewish commentators as 'the all-sufficient' (*hikanos* in Jewish–Greek OT versions of 2nd century AD and later). Modern scholars offer a wide range of derivations, none certain. Outside the OT the name apparently occurs in the Tell Deir Alla Aramaic text *c.* 700 BC (* WRITING) in the plural form *šdyn*, denoting supernatural beings. Within the OT *šaddai* carries ideas of power to injure and protect (Pss. 68:14; 91:1; Is. 13:6; Joel 1:15). The name is used six times in relation to the Patriarchs, as stated in Ex. 6:3, sometimes in the compound *'ēl šaddai*, 'God Almighty'. Each case concerns the promise of blessing upon Abraham and his descendants, again with the note of power. In Job 'the Almighty' stands as a poetic parallel to 'God', as also in Ruth 1:20–21 to Yahweh, showing their identity for the writers of these books.

Gk. *pantokratōr* ('all-powerful') occurs in 2 Cor. 6:18, and nine times in Rev., where the power of God is stressed (1:8; 4:8; 11:17; 15:3; 16:7, 14; 19:6, 15; 21:22).

BIBLIOGRAPHY. N. Walker, *ZAW* 72, 1960, pp. 64–66; L. Morris in A. E. Cundall and L. Morris, *Judges and Ruth*, *TOTC*, 1968, pp. 264–268; K. Koch, *VT* 26, 1976, pp. 299–332; W. Michaelis, *TDNT* 3, pp. 914–915. A.R.M.

ALMS, ALMSGIVING. From Gk. *eleēmosynē via* eccl. Lat. *eleemosyna* and Old English *ælmysse*. The Gk. word signifies pity, prompting relief given in money or kind to the poor.

Though not explicitly mentioned in the English OT, almsgiving is implied as an expression of compassion in the presence of God. It had a twofold development: (*a*) The Mosaic legislation looked on compassion as a feeling to be cherished in ideal conduct (*cf.* Dt. 15:11); (*b*) The prophets considered almsgiving as a right which the needy might justly claim.

From the fusion of these two concepts there arose in the intertestamental age the idea of righteousness secured through almsgiving as efficacious in annulling the guilt of sin, and as ensuring divine favour in time of trouble (*cf.* Ps. 112:9; Dn. 4:27). Righteousness and almsgiving were at times regarded as synonymous terms, as in the LXX (and in our modern use of 'charity' to denote almsgiving), but this is scarcely justifiable from either the Hebrew OT or the true text of the NT.

After the cessation of sacrifice, almsgiving seems to have ranked among the Jews as the first of religious duties. In every city there were collectors who distributed alms of two kinds, *i.e.* money collected in the synagogue chest every sabbath for the poor of the city, and food and money received in a dish. 'Therefore no disciple should live in a city where there is no alms-box' (*Sanhedrin* 17b). It is significant that in the OT scarcely a trace of beggars and begging in the street can be found (but see 1 Sa. 2:36; Ps. 109:10). Ps. 41:1 can be taken as not merely an exhortation to almsgiving, but also as an adjuration to take a personal interest in the poor.

Jesus does not reject almsgiving as futile in the search for right standing with God, but stresses the necessity for right motive, 'in my name'. He rebuked the ostentatious charity of his day (Mt. 6:1–4; note RSV 'piety', translating *dikaiosynēn* for AV 'alms', translating TR *eleēmosynēn*), and emphasized the blessedness of giving (*cf.* Acts 20:35), and its opportunities.

In the early Christian community the first election of officers was made to ensure a fair distribution of alms; the needs of the poor were met (Acts 4:32, 34); and every Christian was exhorted to lay by on the first day of each week some portion of his profits to be applied to the wants of the needy (Acts 11:30; Rom. 15:25–27; 1 Cor. 16:1–4).

'Alms' are equated with 'righteousness', not because they justify a man (Rom. 3–4), but because they constitute an action which is right and for which our neighbour has a rightful claim on us in the eyes of God who gives us means for this very end (Eph. 4:28).

(* POVERTY; * COMMUNION; * COMPASSION.) J.D.D.

ALPHA AND OMEGA. This juxtaposition of the first and last letters of the Gk. alphabet, corresponding to the Heb. *'ālep̄* and *tāw*, is used in Rev. alone as a self-designation of both God (Rev. 1:8; 21:6, where 'the Alpha and the Omega' is explained by the parallel 'the beginning and the end') and Christ (22:13, with the same parallel, and the additional phrase 'the first and the last'). In Rev. 22:13 the Son's divinity is confirmed by applying to him what is said of the Father. In each of these cases the term refers to the eternal, dynamic and comprehensive activity of God or Christ in creation and salvation; that is, the origin, preservation and goal of all things are to be found in the Godhead (*cf.* Rom. 11:36). The Hebrews, Greeks and Romans all used their alphabetic letters as numerals, so that 'alpha and omega' could easily stand for 'first and last' (*cf.* Is. 44:6, 'Thus says the Lord, . . . "I am the first and I am the last"'; also Rev. 2:8). S.S.S.

ALPHAEUS. 1. The father of Levi, the tax collector (Mk. 2:14), who is generally identified with the apostle Matthew. Nothing else is known about him.

2. The father of the apostle James, who is called 'the son of Alphaeus', to distinguish him from James the son of Zebedee (Mt. 10:3; Mk. 3:18; Lk. 6:15; Acts 1:13). There is no valid reason for identifying him with the father of * Levi **1**. Attempts have also been made to identify him with Cleopas (Lk. 24:18) and Clopas (Jn. 19:25). However, it is improbable that * Cleopas and * Clopas are the same person and that Alphaeus is the same as either of them. The Aramaic of Alphaeus is *Halphai*, which could be transliterated as *Klōpas*, but even if the same indivi-

ALGUM
See Trees, Part 3.

ALLELUIA
See Hallelujah, Part 2.

ALLIANCE
See Covenant, Part 1.

ALMOND
See Trees, Part 3.

ALMUG
See Trees, Part 3.

ALOES
See Herbs, Part 2.

Alpha and Omega as written in ordinary documents of the 1st cent. AD, the time when Revelation was written. (ARM)

dual is signified, we cannot assume from Jn. 19:25 that this James was in any way related to our Lord and certainly not that he was James the Lord's brother. R.E.N.

ALTAR.

I. In the Old Testament

In all but four of the OT occurrences of the word 'altar', the Heb. is *mizbēaḥ*, which means 'place of sacrifice' (from *zāḇaḥ*, 'to slaughter for sacrifice'), and one of the remaining occurrences (Ezr. 7:17) is simply its Aram. cognate *madbaḥ*. While etymologically the term involves slaughter, in usage it was not always so restricted, being applied also to the altar for burning incense (Ex. 30:1). For other occurrences of 'altar' in the EVV, see *g*, below.

a. The Patriarchs

The Patriarchs built their own altars and offered their own sacrifices on them without having any recourse to a priesthood. Noah built one after the flood and made burnt-offerings on it (Gn. 8:20). Abraham built altars to Yahweh at Shechem, between Bethel and Ai, at Hebron and at Moriah, where he offered a ram instead of Isaac (Gn. 12:6–8; 13:18; 22:9). Isaac did likewise at Beersheba (Gn. 26:25), Jacob erected altars at Shechem and Bethel (Gn. 33:20; 35:1–7), and Moses erected one at Rephidim after the victory of the Israelites over Amalek (Ex. 17:15). The altars were evidently erected mainly to commemorate some event in which the principal had had dealings with God. No information is given as to their construction, but it is reasonable to suppose that they were of the same type as those later allowed in the Mosaic law (see *d*, below).

Bronze altar covered with cloth and bearing sacrificial parts of an animal and other gifts of food. Part of a scene in which King Ashurbanipal of Assyria makes a dedication following a lion-hunt. Nineveh. c. 650 BC. (BM)

b. Pre-Israelite altars in Palestine

In the early days of Palestine exploration it was customary to see altars in many things which today are understood as domestic, agricultural or industrial installations. True altars have, however, been uncovered at several sites from different periods. At Ai, Mme J. Marquet-Krause discovered a small temple of the Early Bronze Age in which was an altar of plastered stones, against the wall, on which animal and food-offerings had been made. In Middle Bronze Age *Megiddo (level XV) two temples were found containing rectangular altars, one of mud bricks and the other of lime-plastered stones. Temples of the Late Bronze Age containing altars of similar type have been found at Lachish, Beth-shean and Hazor. In the levels of this period at Hazor a great hewn block of stone was discovered, with two hollowed basins on one face, perhaps for catching the blood of sacrificed animals. At Megiddo and Nahariyeh great platforms of stones which were probably used as places of sacrifice were uncovered, but these were more *'high places' than they were true altars.

A number of hewn limestone altars with four horns at the upper corners, dating from about the period of the conquest, were found at Megiddo. These, however, to judge from their relatively small size (largest *c.* 70 cm high), were probably incense altars. Numerous clay stands which may have been for burning incense have been uncovered at such sites as Megiddo, Beth-shean and Lachish, from Bronze and Iron Age Levels.

Thus altars were in use among

Pillar-like altar from Canaanite Hazor with the emblem of the sun-god carved in relief. Height 1·40 m. 13th cent. BC. (YY)

Altar with projecting horns from Megiddo. Height 0·54 m. 10th–9th cent. BC. (RS)

the Canaanites in the Promised Land, a fact that gives point to the careful regulations on this matter in the Sinai revelation. That altars were not limited to Palestine is shown by the discoveries at such sites as Eridu, Ur, Khafajah and Assur in Mesopotamia, and the episode in which Balaam erected, and offered bullocks on, 7 altars at Kiriath-huzoth (Nu. 23) may perhaps be understood in this light.

c. The altars of the tabernacle

At Sinai God revealed to Moses the specifications for two altars which were to be used in the * tabernacle: the altar of burnt-offering and the altar of incense.

d. Built altars

In Ex. 20:24–26, God instructed Moses to tell the people to make an altar of earth (*mizbaḥ ʾaḏāmâ*) or (unhewn) stones (*mizbaḥ ʾaḇānîm*), upon which to sacrifice their offerings. In neither case were there to be steps, so that the 'nakedness' of the offerer might not be uncovered. The form of this passage, in which God tells Moses to pass on this instruction to the people, suggests that it, like the Ten Commandments at the beginning of the chapter, was addressed to each Israelite individually, rather than to Moses as their representative as in Ex. 27. It may be that under this provision the layman was permitted to perform this himself, and it is perhaps in the light of this that the altars built by Joshua on Mt Ebal (Jos. 8:30–31; *cf.* Dt. 27:5), by Gideon in Ophrah (Jdg. 6:24–26), by David on the threshing-floor of Araunah (2 Sa. 24:18–25) and by Elijah on Mt Carmel (1 Ki. 18), as well as the episodes described in Jos. 22:10–34 and 1 Sa. 20:6, 29, are to be viewed (*cf.* Ex. 24:4).

e. The Temple of Solomon

In building his * Temple, Solomon, though influenced by his Phoenician associates, sought to follow the basic layout of the tabernacle and its court. Though David had already built an altar of burnt-offerings (2 Sa. 24:25), Solomon probably built a new one, as is indicated by 1 Ki. 8:22, 54, 64 and 9:25 (not mentioned in the main description, 1 Ki. 6–7). Altars of this period are well illustrated by the finds (IA II period) at Arad where in the temple courtyard stood an altar made of brick and rubble for burnt-offerings (*cf.* Ex. 20:25) which measured 5 cubits sq. (2·5 m) like that of the tabernacle (Ex. 17:1; *cf.* 2 Ch. 6:13). Two stone incense-altars with concave bowl-shaped tops were found on a step leading up to the 'holy of holies'. Other Israelite incense-altars of the Israelite period have been recovered from Beersheba, *etc.*

f. False altars

Unlawful altars were in use in both Israel and Judah, as is shown by the condemnations of the prophets (Am. 3:14; Ho. 8:11) and the account of Jeroboam's sins in 1 Ki. 12:28–33, as well as by archaeological finds.

g. Ezekiel's vision

During the Exile, Ezekiel had a

Stones from this altar were used to repair a corner of a storehouse at Beersheba, possibly during the Assyrian attack of 701 BC. *The altar was probably used for burnt-offerings. Height c. 1·57 m (to the top of the horns).* (TAU)

vision of Israel restored and the Temple rebuilt (Ezk. 40–44), and while no incense altar is mentioned, the altar of burnt offering in this visionary temple is described in detail (43:13–17). It consisted of 3 stages reaching to a height of 11 cubits on a base 18 cubits square. It was thus in form reminiscent of a Babylonian ziggurat, and this impression is furthered by the names of some of its parts. The base, *ḥêq hā'āreṣ* (Ezk. 43:14, AV 'bottom upon the ground', literally 'bosom of the earth') recalls the Akkadian *irat irṣiti* with the same meaning, and the terms *har'ēl* and *'ᵃri'êl* translated 'altar' in vv. 15–16 may be Hebraized forms of Akkadian *arallu*, one of the names for the underworld, which had the secondary meaning 'mountain of the gods'. Such borrowings from the Babylonian vocabulary, which would be independent of their etymological meaning, would have been normal after an exile of many years in Babylonia. The altar was ascended by a flight of steps, and the 4 upper corners bore horns.

h. The second Temple

When the Temple was rebuilt after the Return it was presumably provided with altars. These are referred to in Josephus (*Contra Apionem* 1. 198) and in the *Letter of Aristeas*, but on this period neither of these authors can be followed uncritically. In 169 BC Antiochus Epiphanes carried off the 'golden altar' (1 Macc. 1:21), and 2 years later he surmounted the altar of burnt offering with a 'desolating sacrilege' (1 Macc. 1:54), probably an image of Zeus. The Maccabees built a new altar and restored the incense altar (1 Macc. 4:44–49), and these must have continued in use when Herod enlarged the *Temple in the latter part of the 1st century BC. In his time the altar of burnt offering was a great pile of unhewn stones, approached by a ramp.

II. In the New Testament

In the NT two words for altar are used, that most frequently found being *thysiastērion*, which is used often in the LXX for *mizbēaḥ*. This word is used of the altar on which Abraham prepared to offer Isaac (Jas. 2:21), of the altar of burnt offering in the Temple (Mt. 5:23–24; 23:18–20, 35; Lk. 11:51; 1 Cor. 9:13; 10:18; Heb. 7:13; Rev. 11:1), and of the altar of incense, not only in the earthly Temple (Lk. 1:11) but also in the heavenly (Rev. 6:9; 8:5; 9:13; 14:18; 16:7; *cf.* also Rom. 11:3; Heb. 13:10). The other word, *bōmos*, is used once (Acts 17:23). It was employed in the LXX for both *mizbēaḥ* and *bāmâ* (*HIGH PLACE), and had primarily the meaning of a raised place.

BIBLIOGRAPHY. R. de Vaux, *Ancient Israel. Its Life and Institutions*, 1961, pp. 406–414, 546; B. F. Westcott, *The Epistle to the Hebrews*, 1889, pp. 453ff.; A. Edersheim, *The Temple, Its Ministry and Services as they were at the Time of Jesus Christ*, 1874, pp. 32–33. T.C.M.

AMALEK, AMALEKITES. Amalek (Heb. *ᵃmālēq*) was the son of Eliphaz and the grandson of Esau (Gn. 36:12, 16). The name is used as a collective noun for his descendants, Amalekites (Ex. 17:8; Nu. 24:20; Dt. 25:17; Jdg. 3:13, *etc.*).

Some writers distinguish the nomadic Amalekites normally found in the Negeb and Sinai area, from the descendants of Esau, because Gn. 14:7, which pre-dates Esau, refers to 'the country of the Amalekites' (Heb. *ᵃmālēqî*). The distinction is unnecessary if we regard the phrase as a later editorial description.

Israel first met the Amalekites at Rephidim in the wilderness of Sinai (Ex. 17:8–13; Dt. 25:17–18). Because of this attack, the Amalekites came under a permanent ban and were to be destroyed (Dt. 25:19; 1 Sa. 15:2–3). On that occasion Aaron and Hur held up Moses' hands and Israel prevailed. A year later, after the report of the spies, Israel ignored Moses' command and sought to enter S Palestine. The Amalekites defeated them at Hormah (Nu. 14:43, 45).

From the days of the Judges two encounters are recorded. The Amalekites assisted Eglon, king of Moab, to attack Israelite territory (Jdg. 3:13), and later combined forces with the Midianites and the children of the E to raid Israelite crops and flocks. Gideon drove them out (Jdg. 6:3–5, 33; 7:12; 10:12).

From the Exodus onwards, Amalekites were to be found in the Negeb, but for a time they gained a foothold in Ephraim (Jdg. 12:15). Balaam, the foreign prophet, looked away to their lands from his vantage-point in Moab, and described them as 'the first of the nations' (Nu. 24:20), which may mean in regard either to origin or to status.

Samuel commanded Saul to destroy the Amalekites in the area S of *Telaim. Booty was forbidden. Saul pursued them from Havilah to Shur but captured their king alive. Later, Samuel slew Agag and rebuked Saul (1 Sa. 15).

David fought the Amalekites in the area of Ziklag which Achish, king of Gath, had given him (1 Sa. 27:6; 30:1–20). The Amalekites declined later, and in Hezekiah's day the sons of Simeon attacked 'the remnant of the Amalekites that had escaped', taking their stronghold in Mt Seir (1 Ch. 4:43).

BIBLIOGRAPHY. F. M. Abel, *Géographie de la Palestine*, 2, 1933, pp. 270–273; D. Baly, *The Geography of the Bible*², 1974. J.A.T.

AMARNA. (Tell) el-Amarna is the modern name of Akhetaten, capital of Egypt under Amenophis IV (Akhenaten) and his immediate successors, *c.* 1375–1360 BC. The ruins lie some 320 km S of Cairo on the E bank of the river Nile. The site extends about 8 × 1 km and has been partially excavated. The impressive remains include temples, administrative buildings, tombs with wall paintings as well as the buildings of many prosperous estates with houses often of uniform plan.

The importance of Amarna for biblical studies lies in the series of letters written in cuneiform on clay tablets found by chance in 1887. With subsequent discoveries, the number of documents recovered now totals about 380. The majority are letters from various Asiatic rulers to the pharaohs Amenophis III and IV in the period *c.* 1385–1360 BC; nearly half come from Palestine and Syria. They supply important information concerning the history of the area, providing a vivid picture of the intrigues and inter-city strife which followed the weakening of Egyptian control shortly before the Israelites entered the land.

In S Syria, Abdi-ashirta and his son Aziru, though protesting their loyalty to their Egyptian overlords, were in reality increasing their own domains with the connivance of the Hittites of N Syria, and thus preparing the way for the eventual conquest of all Syria by the Hittite Suppiluliuma. Rib-ḫaddi of Byblos, a loyalist who wrote 53 letters to the

Inscribed clay tablet from Amarna, part of the correspondence from Tushratta, king of Mitanni, to Amenophis III of Egypt. The cuneiform inscription records his defeat of the Hittites and gifts of horses and chariots to the Egyptian king and of jewellery to his sister, a wife of Amenophis. Beneath this are notes in hieratic script made by the Egyptian clerk. Height 4·1 cm. c. 1400–1360 BC. (BM)

Egyptian court, describes the uncertainty and chaos which followed his unanswered pleas for military assistance. He reports the capture by Aziru of an adjacent town, where the Egyptian resident had been slain, and the attack on Byblos from which he was forced to flee.

Similarly Lab'ayu of Shechem, despite his protests of innocence (EA 254), was increasing his hold in the central hills in league with the semi-nomadic 'Apiru, who are frequently named in the texts, mainly as small armed bands (* HEBREWS). The activities of these 'Apiru are reported by many cities. When Lab'ayu threatened Megiddo, its ruler, Biridiya, begged Egypt for help.

Abdi-ḫeba of Jerusalem makes frequent reports, complaining that Milkilu of Gezer and others are engaged in raids. He cannot, therefore, understand why the pharaoh should allow Gezer, Lachish and Ashkelon to escape from the duty of providing the Egyptian garrison with food when they have plenty. He himself has been robbed by Egyptian troops and warns the pharaoh that his tribute and slaves being sent to Egypt will probably not arrive, as Lab'ayu and Milkilu have planned an ambush (EA 287). The latter might be a ruse to avoid sending any gifts, for in another letter Shuwardata of Hebron warns the pharaoh that Abdi-ḫeba of Jerusalem is a rogue.

Our knowledge of the political geography of Palestine at this time is helped by references to various local rulers, such as Ammunira of Beirut, Abimilki of Tyre, Akizzi of Qatna and Abdi-tirši of Hazor. Some of these names can be correlated with contemporary texts from Ugarit (* RAS SHAMRA). In addition to the local historical evidence, these letters are important for the wider implications of alliances between Egypt and the rulers of Mitanni and Babylon, often concluded, or supported, by marriages between the ruling families.

References to an Egyptian official named Yanḫamu, who attained high office, remind one of the position of Joseph, though the two cannot be identified. Yanḫamu's name is a Semitic form, and one of his functions was the supervision of the grain supply during a time of scarcity for the pharaoh's Syrian subjects.

The tablets are also of great linguistic importance. All but two are written in Akkadian, the *lingua franca* of the whole ancient Near East in this period. The presence at Amarna of Mesopotamian literature (myths of Nergal and Adapa, a story of Sargon of Akkad) and lexical texts including a list of Egyptian and Akkadian words indicates the influence of Akkadian, and this is supported by the discovery in 1946 of a fragment of the Gilgamesh Epic (*c.* 1400 BC) at Megiddo. The letters from Palestine and Syria are written mainly in local W Semitic dialects of Akkadian, and they provide valuable information about the Canaanite language in its various local forms before the arrival of the Israelites. Letters from King Tushratta of Mitanni have also added considerably to our knowledge of the non-Semitic Hurrian language (* HORITES).

Since some have argued that the 'Apiru of these texts are to be identified with the Hebrews under Joshua, instead of being evidence of the state of the land prior to the Conquest, the following aspects of the Amarna evidence should perhaps be stressed. The *ḫab/piru* (SA.GAZ) (= 'Apiru) here, as indicated also by the Ras Shamra and *Alalaḫ texts, were occupying the areas not strictly controlled by the larger towns; they operated usually in small numbers throughout Palestine and Syria, and do not appear as besiegers of cities. Moreover, these texts show a situation different from that under

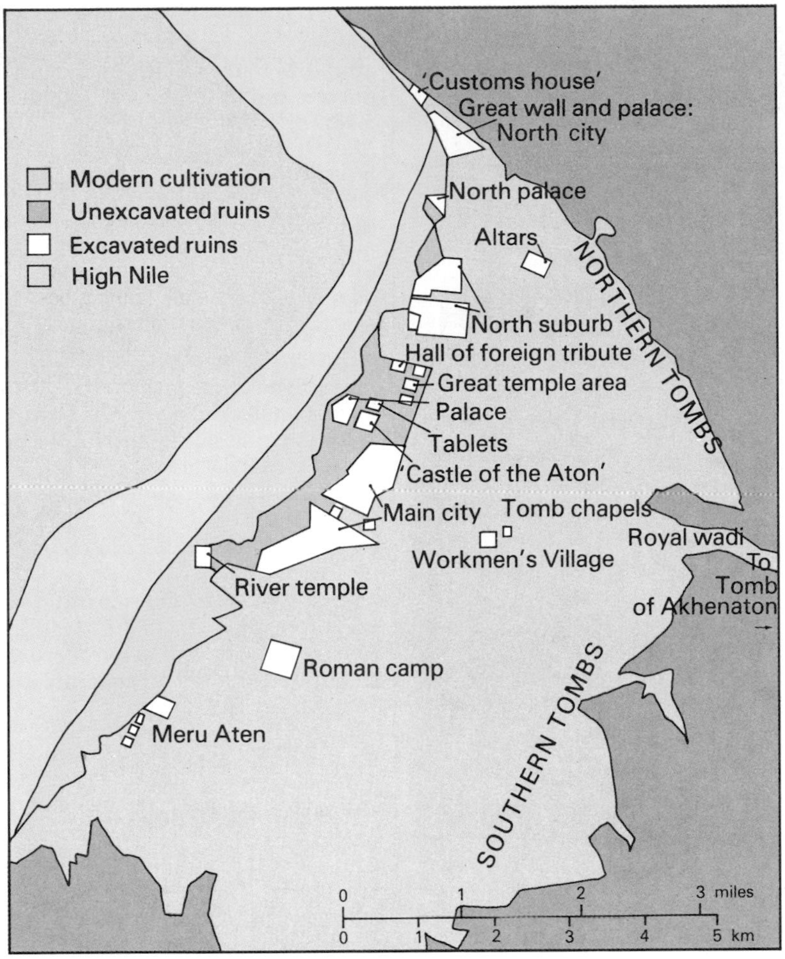

Sketch-map of the site of Amarna, showing areas of excavations.

Egyptian queen offering flowers to the king; probably Merit-Aton and Smenkh-ka-Rēʿ. Painted limestone. Height 23 cm. c. 1360 BC. (PAC)

Joshua: Lachish and Gezer, far from being destroyed (Jos. 10), are in active support of the ʿApiru. The names of the rulers also differ, the king of Jerusalem at this time being Abdi-ḫeba, and whereas the Apiru were very active in the Jerusalem area, the city did not become Israelite until the time of David. Finally, the ʿApiru made use of chariots, but the Israelites knew nothing of this method of warfare until David's reign.

BIBLIOGRAPHY. J. A. Knudtzon, *Die El-Amarna-Tafeln*, 2 vols., 1907, 1915 (=EA); A. F. Rainey, *El Amarna tablets 359–379*², 1978; W. F. Albright in *ANET*, pp. 483–490; C. J. M. Weir in *DOTT*, pp. 38–45; W. F. Albright, *The Amarna letters from Palestine*, *CAH*, 2/2, 1975, pp. 98–116; F. F. Bruce in *AOTS*, pp. 1–20; K. A. Kitchen, *Suppiluliuma and the Amarna Pharaohs*, 1962. M.J.S.

AMASA. 1. Son of Jether (or Ithra) an Ishmaelite, and of David's sister Abigail, Amasa commanded Absalom's rebel army (2 Sa. 17:25), was defeated by Joab (2 Sa. 18:6–8), pardoned by David, and replaced Joab as commander of the army (2 Sa. 19:13). Taken off his guard, he was slain by the double-dealing Joab at 'the great stone of Gibeon' (2 Sa. 20:9–12). Amasa may possibly be the Amasai of 1 Ch. 12:18, but the evidence is inconclusive.

2. An Ephraimite who, among others, obeyed the prophet Oded and opposed the entry into Samaria of the Jewish prisoners taken by Pekah, king of Israel, in his campaign against Ahaz (2 Ch. 28:9–15). J.D.D.

AMAZIAH (Heb. *ʾamaṣyâ* or *ʾamaṣyāhû*, 'Yahweh is mighty'). **1.** Son and successor of Joash, king of Judah (2 Ki. 14:1–20; 2 Ch. 25). He inflicted a severe defeat on Edom, which had previously regained its independence from Judah (2 Ki. 8:20–22), though apparently without subduing it completely (*cf.* 2 Ki. 14:22). Elated with his success, and perhaps also angered by the raiding of some dismissed Israelite mercenaries, he challenged Joash of Israel to a battle which proved his undoing. His overwhelming defeat led to the dismantling of part of Jerusalem's defences and the plundering of the Temple and palace. He himself was cap-

Two ambassadors (in tasselled caps) from Rusa, king of Urartu, at the court of Ashurbanipal, king of Assyria. Bas-relief from Nineveh. c. 640 BC. (BM)

AMETHYST
See Jewels, Part 2.

AMMAH
See Metheg-ammah, Part 2.

AMMAN
See Rabbah, Part 3.

tured (2 Ki. 14:13). It has been suggested that at this time his son Azariah began to rule as co-regent, a suggestion which certainly eases some of the difficulties of the *chronology of his reign. He was eventually assassinated for reasons which are not disclosed.

2. The priest of Jeroboam II who sought to silence the prophet Amos at Bethel (Am. 7:10–17).

3. A Simeonite (1 Ch. 4:34).

4. A Levite of the family of Merari (1 Ch. 6:45). H.G.M.W.

AMBASSADOR (Heb. *mal'āḵ*, 'messenger'; *lûṣ*, 'interpreter'; *ṣîr*, 'to go'). A term used to describe envoys sent to other nations on special occasions, *e.g.* to congratulate (1 Ki. 5:1; 2 Sa. 8:10), solicit favours (Nu. 20:14), make alliances (Jos. 9:4), or protest against wrongs (Jdg. 11:12). Usually men of high rank, ambassadors became more common after Israel had developed relations with Syria, Babylon, *etc.* They did not represent the person of their sovereign, nor, as a general rule, were they empowered to negotiate (but see 2 Ki. 18:17–19:8). They were nevertheless treated with respect, and the only biblical infringement of this brought severe retribution (2 Sa. 10:2–5). The word (Gk. *presbeuō*, 'to be a senior') occurs metaphorically in the NT (2 Cor. 5:20; Eph. 6:20), applied to the representative of Christ in carrying his message of reconciliation. The collective term 'ambassage' is found in Lk. 14:32 (AV; RSV 'embassy'). J.D.D.

AMBER. Heb. *ḥašmal*, occurring only in Ezk. 1:4, 27; 8:2 (AV). The context requires *ḥašmal* to be something shining, but the exact denotation of the word has puzzled scholars from the rabbinic to present times. LXX renders *ēlektron*, meaning 'amber' or 'an alloy of gold and silver' (*LSJ*). Delitzsch suggests the Assyrian *ešmaru* as a cognate, which is phonologically possible, and which denotes a shining metallic alloy. G. R. Driver suggests 'brass', comparing Akkadian *elmešu*. See *VT* 1, 1951, pp. 60–62; *VT Supp*. 16, pp. 190–198. R.J.W.

AMEN. Heb. *'āmēn*, 'surely', from a root meaning 'to be firm, steady, trustworthy'; *cf.* *'^{e}mûnâ*, 'faithfulness', *'^{e}meṯ*, 'truth'. It is used in the OT as a liturgical formula in which a congregation or individual accepts both the validity of an oath or curse and its consequences (Nu. 5:22; Dt. 27:15ff.; Ne. 5:13; Je. 11:5). It was also the response to a benediction (1 Ch. 16:36; Ne. 8:6), and is found incorporated in the doxologies which conclude the first four books of Psalms (Ps. 41:13; 72:19; 89:52; 106:48). Other uses are Jeremiah's ironic response to Hananiah's prophecy of a brief exile (Je. 28:6) and Benaiah's willing acceptance of David's command to make Solomon king (1 Ki. 1:36); in both cases it introduces a prayer for God's blessing on the proposal. Its connection with both blessings and cursings is sufficient explanation for the description of God as 'the God of truth (lit. amen)' in Is. 65:16. Outside the OT, the word is used in a 7th-century BC document to introduce a sworn declaration of innocence: 'Amen, I am free of guilt . . .'

By NT times the word is regularly used at the close of prayers and doxologies and is a natural response to be expected in public worship (1 Cor. 14:16). Christ's use of it in the introductory 'Amen, I say to you' was probably peculiar to himself, there being no evidence that the apostles followed his example, and gave his words their distinctive Messianic authority. Hence the association of the term with the promises of God, uniquely fulfilled in him (2 Cor. 1:20), and the attribution to him of the title 'the Amen' (Rev. 3:14).

BIBLIOGRAPHY. H. Bietenhard, *NIDNTT* 1, pp. 97–99; S. Talmon, *Textus* 7, 1969, pp. 124–129. J.B.Tr.

AMMON, AMMONITES. Ammon (Heb. *'ammôn*) was the name of the descendants of Benammi, Lot's younger son by his daughter, born in a cave near Zoar (Gn. 19:38). They were regarded as relatives of the Israelites, who were commanded to treat them kindly (Dt. 2:19).

At an early date the Ammonites occupied the territory of the Zamzummim between the Arnon and Jabbok rivers (Dt. 2:20–21, 37; 3:11). Later, part of this territory was taken from them by the Amorites, and they were confined to an area to the E of the Jabbok (Nu. 21:24; Dt. 2:37; Jos. 12:2; 13:10, 25; Jdg. 11:13, 22). Archaeology shows that the Ammonites, like others, surrounded their territories by small fortresses (Nu. 21:24).

At the time of the Exodus, Israel did not conquer Ammon (Dt. 2:19, 37; Jdg. 11:15). However, the Ammonites were condemned for joining the Moabites in hiring Balaam, and were forbidden to enter the congregation of Israel to the 10th generation (Dt. 23:3–6).

Their chief town was Rabbath Ammon, mod. Amman (* RABBAH), where the ironstone sarcophagus ('bedstead of iron') of Og, the king of Bashan, rested (Dt. 3:11).

In the days of the Judges, the Ammonites assisted Eglon of Moab to subdue Israelite territory (Jdg. 3:13). Again, at the time of Jephthah they encroached on Israelite lands E of Jordan (Jdg. 11) and were driven out. Their religion influenced some of the Israelites (Jdg. 10:6), and this caused the Ammonite oppression in Gilead which led to Jephthah's campaign (Jdg. 10). Later Nahash, king of the Ammonites, besieged Jabesh-gilead just before Saul became king. Saul rallied Israel and drove off Nahash (1 Sa. 11:1–11; 12:12; 14:47). A few years later Nahash was a friend of David (2 Sa. 10:1–2), but his son Hanun rejected a kindly visit of David's ambassadors and insulted them. He hired Syrian mercenaries and went to war, but David's generals Joab and Abishai defeated them (2 Sa. 10; 1 Ch. 19). A year later the Israelites captured Rabbah, the Ammonite capital (2 Sa. 12:26–31; 1 Ch. 20:1–3) and put the people to work. Some Ammonites befriended David, however, *e.g.* Shobi son of Nahash, who cared for him when he fled from Absalom (2 Sa. 17:27, 29) and Zelek, who was one of his 30 mighty men (2 Sa. 23:37; 1 Ch. 11:39).

Solomon included Ammonite women in his harem, and worshipped Milcom (Molech) their god (1 Ki. 11:1, 5, 7, 33). An Ammonitess, Naamah, was the mother of Rehoboam (1 Ki. 14:21, 31; 2 Ch. 12:13).

In the days of Jehoshaphat, the Ammonites joined Moabites and Edomites in a raid on Judah (2 Ch. 20:1–30). About 800 BC, Zabad and

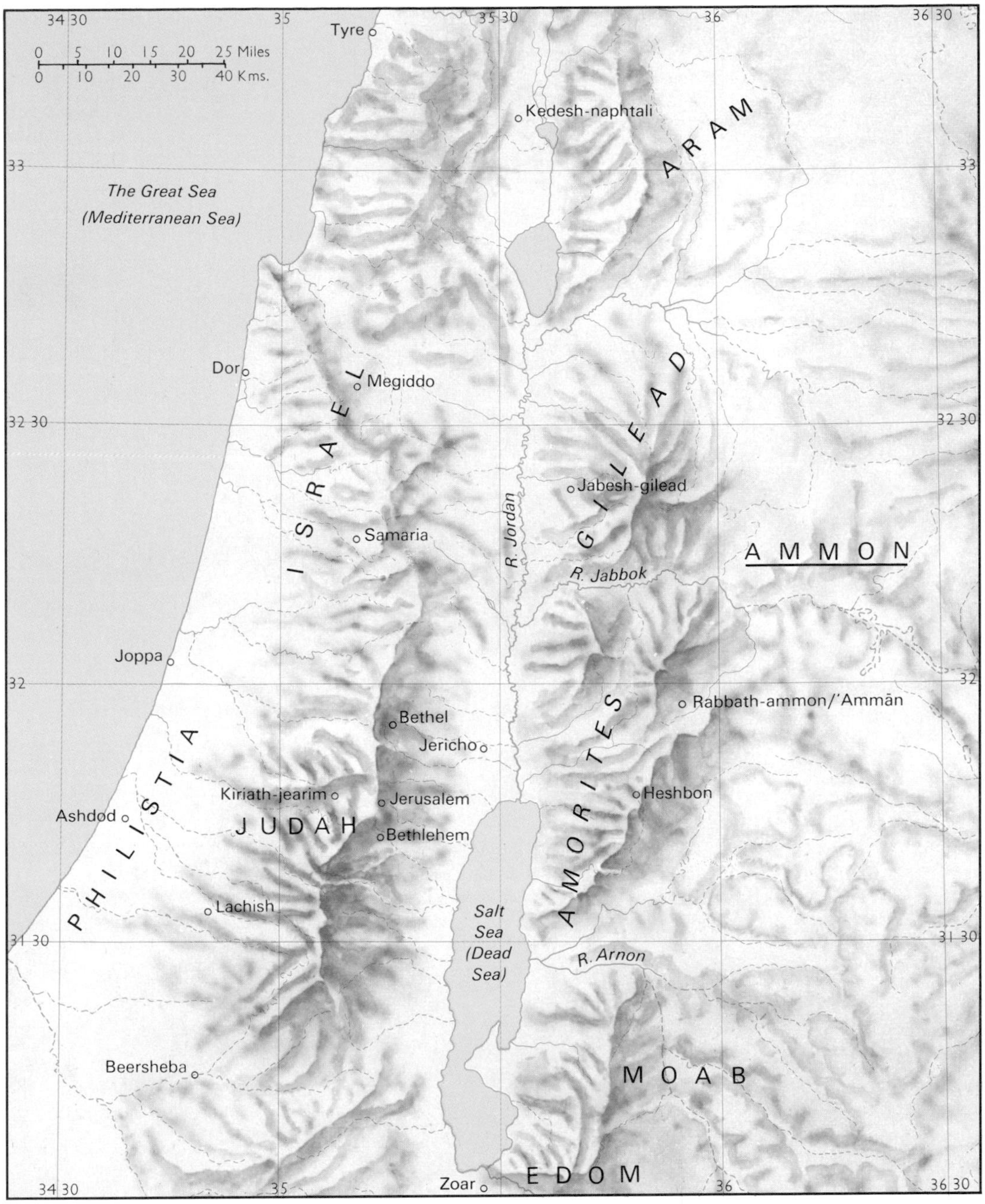

The territory of the Ammonites, to the E of the river Jabbok.

Stone statue of a king, wearing a ceremonial tasselled dress and heavy crown, from Amman. Height 80 cm. c. 800 BC. (DAA)

The Egyptian god Amen-Rē'. A statuette of silver, partly overlaid with gold foil. Late period. c. 900 BC. (BM)

Jehozabad, both sons of an Ammonitess, conspired to slay Joash king of Judah (2 Ch. 24:26). Later in the century, both Uzziah and Jotham of Judah received tribute from the Ammonites (2 Ch. 26:8; 27:5). Josiah defiled the high place that Solomon erected (2 Ki. 23:13). Ammonites joined others in troubling Jehoiakim (2 Ki. 24:2), and after the fall of Jerusalem in 586 BC, Baalis their king provoked further trouble (2 Ki. 25:25; Je. 40:11–14). They were bitterly attacked by the prophets as inveterate enemies of Israel (Je. 49:1–6; Ezk. 21:20; 25:1–7; Am. 1:13–15; Zp. 2:8–11).

After the return from exile Tobiah, the governor of Ammon, hindered the building of the walls by Nehemiah (Ne. 2:10, 19; 4:3, 7). Intermarriage between the Jews and the Ammonites was censured by both Ezra and Nehemiah (Ezr. 9:1–2; Ne. 13:1, 23–31). The Ammonites survived into the 2nd century BC at least, since Judas Maccabaeus fought against them (1 Macc. 5:6).

Sedentary occupation of the area was resumed about the beginning of the 13th century BC after an almost complete break of some centuries. A few Middle Bronze tombs from the 17th to 16th century BC, a shrine near Amman and occupation levels in the city of the Late Bronze Age suggest some limited occupation, prior to the 13th century. There was a vigorous resurgence of urban life at the start of the Iron Age which is evidenced by a string of small circular tower fortresses built of large stones. Other structures from the period were square or rectangular. Several settlements have been investigated, each consisting of several flint-block houses together with one or more towers, *e.g.* Khirbet Morbat Bedran. Clearly Ammonite occupation was vigorous during the Iron II period (840–580 BC). During the 7th century BC Ammon flourished under Assyrian control, as numerous references in Assyrian documents show. Ammon paid considerable tribute to Assyria. Tombs found in the region of Amman give evidence of a high material culture, to judge from the pottery, anthropoid coffins, seals, statues, figures, *etc.* A growing volume of written material including seals (7th century BC), an inscribed copper bottle from Siran (*c.* 600 BC) and an eight-line fragmentary inscription from the Amman citadel (9th century BC) display a language similar to Heb., but a script influenced by Aram. The copper bottle contained seeds of emmer wheat, bread wheat and hulled six-row barley, three domesticated grasses in use by the Ammonites of the 6th century BC. At least eleven Ammonite kings can now be listed from various sources.

Archaeological work suggests that sedentary occupation was interrupted by the Babylonian campaigns of the 6th century BC and did not resume until the 3rd century. Bedouin groups occupied the area until the Tobiads (4th–2nd century BC), the Nabataeans (1st century BC) and the Romans (1st century BC–3rd century AD).

BIBLIOGRAPHY. W. F. Albright, *Miscellanea Biblica B. Ubach*, 1953, pp. 131ff.; P. Bordreuil, *Syria* 50, 1973, pp. 181–195 (seals); G. Garbini, *Ann. de l'Inst. Or. Napoli* 20, 1970, pp. 249–257; *idem, JSS* 19, 1974, pp. 159–168; N. Glueck, *The Other Side of Jordan*, 1940; *idem, AASOR* 18, 19, 25–28; P. C. Hammond, *BASOR* 160, 1960, pp. 38–41; S. H. Horn, *BASOR* 193, 1967, pp. 2–13; G. M. Landes, *BA* 24.3, 1961, pp. 66–86; H. O. Thompson, *AJBA* 2.2, 1973, pp. 23–38; *idem* and F. Zayadine, *BASOR* 212, 1973, pp. 5–11.

J.A.T.

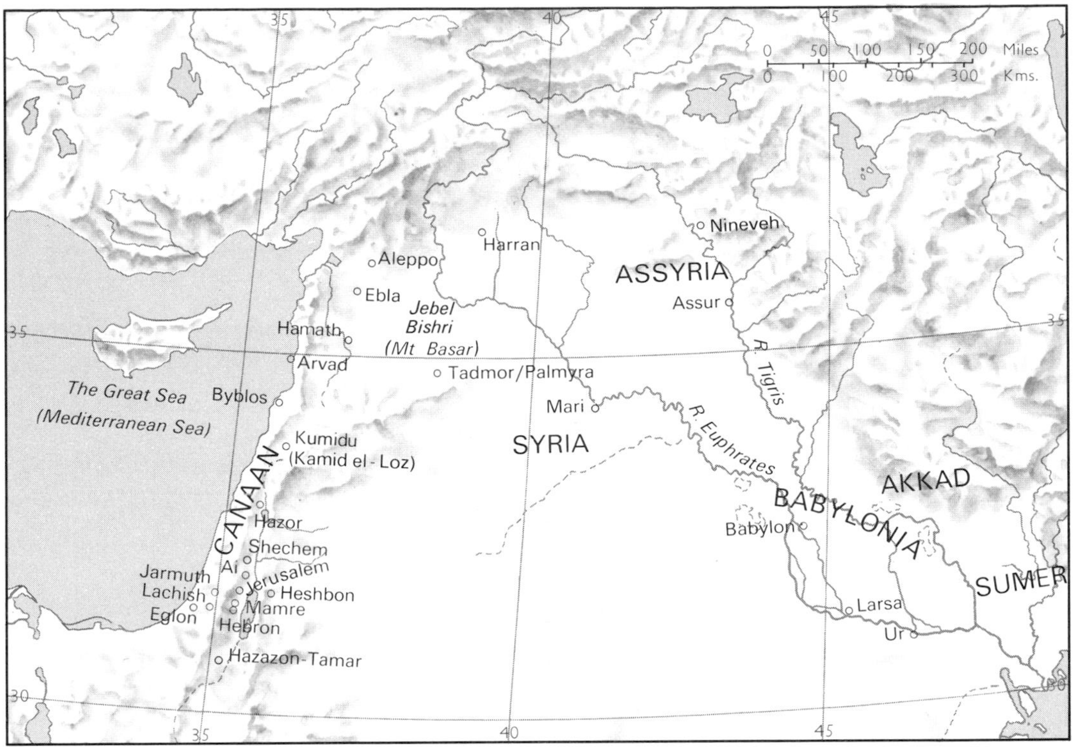

Amorite towns and areas of settlement.

AMON. The son of Manasseh, Amon reigned for 2 years over Judah (2 Ki. 21:19–26; 2 Ch. 33:21–25). Before his reign was cut short by assassination, he gave the clearest evidence of his complete acceptance of the gross idolatry of his father's earlier years. It is not certainly known what motive inspired his assassins, but the fact that they were in turn put to death by 'the people of the land' suggests that Amon was the victim of court intrigue rather than of a popular revolution. J.C.J.W.

AMON (Egyp. *Amūn*, 'the hidden'). An Egyptian god whose essential nature is as unclear as his name indicates. Often associated with the wind, and in certain forms embodying the power of generation, he was first prominent as a local god of *Thebes, whence came the powerful 12th Dynasty pharaohs (1991–1786 BC). Through union with the cosmic and royal sun-god Rē' as Amen-Rē', Amūn became chief god. Later, when the 18th Dynasty Theban pharaohs established the Egyptian Empire (1552 BC ff.), Amūn became state god, 'king of the gods', gathering up many of their powers and attributes, while his priesthood accumulated vast wealth and lands. Hence, the fall of Thebes (No) and the wealth of its priesthoods to the Assyrians in 663 BC was fittingly selected by Nahum (3:8) in prophesying the crash of equally mighty Nineveh. After this, Amūn and Thebes, still his holy city, regained some measure of prosperity, but even this was doomed by prophecy of Jeremiah (46:25). (*EGYPT.)

K.A.K.

AMORITES. A people of Canaan (Gn. 10:16) often listed with the Hittites, Perizzites, *etc.*, as opponents of Israel (Ex. 33:2). They were scattered throughout the hill country on either side of the Jordan (Nu. 13:29). Abraham had an alliance with the Amorites of Hebron and, with their aid, routed the four kings who had attacked the Dead Sea plain, including the Amorite town of Hazazon-tamar (Gn. 14:5–7). The name was also used as a general term for the inhabitants of Canaan (Gn. 48:22; Jos. 24:15). Ezekiel well indicates the mixed population of Palestine (caused largely by continuous infiltrations from the eastern steppes), describing Jerusalem as the offspring of Amorite and Hittite (Ezk. 16:3, 45).

During the latter half of the 3rd millennium BC, Sumerian and Akkadian inscriptions refer to the Amorites (Sum. *mar-tu*, Akkad. *amurru*) as a desert people unacquainted with civilized life, grain, houses, cities, government. Their headquarters were in the mountain of Basar, probably Jebel Bishri N of Palmyra. About 2000 BC these people, who had been infiltrating for centuries, moved into Babylonia in force. They were partly responsible for the collapse of the powerful 3rd Dynasty of Ur and took over the rule of several towns (*e.g.* Larsa). An 'Amorite' dynasty was established at *Babylon, and its most powerful king, Hammurapi, conquered the two other important 'Amorite' states of Assur and Mari (*c.* 1750 BC). Amorites are traceable by linguistic, mainly onomastic, evidence. Such is not always reliable or conclusive, but these dynasties were clearly of western origin, Hammurapi's being termed Amorite in a contemporary text. The 20,000 texts found at *Mari are mostly written in Akkadian with many W Semitic features. Personal name forms common in these texts show that the names of the Patriarchs followed well-known styles. The Mari texts give information about nomadic tribes in Syria, notably the *Mare-Yamina* (or possibly *Bene-*

Yamina) connected with the area of Mt Basar. Another group had settled in the Lebanon and engaged in the trading of horses. This kingdom survived into the period of the Amarna letters and the 19th Dynasty of Egypt when tribute is recorded from the state of Amor. The capital of this seems to have been the port of Ṣumur (modern Tell Kazel) S of Arvad. This is the country mentioned in Jos. 13:4.

The general unrest of the years *c.* 2100–1800 BC both in Mesopotamia and in Palestine was closely connected with increased Amorite movement. The break in occupation of several Palestinian cities between the Early and Middle Bronze Age was caused by an influx of nomadic folk who left many graves behind them, but little trace of buildings. The pottery of these people has clear affinities with pottery from Syria, which may indicate that they were related 'Amorites' (see K. M. Kenyon, *Amorites and Canaanites*, 1966; W. G. Dever, *HTR* 64, 1971, pp. 197–226). The journeys of Abraham may be associated with the latter part of this period.

At the time of the Israelite invasion of Palestine, Amorite kings (Sihon of Heshbon and Og of Bashan) ruled most of Transjordan (Jos. 12:1–6; Jdg. 1:36). The conquest of these two kings was the first stage of the possession of the Promised Land and was looked upon as a most important event in Israelite history (Am. 2:9; Pss. 135:11; 136:19). Gad, Reuben and half of Manasseh occupied this territory (Nu. 32:33), and it later formed one of the twelve regions supporting Solomon's court (1 Ki. 4:19). The men of Ai are called Amorites (Jos. 7:7) and Jerusalem, Hebron, Jarmuth, Lachish and Eglon were Amorite principalities which Israel overcame (Jos. 10:1–27). Northern Amorites aided the king of *Hazor (Jos. 11:1–14). After the land was settled, the Amorites became menials and were gradually absorbed (1 Ki. 9:20). Their evil memory remained, providing comparison for the idolatry of Ahab and Manasseh (1 Ki. 21:26; 2 Ki. 21:11; *cf.* Gn. 15:16).

Invasions of other peoples, the Kassites, Hurrians and Indo-Europeans in Mesopotamia, the Israelites in Palestine and the Aramaeans in Syria weakened the Amorites as a power by 1000 BC. The name survived in Akkadian as a designation for Syria–Palestine until superseded by *Ḫatti* (Hittite), and was also a word for 'West'.

BIBLIOGRAPHY. S. Moscati, *The Semites in Ancient History*, 1959; J. R. Kupper, *Les Nomades en Mésopotamie au temps des Rois de Mari*, 1957; review by A. Goetze, *JSS* 4, 1959, pp. 142–147; I. J. Gelb, *JCS* 15, 1961, pp. 24–47; M. Liverani in *POTT*, pp. 100–133.

A.R.M.

AMOS, BOOK OF.

I. Outline of contents

On the whole the Hebrew text of Amos' prophecies has been well preserved. In addition, the progressive orderliness of his writings makes it possible to divide the book up into sections which are not artificial. It falls into four parts.

a. 1:1–2:16. After a simple introduction (1:1f.) in which Amos tells who he is, when he prophesied and wherein resided his authority to preach, he announces judgment upon the surrounding peoples (1:3–2:3), upon his native Judah and upon Samaria (2:4–16). Judgment falls on Gentile nations for offences against humanity, violations of those conscience-taught standards which make people human; Judah and Israel are judged for turning away from divine revelation (2:4, 11–12) with consequent moral and social collapse.

b. 3:1–6:14. The series of addresses in this section are each introduced by a clearly defined formula (3:1; 4:1; 5:1; 6:1). Here the emphasis is upon Samaria's privileges, but the nation's sinfulness has turned privilege into a ground upon which Amos bases his doctrine of judgment. Privilege involves God's people in penalty, hence Amos' insistence that status does not save (3:1–2) and that the 'day of Yahweh' will bring darkness and not the light complacently expected (5:16–20).

c. 7:1–9:10. A series of five visions of judgment, in each of which the judgment is set forth under a symbol: locusts (7:1–3), fire (7:4–6), a plumbline (7:7–9), summer fruit (8:1–14) and a smitten sanctuary (9:1–10). In 7:10–17 Amos displays his credentials for thus addressing the people of God.

d. 9:11–15. An epilogue which describes the restoration of the Davidic kingdom.

II. Authorship and date

Nothing is known of the prophet Amos outside of his writings. He was a native of Tekoa (1:1; *cf.* 2 Sa. 14:2; 2 Ch. 11:6), situated about 16 km S of Jerusalem. The surrounding countryside yielded pasture for the flocks, to tend which was part of Amos' calling (1:1). In addition, he was a fig farmer (*TREES, Sycomore; 7:14). The significance of this information is that Amos had no background in prophetic activity: he had not previously considered himself a prophet, nor was he trained in the prophetic schools (7:14f.). We know from 1:1 that he lived during the reigns of Uzziah, king of Judah (779–740 BC) and Jeroboam II, king of Samaria (783–743 BC). Uzziah and Jeroboam II reigned concurrently for 36 years (779–743). We do not know the date of the earthquake (1:1) and can place the ministry of Amos only by general indications. The level of prosperity and security which seems to have been enjoyed by Israel would indicate a date possibly about the middle of the reign of Jeroboam, *c.* 760 BC.

III. Circumstances

A Hebrew prophet's ministry and message were intimately bound up with the conditions in which the people to whom he preached lived, and in this Amos' book is no exception.

a. Political and social conditions. Over 40 years before Amos' ministry Assyria had crushed Syria, Samaria's N neighbour. This permitted Jeroboam II to extend his frontiers (2 Ki. 14:25), and to build up a lucrative trade which created a powerful merchant class in Samaria. Unfortunately the wealth that came to Samaria was not evenly distributed among the people. It remained in the hands of the merchant princes, who spent the newfound riches on improving their own living standards (3:10, 12, 15; 6:4), and neglected completely the peasant class which had hitherto been the backbone of Samaria's economy. The unmistakable symptoms of a morally sick society began to declare themselves in Samaria. In Amos' day oppression of the poor by the rich was common (2:6f.), and heartless indifference among the wealthy towards the affliction of the hungry (6:3–6). Justice went to the highest bidder (2:6; 8:6). In drought (4:7–9) the poor had recourse only to the moneylender (5:11f.; 8:4–6), to whom he was often compelled to mortgage both his land and his person.

b. The state of religion. Naturally the social conditions in Samaria affected religious habits. Religion was being not neglected but perverted. At the national religious shrines (5:5) ritual was being maintained (4:4f.), but it went hand in hand with godlessness and immorality. Far from pleasing Yahweh it invited his judgment (3:14; 7:9; 9:1–4); it did not remove but increased transgression (4:4). God was not to be found at the national shrines (5:4f.) because he could not accept the worship there (5:21–23); the true preoccupations of the people were with other gods (8:14). In addition, this rich ceremonial and the costly sacrifices were being offered at the expense of the poor (2:8; 5:11).

IV. Amos and the sacrificial system

Amos was well aware of the traditions of his own nation, historical (2:9ff.; 3:1, 13; 4:11; 5:6, 25; 7:16), religious (4:4ff.; 5:22; 8:5) and legal (2:8, *cf.* Ex. 22:26; Am. 8:5, *cf.* Lv. 19:35; Am. 2:4, *cf.* Dt. 17:19). This helps to give background to an understanding of his apparently hostile attitude to the religion he saw around him, and particularly to what is often thought of as his rejection of the whole system of sacrifices as lacking divine authorization (5:25). In company with other occasional verses in the pre-exilic prophets (*cf.* Is. 1:10–15; Je. 7:21f.; Ho. 6:6; Mi. 6:7f.) we have here, however, not a condemnation of the sacrificial code as such but of the way in which it was currently abused (*PROPHECY). On any reading of the Pentateuch, the people of Amos' day would have been instructed in the patriarchal and Mosaic traditions that sacrifice had ever been part of the religion of God's people and that he had accepted this with approval. Bearing in mind, then, that in 5:25 Amos does not make an assertion but asks a rhetorical question, only one answer is possible: an immediate affirmative. The balance of the Hebrew, however, suggests that Amos did not aim his question at the institution of sacrifice but at the prominence currently given to it: 'Was it sacrifices and offerings you brought me . . .?' The implication ('Was that the sum total of your religion then as it is now?') suits the context in Amos. Vv. 22–23 and v. 24 are an either/or in appearance only (a frequent biblical mode of emphasizing a due priority in things, *e.g.* Pr. 8:10a, 10b; Lk. 14:26); they are at heart an appeal for the restoration of a true balance wherein, as in the Mosaic norm, the sacrifices act as a divine provision for the lapses of a people committed to a life of ethical obedience to the law of God.

V. The prophet's message

a. Amos' concept of God is fundamental to an understanding of his message to Samaria. The Lord is the Creator of the world (4:13), but he is still actively present as its Sustainer. He it is who brings day and night to pass, and controls the waves of the sea (5:8; 9:6). He determines whether famine (4:6–11) or plenty (9:13) shall prevail. In the light of this knowledge of the God of creation there is no need to reject as later insertions 4:13; 5:8–9; 9:5–6. They are neither theologically premature, as used to be asserted, nor contextually misplaced: each in turn relates the foregoing declaration of judgment to a clear understanding of the divine nature and capability. The Lord also controls the destinies of the nations. He restrains this nation (1:5), raises up that (6:14) and puts down another (2:9). He also controls their distribution (9:7). He is therefore their Judge (1:3–2:3) when they offend against his moral laws.

b. Naturally Amos' message betrays a particular interest in Israel. In a quite special sense it was Yahweh's will to elect her to covenant relation with himself (3:2). Through his servants he has made known his will to her (2:11; 3:7). But these high privileges involve Israel in heavy responsibility; and failure to accept this brings upon his people a far more severe judgment than that which was to fall upon pagan nations. When Israel broke Yahweh's laws (2:4) there could be only a fearful looking forward to judgment (4:12).

c. Amos was also concerned to proclaim that a law broken through unrighteousness could not be mended by means of ritual, festival or offering alone. Indeed, Yahweh was already standing at the altar waiting to smite it (9:1–4). The most elaborate ritual was an abomination to him so long as it was offered by a people who had no intention of measuring up to the ethical standards laid down in his holy laws. Such a religion of ceremonial and ritual was divorced from morality, and this Yahweh could only hate (5:21f.).

d. The foregoing means that Amos' main concern was to demand righteousness in the name of the Lord from the people of the Lord (5:24). Righteousness was for Amos the most important moral attribute of the divine nature. Every outrage of the moral law, whether perpetrated by pagan nations (1:3–2:3) or by Israel (2:4–16), was an outrage upon the nature of God and was, therefore, a provocation of divine justice. If Yahweh is righteous, then injustice, dishonesty, immorality, cannot be tolerated by him, and must receive stern retribution from him.

e. But judgment was not Amos' final word to Samaria (5:4). Indeed, he closes with a promise of a brighter day for her (9:11–15). The prevailing fashion for refusing these verses to Amos ought to be resisted. It is not out of place for a Judahite to assert the Davidic hope nor inappropriate for Amos (notwithstanding his stress on judgment) to crown the negative ruling out of final loss (7:1–6) with a matching positive statement of final glory.

BIBLIOGRAPHY. W. R. Harper, *A Critical and Exegetical Commentary on Amos and Hosea*, 1910; S. R. Driver, *Joel and Amos*, 1915; R. M. Gwynn, *The Book of Amos*, 1927; R. S. Cripps, *A Critical and Exegetical Commentary on the Book of Amos*, 1929; E. A. Edghill, *The Book of Amos*, 1914; J. Marsh, *Amos and Micah*, 1959; J. L. Mays, *Amos*, 1969; J. A. Motyer, *NBCR*, 'Amos', 1970; *idem, The Day of the Lion, The Message of Amos*, 1974; H. W. Wolff, *Amos the Prophet*, 1973; R. Gordis, 'The Composition and Structure of Amos', *HTR* 33, 1940, pp. 239–251; H. H. Rowley, 'Was Amos a Nabi?' Eissfeldt *Festschrift*, 1947; J. D. Watts, *Vision and Prophecy in Amos*, 1958; E. Hammershaimb, *The Book of Amos*, 1970.

J.G.S.S.T.
J.A.M.

AMPHIPOLIS. An important strategic and commercial centre at the N of the Aegean, situated on the river Strymon (Struma) about 5 km inland from the seaport Eion. Prized by the Athenians and Macedonians as the key both to the gold, silver and timber of Mt Pangaeus and also to the control of the Dardanelles, it became under the Romans a free town and the capital

AMPLIAS
See Ampliatus, Part 1.

AMUN
See Thebes, Part 3.

ANA
See Hena, Part 2.

of the first district of Macedonia. Amphipolis is about 50 km WSW of Philippi on the Via Egnatia, a great Roman highway, and Paul passed through it on his way to Thessalonica (Acts 17:1).

K.L.McK.

AMPLIATUS. Paul's friend, affectionately greeted (Rom. 16:8). The best MSS show 'Ampliatus', a Latin slave name: 'Amplias' (AV) is a Gk. pet-form. Lightfoot (*Philippians*, p. 174) finds the name in inscriptions of 'Caesar's household' (*cf.* Phil. 4:22); but it was common. Those addressing Rom. 16 to Ephesus can find one there (*CIL*, 3, 436). A tomb-inscription 'Ampliati', perhaps late 1st century, in the catacomb of Domitilla, is ornate for a slave, perhaps reflecting his honour in the church (*cf.* Sanday and Headlam, *Romans*, p. 424). A connection with Paul's Ampliatus or his family is not impossible (*cf.* R. Lanciani, *Pagan and Christian Rome*, 1895, pp. 342ff.). Ampliatus, Stachys and Urbanus (*cf.* v. 9) were commemorated together as martyrs (*Acta Sanctorum*, Oct. 13, p. 687).

A.F.W.

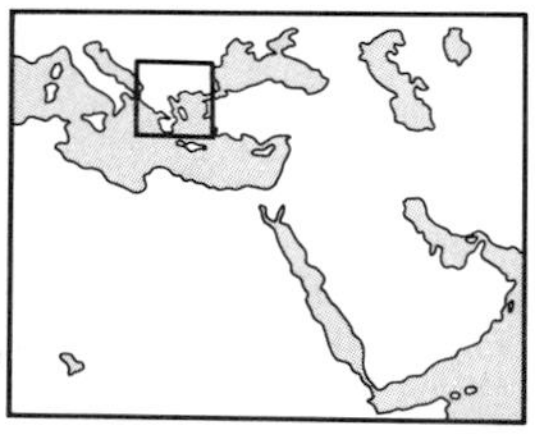

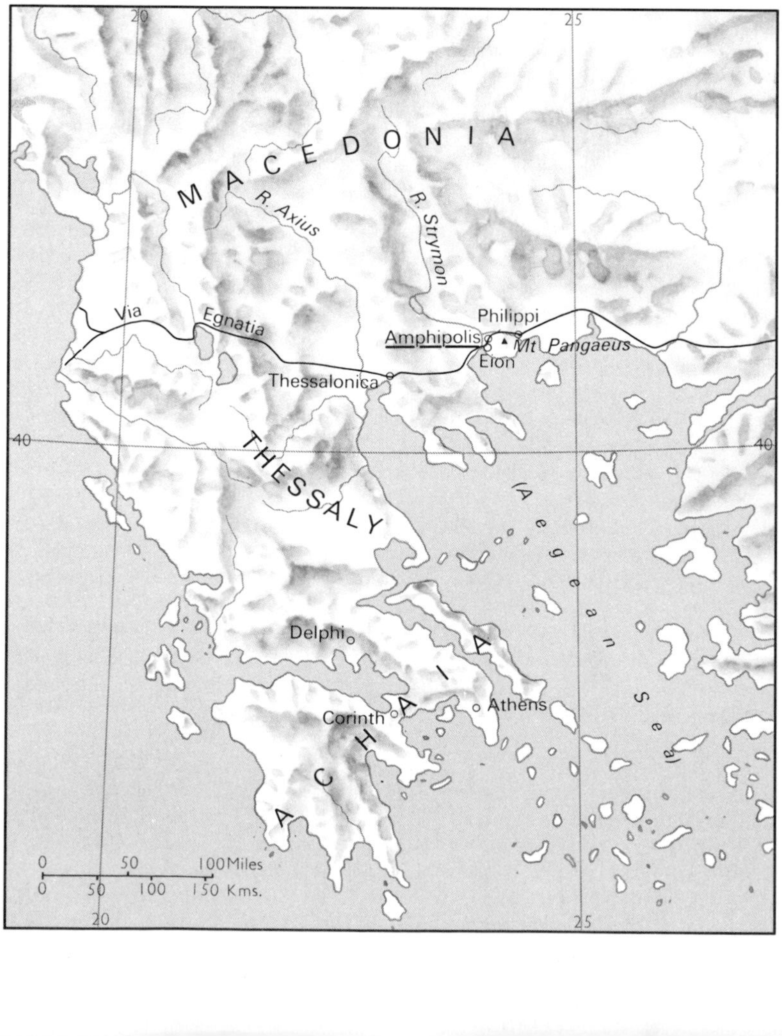

The situation of Amphipolis.

AMRAM (Heb. *'amrām*, 'people exalted'). **1.** The husband of Jochebed, and father of Moses, Aaron and Miriam (Ex. 6:20; Nu. 26:59; 1 Ch. 6:3; 23:13). He was a 'son' (*i.e.* probably descendant, *cf.* 1 Ch. 7:20–27) of Kohath (Ex. 6:18; Nu. 3:19), and so of Levi. **2.** An Amram is mentioned in Ezr. 10:34 as having taken a foreign wife.

E.J.Y.

AMRAPHEL. A king of *Shinar who attacked Sodom and its neighbours with the aid of *Chedorlaomer and other kings, but was repulsed by Abram (Gn. 14:1ff.). His identity is uncertain. The equation with *Hammurapi is unlikely.

D.W.B.

AMULETS. The practice of wearing on the person a small symbolic object as a charm or protection against evil was common throughout the ancient Near East. Such amulets were usually in the form of small ornaments, gems, stones, seals, beads, plaques or emblems, sometimes inscribed with an incantation or prayer. The Hebrews were unique in condemning their use and Is. 3:18–23 gives a list of such trinkets worn by women. These include 'soul boxes' and 'amulets' (*l^ehāšîm* —a word meaning 'whisper', either an incantation or perhaps snake-charming) (Is. 3:20, AV 'earrings'; *cf.* Ps. 58:5; Ec. 10:11; Je. 8:17). The presence of amulets may also be inferred in 'stones conferring favour' (Pr. 17:8; AVmg. 'stones of grace') for most stones were thought to have magical properties. Thus all stones and rings used as *seals were considered as amulets (*cf.* Je. 22:24; Hg. 2:23), as were most personal ornaments like those used to make the golden calf (Ex. 32:2) or buried by Jacob (Gn. 35:4). In common with the condemnation of those who employed charms (as Is. 3:3, RSV), the bronze serpent made by Moses was destroyed as soon as it became an object of superstitious reverence in itself (2 Ki. 18:4).

Archaeological evidence reveals the common use of ornaments in the shape of the sun disk or inverted moon crescent, a symbol of the goddess Ishtar-Astarte, worn by women or animals to increase their fertility (Jdg. 8:21). Egyptian-style figurines, and animal and fruit symbols (*ankh* for life, sacred eye) also generally relate to fertility and protection. The frontlets between the eyes (*ṭôṭāpôṯ*, Ex. 13:16; Dt. 6:8; 11:18) and fringes (*ṣîṣîṯ*, Nu. 15:38–39; Mt. 23:5) on garments were designed to act as a reminder of the law and as a deterrent to superstition and idolatry, which it condemned (Ex. 13:9; Dt. 6:8ff.; Pr. 3:3). These crimson cords have been compared with the Hittite use of blue and red cords as amuletic fringes, and some have thought that the bells on the fringe of the high priest's garment had a similar function (Ex. 28:33) as they had on horses in Assyria (*cf.* Zc. 14:20). Judas Maccabeus found amulets on the bodies of his dead soldiers (2 Macc. 12:40), presumably used as *phylacteries (Gk. *phylaktērion*, 'safeguard'), much as the small box containing a tiny scroll with a biblical passage and fixed to the doorpost (*m^ezûzâ*; Dt. 6:9) came to be regarded by later Jews.

D.J.W.

ANAH. 1. RSV, following Samaritan LXX, and Syr. Pesh., reads 'son' (AV, with Heb., 'daughter') of Zibeon, the Hivite, and father of Oholibamah, one of Esau's

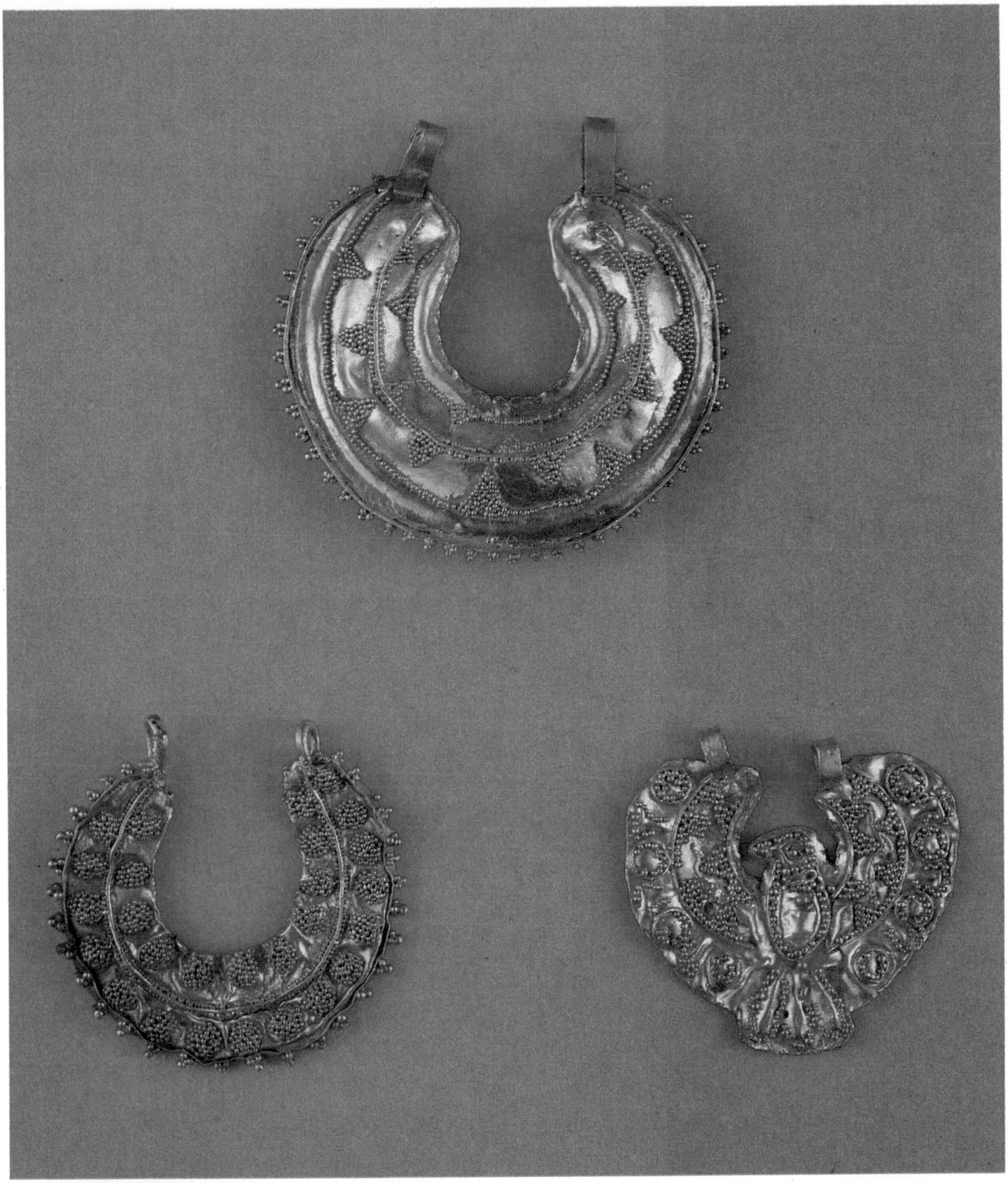

Gold amulets in the shape of crescent moons, worn as ear-rings or pendants. From Tell-el-Ajjul, Palestine. 14th–13th cent. BC. (BM)

Bottom left:
Three Phoenician multi-coloured glass amulets, possibly worn as part of a necklace. 5th–4th cent. BC. (AMO)

Bottom right:
Egyptian 'udjat' or Eye of Horus, open-work and inlay. Probably New Kingdom. c. 1600–1000 BC. (MH)

Canaanite wives (Gn. 36:2, also vv. 14, 18, 24–25; 1 Ch. 1:40). If in Gn. 36 Hivite and Horite (Hurrian) may be equated, Anah found the hot springs in the wilderness as he pastured his father's asses (v. 24). Further, if Oholibamah of Gn. 36:2 may be identified with Judith (Gn. 26:34), Beeri the Hittite of this verse will be another name for Anah, and commemorates the discovery of the hot springs, Heb. *be'ēr* meaning 'well'.

2. A Horite chief, brother of Zibeon and son of Seir (Gn. 36:20, 29; 1 Ch. 1:38). R.A.H.G.

ANAK, ANAKIM. The Anakim (Heb. *'anâqîm*), descendants of an eponymous ancestor Anak, were among the pre-Israelite inhabitants of Palestine. The name Anak occurs without the article only in Nu. 13:33 and Dt. 9:2, but elsewhere it appears in the form 'the Anak' (*hā 'anāq*), where it is presumably to be taken as the collective, equivalent to Anakim. The phrase 'the city of Arba (*qiryat 'arba'*, *KIRIATH-ARBA), father of Anak' in Jos. 15:13 apparently indicates that an individual named Arba was the ultimate ancestor of the Anakim, unless the noun 'father' is taken to qualify the city, in which case this city, later known as *Hebron, was considered the ancestral home of the Anakim.

The stature and formidable nature of the Anakim were almost proverbial, for they were taken as a standard for comparison to stress the size of such other peoples as the Emim (Dt. 2:10) and the Rephaim (Dt. 2:21), and there was a saying, 'Who can stand before the sons of Anak?' (Dt. 9:2). In the account of the Promised Land brought back by the ten faint-hearted spies, emphasis was laid on the fact that the Anakim were there (Dt. 1:28; the LXX here renders *'anāqîm* by *gigantes*, *GIANT). It was even stated that they were descended from the Nephilim, who were also claimed as sons of Anak, and the spies said that they felt like grasshoppers beside them (Nu. 13:33). They were settled in the hill-country, particularly at Hebron (Nu. 13:22), where Ahiman, Sheshai and Talmai, 'descendants of Anak', were found. Joshua cut off the Anakim from the hill-country (from Hebron, Debir and Anab), but some were left in Gaza, Gath and Ashdod (Jos. 11:21f.), and it fell to Caleb finally to drive them out from Hebron, which had been allotted to him. Nothing is known of these people outside the Bible, unless they are, as some scholars hold, among the peoples mentioned in the Egyp. 18th-century Execration Texts, or they represent an early 'Philistinian-type' title.

BIBLIOGRAPHY. *ANET*, p. 328; *VT* 15, 1965, pp. 468–474. T.C.M.

ANAMMELECH. A deity worshipped, with *Adrammelech, by Sepharvaim colonists placed in Samaria by the Assyrians (2 Ki. 17:31). If *Sepharvaim is interpreted as Babylonian Sippar the name is 'Anu is king'. However, as the name has initial ' the link with Anu is unlikely, because Akkadian divine names with initial vowels are written with ' in Aramaic transcriptions (as is Anu in 3rd century BC Uruk). More probable is identification with 'An, male counterpart of 'Anat, known in Ugaritic and Phoenician (F. Gröndahl, *Die Personennamen der Texte aus Ugarit*, 1967, pp. 83, 110). D.J.W.

ANANIAS, Gk. form of Hananiah ('Yahweh has dealt graciously'). **1.** In Acts 5:1ff. a member of the primitive church of Jerusalem whose contribution to the common fund was less than he pretended; he fell dead when his dishonesty was exposed. **2.** In Acts 9:10ff. a follower of Jesus in Damascus, 'a devout man according to the law', who befriended Saul of Tarsus immediately after his conversion and conveyed Christ's commission to him. **3.** In Acts 23:2; 24:1, Ananias the son of Nedebaeus, high priest AD 47–58, president of the Sanhedrin when Paul was brought before it, notorious for his greed; killed by Zealots in 66 for his pro-Roman sympathies. F.F.B.

ANATHEMA. 1. Gk. *anathēma* originally meant 'something set up (in a temple)', hence a votive offering, a form and sense preserved in Lk. 21:5 (AV 'gifts').

2. Gk. *anathema* (short *e*) is later; the forms are distinguished by lexicographers such as Hesychius, but are related in meaning and often confused in practice.

The LXX often uses *anathema* to represent Heb. *ḥērem*, *curse, 'the devoted thing', the thing to be put to the *ban, involving total destruction (*e.g.* Lv. 27:28f.; Nu. 21:3, of Hormah; Dt. 7:26, and *cf.* the striking Judith 16:19). Pagan imprecatory texts show that the word was used as a cursing formula outside Judaism (see Deissmann, *LAE*, pp. 95ff.; and *MM*).

So it was that Christians might hear, Hellenistic syncretism being what it was, the horrid blasphemy 'Anathema Jesus' from the lips of apparently 'inspired' preachers (1 Cor. 12:3): whether as an abjuration of allegiance (Pliny, *Ep.* 10. 96 and other sources show persecuted Christians were called on to 'curse Christ'), or by way of disparaging the earthly Jesus in contrast to the exalted Christ. Whatever the condition of the speaker, no message degrading Jesus came from the Holy Spirit. Again, Paul could wish himself for the sake of his unconverted brethren 'under the ban', involving separation from Christ (Rom. 9:3), and could call the ban, involving the abolition of Christian recognition, on preachers of 'any other gospel' (Gal. 1:8–9). In all these cases RV transliterates *anathema*, while AV and RSV render it 'accursed' or 'cursed'.

In one place, 1 Cor. 16:22, AV has transliterated *anathema* putting haters of Christ under the ban, attaching the following *maranatha* to it. This would perhaps give the general sense 'and may our Lord swiftly execute his judgments' (*cf.* C. F. D. Moule, *NTS* 6, 1960, pp. 307ff.). But *maranatha* may be a separate sentence (*cf.* RSV). In view of the contents of 1 Cor., these words amid the affectionate closing greetings are quite appropriate, without any special connection of the anathema with the dismissal before the Eucharist, which some find (*cf.* G. Bornkamm, *ThL* 75, 1950, pp. 227ff.; J. A. T. Robinson, *JTS* n.s. 4, 1953, pp. 38ff.).

The conspirators in Acts 23:14 put themselves under an *anathema* (RSV 'oath'; AV, RV 'curse'): *i.e.* they called the curse upon themselves if they failed (*cf.* the OT phrase 'May the Lord do so to me and more also if I do not . . .').

The ecclesiastical sense of excommunication is an extension, not an example, of biblical usage, though it is not impossible that synagogue practice (*cf. SB*, 4, pp. 293ff.) gave some early colouring to it.

The cognate verb appears in Mk. 14:71; Acts 23:12, 14, 21.

BIBLIOGRAPHY. H. Aust, D.

Müller, *NIDNTT* 1, pp. 413–415; J. Behm, *TDNT* 1, pp. 354f.

A.F.W.

ANATHOTH. Town in the territory of Benjamin assigned to Levites (Jos. 21:18). The home of Abiathar (1 Ki. 2:26) and Jeremiah (Je. 1:1; 11:21), Abiezer (2 Sa. 23:27; 1 Ch. 11:28; 27:12) and Jehu (1 Ch. 12:3). Conquered by Sennacherib (Is. 10:30). Repopulated after the Exile (Ne. 11:32). The modern site, Ras el-Ḥarrūbeh, *c.* 5 km N of Jerusalem, lies near the village of 'Anāta (Photo. Grollenberg, *Atlas*, pl. 250). D.J.W.

ANCESTOR WORSHIP. Most primitive pagan peoples believe in the existence of spirits, good and evil, and many consider that among these are the spirits of the dead. The desire to provide for the comfort of the benevolent, and to placate the ill-will of the malevolent, among these, often leads to a 'cult of the dead', where such services as fitting burial and provision of food and drink are performed to achieve these ends. The overt worship of the dead in the sense of adoration or even deification is, however, comparatively rare; the best-known example is that of Confucian China. It is more appropriate therefore to speak of a 'cult of the dead' than of 'ancestor worship', since there is no question of the latter's being found in the Bible.

In the latter part of the 19th and early years of the 20th century the reports of travellers and missionaries of the beliefs of modern primitive peoples gave material for anthropologists to speculate on the 'development' of religion. In the light of the resultant theories the Bible was re-examined, and the supposed traces of early stages in the development of Israelite religion detected. Among these traces were indications of ancestor worship. Thus it was claimed that evidence of this was to be found in the translation of *Enoch to be with God (Gn. 5:24), an indication that he was deified, but this is entirely gratuitous. It was suggested likewise that the *teraphim were originally worshipped as ancestor images, but there is again no foundation for such a view.

With the rediscovery of the civilizations of the ancient Near East, which formed the *milieu* of the OT, the customs of modern primitive peoples were seen to be largely irrelevant, but many of the theories of the development of religion remained, though now the religion of the OT was viewed as something of an amalgam of the beliefs and practices of the surrounding peoples.

In the ancient Near East belief in the after-life led to widespread cult practices connected with the dead. The provisions by the Egyptians for the comfort of the deceased, in what was believed to be a basically enjoyable future existence, were elaborate. In Mesopotamia less is known of the funeral rites of individuals, but a gloomy view was taken of the life to come, and it was in consequence important to ensure, by the provision of necessities as well as by ritual and liturgy, that the dead did not return as dissatisfied spirits to molest the living. The case of kings was different, and there was a tendency, in form at least, to their deification. The names, for example, of such early rulers as Lugalbanda and Gilgamesh were written with the divine determinative, an honour also accorded particularly to the kings of the 3rd Dynasty of Ur, and prayers were on occasion offered to them. In Syria also a cult of the dead is well attested, as, for instance, in the discoveries at Ras Shamra, where tombs were found provided with pipes and gutters to make it possible for libations to be poured from the surface into the tomb vaults.

Few cemeteries or tombs of the Israelite period have been excavated in Palestine, but those which have show, perhaps, a decline in furniture from the Canaanite Bronze Age or, in other words, a decline in the cult of the dead. That the Israelites, however, were continually falling away from the right path and adopting the religious practices of their neighbours is clearly stated by the Bible. It is to be expected that among these practices should have been some associated with the cult of the dead. Thus, the declarations in Dt. 26:14 suggest that it was necessary to prohibit offerings to the dead; it appears that it was expected that incense would be burned for (*lᵉ*) Asa at his burial (2 Ch. 16:14), and at Zedekiah's funeral (Je. 34:5); and Ezk. 43:7–9 implies that there was worship of the dead bodies of kings. The practice of necromancy (*DIVINATION) is also attested (1 Sa. 28:7), though clearly condemned (Is. 8:19; 65:4).

Other biblical passages are sometimes cited as evidence that such practices were acquiesced in, or accepted as legitimate. Thus, in Gn. 35:8 it is described how the oak under which Rebekah's nurse was buried was called Allon-bacuth, 'Oak of weeping', and again in Gn. 35:20 Jacob set up a *maṣṣēḇâ* (*PILLAR) over Rachel's grave. These actions have been taken to indicate a belief in the sanctity of graves, and, as a consequence, cult practices associated with the dead. But weeping over the dead may just as well be genuine as ritual, and there is no evidence to suggest that the raising of a memorial pillar necessarily implies a cult practice. The custom of levirate marriage (Dt. 25:5–10; *MARRIAGE, **IV**) has been interpreted as partly aimed at providing someone to carry out the cult of the dead for the deceased. This interpretation, however, is again one which exceeds the simple testimony of the text. Despite various theories, the participation in family sacrifices (*e.g.* 1 Sa. 20:29) provides no evidence of a cult of the dead. It has been further suggested that some of the mourning customs (*BURIAL AND MOURNING) show signs of a cult of, or even worship of, the dead. But such of these practices as were legitimate (*cf.* Lv. 19:27–28; Dt. 14:1) may just as well be explained as manifestations of sorrow over the loss of a dear one.

It is thus clear that neither ancestor worship nor a cult of the dead played any part in the true religion of Israel.

BIBLIOGRAPHY. R. H. Lowie, *An Introduction to Cultural Anthropology*, 1940, pp. 308–309 (modern primitives); J. N. D. Anderson (ed.), *The World's Religions*⁴, 1975, pp. 40 (modern primitives), 202–203 (Shinto), 223–224 (Confucian); A. H. Gardiner, *The Attitude of the Ancient Egyptians to Death and the Dead*, 1935; H. R. Hall in *ERE*, 1, pp. 440–443 (Egypt); A. Heidel, *The Gilgamesh Epic and Old Testament Parallels*², 1949, pp. 137–223; H. W. F. Saggs, 'Some Ancient Semitic Conceptions of the Afterlife', *Faith and Thought* 90, 1958, pp. 157–182; C. F. A. Schaeffer, *The Cuneiform Texts of Ras Shamra*, 1939, pp. 49–54; G. Margoliouth in *ERE*, 1, pp. 444–450; M. Burrows, *What Mean These Stones?*, 1941, pp. 238–242; R. de Vaux, *Ancient Israel*, E.T. 1961, p. 38.

T.C.M.

ANDREW. One of the twelve apostles. The name is Greek (meaning 'manly'), but it may have been a 'Christian name' like 'Peter'. He was the son of Jonas or John and came from Bethsaida in Galilee (Jn. 1:44), but afterwards went to live with his brother Simon Peter at Capernaum (Mk. 1:29), where they were in partnership as fishermen (Mt. 4:18). As a disciple of John the Baptist (Jn. 1:35–40) he was pointed by him to Jesus as the Lamb of God. He then found Simon and brought him to Jesus (Jn. 1:42). Later he was called to full-time discipleship (Mt. 4:18–20; Mk. 1:16–18) and became one of the twelve apostles (Mt. 10:2; Mk. 3:18; Lk. 6:14). His practical faith is shown in Jn. 6:8–9; 12:21–22. He was one of those who asked about the judgment coming on Jerusalem (Mk. 13:3–4). He is last mentioned as being with the other apostles after the ascension of Jesus (Acts 1:13).

It is probable that he was crucified in Achaia. The Synoptic Gospels say little about him, but in John he is shown as the first home missionary (1:42) and the first foreign missionary (12:21–22). Of the former, William Temple wrote, 'Perhaps it is as great a service to the Church as ever any man did' (*Readings in St John's Gospel*, p. 29). R.E.N.

ANDREW, ACTS OF
See New Testament apocrypha, Part 2.

ANDRONICUS AND JUNIAS, JUNIA. (AV 'Junia' is feminine—perhaps Andronicus' wife? RSV 'Junias' would be masculine, contracted from Junianus.) Affectionately greeted by Paul (Rom. 16:7) as (1) 'kinsmen', *i.e.* probably fellow-Jews, as in Rom. 9:3 (but see *MM*, *syngenēs*, for this word as a title of honour); Ramsay (*Cities of St Paul*, pp. 176ff.) infers membership of the same Tarsian civic tribe; (2) 'fellow-prisoners of war', probably to be understood of literal imprisonment (see Abbott, *ICC*, on Col. 4:10), but at what time this occurred is unknown; (3) 'distinguished among the apostles' ('well known *to* the apostles' is improbable): on this see *Apostle, and (4) Christians before him, as one might expect of apostles. For hypotheses connecting them with the foundation of the Ephesian or Roman churches, see B. W. Bacon, *ExpT* 42, 1930–1, pp. 300ff., and G. A. Barton, *ibid.*, 43, 1931–2, pp. 359ff. A.F.W.

ANGEL. A biblical angel (Heb. *mal'āḵ*, Gk. *angelos*) is, by derivation and function, a messenger of God, familiar with him face to face, therefore of an order of being higher than that of man. He is a creature certainly, holy and uncorrupted spirit in original essence, yet endowed with free will, therefore not necessarily impervious to temptation and sin. There are many indications of an angelic fall, under the leadership of Satan (Jb. 4:18; Is. 14:12–15; Ezk. 28:12–19; Mt. 25:41; 2 Pet. 2:4; Rev. 12:9), though this belongs properly to the realm of demonology. The Qumran Scrolls have a double hierarchy of angels, with associated mortals, those from the respective realms of light and darkness. Both Testaments use the selfsame word for mortal and for quite mundane messengers. The biblical material will be considered roughly in its time order, but without discussing chronological problems.

I. In the Old Testament

Apart perhaps from the *angel of the Lord, the executive or even manifestation of Yahweh, angels are spiritual beings separate from God, yet, unless they be fallen, of unquestioned integrity, goodwill and obedience to him (*cf.* 1 Sa. 29:9; 2 Sa. 14:17, 20; 19:27). Angels may appear to men as bearers of God's specific commands and tidings (Jdg. 6:11–23; 13:3–5, *etc.*; see **II**, below). They may bring specific succour to needy mortal servants of God (1 Ki. 19:5–7; see **II**, below). They may undertake commissions of military assistance (2 Ki. 19:35, *etc.*) or, more rarely, active hostility (2 Sa. 24:16f.) towards Israel. The men of Sodom (Gn. 19 *passim*) or any other evildoers may be smitten by them. Their warlike potential, implied in Gn. 32:1f.; 1 Ki. 22:19, is more specific in Jos. 5:13–15; 2 Ki. 6:17—hence the familiar title of deity, Lord God of hosts.

Man's early thinking associated angels with stars. This prompted one of the poetic thoughts of Job, where the angels are also witnesses of creation (Jb. 38:7, see below; *cf.* Jdg. 5:20; Rev. 9:1). Balaam's ass is more aware of the presence of the angel of the Lord than her greedy, blinded master, who merits divine rebuke (Nu. 22:21–35). Very familiar are the angels in converse with Abraham (Gn. 18:1–16) or on Jacob's ladder (Gn. 28:12). Individual guardian angels are probably reflected in Ps. 91:11; some discern the angel of death in Jb. 33:23 (*cf.* *ICC*, *ad loc.*). These ideas, rudimentary in OT, become strong speculative tenets in the uninspired rabbinic literature. The term 'sons of God' means simply angels—the descent implied is mental or spiritual, not physical. The beings thus denoted may be clearly good angels (Jb. 38:7; see above), possibly good angels (Jb. 1:6; 2:1) or clearly fallen angels (Gn. 6:4). Another special term is *qᵉḏôšîm*, 'holy ones', AV 'saints' (Jb. 5:1; Ps. 89:5, 7; Dn. 8:13, *etc.*). This latter term is perhaps a little technical, for it may be used even in a context of potential criticism (*cf.* Jb. 15:15). The word *'ᵉlōhîm* (Ps. 8:5; *cf.* Heb. 2:7) is rendered 'God' (RSV) or 'divine' (Moffatt), yet the familiar AV rendering 'angels' remains arguable. Noteworthy also is Nebuchadrezzar's Aram. term 'wakeful one' or 'watcher', *'îr*; *cf.* Dn. 4:13, 17. *Cf.* also *Cherubim, *Seraphim.

Excepting minor references to Dn., the material so far examined is broadly pre-exilic, in origin at least. Here the angels still remain echoes of a higher will, lacking in that independent personality which will broaden in the later writings.

In the post-exilic books, the angel unquestionably gains in firmness and contour. The 'man' who acts as Ezekiel's divinely appointed guide to the ideal temple is a midway concept (chs. 40ff.), his counterpart becomes explicitly an interpreting angel in Zc. 1–6. The intercessory ministry on behalf of Israel in Zc. 1:12 calls for special mention. If it be remembered that 'saints' means 'angels' in that context, the last words of Zc. 14:5 make interesting reading in the light of the Synoptic predictions of the second coming.

OT angelology reaches its fullest development in Daniel, the earliest Jewish apocalypse. Here angels are first endowed with proper names, and attain to something like personality. Gabriel explains many things to Daniel, much in the spirit of Zechariah's divine visitant (Dn. 8:16ff.; 9:21ff.). In both books the angel is the fluent mouthpiece of God, and may be questioned, but Daniel's Gabriel is more rounded and convincing. Michael has a special function as guardian angel of Israel (Dn. 10:13, 21; 12:1), and other nations are similarly equipped (Dn. 10:20). This became rabbinic commonplace. There is a visionary glimpse into the heavenly places, where there are countless myriads of throne angels (Dn. 7:10; *cf.* Dt. 33:2; Ne. 9:6; Ps. 68:17 for slighter echoes).

II. In the New Testament

The NT largely endorses and underlines the OT, though developments in the intervening uninspired literature are historically important. Heb. 1:14 defines the angel both as messenger of God and as minister to man; the NT as a whole suggests a deepening bond of sympathy and service (*cf.* Rev. 19:10; Lk. 15:10). The concept of the personal guardian angel has sharpened, as in the rabbinic literature (Mt. 18:10; *cf. SB, ad loc.*; and on Acts 12:15). Special missions of communication to individuals are not lacking: the visitation of Gabriel to Daniel may be compared with that to Zechariah (Lk. 1:11–20) and Mary (Lk. 1:26–38; *cf.* also Mt. 1–2 *passim*; Acts 8:26; 10:3ff.; 27:23, *etc.*). The role of active succour to humanity is perceived in Acts 5:19f.; 12:7–10, which recalls Elijah under the juniper tree. God's throne is surrounded by countless myriads of angels, as Daniel had already declared (Heb. 12:22; Rev. 5:11, *etc.*).

The OT implies that angels were the joyful witnesses of, though not necessarily active participants in, God's act of creation (Jb. 38:7). In the NT they are closely associated with the giving of the law (Acts 7:53; Gal. 3:19; Heb. 2:2), and it is not inconsistent that they should be coupled with final judgment (Mt. 16:27; Mk. 8:38; 13:27; Lk. 12:8f.; 2 Thes. 1:7f., *etc.*). It may be their special task also to carry the righteous dead into Abraham's bosom (Lk. 16:22f.). Little is attempted by way of direct description of the angelic form. There are hints of lustrous countenance and apparel, of awesome, other-worldly beauty, which Christian art has attempted to express in its own way (Mt. 28:2f. and parallels; Lk. 2:9; Acts 1:10). The OT shows a comparable restraint in dealing with the *cherubim (Ezk. 10) and *seraphim (Is. 6). The splendour on the face of the condemned Stephen reflects the angelic loveliness (Acts 6:15).

The incarnate Christ received the angelic ministry on several occasions (Mt. 4:11; Lk. 22:43), and he could have commanded thousands of angels, had he been prepared, at Gethsemane or anywhere else, to deviate from the appointed sacrificial path (Mt. 26:53).

There is a strange undertone of hostility or suspicion towards angels in certain passages. This has interesting though unconnected parallels in the rabbinic literature. Rom. 8:38 refers to fallen angels, and this explains also the puzzling passage 1 Cor. 11:10, which should be read in the light of Gn. 6:1ff. Some special exegesis is still necessary for Gal. 1:8 and 1 Cor. 13:1, also for the stern warning of Col. 2:18. It was doubtless through doctrinal errors on the part of his readers that the writer to the Hebrews urged so forcefully the superiority of the Son to any angel (Heb. 1).

The essential meaning of Jude 9 (partial parallel 2 Pet. 2:10f.) would seem to be that fallen angels retain from their first condition a status and dignity such that even their unfallen former companions may not revile them, but must leave the final condemnation to God. The incident referred to by Jude is said to have been recorded in the *Assumption of Moses*, a fragment of apocalyptic midrash. There Satan claims the body of Moses for his kingdom of darkness, because Moses killed the Egyptian (Ex. 2:12), and was therefore a murderer, whatever his subsequent virtues may have been. The final honours do not go to Satan, but even Michael the archangel must bridle his tongue before the foe of mankind.

BIBLIOGRAPHY. L. Berkhof, *Systematic Theology*, 1949, pp. 141–149, and similar manuals; H. Heppe, *Reformed Dogmatics*, 1950, pp. 201–219; *TDNT* 1, pp. 74–87; *NIDNTT* 1, pp. 101–105, 449–454 (with biblios.). For rabbinic background, see *SB*, under particular NT passages; R. A. Stewart, *Rabbinic Theology*, 1961. For Qumran aspect, Y. Yadin, *The Scroll of the War of the Sons of Light against the Sons of Darkness*, 1962, pp. 229–242. R.A.S.

ANGEL OF THE LORD. The angel of the Lord, sometimes 'the angel of God' or 'my (or 'his') angel', is represented in Scripture as a heavenly being sent by God to deal with men as his personal agent and spokesman. In many passages he is virtually identified with God and speaks not merely in the name of God but as God in the first person singular (*e.g.* with Hagar, Gn. 16:7ff.; 21:17f.: at the sacrifice of Isaac, Gn. 22:11ff.; to Jacob, Gn. 31:13, 'I am the god of Beth-el'; to Moses at the burning bush, Ex. 3:2; with Gideon, Jdg. 6:11ff.). Sometimes he is distinguished from God, as in 2 Sa. 24:16; Zc. 1:12f.; but Zechariah does not consistently maintain the distinction (*cf.* Zc. 3:1f.; 12:8).

In the NT there is no possibility of the angel of the Lord being confused with God. He appears as *Gabriel in Lk. 1:19, though from Acts 8:26, 29 some would infer an identification with the Holy Spirit.

In function, the angel of the Lord is the agent of destruction and judgment (2 Sa. 24:16; 2 Ki. 19:35; Ps. 35:5f.; Acts 12:23); of protection and deliverance (Ex. 14:19; Ps. 34:7; Is. 63:9, 'the angel of his presence'; Dn. 3:28; 6:22; Acts 5:19; 12:7, 11); he offers guidance and gives instructions (Gn. 24:7, 40; Ex. 23:23; 1 Ki. 19:7; 2 Ki. 1:3, 15; Mt. 2:13, 19; Acts 8:26); he gives advance warning about the birth of Samson (Jdg. 13:3ff.), John the Baptist (Lk. 1:11ff.) and Jesus (Mt. 1:20, 24; Lk. 2:9). He is not recognized at once in Jdg. 13:3ff. and is not even visible to Balaam (Nu. 22:22ff.); but mostly when appearing to men he is recognized as a divine being, even though in human form, and is addressed as God (Gn. 16:13, *etc.*).

J.B.Tr.

ANGELS OF THE CHURCHES. The 'seven stars' of the Patmos vision are explained as referring to 'the angels (*angeloi*) of the seven churches' (Rev. 1:20), to whom the letters of Rev. 2 and 3 are then addressed. The 'angel' concept is problematic. It is often taken either of guardian angels or of human leaders or bishops of the churches. Both suggestions involve difficulty. Elsewhere in Rev. *angelos* certainly means 'angel', but the 'angel' can scarcely be made to share responsibility for the sins of the church. The interpretation 'bishop' seems contrary to usage, and unsupported by effective parallels. There is no such emphasis on episcopacy as later in Ignatius. Nor can this view be based on the inferior reading 'your wife' in 2:20 (*sou* inserted by dittography). And again it would be strange to hold one man individually and absolutely responsible for the church. *angelos* is literally 'messenger', but the initially attractive idea that the *angeloi* might be messengers appointed by the churches breaks down for a com-

Assyrian royal war-horses being tended. Bas-relief from the palace of Ashurnasirpal II at Calah (Nimrud). 883–859 BC. (BM)

bination of similar reasons.

The real difficulty is probably that the image belongs to a context and genre which eludes the logic of modern categories. *angelos* must be rendered verbally as 'angel', but the verbal equivalence does not sufficiently explain the underlying thought. The 'angel' is perhaps something like a heavenly counterpart of the church. In practice we may visualize this as amounting to a personification of the church, even if this does less than justice to the connotations of the original concept. C.J.H.

ANIMALS OF THE BIBLE. Both early and modern EVV mention a wide range of animal names. In the earliest EVV, especially AV, lack of precise knowledge of the Palestine fauna was a major reason for inaccuracy and it is not surprising that translators used the names of European species with which they were familiar. The precise study of animal life began only in the 19th century, and it was formerly usual to give names only to animals which were obvious or of practical importance. Animals resembling each other in general appearance or usage would thus be called by the same or by similar names. These general principles apply to animal life as a whole. There is usually little difficulty in identifying animals mentioned several times in varying contexts likely to provide clues, but the correct translation of many names found only in the various lists of Lv. and Dt. will always be difficult. EVV published since about 1900 have corrected some early mistakes, but there is lack of uniformity within and among the EVV and most include some strange translations. Not all of these names, some now obsolete or indefinite, are mentioned below but most are discussed. Two major sections may be recognized—the wild animals that usually form part of the incidental background, and the domestic animals that were a basic part of daily life. The latter is the more important and is treated first.

Two Heb. words are translated **ASS**: *'āṯôn*, referring to its endurance, and *ḥ^{a}môr* from the reddish coat of the most usual colour form. The latter is used much more frequently than the former, which is found mainly in the two incidents of Balaam's ass (Nu. 22) and the asses of Kish (1 Sa. 9–10). These words refer only to the domesticated ass. **DONKEY**, of unknown origin, is not found before the end of the 18th century: applied only to the domesticated form, it is used in some modern EVV, including JB and NEB.

In addition, two words are generally translated **WILD ASS**—*'ārôḏ* and *pere'*. The former is found both in the Aram. form *^{a}rād* (Dn. 5:21), and as Heb. *'ārôḏ* (Jb. 39:5), but the translation is questioned by some authorities. *pere'* occurs 9 times and its translation 'wild ass' in Jb. 39:5–8 is well endorsed by the context. This species is known today as the **ONAGER** (*Equus onager*) and it is still found in parts of W and Central Asia. A form closely related to the sub-species that became extinct about mid-19th century has now been successfully introduced into the Hay Bar Nature Reserve in the S Negeb.

The **ASS** is descended from the Nubian wild ass (*Equus asinus*) and is thought to have been domesticated in Neolithic times in NE Africa. The first biblical mention is during Abram's stay in Egypt (Gn. 12:16), but he had probably used asses as transport from Mesopotamia, where several distinct breeds were recognizable by *c.* 1800 BC. 'Asses' which drew wheeled carts in ancient Mesopotamia more than 1,000 years earlier are now known from stone carvings and drawings to have been onagers, but this species was never fully domesticated. Asses were vitally important to poor nomadic peoples and provided their basic transport, allowing an average journey of about 30 km a day. A text from Mari shows that as early as the 17th century BC it was considered improper for royalty to ride a horse rather than an ass. The biblical picture is consistent, that royal persons rode asses on peaceful occasions, while horses are associated with war. In the light of this, *cf.* Zc. 9:9 and Mk. 21:2f.

Both **COLT** and **FOAL** are correctly used for the young of members of the horse tribe; in EVV they refer only to the ass, except for Gn. 32:15 where colt applies to a young camel.

The OT contains numerous references to the **HORSE** (*sûs*), many of them figurative, and its use is especially frequent in the prophetic literature and poetic books. Throughout OT and NT the horse is regularly associated with war and power, and very seldom mentioned singly. A further word, *pārāš*, translated 'horseman' in most EVV, could mean a mounted horse of the cavalry or perhaps a horse with rider; *sûs* is a more general word, used in particular for horses drawing chariots.

Of all the animals that have become beasts of burden, the horse is the most important, though it was domesticated long after cattle and the ass. In contrast to the wild ass, which lived in the semi-desert of N Africa, the ancestors of the horse were native to the grasslands of Europe and Asia. It is likely that domestication took place independently in several different areas —W Europe, SW Asia and Mongolia. Horses in the biblical record presumably come from the second of these.

A Bab. tablet of the period of Hammurapi, *c.* 1750 BC, gives the first record of the horse, referred to as 'the ass from the east'. Horses were already in Egypt when Joseph was in power, and they were used in pursuit at the Exodus. It is unlikely that the children of Israel owned horses, but in any case they would have been unsuited to a desert journey.

The nations living in Canaan had horses and rode them in battle (Jos. 11:4, *etc.*). David frequently fought against them: 'David hamstrung all the chariot horses (of 1,700 horsemen), but left enough for 100 chariots' (2 Sa. 8:4), which seems to be the first record that he owned any. (In AV the obsolete word 'hough' is used for hamstring; now spelt, as pronounced, 'hock', it is the joint between knee and fetlock in the hind leg. Cutting this tendon permanently crippled a horse.) David's sons ignored the prohibition in Dt. 17:16 (referring to the time when the people would demand a king), 'He must not multiply horses for himself'; *e.g.* 'Absalom got himself a chariot and horses' (2 Sa. 15:1), while Solomon later had great numbers of horses, kept in special establishments at Hazor, Megiddo and Gezer. These were imported from Egypt and Kue (S Anatolia) and exported to neighbouring states, the price of a horse being 150 shekels of silver (1 Ki. 10:28f.).

Although the Eng. word **MULE** has a number of other meanings it was first, and still is primarily, applied to the offspring of a horse by a donkey. These hybrids were probably first bred soon after the horse was introduced into areas where the donkey was kept, although such breeding seems to be specifically forbidden by Lv. 19:19, 'You shall not let your cattle breed with a different kind' (cattle, *b^ehēmâ*, here means any domesticated stock). This may explain why it was not until towards the end of David's reign (2 Sa. 13:29) that mules appear in the record. It is generally agreed that Heb. *yēmîm* (Gn. 36:24) should be translated 'hot springs' (RSV) and not 'mule' (AV). *pereḏ* and *pirdâ* are used for the male and female, but this hybrid is always sterile. Mules are valuable in that they combine the strength of the horse with the endurance and sure-footedness of the donkey, as well as its ability to thrive on poorer food; they also have the extra vigour characteristic of hybrids, both plant and animal.

In Est. 8:14 Heb. *reḵeš* is better translated 'swift horses' (RSV).

Although the early history of the **CAMEL** (Heb. *gāmāl*; Gr. *kamēlos*) has major gaps and its wild ancestor is unknown, there is ample evidence of early domestication. The one-humped camel, usually known as Arabian, is often called dromedary, though this name strictly refers to the fast riding breed; it is typical of the deserts of the Middle East and features in the biblical narrative. The two-humped, or Bactrian, camel (named after Bactria, probably near the Oxus river in SW Asia) is now associated with Central and NE Asian deserts, where winters are very cold. This form was sometimes brought farther S and an obelisk at Nimrod (841 BC) shows it as part of the booty taken by Shalmaneser III. Anatomically there is little difference between the two and they are known to interbreed.

The camel is wonderfully fitted to life in dry zones. The hump is a storage organ which is drawn on when food is short, as it often is on desert crossings. Its water economy allows it to go for a week without drinking, a feat made possible by a camel's ability to lose up to one-third of its body weight without danger; when given access to water this is replaced in about 10 minutes. There is also an unusual physiological mechanism whereby body temperature rises from a morning reading of 34°C to 40°C in the afternoon, thus avoiding water loss through sweating. Mouth, nose, eyes and feet are all anatomically adapted to desert life. The camel's products are widely used; the winter hair is woven into rough cloth and the droppings are collected for fuel. The camel chews the cud but is not cloven-hoofed, so under Mosaic law it was unclean; it is not certain that this ban applied to the milk, which is a valuable source of food, for the cow may stay in milk for nearly 2 years. Camel hides are made into leather. Camels can live on poor vegetation, of which the high fibre content makes the droppings useful.

A camel can carry about 200 kg and its rider, but only half that for desert reaches. Freight camels can average 45 km a day but a fast riding camel has covered 150 km in 13 hours.

There has been much argument about the use of camels by the Patriarchs, but archaeology has now shown that there were domesticated camels in Egypt at least 1,200 years earlier. The problem arises largely because there were long periods when the camel seems to have been unknown in Egypt, possibly for reasons of taboo; it was in one such period that Abram went there (Gn. 12:16), and the inclusion of camels in the list of presents from the pharaoh is considered a scribal addition, but there is no reason to reject later mentions. The evidence for the camel's early use is detailed in Zeuner (ch. 13) and Cansdale (ch. 4). More recent excavations in Oman confirm its occurrence there *c.* 2500 BC.

In the narrative from Gn. 24:35 onwards camels formed an important part of wealth and were also used for long-distance transport (Gn. 24:10ff. and 31:34), but camel nomadism and the regular use of camels did not become general until *c.* 16th century BC. David appointed an Ishmaelite as his camel master (1 Ch. 27:30) and the Queen of Sheba's baggage was carried on camels from SW Arabia (1 Ki. 10:2).

Camels were valuable for transport in and around deserts but were never popular with the Hebrews. There is no clear biblical reference to camels as draught animals, but they have been widely used in cultivation, sometimes paired oddly with a donkey. In contrast to the 57 wholly literal OT mentions only two of the six NT references are literal—the material for John the Baptist's clothes in Mt. 3:4 and Mk. 1:6. The others are in colourful comments by Christ which are perhaps proverbial in origin—'straining out a gnat' (Mt. 23:24) and 'the eye of a needle' (Mt. 19:24). See also separate article on *Camel.

The importance of the domestic **SHEEP** to the Israelites is shown by its being mentioned some 400 times, with 12 Heb. words. Of these some are simple alternatives; others refer to age and sex, while at least one word (*kar*, Aram. *d^ekar*) may denote a separate breed. *ṣō'n*, the most common word, is a collective term, discussed under 'Goat', to which it refers equally. *keḇeś* occurs over 100 times and with

Assyrian shepherd with his flock of sheep and goats, from the palace of Tiglath-pileser III at Calah (Nimrud). 744–727 BC. (BM)

only 5 exceptions applies to sacrificial animals; the frequent qualification 'a year old' suggests that it may refer to a lamb of 1 year and upwards. Four Gk. words cover the more than 70 NT occurrences, in which *probaton* is most used. For a complete list of Heb. and Gk. words and their usage, see Cansdale, pp. 53–55.

The origins and early history of the sheep are complex and disputed. It was kept by Neolithic man *c.* 5000 BC and by 2000 BC at least five different breeds had reached Mesopotamia. Its ancestors were probably mountain sheep, perhaps from more than one source; a wide range of breeds has now been developed which serve many purposes and utilize habitats ranging from marshland to near desert. Sheep were first domesticated for their meat and fat, especially the latter, of which the earlier goat provided little. The wool was developed by careful breeding and became very valuable, being the most useful and easily available fibre for clothing. Mesha, king of Moab (2 Ki. 3:4), paid as annual tribute the wool of 100,000 rams, with fleeces perhaps averaging 1 kg. The tanned skins were used for clothes and also for the inner covering of the tabernacle (Ex. 25:5, *etc.*). The milk was mostly used in the form of curds and as a basic food it was probably more important than the meat, which was usually eaten only as part of sacrificial meals.

The sheep is mainly a grazer, *i.e.* it feeds on grasses and is thus more selective than the grazing goat. The fat-tailed breed is now the most common in Palestine. This strange feature, which may weigh 5 kg, is known from Egyp. mummies of *c.* 2000 BC; it is a storage organ, analogous to the camel's hump, and is useful in the hot dry summer and cold winter. The main limiting factor was probably winter feed, and in NT times flocks were often kept under cover from the November rains until Passover and fed on chaff and barley.

It is clear from Gn. 30:32 that both sheep and goats were already in various colours and patterns, and possibly few were pure white. This suggests that the correct translation of Heb. *tāmîm* (Nu. 28:3) is 'without blemish' (most modern EVV) and not 'without spot' (AV), referring to general imperfections rather than to colour markings.

Although archaeological material is rich in tools and other objects made from sheep bones, there is no biblical reference other than to the use of rams' horns as containers of oil (1 Sa. 16:1) and as musical instruments (Jos. 6:4, *etc.*).

Throughout the Bible the sheep has deep metaphorical significance and in the NT the only entirely non-figurative references are to their being sold in the Temple (Jn. 2:14, *etc.*). Sheep were always a familiar part of the scene, with the shepherd leading and protecting his sheep and building folds for them. It is therefore not surprising that the sheep is consistently a picture of man—helpless, easily led astray and lost, essentially sociable, unable to fend for itself or find its way home, *e.g.* Is. 53:6, 'All we like sheep have gone astray; we have turned every one to his own way.' The alternative, of man restored, is stated in Ps. 23, written by David from his early experience as a shepherd. The NT unfolds the great paradox of Jn. 1:29, ‘Behold, the Lamb of God, who takes away the sin of the world!’ and Jn. 10:14, ‘I am the good shepherd’, with Rev. 5:6, ‘a lamb standing, as though it had been slain’.

The meaning of separating the sheep from the goats (Mt. 25:32) becomes clear when a mixed flock is inspected; the two may look alike, and close scrutiny is needed to distinguish them. Of the highly figurative passage in Ct. 4:2 it is enough to say that although the phrase ‘all of which bear twins’ is a disputed translation, the shepherd’s ambition is for all ewes to have twin lambs and lose none by abortion.

CATTLE (from OE *catel*) first meant property, of which livestock was then a major part. This usage is close to Heb. *miqneh*. Today cattle are wild and domesticated bovines, *i.e.* members of the ox tribe, but biblical reference is confined to domestic animals. Ten Heb. words apply to cattle, which between them are mentioned over 450 times. The following are the most important: *b^{e}hēmâ* (sing. and collective) denotes larger domestic animals and not only bovines. *šôr*, usually a bull, though occasionally female, is the basic word for a single animal. *bāqār* is another collective term for adult horned cattle, often translated herd, while *b^e‘îr* is a collective term used mostly for beasts of burden, which could include oxen. *par* is a bull; its feminine, *pārâ*, is used of the red heifer of Nu. 19. *‘ēḡel* and *‘eglâ* (fem.) (from a root ‘to roll’) are used of young animals. *m^{e}rî’*, translated fat beast, almost always refers to animals for sacrifice.

Six Gk. words are used. *damalis*, the (red) heifer; *thremma*, *moschos* and *sitistos* mostly refer to fattened cattle; *tauros*, ox; and *bous*, bull.

All domestic cattle are thought to be derived from the aurochs or wild ox (see below). It was first tamed in Neolithic times, probably in several different parts of the world independently, and later than sheep and goats. The primary reason for domestication was for meat; later the cows were used for milking and the bulls for draught purposes, which greatly increased the area of land that could be cultivated. Their size and the need for good grazing limited the range of cattle-keeping and they did best in the hilly country of Upper Galilee. However, they seem to have been widely kept in small numbers and were everywhere used as multipurpose animals.

Several humanitarian rules about oxen are recorded in both OT and NT. They were included in the sabbath rest (Ex. 23:12). A straying ox should be led to safety (Ex. 23:4). Watering cattle was permitted on the sabbath (Lk. 13:15). Paul twice quoted the Mosaic injunction (Dt. 25:4) not to muzzle the ox treading out corn (1 Cor. 9:9; 1 Tim. 5:18). These and other precepts show a concern for animal welfare still unknown in many countries and not recognized in the West until well into the 19th century.

Domesticated in antiquity—from the **WILD GOAT** (*Capra aegagrus*)—the **GOAT** was useful to the Patriarchs (Gn. 15:9), for though kept with sheep it had the advantage of being able to thrive on poorer ground. The story of Jacob and Esau (Gn. 27:9) stresses its value as meat, but normally only kids were used for food. The she-goats provided milk, skins were used for leather and as bottles, and the hair of some varieties was woven into cloth; but goats have also done untold damage to the habitat of lands where they have been introduced and not properly controlled. This is especially true of hilly terrain of the E Mediterranean, with hot, dry summers and winter rains.

As would be expected, such an important animal has a range of Heb. names for male (*ṣāp̄îr*, *śā‘îr*, *tayiš*), female (*‘ez*, *ś^e‘îrâ*), young (*g^{e}dî*, *g^{e}ḏî ‘izzîm*, pl. *b^{e}nê ‘izzîm*), *etc.* In addition, two collective nouns, *ṣō’n* or *ṣ^e’ôn* ‘flock’ and *śeh* or *śê* ‘member of the flock’, are found more often than any other names. Unless specified by attaching *‘ez*, ‘goat’, or *keḇeś*, ‘sheep’, these words may refer equally to either sheep or goats, or to a mixture of both. It is therefore often difficult to speak of relative numbers.

The domestic **SWINE** of Palestine was derived from *Sus scrofa*, the wild boar of Europe and W Asia. The children of Israel were divinely prohibited from eating swine (*ḥ^{a}zîr*, Lv. 11:7; Dt. 14:8). This was for two hygienic reasons. First, the pig, as a frequent scavenger, may pick up diseased material and either carry infection mechanically or itself become infected. Secondly, the pig is host of the tapeworm causing trichinosis; this passes one stage in the muscles of a pig and can be transmitted only by being eaten. The tape worms then invade various tissues in man and

Weights in the form of a cow and a goat, from Ras Shamra (Ugarit). Both are 3 cm long. c. 1300 BC. (MC)

can even cause death. Thorough cooking kills the worms but this is not always possible when firewood is scarce, so that only a complete ban is safe. This relationship was proved only in the 20th century.

This prohibition became a national loathing with the Jews, with the pig standing for what is despicable and hated. Thus in Pr. 11:22 a woman of doubtful character is associated with a swine, and the prodigal son had reached the

A wild sow and her young in the marshlands of S Mesopotamia. Relief from the palace of Sennacherib at Nineveh. c. 690 BC. (BM)

Dogs on leashes, from Ashurbanipal's palace reliefs at Nineveh. c. 640 BC. (BM)

utter depths when feeding the swine (*choiros*) of a Gentile (Lk. 15:15). Herds were kept by local Gentile communities in NT times (Mt. 8:30ff., *etc*.). The demons' plea to be sent into a nearby herd of swine would not appear strange to a Jew, who considered swine and demons of the same order. Similarly, in Mt. 7:6 Jesus warns his followers not to throw pearls before swine. The author of 2 Pet. 2:22 regards false teachers as those who will return to their (swinish) pagan nature.

Pig, which once meant young swine, is now the name in general use; swine is obsolete other than in some technical terms, but is still retained in most EVV.

The contempt and disgust with which the **DOG** is regarded in the OT cannot easily be understood by Western people, to whom the dog is a companion and auxiliary. It is generally agreed that it was the first animal to be domesticated and that by the late Stone Age it was being kept in many parts of the world. Most authorities regard the wolf as the ancestor of all the many and varied breeds of domestic dog.

In many parts of the East the dog is still basically a scavenger. It was useful in disposing of refuse but was by its very nature unclean and a potential carrier of disease, and therefore could not be touched without defilement. Heb. *keleḇ* and Gr. *kyōn* are without doubt the semi-wild dogs which roamed outside the city walls waiting for rubbish or dead bodies to be thrown over. Dogs were differently regarded in other lands, especially in Egypt, where they were used in hunting and also held in reverence. A second Gk. word, the diminutive *kynarion*, is used in the incident of the Syro-Phoenician woman (Mt. 15:26ff.). The context suggests that this was a pet dog allowed about the house.

The 'dogs' of Phil. 3:2 are Judaizing intruders who disturb the peace of the church; the 'dogs' who are excluded from the new Jerusalem in Rev. 22:15 are people of unclean lives, probably an echo of Dt. 23:18, where 'dog' seems to be a technical term for a male temple prostitute.

In OT times Palestine was fairly rich in wild **RUMINANTS** (animals that chew the cud) that were allowed as food. There is frequent mention of *hunting and hunting methods, with a wide range of nets, traps, pitfalls, *etc*. Many of these are in figurative contexts and cannot always be identified exactly, but they were certainly the tools of the hunter, and it must be assumed that hunting yielded useful meat. It seems likely that all the major species find mention in the Heb. text, but there has been no consistency in the EVV, only in part because the Palestine fauna was not known when the early translations were made, for even in modern EVV the treatment is often erratic. The wild ruminants known to have occurred in Palestine will be listed, with brief notes, but there is no point in tabulating all the EVV translations. For a fuller discussion see Cansdale, ch. 5, 'Beasts of the Chase'.

Heb. *r*ᵉ*'ēm* is without doubt the **AUROCHS** or **WILD OX**, ancestor of domestic cattle. It had disappeared from Palestine before the Christian era, and the last-known specimen was killed in Poland early in the 17th century. EVV now generally translate 'wild ox', and the AV 'unicorn' is rightly dropped. Heb. *te'ô* is translated 'wild ox' and 'wild bull' (AV) and more widely 'antelope'. JB has **ORYX**, which is correct. Properly called the Arabian or desert oryx, it is a specialized desert animal able to survive long periods without water; almost white in coat, it stands 1 m high and both sexes have long, straight horns. Modern weapons and transport brought disaster and this oryx may already be extinct in the wild. Is. 51:20 speaks of its being taken in a net, a method of hunting practised by Arabs up to the end of the 19th century.

The **ADDAX** is another rare desert antelope; it still survives in the Sahara, but was lost to Bible lands before 1900. Heb. *dîšôn* is translated 'pygarg' (AV) via the Gk. in LXX. Long tradition, and its placing between two desert species in the food lists suggest that this is probably the addax. 'Ibex' (RSV) cannot be right.

Heb. *yaḥmûr* is the most difficult in the list of clean animals in Dt. 14:5. Tradition, backed by LXX, suggests the **BUBAL HARTEBEEST**, now extinct in the N part of its range, but this is made less likely by its inclusion in Solomon's daily provision for the table (1 Ki. 4:23), for this seems to imply a herd animal or one that could be penned. 'Fallow deer' (AV) and 'roedeer' (RSV) are unlikely.

The last name in this food list is also difficult. *zemer* ('leaper') is translated 'chamois' (AV, RV), which cannot be right, for this is an animal of the high mountains. **MOUNTAIN SHEEP** (RSV) is acceptable but this name is not precise. It cannot be the Barbary sheep, confined to N Africa and the Sahara, but it would be one of the now extinct forms of **MOUFLON**, of which other sub-species are still found in S Europe and SW Asia.

The **NUBIAN IBEX** can be seen today in its true habitat on the rocky slopes above the oasis of En-gedi—the 'spring of the wild kid'. There is no doubt that this is the correct translation of *y*ᵉ*'ēlîm*, 'wild goats' (AV). The root means 'climber'; it is always associated with mountains and the name is always plural, as befits a herd animal: 'The high mountains are for the wild goats' (Ps. 104:18). It seems probable that Heb. *'aqqô* (Dt. 14:5) is a synonym for *yā'ēl*, the singular form; it is not unusual for well-known animals to have two names.

To many Eng.-speaking people any hoofed animal with horns or antlers is just a **DEER**. In fact, deer form a large well-defined group of ruminants; they are distinguished by having antlers that are shed and regrown annually, and most typical of the N temperate regions. There are many species and to be meaningful the word must be qualified.

Red deer stag. (AA)

Three kinds once lived in Palestine. The **RED DEER**, the species found commonly through much of Europe and SW Asia, is the largest, standing about 1·5 m. It could not have been common, for Palestine offered little shelter, and it disappeared early, perhaps before the arrival of the Israelites. The **FALLOW DEER**, which is a common park deer in many countries today, stands only 1 m at the shoulder and is distinguished by having a coat more or less spotted at all ages and not just when young. This kind was lost to Palestine by about 1922. The **ROE DEER** is no taller than 80 cm; unlike the other two it is found only in ones and

Herd of gazelle, from Ashurbanipal's palace at Nineveh. c. 640 BC. (BM)

twos, and it is hard to see, so its presence may not be noticed. The last Palestine specimen was reported on Mt Carmel early in the 20th century. It is likely that Heb. *'ayyāl* and its feminine forms, translated stag, hart, hind, *etc.*, in most EVV, refer to both fallow and roe deer generally and are therefore best translated deer.

The key to Heb. *ṣ^eḇî* is found in Acts 9:36, 'Tabitha, which means Dorcas' (*dorkas*, **GAZELLE**). This latter word had not reached England when the AV translated 'roe' and 'roedeer', but later EVV are fairly consistent with gazelle. Two species are found in Palestine: the dorcas and Palestine gazelles, both standing under 70 cm. Once seriously in danger of extermination, they have recovered under protection, and today can be seen in the Judaean hills and the central plains, as well as around the desert. Gazelles are typically dry-zone antelopes, pale coloured and often with forward-pointing horns.

The **WILD BOAR** is mentioned above as the ancestor of the domestic pig. Heb. *ḥ^azîr* refers to both forms. The wild boar is still common in parts of the Middle East, where the food habits of both Jew and Muslim give no extra incentive for control. Its main habitat is forest and reed beds; *e.g.* Ps. 80:13, 'the boar from the forest ravages it'. In Ps. 68:30 'the beasts that swell among the reeds' are thought to be wild boars.

The **ELEPHANT** is not directly mentioned in Scripture but there are 12 references to *ivory, which came from both African and Asiatic species. Methods of taming and training elephants were worked out in India in the 3rd millennium BC. But this was not true domestication, for the animals were caught young and reared to become beasts of burden or, frequently, for use in war. The books of Maccabees (*e.g.* 1 Macc. 6:30, 35) have several references to the fighting elephants used against the Jews by the Seleucid, Antiochus Epiphanes. The Asiatic elephant was once found as far W as the upper reaches of the Euphrates where, according to Assyrian records, it was taken in pits; in such country it is not likely to have been common and it was killed out late in the 1st millennium BC.

At one time **LIONS** were found from Asia Minor through the Middle East and Persia to India, with a similar form in Greece up to nearly AD 100. This European/Asiatic lion resembles the African lion closely. Of all the carnivorous animals only the lion has certainly disappeared from Bible lands, though the cheetah and bear have almost gone. The last Palestine lion was probably killed near Megiddo in the 13th century; lions were still known in Persia in 1900; they had gone by 1930 at the latest. Lions were reported in Syria up to 1851 by Burton (*Travels in Syria*) and in parts of Iraq up to the early 1920s. The few Asiatic lions surviving today are in a small patch of forest in the Kathiawar peninsula of India.

The word 'lion' occurs some 130 times in AV/RSV, with one general Heb. word *'aryeh* and 8 other words, perhaps applied to various ages of the two sexes, though at least some are probably poetical names. This rich vocabulary suggests that the lion was common and well known in OT times, and many contexts confirm this, even though the usage is largely metaphorical for strength. The lion was also a symbol of royalty in the an-

Lion from the Processional Way, Babylon. Enamelled brick. c. 580 BC. (SMB)

Elephant and monkeys, part of the tribute being brought to Shalmaneser III, king of Assyria, as depicted on his Black Obelisk. Calah (Nimrud). c. 830 BC. (BM)

cient Near East (*Lion of Judah). Lions were frequently kept in captivity (*cf.* Dn. 6:7ff.). They were being bred by Ashurnasirpal II (883–859 BC) at Nimrud (*Calah) and kept in large numbers (E. W. Budge and L. W. King, *Annals of the Kings of Assyria*, 1901).

In popular Eng. usage the word **LEOPARD**, usually with a qualifying word, stands for a number of different spotted cats. It is possible that Heb. *nāmēr* refers to both the true leopard and the **CHEETAH**, or hunting leopard, and also to one or two other spotted wild cats of Palestine. All the few references are proverbial and figurative, and the precise species is therefore immaterial. Perhaps the most familiar use of the word is in the proverb of Je. 13:23, 'Can the Ethiopian change his skin or the leopard his spots?'

The **JUNGLE CAT** (*Felis chaus*) still lives in the more wooded parts, especially in Galilee. The leopard (*Panthera pardus*) is now very rare in Israel and Jordan, but several were seen or killed in the late 1960s, including two near the shore of the Dead Sea and one in Galilee.

Heb. *z^{e}'ēḇ* (Is. 11:6, *etc.*) and Gk. *lykos* (Mt. 7:15, *etc.*) refer to the SE Asiatic form of the **WOLF**. Its range and numbers have been drastically reduced by the growth of population and modern methods of control, but up to NT times it was common enough to be a menace to livestock, though it is now agreed that wolves have never been the danger to man that popular legend suggested. Their carnivorous nature is implied in most passages but the wolf is mentioned only metaphorically throughout. It is notable that in more than half the references the wolf stands for someone in authority who is misusing his position, *e.g.* Zp. 3:3, 'Her judges are evening wolves'. The wolf of Palestine is similar to, though rather smaller than, the wolf that is found in Central and N Europe.

Both **FOXES** and **JACKALS** are found throughout the Middle East. They are members of the *Canidae*, the dog family, and closely related, but the fox is usually solitary, whereas jackals often go in packs. It is likely that Heb. *šû'āl* and Gk. *alōpēx* include both fox and jackal, and modern EVV translate fox in some passages and jackal in others. Both species eat fruit and other vegetable matter, including grapes (Ct. 2:15). In Jdg. 15:4 the 300 animals caught by Samson were probably jackals.

Another Heb. word *tannîm*, always plural, which AV translates 'dragon' is now translated 'jackal' in RV/RSV. It is possible that this is a poetical name used to suggest desolation.

The Syrian form of the widely distributed **BROWN BEAR** may still be found in parts of the Middle East though no longer within the actual area of Palestine, but its status is doubtful and it may already be extinct. The last bear in Palestine was killed in Upper Galilee in the 1930s but a few lived around Mt Hermon for a further 10 years or so. It is clearly Heb. *dōḇ* (Arab. *dub*). It is paler than the typical race and usually referred to as a sub-species *Ursus arctos syriacus*. Like most bears other than the polar bear, the brown bear

Syrian rock hyrax in its natural rocky environment. (AA)

is omnivorous or vegetarian for most of the year, so its attacks on livestock, especially sheep, would be most likely during winter when wild fruits are scarce.

The term 'bear robbed of her cubs' (2 Sa. 17:8; Pr. 17:12) seems to be proverbial; also the expression in Am. 5:19, 'as if a man fled from a lion and a bear met him'. The bear is more feared than the lion because its strength is greater and its actions are less predictable.

The **WEASEL** is mentioned only in Lv. 11:29, translating *ḥōleḏ*. Several members of the weasel tribe are found in Palestine, and also a mongoose; there is nothing to confirm that *ḥōleḏ* refers to all or any of them but it is widely thought to refer to the actual weasel.

It is obvious that smaller animals are hard to identify unless the context includes some clues. Heb. *šāp̄ān* is clearly recognizable from its 4 OT occurrences (Lv. 11:5; Dt. 14:7; Ps. 104:18; Pr. 30:26) as the **SYRIAN ROCK HYRAX**. This belongs to a small order classified nearest to the elephants and is about the size of a rabbit, 30–40 cm long. It feeds on a variety of plants and lives in rocky hills where it can shelter in crevices. This identification was clearly made last century and confirmed by Tristram in his *The Natural History of the Bible* (1867). It is thus hard to understand why modern EVV, though rightly dropping 'coney' because of its confusion with 'rabbit', use such non-names as 'rock-rabbit' and 'rock-badger'. JB gives 'hyrax' in the Mosaic lists, though 'rock-badger' elsewhere, and is one of the few EVV to translate *šāp̄ān* correctly.

Heb. *taḥaš* is the material used for covering the tabernacle when erected (Ex. 25) and the Ark of the Covenant when being carried (Nu. 4). This is translated badgers' skin (AV), sealskin (RV), goatskin (RSV). Tristram (1867) seems to have been the first to suggest that the most likely source of this skin was the **DUGONG**, a large marine mammal belonging to the *Sirenia* which, until the early 19th century, was fairly common in the Gulf of Aqaba. NEB translates 'porpoise hide', with mg. note '*strictly* sea-cow'. The latter is a popular name for dugong, which is not at all related to the porpoise, one of the toothed whales.

Heb. *'aḵbār* is found 6 times in OT and uniformly translated **MOUSE**. In popular usage this name is applied to a wide range of small rodents, and one would expect *'aḵbār* to have this force when used as a prohibited item of food in Lv. 11:29, *i.e.* it probably covered voles, jerboas, gerbils, *etc.*, as well as true rats and mice. Four occurrences are in 1 Sa. 6, the incident of the pestilence that struck the Philistines. The symptoms seem to fit bubonic plague precisely, which suggests that *'aḵbār* here refers to the **BLACK RAT** (*Rattus rattus*) whose flea is the main carrier for this lethal disease, which was the black death of the Middle Ages in Europe.

Heb. *'arneḇeṯ* is mentioned only as a forbidden food but the similarity to Arab. *'arneb* and the reason for the ban suggests that this is the Palestine **HARE**. Lv. 11:6, 'because it chews the cud but does not part the hoof' (*i.e.* is not cloven-hoofed), was long misunderstood, for clearly the hare, related to rodents, does not really chew the cud. However, it is now known that hares, like the closely related rabbit, pass two different kinds of droppings, one of which is chewed and swallowed again, giving the appearance of cud-chewing. This strange habit serves somewhat the same purpose as rumination, for it allows digestion of material otherwise hard to utilize.

BAT is a reasonable translation for *ʿᵃṭallēp̄* (Lv. 11:19 and Dt. 14:18) among the flying animals in the Mosaic lists. Many species are found abundantly throughout the Middle East, some of which roost communally in large numbers in caves, either hanging from the roof or clustering in crevices. They would have been some of the most obvious animals at certain seasons and logically included in the forbidden foods, for most species are insectivorous. The only other mention of bats is in Is. 2:20, 'men will cast forth their idols . . . to the bats', where this unclean animal is used almost to signify desolation.

Heb. *qôp̄*, generally translated **APE**, is usually taken to be a loanword from Egyp. *g(i)f*, *gwf*, **MONKEY**. These animals were included in cargoes brought to Egypt by her Red Sea fleets from 'Punt', a land possibly located in SE Sudan and Eritrea. These would have been baboons or vervet monkeys. Another suggestion is that this word is derived from Tamil and therefore indicates an E origin, in which case the monkeys would have been **MACAQUES** or **LANGURS**. None of these is, technically, an ape.

Heb. *tannîn* is discussed under ***DRAGON**, which is the commonest translation in most EVV, though serpent, whale and sea monster are also found. (See Cansdale, Appendix B, for detailed analysis.) There has been some confusion with Heb. *tannîm*, which is probably a poetic name for jackal, but it is unlikely that the two words are related. *tannîn* is mostly found in wholly figurative contexts and it is not at all certain that a living animal is intended; these therefore merit no comment here. However, *tannîn* is also found in the creation narrative, 5th day (Gn. 1:21), 'great whales' (AV), 'sea monsters' (RSV). In this context it is a general word and not specific, and 'giant marine animals' is perhaps the best translation. It is also translated 'serpent' in the incident where the rods became serpents (Ex. 7:9–10, 12). In two other vv. AV has 'whale' where the context is clearly figurative.

In Mt. 12:40 Gk. *kētos* is translated **WHALE** (most EVV) referring to the great fish (Heb. *dāg*) of Jon. 1:17. For anatomical reasons it seems most unlikely that 'fish' is correct, but several toothed whales are recorded from the E Mediterranean, including some that are capable of swallowing a man. In the early part of this century there were one or two reasonably authenticated cases of men surviving after being swallowed (*PTR* 25, 1927, pp. 636ff.). This is the only NT occurrence of *kētos*, which is used by Homer and Herodotus for a wide range of sea animals, real and mythical, and the precise meaning must remain in doubt.

The word **BEHEMOTH** came into the Eng. language when the early translators failed to find an animal that seemed to fit the context of Jb. 40:15. It is the plural of Heb. *b^{e}hēmâ*, a common general word for beast. This is found 9 times and in all but one it has the normal plural meaning of animals or cattle. The passage in Jb. 40, however, is a special case, for the plural seems to be used for intensive effect and a specific animal is probably meant. Although various suggestions have been made, the opinion of most scholars over the years is that Job was writing about the **HIPPOPOTAMUS**, an animal that received its Eng. name after the AV appeared. This comes from the Gk., meaning 'river horse', though the two species are not at all related. This huge water animal lived in the lower Nile until the 12th century AD and, much earlier, in the Orontes river in Syria (and perhaps elsewhere in SW Asia) until after the time of Joseph, so it was well known in Bible lands. This passage is a difficult one, but several points in the RSV translation seem helpful. It is aquatic and powerful (vv. 21–23) and vegetarian (v. 15). 'The mountains yield food for him' (v. 20). It is true that hippos can climb steep slopes as they leave the water in search of food. This problem is discussed fully in Cansdale, pp. 100f.

Heb. *qippōḏ* is one of a number of difficult words applied to creatures of desolation, and it is found 3 times in connection with God's judgment on Babylon (Is. 14:23), Idumaea (Is. 34:11) and Nineveh (Zp. 2:14). Numerous alternatives have been suggested, such as bittern, heron, bustard, porcupine, hedgehog and lizard. Neither philology nor the context gives much help. Bittern and heron are marsh and water birds, and most unlikely, while the bustards are rarely seen in the region. Perhaps **HEDGEHOG** is the most probable. In Zp. 2:14 Nineveh was to become a waste and the city has actually been buried in sand, so it is literally possible for hedgehogs to 'lodge in her capitals'. Three kinds of hedgehog live in the region, two being desert or semi-desert forms, with one in the N of Palestine similar to the British species.

The **PORCUPINE** is still found in Israel, where it is by far the largest rodent, with a weight of some 20 kg. Nothing connects it with *qippōḏ* or any other Heb. word in the Bible.

Palestine is a land very rich in **BIRDS**. It has a great range of habitats, varying from semi-tropical to true desert; moreover, one of the main migration routes from Africa into Europe and W Asia runs from the N point of the Red Sea through the whole length of Israel. The resident birds therefore are augmented by numerous migrants, and there is some movement in progress in almost every month.

This wealth of bird life makes it difficult to identify with certainty some of the birds named in the Bible, and in some cases it is not possible to state whether the Heb. words refer to birds or other classes of animals. With the exception of 'hawk', which is also mentioned in Jb. 39:26, the following birds are found only in the food lists of Lv. and Dt.: **SEA GULL** (*šaḥap̄*), **HAWK** (*nēṣ*), **NIGHT-HAWK** (*taḥmās*), **CORMORANT** (*šālāḵ*), **HOOPOE** (*dûḵîp̄eṯ*), **OSPREY** (*'ozniyyâ*) and **WATER HEN** (*tinšemeṯ*). These may not indicate even the major group to which each bird belongs, and Driver (1955) gives an interesting new list of translations.

Palestine is still rich in large birds of prey, and outside the main towns the traveller is likely to see some of them in the air almost every day.

Heb. *rāḥām* (Lv. 11:18; Dt. 14:17), 'gier eagle' (AV), 'vulture' (RSV), rendered by R. Young as 'parti-coloured vulture', is likely to be the Egyp. **VULTURE**, a conspicuous black-and-white bird frequently seen scavenging on garbage tips.

Among several birds of prey forbidden as food (Lv. 11:13) is the **OSSIFRAGE** or bone-breaker (Heb. *peres*). This accurately describes the **LAMMERGEIER** or **BEARDED VULTURE**, which drops bones from a height on to rocks in order to break them and get the marrow within.

Some true **EAGLES** are still found in, or travel through, Palestine: Heb. *nešer* is probably as much a generic term as the Eng. word 'eagle'. It could include all large birds of prey, and the many references, most of them figurative, give few clues to the species. Mi. 1:16, 'make yourselves as bald as the eagle', clearly suggests the **GRIFFON VULTURE**, whose pale down-covered head contrasts with the well-feathered heads of all eagles. Some authorities consider that in all cases *nešer* should be the griffon vulture, just as Gk. *aetos*, translated 'eagle' in Mt. 24:28 ('there the eagles will be gathered together'), should be so rendered. This clearly describes the flocking of vultures to a carcass.

Heb. *'ayyâ* (Jb. 28:7), *dā'â* (Lv. 11:14) and *dayyâ* (Dt. 14:13; Is. 34:15) is probably the **KITE**, of which both the black and the red species are common.

OWLS are referred to 8 times in the OT by 4 Heb. words. The translation is probably correct, and several different species may be intended.

Heb. *lîlîṯ* is found only in Is. 34:14 among several other much disputed names which together seem to signify a setting of desolation. It is thought to be a loan-word from the Assyr. female demon of the night, *lilitu*. The following translations have been suggested—screech owl (AV), night monster (AVmg., RV), night hag (RSV), nightjar (NEB), *Lilith (JB). According to rabbinical tradition it was a ghost in the form of a well-dressed woman which lay in wait at night. Israeli zoologists suggest 'tawny owl'. *lîlîṯ* may be a real animal, but in the absence of further evidence it must be left as 'unidentified'.

The **WHITE STORK** is one of the most striking migratory birds of Palestine, slowly travelling N, especially along the Jordan valley in March and April. Je. 8:7, 'the stork in the heavens knows her times', suggests *ḥ^{a}sîḏâ* may well be the stork, though it could refer to several other large birds, including the kite and heron.

The **CRANE** is a bird of similar build to the white stork and is also a migrant. It is thought that in Is. 38:14 and Je. 8:7 *'āḡûr* should be translated 'crane' and *sûs* 'swallow', from its note. Both are migrants as Je. 8:7 suggests. Another word, *d^{e}rôr*, is translated **SWALLOW** in Ps. 84:3 and Pr. 26:2, and in the former it is implied that it nests within the temple buildings. This would be true of several species of swallow and also of the **SWIFT**, a bird of similar build and habits, but unrelated to the swallow. At least 4 species of swallow, 4 species of **MARTIN** and 3 species of swift occur in Palestine.

SPARROWS are associated with human habitations in many parts of the world, and the house sparrow so common in Palestine today is almost identical with the W European form. This could well have been the bird to which our Lord referred (Mt. 10:29, *etc.*), though Gk. *strouthion* implies assorted small birds such as were, and still are, killed and offered for sale in Palestine. In Ps. 84:3 Heb. *ṣippôr* is translated 'sparrow'; Ps. 102:7, 'a sparrow alone upon the house top' (AV) hardly suggests the sociable house sparrow, and it could refer to the **BLUE ROCK THRUSH**, a solitary bird which sometimes perches on houses.

The absence of any mention of the **DOMESTIC FOWL** from the OT is at first surprising, since there is some evidence that Assyria paid tribute to Egypt in the form of **HENS**, *c.* 1500 BC, and **COCKS** are shown on seals of the 7th century BC. However, Homer (*c.* 9th century BC) does not refer to hens, though he mentions **GEESE**. Some authorities consider that the fatted fowl of 1 Ki. 4:23 could be domestic fowls. The importation of **PEACOCKS** (1 Ki. 10:22), if this translation is correct, suggests that Solomon had traffic with Ceylon or India, the original home of the domestic fowl, and he could therefore have introduced them.

The only mention of the hen in the NT is in Mt. 23:37 and Lk. 13:34, where in one of our Lord's most poignant similes it is obvious that Gk. *ornis* is the domestic hen. The cock (*alektōr*) is mentioned in two incidents. In Mk. 13:35 Jesus mentioned the four night-watches, including 'at cockcrow' (midnight to 3 a.m. by Roman reckoning). The crowing of the cock was thought to take place at set times, and in many countries the domestic cock was regarded as an alarm clock, but it would be unwise to read any specific hours into the incident of Peter and the cock-crowing, Mt. 26:74–75, *etc.* See W. L. Lane, *The Gospel according to Mark*, *NIC*, 1974, p. 512, n. 69, and p. 543, for some remarkable observations on the conscientious time-keeping of cocks in Jerusalem.

The **PEACOCK** is native to the jungles of the Indo-Malayan region. There is no independent evidence to confirm the identification *tukkiyyim*; it is suggested that this word is derived from the Tamil *tokai*, but this means 'tail' and is not now known to refer to the peacock itself. This splendid bird had reached Athens by 450 BC, and had been kept on the island of Samos earlier still.

The **QUAIL**, almost the smallest of the game birds, features in only one incident, Ex. 16:13, *etc.*, 'In the evening quails (*ś^{e}lāw*) came up and covered the camp'. There has been speculation as to the correct translation, but the quail fits better than any other. Ps. 78:27, 'winged birds', confirms that *ś^{e}lāw* were birds; they also belonged to one of the few groups regarded as clean. Quails are migrants, and at certain seasons travel in large flocks a metre or two above the ground. Their migrations take them across the route followed after the Exodus.

The only other gallinaceous bird identifiable is the **PARTRIDGE**: 1 Sa. 26:20, 'like one who hunts a partridge in the mountains'. Heb. *qōrē'* is the rock partridge (*Alectoris graeca*), which is hunted regularly in many parts of the Middle East and SE Europe. It is similar to the red-legged partridge (*A. rufa*) of SW Europe. The significance of the proverb in Je. 17:11 is not clear.

Two members of the **CROW** family can be seen very frequently in Palestine—the **RAVEN** and the hooded crow. Heb. *'ōrēḇ* and Gk. *korax* are analagous to the Eng. 'crow' in that they probably refer primarily to the raven but are also used of crows as a whole. Both raven and hooded crow are similar in appearance and habits to the British birds.

The **OSTRICH** finds mention in several passages, but the general view is that *baṯ ya'^{a}nâ* should be 'ostrich' and not 'owl' (AV) in 8 passages. Jb. 39:13–18 is clearly a description of the ostrich, a bird which once lived in the Middle East. Heb. *y^e'ēnîm* is also trans-

Two ostriches fleeing from a winged genius. Impression from an Assyrian cylinder seal. 12th–11th cent. BC. (PML)

White stork at nest. (AA)

lated 'ostriches' in La. 4:3, but a bird such as an ostrich may well have several native names.

'A **PELICAN** of the wilderness' (Ps. 102:6) (most EVV except RSV, 'vulture') has been thought a contradiction, but *wilderness does not always connote desert. A swamp could also be described in this way, and the drained swamps of the N Jordan valley are still visited by flocks of white pelicans passing on migration.

Several species of **DOVES** and **PIGEONS** are found in Palestine, and there is some confusion of names (so the Eng. wood-pigeon is also known as ring-dove). Heb. *yônâ* is usually translated 'dove', but in the sacrificial passages of Lv. and Nu. it is always translated '(young) pigeon'. In the same verses is the *tôr*, turtle or turtle dove; this has the scientific generic name *Turtur*, from its call, and this can be identified with both the common turtle dove and the collared turtle dove, mostly the latter, which has long been domesticated with the name Barbary dove. Heb. *yônâ* is therefore the rock dove (*Columba livia*), which was domesticated in antiquity and has been used widely as a source of food and for message-carrying.

Speckled bird (*ṣāḇûa'*), Je. 12:9, is considered by many authorities to be better rendered **'HYENA'**.

BIBLIOGRAPHY. G. R. Driver, 'Birds in the Old Testament', *PEQ* 86, 1954, pp. 5ff.; 87, 1955, pp. 129ff.; 'Once Again, Birds in the Bible', *PEQ* 90, 1958, pp. 56ff.; G. S. Cansdale, *Animals of Bible Lands*, 1970, chs. 10–15.

LIZARDS are by far the most conspicuous reptiles in Palestine, with some 40 species, and they are the only reptiles that the traveller can be sure of seeing. The two most obvious are the **AGAMA** or **RAINBOW LIZARD**, which frequents roadsides and the vicinity of humans; it is easily recognized by its habit of doing 'press-ups'; and the **ROCK GECKO** that often basks on boulders in the early morning. Mention of lizards may therefore be expected and there are, in fact, 6 Heb. words that EVV generally translate lizard. Each occurs only in the food list of Lv. 11:29f., with no help from the context other than that they are unclean; this suggests that they are carnivorous but any identification is largely conjecture, from slender philologi-

Rock partridge. (GSC)

cal evidence and tradition, that this is a series of reptiles.

1. *ṣāḇ*. Tortoise (AV) is incorrect. RV, RSV translate 'great lizard', a non-specific name. Tradition identifies this with the spiny-tailed lizards, reaching some 50 cm. Arab. *dhubb* or *dhabb* may be sufficiently alike to give some confirmation.

2. *'ᵃnāqâ*. Ferret (AV) is not correct. **GECKO** (RV, RSV) is more probable.

3. *kōaḥ*. Chameleon (AV) and crocodile (RV, RSV). The latter expression is meaningless but was once applied to the desert monitor, the largest lizard of the region.

4. *lᵉṭā'â*. Lizard (most EVV). Perhaps lizards of the *Lacertid* family.

5. *ḥōmeṭ*. Snail (AV) is not correct. RV, RSV translate 'sand lizard'. Perhaps the fast, streamlined **SKINKS** so typical of sandy areas.

6. *tinšemeṯ* is very difficult. Mole (AV) is not correct. RV, RSV translate chameleon.

In addition *śᵉmāmîṯ* (Pr. 30:28) is translated spider (AV) or lizard (RV, RSV). This could well be a **GECKO**, or house lizard; several species, some of which live on and inside buildings, are found in Palestine. The specially modified feet allow them to cling to smooth walls and even ceilings.

One of the geckos, *Ptyodactylus hasselquisti*, was called *abubrais* (Arab.), 'father of leprosy', perhaps because of its fleshy colour, perhaps because of (incorrectly) supposed poisonous qualities. The **CHAMELEON** is small (up to 15 cm) and rather uncommon, living in the more wooded areas of Palestine. Its colour, shape and habits make it inconspicuous and one would not expect it to feature in the food lists.

Several species of **TORTOISE** are found in the Middle East. The tortoise could be the *ṣāḇ* (AV) in Lv. 11:29, for it is a reptile that would be seen from time to time, but other authorities translate 'lizard' and the identity must be considered doubtful. Tortoises were known in ancient Assyria, whence a curse runs, 'May you be turned upside down like a tortoise (and die)' (*Iraq* 20, 1958, p. 76).

The words ***SERPENT** and **SNAKE** are of roughly equal age: snake has always had a specific meaning, a member of the suborder of reptiles known as *Ophidia*, but serpent, while having been popularly used for snake, also had a wide application, including many mythical creatures. Although serpent is obsolescent it is retained generally by modern EVV, even in literal passages. NEB and JB use both snake and serpent.

Three Heb. words are translated serpent (RSV) of which *nāḥāš* occurs most often and is a general word, probably including other creeping reptiles also. The Heb. word translated 'divination' *etc.* is from the same root—to foretell by observing serpents. The first mention of *nāḥāš* is in Gn. 3:1, introducing the fall of man. *śārāp̄* is a common root usually translated fiery or burning; in Nu. 21:6 it qualifies *nāḥāš* and is translated fiery serpent, but stands alone in vv. 8 and 9 for the bronze serpent cast by Moses. It is translated flying serpent in Is. 14:29; 30:6. *tannîn*, usually translated dragon, is translated serpent only in the incident of Aaron's rod (Ex. 7:9ff.).

Gk. *ophis*, specific for snake, is found 14 times in a variety of NT contexts, including the reference to the serpent in the wilderness (Jn. 3:14) and the serpent of Gn. 3 (Rev. 12:9).

Snakes are found in all habitats from desert to closed woodland and marsh, with a wide range of species, some under 30 cm while others may reach 2 m. Most are harmless; about 6 species are potentially lethal, but only a low percentage of bites prove fatal if given any treatment. All feed only on animals, from insects to mammals, which they swallow whole with no chewing. They can pass long periods, sometimes over one year, without food but need water more often.

Snakes are today widely regarded with terror and are a common object of phobias. This has probably always been true. One cannot expect snakes to be clearly identified in the Bible or their habits described, but contexts and roots sometimes allow deductions to be made.

Heb. *peṯen* must represent a poisonous species. It occurs 6 times and while most EVV, including RSV, translate adder and asp, NEB has cobra twice and asp 4 times. There is general agreement that **COBRA** is correct, since the bite of the **ASP** (now obsolete) was used in Egypt to commit suicide; a cobra's neurotoxic venom would usually cause a quick death. Is. 11:8 speaks of the 'hole of the asp'; cobras typically live in holes. Snake-charming is clearly mentioned in Ps. 58:4–5, 'the voice of charmers', referring to *peṯen*; cobras are traditionally used for this purpose.

The figurative importance of the fiery serpent is emphasized by our Lord's reference to it in Jn. 3:14. The context of Nu. 21, where both *nāḥāš* and *śārāp̄* are used, allows some deductions, and 4 facts suggest the **CARPET VIPER** *Echis*. It is notorious for striking without provocation, which is rare in snakes; its venom is largely haemolytic, causing death after several days; it is more active by day than other desert vipers; in parts of Asia and Africa it is known to become very numerous over limited areas. When the Israelites cried for help God told Moses to cast a serpent in bronze and put it on a pole so that those who looked in faith would live. It seems that the brazen serpent, or a copy of it, later became a focus for heathen worship, so that Hezekiah destroyed it in his reformation (2 Ki. 18:4). There is evidence of a snake-cult in early Palestine and a direct statement in Wisdom 11:15 that they worshipped 'irrational serpents'. A flat relief stela of the serpent goddess was found at Beit Mirsin. A bronze snake, *c.* 15th century BC, from Gezer has the expanded neck of a cobra and there are many examples of jars and incense vessels with relief patterns of snakes. It is likely that snakes were among 'all kinds of creeping things' worshipped by the Jerusalem elders (Ezk. 8:10).

Five further Heb. words are translated **ADDER** and **VIPER**. *ṣip̄'ônî* (Pr. 23:32) translated adder (RSV), adder, asp, basilisk (RV), is found only in figurative passages from which little can be inferred; but in Je. 8:17 'adders which cannot be charmed' suggest **DESERT VIPERS**. *ṣep̄a'* (Is. 14:29) was earlier translated cockatrice (AV) and basilisk (RV), both words indefinite and now obsolete; RSV now translates adder. *šᵉp̄îp̄ôn* is found only in Gn. 49:17, 'a viper by the path that bites the horses' heels'. (Arrowsnake [AVmg.] has no known meaning.)

The desert vipers *Cerastes cerastes* and *C. vipera* became the Egyp. hieroglyph for 'f' from the onomatopoeic *fy*, *fyt*; the above 3 names may be related to this. Tristram notes that *shiphon* is Arab. for the horned viper. Although the words adder and viper are nearly synonymous and refer to the Old World viperine snakes, adder first referred to snakes generally (a **NADDER** [OE] became an adder). Viper, derived from viviparous (live-bearing), was first used by Tyndale in the early 16th century.

Both *'ep̄'eh* and *'aḵšûḇ* are translated viper (RSV) in figurative passages. The former is identical with Arab. *afa'â*, used sometimes of snakes generally, sometimes of vipers. *'aḵšûḇ* is related to an Arab. root 'to coil itself', which describes a habit of the desert vipers.

Palestine's largest viper (*Vipera palestina*) is found over much of the country except the desert; it cannot be identified with any of the above but it is common in Galilee and Judaea and could be the species to which Gk. *eḥidna* largely refers. Four of its 5 mentions are to a 'brood of vipers' used by Christ and John the Baptist of the Pharisees. This is apt, for these vipers bear live young in batches. The fifth mention is the only literal one, in Acts 28:3; the snake which bit Paul is traditionally held to be the common viper, which is still found on Sicily and other islands, though not on Malta.

For further details on biology and distribution see Cansdale, pp. 202–210.

The word **CROCODILE** is not found in any EV other than RSVmg. where it translates leviathan (Jb. 41:1) and though this passage is wholly figurative there are several points suggesting crocodile is correct: *e.g.* vv. 13 and 15, 'Who can penetrate his double coat of mail? . . . his back is made of rows of shields.' The precise setting of Job is uncertain but it is likely to have been somewhere around the E Mediterranean. In biblical times the Nile crocodile was found from source to mouth of the Nile. While its distribution N of Egypt in that period is unknown, returning Crusaders reported crocodiles in the Zerka river, which runs into the Mediterranean near Caesarea and is still known locally as the Crocodile river. Crocodilians are eaten in various parts of the world and though they cannot be identified in the Mosaic food lists it is certain that their carnivorous habits would make them unclean.

Apart from one figurative use in Rev. 16:13 (Gk. *batrachos*), the word **FROG** (Heb. *ṣ*ᵉ*p̄ardēa'*) occurs only in connection with the second of God's plagues upon Egypt (Ex. 8:2ff.). Frogs belong to the class *Amphibia*, all members of which must pass their early stages in water. Several frogs, especially of the genus *Rana*, are common in the Nile valley, and more than one species could have been the *ṣ*ᵉ*p̄ardēa'* which caused this plague.

LOCUSTS are the most important biblical insects, with some 56 appearances under 9 Heb. names and one Gk. To the ancient Heb. the locust was primarily a destroyer but it was also a useful source of animal protein. Three suggestions for interpreting the Heb. names are:

1. They refer to different species. This cannot be wholly true, for only 3 species of true locust are involved—migratory, desert and Moroccan locusts.

2. They represent various colour phases and/or the stages through which locusts pass as they mature. The list in Joel 1:4 is sometimes taken to describe such a series.

3. These names are descriptive nicknames, for all with identifiable roots refer to one or other attribute of locusts. This is most likely, though (1) and (2) may be true in part.

Locusts, of the section *Saltatoria* (leapers) of the order *Orthoptera*, were the only insects regarded as 'clean', described vividly as having 'legs above their feet, with which to leap on the earth' (Lv. 11:21). Locusts are, in fact, **GRASSHOPPERS** and 2 of the Heb. words may refer to species other than true locusts—*ḥag̱āḇ*, from a root 'to hide', could have been a recognizable smaller species, for 3 of its 5 occurrences refer to smallness. *sol'ām*, from a root 'to swallow up or destroy', is sometimes translated 'bald locust' from old Talmudic statements that its head is smooth in front, which would well fit the *Tryxalinae*, a distinct family of grasshoppers.

The EVV handle these names so variously, especially in the food lists and Joel 1:4, that it is not useful to tabulate them. *'arḇeh* (24 times) is the general term, from a root 'to multiply', always used of the 8th plague and often considered to be specific for migratory locust. The other Heb. words are *ḥargôl*, incorrectly beetle (AV) and cricket (RSV), probably from root 'to run swiftly'; *gāzām*, from root 'to cut off'; *yeleq*, perhaps from root 'to lick or eat up'; *ḥāsîl*, from root 'to consume'; *ṣ*ᵉ*lāṣal* from root 'to whir'; and *gôḇ*, literally 'a swarm'.

Locusts are typically highly gregarious but there is now evidence that they also have solitary phases and that swarming is probably a physiological response to conditions. Migrations follow no precise pattern and swarms are largely wind-driven, certainly over long distances ('the east wind had brought the locusts', Ex. 10:13). The biology of all species is roughly the same. The female lays packets of eggs just beneath the surface of the soil where they may stay for many months before moisture allows them to hatch. The locust does not pass through the 3 distinct stages of a typical insect; when the egg hatches, the larva has the general shape of the adult, but without wings, which it acquires gradually over the 5 or 6 moults. The young are often known as hoppers. Locusts are wholly vegetarian and exist in such numbers that disastrous damage is done to crops; in 1889 a desert locust swarm that crossed the Red Sea was reckoned to cover 5,000 sq. km.

Desert locust (Chistocerca gregario). (RH)

There is no direct statement that the Israelites ate locusts, but the reference in the food lists implies it. Their potential food value in ancient times is often forgotten but there is much evidence in the literature for their wide use. Until recent years large numbers have been eaten by desert and other tribes and at some seasons it was probably a main source of protein, as well as of fat and minerals.

The locust was almost synonymous with 'destroyer' and a plague of locusts was often regarded as God's judgment; in 3 cases, apart from the 8th plague, locusts were sent or threatened by God as

Hieroglyphs of reed and bee, signifying 'King of Upper and Lower Egypt', from the Kiosk of Sesostris I at Karnak. c. 1940 BC. (PAC)

punishment.

ANTS, BEES and **WASPS** form the insect order *Hymenoptera* (membranous-winged), many of whose species have complex social organization. Numerous kinds are found in Palestine and of these the most important is the honey bee, for until the 18th century honey was the basic material for sweetening. The general name **BEE** is properly given today to several families of this order, including solitary and bumble bees as well as honey bees. Heb. *d*ᵉ*ḇôrâ* could have covered an even larger range of insects, including bee-like flies, but it is clear from their contexts that 3 out of 4 OT occurrences refer to the honey bee (Jdg. 14:8; Ps. 118:12; Dt. 1:44). The fourth passage using this word

Colony of harvester ants in the Negeb. (FNH)

Israeli scorpion. (AA)

is a figurative one—Is. 7:18, 'The Lord shall whistle . . . for the bee that is in the land of Assyria.' This translation for *šāraq* is preferred to 'hiss' (AV). A tradition that the natives of Palestine called their bees by making a whistling or hissing sound suggests that *d^eḇōrâ* here also refers to the honey bee.

The numerous references to *honey in OT and NT imply that its use was common and widespread. It is likely that much of the honey was produced by wild bees nesting in hollow trees or rocky holes, but from very early times bees have been encouraged to occupy simple hives of basket or earthenware.

All EVV translate Heb. *ṣir'â* as **HORNET**, which is a large colonial wasp with a very painful or even dangerous sting, still common in parts of Palestine, including the desert around the Dead Sea. All the mentions are in rather similar contexts, as Ex. 23:28, 'I will send hornets before you'. The reference could be literal, for there are records of hornets, and even bees, causing horses and cattle to panic and stampede. J. Garstang's suggestion (*Joshua–Judges*, 1931, pp. 112ff., 285ff.) that the hornet of Jos. 24:12, *etc*., represents the Egyptian empire in Canaan has not found much acceptance.

The **ANT** (Heb. *n^emālâ*) is mentioned only in Pr. 6:6 and 30:25. Ants vary widely in size and habits, but all are social, living in colonies of a dozen or so to hundreds of thousands. Many types of ants occur in Palestine, but the context clearly identifies this as the harvester ant, sometimes called the agricultural ant, which is about 6 mm long. Its colonies are common and conspicuous in many parts of Israel outside the actual desert. It collects seeds of many kinds, especially grasses, during spring and early summer and stores them in underground galleries, often after removing the husks and letting them blow away in the wind, which clearly indicates the nest entrance.

MOTH is the name given correctly to the larger section of the order *Lepidoptera* (scale-winged insects) which includes the most colourful and conspicuous insects. Palestine has many species of both butterfly and moth, but the only biblical reference is to the atypical clothes moth, Heb. *'āš* and Gk. *sēs* (Jb. 4:19; Lk. 12:33, *etc*.). The contexts all confirm identification of this pest, which is always associated with man and his goods. In countries with fairly high average temperatures for much of the year, where clothes were regarded as a form of wealth and therefore stored in quantity, damage by the larvae of these clothes moths could be serious. When the moths emerge the damage has already been done, for the adults do not feed.

FLEAS, belonging to a wingless insect order, have always been parasitic on man and his domestic stock and they are particularly numerous among nomadic peoples. Heb. *par'ōš* occurs only in 1 Sa. 24:14; 26:20. The metaphor is clear and the jumping habit of the flea confirms the translation. Although mostly known just as nuisances, fleas are also potential carriers of serious diseases, notably bubonic plague (see 'Mouse', above).

Although the word **FLY** is widely and loosely used it is strictly applied only to *Diptera*, a large insect order having only one pair of wings. The word occurs only twice in AV/RSV, each time translating Heb. *z^eḇûḇ*, but nothing in the context of either allows more precise identification. In Is. 7:18 it is used figuratively, while Ec. 10:1 is the familiar proverb, 'Dead flies cause the ointment of the apothecary to send forth a stinking savour' (AV). A wide variety of insects, and not only true flies, might be attracted to embalmers' spices and unguents. Heb. *'ārōḇ* is translated 'swarms of flies' (Ex. 8:21ff.; Pss. 78:45; 105:31). These passages refer to the plague of flies in Egypt; many species have mass hatchings into profuse swarms that are dangerous or gravely inconvenient from sheer weight of numbers. These swarms could well have consisted of 'divers sorts of flies' (AV).

GNAT is an imprecise word given to several groups of small two-winged insects, similar to and sometimes including midges and mosquitoes. The only NT occurrence of Gk. *kōnōps* is in Mt. 23:24, which should be read as in RSV 'straining out a gnat'. (AV 'strain *at* a gnat' seems to be a printer's error.) This comment was based on the Pharisaic practice of drinking water through a straining cloth to avoid swallowing an insect regarded as unclean. Many small insects breed in and near water and their larval forms are common in stagnant water. *kōnōps* probably had as wide an application as the Eng. 'gnat'.

RSV prefers 'gnat' to 'louse' (Heb. *kinnām*) in Ex. 8:16–18, but the most probably translation is **TICK**. The louse is a wingless insect but the tick is an eight-legged arthropod more nearly related to spiders. Both are specialized blood-sucking parasites and vectors of dangerous human diseases. This problem is discussed in Cansdale, p. 229.

The **SCORPION** (Heb. *'aqrāḇ*; Gk. *skorpios*) is one of the arthropods that can be identified with certainty. Members of this order vary widely in size and toxicity; though the largest of the Palestine species is up to 15 cm, most of the 12 species are much smaller and none has a sting likely to be fatal under normal conditions. All have the typical scorpion shape—heavy pincers, 4 pairs of legs and a long up-turned tail ending in a sting. Scorpions are largely nocturnal, especially in desert country, spending the day hidden under stones or in holes and emerging at night to hunt the small animals on which they feed. Several mentions in the OT and NT are in proverbial form, *e.g*. 1 Ki. 12:11, 'I will chastise you with scorpions', possibly a reference to a many-tailed whip, loaded with hooked knobs of metal and known as a scorpion (*cf*. 1 Macc. 6:51; 'machines [Gk. *skorpidia*] to shoot arrows'). Our Lord vividly likens a scorpion to an egg in Lk. 11:12; the main segment of some scorpions is fat and almost egg-shaped.

Palestine has a large range of **SPIDERS**, another order of eight-legged arthropods, of which the web-spinners are clearly referred to in Jb. 8:14 and Is. 59:5–6 (Heb. *'akkāḇîš*). *ś^emāmîṯ* also is translated 'spider' in Pr. 30:28, 'The spider taketh hold with her hands' (AV). A more likely translation is **GECKO**.

Finally, there is a series of names that refer to less easily identified invertebrates (animals without backbones). The context clearly confirms **SNAIL** as the translation for Heb. *šaḇlûl* 'as a snail which melteth' (AV), 'like the snail which dissolves into slime' (RSV), Ps. 58:8. Both translations reflect an ancient belief that in leaving a visible trail behind it the snail was gradually melting away. There is nothing to confirm 'snail' as the translation of Heb. *ḥōmeṭ* in the list of forbidden meats in Lv. 11:30. RSV renders it 'sand lizard' and there is general agreement in modern EVV that it is a **LIZARD** of some kind.

■ **ANKLE CHAIN**
See Ornaments, Part 2.

The word **WORM** is technically correct only for several phyla of invertebrate animals, but popular language uses it much more widely. Wire-worms and wood-worms are beetles; cut-worms are moth caterpillars; slow-worms are lizards, and so on. In ancient times and among less-developed peoples the usage is even more vague. Five Heb. words are translated 'worm' and in the popular sense this translation can be accepted. In most passages the use is solely figurative and more precise identification is difficult, but see Cansdale, pp. 235f., for discussion. There is no word for 'worms' in the Heb. text of the well-known passage in Jb. 19:16 and the AVmg. and RSV should be followed: 'after my skin has been destroyed'.

Found only in Pr. 30:15 the word 'horseleach' (AV), 'leech' (RSV), is a translation of Heb. *'^{a}lûqâ*, 'sucking'; but in most EVV there is mg. comment that the text is obscure. Two interpretations are found. 1. Most scholars, following AV, RSV, assume a reference to the **LEECH**, probably of some aquatic type such as the horse leech (*Limnatis nilotica*), still found in stagnant waters of Egypt and the Near East, which is a serious menace to men and animals when swallowed with drinking-water. Leeches belong to the world-wide *Phylum Annelida*, or segmented worms. 2. Others, noting the similarity to the Arab. word *'alaqeh*, identify it with a female demon, perhaps a blood-sucking vampire (*cf.* RVmg.) which the Arabs call *'Alūq*; this latter cannot be accepted, for blood-sucking bats, the true vampires, are found only in Central and S America.

The phrase **CREEPING THINGS** is a non-specific term in EVV translating two Heb. words which are used particularly in the *creation narrative. The comments below refer mainly to AV. In RSV the translation of these two words is not uniform and in one case (1 Ki. 4:33) *šereṣ* is translated reptiles.

1. *remeś*, from the verb *rāmaś*, to creep, move', and having, with *rōmēś*, the participle of that verb, the meaning 'creeping or moving thing'. It is apparently applied to all animals in Gn. 9:3, but is sometimes used of sea (Gn. 1:21; Ps. 104:25) or land (Gn. 1:24–25; 6:20; 7:8, 14, 21, 23) creatures exclusively, and in 1 Ki. 4:33 and Ezk. 38:20 it is distinguished from beasts (*b^{e}hēmâ*), fowls (*'ôp̄*) and fishes (*dāḡ*). Though some commentators have argued that in the creation account it refers to reptiles, it cannot correspond exactly to any modern scientific category, referring rather to all creatures moving close to the ground.

2. *šereṣ*, from the verb *šāraṣ*, 'to swarm, teem', and meaning 'swarming thing', translated in the AV as 'creeping thing' (Gn. 7:21; Lv. 5:2; 11:21, 23, 29, 41–44; 22:5; Dt. 14:19) and 'moving creature' (Gn. 1:20; *CREATION). It could be applied to water (Gn. 1:20; Lv. 11:10) and land (Gn. 8:21) creatures, and in Lv. 11:29 is specifically defined as including weasels, mice and lizards. In short, *šereṣ*, like *remeś*, seems to refer to creatures which appear to move close to the ground with a range of possibilities according to the context.

In NT Gk. *herpeton*, derived from *herpō*, 'to creep, crawl' (not in the Bible), and therefore meaning 'creeping thing', is used 4 times (Acts 10:12; 11:6; Rom. 1:23; Jas. 3:7), probably meaning 'reptile' in each case. In the LXX it is used chiefly as a translation for *remeś* and *šereṣ*.

BIBLIOGRAPHY. G. S. Cansdale, *Animals of Bible Lands*, 1970; F. E. Zeuner, *A History of Domesticated Animals*, 1963. G.S.C.

ANNA (Gk. form of Heb. *ḥannâ*, 'grace'). An aged widow, daughter of Phanuel, of the tribe of Asher (Lk. 2:36–38). Like Simeon, who also belonged to the remnant which 'waited for the consolation of Israel', she had prophetic insight, and was a regular attender at the morning and evening services in the Temple. On hearing Simeon's words at the presentation of Jesus, she commended the child as the long-awaited Messiah, and praised God for the fulfilment of his promises. J.D.D.

ANNAS. Annas or Ananos, son of Seth, was appointed high priest in AD 6 and deposed in AD 15. In the NT he is still referred to as high priest after AD 15. This may be for one of three reasons. First, though the Romans deposed high priests and appointed new ones, the Jews thought of the high priesthood as a life office. The Mishnah (*Horayoth* 3. 4) says: 'A high priest in office differs from the priest that is passed from his high priesthood only in the bullock that is offered on the Day of Atonement and the tenth of the ephah.' Secondly, the title 'high priest' is given in Acts and Josephus to members of the few priestly families from which most high priests were drawn, as well as to those exercising the high-priestly office. Thirdly, Annas had great personal influence with succeeding high priests. Five of his sons and Caiaphas his son-in-law became high priest. At the trial of Jesus we find Annas conducting a preliminary investigation before the official trial by Caiaphas (Jn. 18:13–24). When Lk. 3:2 says that the high priest was Annas and Caiaphas, the singular is probably deliberate, indicating that, though Caiaphas was the high priest officially appointed by Rome, his father-in-law shared his high-priestly power, both *de facto* by his personal influence and, according to strict Jewish thought, also *de jure* (*cf.* Acts 4:6). D.R.H.

ANNUNCIATION. The vision of Mary (Lk. 1:26–38) 'announces' the conception of a Messiah-Son and describes with poetic imagery Messiah's human (Lk. 1:32) and divine (Lk. 1:34f.) character and the eternal nature of his kingdom (Lk. 1:33). Machen and Daube give the most helpful treatment of the literary questions. See also *VIRGIN BIRTH, *INCARNATION.

BIBLIOGRAPHY. R. E. Brown, *The Birth of the Messiah*, 1977; D. Daube, *The New Testament and Rabbinic Judaism*, 1956; E. E. Ellis, *The Gospel of Luke*², 1974; J. G. Machen, *The Virgin Birth*, 1931; J. McHugh, *The Mother of Jesus in the New Testament*, 1975; *DCG*; *ODCC*. E.E.E.

ANOINTING, ANOINTED. Persons and things were anointed, in the OT, to signify holiness, or separation unto God: pillars (*cf.* Gn. 28:18); the tabernacle and its furniture (Ex. 30:22ff.); shields (2 Sa. 1:21; Is. 21:5: probably to consecrate them for the 'holy war', see Dt. 23:9ff.); kings (Jdg. 9:8; 2 Sa. 2:4; 1 Ki. 1:34); priests (Ex. 28:41); prophets (1 Ki. 19:16). The importance and solemnity of the anointing is shown, first, by the fact that it was an offence meriting excommunication to compound the holy oil for a common purpose (Ex. 30:32–33); secondly, by the authority which the anointing carried, such that, for example, while

Jehu's fellow-commanders scorned the prophet as a 'madman', they did not dare resist the implications of his action, but accepted without question that he who was anointed as king must indeed be king (2 Ki. 9:11–13); thirdly, by the effect produced in the anointed, the person or thing becoming holy (Ex. 30:22–33) and sacrosanct (1 Sa. 24:7, *etc.*). Fundamentally the anointing was an act of God (1 Sa. 10:1), and the word 'anointed' was used metaphorically to mean the bestowal of divine favour (Pss. 23:5; 92:10) or appointment to a special place or function in the purpose of God (Ps. 105:15; Is. 45:1) (* MESSIAH). Further, the anointing symbolized equipment for service, and is associated with the outpouring of the Spirit of God (1 Sa. 10:1, 9; 16:13; Is. 61:1; Zc. 4:1–14). This usage is carried over into the NT (Acts 10:38; 1 Jn. 2:20, 27). The use of oil in anointing the sick (Jas. 5:14) is best understood thus, as pointing to the Holy Spirit, the Lifegiver. Or, on the OT model of setting aside kings by anointing, the oil may signify a separating off of the sickness from the patient to Christ (*cf.* Mt. 8:17).

BIBLIOGRAPHY. E. Kutsch, *Salbung als Rechtsakt im A.T.* (*ZAW* Beiheft 87), 1963; W. Brunotte, D. Müller, *NIDNTT* 1, pp. 119–124.

J.A.M.

ANTICHRIST. The expression *antichristos* is found in the Bible only in the Johannine Epistles (1 Jn. 2:18, 22; 4:3; 2 Jn. 7), but the idea behind it is widespread. We should probably understand the force of *anti* as indicating opposition, rather than a false claim, *i.e.* the antichrist is one who opposes Christ rather than one who claims to be the Christ. If this is so, then we should include under the heading 'antichrist' such OT passages as Dn. 7:7f., 21f., and those in 2 Thes. 2 and Revelation which deal with the strong opposition that the forces of evil are to offer Christ in the last days.

The concept is introduced in John as already well known ('you have heard that antichrist is coming', 1 Jn. 2:18). But though he does not dispute the fact that at the end of this age there will appear an evil being, called 'antichrist', John insists that there is a temper, an attitude, characteristic of antichrist, and that already exists. Indeed, he can speak of 'many antichrists' as already in the world (1 Jn. 2:18). He gives something in the nature of a definition of antichrist when he says, 'This is the antichrist, he who denies the Father and the Son' (1 Jn. 2:22). This becomes a little more explicit when the criterion is made the refusal to acknowledge 'the coming of Jesus Christ in the

ANT
See Animals, Part 1.

ANTELOPE
See Animals, Part 1.

ANTHRAX
See Jewels, Part 2.

Anointing-horn carried by a Semitic envoy as part of his tribute. Tomb of Sebekhotep, Thebes. c. 1420 BC. (BM)

flesh' (2 Jn. 7). For John it is basic that in Jesus Christ we see God acting for man's salvation (1 Jn. 4:9f.). When a man denies this he is not simply guilty of doctrinal error. He is undercutting the very foundation of the Christian faith. He is doing the work of Satan in opposing the things of God. At the end of the age this will characterize the work of the supreme embodiment of evil. And those who in a small way do the same thing now demonstrate by that very fact that they are his henchmen.

Paul does not use the term 'antichrist', but the 'man of lawlessness' of whom he writes in 2 Thes. 2:3ff. clearly refers to the same being. The characteristic of this individual is that he 'opposes and exalts himself against every so-called god or object of worship' (v. 4). He claims to be God (*ibid.*). He is not Satan, but his coming is 'by the activity of Satan' (v. 9). It cannot be said that all the difficulties of this passage have been cleared up, and, in particular, the identification of the man of lawlessness is still hotly debated. But for our present purpose the main points are clear enough. Paul thinks of the supreme effort of Satan as not in the past, but in the future. He does not think of the world as gradually evolving into a perfect state, but of evil as continuing right up till the last time. Then evil will make its greatest challenge to good, and this challenge will be led by the mysterious figure who owes his power to Satan, and who is the instrument of Satan's culminating challenge to the things of God. Paul is sure of the outcome. Christ will consume the man of lawlessness 'with the breath of his mouth' (v. 8). The last, supreme challenge of Satan will be defeated.

That is surely the meaning of some, at least, of the imagery of the book of Revelation. Biblical students are far from unanimous about the right way to interpret this book, but nearly all are agreed that some of the visions refer to the final struggle of the forces of evil with Christ. Sometimes the symbolism refers plainly to Satan. Thus the 'great red dragon' of Rev. 12:3 is expressly identified with Satan (v. 9). But the 'beast' of Rev. 11:7 is not. He is closely related to Satan, as his works show. Other similar figures appear (Rev. 13:11, *etc.*). It is not our purpose here to identify any particular one with the antichrist, but simply to point to the fact that this book too knows of one empowered by Satan who will oppose Christ in the last days. This may fairly be said to be characteristic of the Christian view of the last days.

BIBLIOGRAPHY. W. Bousset and A. H. Keane, *The Antichrist Legend*, 1896; art. 'Antichrist' in *EBi*; M. R. James, art. 'Man of Sin and Antichrist' in *HDB*; G. Vos, *The Pauline Eschatology*², 1961, pp. 94–135; *NIDNTT* 1, pp. 124–126; G. C. Berkouwer, *The Return of Christ*, 1972, pp. 260–290. L.M.

ANTIOCH (PISIDIAN). This Asia Minor city located in Phrygia towards Pisidia, according to Strabo, was one of a number of Antiochs founded by a Macedonian cavalry leader, Seleucus I Nicator (312–280 BC), probably on the site of a Phrygian temple-village. Situated astride a main trading route between Ephesus and Cilicia, it became a prominent centre of Hellenism in the pre-Christian period. The Seleucids brought Jewish colonists into Phrygia for political and commercial reasons, and the more tolerant descendants of these settlers received Paul kindly on his first missionary journey (Acts 13:14). The Romans included Pisidian Antioch in the province of Galatia, and Augustus made it one of a series of Roman colonies in Pisidia.

In Phrygia, women enjoyed considerable prestige and sometimes occupied civic offices. Paul's enemies employed some of these to obtain his expulsion from Antioch (Acts 13:50). The ruined site is near Yalvaç in modern Turkey, and from that locality have come inscriptions, damaged stelae and other artifacts relating to the cult of the god Mên, which was prominent in Pisidian Antioch in the 1st century AD.

BIBLIOGRAPHY. B. Levick, *JHS* 91, 1971, pp. 80–84. R.K.H.

ANTIOCH (SYRIAN). Antioch on the Orontes, now Antakya in SE Turkey, some 500 km N of Jerusalem, was founded *c.* 300 BC by Seleucus I Nicator after his victory over Antigonus at Issus (310 BC). It was the most famous of sixteen Antiochs established by Seleucus in honour of his father. Built at the foot of Mt Silpius, it overlooked the navigable river Orontes and boasted a fine seaport, Seleucia Pieria. While the populace of Antioch was always mixed, Josephus records that the Seleucids encouraged Jews to emigrate there in large numbers, and gave them full citizenship rights (*Ant.* 12. 119).

Antioch fell to Pompey in 64 BC, and he made it a free city. It became the capital of the Roman province of Syria, and was the third largest city of the empire. The Seleucids and Romans erected magnificent temples and other buildings.

Even under the Seleucids the inhabitants had gained a reputation for energy, insolence and instability, which manifested itself in a series of revolts against Roman rule. Nevertheless, Antioch was renowned for its culture, being commended in this respect by no less a person than Cicero (*Pro Archia* 4). Close by the city were the renowned groves of Daphne, and a sanctuary dedicated to Apollo, where orgiastic rites were celebrated in the name of religion. Despite the bad moral tone, life in Antioch at the beginning of the Christian era was rich and varied.

Apart from Jerusalem itself, no other city was so intimately connected with the beginnings of Christianity. Nicolas, one of the seven 'deacons' of Acts 6:5, was of Antioch, and had been a Gentile convert to Judaism. During the persecution which followed the death of Stephen, some of the disciples went as far north as Antioch (Acts 11:19), and preached to the Jews. Later arrivals also took Christianity to the Greek populace, and when numerous conversions occurred the Jerusalem church sent Barnabas to Antioch. When he had assessed the situation he went to Tarsus and brought Saul back with him, and both of them taught in Antioch for a whole year. The disciples were first called 'Christians' there (Acts 11:26).

The energetic nature of the Christians in Antioch was displayed in the way in which alms were sent to the mother church in Jerusalem when famine struck (Acts 11:27–30). It was fitting that the city in which the first Gentile church was founded, and where the Christians were given, perhaps sarcastically, their characteristic name, should be the birthplace of Christian foreign missions (Acts 13:1–3). Paul and Barnabas set out from the seaport of Antioch and sailed for Cyprus. This first journey into Asia Minor concluded when Paul and Barnabas returned to Antioch and reported to the assembled church.

Some of the refugees from the persecution over Stephen had taken the lead in preaching at Antioch to Gentiles equally with Jews (Acts 11:20). The Gentile problem came to a head when some Jews visited Antioch and proclaimed the necessity of circumcision for Gentiles as a prerequisite to becoming Christians. Resisting this principle, the church at Antioch sent a deputation headed by Paul and Barnabas to Jerusalem to debate the matter (Acts 15:1–2).

With James presiding, the question of whether or not circumcision was to be obligatory for Gentile Christians was thoroughly discussed. Peter had already encountered the difficulties involved in the relationships between Jews and Gentiles at other than commercial levels (Acts 10:28). Although appearing favourable to such contacts, he had been censured by the Jerusalem church for eating in uncircumcised company (Acts 11:3; *cf.* Gal. 2:12). He now acknowledged that God had not differentiated between Jew and Gentile after Pentecost.

After Paul had related the blessings which the Gentiles had received, James gave his opinion that abstinence from blood, things strangled, idolatry and immorality should alone be required of Gentile converts. These provisions were written into the apostolic letter to the churches of Antioch and its province. Paul returned to Antioch as the recognized apostle to the uncircumcision (Acts 15:22–26). There is good reason for the view that *Galatians was written on the eve of this Jerusalem Council, possibly from Antioch. It appears that the Council settled in principle the contentions for which Paul had to battle in Galatians.

Paul began and ended his second missionary journey at Antioch. This notable city saw also the start of his third missionary visitation. Its evangelistic zeal afforded Antioch great status in the subsequent history of the church. Archaeological excavations at the site have unearthed over twenty ruined churches dating from the 4th century AD.

See G. Downey, *Ancient Antioch*, 1963.

R.K.H.
C.J.H.

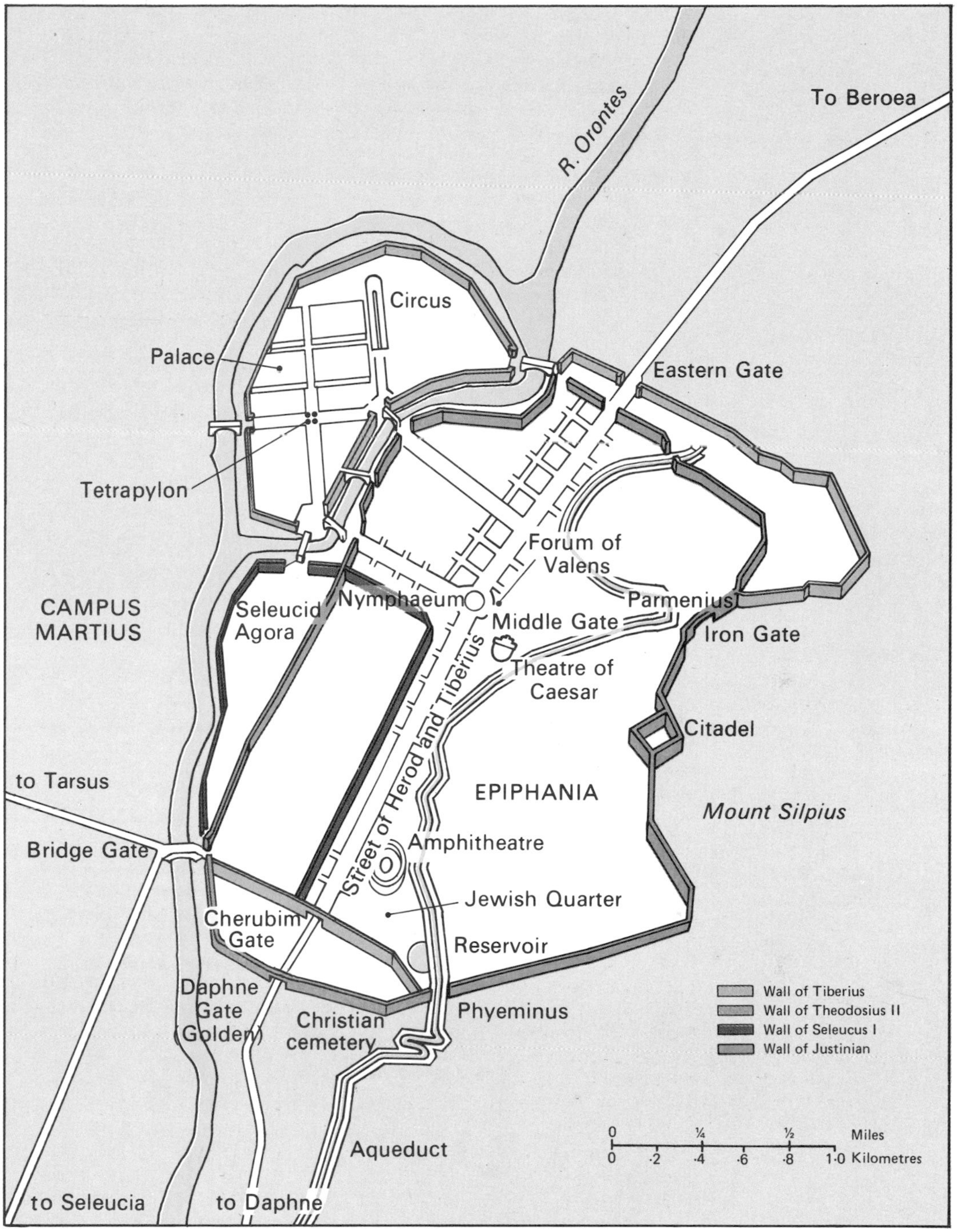

Plan of the city of Antioch in the 1st cent. AD.

ANTIOCHUS. The name of 13 kings of the Seleucid dynasty which in the 40 years following the death of Alexander the Great in 323 BC had become master of Asia Minor, Syria and the more westerly of Alexander's E dominions. Being a Hellenistic dynasty, they sought to maintain hold of this vast empire by founding or resettling a chain of Graeco-Macedonian cities throughout its length and breadth. *Antioch on the Orontes was their capital, with Seleucia on the Tigris a second capital administering the eastern provinces.

Antiochus I was the son of Seleucus I, founder of the dynasty, and Apama I. Joint-king with his father from 292, he succeeded him early in 280 and ruled until his death on 1 or 2 June 261. About 275 he was honoured with the title *Sōtēr* ('saviour') for delivering several cities of Asia Minor from the Gauls: he founded many Hellenistic cities. During his reign there was much conflict with the Ptolemaic dynasty of Egypt.

Antiochus II, the younger son of Antiochus I and Stratonice, succeeded his father in 261. He liberated Ephesus, Ionia, Cilicia and Pamphylia from Egyptian domi-

ANTIPATER
See Antipas, Part 1.

ANTITYPE
See Typology, Part 3.

APE
See Animals, Part 1.

nation, and in return for their autonomy the cities of Asia Minor gave him the title *Theos* ('god'). He banished his first wife, his cousin Laodice and her two sons and two daughters, and in 252 married Berenice, daughter of Ptolemy II Philadelphus of Egypt. He died in 246.

Antiochus III, the younger son of Seleucus II and grandson of Antiochus II and Laodice, succeeded his older brother Alexander Seleucus III Soter on the latter's assassination in 223. While reducing S Syria and Palestine in 217 he was defeated at Raphia by Ptolemy IV Philopator of Egypt, but a victory at Panion (the NT Caesarea Philippi) in 198 BC gave him secure control of those regions, formerly part of the empire of the Ptolemies. After putting down two domestic revolts, he led a victorious army E as far as Bactria to regain the old Seleucid empire: for this he was called by the Greeks 'the Great' as he had assumed the Achaemenid title of the 'Great King'. Campaigns in Asia Minor and Greece resulted in successive defeats by Rome, culminating in the battle of Magnesia (189) and the subsequent Treaty of Apamea, by which he ceded to Rome all Asia Minor N and W of the Taurus Mountains. In 187 he died and was succeeded by his son Seleucus IV Philopator.

Coin, the 'Lily of Judaea', struck at the Jerusalem mint after the decree of Antiochus VII enabled the Jews to coin their own money. 132–131 BC. (BM)

Antiochus IV, the youngest son of Antiochus III and Laodice III, succeeded his brother Seleucus IV in 175. Until 170/169 he reigned with his nephew Antiochus, Seleucus' baby son, who was murdered in Antiochus' absence by Andronicus, who arranged also the assassination of Onias III, the illegally deposed high priest, and was himself rewarded with execution (2 Macc. 4:32–38). During his reign there was much intrigue for the high priesthood on the part of Jason and Menelaus, and because of their misbehaviour Antiochus visited Jerusalem in 169 and insisted on entering the holy of holies, and carried off some of the gold and silver vessels. Pressure from Egypt convinced him of the necessity to hellenize Palestine, and measures against the old religion resulted in the cessation of the sacrifices in the Temple and the erection of a Greek altar on the site of the old one on 25 December 167. The revolt led by Mattathiah of the house of Hashmon and his 5 sons led to the reconsecration of the Temple just 3 years later. Antiochus, who on coins of the later years of his reign called himself (*Theos*) *Epiphanēs*, '(god) manifest', died on campaign in Media in 164.

Antiochus V Eupator, son of Epiphanes and Laodice, was put to death by the army in 162 on the arrival in Syria of his cousin Demetrius I Soter, the younger son of Seleucus IV and Epiphanes' rightful successor.

Antiochus VI Epiphanes Dionysus, the infant son of the pretender Alexander Balas (ruled 150–145), was put forward as king by Diodotus (Tryphon) in 143, dethroned by him in 142 and murdered by him in 138.

Antiochus VII Sidetes, son of Demetrius I Soter, deposed Tryphon in 139 and ruled until 130/129. After his decree to the Jews (1 Macc. 15:1–9), permitting them to coin their own money for the first time, he invaded and subdued Judaea in 134, granting the people religious freedom.

The rest of the history of the dynasty is a story of constant rivalry for the throne. Antiochus VIII Grypus (nephew of Sidetes) ruled from 125 to 115, when he was expelled by Antiochus IX Philopator (Cyzicenus), son of Grypus' mother, Cleopatra Thea, and Sidetes. Grypus returned in 111 and regained all except Coele-Syria, which Cyzicenus ruled until his death in 95. In 96 Grypus died, and among subsequent contestants for the throne bearing this name were two sons of Grypus (Antiochus XI Epiphanes Philadelphus and Antiochus XII Dionysus), and a son and grandson of Cyzicenus (Antiochus X Eusebes Philopator and Antiochus XIII Asiaticus). The last-named ruled from 69 to 65 and was the last of the Seleucid monarchs: in his settlement of the E in 64 Pompey annexed Syria to Rome.

BIBLIOGRAPHY. *CAH*, 6–9, *passim*; J. Bright, *History of Israel*, chs. 11–12; D. J. Wiseman in *Iraq* 16, 1954, pp. 202–211. D.H.W.

ANTIPAS. An abbreviation of Antipater. **1.** *Herod Antipas, who ordered the execution of John the Baptist. **2.** A martyr of the church of Pergamum (Rev. 2:13), who tradition states was roasted in a brazen bowl during Domitian's reign.

Bronze coin of Herod Antipas, titled Tetrarch, minted during the time of Tiberius. The palm frond may indicate agricultural prosperity or the Tree of Wisdom. (RG)

BIBLIOGRAPHY. H. Hoehner, *Herod Antipas*, 1972. J.D.D.

ANTIPATRIS. Formerly Kaphar-Saba, the modern Ras el-Ain, this city, about 42 km S of Caesarea on the road to Lydda, was rebuilt by Herod the Great in memory of his father Antipater (Josephus, *Ant.* 16. 143; *BJ* 1. 417). Paul was taken there on his way from Jerusalem to Caesarea (Acts 23:31). Vespasian occupied it in AD 68 (*BJ* 4. 443). Codex Sinaiticus reads *Antipatris* instead of *patris* (home-country) in Mt. 13:54, with *anti-* subsequently crossed out. (*APHEK.) D.H.W.

APELLES. Greeted by Paul as a tried Christian (Rom. 16:10). Lightfoot (*Philippians*, p. 174) found the name—which was often adopted by Jews (*cf.* Horace, *Sat.* 1. 5. 100)—in Imperial household circles: Lagrange *in loc.* notes the sculptured contemporary Apelles in *CIL*, VI, 9183, just possibly Christian. Some MSS have 'Apelles' for 'Apollos' at Acts 18:24; 19:1, perhaps through Origen's guess that they may have been identical.
A.F.W.

APHEK, APHEKAH (Heb. *ʾᵃp̄ēq*[*â*], 'fortress'). Name of several places in Palestine. **1.** Jos. 13:4. Defining the land remaining to be

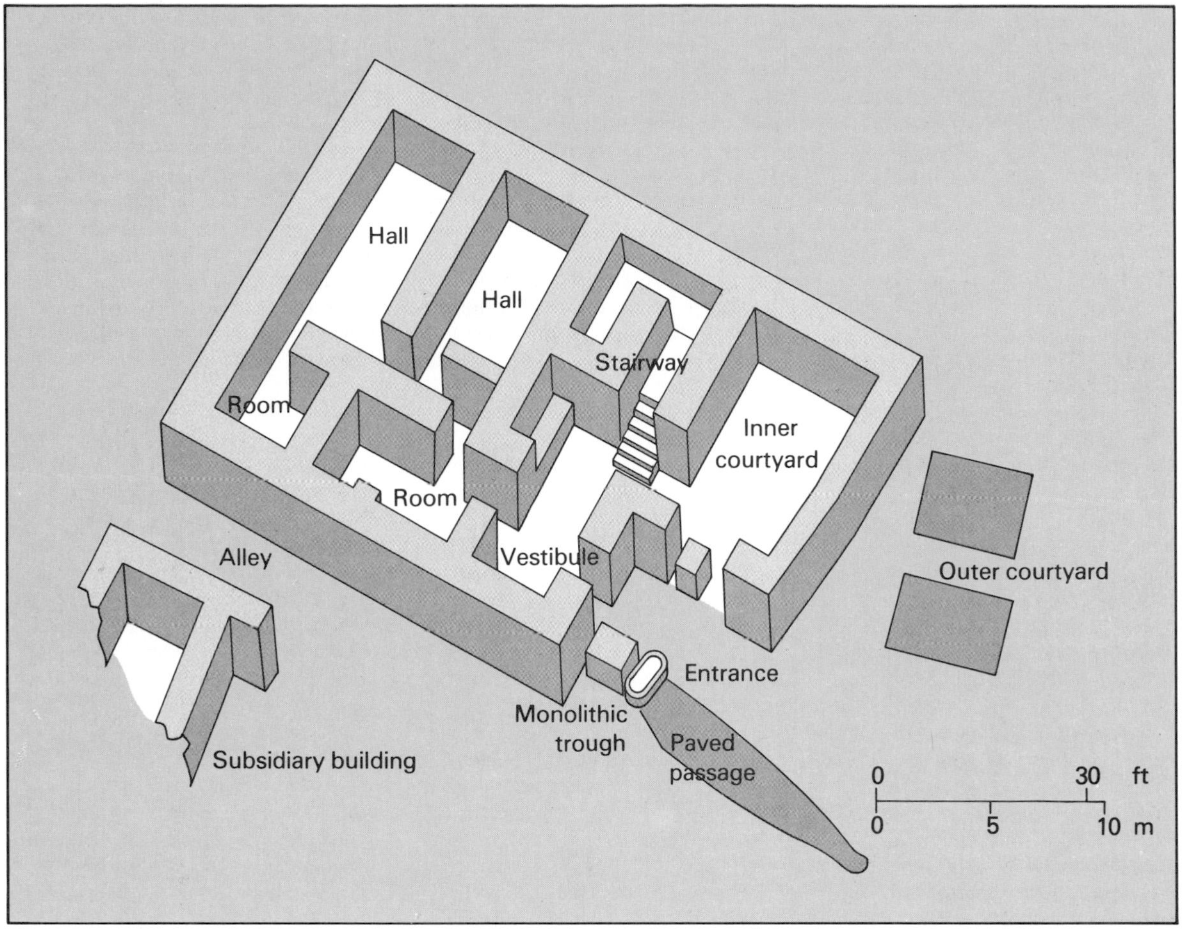

Isometric reconstruction of the Late Bronze Age acropolis (citadel) encountered at Aphek-Antipatris.

occupied to the N. Probably Afqa, NE of Beirut at the source of Nahr Ibrahim (*BDB*; Abel, *Géographie de la Palestine*, p. 247; *LOB*, p. 217). A different view places it at * Ras el-'Ain (*cf. GTT*, p. 110).

2. Jos. 12:18; 1 Sa. 4:1; 29:1. Later *Antipatris, now Ras el-Ain, Heb. Tel Afeq, at the source of Nahr el-Auga (Jarkon, Jos. 19:46) on the trunk road to Egypt. Listed by Tuthmosis III, Amenophis II, Ramesses II and III, probably the Execration Texts. Esarhaddon mentions '*Apku* in the territory of Samaria', and it occurs in the Aramaic letter of Adon, *c.* 600 BC (see *ANET*, 242, 246, 292, 329). Excavations by Tel Aviv University since 1972 have found important Late Bronze Age and Philistine remains.

3. Jos. 19:30; Jdg. 1:31 (Aphik). In Asher, modern Tell Kurdaneh, Heb. Tel Afeq, at the source of Nahr Na'amein which flows into the Bay of Haifa.

4. 1 Ki. 20:26, 30; 2 Ki. 13:17. Fīq or Afīq at the head of Wadi Fīq, E of the sea of Galilee may preserve the name, the place being 'En-Gev, a tell on the shore (*LOB*, p. 304, n. 60).

5. Jos. 15:53 (Aphekah). SW of Hebron, either Khirbet eḍ-ḍarrame (A. Alt, *Palästinajahrbuch*, 28, pp. 16f.) or Khirbet Kana'an (Abel, *op. cit.*, p. 247). A.R.M.

APOCALYPTIC. The word designates both a genre of literature (the Jewish and Christian apocalypses) and also the characteristic ideas of this literature. Within the Canon apocalyptic is represented especially by the books of * Daniel and * Revelation, but there are many other apocalypses from the inter-testamental and early Christian periods.

Already within the OT prophetic books there are passages which must be classified as apocalyptic in some respects at least. Apocalyptic *eschatology can be found especially in Is. 24–27; 56–66; Joel; Zc. 9–14. In these passages the eschatological future is envisaged in terms of direct divine intervention, a universal judgment of the nations and a new age of salvation, in which the cosmos will be radically transformed. This transcendent eschatology is the central core of apocalyptic belief. The apocalyptic doctrine of the resurrection of the dead is also probably found already in Is. 26:19, as well as in Dn. 12:2. The literary forms of the apocalypse, however, are anticipated especially in the visions of Ezekiel and Zc. 1–6.

It was after the cessation of prophecy that apocalyptic flourished as a literature distinct from prophecy. Its first great flowering was in the mid-2nd-century crisis of Jewish faith under Antiochus Epiphanes, when apocalyptic was the literary vehicle of the Hasidic movement, which stood for national repentance, uncompromising opposition to hellenization and eschatological faith in God's imminent intervention on behalf of his people. Thereafter apocalyptic probably characterized various groups within Judaism, including Essenes, Pharisees, Zealots, Jewish Christians. (The *variety* of the apocalyptic literature should be remembered whenever generalizations about apocalyptic are attempted.) Apocalyptic flourished especially in times of national crisis, and the last great Jewish eschatological apocalypses come from the period between the fall of Jerusalem in AD 70 and the failure of Bar Kokhba's revolt.

The most important post-canonical Jewish apocalypses are: * *1 Enoch*, a collection of writings of which the earliest may date from the 5th century BC and the latest from the 1st century AD; *The Testament of Moses* (also called *Assumption of Moses*), which should be dated either *c.* 165 BC or early 1st century AD; *4 Ezra* (or *2 Esdras*, in the English Apocrypha), *2 Baruch* and the *Apocalypse of Abraham*, all from the period AD 70–140. The Jewish *Sibylline Oracles* contain apocalyptic material cast in the style of the pagan oracles of the Sibyls. Other works, such as * *Jubilees* and *The Testaments of the Twelve Patriarchs*, contain apocalyptic passages, and some new apocalyptic texts have been found at Qumran.

The apocalypses just listed are largely eschatological in content, continuing, in some sense, the tradition of OT prophecy. They reveal (Gk. *apokalyptō*) the secrets of God's plans for history and for his coming triumph at the end of history. But the apocalyptic literature also includes a tradition of *cosmological apocalyptic*, which reveals the mysteries of the cosmos. This tradition has its origin in parts of *1 Enoch*, where Enoch is taken by angels on journeys through the heavens and the realms of the dead. Cosmology really comes into its own in hellenistic apocalypses of the Christian era, such as *2 Enoch* and *3 Baruch*, where the eschatological hope has largely faded. In the rest of this article we confine our attention to *eschatological* apocalyptic.

In *literary* terms, apocalyptic is a highly stylized form of literature, with its own conventions of symbolism and terminology, continually feeding on OT sources. It is a literature of dreams and visions, often centred on a vision of the heavenly throne-room. Eschatological prophecy may take the form of long discourses or of symbolic imagery, which is sometimes very artificial, sometimes vivid and effective. Probably the apocalyptists never intended to depict the End in literal terms. In their attempt to portray a future salvation which transcends ordinary historical experience, they seem to have borrowed symbols from Canaanite myth and from the mythology they encountered in the Eastern Diaspora and in hellenistic Palestine. Apocalyptic literature often exhibits a close but critical interaction with the international culture of its time.

If Jewish apocalyptic was often indebted for its imagery and forms to its non-Jewish environment, its eschatological content derived from OT prophecy. In this respect apocalyptic was the *heir of prophecy*. Its role was to reassert the prophetic promises for the future in their relevance to the apocalyptist's own generation. The apocalyptists were not themselves prophets. They lived in an age when prophecy had ceased, and probably for that reason they adopted the device of *pseudonymity*, writing under the name of an OT saint from the period of prophetic revelation. This need not be regarded as a fraudulent device, as though they wished to pass off their work as belonging to the age of prophecy; rather it should be seen as a literary form expressing the apocalyptists' role as interpreters of the revelation given in the prophetic age.

From this fictional standpoint in the past, the apocalyptists often give reviews of history up to their own time in the form of predictive prophecy. Again, this device need not be intended to deceive. It is the apocalyptist's means of penetrating the divine plan of history and presenting an interpretation of the prophecies of the past, which he rewrites in the light of their fulfilment in order to show how they have been fulfilled and what still remains to be fulfilled.

The apocalyptists, then, are interpreters of OT prophecy. This does not mean they do not claim inspiration. There is good reason to think that the visionary experiences attributed to the pseudonym often reflect the real experience of the apocalyptist himself. The apocalyptist's inspiration, however, was the source not so much of fresh prophetic revelation as of interpretation of the revelation already given through the prophets. The authority of his message is thus derivative from that of the prophets.

If this view of the apocalyptists' self-understanding is adopted, it will be seen that they occupy an essentially *intertestamental* position. They interpret the prophets to an age when prophecy has ceased but fulfilment is still awaited. Their exclusion from the Canon is not therefore a negative judgment on their value for the intertestamental development of Jewish religion. On the contrary, by sustaining and intensifying the eschatological hope they played a decisively important role as a bridge between the Testaments.

The apocalyptic understanding of *history and eschatology* developed in the context of the post-exilic experience of history, in which Israel remained under the domination of the Gentile powers and the prophetic promises of glorious restoration remained largely unfulfilled. In the extended period of contradiction between God's promises and the reality of Israel's historical experience, the apocalyptists sought to assure the faithful that God had not abandoned his people, that the promised salvation was coming. To this end they stressed the divine *sovereignty over history*: God has predetermined the whole course of world history and the End will come at the time he has appointed. The power of the pagan empires survives only so long as he permits. This strongly deterministic view of history does not, however, become a fatalism which contradicts human freedom and responsibility, for the apocalyptists also call their readers to repentance and intercession and ethical action. Only rarely do they venture to set a date for the End.

The coming eschatological salvation is envisaged in transcendent and universal terms. It is an event which far transcends the great events of the salvation-history of the past. It amounts to a new creation, in which all forms of evil and suffering will be eliminated. It is characteristic of the apocalyptists to believe that even death will be conquered: this belief appears in the form both of bodily resurrection and of spiritual immortality. The eschatological age will be the kingdom of God, replacing all earthly empires for ever. Expectations of the fate of the Gentiles vary. The oppressors of Israel will be condemned, but frequently the nations may come to share in the salvation of the righteous in Israel, while the apostates in Israel will be judged. The universalism of apocalyptic results both from post-exilic Israel's involvement in the history of the world-empires, and from the apocalyptists' intense awareness of the universal problem of evil.

The negative experience of present history, in which apocalyptic arose, contrasted with the transcendent future salvation, gives rise to the *temporal dualism* of apocalyptic: its distinction between this age and the age to come which follows the new creation. This dualism became fully developed only at a late stage. The terminology of the two ages appears only in the 1st century AD (when it is also found in the NT). It is never an absolute dualism, for although the powers of evil have become dominant in this age, God remains in sovereign control over them. The new creation is seen as a renewal of *this* world (though the degree of continuity envisaged seems to vary). Apocalyptic dualism is at its starkest in *2 Baruch* and *4 Ezra*, where there is a deepening pessimism and a strong tendency to view the history of this age in wholly negative terms. From this extreme eschatological dualism it is not too great a step to the cosmological dualism of Gnosticism.

The relation between *apocalyptic and the NT* has been much debated. There are passages which strongly resemble the Jewish apocalypses in both form and content: especially Mt. 24; Mk. 13; Lk. 21; 1 Thes. 4:16f.; 2 Thes. 2; Rev. But even apart from these apocalyptic passages it is clear that both Jesus and the early church were broadly indebted to the apocalyptic world of thought, as is evident from their use of such apocalyptic concepts as resurrection, the two ages, the Son of man, the time of tribulation, the kingdom of God.

On the other hand, the purely future orientation of Jewish apocalyptic is modified in the NT by the conviction that eschatological *fulfilment has already begun* in the historical event of Jesus Christ. Christians live between the 'already' and the 'not yet'. In this way the apocalyptic tendency to a negative evaluation of present history is superseded by the conviction that God's redemptive purpose is already at work within the history of this age.

Moreover, NT apocalyptic is *Christ-centred.* God's decisive act of eschatological salvation has taken place in the history of Jesus, and Jesus is therefore also the focus of the future hope of Christians. For NT writers apocalyptic becomes primarily a means of declaring the significance of Jesus Christ for the destiny of the world.

One aspect of eschatological fulfilment is the renewal of prophecy, and so NT apocalyptic is a form of fresh prophetic revelation. It is no longer pseudonymous and no longer takes a fictional standpoint in the past: the prophet John, for example, writes in his own name (Rev. 1:1) and abandons the convention of writing for the distant future (22:10).

BIBLIOGRAPHY. G. R. Beasley-Murray, *Jesus and the Future*, 1954; P. D. Hanson, *The Dawn of Apocalyptic*, 1976; M. Hengel, *Judaism and Hellenism*, 1974; K. Koch, *The Rediscovery of Apocalyptic*, 1970; L. Morris, *Apocalyptic*, 1973; H. H. Rowley, *The Relevance of Apocalyptic*, 1944; R. J. Bauckham, *Them* 3.2, Jan. 1978, pp. 10–23; D. Russell, *The Method and Message of Jewish Apocalyptic*, 1964. R.J.B.

APOCRYPHA.

I. Definition

The term 'apocrypha' (neuter plural of the Gk. adjective *apokryphos*, 'hidden') is a technical term concerning the relation of certain books to the OT Canon, signifying that, while they are not approved for public lection, they are nevertheless valued for private study and edification. The term covers a number of additions to canonical books in their LXX form (*viz.* Esther, Daniel, Jeremiah, Chronicles), and other books, legendary, historical or theological, many originally written in Hebrew or Aramaic but preserved or known until recently only in Greek; these figure in the loosely defined LXX Canon, but were rejected from the Hebrew *Canon at Jamnia. Christian usage and opinion about their status were somewhat ambiguous until the 16th century, when twelve works were included in the Canon of the Roman Church by the Council of Trent; but Protestant thought (*e.g.* Luther, and the Anglican Church in the Thirty-Nine Articles) admitted them only for private edification. Works other than the twelve here under discussion are nowadays usually termed *'pseudepigrapha'. These, too, were freely drawn upon before the 16th century in the outlying Eastern churches in whose languages alone they have been preserved (*e.g.* Ethiopic, Armenian, Slavonic).

II. Contents

We may proceed to summarize the contents and chief critical problems of the twelve books which go to make up what we know today as the Apocrypha.

1 Esdras in EVV is called *2 Esdras* in the Lucianic recension of the LXX, and *3 Esdras* in Jerome's Vulg. This gives a parallel account of events recorded in Chronicles–Ezra–Nehemiah, with one large addition (*viz.* the 'Debate of the Three Youths' in 3:1–5:6). 1:1–20, 23–25 = 2 Ch. 35:1–36:21; 2:1–11 = Ezr. 1:1–11; 2:12–26 = Ezr. 4:7–24; 5:7–71 = Ezr. 2:1–4:5; 6:1–9:36 = Ezr. 5:1–10:44; 9:37–55 = Ne. 7:72–8:13. The 'Debate of the Three Youths' is an adaptation of a Persian tale, and in its details evidence of this may still be discerned: it is adapted as the means whereby Zerubbabel, guardsman of Darius, by winning a debate on the strongest power (wine, women or Truth?), gains opportunity to remind the Persian monarch of his obligation to allow the Temple to be rebuilt. Detailed comparison of it with the LXX Ezra shows that the two are independent translations from the *MT*: 1 Esdras is probably the earlier of the two. They present contrasts not only of text but also in chronological order of events and of the Persian kings. In a number of these cases scholarship is still undecided as to which work to follow. Certainly in some cases 1 Esdras provides good textual evidence. It is a free and idiomatic translation, and was known to Josephus.

2 Esdras in EVV is *4 Esdras* in the Vulg.; it is also called the *Apocalypse of Ezra* or *4 Ezra*. This version, as it now stands in the Old Latin, is an expansion by Christian writers of an original Jewish apocalyptic work found in chs. 4–14. The other chapters, *i.e.* the Christian additions, are lacking in some oriental versions. The original body of the book consists of seven visions. In the first (3:1–5:19) the seer demands an explanation of the suffering of Zion, whose sin is not greater than that of her oppressor. The angel Uriel answers that this cannot be understood, but that the era shortly to dawn will bring salvation. The second (5:20–6:34) deals with a similar problem—why Israel, God's chosen, has been delivered up to other nations; this, too, is declared to be incomprehensible to men. The age to come will follow this age without interval, preceded by signs of the end and a time of conversion and salvation. This should give comfort to the seer. The third vision (6:35–9:25) asks why the Jews do not possess the earth; the answer is given that they will inherit it in the age to come. Various other matters about the after-life and the age to come are dealt with, including the fewness of the elect. The fourth vision (9:26–10:59) is of a mourning woman who recounts her woes, and is thereupon transformed into a glorious city. This is a symbol of Jerusalem. The fifth vision (10:60–12:51) is of a twelve-winged and three-headed eagle—the symbol of Rome, which is explicitly declared by the interpreting angel to be the fourth kingdom of Dn. 7. The Messiah is to supplant it. By the most probable interpretation, this vision is to be dated in the reign of Domitian. The sixth vision (13:1–58) is of a man arising from the sea, and annihilating an antagonistic multitude. This is an adaptation of the Son of man vision of Dn. 7. The final vision (14) deals with the distinct topic of Ezra's restoration of the sacred books of the Hebrews, by means of a vision and with the help of supernaturally aided scribes. There are 94 such books, *viz.* the 24 of the Hebrew Canon and 70 esoteric or apocalyptic works.

Tobit is a pious short story of a righteous Hebrew of the northern captivity, Tobit, and his son Tobias. Tobit suffers persecution and privations because of his succour of fellow Israelites under the tyranny of Esarhaddon. At length he is blinded accidentally; and to his shame, his wife is obliged to support him. He prays that he may die. At the same time, prayer is offered by Sarah, a young Hebrew woman in Ecbatana, who is haunted by the demon Asmodaeus, who has slain seven suitors on their wedding night with her. The angel Raphael is sent 'to heal them both'. Tobias is sent by his father to collect 10 silver talents left in Media. Raphael takes on the form of Azariah, who is hired as a travelling companion. In the Tigris a fish is caught, and its heart, liver and gall are preserved by Tobias on Azariah's advice. Tobias arrives in Ecbatana and becomes betrothed to Sarah, who is found to be his cousin. On the bridal night he burns the heart and liver of the fish, the stench of which drives the demon away to Egypt. On his return home (preceded by his dog), where he had been given up as lost, Tobias anoints his father's eyes with the fish-gall and restores his sight. The story apparently originated in the Babylonian or Persian Exile, and its original language is likely to have been Aramaic. Three Greek recensions are known, and fragments in Hebrew and Aramaic have been found by the Dead Sea.

Judith tells the story of a courageous young Jewess, a widow, and the overthrow of Nebuchadrezzar's host by her guile. A native of Bethulia, besieged by Holofernes, she visits him in his camp, under the ruse of giving military secrets away: she then begins to entice him by her charms, until at length, banqueting with him alone at night, she is able to behead him. She then returns with his head to the city, greeted by rejoicing. The Assyrian(!) host retreats on the discovery of its general's assassination. Judith and the women of Bethulia rejoice in a psalm before God. The story is frank fiction—otherwise its inexactitudes would be incredible—and dates from the 2nd century BC. Its original was Hebrew, and a Greek translation in 4 recensions has preserved the tale for us.

Additions to Daniel are found in the LXX and Theodotion's translation. To chapter 3 is added the **Prayer of Azariah** uttered in the furnace and the **Song of the Three Holy Children** (*i.e. paidōn*, 'servants') sung to God's praise as the three walk about in the fire. This is the Benedicite of Christian worship. These two additions evidently existed in a Hebrew original. Prefaced to Daniel in Theodotion but following in LXX, is the story of **Susanna**. She is the beautiful and virtuous wife of a wealthy Jew in Babylon. Two elders of the people who lust after her come upon her bathing and offer her the alternatives of yielding to their desire or facing false accusation as an adulteress. She chooses the latter: her detractors are believed, and she is condemned protesting her innocence. Daniel, though but a mere youth, cries out against the injustice of this, and in a second trial before him the lie is uncovered and the woman justified.

The stories of **Bel and the Dragon** are plainly written to ridicule idolatry. Daniel shows that the priests of Bel, and not the image of the god, devour the nightly offering of food; the king thereupon destroys the image. A mighty dragon worshipped in Babylon is destroyed by Daniel. He is thrown into the lions' den and is preserved alive for 6 days; on the 6th the prophet Habakkuk is miraculously transported from Judaea to give him food; on the 7th he is released by the king. These two stories are probably translated from a Semitic original, but the matter is not finally decided. These additions are examples of pious legendary embroidery of the Daniel story and date from about 100 BC.

Additions to Esther considerably increase the size of the Greek version of the book. There are 6 additional passages. The first deals with Mordecai's dream and his prevention of a conspiracy against the king; it precedes chapter 1. The second is the king's edict for the destruction of all Jews in his realm. This follows 3:13 of the Hebrew. The third comprises prayers of Esther and Mordecai to follow chapter 4. The fourth describes Esther's audience with the king, to supplement 5:12. The fifth is the king's edict permitting Jewish self-defence, to follow 8:12. The sixth includes the interpretation of Mordecai's dream; and a historical note giving the date of the bringing of the Greek version into Egypt. The majority of scholars consider that all this is in fact addition to the shorter work of the Hebrew Canon, and that some, if not all, was composed in Greek. Scholars of the Roman obedience and a minority of others (including C. C. Torrey) argue, however, that the Hebrew is an abbreviation of a larger work, in Hebrew or Aramaic, of which the Greek is a translation. The colophon claims that the work was translated in Palestine some time before 114 BC, by one Lysimachus, son of Ptolemy, a Jerusalemite.

The Prayer of Manasses claims to give the prayer of which record is made in 2 Ch. 33:11–19. In the opinion of most scholars it is a Jewish composition and probably was written originally in Hebrew. However this may be, it is first attested in the Syriac Didascalia (3rd century AD), and found also among the Odes (*i.e.* hymns from OT and NT used in Christian worship) appended to the Psalms in some LXX MSS, such as the Codex Alexandrinus.

The Epistle of Jeremiah is a typical Hellenistic–Jewish attack on idolatry in the guise of a letter from Jeremiah to the exiles in Babylon, similar to that mentioned in Je. 29. Idols are ridiculed; the evils and follies connected with them are exposed, and the captive Jews are told neither to worship nor to fear them. It is written in good Greek, but it may have had an Aramaic original.

The Book of Baruch is allegedly the work of the friend and scribe of Jeremiah. The work is brief, but, in the opinion of most scholars, it is a composite work, variously attributed to two, three or four authors. It falls into the following sections. (*a*) 1:1–3:8. In the setting of the Babylonian Exile of 597, Baruch is depicted as addressing the exiles, setting out a confession of sins, a prayer for forgiveness and a prayer for salvation. (*b*) 3:9–4:4. This section sets out the praises of Wisdom which may be found in the law of Moses, and without which the heathen have come to naught, but with which Israel will be saved. (*c*) 4:5–5:9. A lament of Jerusalem over the exiles, followed by an exhortation to Jerusalem to be comforted, since her children will be brought back to their home. The first part was patently written in Hebrew, and, although the Greek of the two later sections is more idiomatic, a plausible case for a Hebrew original can be made.

Ecclesiasticus is the name given in its Greek dress to the Wisdom of Joshua ben-Sira. He was a Palestinian living in Jerusalem, and parts of his work survive in the original Hebrew in MSS of the Cairo Geniza. The work figures in Greek among the apocrypha in the translation made by his grandson, who furnishes chronological details in a preface. The most likely date for Ben-Sira himself is *c.* 180 BC, since his grandson apparently migrated to Egypt in the reign of Ptolemy VII Euergetes (170–117 BC). The author composed his work in two parts, chapters 1–23 and 24–50, with a short appendix, chapter 51. Like the Wisdom books, it is advice for a successful life conceived in the widest sense; fear of the Lord and the observance of his law are allied in the author's experience and teaching with practical 'wisdom' drawn from observation and his own life. Personal piety will express itself in the observance of the law, in which Wisdom is revealed; and in daily living moderation will be the keynote of all aspects of life. The second book concludes with the praise of famous men, a list of the worthies of Israel, ending with Simon II the high priest (*c.* 200 BC), who is known also from the Mishnah (*Aboth* 1:2) and Josephus (*Ant.* 12. 224). The book represents the beginnings of the ideal of the scribe, such as Ben-Sira himself, which became the type of orthodox Jewry—devoted to God, obedient to the law, sober in living and setting the highest value on learning in the law. It became a favourite Christian book, as its title ('The Church-book') shows; and though never canonical among the Jews, it was held in high honour by them, being occasionally cited by the Rabbis as if it were Scripture. The Syriac version is of Jewish origin and is based upon the Hebrew text.

The Wisdom of Solomon is perhaps the highlight of Jewish Wisdom writing. Its roots are in the stream of Wisdom literature which is to be found in the OT and Apocrypha, but here under the influence of Greek thought the book achieves a greater formality and precision than other examples of this literary type. The book is an exhortation to seek Wisdom. Chapters 1–5 declare the blessings which accrue upon the Jews who are the seekers after Wisdom; chapters 6–9 speak the praises of the divine Wisdom, hypostatized as a feminine celestial being, foremost of the creatures and servants of God; chapters 10–19 review OT history in illustration of the theme that throughout it Wisdom has helped her friends the Jews, and has brought punishment and damnation upon her adversaries. The work may thus be interpreted as an encouragement to Jews not to forsake their ancestral faith, but the missionary motive so evident in Hellenistic Judaism is not lacking. The author drew on sources in Hebrew, but it appears clear that the work as it stands was composed in Greek, since its prosody is Greek, and it makes use of Greek terms of philosophy and depends on the Greek version of the OT. The description of Wisdom, in which Stoic and Platonic terminology is utilized, and the author's convictions about the immortality of the soul, are the points at which his dependence on Greek thought is most clearly in evidence. In the opinion of most scholars there are no conclusive arguments for subdividing the authorship of the book, but various sources may be discerned. The author of the book is unknown, but an Alexandrian origin is most likely.

Several works are entitled **Maccabees**: of these, two figure in the Apocrypha as printed in the English versions. These are the historical works **1 and 2 Maccabees.** 1 Maccabees covers events between 175 and 134 BC, *i.e.* the struggle with Antiochus Epiphanes, the wars of the Hasmonaeans, and the rule of John Hyrcanus. The book ends with a panegyric on John and was evidently written just after his death in 103 BC. Originally written in Hebrew, it is translated in the literal style of parts of the LXX. The aim of the work is to glorify the family of the Maccabees seen as the champions of Judaism. **2 Maccabees** is a work of different origin: its subject-matter covers much of the same history as its namesake, but does not continue the history beyond the campaigns and defeat of Nicanor. Its unknown author is sometimes called the 'epitomist', since much of his book is excerpted from the otherwise unknown work of Jason of Cyrene. There are a number of discrepancies in chronological and numerical matters between the two works, and it is customary to place more reliance on 1 Maccabees. There is debate also over the historical value of the letters and edicts which figure in the two works. Nevertheless, neither work is to be discredited as an historical source. **3 and 4 Maccabees** are found in a number of MSS of the LXX. The former is an account of pogroms and counter-pogroms under Ptolemy IV (221–204 BC) not unlike the book of Esther in tone and ethos. 4 Maccabees is not a narrative but a diatribe or tract on the rule of reason over the passions, illustrated from biblical stories and the martyr stories of 2 Macc. 6–7. The writer seeks to enhance the law, though he is greatly influenced by Stoicism. (See also * NEW TESTAMENT APOCRYPHA.)

BIBLIOGRAPHY. R. H. Charles (ed.), *The Apocrypha and Pseudepigrapha of the Old Testament*, 1913; *idem*, *Religious Development between the Old and New Testaments*, 1914; C. C. Torrey, *The Apocryphal Literature*, 1945; R. H. Pfeiffer, *History of New Testament Times with an Introduction to the Apocrypha*, 1949; B. M. Metzger, *An Introduction to the Apocrypha*, 1957. J.N.B.

APOLLO
See Python, Part 3.

APOLLONIA. A town on the Via Egnatia some 43 km WSW of Amphipolis. It lay between the rivers Strymon and Axius (Vardar), but its site is not known for certain. Paul and Silas passed through it on their way from Philippi to Thessalonica (Acts 17:1). There were several other towns named Apollonia in the Mediterranean area.

K.L.MCK.

APOLLOS. An Alexandrian Jew (Acts 18:24). The name is abbreviated from Apollonius. He came to Ephesus in AD 52 during Paul's hasty visit to Palestine (Acts 18:22). He had accurate knowledge of the story of Jesus, which may have come to him (possibly at Alexandria) either from Galilean disciples of our Lord or from some early written Gospel. He combined natural gifts of eloquence (or learning) with a profound understanding of the OT, and he was enthusiastic in proclaiming such truth as he knew (Acts 18:24–25). The conspicuous gap in his knowledge concerned the outpouring of the Holy Spirit and the consequent rite of Christian baptism. This was made good by the patient instruction of Priscilla and Aquila (Acts 18:26). From Ephesus Apollos went on to Corinth, where he showed himself to be an expert at Christian apologetics in dealing with the Jews (Acts 18:27–28). At Corinth there sprang up factions in the names of Paul, Apollos, Cephas and Christ himself (1 Cor. 1:12). Paul seeks to show that this was not due to himself or Apollos, who were both working together under the hand of God (1 Cor. 3:4–6). All belonged to the Corinthians, including himself and Apollos (1 Cor. 3:21–23), and there could be no cause for party spirit (1 Cor. 4:6). The factions were probably due to the preference of some for the polished eloquence of Apollos. His desire to lessen the controversy may be the reason for his not returning to Corinth despite Paul's request (1 Cor. 16:12). He is last mentioned in Tit. 3:13 as making some sort of journey.

Since the time of Luther, Apollos has often been suggested as the author of the Epistle to the Hebrews. This is possible, if he used the allegorical exegesis of his native Alexandria, but it is by no means proved.

BIBLIOGRAPHY. H. W. Montefiore, *A Commentary on the Epistle to the Hebrews*, 1964, pp. 9ff.; F. F. Bruce, *New Testament History*, 1969, pp. 304ff.; *idem*, 'Apollos in the NT', *Ekklesiastikos Pharos* 57, 1975, pp. 354ff.

R.E.N.

APOLLYON
See Abaddon, Part 1.

APOSTASY. In classical Gk. *apostasia* is a technical term for political revolt or defection. In LXX it always relates to rebellion against God (Jos. 22:22; 2 Ch. 29:19), originally instigated by Satan, the apostate dragon of Jb. 26:13.

There are two NT instances of the Gk. word. Acts 21:21 records that Paul was maliciously accused of teaching the Jews to forsake Moses by abandoning circumcision and other traditional observances. 2 Thes. 2:3 describes the great apostasy of prophecy, alongside or prior to the revelation of the man of lawlessness (*cf.* Mt. 24:10–12). The allusion is neither to the political nor to the religious infidelity of the Jews, but is entirely eschatological in character and refers to 'the final catastrophic revolt against the authority of God which in apocalyptic writings is a sign of the end of the world' (E. J. Bicknell, *The First and Second Epistles to the Thessalonians*, 1932, p. 74). It may be regarded as the earthly counterpart of the heavenly rebellion in Rev. 12:7–9.

Apostasy is a continual danger to the church, and the NT contains repeated warnings against it (*cf.* 1 Tim. 4:1–3; 2 Thes. 2:3; 2 Pet. 3:17). Its nature is made clear: falling 'from the faith' (1 Tim. 4:1) and 'from the living God' (Heb. 3:12). It increases in times of special trial (Mt. 24:9–10; Lk. 8:13) and is encouraged by false teachers (Mt. 24:11; Gal. 2:4), who seduce believers from the purity of the Word with 'another gospel' (Gal. 1:6–8; *cf.* 2 Tim. 4:3–4; 2 Pet. 2:1–2; Jude 3–4). The impossibility of restoration after deliberate apostasy is solemnly urged (Heb. 6:4–6; 10:26).

BIBLIOGRAPHY. *NIDNTT* 1, pp. 606–611; I. H. Marshall, *Kept by the Power of God: A Study of Perseverance and Falling Away*, 1969.

A.S.W.

APOSTLE. There are over 80 occurrences of the Gk. word *apostolos* in the NT, mostly in Luke and Paul. It derives from the very common verb *apostellō*, to send, but in non-Christian Gk., after Herodotus in the 5th century BC, there are few recorded cases where it means 'a person sent', and it generally means 'fleet', or perhaps occasionally 'admiral'. The sense of 'sent one, messenger' may have survived in popular speech: at least, isolated occurrences in the LXX and Josephus suggest that this meaning was recognized in Jewish circles. Only with Christian literature, however, does it come into its own. In NT it is applied to Jesus as the Sent One of God (Heb. 3:1), to those sent by God to preach to Israel (Lk. 11:49) and to those sent by churches (2 Cor. 8:23; Phil. 2:25); but above all it is applied absolutely to the group of men who held the supreme dignity in the primitive church. Since *apostellō* seems frequently to mean 'to send with a particular purpose', as distinct from the neutral *pempō* (save in the Johannine writings, where the two are synonyms), the force of *apostolos* is probably 'one commissioned'—it is implied, by Christ.

It is disputed whether *apostolos* represents in NT a Jewish term of similar technical force. Rengstorf, in particular, has elaborated the theory that it reflects the Jewish *šālîaḥ*, an accredited representative of religious authority, entrusted with messages and money and empowered to act on behalf of the authority (for the idea, *cf.* Acts 9:2); and Gregory Dix and others have applied ideas and expressions belonging to the *šālîaḥ* concept (*e.g.* 'a man's *šālîaḥ* is as himself') to the apostolate and eventually to the modern episcopate. Such a process is full of perils, and not least because there is no clear evidence that *šālîaḥ* was used in this sense until post-apostolic times. *apostolos*, in fact, may well be the earlier as a technical term, and it is safest to seek its significance in the meaning of *apostellō* and from the contexts of the NT occurrences.

a. The origin of the Apostolate

Essential to the understanding of all the Gospels as they stand is the choice by Jesus, out of the wider company of his followers, of a group of 12 men whose purpose was to be with him, to preach, and to have authority to heal and to exorcize (Mk. 3:14f.). The only occasion on which Mark uses the word 'apostle' is on the successful return of the Twelve from a mission of preaching and healing (Mk. 6:30; *cf.* Mt. 10:2ff.). This is usually taken as a non-technical use (*i.e.* 'those sent on this particular assignment'), but it is unlikely that Mark would use it without evoking other associations. This preparatory mission is a miniature of their future task in the wider world. From this preliminary training they return 'apostles' indeed. There is then nothing incongruous in Luke (who speaks of the 'apostles' in 9:10; 17:5; 22:14; 24:10) declaring that Jesus conferred the title (already in Gk.?) himself (6:13).

b. The functions of the Apostolate

Mark's first specification on the choice of the Twelve is for them 'to be with him' (Mk. 3:14). It is no accident that the watershed of Mark's Gospel is the apostolic confession of the Messiahship of Jesus (Mk. 8:29), or that Matthew follows this with the 'Rock' saying about the apostolic confession (Mt. 16:18f.; * PETER). The primary function of the apostles was witness to Christ, and the witness was rooted in years of intimate knowledge, dearly bought experience and intensive training.

This is complementary to their widely recognized function of witness to the resurrection (*cf.*, *e.g.*, Acts 1:22; 2:32; 3:15; 13:31); for the special significance of the resurrection lies, not in the event itself, but in its demonstration, in fulfilment of prophecy, of the identity of the slain Jesus (*cf.* Acts 2:24ff., 36; 3:26; Rom. 1:4). Their witness *of* the resurrection of Christ made them effective witnesses *to* his Person, and he himself commissions them to world-wide witness (Acts 1:8).

The same commission introduces a factor of profound importance for the apostolate: the coming of the Spirit. Curiously enough, this is most fully treated in Jn. 14–17, which does not use the word 'apostle' at all. This is the great commissioning discourse of the Twelve (*apostellō* and *pempō* are used without discrimination): their commission from Jesus is as real as his from God (*cf.* Jn. 20:21); they are to bear witness from their long acquaintance with Jesus, yet the Spirit bears witness of him (Jn. 15:26–27). He will remind them of the words of Jesus (Jn. 14:26), and guide them into all the truth (a promise often perverted by extending its primary reference beyond the apostles) and show them the age to come (of the church) and Christ's glory (Jn. 16:13–15). Instances are given in the Fourth Gospel of this process, where the significance of words or actions was recalled only after Christ's 'glorification' (Jn. 2:22; 12:16; *cf.* 7:39). That is, the witness of the apostles to Christ is not left to their impressions and recollections, but to the guidance of the Holy Spirit, whose witness it is also—a fact of consequence in assessing the recorded apostolic witness in the Gospels.

For this reason the apostles are the norm of doctrine and fellowship in the NT church (Acts 2:42; *cf.* 1 Jn. 2:19). In their own day they were regarded as 'pillars' (Gal. 2:9—*cf.* C. K. Barrett in *Studia Paulina*, 1953, pp. 1ff.)—perhaps translate 'marking posts'. The church is built on the foundation of the apostles and prophets (Eph. 2:20; probably the witness of the OT is intended, but the point remains if Christian prophets are in mind). The apostles are the assessors at the Messianic judgment (Mt. 19:28), and their names are engraved on the foundation stones of the holy city (Rev. 21:14).

Apostolic doctrine, however, originating as it does with the Holy Spirit, is the *common* witness of the apostles, not the perquisite of any individual. (For the common preaching, *cf.* C. H. Dodd, *The Apostolic Preaching and its Developments*, 1936; for the common use of the OT, C. H. Dodd, *According to the Scriptures*, 1952.) The chief apostle could by implication betray a fundamental principle he had accepted, and be withstood by a colleague (Gal. 2:11ff.).

The Synoptists, as already noted, view the incident of Mk. 6:7ff. and parallels as a miniature of the apostolic mission, and healing and exorcism, as well as preaching, were included. Healing, and other spectacular gifts, such as prophecy and tongues, are abundantly attested in the apostolic church, related, like the apostolic witness, to the special dispensation of the Holy Spirit; but they are strangely missing in the 2nd-century church, the writers of those days speaking of them as a thing in the past—in the apostolic age, in fact (*cf.* J. S. McEwan, *SJT* 7, 1954, pp. 133ff.; B. B. Warfield, *Miracles Yesterday and Today*, 1953). Even in the NT, we see no signs of these gifts except where apostles have been at work. Even where there has previously been genuine faith, it is only in the presence of apostles that these gifts of the Spirit are showered down (Acts 8:14ff.; 19:6—the contexts show that visual and audible phenomena are in question).

By contrast, the NT has less to say than might be expected of the apostles as ruling the church. They are the touchstones of doctrine, the purveyors of the authentic * tradition about Christ: apostolic delegates visit congregations which reflect new departures for the church (Acts 8:14ff.; 11:22ff.). But the Twelve did not appoint the Seven; the crucial Jerusalem Council consisted of a large number of elders as well as the apostles (Acts 15:6; *cf.* 12, 22): and two apostles served among the 'prophets and teachers' of the church at Antioch (Acts 13:1). Government was a distinct gift (1 Cor. 12:28), normally exercised by local elders: apostles were, by virtue of their commission, mobile. Nor are they even prominent in the administration of the sacraments (*cf.* 1 Cor. 1:14). The identity of function which some see between apostle and 2nd-century bishop (*cf.* K. E. Kirk in *The Apostolic Ministry*, p. 10) is by no means obvious.

c. Qualifications

It is obvious that the essential qualification of an apostle is the divine call, the commissioning by Christ. In the case of the Twelve, this was given during his earthly ministry. But with Matthias, the sense of the divine commissioning is not less evident: God has already chosen the apostle (Acts 1:24), even though his choice is not yet known. No laying on of hands is mentioned. The apostle, it is assumed, will be someone who has been a disciple of Jesus from the time of John's baptism ('the beginning of the gospel') to the ascension. He will be someone acquainted with the whole course of the ministry and work of Jesus (Acts 1:21–22). And, of course, he must be specifically a witness of the resurrection.

Paul equally insists on his direct commission from Christ (Rom. 1:1; 1 Cor. 1:1; Gal. 1:1, 15ff.). He in no sense derived his authority from the other apostles; like Matthias, he was accepted, not appointed by them. He did not fulfil the qualifications of Acts 1:21f., but the Damascus road experience was a resurrection appearance (*cf.* 1 Cor. 15:8), and he could claim to have 'seen the Lord' (1 Cor. 9:1); he was thus a witness of the resurrection. He remained conscious that his background—an enemy and persecutor, rather than a disciple—was different from that of the other apostles, but he counts himself with their number and associates them with his own gospel (1 Cor. 15:8–11).

■ **APOSTOLIC FATHERS**
See Patristic literature, Part 3.

■ **APPAREL**
See Vesture, Part 3.

d. The number of the apostles

'The Twelve' is a regular designation of the apostles in the Gospels, and Paul uses it in 1 Cor. 15:5. Its symbolic appropriateness is obvious, and recurs in such places as Rev. 21:14. The whole Matthias incident is concerned with making up the number of the Twelve. Yet Paul's consciousness of apostleship is equally clear. Further, there are instances in the NT where, *prima facie*, others outside the Twelve seem to be given the title. James the Lord's brother appears as such in Gal. 1:19; 2:9, and, though he was not a disciple (*cf.* Jn. 7:5), received a resurrection appearance personal to himself (1 Cor. 15:7). Barnabas is called an apostle in Acts 14:4, 14, and is introduced by Paul into an argument which denies any qualitative difference between his own apostleship and that of the Twelve (1 Cor. 9:1–6). The unknown *Andronicus and Junias are probably called apostles in Rom. 16:7, and Paul, always careful with his personal pronouns, may so style Silas in 1 Thes. 2:6. Paul's enemies in Corinth evidently claim to be 'apostles of Christ' (2 Cor. 11:13).

On the other hand, some have argued strongly for the limitation of the title to Paul and the Twelve (*cf.*, *e.g.*, Geldenhuys, pp. 71ff.). This involves giving a subordinate sense ('accredited messengers of the church') to 'apostles' in Acts 14:14 and Rom. 16:7, and explaining otherwise Paul's language about James and Barnabas. Some have introduced more desperate expedients, suggesting that James replaced James bar-Zebedee as Matthias replaced Judas, or that Matthias was mistakenly hurried into the place which God intended for Paul. Of such ideas there is not the remotest hint in the NT. However it may be explained, it seems safest to allow that there *were*, at an early date, apostles outside the Twelve. Paul's own apostleship makes such a breach in any more restrictive theory that there is room for others of God's appointment to pass with him. A hint of this may be given in the distinction between 'the Twelve' and 'all the apostles' in 1 Cor. 15:5, 7. But everything suggests that an apostle was a witness of the resurrection, and the resurrection appearance to Paul was clearly exceptional. Whether, as old writers suggested, some who are later called 'apostles' belonged to the Seventy sent out by the Lord (Lk. 10:1ff.), is another matter. The special significance of the Twelve for the first establishment of the church is beyond question.

e. Canonicity and continuity

Implied in apostleship is the commission to witness by word and sign to the risen Christ and his completed work. This witness, being grounded in a unique experience of the incarnate Christ, and directed by a special dispensation of the Holy Spirit, provides the authentic interpretation of Christ, and has ever since been determinative for the universal church. In the nature of things, the office could not be repeated or transmitted: any more than the underlying historic experiences could be transmitted to those who had never known the incarnate Lord, or received a resurrection appearance. The origins of the Christian ministry and the succession in the Jerusalem church are beyond the scope of this article; but, while the NT shows the apostles taking care that a local ministry is provided, there is no hint of the transmission of the peculiar apostolic functions to any part of that ministry.

Nor was such transmission necessary. The apostolic witness was maintained in the abiding work of the apostles and in what became normative for later ages, its written form in the NT (see Geldenhuys, pp. 100ff.; O. Cullmann, 'The Tradition', in *The Early Church*, 1956). No renewal of the office or of its special gifts has been called for. It was a foundational office: and church history ever since has been its superstructure. (*Bishop; *Tradition.)

Bibliography. K. H. Rengstorf, *TDNT* 1, pp. 398–447; J. B. Lightfoot, *Galatians*, pp. 92ff.; K. Lake in *BC*, 5, pp. 37ff.; K. E. Kirk (ed.), *The Apostolic Ministry*², 1957, especially essays 1 and 3; A. Ehrhardt, *The Apostolic Succession*, 1953 (see ch. 1 for a trenchant criticism of Kirk); J. N. Geldenhuys, *Supreme Authority*, 1953; W. Schneemelcher, *etc.*, 'Apostle and Apostolic', in *New Testament Apocrypha*, ed. E. Hennecke, W. Schneemelcher, R. McL. Wilson, 1, 1965, pp. 25–87; C. K. Barrett, *The Signs of an Apostle*, 1970; R. Schnackenburg, 'Apostles before and during Paul's time', in *Apostolic History and the Gospel*, ed. W. W. Gasque and R. P. Martin, 1970, pp. 287–303; W. Schmithals, *The Office of Apostle in the Early Church*, 1971; J. A. Kirk, 'Apostleship since Rengstorf: Towards a Synthesis', *NTS* 21, 1974–5, pp. 249–264; D. Müller, C. Brown, *NIDNTT* 1, pp. 126–137. A.F.W.

APPEAL TO CAESAR. When *Festus succeeded *Felix as Roman procurator of Judaea in AD 59 (Acts 24:27) and re-opened Paul's case, which Felix had left unsettled, Paul soon had reason to fear that the new governor's inexperience might be exploited by the high priest to his own disadvantage. Accordingly, he availed himself of his privilege as a Roman citizen and 'appealed to Caesar'—*i.e.* appealed for the transfer of his case from the provincial court to the supreme tribunal in Rome (Acts 25:10f.).

The citizen's right of appeal (*prouocatio*) to the emperor appears to have developed from the earlier right of appeal in republican times to the sovereign Roman people. According to Dio Cassius (*Hist.* 51. 19), Octavian in 30 BC was granted the right to judge on appeal. It was in this period, too, that the *lex Iulia de ui publica* (Julian law on the public use of force) was enacted, which forbade any magistrate vested with *imperium* or *potestas* to kill, scourge, chain or torture a Roman citizen, or to sentence him *aduersus prouocationem* ('in the face of an appeal') or prevent him from going to Rome to lodge his appeal there within a fixed time. A. H. M. Jones (*Studies in Roman Government and Law*, 1960, p. 96) concluded that, from the date of this enactment, a Roman citizen anywhere in the empire was protected against summary magisterial punishment (*coercitio*), although the provincial magistrate might deal with cases which involved a plain breach of established statute law (which Paul's case manifestly did not). By the beginning of the 2nd century AD it evidently became the regular practice for Roman citizens in the provinces, charged with offences *extra ordinem* (not covered by the standard code of procedure), to be sent to Rome almost automatically, without going through the formality of appealing to Caesar. In this, as in many other respects, the picture of Roman practice given in Acts is true to the dramatic date of the book; the case of Paul's appeal fits in with what we know of conditions in the late fifties of the 1st Christian century, and Luke's account of it is a substantial contribution to the available evidence.

It was with some relief that Festus heard Paul's appeal to Caesar: he himself would now be quit of the responsibility of adjudicating in a case where he knew himself to be out of his depth. One responsibility remained, however: he had to send to Rome along with the accused man an explanatory statement (*litterae dimissoriae*) outlining the nature of the case and its history to date. In drafting this statement he was glad to have the timely aid of one who was reputed to be an expert in Jewish religious affairs, the younger Agrippa, who came to Caesarea about this time with his sister Bernice to greet the emperor's new representative.

After the normal exchange of courtesies, Festus acquainted Agrippa with his problem. The charges against Paul, he said, seemed to revolve around 'one Jesus, who was dead, but whom Paul asserted to be alive' (Acts 25:19). Agrippa's interest was immediately aroused and he expressed a desire to meet Paul. Festus was only too glad to arrange an interview. After listening to Paul, Agrippa agreed with Festus that he could not reasonably be convicted on any of the serious charges brought against him. Indeed, said the king, Paul might have been discharged on the spot had he not appealed to Caesar, but for Festus to prejudge the issue now by releasing him would have been *ultra vires* (Acts 26:30–32). But Agrippa presumably gave Festus the help he required in drafting the *litterae dimissoriae*.

Paul did not appeal to Caesar while Felix was in office, presumably because Felix had virtually decided on his innocence and was simply postponing his formal acquittal and release. One day (Paul might have hoped) Felix's procrastination would come to an end and Paul would be discharged and be able to carry out his long-cherished plan of travelling to Rome and the West. But with the recall of Felix and his supersession by Festus a new and dangerous situation was developing for Paul; hence his decision to appeal.

The uppermost consideration in Paul's appeal to Caesar was not his own safety, but the interests of the gospel. 7 or 8 years previously he had experienced the benevolent neutrality of Roman law in the tacit decision of *Gallio, proconsul of Achaia, that there was nothing illegal in his preaching (Acts 18:12–16). He might reasonably expect a similarly favourable verdict from the supreme court in Rome. Not only so: even a man of smaller intelligence than Paul must have realized that the consideration which moved Gallio would not be valid much longer. Gallio had ruled in effect that what Paul preached was a variety of Judaism, and therefore not forbidden by Roman law. But, thanks in large measure to Paul's own activity, it would soon be impossible to regard Christianity as a variety of Judaism, since it was now manifestly more Gentile than Jewish. A favourable hearing from the emperor in Rome might win recognition for Christianity, if not as the true fulfilment of Israel's ancestral religion (which Paul believed it to be), at least as a permitted association (*collegium licitum*, or group of *collegia licita*) in its own right. Besides, if Caesar in person heard Paul's defence, what might the outcome not be? The younger Agrippa had politely declined to admit the logic of Paul's argument, but Gentiles had regularly shown themselves more amenable to the gospel than Jews, and a Roman emperor might be more easily won than a Jewish client-king. It would be precarious to set limits to Paul's high hopes, however impracticable they may appear to us in retrospect.

But the fact that it was to Caesar that Paul appealed does not necessarily mean that Caesar would hear the case personally. According to Tacitus (*Annals* 13. 4. 2), Nero announced at the beginning of his principate that he would not judge cases *in propria persona*, as his predecessor Claudius had done; and indeed, during his first 8 years he generally delegated them to others. Thus, 'if Paul came to trial some time after the period of 2 years mentioned in Acts 28:30, it is probable that his case was heard by someone other than the Princeps' (A. N. Sherwin-White, *Roman Society and Roman Law in the New Testament*, 1963, p. 366). This 'someone other' might be the prefect of the praetorian guard, 'representing the Emperor in his capacity as the fountain of justice, together with the assessors and high officers of the court' (W. M. Ramsay, *SPT*, p. 357). But this is a matter on which we have no information.

Neither have we any information on the outcome of the appeal—whether Paul was heard and condemned, or heard and acquitted. We do not even know whether his appeal was ever heard. The prolongation of his stay in Rome over 2 full years could have been due to congestion of court business as much as anything else; and if indeed he was discharged without coming to trial, this would probably have been the result of an act of *imperium* on Caesar's part. 'Perhaps Paul benefited from the clemency of Nero, and secured a merely casual release. But there is no necessity to construe Acts to mean that he was released at all' (A. N. Sherwin-White, *op. cit.*, p. 109). By the account of Paul's night vision at sea, in which he was assured that he would stand before Caesar (Acts 27:23f.), Luke probably implies that Paul's appeal did at length come up for hearing, whatever the outcome was.

BIBLIOGRAPHY. H. J. Cadbury, 'Roman Law and the Trial of Paul', *BC* 5, pp. 297ff.; A. H. M. Jones, *Studies in Roman Government and Law*, 1960; T. Mommsen, *Römisches Strafrecht*, 1899; A. N. Sherwin-White, *Roman Society and Roman Law in the New Testament*, 1963; *idem*, *The Roman Citizenship*², 1973. F.F.B.

APPHIA. Addressed in Phm. 2 in a manner suggesting that she was Philemon's wife, and hostess to the Colossian church (but see *PHILEMON, EPISTLE to). RSV's text 'our sister' is probably to be preferred to AV's 'our beloved'. The name was common in W Asia and is probably native Phrygian. (See examples in Lightfoot, *Colossians*, p. 304, *MM*, and the Colossian inscription, *CIG*, 3, 4380K, 3.) A.F.W.

APPLE
See Trees, Part 3.

APRICOT
See Trees (Apple), Part 3.

AQUAMARINE
See Jewels, Part 2.

AQUILA AND PRISCA, PRISCILLA. A Jewish leather-worker (RSV 'tent-maker', Acts 18:3) and his wife, staunch friends of Paul. Aquila came from Pontus, but the couple were in Rome when Claudius' edict of *c.* AD 49 expelled all Jews from the city. Obscure words of Suetonius (*Claudius* 25. 4) suggest that the purge followed disturbances in the Roman Jewish community over Christianity, and there is every likelihood that Aquila and Prisca were already Christians on meeting Paul in Corinth. He stayed with them and shared in

A dry wadi (river-bed) in the Arabah. (FNH)

Rom. 16:3 shows how widely this peripatetic and ever-hospitable Jewish couple were known and loved in the Gentile churches, and the temptation to fill in the blanks in our knowledge about them has proved irresistible. The curious fact that Prisca is usually named first has been interpreted as indicating that she was a Roman lady of higher rank than her husband (*cf.* Ramsay, *CBP*, 1, p. 637, for a contemporary analogy), or that she was more prominent in the church. The true reason is undiscoverable. Attempts have been made to trace their final return to Rome (*cf.* Sanday and Headlam, *Romans*, pp. 418ff., for archaeological data), or even Pontus, or to show that Aquila was a member or freedman of the *gens Pontia* or the *gens Acilia.* While some are attractive, none is conclusive; and still less is Harnack's attribution to the couple, with the lady in the lead, of the Epistle to the Hebrews.

their craft (Acts 18:1–3; an inferior reading in v. 7 adds that Paul left them after the split in the synagogue). It was doubtless in this period that they endangered their lives for his sake (Rom. 16:3); perhaps, too, they turned the apostle's mind to the needs and opportunities of Rome.

When Paul left, they accompanied him as far as Ephesus, where they received and assisted to a fuller faith the very influential *Apollos (Acts 18:18–28). They were still at Ephesus, and a church was meeting in their house, when 1 Cor. was written, and they had not forgotten their Corinthian friends (1 Cor. 16:19—a gloss claims that Paul was again their guest). Not long afterwards, perhaps taking advantage of relaxations towards Jews after Claudius' death, they seem to be back in Rome (Rom. 16:3). Since 2 Tim. 4:19 evidently indicates a renewal of the Ephesian residence, the references to the couple have been a primary argument for regarding Rom. 16 as a separate letter to Ephesus (*cf.* especially K. Lake, *EEP*, pp. 327ff.); but the force of it is much reduced by the obvious propensity of Aquila and Prisca for travel.

Aquila's name is attested in Pontus (*cf. MM*)—his namesake, the translator, also came from there. The best MSS indicate that Paul uses the proper form, Prisca, for the lady, Luke, characteristically, the diminutive, Priscilla.

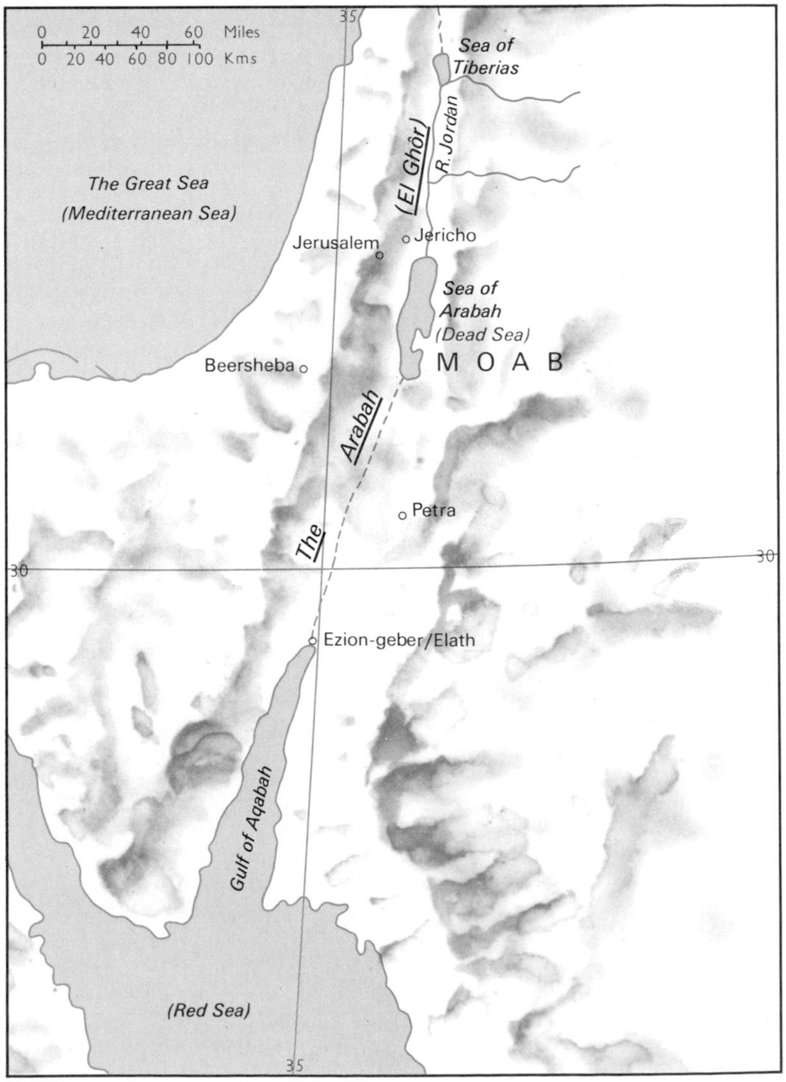

The Arabah; the rift valley running from the Sea of Tiberias to the Gulf of Aqabah.

BIBLIOGRAPHY. A. Harnack, *ZNW* 1, 1900, pp. 16ff.; Ramsay, *SPT*, pp. 241, 253ff. A.F.W.

AR. The chief city of Moab, E of the Dead Sea near the Arnon river (site unknown). Something of the early history of the city was known to the Hebrews from records in the Book of the Wars of the Lord (Nu. 21:15), and popular proverbs (Nu. 21:28). Isaiah appears to have had access to similar sources (Is. 15:1). In the later stages of the wilderness wanderings the Hebrews were forbidden to dispossess the Moabite inhabitants of the city and settle there themselves, for this was not the land which the Lord their God had given them. (Dt. 2:9, 18, 29; LXX 'Seir'.) R.J.W.

ARABAH (Heb. *ᵃrāḇâ*). In the AV the word is used only once in its original form (Jos. 18:18), although it is of frequent occurrence in the Hebrew text.

1. The root *rb*, meaning 'dry', 'burnt up' and therefore 'waste land', is used to describe the desert steppe (Jb. 24:5; 39:6; Is. 33:9; 35:1, 6; Je. 51:43; RSV usually translates as 'wilderness' or 'desert').

2. Used with the article (*hā-ᵃrāḇâ*), the name is applied generally to the rift valley which runs from the Sea of Tiberias to the Gulf of Aqabah. Although the topographical significance of this word was ignored by the earlier commentators, it has a precise connotation in many OT references. Its location is connected with the lake of Tiberias (Dt. 3:17; Jos. 11:2; 12:3) and as far S as the Red Sea and Elath (Dt. 1:1; 2:8). The Dead Sea is called the Sea of Arabah (Jos. 3:16; 12:3; Dt. 4:49; 2 Ki. 14:25). Today, the valley of the Jordan downstream to the Dead Sea is called the Ghôr, the 'depression', and the Arabah more properly begins S of the Scorpion cliffs and terminates in the Gulf of Aqabah. For its physical features see *JORDAN.

3. The plural of the same word, 'Araboth, without the article, is used in its primary meaning to describe certain waste areas within the Arabah, especially around Jericho (Jos. 5:10, RSV 'plains'; 2 Ki. 25:5; Je. 39:5, RSV 'plains'), and the wilderness of Moab. The Araboth Moab ('plains of Moab', RSV) is plainly distinguished from the pastoral and cultivated lands of the plateaux above the Rift Valley, the Sede-Moab (see Nu. 22:1; 26:3, 63; 31:12; 33:48–50; Dt. 34:1, 8; Jos. 4:13; 5:10, *etc.*).

4. Beth-arabah (the house of Arabah) refers to a settlement situated near Ain el-Gharba (Jos. 15:6, 61; 18:22).

BIBLIOGRAPHY. D. Baly, *Geography of the Bible*², 1974, pp. 191–209. J.M.H.

ARABIA.

I. In the Old Testament

a. Geography

In structure the Arabian peninsula consists of a mass of old crystalline rock which forms a range of mountains on the W, rising above 3,000 m in places, with a series of strata of younger formation uptilted against its E side. In the W mountains, and particularly in the SW corner of the peninsula, where the annual rainfall exceeds 500 mm in parts, settled life based on irrigation is possible, and it was in this area, the modern Yemen Arab Republic and the People's Democratic Republic of Yemen, that the ancient kingdoms of S Arabia chiefly flourished. The capitals of three of these, Qarnāwu (of Maʿīn), Mārib (of Saba') and Timnaʿ (of Qatabān), were situated on the E slopes of the mountain range, on watercourses running off to the E, and Shabwa the capital of Ḥaḍramaut lay farther to the SE on a watercourse running NW off the Ḥaḍramaut table-land. An area of rainfall of 100–250 mm extends N along the W mountains and E along the coast, and here settled life is also possible. In the whole of the rest of the peninsula the annual rainfall is negligible and life depends upon oases and wells.

Between the escarpments formed by the uptilted strata and the E coast the scarp slope of the uppermost provides level areas ranging from steppe to sandy desert. The zones of desert which exist in this area and between the central escarpments widen out in the S into the barren sand desert of al-Rubʿ al-Ḫāli ('the empty quarter'), and in the N to the smaller desert of al-Nafud. At various points along the foot of the escarpments springs provide oases, and consequent trade routes. Apart from the areas of sandy and rocky desert, the terrain of the peninsula is largely steppe, yielding grass under the sporadic annual rains, and supporting a poor nomadic population (*NOMADS), particularly in the N area between Syria and Mesopotamia. It was where this zone graded into the settled areas of Syria that such metropolises as Petra, Palmyra and Damascus flourished.

b. Exploration

The first notable European explorer in the Arabian peninsula was the Danish orientalist, Carsten Niebuhr, who visited the Yemen in 1763. In the N, J. L. Burckhardt rediscovered Petra in 1812, but interest was focused on the S when J. R. Wellsted published in 1837 the first S Arabian inscriptions to be seen in Europe, an event which led to their decipherment in 1841 by W. Gesenius and E. Rödiger. These inscriptions were known as 'Ḥimyaritic', from the name of the kingdom which dominated the whole of the SW of the peninsula in the last centuries BC, and was therefore considered by later historians to be the source of the inscriptions, though in fact they stemmed from the earlier kingdoms. Some thousands of these inscriptions are now known, chiefly as a result of the explorations of J. Halévy and E. Glaser in the second half of the last century, but also from numerous individual explorers, and recently from the investigations of the American Foundation for the Study of Man in Aden and the Yemen. Excavations in S Arabia have been few. In 1928 C. Rathjens and H. v. Wissmann excavated at Ḥugga near Sanʿâ in the Yemen, and in 1937–8 Miss G. Caton Thompson uncovered a temple of the moon god (*syn*) at Ḥureyḍa in the Ḥaḍramaut. Since World War II the American Foundation for the Study of Man has excavated at Timnaʿ and surrounding sites (1950–1), at Mārib, where the temple of the Sabaean moon god *'lmqh* was uncovered (1952), and in subsequent expeditions in Oman. More recently a French expedition has worked at Shabwa.

Many explorations have been made in other parts of Arabia, notable among which are those of the Czech orientalist A. Musil, who travelled extensively in central and N Arabia (1909–14), those of N. Glueck, who made exhaustive surveys in Transjordan and Sinai (1932–71), and those of G. Ryckmans and H. St J. Philby, who collected some thousands of Arabic inscriptions from Sa'udi Arabia in 1951–2, not to mention the travels on a lesser scale of such men as Burton, Hurgronje, Doughty, Rutter and Thomas. Important among inscriptions from the N is the Taima' Stone, which bears an Aramaic inscription of about the 5th century BC, obtained by Huber in 1883 (*TEMA).

c. History and civilization

Apart from the *nomads of the steppe lands of Arabia, whose life has continued with little change for millennia, the main areas of historical civilization were in the SW corner of the peninsula, and in the zone to the N where the steppe merges into the settled regions of Syria.

In the 2nd millennium BC various Semitic-speaking tribes arrived from the N in the area of modern Yemen and W Aden, and formed the settlements which were later to emerge as the kingdoms of Saba' (*SHEBA, 7), Ma'īn (*MINAEANS), Qatabān and Ḥaḍramaut (Hazarmaveth, Gn. 10:26). The main cause of their prosperity was their intermediate position on the trade routes from the frankincense lands of the S coast and Ethiopia (*HERBS, Frankincense), to the civilizations in the N. The first of these kingdoms to emerge was Saba', as revealed by the appearance in the 8th century of native inscriptions which indicate a well-organized polity under a ruler (*mkrb*) who evidently combined certain priestly functions in his office. Its prosperity is indicated by the fact that it paid tribute to Sargon and Sennacherib. In *c.* 400 BC the neighbouring kingdom of Ma'īn came into prominence and infringed on much of Sabaean authority. In the 4th century the monarchy was founded at Qatabān, and in the last quarter of the 1st millennium the dominion of Saba', Ma'īn, Qatabān and Ḥaḍramaut fluctuated with turn of fortune, until the area came under the control of the Ḥimyarites. At their height, the S Arabian kingdoms had colonies as far afield as N Arabia, and inscriptions in their characters have been found on the Persian Gulf and in Mesopotamia (Ur, Uruk). The alphabets of the Thamūdic, Liḥyānite and Ṣafāitic inscriptions also show their influence in the N, and the Ethiopic language and script offer similar evidence from Africa.

In the N the history is one of the contacts made by nomads with the settled civilizations of Mesopotamia and Syria. In Transjordan the process of infiltration and settlement is evident, thoough there were periods when this was very sparse. In the early part of the Middle Bronze Age the whole of Transjordan was dotted with settlements (*ABRAHAM), but this was followed by a barren period, *c.* 1900–1300 BC, until settlement was increased

Two Arabs, mounted on a camel, flee from pursuing Assyrians, while a third lies dead. Part of a relief illustrating the desert campaign of Ashurbanipal, from the king's palace at Nineveh. c. 640 BC. (BM)

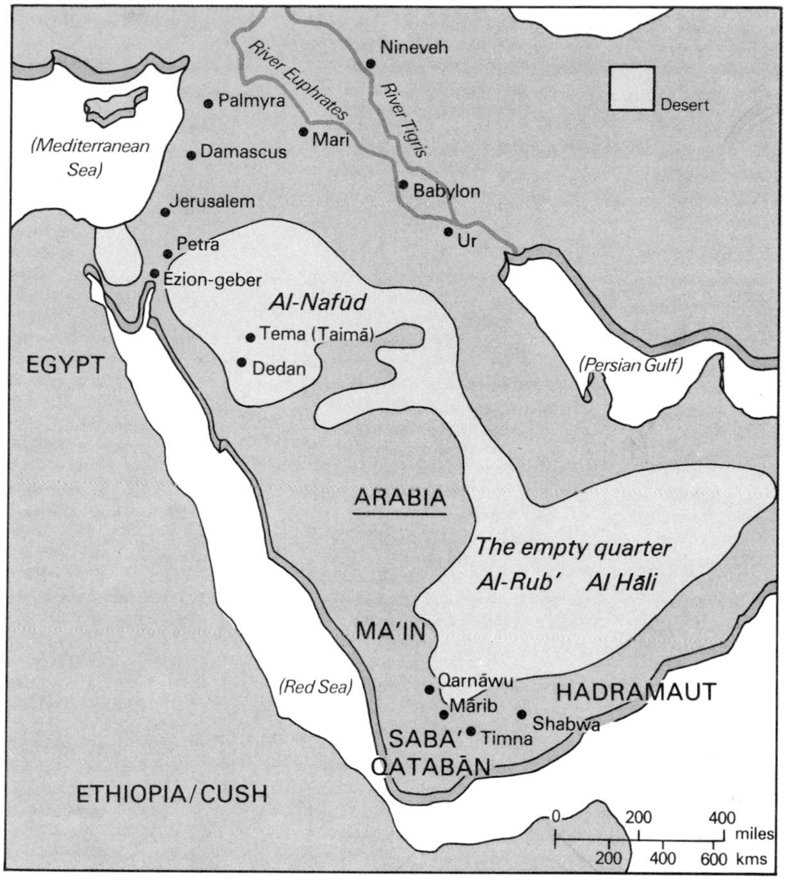

Ancient Arabia.

again in the 13th century. The name 'Arab' first appears in the contemporary inscriptions in the annals of Shalmaneser III, when one Gindibu ([*m*]*gin-in-di-bu-'* [*mât*]*ar-ba-a-a*; Kurkh Stele 2. 94) fought against him at Qarqar (853 BC), and thereafter they frequently appear in the Assyrian inscriptions as camel-borne raiding nomads, and they are so depicted in the bas-reliefs of Ashurbanipal at Nineveh (*CAMEL). One of the unusual episodes in Mesopotamian history was the sojourn of Nabonidus, king of Babylon (556–539 BC) at Taima' (*TEMA) in the N. He stayed there for 10 years while his son Bel-šar-uṣur (*BELSHAZZAR) ruled for him in Babylon.

In the latter part of the 4th century BC the Aramaic-speaking Arab kingdom of the *Nabataeans, with its capital at Petra, began to emerge, and it flourished as a trading state from the 2nd century until well into the Roman period. Farther S in the same period the Liḥyānite kingdom of *Dedan was formed by Arabs settling at an ancient Minaean colony. In the 1st century BC another Arab state, which adopted Aramaic as its official language, began to come to prominence at Palmyra (*TADMOR), and in the Christian era it largely eclipsed Petra as a trading state, and became a serious rival to Rome.

d. Biblical references

Arabia is not often referred to by this name in the Bible, since its inhabitants were generally known by the political or tribal names of the smaller groups to which they belonged. The Table of the *Nations in Gn. 10 lists a number of S Arabian peoples as the descendants of *Joktan and of *Cush. A number of mainly N Arabian tribes are listed as being descendants of Abraham through *Keturah and *Hagar (Gn. 25). Again among the descendants of Esau (Gn. 36) a number of Arabian peoples are mentioned. In the time of Jacob two groups of Abraham's descendants, the Ishmaelites (*ISHMAEL) and the *Midianites, are found as caravan merchants (Gn. 37:25–36; *NOMADS). It is, however, in the time of Solomon that contacts with Arabia become prominent in the OT narrative, mainly as a result of his extensive trade relations, particularly from his port of Ezion-geber on the Red Sea. This is emphasized by the famous visit of the Queen of *Sheba (1 Ki. 9:26–28; 10), and nearer home by the tribute he received from the *malᵉḵê ᵃraḇ* (2 Ch. 9:14) which the EVV render 'kings of Arabia'. The name *ᵃrāḇ*, *ᵃrāḇî* seems to have originally meant 'desert' or 'steppe' and by extension 'steppe dweller', and therefore in the biblical context it referred chiefly to those people who occupied the semi-desert areas to the E and S of Palestine (*EAST, CHILDREN OF). It is not possible, however, to say whether the word is always to be taken as a proper name 'Arab', or as a collective noun 'steppe dweller'. The matter is further complicated by the fact that there is an etymologically distinct root *'rb*, 'to intermix', one of whose forms is vocalized *'ēreḇ*, which is taken in some contexts to mean 'mixed multitude'. Indeed, this is the form that occurs in 1 Ki. 10:15, the parallel passage to 2 Ch. 9:14, the distinction depending entirely upon the Massoretic vocalization. Each occurrence of the word has therefore to be judged from its context rather than its form, and in this case there is no reason why it should not be taken as 'Arabia', or perhaps better 'Arabs'.

In the 9th century, Jehoshaphat of Judah received tribute from the '*ᵃrāḇî* (2 Ch. 7:11), but his successor Jehoram suffered a raid in which the '*ᵃ rāḇî* carried off his wives and sons (2 Ch. 21:16–17), and only Ahaziah, the youngest, was left (2 Ch. 22:1). In the 8th century Uzziah reversed the situation and restored *Elath to his dominion (2Ki. 14:22).

Though the S Arabian kingdoms were known (*e.g.* Joel 3:8), most of the contacts of Israel with Arabia were with the nomadic tribes of the N. In the time of Hezekiah these people were very familiar (Is. 13:20; 21:13), and some even served as mercenaries in the defence of Jerusalem against Sennacherib ([*amêl*]*ur-bi*; Taylor Prism 3. 31). In the time of Josiah (Je. 3:2), and in the closing days of the kingdom of Judah, the Arabians were coming to prominence as traders (Je. 25:23–24; Ezk. 27; *KEDAR).

The growing tendency of the Arabs to settle and build trading centres is illustrated by *Geshem, the Arab who tried to hinder Nehemiah rebuilding Jerusalem (Ne. 2:19; 6:1), presumably because he feared trade rivals. The kingdom of the Nabataeans was to follow, and in the Apocrypha the term 'Arab' usually refers to these people (1 Macc. 5:39; 2 Macc. 5:8), and indeed the 'Arabian' desert to which Paul retired (Gal. 1:17) was probably part of the Nabataean dominion.

BIBLIOGRAPHY. (*a*) General: J. Bright, *A History of Israel*[2], 1972; I. Eph'al, *JAOS* 94, 1974, pp. 108–115; W. C. Brice, *South-West Asia*, 1966, pp. 246–276; W. B. Fisher, *The Middle East. A . . . Geography*[6], 1971, pp. 441–478; H. Field, *Ancient and Modern Man in South-western Asia*, 1956, pp. 97–124, and folding pocket map; P. K. Hitti, *History of the Arabs*[6], 1956, pp. 1–86; J. A. Montgomery, *Arabia and the Bible*, 1934, reprinted 1969 with introduction by G. W. van Beek; A. Grohmann, *Arabien*, 1963; G. W. van Beek in G. E. Wright (ed.), *The Bible and the Ancient Near East*, 1961, pp. 229–248; A. K. Irvine in *POTT*, pp. 287–311; S. Moscati, *Ancient Semitic Civilizations*, 1957, pp. 181–207, 243; *The Semites in Ancient History*, 1959, pp. 104–132; G. Ryckmans, *Les religions arabes préislamiques*, 1951.

(*b*) S Arabia: A. F. L. Beeston, *A Descriptive Grammar of Epigraphic South Arabian*, 1962; B. Doe, *Southern Arabia*, 1971; on the American excavations in S Arabia, R. le B. Bowen and F. P. Albright, *Archaeological Discoveries in South Arabia*, 1958; and a number of other volumes published for the American Foundation for the Study of Man by the Johns Hopkins Press, Baltimore; R. L. Cleveland, *An Ancient South Arabian Necropolis*, 1965.

(*c*) N Arabia: W. Wright, *A Grammar of the Arabic Language*[3], rev. by W. R. Smith and M. J. de Goeje, 1896; A. Musil, *Oriental Explorations and Studies*, 1–6, 1926–8; N. Glueck, *Explorations in Eastern Palestine*, I–IV (*AASOR* 14, 15, 18, 19, 25, 28), 1934–51; and more popular accounts—*The Other Side of the Jordan*[2], 1970; *The River Jordan*, 1946; and *Rivers in the Desert*, 1959; see also *BA* 22, 1959, pp. 98–108; B. Dee, *Southern Arabia*, 1977; F. V. Winnett and W. L. Reed, *Ancient Records from North Arabia*, 1970; on Tema, see R. P. Dougherty, *Nabonidus and Belshazzar*, 1929, pp. 105–166; C. J. Gadd, in *Anatolian Studies* 8, 1958, pp. 79–89. T.C.M.

II. In the New Testament

Arabia did not, as it does today, denote the whole of the great peninsula between the Red Sea and the Persian Gulf, but only the area to the immediate E and S of Palestine. This territory was occupied by an Arab tribe or tribes called the *Nabataeans, who had settled in the area during the 3rd century BC. By the 1st century they had established their control over an area which stretched from Damascus on the N to Gaza to the S and far into the desert to the E. Their capital was the red-rock city of Petra.

Arabia is mentioned only twice in the NT. Paul relates how, after his conversion, he went away into Arabia (Gal. 1:17). No other account of this incident occurs in the NT. The exact location of this event is very uncertain. Since Arabia to the Graeco-Roman mind meant the Nabataean kingdom, it is likely that he went there, possibly to Petra, the capital city. Why he went is not revealed. Perhaps his purpose was to be alone to commune with God. K. Lake suggests that Paul conducted a preaching mission there, because in the Epistle to the Galatians, where he mentions this incident, the antithesis is not between conferring with the Christians at Jerusalem and conferring with God in the desert, but between obeying immediately his commission to preach to the Gentiles and going to Jerusalem to obtain the authority to do this (*The Earlier Epistles of St Paul*, 1914, pp. 320f.).

In the only other occurrence of the word Arabia in the NT (Gal. 4:25) it is used in the narrower sense to denote the Sinai Peninsula, or the territory immediately to the E, across the Gulf of Aqabah.

BIBLIOGRAPHY. G. A. Smith, *The Historical Geography of the Holy Land*, 1931, pp. 547f., 649; *HDAC*; *IDB*; J. A. Montgomery, *Arabia and the Bible*, 1934. W.W.W.

Two stone incense-altars which stood at the entrance to the holy of holies in the temple at Arad. Late 9th cent. BC. (ZR)

ARAD. 1. A Canaanite town in the wilderness of Judah whose king vainly attacked Israel during the Wandering. Arad was destroyed, and renamed *Hormah (Nu. 21:1–3; 33:40). Jos. 12:14 lists a king of Arad and a king of Hormah amongst the conquered, while Jdg. 1:16f. tells of Kenites settling in the area, and of Judah and Simeon destroying Zephath, renamed Hormah. Now Tell Arad 30 km NE of Beersheba, excavated from 1962 to 1974 by Y. Aharoni and R. B. K. Amiran. A large fortified city existed in the Early Bronze Age (Lower City), then the site was deserted until Iron Age I, when a mound at one side was occupied. Here a fortress was built in the 10th century BC that was used until the 6th century. During several phases of remodelling a shrine with stone altars and pillars existed in one corner. Potsherds inscribed in Hebrew found there include the names of the priestly families Pashhur and Meremoth. More texts were recovered from other parts of the fort, dealing with military affairs and supplies in the troubled years about 600 BC. One mentions 'the house of YHWH'. Arad of the Late Bronze Age (Canaanite Arad) may have been the present Tell Malḥatah, 12 km to the SW. Two Arads, Arad Rabbat and Arad of Yeruham, were listed by * Shishak after his invasion. See *EAEHL*, 1, *s.v.*; and *K^{e}tuvot 'Arad*, 1975.

2. A Benjaminite, son of Beriah (1 Ch. 8:15–16). A.R.M.

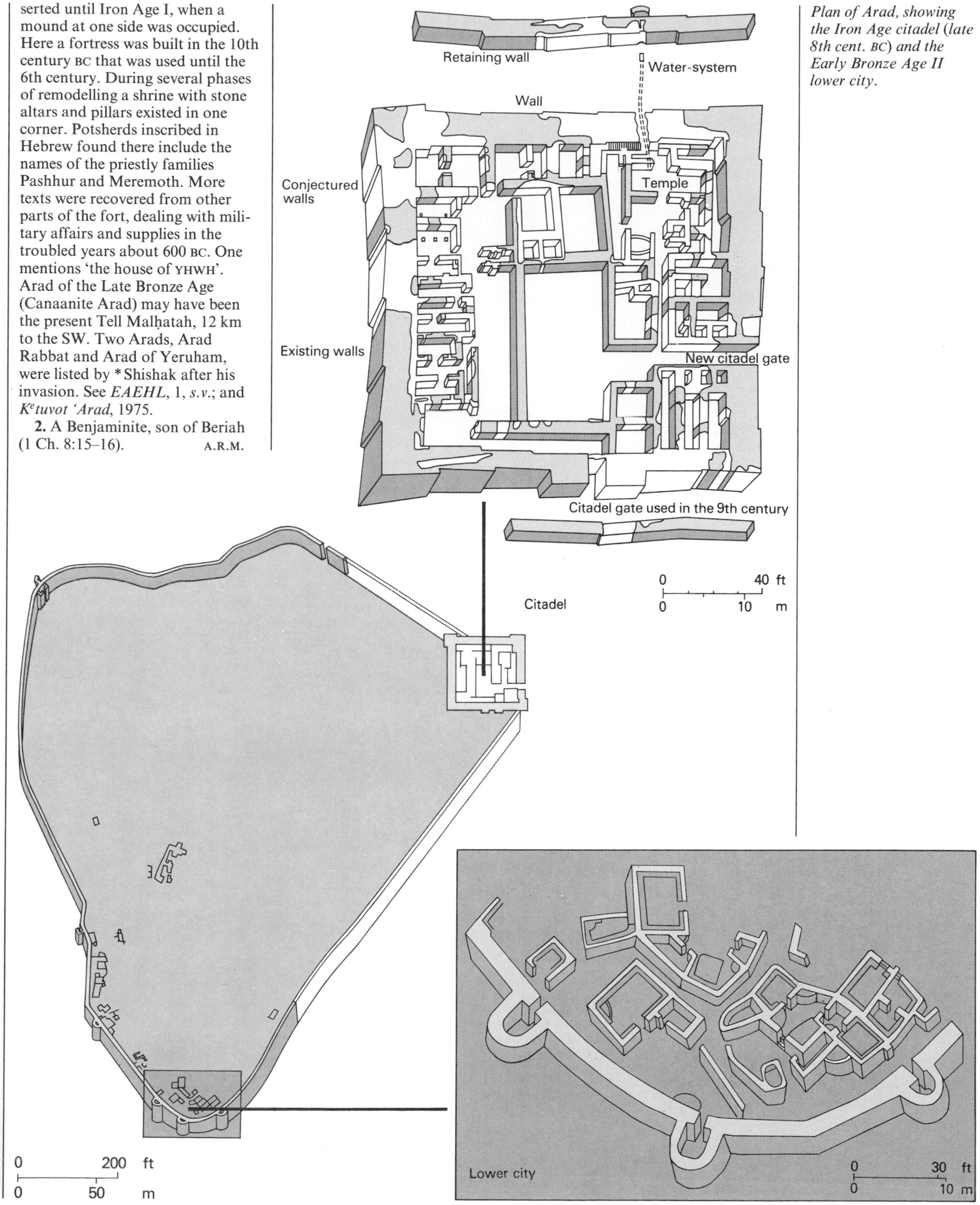

Plan of Arad, showing the Iron Age citadel (late 8th cent. BC) and the Early Bronze Age II lower city.

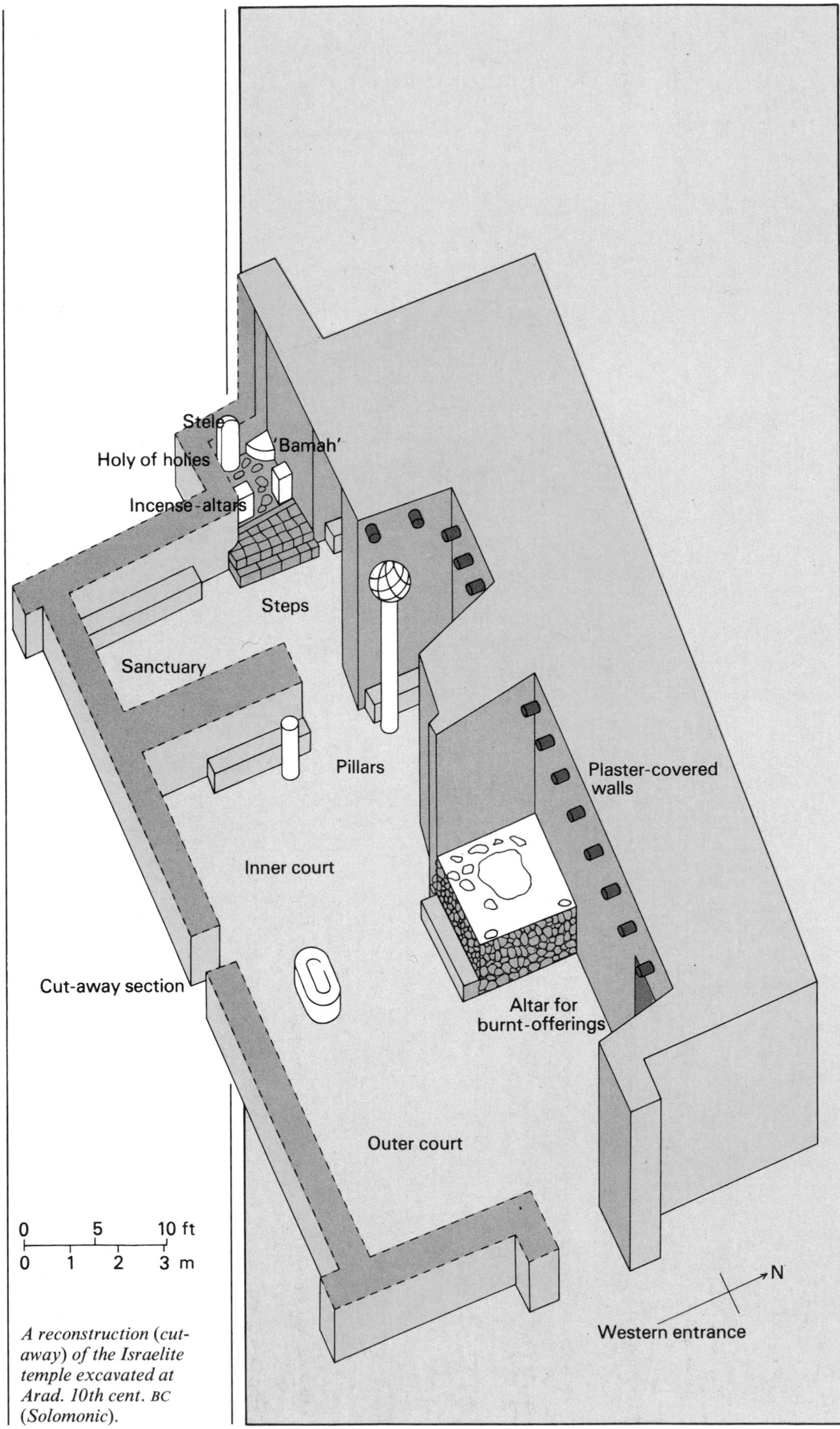

A reconstruction (cut-away) of the Israelite temple excavated at Arad. 10th cent. BC *(Solomonic).*

ARAM, ARAMAEANS.

I. Ancestral and personal

a. The son of Shem, so named with Elam, Assyria and others in Gn. 10:22–23 and 1 Ch. 1:17, having four others grouped under him. On this association of Aram with the E and NE parts of the ancient East, see section **II.***a*, below.

b. A personal name borne by individuals and heads of later clans in the patriarchal age and after, thus: Aram, grandson of Nahor, Abraham's brother (Gn. 22:21); an 'Aramitess' was mother of Machir by Manasseh (1 Ch. 7:14); another Aram is mentioned as a descendant of Asher (1 Ch. 7:34).
In the genealogies of Mt. 1:3–4 and Lk. 3:33 (AV) the name Aram is simply the misleading Gk. form of Ram (RSV), an entirely different name.

II. People, lands and language

a. Origins

Aram and Aramaeans are usually called 'Syria(ns)' in the English OT—a misleading appellation when applied to the period before *c.* 1000 BC. From the 3rd millennium BC, W Semitic-speaking semi-nomadic peoples are known from cuneiform sources to have been constantly infiltrating into Syria and Mesopotamia from almost the whole of the Arabian desert-fringe. In Mesopotamia under the kings of Akkad and of the 3rd Dynasty of Ur (*c.* 2400–2000 BC) these 'Westerners' (*MAR.TU* in Sumerian, *Amurru* in Babylonian) eventually penetrated right across the Tigris to the steppelands farther E, reaching the Iranian mountains. Evidence shows that they became well established there. (For a good discussion of this see J.-R. Kupper, *Les Nomades en Mésopotamie au Temps des Rois de Mari*, 1957, pp. 147f., 166, 177f., 196.) But these NE regions were no empty land. In the steppes and hills beyond, the Hurrians were at home, and the two populations doubtless mingled. These facts provide an illuminating background for the origins of the Aramaeans of biblical and external sources.

At this period mention is made of a settlement called Aram(e·i) in the E Tigris region N of Elam and ENE of Assyria. If this fact is linked with the presence of W Semitic-speaking settlers there, these may justifiably be considered as proto-Aramaeans. Kupper rejects this interpretation, but has apparently overlooked the importance of some OT passages here.

This association of the earliest 'Aramaeans' with the E and NE is evident in Gn. 10:22–23, where Aram, Elam and Assyria occur together—a mark of very early date. Am. 9:7 carries on this tradition in later times: God brought Israel from Egypt (S), the Philistines from Caphtor (W) and the Aramaeans from Qir (NE). Qir occurs only once more (Is. 22:6)—standing for Assyria-along with Elam, so Amos is in line with Gn. 10 and with the ascertainable NE occurrences of proto-Aramaeans. On the cuneiform evidence (but not using the biblical passages adduced here), these earliest Aramaeans were accepted by A. Dupont-Sommer, *VT Supp*. Vol. I, 1953, pp. 40–49; by S. Moscati, *The Semites in Ancient History*, 1959, pp. 66–67, and in earlier works; and by M. McNamara, *Verbum Domini* 35, 1957, pp. 129–142; but rejected (*e.g.*) by I. J. Gelb, *JCS* 15, 1961, p. 28, n. 5; D. O. Edzard, *Die zweite Zwischenzeit Babyloniens*, 1957, p. 43, n. 188.

Aramu is attested as a personal name in the 3rd Dynasty of Ur (*c.* 2000 BC) and at Mari (18th century BC); at Alalaḫ in N Syria about this time occurs the form Arammú for the doubled 'm' *cf.* the Heb. *'ᵉrammî*, 'Aramaean'. This corresponds with Aram as an OT personal name about that time. The name Aram may even be Hurrian; at Alalaḫ and at Nuzi appear a series of Hurrian-type names compounded with initial Aram- or Arim- (Kupper, *Nomades*, p. 113). 'Aram– may have been the name of a tribal group that first crossed the Tigris into the Hurrian regions, and its name has been applied by the Hurrians to all such W Semitic-speaking infiltrators and settlers (*cf.* Sumerian and Babylonian use of terms *MAR.TU* and *Amurru*, above)—hence its occurrence in place-names, or it might even have been a Hurrian epithet, which would better explain its occurrence in personal names. As the Hurrians spread right across upper Mesopotamia and into Syria by the beginning of the 2nd millennium, they would then perhaps use this term of the many W Semitic settlers in these regions—known from non-Hurrian cuneiform sources (*e.g.* Mari), Haneans, Suteans and others; but this remains wholly uncertain.

b. Early history, 19th–12th centuries BC

The Hebrew Patriarchs, after leaving Ur, first settled in this upper Mesopotamian area, at Harran (Gn. 11:28–32), in 'Aram-naharaim' (see below). One part of the family stayed on here (Nahor, Bethuel, Laban) as 'Aramaeans' (*i.e.*, named after the place where they lived), while the other (Abraham) went on to Canaan. But the wives of both Isaac and Jacob came from the Aramaean branch of the family (Gn. 24:28ff.), thoroughly justifying the later Israelite confession of descent from 'a wandering Aramaean' (= Jacob) in Dt. 26:5. The speech of Jacob's and Laban's families already showed dialectal differences ('Canaanite' and 'Aramaic'), see Gn. 31:47; note the early form of this Aramaic phrase, using direct (construct) genitive and not circumlocution with *dî*.

Aram-naharaim ('Aram of the two rivers') or Paddan-aram was basically the area within the great bend of the river Euphrates past Carchemish bounding it on the W, with the river Habur as limit in the E. In this area arose the Hurrian kingdom of Mitanni (16th–14th centuries BC). In the *Amarna Letters (*c.* 1360 BC) it is called *Naḫrima* with Canaanitic dual in 'm' (like Heb.), while in Egyptian texts of *c.* 1520–1170 BC appears the form *Nhrn*, clearly exhibiting an Aramaic-type dual in 'n', not assimilated to Canaanite as in the Amarna Letters. The form in Egyptian is clear evidence—deriving directly from Egyptian military contact with Aram-naharaim—for Aramaic dialect-forms there from the 16th century BC. The forms *Naḫrima*/*Nhrn* are mentioned briefly in Gelb, *Hurrians and Subarians*, 1944, p. 74 and n. 208. Further hints of (proto-)Aramaic forms in the early 2nd millennium in this area are found in Albright, *AfO* 6, 1930–1, p. 218, n. 4.

From Ugarit (14th–13th centuries BC) come personal names Armeya and B(e)n-Arm(e)y(a), and a plot of land called 'fields of Aramaeans' (Kupper, *Nomades*, p. 114), which continue the story. An Egyptian mention of Aram occurs under Amenophis III (*c.* 1370 BC), *cf.* E. Edel, *Die Ortsnamenlisten aus dem Totentempel Amenophis III*, 1966, pp. 28f. Thus the place-name 'the Aram' or 'Pa-Aram' in the Egyptian Papyrus Anastasi III (13th century BC) probably stands for Aram, not Amurru. It was in the 13th century BC that Balaam was hired from *Pethor (in 'Amaw?) by the Euphrates in Aram (-naharaim) and the 'mountains of the east', in order to curse Israel (Nu. 22:5, RSV; 23:7; Dt. 23:4).

In the chaos that befell the W part of the ancient E just after *c.* 1200 BC when the sea peoples destroyed the Hittite empire and

King Bar Rakab of Sam'al (Zincirli) seated on his throne, with a scribe in attendance. The Aramaic inscriptions read 'I am Bar Rakab, son of Panammu' and 'My Lord is Baal Harran'. Height 1·12 m. c. 800–750 BC. (SMB) (AMM)

disrupted Syria-Palestine (*CANAAN; *EGYPT, History), one of Israel's oppressors was the opportunist *Cushan-rishathaim, king of Aram-naharaim, whose far-flung but fragile dominion lasted only 8 years (Jdg. 3:7–11). Still later in the Judges' period, the gods of Syria proper could already be called 'the gods of Aram' (*c.* 1100 BC?) in Jdg. 10:6 (Heb.); this ties up with the accelerating inflow of Aramaeans and settling in the later 12th and 11th centuries BC in Syria and Mesopotamia, culminating in the founding of Aramaean states. Just at this time, Tiglath-pileser I of Assyria (1100 BC) was trying unavailingly to stem the advance of 'Akhlamu, Aramaeans' across the length of the middle Euphrates (*ANET*, p. 275). The Akhlamu occur in the 13th, 14th and (as personal name) 18th centuries BC as Aramaean-type people, thus further witnessing to an Aramaean continuity from earlier to later times. On this section see also Kupper, *Nomades*; R. T. O'Callaghan, *Aram Naharaim*, 1948; A. Malamat, *The Aramaeans in Aram Naharaim and the Rise of Their States*, 1952 (Hebrew); M. F. Unger, *Israel and the Aramaeans of Damascus*, 1957; *ANET*, p. 259 and n. 11.

An Aramaean prince, seated, with his feet resting on a footstool, wearing a dagger and a necklace with emblems of the sun and moon. From Ain et-Tell, near Aleppo. Height c. 2 m. c. 800 BC. (ARM)

c. Israel and the Aramaean States (c. 1000–700 BC)

(i) *Saul* (*c. 1050–1010 BC*). During his reign, Saul had to fight many foes for Israel: Moab, Ammon and Edom in the E, the Philistines in the SW and the 'kings of Zobah' in the N (1 Sa. 14:47; or 'king', if LXX be followed). This was probably at the height of his power (*c.* 1025 BC?), before the final disasters of his reign.

(ii) *David* (*c. 1010–970 BC*). David's first known Aramaean contact is with Talmai son of Ammihur, king of Geshur, whose daughter he married (Absalom being her son by him) within his first 7 years' reign at Hebron (1010–1003 BC), 2 Sa. 3:3, 5. Talmai still ruled Geshur late in David's reign when Absalom fled there for 3 years (2 Sa. 13:37–39). In the second half of his reign, David clashed with Hadadezer son of Rehob, king of Aram-zobah (N of Damascus). This king had already extended his rule as far as the Euphrates (subduing the hostile Toi, king of Hamath, 2 Sa. 8:10), but his N subjects must have revolted, for when David attacked him Hadadezer was then going to 'restore' his conquests there (2 Sa. 8:3). Perhaps David and Toi found Hadadezer too dangerous; at any rate, David annexed Damascus and Toi of Hamath became his (subject-) ally, 2 Sa. 8:5–12. The revolt against Hadadezer probably followed the two heavy defeats that David inflicted on him as ally of Ammon (2 Sa. 10; 1 Ch. 19) with other Aramaean states (see Unger, pp. 42–46). No direct time-relation between 2 Sa. 8:3–12 and 2 Sa. 9–12 is stated—but the Ammonite war probably preceded that of 2 Sa. 8. Henceforth, David was doubtless overlord of Hadadezer and all Syria. The earlier wide but ephemeral power of Hadadezer may be reflected in later Assyrian texts which report how, under Ashur-rabi II (*c.* 1012–972 BC), 'the king of Aram' gained control of Pethor (Pitru) and Mutkinu on either side of the Euphrates; this may mark the foundation there of the Aramaean kingdom of Bit-Adini—perhaps the source of Hadadezer's troops from beyond the Euphrates. For further discussion, see Landsberger, *Sam'al I*, 1948, p. 35, n. 74; and Malamat, *BA* 21, 1958, pp. 101–102.

(iii) *Solomon* (*c. 970–930 BC*). Probably it was in the first half of his reign that Solomon overcame 'Hamath-zobah', *i.e.* presumably crushed a revolt in the S part of the country of Hamath that adjoined Zobah—perhaps a rising against Hamath's subject-ally status? At any rate Solomon's overlordship was effective enough for him to have store-cities built there (2 Ch. 8:3–4). But in the last part of David's reign, after the discomfiture of Hadadezer of Zobah, a mere youth, Rezon, went off and gathered a marauding band around himself. For some time, into Solomon's earlier years, he was probably little more than a petty, roving insurgent. But for the latter half of Solomon's reign he gained control of Damascus and became king there, briefly surviving Solomon, whom he had always opposed (1 Ki. 11:23–25); Rezon, it seems, played bandit till *c.* 955 BC, reigning in Damascus perhaps *c.* 955–925 BC, till at last—full of years—he passed away, and a new 'strong man', Hezion, seized the Damascus throne.

(iv) *The Dynasty of Hezion.* The new opportunist founded a dynasty that lasted a century. Hezion (*c.* 925–915?), his son Tabrimmon (*c.* 915–900?) and grandson Ben-hadad I (*c.* 900–860?) are attested in this order and relationship, from 1 Ki. 15:18. (The Melqart Stele, commonly held to show the same line (*DOTT*, pp. 239–41; *ANET*, p. 501), is in fact impossible to read with confidence.) These kings speedily made of Damascus the paramount kingdom in Syria proper, rivalled only by Hamath. When attacked by Baasha of Israel, Asa of Judah sought aid from Ben-hadad I (1 Ki. 15:18ff.).

The *Ben-hadad who clashed with Ahab (1 Ki. 20) and was murdered by Hazael in Joram's time, *c.* 843 BC (2 Ki. 6:24ff.; 8:7–15) is probably a different king, a Ben-hadad II (*c.* ?860–843), but it

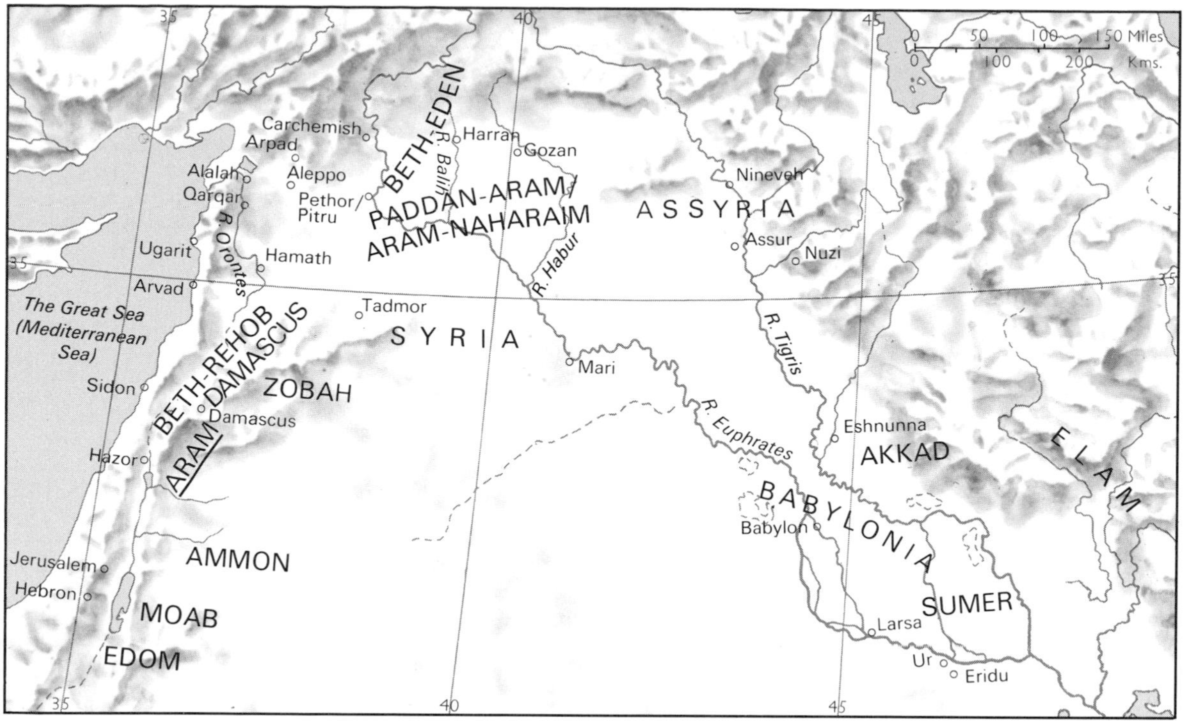

Centres of Aramaean settlement.

is possible to argue, with Albright, that this is still Ben-hadad I (then, *c.* 900–843 BC—a long reign but not unparalleled). This Ben-hadad II/I is almost certainly the Adad-idri ('Hadad-ezer') of Damascus whom Shalmaneser III attacked in 853, 849, 848 and 845 BC, and whose murder and replacement by *Hazael are also alluded to by the Assyrian. Double names are common among ancient Near Eastern rulers; Ben-hadad/Adad-idri is but one more example. It was Ben-hadad of Damascus and Urhileni of Hamath who led the opposition to Assyria and contributed the largest armed contingents, though their efforts were handsomely matched in this respect by Ahab of Israel in 853 BC at Qarqar (*ANET*, pp. 278–281; Wiseman in *DOTT*, p. 47).

(v) *Hazael to Rezin.* The usurper *Hazael (*c.* 843–796 BC) almost immediately clashed with Joram of Israel (842/1 BC), *cf.* 2 Ki. 8:28–29; 9:15. Jehu gained the Israelite throne at this time, but he and others paid tribute to Assyria (*ANET*, p. 280; *DOTT*, p. 48; *IBA*, p. 57, fig. 51), leaving Hazael of Damascus to oppose Assyria alone in 841 and 837 BC (Unger, *op. cit.*, pp. 76–78). Thereafter, Hazael savagely attacked Israel under Jehu, seizing Transjordan (2 Ki. 10:32–33), and throughout the reign of Jehoahaz, *c.* 814/3–798 BC (2 Ki. 13:22). But temporary relief did occur; the 'deliverer' sent by God then (2 Ki. 13:5) may have been Adad-nirari III of Assyria who intervened against Hazael (called 'Mari') about 805–802 BC.

In the Israelite Joash's early years the pressure was at first maintained by Hazael's son Ben-hadad III (2 Ki. 13:3). But as promised by God through Elisha, Joash (*c.* 798–782/1 BC) was able to recover from Ben-hadad the lands previously lost to Hazael (2 Ki. 13:14–19, 22–25). Ben-hadad acceded *c.* 796 BC, and reigned till roughly 770 BC on evidence of Zakur's stele (see Unger, *op. cit.*, pp. 85–89; *DOTT*, pp. 242–250). Ben-hadad headed a powerful coalition against Zakur of Hamath, a usurper from Lu'ash who had seized control of the whole kingdom Hamath-Lu'ash. But Zakur and his allies defeated Ben-hadad's coalition and so spelt the end of the dominance in Syria of the Aramaean kingdom of Damascus.

Shortly after this, discredited Damascus came under the overlordship of Jeroboam II of Israel (2 Ki. 14:28). Still later, perhaps after Jeroboam II's death in 753 BC, a king *Rezin (Assyrian *Raḫianu*) appeared in Damascus and menaced Judah as Israel's ally, even (like Hazael) conquering Transjordan again; but Ahaz of Judah appealed to Tiglath-pileser III of Assyria, who then in 732 BC defeated and slew Rezin (2 Ki. 16:5–9; *ANET*, p. 283), deporting the unhappy Aramaeans to Qir, ironically their ancient homeland, as prophesied by Amos (1:4–5).

(vi) *Other Aramaean kingdoms* are rarely mentioned in Scripture. Sennacherib in 701 BC mocked Hezekiah over the impotence of the kings and gods of *Arpad, *Hamath, *Gozan, *Harran, *Rezeph (Assyr. *Raṣappa*) and the 'children of Eden in Telassar' (2 Ki. 18:34; 19:12–13). The last-named are the people of the Aramaean province (former kingdom) of Bit-Adini, the 'House of Eden' or Beth-eden of Am. 1:5.

BIBLIOGRAPHY. M. F. Unger, R. T. O'Callaghan, A. Malamat (works cited at end of **II.***b*); A. Dupont-Sommer, *Les Araméens*, 1949. Specific studies include: R. de Vaux, *RB* 43, 1934, pp. 512–518, and A. Jepsen, *AfO* 14, 1941–4, pp. 153–172, and *ibid.* 16, 1952–3, pp. 315–317; B. Mazar, *BA* 25, 1962, pp. 98–120, for Aram-Damascus and Israel; E. O. Forrer, in Ebeling and Meissner, *Reallexikon der Assyriologie*, 1, 1932, pp. 131–139 (*Aramu*), and B. Landsberger, *Sam'al I*, 1948; W. F. Albright in *AS* 6, 1956, pp. 75–85, on Assyrian penetration of Aramaean politics and art; A. Malamat, in *POTT*, pp. 134–155. Inscriptions, *cf.* J. C. L. Gibson, *Textbook of Syrian Semitic Inscriptions*, 2, 1975.

d. Language

See *LANGUAGE OF THE OLD TESTAMENT.

It should be recognized that the

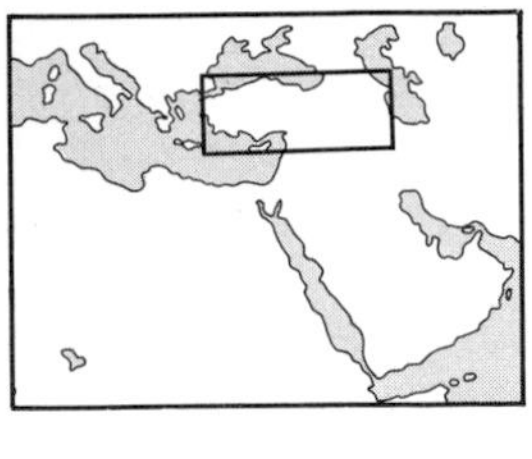

The location of Ararat in Armenia.

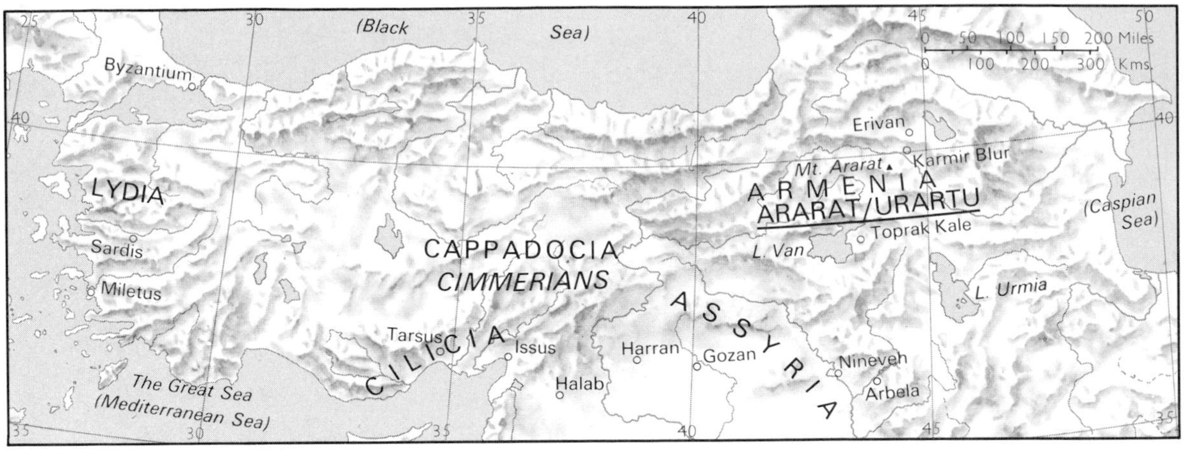

occurrence of Aramaisms in OT Hebrew often indicates an *early*, not a late, date. Note the 2nd-millennium traces of Aramaic forms (**II.***b*, above). Aramaean states in Syria which existed from at least Saul's reign, and marriages in the time of David (Talmai), imply Aramaic linguistic influence in Palestine then. Finally, some 'Aramaisms' are actually Hebraisms (or Canaanisms) in Aramaic (*cf.* K. A. Kitchen, *Ancient Orient and Old Testament*, 1966, pp. 143–146; A. Hurwitz, *IEJ* 18, 1968, pp. 234–240).

e. Aramaean culture

The Aramaeans' one major contribution to ancient Oriental culture was their language: at first, in commerce and diplomacy, then for communication over wide areas (see above), but also as a literary medium (see R. A. Bowman, 'Aramaic, Arameans and the Bible', *JNES* 7, 1948, pp. 65–99). The story and proverbs of Ahiqar are set in the Assyria of Sennacherib and certainly go back in origin to almost that time; from the 5th century BC come the religious texts in demotic (Egyptian) script (Bowman, *JNES* 3, 1944, pp. 219–231) and the Papyri Blacassiani (G. A. Cooke, *A Textbook of North-Semitic Inscriptions*, 1903, pp. 206–210, No. 76). Still later come magical texts, including one in cuneiform script of the Seleucid era (C. H. Gordon, *AfO* 12, 1937–9, pp. 105–117). Syriac in the Christian epoch was a great province of Christian literature. The chief gods of the Aramaeans were Baal-shamain and other forms of Baal, Hadad the storm-god, Canaanite deities such as Ashtar, and Mesopotamian ones, including Marduk, Nebo, Shamash, *etc.* (J. A. Fitzmyer, *The Aramaic Inscriptions of Sefîre*, 1967, pp. 33ff.). See Dupont-Sommer, *Les Araméens*, pp. 106–119; Dhorme and Dussaud, *Religions, Babylonie, etc.*, 1949, pp. 389ff. K.A.K.

ARARAT.

I. Biblical evidence

The name Ararat occurs four times in the Bible. It was the mountainous or hilly area (*hārê ʾᵃrārāṭ*, 'mountains of Ararat') where Noah's ark came to rest (Gn. 8:4. Reports linking supposed remains of wood from Lake Kop on Mt Ararat with the ark of Noah's *flood have not been confirmed archaeologically nor dated prior to *c.* 2500 BC); the land (*ʾereṣ*) to which Adrammelech and Sharezer, the parricides of Sennacherib, fled for asylum (2 Ki. 19:37 = Is. 37:38); and a kingdom (*mamlāḵâ*) grouped by Jeremiah with Minni and Ashkenaz in a prophetic summons to destroy Babylon (Je. 51:27). The AV reads 'Armenia' in both Kings and Isaiah, following *Armenian* in the LXX of Isaiah.

II. Extra-biblical evidence

There is little doubt that biblical *ʾᵃrārāṭ* was the *Urarṭu* of the Assyrian inscriptions, a kingdom which flourished in the time of the Assyrian empire in the neighbourhood of Lake Van in Armenia. While it is frequently mentioned by the Assyrian kings as a troublesome N neighbour, it was much influenced by Mesopotamian civilization, and in the 9th century the cuneiform script was adopted and modified for writing Urarṭian (also called 'Vannic' or 'Chaldian', not to be confused with 'Chaldean'), a language unrelated to Akkadian. Nearly 200 Urarṭian inscriptions are known, and in these the land is referred to as *Biainae* and the people as 'children of Ḫaldi', the national god. Excavations, notably at Toprak Kale, part of the ancient capital, Ṭušpa, near the shore of Lake Van, at Karmir Blur, a town site near Erivan in the USSR, and at Alting Tepe, near Erzincan, have revealed examples of art and architecture.

III. Urarṭu

In the 13th century, when Urarṭu is first mentioned in the inscriptions of Shalmaneser I, it appears as a small principality between the lakes of Van and Urmia, but it seems to have grown in power in the following centuries when Assyria was suffering a period of decline. In the 9th century reports of Assyrian campaigns against Urarṭu, whose territory now extended well to the N and W, become more frequent, and about 830 BC a new dynasty was founded by Sardur I, who established his capital at Ṭušpa. His immediate successors held the frontiers, but the kingdom was badly shaken at the end of the 8th century by the Cimmerian (*GOMER) invasions, and was only briefly revived in the mid-7th century by Rusa II, who may have been the king who gave asylum to Sennacherib's assassins. The end of Urarṭu is obscure, but the Indo-European-speaking Armenians must have been established there by the late 6th century BC, as is shown by the Behistun inscription which gives *arminiya* in the Old Persian version where the Babylonian version reads *urašṭu*, and the Aramaic version from Elephantine gives *ʾrrṭ*. Urarṭu probably disappeared as a state in the early 6th century, at about the time of Jeremiah's prophetic summons.

BIBLIOGRAPHY. A. Goetze, *Kleinasien*², 1957, pp. 187–200,

215–216; F. W. König, *Handbuch der chaldischen Inschriften* (*AfO*, Beiheft 8), I, 1955, II, 1957; M. N. van Loon, *Urartian Art*, 1966.
T.C.M.

ARAUNAH (Heb. *'ᵃrawnâ*, also *hā'ᵃwarnâ*, *'ᵃranyâ*). In 2 Sa. 24:16ff. a Jebusite whose threshing-floor was bought by David when he saw the destroying angel hold his hand there, so that he might build an altar on the spot and offer a sacrifice to check the pestilence which broke out after his numbering of the people. In 1 Ch. 21:18ff. (where Araunah is called Ornan) David buys the area surrounding the threshing-floor too, to be the site of the future Temple which, in due course, Solomon built there (1 Ch. 22:1; 2 Ch. 3:1). Araunah's name has been derived from Hittite *arawanis*, 'freeman', 'noble'. H. A. Hoffner (*POTT*, p. 225) suggests rather reading *'wrnh* (*cf.* Ch. and LXX) = Hurrian *ewri-ne*, 'the lord'. Ugarit supplies both *iwrn* (Hurrian) and *arwn* (Hittite) as personal names (F. Gröndahl, *Die Personennamen der Texte aus Ugarit*, 1967, pp. 224, 272). In 2 Sa. 24:16 the name is preceded by the definite article, and in v. 23 it is glossed by *hammeleḵ* ('the king'), whence it has been conjectured that he was the last king of Jebusite Jerusalem. (*HITTITES.)
F.F.B.

ARCHAEOLOGY.

I. General

Within the rapidly developing science of archaeology the special study of 'Biblical Archaeology' selects those material remains of Palestine and its neighbouring countries which relate to the biblical period and narrative. These include the remains of buildings, art, inscriptions and every artefact which helps the understanding of the history, life and customs of the Hebrews and those peoples who, like the Egyptians, Phoenicians, Syrians, Assyrians and Babylonians, came into contact with and influenced them. Interest in places and times mentioned in the Bible provided the initial incentive to many of the earlier excavations, and the broad picture of the historical, religious and ethical background to the Bible now available from archaeological discoveries has done much to explain, illustrate and sometimes to corroborate biblical statements and counteract theories insufficiently based on facts.

The limitations of archaeology are due to the vast span of time and area to be covered and to the hazards of preservation. Objects of wood, leather or cloth rarely survive and their existence has to be assumed. No biblical site has ever been, or probably can be, completely excavated. Only in recent years have accurate methods of stratification and recording enabled detailed comparisons to be made between sites. This has led to the revision of some earlier conclusions, *e.g.* Garstang's dating of Jericho walls to centuries earlier by Kenyon. Moreover, the dearth of inscriptions from Palestine itself means that direct extra-biblical insight into the thoughts and life of the early peoples is rare. As archaeology, a branch of history, deals primarily with materials, it can never test such great biblical truths as the existence and redeeming activity of God and Christ, the incarnate Word.

In Palestine (taking this term to include the modern states of Israel and Jordan) the archaeological technique of sequence dating was first worked out. At Tell el-Hesi in 1890 Flinders Petrie realized that different levels of occupation could be distinguished by the characteristic pottery and other features found in them. This scheme of stratigraphy and typology is now applied throughout the world; in Palestine it has been improved by later excavators, especially at Tell Beit Mirsim, Samaria, Lachish and Jericho. By comparison between sites within Palestine and farther afield a network of related finds has been established, linking with historical records, to give a remarkably close-knit chronology from the 4th millennium BC. Dates before that time are still imprecise, even when the Carbon 14 method supplies some evidence. The accompanying table gives the currently-accepted designations for these archaeological periods.

II. Prehistory

The Near East was the scene of man's first emergence as a food-gatherer in the Palaeolithic period of which remains are found in the Carmel caves (Wadi al-Mughârah), 'Ekron and 'Oren. After a gap he is traced as a food-gatherer in the so-called 'Neolithic revolution'. Many find early associations with

Bronze lion from Toprak Kale (ancient Ṭušpa), E Turkey, possibly part of an arm-rest for a royal throne. It was originally gilded and decorated with coloured stones. Height c. 10 cm. 9th–8th cent. BC. (BM)

ARBA
See Anak, Part 1.

pre-historic Europe rather than Africa and physical relationships with European Neanderthal types. Open settlements with huts dated *c.* 9000 BC are found at Shanidar (Iraq), ‘Eynan (Lake Huleh), Jericho and Beidha (near Petra). These lead on to the pre-pottery Neolithic B with the development of the economy of production. At Jericho at this time (*c.* 7500 BC) there are found massive defences and unusually plastered skulls and figurines of unidentified purpose. Neolithic sites have been traced in Yarmuk and Galilee (Sha‘ar Haggolan). These are contemporary with settlements in Nile, Cyprus and the Tigris Valley (Jarmo).

In the Chalcolithic period wall paintings, painted pottery and simple copper axeheads come from the Jordan Valley, Telulat Ghassul, Esdraelon, near Gaza, and in the N Negeb. Metal gradually appears in widespread use and clay models show that curved vaulted roofs were a feature of underground stores (Abu Matar), rock cisterns and some dwellings.

The transition to the Early Bronze Age is ill-defined in Palestine. Some trace this at a number of settlements which later grew into city states (Megiddo, Jericho, Beth-shan, Beth-yeraḥ and Tell el-Far‘a near Shechem) or were later abandoned for a time (Samaria and Tell en-Nasbeh). Invaders, probably former nomads from the N or E, brought a new type of pottery and buried their dead in mass graves cut in the rocks. These tombs sometimes included pottery types known from the previous Late Chalcolithic period, Esdraelon burnished wares and painted pottery later found in abundance (EB I). The term Proto-Urban, corresponding to the Protoliterate (Jemdet Nasr) period in Iraq *c.* 3200 BC has been used to describe this phase.

III. The Canaanite (Bronze) Age

Towns with mud-brick walls begin to appear in the Early Bronze Age I. At the same time the pottery in the N (Beth-yeraḥ, level II; Beth-shan, level XI) differs from that in the S, found at Ophel (Jerusalem), Gezer, Ai, Jericho (VI–VII) and Tell en-Nasbeh. The towns in the N continued to flourish in EB II *c.* 2900 BC (Megiddo, XVI–XVII; Beth-yeraḥ, III; Beth-shan, XII) although in the S some Egyptian influence can be seen (Jericho, IV). The well-developed lower city at Arad (IV–I) with its twin temples shows affinities with the N Canaanite towns (*cf.* *AI). Texts from Ebla (Syria) *c.* 2300 BC already mention places known later, *e.g.* Lachish, Hazor, Megiddo, Gaza. There were striking developments, notably in a fine new ‘Khirbet Kerak’ ware which shows the gradual improvement in pottery technique in Palestine and Syria.

About 2200 BC began the arrival of people with distinctive burial customs, pottery and weapons, probably the semi-nomadic Amorites (*e.g.* Tell-Ajjul, Jericho, Megiddo). These were nomadic groups whose presence in the Palestinian hills was later noted by the incoming Israelites (Nu. 13:29; Jos. 5:1; 10:6) and by the Execration Texts from *Egypt.

Other types of pottery, weapons and burial customs show there were people connected with the city-states of Syria and Phoenicia, and soon the numerous city-states begin to appear which are characteristically Canaanite. Their kings probably included the Asiatic ‘Foreign Rulers’ (Hyksos) who overran Egypt *c.* 1730 BC. It was a time of wealth, though of frequent inter-city warfare. Major cities had a citadel and a lower town enclosed by high ramparts (*e.g.* Carchemish, Qatna, Hazor, Tel el-Yahudiyeh, Egypt).

This Middle Bronze Age was a time when semi-nomadic groups, including Habiru, among whom may well have been the Patriarchs, infiltrated the scrub-land between the defended towns (*PATRIARCHAL AGE). The tombs of such people have been found at Jericho. The towns and their houses (*e.g.* Beit Mirsim, Megiddo and Jericho) remained small but with little change until they were violently destroyed (LB) probably by the Egyptians (Tuthmosis III) repulsing the Hyksos, *c.* 1450 BC. Despite trade contacts with the E Mediterranean (Mycenaean pottery), the hill towns of Palestine were now poorer than the neighbouring Phoenician cities.

Once again the major cities were reoccupied, but only to be sacked again later in the 13th century. Traces of the Israelite attack under Joshua have been seen in the burnt ruins of Hazor, Bethel, Beit Mirsim (Debir?) and Lachish, but it is impossible to substantiate this claim. According to the OT, Joshua did not set fire to many places. At Jericho the town has been found to have been abandoned *c.* 1325 BC, but the fallen walls once thought to belong to this LB period (Garstang) are now known to have been destroyed in EB (Kenyon).

Examples of at least six different types of *writing have been found in the LB sites of Canaan: Babylonian cuneiform, Egyp. hieroglyphic and hieratic, the Canaanite linear alphabet (ancestor of the Heb. and Gk. alphabets), and an alphabet of 25 to 30 cuneiform signs related to that of *Ugarit, the syllabic script of Byblos and scripts of Cypriot or Cretan type.

Canaanite religious practices can be glimpsed in the remains of temples and shrines at Hazor, Lachish, Megiddo, Arad and other places, with *altars, offering tables and cultic furniture. Metal figurines represent *Baal, and clay ones Astarte. These are commonly found. Cylinder *seals also show gods and goddesses, one from Bethel bearing the name Astarte in Egyptian.

(For a new statement of the archaeological and other evidence for a 15th-century-BC date for the Exodus, see J. J. Bimson, *Redating the Exodus and Conquest*, 1978.)

IV. The Israelite (Iron) Age

By the 12th century the Philistine settlement in SW Canaan is attested by a new range of decorated pottery inspired by Late Mycenean forms yet with local Palestinian, Cypriote and Egyp. elements. The lack of evidence for this Philistinian pottery at sites hitherto identified as Gath is a problem. This otherwise occurs throughout Philistia, the Shephelah from Debir to Gezer and as far N as Joppa. It is absent from sites occupied by other sea-peoples and, other than small amounts attributable to trade, is not found at first in the central hills (Gibeah, Jerusalem, Beth-zur, Tell en-Nasbeh), but by 1050 BC traces of their inroads to Shiloh and Beth-shan have been discovered. These Philistines were the first people to use iron in Palestine (an iron dagger and knife in a Tell el-Far‘a tomb) and the Israelites were slow to break this monopoly and their consequent economic superiority (1 Sa. 13:18–22). Wealthy and well-constructed Canaanite strongholds held out for at least another century (Beth-shan). The Israelites in the time of the Judges either built poor houses (Bethel), lived on the ground floor of captured Canaanite buildings (Beit Mirsim) or squatted in

Opposite page: Classification of archaeological periods.

Islamic AD 636 →

Byzantine AD 324 – 636

Roman 37 BC – AD 324

Hellenistic 330 – 37 BC

Iron Age 1200 – 330 BC
Sometimes known as Israelite Period

Bronze Age 3150 – 1200 BC
Sometimes known as Canaanite Period

Chalcolithic 4000 – 3150 BC

Stone Age → 4000 BC

Archaeological Periods	Sometimes known as	Approx. Period
Islamic		AD 636 –
Byzantine		AD 324 – 636
Roman III		AD 180 – 324
Roman II		AD 70 – 180
Roman I	Herodian	37 BC – AD 70
Hellenistic II	Hasmonaean/Maccabean	152 – 37 BC
Hellenistic I		330 – 152 BC
Babylonian/Persian	Late Iron (= LI)/Persian	587 – 330 BC
Iron Age III b		720 – 587 BC
Iron Age III a		800 – 720 BC
Iron Age II b	Middle Iron (= MI)	900 – 800 BC
Iron Age II a		1000 – 900 BC
Iron Age I b		1150 – 1000 BC
Iron Age (= IA) I a	Early Iron/Israelite (= EI)	1200 – 1150 BC
Late Bronze II b		1300 – 1200 BC
Late Bronze II a		1400 – 1300 BC
Late Bronze (= LBA) I	(Late Canaanite (= LC))	1550 – 1400 BC
Middle Bronze II c		1600 – 1550 BC
Middle Bronze II b		1750 – 1600 BC
Middle Bronze II a	(Middle Canaanite (= MC))	1950 – 1750 BC
Middle Bronze (= MBA) I	Early – Middle Bronze Age	2200 – 1950 BC
Early Bronze IV	Early Bronze Age III b	2350 – 2200 BC
Early Bronze III	(Early Canaanite III)	2650 – 2350 BC
Early Bronze II	(Early Canaanite II)	2850 – 2650 BC
Early Bronze (= EBA) I	(Early Canaanite (= EC) I)	3150 – 2850 BC
Chalcolithic	Ghassulian	4000 – 3150 BC
Neolithic (Pottery)		5000 – 4000 BC
Neolithic (Pre-Pottery)	New Stone Age	7500 – 5000 BC
Mesolithic	Middle Stone Age/Natufian	10,000 – 7500 BC
Palaeolithic	Old Stone Age	– 10,000 BC

roughly constructed villages of their own (Gat, Raqqat). Their pottery also was rough and poor compared with that of the Canaanites.

Saul's citadel at Gibeah (Tell el-Fûl) shows how the Israelites adopted a N system of casemate walls for their defences which were a characteristic feature of this period in *architecture. Life here was simple, though marked by the importation of a few iron weapons. Similar casemate walls at Shechem may have been built by Abimelech (Jdg. 9), while those at Beit Mirsim and Beth-shemesh may indicate David's work of fortifying Judah against the Philistines. Otherwise, except for the walls and defences at Ophel, no building which can certainly be attributed to David's reign has so far been identified.

The age of Solomon shows an increase in the use of iron and improved building techniques. The same plan was used for city gate-buildings he built at Hazor, Gezer and Megiddo (1 Ki. 9:15). Residences for district-governors were constructed at Megiddo and Hazor, with massive granaries for storing the taxes, paid in grain, at Lachish and Beth-shemesh. There is also evidence of an extensive programme for the building of regional administrative offices. The material prosperity of Solomon's reign must have been largely due to the construction and development of many copper- and iron-smelting *mines. Ezion-geber at Aqabah was used for importing many commodities by *ship. A pot found at Tell Qasileh inscribed 'gold from Ophir' attests this trade.

The defeat of the Philistines opened the way for an undisputed expansion of Phoenician trade, and this is reflected in the building of Solomon's Temple. The plan followed a Syro-Phoenician style already adopted at Hazor and Tell Tainat. The entrance, flanked by twin free-standing pillars (*cf.* *JACHIN AND BOAZ), led by a direct axis through a vestibule into the large sanctuary (*hêkāl*) into the small, inner sanctuary (*dᵉḇîr*). A peculiar Solomonic development was the provision of considerable storage space for the treasuries along the sides of this building. The decoration of the *Temple, with its cherubim, palms, open-work patterns or furnishings, can be paralleled from contemporary ivories found at Samaria, Arslan Tash (Syria) or Nimrud (Iraq), and attested in earlier *art also at *Ugarit. Other items, altars, stands, tongs and utensils, have been found during excavations.

The invasion of Shishak I of Egypt, *c.* 926 BC, resulted in destruction as far N as Tell Abu Hawan and at Beit Mirsim (B) and Beth-shemesh (IIa). The period of the divided Monarchy has been illuminated by a number of excavations. At Tirzah (Tell el-Far'a) de Vaux has shown that after the 10th century the town was abandoned, as would be expected when Omri transferred his capital to Samaria (1 Ki. 16:23–24) which gave him better communications with the Phoenician sea-ports. At Samaria the summit was laid out as a royal quarter surrounded by a wall of fine masonry. Many ivories found in the Omri-Ahab palace may have come from the decorations or furnishings of Ahab's 'ivory house' (1 Ki. 22:39; Am. 6:4), and some are inscribed with Phoenician marks common in the working of *ivory. The script is identical with that of the inscription of Mesha, found at Dibhan, describing relations between him and Israel *c.* 825 BC (*MOABITE STONE). In the palace courtyard at Samaria was an open cistern or 'pool', perhaps that in which Ahab's chariot was washed down (1 Ki. 22:38). Sixty-three inscribed ostraca, accounts of wine and oil brought to the royal stores, testify to the administrative organization, probably under Jeroboam II. Official buildings similar to those at Samaria (I) have been found at Beth-shan (V) and Megiddo (V). At Megiddo, Hazor and Beer-sheba large storehouses have been uncovered where the taxes paid in kind were kept. At Hazor (VIII) Ahab appears to have extended the town by building new fortifications round the whole of the high ground around the citadel. There, as at Samaria (II = Jehu), the solid defence walls now built were to stand until the Hellenistic reconstructions, *c.* 150 BC. About 800 BC Tell el-Far'a was reoccupied as a local residence for a governor with excellent private houses near by. The pottery found there is similar to that at Samaria (IV), where Jeroboam II was in residence.

Tell en-Nasbeh (Mizpah) and Gibeah were strongly refortified as frontier towns during the divided Monarchy. Both sites were reconstructed on an identical plan and with similar material which may show that this was the work of Asa after he had destroyed the nearby fort of Baasha at Ramah (1 Ki. 15). The invasion of Tiglath-pileser III of Assyria, *c.* 734 BC, resulted in the heavy destruction of Hazor (V) and Megiddo (IV). In the debris of the former a sherd inscribed *lpqḥ* ('belonging to Pekah') recalls that, according to 2 Ki. 15:29; 16:5–8 and the Assyrian Annals, Pekah ruled there at this time. The same Assyrian king mentioned (Jeho)-ahaz whose tribute is recorded in 2 Ki. 16:8.

In 722 BC Sargon II concluded the siege of Samaria and, as he claims, removed 27,290 prisoners 'and their gods' from the city and district, importing foreigners to take their place (2 Ki. 17:24). Archaeologically, this can be seen by the poorer and partial habitation of the site, which included imported Assyrian and foreign pottery types. Henceforth Israel was under Assyrian domination and influence. When Judah threatened the Assyrian advance into Egypt, Sennacherib led his army S, sacking Megiddo (IV), Samaria and Gibeah *en route* for Judah in 701 BC. The

Uncovering ivories during excavations at Calah (Nimrud). (DJW)

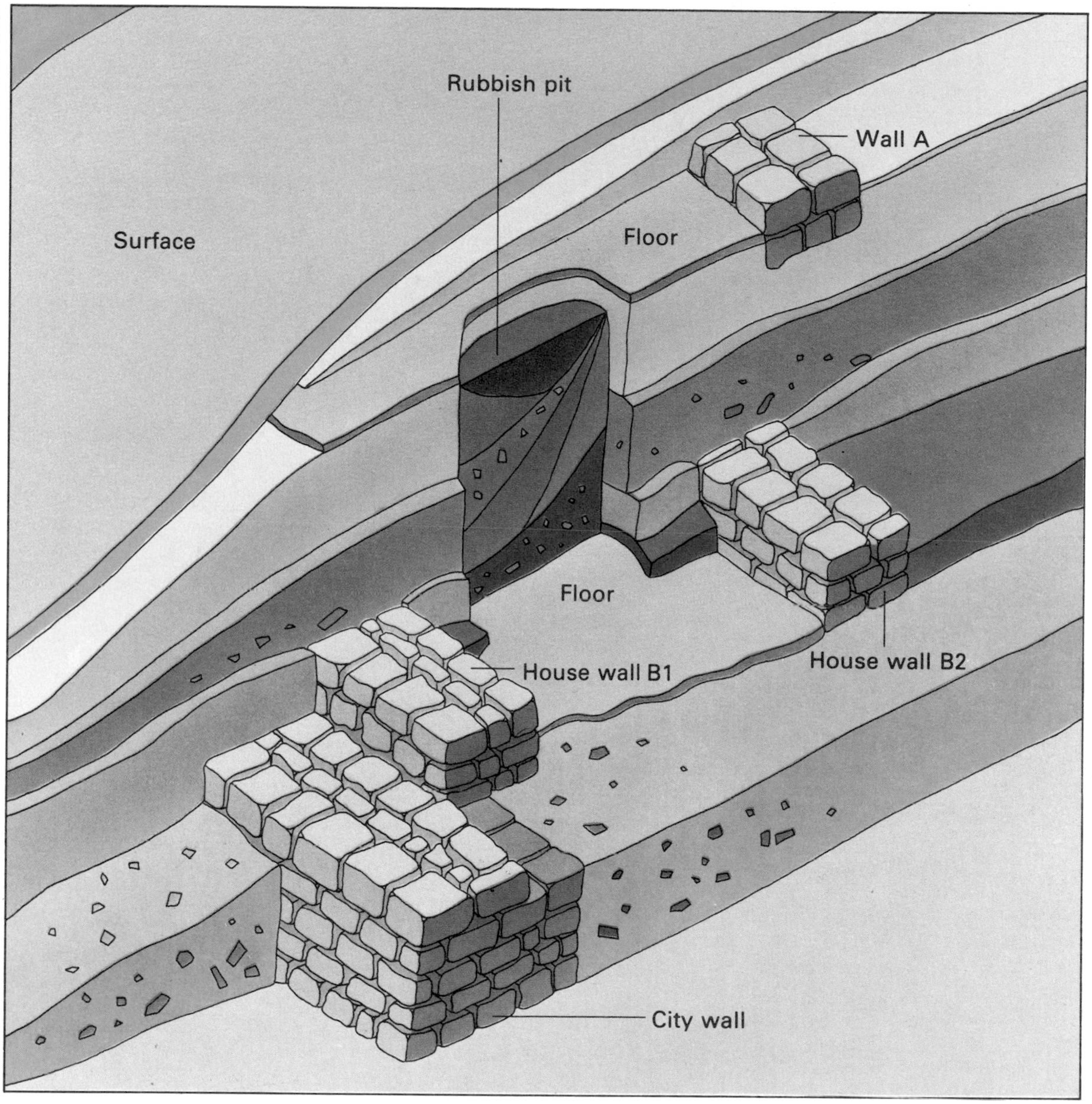

Section through part of a tell *(ruin-mound). The last building in use is represented by one wall (A) and a floor; the wall parallel to A has been destroyed by erosion at the edge of the mound. A rubbish pit cuts through the debris of an earlier house beneath (walls B1, B2), touching its floor.*

fall of Lachish, an event shown on the Assyrian palace reliefs, has been confirmed by the armour, weapons and helmets of fallen attackers near the ramp leading to the main city gate. A communal grave for 1,500 victims may be dated to this time. Hezekiah, whom Sennacherib claims to have 'shut up in his capital Jerusalem like a bird in a cage', was helped to withstand the Assyrian siege of his capital by the tunnel he had had the foresight to have cut to bring water 500 m into the city from the Virgin's Spring (2 Ki. 20:20; 2 Ch. 32:30). The inscription found in the *Siloam tunnel in 1880 is one of the longest monumental Heb. texts extant (*DOTT*, pp. 209–211). Other contemporary Heb. *writing includes a possible inscription of *Shebna.

The ardour of Josiah's opposition to Egypt is seen in the destruction of Megiddo (II) by Neco in 609 BC while on his way to Carchemish, a city which excavation shows to have been destroyed by fire soon afterwards. This was during the battle in 605 BC when Nebuchadrezzar II captured the city and overran Syria and Palestine, which became subject to the Babylonians (so the Babylonian Chronicle). When Judah rebelled, stern punishment was inevitable. The Babylonian Chronicle describes the capture of Jerusalem on 16 March 597 BC. Many towns and fortresses in Judah, but not in the N, show the ravages of the Babylonian attacks at this time and, following Zedekiah's revolt, during the war of 589–587, some were destroyed and never again reoccupied (Beth-shemesh, Tell Beit Mirsim). In the debris at *Lachish (III) 21 inscribed potsherds bear witness to the anxiety of the defenders (*DOTT*, pp. 211–217).

Archaeological surveys show that the country was greatly impoverished during the Exile, although the royal estates in Judah continued to be administered on behalf of Jehoiachin, who is named in texts from his prison in Babylon. Stamp sealings of 'Eliakim, steward of Yaukin'; *seals of Jaazaniah from Tell en-Nasbeh and of Gedaliah from Lachish (2 Ki. 25:22–25) are witnesses to the activities of these leaders.

The resettlement of Judah was slow, and excavations show that it was not until the 3rd century that Judah was repopulated to the same density as in former times. Samaria, Bethel, Tell en-Nasbeh, Beth-zur and Gezer were, however, occupied almost continuously, and cemeteries at 'Athlit (Carmel) and Tell el-Far'a (Negeb) produced Iron Age III pottery and Persian objects. The Persians allowed a measure of local autonomy, and locally minted coins begin to appear in the 5th and are abundant by the 3rd century. Most are imitations of Attic drachmas, but some bear Hebrew–Aramaic inscriptions (*yehud*, 'Judah') similar to those found on the Jewish coin which shows also a male deity seated on a chariot holding a hawk (early 4th century BC; see *IBA*, fig. 96). This may be an early instance of the use of *money. Many jar handles of this period are stamped with inscriptions such as 'Judah' (*yhd*), Jerusalem (*yršlm*) or the place-name Mosah. Gk. influence steadily increased through the imports *via* their coastal trading colonies. Attic red-figured and, later, Ionian and Attic black-figured wares are increasingly found. Trade from Arabia flourished with the establishment of the 'Idumaean' kingdom. S Palestine was controlled by an Arab, Gashmu (Ne. 6:1); the name of this 'king of Kedar' is inscribed on silver bowls, and it is possible that the supposed Persian villa at Lachish, of a design similar to the Parthian palace at Nippur in Babylonia, was a centre of his administration. Persian silver vessels have been unearthed at Gezer and Sharuhen. Carved limestone incense burners of a shape known in Babylonia and S Arabia have been found at Tell Jemmeh, Lachish and other sites.

V. Exploration and excavation

Interest in traditional biblical sites revived after the Reformation, and many wrote of their travels in Palestine. It was not, however, until 1838 that the Americans Edward Robinson and Eli Smith carried out the first planned surface exploration, identifying several ancient sites with places named in the Bible. The first excavation was undertaken by the Frenchman De Saulcy, near Jerusalem in 1863, and this was followed by a series of surveys on behalf of the Palestine Exploration Fund in 1865–1914. The areas visited and mapped included W Palestine, Kadesh (Conder), Galilee and the Arabah (Kitchener), the desert of the Exodus (Palmer) and sites including Capernaum, Samaria and Caesarea (Wilson). Interest centred on Jerusalem itself, where underground tunnelling revealed the foundations of walls, and rock levels and parts of the S wall and gates and Ophel were explored between 1867 and 1928. Following the excavation in 1890 by Sir Flinders Petrie of Tell el-Hesi, which established the first ceramic index and stratigraphical chronology based on comparisons with Egypt, many scientific expeditions led by American, British, French, German and Israeli scholars have worked at a variety of sites, principally *Gezer, *Taanach, *Megiddo, *Samaria, *Shechem and *Beth-shemesh. Subsequent surface surveys by N. Glueck in Jordan (1933–) and the Israelis in the Negeb have made detailed archaeological maps possible.

In 1920 the Department of Antiquities, Palestine, encouraged the development of careful techniques and interpretation, and soon a pottery chronology was established (especially by Albright at Gibeah and Tell Beit Mirsim, and subsequently refined). Comparisons were made with similar finds elsewhere in the ancient Near East. While work continued at pre-World War I sites, others excavated *Ashkelon, *Beth-shan, *Gibeah, Ophel, *Shiloh, *Ai, *Bethel, Beth-eglaim, *Beth-zur, with major effort devoted to *Jericho, *Lachish, Ghassul, Tell en-Nasbeh, Tell Beit Mirsim (*Kirjath-sepher or *Debir) and *Tirzah. Work was resumed at most of these sites after World War II, and begun at *Bethel, *Caesarea, Der 'Alla, *Dothan and *Gibeon. The more recent 'school' of Israeli archaeology, including such scholars as Mazar, Yadin and Aharoni, has led among other things to work at Acco, *Arad, *Ashdod, *Beer-sheba, *Dan, *En-gedi, Masada, Tell ash-Sheriah, Tell Mor, Tell Qasile, Ras-al-'Ain (*Aphek?) and Sinai.

In Jordan important work has been undertaken at Buseirah (*Bozrah), *Heshbon (Hesban), Madeba, Petra and Ezion-geber. The results of all this work have been reported regularly in journals (some listed in the bibliography), encyclopaedias of archaeology and in special volumes devoted to specific sites. A continued enlargement of the knowledge of biblical lands and times is to be expected.

VI. Inscriptions (Old Testament)

Many excavations have resulted in the discovery of documents, both in archives and in isolation. These employ various forms of writing on diverse materials. It is to be expected that such inscriptions, especially those from *Egypt, *Assyria and *Babylonia which can be closely dated, will be of much value in comparison with the documents preserved in the OT. Some bring direct reference, others illustrate the

widespread nature of literacy and literary styles spread through the whole of the ancient Near East. Products of these schools of writing are also found in Palestine in addition to indigenous and local writing on papyri and ostraca, *seals, and *money in the form of coins, stone, wood and other surfaces.

Some collections of documents or archives are of particular importance for comparison with the OT. These include for *Egypt the Execration Texts (*c.* 1800 BC) and for Syria the texts from *Ebla (*c.* 2300 BC), *Mari and *Ugarit (Ras Shamra). While these, and the texts from *Nuzi (15th century) and *Amarna (14th century), illustrate the early history down to the patriarchal period, later ostraca from *Samaria and *Lachish give background to the later kingdoms of Israel and Judah. Other inscriptions illustrate the development of *writing throughout the OT period.

The study of biblical (Palestinian) archaeology requires comparisons to be made with both the general evidence of neighbouring *Egypt, *Syria, *Assyria and *Babylonia, and with the particular

Aerial view of Tell Beersheba, showing excavations on the mound. (TAU)

aspects, *e.g.* *art and *architecture, and its specific aspects, building, *palace, *house and artefacts (*e.g.* *altar, *amulets, *glass, *pottery, *money) and sites (*e.g.* *Jerusalem, *etc.*).

BIBLIOGRAPHY. *Sites:* E. K. Vogel, *Bibliography of Holy Land Sites*, 1972; Current details are given in such periodicals as *The Biblical Archaeologist* (American Schools for Oriental Research); *Israel Exploration Journal, Iraq, Levant, Palestine Exploration Quarterly*.

Texts: ANET, ANEP, DOTT.

Selected bibliography: W. F. Albright, *The Archaeology of Palestine*, 1960; E. Anati, *Palestine before the Hebrews*, 1962; M. Avi-Yonah, *Encyclopedia of Archaeological Excavations in the Holy Land*, 1976–7; M. Burrows, *What Mean these Stones?*, 1957; H. J. Franken and C. A. Franken-Battershill, *A Primer of Old Testament Archaeology*, 1963; G. L. Harding, *The Antiquities of Jordan*, 1959; K. M. Kenyon, *Archaeology in the Holy Land*, 1960; K. A. Kitchen, *Ancient Orient and Old Testament*, 1966; A. R. Millard, *The Bible BC; What can archaeology prove?*, 1977; P. R. S. Moorey, *The Bible Lands*, 1975; S. M. Paul and W. G. Devers, *Biblical Archaeology*, 1973; J. A. Sanders, *Near Eastern Archaeology in the Twentieth Century*, 1969; D. Winton Thomas (ed.), *Archaeology and Old Testament Study*, 1967; D. J. Wiseman, *Illustrations from Biblical Archaeology*, 1962; *Peoples of Old Testament Times*, 1973; G. F. Wright, *Biblical Archaeology*, 1962; E. Yamauchi, *The Stones and the Scriptures*, 1973. D.J.W.

VII. The Hellenistic–Roman period

When the Macedonian Alexander the Great won Palestine as part of the former Persian empire in 332 BC, the country was yet further opened to Hellenistic influence. However, after his death internecine warfare between his generals retarded this development. Only isolated pottery and coins can be assigned with confidence to the ruling Lagides in 332–200 BC. At Mareshah (Marisa) in Idumaea a carefully laid-out Greek town has been uncovered. The streets set at right angles and parallel to each other led near the city gate to a market square (*agora*), round three sides of which were shops. Near the city were tombs of Greek, Phoenician and Idumaean traders (*c.* 250–200 BC).

The stern days in which the Maccabees fought for Jewish independence (165–37 BC) are attested by refugee camps and caves (Wadi Ḥabsa) and forts like that built at Gezer by Simon Maccabaeus. Traces of the N line of forts said to have been created by Alexander Jannaeus (Jos., *BJ* 7. 170) have been found near Tel Aviv-Jaffa. At Beth-zur, commanding the road from Hebron to Jerusalem, Judas (165–163 BC) had built a fort on top of an earlier Persian structure, and this in turn was later rebuilt by the general Bacchides. Shops, houses, fortifications, reservoirs, Rhodian stamped jar handles and coins help to illustrate the life of the Hasmonaean princes, one of whom, John Hyrcanus (134–104 BC), destroyed the pagan Greek cities of Samaria and Marisa.

Herod the Great (37–4 BC), an able and ambitious ruler, carried through many grandiose building projects. At Jerusalem the massive walls which he built around the Temple Mount, enlarged and embellished, have been found *in situ* on bedrock and rising above the present ground-level to a considerable height. The upper parts of the wall were surrounded by pilasters, and would have looked exactly like the wall—still standing—at Hebron (Machpelah). This wall too surrounded a sacred place, where the Patriarch Abraham and his wife Sarah had been buried. Recent work around the Temple Mount at Jerusalem has also located a complex of streets and terraces, as well as ornamental fragments from gates and cloisters (reconstructions and plans on pp. 26–31, 34–35 in *Jerusalem Revealed*). In the Upper City remains of wall-paintings and polychrome mosaics from luxurious upper-class houses have been excavated by Avigad (*ibid.*, pp. 41–51; colour-plate before p. 41) together with various items of furniture, tableware and so on. The so-called *Tower of David* in the Upper City, excavated long ago by Johns, is also Herodian work *in situ*, built over Hasmonaean walls. This was one of three Herodian towers which defended the NW angle of the city; just inside the city-wall at this point was the palace of Herod (in the Upper City), and the substructures of this too have recently been excavated. Outside the palace was the site of *Gabbatha*, and the Pavement where Jesus was tried by Pilate. On the other side of the city, at the N end of the Temple Mount, was the Antonia tower. The various remains at the Convent of the Sisters of Zion are now thought to be too far N to come from the Antonia; they are probably from the refounded Hadrianic city, Aelia Capitolina. The Pools of Bethesda were outside the city-wall just N of the Temple Mount in the time of Jesus; they were brought into the city by Agrippa's Wall (the 3rd N Wall of Jerusalem) *c.* AD 41–44. The respective lines of the 2nd and 3rd N Walls of Jerusalem are not agreed by scholars; but certainly, whether one assumes the Sukenik/Mayer line or the British School line, the sites of Golgotha and the tomb at the traditional *Holy Sepulchre* were outside the 2nd N Wall. These have a strong claim to be the sites of the crucifixion and burial of Jesus, supported by a tradition which seems to go back at least to Hadrian (AD 135). But the form of the burial-chamber with its trough-arcosolium, as described by the pilgrim Arculf, is atypical for the period, and constitutes a problem. The other site which attracts pilgrims, the *Garden Tomb*, is a congenial one, but has no claim to be authentic. Very many tombs of the 1st century BC/AD have been located at Jerusalem, some of them monumental. The groups at 'Dominus Flevit' (Mt of Olives) and at Sanhedria are interesting; the tomb of a convert to Judaism, Queen Helena of Adiabene, is the most impressive. The ossuaries (small chests for bones) from these tombs are often inscribed. Recently an ossuary was found which contained the bones of a crucified man; a nail still transfixed two of the bones. Various attempts to restore the position of the body at crucifixion have followed (*e.g. IEJ* 1970, pl. 24).

Outside Jerusalem the most important Herodian remains have been found in cities established by King Herod (Sebaste, Caesarea Maritima), at his winter-resort (Jericho) and in his fortresses (Masada, Herodium). In the Samaritan hills the old city of Samaria was re-founded by Herod as Sebaste in honour of the Roman emperor Augustus (the Gk. equivalent of Lat. *augustus* is *sebastos*). Ancient Israelite walls were rebuilt and reinforced with round towers, a temple of Augustus was dedicated and a sports-stadium founded; all have been located by excavation, including painted wall-panels in the stadium just like other wall-paintings at Jericho, Masada and Herodium. At Caesarea the great Herodian harbour or mole has been explored by an underwater team; its lines are clearly visible in air-photographs. Italian excavators have found part of the city-wall of Strato's Tower and the Herodian theatre with its seats and stage and a series of painted-plaster floors (almost unique). At Jericho the Herodian palace is on both sides of the Wadi Qelt with a sunken garden and a pool between the two wings, a magnificent conception. Even more unusual is the use of the native technique of building in dried brick together with special Roman concrete techniques characteristic of Augustan Italy. Only at Jericho has this Roman technique been found; so far as is known Herod used it nowhere else. At Jericho even the flower-pots from the garden were still there! Interior embellishments of the Herodian palaces include painted wall-panels, marquetry floors and mosaics. Open or vaulted pools, stepped and plastered, are present on many Herodian sites, but together with these one finds the Roman technique of underfloor heating and a steam-room. Such baths are found in Herod's fortresses, which were also provided with luxurious dwelling-space. The polychrome mosaics are perhaps the most interesting feature of the administrative palace at Masada. The small palace (villa) at the N end of Masada perches on terraces at the edge of sheer cliffs; again the painted Herodian wall-panels are there. In the fortresses at Masada and at Herodium Israeli archaeologists claim to have found at last the remains of 1st century AD synagogues (otherwise the earliest known are usually dated to the late 2nd century AD or 3rd century AD). In all this Herodian art human and animal motifs have never been found until very recently in Broshi's excavations near the Zion Gate at Jerusalem.

VIII. Other inscriptions (New Testament)

Certain inscriptions found at Jerusalem are to be connected with Herod's Temple. Some of these occur on the small stone chests (ossuaries) in which the dry bones of the dead were re-buried (1st century BC/AD). One such ossuary contained the bones of 'Simon, builder of the Temple', presumably a mason rather than Herod's architect. On another ossuary one reads 'Bones of the sons of Nikanor the Alexandrian, who provided the gates'; this must refer to the Jew, famed for his piety, who paid for the most splendid of the gates within the new Temple. An important inscription which was actually set up within the Temple enclosure has been found. Two examples are known, both in Gk., one fragmentary. The text (1st century BC/AD) reads: 'No non-Jew to proceed beyond the barrier and enclosure which surrounds the Sacred Place; any man who [does so and] is caught is himself responsible for his death, which is the consequence.' Josephus refers to these plaques, which were set up in Gk. and Lat. round the Sacred Place (Inner Temple); he uses almost the same words as one finds in the inscriptions (*BJ* 5. 194; *Ant.* 15. 417). The incidents of Acts 21:26–29 must be connected with the same prohibition. The riot which broke out was caused by pious Jews who believed that Paul had brought a Greek within the forbidden area.

Other ossuary-inscriptions are also relevant. One must now discount the words said to be 'Jesus! Woe!', which many have connected with the crucifixion. These words, written on the ossuary of a Jew within his family tomb, are in fact merely his name, 'Jesus, son of Judas' (identifying the bones of the dead as usual). It may be of interest to note the combination 'Jesus, son of Joseph', which occurs on another ossuary; both names were common ones of the period. Indeed the list of names derived from these ossuaries is much as one would expect from reading the NT: John, Judas, Lazarus (Eliezer), Jesus, Mary, Martha, *etc.* Finally, one may mention the tomb and ossuaries of 'Alexander, son of Simon, of Cyrene' and his sister Sarah from Cyrenaican Ptolemais. It seems quite possible that this man's father was the 'man called Simon, from Cyrene, the father of Alexander and Rufus' (Mk. 15:21).

The ruins of many ancient synagogues are to be found in Palestine. For a long time the earliest were thought to be those at Capernaum, Chorazin and Kefar Biram in Galilee (usually dated late 2nd/ early 3rd century AD). Now it is claimed that assembly-halls of the 1st century AD in Masada and Herodium were synagogues; and Franciscan excavators have argued that the ruins at Capernaum are later than was thought (late 4th/ early 5th century AD). Be all this as it may, the earliest certain evidence for a synagogue in Palestine comes from Jerusalem, and is a Gk. inscription (1st century BC/AD). It declares that a certain Theodotus, a priest, paid part of the expenses involved in building a meeting-house (synagogue), over which he presided as 'archisynagogos'. It was a family affair: his father and grandfather before him had also been heads of the same synagogue. The inscription further declares

The 50 m high ruin-mound of Sultan Tepe, Turkey, near ancient Harran, being identified from surface finds. (DJW)

that this place was built 'for the reading of the Law and study of (its) precepts'; and that a hospice was attached to it for visitors from abroad, who had their own baths and chambers.

In Italian excavations at Caesarea, Herod's re-foundation of the old Phoenician strongpoint, Strato's Tower, the ancient theatre was found to have gone through various phases of construction and rebuilding. When in the later Roman period the original Herodian remains were dumped under steps as 'rubble', an inscribed stone was included. The excavators found that this refers to Pontius *Pilate. He is named 'prefect of Judaea', and the wording states that he set up a shrine in honour of Tiberius, the Roman emperor. It must have been about this time that the term 'prefect' was dropping out of use as the title of minor (equestrian) governors like Pilate; the word 'procurator' (formerly reserved for the emperor's fiscal agents) supplanted it.

The inscriptions so far described relate mainly to the Gospels. Others—from Greece, Turkey, *etc.*—are connected with events described in Acts or Paul's Epistles. A decree of Claudius found at Delphi (Greece) describes Gallio as proconsul of Achaia in AD 51, thus giving a correlation with the ministry of Paul in Corinth (Acts 18:12). In Corinth also a door inscription—'Synagogue of the Hebrews'—may indicate the place where Paul preached (Acts 18:4). Excavations there revealed a text naming a benefactor, Erastus, perhaps the city-treasurer of Rom. 16:23; shops similar to those in which Paul worked (Acts 18:2–3), and an inscription of 'Lucius the butcher', which probably marks the site of the 'meat-market' (*makellon*) to which Paul referred in 1 Cor. 10:25.

At Ephesus parts of the temple of Artemis, the 'Diana of the Ephesians', have been recovered together with the agora and open-air theatre capable of seating more than 25,000 persons. A votive text of Salutaris, dedicating a silver image of Artemis 'to be erected in the theatre during a full session of the *ecclēsia*', shows that the full assembly met here as implied by Acts 19:28–41. The historical trustworthiness of Luke has been attested by a number of inscriptions. The 'politarchs' of Thessalonica (Acts 17:6, 8) were magistrates and are named in five inscriptions from the city in the 1st century AD. Similarly Publius is correctly designated *prōtos* ('first man') or Governor of Malta (Acts 28:7). Near Lystra inscriptions record the dedication to Zeus of a statue of Hermes by some Lycaonians, and near by was a stone altar for 'the Hearer of Prayer' (Zeus) and Hermes. This explains the local identification of Barnabas and Paul with Zeus (Jupiter) and Hermes (Mercury) respectively (Acts 14:11). Derbe, Paul's next stopping-place, was identified by Ballance in 1956 with Kaerti Hüyük near Karaman (*AS* 7, 1957, pp. 147ff.). Luke's earlier references to *Quirinius as governor of Syria before the death of Herod I (Lk. 2:2) and to *Lysanias as tetrarch of Abilene (Lk. 3:1) have likewise received inscriptional support.

BIBLIOGRAPHY. Only recent, non-technical works in English are listed. Y. Yadin, *Masada*, 1966; K. M. Kenyon, *Jerusalem: Excavating 3,000 Years of History*, 1967 (chs. 6–11); P. Benoit, *HTR* 1971, pp. 135–167 (Antonia); *Inscriptions Reveal*, 1973, incl. nos. 169–170, 182, 216 (published by the Israel Museum, Jerusalem); K. M. Kenyon, *Digging Up Jerusalem*, 1974 (chs. 1–3, 10–15); B. Mazar, *The Mountain of the Lord*, 1975; L. I. Levine, *Roman Caesarea: an Archaeological-Topographical Study*, 1975; Y. Yadin, *Jerusalem Revealed: Archaeology in the Holy City*, 1968–74, pp. 1–91; *EAEHL*, *s.v.* Caesarea, Herodium, Jericho, Jerusalem. J.P.K.

ARCHELAUS
See Herod, Part 2.

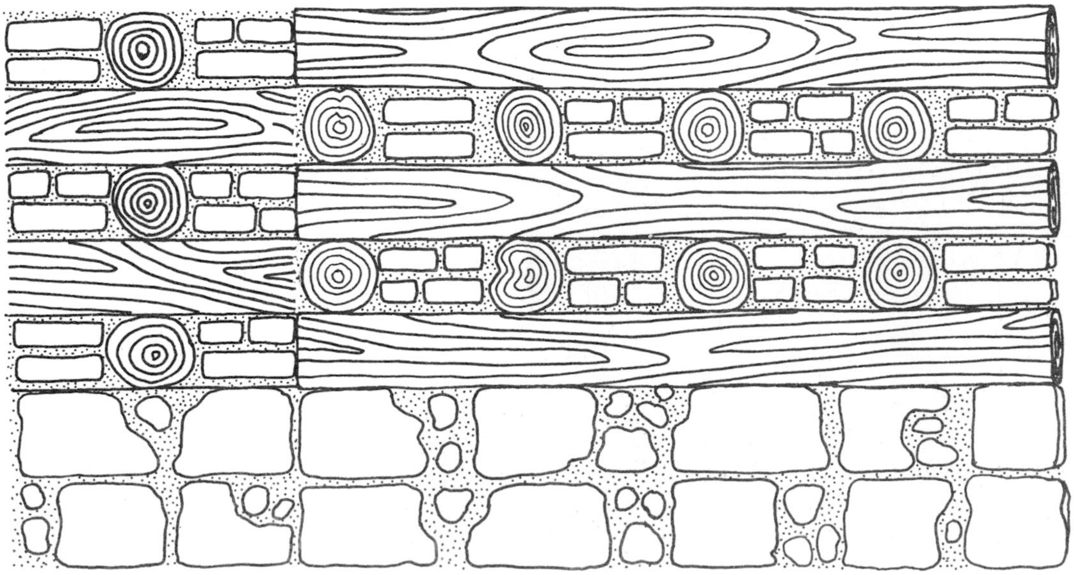

The Syrian technique of stone, mudbrick and wood in wall construction. (PS)

ARCHIPPUS. 'Fellow soldier' of Paul and Timothy (Phm. 2); the phrase implies previous service together (*cf.* Phil. 2:25). He is addressed with Philemon and Apphia in a manner suggesting that he may have been their son. This does not necessarily exclude the early suggestion (*cf. Theodore of Mopsuestia*, ed. Swete, I, p. 311) based on the context of Col. 4:17, and adopted with divergent conclusions by Lightfoot and Goodspeed, that the 'ministry' that the Colossians must exhort him to fulfil was exercised in nearby Laodicea; but the context does not demand, and may not support, this. Even if he ministered at Colossae, and the charge is to root out the heresy there (*cf.* W. G. Rollins, *JBL* 78, 1959, pp. 277f.), it is curious that the *church* is bidden to convey it. Even more dubious is J. Knox's suggestion that Archippus was host to the Colossian house-church, the owner of Onesimus and the principal addressee of Philemon. The expressions in Col. 4:17 imply the reception of a tradition, and can hardly be interpreted in terms of the release of Onesimus. The precise nature of the ministry is unknown, but perhaps Paul's old comrade-in-arms, while still linked with his home church, was again on missionary service. The solemn charge need not imply actual dereliction (*cf.* 2 Tim. 4:5). (*PHILEMON, EPISTLE TO.)

BIBLIOGRAPHY. J. Knox, *Philemon among the Letters of Paul*^{2}, 1960. A.F.W.

ARCHITECTURE. Compared with many ancient cultures, the architectural remains of Palestine are for most of its history unim-

Architectural plan, showing crenellated walls with projecting towers and possibly a two-horned altar (on the left), on the knees of a statue of Gudea of Telloh (S Babylonia). Height 73 cm. Early 21st cent. BC. (MC)

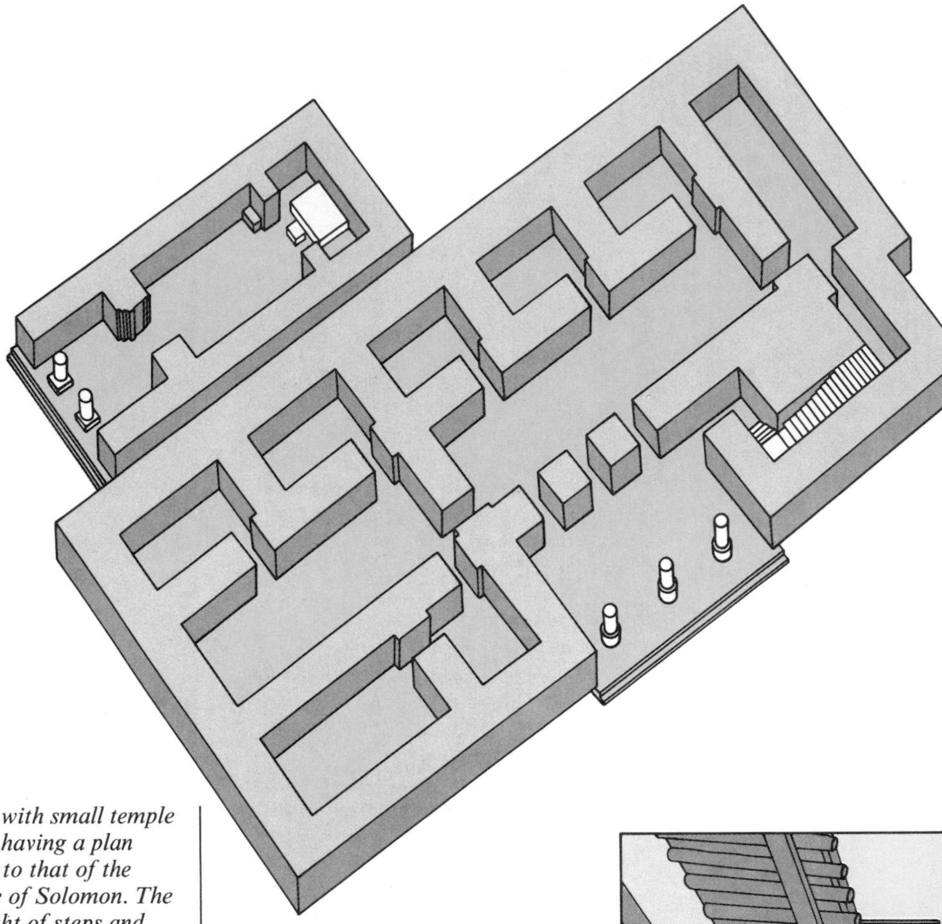

Palace with small temple at rear having a plan similar to that of the Temple of Solomon. The low flight of steps and three-columned portico of the palace are characteristic of Syrian architecture. Tell Taanach, Syria. c. 743 BC, built by Tiglath-pileser III.

pressive. The perishable nature of the normal building materials used is partly to blame for this deficiency as is the frequent lack of indigenous prosperity, without which monumental structures cannot be attempted. While most building in Palestine was performed on a non-professional basis, a few periods are outstanding for their architectural splendour: the Middle Bronze II, Solomonic, Herodian and Omayyad periods. The biblical account includes Egypt, Mesopotamia, Persia and the classical world, which together possess the most imposing ancient architectural remains.

a. Materials and construction

Because of the quantities involved, it was not normal for building materials to be transported long distances. This is true of most stone, although not marble which during the Roman period was transported up to 1500 km. The base rock of the hill country of *Palestine is limestone and the normal building stone for that area. It may even have been quarried on the building site itself, as at *Samaria and Ramat Raḥel (*BASOR* 217, 1975, p. 37). Sandstone was used in the coastal areas of Palestine, while in S Syria, basalt is a common building stone. The comparatively wet climate of Palestine necessitated the laying of *foundations consisting of rubble walls, which were erected above ground level to protect the mud-brick structure from rising damp. Some *fortifications were constructed almost entirely of rubble; the earliest known example is a Neolithic tower at *Jericho (*c.* 7000 BC). It was, however, not until *c.* 1400 BC that squared masonry was employed for building in Palestine. Solomon used coursed rectangular masonry in many of his buildings, examples of which are the gates at *Megiddo and Gezer. The production of this building stone was expensive and required a large workforce (2 Ch. 2:18). Later examples of fine masonry have been found at Samaria and Ramat Raḥel, and can be seen in the 'wailing wall' in Jerusalem built by *Herod the Great. During the Israelite monarchy, stone was carved into a variety of architectural elements such as the

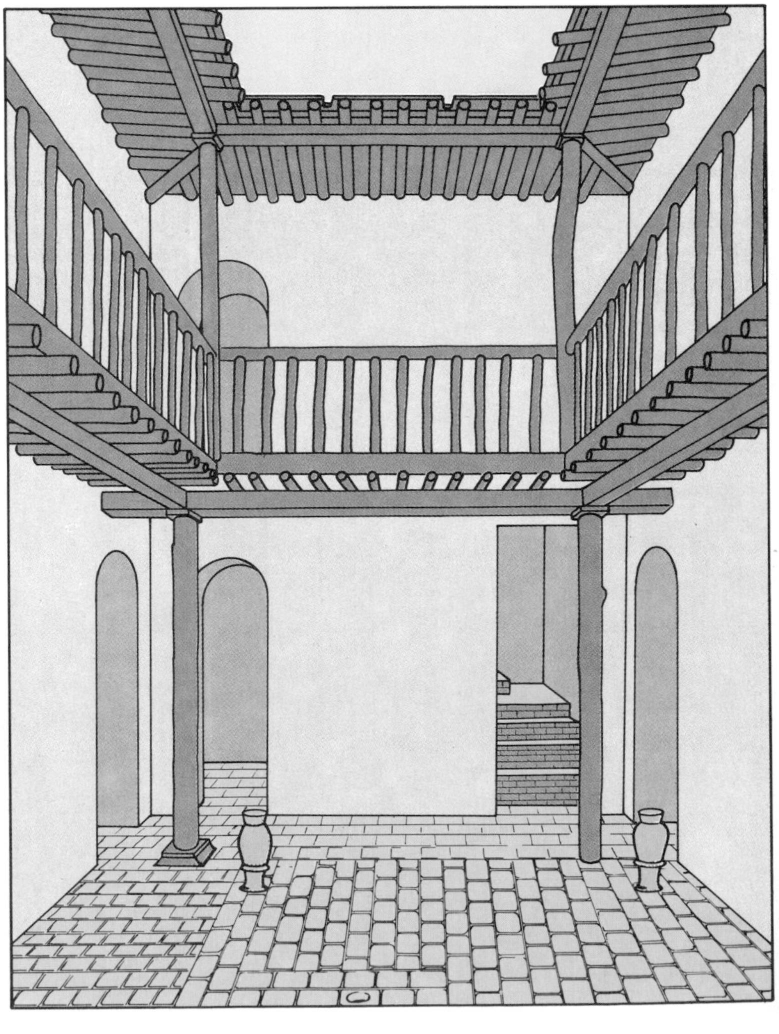

Reconstruction of a private house excavated at Ur. The living quarters were on the first floor, the ground floor being used for servants and storage. c. 1900 BC.

Reconstruction of the monumental entrance to the citadel at Hazor, showing proto-Aeolic capitals and a monolithic lintel. 9th cent. BC. (IM)

proto-aeolic *pillars (*PEQ* 109, 1977, pp. 39–52) and the balustrade from Ramat Raḥel which probably formed the lower part of a window. (*ARTS AND CRAFTS.)

Most types of stone were used for building somewhere in the ancient world. From the classical period marble was one of the most valued building stones and the remains of *Corinth, *Ephesus, *Pergamum and *Athens give a good impression of the magnificence of architecture which employed it during the NT age.

Timber was also a plentiful commodity in Palestine (Jos. 17:15, 18). Royal buildings were constructed and decorated with expensive woods such as cedar and fir (1 Ki. 5:6, 8) imported from Lebanon, almug (1 Ki. 10:11–12) from Ophir and the local olive (1 Ki. 6:23, 31, 33). (*TREES.) General work was normally done with the most suitable local wood, which may have been sycamore (Is. 9:10), pine or oak. The excavation of a small fortress at *Gibeah from *c.* 1000 BC showed that cypress and pine were used in the first construction, but, possibly because of deforestation, almond was used in later rebuilding. The large amount of charred wood found may indicate that the superstructure was predominantly wood. Because of its tensile strength, wood performed such vital architectural functions as roof support, wall stresses, door and window frames (1 Ki. 6:31, 34),

Model of the fortress Antonia *at Jerusalem, built by King Herod before 31 BC. This reconstruction embodies the work of Vincent and Marie-Aline who wrongly attributed to Herod remains from Hadrian's* Aelia Capitolina (*after AD 135*). (JPK) (HC)

doors and as support for overhanging towers. Reeds are the only other building material that offer tensile strength and they may therefore have been used to strengthen mudbrick walls. The major value of reeds, however, is in roof construction, where they are laid across the wooden rafters to form a secure base for a plaster covering. This could easily be removed (*cf.* Mk. 2:4).

Preparations involving earth were the most common materials used for building in the ancient world. Early attempts at wall-building with solid masses of mud would have been unsuccessful, as shrinkage of the mud while drying would have resulted in severe cracking. Instead it became normal practice to make the mud into lumps or *bricks which would be dried in the sun before being incorporated into the building. A brickyard with bricks laid out to dry was found at Tell el-Kheleifeh near the Red Sea and has been dated *c.* 850 BC. Mud for bricks was mixed with chopped straw which not only provided coherence, but also accelerated drying and prevented the mud from adhering to the mould during casting. Rectangular wooden moulds were used from *c.* 4000 BC in Mesopotamia, and sometime later in Palestine.

The 'Great join' discovered by Warren near the S end of the E wall enclosing the Temple Mount. King Herod added the southernmost part of this wall (left of the join) to earlier masonry (right of the join) which probably dates from Zerubabbel's rebuilding (so Kenyon) or possibly even from Solomon's Temple (so Laperrousaz). (JPK)

Mudbricks were generally mortared to each other with mud and then coated with a mud plaster. Each year the entire building would be replastered on the outside, and perhaps also on the inside, in order to keep it waterproof. Without this maintenance, mudbrick buildings soon decay. At *Shechem a slab of roofing material showing the successive replasterings was found in the debris of a house dating from *c.* 730 BC (G. E. Wright, *Shechem*, 1965). Excavations at Tell Jemmeh have revealed an Assyrian residence of *c.* 700 BC with a vaulted mudbrick roof. This form of architecture was common in Mesopotamia and Egypt from the 3rd millennium, but no earlier example is known in Palestine.

Baked bricks and tiles were not used except in special circumstances before the Roman period in Palestine, and even then only by the wealthy.

b. General survey

The efficiency of community life produces wealth which must be protected, and so as soon as man began living in settlements, *fortifications were required. The walls of houses on the perimeter of the village were strengthened as the earliest form of defence. The gate was always the most vulnerable feature of fortification and the special attention given to it can be seen at Jawa in the Syrian desert where all the basic plans of gates later employed in Palestine were in use by *c.* 3200 BC. After 3000 BC it was common for cities to have secondary walls to cover the base of the main wall, as well as towers situated at all strategic points along the main wall. Earth embankments were also used, but were not utilized to their full potential until after 2000 BC, when steep slopes outside the city walls were built up and stabilized with consolidated limestone chips.

Cities in this period were large. The walls of *Hazor enclosed *c.* 700,000 sq. m; this included an upper town area (or tell), enclosed within a second main wall. It continued to be normal for cities to have a number of lines of defence, either enclosing the entire city as at *Lachish (*c.* 700 BC), or protecting different sections, as in NT *Jerusalem. During the Assyrian expansion (after *c.* 850 BC) city gates were enlarged with additional gatehouses planned to foil carriage-mounted battering rams. In the Roman period, Palestine was a frontier area and was defended with many forts; one such was the Fortress of Antonia (*PRAETORIUM) in Jerusalem, where Jesus may have been imprisoned (Mt. 27:27; Mk. 15:16).

Architecturally, *temples and shrines are often hard to distinguish from palaces or large houses, and unless the objects found within them indicate religious practice, identification is difficult. After 2000 BC there was in Palestine a great variety of religious buildings. At *Hazor alone, four separate temples and shrines have been found. Other significant Canaanite temples have been excavated at Megiddo and at Shechem, where a structure of the 'Migdol' (tower) type is identified by some as the temple of El-be'rith (Jdg. 9:46). This building had thick walls (5·1 m) with a porch at its entrance. At *Bethshean two temples were uncovered revealing Egyptian styles of design and construction, although they were devoted to the Canaanite deities, *Dagon and *Ashtaroth. Religious buildings have also been found away from towns, such as at Nahariyah where an altar (*HIGH PLACE) and temple were excavated. Canaanite temples display no uniformity of design. This may reflect their religious variety, which the Israelites were to fight against (Dt. 7:1–5). A temple most prob-

Tower forming part of the fortifications of the Judaean city of Lachish. The disc-like objects on the parapet are probably shields. From relief of Sennacherib's attack on Lachish, Nineveh. 701 BC. (BM)

ably used by Israelites has been excavated at *Arad. It consisted of a broad room sanctuary containing a niche and a courtyard in which an altar 2·5 × 2·5 m was situated. One of its few similarities with the Temple of Solomon (as described in 1 Ki. 6 and 7) was the two-column bases situated on each side of the sanctuary-entrance like Jachin and *Boaz (1 Ki. 7:15–22). An 8th-century BC temple associated with a Hittite-style palace at Tell Tainat in N Syria is the only known temple with a plan similar to that of Solomon's *Temple. The design has often been thought to be *Phoenician in origin, but a recently excavated Phoenician temple at Kition, Cyprus, is completely different. A Philistine temple found at Tell Qasile (*c.* 1000 BC) had wooden columns to support the roof (*cf.* Jdg. 16:29) and a platform. The Temple of *Herod was described by Josephus and with reference to the present remains, a reasonable reconstruction can be made. The massive stonework of Herod's substructure is still visible in the Haram esh-Sherif (*cf.* Mk. 13:1–2).

Substantial *palaces are not common in Palestine. One building which may have been a local monarch's residence was uncovered at Megiddo, near the gate. It had a number of storeys arranged around a courtyard and was in use between *c.* 1500 and 1200 BC, during which time it was reconstructed at least once. Solomon's palaces in Jerusalem are undiscovered and little has been found of the palaces of *Omri and *Ahab at *Samaria. The palace of *Jehoiakim at Ramat Raḥel, probably referred to by Jeremiah (22:13–19), has been excavated, but no precise plan could be determined. The vast palaces of the Assyrian and Babylonian kings have been excavated extensively at *Nineveh, Nimrud, Khorsabad and *Babylon. These were considerable administrative complexes, having large state rooms richly decorated with relief sculpture, and also numerous offices and official residences. The spectacularly sited N palace of Herod the Great at Masada has been uncovered revealing its imitation marble decoration.

The normal *house plan in Palestine has always been of the courtyard variety. Houses at Arad (*c.* 2800 BC) consisted of a main room and one or two smaller rooms built round an irregular walled courtyard. The Israelites used a very regular form of courtyard house in which a number of rooms were built around three sides of a rectangular courtyard. On the fourth side was a doorway leading to the street. This design used space economically and provided the protection and warmth required in the hill country of Palestine. Upper storeys were added when required (2 Ki. 4:10). Some of the largest and most comfortable ancient houses were excavated at *Ur. They were in use *c.* 1900 BC and consisted of two storeys arranged around a courtyard.

A common building in Israelite cities is the store-house. (*BARN.) When these were first excavated at Megiddo they were thought to be stables.

BIBLIOGRAPHY. H. J. Franken and C. A. Franken-Battershill, *A Primer of Old Testament Archaeology*, 1963; S. M. Paul and W. G. Dever, *Biblical Archaeology*, 1973; H. and R. Leacroft, *The Buildings of Ancient Mesopotamia*, 1974.

C.J.D.

ARCTURUS
See Stars, Part 3.

The rocky Areopagus, original meeting-place of the Areopagus Council. In the background is the Acropolis, Athens. (BPL)

AREOPAGUS (Gk. *Areios pagos*, 'the hill of Ares', the Greek god of war, corresponding to the Roman Mars).

1. A little hill NW of the Acropolis in Athens, called 'Mars' hill' in Acts 17:22 (AV).

2. The Council of the Areopagus, so called because the hill of Ares was its original meeting-place. In NT times, except for investigating cases of homicide, it met in the 'Royal Porch' (*stoa basileios*) in the Athenian market-place (*agora*), and it was probably here that Paul was brought before the Areopagus (Acts 17:19) and not, as AV puts it, 'in the midst of Mars' hill' (v. 22). It was the most venerable institution in Athens, going back to legendary times, and, in spite of the curtailment of much of its ancient powers, it retained great prestige, and had special jurisdiction in matters of morals and religion. It was therefore natural that 'a preacher of foreign divinities' (Acts 17:18) should be subjected to it adjudication.

The Areopagus address delivered by Paul on the occasion referred to (Acts 17:22–31) is a discourse on the true knowledge of God. Taking as his point of departure an altar inscription 'To an *unknown god', he tells his audience that he has come to make known to them the God of whose nature they confess themselves ignorant. The true God is Creator and Lord of the universe; he does not inhabit material shrines; he is not dependent on the offerings of his creatures but bestows on them life and everything else that they need. He who is Creator of all things in general is Creator of mankind in particular; and so the speech goes on to make certain affirmations about man in relation to God. Man is one; the habitable zones of earth and the seasons of the year have been appointed for his advantage; God's purpose in these appointments is that men might seek and find him, the more so because they are his offspring. While the wording and citations of the speech are Hellenistic, the emphases are thoroughly biblical. In the peroration Paul calls his hearers to repent and submit to the knowledge of

God, since he is not only Creator of all but Judge of all; the pledge of his coming judgment has been given in his raising from the dead the Man empowered to execute that judgment. Hearing this reference to resurrection, the Council dismissed Paul as unworthy of serious consideration.

BIBLIOGRAPHY. N. B. Stonehouse, *Paul before the Areopagus*, 1957; M. Dibelius, *Studies in the Acts of the Apostles*, 1956, pp. 26–83; B. Gärtner, *The Areopagus Speech and Natural Revelation*, 1955; H. Conzelmann, 'The Address of Paul on the Areopagus', in L. E. Keck and J. L. Martyn (eds.), *Studies in Luke–Acts*, 1966, pp. 217–230; T. D. Barnes, 'An Apostle on Trial', *JTS* n.s. 20, 1969, pp. 407–419; C. J. Hemer, 'Paul at Athens: A Topographical Note', *NTS* 20, 1973–4, pp. 341–349.

F.F.B.

ARETAS. The reference in 2 Cor. 11:32 is to Aretas IV Philopatris, the last and most famous *Nabataean king of that name (*c.* 9 BC–AD 40). He was confirmed in the tenure of his client kingdom by Augustus, albeit somewhat reluctantly, for he had seized it without permission. His daughter married *Herod Antipas, who divorced her when he wanted to marry *Herodias (Mk. 6:17). Aretas declared war on Herod and defeated him in AD 36. Rome sided with Herod, but the punitive expedition which was eventually despatched under Vitellius, governor of Syria, had reached only Jerusalem when news of the death of the emperor Tiberius in AD 37 caused it to be abandoned.

From 2 Cor. 11:32 it seems probable, though very surprising, that Aretas had at some stage held Damascus, the old Syrian capital. It is commonly assumed that he was given the city by Gaius (AD 37–41), whose policy it was to encourage client kingdoms. In fact no Roman coinage is known to have been minted at Damascus between AD 34 and AD 62. This gap may or may not be significant. An occupation by Aretas may well have intervened at some stage between 34 (or 37) and 40, or the activity of his 'ethnarch' may possibly admit of some other explanation. The reference is potentially important for Pauline chronology, but on the evidence now available the indications are too uncertain and the possibilities too various to permit any conclusion. If we may equate the occasion of 2 Cor. 11:32 with the events both of Gal. 1:17–18 and Acts 9:23–29, this may be set '3 years' after Paul's conversion. This option might, on some readings of the case, accord more easily with the early dating of the apostle's conversion which seems probable on other grounds.

E.M.B.G.
C.J.H.

ARGOB. A district of Transjordan which was ruled over by Og, king of Bashan, before the Israelite conquest under Moses (Dt. 3:3–5). It contained sixty strongly fortified, walled cities and many unwalled towns. The exact location of the areas has been a matter of dispute. One view which had the support of Jewish tradition and derived additional weight from an unlikely etymology of Argob identified the region with the volcanic tract of land known as el-Leja (*TRACHONITIS). This view is no longer favoured. The name probably indicates a fertile area of arable land (*'argōḇ* probably from *reḡeḇ*, 'a clod'. *Cf.* Jb. 21:33; 38:38). Its W extent is given as the border of the petty kingdoms of Geshur and Maacah (Dt. 3:14), *i.e.* the Golan Heights. Some difficulty arises over the reference to the renaming of the cities of Argob, *Havvoth-jair, by Jair the Manassite. In 1 Ki. 4:13 the towns of Jair are located in Gilead (*cf.* Jdg. 10:3–4).

J.C.J.W.

ARIEL (Heb. *'ᵃrî'ēl*, 'hearth of El [God]'). **1.** A name for the altar of burnt-offering described by Ezekiel (43:15–16). Several interpretations of this name have been given; 'altar-hearth' (RV); 'mount of God' (*cf.* Ezk. 43:15–16) or, less likely, 'Lion of God'. In this sense *'r'l* is named on the *Moabite Stone (1:12, *c.* 830 BC). **2.** A cryptic name applied to Jerusalem (Is. 29:1–2, 7) as the principal stronghold and centre of the worship of God (see **1** above). **3.** A Moabite whose sons were slain by Benaiah, one of David's warriors (2 Sa. 23:20; 1 Ch. 11:22). AV translates 'lionlike man' (see **1** above). **4.** A delegate sent by Ezra to Casiphia to bring men to accompany him to Jerusalem for the Temple ministry (Ezr. 8:16).

D.J.W.

ARIMATHEA. 'A city of the Jews', and home of *Joseph, in whose sepulchre the body of Jesus was laid (Mt. 27:57; Mk. 15:43; Lk. 23:51; Jn. 19:38). Identified by Eusebius and Jerome with *Ramah or Ramathaim-zophim, the birthplace of Samuel (1 Sa. 1:19). It is probably identical with the Samaritan toparchy called Rathamein (1 Macc. 11:34) or Ramathain (Jos., *Ant.* 13. 127), which Demetrius II added to Jonathan's territory. Possibly the modern Rentis, *c.* 15 km NE of Lydda. See K. W. Clark, 'Arimathaea', in *IDB*.

J.W.M.
F.F.B.

ARIOCH. 1. Name of the king of *Ellasar, an ally of *Chedorlaomer of Elam and *Amraphel of Shinar, who warred against Sodom and Gomorrah (Gn. 14:1, 9) and was defeated by Abraham. Although this person is unidentified, the name can be compared with *Arriwuk*, a son of Zimri-Lim, mentioned in the Mari letters (*c.* 1770 BC) or with the later Hurrian *Ariukki* of the Nuzi texts (15th century BC).

2. The Babylonian king's bodyguard in 588 BC (Dn. 2:14–15). He was commanded to slay the 'wise men' who had failed to interpret the royal dream but avoided this command by introducing Daniel to King Nebuchadrezzar II.

D.J.W.

ARISTARCHUS. All the references undoubtedly relate to the same person. The first, Acts 19:29, describes him as already Paul's fellow-traveller when seized by the Ephesian mob (though it has been argued that this is proleptic). In Acts 20:4 he accompanies Paul to Jerusalem, probably as an official Thessalonian delegate with the collection; and in Acts 27:2 he is on Paul's ship from Caesarea. W. M. Ramsay argued that he could have travelled only as Paul's slave (*SPT*, pp. 315f.), though Lightfoot's suggestion still deserves mention, that the manner of reference indicates that he was on his way home to Thessalonica. However (assuming a Roman origin for Colossians), he rejoined Paul, and became his 'fellow prisoner-of-war' (Col. 4:10), possibly alternating with Epaphras in voluntary imprisonment (*cf.* Col. 4:10–12 with Phm. 23–24). On the 'Ephesian imprisonment' theory he will have gone home after the riot and the writing of Colossians (*cf.* G. S. Duncan, *St Paul's Ephesian Ministry*, 1929, pp.

196, 237ff.). His association with the collection has suggested an identification with the 'brother' of 2 Cor. 8:18 (Zahn, *INT*, 1, p. 320). The most natural reading of Col. 4:10–11 implies a Jewish origin.

A.F.W.

ARK. 1. The ark of Noah (Heb. *tēḇâ*, probably from Egyp. *ḏb'.t*, 'chest, coffin', Gn. 6–9; *kibōtos*, 'box, chest' in the NT) was evidently intended to be no more than a floating repository, measuring, if the cubit is taken at *c.* 46 cm (* WEIGHTS AND MEASURES), about 150 × 25 × 15 m (Gn. 6:15). It is possible to read *qānîm*, 'reeds', for *qinnîm*, 'nests', in Gn. 6:14, without interfering with the consonantal text, giving the sense that the gopher wood components were bound together and caulked with reeds, and the whole then finished off with * bitumen. While the statement in 6:16 (literally, 'thou shalt make it lower, second, and third') can be taken in the traditional sense as describing three storeys, it is also possible to understand it to indicate three layers of logs laid cross-wise, a view which would accord well with a construction of wood, reeds and bitumen. The ark also had an opening (*peṯaḥ*) in the side, and a *ṣōhar*, a word not properly understood, but most commonly taken to mean an opening for light, running right round the vessel just below the roof.

The ark came to rest on 'one of the mountains of * Ararat' (Gn. 8:4) or, according to the Babylonians, Mt Niṣir ('Salvation') in NW Persia. Attempts to find the remains of the Noahic ark and prove its existence from wood fragments found in E Turkey are as yet unconfirmed (*cf.* J. A. Montgomery, *The Quest for Noah's Ark*, 1972).

2. The ark of Moses (Heb. *tēḇâ*, Ex. 2:3–6) may perhaps be pictured as a miniature version of that of Noah, but only of sufficient size to take a small infant. It was made of reeds (*gōme'*, * PAPYRI), and sealed with bitumen (*ḥēmār*) and pitch (*zep̄eṯ*, * BITUMEN) and from the fact that it was necessary to open it (Ex. 2:6) it was apparently, as was probably Noah's ark, completely closed in.

BIBLIOGRAPHY. A. Heidel, *The Gilgamesh Epic and Old Testament Parallels*[2], 1949, pp. 232–237; E. Ullendorff, *VT* 4, 1954, pp. 95–96.

T.C.M.

ARK (MOSES)
See Papyri, Part 2.

ARK OF THE COVENANT. Called also 'ark of the Lord', 'ark of God', 'ark of the covenant of the Lord' (Dt. 10:8) and 'ark of the testimony' (*ēḏûṯ* = covenant-terms: * WITNESS). The ark was a rectangular box (*'ārôn*) made of acacia wood, and measured $2\frac{1}{2} \times 1\frac{1}{2} \times 1\frac{1}{2}$ cubits (*i.e. c.* 4 × $2\frac{1}{2}$ × $2\frac{1}{2}$ feet or *c.* 1·22 m × 76 cm × 76 cm). The whole was covered with gold and was carried on poles inserted in rings at the four lower corners. The lid, or 'mercy-seat', was a gold plate surrounded by two antithetically-placed cherubs with outspread wings.

The ark served (i) as receptacle for the two tablets of the Decalogue (Ex. 25:16, 21; 40:20; Dt. 10:1–5) and also for the pot of manna and Aaron's rod (Heb. 9:4–5); (ii) as the meeting-place in the inner sanctuary where the Lord revealed his will to his servants (Moses: Ex. 25:22; 30:36; Aaron: Lv. 16:2; Joshua: Jos. 7:6). Thus it served as the symbol of the divine presence guiding his people. The ark was made at Sinai by Bezalel to the pattern given to Moses (Ex. 25:8ff.). It was used as a depository for the written law (Dt. 31:9; Jos.

Tutankhamun's cedar-wood chest, decorated with ebony and ivory. Underneath, four poles slide through bronze rings attached to boards at the base of the box and are secured by flanges at the inner ends. This idea may be compared with the means by which the ark was carried. 63·5 cm × 83 cm × 60·5 cm. 18th Dynasty, c. 1400 BC. (GIO)

24:26) and played a significant part at the crossing of Jordan (Jos. 3–4), the fall of Jericho (Jos. 6) and the ceremony of remembering the covenant at Mt Ebal (Jos. 8:30ff.).

From Gilgal the ark was moved to Bethel (Jdg. 2:1; 20:27), but was taken to Shiloh in the time of the Judges (1 Sa. 1:3; 3:3), remaining there till captured by the Philistines on the battlefield at Ebenezer (1 Sa. 4). Because its presence caused 7 months of plagues, the Philistines returned it to Kiriath-jearim, where it remained for 20 years (2 Sa. 5:1–7:2), except possibly for a temporary move to Saul's camp near Bethaven (1 Sa. 14:18—where, however, LXX indicates that the original reading was probably 'ephod').

David installed the ark in a tent at Jerusalem (2 Sa. 6), and would not remove it during Absalom's rebellion (2 Sa. 15:24–29). It was placed in the Temple with great ceremony in the reign of Solomon (1 Ki. 8:1ff.), and re-sited in the sanctuary during Josiah's reforms (2 Ch. 35:3) when Jeremiah anticipated an age without its presence (3:16). It was presumably lost during the destruction of Jerusalem by the Babylonians in 587 BC. There was no ark in the second Temple (Josephus, *BJ* 5. 219).

Gold-overlaid wooden receptacles or portable shrines are known from the ancient Near East in pre-Mosaic times. The ark is unique, however, as the repository of the covenant-tablets, *i.e.* documents bearing the 'covenant-stipulations' (*'ēḏûṯ*). K.A.K.

ARKITE. Gn. 10:17; 1 Ch. 1:15. A descendant of Ham through Canaan, and the eponymous ancestor of the inhabitants of a Phoenician city, modern Tell 'Arqa, 20 km NE of Tripolis. The place is mentioned in Egyptian records, including the *Amarna letters, and by Shalmaneser III (853 BC) and Tiglath-pileser III. Called Caesari Libani in Roman times. G.G.G.

ARM (Heb. *z^{e}rōa'*, common throughout the OT, with parallels in other Near Eastern languages, of the human arm or shoulder as a symbol of strength: paralleled, less frequently, in the NT by Gk. *brachiōn*).

The symbol of the arm outstretched, or made bare (much the same idea in view of E dress), is used especially of the Lord to portray his mighty acts, referring often to the deliverance of Israel from Egypt (Ex. 6:6, *etc.*), also to other acts of judgment or salvation evidenced or sought (Is. 51:9; Ezk. 20:33). Thus, logically, the arm or arms of the Lord become the symbol of safe refuge (Dt. 33:27). The powerful arm of the Lord is contrasted with the puny arm of man, 'an arm of flesh' (2 Ch. 32:8). The arms of the wicked are broken, or withered (Ps. 37:17; Zc. 11:17), but the Lord can strengthen the arms of those whom he chooses to enable them to do wonders (Ps. 18:34).

In Dn. 11:22 (AV) the symbol is used of impersonal force, 'the arms of a flood'. The parallelism with *'hand' or 'right hand' is natural (Ps. 44:3). B.O.B.

ARMAGEDDON (*WH*, RV, *Har Magedon*; TR *Armageddon*; Lat. *Hermagedon*; Syr.$^{Gwy.}$ *Magedon*). The assembly-point in the apocalyptic scene of the great Day of God Almighty (Rev. 16:16; unknown elsewhere). If it is symbolic, geographical exactness is unimportant. The earliest known interpretation, extant only in Arabic, is 'the trodden, *level* place (Arab. *'lmwḍ' 'lwṭv* = the Plain?)' (Hippolytus, ed. Bonwetsch). Of four modern interpretations, namely, 'mountain of Megiddo', 'city of Megiddo', 'mount of assembly' (C. C. Torrey) and 'his fruitful hill', most scholars prefer the first. The fact that the tell of Megiddo was about 21 m high in John's day, and was in the vicinity of Carmel Range, justifies the use of Heb. *har*, used loosely in the OT for 'hill' and 'hill country' (*BDB*, p. 249; *cf.* Jos. 10:40; 11:16). The 'waters of Megiddo' (Jdg. 5:19) and the 'valley-plain of Megiddo' (2 Ch. 35:22) have witnessed important battles, from one fought by Tuthmosis III in 1468 BC to that of Lord Allenby of Megiddo in 1917. The 'mountains of Israel' witness Gog's defeat in Ezk. 39:1–4. This may be in the writer's mind. R.J.A.S.

ARMOUR AND WEAPONS. The comprehensive terms in Hebrew and Greek are *kēlîm* (Gn. 27:3; 1 Sa. 17:54; more specifically *k^{e}lê milḥāmâ*, 'weapons of war', as Dt. 1:41, *etc.*) and *hopla* (LXX *passim*; 2 Cor. 10:4). References to armour-bearers in Jdg. 9:54; 1 Sa. 14:1; 17:7, and to armouries in 1 Ki. 10:17; Ne. 3:19. The Qumran *War Scroll* furnishes a detailed description of the armour to be used by the 'sons of light' in their eschatological war with the 'sons of darkness'. Yadin (see bibliography) maintains that the descriptions reflect Roman military practice in the second half of the 1st century BC. Various items of armour are given a figurative, spiritual significance in Is. 59:17; Eph. 6:10–17, *etc.*

ARMLET See Ornaments, Part 2.

Shield of Ionian type, probably carried by an Ionian mercenary fighting for the Egyptians at the battle of Carchemish in 605 BC. (BM)

I. Armour (defensive)

a. Shield

The use of shields in battle is attested in the earliest battle scenes from Egypt and Mesopotamia; for Egypt *cf.* the pre-dynastic mural from Hierakonpolis, now in Cairo Museum, and, for Mesopotamia, Eannatum's Stele of the Vultures (*c.* 2500 BC). Various shapes and sizes were in vogue depending on the country and period in question. The advent of the smaller, circular shield is associated with the appearance of the Sea Peoples in the Levant in the late 2nd millennium BC. In Hebrew the commonest term is *māgēn*, often denoting this type of shield; *ṣinnâ* is used for the larger version. It was the latter which was used by Goliath, who had his own shield-bearer (1 Sa. 17:7). The smaller shield was carried by archers such as the Benjaminites in Asa's army (2 Ch. 14:8, 'bucklers'). Shields commonly consisted of a wooden frame covered with hide which was oiled before use in battle (*cf.* 2 Sa. 1:21; Is. 21:5). Metal provided greater protection, but impeded movement; for its use *cf.* 1 Ki. 14:27. As a compromise, leather shields might be studded with metal discs to increase their effectiveness.

Electrum helmet of Meskalamdug, from Ur, Iraq, worn over a cloth and wool inner cap attached by laces which passed through the holes around the rim. Height 23 cm. c. 2500 BC. (SAOB)

b. Helmet

Metal helmets were worn by Sumerian and Akkadian soldiery in the 3rd millennium BC. The Hebrew term is *qôḇa'/kôḇa'*, and may be of foreign origin. Metal helmets were expensive to make, and in some periods their use was restricted to kings and other military leaders; Saul offered David his own bronze helmet for the contest with Goliath (1 Sa. 17:38). 2 Ch. 26:14 could be interpreted to mean that (leather?) helmets were general issue in the army of Judah in the time of Uzziah. According to 1 Macc. 6:35 the rank and file were supplied with bronze helmets in the Seleucid period. The Assyrian army attacking Palestine often wore the conical, reinforced helmet with an elongation to protect the neck.

c. Coat of mail

The coat of mail was worn in the first instance by charioteers (*cf.* Je. 46:4) and archers (*cf.* Je. 51:3), who were not in a position to protect themselves with shields. Scale armour, more protective than leather and lighter than plate-armour, was in widespread use in the Near East by the middle of the 2nd millennium BC. It was expensive, and Tuthmosis III (1490–1436 BC) was pleased to include more than 200 coats of mail in the spoil taken by his army after the battle of Megiddo. Nuzi (15th century BC) provides both material and textual evidence for the composition of the coat of mail. One text mentions a coat consisting of 680 scales and another of 1,035 scales. The size of the scales depended on their place in the coat; they were affixed to the leather or cloth by means of thread which was inserted in holes pierced in them for this purpose. The joins of the sleeves were weak points, as is illustrated by the story of Ahab (1 Ki. 22:34f.) and by a relief on a chariot belonging to Tuthmosis IV. In Hebrew the usual term is *širyôn*, which probably comprised both breastplate and back-plate. One such was worn by Goliath (1 Sa. 17:5), while coats of mail also provided protection for Nehemiah's workmen (Ne. 4:16).

The Greek equivalent was the *thōrax*, also used in 1 Macc. 6:43 of armour protecting the Seleucid war-elephants.

Targum Onkelos' translation of *taḥrā'* in Ex. 28:32; 39:23 by 'coat of mail' has been shown to be correct in the light of the Samaritan use of *taḥrā'* with precisely this meaning; see J. M. Cohen, *VT* 24, 1974, pp. 361–366.

d. Greaves

It is said in 1 Sa. 17:6 that Goliath wore *miṣḥôṯ* (*MT miṣḥaṯ*) of bronze upon his legs, and LXX translates by *knēmides*, 'greaves' (armour for shins). The Hebrew word is a *hapax legomenon*, but the sense does not seem to be in doubt. Greaves were commonly used by Greek and Roman soldiers at a later date.

II. Weapons (offensive)

a. Sword

The sword (Heb. *ḥereḇ*) is the most frequently mentioned weapon in the Bible. The earliest swords in the ancient world were usually straight, double-edged and more akin to daggers, being used for stabbing (*cf.* the examples from the Royal Cemetery at Ur and from Dorak (Anatolia), all dated *c.* 2500 BC). About the middle of the 3rd millennium the sickle-shaped sword begins to appear; examples from somewhat later have been found at Byblos, Shechem and Abydos. In the first half of the 2nd millennium blades were still quite short, and it was only in the time of the Egyptian New Kingdom that the longer-bladed sword began to be used widely. With the arrival of the Sea Peoples the long, straight sword began to enjoy popularity; *cf.* the sword bearing the name of Pharaoh Merenptah discovered at Ugarit (late 13th century BC). The sword played no small part in the Israelite conquest of Canaan just about this time (*cf.* Jos. 10:11; 11:11, *etc.*). It was usually housed in a sheath which was suspended from a belt (*cf.* 2 Sa. 20:8); hilts were often ornamented, to judge from the various finds in Egypt and Mesopotamia.

The word most often used in the NT is *machaira* (*cf.* Mt. 26:47). The *rhomphaia*, occurring, with one exception, only in Revelation, was a large, broad sword, used originally by the Thracians. The revolutionary Jewish assassins, the *sicarii*, carried short, slightly curved daggers under their clothing (Jos., *BJ* 2. 255). In both Testaments the sword is frequently used, by metonymy, for war, or as a symbol for the word of God (*cf.* Ezk. 21:9; Eph. 6:17).

b. Spear and javelin

The spear (Heb. *ḥ^{a}nîṯ*), consisting of a wooden shaft and a metallic head, in later times of iron (*cf.* 1 Sa. 13:19; 17:7), was greatly favoured by the Sumerians in the 3rd millennium. It remained the basic weapon of the infantry, the lighter javelin or lance being used by the charioteers (*cf.* the Egyptian practice in the 19th Dynasty and subsequently). Hebrew also has the word *rōmaḥ* (*e.g.* Jdg. 5:8), by which a light spear or lance (*cf.* Nu. 25:7) may be intended. The Hebrew *kîḏôn* has traditionally been rendered 'javelin' (*e.g.* 1 Sa. 17:6), but the translation has been disputed (*cf.* NEB 'dagger'), and the evidence of the Qumran *War Scroll* supports the meaning 'sword'. In certain circumstances the spear was a symbol of royal authority (*cf.* 1 Sa. 22:6; 26:7). Pikes and throw-spears were also used by the Assyrian *army.

The Greek *longchē* of Jn. 19:34 is the equivalent of the Hebrew *ḥ^{a}nîṯ*.

Coat of mail made of overlapping bronze scales, laced together with leather thongs. From Nuzi, Iraq. c. 1400 BC. (SAOB)

Persian soldiers carrying spears and round, concave shields. From the palace at Persepolis. 5th cent. BC. (SMB)

It has been conjectured that 'hyssop' in Jn. 19:29 has replaced an original reading 'javelin' (*hyssōpos* for *hyssos*), but there is good reason to retain the traditional text.

c. Bow and arrow

The basic Hebrew words are *qešeṯ* and *ḥēṣ*. The ancient bow could have a single curve or be double-convex (examples of the latter from as early as pre-dynastic Egypt). Development of the composite bow meant a considerable increase in power and range, and may partly account for the military superiority of the Semitic Akkadians over the Sumerians in the late 3rd millennium BC. However, it was fully another millennium before the composite bow came into more general use. Animal horn and sinews were bonded with strips of wood to make up the frame (*cf.* the description of Anat's bow in the Ugaritic Aqhat legend); bronze might also be used as a strengthener (*cf.* Ps. 18:34). Arrows were usually made of reed and fitted with metal heads; they might

Eannatum, king of Lagash, leading his troops in a charge; the first known depiction of soldiers fighting in a phalanx. The men are protected by large shields, carry spears, and wear round Sumerian helmets. Limestone 'Stele of the Vultures', from Telloh (Lagash). Height c. 75 cm. c. 2500 BC. (RS)

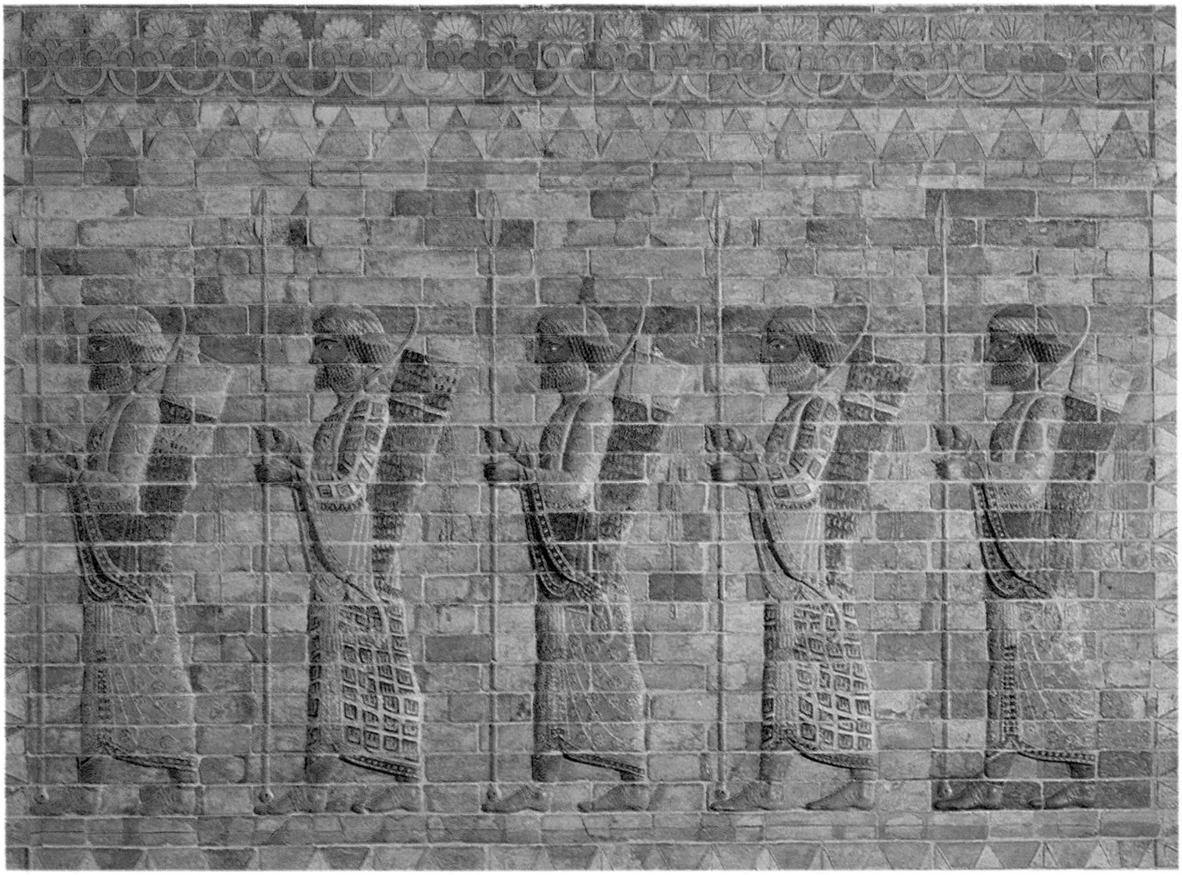

Armed Elamite soldiers. Frieze of enamelled brick from the palace of Darius I at Susa (Shushan), Persia. 5th cent. BC. (MC)

Ashurbanipal's servants stringing bows for hunting. Nineveh. c. 650 BC. (BM)

be carried in leather quivers, and sometimes chariots were also fitted with quivers. A quiver is usually depicted as holding thirty arrows (Amarna, Nuzi), or fifty when attached to a chariot (Assyrian reliefs). To string the bow the lower end was pressed down by the foot, while the upper end was bent so as to permit the string to be fastened in a notch, hence the Hebrew expression 'to tread the bow'; archers were called 'bow-treaders' (Je. 50:14). Among the Israelites the tribes of Benjamin, Reuben, Gad and Manasseh were especially famed for their bowmen (*cf.* 1 Ch. 5:18; 12:2; 2 Ch. 14:8).

d. The sling

The sling (*qela*) was carried chiefly by shepherds (*e.g.* David, 1 Sa. 17:40), to ward off wild beasts from their flocks or to prevent animals

Assyrian archers shooting from behind large reed shields. Relief from Sennacherib's palace at Nineveh. c. 690 BC. (BM)

Assyrian slingers, wearing copper helmets and coats of mail, from Sennacherib's palace at Nineveh. c. 690 BC. (BM)

from straying. It was used as a weapon of war by the Egyptian, Assyrian and Babylonian armies, though monumental evidence in the case of the Assyrians begins only in the 8th century BC. The Israelites also employed companies of slingers in their armies, the ambidextrous Benjaminites being the leading exponents of this method of warfare (1 Ch. 12:2). The sling consisted of a patch of cloth or leather with cords attached at opposite ends. The ends of the cords were held firmly in the hand as the loaded sling was whirled above the head, until one end was suddenly released. Graphic metaphorical use of this is made in Je. 10:18. Sling-stones (pointed or round pebbles) fired by Assyrian besiegers were found in the Lachish excavations.

Bottom left: Sling-stones found at the main gate of Lachish. Probably used either during Sennacherib's siege of the city in 701 BC, *or during the Babylonian attack c. 588/7* BC. (BM)

e. The battle-axe

The battle-axe, like the mace, was designed for hand-to-hand combat and varied greatly in shape and size. Biblical references are few. In Je. 51:20 *mappēṣ* (lit. 'shatterer',

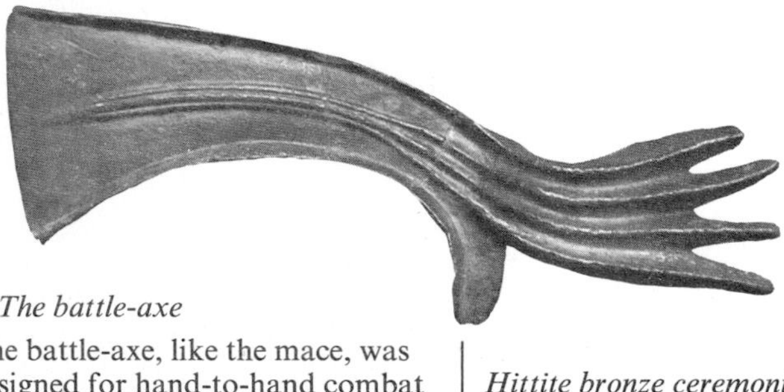

Hittite bronze ceremonial axe-head. From Beth-shean. Length 20·5 cm. 18th cent. BC. (ZR)

BDB) is translated 'hammer' in RSV and 'battle-axe' in NEB. A similar word occurs in the expression 'weapon for slaughter' in Ezk. 9:2. (*ARMY, *WAR.)

BIBLIOGRAPHY. Y. Yadin, *The Scroll of the War of the Sons of Light against the Sons of Darkness*, 1962; *idem*, *The Art of Warfare in Biblical Lands in the Light of Archaeological Discovery*, 1963; K. Galling, *SVT* 15, 1966, pp. 150–169. R.P.G.

View of the encampment of the 10th Roman legion under Flavius Silva at Masada. AD 72–73. (RP)

ARMY. Unlike their Egyptian and Mesopotamian counterparts, the monarchs of Israel appear not to have been interested in having their military exploits commemorated in propagandist reliefs and paintings. Our description of the Israelite military machine must therefore largely be dependent on the verbal accounts of battles and the incidental references which the OT offers.

a. Composition

As the story of Deborah and Barak well illustrates, the Israelite army began as a tribal militia assembled in times of crisis and led by someone of charismatic stamp. The basis of organization was the tribal clan which, in theory, provided a contingent of a thousand men (1 Sa. 10:19). Certain tribes gained reputations for proficiency in the use of particular weapons (*e.g.* Jdg. 20:16; *cf.* 1 Ch. 12). It was Saul who provided Israel with the nucleus of a standing army, numbering in the first instance no more than 3,000 (1 Sa. 13:2). Like the institution of kingship itself, the creation of this regular force owed much to the continuing menace of the Philistines. Duels between champions as a means of avoiding excessive bloodshed seem to have been more familiar to the Philistines than to the Israelites (1 Sa. 17), but we do read of a representative encounter between two groups of *nᵉʿārîm* (lit. 'young men', but occasionally used as a technical term meaning 'picked troops') from the armies of David and Ishbosheth (2 Sa. 2:12–17). David's army comprised both regular contingents (2 Sa. 15:18) and a militia force. 2 Sa. 23:8ff. lists the commanding officers in David's army—'The Three' and 'The Thirty'. In the main these were men who had distinguished records from the days when David was in hiding from Saul and at the head of

The Assyrian king's tent in an army encampment. He is offered a drink while a couch is made ready for him and a butcher prepares a carcass in the adjoining tent. (SMB) (AMM)

a band of freebooters. Included in the regular contingents were Aegean mercenaries (Cherethites and Pelethites) who acted as the royal bodyguard (2 Sa. 15:18–22, mentioning also Philistines of Gath). The militia was divided into twelve battalions each of which served for a month at a time (1 Ch. 27:1–15). If David had a chariot force it must have been quite small (*cf.* 2 Sa. 8:3–4); it is in Solomon's reign that chariots come into their own (1 Ki. 4:26; 10:26). There is little evidence to suggest that Israel ever had a cavalry force worthy of the name. Most of the chariots were appropriated by the N kingdom after the Disruption but, thanks to the Syrian depredations, the advantage had largely been lost by the end of the 9th century (2 Ki. 13:7). (*CAPTAIN.)

b. Camp

The camp (Heb. *maḥ^aneh*) was probably in the shape of a circle or square (*cf.* Nu. 2); the king and his commanding officers would in any case be in the centre (1 Sa. 26:5). That the soldiers slept in booths (Heb. *sukkôṯ*; *cf.* 2 Sa. 11:11; 1 Ki. 20:12, 16) is disputed by Yadin (pp. 274–275, 304–310) who prefers to read Succoth, *i.e.* the place-name. During an engagement the baggage at base would be guarded by a detachment (1 Sa. 25:13). It was possible for civilians to visit the camp and bring supplies of food—as well as exchange news (1 Sa. 17:17–30).

c. Roman army

The main division was the *legion, in theory numbering 6,000 men but actually somewhere between 4,000 and 6,000. There were ten cohorts to a legion and each cohort was made up of six centuries; each centurion commanded between seventy and a hundred men. There were also auxiliary cohorts and small cavalry units called *alae*, these mainly composed of provincials, though not Jews (Josephus, *Ant.* 14. 204). There is inscriptional evidence for the presence of an 'Italian Cohort' (Acts 10:1) in Syria *c.* AD 69; this was an auxiliary cohort and was composed of Roman freedmen.

d. Spiritual armies

The original sense of the OT expression 'Lord of hosts' (*Yahweh ṣ^eḇā'ôṯ*) is uncertain; the title may refer to God's sovereignty over the armies of Israel (1 Sa. 17:45) or to spiritual armies under his command (Jos. 5:13–15; 1 Ki. 22:19; 2 Ki. 6:17). It is the latter sense which predominates in the OT. In the final battle between good and evil Christ appears as leader of the armies of heaven (Rev. 19:14), defeating the armies of the beast and of the kings of the earth (Rev. 19:19).

BIBLIOGRAPHY. Y. Yadin, *The Art of Warfare in Biblical Lands*, 1963; R. de Vaux, *Ancient Israel*², 1965, pp. 213–228; A. F. Rainey in L. R. Fisher (ed.), *Ras Shamra Parallels*, 2, 1975, pp. 98–107.

R.P.G.

ARNON. A wadi running into the E side of the Dead Sea opposite En-gedi. This formed the S border of Reubenite territory at the time of the settlement (Dt. 3:12, 16), and previously marked the boundary between Moab to the S and Ammon to the N (Jdg. 11:18–19). The invading Hebrews crossed the Arnon from S to N, and this proved a turning-point in their career, for they took their first territorial possessions on the N side (Dt. 2:24). However, the *Moabite Stone (line 10) mentions Moabites living in Ataroth, which is to the N of the wadi, suggesting either incomplete conquest on the part of the settlers or later Moabite infiltration. The importance of the river is confirmed by the number of forts and fords which are found there, the latter being mentioned by Isaiah (Is. 16:2).

R.J.W.

AROER. 1. In Transjordan, on the N bank of the river Arnon (Wadi Môjib) overlooking its deep gorge (D. Baly, *The Geography of the Bible*, 1957, fig. 72 on p. 237), at modern 'Ara'ir (N. Glueck, *Explorations in Eastern Palestine* I (= *AASOR* 14, 1934, pp. 3, 49–51 with fig. 21a and Plate 11), *c.* 22 km E of the Dead Sea (Dt. 2:36; 3:12; 4:48; Jos. 12:2). It symbolized the S limit, first, of the Amorite kingdom of Sihon, second, of the tribal territory of Reuben (Jos. 13:9, 16; Jdg. 11:26 and probably 33) being the seat of a Reubenite family (1 Ch. 5:8), and third, of the Transjordanian conquests of Hazael of Damascus in Jehu's time (2 Ki. 10:33). About this time,

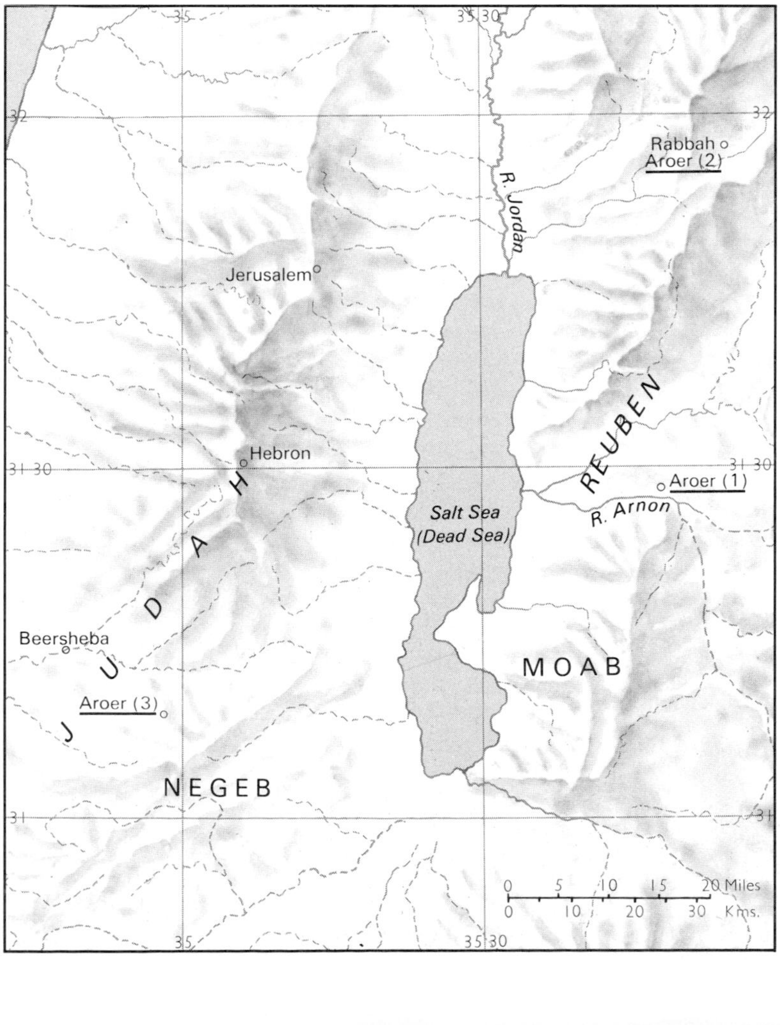

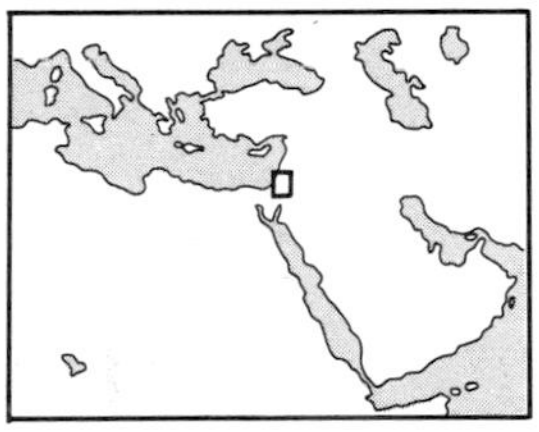

Locations of the three OT towns bearing the name Aroer.

ARPHAD
See Arpad, Part 1.

ARPHAXAD
See Arpachshad, Part 1.

ARROW
See Armour, Part 1.

ARROWSNAKE
See Animals, Part 1.

Mesha, king of Moab, 'built Aroer and made the road by the Arnon' (Moabite Stone, line 26); Aroer remained Moabite down to Jeremiah's time (Je. 48:18–20). In Nu. 32:34 Gad apparently helped to repair newly conquered cities, including Aroer, before formal allotment of Reubenite and Gadite territories by Moses. In 2 Sa. 24:5 probably read with RSV that Joab's census for David started from Aroer and the city in the valley *towards* Gad and on to Jazer. Isaiah (17:1–3) prophesied against (Moabite-held) Aroer, alongside Damascus and Ephraim. The 'city that is in the valley' (Dt. 2:36; Jos. 13:9, 16, all RV [but not 12:2, see AV, RSV]; 2 Sa. 24:5, RV) may be present Khirbet el-Medeiyineh *c.* 11 km SE of Aroer (Simons, *Geographical and Topographical Texts of the Old Testament*, 1959, § 298, pp. 116–117; for a description, see Glueck, *op. cit.*, p. 36, No. 93).

2. In Transjordan, 'before Rabbah' (Jos. 13:25, AV, RV, against RSV); could be modern es-Ṣweiwinā, *c.* 3½ km SW of Rabbah (Glueck, *Explorations in Eastern Palestine* III (= *AASOR* 18, 19), 1939, pp. 247, 249; for a description, see *ibid.*, pp. 168–170 and fig. 55). But the existence of this Aroer separate from **1** above is doubtful, as Jos. 13:25 might perhaps be rendered '. . . half the land of the Ammonites unto Aroer, which (land is/extends) towards/as far as Rabbah' (Glueck, *op. cit.*, p. 249).

3. In Negeb (southland) of Judah, 19 km SE of Beersheba, present Khirbet Ar'areh (N. Glueck, *Rivers in the Desert*, 1959, pp. 131–132, 184–185). Among the Judaeans receiving presents from David at Ziklag (1 Sa. 30:26–28) were 'them which were in Aroer'; among his mighty men were two sons of 'Hotham the Aroerite' (1 Ch. 11:44). K.A.K.

ARPACHSHAD, ARPHAXAD (Heb. *'arpak̲šad̲*; LXX and NT *Arphaxad*). A son of Shem (Gn. 10:22; 1 Ch. 1:17, 24), who was born 2 years after the Flood (Gn. 11:10). The *MT* states that he was the father of Shelah, who was born when he was 35 years old (Gn. 10:24; 11:12; 1 Ch. 1:18, 24; LXX and Samaritan Pentateuch read 135), but some MSS of the LXX interpose a *Kainan* between Arpachshad and Shelah, and this has evidently been followed by Lk. 3:36. Arpachshad lived for a total of 438 years (Gn. 11:13; LXX gives 430, but the Samaritan Pentateuch agrees in the total in spite of disagreement on the component figures). Several theories about the identification of the name have been put forward, perhaps the commonest connecting it with *Arrapḫu* of the cuneiform inscriptions, Gk. *Arrapachitis*, probably modern Kirkuk. Other theories see the end of the name, *-kšad*, as a corruption from *keśed̲, kaśdîm*, *'Chaldeans', therefore referring to S Mesopotamia. An Iranian etymology has also been suggested, in which connection it is to be noted that it is stated in the Apocrypha (Judith 1:1) that one Arphaxad (*cf.* LXX *Arphaxad*) ruled over the Medes in Ecbatana. This book is, however, largely fiction, and in the absence of a Hebrew original there is no guarantee that the name is the same. The name continues therefore to be unknown outside the Bible.

BIBLIOGRAPHY. J. Skinner, *ICC, Genesis*², 1930, pp. 205, 231, 233; W. F. Albright, *JBL* 43, 1924, pp. 388–389; W. Brandenstein, in *Sprachgeschichte und Wortbedeutung: Festschrift Albert Debrunner*, 1954, pp. 59–62; and for another theory G. Dossin, *Muséon* 47, 1934, pp. 119–121; *KB*, p. 87. T.C.M.

ARPAD. Name of city and Aramaean province in N Syria, now Tell Rif'at, *c.* 30 km NW of Aleppo, excavated in 1956–64. From *c.* 1000 BC Arpad (Akkad. *Arpaddu*, Old Aram. *'rpd*), capital of an *Aramaean tribal territory known as Bit Agusḫ, opposed Assyria as an ally of Hamath, Damascus, and in 743 BC Urartu. (*ARARAT.) Annexed by *Tiglath-pileser III after a 2-year siege in 740 BC, it rebelled with Hamath, Damascus and Samaria in 720, and was reconquered by Sargon II. This lies behind the boast of *Rabshakeh to Jerusalem (2 Ki. 18:34; Is. 36:19; 37:13, AV 'Arphad'). Its destruction symbolized the overwhelming might of Assyria (Is. 10:9; Je. 49:23). The last ruler of Arpad, Mati'el, signed a vassal treaty under Ashur-nirari V of Assyria in 754 BC, which survives in Assyrian, and another with an unidentified king, 'Bar-Ga'yah of KTK', which was inscribed on stone stelae found at Sefire (*cf.* Jos. 8:32).

BIBLIOGRAPHY. *Excavations:* V. M. S. Williams, *Iraq* 23, 1961, pp. 68–87; *idem*, *AASOR* 17, 1967, pp. 69–84; *Iraq* 29, 1967, pp. 16–33; *Treaty: ANET*, pp. 532f., 659–661; J. A. Fitzmyer, *The Aramaic Inscriptions of Sefire*, 1967. D.J.W.

ART. Throughout their long history Palestine and Syria were occupied by mixed peoples and cultures, and it is not easily possible to distinguish Heb. or Jewish art from the contemporary Egyp., Syrian, Mesopotamian or Phoenician art, or the later Jewish art from the Hellenistic and Graeco-Roman importations, imitations or influences. In each period, however, certain local styles found in a defined context supplied by *archaeology can be traced.

a. Prehistoric art

Natufian bone carvings from the Carmel region (*c.* 8000 BC), carved sickle handle or red ochre painting of a gazelle on limestone or the decoration of skulls with cowrie shells, a practice followed in prepottery Neolithic Jericho (*c.* 6500 BC), are, with figurines and votive figures, a portent of a long history of art. The earliest extant wall-painting comes from Teleilat Ghassul in the Jordan valley (*c.* 3500 BC). One polychrome fresco uses geometrical patterns centring on an eight-pointed star encircled by figures and dragons(?). Others depict a bird or a group of figures, possibly worshippers. The style is reminiscent of contemporary Assyria (Tell Halaf). The Neolithic people of Jericho also decorated red burnished pottery with geometric designs. Elsewhere *ivory and bone was worked to make precious objects like figurines and furniture (*e.g.* Abu Matar, *c.* 3900–3300 BC).

b. Canaanite art (3000–*c.* 1200 BC)

This now has to be studied according to its regional developments which range from the fine engraved statue from Tell Mardiḫ (*EBLA) and the engraved silver cup from Ain Samiyeh (both reflecting Mesopotamian influence) to the more common local versions of figurines and images. Metal figurines from Byblos, inlaid and silhouette ivories from an El Jisr tomb (MB II) show strong Egyptian inspiration, while the basalt relief orthostats from the 18th-century palace of Yarimlim of *Alalah are not dissimilar to those

The mound of Arpad (modern Tell Rif'at). (ARM)

also found in Anatolia and Palestine (Hazor). The figure of Yarim-lim, like that of the later sculpture of the seated figure of Idrimi of Alalaḫ (*c.* 1460 BC), seems to show a Sumerian-type ancestry.

By the Late Bronze Age there are many local composite art forms in sculpture, as on the Baal stela, which is a cross between Egyptian (stance and part dress), Anatolian (helmet and hairstyle) and Syrian (dress). Ivory carvings from this period have been compared with both Mycenean and Mesopotamian art. A finely-worked gold plate from *Ugarit uses mythological motifs. Towards the end of this period come a number of reliefs following the tradition of the Beth-shean sculptured stela (MN II under Egyp. influence) and votive plaques dedicated to the local god Mekal of Khirbet Balu'a (Transjordan). Such images of *idols include a gold-covered bronze statue from Megiddo and ivory carvings, ably executed, from Lachish, Tell el-Farah or Megiddo (12th century). From this period also comes a steady flow of painted pottery using local motifs though some were already known from Syria and Mesopotamia. A characteristic spiral and 'bird' decoration marks out the jugs and craters of the Philistines in the coastal area.

c. Hebrew art (*c. 1200–586 BC*)

There seems to be little change in the local products, which were in a period of decline throughout the ancient Near East, when the Israelites entered the land. They do not appear to have imported indigenous forms, though they were not devoid of appreciation of art or its employment in *arts and crafts. They had accepted fine Egyp. jewellery as gifts (Ex. 12:35) and had used gold and silver for fashioning an Egyptianizing bull-calf in the round after the Exodus (Ex. 32:2–4). The Israelites gave their finer possessions to adorn the *tabernacle which was constructed under the direction of a native of Judah, Bezalel, himself capable of designing and working in wood, metal and *embroidery (Ex. 35:30–33).

Open-work ivory plaque with inlaid glass eyes. Probably used as an inlay in furniture. From Megiddo. Height c. 20 cm. Early 12th cent. BC. (OIUC)

With increasing prosperity under David and Solomon the Hebrews turned to Phoenician artists to train their native workers. Since the plans for the *architecture and building of David's *palace and Solomon's *Temple in Jerusalem received royal approval, it may be indicative that local Heb. tastes did not differ significantly from their neighbours in Syro-Phoenicia.

The second commandment forbidding the making of 'a graven

Wall-painting of two Assyrian royal officials, from Til Barsip, Syria. 8th cent. BC. (AP)

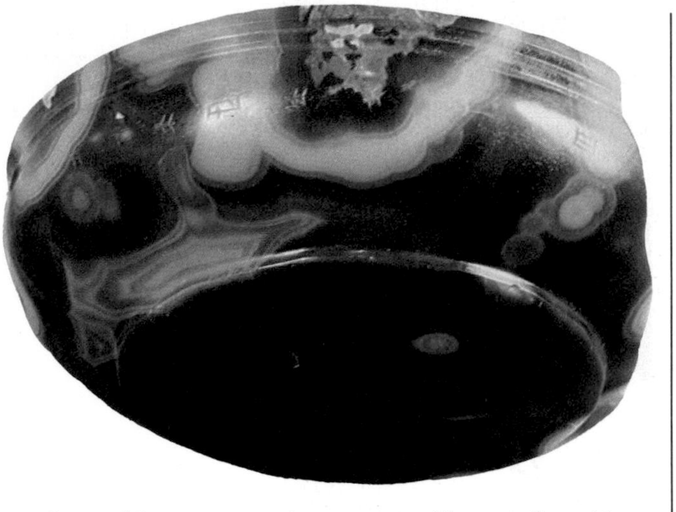

Bowl carved from onyx and inscribed with the name of Esarhaddon king of Assyria. c. 675 BC. (BM)

image, or any likeness of anything that is in heaven . . . earth . . . or the water' (Ex. 20:4) did not condemn art but the practice of idolatry to which it might lead (v. 5). In practice it seems to have been interpreted as precluding only the representation of the human form and significantly none such which can be said to be indubitably Heb. or Jewish has yet been discovered. The Temple, as the tabernacle, was decorated with winged human-headed lions (*CHERUBIM), winged griffins, palmettes, and floral and arboreal patterns. Elsewhere Egyptianized figures and symbols, as well as birds and reptiles and a variety of animals (lions, bulls) and patterns (*e.g.* guilloche), are found on temple decoration (1 Ki. 6:18) and on contemporary ivories from Samaria and Hazor, drawn on pottery and engraved on seals.

Both kings and the wealthy employed craftsmen to beautify their homes (1 Ki. 22:39), and where this is condemned it is on the grounds of the inappropriateness of such luxury, an expression of self-interest, while God's house and work lie neglected (Am. 3:15; Ps. 45:8; Hg. 1:4). It must always be remembered that the Hebrews, by their encouragement of *music, literature (both prose and poetry) and speech, set a high standard of 'artistic expression' which has profoundly influenced later art.

d. Media

(i) *Painting*. Since the Egyptians and Amorites (*e.g.* the Investiture fresco from Mari) commonly painted scenes on plastered walls, it is possible that the Hebrews may have done so, though few examples are yet known. Pigments have been found in excavations (see also Dyer under *ARTS AND CRAFTS) and red ochre (Heb. *šāšēr*) was used for painting on walls and wood (Je. 22:14; Ezk. 23:14). Oholibah in the 6th century saw Chaldeans painted (*māšaḥ*, 'to smear, anoint') on a wall in vermilion (Ezk. 23:14).

(ii) *Wood-carving*. Bezalel and his assistant Aholiab directed the wood-cutting (*ḥᵃrōšeṯ ʿēṣ*) for the tabernacle, which included pillars with curved capitals (Ex. 36:38; 35:33), and a horned altar recessed to take a grating (38:2–4). The Temple built by Solomon was roofed with pine with appliqué palmettes and guilloche borders (2 Ch. 3:5) and panelled in cedar (1 Ki. 6:15–16). The walls and doors were sculptured in bas-relief with carvings (*miqlāʿôṯ*) of lotus buds and 'fleur-de-lis' or 'Prince-of-Wales' feathers' forming a triple flower (AV 'knops and open flowers'), palm designs and representations of *cherubim (1 Ki. 6:18, 29). The doors of olive-wood had similar designs etched (*ḥāqâ*) and in intaglio work (vv. 32–35); the whole, as so often with fine wood or ivory work, was overlaid with gold. Since hard woods, such as almug (sandalwood) and ebony, had to be imported (1 Ki. 10:11), and skilled carvers were rare, the use of panelling (*sāpan*), elaborate woodwork, and carved windows was considered an extravagant display of wealth (Je. 22:14; Hg. 1:4). Ezekiel's Temple was conceived as having carved panels of two-faced cherubim alternating with palm-trees and young lions, the outer doors being veneered (*šᵉḥîp*) with wood (Ezk. 41:16–26).

Elaborately carved furniture and other objects of wood, boxes, spoons and vessels have been found in the 'Amorite' tombs at *Jericho. Since ancient Egyp. wood-carving (*c.* 2000–500 BC) 'both on a large and miniature scale reached a standard not equalled in Europe until the Renaissance', something of this work must have been known to wealthy Hebrews. See also Carpenter under *ARTS AND CRAFTS.

(iii) *Ivory-carving*. As early as 34th–33rd centuries BC (Abu Matar) ivory and bone was worked in Palestine to make precious objects, figurines and furniture. It was incised (mostly in panels), sculptured in the round, or cut as open work, or relief. 'Canaanite'

Bronze stand for a large basin or brazier, showing a man carrying an ingot of copper in the shape of an animal hide. Cyprus. 12th cent. BC. (MH)

Mosaic standard of shell, red limestone and lapis lazuli inlaid in bitumen. Detail from scenes of war showing a Sumerian chariot. From the Royal Cemetery at Ur, Mesopotamia. c. 2500 BC. (BM)

ivories include an ointment vase in female form with a hand-shaped (Lachish, 14th century BC) or Hathor-headed stopper (Hazor, 13th century BC), an unguent spoon shaped as a swimming lady catching a duck (Tell Beit Mirsim) and several pyxides show human figures. After a period of decline in the art, incised panels from Megiddo, probably of local workmanship in the 12th to 10th centuries, show lively scenes in one of which the king seated on a throne, which must have been similar to that later made for Solomon (2 Ch. 9:17–18), receives tribute.

Ivories found at Samaria, of the time of Ahab, show the influence of Phoenician art with its Egyp., Syro-Hittite and Assyr. elements. They compare closely with contemporary ivories found at Arslan Tash (Syria) and Nimrud (Iraq), and may have been from the same 'school' or guild of craftsmen. Some are overlaid with gold or inlaid with gold, lapis-lazuli, coloured stones and glass. Commonly recurring designs include the 'lotus' patterns and cherubim already noted in a wood-carving and allied art; also panels with a woman's head (Astarte?) at a window, couchant and suckling animals, and 'Egyptian' figures and symbols, especially the kneeling infant Horus. A matching cosmetic palette and jar from Hazor (8th century) bears a

Fragment of a wall-painting from the palace of Zimri-Lim at Mari. A gigantic divine figure heads a procession in which the king leads a sacrificial ox. (MC)

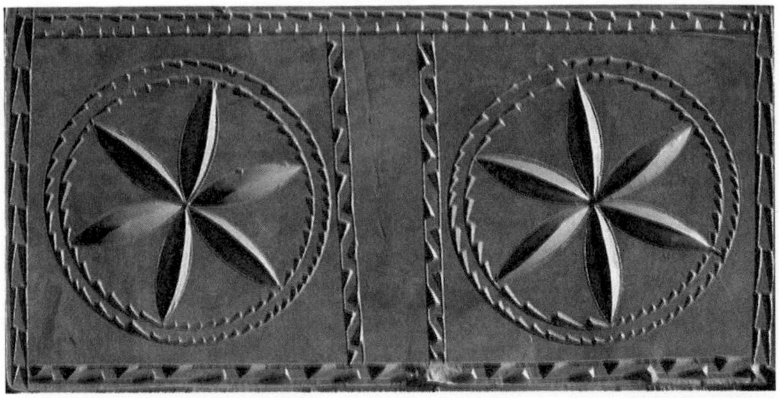

Ossuary (bone-chest) from Jerusalem with typical ornament of zig-zag frames and hexagons (so-called 'rosettes'). Such finds indicate clearly that Jewish burial at Jerusalem in this period involved the further stage of gathering of the dry bones of the dead. Between 40 BC and AD 135. (JPK)

simple hatched pattern and is of Israelite manufacture.

(iv) *Sculpture*. A few sculptures from the 'Canaanite' period in Palestine have been recovered. The seated basalt figure of a Baal, the roughly engraved stele with its pair of upraised hands and the altars from Hazor, and the serpent-coiled goddess on a stele from Beit Mirsim must be considered alongside the well-sculptured feet of a statue from Hazor (13th century BC) to show that good as well as moderate artists were at work there. A stone incense ladle in the form of a hand clasping a bowl from the same city (8th century) shows affinities with contemporary Assyr. art. The boulder in the Lachish water-shaft (9th century BC) worked into the likeness of a bearded man shows that the people of Palestine were never without an inventive spirit. But little has so far survived, and the work of their neighbours (*e.g.* the sculptured sarcophagus of Ahiram from Byblos) is better known. Volute capitals, forerunners of the Ionic type, found at Megiddo and Samaria, were probably similar to those used in the Temple. In the Maccabean period Hellenistic–Jewish ornamentalists of stone carved the fruits of the land (grapes, ethrog and acanthus leaves), symbols which are also found on coins used for *money.

A special guild of ossuary workers at Jerusalem has bequeathed us several chests engraved with six-pointed stars, rosettes, flowers and even architectural designs.

(v) *Seal-engraving*. Cylinder, scarab, stamp and cylinder seals from Palestine bear typical 'Phoenician' motifs as found on ivories, though here the winged disc and winged scarab occur more frequently. The human figure is often engraved up to the Monarchy, and the inclusion of personal names seems to be more customary in Israel than among her neighbours. Pictorial representations are rare on Judaean seals, which may show a growing awareness of the religious prohibition (see section *c*, above).

(vi) *Metal-work*. There is every indication that the Hebrews were expert metal-workers, but little has survived. This impression is borne out by the miniature bronze stand from Megiddo in open-work style showing the invocation of a seated god (*c*. 1000 BC). The bronze 'sea' of Solomon's Temple is computed to have weighed about 23,000 kg and have been of cast bronze 8 cm thick with a bowl 4·6 m in diameter and 2·3 m high with a 'petalled' rim. The whole rested on the backs of twelve oxen separately cast and arranged in four supporting triads (1 Ki. 7:23ff.). It held about 50,000 litres of water and must have been a remarkable technological achievement (*JACHIN AND BOAZ).

Many of the motifs in the materials used in i–vi are similar to those employed in other *arts and crafts such as metal-working and are known from representations of art from outside Palestine. It is not possible to judge how far *dance was considered an art form so much as part of sacred ritual.

BIBLIOGRAPHY. A. Reifenberg, *Ancient Hebrew Arts*, 1950; H. H. Frankfort, *The Art and Architecture of the Ancient Orient*, 1963; A. Moortgart, *The Art of Ancient Mesopotamia*, 1969. D.J.W.

Dying lioness, paralysed during the hunt by an arrow in her back. A prime example of Assyrian skill in depicting animals. Palace of Ashurbanipal, Nineveh. c. 640 BC. (BM)

ARTAXERXES (Heb. *'artaḥšastâ'*, with variant vocalizations, from Old Persian *arta-xša ra*, 'kingdom of righteousness'). **1.** Artaxerxes I (Longimanus), 464–424 BC. In his reign Ezra and Nehemiah came to Jerusalem, according to Ezr. 7:1; Ne. 2:1; *etc*. It has been argued that in the former case the Chronicler has confused him with Artaxerxes II (Mnemon), 404–359 BC, but there is no need to doubt the biblical record. (See J. Stafford Wright, *The Date of Ezra's Coming to Jerusalem*, 1958.)

2. Ezr. 4:7. This also is likely to be Artaxerxes I, and the date is shortly before Ne. 1:1f., when the king reverses the edict of Ezr. 4:21. Others (improbably) identify him with the pseudo-Smerdis, who reigned for a few months in 522–521 BC.

3. The LXX has Artaxerxes in

place of *Ahasuerus in *Esther and some believe that the king here is Artaxerxes II, 404–359 BC.

BIBLIOGRAPHY. A. T. Olmstead, *History of the Persian Empire*, 1948. J.S.W.

ARTEMIS. This was the Greek name of the goddess identified with the Latin Diana of classical mythology. The name Artemis is pre-Greek. She first appears in Greek literature as mistress and protectress of wild life. (*Cf.* W. K. C. Guthrie, *The Greeks and their Gods*, 1950, pp. 99ff.) In Greece proper she was worshipped as the daughter of Zeus and Leto, and twin sister of Apollo. Horror at the pains her mother endured at her birth is supposed to have made her averse to marriage. She was goddess of the moon and of hunting, and is generally portrayed as a huntress, with dogs in attendance. Her temple at *Ephesus was one of the seven wonders of the world, and here worship of the 'virgin goddess' appears to have been fused with some kind of fertility-cult of the mother-goddess of Asia Minor. The temple was supported on 100 massive columns, some of which were sculptured. Tradition claims that her image fell there from the sky (Acts 19:35), and is thought to refer to a meteorite; Pliny tells of a huge stone above the entrance, said to have been placed there by Diana herself. Her worship was conducted by eunuch priests, called *megabyzoi* (Strabo, 14. 1. 23), and archaeologists have discovered statues depicting her with many breasts. The silversmiths who made small votary shrines, portraying the goddess in a recess with her lions in attendance, or possibly souvenir models of the temple, caused the riot when Paul was ministering there (Acts 19:23–20:1). Their cry of 'Great is Artemis of the Ephesians!' (Acts 19:28, 34) is attested by inscriptions from Ephesus which call her 'Artemis the Great' (*CIG*, 2963c; *Greek Inscriptions in the British Museum*, iii, 1890, 481. 324).

See also *DEMETRIUS; Conybeare and Howson, *Life and Epistles of St Paul*, 1901, ch. 16; J. T. Wood, *Discoveries at Ephesus*, 1877. D.H.W.

Statue of Artemis, symbolizing fertility, from Ephesus. (BPL)

ARTS AND CRAFTS. Throughout their history the inhabitants of Palestine maintained the same basic trades as their neighbours and were able to make most of their artefacts by the use of clay, metal, fibres, wood and stone. Working with these materials was the task of any able-bodied peasant, supported by the women in the home spinning and weaving cloth and cooking. Contacts with countries which were more advanced technologically meant that the Hebrews were quick to learn and adapt for their own use more specialized crafts, and were thus probably never without some outstanding craftsmen, though archaeology has revealed few examples of their work.

There is evidence that the Israelites, while not of outstanding inventiveness or artistry, themselves appreciated good workmanship. The possession of such skill by the Judaean Bezalel was considered a divine gift (Ex. 31:3; 35:31; 28:3). Iron-working was learnt from the Philistines (1 Sa. 13:20) and the secrets of dyeing from the Phoenicians, who supplied designers, foremen and craftsmen to supplement the local labour force available for work on such major projects as the building of David's royal palace and the Temple at Jerusalem (see section **III.***c*, below). In the 1st century BC the art of glass-making was similarly imported from Tyre.

I. Trades and trade guilds

For reasons of economy and supply the more skilled artisans lived in the larger towns and cities, usually working in special quarters, as in the modern bazaar (*sūq*). This led to the organization of craft unions or guilds called 'families' which were sometimes located at a town where their work was centred, as the scribes at Jabez (1 Ch. 2:55) or dyers and weavers at Tell Beit Mirsim (Debir?; 1 Ch. 4:21). At Jerusalem certain areas were allotted to the wood- and stone-workers (1 Ch. 4:14; Ne. 11:35); potters (Mt. 27:7) and fullers (2 Ki. 18:17) had fields of their own outside the city walls. A guild member was called 'a son' of his craft (*e.g.* the goldsmiths in Ne. 3:8, 31). By NT times the guilds were powerful political groups working under imperial licence. Demetrius led the guild of silversmiths at Ephesus (Acts 19:24), and the designation of Alexander as coppersmith (Gk. *chalkeus*) implies his membership of such a union (2 Tim. 4:14).

A general term (Heb. *ḥārāš*, 'one who cuts in, devises') is used both of craftsmen (AV 'artificers') in general (Ex. 38:23; 2 Sa. 5:11) or of a skilled worker in metal, whether copper (2 Ch. 24:12; Is. 40:19) or iron (Is. 44:12; 2 Ch. 24:12). It includes those who prepared and refined the basic metal (Je. 10:9) and was also applied to wood-workers (Is. 44:13; 2 Ki. 12:12), stonemasons (2 Sa. 5:11), engravers of gems (Ex. 28:11) or those specially devoted to manufacturing idols (Is. 44:9–20).

II. Basic tools

From prehistoric times in Palestine worked flint knives, scrapers and hoes have been found, and these long continued in use for rough tools, for reaping-hooks, in which the flints are set in a semicircle of plaster, or for striking lights. Wooden implements and stone hammers and pestles were of early origin. Meteoric iron was utilized when available (Gn. 4:22), as was native copper from *c.* 6000 BC. In Palestine copper was regularly employed from 3200 BC, and iron tools were plentiful after the arrival of the Philistines, *c.* 1190 BC (*cf.* 1 Ki. 6:7). Axe-heads, fitted on wooden handles, were used for felling trees (Dt. 19:5), and knives (Gn. 22:6) for a variety of purposes, including eating (Pr. 30:14). Tools are sometimes mentioned under the collective Heb. *kᵉlî*, 'vessels, instruments', or *ḥereḇ*, which includes the sword, knife or any sharp cutter. Iron axe-heads (2 Ki. 6:5), saws (1 Ki. 7:9), adzes, hoes, scrapers, chisels, awls, bow-drills and nails (Je. 10:3–4) were in constant use and have left their traces on objects recovered by excavation.

Assyrian workmen carrying tools. Relief from Sennacherib's palace at Nineveh. c. 690 BC. (BM)

III. Archaeological evidence

a. The potter

The earliest known pottery comes from N Syria and is dated *c.* 8000 BC. It was, however, not until *c.* 4000 BC that a slow wheel was used by the potter and *c.* 3000 BC before the fast wheel was developed. The *potter, whose work is described in Je. 18:3–4, sat on a stone seat with his feet working a large stone or wooden wheel, set in a pit, which turned an upper stone on which the vessel was thrown. A potter's workshop, with its 'two stones' (v. 3), has been found at Lachish (*c.* 1200 BC). Smaller wheels of stone

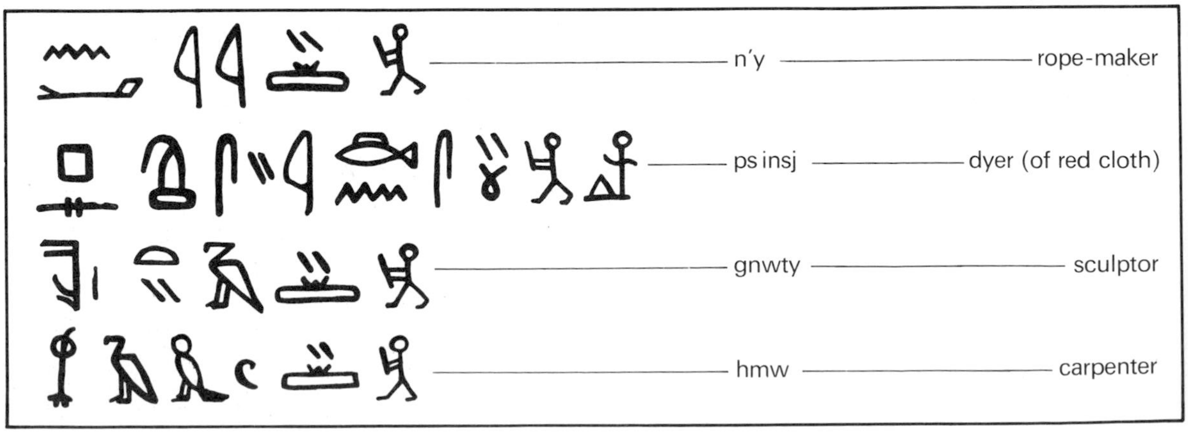

Various occupations of Ancient Egypt with their names in hieroglyphs and transliteration.

or clay which revolve in a socketed disc date from the time of the monarchy at Megiddo, Gezer and Hazor. The clay used for finer vessels or slips was prepared by treading out coarser clay in water with the feet (Is. 41:25). For the development and types of pottery in use, see *POTTER. Pottery kilns have been found at many sites in Palestine, although only rarely does more than the 'fire-box' remain. Outside a potter's shop at Megiddo lay three U-shaped *furnaces (8th–7th century BC).

b. The builder

The manufacture of sun-dried *brick for use in building the ordinary dwelling was part of the seasonal work of the peasant, who covered his house with clay or thatch spread over roof timbers. Such buildings require constant attention. In a few cases bricks made in a mould were fired, and this was probably the potters' work.

The Heb. *bānâ*, meaning 'to build' and 'to rebuild, to repair' and 'builder' (so AV), is used both of skilled and unskilled workmen (2 Ch. 34:11) who were needed for work on any large project which involved the labours of stonemasons, carpenters, and many porters and untrained men. Large buildings were both planned and constructed under the close supervision of a master-builder (Gk. *architektōn*; 1 Cor. 3:10).

A site was first surveyed with a measuring-line consisting of a rope or cord (2 Sa. 8:2; Zc. 2:1), string (1 Ki. 7:15), or twisted linen thread (Ezk. 40:3) marked in cubits (1 Ki. 7:15, 23). In Hellenistic times a reed rod marked in furlongs was similarly used (Rev. 11:1; 21:15). More than one line might be used to mark out a site (2 Sa. 8:2), the survey of which was recorded in plan and writing. The work of the surveyor was taken as a symbol of divine judgment (Is. 28:17; Je. 31:39).

The progress of the building was checked by the chief builder using a 'plumb-line', or cord weighted with lead or tin (*'ᵃnāḵ*; Am. 7:7–8), a stone (Zc. 4:10), or any heavy object (Heb. *mišqeleṯ*, AV 'plummet'; 2 Ki. 21:13), to test any vertical structure. This was a symbol of testing the truth (Is. 28:17). The metaphor of building is frequently used, for God as Builder establishes the nation (Ps. 69:35), the house of David (Ps. 89:4) and his city of Jerusalem (Ps. 147:2). So the church is compared to a building (1 Cor. 3:9; 1 Pet. 2:4–6). Paul uses the word 'to build (up), edify' (Gk. *oikodomeō*) about 20 times. The believers are both built up (*epoikodomeō*) into Christ (Col. 2:7) and exhorted to build themselves up in their faith (Jude 20).

c. The carpenter

Both Joseph (Mt. 13:55) and Jesus (Mk. 6:3) followed the ancient trade of carpenter (Gk. *tektōn*). A skilled worker in wood (Heb.

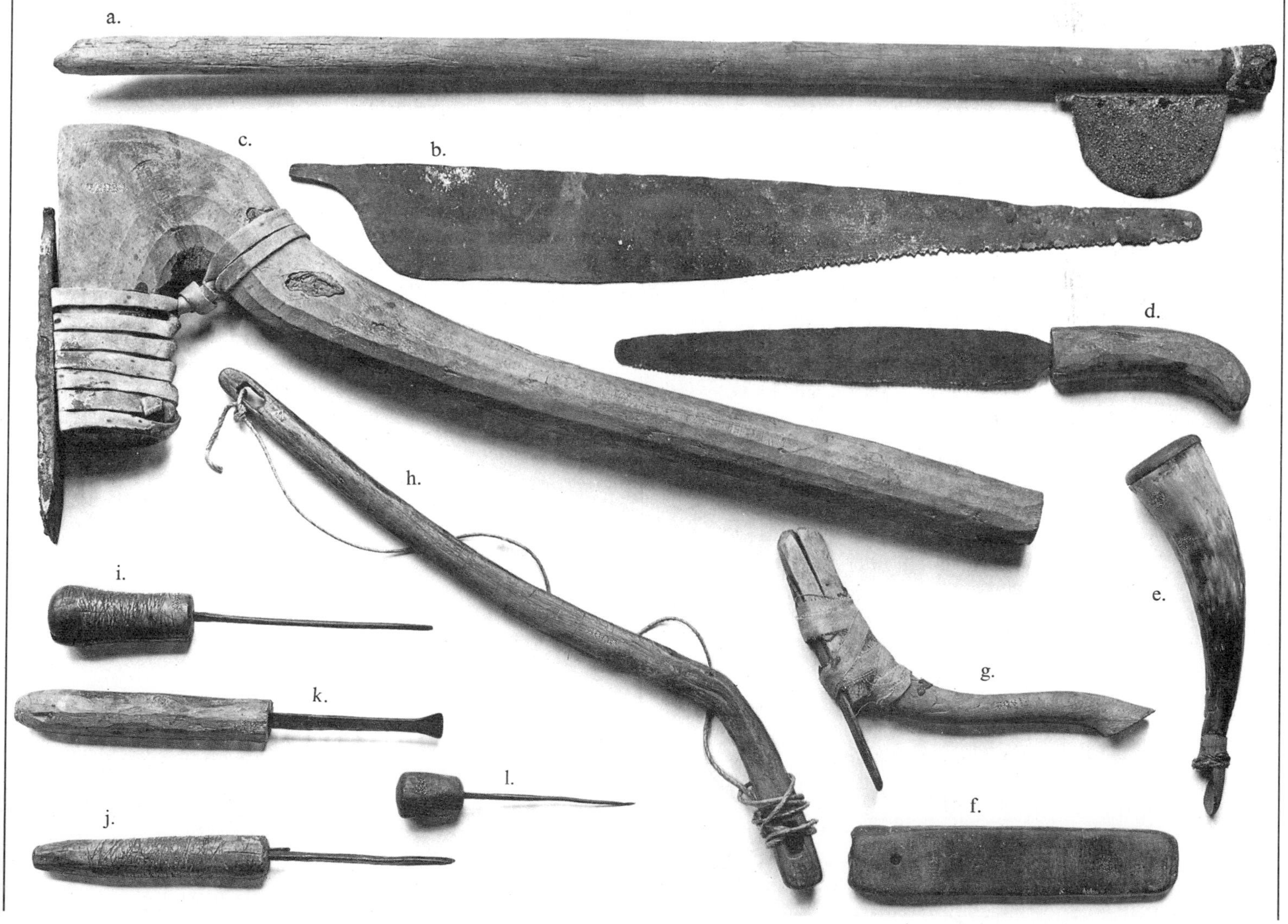

Egyptian carpenter's tools, from Thebes.
a. *Bronze-headed axe.*
b. *Bronze saw blade.*
c. *Large adze, with bronze blade held in place by leather thongs.*
d. *Small handsaw with bronze blade.*
e. *Horn fitted with a lip for pouring, used as an oil-flask.*
f. *Green slate hone for sharpening tools.*
g. *Model bronze-bladed adze.*
h, i, j. *Wooden bow-drill with two metal tools possibly used as drilling bits.*
k. *Bronze chisel with wooden handle.*
l. *Bronze bradawl.* (BM)

Egyptian stonemason's mallet. New Kingdom. (BM)

ḥāraš 'ēṣîm) undertook all the carpentry tasks required in building operations, making roof, door, window and stair fittings. Of the furniture he constructed couches, beds, chairs, tables and footstools. Examples of some of these and of finely carved bowls, spoons and boxes have survived in the tombs at Jericho (*c.* 1800 BC). The same carpenter would manufacture agricultural implements, ploughs, yokes, threshing instruments (2 Sa. 24:22) or boards (Is. 28:27–28) and irrigation machines. In the large cities groups of carpenters who made carts would, in time of war, build chariots (Ct. 3:9). In the Levant ship-building seems to have remained a Phoenician monopoly centred at Tyre, where boats were constructed of local cypress with masts of cedar and oars of oak (Ezk. 27:5–6). (*Ships.) Some carpenters made idols (Is. 44:13–17). Though the Israelites undertook their own wood-working for the tabernacle fitments (Ex. 25), wood and experienced carpenters were supplied by agreement with Tyre for the construction of David's palace (2 Sa. 5:11) and the Temple built by Solomon. The same practice was followed for the later Temple (Ezr. 3:7) and possibly for the repair of the Temple recorded in 2 Ch. 24:12.

Wood-carving was undertaken by a few specialists (Ex. 31:5; 35:33), who may have also worked on bone and ivory. These worked the cherubim for the first Temple (1 Ki. 6:23) and other *objets d'art*. For this hard woods, ebony, sandal- and boxwood, were imported, while the local woods, cedar, cypress, oak, ash (Is. 44:14) and acacia (AV 'shittim') were used for most joinery, the mulberry being commonly worked for agricultural implements. (*Trees.)

The carpenter's special tools included a marking tool (*śereḏ*, AV 'rule'), compass or dividers (*meḥûḡâ*), an adze (*maqṣu'â*—'a scraping instrument', AV 'plane', Is. 44:13), small chopper (*ma'aṣāḏ*), iron saw (some two-edged), and files (Je. 10:4), bow-drill and wooden mallet (*halmûṯ*, Jdg. 5:26, AV 'hammer') and hammer (*maqqāḇâ*, Is. 44:12) as well as the various chisels and awls, examples of which have been recovered. Both nail and dowel joints can be seen on wooden objects from Middle Bronze Age and Monarchy period sites. By Roman times various types of wood plane and spoke-shave were also in use.

d. The mason

Stone, being costly to transport and work, was considered an extravagance in a private house (Am. 5:11), and for the more important public buildings would be used only sparingly for essential constructional features. (*Cornerstone, *Architecture.) While in Egypt, granite, sandstone, quartzite and limestone were quarried for building stone, only limestone was available in Palestine for this purpose. Blocks of harder stones for the Temple and other splendid buildings were worked in the Lebanon prior to importation (1 Ki. 6:7). The stonemason used many of the same tools as the carpenter, sawing the limestone (1 Ki. 7:9) and trimming it with a mallet and chisel or walling hammer. In quarrying large blocks of stone wooden wedges were knocked in with wooden hammers and soaked until the stone cracked under the force of their expansion; a method commonly used in the ancient Near East. Hard stone was shaped by repeated pounding with a large metal forge-hammer (Heb. *paṭṭîš*). Such a hammer is used to describe the action of the divine Word (Je. 23:29) and of mighty Babylon (Je. 50:23).

The mason also quarried out tombs in the natural caves in the hills or drove shafts into the hillside off which chambers were excavated (Is. 22:16). Particularly fine examples of such family mausolea have been found at Bethshemesh (8th century) and round Jerusalem (both 8th century BC and 1st century BC–2nd century AD). Deep silos or cisterns as cut at Lachish, Megiddo and Gibeon involved the removal of as much as 400,000 cubic m of limestone by hand. There, and in the water tunnels cut by masons and miners, the marks of their chisels remain visible. (*Mining, *Architecture, *Siloam.)

In the Monarchy large stone pillar bases were cut, and from the 10th century BC pecked and marginally drafted masonry was used. By the Hellenistic period Herodian buildings at Jerusalem, Machpelah and other sites show the use of immense blocks of stone so carefully dressed as to be aligned without mortar, and it is still impossible to insert a knife blade between the joins. Such careful work can also be seen at Megiddo in the 9th century BC. Masons' marks can be seen on a number of constructions such as the steps of the Capernaum synagogue. Masons were also employed to cut inscriptions on rock surfaces, and for this seem to have copied cursive inscriptions, for surviving examples at Shebna's tomb, the Siloam tunnel and the Samaria fragment show no adaptation to the *writing material. Finer engraving can be seen on *seals.

e. The metalworker

Copper was regularly smelted and cast in Palestine from *c.* 3200 BC. After *c.* 2000 BC it was normal to use bronze rather than copper and this material remained popular even after the introduction of iron. Solomon had large objects, such as the pillars for the Temple, made from bronze by a Tyrian smith who cast them in the clay of the Jordan valley between Succoth and Zarethan (1 Ki. 7:46; 2 Ch. 4:17). Because of its strength iron was preferred for agricultural tools and weapons, but it required more sophisticated techniques of manufacture and maintenance. Initially Israel was without the knowledge of iron-working and relied on the Philistines for their iron tools (1 Sa. 13:19–22).

The smith worked within the city with the aid of a furnace supplied with a forced draught provided by skin or pottery bellows (Heb. *mappuaḥ*, 'a blowing instrument'). Thus the smith was commonly designated as 'he who blows (the coals)', a title akin to the common Akkadian *nappāḫu* (Is. 54:16). Copper and bronze were refined in crucibles (Heb. *maṣrēp̄*, Pr. 17:3; 27:21), and then poured into stone or clay moulds. Iron, on the other hand, was forged by being beaten on an anvil (Heb. *pa'am*, Is. 41:7). The ironsmith is naturally called 'he who strikes the anvil', while the bronze-worker, who had to trim rough castings by hammering, is called 'he who smooths with the hammer' (Is. 41:7). Techniques of soldering, riveting and casting-on were practised by these craftsmen, enabling them to manufacture intricate objects. Such an object is the small bronze stand from Megiddo which, if Israelite, indicates that their technical skill was as good as any of their neighbours.

The smiths manufactured a variety of metal vessels and implements, plough-blades, tips for ox-goads, forks, axle-trees and axes, as well as the smaller pins, fibulae

Joiners and other craftsmen at work. Copy of Egyptian wall-painting. Tomb of Nebamun and Ipuky, Thebes. c. 1380 BC. (BM)

(from 10th century BC), images, figurines and small instruments. The manufacture of knives, which were a close relation to daggers and swords, lance and spear-heads, and other weapons of war (*ARMOUR AND WEAPONS), reminds us how easily these same craftsmen could turn their hand to making implements for war or peace (Is. 2:4; Joel 3:10; Mi. 4:3).

Jewellery was possessed from an early period by women for whom it was the only method by which they could possess and preserve their personal wealth. Gold- and silver-smiths used blow-pipes to ventilate their small furnaces and cast their products with the aid of steatite or clay moulds. *Cire perdue*, granulation, filigree and *cloisonné* inlay were all techniques practised by early gold- and silver-smiths.

f. The tanner

Leather, the treated skins of sheep and goats, was used for certain items of clothing (Lv. 13:48; Nu. 31:20), including sandals and girdles (2 Ki. 1:8; Mt. 3:4). The sewn skins were specially suitable at low cost for vessels or containers for water (Gn. 21:14), wine (Mt. 9:17) or other liquids (Jdg. 4:19). Sometimes the skins were sewn into true 'bottle' shapes. Leather was rarely used for tents (Ex. 25:5; Nu. 4:6) but commonly for military articles, such as helmets, quivers, chariot fittings, slings and shields, the latter well oiled to prevent cracking or the penetration of missiles (2 Sa. 1:21; Is. 21:5). Sandals of seal or porpoise skin (AV 'badgers' skin') were a sign of luxury (Ezk. 16:10), though it is likely that, as in Egypt and Assyria, fine leather was used for beds, chair covers and other furnishings.

Since tanning was a malodorous task, it was usually undertaken outside a town and near abundant water. Peter's visit to Simon the tanner outside Joppa (Acts 9:43; 10:6, 32) illustrates how far he had overcome his scruples against contact with what was ceremonially unclean. The process began by removing the animal fat from the skin by stone scrapers or metal knives. The hair was removed by scraping, soaking in urine or rubbing with lime. The skin was then either dressed by smoking or by being rubbed with an oil, or tanned with suitable wood, bark or leaves. If the hair or fur was not removed, the skin was dressed with alum which was obtained from the Dead Sea or Egypt, sun-dried and then oil-dressed to alleviate the stiffness.

g. The dyer

The ancient craft of dyeing was known to the Israelites at the Exodus, when skins used for the tabernacle were dyed scarlet by the juices of crushed cochineal insects found in oak-trees (Ex. 26:1, 31;

Egyptian carpenter working with an adze. c. 1400 BC. (SMB)

36:8; Lv. 14:4). The black-purple or red-violet 'Tyrian' or 'Imperial' dye, prepared from the molluscs *purpura* and *murex* found on the E Mediterranean coast, was mainly a Phoenician monopoly and used for dyeing the highly-priced garments which were a mark of rank and nobility (Jdg. 8:26; Pr. 31:22; Lk. 16:19; Rev. 18:12, 16). The trade is attested in Ras Shamra texts (*c.* 1500 BC). This was also the 'purple' used in the tabernacle fabric (Ex. 26:31, 28:5), for the Temple veil, the 'blue and purple and crimson' being variants of the same dye (2 Ch. 3:14), and for the garment put upon Jesus at his trial (Jn. 19:2, 5). Native Israelites were taught the trade by Tyrian workmen at Solomon's request (2 Ch. 2:7). Lydia traded in cloth similarly treated in Thyatira (Acts 16:14). See *JNES* 22, 1963, pp. 104ff.

ARUMAH
See Rumah, Part 3.

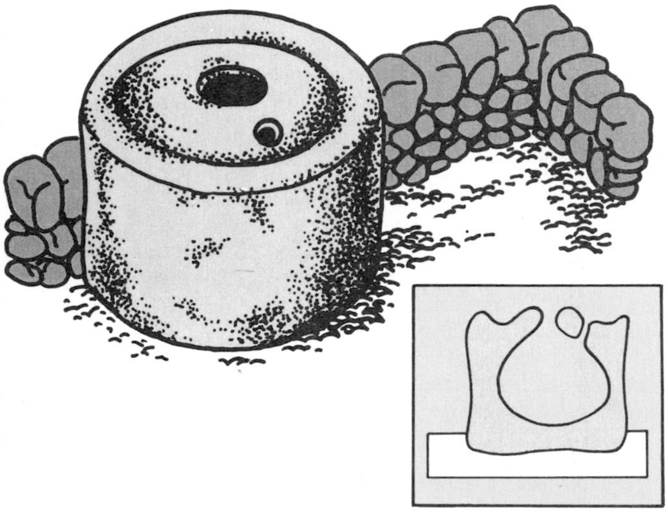

Stone dye vat from Tell beit Mirsim (Debir?). The small size of the round hole in the top indicates that the woven cloth was dyed in threads or strands. 7th cent. BC.

In Palestine yellow dyes were made from ground pomegranate rind, the Phoenicians also using safflower and turmeric. Blue was obtained from indigo plants (*Indigofera tinctoria*) imported from Syria or Egypt, where it had been originally transplanted from India. Woad was known after 300 BC.

At Tell Beit Mirsim (= Debir?) six or seven dye-plants were excavated indicating that textile-fabrication was a major industry at that site. At Tell Amal near Beth-shean many pottery vessels, in which skeins of thread were dyed, have been found, together with weaving artefacts such as loom weights.

h. The fuller

The art of fulling, cleansing and bleaching cloth was of importance because of the high cost of clothing and the need to cleanse the fibres of their natural oil or gums before dyeing. In some places the fuller was also the dyer.

It was customary for a fuller to work outside a town within reach of water in which clothes could be cleaned by treading them on a submerged stone. Hence the fuller was characteristically called a 'trampler' (Heb. *kāḇas*). At Jerusalem the locality outside the E wall where garments were spread to dry in the sun was called the 'fuller's field' (2 Ki. 18:17; Is. 7:3; 36:2). Christ's garments at the transfiguration were described as brighter than it was possible for any fuller (Gk. *gnapheus*, 'cloth dresser') to whiten them (Mk. 9:3).

For cleansing, natron (nitre) was sometimes imported from Egypt, where, mixed with white clay, it was used as soap (Pr. 25:20; Je. 2:22). Alkali was plentifully available in plant ash, and 'soap' (Heb. *bōrîṯ*, *kâlî*) was obtained by burning the soda plant (*Salsola kali*). The 'fullers' soap' of Mal. 3:2 was probably 'cinders of *bōrîṯ*', since potassium and sodium nitrate do not seem to have been known in Syria or Palestine, though found in Babylonia.

Other crafts, *ART, *COSMETICS AND PERFUMERY, *IVORY, *SPINNING AND WEAVING, *EMBROIDERY; glass-making, *GLASS; other references to crafts, *MUSIC, *EGYPT, *ASSYRIA and *BABYLONIA.

BIBLIOGRAPHY. C. Singer (ed.), *A History of Technology*, 1, 1958; G. E. Wright, *Biblical Archaeology*, 1957, pp. 191–198; R. J. Forbes, *Studies in Ancient Technology*, 1–8, 1955–64; A. Reifenberg, *Ancient Hebrew Arts*, 1950; A. Lucas, *Ancient Egyptian Materials and Industries*, 1962; J. Jeremias, *Jerusalem in the Time of Jesus*, 1969; D. Strong and D. Brown, *Roman Crafts*, 1976. D.J.W.

ARVAD. Ezk. 27:8, 11; 1 Macc. 15:23 (Aradus) and its inhabitants, the Arvadites, Gn. 10:18; 1 Ch. 1:16. Modern Ruād, a small island 3 km off the coast of Syria (anciently Phoenicia) and about 80 km N of Byblos. The most N of the four great Phoenician cities, it paid tribute to some Assyrian kings, who noted its seafaring skills. A period of independence from *c.* 627 BC was ended by Nebuchadrezzar (*ANET*, p. 308). During these eras it was secondary to Tyre and Sidon. Its commercial fortunes revived under the Persians and Seleucids, but it was displaced by Antaradus (mod. Tartûs) in Roman times. G.G.G.

ASA (Heb. *'āsā'*). **1.** Third king over the independent state of Judah, reigned 41 years (*c.* 911–870 BC). The problem of synchronizing his reign with that of *Baasha (1 Ki. 16:8, Baasha dies in 26th year of Asa; 2 Ch. 16:1, Baasha attacks Judah in Asa's 36th year) is at present most plausibly solved by assuming Chronicles is computing from the disruption of the united monarchy. The early part of his reign was characterized by religious zeal which led to the abolition of heathen gods and cultic prostitution. The extent of his zeal and of the pervasiveness of pagan cults is indicated by Asa's removal of his (grand-)mother *Maacah from her official postion (1 Ki. 15:13). He did not destroy all the high places in Israel, but his devotion was said to be the reason for a period of peace in the country (2 Ch. 15:15, 19). The Chronicler contrasts his notable victory over *Zerah the Ethiopian (2 Ch. 14:9), attributed to his faith in Yahweh, with his dependence on Syrian aid to overcome Baasha. This latter action, which may have been sparked off by defection of large numbers of Israelites to Asa (2 Ch. 15:9), enabled him to fortify Mizpah and Geba (not Gibea with LXX), which thereafter became the N border of Judah. The latter part of his reign was marred by illness (2 Ch. 16:12) and continued warfare, which were viewed by Chronicles as the outcome of his failure to continue in dependence on Yahweh (2 Ch. 16:7ff.).

2. A Levite, son of Elkanah, among the first to return from the Exile and settle again in Palestine. W.O.

ASAHEL (Heb. *ʿaśāh'ēl*, 'God has made'). **1.** A son of David's sister Zeruiah, and brother of Joab and Abishai (1 Ch. 2:16). He was famous for his amazing speed, but when he used it to pursue *Abner following the clash at Gibeon, the latter was forced to use his greater experience in warfare to kill him (2 Sa. 2:18ff.). This gave rise to a blood feud in which Abner was treacherously murdered by Joab (2 Sa. 3:27ff.). He is among David's thirty select warriors (2 Sa. 23:24), and is listed as being in charge of 24,000 men appointed to serve David during the fourth month (1 Ch. 27:7). This list may originally have been drawn up in outline early in David's reign, so that Asahel is now represented by his son Zebadiah.

2. One of nine Levites whom Jehoshaphat sent together with priests and officials on a teaching mission throughout the cities of Judah (2 Ch. 17:8). **3.** An overseer assisting in the control of tithes for the Temple in Hezekiah's time (2 Ch. 31:13). **4.** Father of Jonathan who opposed the appointment of a select body to represent the returned Exiles in determining the removal of foreign wives (Ezr. 10:15). W.O.

ASAPH (Heb. *'āsāp̄*). **1.** A descendant of Gershom, son of Levi (1 Ch. 6:39); nominated by the chief Levites as a leading singer, using cymbals, when the ark was brought to Jerusalem (1 Ch. 15:17, 19). David made him leader of the choral worship (16:4–5). The 'sons of Asaph' remained the senior family of musicians until the Restoration (1 Ch. 25; 2 Ch. 20:14; 35:15; Ezr. 3:10; Ne. 11:17, 22; 12:35), primarily as singers and cymbalists. Asaph himself had a reputation as a seer, and was recognized as the author of psalms used when Hezekiah revived the Temple-worship (2 Ch. 29:30; *cf.* the traditional ascriptions of Pss. 50, 73–83; *cf.* also the prophecy of Jahaziel, 2 Ch. 20:14ff.). It is not clear whether Asaph lived to see the Temple consecrated, or if 2 Ch. 5:12 simply means 'the families of Asaph', *etc.* **2.** Warden of forests in Palestine under the Persian king Artaxerxes (Ne. 2:8). J.P.U.L.

ASCENSION. The story of the ascension of the Lord Jesus Christ is told in Acts 1:4–11. In Lk. 24:51 the words 'and was carried up into heaven' are less well attested, as is also the description in Mk. 16:19. There is no alternative suggestion in the NT of any other termination to the post-resurrection appearances, and the fact of the ascension is always assumed in the frequent references to Christ at the right hand of God, and to his return from heaven. It would be unreasonable to suppose that Luke would be grossly mistaken or inventive about such an important fact so long as any of the apostles were alive to note what he had written. For other allusions to the ascension see Jn. 6:62; Acts 2:33–34; 3:21; Eph. 4:8–10; 1 Thes. 1:10; Heb. 4:14; 9:24; 1 Pet. 3:22; Rev. 5:6.

Objections are made to the story on the ground that it rests upon out-dated ideas of heaven as a place above our heads. Such objections are beside the point for the following reasons:

1. The act of ascension could have been an acted parable for the sake of the disciples who held this idea of heaven. Jesus thus indicated decisively that the period of post-resurrection appearances was now over, and that his return to heaven would inaugurate the era of the presence of the Holy Spirit in the church. Such acted symbolism is perfectly natural.

2. The terms 'heaven' and 'the right hand of the Father' have some necessary meaning in relation to this earth, and this meaning can best be expressed with reference to 'above'. Thus Jesus lifted up his eyes to heaven when he prayed (Jn. 17:1; *cf.* 1 Tim. 2:8), and taught us to pray, 'Our Father who art in heaven . . . Thy will be done on earth, as it is in heaven.' In one sense heaven is away from this earth, whatever may be its nature in terms of a different dimension. In passing from the earthly space-time to the heavenly state, Jesus was observed to move away from the earth, just as at his second coming he will be observed to move towards the earth. This doctrine of bodily absence is balanced in the NT by the doctrine of spiritual presence. (*Spirit, Holy.) Thus the Lord's Supper is in memory of One who is bodily absent 'until he comes' (1 Cor. 11:26), yet, as at all Christian gatherings, the risen Lord is spiritually present (Mt. 18:20).

The concept of God above on the throne has special reference to the difference between God and man, and to the approach to him by the sinner, whose sin bars access to the King. Thus we may see the purpose of the ascension as follows:

1. 'I go to prepare a place for you' (Jn. 14:2).

2. Jesus Christ is seated, a sign that his atoning work is complete and final. Those who believe that as Priest he continues to offer himself to the Father, say that one must not mix together the two metaphors of king and priest. Yet this is precisely what is done in Heb. 10:11–14 to show the finality of Christ's offering.

3. He intercedes for his people (Rom. 8:34; Heb. 7:25), though nowhere in the NT is he said to be offering himself in heaven. The Greek word for intercede, *entynchanō*, has the thought of looking after someone's interests.

4. He is waiting until his enemies are subdued, and will return as the final act in the establishment of the kingdom of God (1 Cor. 15:24–26).

Bibliography. W. Milligan, *The Ascension and Heavenly Priesthood of our Lord*, 1891; H. B. Swete, *The Ascended Christ*, 1910; C. S. Lewis, *Miracles*, ch. 16, 1947; M. L. Loane, *Our Risen Lord*, ch. 9, 1965.

J.S.W.

ASENATH. Daughter of 'Poti-phera priest of On' in Egypt, given in marriage to Joseph by Pharaoh (Gn. 41:45) and so mother of Manasseh and Ephraim (Gn. 41:50–52; 46:20). The name Asenath (Heb. *'āsᵉnaṯ*) is good Egyptian, of the pattern *'I(w).s-n-X*, 'she belongs to X', X being a deity or parent, or a pronoun referring to one of these. Three equally good possibilities would be: *'Iw.s-(n)-Nt*, 'she belongs to (the goddess) Neit', *'Iw.s-n-'t*, 'she belongs to (her) father', or *'Iw.s-n.t* (*t* for *ṯ*), 'she belongs to thee' (fem., either a goddess or the mother). Such names are well attested in the Middle Kingdom and Hyksos periods (*c.* 2100–1600 BC) of Egyptian history, corresponding to the age of the Patriarchs and Joseph. K.A.K.

ASHDOD. Tel Ashdod, 6 km SE of the modern village, was a major Philistinian city, first mentioned in Late Bronze Age texts (Jos. 11:22) dealing with Ugarit. It may have withstood attempts by Judah to conquer it and settle there (Jos. 13:3; 15:46–47). It had a principal port (Ashdod-Yam; in Akkadian sources *Asdudimmu*; *cf. ANET*, p. 286) and a temple of Dagon to which the ark was taken (1 Sa. 5:1ff.). It was attacked by Uzziah of Judah (2 Ch. 26:6). When it rebelled against Assyria, who replaced King Azuri by his brother, *Asdudu* was sacked, according to Assyr. inscriptions, by Sargon II in 711 BC. These calamities were noted by Amos (1:8) and Isaiah (20:1). Later besieged by Psamtik I of Egypt for 29 years (Herodotus 2. 157), it became a Bab. province

---

ASH
See Trees (Pine), Part 3.

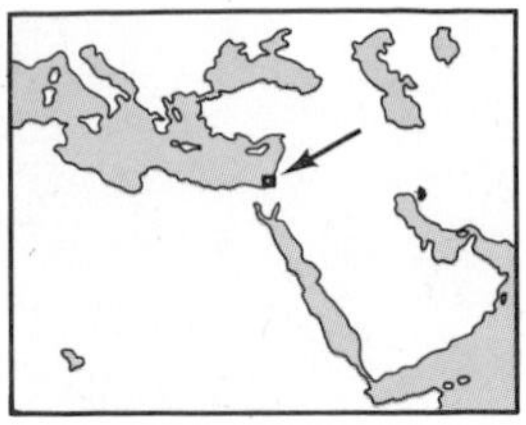

The location of the Philistinian city of Ashdod.

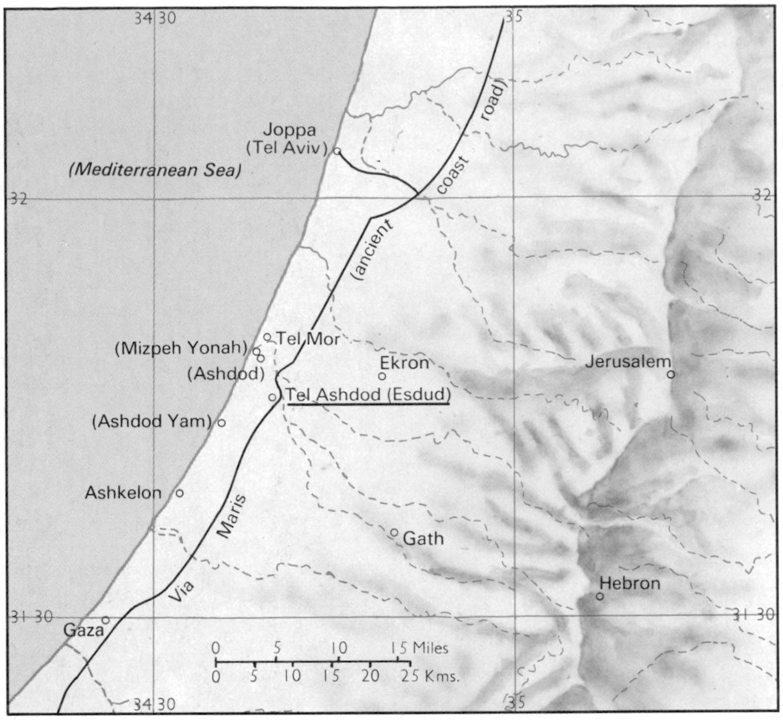

and was weak (Je. 25:20) and derelict (Zp. 2:4; Zc. 9:6). It was partially repopulated after the Exile (Ne. 13:23–24). As Azotus, its idolatry provoked attacks by the Maccabeans (John the Hasmonean and John Hyrcanus, 1 Macc. 5:68; 10:84). Separated from Judaea by Pompey (Jos., *BJ* 1. 156), reconstructed by Gabinius, and given to Salome, Herod's sister, by Augustus, it flourished (Acts 8:40) until it surrendered to Titus.

Excavations (1962–72) confirm this history and show Canaanite, Philistinian (temple) and possibly Solomonic occupation (gateway).

BIBLIOGRAPHY. *EAEHL*, 1, pp. 103–119; F. M. Cross, Jr. and D. N. Freedman, *BASOR* 175, 1964, pp. 48f. (on name). D.J.W.

Part of the excavated area of the Philistine city of Ashdod. (JLH)

ASHDOTH-PISGAH
See Pisgah, Part 3.

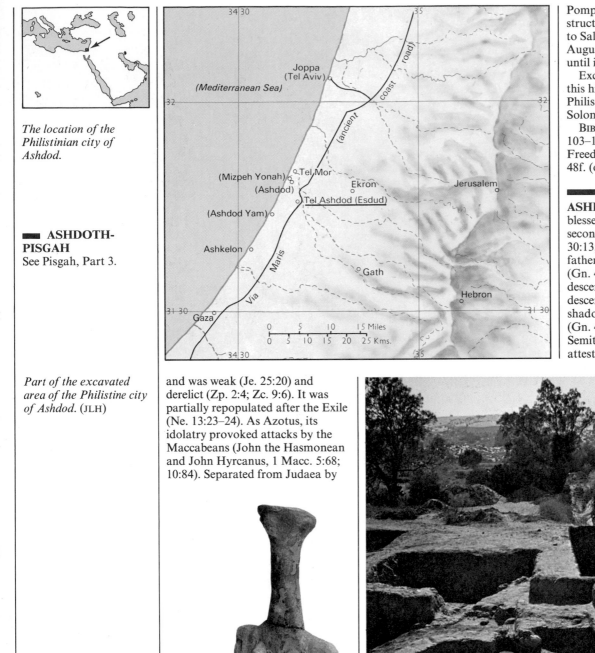

Fertility figurine in the form of a mother goddess and bed, from Ashdod. 12th cent. BC. (ZR)

ASHER (Heb. *'āšēr*, 'happy, blessed'). **1.** Jacob's eighth son, his second by Leah's maid Zilpah (Gn. 30:13; 35:26). Asher himself fathered four sons and a daughter (Gn. 46:17; Nu. 26:46; with descendants, 1 Ch. 7:30–40). His descendants' prosperity was foreshadowed in Jacob's last blessing (Gn. 49:20). As an authentic NW Semitic personal name Asher is attested at precisely Jacob's period, as that of a female servant (*c.* 1750 BC in an Egyptian papyrus list; see W. C. Hayes, *A Papyrus of the Late Middle Kingdom in the Brooklyn Museum*, 1955, pp. 88, 97, and especially W. F. Albright, *JAOS* 74, 1954, pp. 229, 231: *išr*, *'šra*). This particular philological discovery rules out the commonly adduced equation of biblical Asher with the *isr* in Egyptian texts of the 13th century BC as a Palestinian place-name: *isr* would represent *'ṯr* not *'šr* (*cf.* Albright, *loc. cit.*). This eliminates the consequent suggestion that the Egyptian *isr* of 1300 BC (Sethos I) indicated an 'Asher'-settlement in Palestine prior to the Israelite invasion later in the 13th century BC.

2. An Israelite tribe descended from **1**, and its territory. Consisting of five main families or clans (Nu. 26:44–47), Asher shared the organization and fortunes of the tribes in the wilderness journeyings (Nu. 1:13; 2:27; 7:72; 13:13, *etc.*), and shared in Moses' blessing (Dt. 33:24). Asher's territory as assigned by Joshua was principally the Plain of Acre, the W slopes of the Galilean hills behind it and the coast from the tip of Carmel N to Tyre and Sidon (Jos. 19:24–31, 34). On the S, Asher bordered on Manasseh, *ex*cluding certain border cities (Jos. 17:10–11; translate v. 11, 'Manasseh had *beside* Issachar and *beside* Asher . . . (various towns) . . .'). See Y. Kaufmann, *The Biblical Account of the Conquest of Palestine*, 1953, p. 38. (*Cf.* also *HELKATH and *IBLEAM.) In Asher the Gershonite Levites had four cities (1 Ch. 6:62, 74–75). However, the Asherites failed to expel the Canaanites, and merely occupied parts of their portion among them (Jdg. 1:31–32). On topography and resources of Asher's portion, *cf.* D. Baly, *The Geography of the Bible*, 1974, pp. 121–127. In the Judges' period Asher failed to help Deborah but rallied to Gideon's side (Jdg. 5:17; 6:35; 7:23). Asher provided warriors for David (1 Ch. 12:36) and formed part of an administrative district of Solomon (1 Ki. 4:16). After the fall of the N kingdom some Asherites responded to Hezekiah's call to revive the Passover at Jerusalem (2 Ch. 30:11). In much later times the aged prophetess Anna, who rejoiced to see the infant Jesus, was of the tribe of Asher (Lk. 2:36).

3. Possibly a town on the border of Manasseh and Ephraim, location uncertain (Jos. 17:7). K.A.K.

ASHERAH. A Canaanite mother-goddess mentioned in the Ras Shamra texts (*'aṯrt*) as a goddess of the sea and the consort of El, but associated in the OT with Baal (*e.g.* Jdg. 3:7). While the OT sometimes refers to Asherah as a goddess (*e.g.* 1 Ki. 18:19; 2 Ki. 23:4; 2 Ch. 15:16), the name is used also of an image made for that goddess (*e.g.* 1 Ki. 15:13) which consequently came to represent her. The Israelites were commanded to cut down (*e.g.* Ex. 34:13) or burn (Dt. 12:3) the *asherim* of the Canaanites, and were likewise forbidden themselves to plan 'an Asherah of any kind of tree' beside God's altar (Dt. 16:21). From these references it appears that the object was of wood, and was presumably an image of some kind. A piece of carbonized wood about 1·2 m long, discovered in the Early Bronze Age shrine at Ai, has been interpreted as a possible asherah, but many scholars would now reject the view that the object was a post, and would give the translation 'Asherah-image' in all occurrences. In the AV the word is consistently translated 'grove'.

BIBLIOGRAPHY. W. L. Reed, *The Asherah in the Old Testament*, 1949; A. Caquot, M. Sznycer and A. Herdner, *Textes Ougaritiques*, 1, 1974, pp. 68–73; J. C. de Moor in *TDOT* I, pp. 438–444; R. Patai, *JNES* 24, 1965, pp. 37–52; W. F. Albright, *Archaeology and the Religion of Israel*³, 1953, pp. 77–79; J. Marquet-Krause, *Les Fouilles de 'Ay (et-Tell) 1933–1934* . . ., 1949, p. 18. T.C.M.

ASHES. 1. Heb. *'ēper*. This is the most commonly used term to indicate powdery ashes. As such it occurs alone or in connection with *sackcloth as a symbol of mourning (2 Sa. 13:19; Est. 4:3; Is. 58:5; Je. 6:26; Dn. 9:3). It also signifies worthless or debased objects or ideas (Ps. 102:9; Is. 44:20), and in this connection it is linked with *'dust', *'āpār* (Gn. 18:27; Jb. 13:12; 30:19). *'āpār*, 'dust', is translated 'ashes' in Nu. 19:17, and 2 Ki. 23:4, where it refers to the ashes of a burnt sin offering and those of pagan vessels respectively. **2.** Heb. *dešen*, 'fatness', is translated 'ashes' referring to the admixture of the fat of sacrifices and the fuel used to consume them (Lv. 1:16; 6:10; 1 Ki. 13:3, 5). It is used also of burnt corpses. **3.** Heb. *pîaḥ*, 'soot', is rendered 'ashes' in reference to the residual deposits of a kiln, used by Moses to create the plague of boils (Ex. 9:8, 10). **4.** Gk. *spodos* is used in the NT for ashes employed in mourning (Mt. 11:21; Lk. 10:13) or purification (Heb. 9:13). W.O.

Stone mould, with modern cast, for making figurines of a fertility goddess with a horned hat, probably Asherah. Height 22 cm. Middle Bronze II. c. 1900 BC. (ZR)

ASHIMA. The god or idol of the people of Hamath (2 Ki. 17:30), which they made in the territory of Samaria, whence they had been deported by the Assyrians. Not known outside the OT, though some have suggested identity with the Syrian Semios or the *'šm* of the Elephantine papyri. See A. Vincent, *La Religion des Judéo-Araméens d'Elephantine*, 1937, pp. 654ff.; P. Grelot, *Documents Araméens d'Égypte*, 1972, pp. 353, 464. T.C.M.

ASHKELON. Mod. Asqalōn lies on the S Palestinian coast between Jaffa and Gaza. The site shows occupation from Neolithic times to the 13th century AD (*IEJ* 5, 1955, p. 271). It is named in Egyp. texts (19th–15th centuries BC) and in the *Amarna letters (14th century BC) when its ruler Widiya helped the Habiru. A pre-Philistinian occu-

Ashkelon besieged by Egyptian troops shown brandishing their weapons and mounting ladders for a final assault. Relief from Karnak, Egypt (probably Merenptah). 13th cent. BC. (KAK)

pation may be referred to in Dt. 2:23. It was sacked by Ramses II (*ANET*, p. 256, *cf.* Merenptah stele, *ANET*, p. 378).

It was captured by Judah (Jdg. 1:18), but regained independence as one of five major Philistine cities (Jos. 13:3); associated with *Gaza, *Ashdod and *Ekron (Am. 1:1–7) and sometimes with Gath (2 Sa. 1:20). *Tiglath-pileser III made *Asqaluna* a vassal of Assyria in 733 BC until it was captured by Sennacherib of Assyria, who suppressed the revolt of Sidqa and set Sharruludar on the throne (701 BC).

Ashkelon came under Egyp. domination again, *c.* 630 BC, but was attacked for resisting Nebuchadrezzar in 604 BC (Bab. Chronicle). Its king, Aga', was killed and prisoners were taken to Babylon in 598 BC (*Mélanges Dussaud* 2, 1939, p. 298). This event, predicted by Jeremiah (47:5–7) and Zephaniah (2:4–7), had a profound effect on Jerusalem, which was to suffer a similar fate a few years later (Je. 52:4–11). Subordinated to Tyre in Persian times Ashkelon became a free Hellenistic city in 104 BC. It was captured by Jonathan (1 Macc. 10:86). Herod the Great embellished the city, which was his birthplace. Excavations (1921–76) have uncovered successive Canaanite, Philistinian, Persian, Hellenistic and predominantly Roman remains.

BIBLIOGRAPHY. *EAEHL*, 1, 1975, pp. 121–130. D.J.W.

ASHKENAZ. A descendant of Noah through Japheth and Gomer (Gn. 10:3; 1 Ch. 1:6). Eponymous ancestor of the successive inhabitants of an area between the Black and Caspian Seas. *Ascanius* occurs as the name of a Mysian and Phrygian prince, while elsewhere these people are said to live in the district of *Ascania*. Assyrian texts tell of *Aškuzai* in the NE from *c*. 720 BC onwards. Later they joined other tribes in the conquest of Babylon reflected in Je. 51:27. The Ashkenaz are to be identified with the *Skythai* (*SCYTHIANS) mentioned by Herodotus (1. 103–107; 4. 1). R.J.W.

ASHTAROTH, ASHTORETH.
1. Heb. *'aštōreṯ*, *'aštārôṯ*, a mother goddess with aspects as goddess of fertility, love and war, known to the Israelites through the Canaanites (1 Ki. 11:5). The name was common in one form or another, among many of the Semitic-speaking peoples of antiquity. In Mesopotamia Ištar was identified with the Sumerian mother goddess Inanna. The name occurs in the form *'ṯtrt* in the Ugaritic texts, and as *'štrt* in the (later) Phoenician inscriptions, transcribed in the Gk. script as *Astartē*. It has been suggested that the Heb. *'aštōreṯ* is an artificial form created from *'štrt*, by analogy with the vowel pattern of *bōšeṯ* 'shame', to show a fitting attitude among the Israelites to the goddess, whose cult as practised by the Canaanites was depraved in the extreme. *'aštārôṯ* is the plural form of the name. The Israelites turned to the worship of Ashtoreth soon after arriving in the land (Jdg. 2:13; 10:6); it was rife in the time of Samuel (1 Sa. 7:3–4; 12:10) and was given royal sanction by Solomon (1 Ki. 11:5; 2 Ki. 23:13). After Saul had been killed by the Philistines, his armour was placed in the temple of Ashtaroth at Beth-shan (1 Sa. 31:10), and the excavators of this site have suggested that the N temple in level V there may have been the one in question, though this remains an inference. Numerous clay plaques depicting naked female images have been discovered in Palestinian sites of the Bronze and Iron Ages, and it is probable that some of these are representations of the goddess Ashtoreth-Astarte.

Terracotta mould and impression of figurine, possibly representing Ashtoreth-Astarte. (BM)

BIBLIOGRAPHY. J. B. Pritchard, *Palestinian Figurines in Relation to Certain Goddesses Known through Literature*, 1943, esp. pp. 65–72; W. F. Albright, *Mélanges Syriens . . . Dussaud*, 1, 1939, pp. 107–120; *Archaeology and the Religion of Israel*, 1953, pp. 74ff.; A. Caquot, M. Sznycer and A. Herdner, *Textes Ougaritiques*, I, 1974, pp. 92–95; H. Ringgren, *Religions of the Ancient Near East*, 1973, pp. 141–142; A. Rowe, *The Four Canaanite Temples of Beth-Shan*, Part I, 1940, pp. 31–34.

2. *'ašteroṯ ṣō'neḵā*, a phrase occurring in Dt. 7:13; 28:4, 18, 51 and rendered variously 'flocks of thy sheep' (AV) and 'young of thy flock' (RV, RSV). It may be that from her fertility aspect the name of Astarte was associated by the Canaanites with sheep-breeding, and came to mean 'ewe' or something similar, the word being later borrowed by the Israelites without the cultic overtones.

BIBLIOGRAPHY. W. F. Albright, *Archaeology and the Religion of Israel*, 1953, pp. 75, 220.

3. *'aštarôṯ*. A city, presumably a centre of the worship of the goddess Ashtaroth, which is probably to be identified with Tell Ashtarah some 30 km E of the Sea of Galilee. The city, probably *Ashteroth-karnaim of Abraham's day, was the capital of Og, king of Bashan (Dt. 1:4). It was in the territory allotted to Manasseh by Moses (Jos. 13:31), but, though Joshua conquered Og (Jos. 9:10) and took Ashtaroth (Jos. 12:4), it was evidently not held, for it remained among the territories yet to be possessed when Joshua was an old man (Jos. 13:12). It later became a levitical city (1 Ch. 6:71; Jos. 21:27, *be'ešterâ*, possibly a contraction of *bêṯ 'aštārâ*, which appears in EVV as Beeshterah), and is only subsequently mentioned in the Bible as the home of Uzzia, one of David's mighty men (1 Ch. 11:44). It is perhaps to be identified with the *'s[t']rtm* ('As[ta]rtum?) in the Egyp. Execration Texts of about the 18th century, and with more certainty with the *strt* of the records of Tuthmosis III, the *aš-tar-te* of the Amarna Letters and the *as-tar-tu* of the Assyr. inscriptions. A stylized representation of a city with crenellated towers and battlements standing on a mound below the name

Gold Astarte pendant, emphasizing her role in the fertility cult. From Tell el-Ajjul. 10 cm. c. 1600 BC. (RS)

Battlements of Astartu, possibly biblical Ashtaroth, captured by Tiglath-pileser III of Assyria. Calah (Nimrud). 745–727 BC. (BM)

as-tar-tu is given on a bas-relief of Tiglath-pileser III which was discovered at Nimrud (BM 118908; *ANEP*, no. 306). G. Pettinato (*BA* 39, 1976, p. 46 and n. 7) reports that the 3rd-millennium *Ebla texts repeatedly refer to the place Ashtaroth.

Bibliography. N. Glueck, *AASOR* 18–19, 1937–9, p. 265; F. M. Abel, *Géographie de la Palestine*, 2, 1938, p. 255; W. F. Albright, *BASOR* 83, 1941, p. 33; J. A. Knudtzon, *Die el-Amarna Tafeln*, 1, 1907, pp. 726, 816; 2, 1915, p. 1292; Honigman, *Reallexikon der Assyriologie*, 1, 1932, p. 304; W. Helck, *Die Beziehungen ägyptens zu Vorderasien*, 1962, p. 57; R. D. Barnett and N. Falkner, *The Sculptures of Tiglath-Pileser III (745–727 BC)*, 1962, pl. LXIX, p. 30. T.C.M.

ASHTEROTH-KARNAIM. A city inhabited by the Rephaim, sacked by Chedorlaomer in the time of Abraham (Gn. 14:5). Some scholars interpret the name as 'Astarte of the Two Horns' and identify this goddess with representations in art of a female with two horns of which Palestinian examples have been found at Gezer and Beth-shan. It is more probable, however, that the name is to be taken as 'Ashteroth near Karnaim' and identified with the city of *Ashtaroth (**3**), which lies in the vicinity of Karnaim (mentioned in 1 Macc. 5:43–44).

Bibliography. F. M. Abel, *Géographie de la Palestine*, 2, 1938, p. 255; D. Baly, *The Geography of the Bible*, 1974, pp. 97, 216; H. Tadmor, *IEJ* 12, 1962, p. 121 and n. 30; W. C. Graham and H. G. May, *Material Remains of the Megiddo Cult*, 1935, p. 12. T.C.M.

ASHTORETH See Ashtaroth, Part 1.

ASHURBANIPAL (Assyr. *Aššur-bān-apli*, 'Ashur has made a son'). He was created crown prince in May 672 BC by his father Esarhaddon whom he succeeded in 669 BC as king of *Assyria. Early in his reign he warred against Egypt, where he captured *Thebes in 663 BC (*cf.* Na. 3:8), and to hold this distant land had to make a number of punitive raids against the Syrians, Phoenicians and Arabs. He is probably the king who freed Manasseh from exile in Nineveh (2 Ch. 33:13) and thus had a vassal king serving him in Judah. About 645 BC Ashurbanipal sacked *Susa, capital of Elam, and for this reason is thought to be the 'great and noble Osnappar (AV Asnappar)', whom the Samaritans claimed had brought men from Susa and Elam to their city (Ezr. 4:9–10). Since this is a reference in an Aramaic letter more than 200 years after the event, the rendering of the Assyrian royal name as *'as(rb)npr* (LXX *Asennaphar*; Gk. [Lucian] interprets as *Shalmaneser) is not unlikely.

From 652 to 648 BC the last of the great Assyrian kings was at war with his twin brother Šamaš-šum-ukin of Babylon and the Assyrian hold on Palestine weakened. The end of his reign is obscure for *c.* 627 BC he died or had his son Aššur-eṭil-ilāni as co-regent. Ashurbanipal is well known for his library of Akkadian literature collected at Nineveh.

Bibliography. *CAH*, 3, 1978. D.J.W.

ASHURITES. The translation of *Ashuri* (2 Sa. 2:9) by Ashurites, taking it as a gentilic collective, has raised problems. It seems clear that there is no connection with the Ashurites of Gn. 25:3. Some would read Asherites and connect it with Jdg. 1:32, since the Targum of Jonathan reads Beth-Asher. Some scholars would emend to Geshurites, finding support (*cf. POTT*, p. 26, n. 45) in the Syr. and Vulg. The objection to this reading is that Geshur had its own king Talmai (*cf.* 2 Sa. 13:37), whose daughter David had married (1 Ch. 3:2). The LXX has *thaseiri*, possibly due to the misreading of the definite article *h* as a *t*.

The use, however, of the preposition *'el* in 2 Sa. 2:9 with the names Gilead, Ashuri and Jezreel rather indicates place-names, as this preposition can have the sense of 'at'. The meaning would then be that these are the names of three administrative centres. In the choice of such centres consideration would be given to geographical accessibility. In the case of Ashuri, otherwise unknown, this could have been the decisive factor. With the following three names the preposition *'al* is used, as commonly with 'people' in the phrase 'to reign over', thus, and over Ephraim, and over Benjamin, even over all Israel'. The use of the definite article with Ashuri is not unusual with proper names (*cf.* Gilead), and there are other examples of place-names with the ending *i* (*e.g.* Edrei, Ophni). If the three towns formed a triangle, then Ashuri would be the S point, with Jezreel N and Gilead E. Thus geographically an identifi-

King Ashurbanipal participating in the ritual for the rebuilding of the temple Esagila at Babylon, by carrying a basket of building materials. Height 36·8 cm. 668–633 BC. (BM)

cation with Asher (Jos. 17:7) might be possible. W.J.M.

ASIA. To Greeks the name either of the continent or more commonly of the region in Asia Minor based on Ephesus. The latter embraced a number of Greek states which in the 3rd century BC fell under the control of the kings of Pergamum. In 133 BC the royal possessions were bequeathed to the Romans, and the area was subsequently organized as a province including the whole W coast of Asia Minor together with adjacent islands, and stretching inland as far as the Anatolian plateau. There was a galaxy of wealthy Greek states which suffered at first from Roman exploitation, but recovered in the NT period to become the most brilliant centres of Hellenism in the world. The Roman jurisdiction was exercised through nine or more assizes (*agoraioi*, Acts 19:38) presided over by the senatorial proconsul or his legates (*anthypatoi*, *ibid.*). The Greek republics formed a confederation whose chief expression was the cult of Rome and Augustus established initially at Pergamum. It is not certain whether the 'Asiarchs' (Acts 19:31) were the ex-high priests of the cult or the members of the federal assembly. In either case they represent a pro-Roman political élite. (J. A. O. Larsen, *Representative Government in Greek and Roman Antiquity*, 1955, pp. 117–120.)

Churches were established only in the administrative heart of the province at first. All three metropolitan centres, Pergamum, Smyrna and Ephesus, had churches. Beyond that we know for certain of churches in only two of the nearer assize centres, Sardis in the Hermus valley (Thyatira and Philadelphia being important cities in the same region) and Laodicea (on the Lycus) at the head of the Maeander valley (with the smaller towns of Colossae and Hierapolis near by).

BIBLIOGRAPHY. Pliny, *NH* 5. 28–41; Strabo 12–14; J. Keil, *CAH*, 11, pp. 580–589; A. H. M. Jones, *Cities of the Eastern Roman Provinces*[2], 1971, pp. 28–94; D. Magie, *Roman Rule in Asia Minor*, 2 vols., 1950.

E.A.J.

ASIARCH. In Acts 19:31 some of the Asiarchs (Gk. *asiarchēs*), described as friends of Paul, warn him

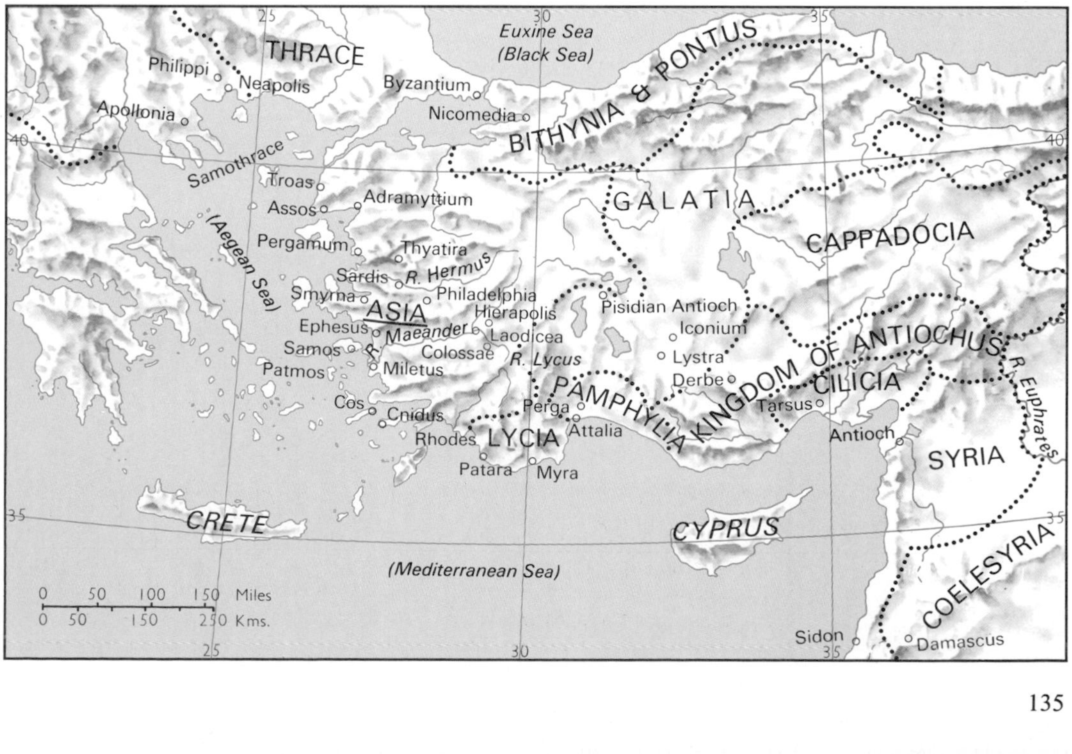

The Roman province of proconsular Asia (after 133 BC*).*

not to risk his life by going into the Ephesian theatre during the riotous demonstration in honour of Artemis. The league (*koinon*) of cities of the province of Asia was administered by the Asiarchs, who were chosen annually from the wealthiest and most aristocratic citizens. From their ranks were drawn the honorary high priests of the provincial cult of 'Rome and the Emperor', established by the league with its headquarters at Pergamum in 29 BC. They are further mentioned by Strabo (*Geography* 14. 1. 42) and in inscriptions.

BIBLIOGRAPHY. L. R. Taylor, 'The Asiarchs', in *BC*, 5, 1933, pp. 256–262. F.F.B.

ASIBIAS
See Malchijah, Part 2.

ASNAPPAR
See Ashurbanipal, Part 1.

ASP
See Animals, Part 1.

ASPHODEL
See Plants (Crocus), Part 3.

ASSASSINS. A term in Acts 21:38 to render the Gk. *sikarioi*, here used of the followers of an * Egyptian impostor. The term was applied specially to groups of militant Jewish nationalists in the middle years of the 1st century AD who armed themselves with concealed daggers (Lat. *sicae*, whence *sicarii*, 'dagger-men') to despatch unawares men whom they regarded as enemies of the nation (Josephus, *BJ* 2. 254–257; *Ant*. 20. 163–165, 186–188). F.F.B.

ASSOS. A seaport of NW Asia Minor, at the modern Behram Köy on the S coast of the Troad, directly opposite the island of Lesbos. The city was built on a commanding cone of rock over 230 m high and impressive remains survive of its superb 4th-century-BC fortifications. The shore below is sheltered from the prevalent northerlies, but the harbour was artificial, protected by a mole (Strabo 13. 1. 57 = p. 610). Acts 20:13–14 records that Paul's companions sailed ahead of him from * Troas to Assos, where he rejoined them after making the swifter 30 km land journey, perhaps wishing to spend as long as possible at Troas without deferring his voyage to Jerusalem. A harbour village with dwindling trade persisted at Assos into modern times. C.J.H.

ASSURANCE. 1. Grounds for certainty (a pledge, token or proof). **2.** The state of certainty. Both Testaments depict faith as a state of assurance founded upon divinely given assurances.

Sense **1** is found in Acts 17:31, where Paul says that by raising Jesus God has 'given assurance to all men' (*pistis*, objectively adequate grounds for belief) that Jesus will judge the world. *Cf.* 2 Tim. 3:14 AV, where Timothy is told to continue in what he has 'been assured of' (passive of *pistoō*, render certain)—the assurance deriving in this case from Timothy's knowledge of his teachers and of the Scriptures.

Sense **2** is regularly expressed by the noun *plērophoria* (fullness of conviction and confidence), which EVV translate 'full assurance'. We read of the 'riches of the *plērophoria* of understanding' ('a wealth of assurance, such as understanding brings', Arndt) (Col. 2:2); of approaching God with *plērophoria* of faith (Heb. 10:22); of maintaining *plērophoria* of hope (Heb. 6:11); and of the gospel being preached 'in the Holy Spirit and with full *plērophoria*'—*i.e.* with strong, Spirit-wrought conviction in both preacher and converts (1 Thes. 1:5). Paul uses the passive of the corresponding verb *plērophoreō* (lit., 'be filled full; be fully resolved', Ec. 8:11, LXX; 'be fully satisfied', papyri [see *LAE*, p. 82]) to denote the state of being fully assured as to God's will (Rom. 14:5) and his ability to perform his promises (Rom. 4:21). Another passive (*pepeismai*, 'I am persuaded') introduces Paul's conviction that God can guard him (2 Tim. 1:12), and that nothing can separate him from God's love (Rom. 8:38f.). This passive points to the fact that

The agora (market-place) of Assos from the south. (FNH)

Christian assurance is not an expression of human optimism or presumption, but a persuasion from God. It is, indeed, just one facet of the gift of *faith (*cf.* Heb. 11:1). God's witness is its ground and God's Spirit its author.

Assured faith in the NT has a double object: first, God's revealed truth, viewed comprehensively as a promise of salvation in Christ; second, the believer's own interest in that promise. In both cases, the assurance is correlative to and derived from divine testimony.

1. God testifies to sinners that the gospel is his truth. This he does, both by the miracles and charismata which authenticated the apostles as his messengers (Heb. 2:4), and by the Spirit-given illumination which enabled their hearers to recognize and receive their message 'not as the word of men but as what it really is, the word of God' (1 Thes. 2:13, *cf.* 1:5).

2. God testifies to believers that they are his sons. The gift to them of the Spirit of Christ (see Acts 2:38; 5:32; Gal. 3:2) is itself God's testimony to them that he has received them into the Messianic kingdom (Acts 15:8), and that now they know him savingly (1 Jn. 3:24). This gift, the 'guarantee of our inheritance' (Eph. 1:14), seals them as God's permanent possession (Eph. 1:13; 4:30), and assures them that through Christ they are now his children and heirs. The Spirit witnesses to this by prompting them to call God 'Father' (Rom. 8:15f.; Gal. 4:6) and giving them a sense of his fatherly love (Rom. 5:5). Hence the boldness and joy before God and men that everywhere characterize NT religion.

Self-deception is, however, a danger here, for strong persuasions of a saving relationship with God may be strong delusions of demonic origin. Inward assurance must therefore be checked by external moral and spiritual tests (*cf.* Tit. 1:16). John's Epistles deal directly with this. John specifies right belief about Christ, love to Christians and righteous conduct as objective signs of being a child of God and knowing him savingly (1 Jn. 2:3–5, 29; 3:9f., 14, 18f.; 4:7; 5:1, 4, 18). Those who find these signs in themselves may assure (lit., persuade) their hearts in the presence of God when a sense of guilt makes them doubt his favour (1 Jn. 3:19). But absence of these signs shows that any assurance felt is delusive (1 Jn. 1:6; 2:4, 9–11, 23; 3:6–10; 4:8, 20; 2 Jn. 9; 3 Jn. 11).

BIBLIOGRAPHY. L. Berkhof, *The Assurance of Faith*; G. Delling, *TDNT* 6, pp. 310f.; R. Schippers, *NIDNTT* 1, pp. 733ff.; and, among older works, W. Guthrie, *The Christian's Great Interest*, 1658.

J.I.P.

ASSYRIA. The name of the ancient country whose inhabitants were called Assyrians. It lay in the upper Mesopotamian plain, bounded on the W by the Syrian desert, on the S by the Jebel Hamrin and Babylonia, and on the N and E by the Urarṭian (Armenian) and Persian hills. The most fertile and densely populated part of Assyria lay E of the central river Tigris ('Hiddekel', Gn. 2:14, AV). The Heb. *'aššûr* (Assyr. *aššur*) is used both of this land and of its people. The term Assyria was sometimes applied to those territories which were subject to the control of its kings dwelling at Nineveh, Assur and Calah, the principal cities. At the height of its power in the 8th–7th centuries BC, these territories included Media and S Anatolia, Cilicia, Syria, Palestine, Arabia, Egypt, Elam and Babylonia.

In the OT Asshur was considered the second son of Shem (Gn. 10:22) and was distinct from Ashuram ('Asshurim'), an Arab tribe descended from Abraham and Keturah (Gn. 25:3), and from the *Ashurites of 2 Sa. 2:9 (where 'Asherites' or 'Geshur' is perhaps to be read; *cf.* Jdg. 1:31–32). Assyria, which is always carefully distinguished from Babylonia, stands for the world power whose invasions of Israel and Judah were divinely permitted, though later it too suffered destruction for its godlessness. There are frequent references to the land (Is. 7:18; Ho. 11:5) and to the kings of Assyria (Is. 8:4; 2 Ki. 15–19).

I. History

a. Early history down to 900 BC

Assyria was inhabited from prehistoric times (*e.g.* Jarmo, *c.* 5000 BC) and pottery from the periods known as Hassuna, Samarra, Halaf and 'Ubaid (*c.* 5000–3000 BC) has been found at a number of sites, including Assur, Nineveh and Calah, which, according to Gn. 10:11–12, were founded by immigrants from Babylonia. Although the origins of the Assyrians are still disputed, the Sumerians were present at Assur by 2900 BC and Assyrian language and culture owes much to the southerners. According to the Assyrian king list, the first seventeen kings of Ashur 'lived in tents'. One of these, Tudiya, made a treaty with *Ebla *c.* 2300 BC, so cannot be a mere 'eponymous ancestor'.

The kings of Babylonia, including Sargon of Agade (*ACCAD), *c.* 2350 BC built in Assyria at Nineveh, and a building inscription of Amar-Su'en of Ur (*c.* 2040 BC) has been found at Assur. After the fall of Ur to Amorite invaders Assur, according to the Assyrian king list, was ruled by independent princes. These established trade connections with Cappadocia (*c.* 1920–1870 BC). Šamši-Adad I (1813–1781 BC) gradually increased his lands, his sons Yasmaḫ-Adad and Zimrilim ruling at *Mari until

Assyrian bronze demon, Pazuzu, who was thought to carry disease. Height 15 cm. c. 800 BC. (MC)

Reconstruction of the façade of the Assyrian temple of the moon-god Sin at Khorsabad (Dur-Šharrukin). 8th cent. BC. (AP)

Silver beaker decorated with bands of gold leaf at the neck, shoulder and base. From Fort Shalmaneser, Calah (Nimrud). 7th cent. BC. (BM)

that city was captured by *Hammurapi of Babylon. With the advent of the Mitanni and Hurrian groups in the Upper Euphrates the influence of Assyria declined, though it remained a prosperous agricultural community whose typical life and customs can be seen in the tablets recovered from *Nuzi. Under Ashur-uballiṭ I (1365–1330 BC) Assyria began to recover something of its former greatness. He entered into correspondence with Amenophis IV of Egypt whereupon Burnaburias II of Babylon objected, declaring him to be his vassal (Amarna letters). However, the decline of the Mitanni allowed the trade routes to the N to be reopened and in the reigns of Arik-den-ili (1319–1308 BC) and Adad-nirari I (1307–1275 BC) territories as far W as Carchemish, lost since the days of Šamši-Adad, were recovered.

Shalmaneser I (1274–1245 BC) made constant expeditions against the tribes in the E hills and against new enemies in Urarṭu. He also sought to contain the Hurrian forces by campaigns in Hanigalbat to the NW. He rebuilt *Calah as a new capital. His son Tukulti-Ninurta I (1244–1208 BC) had to devote much of his attention to Babylonia, of which he was also king for 7 years until murdered by his son Aššurnadinapli. Soon afterwards Babylonia became independent again and there was a revival of fortune for a while under Tiglath-pileser I (1115–1077 BC). He vigorously campaigned against the Muški (*MESHECH) and Subarian tribes, thrusting also as far as Lake Van in the N and to the Mediterranean, where he received tribute from Byblos, Sidon and Arvad, and making expeditions as far as Tadmor (Palmyra) in his efforts to control the Aramaean (Aḫlame) tribes of the desert. It was the activities of these latter tribes which contained Assyria from *c.* 1100 to 940 BC and left David and Solomon free to strike into Syria (Aram).

b. The Neo-Assyrian period (900–612 BC)

The Assyrians under Tukulti-Ninurta II (890–884 BC) began to take more vigorous military action against the tribes oppressing Assyria.

His son, Ashurnasirpal II (883–859 BC), in a series of brilliant campaigns subdued the tribes on the Middle Euphrates, and reached

Glazed brick showing an Assyrian king carrying a libation cup, followed by attendants with bows and arrows. Calah (Nimrud). 23 cm × 30 cm. Early 9th cent. BC. (BM)

the Lebanon and Philistia, where the coastal cities paid him tribute. He also sent expeditions into N Babylonia and the E hills. His reign marked the commencement of a sustained pressure by Assyria against the W which was to bring her into conflict with Israel. More than 50,000 prisoners were employed on the enlargement of Calah, where Ashurnasirpal built a new citadel, palace and temples, and commenced work on the ziggurat. He employed artists to engrave sculptures in his audience chambers and skilled men to maintain botanical and zoological gardens and a park.

Ashurnasirpal's son Shalmaneser III (858–824 BC) continued his father's policy and greatly extended Assyria's frontiers, making himself the master from Urarṭu to the Persian Gulf and from Media to the Syrian coast and Cilicia (Tarsus). In 857 BC he captured Carchemish and his attack on Bit-Adini (*EDEN, HOUSE OF) alerted the major city-states to the SW. Irhuleni of Hamath and Hadadezer of Damascus formed an anti-Assyrian coalition of 10 kings who faced the Assyrian army in the indecisive battle of Qarqar in 853 BC. According to the Assyrian annals, 'Ahab the Israelite (*sirla'aia*)' supplied 2,000 chariots and 14,000 men on this occasion. 3 years later Shalmaneser undertook a further series of operations directed mainly against Hadadezer (probably *BEN-HADAD I). By 841 BC, Shalmaneser's 18th year, the coalition had split up, so that the full force of the Assyrian army could be directed against *Hazael of Damascus who fought a rearguard action in the Anti-Lebanon mountains and withdrew into Damascus. When the siege of this city failed, Shalmaneser moved through the Hauran to the Nahr el-Kelb in the Lebanon and there received tribute from the rulers of Tyre, Sidon and 'Jehu (*Ya-ú-a*), son of Omri', an act, in the reign of Jehu, rather than Jehoram, not mentioned in the OT but depicted on Shalmaneser's 'Black Obelisk' at Nimrud (Calah). He had scenes from the other campaigns engraved on the bronze plating of the gates of the temple at Imgur-Bel (Balawat). (These are now in the British Museum.)

Šamši-Adad V (823–811 BC) was obliged to initiate reprisal raids in Nairi to counteract the plots of the rebel Ispuini of Urarṭu, and also launched three campaigns against Babylonia and the fortress Der on the Elamite frontier. Šamši-Adad died young, and his influential widow Sammuramat (Semiramis) acted as regent until 805 BC, when their son Adad-nirari III was old enough to assume authority. Meanwhile the army undertook expeditions in the N and W, and Guzana (*GOZAN) was incorporated as an Assyrian province. Adad-nirari set out to support Hamath in 804 by attacking Damascus, where *Hazael, son of Ben-hadad II—whom he called by his Aramaic title *Mari'*—was ruling. This gave Israel a respite from the attacks from Aram (2 Ki. 12:17; 2 Ch. 24:23f.), and many rulers brought the Assyrian gifts in recognition of his aid. He claims that among those bringing tribute were 'Hatti (N Syria), Amurru (E Syria), Tyre, Sidon, Omri-land (Israel), Edom and Philistia as far as the Mediterranean'. A stela from Rimah (Assyria) names 'Joash of Samaria' (*Ya'usu samerinaia*) among these, *c.* 796 BC. The Assyrian action seems to have enabled Joash to recover towns on his N border which had previously been lost to Hazael (2 Ki. 13:25). Affairs at home appear to have been peaceful, for the Assyrian king built a new palace outside the citadel walls at Calah.

Shalmaneser IV (782–773 BC), though harassed by the Urarṭian Argistis I on his N border, kept up the pressure against Damascus, and this doubtless helped Jeroboam II to extend the boundaries of Israel to the Beqa' ('entrance of Hamath', 2 Ki. 14:25–28). But Assyria was now being weakened by internal dissension, for the succession was uncertain, since Shalmaneser had died when young and childless. A notable defeat in the N was marked by that 'sign of ill omen', an eclipse of the sun, in 763 BC, a date of importance in Assyrian chronology. Once again the W was free to re-group to withstand further attacks, as indicated by the Aramaic treaty of Mati'el of Bit-Agusi (Arpad) with Barga'ayah.

The records of Tiglath-pileser III (744–727 BC) are fragmentary, and the order of events in his reign uncertain. He was, however, a strong ruler who set out to regain, and even extend, the territories which owed allegiance to the national god Ashur. Early in his reign he was proclaimed king of Babylon under his native name Pul(u) (2 Ki. 15:19; 1 Ch. 5:26). In the N he fought Sardur II of Urarṭu, who was intriguing with the Syrian states. By relentless campaigning Tiglath-pileser defeated the rebels in towns along the Anti-Taurus (Kashiari) mountains as far as Kummuḫ, organizing the subdued country in a series of provinces owing allegiance to the king. *Arpad was besieged for 2 years (742–740 BC), and during this time Rezin of Damascus and other neighbouring rulers brought in their tribute. While Tiglath-pileser was absent in the N hills in 738 a revolt was stimulated by 'Azriau of Yaudi' in league with Hamath. Yaudi was a small city-state in N Syria, though there is a possibility that the reference is to Azariah of Judah. At this time Tiglath-pileser claims to have received tribute from Menahem (*Meni ḫimmu*) of Samaria and Hiram of Tyre. This event is not mentioned in the OT, which records a later payment. Then the amount of 50 shekels of silver extorted from the leading Israelites to meet this demand is shown by contemporary Assyrian contracts to be the price of a slave. It was evidently a ransom to avoid deportation (2 Ki. 15:20).

A series of campaigns 2 years later ended with the capture of Damascus in 732 BC. Tiglath-pileser, according to his annals, replaced Pekah, the murderer of Pekahiah, son of Menahem, by 'Ausi (Hoshea). *Cf.* 2 Ki. 15:30. This was probably in 734 BC, when the Assyrians marched down the Phoenician coast and through 'the border of Israel' as far as Gaza, whose king, Hanunu, fled across the 'River of *Egypt'. This action in Palestine was at least in part a response to the appeal of *Iauḫazi* ([Jeho]Ahaz) of Judah, whose tribute is listed with that of Ammon, Moab, Ashkelon and Edom, for help against Rezin of Damascus and Pekah of Israel (2 Ki. 16:5–9). Israel (*Bit-Humria*) was attacked, Hazor in Galilee destroyed (2 Ki. 15:29), and many prisoners taken into exile. Ahaz, too, paid dearly for this bid and had to accept religious obligations (2 Ki. 16:10ff.), the imported altar being but one symbol of vassalage, another being an image of the king such as Tiglath-pileser set up in conquered Gaza.

Shalmaneser V (726–722 BC), son of Tiglath-pileser III, also warred in the W. When the Assyrian vassal

Hoshea failed to pay his annual tribute after listening to overtures of help promised by Egypt (2 Ki. 17:4), Shalmaneser laid siege to Samaria (v. 5). After 3 years, according to the Babylonian Chronicle, 'he broke the resistance of the city of *Šamara'in'* (Samaria?) so 'the king of Assyria (who) took Samaria' (v. 6) and carried off the Israelites to exile in the Upper Euphrates and Media may be this same Assyrian king. However, since his successor Sargon II later claims the capture of Samaria as his own act, it may be that the unnamed king of v. 6 was Sargon, who could have been associated with Shalmaneser in the siege and have completed the operation on the latter's death.

Sargon II (721–705 BC) was a vigorous leader like Tiglath-pileser III. He records that, when the citizens of Samaria were led by Iau-bi'di of Hamath to withhold their taxes, he removed 27,270 (or 27,290) people from the area of Samaria, 'with the gods in which they trusted'. The exact date of this exile, which broke Israel as an independent nation, cannot be determined as yet from Assyrian records. Hanunu of Gaza had returned from Egypt with military support so Sargon marched to Raphia, where, in the first clash between the armies of the two great nations, he defeated the Egyptians. Despite this, the Palestinian rulers and peoples still leaned on Egypt for support, and the history of this period is an essential background for the prophecies of Isaiah. In 715 Sargon intervened once more, sacking Ashdod and Gath and claiming to have 'subjugated Judah'; but there is no evidence in the OT that he entered the land at this time. Sargon defeated Pisiris of Carchemish in 717 and campaigned in Cilicia. He continued Assyrian raids on the Mannai and tribes in the Lake Van area (714 BC) who were restless under Cimmerian pressure. In the S he invaded Elam, sacked Susa and drove Marduk-apla-iddina II (*MERODACH-BALADAN) back into the marshland at the head of the Persian Gulf. Sargon died before his new palace at Dur-Šarrukin (Khorsabad) could be completed.

The first years of Sennacherib (704–681 BC) were occupied in suppressing revolts which broke out on his father's death. While crown-prince he had been responsible for safeguarding the N frontier, and this knowledge proved invaluable in his dealings with Urarṭu and Media, and in his military expeditions, which reached as far W as Cilicia, where Tarsus was captured in 698 BC. Marduk-apla-iddina seized the throne of Babylon (703–701 BC), and it required a concentrated military expedition to dislodge him. It was probably during these years that the Chaldean asked Hezekiah for help (2 Ki. 20:12–19). Isaiah's disapproval of this alliance was justified, for by 689 BC the Assyrians had driven Merodach-baladan out of the country and sacked Babylon. A naval operation which was planned to cross the Gulf in pursuit of the rebel was called off on receipt of the news of his death in Elam. Moreover, in 701 BC Sennacherib had marched to Syria, besieged Sidon and moved S to attack rebellious Ashkelon. It was probably at this time that the Assyrians successfully besieged Lachish (2 Ki. 18:13–14), a victory depicted on the bas-reliefs in Sennacherib's palace at Nineveh. The army next moved to meet the Egyptians at Eltekeh. During these moves in Judah, Hezekiah paid tribute (2 Ki. 18:14–16), an act which is recorded in the Assyrian annals. The majority opinion is that it was later in this same campaign and year that Sennacherib 'shut up Hezekiah the Judaean in Jerusalem as a bird in a cage', and demanded his surrender (2 Ki. 18:17–19:9). On any interpretation, the Assyrians raised the siege suddenly and withdrew (2 Ki. 19:35–36, *cf.* Herodotus, 2. 141). Another view connects the siege of Jerusalem with a later campaign, perhaps that against the Arabs in 686 BC. This minority view assumes no time lapse, as is probable between the return to Nineveh and the assassination of *Sennacherib by his sons in the month Tebet 681 BC (Is. 37:38; 2 Ki. 19:37). The Babylonian Chronicle states that Sennacherib was murdered by 'his son', and Esarhaddon, his younger son and successor, claimed to have pursued his rebel brothers, presumably the murderers, into S Armenia (for a fuller discussion of the seeming discrepancy between the OT and Assyrian texts on the place and number of the assassins, see *DOTT*, pp. 70–73).

Sennacherib, with his W Semitic wife Naqi'a-Zakutu, extensively rebuilt Nineveh, its palaces, gateways and temples, and to ensure water-supplies aqueducts (Jerwan) and dams were built. This was also used to irrigate large parks around the city. Prisoners from his campaigns, including Jews, were used on these projects and are depicted on the palace reliefs.

Esarhaddon (680–669 BC) had been designated crown-prince by his father 2 years before he came to the throne, and had served as viceroy in Babylon. When the S Babylonians rebelled, a single campaign sufficed to subdue them, and Na'id-Marduk was appointed as their new chief in 678. But a series of campaigns was needed to counteract the machinations of their neighbours, the Elamites. In the hills farther N also periodic raids kept the tribesmen of Zamua and the Median plain subject to Assyrian overlordship. The N tribes were more restless, due to the plotting of Teušpa and the Cimmerians. Esarhaddon also came into conflict with Scythian tribes (*Išguzai*).

In the W Esarhaddon continued his father's policy of exacting tribute from the city-states, including those in Cilicia and Syria. Baal of Tyre refused payment and was attacked, and Abdi-Milki was besieged in Sidon for 3 years from 676. This opposition to Assyrian domination was incited by Tirhakah of Egypt and provoked a quick reaction. Esarhaddon increased the amount payable, collecting in addition wood, stone and other supplies for his new palace at *Calah and for his reconstruction of Babylon. It may have been in connection with the latter that Manasseh was taken there (2 Ch. 33:11). 'Manasseh (*Menasi*) of Judah' is named among those from whom Esarhaddon claimed tribute at this time. These included 'Baal of Tyre, Qauš-(Chemosh)-gabri of Edom, Muṣuri of Moab, Ṣili-Bel of Gaza, Metinti of Ashkelon, Ikausu of Ekron, Milki-ašapa of Gebel, . . . Aḫi-Milki of Ashdod as well as 10 kings of Cyprus (*Iadnana*)'.

With these states owing at least a nominal allegiance, the way was open to the fulfilment of Assyria's ambition to control the Egyptian Delta from which so much opposition was mounted. This was accomplished by a major expedition in 672 BC, which resulted in Assyrian governors being installed in Thebes and Memphis. In this same year Esarhaddon summoned his vassals to hear his declaration of Ashurbanipal as crown-prince of Assyria and Šamaš-šum-ukin as crown-prince of Babylonia. In this way he hoped to avoid disturbances similar to those which marked his own succession to the throne. Copies of the terms and oaths imposed at this ceremony are of interest as indicative of the *'covenant' form of relationship between a suzerain and his vassals. Many parallels can be drawn between this and OT terminology (D. J. Wiseman, *Vassal-Treaties of Esarhaddon*, 1958). It shows that Manasseh, as all the other rulers, would have had to swear eternal allegiance to Ashur, the national god of his overlord (2 Ki. 21:2–7, 9). The end of Esarhaddon's reign saw the beginning of the very revolts these 'covenants' were designed to forestall. Pharaoh Tirhakah incited the native chiefs of Lower Egypt to break away. It was at Harran, while on his way to crush this insurrection, that Esar-

Neo-Assyrian cylinder-seal with its imprint, showing the king and a bird-headed figure flanking a sacred tree. The duplicates of the king and the figure may represent different aspects of authority, royal and religious. The inscription names the owner (the priest Mushezib-Ninurta), his father and grandfather. Height 4·9 cm. (BM)

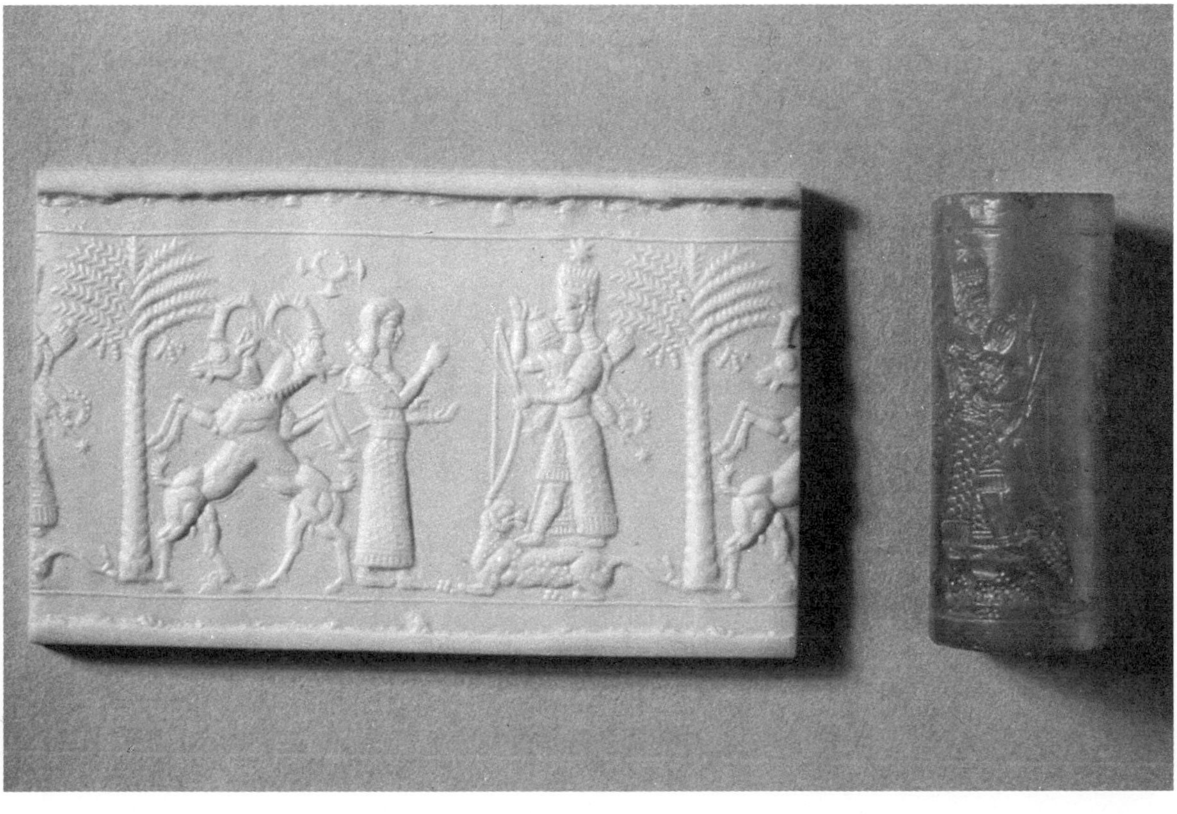

Assyrian seal and imprint showing Ishtar, goddess of war and love, standing on a lion. Height 4·3 cm. 7th–6th cent. BC. (BM)

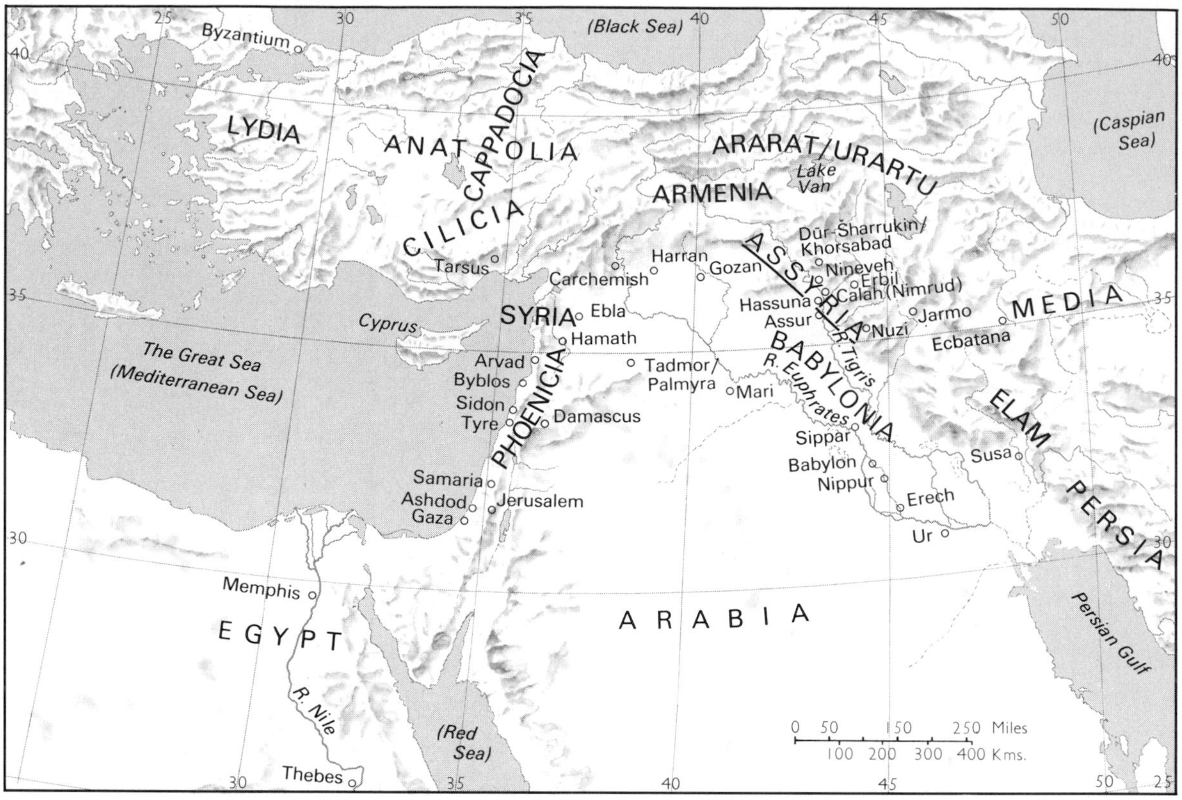

Assyria and surrounding regions.

haddon died and was succeeded by his sons as planned.

Ashurbanipal (668–*c.* 627 BC) immediately took up his father's unfinished task and marched against Tirhakah (*Tarqu*); but it required three hard campaigns and the sack of Thebes in 663 (Na. 3:8, 'No' AV) to regain control of Egypt. In his reign Assyria reached its greatest territorial extent. Punitive raids on the rebels in Tyre, Arvad and Cilicia brought Assyria into contact with another rising power—Lydia, whose king Gyges sent emissaries to Nineveh seeking an alliance against the Cimmerians. The raids on the Arab tribes and the restoration of Manasseh of Judah, called *Minse* by Ashurbanipal, probably had the one aim of keeping the route open to Egypt. Nevertheless, Assyria was doomed to fall swiftly. The Medes were increasing their hold over neighbouring tribes and threatening the Assyrian homeland. By 652 BC Šamaš-šum-ukin had revolted and the resultant struggle with Babylonia, which restrained the army from needed operations farther afield, ended in the sack of the S capital in 648 BC. This rebellion had been supported by Elam, so Ashurbanipal marched in to sack *Susa in 645 and henceforth made it an Assyrian province. Free from the frequent incursions of the Assyrian army in support of its local officials and tax-collectors, the W city-states gradually loosed from Assyria, and in Judah this new-found freedom was to be reflected in the reforms initiated by Josiah. Once again Egypt was independent and intriguing in Palestine.

The date of Ashurbanipal's death is uncertain (*c.* 631–627 BC), and very few historical texts for this period have yet been found. The hordes of the Scythians (Ummanmanda) began to dominate the Middle Euphrates area and Kyaxares the Mede besieged Nineveh. Ashurbanipal may have delegated power to his sons Aššur-eṭel-ilāni (632–628 BC) and Šin-šar-iškun (628–612 BC). Ashurbanipal himself was interested in the arts. He built extensively in *Nineveh, where in his palace and in the Nabu temple he collected libraries of tablets (see section **III,** Literature, below).

With the rise of Nabopolassar, the *Chaldeans drove the Assyrians out of Babylonia in 625 BC. The Babylonians joined the Medes to capture Assur (614 BC) and in July/August 612 BC, as foretold by Nahum and Zephaniah, Nineveh fell to their attack. These campaigns are fully told in the Babylonian Chronicle. The walls were breached by floods (Na. 1:8; Xenophon, *Anabasis* 3. 4) and Šin-šar-iškun (Sardanapalus) perished in the flames. For 2 years the government under Ashur-uballiṭ held out at Harran, but no help came from Egypt, Neco marching too late to prevent the city falling to the Babylonians and Scythians in 609 BC. Assyria ceased to exist and her territory was taken over by the Babylonians.

In later years 'Assyria' formed part of the Persian, Hellenistic (Seleucid) and Parthian empires, and during this time 'Assyria' (Persian *Athura*) continued to be used as a general geographical designation for her former homelands (Ezk. 16:28; 23:5–23).

II. Religion

The Assyrian king acted as regent on earth for the national god Ashur, to whom he reported his activities regularly. Thus Assyrian campaigns were conceived, at least in part, as a holy war against those who failed to avow his sovereignty or breached the borders of his land, and were ruthlessly pursued in the event of rebellion. Ashur's primary temple was at the capital Assur, and various deities were thought to guard the interests of the other cities. Anu and Adad resided at Assur, having temples and associated ziggurats there, while Ishtar, goddess of war and love, was worshipped at Nineveh, though as 'Ishtar of Arbela' she also held sway at

Erbil. Nabu, god of wisdom and patron of the sciences, had temples at both Nineveh and Calah (Nimrud), where there were libraries collected by royal officials and housed in part in the Nabu (*NEBO) temple. Sin, the moon-god, and his priests and priestesses had a temple and cloisters at Ehulhul in Harran and were in close association with their counterpart in Ur. In general, divine consorts and less prominent deities had shrines within the major temples; thus at Calah, where the temples of Ninurta, god of war and hunting, Ishtar and Nabu have been discovered, there were places for such deities as Shala, Gula, Ea and Damkina. In most respects Assyrian religion differed little from that of *Babylonia, whence it had been derived. For the part played by religion in daily life, see the next section.

Clay foundation-figurine, one of several found in boxes laid under the floor at the dedication of an Assyrian palace or temple. Nineveh. Height 11·4 cm. 7th cent. BC. (BM)

III. Literature

The daily life and thought of the Assyrians is to be seen in the many hundreds of letters, economic and administrative documents, and literary texts found during excavations. Thus the early 2nd millennium BC is illuminated by the letters from Mari and Shemshara and *c.* 1500, during the period of Hurrian influence, from *Nuzi. The best-known period is, however, that of the Neo-Assyrian empire, when many texts, including some copied from the Middle Assyrian period, enable a detailed reconstruction to be made of the administration and civil service. Thus the historical annals, recorded on clay prisms, cylinders and tablets, though originally intended as introductions to inscriptions describing the king's building operations, can be supplemented by texts which record the royal requests to a deity (often Shamash) for oracles to guide in decisions concerning political and military affairs. A number of the letters and legal texts, as well as the annals, make reference to Israel, Judah and the W city-states (*DOTT*, pp. 46–75; *Iraq* 17, 1955, pp. 126–154).

Ashurbanipal, an educated man, created a library by importing or copying texts both from the existing archives at Nineveh, Assur and Calah and from Babylonian religious centres. Thus, in 1852/3 in his palace at Nineveh and in the Nabu temple there, Layard and Rassam discovered 26,000 fragmentary tablets, representing about 10,000 different texts. This find and its subsequent publication laid the foundation for the study of the Semitic Assyrian language and of Babylonian, from which it differs mainly dialectally. The cuneiform script, employing 600 or more signs as ideographs, syllables or determinatives, was taken over from the earlier Sumerians. Assyro-Babylonian (Akkadian) now provides the major bulk of ancient Semitic inscriptions. Since some texts had interlinear Sumerian translations, this find has been of importance in

The god Ashur in the sun-disc beneath stylized rain-clouds. Fragment of glazed brick from Assur. c. 890–884 BC. (BM)

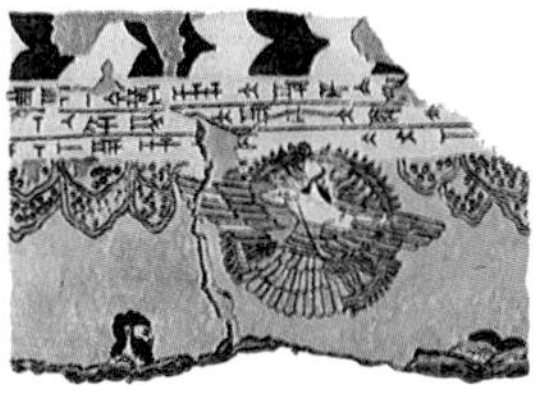

Artist's representation of the glazed brick in its undamaged state. (AP)

the study of that non-Semitic tongue which survived, as did Latin in England, for religious purposes.

The discovery among the Nineveh (Kuyunjik) collection, now housed in the British Museum, of a Babylonian account of the flood (Gilgamesh XI), later published by George Smith in December 1872, proved a stimulus to further excavations, and much has been written with special reference to the bearing of these finds on the OT. The library texts represent scholarly handbooks, vocabularies, sign and word lists, and dictionaries. The mythological texts written in poetic form include the series of twelve tablets now called the 'Epic of Gilgamesh' which describes his quest for eternal life and the story he was told by Uta-napishtim of his own survival of the *Flood in a specially constructed ship. The Epic of *Creation, called *Enuma eliš* after the opening phrase, is principally concerned with the exaltation of Marduk as the head of the Babylonian pantheon. An old Babylonian epic (*Atra-hasīs*) describes the creation of man following a strike against the gods and also the Flood. This provides closer parallels with OT than either *Enuma eliš* or Gilgamesh epics. Other epics include the Descent of Ishtar into the underworld in search of her husband Tammuz. Contrary to many recent theories, no text describing the resurrection of Tammuz has yet been found. Legends, including that of Sargon of Agade, who was saved at birth by being placed in a reed basket on the river Euphrates until rescued by a gardener, who brought him up to be king, have been compared with OT incidents. These Akkadian literary texts also contain the legend of Etana, who flew to heaven on an eagle, and that of the plague god Era, who fought against Babylon. Wisdom literature includes the poem of the righteous sufferer (*Ludlul bēl nēmeqi*) or the so-called 'Babylonian Job', the Babylonian theodicy, precepts and admonition, among which are counsels of wisdom, sayings and dialogues of a pessimist, and advice to a prince of the same *genre*, but not spirit, as OT Wisdom literature. There are also collections of hymns, fables, popular sayings, parables, proverbs and tales ('The poor man of Nippur') which are precursors of later literary forms.

Religious literature is also well represented by tablets grouped in series of up to ninety with their number and title stated in a colophon. The majority are omens derived from the inspection of the liver or entrails of sacrificial animals, or the movements and features of men, animals, birds, objects and planets. Many tablets give instructions for rituals to ensure the king's welfare and that of his country. Closely allied to these texts are the carefully recorded observations which formed the basis of Akkadian science, especially medicine (prognosis and diagnosis), botany, geology, chemistry, mathematics and law. For chronological purposes lists covering many of the years from *c.* 1100 to 612 BC gave the name of the eponym or *limmu*-official by whom each year was designated. These, together with the recorded king lists and astronomical data, provide a system of dating which is accurate to within a few years.

IV. Administration

The government derived from the person of the king who was also the religious leader and commander-in-chief. He exercised direct authority, although he also delegated local jurisdiction to provincial governors (*e.g.* *RAB-SHAKEH, *RAB-SARIS) and district-governors who collected and forwarded tribute and taxes, usually paid in kind. They were supported by the expeditions of the Assyrian army, the nucleus of which was a highly-trained and well-equipped regular force of chariots, siege-engineers, bowmen, spearmen and slingers. Conquered territories were made vassal-subjects of the god Ashur on oath and forced to render both political and religious allegiance to Assyria. Offenders were punished by reprisals and invasion, which resulted in the loot and destruction of their cities, death to the rebel leaders, and slavery and exile for the skilled citizens. The remainder were subjected to the surveillance of pro-Assyrian deputies. This helps to explain both the attitude of the Hebrew prophets to Assyria and the fear of 'this cauldron boiling over from the north' (*cf.* Je. 1:13) by the small states of Israel and Judah.

V. Art

Many examples of Assyrian art, wall-paintings, painted glazed panels, sculptured bas-reliefs, statues, ornaments, cylinder seals, ivory carvings, as well as bronze and metal work, have been preserved following excavation. Some of the reliefs are of particular interest in that the stele and obelisk of Shalmaneser III from Nimrud mention Israel and may portray Jehu. Sennacherib, on his palace sculptures at Nineveh, depicts the siege of Lachish and the use of Judaean captives to work on his building projects; while the bronze gates at Balawat show the Assyrian army engaged in Syria and Phoenicia. Other reliefs of Ashurnasirpal II at Nimrud and Ashurbanipal in the 'Lion Hunt' from Nineveh are a pictorial source for the costume, customs, and military and civilian operations of the Assyrians from the 9th to the 7th centuries BC.

VI. Excavations

Early explorers searched for biblical *Nineveh (Kuyunjik and Nebi Yunus) opposite Mosul, which was surveyed by C. J. Rich in 1820 and excavated in 1842–3 by Botta, in 1846–7, 1849–51 and 1853–4 by Layard and Rassam, by the British Museum in 1903–5, 1927–32 and subsequently by Iraqi archaeologists. Other major cities excavated include Assur (Qala'at Shergat) by German expeditions (1903–14); *Calah (Nimrud) by the British—Layard (1842–52), Loftus (1854–5), Mallowan and Oates (1949–63)—and by Iraqis and Poles (1969–76); and Dūr-Sharrukīn (Khorsabad) by the French (1843–5) and Americans (1929–35). Outlying prehistoric sites include Jarmo, Hassuna, Thalathat, Umm Dabaghiyah, Arpachiyah and Tepe Gawra. The principal Middle Assyrian occupations uncovered in addition to Assur are Tell Rimah and Billa (Shibaniba). Later Assyrian sites of note include Balawat (Imgur-Bēl).

For sites explored 1842–1939, see S. A. Pallis, *The Antiquity of Iraq*, 1956; for 1932–56 see M. E. L. Mallowan, *Twenty-Five Years of Mesopotamian Discovery*, 1956; and subsequently, reports in the journals *Iraq*, *Sumer* (*passim*).

BIBLIOGRAPHY. *History: CAH*, 1, 1971, pp. 729–770; 2, 1975, pp. 21–48, 274–306, 443–481; 3, 1978. *Inscriptions:* A. K. Grayson, *Assyrian Royal Inscriptions*, 1975–6; W. W. Hallo and W. K. Simpson, *The Ancient Near East; A History*, 1971, ch. 5; A. L. Oppenheim, *Letters from Mesopotamia*, 1967; *Ancient Mesopotamia*, 1964. *Relation to OT: ANET, DOTT. General: Reallexikon der Assyriologie*, 1932–78. *Art:* R. D. Barnett, *The Assyrian*

Palace Reliefs, 1976; *The Sculptures of Ashurbanipal*, 1976; M. E. L. Mallowan, *Nimrud and its Remains*, 1966. *Various:* G. van Driel, *The Cult of Aššur*, 1976; J. N. Postgate, *Taxation and Conscription in the Assyrian Empire*, 1974. D.J.W.

ATAROTH (Heb. *ᵃṭārôṯ*, lit. 'crowns'). **1.** A city on the E of Jordan in Reubenite territory (Nu. 32:3, 34), modern Khirbet 'Attarus; *cf.* *ARNON. A city called Atroth occurs in Nu. 32:35, but this may be an accidental repetition from the previous verse, or else should be taken with the following word, giving the otherwise unknown place-name Atroth-Shophan. **2.** A city in Ephraim, perhaps the same as Ataroth-Addar (Jos. 16:2, 5, 7;

ASTRONOMY
See Stars, Part 3.

ASWAN
See Seveneh, Part 3.

ATARGATIS
See Tartak, Part 3.

Winged human-headed bull, pairs of which guarded the entrance to the palace at Calah (Nimrud). Height 3·15 m. c. 870 BC. (BM)

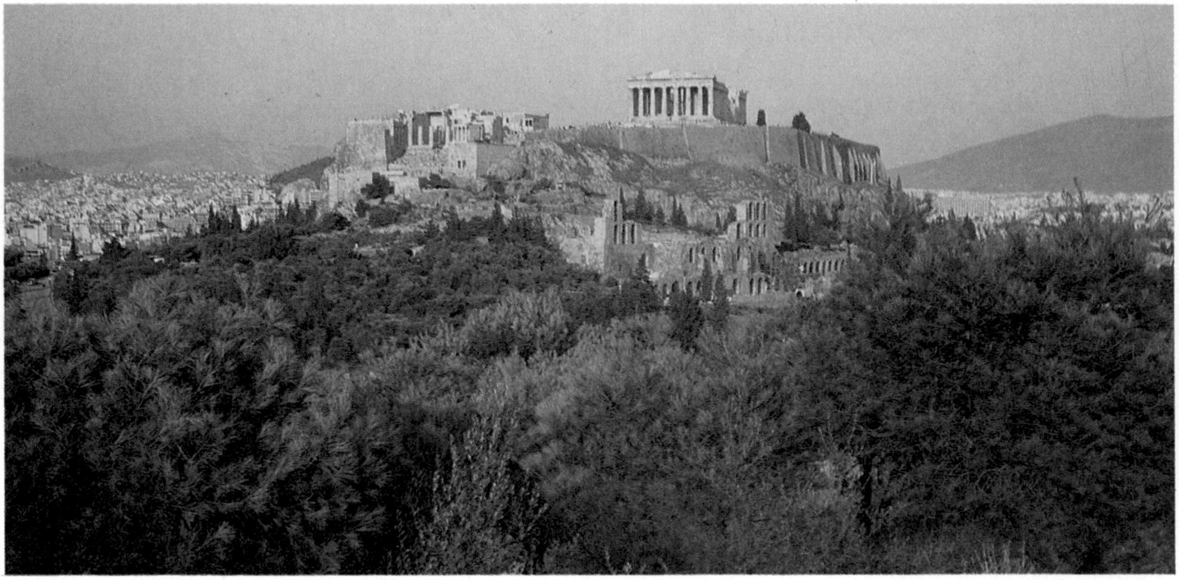

Athens. The Acropolis, showing the dominant position of the Parthenon, built between 447 and 438 BC. (MH)

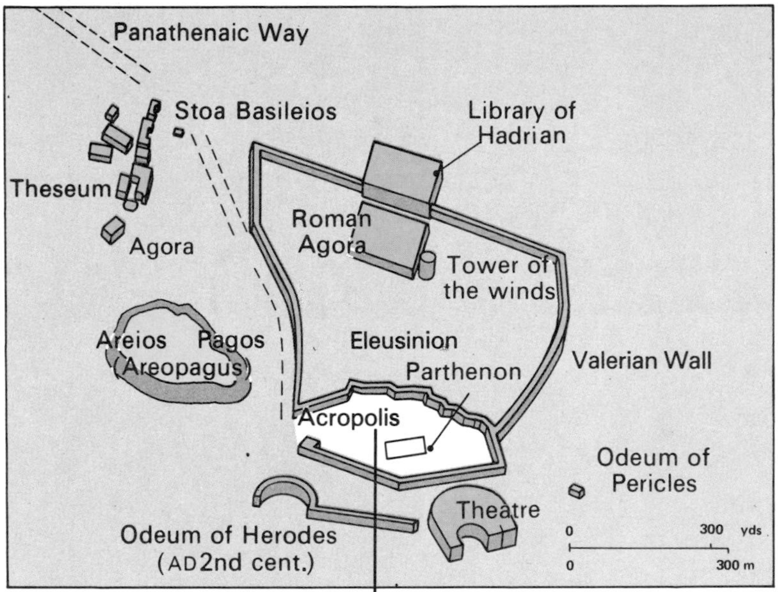

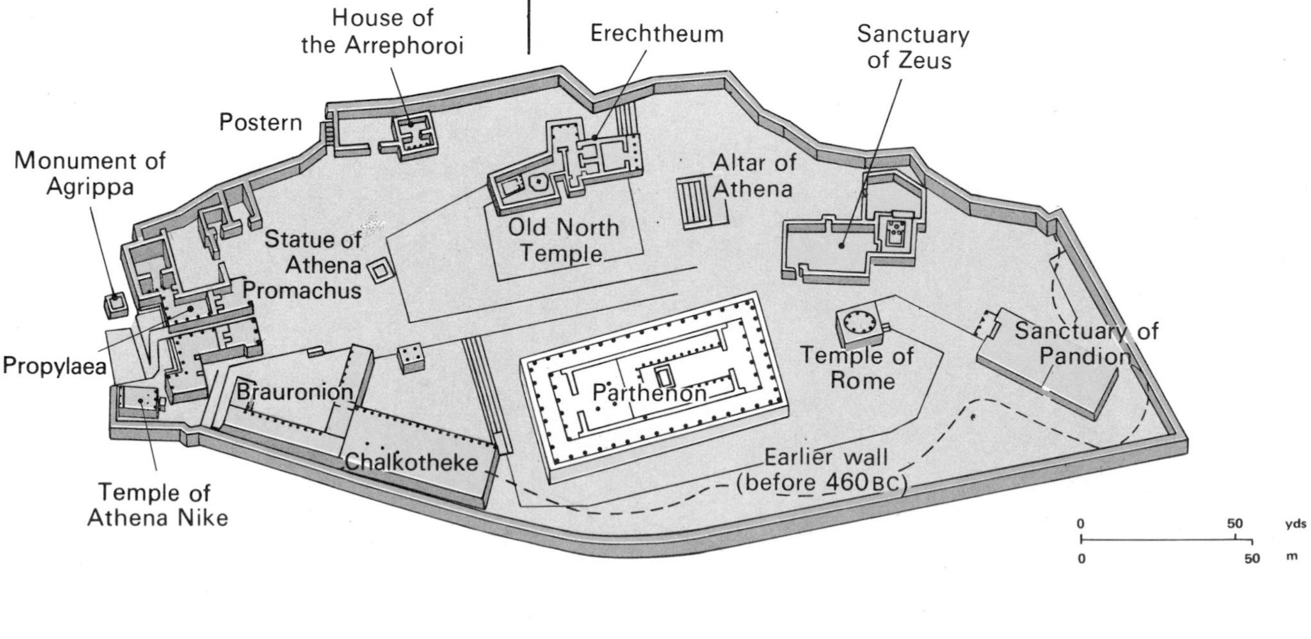

Ancient Athens incorporating the Acropolis.

18:13). **3.** 'Ataroth, the house of Joab' is mentioned in a Judaean genealogy (1 Ch. 2:54). This may be understood as 'the crowns (scions, chiefs) of the house of Joab', a description of Bethlehem and Netophathi, whose names immediately precede. See *LOB*.

R.J.W.

ATHALIAH (Heb. *ᵃṯalyāhû*, 'Yahweh is exalted'). **1.** The daughter of Ahab, and the granddaughter of Omri (2 Ki. 8:26). Her marriage with Jehoram, king of Judah, marked an alliance between N and S, and implied the superiority of Israel. The death of her son, Ahaziah, after a reign of 1 year, at the hand of Jehu, in the 'Prophetic Revolution' (2 Ki. 8:25–10:36), revealed her as 'that wicked woman' (2 Ch. 24:7). To retain the power she had enjoyed as queen-mother, she 'destroyed all the royal family' (2 Ki. 11:1); and began to reign (*c.* 842 BC). For 6 years her authority was unchallenged, then the priest Jehoiada put thc child Joash on the throne. She came out to meet her enemies, and was put to death outside the Temple.

2. A person named in the genealogy of Benjamin (1 Ch. 8:26).

3. One of the exiles who returned from Babylon with Ezra (Ezr. 8:7).

M.B.

ATHENS. Acts 17:15–34; 1 Thes. 3:1. In the 5th and 4th centuries BC Athens was famous for its culture, the home of great dramatists, and of great philosophers like Plato and Aristotle. After the Roman conquest of Greece, Athens became a *civitas foederata* (a city linked to Rome by treaty), entirely independent of the governor of Achaia, paying no taxes to Rome and with internal judicial autonomy. Of the three great university cities Athens, Tarsus and Alexandria, Athens was the most famous. Philo the Alexandrian said that the Athenians were the keenest-sighted mentally of the Greeks. It was also famous for its temples, statues and monuments. The first 168 pages of the Loeb edition of the *Description of Greece*, by Pausanias, written a century after Paul's visit, are a good tourists' guide to the antiquities of Athens. Though the Athenians were religious and eager to discuss religion, their spiritual level was not exceptionally high. Apollonius the philosopher, a contemporary of Paul, rebuked them for their lascivious jigs at the festival of Dionysus and for their love of human slaughter in the gladiatorial games.

D.R.H.

ATONEMENT. The word 'atonement' is one of the few theological terms which derive basically from Anglo-Saxon. It means 'a making at one', and points to a process of bringing those who are estranged into a unity. The word occurs in the OT to translate words from the *kpr* word group, and it is found once in the NT (AV), rendering *katallagē* (which is better translated 'reconciliation' as RSV). Its use in theology is to denote the work of Christ in dealing with the problem posed by the sin of man, and in bringing sinners into right relation with God.

The Stoa (roofed colonnade) of Attalos II (159–138 BC) at Athens, looking across the agora (market-place). (RP)

I. The need for atonement

The need for atonement is brought about by three things, the universality of sin, the seriousness of sin and man's inability to deal with sin. The first point is attested in many places: 'there is no man who does not sin' (1 Ki. 8:46); 'there is none that does good, no, not one' (Ps. 14:3); 'there is not a righteous man on earth, who does good and never sins' (Ec. 7:20). Jesus told the rich young ruler, 'No one is good but God alone' (Mk. 10:18), and Paul writes, 'all have sinned and fall short of the glory of God' (Rom. 3:23). Much more could be cited.

The seriousness of sin is seen in passages which show God's aversion to it. Habakkuk prays 'Thou who art of purer eyes than to behold evil and canst not look on wrong' (Hab. 1:13). Sin separates from God (Is. 59:2; Pr. 15:29). Jesus said of one sin, blasphemy against the Holy Spirit, that it will never be forgiven (Mk. 3:29), and of Judas he said, 'It would have been better for that man if he had not been born' (Mk. 14:21). Before being saved men are 'estranged and hostile in mind, doing evil deeds' (Col. 1:21). There awaits the unrepentant sinner only 'a fearful prospect of judgment, and a fury of fire which will consume the adversaries' (Heb. 10:27).

And man cannot deal with the situation. He is not able to keep his sin hidden (Nu. 32:23), and he cannot cleanse himself of it (Pr. 20: 9). No deeds of law will ever enable man to stand before God justified (Rom. 3:20; Gal. 2:16). If he must depend on himself, then man will never be saved. Perhaps the most important evidence of this is the very fact of the atonement. If the Son of God came to earth to save men, then men were sinners and their plight serious indeed.

II. Atonement in the Old Testament

God and man, then, are hopelessly estranged by man's sin, and there is no way back from man's side. But God provides the way. In the OT atonement is usually said to be obtained by the sacrifices, but it must never be forgotten that God says of atoning blood, 'I have given it for you upon the altar to make atonement for your souls' (Lv. 17:11). Atonement is secured, not

ATHLETICS See Games, Part 1.

by any value inherent in the sacrificial victim, but because sacrifice is the divinely appointed way of securing atonement. The sacrifices point us to certain truths concerning atonement. Thus the victim must always be unblemished, which indicates the necessity for perfection. The victims cost something, for atonement is not cheap, and sin is never to be taken lightly. The death of the victim was the important thing. This is brought out partly in the allusions to *blood, partly in the general character of the rite itself and partly in other references to atonement. There are several allusions to atonement, either effected or contemplated by means other than the cultus, and where these bear on the problem they point to death as the way. Thus in Ex. 32:30–32 Moses seeks to make an atonement for the sin of the people, and he does so by asking God to blot him out of the book which he has written. Phinehas made an atonement by slaying certain transgressors (Nu. 25:6–8, 13). Other passages might be cited. It is clear that in the OT it was recognized that death was the penalty for sin (Ezk. 18:20), but that God graciously permitted the death of a sacrificial victim to substitute for the death of the sinner. So clear is the connection that the writer of the Epistle to the Hebrews can sum it up by saying 'without the shedding of blood there is no forgiveness of sins' (Heb. 9:22).

III. Atonement in the New Testament

The NT takes the line that the sacrifices of old were not the root cause of the putting away of sins. Redemption is to be obtained even 'from the transgressions under the first covenant' only by the death of Christ (Heb. 9:15). The cross is absolutely central to the NT, and, indeed, to the whole Bible. All before leads up to it. All after looks back to it. Since it occupies the critical place, it is not surprising that there is a vast volume of teaching about it. The NT writers, writing from different standpoints, and with different emphases, give us a number of facets of the atonement. There is no repetition of a stereotyped line of teaching. Each writes as he sees. Some saw more and more deeply than others. But they did not see something different. In what follows we shall consider first of all what might be termed the common, basic teaching about the atonement, and then some of the information that we owe to one or other of the NT theologians.

a. It reveals God's love for men

All are agreed that the atonement proceeds from the love of God. It is not something wrung from a stern and unwilling Father, perfectly just, but perfectly inflexible, by a loving Son. The atonement shows us the love of the Father just as it does the love of the Son. Paul gives us the classic exposition of this when he says, 'God shows his love for us in that while we were yet sinners Christ died for us' (Rom. 5:8). In the best-known text in the Bible we find that 'God so loved the world that he gave his only Son . . .' (Jn. 3:16). In the Synoptic Gospels it is emphasized that the Son of man 'must' suffer (Mk. 8:31, *etc.*). That is to say, the death of Christ was no accident: it was rooted in a compelling divine necessity. This we see also in our Lord's prayer in Gethsemane that the will of the Father be done (Mt. 26:42). Similarly, in Hebrews we read that it was 'by the grace of God' that Christ tasted death for us all (Heb. 2:9). The thought is found throughout the NT, and we must bear it well in mind when we reflect on the manner of the atonement.

b. The sacrificial aspect of Christ's death

Another thought that is widespread is that the death of Christ is a death for sin. It is not simply that certain wicked men rose up against him. It is not that his enemies conspired against him and that he was not able to resist them. He 'was put to death for our trespasses' (Rom. 4:25). He came specifically to die for our sins. His blood was shed 'for many for the forgiveness of sins' (Mt. 26:28). He 'made purification for sins' (Heb. 1:3). He 'bore our sins in his body on the tree' (1 Pet. 2:24). He is 'the propitiation for our sins' (1 Jn. 2:2; so, rightly, AV). The cross of Christ will never be understood unless it is seen that thereon the Saviour was dealing with the sins of all mankind.

In doing this he fulfilled all that the old sacrifices had foreshadowed, and the NT writers love to think of his death as a sacrifice. Jesus himself referred to his blood as 'blood of the covenant' (Mk. 14:24), which points us to the sacrificial rites for its understanding. Indeed, much of the language used in the institution of the Holy Communion is sacrificial, pointing to the sacrifice to be accomplished on the cross. Paul tells us that Christ 'loved us and gave himself up for us, a fragrant offering and sacrifice to God' (Eph. 5:2). On occasion he can refer, not to sacrifice in general, but to a specific sacrifice, as in 1 Cor. 5:7, 'For Christ our paschal lamb (better, passover) has been sacrificed.' Peter speaks of 'the precious blood of Christ, like that of a lamb without blemish or spot' (1 Pet. 1:19), which indicates that in one aspect Christ's death was a sacrifice. And in John's Gospel we read the words of John the Baptist, 'Behold, the Lamb of God, who takes away the sin of the world' (Jn. 1:29). Sacrifice was practically the universal religious rite of the 1st century. Wherever men were and whatever their background, they would discern a sacrificial allusion. The NT writers made use of this, and employed sacrificial terminology to bring out what Christ had done for men. All that to which the sacrifices pointed, and more, he had fully accomplished by his death.

c. The representative nature of Christ's death

It is agreed by most students that Christ's death was vicarious. If in one sense he died 'for sin', in another he died 'for us'. But 'vicarious' is a term which may mean much or little. It is better to be more precise. Most scholars today accept the view that the death of Christ is representative. That is to say, it is not that Christ died and somehow the benefits of that death become available to men (did not even Anselm ask to whom more fittingly than to us could they be assigned?). It is rather that he died specifically for us. He was our representative as he hung on the cross. This is expressed succinctly in 2 Cor. 5:14, 'one died for all; therefore all have died'. The death of the Representative counts as the death of those he represents. When Christ is spoken of as our 'advocate with the Father' (1 Jn. 2:1) there is the plain thought of representation, and as the passage immediately goes on to deal with his death for sin it is relevant to our purpose. The Epistle to the Hebrews has as one of its major themes that of Christ as our great High Priest. The thought is repeated over and over. Now whatever else may be said about a High Priest, he represents men. The thought of representation may thus be said to be very strong in this Epistle.

d. Substitution taught in the New Testament

But can we say more? There is a marked disinclination among many modern scholars (though not by any means all) to use the older language of substitution. Nevertheless, this seems to be the teaching of the NT, and that not in one or two places only, but throughout. In the Synoptic Gospels there is the great ransom saying, 'the Son of man also came not to be served but to serve, and to give his life as a ransom for many' (Mk. 10:45). Both the details ('ransom' has a substitutionary connotation, and *anti*, 'for', is the preposition of substitution) and the general thought of the passage (men should die, Christ dies instead, men no longer die) point to substitution. The same truth is indicated by passages which speak of Christ as the suffering Servant of Is. 53, for of him it is said, 'he was wounded for our transgressions, he was bruised for our iniquities; upon him was the chastisement that made us whole, and with his stripes we are healed . . . the Lord has laid on him the iniquity of us all' (Is. 53:5f.). The shrinking of Christ in Gethsemane points in the same direction. He was courageous, and many far less worthy than he have faced death calmly. The agony seems to be inexplicable other than on the grounds disclosed by Paul, that for our sake God 'made him to be sin, who knew no sin' (2 Cor. 5:21). In his death he took our place, and his holy soul shrank from this identification with sinners. And it seems that no less than this gives meaning to the cry of dereliction, 'My God, my God, why hast thou forsaken me?' (Mk. 15:34).

Paul tells us that Christ 'redeemed us from the curse of the law, having become a curse for us' (Gal. 3:13). He bore our curse, which is but another way of saying substitution. The same thought lies behind Rom. 3:21–26, where the apostle develops the thought that God's justice is manifested in the process whereby sin is forgiven, *i.e.* the cross. He is not saying, as some have thought, that God's righteousness is shown in the *fact* that sin is forgiven, but that it is shown in the *way* in which sin is forgiven. Atonement is not a matter of passing over sin as had been done previously (Rom. 3:25). The cross shows that God is just, at the same time as it shows him justifying believers. This must mean that God's justice is vindicated in the way sin is dealt with. And this seems another way of saying that Christ bore the penalty of men's sin. This is also the thought in passages dealing with sin-bearing as Heb. 9:28; 1 Pet. 2:24. The meaning of bearing sin is made clear by a number of OT passages where the context shows that the bearing of penalty is meant. For example, in Ezk. 18:20 we read, 'The soul that sins shall die. The son shall not suffer for (Heb. 'bear') the iniquity of the father . . .', and in Nu. 14:34 the wilderness wanderings are described as a bearing of iniquities. Christ's bearing of our sin, then, means that he bore our penalty.

Substitution lies behind the statement in 1 Tim. 2:6 that Christ gave himself 'a ransom for all'. *antilytron*, translated 'ransom', is a strong compound meaning 'substitute-ransom'. Grimm–Thayer define it as 'what is given in exchange for another as the price of his redemption'. It is impossible to empty the word of substitutionary associations. A similar thought lies behind John's recording of the cynical prophecy of Caiaphas, 'it is expedient for you that one man should die for the people, and that the whole nation should not perish' (Jn. 11:50). For Caiaphas the words were sheer political expediency, but John sees in them a prophecy that Christ would die instead of the people.

This is a formidable body of evidence (and is not exhaustive). In the face of it it seems impossible to deny that substitution is one strand in the NT understanding of the work of Christ.

e. Other NT aspects of the atonement

Such are the main points attested throughout the NT. Other important truths are set forth in individual writers (which does not, of course, mean that they are any the less to be accepted; it is simply a method of classification). Thus Paul sees in the cross the way of deliverance. Men naturally are enslaved to sin (Rom. 6:17; 7:14). But in Christ men are free (Rom. 6:14, 22). Similarly, through Christ men are delivered from the flesh, they 'have crucified the flesh' (Gal. 5:24), they 'do not war after the flesh' (2 Cor. 10:3, AV), that flesh which 'lusteth against the Spirit' (Gal. 5:17, AV), and which apart from Christ spells death (Rom. 8:13). Men are under the wrath of God on account of their unrighteousness (Rom. 1:18), but Christ delivers from this, too. Believers are 'justified by his blood', and thus will 'be saved by him from the wrath of God' (Rom. 5:9). The law (*i.e.* the Pentateuch, and hence the whole Jewish Scripture) may be regarded in many ways. But considered as a way of salvation it is disastrous. It shows a man his sin (Rom. 7:7), and, entering into an unholy alliance with sin, slays him (Rom. 7:9–11). The end result is that 'all who rely on works of the law are under a curse' (Gal. 3:10). But 'Christ redeemed us from the curse of the law' (Gal. 3:13). Death to men of antiquity was a grim antagonist against whom none might prevail. But Paul sings a song of triumph in Christ who gives victory even over death (1 Cor. 15:55–57). It is abundantly plain that Paul sees in Christ a mighty Deliverer.

The atonement has many positive aspects. It must suffice simply to mention such things as redemption, reconciliation, justification, adoption and propitiation. These are great concepts and mean much to Paul. In some cases he is the first Christian of whom we have knowledge to make use of them. Clearly he thought of Christ as having wrought much for his people in his atoning death.

For the writer to the Hebrews the great thought is that of Christ as our great High Priest. He develops thoroughly the thought of the uniqueness and the finality of the offering made by Christ. Unlike the way established on Jewish altars and ministered by priests of the Aaronic line, the way established by Christ in his death is of permanent validity. It will never be altered. Christ has dealt fully with man's sin.

In the writings of John there is the thought of Christ as the special revelation of the Father. He is One sent by the Father, and all that he does must be interpreted in the light of this fact. So John sees Christ as winning a conflict against the darkness, as defeating the evil one. He has much to say about the working out of the purpose of God in Christ. He sees the true glory in the lowly cross whereon such a mighty work was done.

From all this it is abundantly apparent that the atonement is vast and deep. The NT writers strive with the inadequacy of language as they seek to present us with what this great divine act means. There is more to it by far than we have been able to indicate. But all the points we have made are important, and none is to be neglected. Nor are we to overlook the fact that the atonement represents more than something negative. We have been concerned to insist on the place of Christ's sacrifice of himself in the putting away of sin. But that opens up the way to a new life in Christ. And that new life, the fruit of the atonement, is not to be thought of as an insignificant detail. It is that to which all the rest leads. (*Expiation, *Forgiveness, *Propitiation, *Reconciliation, *Redeemer, *Sacrifice.)

Bibliography. D. M. Baillie, *God was in Christ*, 1956; J. Denney, *The Death of Christ*, 1951; *The Christian Doctrine of Reconciliation*, 1917; G. Aulen, *Christus Victor*, 1931; E. Brunner, *The Mediator*; K. Barth, *Church Dogmatics*, 4, i; *The Doctrine of Reconciliation*; J. S. Stewart, *A Man in Christ*; Anselm, *Cur Deus Homo*; L. Morris, *The Apostolic Preaching of the Cross*, 1965; *The Cross in the New Testament*, 1967; J. Knox, *The Death of Christ*; J. I. Packer, 'What did the Cross achieve? The Logic of Penal Substitution', *TynB* 25, 1974, pp. 3–45.

L.M.

ATONEMENT, DAY OF (Heb. *yôm hakkippurîm*). On the 10th day of the 7th month (Tishri, September/October), Israel observed its most solemn holy day. All work was forbidden and a strict fast was enjoined on all of the people.

I. Purpose

The Day of Atonement served as a reminder that the daily, weekly and monthly sacrifices made at the altar of burnt offering were not sufficient to atone for sin. Even at the altar of burnt offering the worshipper stood 'afar off', unable to approach the holy Presence of God, who was manifest between the cherubim in the holy of holies. On this one day in the year, atoning blood was brought into the holy of holies, the divine throne-room, by the high priest as the representative of the people.

The high priest made atonement for 'all the iniquities of the children of Israel and all their transgressions in all their sins'. Atonement was first made for the priests because the mediator between God and his people had to be ceremonially clean. The sanctuary was also cleansed, for it, too, was ceremonially defiled by the presence and ministration of sinful men.

II. Ancient observance

To prepare for the sacrifices of the day, the high priest put aside his official robes and dressed in a simple white garment. He then offered a bullock as a sin-offering for himself and the priesthood. After filling his censer with live coals from the altar, the high priest entered the holy of holies, where he placed incense on the coals. The incense sent forth a cloud of smoke over the mercy seat, which served as a covering for the ark of the covenant. The high priest took some of the blood of the bullock and sprinkled it on the mercy seat and on the ground in front of the ark. In this way atonement was made for the priesthood.

The high priest next sacrificed a he-goat as a sin offering for the people. Some of the blood was taken into the holy of holies, and it was sprinkled there in the manner in which the sin offering for the priests had been sprinkled (Lv. 16:11–15).

After purifying the holy place and the altar of burnt offering with the mingled blood of the bullock and the goat (Lv. 16:18–19) the high priest took a second goat, laid his hands upon its head and confessed over it the sins of Israel. This goat, commonly called the *scapegoat (*i.e.* escape goat), was then driven into the desert, where it symbolically carried away the sins of the people.

The carcasses of the two burnt offerings—the bullock and the he-goat—were taken outside the city and burnt. The day was concluded with additional sacrifices.

III. Significance

The Epistle to the Hebrews interprets the ritual of the Day of Atonement as a type of the atoning work of Christ, emphasizing the perfection of the latter by contrast with the inadequacy of the former (Heb. 9–10). Jesus himself is termed our 'great high priest', and the blood shed on Calvary is seen as typified in the blood of bulls and goats. Unlike the OT priesthood, the sinless Christ did not have to make sacrifice for any sins of his own.

As the high priest of the OT entered the holy of holies with the blood of his sacrificial victim, so Jesus entered heaven itself to appear before the Father on behalf of his people (Heb. 9:11–12).

The high priest had to offer sin offerings each year for his own sins and the sins of the people. This annual repetition of the sacrifices served as a reminder that perfect atonement had not yet been provided. Jesus, however, through his own blood effected eternal redemption for his people (Heb. 9:12).

The Epistle to the Hebrews notes that the levitical offerings could effect only 'the purification of the flesh'. They ceremonially cleansed the sinner, but they could not bring about inward cleansing, the prerequisite for fellowship with God. The offerings served as a type and a prophecy of Jesus, who, through his better sacrifice, cleanses the conscience from dead works (Heb. 9:13–14).

The OT tabernacle was designed, in part, to teach Israel that sin hindered access to the presence of God. Only the high priest, and he only once a year, could enter the holy of holies, and then 'not without taking blood' offered to atone for sins (Heb. 9:7). Jesus, however, through a 'new and living way' has entered heaven itself, the true holy of holies, where he ever lives to make intercession for his people. The believer need not stand afar off, as did the Israelite of old, but may now through Christ approach the very throne of grace.

In Heb. 13:11–12 we are reminded that the flesh of the sin offering of the Day of Atonement was burnt outside the camp of Israel. Jesus, also, suffered outside the gate of Jerusalem that he might redeem his people from sin.

IV. Modern observance

In modern Jewish usage the Day of Atonement, *Yom Kippur*, is the last of the '10 Days of Penitence' which begin with *Rosh Hashanah*—the Jewish New Year's Day. This 10-day period is devoted to the spiritual exercises of penitence, prayer and fasting in preparation for the most solemn day of the year, *Yom Kippur*. Although the sacrificial aspects of the Day of Atonement have not been in effect since the destruction of the Temple, Jews still observe the day by fasting and refraining from all types of work.

The shophar, or ram's horn, is blown to assemble the people for worship in the synagogue on the eve of *Yom Kippur*. At this time the impressive *Kol Nidre* ('all vows') service is chanted. The congregation penitently asks God to forgive them for breaking the vows which they were unable to fulfil.

Services are held on the next day from early morning until nightfall. At sunset the Day of Atonement is ended by a single blast of the shophar, after which the worshippers return to their homes.

BIBLIOGRAPHY. M. Noth, *Leviticus*, 1965, pp. 115–126; N. H. Snaith, *The Jewish New Year Festival*, 1947, p. 121 *et passim*; *idem, Leviticus and Numbers*, 1967, pp. 109–118; R. de Vaux, *Ancient Israel*, 1961, pp. 507–510; *idem, Studies in Old Testament Sacrifice*, 1964, pp. 91–97. C.F.P.

ATTALIA, modern Antalya, near the mouth of the river Cataractes (mod. Aksu), was the chief port of Pamphylia. Founded by Attalus II of Pergamum (159–138 BC), it was bequeathed by Attalus III to Rome. Paul and Barnabas returned from their missionary journey through Attalia (Acts 14:25). There was another Attalia in N Lydia. K.L.McK.

AUGUSTUS. An additional name adopted by *Caesar Octavianus upon the regularization of his position in 27 BC, and apparently intended to signalize that moral authority in terms of which he defined his primacy in the Roman republic (*Res Gestae* 34). It passed to his successors as a title of office rather than a name, and was hence translated into Greek (*sebastos*, 'His Reverence', Acts 25:21, 25: RSV 'the emperor') when referring to them, though transliterated when referring to him (Lk. 2:1).

Augustus embodied the Roman ideal: personal merit should win dignity and power. But his success put an end to competition, and left him with the burden of universal responsibility. His 57 years of rule (43 BC to AD 14) saw the foundation of a new era of peace under the *Roman empire.

BIBLIOGRAPHY. A. H. M. Jones, *Augustus*, 1970. E.A.J.

AUTHORITIES, CITY. The senior board of magistrates, five in number and later six, at Thessalonica. Their title (Gk. *politarchai*) is epigraphically attested for a number of Macedonian states (E. D. Burton, *American Journal of Theology* 2, 1898, pp. 598–632). As is nicely illustrated by the Acts (17:6–9), they controlled the republic under Roman supervision. E.A.J.

AUTHORITY. The NT word is *exousia*, meaning rightful, actual and unimpeded power to act, or to possess, control, use or dispose of, something or somebody. Whereas *dynamis* means physical power simply, *exousia* properly signifies power that is in some sense lawful. *exousia* may be used with the stress on either the rightfulness of power really held, or the reality of power rightfully possessed. In the latter case, EVV often translate it as 'power'. *exousia* sometimes bears a general secular sense (*e.g.* in 1 Cor. 7:37, of self-control; Acts 5:4, of disposing of one's income), but its significance is more commonly theological.

The uniform biblical conviction is that the only rightful power within creation is, ultimately, the Creator's. Such authority as men have is delegated to them by God, to whom they must answer for the way they use it. Because all authority is ultimately God's, submission to authority in all realms of life is a religious duty, part of God's service.

I. The authority of God

God's authority is an aspect of his unalterable, universal and eternal dominion over his world (for which see Ex. 15:18; Pss. 29:10; 93:1f.; 146:10; Dn. 4:34f., *etc.*). This universal Kingship is distinct from (though basic to) the covenanted relationship between himself and Israel by which Israel became his people and kingdom (*cf.* Ex. 19:6), and so heirs of his blessing. His regal authority over mankind consists in his unchallengeable right and power to dispose of men as he pleases (compared by Paul to the potter's *exousia* over the clay, Rom. 9:21; *cf.* Je. 18:6), plus his indisputable claim that men should be subject to him and live for his glory. Throughout the Bible, the reality of God's authority is proved by the fact that all who ignore or flout this claim incur divine judgment. The royal Judge has the last word, and so his authority is vindicated.

In OT times, God exercised authority over his people through the agency of prophets, priests and kings, whose respective work it was to proclaim his messages (Je. 1:7ff.), teach his laws (Dt. 31:11; Mal. 2:7) and rule in accordance with those laws (Dt. 17:18ff.). So doing, they were to be respected as God's representatives, having authority from him. Also, written Scripture was acknowledged as God-given and authoritative, both as instruction (*tôrâ*) to teach Israelites their King's mind (*cf.* Ps. 119) and as the statute-book by which he ruled and judged them (*cf.* 2 Ki. 22–23).

II. The authority of Jesus Christ

The authority of *Jesus Christ is also an aspect of kingship. It is both personal and official, for Jesus is both Son of God and Son of man (*i.e.* the Messianic man). As man and Messiah, his authority is real because delegated to him by the God at whose command he does his work (Christ applauded the centurion for seeing this, Mt. 8:9f.). As the Son, his authority is real because he is himself God. Authority to judge has been given him, both that he may be honoured as the Son of God (for *judgment is God's work), and also because he is the Son of man (for judgment is the Messiah's work) (Jn. 5:22f., 27). In short, his authority is that of a divine Messiah: of a God-man, doing his Father's will in the double capacity of (*a*) human servant, in whom meet the saving offices of prophet, priest and king, and (*b*) divine Son, co-creator and sharer in all the Father's works (Jn. 5:19ff.).

This more-than-human authority of Jesus was manifested during his ministry in various ways, such as the finality and independence of his teaching (Mt. 7:28f.); his exorcizing power (Mk. 1:27); his mastery over storms (Lk. 8:24f.); his claiming to forgive sins (a thing which, as the bystanders rightly pointed out, only God can do) and, when challenged, proving his claim (Mk. 2:5–12; *cf.* Mt. 9:8). After his resurrection, he declared that he had been given 'all *exousia* in heaven and on earth'—a cosmic Messianic dominion, to be exercised in such a way as effectively to bring the elect into his kingdom of salvation (Mt. 28:18ff.; Jn. 17:2; *cf.* Jn. 12:31ff.; Acts 5:31; 18:9f.). The NT proclaims the exalted Jesus as 'both Lord and Christ' (Acts 2:36)—divine Ruler of all things, and Saviour-king of his people. The gospel is in the first

ATTRIBUTES OF GOD
See God, Part 1.

AUGURY
See Divination, Part 1.

AUGUSTAN COHORT
See Julius, Part 2.

AUROCH
See Animals, Part 1.

AUTHENTICATION
See Seal, Part 3.

Bust of the Emperor Augustus (63 BC–AD 14). (MuC)

instance a demand for assent to this estimate of his authority.

III. Apostolic authority

Apostolic authority is delegated Messianic authority; for the *apostles were Christ's commissioned witnesses, emissaries and representatives (*cf.* Mt. 10:40; Jn. 17:18; 20:21; Acts 1:8; 2 Cor. 5:20), given *exousia* by him to found, build up and regulate his universal church (2 Cor. 10:8; 13:10; *cf.* Gal. 2:7ff.). Accordingly, we find them giving orders and prescribing discipline in Christ's name. *i.e.* as his spokesmen and with his authority (1 Cor. 5:4; 2 Thes. 3:6). They appointed deacons (Acts 6:3, 6) and presbyters (Acts 14:23). They presented their teaching as Christ's truth, Spirit-given in both content and form of expression (1 Cor. 2:9–13; *cf.* 1 Thes. 2:13), a norm for faith (2 Thes. 2:15; *cf.* Gal. 1:8) and behaviour (2 Thes. 3:4, 6, 14). They expected their *ad hoc* rulings to be received as 'the commandment of the Lord' (1 Cor. 14:37). Because their authority depended on Christ's direct personal commission, they had, properly speaking, no successors; but each generation of Christians must show its continuity with the first generation, and its allegiance to Christ, by subjecting its own faith and life to the norm of teaching which Christ's appointed delegates provided and put on record for all time in the documents of the NT. Through the NT, apostolic *exousia* over the church has been made a permanent reality.

IV. Authority delegated to man

Besides the church, where 'leaders' (presbyters) may claim obedience because they are Christ's servants, tending his flock under his authority (Heb. 13:17; 1 Pet. 5:1f.), the Bible mentions two other spheres of delegated divine authority.

a. Marriage and the family

Men have authority over women (1 Cor. 11:3; *cf.* 1 Tim. 2:12) and parents over children (*cf.* 1 Tim. 3:4, 12). Hence, wives must obey their husbands (Eph. 5:22; 1 Pet. 3:1–6) and children their parents (Eph. 6:1ff.). This is God's order.

b. Civil government

Secular (Roman) governors are called *exousiai*, and described as God's servants to punish evil-doers and encourage law-abiding citizens (Rom. 13:1–6). Christians are to regard the 'powers that be' as God-ordained (see Jn. 19:11), and dutifully subject themselves to civil authority (Rom. 13:1; 1 Pet. 2:13f.; *cf.* Mt. 22:17–21) so far as is compatible with obedience to God's direct commands (Acts 4:19; 5:29).

V. Satanic power

The exercise of *power by Satan and his hosts is sometimes termed *exousia* (*e.g.* Lk. 22:53; Col. 1:13). This indicates that, though Satan's power is usurped from God and hostile to him, Satan holds it only by God's permission and as God's tool.

BIBLIOGRAPHY. Arndt; *MM*; T. Rees in *ISBE* and J. Denney in *DCG*, *s.v.* 'Authority'; N. Geldenhuys, *Supreme Authority*, 1953; O. Betz, *NIDNTT* 2, pp. 606–611; W. Foerster, *TDNT* 2, pp. 562–575.

J.I.P.

AVA
See Ivah, Part 2.

AVARICE
See Covetousness, Part 1.

AVEN. 1. Abbreviated (Ho. 10:8) for *Beth-aven, epithet of Bethel (Ho. 4:15, *etc.*). **2.** In Am. 1:5, probably the Beqaʿ valley between Lebanon and Anti-lebanon in the Aramaean kingdom of Damascus. **3.** For Ezk. 30:17, see *On.

K.A.K.

AVENGER OF BLOOD (Heb. *gō'ēl haddām*, lit. 'redeemer of blood'). Even before the time of Moses, a basic feature of primitive life was the system of blood revenge for personal injury. It is mentioned with approval as early as Gn. 9:5. All members of the clan were regarded as being of one blood, but the chief responsibility for avenging shed blood devolved upon the victim's next-of-kin, who might under other circumstances be called on to redeem the property or person of a poor or captive relative (Lv. 25:25, 47–49; Ru. 4:1ff., though in the latter case other factors were involved also). The Mosaic penal code authorized the avenger to execute the murderer but no-one else (Dt. 24:16; 2 Ki. 14:6; 2 Ch. 25:4), and made provision for accidental homicide. Blood revenge seems to have persisted into the reigns of David (2 Sa. 14:7–8) and Jehoshaphat (2 Ch. 19:10). (*KIN, *CITIES OF REFUGE.)

J.D.D.

AVVA
See Tartak, Part 3.

AWE
See Fear, Part 1.

AZARIAH (Heb. *ᵃzaryāhû*, *ᵃzaryâ*, 'Yahweh has helped'). **1.** One of Solomon's ministers, son of Zadok (1 Ki. 4:2; *cf.* 1 Ch. 6:9). **2.** Another of Solomon's ministers, son of Nathan; he was over the officers (1 Ki. 4:5). **3.** Alternative name for King *Uzziah (2 Ki. 14:21, *etc.*). Montgomery (*Kings*, *ICC*, p. 446) calls it the 'throne-name', Uzziah representing the popular or adopted name. For his reign, see H. Tadmor, 'Azriyau of Yaudi', *Scripta Hierosolymitana* 8, 1961, pp. 232–271. **4, 5.** Son of Ethan (1 Ch. 2:8) and son of Jehu (1 Ch. 2:38) in the genealogical table of Judah.

6–8. Son of Johanan (1 Ch. 6:10; *cf.* Ezr. 7:3), son of Hilkiah (1 Ch. 6:13; *cf.* 9:11; Ezr. 7:1) and son of Zephaniah (1 Ch. 6:36) in the genealogical table of Levi. **9.** The prophet, son of Oded, who encouraged Asa in his reformation (2 Ch. 15:1–8). **10, 11.** Two of Jehoshaphat's sons, slain by Jehoram on his accession (2 Ch. 21:2, 4). **12.** Scribal error for Ahaziah (2 Ch. 22:6).

13, 14. Two of the 'centurions' who helped to restore Joash (2 Ch. 23:1). **15.** High priest who withstood Uzziah's attempt to offer incense in the Temple (2 Ch. 26:16–20). **16.** An Ephraimite chief who supported the prophet Oded's plea for clemency (2 Ch. 28:12). **17, 18.** Two Levites connected with Hezekiah's cleansing of the Temple (2 Ch. 29:12). **19.** A chief priest in Hezekiah's reign (2 Ch. 31:10).

20. A workman repairing the city wall (Ne. 3:23). **21.** One of Zerubbabel's companions (Ne. 7:7; *cf.* Ezr. 2:2—'Seraiah'). **22.** One who expounded the law after Ezra had read it (Ne. 8:7). **23.** A priest who sealed the covenant with Nehemiah (Ne. 10:2; *cf.* Ne. 12:33). **24.** Son of Hoshaiah and supporter of Gedaliah, who later rejected Jeremiah's advice to remain in Palestine (Je. 43:2). Called Jezaniah in Je. 42:1

The mound of Azekah, from the valley of Elah. (AIA)

(*cf.* Je. 40:8; 2 Ki. 25:23). **25.** Heb. name of Abed-nego (Dn. 1:6f., 11, 19; 2:17). J.G.G.N.

AZEKAH. A Judaean conurbation (Jos. 15:35), lying in the low agricultural plains along the W coast, perhaps modern Tell ez-Zahariyeh. Joshua pursued the Amorites as far as Azekah on the day they attacked the newly settled Gibeonite group (Jos. 10:10–11). In the days of Rehoboam it was a fortified border city (2 Ch. 11:5ff.), and in later times was one of the few strong points to resist the Babylonian incursion under Nebuchadrezzar (Je. 34:7). Azekah is mentioned, and its capture by Nebuchadrezzar probably implied, in one of the Lachish Letters (*DOTT*, pp. 216f.). R.J.W.

BAAL. The Hebrew noun *ba'al* means 'master', 'possessor' or 'husband'. Used with suffixes, *e.g.* Baal-peor or Baal-berith, the word may have retained something of its original sense; but in general Baal is a proper name in the OT, and refers to a specific deity, Hadad, the W Semitic storm-god, the most important deity in the Canaanite pantheon. It is not clear to what extent local Baals were equated with or distinguished from Hadad. The Baal confronted at Mt Carmel (1 Ki. 18) was probably Melqart, the god of Tyre. The OT use of the plural (*e.g.* 1 Ki. 18:18) may suggest that more Baals than one were clearly distinguished; but in any case there was fluidity in the pagan conception of deities.

The Baal cults affected and challenged the worship of Yahweh throughout Israelite history. The limited OT data about Baal can now be supplemented by the information from the Ras Shamra documents. One of his consorts was *Ashtaroth, another *Asherah; and Baal is called the son of *Dagon. The texts reveal him as a nature deity; myths describe him in conflict with death, infertility and flood waters, emerging victorious as 'king' of the gods.

Yahweh was 'master' and 'husband' to Israel, and therefore they called him 'Baal', in all innocence; but naturally this practice led to confusion of the worship of Yahweh with the Baal rituals, and presently it became essential to call him by some different title; Hosea (2:16) proposed *'îš*, another word meaning 'husband'. Once the title 'Baal' was no longer applied to Yahweh, personal names incorporating the word were likely to be misunderstood. So *bōšeṯ* ('shame') tended to replace *ba'al* in such names. Thus Esh-baal and Merib-baal (1 Ch. 8:33f.) are better known as Ish-bosheth (2 Sa. 2:8) and Mephibosheth (2 Sa. 9:6).

The word Baal also occurs once or twice as a man's name and as a place-name (*cf.* 1 Ch. 5:5; 4:33).

BIBLIOGRAPHY. H. Ringgren, *Religions of the Ancient Near East*, E.T. 1973, ch. 3; A. S. Kapelrud, *Baal in the Ras Shamra Texts*, 1952; W. F. Albright, *Yahweh and the Gods of Canaan*, 1968; N. C. Habel, *Yahweh versus Baal*, 1964; and see *CANAAN. D.F.P.

BAAL-BERITH (Heb. *ba'al bᵉrîṯ*, 'Lord of the covenant'). The Canaanite Baal-deity worshipped

AZAZEL
See Scapegoat, Part 3.

Baal as storm-god, brandishing a club and grasping a thunderbolt. Before him stands the king of Ugarit. Limestone stele from Ras Shamra (Ugarit). Height 1·5 m. Mid-2nd millen. BC. (MC)

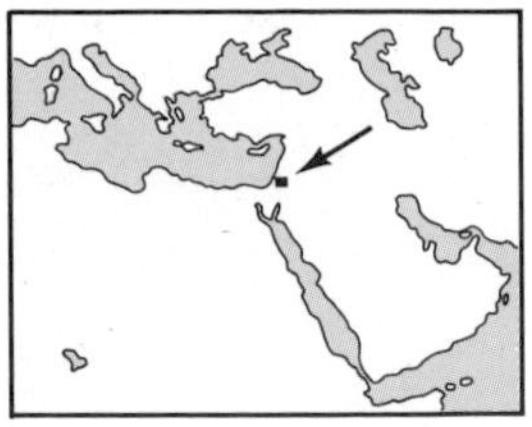

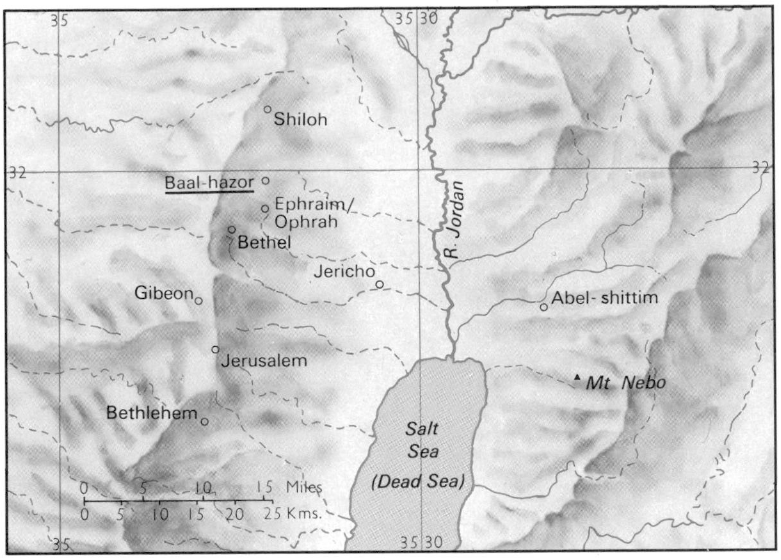

The location of Baal-hazor, near Bethel.

BAALI
See Ishi, Part 2.

BAAL-PEOR
See Peor, Part 3.

BAAL-SHALISHAH
See Shalisha, Part 3.

originally at Shechem (Jdg. 8:33; 9:4), probably to be equated with El-berith (Jdg. 9:46). The capture of Shechem by Joshua is nowhere recorded; it came under Habiru control in the 14th century BC and was probably incorporated into Israel by treaty. The Abimelech episode (Jdg. 9) illustrates the tension between the true Israelites and this basically Canaanite enclave. The Shechemites are called 'the sons of Hamor' ('ass', Jdg. 9:28) which is equivalent to 'the sons of the covenant' since the sacrifice of an ass was essential to the ratification of a treaty amongst the Amorites. A.E.C.

BAAL-GAD. The N limit of Israelite conquest lying at the foot of and to the W of Mt Hermon (Jos. 11:17; 13:5; 21:7). It may be Hasbeiyah (so F. M. Abel, *Géographie de la Palestine*, 2, 1938, p. 258) or Tell Hauš (so *GTT*, 509), 19 km farther N, both in the Wadi et-Teim. Archaeological evidence favours the latter. A.R.M.

BAAL-HAZOR. A mountain 1,016 m high, 9 km NNE of Bethel, mod. Jebel el-'Aṣûr. Absalom gathered his half-brothers to this mountain, perhaps to a settlement of the same name at its foot, at sheep-shearing time and killed Amnon (2 Sa. 13:23). (*OPHRAH.) A.R.M.

BAAL-MEON, known also as Beth-baal-meon (Jos. 13:17), Beth-meon (Je. 48:23) and Beon (Nu. 32:3), was one of several towns built by the Reubenites in the territory of Sihon the Amorite (Nu. 32:38). It was later captured by the Moabites and was still in their hands in the 6th century BC (Je. 48:23; Ezk. 25:9). Today the site is known as Ma'în. (*MOABITE STONE.) J.A.T.

BAAL-ZEBUB, BEELZEBUL. **1.** In OT Heb. *ba'al zᵉḇûḇ* ('lord of flies'), probably a mocking alteration of *ba'al zᵉḇûl* ('Prince *Baal'), appears as the name of the god of Ekron, whom Ahaziah, king of Israel, tried to consult in his last illness (2 Ki. 1:1–6, 16).

2. In NT Gk. *beelzeboul, beezeboul* (Beelzebub in TR and AV) is the prince of the demons (Mt. 12:24, 27; Mk. 3:22; Lk. 11:15, 18f.), identified with Satan (Mt. 12:26; Mk. 3:23, 26; Lk. 11:18). In contemporary Semitic speech it may have been understood as 'the master of the house'; if so, this phrase could be used in a double sense in Mt. 10:25b. F.F.B.

BAAL-ZEPHON ('Baal [lord] of the north'). The name of a place in the Egyptian E Delta near which the Israelites camped during their Exodus (Ex. 14:2, 9; Nu. 33:7), deriving from the name of the Canaanite god Baal-Zephon. The 'waters of Baal' were in the general area of the Delta residence Pi-R'messē (Qantir) in the 13th century BC; a Phoen. letter of the 6th century BC alludes to 'Baal-Zephon and all the gods of Tahpanhes'. This has led to the suggestion that Tahpanhes, modern Tell Defneh some 43 km SSW of Port Said, was earlier the Baal-Zephon of the 'waters of Baal' near Ra'amses and of the Israelite Exodus. Eissfeldt and Cazelles identify Baal-Zephon and Baal-Hasi (in Ugaritic; later Zeus Casios) and place the Egyptian Zephon/Casios at Ras Qasrun on the Mediterranean shore some 70 km due E of Port Said, backed by Lake Serbonis. However, the deity Baal-Zephon/Casios was worshipped at various places in Lower Egypt, as far S as Memphis, which leaves several possibilities open.

BIBLIOGRAPHY. R. A. Caminos, *Late-Egyptian Miscellanies*, 1954; N. Aimé-Giron, *Annales du Service des Antiquités de l'Égypte* 40, 1940/41, pp. 433–460; W. F. Albright in *BASOR* 109, 1948, pp. 15–16, and in *Festschrift Alfred Bertholet*, 1950, pp. 1–14; *RB* 62, 1955, pp. 332ff. C.D.W.

BAASHA. The founder of the second brief dynasty of N Israel (*c.* 900–880 BC). Though of humble origin (1 Ki. 16:2), Baasha usurped the throne following his assassination of Nadab, son of Jeroboam I, during the siege of the Philistine town of Gibbethon (1 Ki. 15:27ff.). His extermination of the entire house of Jeroboam fulfilled the prophecy of Ahijah (1 Ki. 16:5ff.). Active hostility between Israel and Judah continued steadily throughout the 24 years of his reign (1 Ki. 15:32). His provocative action in fortifying Ramah, 6 km N of Jerusalem, prompted Asa's appeal for Syrian intervention. He continued the religious policy of Jeroboam and earned a stern prophetic rebuke (1 Ki. 16:1ff.). J.C.J.W.

BABEL (Heb. *Bāḇel*, 'gate of god'; also *BABYLON). The name of one of the chief cities founded by Nimrod in the land of Shinar (Sumer), ancient Babylonia. It is named with Erech and Accad (Gn. 10:10) and according to Babylonian tradition was founded by the god Marduk and destroyed by Sargon *c.* 2350 BC when he carried earth from it to found his new capital Agade (*ACCAD). The history of the building of the city and its lofty tower is given in Gn. 11:1–11, where the name Babel is explained by popular etymology based on a similar Heb. root *bālal*, as 'confusion' or 'mixing'. Babel thus became a synonym for the confusion caused by language differences which was part of the divine punishment for

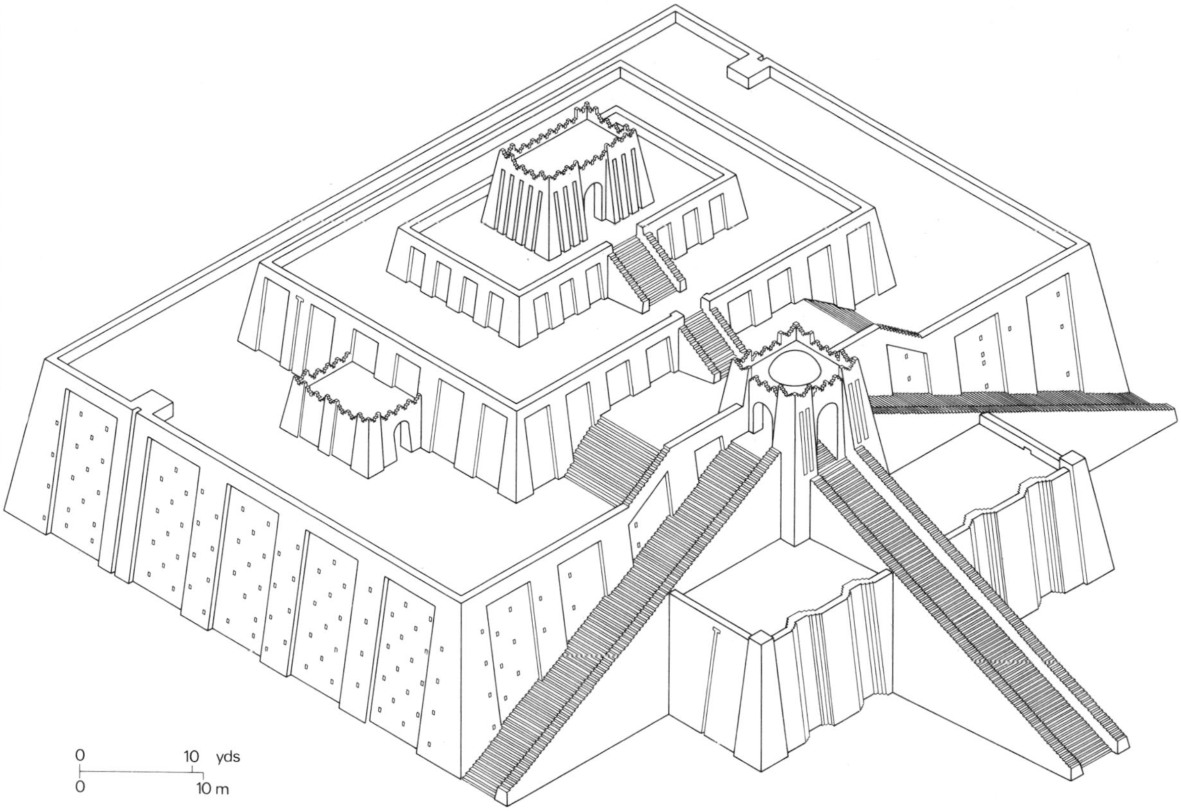

Isometric drawing of the restored temple-tower of the moon-god Nanna, built by King Ur-Nammu of Ur. (BM)

the human pride displayed in the building.

There is as yet no archaeological evidence to confirm the existence of a city at Babylon prior to the 1st Dynasty (*c.* 1800 BC) but Babylonian tradition and a text of Sharkalisharri, king of Agade *c.* 2250 BC, mentioning his restoration of the temple-tower (*ziggurat*) at Babylon, implies the existence of an earlier sacred city on the site. Sargon's action would confirm this. The use of burnt clay for bricks and of bitumen (AV 'slime') for mortar (Gn. 11:3) is attested from early times. The latter was probably floated down the Euphrates from Hit.

The 'Tower of Babel', an expression not found in the OT, is commonly used to describe the tower (*migdōl*) intended to be a very high landmark associated with the city and its worshippers. It is generally assumed that, like the city, the tower was incomplete (v. 8), and that it was a staged temple tower or multi-storeyed *ziggurat* first developed in Babylonia in the early 3rd millennium BC from the low temenos or platform supporting a shrine set up near the main city temples (as at Erech and 'Uqair). After Sharkalisharri the earliest reference to the *ziggurat* at Babylon is to its restoration by Esarhaddon in 681–665 BC.

Remains of the ziggurat at Borsippa, dated to the reign of Nebuchadrezzar II. (DJW)

This was named in Sumerian 'Etemenanki'—'the Building of the Foundation–platform of Heaven and Earth' whose 'top reaches to heaven' and associated with the temple of Marduk Esagila, 'the Building whose top is (in) heaven'. It is very probable that such a sacred edifice followed an earlier plan. The tower was severely damaged in the war of 652–648 BC but restored again by Nebuchadrezzar II (605–562 BC). It was this building, part of which was recovered by Koldewey in 1899, which was described by Herodotus on his visit *c.* 460 BC and is discussed in a cuneiform tablet dated 229 BC (Louvre, AO 6555). These enable an approximate picture of the later tower to be given. The base stage measured 90 × 90 m and was 33 m high. Above this were built five platforms, each 6–18 m

Remains of the ziggurat (temple-tower) of Nanna at Ur, built by King Ur-Nammu. (DJW)

high but of diminishing area. The whole was crowned by a temple where the god was thought to descend for intercourse with mankind. Access was by ramps or stairways. A late Babylonian plan of a seven-staged *ziggurat* shows that the architectural form was a height equal to the width at base with a cubic temple on the summit. Among others, ziggurats were found in *UR, *ERECH, *NINEVEH and elsewhere in *ASSYRIA and *BABYLONIA.

The *ziggurat* at Babylon was demolished by Xerxes in 472 BC, and though Alexander cleared the rubble prior to its restoration this was thwarted by his death. The bricks were subsequently removed by the local inhabitants, and today

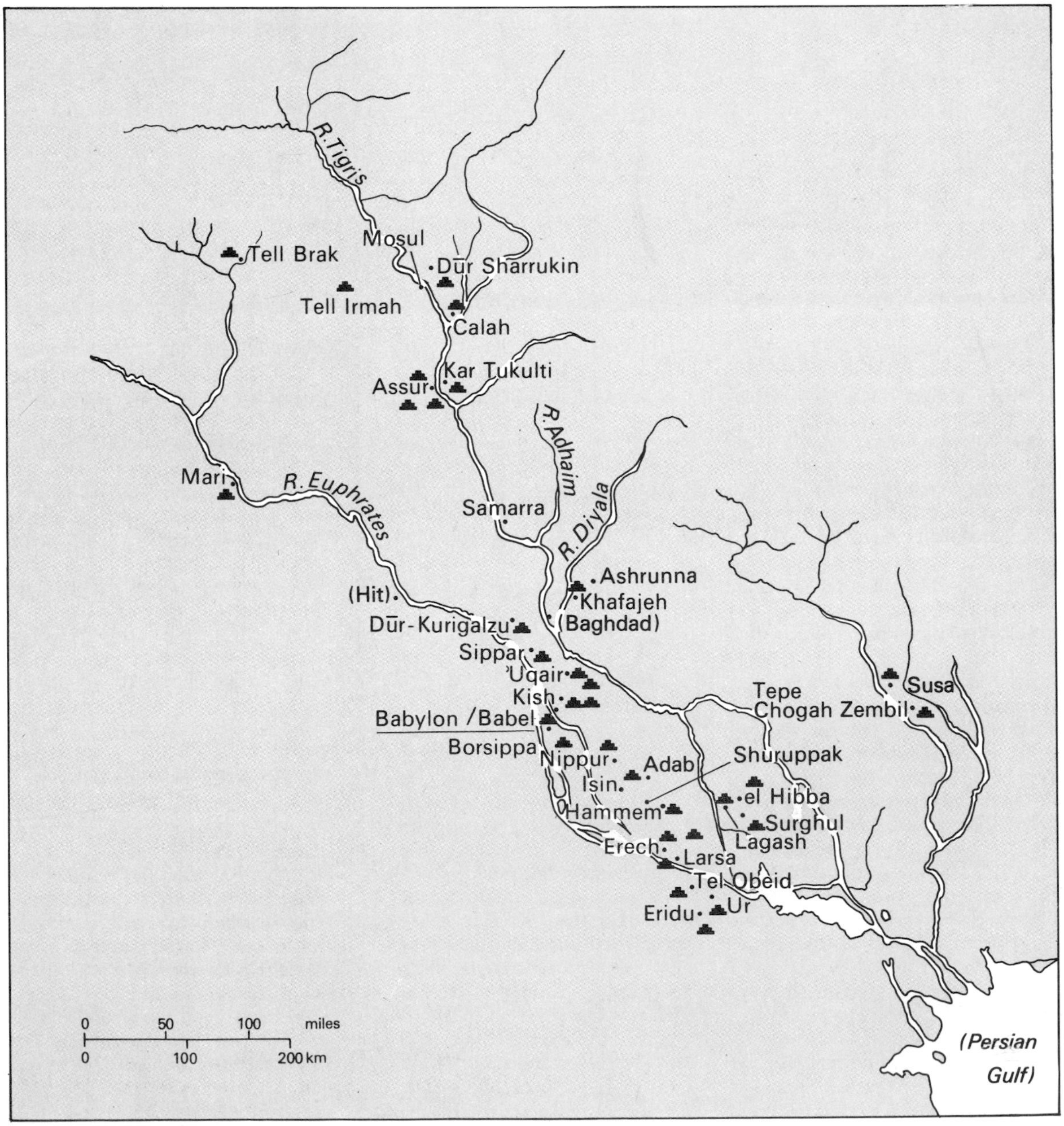

Sites of Mesopotamian ziggurat towers.

Late-Babylonian plan of a seven-staged ziggurat, with measurements. Obverse and one side of the tablet. (DJW)

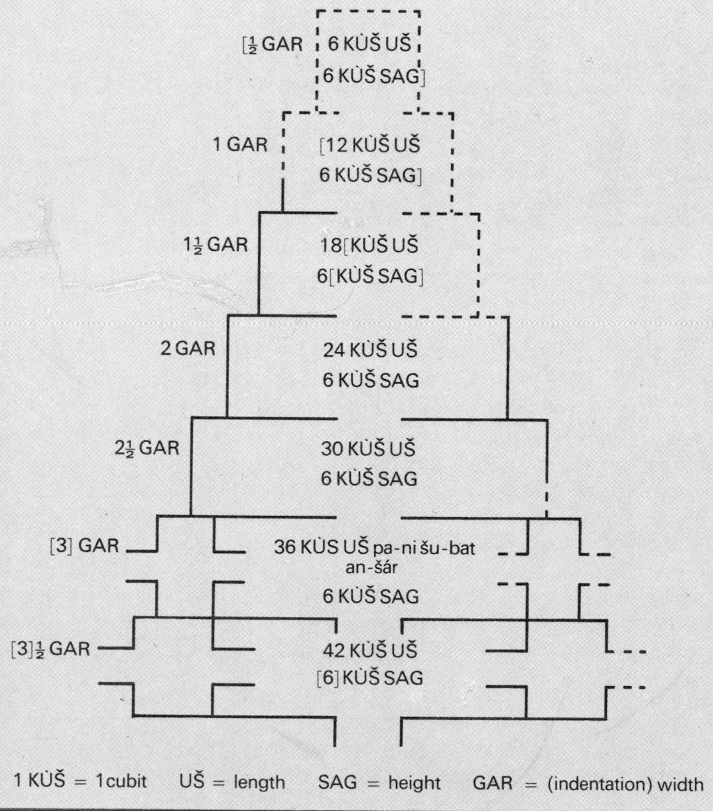

Drawing from the Babylonian tablet. (DJW)

the site of Etemenanki is a pit (*Es-Saḫn*) as deep as the original construction was high.

Travellers of all ages have sought to locate the ruined tower of Babel. Some identify it with the site described above and others with the vitrified remains of a *ziggurat* still visible at Borsippa (mod. Birs Nimrūd) 11 km SSW of Babylon, which is probably of Neo-Babylonian date. Yet others place the biblical tower at Dūr-Kurigalzu (Aqar Quf), W of Baghdad, a city which was, however, built *c.* 1400 BC. All that can certainly be said is that the Gn. 11 account bears all the marks of a reliable historical account of buildings which can no longer be traced.

Some scholars associate Jacob's vision of a ladder and a 'gate of heaven' (Gn. 28:11–18) with a *ziggurat* of the kind once built at Babel.

According to Gn. 11:9, the intervention of Yahweh at the building of Babel led to the confusion of tongues and the subsequent dispersion of mankind, possibly in the days of Peleg (Gn. 10:25). (*NATIONS, TABLE OF; Gn. 10.)

Babel, as *Babylon throughout its history, became a symbol of the pride of man and his inevitable fall. Babel was also theologically linked with the confusion and broken fellowship between men and nations when separated from God. Its effects are to be reversed in God's final kingdom, but there is no certainty that the *tongues or glossolalia of Acts 2:4 (*cf.* the interpretation of Joel in vv. 16–21), which were confined to Jews and proselytes and largely Aramaic- and Greek-speaking peoples, were other than known 'foreign languages' (*JTS* n.s. 17, 1966, pp. 299–307).

BIBLIOGRAPHY. A. Parrot, *The Tower of Babel*, 1955; D. J. Wiseman, *AS* 22, 1972, pp. 141ff.

D.J.W.

BABOON
See Animals, Part 1.

BABYLON.

I. In the Old Testament

The city on the river Euphrates (80 km S of modern Baghdad, Iraq) which became the political and religious capital of Babylonia and of the empire and civilization based upon it.

a. Name

The Heb. *Bāḇel* is translated by EVV as Babylon (except Gn. 10:10; 11:9, *BABEL) based on the Gk.

The ruins of Babylon.
(DJW)

Model reconstruction of the Procession Way, leading to the Ishtar gate at Babylon. (SAOB)

Babylōn. These are renderings of the Babylonian *bâb-ili*; pl. *bâb-ilāni*, which in its turn translates the earlier Sumerian name *kà-dingir-ra*, 'gate of god'. The Egyptians wrote the name *b-bī-r'* (= *bbr* or *bbl*) and the Achaemenids Old Pers. *babiruš*. Other common names for the city in the Babylonian texts are *tin-tir* (*ki*), 'life of the trees', explained by them as 'seat of life' and *e-ki*, 'place of canals'. *Šešak̠* of Je. 25:26; 51:41 is generally taken to be an '*atbash*' cypher rendering of Babel, but may be a rare occurrence of an old name *šeš-ki*.

b. Foundation

According to Gn. 10:10, *Nimrod founded the city as his capital, while Babylonian religious tradition gives the credit to the god Marduk (otherwise apart from the reference to the building of the Tower of *Babel (the *ziggurat*) there are no records of its foundation).

c. History

Sargon I of Agade (*c*. 2400 BC) and his successor Sharkalisharri built temples for the gods Anunitum and Amal and restored the temple-tower according to tradition. It is possible that their city of Agade was built on part of the ruins of the earlier city of Babylon. In the time of Shulgi of Ur (*c*. 2000 BC) Babylon was attacked and then ruled by governors (*patensi*) appointed from Ur. With the advent of the Amorite 1st Dynasty of Babylon under Sumu-abum the city walls were restored and Hammurapi and his successors enlarged the town, which flourished as capital of their realm until its overthrow by the Hittites *c*. 1595 BC. After a period under Kassite domination the city revolted and was attacked on several occasions, notably by Tiglath-pileser I of Assyria *c*. 1100 BC. Babylon repeatedly strove for its independence, and once a Chaldean ruler, Marduk-apla-iddina II (722–710, 703–702 BC), sent embassies to enlist the help of Judah (2 Ki. 20:12–18). Isaiah's account of the fate of the city (Is. 13) is very similarly worded to the account by Sargon II of Assyria of his sack of the place. In an attempt to remove the chief rebels, some of the leading citizens were deported to Samaria, where they introduced the worship of local Babylonian deities (2 Ki. 17:24–30). Sennacherib made his son king of Babylon but he was killed by pro-Baby-

Bull, possibly representing the god Marduk, one of over 200 decorating the Ishtar gate at Babylon. 7th–6th cent. BC. (SMB) (AMM)

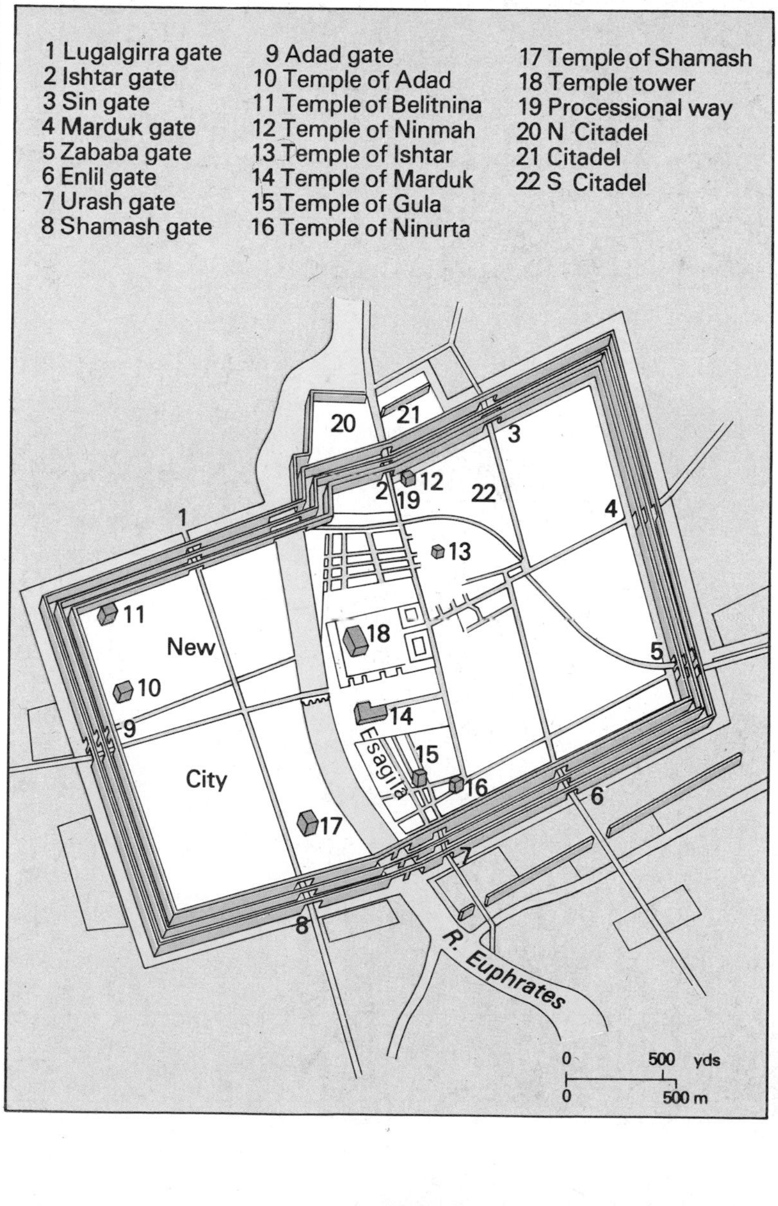

Plan of Babylon at the time of Nebuchadrezzar II, 605–582 BC.

lonian Elamites in 694 BC. In an attempt to end this upsurge of Babylonian nationalism Sennacherib sacked the city in 689 BC and removed the sacred statues. His son, Esarhaddon, sought to restore the holy city to which he transported Manasseh as prisoner (2 Ch. 33:11). He made Babylon a vassal-city under a son, Šamaš-šum-ukin, who, however, quarrelled with his brother *Ashurbanipal of Assyria. In the subsequent war of 652–648 BC Babylon was severely damaged by fire, and once again the Assyrians tried appointing a local chief, Kandalanu, as governor.

The decline of the Assyrian empire enabled Nabopolassar, a Chaldean, to recover the city and found a new dynasty in 626 BC. His work of restoring the city was ably continued by his successors, especially his son, Nebuchadrezzar II, king of Babylonia (2 Ki. 24:1), whose boast was of the great city he had rebuilt (Dn. 4:30). It was to Babylon that the victorious Babylonian army brought the Jewish captives after the wars against Judah. Among these was Jehoiachin, whose captivity there is confirmed by inscriptions found in the ruins of Babylon itself. The plunder from the Temple at Jerusalem, brought with the blinded king Zedekiah (2 Ki. 25:7–13), was stored in the main temple of the city, probably that of the god Marduk (2 Ch. 36:7). The city was later ruled by Amēl-Marduk (*EVIL-MERODACH) and was the place where Daniel served the last Chaldean ruler *Belshazzar, co-regent of Nabonidus.

As predicted by Isaiah (14:1–23; 21:1–10; 46:1–2; 47:1–5) and Jeremiah (50–51), Babylon was to fall in its turn and be left a heap of ruins (see *d*). In October 539 the Persians under Cyrus entered the city and Belshazzar was slain (Dn. 5:30). The principal buildings were spared and the temples and their statues restored by royal decree. There is no extra-biblical record of the government of the city, which now became a subsidiary Persian capital with an Achaemenid palace there. The temple vessels were delivered to Sheshbazzar for restoration to Jerusalem, and the discovery of the record of this, probably in the record office at Babylon, in the reign of Darius I (Ezr. 5:16ff.) was the cause of a further return of exiles rallied at Babylon by Ezra (8:1). Babylon, as

Palace of Nabopolassar, restored by Nebuchadrezzar. Reconstruction (with some original glazed bricks) of a part of the wall of the throne-room facing on to the principal courtyard. Height 12·40 m. c. 600 BC. Decoration includes motifs also found elsewhere in the city. Compare the procession of lions on the Ishtar Gate and the Procession Way. (SMB)

Part of the ruins of Babylon, with the reconstructed Ninmah temple in the background. (DJW)

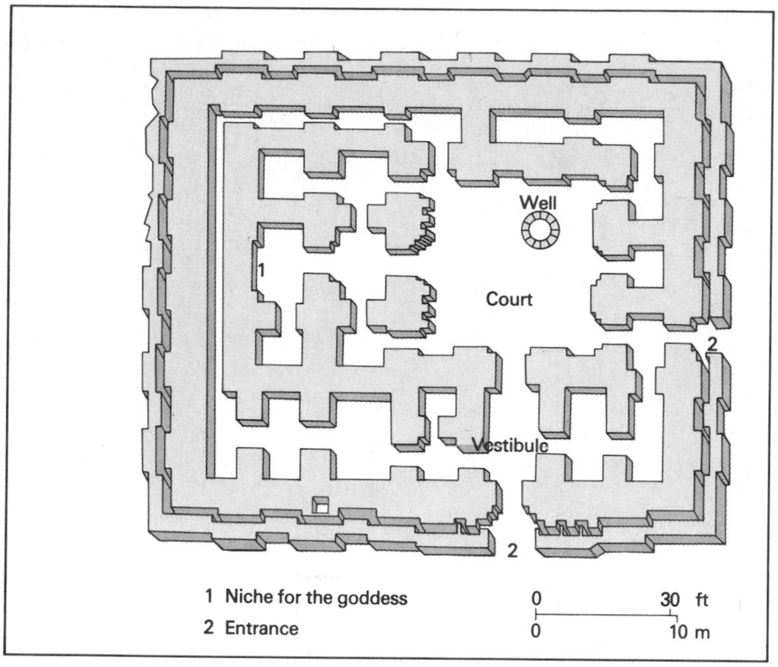

of old, was the centre of a number of rebellions, by Nidintu-Bēl in 522 BC, and Araka (521 BC), and by Bel-shimanni and Shamash-eriba in 482 BC. In suppressing the latter, Xerxes destroyed the city (478 BC); although Alexander planned to restore it, he met his death there before work had progressed far, and with the founding of Seleucia on the river Tigris as the capital of the Seleucid rulers after the capture of Babylon in 312 BC, the city once again fell into disrepair and ruins, although, according to cuneiform texts, the temple of Bel continued in existence at least until AD 75.

d. Exploration

Many travellers since Herodotus of Halicarnassus *c.* 460 BC (*History* 1. 178–188) have left accounts of their visits to Babylon. Benjamin of Tudela (12th century), Rauwolf (1574), Niebuhr (1764), C. J. Rich (1811–21) and Ker Porter (1818) were among those who were followed by the more scientific explorers who made soundings and plans of the ruins. The preliminary work by Layard (1850) and Fresnel (1852) was succeeded by systematic excavation of the inner city by the Deutsche Orient-Gesellschaft under Koldewey (1899–1917) and more recently by Lenzen in 1956–8 and since 1962 by the Iraqis (including the preservation and restoration of the Ninmah temple).

This work, combined with evidence of more than 10,000 inscribed tablets, recovered from the site by natives digging for bricks, enables a fair picture of the city of Nebuchadrezzar's day to be reconstructed. The deep overlay of debris, the frequent destruction and rebuilding, together with the change in the course of the river Euphrates and a rise in the water-table, means that, excepting only a few parts of it, the city of the earlier period has not been uncovered.

The site is now covered by a number of widely scattered mounds. The largest, Qasr, covers the citadel, Merkes a city quarter; to the N, Bāwil the N or summer palace of Nebuchadrezzar; Amran ibn 'Ali the temple of Marduk; and Saḥn the site of the *ziggurat* or temple-tower.

The city was surrounded by an intricate system of double walls, the outer range covering 27 km, strong and large enough for chariots to pass upon the top, buttressed by defence towers and pierced by 8 gates. On the N side the massive Ishtar gates marked the procession way leading S to the citadel to Esagila, the temple of Marduk and the adjacent *ziggurat* Etemenanki. This paved roadway was *c.* 920 m long, its walls decorated with enamelled bricks showing 120 lions (symbol of Ishtar) and 575 *mušruššu*—dragons (Marduk) and bulls (Bel) ranged in alternate rows. From this road another ran W to cross the river Euphrates by a bridge which linked the New Town on the W bank with the ancient capital. The main palaces on which successive kings lavished attention are now represented by the complex of buildings in the citadel, among which the throne-room (52 × 17 m) may have been in use in the time of Daniel. At the NE angle of the palace are the remains of vaults thought by Koldewey to be supports for the terraced 'hanging gardens' built by Nebuchadrezzar for Amytis, his Median wife, as a reminder of her homeland.

The temple-tower of Babylon became famous as the Tower of *Babel.

Many details of the city quarters and their temples, of which 53 are now known, have been recovered. The names of these quarters were used on occasions to designate the city as a whole (Šu'ana [*JCS* 23, 1970, p. 63], Shushan, Tuba, Tintir, Kullab). The frequent destructions of the city left few of the contents of the temples *in situ*. The pos-

Aerial view of part of the ruins of Babylon, with the temple complex Etemenanki in the foreground and the river Euphrates in the background. (JLH)

Top left: Plan of the temple of Ishtar, Babylon. The open inner court was surrounded by rooms, one of which led into the 'holy of holies', which contained a statue of the goddess.

Restored interior of the temple of the goddess Ninmah (Ishtar) at Babylon. (DJW)

session of the statue of Marduk, housed in Esagila, was a mark of victory, and it was carried off to the conqueror's capital. The religion and civilization were largely synonymous with those of *Assyria and *Babylonia.

BIBLIOGRAPHY. R. Koldewey, *The Excavations at Babylon*, 1914; E. Unger, *Babylon, Die Heilige Stadt*, 1931; art. 'Babylon' in *Reallexikon der Assyriologie*, 1932, pp. 330–369; A. Parrot, *Babylon and the Old Testament*, 1958; O. E. Ravn, *Herodotus' Description of Babylon*, 1932; I. J. Gelb, *Journal of Inst. of Asian Studies* 1, 1955, on name of Babylon. D.J.W.

II. In the New Testament

1. Babylon on the Euphrates, with special reference to the Babylonian Exile (Mt. 1:11–12, 17 (2); Acts 7:43).

2. In Rev. 14:8; 18:2, 'Fallen, fallen is Babylon the great' is an echo of Is. 21:9 (*cf.* Je. 51:8), but refers no longer to the city on the Euphrates but to Rome, as is made plain by the mention of seven hills in Rev. 17:9 (*cf.* also Rev. 16:19; 17:5; 18:10, 21). The scarlet woman of Rev. 17, enthroned upon the seven-headed beast and bearing the name of mystery, 'Babylon the great', is the city of Rome, maintained by the Roman empire. The seven heads of the imperial beast are interpreted not only of the seven hills of Rome but also of seven Roman emperors—of whom the five already fallen are probably Augustus, Tiberius, Gaius, Claudius and Nero, and the one currently reigning is Vespasian (Rev. 17:10).

3. In 1 Pet. 5:13, 'she who is at Babylon, who is likewise chosen', who sends her greetings to the Christians addressed in the Epistle, is most probably a Christian church. 'Babylon' here has been identified with the city on the Euphrates, and also with a Roman military station on the Nile (on the site of Cairo); but it is best to accept the identification with Rome.

BIBLIOGRAPHY. E. G. Selwyn, *The First Epistle of St Peter*, 1946, pp. 243, 303ff.; O. Cullmann, *Peter: Disciple, Apostle, Martyr*, 1953, pp. 70ff. *et passim*; R. E. Brown, K. P. Donfried, J. Reumann, *Peter in the New Testament*, 1973; I. T. Beckwith, *The Apocalypse of John*, 1919, pp. 284ff., 690ff.; G. B. Caird, *The Revelation of St John the Divine*, 1966, pp. 211ff. F.F.B.

BABYLONIA. The territory in SW Asia, now S Iraq, which derived its name from the capital city of *Babylon. It was also called *Shinar (Gn. 10:10; 11:2; Is. 11:11; Jos. 7:21, AV 'Babylonish') and, later, 'the land of the Chaldeans' (Je. 24:5; Ezk. 12:13). In earlier antiquity it bore the name of Akkad (Gn. 10:10, AV *ACCAD) for the N reaches and Sumer for the S alluvium and the marshes bordering the Persian Gulf; a territory which was later strictly called 'Chaldaea', a term for the whole country after the rise of the 'Chaldean' dynasty (see **I.***h*, below). Thus the Babylonians (*bᵉnê bāḇel*, 'sons of Babylon') are also qualified as Chaldeans (Ezk. 23:15, 17, 23). Babylonia, watered by the Tigris and Euphrates rivers, was the probable site of Eden (Gn. 2:14) and of the tower of *Babel, and the country to which the Jews were exiled.

This small flat country of about 20,000 sq. km was bounded on the N by *Assyria (Samarra–Jebel Hamrîn as border), on the E by the hills bordering *Elam, on the W by the Arabian desert and on the S by the shores of the Persian Gulf. There is debate whether the latter coastline has changed appreciably since ancient times (*Geographical Journal* 118, 1952, pp. 24–39; *cf. JAOS* 95, 1975, pp. 43–57). The principal cities, of which Babylon, Warka (Erech) and Agade are the first mentioned in the OT (Gn. 10:10), with Nippur, Ur, Eridu and Lagash, were all located on or near the Euphrates.

I. History

a. Pre-history

There is still much discussion regarding the relation of the earliest discoveries in S Mesopotamia to those in the N. The earliest types of pottery from the lowest level at Eridu (levels XV–XVII) imply very early settlement, while the pottery which lay above it (Haji Muhammad) is of a type known from near Kish and Warka which has affinities with Halaf and Hassuna in the N. The pre-'Ubaid culture is to be dated *c.* 4000 BC. The 'Ubaid culture, which is also found in the N, appears to have been introduced by new immigrants. There is as yet no sure means of identifying the inhabitants of Sumer (possibly biblical *SHINAR), though in the succeeding 'Proto-literate period' (*c.* 3100–2800 BC) pictographic writing is found on clay tablets (Uruk, levels III–IV). Since the language appears to be an early non-Semitic agglutinative Sumerian, employing names for older cities and technical terms in a different language, perhaps Semitic, it is likely that Semites and Sumerians were the earliest, or among the early, settlers. The highly developed art, in pottery, seals and architecture, is generally attributed to the influx of the Sumerians, so that the present evidence points to the presence of both Semites and Sumerians in the land from early times.

b. The Early Dynastic period (c. 2800–2400 BC)

This period saw the advent of kingship and the foundation of great cities. According to the Sumerian king list, 8 or 10 kings ruled before the Flood at the cities of Eridu, Badtibirra, Larak, Sippar and Shuruppak. The governor of the latter was the hero of the Sumerian flood story (*cf.* *NOAH). The 'flood' deposit found by Woolley at Ur is dated in the 'Ubaid period, and therefore does not correspond with similar levels found at Kish and Shuruppak (Proto-literate—Early Dynastic I; *cf. Iraq* 26, 1964, pp. 62–82). There was, however, a strong literary tradition of a *flood in Babylonia from *c.* 2000 BC.

After the Flood 'kingship came down again from heaven' and the rulers at Kish and Uruk (Erech) include Gilgamesh and Agga, the heroes of a series of legends, who may well be historical characters. City-states flourished with centres at Uruk, Kish, Ur (Royal Graves), Lagash, Shuruppak, Abu Ṣalabīkh and as far N as Mari. Often more than one powerful ruler sought to dominate Babylonia at the same time, and clashes were frequent. Thus the 1st Dynasty at Lagash founded by Ur-Nanše ended when Urukagina, a social reformer (*c.* 2351 BC), defeated Enannatum and soon afterwards Lugalzagesi of Umma, who had taken over the cities of Lagash, Ur and Uruk, established the first or 'proto-' imperial domination of Sumer as far as the Mediterranean.

c. The Akkadians (c. 2400–2200 BC)

A strong Semitic family founded a new city at Agade and about this time may have restored Babylon. This 'Akkadian' or Sargonid dynasty (2371–2191 BC), so called after the name of its founder *Sargon, developed a new technique of war with the bow and arrow and soon defeated the despot Lugalzagesi of Umma, Kish and Uruk to gain the whole of Sumer. This king carried his arms to the Mediterranean and Anatolia. His widespread authority was maintained by his grandson Naram-Sin before the Gutians from the E hills overran N Babylonia (2230–2120 BC) and kept their hold over the economy until defeated by a coalition led by Utuḫegal of Uruk. Their rule was, however, somewhat local and strongest E of the river Tigris. Lagash under its *ensi*, or ruler, Gudea (*c.* 2150 BC) remained independent and dominated Ur and the S cities. Gudea gradually extended his territory and expeditions as far as Syria (*EBLA) to win wood, precious stones and metals, and so increased the prosperity of his city. The Sumerian renaissance or 'Golden Age' which followed was one of economic and artistic wealth.

d. 3rd Dynasty of Ur (2113–2006 BC)

Following the reign of Utuḫegal of Uruk and Namaḫani, the son-in-law of Gudea, in Lagash, Ur once more became the centre of power. Ur-Nammu (2113–2096 BC) rebuilt the citadel with its ziggurat and temples at *Ur and in Uruk, Isin and Nippur set up statues of himself in the temples which were controlled by his nominees. Gradually Ur extended its influence as far as Assur and Byblos, and for a while his successors were accorded divine honours, depicted on their monuments and seals by the horned headgear of divinity (C. J. Gadd, *Ideas of Divine Rule in the Ancient Near East*, 1944). Similar honours appear to have been granted to Naram-Sin earlier. Many thousands of documents reveal the administration and religion of this period when Ur traded with places as far distant as India. The end came after severe famines, and the Sumerian rulers were displaced by invaders from Elam and Semitic semi-nomads from the W deserts. It is possible that the migration of Terah and Abraham (Gn. 11:31) took place at this time of change in Ur's fortune.

e. The Amorites (2000–1595 BC)

The territories formerly controlled by Ur were divided among the local chiefs at Assur, Mari on the Upper Euphrates and Eshnunna. Independent rule was established by Ishbi-Irra in Isin and Naplanum in Larsa, thus dividing the loyalties of the previously united Sumerians. Then Kudurmabug of Yamutbal, E of the river Tigris, made his son Warad-Sin ruler of Larsa. He was followed by Rim-Sin, who took over Isin but failed to make headway against the growing power of Babylon, where a series of vigorous rulers in the 1st (Amorite) Dynasty of Babylon (1894 1595 BC) held sway. The sixth of the line, *Hammurapi (1792–1750 BC; according to the most accepted *Chronology), eventually defeated Rim-Sin and for the last decade of his reign ruled from the Persian Gulf to *Mari, where he defeated Zimrilim, a Semite who had previously driven out Yasmaḫ-Adad, son of Shamshi-Adad I of Assyria. Despite this victory, Hammurapi was not as powerful as his namesake in Aleppo, and the Mari letters, which afford a remarkable insight into the diplomacy, trade, history and religion of those days, show that he did not subdue Assyria, Eshnunna or other cities in Babylonia (*ARCHAEOLOGY). The relations between Babylon, Elam and the W at this time made possible a coalition such as that described in Gn. 14. With the decline of Sumerian influence the increasing power of the Semites was emphasized by the place given to Marduk (*MERODACH) as the national god, and this encouraged Hammurapi to revise the laws of Babylon to accommodate both traditions. The text bearing this 'code' of 282 laws is based on the earlier reforms of Urukagina, Ur-Nammu and Lipit-Ishtar.

f. The Kassites (1595–1174 BC)

Babylon, as often in its history, was to fall by sudden assault from the N. About 1595 BC the Hittite Mursili I raided the city and the Kassites from the E hills gradually took over the country, later ruling from a new capital (Dur-Kurigalzu) built by Kurigalzu I (*c.* 1450 BC). In the centuries which followed Babylonia was weak, though independent except for brief periods when under direct Assyrian control (*e.g.* Tukulti-Ninurta I, 1244–1208 BC). Aramaean incursions were frequent, and these raids may well have left the Israelites free to settle in S Palestine and later to expand their borders under Solomon with little opposition from these desert peoples (*ASSYRIA). Periodically national heroes were able to maintain local control and trade, as when Nebuchadrezzar I (1124–1103 BC) defeated Elam, but soon Tiglath-pileser I re-established Assyrian overlordship.

g. Assyrian domination (*745–626* BC)

About the time of Nabû-naṣir (Nabonassar), whose reign (747–735 BC) marked the beginning of a new era, there began a prolonged struggle for independence from *Assyria. Tiglath-pileser III of Assyria proclaimed himself 'King of Sumer and Akkad', took the hands of Bel(= Marduk) and thus claimed the throne in Babylon in 745 BC, using his other name Pul(u) (1 Ch. 5:26). 15 years later he had to bring the Assyrian army to fight the rebel Ukin-zēr of Bît-Amukkani. He defeated him in Sapia and deported many prisoners. A rival sheikh, Marduk-apla-iddina II, of the S district of Bît-Yakin, paid Tiglath-pileser tribute at this time (*Iraq* 17, 1953, pp. 44–50). However, the preoccupation with the siege of *Samaria by *Shalmaneser V and *Sargon II in 726–722 gave Marduk-apla-iddina (*MERODACH-BALADAN) his opportunity for intrigue. For 10 years (721–710 BC) he held the throne in Babylon until the Assyrian army attacked Der, defeated Ḫumbanigaš of Elam and occupied Babylon. The Assyrian army moved S, but Merodach-baladan was retained as local ruler. It says much for Sargon's diplomacy that he kept him a loyal subject for the rest of his reign.

On Sargon's death in 705 BC, however, Merodach-baladan again plotted against his masters, and it is likely that it was he, rather than Hezekiah, who initiated the overtures for an alliance against Assyria (2 Ki. 20:12–19; Is. 39). Isaiah's opposition was well founded, for the Babylonians themselves set their own citizen Marduk-zakir-šum on the throne in 703 BC. This freed Merodach-baladan's hand and he had himself proclaimed king of Babylon, though he lived in the more friendly city of Borsippa. Sennacherib marched against him, defeated the rebels and their Elamite supporters in battles at Kutha and Kish, and entered Babylon, where he set a pro-Assyrian, Bel-ibni, on the throne. Bît-Yakin was ravaged, but Merodach-baladan had already fled to Elam, where he died before Sennacherib was able to assemble a Punic naval force in 694 BC.

For a while Sennacherib's son Esarhaddon had special responsibilities as viceroy at Babylon, and when he came to the throne in 681 did much to repair the city's temples and to restore its fortunes. It may be in conjunction with this that he temporarily deported Manasseh there (2 Ch. 33:11). Since the Elamites continued to stir up the Babylonian tribes, Esarhaddon led a campaign into the 'sea-lands' in 678 BC and installed Na'id-Marduk as chief. In May 672 Esarhaddon made all his vassals swear to support his son Ashurbanipal as crown-prince of Assyria, and his son Šamaš-šum-ukin as crown-prince of Babylonia (*Iraq* 20, 1958). On his death in 669 this arrangement came into force and worked well under the influence of the queen-mother. Nevertheless, by 652 BC the twin brother in Babylon was in open revolt against the central government, and his death followed the sack of Babylon in 648. Ashurbanipal struck at Elam also and captured Susa, from which prisoners were taken with Babylonian rebels to be settled in Samaria (Ezr. 4:2). Kandalanu was made viceroy

Babylonia and the areas under its influence.

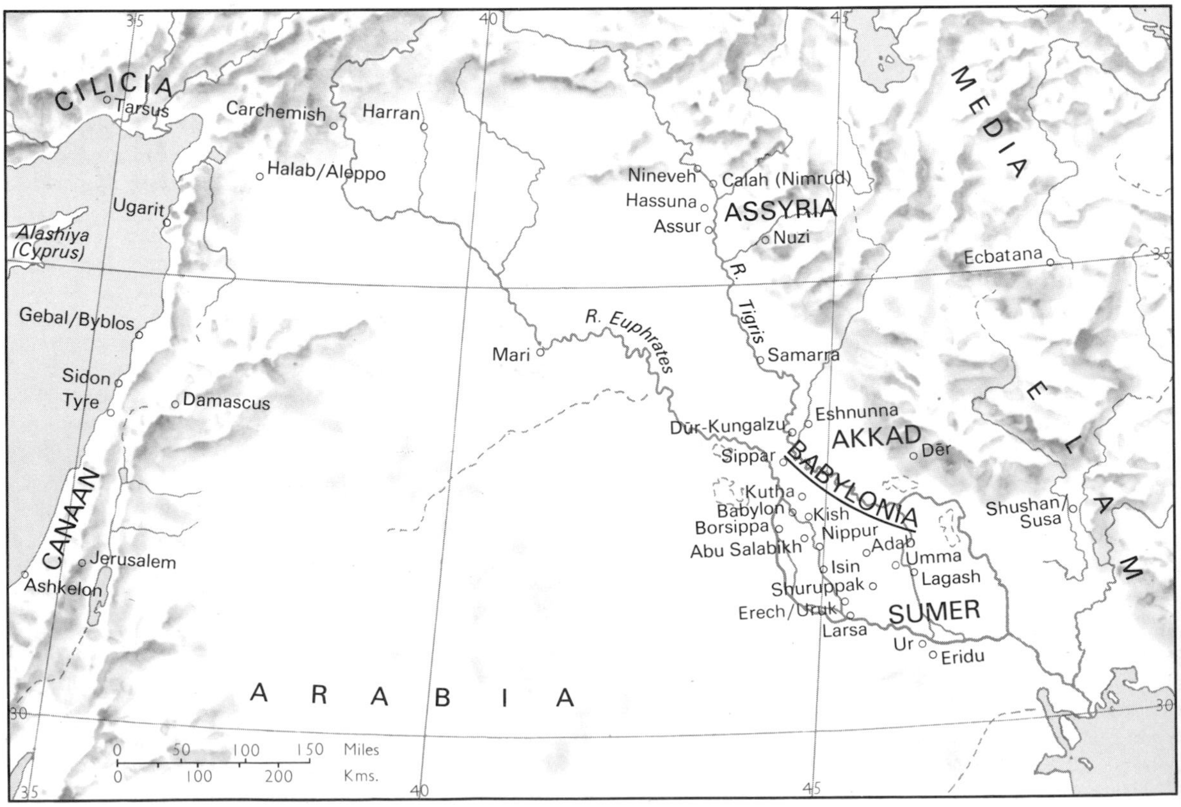

of Babylonia (648–627 BC), while *Ashurbanipal kept direct control of the religious centre of Nippur. These preoccupations in the S diverted Assyrian attention from the W, and the city-states in Palestine were able to take steps towards independence under *Josiah. The end of Ashurbanipal's reign is obscure, but may have followed soon after the death of Kandalanu. In the interregnum which followed, the local tribes rallied to support the Chaldean Nabopolassar against the Assyrian Sin-šar-iškun.

h. The Neo-Babylonian (*Chaldean*) *period* (*626–539 BC*)

Nabopolassar, a governor of the 'sea-lands' near the Persian Gulf, was a Chaldean (*kaldu* hence *CHALDEA), occupied the throne in Babylon on 22 November 626, and at once made peace with Elam. In the following year he defeated the Assyrians at Sallat, and by 623 Der had broken from their yoke. The Babylonian Chronicle, the principal and reliable source for this period, is silent on the years 623–616 BC, by which time Nabopolassar had driven the Assyrians back along the rivers Euphrates and Tigris. In 614 the Medes joined the Babylonians to attack Assur, and the same allies, perhaps with Scythian support, captured Nineveh in the summer of 612 BC, the Babylonians pursuing the refugees westwards. Babylonian campaigns in Syria were followed by the assault on Harran in 609 and raids on the N hill-tribes in 609–606 BC. Nabopolassar, now aged, entrusted the Babylonian army to his crown-prince Nebuchadrezzar, who fought the Egyptians at Kumuḫi and Quramati (Upper Euphrates).

In May–June 605 BC Nebuchadrezzar made a surprise attack on Carchemish, sacked the city and annihilated the Egyptian army at Hamath. Thus the Babylonians now overran all Syria as far as the Egyptian border but do not appear to have entered the hill-country of Judah itself (2 Ki. 24:7; Jos., *Ant.* 10. 6; *cf.* Dn. 1:1). Jehoiakim, a vassal of Neco II, submitted to Nebuchadrezzar, who carried off hostages, including Daniel, to Babylon. While in Palestine, Nebuchadrezzar heard of the death of his father (15 August 605 BC) and at once rode across the desert to 'take the hands of Bel', thus claiming the throne, on 6 September 605 BC.

In 604 BC Nebuchadrezzar received the tribute of 'all the kings of Hatti-land (Syro-Palestine)', among whom must have been Jehoiakim. Ashkelon, however, refused and was sacked, an event which had a profound effect on Judah (Je. 47:5–7). An Aramaic letter appealing for help from the pharaoh against the advancing Babylonian army may be assigned to this time (*cf. DOTT*, pp. 251–255). In 601 the Babylonians fought the Egyptians, both sides sustaining heavy losses; the Babylonians remained at home to re-equip the army during the next year. It was probably as a result of this that Jehoiakim, contrary to the word of Jeremiah (Je. 27:9–11), transferred his allegiance to Neco II after submitting to Babylon for 3 years (2 Ki. 24:1).

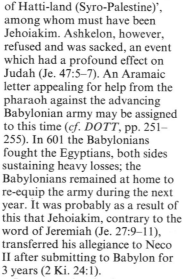

The god Shamash enthroned within his shrine, to whom King Nabu-apla-iddina is presented. The Babylonian tablet records the king's endowment of the sun temple at Sippar (Abu Habbah). c. 870 BC. (BM)

In preparation for further campaigns the Babylonian army raided the Arab tribes in 599/8 (Je. 49:28–33). In the month Kislev in his 7th year (December 598) Nebuchadrezzar called out his army once more and, according to the Babylonian Chronicle, 'besieged the city of Judah, capturing it on the second day of Adar. He captured its king, appointed a ruler of his own choice and, having taken much spoil from the city, sent it back to Babylon' (BM 21946). The fall of Jerusalem on 16 March 597, the capture of Jehoiachin, the appointment of Mattaniah-Zedekiah and the commencement of the Jewish Exile are thus recorded as in the OT (2 Ki. 24:10–17; 2 Ch. 36:8–10).

In the following year Nebuchadrezzar appears to have marched

Nabonidus of Babylonia standing before the symbols of the moon-god Sin, the sun-god Shamash, and Ishtar, the goddess of war and love. (BM)

against Elam (*cf.* Je. 49:34–38). The Babylonian Chronicle is missing from 595 BC, but further Babylonian operations against Judah when Zedekiah rebelled are recorded by Jeremiah (52:3ff.; 2 Ki. 25:7). Jerusalem was destroyed in 587 BC and a further deportation effected in 581 (2 Ki. 25:8–21), leaving Judah a dependent province under Gedaliah (vv. 22–26). A Babylonian text gives a glimpse of an invasion of Egypt in 568/7 BC (Je. 46). The exiled Jehoiachin, who is named in ration-tablets from Babylon (dated 595–570 BC), was favourably treated by Nebuchadrezzar's successor Amēl-Marduk (* EVIL-MERODACH, 562–560 BC; 2 Ki. 25:27). This king was assassinated by Nebuchadrezzar's son-in-law Neriglissar (* NERGAL-SHAREZER, 560–556 BC), who campaigned in Cilicia in an effort to stem the rising power of Lydia. His son, Labaši-Marduk, reigned only 9 months before Nabonidus took the throne and immediately marched to Cilicia, where, according to Herodotus, he mediated between the Lydians and Medes. The latter now threatened Babylonia, from which Nabonidus was driven by the people's unwillingness to accept his reforms. He campaigned in Syria and N Arabia, where he lived at Tema for 10 years while his son * Belshazzar acted as co-regent in Babylon. About 544 his people and the kings of Arabia, Egypt and the Medes being favourably disposed, Nabonidus returned to his capital (*AS* 8, 1958), but by this time the country was weak and divided.

i. The Achaemenids (539–332 BC)

Cyrus, who had taken over Media, Persia and Lydia, entered Babylon on 16 October 539 BC, following its capture by his general Gobryas. The course of the river Euphrates had been diverted at Opis to enable the invaders to penetrate the defences along the dried-up river-bed. Belshazzar was killed (Dn. 5:30) and Nabonidus was exiled to Carmania. The identity of * Darius the Mede with Cyrus (as Dn. 6:28) or with Gubaru has been proposed.

The rule of Cyrus in Babylon (539–530 BC) was just and favourable to the Jews, whose return from exile he encouraged (Ezr. 1:1–11; *cf.* Is. 44:24–28; 45:13; Mi. 5). For a brief time his son Cambyses acted as co-regent until his father died fighting in the NE hills. He invaded Egypt but his death (522 BC) brought insurgence, and pretenders seized the throne (*AJSL* 58, 1941, pp. 341ff.), until in December 522 Darius I restored law and order. During his reign (522–486 BC) he allowed the Jews to rebuild the Temple at Jerusalem under Zerubbabel (Ezr. 4:5; Hg. 1:1; Zc. 1:1).

Henceforth Babylonia was ruled by kings of * Persia; Xerxes (*AHASUERUS, 486–470 BC), Artaxerxes I (464–423 BC) and Darius II (423–408 BC), who may be the 'Darius the Persian' so named in Ne. 12:22 to distinguish him from 'Darius the Mede'.

Following the capture of Babylon, which he planned to rebuild, Alexander III (the Great) ruled the city (331–323 BC) and was followed by a Hellenistic line; Philip Arrhidaeus (323–316 BC) and Alexander IV (316–312 BC). The country then passed in turn into the hands of the Seleucids (312–64 BC) and then of the Parthians (Arsacids) and Sassanians until its conquest by the Arabs in AD 641.

From the Neo-Babylonian period onwards there were a number of Jewish settlements in Babylonia maintaining links with Judaea (Acts 2:9), and after the fall of Jerusalem in AD 70 these became influential in the *diaspora.*

II. Religion

From the 3rd millennium BC onwards lists of the names of deities with their titles, epithets and temples were compiled. Although in the final library version at Nineveh in the 7th century BC these numbered more than 2,500, many can be identified as earlier Sumerian deities assimilated by the Semites after the time of the 1st Dynasty of Babylon (*c.* 1800 BC), so that the actual number of deities worshipped in any one period was considerably less.

a. The Pantheon

The chief gods were Anu (Sumerian *An*) the heaven-god, with his principal temple É.anna at Uruk (* ERECH). He was the Semitic 'El, and his wife Innana, or Innin, was later confused with Ishtar. Similar syncretistic tendencies can be traced over Enlil, the air-god, whose attributes were later taken over by Bel (Baal) or Marduk (* MERODACH). His wife, called Ninlil or Ninhursag, was later identified also with Ishtar. The third deity of the supreme triad was Ea (Sum. *Enki*), 'lord of the deep waters', god of wisdom and thus especially favourable to mankind, to whom he revealed the means of learning the mind of the gods through divination, and for whom he interceded. His temple É.abzu was at Eridu, and his wife bore the names of Dam-gal, Nin-mah or Damkina, the great wife of earth and heaven.

Among the other principal deities was the Semitic Ishtar, at first perhaps a male deity (*cf.* Arab. *'Athtar*). But later, by the assumption of the powers of Innana through the same process of syncretism, Ishtar became supremely the goddess of love and the heroine of war and was considered to be the daughter of Sin. Sin, the Babylonian moon-god (Sum. *su'en*), was worshipped with his wife Ningal in temples at Ur and Harran. He was said to be the son of Anu or of Enlil. Shamash, whose wife Aya was also later considered to be a form of Ishtar, was the sun in his strength (Sum. *utu*), the son of Sin, the god of power, justice and of war. His main temples (É.babbar, 'the House of the Sun') were at Sippar and Larsa, though like that of all the principal deities his worship was perpetuated in shrines in other cities.

Adad, of W Semitic origin, was the god of storms, the Canaanite-Aramaean Addu or *Hadad. Nergal and his wife Ereshkigal ruled the underworld, and thus he was the lord of plagues (Irra), fevers and maladies. With the rise of the Amorites the worship of Marduk (Sum. *amar.utu*, 'the young bull of the sun'?), the eldest son of Enki, became paramount in Babylon. The Epic of Creation

Babylonian Chronicle for the years 616–609 BC, *including an account of the capture of Assur by the Medes (614* BC*) and the fall of Nineveh to the Medes, Scythians and Babylonians. 13·6 cm × 7·1 cm* (BM)

Early Babylonian seal and impression. Utu Shamash, the sun-god, rises between two mountains. The presence with him of Ea, god of the deep, wisdom and incantation, and other deities may show that this scene may represent an ancient epic or myth. Height 3·8 cm. Akkadian period. c. 2360–2180 BC. (DJW)

This tablet outlines the world of the time of Sargon of Agade, c. 2300 BC, depicted as a circle surrounded by water, with Babylon at its centre. This is possibly the oldest 'map' yet found. 8·2 cm × 11·7 cm. Tablet from 7th/6th cent. BC. (BM)

(*enuma eliš*) is a poem concerning the creation of the universe and of order restored by Marduk, whose 50 titles are given. Nabu (*NEBO), god of science and writing, had his temple (É.zida) in many cities, including *Nineveh, *Calah and Borsippa. Many deities were of importance in certain localities. Thus Ashur (*an.šar*) became the national god of Assyria. Amurru (*mar.tu*, 'the west'), who is identified with Anu, Sin and Adad, was a W Semitic deity as was *Dagon (*TAMMUZ). Dummuzi was a god of vegetation whose death, but not resurrection, forms the subject of an Ishtar myth. Ninurta was the Babylonian and Assyrian god of war and hunting (perhaps reflected in the biblical *NIMROD).

The upper world was peopled with Igigu-gods and the lower by Annunaku. The whole spiritual and material realm was regulated by divine laws (*me*), over a hundred of which are known, ranging from 'godship' to 'victory' and 'a musical instrument', *i.e.* cultural traits and complexes. The gods were immortal yet of limited power. The myths, in which but few of the principal deities figure, illustrate their anthropomorphic character and the conception of any object (*e.g.* a stone) being imbued with 'life'. Spirits and demons abound. The Sumerians sought by various theological devices to resolve the problems inherent in their polytheistic system. Thus the myths are primarily concerned with such questions as the origin of the universe, the foundation and government of the world and the *creation of man and the search for immortality, as in the Epic of the Flood, and man's relationship to the spiritual world.

b. Priesthood

There were many classes of temple servants, with the king or ruler as the supreme pontiff at certain solemn festivals. In early Sumerian times the whole economy was centred on the temple, where the chief official (*ênû*) was 'the lord of the manor'. In the worship of Sin, the high-priestess (*entu*) was usually a royal princess. The chief priests (*maḫḫu*) had many priests (*šangu*), males of sound body and often married, to assist them. The chief liturgist (*urigallu*) was supported by a host of minor officials who had access to the temple (*ēreb bīti*). In the ceremonial, chanters, psalmists, dirge-singers and musicians played a great part.

In man's approach to the god many specialists might play a role. The exorcist (*ašipu*) could remove the evil spirit or spell with the incantations or ritual prescribed in the texts (*šurpu*; *maqlu*) involving symbolic substitutions (*kuppuru*), purification by *mašmašu*-priests or by those who cleansed by water (*ramku*). There are many documents describing the action to be taken against evil spirits (*utukki limnūti*), demons of fate (*namtaru*), demons plaguing women (*lamaštu*) or taboos. The extensive medical literature of the early period was closely allied to religion, as was the astronomy or astrology of the later 'Chaldean' dynasty. The latter was based on the equation of deities with planets or stars (*e.g.* Nabu = Mercury), or with parts of the heavens ('The Way of Anu' = fixed stars).

Others were engaged in ascertaining the will of the gods by omens from livers (the *barû*-priest or 'seer'), or by inquiry by oracle (*ša'ilu*), or by offering prayers. Many women, including sanctuary prostitutes, were attached to the temples (H. A. Hoffner, *Orient and Occident*, 1973, pp. 213–222) and local shrines where travellers prayed have been found at Ur (*Iraq* 22, 1960).

The regular service (*dullu*) included giving the gods something to eat and drink. Statues were dressed and ornamented and votive figures of worshippers set near by. Sacrifices placed on altars were subsequently allocated, wholly or in part, to the priests. The gods had their own chairs, chariots and boats for use in processions.

c. Festivals

Most cities and temples had their own distinctive festivals and sacred days. At Babylon, Erech and Ur, as at Assur, Nineveh and Calah, the New Year Festival (*akitu*) was the most outstanding, held in the spring, but not exclusively, and with varying practices at different centres and periods. At Babylon the ceremonies lasted 2 weeks with numerous rites including a procession of gods to Marduk's temple, the humiliation and restoration of the king who later 'took the hand of Bēl' to lead him in procession to the *akitu*-house outside the city where a re-enactment of the assembly of the gods, the creation debate and struggle (in ritual combat?) and the fixing of the fates for the ensuing year took place. This was sometimes followed by a 'sacred marriage' (king and priestess representing the god) and days of general rejoicing. The Epic of Creation was recited during this time and also at other times later in the year.

Royal festivals included the coronation of the king (texts of Ur-Nammu, Nabopolassar, *etc.*, survive), celebration of victories and the inauguration of a city or temple. Personal festivals include celebration of birth, marriage and the installation of girls as priestesses.

d. Literature

Babylonian literature is already well developed in the Abū Ṣalabīkh tablets (*c.* 2800–2500 BC) with evidence of Semitic scribes copying earlier Sumerian texts and using literary techniques (colophons, *etc.*) commonly taught in schools. Throughout its long history (to AD 100) this literature was influential throughout the ancient Near East, copies being found in Anatolia (*HITTITE), Syria (*EBLA, *UGARIT), Palestine (Megiddo, Hazor, *etc.*), Egypt (*AMARNA) and later even Greece. Originals or copies were taken to, or made for, the royal libraries of *Assyria at Assur, Nineveh and Calah.

The range covered some 50 epics about ancient heroes and myths in Akkadian (some translated from Sumerian, and relating to creation, the flood and establishment of civilization). 'Wisdom literature' includes compositions about 'man and his god', the Babylonian 'Job' (*ludlul bēl nēmeqi*), theodices, disputations, dialogues, practical instructions, proverbs, parables, fables and folk-tales, miniature essays and love-songs. These are also found as part of the school curriculum besides the series of handbooks necessary to a skilled scribe (sign-lists, syllabaries, grammatical paradigms, phrase books, dictionaries and numerous lists, *e.g.* personal and place-names).

'Religious' literature includes psalms, hymns and prayers (to gods and some kings), rituals, incantations, as well as catalogues of such literature, much of which is still lost. 'Scientific' literature covers medicine (prognosis, diagnosis, prescriptions, *vade mecum*, surgery and veterinary texts), chemistry (mainly perfume and glass-making), geology (lists of stones with colour and hardness), alchemy, botany (drug and plant lists) and zoology (lists of fauna). Mathematics (including geometry and algebra) is represented by both problem and practical texts and is closely related also to astronomy with its tables, procedure, ephemerides and goal-year texts, almanacs and diaries. Texts include predictions for intercalated months to maintain the *calendar.

In Babylonia the historical Chronicle was highly developed; extracts from it were included in a whole range of literature (epics, 'dynastic prophecies' and astronomical diaries). Collections of laws (but not law codes) from the 2nd millennium BC (*e.g.* Eshnunna, Hammurapi) are well known and can be compared with practice in more than a quarter of a million texts—letters, legal, economic and administrative from *c.* 3000 to 300 BC. From the 4th century BC developments include horoscopes, the zodiac, and texts written in Greek letters on clay tablets, among other *writing materials.

III. Exploration and excavation

Many travellers, from the time of Herodotus in the 5th century BC, have described their journeys in Babylonia. From the 19th century AD interest in the location of Babylon and the 'Tower of Babel' was increased by the objects and drawings brought to Europe by travellers such as C. J. Rich (1811–25), Ker Porter (1818) and Costin and Flandin (1841). Excavation soon followed at Babylon, Erech and Borsippa (Layard, Loftus), and the good results led to more scientific expeditions, notably at Erech (Warka), *Kish, *Babylon, *Ur, Lagash and Nippur from 1850 onwards. More recent and still continuing excavation has added largely to our knowledge of all periods, *e.g.* the Early Dynastic period—Erech (Warka), Abū Ṣalabīkh, Girsu (Telloh), Lagash (Tell Hiba); Ur III (Adab, Drehem and Ur); Old Babylonian (Tell Harmal, Dēr, Sippar (Abu Habbah), Larsa, Eshnunna, Umma); Kassite (Dūr-Kurigalzu); Neo-Babylonian (Erech, Nippur, Kutha, Sippar) and later periods (Dilbat, Seleucia). Reports and texts are published regularly in the journals *Archiv für Orientforschung*, *Orientalia*, *Iraq*, *Sumer*, *Journal of Cuneiform Studies*.

The Babylonian Chronicle for the years 605–594 BC. *The events recorded include the battle of Carchemish in 605* BC, *the accession of Nebuchadrezzar II as king of Babylon, and the appointment of Zedekiah as king of Judah after the capture of Jerusalem on 16 March 597* BC *and the removal of the Judaeans to exile in Babylon. Height 8 cm. 6th cent.* BC. (BM)

BIBLIOGRAPHY. *General and History:* S. N. Kramer, *History Begins at Sumer*, 1958; H. W. F. Saggs, *The Greatness that was Babylon*, 1961; D. J. Wiseman, *Chronicles of Chaldaean Kings*, 1956; A. L. Oppenheim, *Ancient Mesopotamia*, 1964; J. A. Brinkman, *A Political History of Post-Kassite Babylonia*, 1968; W. W. Hallo and W. K. Simpson, *The Ancient Near East*, 1971; *CAH*, 1/2, 1971–2/2, 1975, 3 (forthcoming). *Texts:* A. K. Grayson, *Assyrian and Babylonian Chronicles*, 1975; *Babylonian Historical-Literary Texts*, 1975; *ANET* for translations of historical, religious, law and other texts. *Religion:* J. Bottéro, *La religion babylonienne*, 1952; T. Jacobsen, *Treasures of Darkness*, 1976; H. Ringgren, *Religions of the Ancient Near East*, 1967. *Art:*

ANEP; H. Frankfort, *The Art and Architecture of the Ancient Orient*, 1954; Seton Lloyd, *The Archaeology of Mesopotamia*, 1978. *Other:* R. S. Ellis, *A Bibliography of Mesopotamian Sites*, 1972. D.J.W.

BABYLONIAN TALMUD
See Talmud, Part 3.

BACHELOR
See Marriage, Part 2.

BACTRIAN CAMEL
See Animals, Part 1.

BAGPIPE
See Music, Part 2.

BAKER, BAKING
See Bread, Part 1.

BACA, VALLEY OF (Heb. *'ēmeq habbāḵā'*), a place near Jerusalem mentioned in Ps. 84:6, so translated in AV, RSV. The traditional rendering 'valley of Weeping' (RV; *cf.* 'Valley of the Weeper', JB), as though from *beḵeh* (*cf.* Ezr. 10:1), goes back through Jerome's Gallican Psalter to LXX; it is accepted by G. R. Driver, who suggests the valley may have been so called because it was lined with tombs. Other renderings are 'valley of mulberry (balsam) trees' (AVmg., RVmg.), as though from *b^{e}ḵā'îm* (2 Sa. 5:23f.); these are supposed to grow in arid districts, whence perhaps the paraphrase 'thirsty valley' (NEB).

BIBLIOGRAPHY. G. R. Driver, 'Water in the Mountains!', *PEQ* 102, 1970, pp. 87ff. F.F.B.

BADGERS' SKINS (Heb. *taḥaš*, probably from Egyp. *ṯḥś*, 'leather', and Arab. *tuḫasun*, 'dolphin'). Mentioned in AV as the upper covering of the tabernacle, *etc.* (Ex. 25:5; 26:14, *etc.*, in all of which cases RSV has 'goatskins'), and as the material used in making sandals (Ezk. 16:10, where RV has 'sealskin', RVmg. 'porpoise-skin', NIV 'hides of sea cows', ASV 'sealskin', RSV 'leather'). LXX has *hyakinthos*, probably meaning 'skins with the colour of the hyacinth', the colour of which is difficult to ascertain because classical authors differ about it. The common opinion of modern scholars is that *taḥaš* means 'dolphin' or 'porpoise'. (*ANIMALS.)

The *taḥaš*-skin was precious in OT times as is indicated by Ezk. 16:10, where it is mentioned along with embroidered cloth, fine linen and silk. The skins are included among the gifts for the erecting of the sanctuary (Ex. 25:5); they were used with tanned rams' skins for the covering of the tent of the tabernacle and the ark (*e.g.* Nu. 4:6). F.C.F.

BAG. 1. Heb. *kîs* (similarly Arab.) is a bag for money, or shopkeeper's stone weights, the latter sometimes used deceitfully (Dt. 25:13; Mi. 6:11). In Is. 46:6; Pr. 1:14, AV uses bag, RSV purse.

2. Heb. *ḥārîṭ* (rare word; used in Arabic), 2 Ki. 5:23; Is. 3:22. In the latter passage, AV has crisping pins, RSV handbags, which may be a good approximation. Arabic Bible uses *kîs* in both contexts.

3. Heb. *yalqûṭ* (1 Sa. 17:40) is a shepherd's bag or wallet, synonymous with *k^{e}lî hārō'îm*, lit. bag of shepherds (1 Sa. 17:40, 49). *k^{e}lî* can mean article, utensil, vessel, sack, bag, according to context. *Cf.* Mt. 10:10 and parallels, where Gk. has *pēra*.

4. Heb. *ṣ^{e}rôr* sometimes means bag (Jb. 14:17; Pr. 7:20; Hg. 1:6), quite often bundle (*e.g.* Gn. 42:35; Ct. 1:13; metaphorically, 1 Sa. 25:29).

5. Gk. *ballantion* (Lk. 10:4; 12:33, *etc.*) is a money-bag or purse.

6. Gk. *glōssokomon*, Jn. 12:6, is a moneybox (RSV), rather than bag (AV). LXX uses it for the Temple tax chest of Joash (2 Ch. 24:8, 10–11), Aquila's Gk. version for the ark of the covenant (Ex. 37:1; 1 Sa. 6:19). The Mishnah uses the Gk. loan-word for bookcase or coffin. R.A.S.

BAHURIM. Modern Ras eṭ-Ṭmim, to the E of Mt Scopus, Jerusalem. Phaltiel, the husband of Michal, accompanied his wife as far as Bahurim when she went to David to become his wife (2 Sa. 3:14–16). Shimei, a man of Bahurim, met and cursed David as he reached this locality in his flight from Jerusalem before Absalom (2 Sa. 16:5), and David's soldiers hid in a well in Bahurim when pursued by Absalom's men (2 Sa. 17:17–21). R.J.W.

BALAAM. The name *Bilām* occurs 50 times in Nu. 22–24; it is mentioned also in Nu. 31:8, 16; Dt. 23:4–5; Jos. 13:22; 24:9–10; Ne. 13:2; Mi. 6:5. In the Greek of the NT the name is written *Balaam* (2 Pet. 2:15; Jude 11; Rev. 2:14). Whereas Albright, in his attempt to date the oracles of Balaam in the 12th century, tried to explain the name as derived from Amorite *Yabilammu*, 'the (divine) uncle brings', most scholars derive the name from Hebrew *bāla*, 'to swallow down', comparing Arabic *balam*, 'glutton'. Taking the last two consonants as representing *am*, 'nation', Rev. 2:6, 15 translated the name as *Nicolas, 'he that inflicts defeat on the nation'.

Balaam's father is called Beor, but against his identification with Bele the son of Beor, a king in Edom (Gn. 36:32), there are serious objections: the one is a seer, the other is a king; the one lives in Dinhaba, the other in Pethor (Akkad. *Pitru*, on the river Euphrates, 20 km S of Carchemish); the one is connected with Edom, the other with Moab and Midian.

The narrative in Nu. 22 is rather intricate. Balak, king of Moab, summons Balaam from the land of Amaw or Amae (*BASOR* 118, 1950, p. 15). The elders of Midian in vv. 4, 7 are perhaps mentioned to prelude on Nu. 31:16; they play no role in the further story. God first forbids and later on allows Balaam to follow the summons; still later God's angel opposes his going, and after the show-down between man, beast and angel, Balaam is again allowed to proceed on his voyage. It is a total misconception of ancient oriental story-telling to unravel the story into different strands. The author wants to heighten the suspense of his hearers, for whom the arrival of a soothsayer (Jos. 13:22), whose *curses might have a fatal effect on the future of Israel, represented a lethal danger. Such belief in the magical working of curses (*cf.* the Egyptian execration texts, *ANET*, pp. 328ff.) was widespread, but the faithful worshippers of the Lord believed that God could turn a human curse into a blessing; Ps. 109:28, *cf.* 2 Sa. 16:12; 1 Ch. 4:9–10; Pr. 26:2. According to Dt. 23:5 and Ne. 13:2 this was what happened with Balaam's curses, and the story in Nu. 22–24 illustrates Israel's belief that under the protection of the Lord no human curse or other form of magic is to be feared. It is therefore, also, that both Balak and Balaam are ridiculed, the latter especially in the episode with the ass.

The oracles of Balaam, embedded in a poetical form reminiscent of 2 Sa. 23:1–7, predict Israel's future greatness under David, who is meant by the star that should come forth out of Jacob (24:17). As there is a very strong relation between the story in prose and the oracles in poetry, it looks improbable that the oracles were older than the prose-narrative. The whole is best placed under David, who made Moab subject (2 Sa. 8:2). In that case Asshur in Nu. 24:22, 24 is to be understood not as the Assyrian empire, but as the Arabian tribe of Gn. 25:3; *cf.* Ps. 83:8.

Though Nu. 24:25 seems to indicate that Balaam returned to his town, we find him later (Nu. 31:8, 16) among the Midianites, whom he advised to lure the Israelites into the cult of Baal of Peor (*cf.* Nu. 25). For this reason he was killed, together with the kings of the Midianites, by Israel. In the NT his name is a symbol of avarice (2 Pet. 2:15; Jude 11) and of participation in pagan cult and immorality (Rev. 2:14).

A fragmentary Aramaic text written on wall-plaster at Tell Deir 'Alla in the Jordan valley about 700 BC relates another story about Balaam. Here he is involved with several gods and goddesses whose will he conveys to a disobedient audience. This text reveals the seer's wider fame.

BIBLIOGRAPHY. M. Burrows, *The Oracles of Jacob and Balaam*, 1938; O. Eissfeldt, 'Die Komposition der Bileam-Erzählung', *ZAW* 57, 1939, pp. 212–241; W. F. Albright, 'The Oracles of Balaam', *JBL* 63, 1944, pp. 207–233; A. H. van Zyl, *The Moabites*, 1960, pp. 10–12, 121–125; J. Hoftijzer and G. van der Koolj, *Aramaic Texts from Deir 'Alla*, 1976.

A.van S.

BALAK. The king of Moab who employed *Balaam to put a curse on the Israelites (Nu. 22–24). He was remembered as an example of the folly of seeking to thwart God's will (Jos. 24:9; Jdg. 11:25).

N.H.

BAMOTH, BAMOTH-BAAL. Bamoth (lit. 'heights') is mentioned as a stage in Israel's journey (Nu. 21:19–20). The important shrine on the height was known as Bamoth-baal (Nu. 22:41) and the settlement is later given among the cities of Reuben (Jos. 13:17). The exact location is unknown but the site was near the river Arnon and on a commanding position for, from it, *Balaam could 'see the full extent of the Israelite host'. *Baal is probably used here in the general sense of 'lord' relating to the Moabite god Chemosh. Balaam built his own altars on which to invoke God. The *Moabite Stone refers to another Moabite *'high place'. ('bamah').

J.T.W.

BAN. The OT ban (Heb. *ḥerem*) denotes in practice to 'ban, exterminate, consecrate to God'. Thus people devoted to idolatry as the *Canaanites (Ex. 23:31; 34:13; Dt. 7:2; 20:10–17) or places (Jericho, Jos. 6:17–21; *cf.* Dt. 2:34f.; Jos. 11:14) were to be destroyed. The ban was extended to an Israelite household (Achan, Jos. 7:24–26; *cf.* Dt. 20:10ff.) and threatened against Israel for her idolatry (Dt. 8:19; Jos. 23:15). The ban involves an aspect of taboo forbidding contact with an abomination (Dt. 7:26) or holy thing (Lv. 27:28). In Israel it was primarily religious, objects being devoted to the Lord and his service (Nu. 18:14).

Similar impositions of taboo on spoils of war to be devoted to the deity are known from extra-biblical sources from *Mari and the *Moabite Stone. The practice seems to have been neglected after the monarchy, though the prophets called for it (1 Sa. 15:9; 1 Ki. 20:31, 42; Mi. 4:13; Is. 34:5). The English 'ban' is used only in Ezr. 10:8 (AV 'separate') where the idea of excommunication or banishment is introduced. Thus Christians were banned from synagogues (Jn. 9:22; 12:42; 16:2; *cf.* Acts 28:16–22). The NT instances reinforce the view that such a ban or exclusion was for the ultimate welfare of the banned person also (1 Cor. 5:1–5).

BIBLIOGRAPHY. A. Malamat, 'The Ban in Mari and the Bible', *Biblical Essays* (South Africa), 1966, pp. 40–49.

D.J.W.

BANK, BANKER. There was no bank in Israel in the sense of an establishment for the custody of private money or the granting of commercial credit. For safe keeping a private person would either bury his valuables (Jos. 7:21) or deposit them with a neighbour (Ex. 22:7). Commerce remained largely a royal monopoly (2 Sa. 5:11; 1 Ki. 10:14–29; *cf.* 2 Ch. 20:35ff.). The palace and the Temple were the repositories of the national wealth (1 Ki. 14:26); later private property also was deposited for safe keeping in temples (2 Macc. 3:6, 10ff.). A banking system existed in Babylonia in 2000 BC, but the Jews did not use it until the Exile. The money-changers in Mt. 21:12; Mk. 11:15; Jn. 2:14–15 converted Roman money into orthodox coinage for the Temple half-shekel (Mt. 17:24). Mt. 25:27 (Lk. 19:23) refers to a money-lender.

A.E.W.

BANNER. 1. Heb. *deḡel*, meaning 'standard' or 'flag', is rendered 'banner' 4 times and 'standard' 14 times in RSV. In the wilderness each tribe was marked by its own banner (Nu. 1:52; 2:2–3, *etc.*). In Ps. 20:5 the word is used for a flag of battle. In the Song of Solomon it is used figuratively by the Shulammite to denote the distinguished appearance of her beloved (Ct. 5:10, AVmg.), and by him in referring to her overpowering beauty (Ct. 6:4, 10; *cf.* 2:4).

2. Heb. *nēs*, meaning 'ensign', is often rendered 'banner' in RSV. It is usually employed to designate a rallying-standard. In Is. 11:12 the Messiah is said to raise up such a standard, while in v. 10 he is himself said to be one. Perhaps this

BALADAN
See Merodach-baladan, Part 2.

BALANCES
See Weights and measures, Part 3.

BALDNESS
See Hair, Part 2.

BALM
See Herbs, Part 2.

BALSAM
See Trees (Poplar), Part 3.

BAMAH
See Bamoth, Part 1.

BAND
See Army, Part 1.

BANK
See Fortification and siegecraft, Part 1.

Egyptian soldiers carrying branches, bone-sticks, axes and a semi-circular fan, from the temple of Queen Hatshepsut, Deir-el-Bahri, Thebes. c. 1480 BC. (SMB)

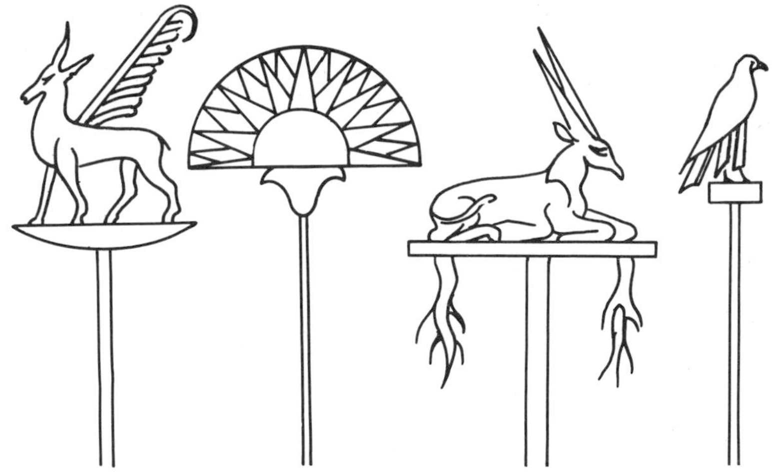

Four banners, three of them Egyptian, including a feather fan, sometimes used as a standard. Second from the right is an Assyrian standard. 9th–8th cent. BC.

Assyrian military standard bearing the figure of Ashur or Ninurta as the god of war.

latter reference is intended to be a link with 'The Lord is my banner' (Jehovah-nissi, AV) in Ex. 17:15. The RSV is probably correct in removing references to a banner in Is. 10:18 and 59:19. G.W.G.

BANQUET. The words translated 'banquet' in AV (variously in RSV, as 'dinner', 'banquet(ing)', '(to) feast', 'carousing') are *mišteh* (*e.g.* Est. 5:4ff.; Dn. 5:10), *šāṯâ* (Est. 7:1), *yayin* (Ct. 2:4) and *potos* (1 Pet. 4:3). These terms refer primarily to wine-drinking; in the 1 Pet. reference *potos* means precisely this. In the OT the 'banquet' motif is used to represent the happiness of the coming Messianic kingdom (so Is. 25:6; *cf.* Mt. 8:11; Lk. 14:15ff.). Similarly, the 'common meal' of the Qumran sectarians seems to have been a ritual anticipation of the Messianic banquet (*cf.* 1QS 2). Such a banquet is also alluded to in the NT at the Last Supper, where Jesus tells the disciples that the meal which they were sharing was a foretaste of the true Messianic glory to come, made possible by his death (Mt. 26:27–29; *cf.* Lk. 22:29f.; Rev. 3:20; 19:9). S.S.S.

BAPTISM.

I. The baptism of John

There have been various suggestions as to the origins of Christian baptism—Jewish ceremonial washings, Qumran purification rites, proselyte baptism, the baptism of John. The last of these, the ritual act which gave John the Baptist his nickname, is the most likely candidate: as John is the forerunner of Jesus, so his baptism is the forerunner of Christian baptism. A direct link is established through Jesus' own baptism by John; some of Jesus' earliest disciples had almost certainly been baptized by John (Jn. 1:35–42); Jesus, or some of his disciples, seems to have continued John's practice at the beginning of Jesus' own ministry (Jn. 3:22f., 26; but 4:1f.); and in the cases of the disciples at Pentecost and of Apollos, it was evidently not thought necessary to supplement their Johannine baptism by baptism in the name of Jesus (Acts 2; 18:24–28). Most likely then it was this earlier practice which was resumed from Pentecost onwards, as ratified by the risen Christ and in his name (Mt. 28:19; Acts 2:38; *etc.*). John's baptism itself is probably best understood as an adaptation of Jewish ritual washings, with some influence from Qumran in particular.

John's baptism was primarily a baptism of *repentance* (Mt. 3:11; Mk. 1:4; Lk. 3:3; Acts 13:24; 19:4). By accepting baptism at John's hands the baptisands were expressing their repentance (Mt. 3:6; Mk. 1:5) and their desire for forgiveness.

It was also *a preparatory and symbolical act*: it prepared the baptisand for the ministry of the Coming One; and it symbolized the judgment he would bring. In John's vivid language that judgment would be like a pruning or a winnowing (Mt. 3:10, 12; Lk. 3:9,

King Ashurbanipal and his queen feasting in a garden. Relief from his palace at Nineveh. c. 640 BC. (RS)

17), or like a baptism in Spirit and fire (Mt. 3:11; Lk. 3:16). It is most unlikely that the Baptist was referring here to another ritual act much like his own. Rather he was probably drawing on the powerful imagery of such passages as Is. 4:4; 30:27f.; 43:2; Dn. 7:10 (possibly again under the influence of Qumran—*cf.* 1QS 4. 21; 1QH 3. 29ff.). If divine judgment could be likened to a stream of God's fiery breath (= Spirit—same word in Hebrew and Greek), then the Coming One's ministry of judgment could appropriately be likened to an immersion in that stream. Those who submitted themselves to an act symbolizing that judgment, as an expression of their repentance in face of that judgment, would find it a judgment that purified and cleansed. Those who refused John's baptism and refused to repent would experience the Coming One's 'baptism' in all its fierceness and, like the barren trees and the chaff, would be burnt up by it (Mt. 3:10–12).

II. Jesus' baptism by John

That Jesus should have undergone a baptism of repentance caused early Christians some difficulty (*cf.* Mt. 3:14f.; Jerome, *contra Pelag.* 3. 2). At the very least it must have been for Jesus an expression of his dedication to God's will and to ministry, perhaps too an expression of his whole-hearted identification with his people before God.

After his baptism the *Spirit* came upon Jesus (Mt. 3:16; Mk. 1:10; Lk. 3:21f.). Many would see here the archetype of Christian baptism—baptism in water and Spirit. But while the Evangelists link the descent of the Spirit closely with Jesus' baptism (immediately after his baptism), they do not equate the two or tie them together under the single term 'baptism'. Nor indeed does any NT writer speak of Jesus' baptism as the pattern of Christian baptism. In each case the Evangelist focuses the readers' attention on the anointing of the Spirit and on the heavenly voice (Jn. 1:32f. does not even mention Jesus' baptism; *cf.* Acts 10:37f.; 2 Cor. 1:21—God establishes us in Christ and has christed/anointed us; 1 Jn. 2:20, 27).

Why Jesus did not continue with John's baptism is not clear. Perhaps because as a symbol of judgment it was less appropriate to the emphasis of Jesus' ministry as one of fulfilment and eschatological blessing, of judgment delayed rather than of judgment itself (*cf.*, *e.g.*, Mt. 11:2–7; Mk. 1:15; Lk. 4:16–21; 13:6–9). The baptism of fiery judgment, the cup of divine wrath, was something which he himself would have to endure (on behalf of others) to the death (Mk. 10:38; 14:24, 36; Lk. 12:49f.).

III. Baptism in earliest Christianity

Whatever its precise background, baptism has been an integral part of Christianity from the first. The earliest converts were baptized (Acts 2:38, 41). Paul, converted within 2 or 3 years of the resurrection, takes it for granted that baptism marks the beginning of the Christian life (see below, **IV**). And we know of no Christian in the NT who had not been baptized, either by John or in the name of Jesus.

As with John's baptism, so earliest Christian baptism was an expression of *repentance and faith* (Acts 2:38, 41; 8:12f.; 16:14f., 33f.; 18:8; 19:2f.; *cf.* Heb. 6:1f.). Many would say that forgiveness of sins was thought of as mediated through baptism from the first (Acts 2:38; 10:43; 22:16; 26:18). Others maintain that earliest Christian baptism was seen more as the baptisand's 'appeal to God for a clear conscience' (1 Pet. 3:21), with the gift of the Spirit recognized as God's act of acceptance and renewal (particularly Acts 10:43–45; 11:14f.; 15:8f.). Certainly it was a decisive step of commitment for the would-be Christian which must often have resulted in his being ostracized and even persecuted by his former fellows.

Unlike John's baptism, Christian baptism was from the first administered '*in the name of Jesus*' (Acts 2:38; 8:16; 10:48; 19:5). This phrase probably indicates either that the one who baptized saw himself acting as a representative of the exalted Jesus (*cf.* particularly 3:6, 16 and 4:10 with 9:34), or that the baptisand saw his baptism as his act of commitment to discipleship of Jesus (*cf.* 1 Cor. 1:12–16 and below, **IV**). It is quite likely that the phrase was understood to embrace both aspects.

It is clear then that, from the first, baptism in the name of Jesus functioned as the *rite of entry* or initiation into the new sect of those who called upon the name of Jesus (Acts 2:21, 41; 22:16; *cf.* Rom. 10:10–14; 1 Cor. 1:2). Sometimes supplemented by laying on of hands, it must also have expressed vividly the baptisand's acceptance by the community of those who like him believed in Jesus (Acts 8:14–17; 10:47f.; 19:6; Heb. 6:2).

The relation between baptism and *the gift of the Spirit* in Acts is greatly disputed. Some argue that the Spirit was given (*a*) through baptism, or (*b*) through the laying on of hands, or (*c*) through both, with the two ritual acts seen as integral parts of a single sacramental whole. Each can claim possible support at some point within Acts: (*a*) 2:38; (*b*) 8:17; *cf.* 9:17; (*c*) 19:6. But without stronger support it is very difficult to maintain that there was a consistent view on this subject in earliest Christianity or that Luke was trying to promote a particular view. It is more probable that for Luke and the first Christians the really crucial factor in demonstrating the reality of a person's commitment to and acceptance by God was the gift of the Spirit; the Spirit's presence being readily discernible by the effects of his coming on the recipient (Acts 1:5; 2:4; 2:38; 4:31; 8:17f.; 10:44–46; 11:15–17; 19:2). In this divine-human encounter, baptism (and sometimes laying on of hands) had an important role, particularly at least as the expression of repentance and commitment, as the sign of entering into discipleship of Jesus and into the company of his disciples, and usually as the context of the divine-human encounter in which the Spirit was given and received. A 'higher' view of baptism has disturbingly little to build on.

IV. Baptism in the Pauline Letters

The only certain references to baptism in Paul are Rom. 6:4; 1 Cor. 1:13–17; 15:29; Eph. 4:5; and Col. 2:12. The clearest of these is 1 Cor. 1:13–17, where Paul obviously takes it for granted that baptism was performed 'in (*eis*) the name of Jesus'. Here he probably uses a formula familiar in accountancy of the time, where 'in/into the name of' meant 'to the account of'. That is, baptism was seen as a deed of transfer, an act whereby the baptisand handed himself over to be the property or disciple of the one named. The problem at Corinth was that too many were behaving as though they had become disciples of Paul or Cephas or Apollos, that is, as though they had been baptized in their names rather than in the name of Jesus.

Of the other references, Eph. 4:5 confirms that baptism was one of the foundation-stones of Christian community. And 1 Cor. 15:29 probably refers to a practice of vicarious baptism, whereby a Christian would undergo baptism in place of someone already dead (Paul does not indicate whether he approves or disapproves).

Most intriguing are Rom. 6:4 and Col. 2:12, both of which speak of baptism as a means of or instrument to being buried with Christ, or as the context in which the would-be Christian was buried with Christ. Paul is here clearly evoking the powerful symbolism of baptism (probably by immersion) as a burying (out of sight) of the old life. In Rom. 6:4 he does not identify emerging from the water as a symbol of resurrection—resurrection with Christ is still something future (6:5). He may make this association in Col. 2:12, since there resurrection with Christ is seen as something past (Col. 3:1), but the Greek of 2:12 does not require it. We should also recall that Paul sees dying with Christ not as a single event of the past; identification with Christ in his sufferings and death is a life-long process (Rom. 6:5; 8:17; 2 Cor. 1:5; 4:10; Gal. 2:20; 6:14; Phil. 3:10). So it may be that Paul thought of baptism as the continuing symbol of this aspect of Christian existence, while the Spirit denoted the new life in Christ (Rom. 8:2, 6, 10f., 13; 1 Cor. 15:45; 2 Cor. 3:3, 6; Gal. 5:25; 6:8).

Many other references to baptism in the Pauline Epistles have been proposed. Most would hold that the phrase 'baptized into Christ' refers directly to baptism (Rom. 6:3; 1 Cor. 10:2; 12:13; Gal. 3:27). A strongly held view here is that 'into Christ' is an abbreviation of 'in/into the name of Christ'. If so then Paul understood the baptismal act to be rich in sacramental meaning and efficacy. Others argue that 'baptized into Christ' is an abbreviation instead for 'baptized in Spirit into Christ' (as explicitly in 1 Cor. 12:13). In this case Paul would be echoing the metaphor which began with John the Baptist, whereby the phrase does not denote the ritual act but that union with Christ (in his death) which baptism (by immersion) so vividly symbolizes (*cf.* Mk. 10:38; Lk. 12:50).

Other passages strongly urged as references to baptism are the washing language of 1 Cor. 6:11; Eph. 5:26; and Tit. 3:5, and the seal of the Spirit talk of 2 Cor. 1:22 and Eph. 1:13; 4:30. If Paul's view of baptism was strongly sacramental, then the allusion to baptism would be convincing, all the more so if Paul was influenced by the mystery cults at this point. On the other hand, 1 Cor. 1:13–17 and 10:1–12 show Paul resisting this kind of sacramentalism. Moreover, against those who insist that Christians should be circumcised he sets not baptism (as a more effective Christian alternative) but their faith and the reality of the Spirit they received through faith (Gal. 3:1–4:7; Phil. 3:3). So Paul may well have understood the washing as directly spiritual and not in sacramental terms (*cf.* Acts 15:9; Tit. 2:14; Heb. 9:14; 10:22; 1 Jn. 1:7, 9). And when we recall the tangible character of the Spirit's presence in earliest Christianity it becomes unnecessary to refer 'the seal of the Spirit' to anything other than the gift of the Spirit itself.

V. Baptism in the Johannine Writings

It is difficult to assess John's views on baptism, since the rich symbolism of the Gospel is open to different interpretations. Some would see sacramental allusions throughout (in every reference to 'water'). Others maintain that John is anti-sacramentalist (*e.g.* 6:63 as qualifying any allusion to the Lord's Supper in 6:51–58).

In Jn. 3:5 ('born of water and Spirit'—the most likely reference to baptism) the beginning of new life in Christ is thought of either as emerging from baptism in water and the gift/power of the Spirit; or as emerging from the cleansing, renewing power of the Spirit (*cf.* Is. 44:3–5; Ezk. 36:25–27); or possibly as requiring birth from the Spirit (3:3, 6–8) in addition to natural birth (3:4). It is clear however that the dominant thought is the work of the Spirit. And in view of the contrast between baptism in water and baptism in Spirit in 1:33 we should hesitate to substitute 'baptized in' for 'born from' in 3:5. There is nothing to suggest that an equation between baptism and new birth existed for any NT writer (*cf.* Jas. 1:18; 1 Pet. 1:3, 23; 1 Jn. 3:9).

Elsewhere in John 'water' probably symbolizes either the Holy Spirit given by Jesus (4:10–14; 7:37–39; 19:34—the only other plausible allusion to baptism), or the old age in contrast to the new (1:26, 31, 33; 2:6ff.; 3:23–36; 5:2–9). In 1 Jn. 5:6–8 'water' refers to Jesus' own baptism as a continuing witness to the reality of Jesus' incarnation.

VI. Infant baptism

Was *infant baptism* practised within 1st-century Christianity? There are no direct references to infant baptism in the NT, but the possibility of there being children within the households baptized in Acts 16:15, 33; 18:8; and 1 Cor. 1:16 cannot be finally excluded. That infants of believers are part of the household of faith can readily be maintained on the basis of 1 Cor. 7:14, not to mention Mk. 10:13–16. On the other hand, in Gal. 3 Paul specifically argues that membership of Christ does not derive from physical descent or depend on a ritual act (circumcision), but comes through faith and is dependent on nothing other than faith and on the gift of the Spirit received through faith.

In short, the more baptism is seen as the expression of the baptisand's faith, the less easy is it to hold to infant baptism. Whereas the more baptism is seen as the expression of divine grace, the easier is it to argue for infant baptism. Either way, Christians should beware of overvaluing baptism in the way that the Judaizers overvalued circumcision. (*Burial, *Circumcision, *Faith, *Judgment, *Laying on of Hands, *Repentance, *Sacrament, *Spirit, *Water.)

Bibliography. K. Aland, *Did the Early Church Baptize Infants?*, 1963; J. Baillie, *Baptism and Conversion*, 1964; K. Barth, *Church Dogmatics*, IV/4, 1970; G. R. Beasley-Murray, *Baptism in the New Testament*, 1962; *Baptism Today and Tomorrow*, 1966; C. Buchanan, *A Case for Infant Baptism*, 1973; J. D. G. Dunn, *Baptism in the Holy Spirit*, 1970; A. George, *et al.*, *Baptism in the New Testament*, 1964; J. Jeremias, *Infant Baptism in the First Four Centuries*, 1960; *The Origins of Infant Baptism*, 1963; G. W. H. Lampe, *The Seal of the Spirit*, 1967; J. Murray, *Christian Baptism*, 1962; J. K. Parratt, 'Holy Spirit and Baptism', *ExpT* 82, 1970–71, pp. 231–235, 266–271; A. Schmemann, *Of Water and the Spirit*, 1976; R. Schnackenburg, *Baptism in the Thought of St Paul*, 1964; G. Wagner, *Pauline Baptism and the Pagan Mysteries*, 1967; G. Wainwright, *Christian Initiation*, 1969; G. R. Beasley-Murray, R. T. Beckwith, in

NIDNTT 1, pp. 143–161.

J.D.G.D.

BARABBAS. A bandit (Jn. 18:40), arrested for homicidal political terrorism (Mk. 15:7; Lk. 23:18f.). Mark's language could indicate a well-known incident, and the epithet 'notable' (Mt. 27:16, AV) some reputation as a species of hero. The priests, possibly taking up an initial demand from his supporters (*cf.* Mk. 15:8), engineered a movement for his release to counter Pilate's intended offer of that of Jesus (Mt. 27:20; Mk. 15:11) and Barabbas became an exemplification of the effects of substitutionary atonement.

The name is a patronymic ('son of Abba'). It occurs as 'Jesus Barabbas' (*cf.* 'Simon Barjonah') in some authorities at Mt. 27:16f., and Origen *in loc.* notes this reading as ancient. It adds pungency to Pilate's offer. 'Jesus Barabbas or Jesus Christ?', but, however attractive, this must remain uncertain.

The privilege of the release of a prisoner at Passover time is independently attested by Mark and John, but remains obscure. Blinzler associates it with Mishnah *Pesaḥim* 8. 6, which ordains that the Passover lamb may be offered 'for one whom they have promised to bring out of prison'.

BIBLIOGRAPHY. Deissmann in G. K. A. Bell and A. Deissmann, *Mysterium Christi*, pp. 12ff. (for the text: *contra*, *cf.* M. J. Lagrange, *S. Matthieu*, pp. 520ff.); H. A. Rigg, *JBL* 64, 1945, pp. 417ff. (a romance with footnotes); C. E. B. Cranfield, *St Mark*, pp. 449ff. (a sensitive reading of the incident); J. Blinzler, *The Trial of Jesus*, 1959, pp. 218ff.; F. F. Bruce, *New Testament History*, 1971, pp. 203ff.

A.F.W.

BARAK (Heb. *bārāq*, 'lightning'; *cf.* Carthaginian *Barca*). In Jdg. 4:6ff. the son of Abinoam, from Kedesh in Naphtali, summoned by the prophetess *Deborah to muster the tribes of Israel and lead them to battle against *Sisera, commander-in-chief of the confederate Canaanite forces. He consented to act on condition that Deborah accompanied him, for which reason he was told that not he, but a woman, would have the honour of despatching Sisera. The details of his victory, when a sudden downpour flooded the river *Kishon and immobilized Sisera's chariotry, are graphically depicted in the Song of Deborah (Jdg. 5:19–22). In Heb. 11:32 Barak is listed among the 'elders' whose faith is attested in the sacred record. In 1 Sa. 12:11 'Bedan' should perhaps be emended to 'Barak', following LXX and Syr. (so RSV, NEB).

F.F.B.

BARBARIAN. A term applied by the Greeks to all non-Greek-speaking peoples. It was not originally, or necessarily, pejorative. Luke actually praises the 'barbarians' of *Malta for their exceptional kindness (Acts 28:2–4). Inscriptions show that a Phoenician dialect was spoken on Malta. Perhaps Luke recalls the first frustration of failure to communicate in the cosmopolitan Latin and Greek. In 1 Cor. 14:11 the use of uninterpreted tongues is seen ironically as creating linguistic barriers. 'Greeks and barbarians' together (Rom. 1:14) comprise all kinds of men without discrimination (*cf.* Col. 3:11).

C.J.H.

BAR-JESUS ('son of Joshua' or 'son of Ishvah'). In Acts 13:6ff. a magician and false prophet, attached to the court of Sergius Paulus, proconsul of Cyprus. He is given the alternative name Elymas in v. 8, possibly from a Semitic root meaning 'sage', 'wise man'. In the Western Text his names appear as Bariesouan and Hetoimas. He tried to dissuade Sergius Paulus from paying attention to Paul and Barnabas, but came off worse in an encounter with Paul. His temporary blinding may have been intended to have the same salutary effect as Paul's similar experience on the Damascus road.

F.F.B.

BARN. The AV rendering of 4 Heb. words, each of them used only once. They are: **1.** *gōren*, 'an open threshing-floor' (Jb. 39:12). RV renders 'threshing-floor' (*AGRICULTURE). **2.** *m^e^gūrâ*, 'a granary' (Hg. 2:19). **3.** *'āṣām*, 'a storehouse' (Pr. 3:10). **4.** *mamm^e^gōrâ*, 'a repository' (Joel 1:17). Often a dry cistern in the ground was used, covered with a thick layer of earth. Grain could keep for years under such conditions. (*STORE-CITIES.)

In the NT, Gk. *apothēkē*, 'a place for putting away', is used literally (Mt. 6:26; Lk. 12:18, 24), and metaphorically to signify heaven (Mt. 13:30).

J.D.D.

BARNABAS. The cognomen of Joseph, a foremost early missionary. Luke (Acts 4:36) interprets 'son of *paraklēsis*', 'one who encourages, or exhorts' (*cf.* 'son of peace' in Lk. 10:6). *Nabas* may reflect Aramaic *n^e^waḥâ*, 'pacification', 'consolation' (the abnormal Greek transcription being eased by the contemporary soft pronunciation of *b*), or some derivative of the root *nb'*, 'to prophesy'. Strictly, this would be 'son of a prophet' or 'of prophecy', but exhortation was supremely a prophetic function (Acts 15:32; 1 Cor. 14:3), and Luke is concerned, not to provide a scientific etymology, but to indicate the man's character. We find him engaged in *paraklēsis* in Acts 11:23. Deissmann equates the name with *Barnebous* (Aramaic *Barn^e^bō*, 'son of Nebo') found in Syrian inscriptions; but Luke states that the apostles gave it, and they would hardly confer a name redolent of a pagan deity.

He came from a Jewish–Cypriot priestly family, but the Jerusalemite John Mark was his cousin (Col. 4:10), and he himself an early member of the Jerusalem church, selling his property (in Cyprus?) for the common good (Acts 4:36ff.). Clement of Alexandria calls him one of the Seventy (*Hypot.* 7; *Stromateis* 2. 20. 116). The Western Text of Acts 1:23 confounds him with Joseph-Barsabas in the apostolic election; but later Luke (Acts 14:4, 14) and Paul (1 Cor. 9:6, in context) regard him as an *apostle.

'A good man,' says Luke, 'full of the Holy Spirit and of faith' (Acts 11:24), and on at least four occasions his warm-heartedness and spiritual insight, and the apparently universal respect for him, had momentous results.

a. When the converted Saul arrived in Jerusalem only to discover that the Christians thought him a spy, it was Barnabas who introduced him to the 'pillar' apostles and convinced them of his conversion and sincerity (Acts 9:27; *cf.* Gal. 1:18).

b. It was Barnabas who represented the apostles at Antioch when, for the first time, Gentiles had been evangelized in significant numbers, and where fellow-Cypriots had been prominent (Acts 11:19ff.). He saw the movement as a work of God—and as a fitting sphere for the forgotten Saul, whom he brought to share his labours. On their visiting Jerusalem

BARACHIAH
See Zechariah, Part 3.

BARBARY DOVE
See Animals, Part 1.

BARREL
See Vessels, Part 3.

with famine-relief, their call to Gentile missionary work was recognized (Gal. 2:9; *CHRONOLOGY OF THE NEW TESTAMENT). But Barnabas was not the man to withstand Peter to his face when he succumbed to Judaizing pressure: 'even Barnabas' temporarily broke table-fellowship with the Antiochene Gentiles (Gal. 2:13).

c. Barnabas' third great contribution, however, showed him committed to full acceptance of Gentiles on faith in Christ (*cf.* Acts 13:46). The journey with Paul (Acts 13–14), beginning in his own Cyprus, resulted in a chain of predominantly Gentile churches far into Asia Minor and a surging Jewish opposition.

For the church and for Barnabas it was a milestone. Hitherto he had been leader, Paul his protégé. Luke's consistent order up to the departure from Cyprus is 'Barnabas and Saul'. Thereafter he usually says, 'Paul and Barnabas'. (Acts 13:43, 46, 50; 15:2, twice, 22, 35. The order in 14:14 is probably due to the order of the deities.) This doubtless reflects the progress of events.

d. But Barnabas had another crucial task. Back at Antioch, the circumcision question became so acute that he and Paul were appointed to bring the matter before the Jerusalem Council. Their policy was triumphantly vindicated (Acts 15:1–29). Significantly, Barnabas stands before Paul both in the account of the proceedings (v. 12) and in the Council's letter (v. 25, contrast 22); probably the words of the original apostolic representative in Antioch carried greater weight with many in the Council. Barnabas insisted on including Mark, who had previously deserted them, on a proposed second journey. Paul refused, and the itinerary was divided, Barnabas taking Cyprus (Acts 15:36–40). Paul's later testimonies to Mark (*e.g.* 2 Tim. 4:11) may mean that the latter greatly profited from working under his cousin. The close partnership was broken, but not the friendship. 'Whenever Paul mentions Barnabas, his words imply sympathy and respect' (Lightfoot on Gal. 2:13). In principles and practice they were identical, and we shall never know how much Paul owed to Barnabas. When 1 Corinthians was written, Barnabas was still alive, and, like Paul and unlike most of their colleagues, supporting himself without drawing on the churches (1 Cor. 9:6). After this, we hear only insubstantial traditions associating him with Rome and Alexandria.

His name was early attached to an anonymous letter of Alexandrian provenance, but there is nothing else to connect it with him (*PATRISTIC LITERATURE). The Epistle to the Hebrews has often been ascribed to him, at least from Tertullian's time (Tert., *De pudicitia* 20; *cf.* Zahn, *INT*, 2, pp. 301ff.), and 1 Peter by A. C. McGiffert (*Christianity in the Apostolic Age*, 1897, pp. 593ff.). There is a late Cypriot martyrology (see James, *ANT*, p. 470). The *Gospel of Barnabas* (ed. L. Ragg, 1907) is a medieval work in Muslim interest.

BIBLIOGRAPHY. A. Klostermann, *Probleme im Aposteltexte neu erörtert*, 1883; A. Deissmann, *Bible Studies*, pp. 307ff.; H. J. Cadbury in *Amicitiae Corolla* (Rendel Harris Festschrift), 1933, pp. 45ff.; *BC*, 4; F. F. Bruce, *Acts, passim.* A.F.W.

BARRENNESS. To be a wife without bearing children has always been regarded in the East, not only as a matter of regret, but as a reproach which could lead to divorce. This is the cause of Sarah's despairing laughter (Gn. 18:12), Hannah's silent prayer (1 Sa. 1:10ff.), Rachel's passionate alternative of children or death (Gn. 30:1) and Elizabeth's cry that God had taken away her reproach (Lk. 1:25). The awfulness of the coming judgment on Jerusalem is emphasized by the incredible statement, 'Blessed are the barren . . .' (Lk. 23:29). It was believed that the gift of children or the withholding of them indicated God's blessing or curse (Ex. 23:26; Dt. 7:14), as also did the barrenness or fruitfulness of the land (Ps. 107:33–34). J.W.M.

BARTHOLOMEW (Gk. *bartholomaios*, 'son of Talmai' or, in Graeco-Roman times, 'son of Ptolemy'). The bearer of this patronymic appears in each list of the Twelve (Mt. 10:3; Mk. 3:18; Lk. 6:14; Acts 1:13), but is otherwise unmentioned in NT. His association in all lists but the last with Philip has suggested to many readers from the 9th century onwards that he may be identical with Philip's friend *Nathanael of Cana (Jn. 1:45ff.; *cf.* 21:2); on this certainty is unattainable. F.F.B.

BARTIMAEUS. A blind beggar who was healed by Jesus (Mk. 10:46–52). The name means 'Son of Timaeus' and may have been recorded by Mark because he was a well-known figure in the early church. The incident took place on Jesus' last journey to Jerusalem as he left Jericho, and is found in the other Synoptic Gospels, though with a number of differences. In Mt. 20:29–34 there are two blind men, while in Lk. 18:35–43 the healing takes place as Jesus is approaching Jericho. The story has been variously reconstructed, and it may be that Matthew and Mark refer to Old Jericho and Luke to New Jericho, which was to the S of it. The incident is remarkable for the persistence of Bartimaeus' faith in Jesus as the Messiah. R.E.N.

BARUCH (Heb. *bārûḵ*, 'blessed'). **1.** The son of Neriah (Je. 36:4), and brother of Seraiah, quartermaster to King Zedekiah (Je. 51:59). He was a faithful attendant on the prophet Jeremiah (36:10), wrote his master's prophecies (36:4, 32) and read them to the people (vv. 14–15). He acted as witness to the purchase by the imprisoned prophet of his family estate at Anathoth (Je. 32). Following the sack of Jerusalem, he is said to have resided with Jeremiah at Masphatha (Mizpah, Josephus, *Ant.* 10. 158) but after the murder of Gedaliah was arrested for influencing Jeremiah's departure (43:3). He was taken with Jeremiah to Egypt (43:6), where according to one tradition he and Jeremiah died (Jerome on Is. 30:6). Josephus, however, implies that they were both carried captive to Babylon after Nebuchadrezzar had invaded Egypt in 583 BC (*Ant.* 10. 182). Josephus also says that Baruch was of noble family (as Baruch 1:1). His association with Jeremiah resulted in his name being given to a number of apocryphal books, notably *The Apocalypse of Baruch*, a work probably of Heb. or Aram. origin of which Gk. (2nd century AD) and Syr. versions survive; *The Book of Baruch*, a deutero-canonical book found in LXX between Jeremiah and Lamentations, of which various VSS (Lat. and Gnostic) are known; and *The Rest of the Works of Baruch.* Jewish tradition (*Mid. Rabba* on Ct. 5:5) speaks of Baruch as Ezra's teacher.

2. A priest, son of Zabbai, who

assisted Nehemiah in rebuilding work (Ne. 3:20) and as witness to a covenant (10:6).

3. Son of Col-hozeh, a Judaean, father of Maaseiah (Ne. 11:5).

D.J.W.

Clay bulla (enlarged 3 ×), bearing the impression of the inscribed seal of 'Berechiah (Baruch), son of Neriah the scribe' (lbrkyhw bn nryhw hspr). *Late 7th cent.* BC. (NA)

BARZILLAI ('Man of iron'). **1.** 'The Gileadite of Rogelim' (2 Sa. 17:27, *etc.*), a faithful follower of David. **2.** A relation of the above by marriage who took the family name (Ezr. 2:61), and is called 'Jaddus' in 1 Esdras 5:38. **3.** 'The Meholathite', whose son Adriel married Saul's daughter Merab (1 Sa. 18:19; 2 Sa. 21:8; LXX and two Heb. MSS), or Michal (2 Sa. 21:8, RSVmg., *MT*).

G.W.G.

BASEMATH (Bashemath, AV). Probably from Semitic stem *bsm*, 'fragrant'. **1.** According to Gn. 26:34, Esau married Basemath, the daughter of Elon, the Hittite. According to Gn. 36:3, he was married to a certain Basemath who was the daughter of Ishmael and the sister of Nebaioth. *Cf.* Gn. 28:9, where she is called Mahalath, and Gn. 36:2, where Elon's daughter is called Adah. It is possible that both Mahalath and Adah were given the nickname Basemath, 'fragrant', or else it is a scribal error (*cf.* some MSS of the LXX). **2.** Basemath, daughter of Solomon, married Ahimaaz of Naphtali (1 Ki. 4:15).

BIBLIOGRAPHY. C-F. Jean, *Dictionnaire des Inscriptions Sémitiques de l'Ouest*, 1954.

F.C.F.

BASHAN. A region E of Jordan lying to the N of Gilead, from which it was divided by the river Yarmuk. Its fertility was famous; see Ps. 22:12; Ezk. 39:18; Am. 4:1; and Is. 2:13; Je. 50:19; Ezk. 27:5–6. The name, nearly always written with the article (*habbāšān*), had varying connotations. In the wide sense it was counted as extending N to Mt Hermon and E to *Salecah; and in the narrower sense it comprised roughly the area called today en-Nuqra. It included the cities of *Ashtaroth, *Golan and *Edrei, and the regions of *Argob and *Havvoth-jair. At the time of the conquest Bashan was under the rule of Og, who had his capital at Ashtaroth. He was defeated by the Israelites at Edrei (Dt. 1:4; 3:1–3) and the territory fell to the lot of Manasseh. It formed part of the dominions of David and Solomon, falling within the sixth administrative district of the latter (1 Ki. 4:13). It was lost during the Syrian wars, but was regained by Jeroboam II (2 Ki. 14:25), only to be taken by Tiglath-pileser III (2 Ki. 15:29), after which it formed part of the successive Assyrian, Babylonian and Persian empires. Under the Persians it roughly coincided with the district of Qarnaim, and in the Greek period with that of Batanaea.

BIBLIOGRAPHY. G. A. Smith, *The Historical Geography of the Holy Land* [11], 1904, pp. 542, 548–553, 575ff.; F. M. Abel, *Géographie de la Palestine*, 1, 1933, pp. 274f.

T.C.M.

BASKET. The following Heb. words are translated 'basket'.
1. *dûḏ*, a round basket large enough to hold a human head (2 Ki. 10:7), but normally used for carrying figs, *etc.* (Ps. 81:6; Je. 24:1–2).
2. *ṭene'* (loan-word from Egyp.

BASILISK
See Animals, Part 1.

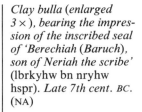

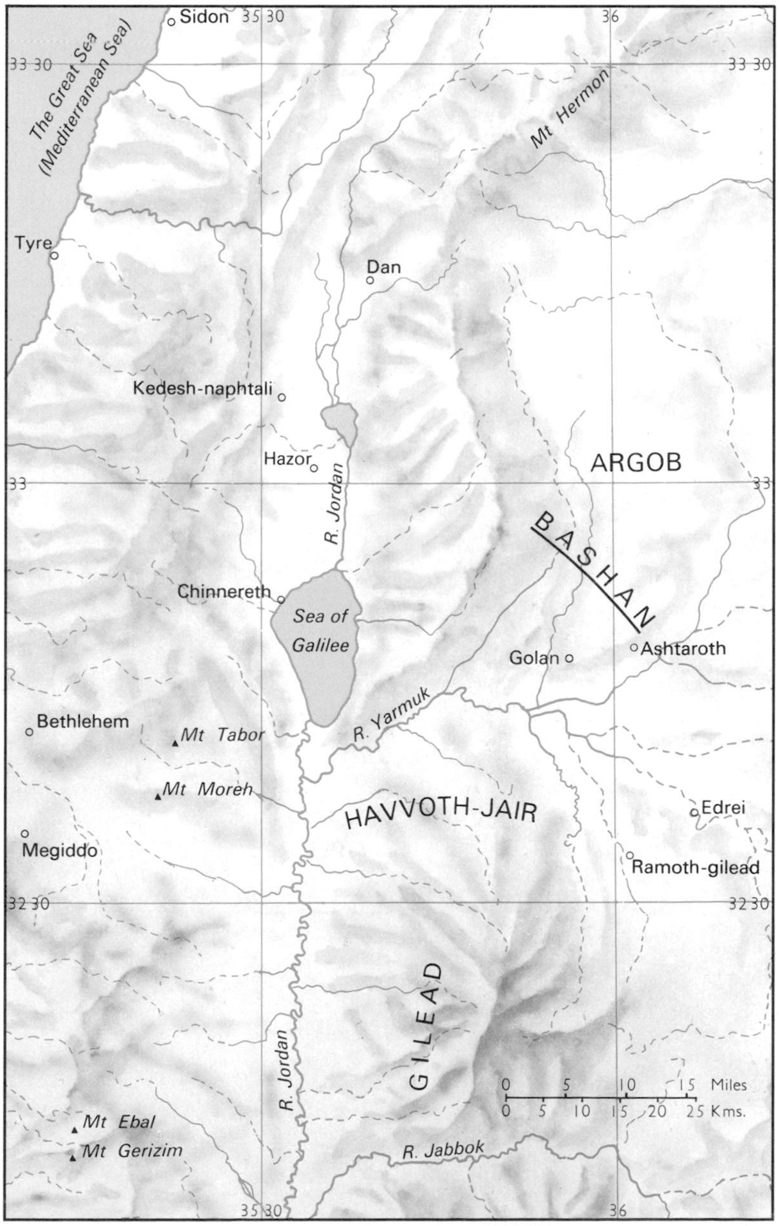

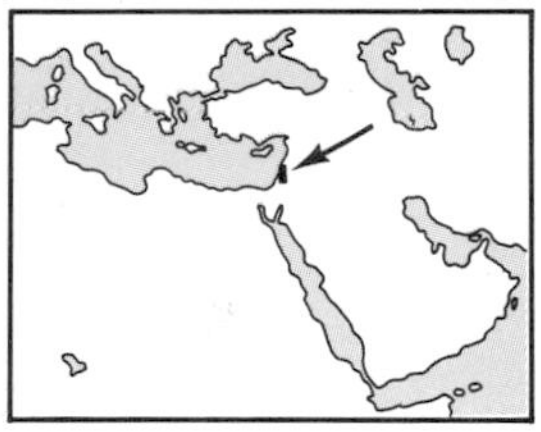

The location of Bashan.

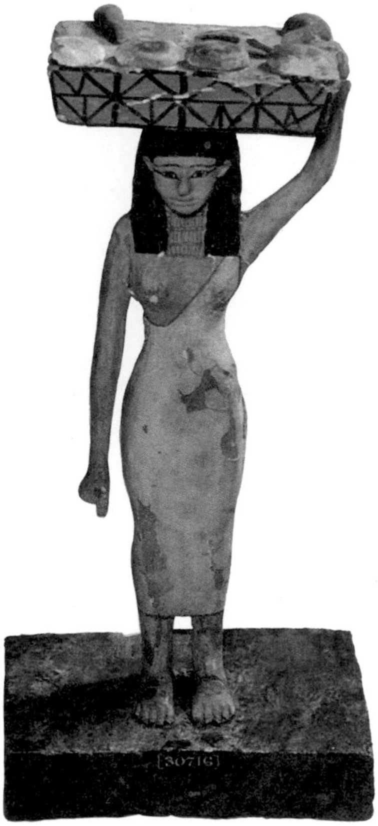

Top left:
Basket full of loaves, carried by an Egyptian servant girl as provision for the dead. Wooden tomb model. Height 38 cm. Middle Kingdom, c. 1900 BC. (BM)

Top right:
Basket containing wig, comb and dipper jug found in a Middle Bronze Age tomb in Jericho. 1900–1600/1550 BC. (JEF)

dnyt, 'basket'), used for storing produce (Dt. 26:2, 4) parallel to kneading-trough (Dt. 28:5, 17) as an item in the household. **3.** k^{e}*lûḇ*, which held fruit in Amos' vision (8:1) but was originally used for trapping birds, as in Je. 5:27 and the Canaanite letters from Amarna. **4.** *sal*, a flat, open basket for carrying bread (unleavened, Ex. 29:3, 23, 32; Lv. 8:2, 26, 31; Nu. 6:15, 17, 19; Jdg. 6:19). Pharaoh's baker dreamt he was carrying three full of white *bread (Heb. *ḥōrî*) on his head (Gn. 40:16; *cf. IBA*, fig. 28). **5.** *salsillôṯ* (Je. 6:9, AV) are more probably branches (RSV)

BAS-RELIEF
See Ornaments, Part 2.

Opposite:
Egyptian fruit basket, 17th Dynasty. Length c. 20 cm. c. 1400 BC. (BM)

Bottom left:
Pottery model of a woman bathing, from a cemetery at Achzib. 8·3 cm × 10·8 cm. 8th–7th cent. BC. (IM)

Bottom right:
The large W palace, built by Herod at Masada, includes this luxurious private bathroom. Hot water was piped in from a furnace behind the bath which is set within a vaulted recess in the wall. The king stepped out on to a fine mosaic floor. (JPK)

which are being thoroughly plucked, rather than 'baskets'.

The distinction between the feeding of the four thousand and of the five thousand is emphasized by the Gospel writers' use of Gk. *kophinos* for basket in the former miracle (Mt. 14:20; 16:9; Mk. 6:43; 8:19; Lk. 9:17; Jn. 6:13), but Gk. *spyris* in the latter (Mt. 15:37; 16:10; Mk. 8:8, 20). Both words denote a hamper, *kophinos* appearing elsewhere in a Jewish context, and *spyris*, in which Paul was lowered from the wall of Damascus, being the larger (Acts 9:25; parallel to Gk. *sarganē*, a plaited container, 2 Cor. 11:33). A.R.M.

BATH, BATHING (Heb. *rāḥaṣ*, 'to wash', 'to rub'; Gk. *louō*, *niptō* [distinguished in Jn. 13:10]). The heat and dust of E lands make constant washing necessary for both health and refreshment. It is likely that the bathing in the Nile of Pharaoh's daughter (Ex. 2:5) was typical of a nation whose priests, according to Herodotus (2.27), bathed four times a day. A host was expected to provide newly arrived travellers with water for their feet (Gn. 18:4; 19:2; 1 Sa. 25:41; *cf.* Jn. 13:1–10; *FOOT). Bathsheba was bathing when David first saw her (2 Sa. 11:2); Naomi's words to Ruth (Ru. 3:3) suggest that it was customary to bathe before calling on one of superior rank; and there is an obscure allusion to bathing in 1 Ki. 22:38.

Nevertheless, bathing as we know it is rarely mentioned in the Bible. Bodily cleanliness was, however, greatly furthered by the injunctions of the law, and most biblical allusions to washing are bound up with ceremonial occasions (*CLEAN AND UNCLEAN). Reference is made to bathing for curative purposes (2 Ki. 5:14; *cf.* Jn. 9:11), though here faith is a necessary part.

Josephus mentions hot springs at Tiberias, Gadara, *etc.*, about the beginning of the Christian era (*Ant.* 17. 171; 18. 36), and also public baths (19. 336), but there is no definite proof of the existence of the latter in Palestine before the Graeco-Roman age. J.D.D.

BATHSHEBA (called, in 1 Ch. 3:5, 'Bathshua, daughter of Ammiel'). She was the daughter of Eliam (2 Sa. 11:3), and, if he is the 'mighty man' of 2 Sa. 23:34, granddaughter of Ahithophel. David took her while her husband, Uriah the Hittite, was in command of the army which was besieging Rabbah, the Ammonite capital. This led to Uriah's murder, Bathsheba's entry into the royal harem and the rebuke by Nathan the prophet (2 Sa. 12). In David's old age Bathsheba allied with Nathan to secure Solomon's accession and become queen-mother. She petitioned Solomon, on Adonijah's behalf, for Abishag, David's concubine (1 Ki. 2:19–21). This was interpreted as a bid for the throne, and resulted in Adonijah's death. M.B.

Head of an Assyrian, showing curled beard and hair. Relief from Khorsabad. 721–705 BC. (BM)

BDELLIUM. A fragrant, transparent, yellowish gum-resin, the sap from trees of the genus *Commiphora*, valued for its use as a perfume. It was found in the land of *Havilah, near Eden (Gn. 2:12), and its colour was the same as that of *manna (Nu. 11:7). The Heb. *b^eḏōlaḥ* was taken over into Gk. as *bdellion*. Although this loan-word is found in the later Gk. translations of the OT, the LXX translates by *anthrax* and *krystallos*, possibly because the hardened gum resembled a precious stone, or because of the associated substances in Gn. 2:11f. (*JEWELS.)

BIBLIOGRAPHY. *KB*; *RAC*, 2, pp. 34f.; *EJ*, 4, p. 354. I.H.M.

BEARD. 1. Heb. *zāqān*. Israelites and their neighbours generally wore full round beards which they tended scrupulously. The beard was a mark of vitality and of manly beauty (Ps. 133:2; *cf.* 2 Sa. 19:24); to shave or cover it was a sign of grief or mourning (Is. 15:2; Je. 48:37, *etc.*; *cf.* Lv. 19:27; 21:5, enacted probably against idolatrous practices), or of leprosy (Lv. 14:9). To mutilate another's beard was to dishonour him (2 Sa. 10:4; Is. 50:6). Jeremiah criticizes those who shave their temples (Je. 9:26, *etc.*). (*HAIR; *BURIAL AND MOURNING.)

2. Heb. *śāp̄ām* (2 Sa. 19:24), denoting the moustache. J.D.D.

BEAST. Although found widely in most modern EVV, including RSV, the word 'beast' is now largely obsolete as a precise term. Coming from Old French, it was in general use when the Bible was first translated into English: 'animal', which has now replaced it, is from Latin and first appeared early 16th century but was not widely used until later. It is still used on farms in a semi-technical way, especially as 'fat beasts' and also, more widely,

BAT
See Animals, Part 1.

BATH
See Weights and measures, Part 3.

BATTERING-RAM
See Fortification and siegecraft, Part 1.

BATTLE
See War, Part 3.

BAY TREE
See Trees (Cedar), Part 3.

BEANS
See Vegetables, Part 3.

BEAR
See Animals, Part 1.

BEAR (constellation)
See Stars, Part 3.

BEARDED VULTURE
See Animals, Part 1.

BEAUTIFUL GATE
See Temple, Part 3.

BED
See House, Part 2.

BEE
See Animals, Part 1.

BEELZEBUB
See Baal-zebub, Part 1.

BEELZEBUL
See Baal-zebub, Part 1.

BEERI
See Anah, Part 1.

as 'beasts of burden'; otherwise it is found only in literary works or used figuratively, *i.e.* a cruel or rough man is a beast and his behaviour is beastly or bestial.

There is little uniformity in its use in EVV. In general both RV and RSV follow AV in the OT, and this is a notable exception to the RV policy of translating Heb. words consistently. Two Heb. words are usually translated 'beast'; *b^{e}hēmâ* (coll.) is also translated *'cattle': *ḥayyâ* is translated 'beast' 96 times (AV), but in 35 other passages it is translated by 10 different Eng. words. *b^{e}'îr* is often translated 'beast' but sometimes 'cattle'.

In some passages *b^{e}hēmâ* and *ḥayyâ* are hard to differentiate as, for instance, where in the same chapter (Lv. 11) and very similar contexts they are both used of clean animals: v. 2 (AV) 'the beasts (*ḥayyâ*) which ye shall eat', but v. 39 'any beast (*b^{e}hēmâ*) of which ye shall eat'. In v. 47 *ḥayyâ* has a wider meaning, so that RV and RSV often translate as 'living thing', but this is reversed in v. 2: 'These are the living things (*ḥay*) which you may eat among all the beasts (*b^{e}hēmâ*) that are on the earth.'

In the NT both RV and RSV follow the Greek more closely than AV. *zōon*, always 'beast' in AV, is translated 'living creature' in RV and RSV in Rev. 4:6. Except for RSV in Acts 23:24 (mounts) and 28:4–5 (creature), Acts 10:12 and 1 Cor. 15:39 (animals), and Rev. 18:13 (cattle), all common EVV retain 'beast' for *ktēnos* (domestic animal, especially beast of burden) and *thērion* (wild beast). RV and RSV thus correctly distinguish between the four living creatures on the one hand and the beast of Rev. 11:7 and all literal passages on the other.

The word 'animal' was current before AV was published but is not used in this or in RV. Animal now has two usages. Strictly it is any living being with sensation and voluntary movement, *i.e.* the animal kingdom in contrast with the plant kingdom; more popularly it refers to four-footed animals, often only to four-footed mammals, in contrast with man, birds, *etc.* As used in RSV the meaning is nearer the latter, but in the 34 OT occurrences there is no uniformity. For instance, the first 12 instances translate 6 different Heb. words, which AV translates 'beast', 'cattle', 'of the herd' and 'of the flock'. The NT pattern is similar; the 7 occurrences are from 4 Greek words: *thērion*, *tetrapous*, *ktēnos* and *zōon*. (*ANIMALS.) G.S.C.

BEAST (APOCALYPSE). 1. The 'beast that ascends from the bottomless pit' (Rev. 11:7) is the apocalyptic symbol of the last anti-Christian power (Rev. 13:1ff.; 17:3ff.; 19:19f.), portrayed as a composite picture of the 4 beasts of Dn. 7:3ff. His 10 horns are borrowed from Daniel's fourth beast; his 7 heads mark his derivation of authority from the dragon of Rev. 12:3, and go back ultimately to Leviathan (*cf.* Ps. 74:14; Is. 27:1); John reinterprets them once of the 7 hills of Rome (Rev. 17:9), otherwise of 7 Roman emperors. The beast is usually the persecuting empire, occasionally the final emperor, a reincarnation of one of the first 7, probably Nero. He claims divine honours, wages war on the saints and is destroyed by Christ at his parousia (*cf.* 2 Thes. 2:8).

2. The 'beast from the earth' (Rev. 13:11ff.), also called the 'false prophet' (Rev. 16:13; 19:20; 20:10), is public relations officer of the former beast, persuades men to worship him and ultimately shares his fate. The imperial cult in the province of Asia (*ASIARCH) evidently suggested some of his features to John. F.F.B.

BEER (*b^{e}'ēr*, lit. 'a well', 'cistern', usually man-made). **1.** Nu. 21:16. A point on the itinerary of the wandering Hebrews, reached soon after leaving Arnon. This verse records an otherwise unknown story of the provision of water; an important event, for v. 18b suggests that Beer was in a desert place. The site is unknown. **2.** Jdg. 9:21. The place to which Jotham fled after having denounced the *coup d'état* of his brother Abimelech. The site is unknown. R.J.W.

BEER-LAHAI-ROI. The name itself and certain elements of Gn. 16:13–14, where it first appears, defy certain translation. As it stands, the name may mean 'The well of the living one who sees me' or 'The well of "He who sees me lives" '. However, the original place-name may have suffered a degree of distortion in transmission, putting the original beyond our discovery. This is not the only proper name in the OT to have suffered in this way. The exact site is not known, but Gn. 16:7, 14 places it towards the Egyptian border, whither Hagar, the Egyptian maid, was fleeing from the wrath of Sarai her mistress. God appeared to Hagar here and announced the birth of Ishmael. Isaac passed through Beer-lahai-roi when waiting for Eliezer to bring him a wife from Mesopotamia (Gn. 24:62), and settled there after the death of Abraham. R.J.W.

BEERSHEBA. The name given to an important well, and also to the local town and district (Gn. 21:14; Jos. 19:2). The present town lies 77 km SW of Jerusalem and approximately midway between the Mediterranean and the S part of the Dead Sea. There are several wells in the vicinity, the largest 3·75 m in diameter. The digging of this well involved cutting through 5 m of solid rock. On one stone of the masonry lining the shaft Conder found a date indicating that repairs had been carried out in the 12th

View of Beersheba, modern Tel es-Seba'. (AIA)

century AD. At the time of his visit in 1874, it was 11 m to the surface of the water.

Excavations at Tel es-Seba', 5 km W of the town, have revealed a planned and fortified town of the Judaean monarchy. A well outside the gateway is dated to the 12th century BC by the excavator, and associated with Abraham, setting the stories of the Patriarchs after the Israelite conquest. There is no evidence to support this speculation. No pottery of Bronze Age date has been found at the site, nor anything to prove the place's ancient name. Iron Age pottery has been found in the modern town (Bir es-Seba'), which was called Berosaba in Roman times, and may yet prove to be the patriarchal site.

The meaning of the name is given in Gn. 21:31, 'The well of seven' (*i.e.* lambs). The alternative interpretation, 'The well of the oath', arises through a misunderstanding of the use of the Heb. word for 'therefore', which can refer only to an antecedent statement (Gn. 11:9 is not really an exception), and a mistranslation of the Heb. particle *kî* by 'because', whereas it here introduces an independent temporal clause and should be rendered 'when', or even 'then'. The antecedent statement tells *why* it was done; this clause, *when* it was done. (For a similar use of *kî*, *cf.* Gn. 24:41; *cf.* König, *Heb. Syntax*, 387 h.) The explanation of the alleged second account of the naming of the well by Isaac (Gn. 26:33) is given in v. 18: 'And Isaac dug again the wells of water which had been dug in the days of

Section of the excavations at Beersheba, showing the store-houses with the city gate in the background. (AIA)

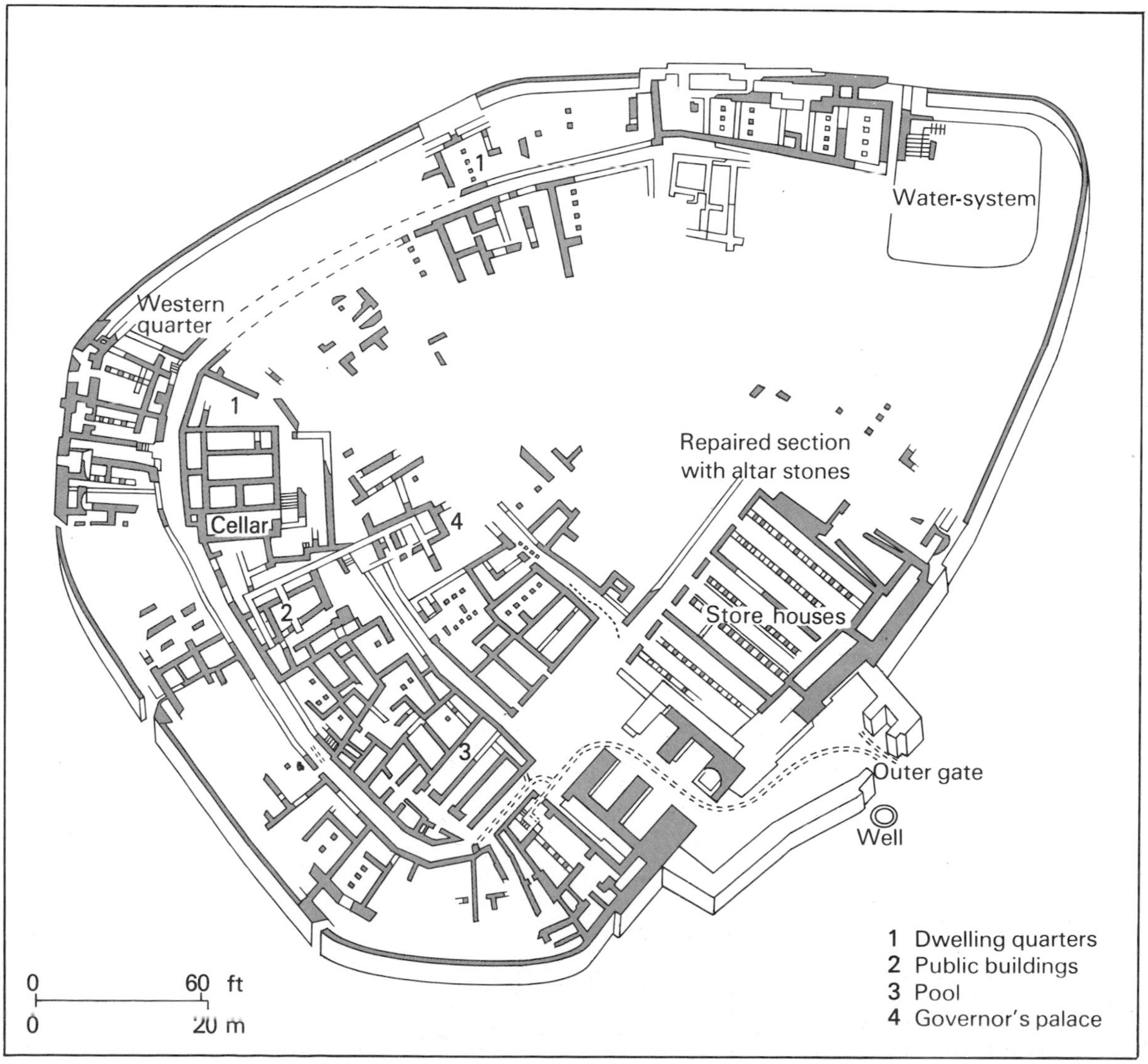

Plan of the excavated sections of the city of Beersheba (Tel es-Seba').

Abraham his father; for the Philistines had stopped them after the death of Abraham; and he gave them the names which his father had given them.' Since the digging of a well was often a major achievement, filial respect alone would insist that the work of a great father would be thus remembered. In v. 33 the actual wording is: 'He called it Shibah.' The use here of the feminine of the numeral may merely express the numerical group, roughly equivalent to 'It, of the seven'.

Beersheba has many patriarchal associations. Abraham spent much time there (Gn. 22:19). It was probably a part of Palestine without an urban population, since the seasonal nature of the pasturage would not have been conducive to settled conditions. From here he set out to offer up Isaac. Isaac was dwelling here when Jacob set out for Harran (Gn. 28:10). On his way through to Joseph in Egypt, Jacob stopped here to offer sacrifices (Gn. 46:1). In the division of the land it went to the tribe of Simeon (Jos. 19:2).

In the familiar phrase 'from Dan to Beersheba' (Jdg. 20:1, *etc.*) it denoted the southernmost place of the land. The town owed its importance to its position on the trade-route to Egypt.

The reference to it in Amos (5:5 and 8:14) indicates that it had become a centre for undesirable religious activities.

Beersheba and its villages (Heb. 'daughters') were resettled after the captivity (Ne. 11:27).

The place referred to by Josephus (*BJ* 2. 573 and 3. 39), which Winckler wanted to identify with the Beersheba of the OT, was a village in lower Galilee (Jos., *Life* 5. 188).

BIBLIOGRAPHY. W. Zimmerli, *Geschichte u. Tradition von Beersheba im A.T.*, 1932. Y. Aharoni, *Beer-sheba*, 1, 1973; *Tel-Aviv*, 1, 1974, pp. 34–42; 2, 1975, pp. 146–168.

W.J.M.
A.R.M.

BEESHTERAH
See Ashtaroth, Part 1.

BEETLE
See Animals, Part 1.

BEGGAR, BEGGING
See Alms, Part 1.

BEKA(H)
See Weights and measures, Part 3.

BELA
See Plain, cities of the, Part 3.

BELIEF
See Faith, Part 1.

BEHEMOTH. Morphologically the Heb. plural of *b*^{e}*hēmâ*, occurring 9 times in the OT (Dt. 32:24; Jb. 12:7; 40:15; Pss. 49:12, 20; 50:10; 73:22; Je. 12:4; Hab. 2:17), and in all but one of these occurrences 'beasts', 'animals' or 'cattle' is apparently the intended meaning. In Jb. 40:15, however, the reference is so qualified in the following verses as to suggest some specific animal, and it is usual to take the plural here as having intensive force, 'great beast', and referring to the hippopotamus which seems to fit the description best. A derivation has been suggested from a hypothetical Egyptian *p'.iḥ.mw*, 'the ox of the water', but the fact that Egyptian has other words for hippopotamus renders this unlikely. While other theories have been put forward, the hippopotamus identification may be tentatively accepted in the present state of knowledge. The LXX renders the word here by *ktēnos*. (*BEAST.)

BIBLIOGRAPHY. S. R. Driver and G. B. Gray, *The Book of Job, ICC*, 1921, 1, pp. 351–358; *KB*, p. 111; for another theory, see G. R. Driver in Z. V. Togan (ed.), *Proceedings of the Twenty-Second Congress of Orientalists . . . Istanbul . . . 1951*, 2, 1957, p. 113; G. S. Cansdale, *Animals of Bible Lands*, 1970, p. 100; J. V. Kinnier Wilson, *VT* 25, 1975, pp. 1–14. T.C.M.

BEL. The name or title of the principal Babylonian deity, Marduk (*MERODACH), whose overthrow was synonymous with the end of Babylon and its domination (Je. 50:2; 51:44). In this connection Bel is named with the god Nabû (*NEBO), who was considered his son (Is. 46:1). Bēl (Sumerian *en*, 'lord'; Heb. *Ba'al*) was one of the original Sumerian triad of deities, with Anu and Enki, his name being a title or epithet of the wind and storm god Enlil. When Marduk became the chief god of Babylon in the 2nd millennium he was given the additional name of Bēl. It was the idol of this god whom Daniel and his companions were commanded to worship (Bel and the Dragon 3ff.). D.J.W.

BELIAL. The sense of this word is generally clear from its context: 'son of' or 'man of' Belial plainly means a very wicked person. The word occurs in Heb. of Ps. 18:4, parallel to the word 'death'; hence the RSV translation 'perdition'. In intertestamental literature and NT it is a synonym for Satan (often spelled 'Beliar'). The derivation is, however, obscure. The Heb. text, with the Massoretic vowels, read *b*^{e}*lîya'al*, apparently from *b*^{e}*lî* ('without') and *ya'al* ('profit'), and so means 'worthlessness'; this is still a strong possibility, although one cannot easily account for its having become a proper name. A number of scholars have sought a mythological background, *e.g.* Baal-yam ('Lord Sea'), but none of the suggestions has been very convincing. A third type of approach is to ignore the Massoretic vowels and derive the word from a Heb. verb *bāla'* ('swallow up, engulf'); the name would then primarily describe Sheol, as 'the Engulfer' (the etymology of English 'infernal' is comparable).

Modern EVV chiefly use such words as 'scoundrel', 'base', 'godless' and 'abominable' to render phrases which contain 'Belial' in Heb.

BIBLIOGRAPHY. D. W. Thomas in *Biblical and Patristic Studies in Memory of R. P. Casey*, 1963, pp.11–19; V. Maag, *TZ* 21, 1965, pp. 287–299; *TDOT*. D.F.P.

BELL. Two Hebrew words are thus translated. **1.** *pa'*^{a}*môn* ('striking', 'beating'). Small gold bells, alternating with pomegranates of blue, purple and scarlet stuff, were attached to the hem of the high priest's ephod (Ex. 28:33–34; 39:25–26), their ringing announced his going into the sanctuary. Bells for religious purposes are known from Assyria (see B. Meissner, *Babylonien und Assyrien*, 1, 1920, p. 268, and photograph, Abb. 142). Bells are also attested for personal adornment in Egypt, from at least the Bubastite period (*c.* 800 BC) to Roman and Coptic times, and were often attached to children to announce their whereabouts. See, with illustrations, Petrie, *Objects of Daily Use*, 1927, pp. 24, 57–58, plates 18:33–37 and 50:292–305. Bells with clappers appear in the 1st millennium BC; earlier small 'bell rattles' were current, openwork metal containers with a small metal ball inside.

2. Heb. *m*^{e}*ṣillâ* ('tinkling'). These are little bells. In Zc. 14:20 they are part of the trappings of horses, prophesied to become 'Holy to the Lord' (and so inscribed). Little bells often appeared among horse-trappings in antiquity; they can be seen at the necks of Assyrian war-horses in Grollenberg, *Shorter Atlas of the Bible*, 1959, p. 113, bottom photograph. See also J. Rimmer, *Ancient Musical Instruments of Western Asia in the British Museum*, 1969, pp. 37ff., pls. xvii–xx. K.A.K.

BELSHAZZAR. The ruler of Babylon who was killed at the time of its capture in 539 BC (Dn. 5). Bēl-šar-uṣur ('Bel has protected the king[ship]') is named in Babylonian documents by his father Nabonidus, king of Babylon in 556–539 BC. Other texts give details of Belshazzar's administration and religious interests in Babylon and Sippar up to the 14th year of his father's reign. He was possibly a grandson of Nebuchadrezzar II and, according to the Nabonidus Chronicle, his father 'entrusted the army and the kingship' to him *c.* 556 BC, while Nabonidus campaigned in central Arabia, where he eventually remained for 10 years. Belshazzar ruled in Babylonia itself. It is possible that Daniel dated events by the years of this co-regency (Dn. 7:1; 8:1), though the official dating of documents continued to use the regnal years of Nabonidus himself. Legal texts dated to the 12th and 13th years of Nabonidus include the name of the Bēl-šar-uṣur, the crown prince, in unique oaths. Since a Harran inscription (*AS* 8, 1958, pp. 35–92; *ANET*^{3}, pp. 562f.) gives 10 years for the exile of Nabonidus, thiss would confirm other sources since the 'king' who died in October 539 BC was Belshazzar (Dn. 5:30), whose father was captured on his subsequent return to the capital (Xenophon, *Cyropaedia*, 7. 5. 29–30, does not give names). Belshazzar (Aram. *Bēlša'ṣṣar*) is also called Balthasar (Gk. Baruch 1:11–12; Herodotus, 1. 188) or Baltasar (Jos., *Ant.* 10. 254).

Belshazzar is named with his father Nabonidus on this clay barrel cylinder which records the king's restoration of the temple of the moon-god Sin, at Ur. 9·5 cm × 4·8 cm. c. 550 BC. (BM)

BIBLIOGRAPHY. R. P. Dougherty, *Nabonidus and Belshazzar*, Yale Oriental Series 15, 1929; A. K. Grayson, *Assyrian and Babylonian Chronicles*, 1975, pp. 104–111 (for Nabonidus Chronicle). D.J.W.

BELTESHAZZAR (Heb. *bēlṭ^{e}ša'aṣṣar*; Gk. *Baltasar*). The name given to Daniel in Babylon (Dn. 1:7; 2:26; 4:8–9, 19; 5:12; 10:1). The Heb. may be a transliteration of the common Babylonian name *Belet/Belti-šar-uṣur* (May the Lady [wife of the god *Bel] protect the king'). For the form of the name, *Belshazzar, *Sharezer, and see A. R. Millard, *EQ* 49, 1977, p. 72. D.J.W.

BENAIAH (Heb. *b^{e}nāyāhû*, *b^{e}nāyâ*, 'Yahweh has built up'). **1.** Son of Jehoiada from Kabzeel in S Judah (2 Sa. 23:20). Captain of David's foreign bodyguard (2 Sa. 8:18; 20:23), he commanded the host for the third month (1 Ch. 27:5–6). He was renowned among 'the thirty' of David's mighty men (2 Sa. 23:20–23; 1 Ch. 11:22 25), and probably accompanied David during Absalom's rebellion (2 Sa. 15:18). He helped to thwart Adonijah and establish Solomon as king (1 Ki. 1) and later executed Adonijah, Joab and Shimei (1 Ki. 2:25, 29ff., 46), replacing Joab as commander-in-chief (1 Ki. 2:35).

2. One of 'the thirty' who formed the second group of David's mighty men, from Pirathon in Ephraim (2 Sa. 23:30; 1 Ch. 11:31), and commanded the host for the eleventh month (1 Ch. 27:14).

Ten other persons bearing this name are known only from the following references: 1 Ch. 4:36; 15:18, 20, 24; 16:5–6; 2 Ch. 20:14; 31:13; Ezr. 10:25, 30, 35, 43 (*cf.* 1 Esdras 9:26, 34–35); Ezk. 11:1, 13. J.G.G.N.

BELLOWS
See Arts and crafts, Part 1.

BELLY
See Stomach, Part 3.

Bronze bells similar to those shown as horse-trappings on contemporary reliefs. Calah (Nimrud). 8th cent. BC. (BM)

BEN-AMMI ('son of my kinship'). The name given to the child born of Lot's incestuous union with his younger daughter (Gn. 19:38), from whom sprang the children of *Ammon. Moses recognized their kinship, through Lot, with the children of Israel; and so directed that they should not be disturbed in the land which had been 'given them for a possession' (Dt. 2:19). Nevertheless, 'the children of Lot' in later times became their enemies (2 Ch. 20:1; Ps. 83:6–8). G.T.M.

BENE-BERAK. A town in the territory of Dan (Jos. 19:45), identified with modern el-Kheirîyeh (till recently Ibn Ibrâq), about 6 km E of Jaffa. According to Sennacherib it was one of the cities belonging to Ashkelon besieged and taken by him (*DOTT*, p. 66; *ANET*, p. 237). J.D.D.

BENEDICTUS. The prophecy of Zechariah (Lk. 1:68–79), named from the first word in the Latin version, is one of six visions (Lk. 1:5–25, 26–38; 2:1–20), and prophecies (Lk. 1:46–56; 2:29–35) in the Lucan infancy narrative. It is a recurrent pattern in Hebrew prophecy to reflect upon or elaborate former revelations (*cf.* Ps. 105; Mi. 4:4; Zc. 3:10). In the NT the Revelation of John is a mosaic of OT language and concepts. Likewise the Benedictus alludes to a number of passages in the Psalms and Isaiah.

The first division of the passage (Lk. 1:68–75), in parallelisms characteristic of Jewish poetry, extols God for his Messianic deliverance and rejoices in its results. The second section (Lk. 1:76–79) describes the place which John will have in this mighty act of God. In the Benedictus Messiah's work is particularly a spiritual deliverance. Does this mean that Zechariah's thought has itself been radically changed in the light of the interpretation of the OT by Christ and his apostles? Not necessarily. While the mass of Jews viewed the Messiah as a political Redeemer, his role as a religious or priestly Redeemer was not absent in Judaism (*cf. Test. Judah* 21. 1–3; *Test. Levi* 18. 2f.; *Test. Simeon* 7. 1f.; 1QS 9. 10f.; CD 19. 10; 20. 1). This would be central in the thoughts of a pious priest; therefore, it is quite in keeping with his personality and background that, 'filled with the Holy Spirit', Zechariah should utter this particular revelation. (*ANNUNCIATION.) E.E.E.

BENEFACTOR. The Gk. *euergetēs* was used as a title by kings of Egypt (*e.g.* Ptolemy IX, 147–117 BC) and of Syria (*e.g.* Antiochus VII, 141–129 BC) and appears on their coins. It occurs also as a laudatory title on inscriptions of the 1st century AD, commemorating services rendered, *e.g.* to the people of Cos (*LAE*, p. 253). Such a title is no honour to any disciple of Jesus (Lk. 22:25). A.R.M.

BENE-JAAKAN. A camping-ground of the Israelites (Nu. 33:31–32; Dt. 10:6). Formally it is a tribal name and refers to one of the clans of Seir (1 Ch. 1:42), which is a name for the mountainous region W of Wadi Arabah. No more exact location is possible, as the section of the itinerary in Nu. 33 in which it occurs could refer to one of a number of routes.

BIBLIOGRAPHY. J. R. Bartlett, *JTS* n.s. 20, 1969, pp. 1–12. G.I.D.

BEN-HADAD. Heb. form of Aramaic Bar- or Bir-Hadad, 'son of Hadad', name of either two or three rulers of the Aramaean kingdom of Damascus.

1. Ben-hadad I is called 'son of Tabrimmon, son of Hezion, king of Aram' in 1 Ki. 15:18. In his 15th year (35th of the divided Monarchy), Asa of Judah vanquished *Zerah the Ethiopian and held a great thanksgiving-feast in Jerusalem, inviting Israelites also (2 Ch. 14:9–15:19); therefore in the 16th (36th) year, Baasha of Israel attacked Judah (2 Ch. 16:1–10), and so Asa sought aid from Ben-hadad I of Aram (1 Ki. 15:18ff., as above). Hence Ben-hadad I was already ruling by *c.* 895 BC, say *c.* 900. For this period, see E. R. Thiele, *Mysterious Numbers of the Hebrew Kings*, 1951, pp. 58–60; 1965 ed., pp. 59–60.

2. Ben-hadad, the opponent of Ahab (*c.* 874/3–853 BC), 1 Ki. 20, died by the hand of *Hazael in the days of Joram (*c.* 852–841 BC) and Elisha (2 Ki. 6:24ff.; 8:7–15). Hazael succeeded Ben-hadad about 843 BC (Shalmaneser III of Assyria already mentions Hazael in 841 BC) (see M. F. Unger, *Israel and the Aramaeans of Damascus*, p. 75). Two problems here arise. First, is the Ben-hadad of Ahab and Joram Asa's Ben-hadad I (implying a long but not unparalleled 57 years' reign, *c.* 900–843 BC), or is he a separate Ben-hadad II? Albright (*BASOR* 87, 1942, pp. 23–29) would identify them as a single Ben-hadad (I), but his only positive reason is a possible date about 850 BC (limits, *c.* 875–825 BC) for the Melqart Stele on the style of its script. But the most natural interpretation of 1 Ki. 20:34 is that Omri had earlier been defeated by Ben-hadad I, father of a Ben-hadad II the contemporary of Ahab; Albright's interpretation of this passage is distinctly forced, and the non-mention by the OT of an event like Omri's discomfiture is well

Drawing of a stele, showing the god Melqart bearing his battle-axe. It is inscribed on the lower part (not shown) with the name of Ben-hadad, king of Aram. c. 860 BC.

paralleled by its similar omission of Jehu's paying tribute to Shalmaneser III. Secondly, Shalmaneser III's annals for 853 BC (Wiseman, in *DOTT*, p. 47) and for 845 BC (*ANET*, p. 280a; *ARAB*, 1, §§ 658, 659) call the king of Damascus ^{d}IM-idri, probably to be read as Adad-idri ('Hadad-ezer'); this must be almost certainly another name for Ben-hadad (I/II), Ahab's contemporary; *cf.* Michel, *Welt des Orients*, 1, 1947, p. 59, n. 14. If two Ben-hadads are admitted, 'I' may be dated roughly 900–860 BC, and 'II' about 860–843 BC. The so-called Melqart Stele dates to this general period; attribution to a specific Ben-hadad is precluded by the illegibility of his ancestry on the monument, despite attempted solutions (*e.g.* Gross, *BASOR* 205, 1972, pp. 36–42).

3. Ben-hadad III, *c.* 796–770 BC, son of Hazael, continued his father's oppression of Israel (*temp.* Jehoahaz, *c.* 814/3–798 BC, 2 Ki. 13:22) into the reign of Jehoash (*c.* 798–782/1 BC), who, in fulfilment of Elisha's dying prophecy, was able successfully to repel Ben-hadad (2 Ki. 13:14–19, 25); this Aramaean king is also mentioned on the contemporary stele of Zakur, king of Hamath and Lu'ash (*cf.* Black, in *DOTT*, pp. 242–250). The unnamed 'deliverer' against Syria at this time (to Israel's benefit) may be a veiled reference to intervention by Adad-nirari III of Assyria against *Aram; *cf.* W. Hallo, *BA* 23, 1960, p. 42, n. 44, following H. Schmökel, *Geschichte* *des Alten Vorderasien*, 1957, p. 259, no. 4. Amos (1:4) prophesied the destruction of the 'palaces of (Hazael and) Ben-hadad', and their memory is evoked by Jeremiah (49:27) in his prophecy against the *Damascus province.

BIBLIOGRAPHY. For these kings, see M. F. Unger, *Israel and the Aramaeans of Damascus*, 1957, chapters V–X; A. Malamat, in *POTT*, pp. 143ff. K.A.K.

BENJAMIN. 1. The youngest son of Jacob, called *binyāmîn* ('son of the right hand', *i.e.* 'lucky') by his father, though his mother Rachel, dying in child-birth, called him *ben-'ônî* ('son of my sorrow') (Gn. 35:18, 24). After Joseph's disappearance, he took first place in his father's affections as the surviving son of Rachel; this was a major factor in bringing about the eventual surrender of Joseph's brothers (Gn. 42:4, 38; 44:1–34).

2. The tribe descended from Benjamin; Heb. *binyāmîn*, as collective, or pl. *b^{e}nê binyāmîn*; also *b^{e}nê y^{e}mînî*, Jdg. 19:16; 1 Sa. 22:7; and sing. *ben y^{e}mînî* or *ben hayy^{e}mînî* (*cf.* *'îš y^{e}mînî*, 1 Sa. 9:1; *'ereṣ y^{e}mînî*, v. 4). A similar name *bīnū* (or *mārū*) *yamina*, possibly meaning 'sons of (dwellers in) the south', is found in the Mari texts (18th century BC), and some scholars, *e.g.* Alt, Parrot, have sought here the antecedents of the biblical tribe; but the difference in time and origin makes this very uncertain.

Much detail is given of Benjaminite genealogies, though they are nowhere complete; ten families are enumerated in Gn. 46:21, but the Chronicler names only three clans (1 Ch. 7:6ff.), of which Jediael does not appear as such in the Pentateuch. The pre-invasion reckoning of 'fathers' houses' is given in Nu. 26:38ff.; for details recorded under the Monarchy, see 1 Ch. 8.

The tribe occupied a strip of land in the passes between Mt Ephraim and the hills of Judah. The boundary with Judah is clearly defined (Jos. 18:15ff.; *cf.* 15:5ff.) and passed S of Jerusalem, which however became a Jebusite town until David captured it. Thence it ran to Kiriath-jearim, at one time in Benjamin (Jos. 18:28; RSV 'and' follows LXX, but the text is unclear). Jos. 15:9 supports this, while identifying with Baalah of Judah; Noth (*Josua*^{2}, *ad loc.*) considers this a gloss, but it is repeated in Jos. 15:60; 18:14; Jdg. 18:12; 1 Ch. 13:6; *cf.* 1 Ch. 2:50ff. The N border ran from Jericho to the N of *Ophrah, then roughly SW to the ridges S of *Beth-horon, leaving Luz in Ephraim (but perhaps originally not the sanctuary of *Bethel; Jos. 18:13). Under the Divided Monarchy, 'Ephraim' (*i.e.* the N kingdom) occupied Bethel and part of E Benjamin, but the border fluctuated; *cf.* 2 Ch. 13:9. The W border is given as a straight line from Beth-horon to Kiriath-jearim, but there was settlement farther W (1 Ch. 8:12f.).

'Benjamin is a ravenous wolf'—so ran the ancient blessing of Jacob (Gn. 49:27). The tribe earned a high reputation for bravery and skill in war, and was noted for its slingers with their traditional left-handed action (Jdg. 3:15; 20:16; 1 Ch. 8:40). Ehud, who delivered Israel from the Moabites, was of Benjamin; so also were Saul, the first king (1 Sa. 9:1), Queen Esther (Est. 2:5) and the apostle Paul (Rom. 11:1). Lying right in the path of Philistine expansion, the tribe played its chief part in Israelite history under Saul's leadership, and on the whole remained loyal to him, though a number came over to David in his exile (1 Ch. 12:2–7, 29). Indeed, the feud was remembered long after (2 Sa. 16:5; 20:1). Such clan loyalty was evident in their disastrous resistance to the national demand for justice in the matter of the Levite's concubine (Jdg. 20–21) many years before the Monarchy (20:26f.).

With the capital established at Jerusalem, Benjamin was drawn closer to Judah (1 Ch. 8:28), and after the division Rehoboam retained its allegiance (1 Ki. 12:21; 2 Ch. 11; note 1 Ki. 11:32, 'for the sake of Jerusalem'). There were two 'Benjamin' gates in the city, one in the Temple (Je. 20:2), the other perhaps the same as the 'sheep gate' in the N city wall (Je. 37:13; Zc. 14:10). Despite the varying fortunes of war, Benjamin remained part of Judah (1 Ki. 15:16ff.; 2 Ki. 14: 11ff.; *cf.* 2 Ki. 23:8, 'Geba'). From the Restoration, the distinction is confined to personal genealogy (*cf.* Ne. 7 with 11:7ff.).

In the vision of Ezekiel, the portion of Benjamin lies just S of the city (Ezk. 48:22ff.).

3. A descendant of Jediael (1 Ch. 7:10).

4. A Benjaminite of the Restoration who took a foreign wife (Ezr. 10:32). Ne. 3:23; 12:34 may refer to the same person.

BIBLIOGRAPHY. *Mari texts:* M. Noth, *JSS* 1, 1956, pp. 322–333;

BEN-HUR
See Hur, Part 2.

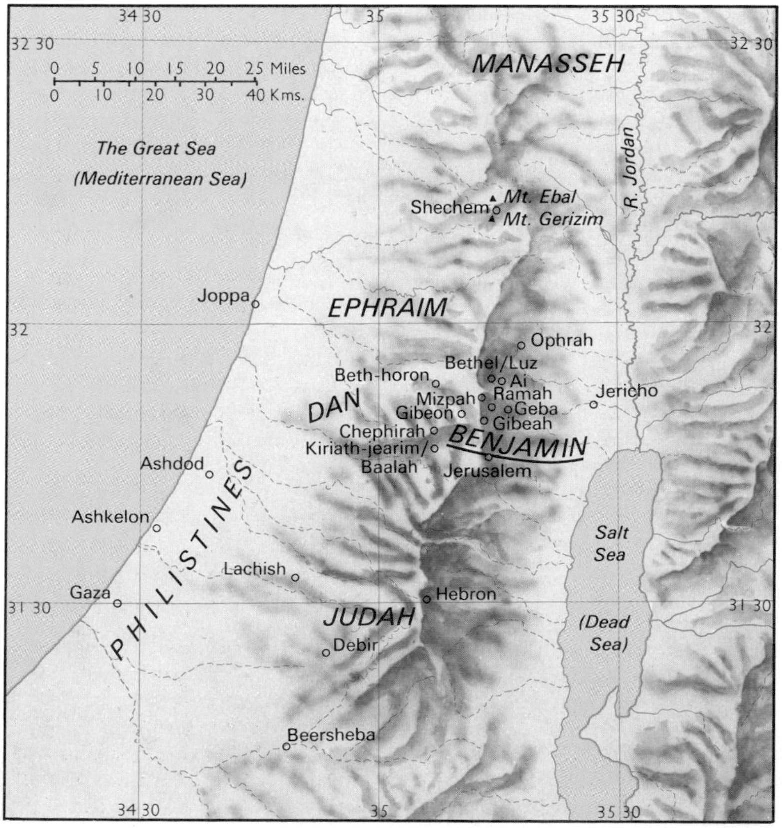

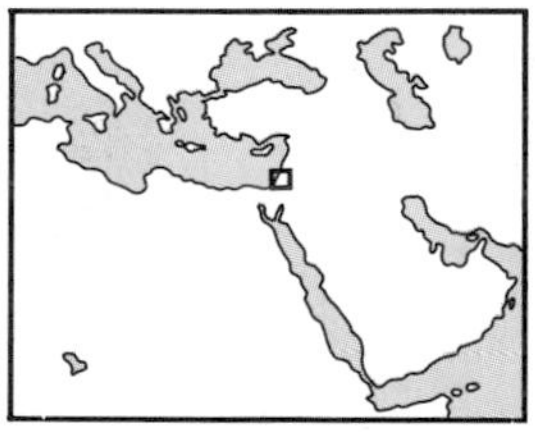

The land occupied by the tribe of Benjamin

BEN-TREE
See Trees (Poplar), Part 3.

BEOR
See Balaam, Part 1.

BEREA
See Beroea, Part 1.

BERODACH-BALADAN
See Merodach-baladan, Part 2.

BERYL
See Jewels, Part 2.

BEST MAN
See Friend of Bridegroom, Part 1.

J. Gibson, *JSS* 7, 1962, pp. 57f. *Topography:* Z. Kallai, *IEJ* 6, 1956, pp. 180–187; *GTT*, pp. 164ff., 170ff. *General:* J. Bright, *History of Israel*², 1972; J. Grønbaek, *VT* 15, 1965, pp. 421–436; K-D. Schunck, *ZAW Suppl.* 86, 1963 (reviewed, *JBL* 83, 1964, p. 207); M. Noth, *History of Israel*², 1960. J.P.U.L.

BERACAH (lit. 'blessing'). **1.** One of the warriors who joined David at Ziklag when he was in straits because of the enmity of Saul (1 Ch. 12:1–3). **2.** A valley where Jehoshaphat and his people gave God thanks for the victory which they had gained over the Ammonites, Moabites and Edomites (2 Ch. 20:26). It is identified with Wadi Bereikūt between Jerusalem and Hebron, and W of Tekoa. The modern name suggests an earlier form which was pronounced slightly differently from that in the Heb. text with the meaning 'water pool' (*berēḵâ*). R.J.W.

BERNICE. The eldest daughter of Herod Agrippa I, and sister of Drusilla, born in AD 28. Having been engaged, if not married, previously, she married at the age of 13 her uncle Herod of Chalcis. Upon his death in AD 48, she went to live with her brother Herod Agrippa II (an incestuous relationship with him is alleged in Juvenal, *Sat.* 6. 156–160). She then married Polemon king of Cilicia, deserted him and returned to her brother, in whose company she heard Paul (Acts 25:13). She subsequently became the mistress of the future emperor Titus. Josephus shows her in a more favourable light: in Jerusalem in AD 66 she intervened courageously in the attempt to prevent a massacre of the Jews by the procurator Florus (*BJ* 2. 309–314). E.M.B.G. C.J.H.

BEROEA, BEREA. 1. The modern Verria, a city of S Macedonia probably founded in the 5th century BC. In NT times it was evidently a prosperous centre with a Jewish colony. When Paul and Silas were smuggled out of Thessalonica to avoid Jewish opposition (Acts 17:5–11), they withdrew to Beroea, 80 km away. Here they received a good hearing until the pursuit caught up with them. Beroea was the home of Sopater (Acts 20:4). **2.** The Hellenistic name of Aleppo (2 Macc. 13:4).

BIBLIOGRAPHY. Strabo 7; *BC*, 4, pp. 188f., 206f. J.H.P.

BETEN. One of the towns of Asher listed in Jos. 19:25. Its location is uncertain. Eusebius's *Onomasticon*, calling it Bethseten, puts it 8 Roman miles E of Ptolemais (Acco). It may be the modern Abtûn, E of Mt Carmel. J.D.D.

BETHABARA (probably from Heb. *bêṯ ʿaḇārâ*, 'house of (the) ford'). This place is read in many Gk. MSS at Jn. 1:28 for *'Bethany beyond Jordan': hence it is found in AV and RVmg. Origen preferred this reading while admitting that the majority of contemporary MSS were against him. He gives its etymology as 'house of preparation', which he associated with the Baptist's 'preparation'. In his day, he says, this place was shown as the place of John's baptism. It is probably the present Qasr el-Yehud, on the right bank of the Jordan, E of Jericho, where a monastery of St John stands.

BIBLIOGRAPHY. F. M. Abel, *Géographie de la Palestine*, 2, 1938, pp. 264–265. J.N.B.

BETH-ANATH (Heb. *bêṯ ʿanāṯ*, 'temple of Anat'). Perhaps Safed el-Battikh, NW of Galilee, and the *bt ʿnt* listed by Seti I and Ramesses II. The city was allotted to Naphtali (Jos. 19:38); the original inhabitants were not expelled, but made tributary (Jdg. 1:33).

BIBLIOGRAPHY. *LOB*, pp. 200, 214. A.R.M.

BETH-ANOTH (Heb. *bêṯ ʿanôṯ*, probably 'temple of Anat'). A conurbation (a city with its villages, Jos. 15:59) which was allotted to Judah. Modern Beit ʿAnûn 6 km NNE of Hebron. J.D.D.

BETHANY. 1. A village (present population 726) on the farther side of the Mount of Olives, about 3 km from Jerusalem on the road to Jericho. It is first mentioned in the Gospels, especially as the home of Jesus' beloved friends, Mary, Martha and Lazarus; hence the modern Arabic name 'el-ʿAzariyeh. Its most central role in the Gospel history is as the place of Jesus' anointing (Mk. 14:3–9). Outside the Gospels it figures largely in Christian itineraries, traditions and legends.

2. The place where John baptized 'beyond the Jordan' (Jn. 1:28). Its identification remains uncertain. Already by the time of Origen (*c.* AD 250) it was unknown (see his *Commentary on John* 6:40, p. 157, ed. Brooke). Origen preferred the reading *Bethabara, since this place was known in his day and, moreover, this choice might in his opinion be corroborated by allegory. 'Bethany', however, should be accepted as the more difficult reading. The mention of a place so soon unknown is frequently adduced as a token of knowledge of 1st-century Palestine by the Evangelist or his source. J.N.B.

BETH-ARBEL. A city described (Ho. 10:14) as having been destroyed by *Shalman in the 'day of battle'. The name is known only from this reference, so that the common identification with modern Irbid, probably the Arbela of Eusebius, some 30 km SE of the Sea of Galilee, remains uncertain.

BIBLIOGRAPHY. W. F. Albright, *BASOR* 35, 1929, p. 10; G. L. Harding, *The Antiquities of Jordan*, 1959, pp. 54–56. T.C.M.

BETH-AVEN (Heb. *bêṯ ʾāwen*, 'house of iniquity'). Lying to the W of Michmash (1 Sa. 13:5) and possibly to be distinguished from the Beth-aven said to lie to the E of Bethel (Jos. 7:2). If these two are to be distinguished, it is impossible to be certain which is referred to as a N boundary mark for Benjamin's allotment (Jos. 18:12). In Hosea (4:15; 5:8; 10:5) the name may be a derogatory synonym for *Bethel, 'House of the false (god)'. R.J.W.

BETH-DAGON (Heb. *bêṯ dāḡôn*). **1.** In the lowland of Judah S of *Azekah (Jos. 15:41). **2.** In Asher, probably N of *Helkath (Jos. 19:27). There were others; that taken by Sennacherib is now Bet Dagan near Tel Aviv (Z. Kallai, *VT* 8, 1958, pp. 53f.; B. Mazar, *IEJ* 10, 1960, p. 72). J.P.U.L.

BETHEL. Identified by most scholars with Tell Beitīn on the watershed route 19 km N of Jerusalem. Although traces of earlier occupation have been found, the city seems to have been established early in the Middle Bronze Age. During this period, Abram camped to the E of Bethel, where he built an altar to Yahweh (Gn. 12:8). After his visit to Egypt, he returned for this site (Gn. 13:3). For Jacob, Bethel was the starting-point of his realization of God, who is for him 'God of Bethel' (Gn. 31:13; 35:7). As a result of his vision of Yahweh he named the place 'House of God' (Heb. *bêṯ 'ēl*) and set up a *pillar (Heb. *maṣṣēḇâ*, Gn. 28:11–22). He was summoned to Bethel on his return from Harran, and both built an altar and set up a pillar, reiterating the name he had given before (Gn. 35:1–15). The site is perhaps Burġ Beitīn, SE of Tell Beitīn, the 'shoulder of Luz' (Jos. 18:13).

Excavations yielded some Early Bronze Age traces, with, the excavator claimed, a blood-stained rock high place. This seems to be an improbable interpretation, and the claim that a Middle Bronze Age shrine replaced it is also dubious. The Middle Bronze Age city was prosperous, destroyed about 1550 BC, and followed by well-built Late Bronze Age houses. These in turn were sacked, and the subsequent Iron Age buildings marked a complete cultural change, which the excavator related to the Israelite conquest (Jos. 12:16; Jdg. 1:22–26). Bethel was allotted to the Joseph tribes who captured it, particularly to Ephraim (1 Ch. 7:28), and bordered the territory of Benjamin (Jos. 18:13). The Israelites soon resettled the town, calling it by the name Jacob had given to the scene of his vision instead of Luz (Jdg. 1:23). When it was necessary for Israel to punish Benjamin, the people sought advice on the conduct of the battle and worshipped at Bethel 'for the ark . . . was there' (Jdg. 20:18–28; 21:1–4). It was a sanctuary too in the time of Samuel, who visited it annually (1 Sa. 7:16; 10:3). The material remains of this period indicate an unsophisticated and insecure community. The settlement was twice burnt, possibly by the Philistines.

Under the early monarchy the city prospered, presently becoming the centre of Jeroboam's rival cult, condemned by a man of God from Judah (1 Ki. 12:28–13:32). The Judaean Abijah captured it (2 Ch. 13:19), and his son, Asa, may have destroyed it (2 Ch. 14:8). Elisha met a group of the 'sons of the prophets' from Bethel but also the mocking boys (2 Ki. 2:3, 23). Amos condemned the rites of the Israelite royal sanctuary (Am. 4:4; 5:5–6; 7:13; *cf.* Ho. 10:15), and Jeremiah showed their futility (Je. 48:13). The priest sent to instruct the Assyrian settlers in Samaria settled at Bethel (2 Ki. 17:28), and worship evidently continued there until Josiah took advantage of Assyrian weakness to invade Israel and destroy its sanctuaries. No traces of Jeroboam's shrine have been unearthed; it may well have been outside the city proper on the site of the patriarchal altars. In the 6th century BC the city was destroyed by fire. Returning exiles settled in Bethel (Ne. 11:31), but their worship was centred on Jerusalem (Zc. 7:2–3). The city grew during the Hellenistic period until it was fortified by Bacchides *c.* 160 BC (1 Macc. 9:50). When Vespasian captured it in AD 69, there was a short break before it was rebuilt as a Roman township. It continued to flourish until the Arab conquest. (*BETH-AVEN.)

BIBLIOGRAPHY. W. F. Albright and J. L. Kelso, 'The Excavation of Bethel (1934–60)', *AASOR* 39, 1968; D. L. Newlands, 'Sacrificial Blood at Bethel?' *PEQ* 104, 1972, p. 155. For identification with modern Bireh, see D. Livingston, *WTJ* 33, 1970, pp. 20–44; 34, 1971, pp. 39–50; criticized by A. F. Rainey, *WTJ* 33, 1971, pp. 175–188. A.R.M.

BETHEL-SHAREZER
See Sharezer, Part 3.

BETHESDA, BETHZATHA. In the TR, the name of a Jerusalem pool (Jn. 5:2), near the Sheep Gate; but there is textual uncertainty about the name itself and about its application. Various names occur

Model of two pools, located N of the Temple Mount at Jerusalem and identified with the Bethesda of Jn. 5:2. The reconstruction is problematic, since no trace has been found of the 'five porticoes' mentioned in the Gospel. (JPK) (HC)

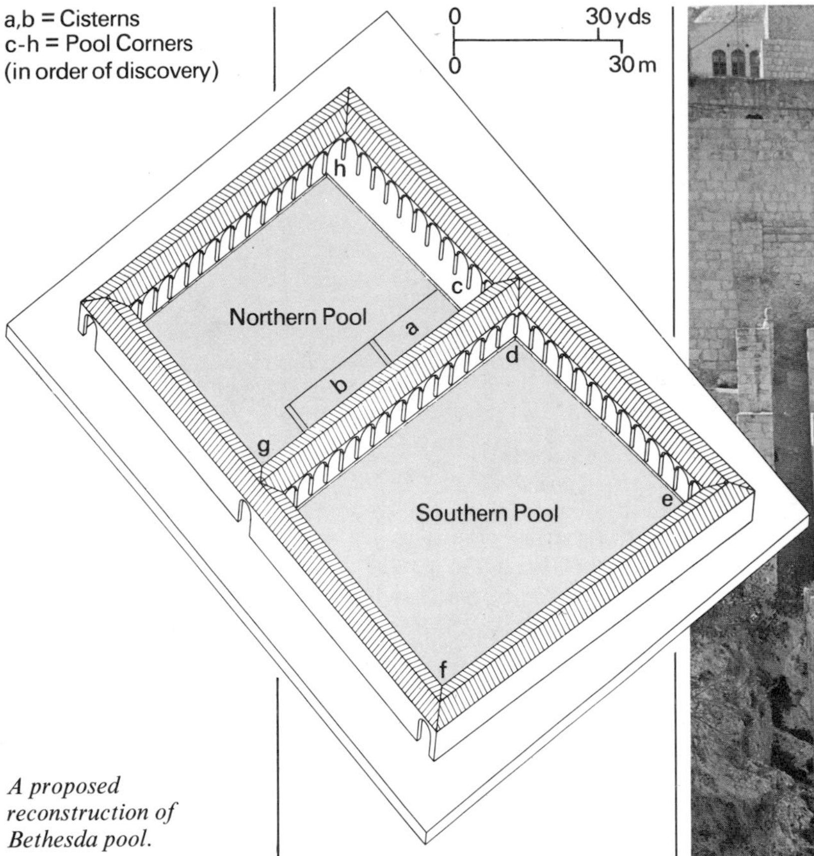

A proposed reconstruction of Bethesda pool.

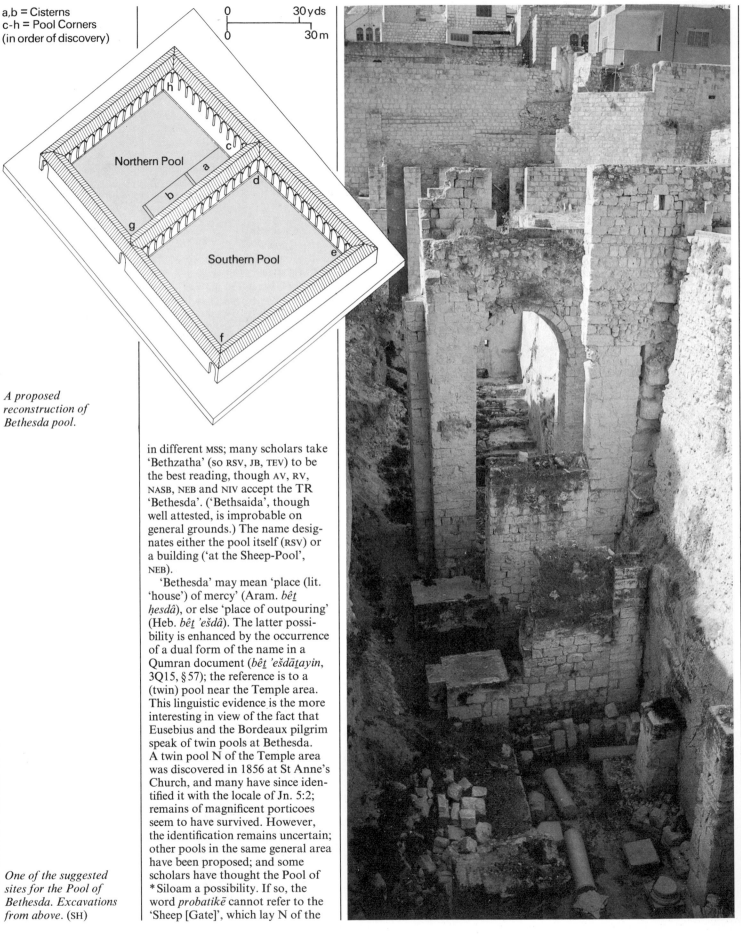

One of the suggested sites for the Pool of Bethesda. Excavations from above. (SH)

in different MSS; many scholars take 'Bethzatha' (so RSV, JB, TEV) to be the best reading, though AV, RV, NASB, NEB and NIV accept the TR 'Bethesda'. ('Bethsaida', though well attested, is improbable on general grounds.) The name designates either the pool itself (RSV) or a building ('at the Sheep-Pool', NEB).

'Bethesda' may mean 'place (lit. 'house') of mercy' (Aram. *bêṯ ḥesdâ*), or else 'place of outpouring' (Heb. *bêṯ 'ešdâ*). The latter possibility is enhanced by the occurrence of a dual form of the name in a Qumran document (*bêṯ 'ešdāṯayin*, 3Q15, § 57); the reference is to a (twin) pool near the Temple area. This linguistic evidence is the more interesting in view of the fact that Eusebius and the Bordeaux pilgrim speak of twin pools at Bethesda. A twin pool N of the Temple area was discovered in 1856 at St Anne's Church, and many have since identified it with the locale of Jn. 5:2; remains of magnificent porticoes seem to have survived. However, the identification remains uncertain; other pools in the same general area have been proposed; and some scholars have thought the Pool of *Siloam a possibility. If so, the word *probatikē* cannot refer to the 'Sheep [Gate]', which lay N of the

Temple area; but other renderings are possible (*cf.*, *e.g.*, NEB).

BIBLIOGRAPHY. J. Jeremias, *The Rediscovery of Bethesda*, E.T. 1966; A. Duprez, *Jésus et les Dieux Guérisseurs*, 1970; B. M. Metzger, *A Textual Commentary on the Greek New Testament*, 1971, *ad loc.*; and standard commentaries.

D.F.P.

BETH-HARAN (Nu. 32:36, to be identified with Beth-aram, Jos. 13:27). This site formed part of the allotment of Gad, and so lay on the E of the Jordan. It was probably a border strong-point which the Gadites built (Nu. 32:36) or else an existing settlement which they fortified (Jos. 13:27) to protect themselves and their cattle. The settlement was in good pasture (Nu. 32:1) but in the valley (Jos. 13:27), and so lacked the security of hill fastnesses which those who crossed the river enjoyed. Identified with modern Tell Iktanû 12 km NE of the mouth of the Jordan.

R.J.W.

BETH-HORON. A Canaanite place-name meaning 'house of Hauron' (a Canaanite god of the underworld). Upper Beth-horon (Jos. 16:5) is modern Beit 'Ûr al-Fôqâ, 617 m above sea-level, 16 km NW of Jerusalem, and Lower Beth-horon (Jos. 16:3) is Beit 'Ûr al-Taḥtâ, 400 m above the sea and 2 km farther NW. These towns were built by Sherah, of the tribe of Ephraim (1 Ch. 7:24). They were within the territory of this tribe, and one of them was assigned to the Levite family of Kohath (Jos. 21:22). They were rebuilt by Solomon (2 Ch. 8:5) and fortified by the Jews after the Exile (Judith 4:4–5) and by Bacchides the Syrian general (1 Macc. 9:50). They controlled the valley of Aijalon, up which went one of the most important ancient routes between the maritime plain and the hill-country. Therefore many armies passed by these towns in biblical times, *e.g.* the Amorites and the pursuing Israelites under Joshua (Jos. 10:10–11), the Philistines (1 Sa. 13:18), and the Egyptian army of Shishak (according to his Karnak inscription), the Syrians under Seron (1 Macc. 3:16, 24) and under Nicanor (1 Macc. 7:39), both of whom Judas defeated at Beth-horon, and the Romans under Cestius (Jos., *BJ* 2. 516).

Sanballat may have been a native of Beth-horon (Ne. 2:10). Pseudo-Epiphanius, in *The Lives of the Prophets*, states that Daniel was born in Upper Beth-horon.

BIBLIOGRAPHY. E. Robinson, *Biblical Researches in Palestine*, 2, 1874, pp. 250–253; G. A. Smith, *Historical Geography of the Holy Land*, 1931, pp. 248–250, 287–292; F. M. Abel, *Géographie de la Palestine*, 2, 1938, pp. 274–275.

J.T.

BETH-JESHIMOTH (Heb. *bêṯ hayšîmôṯ*, 'house of the deserts', AV 'Jesimoth'), a place near the NE shore of the Dead Sea in the plains of Moab (Nu. 33:49; Ezk. 25:9), allocated by Moses to the tribe of Reuben (Jos. 13:20). Eusebius places it 16 km SE of Jericho, and Josephus (*War* 4. 438) mentions it by its Greek name *Bēsimōth* (the nearby Khirbet Sueimeh), captured by the Roman tribune Placidus during the Jewish revolt. A well and some ruins (Tell el-'Azeimeh) remain.

N.H.

BETHLEHEM (Heb. *bêṯ leḥem*, 'house of bread', the latter word probably in the wider sense, 'food'). It has been suggested that the final word *leḥem* is Lakhmu, an Assyrian deity; but there is no evidence that this god was ever revered in Palestine. There are two towns of the name in the OT, both today given the Arabic name Bayt Lahm, the exact equivalent of the Hebrew.

1. The famed city of David, as it came to be styled. It lies 9 km S of Jerusalem. Its earlier name was Ephrath (Gn. 35:19), and it was known as Bethlehem Judah, or Bethlehem Ephrathah, to distinguish it from the other city of the same name. Rachel's tomb was near it; David's ancestors lived there; the Philistines placed a garrison there; and the Messiah was destined to be born there. Jesus was accordingly born there, and the stories of the shepherds and the Magi centre upon it. Bethlehem suffered at the hands of Hadrian in the 2nd century AD, and all Jews were expelled from it; and it seems that the site of the nativity grotto was lost for two centuries; so the Church of the Nativity erected by Helena in the reign of Constantine may or may not mark the true site.

2. The second Bethlehem lay in Zebulunite territory (Jos. 19:15); it is 11 km NW of Nazareth. Most scholars think the judge Ibzan (Jdg. 12:8) was a resident of it, but ancient tradition favours Bethlehem Judah.

BIBLIOGRAPHY. *EAEHL*, 1, pp. 198–206.

D.F.P.

BETH-MARCABOTH (Heb. *bêṯ hammarkāḇôṯ*, 'house of chariots'). A part of the allotment to Simeon (Jos. 19:5; 1 Ch. 4:31). The site is uncertain but, being connected with Ziklag and Hormah, was probably a strong-point on the Judaean–Philistine border. The name suggests that the settlement may have been a Canaanite arsenal in the days of the conquest. The possession of chariots by the Canaanites prevented the unmounted Hebrew soldiers from entirely occupying the land (Jdg. 19).

R.J.W.

BETH-NIMRAH. 'House of pure water' or 'House of leopard', a city in Gad (Nu. 32:36), probably equalling Nimrah (Nu. 32:3) and Nimrim (Is. 15:6; Je. 48:34). By Eusebius, called Betham-Naram and located 8 km N of Livias. Possibly either modern Tell Nimrin beside the Wadi Shaîb or nearby Tell Bileibil, some 24 km E of Jericho.

G.W.G.

BETH-PEOR (lit. 'Temple of Peor'). A place in the hill country in the land of Moab (Jos. 13:20) or of the Amorites (Dt. 4:46), to the E of Jordan, which was part of Reubenite territory. The historical framework of Deuteronomy describes the Hebrews gathering at Mt Pisgah near to Beth-peor to receive their final exhortation before going over into the Promised Land (Dt. 3:29; 4:44–46). Having repeated the law to the immigrants, Moses died, and was buried nearby (Dt. 34:5–6). Beth-peor may be near, or even the same as, Peor, where Balaam built seven altars (Nu. 23:28). Nu. 25:1–5 mentions the worship of a god Baal Peor (Lord of Peor) by the Moabites. The site is uncertain.

R.J.W.

BETHPHAGE (in Aram. 'place of young figs'). A village on the Mount of Olives, on or near the road from Jericho to Jerusalem and near Bethany (Mt. 21:1; Mk. 11:1; Lk. 19:29). Its site is unknown. See *ZPEB*, p. 112.

J.W.M.

BETH-GILGAL
See Gilgal, Part 1.

BETHLEHEM, STAR OF
See Stars, Part 3.

BETH-PELET
See Paltite, Part 2.

BETH-REHOB
See Rehob, Part 3.

BETH-SAIDA. A town on the N shores of Galilee, near the Jordan. The name is Aramaic, meaning 'house of fishing' (if *bêṯ ṣaydâ*) or else 'fisherman's house' (if *bêṯ ṣayyāḏâ*). Philip the tetrarch rebuilt it and gave it the name Julias, in honour of Julia the daughter of Augustus. Pliny and Jerome tell us that it was on the E of the Jordan, and there are two likely sites, al-Tell or Mas'adiya. (The two are close together, the latter being nearer the actual shore.) But in Mk. 6:45 the disciples were sent from E of the Jordan to Beth-saida, towards Capernaum (*cf.* Jn. 6:17); hence a second Beth-saida has been postulated W of the Jordan—perhaps to be located at 'Ayn al-Tabigha. This is also claimed to be Beth-saida 'of Galilee' (Jn. 12:21), since the political division Galilee may not have extended E of the Jordan. But this is unlikely; 'Galilee' is not necessarily used in the technical sense. A suburb of Julias on the W bank may suit Mk. 6:45 best; Capernaum was not far away.

D.F.P.

BETHSHEAN, BETHSHAN. A city situated at the important junction of the Valley of *Jezreel with the Jordan valley. The name occurs in the Bible as *bêṯ šeʾān* (Jos. 17:11, 16; Jdg. 1:27; 1 Ki. 4:12; 1 Ch. 7:29) and *bêṯ šan* (1 Sa. 31:10, 12; 2 Sa. 21:12), but there is little doubt that both names refer to the same place. The name is preserved in the modern village of Beisân, adjacent to which stands Tell el-Ḥosn, the site of the ancient city, which was excavated under the direction of C. S. Fisher (1921–3), A. Rowe (1925–8) and G. M. Fitzgerald (1930–3).

Though a deep sounding was made, revealing settlements of the 4th millennium and an important Canaanite city of the Early Bronze Age, the main excavations were devoted to the 9 upper levels which extended from the 14th century BC to Islamic times. During much of the earlier part of this period, Bethshean was an Egyp. fortified outpost. Already in the 15th century Tuthmosis III mentions it as under his control (scarabs bearing his name were found there), and in the following century one of the Amarna letters speaks of reinforcements sent to garrison *bît-sa-a-ni* on behalf of Egypt. The earliest main level (IX) probably belongs to this century (the levels have been redated on the basis of pottery sequence, since the original dates of the excavators relied on less certain criteria), and in this an extensive temple dedicated to 'Mekal, the Lord (Ba'al) of Bethshan' was uncovered, in which were found the remains of a sacrificed 3-year-old bull (*SACRIFICE AND OFFERING).

Level VIII was comparatively unimportant, dating from about the end of the 14th century, but at this time Sethos (Seti) I was seeking to restore Egyp. control in Asia, which had been largely lost under the later kings of the 18th Dynasty, and in his first year he retook Bethshean. Two of his royal stelae have been found there, one of them recording that he had a clash near by with the *'pr.w* (*HEBREWS). Level VII (*c.* 13th century) contained a temple in which was found a stela depicting a goddess with a two-horned head-dress (*ASHTEROTH-KARNAIM), and in level VI a similar temple was uncovered. This level probably dates to the 12th century, the time of Rameses III, of whom a statue was found there, and the discovery in the city cemetery of anthropoid clay coffins characteristic of the *Philistines suggests that these people were stationed as a mercenary garrison at Bethshean by Rameses. It was not long before this that the Israelites had arrived in Palestine, and Manasseh, being allotted Bethshean (Jos. 17:11), found it too formidable to take (Jos. 17:16; Jdg. 1:27), so that it remained in hostile hands until the time of David. Its importance at this time is suggested by the fact that the Bible refers to it as Beth-shan 'and her daughters' (*i.e.* dependent villages). It was still in Philistine hands at the time of Saul, for it was upon its walls that his body and those of his sons were hung, and from which the men of Jabesh-gilead recovered them (1 Sa. 31:10, 12).

In level V (*c.* 11th century) two

View of the ruin-mound of Bethshean (Tell el-Ḥosn). Height of mound 80 m. (BLS)

The view southwards from the Israelite (possibly Solomonic) gateway at Bethshean. (AIA)

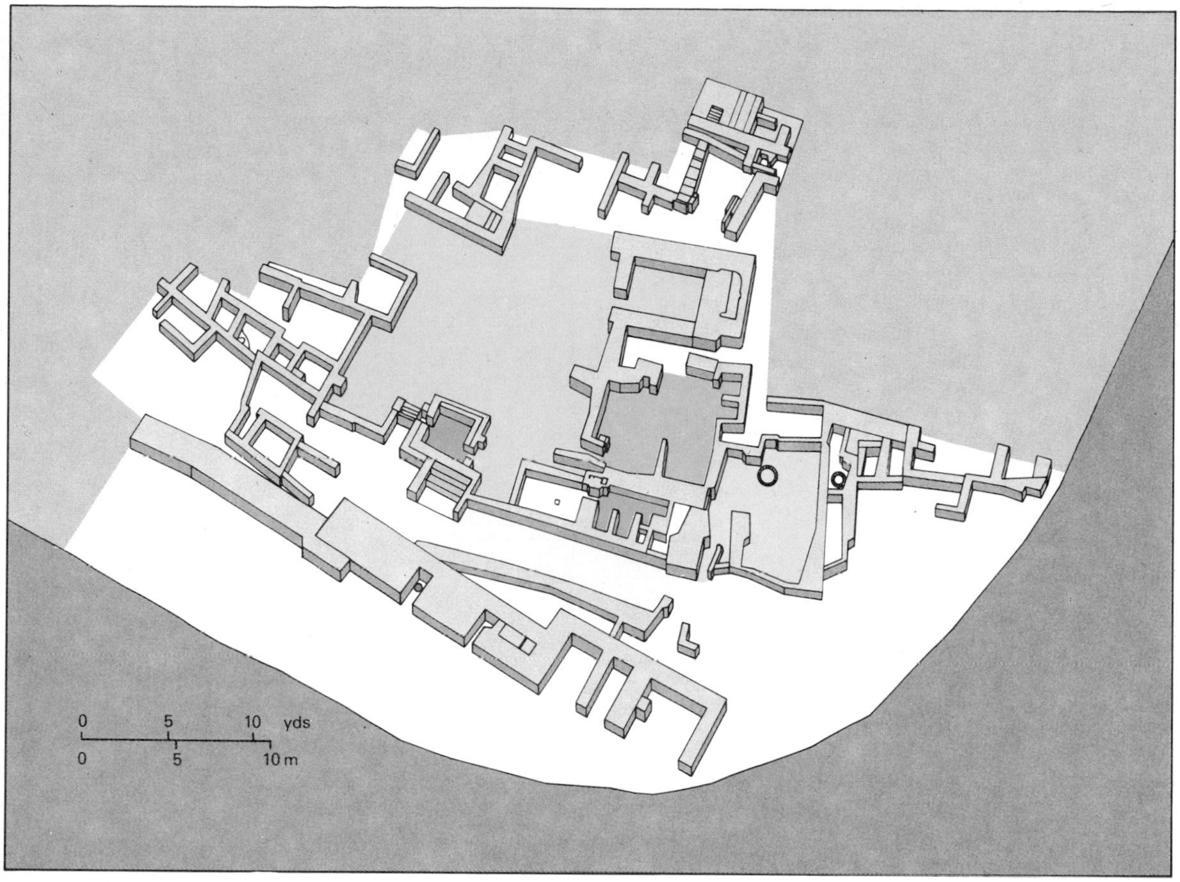

Plan of the temple (level IX) dedicated to 'Mekal, the Lord (Ba'al) of Bethshan'.

Altar court
Inner court
Entrance corridor
Inner courts
Room with oven and well
Room north of the sanctuary
Altar (or steps to the roof?)
Guard room
Water reservoir and well ●

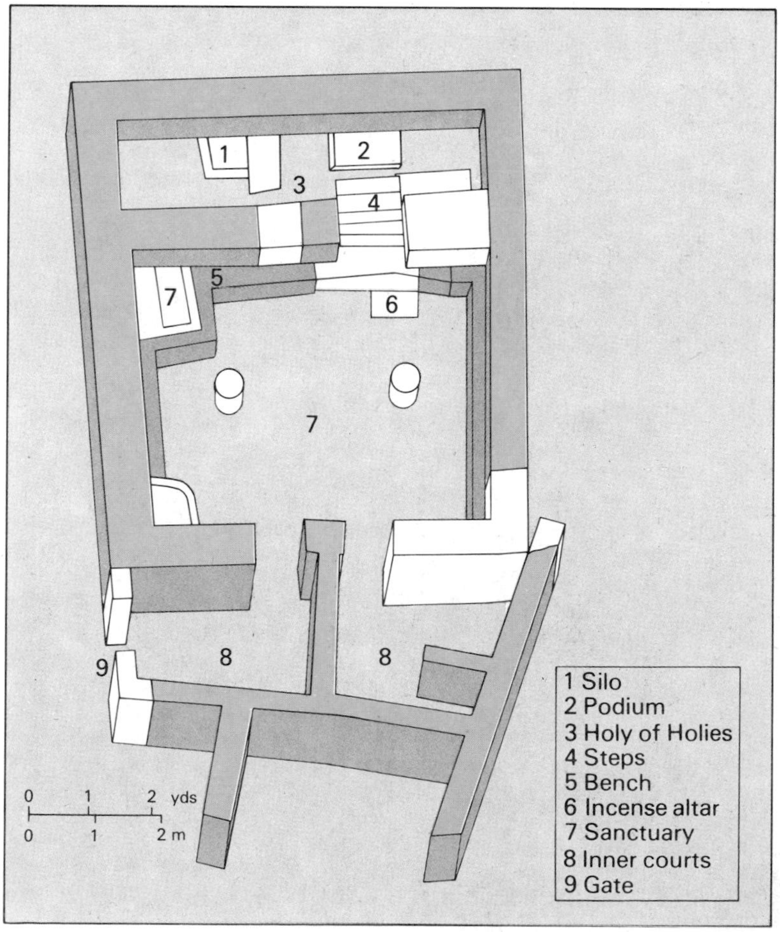

Plan of the temple, level VII, Bethshean.

temples were uncovered, one (the S) dedicated to the god Resheph and the other to the goddess Antit, and Rowe has suggested that these are the temples of Dagon and Ashteroth in which Saul's head and armour were displayed by the Philistines (1 Ch. 10:10; 1 Sa. 31:10). The city must have fallen finally to the Israelites in the time of David, and the excavations have revealed little material settlement (level IV) from then until the Hellenistic Period (level III). During this time it is mentioned with its environs ('all of Bethshean', *kol-bêṯ šᵉʾān*) as belonging to Solomon's fifth administrative district (1 Ki. 4:12), and in the reign of Rehoboam (1 Ki. 14:25) Sheshonq (*SHISHAK) claimed it among his conquests. The city was refounded as the Hellenistic centre of Scythopolis,

Plan of the temple, level VI, Bethshean.

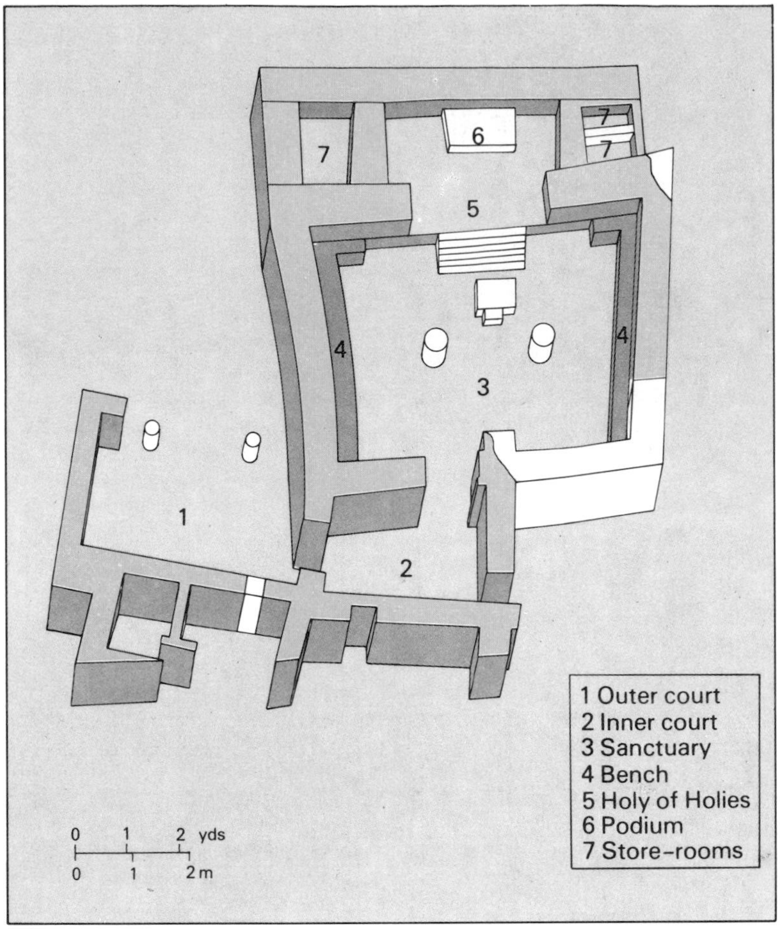

Stele found at Bethshean, recounting the military successes of King Seti I against a coalition of Asiatic princes. Seti is shown making offerings to the hawk-headed god RēʿHarakhti. Height 2·42 m. c. 1300 BC. (ZR)

and this later became a part of the * Decapolis.

BIBLIOGRAPHY. A. Rowe, *Beth-shan*, 1, *The Topography and History of Beth-shan*, 1930; 2, i, *The Four Canaanite Temples of Beth-shan*, 1940; with which see G. E. Wright, *AJA* 45, 1941, pp. 483–485; G. M. Fitzgerald, *Beth-shan*, 2, ii, 1930; 3, 1931; *ANET*, pp. 242, 249, 253; J. Knudtzon, *Die El-Amarna Tafeln* 1, 1907, pp. 874f., no. 289. 20; 2, 1915, p. 1343 (= *ANET*, p. 489); W. F. Albright, 'The Smaller Beth-Shan Stele of Sethos I (1309–1290 BC)', *BASOR* 125, 1952, pp. 24–32; G. Posener in J. Bottéro, *Le Problème des Habiru*, 1954, p. 168 (= *ANET*, p. 255); G. E. Wright, *BA* 22, 1959, pp. 53–56, 65; (on anthropoid coffins) G. M. Fitzgerald, in *AOTS*, pp. 185–196; *EAEHL*, 1, pp. 207–229. T.C.M.

BETH-SHEMESH (Heb. *bêṯ šemeš*, 'house [temple] of the sun'), a name applied to 4 places in the Bible.

1. An important city of Judah (2 Ki. 14:11; 2 Ch. 25:21) on its N border with Dan (Jos. 15:10), situated in a W-facing valley of the hill-country some 24 km W of Jerusalem and consequently commanding a route from the uplands to the coast plain. The site is probably to be identified with modern Tell er-Rumeileh, situated on the saddle of a hill spur to the W of the later settlement of ʿAin Shems. Excavations were conducted in 1911–12, and more extensively in 1928–32. The site was first settled near the end of the Early Bronze Age, some time before 2000 BC, and flourished as a strongly fortified Canaanite city throughout the Middle and Late Bronze Ages, reaching its zenith in the time of the Egyptian domination under the pharaohs of Dynasty 19. Connections with the N are illuminated by the discovery in the Late Bronze Age levels of a clay tablet inscribed in the cuneiform alphabet of Ugarit (* RAS SHAMRA). The close of the Bronze Age is marked by quantities of * Philistine pottery, showing that these people, who settled initially along the coast, also established themselves well inland, where they became the chief rivals of the newly arrived Israelites. The city must have been taken by the Israelites in the period of the Judges, as it was set aside as a levitical city (Jos. 21:16; 1 Ch. 6:59), and was certainly in their hands by the time of Samuel, for thither the captured ark came when the Philistines released it (1 Sa. 6). It is probable that David strengthened this city in the later phases of his struggle with the Philistines, and it is likely that the casemate * walls discovered there date from this period. There is evidence that the city was destroyed in the 10th century, probably at the hands of the Egyptian king * Shishak, who invaded Judah in Rehoboam's fifth year (1 Ki. 14:25–28). About a century after this, Beth-shemesh was the scene of the great victory of Joash of Israel over Amaziah of Judah (2 Ki. 14:11–13; 2 Ch. 25:21–23). In the reign of Ahaz, Beth-shemesh was with other cities again taken by the Philistines (2 Ch. 28:18), but they were driven out by Tiglath-pileser III, to whom Ahaz had appealed and of whom Judah now became a vassal. Life in the city during the period of the monarchy was illuminated by the discovery of a refinery for olive-oil and installations for copper-working, which last had already existed in the Bronze Age. The city was now in decline, however, and it was finally destroyed by Nebuchadrezzar in the 6th century BC.

It is probable that Ir-shemesh, 'city of the sun' (Jos. 19:41), is to be equated with Beth-shemesh.

BIBLIOGRAPHY. D. Mackenzie, 'Excavations at Ain Shems', *Annual Report of the Palestine Exploration Fund*, 1, 1911, pp. 41–94; 2, 1912–13, pp. 1–100; E. Grant (and G. E. Wright), *Ain Shems Excavations*, 1–5, 1931–9; G. E. Wright, *EAEHL*, 1, pp. 248–253; J. A. Emerton, *AOTS*, pp. 197–206.

2. A city on the border of Issachar (Jos. 19:22), from which the Canaanites were not driven out, but became tributary to the Israelites (Jdg. 1:33), perhaps to be identified with modern el-ʿAbēdîyeh, which commands a ford over the Jordan some 3 km S of the Sea of Galilee.

BIBLIOGRAPHY. A. Saarisalo, *The Boundary between Issachar and Naphtali*, 1927, pp. 71–73, 119f.

3. A fortified city allotted to Naphtali (Jos. 19:38), whose site is unknown, unless it is to be identified with **2.**

4. A city in Egypt (Je. 43:13) probably to be identified with Heliopolis (which is here given in RSV) (* ON). T.C.M.

BETH-SHITTAH (Heb. *bêṯ šiṭṭâ*, 'house of [the] acacia'). A town near Abel-meholah, to which the Midianites fled from Gideon (Jdg. 7:22). No definitive identification has yet been made. J.D.D.

BETH-ZUR (Heb. *bêṯ ṣûr*). A city in Judah (Jos. 15:58), not mentioned in the account of the conquest, but settled by the descendants of *Caleb the son of Hezron (1 Ch. 2:45). It was fortified by Rehoboam in the 10th century (2 Ch. 11:7), was of some importance in the time of Nehemiah (3:16), and was a strategic fortified city during the Maccabean wars (1 Macc.).

The name is preserved at the site called Burj eṣ-Ṣur, but the ancient city is represented today by the neighbouring mound of Khirbet eṭ-Ṭubeiqah, about 6 km N of Hebron. The site was identified in 1924, and in 1931 an American expedition under the direction of O. R. Sellers and W. F. Albright carried out preliminary excavations, which, due to the troubled times, were not resumed until 1957, when a further season was undertaken under Sellers.

There was little settlement on the site until Middle Bronze Age II (*c.* 19th–16th century BC), in the latter part of which the Hyksos dominated Palestine, and it is probably to them that a system of massive defensive walls on the slope of the mound is to be attributed. When the Egyptians finally expelled the Hyksos from Egypt and pursued them well into Palestine, Beth-zur was destroyed and largely abandoned, and it evidently remained so throughout the Late Bronze Age (*c.* 1550–1200) and therefore offered no resistance to the armies of Joshua, as indicated by its absence from the conquest narratives. The Israelites evidently settled there, for in the 12th and 11th centuries the city was flourishing, though the population seems to have declined towards the end of the 10th century. No certain evidence of Rehoboam's fortifications has come to light, so it may be that he re-used the Middle Bronze Age walls and stationed only a small garrison there. The site was occupied throughout the Monarchy, abandoned during the Exile and resettled in the Persian period, but its zenith of importance came during the Hellenistic period. It was then a garrison city commanding the Jerusalem–Hebron road at the boundary between Judaea and Idumaea, and figured prominently in the Maccabean wars. A large fortress was uncovered on the summit, in which were found a great number of coins, including many of Antiochus IV Epiphanes, and several stamped Rhodian jar handles, indicating that it had been garrisoned by Greek troops. The fort had seen three main phases, the second probably due to Judas Maccabaeus, who fortified it after having defeated Antiochus' deputy Lysias there (1 Macc. 4:26–34, 61), and the third probably to be ascribed to the Macedonian general Bacchides, who fortified it around 161 BC (1 Macc. 9:52).

BIBLIOGRAPHY. O. R. Sellers, *The Citadel of Beth-zur*, 1933; W. F. Albright, *The Archaeology of Palestine*, revised edition, 1960, *passim*, esp. pp. 150–152; F. M. Abel, *Géographie de la Palestine*, 2, 1938, p. 283; R. W. Funk, *EAEHL*, 1, pp. 263–267. T.C.M.

BEULAH. When the Lord saves Zion, her land shall receive this symbolic name, meaning 'married' (Is. 62:4, AV, RSVmg.). Expressing the closeness of the relation between Zion and her sons (v. 5a), and the restoration of Zion to her God (v. 5b, *cf.* Is. 49:18; 54:1–6; Ho. 2:14–20; contrast Ho. 1:2), the name foretells the fertility of the Messianic age. The Lord will be the *ba'al*, Husband, Guarantor of fruitfulness, on the basis of righteousness (Is. 62:1–2; Dt. 28:1–14). J.A.M.

BEZALEL, BEZALEEL (Heb. *b^{e}ṣal'ēl*, 'in the shadow [protection] of God'). **1.** A Judahite, of Hezron's family in Caleb's house, Uri's son, Hur's grandson; gifted by God as a skilled craftsman in wood, metal and precious stones, and placed in charge of the making of the tabernacle; he also taught other workers. See Ex. 31:1–11; 35:30–35. **2.** A son of Pahath-moab, who was persuaded by Ezra to put away his foreign wife (Ezr. 10:30). D.W.G.

BIBLE. Derived through Latin from Gk. *biblia* ('books'), the books which are acknowledged as canonical by the Christian church. The earliest Christian use of *ta biblia* ('the books') in this sense is said to be *2 Clement* 14:2 (*c.* AD 150): 'the books and the apostles declare that the church . . . has existed from the beginning'. *Cf.* Dn. 9:2, 'I Daniel perceived in the books' (Heb. *bass^{e}pārîm*), where the reference is to the corpus of OT prophetic writings. Gk. *biblion* (of which *biblia* is the plural) is a diminutive of *biblos*, which in practice denotes any kind of written document, but originally one written on papyrus (Gk. *byblos*; *cf.* the Phoen. port of Byblus, through which in antiquity papyrus was imported from Egypt).

A term synonymous with 'the Bible' is 'the writings' or 'the Scriptures' (Gk. *hai graphai*, *ta grammata*), frequently used in the NT to denote the OT documents in whole or in part; *cf.* Mt. 21:42, 'Have you never read in the scriptures?' (*en tais graphais*); the parallel passage Mk. 12:10 has the singular, referring to the particular text quoted, 'have you not read this scripture?' (*tēn graphēn tautēn*); 2 Tim. 3:15, 'the sacred writings' (*ta hiera grammata*), v. 16, 'all scripture is inspired by God' (*pasa graphē theopneustos*). In 2 Pet. 3:16 'all' the letters of Paul are included along with 'the other scriptures' (*tas loipas graphas*), by which the OT writings and probably also the Gospels are meant.

The OT and NT—the *tawrat* (from Heb. *tôrâ*) and the *injīl* (from Gk. *euangelion*)—are acknowledged in the Qur'an (Sura 3) as earlier divine revelations. The OT in Hebrew is the Jewish Bible. The Pentateuch in Hebrew is the Samaritan Bible.

1. Content and authority

Among Christians, for whom the OT and NT together constitute the Bible, there is not complete agreement on their content. Some branches of the Syriac church do not include 2 Peter, 2 and 3 John, Jude and Revelation in the NT. The Roman and Greek communions include a number of books in the OT in addition to those which make up the Hebrew Bible; these additional books formed part of the Christian Septuagint.

While they are included, along with one or two others, in the complete Protestant English Bible, the Church of England (like the Lutheran Church) follows Jerome in holding that they may be read 'for example of life and instruction

BETH-TOGARMAH
See Togarmah, Part 3.

BETHZATHA
See Bethesda, Part 1.

BETROTHAL
See Marriage, Part 2.

BEWITCH
See Magic, Part 2.

BEZER
See Bozrah, Part 1.

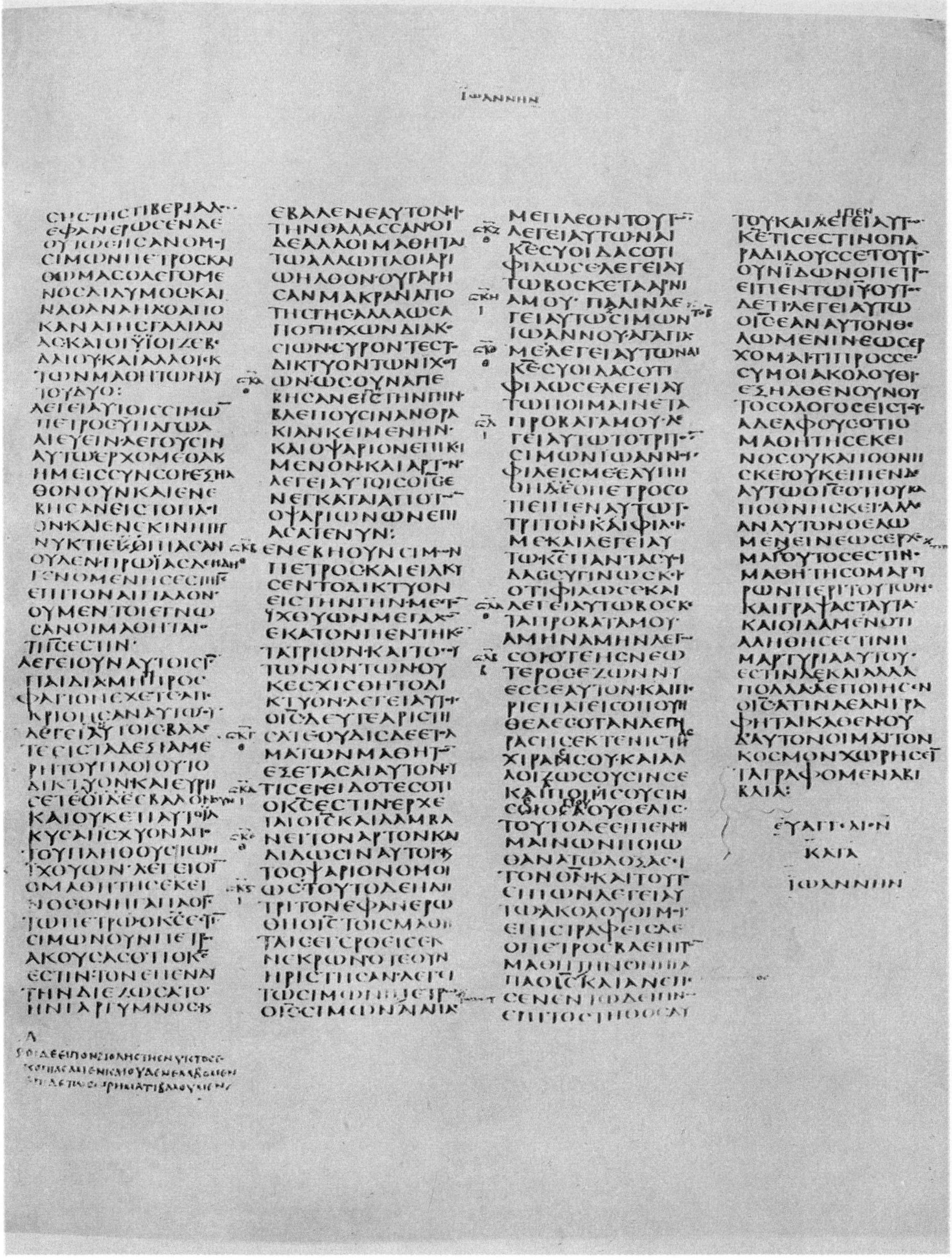

A folio of the Codex Sinaiticus, showing the last page of the Gospel of John. This is one of the early important MSS *of the whole Bible, written in Greek 'biblical uncials' on vellum. Sinai. 4th cent.* AD. (BL)

of manners; but yet doth it not apply them to establish any doctrine' (Article VI). Other Reformed Churches accord them no canonical status at all (*APOCRYPHA). The Ethiopic Bible includes *1 Enoch* and the book of *Jubilees*.

In the Roman, Greek and other ancient communions the Bible, together with the living tradition of the church in some sense, constitutes the ultimate authority. In the churches of the Reformation, on the other hand, the Bible alone is the final court of appeal in matters of doctrine and practice. Thus Article VI of the Church of England affirms: 'Holy Scripture containeth all things necessary to salvation: so that whatsoever is not read therein, nor may be proved thereby, is not to be required of any man, that it should be believed as an article of the Faith, or be thought requisite or necessary to salvation.' To the same effect the *Westminster Confession of Faith*

(1. 2) lists the 39 books of the OT and the 27 of the NT as 'all . . . given by inspiration of God, to be the rule of faith and life'.

II. The two Testaments

The word 'testament' in the designations 'Old Testament' and 'New Testament', given to the two divisions of the Bible, goes back through Latin *testamentum* to Gk. *diathēkē*, which in most of its occurrences in the Greek Bible means 'covenant' rather than 'testament'. In Je. 31:31ff. a new covenant (Heb. *b*^{e}*rîṯ*, LXX *diathēkē*) is foretold which will supersede that which Yahweh made with Israel in the wilderness (*cf.* Ex. 24:7f.). 'In speaking of a new covenant, he treats the first as obsolete' (Heb. 8:13). The NT writers see the fulfilment of the prophecy of the new covenant in the new order inaugurated by the work of Christ; his own words of institution (1 Cor. 11:25) give the authority for this interpretation. The OT books, then, are so called because of their close association with the history of the 'old covenant'; the NT books are so called because they are the foundation documents of the 'new covenant'. An approach to our common use of the term 'Old Testament' appears in 2 Cor. 3:14, 'in the reading of the old covenant', although Paul probably means the law, the basis of the old covenant, rather than the whole volume of Hebrew Scripture. The terms 'Old Testament' (*palaia diathēkē*) and 'New Testament' (*kainē diathēkē*) for the two collections of books came into general Christian use in the later part of the 2nd century; in the W, Tertullian rendered *diathēkē* into Latin now by *instrumentum* (a legal document) and now by *testamentum*; it was the latter word that survived—unfortunately, since the two parts of the Bible are not 'testaments' in the ordinary sense of the term.

III. The Old Testament

In the Hebrew Bible the books are arranged in three divisions—the Law (*tôrâ*), the Prophets (*n*^{e}*ḇî'îm*) and the Writings (*k*^{e}*ṯûḇîm*). The Law comprises the Pentateuch, the five 'books of Moses'. The Prophets fall into two subdivisions—the 'Former Prophets' (*n*^{e}*ḇî'îm rî'šônîm*), comprising Joshua, Judges, Samuel and Kings, and the 'Latter Prophets' (*n*^{e}*ḇî'îm 'aḥ*^{a}*rônîm*), comprising Isaiah, Jeremiah, Ezekiel and 'The Book of the Twelve Prophets'. The Writings contain the rest of the books —first, Psalms, Proverbs and Job; then the five 'Scrolls' (*m*^{e}*ḡillôṯ*), namely Canticles, Ruth, Lamentations, Ecclesiastes and Esther; and finally Daniel, Ezra-Nehemiah and Chronicles. The total is traditionally reckoned as 24, but these 24 correspond exactly to our common reckoning of 39, since in the latter reckoning the Minor Prophets are counted as 12 books, and Samuel, Kings, Chronicles and Ezra-Nehemiah as two each. There were other ways of counting the same 24 books in antiquity; in one (attested by Josephus) the total was brought down to 22; in another (known to Jerome) it was raised to 27.

The origin of the arrangement of books in the Hebrew Bible cannot be traced; the threefold division is frequently believed to correspond to the three stages in which the books received canonical recognition, but there is no direct evidence for this (*CANON OF THE OLD TESTAMENT).

In the LXX the books are arranged according to similarity of subject-matter. The Pentateuch is followed by the historical books, these are followed by the books of poetry and wisdom, and these by the prophets. It is this order which, in its essential features, is perpetuated (*via* the Vulgate) in most Christian editions of the Bible. In some respects this order is truer to chronological sequence of the narrative contents than that of the Hebrew Bible; for example, Ruth appears immediately after Judges (since it records things which happened 'in the days when the judges ruled'), and the work of the Chronicler appears in the order Chronicles, Ezra, Nehemiah.

The threefold division of the Hebrew Bible is reflected in the wording of Lk. 24:44 ('the law of Moses . . . the prophets . . . the psalms'); more commonly the NT refers to 'the law and the prophets' (see Mt. 5:17, *etc.*) or 'Moses and the prophets' (Lk. 16:29, *etc.*).

The divine revelation which the OT records was conveyed in two principal ways—by mighty works and prophetic words. These two modes of revelation are bound up indissolubly together. The acts of mercy and judgment by which the God of Israel made himself known to his covenant people would not have carried their proper message had they not been interpreted to them by the prophets—the 'spokesmen' of God who received and communicated his word. For example, the events of the Exodus would not have acquired their abiding significance for the Israelites if Moses had not told them that in these events the God of their fathers was acting for their deliverance, in accordance with his ancient promises, so that they might henceforth be his people and he their God. On the other hand, Moses' words would have been fruitless apart from their vindication in the events of the Exodus. We may compare the similarly significant role of Samuel at the time of the Philistine menace, of the great 8th-century prophets when Assyria was sweeping all before her, of Jeremiah and Ezekiel when the kingdom of Judah came to an end, and so forth.

This interplay of mighty work and prophetic word in the OT explains why history and prophecy are so intermingled throughout its pages; it was no doubt some realization of this that led the Jews to include the chief historical books among the Prophets.

But not only do the OT writings record this progressive twofold revelation of God; they record at the same time men's response to God's revelation—a response sometimes obedient, too often disobedient; expressed both in deeds and in words. In this OT record of the response of those to whom the word of God came the NT finds practical instruction for Christians; of the Israelites' rebellion in the wilderness and the disasters which ensued Paul writes: 'these things happened to them as a warning, but they were written down for our instruction, upon whom the end of the ages has come' (1 Cor. 10:11).

As regards its place in the Christian Bible, the OT is preparatory in character: what 'God . . . spoke of old to our fathers by the prophets' waited for its completion in the word which 'in these last days' he has 'spoken unto us by a Son' (Heb. 1:1f.). Yet the OT was the Bible which the apostles and other preachers of the gospel in the earliest days of Christianity took with them when they proclaimed Jesus as the divinely sent Messiah, Lord and Saviour: they found in it clear witness to Christ (Jn. 5:39) and a plain setting forth of the way of salvation through faith in him (Rom. 3:21; 2 Tim. 3:15). For their use of the OT they had the authority and example of Christ himself; and the church ever since has done well when it has followed the precedent set by him and his apostles and recognized the OT as Christian scripture. 'What was indispensable to the Redeemer must always be indispensable to the redeemed' (G. A. Smith).

IV. The New Testament

The NT stands to the OT in the relation of fulfilment to promise. If the OT records what 'God . . . spoke of old to our fathers by the prophets', the NT records that final word which he spoke in his Son, in which all the earlier revelation was summed up, confirmed and transcended. The mighty works of the OT revelation culminate in the redemptive work of Christ; the words of the OT prophets receive their fulfilment in him. But he is not only God's crowning revelation to man; he is also man's perfect response to God—the high priest as well as the apostle of our confession (Heb. 3:1). If the OT records the witness of those who saw the day of Christ before it dawned, the NT records the witness of those who saw and heard him in the days of his flesh, and who came to know and proclaim the significance of his coming more fully, by the power of his Spirit, after his rising from the dead.

The NT has been accepted by the great majority of Christians, for the past 1,600 years, as comprising 27 books. These 27 fall naturally into 4 divisions: (*a*) the four Gospels, (*b*) the Acts of the Apostles, (*c*) 21 letters written by apostles and 'apostolic men', (*d*) the Revelation. This order is not only logical, but roughly chronological so far as the subject-matter of the documents is concerned; it does not correspond, however, to the order in which they were written.

The first NT documents to be written were the earlier Epistles of Paul. These (together, possibly, with the Epistle of James) were written between AD 48 and 60, before even the earliest of the Gospels was written. The four Gospels belong to the decades between 60 and 100, and it is to these decades too that all (or nearly all) the other NT writings are to be ascribed. Whereas the writing of the OT books was spread over a period of 1,000 years or more, the NT books were written within a century.

The NT writings were not gathered together in the form which we know immediately after they were penned. At first the individual *Gospels had a local and independent existence in the constituencies for which they were originally composed. By the beginning of the 2nd century, however, they were brought together and began to circulate as a fourfold record. When this happened, *Acts was detached from Luke, with which it had formed one work in two volumes, and embarked upon a separate but not unimportant career of its own.

Paul's letters were preserved at first by the communities or individuals to whom they were sent. But by the end of the 1st century there is evidence to suggest that his surviving correspondence began to be collected into a Pauline corpus, which quickly circulated among the churches—first a shorter corpus of 10 letters and soon afterwards a longer one of 13, enlarged by the inclusion of the 3 *Pastoral Epistles. Within the Pauline corpus the letters appear to have been arranged not in chronological order but in descending order of length. This principle may still be recognized in the order found in most editions of the NT today: the letters to churches come before the letters to individuals, and within these two subdivisions they are arranged so that the longest comes first and the shortest last. (The only departure from this scheme is that Galatians comes before Ephesians, although Ephesians is slightly the longer of the two.)

With the Gospel collection and the Pauline corpus, and Acts to serve as a link between the two, we have the beginnings of the NT *Canon as we know it. The early church, which inherited the Hebrew Bible (or the Greek version of the LXX) as its sacred Scriptures, was not long in setting the new evangelic and apostolic writings alongside the Law and the Prophets, and in using them for the propagation and defence of the gospel and in Christian worship. Thus Justin Martyr, about the middle of the 2nd century, describes how Christians in their Sunday meetings read 'the memoirs of the apostles or the writings of the prophets' (*Apology* 1. 67). It was natural, then, that when Christianity spread among people who spoke other languages than Greek, the NT should be translated from Greek into those languages for the benefit of new converts. There were Latin and Syriac versions of the NT by AD 200, and a Coptic one within the following century.

V. The message of the Bible

The Bible has played, and continues to play, a notable part in the history of civilization. Many languages have been reduced to writing for the first time in order that the Bible, in whole or in part, might be translated into them in written form. And this is but a minor sample of the civilizing mission of the Bible in the world.

This civilizing mission is the direct effect of the central message of the Bible. It may be thought surprising that one should speak of a central message in a collection of writings which reflects the history of civilization in the Near East over several millennia. But a central message there is, and it is the recognition of this that has led to the common treatment of the Bible as a book, and not simply a collection of books—just as the Greek plural *biblia* ('books') became the Latin singular *biblia* ('the book').

The Bible's central message is the story of salvation, and throughout both Testaments three strands in this unfolding story can be distinguished: the bringer of salvation, the way of salvation and the heirs of salvation. This could be reworded in terms of the covenant idea by saying that the central message of the Bible is God's covenant with men, and that the strands are the mediator of the covenant, the basis of the covenant and the covenant people. God himself is the Saviour of his people; it is he who confirms his covenant mercy with them. The bringer of salvation, the Mediator of the covenant, is Jesus Christ, the Son of God. The way of salvation, the basis of the covenant, is God's grace, calling forth from his people a response of faith and obedience. The heirs of salvation, the covenant people, are the Israel of God, the church of God.

The continuity of the covenant people from the OT to the NT is obscured for the reader of the common English Bible because 'church' is an exclusively NT word, and he naturally thinks of it as something which began in the NT period. But the reader of the Greek Bible was confronted by no new word when he found *ekklēsia* in the NT; he had already met it in the LXX as one of the words used to denote Israel as the 'assembly' of

Yahweh. To be sure, it has a new and fuller meaning in the NT. Jesus said 'I will build my church' (Mt. 16:18), for the old covenant people had to die with him in order to rise with him to new life—a new life in which national restrictions had disappeared. But he provides in himself the vital continuity between the old Israel and the new, and his faithful followers were both the righteous remnant of the old and the nucleus of the new. The Servant Lord and his servant people bind the two Testaments together (*CHURCH; *ISRAEL OF GOD).

The message of the Bible is God's message to man, communicated 'in many and various ways' (Heb. 1:1) and finally incarnated in Christ. Thus 'the authority of the holy scripture, for which it ought to be believed and obeyed, dependeth not upon the testimony of any man or church, but wholly upon God (who is truth itself), the author thereof; and therefore it is to be received, because it is the word of God' (*Westminster Confession of Faith*, 1. 4). (*BIBLICAL CRITICISM; *CANON OF NEW TESTAMENT; *CANON OF OLD TESTAMENT; *ENGLISH VERSIONS; *INSPIRATION; *INTERPRETATION (BIBLICAL); *LANGUAGE OF APOCRYPHA, OF OLD TESTAMENT, OF NEW TESTAMENT; *REVELATION; *SCRIPTURE; *TEXTS AND VERSIONS.)

BIBLIOGRAPHY. B. F. Westcott, *The Bible in the Church*, 1896; H. H. Rowley (ed.), *A Companion to the Bible*², 1963; B. B. Warfield, *The Inspiration and Authority of the Bible*, 1948; A. Richardson and W. Schweitzer (eds.), *Biblical Authority for Today*, 1951; C. H. Dodd, *According to the Scriptures*, 1952; H. H. Rowley, *The Unity of the Bible*, 1953; F. F. Bruce, *The Books and the Parchments*, 1953; A. M. Chirgwin, *The Bible in World Evangelism*, 1954; J. Bright, *The Kingdom of God in Bible and Church*, 1955; J. K. S. Reid, *The Authority of the Bible*, 1957; S. H. Hooke, *Alpha and Omega*, 1961; *The Cambridge History of the Bible*, 1–3, 1963–70; J. Barr, *The Bible in the Modern World*, 1973. F.F.B.

BIBLICAL CRITICISM is the application to the biblical writings of certain techniques which are used in the examination of many kinds of literature in order to establish as far as possible their original wording, the manner and date of their composition, their sources, authorship and so forth.

I. Textual criticism

Textual criticism is the discipline by which an attempt is made to restore the original wording of a document where this has been altered in the course of copying and recopying. Even with modern printing methods, where repeated revisions in proof by a number of readers reduce the chance of error to a minimum, it is not often that the printed form reproduces the original copy to the last detail. It was much easier for errors in copying to arise before the invention of printing, when each copy of a document had to be written out by hand. When the author's autograph survives, the copyists' errors can be corrected by reference to it. But when the autograph has disappeared, and the surviving copies differ from one another in various details, the original wording can be reconstructed only by dint of careful study and comparison of these copies. Questions about the scribal habits of this or that copyist, and the remoteness or nearness of this or that copy to the original, must be asked. The types of error most commonly made must be borne in mind. Textual criticism is not a technique that can be learnt overnight; expertise in it comes with long study and practice, although some scholars in addition seem to have a special flair for divining the original text, even where the available copies are almost desperately corrupt.

Since no autograph or original document ('protograph') of any book of the Bible has survived, textual criticism plays an important part in Bible study. The material on which textual critics of the Bible work includes not only manuscript copies of the books of the Bible in their original languages but also ancient translations into other languages and quotations of biblical passages by ancient authors. Since it is important to establish a reliable text before proceeding to further study, textual criticism used to be called 'lower criticism', as though it represented the lower and earlier courses in the structure of critical examination. For further details of biblical textual criticism, see *Texts and Versions.

II. Literary criticism

To distinguish it from textual or 'lower' criticism, literary criticism of the documents was formerly known as 'higher' criticism, because it represented the upper courses of the critical structure, which could not be laid until the lower courses of textual criticism had been placed in position. The phrase 'higher criticism' was first applied to biblical literature by J. G. Eichhorn, in the preface to the second edition of his *Old Testament Introduction* (1787): 'I have been obliged to bestow the greatest amount of labour on a hitherto entirely unworked field, the investigation of the inner constitution of the individual books of the OT by the aid of the higher criticism—a new name to no humanist.' By the 'inner constitution' of a book he meant its structure, including a study of the sources which were used by its author and the way in which these sources were utilized or combined by him. This last aspect of the study is commonly referred to as 'source criticism'. The literary criticism of documents includes also such questions as their date and authorship.

Source criticism can be pursued with greater certainty when a documentary source of a later work has survived along with the work which has drawn upon it. In the OT this is the situation with regard to the books of Chronicles. Prominent among the sources of the Chronicler were the books of Samuel and Kings, and as these have survived we can reach fairly definite conclusions about the Chronicler's use of them. In the NT Mark's Gospel is usually believed to have been a principal source of the other two Synoptic Evangelists; here, too, the source survives alongside the later works which incorporated much of it, so that we can study the way in which Matthew and Luke used Mark.

Where the sources are no longer extant, source criticism is much more precarious. If, for example, our four Gospels in their separate form had disappeared, and we had to depend on Tatian's *Diatessaron*—a 2nd-century compilation which unstitched the contents of the Gospels and rewove them into a continuous narrative—it would have been impossible to reconstruct the four Gospels on its basis. We could certainly recognize that the *Diatessaron* was not a unitary work, and it might not be difficult to distinguish between the Johannine and Synoptic material embodied in it; but to disentangle the three Synoptic narratives would be

BIBLE TRANSLATIONS
See English versions of the Bible, Part 1.

impossible, the more so because of the considerable amount of material common to the three or to two of them. This is the kind of situation we are faced with in the source criticism of the Pentateuch. That a number of sources underlie the Pentateuch as we have it is generally agreed, but what these sources are, what their date and mutual relation may be, and how and when they were utilized in the final recension of the Pentateuch—these are questions on which scholars disagree, more today indeed than they did at the beginning of the 20th century.

The criteria for dating an ancient work are partly internal, partly external. If a work is quoted or otherwise alluded to by a reliable and datable authority we conclude that it must have been composed earlier. It may refer to events which can be dated on the basis of other documents; thus some parts of the OT can be dated because of their references to persons or incidents of Egyptian or Mesopotamian history. It may, of course, date itself; thus some of the prophetical books of the OT indicate the actual year in which this or that oracle was uttered, or the reign or reigns within which a prophet prophesied. And as the history of the ancient Near East is being reconstructed in ever-greater detail, it becomes increasingly possible to put an ancient work into its proper setting in the historical framework.

The predictive element in biblical prophecy, however, involves some modification of the common dating criteria. To interpret all fulfilled predictions as *vaticinia ex eventu* is uncritical. When we are trying to date a genuine piece of predictive prophecy, we shall regard it as earlier than the events it predicts, but not earlier than those which it refers to as having taken place, or presupposes as its historical background. On this basis we should date Nahum's prophecy before the fall of Nineveh in 612 BC, which it foretells, but later than the fall of Thebes in 663 BC, to which it refers as a past event (Na. 3:8f.). Just where within that half-century the prophecy should be located must be decided by a close examination of the wording and a reckoning of probabilities.

Basic to OT literary criticism is the criticism of the *Pentateuch. The continuous modern history of Pentateuchal criticism begins with the work of H. B. Witter (1711) and J. Astruc (1753), who distinguished two documentary sources in the earlier part of the Pentateuch, using as their criterion the alternating use of the divine names Yahweh and *ᵓᵉlōhîm*. J. G. Eichhorn (1780) correlated stylistic variations with the analysis based on the distribution of divine names. This preliminary stage in source criticism was followed by the analysis of the Pentateuch into a large number of smaller units (A. Geddes, 1792, and J. S. Vater, 1802–5). This, in turn, was followed by the 'supplementary hypothesis' (H. Ewald, 1843), which envisaged one basic document (the 'Elohist'), supplemented by a few shorter ones. H. Hupfeld (1853) distinguished two separate sources, both of which used the divine name *ᵓᵉlōhîm* in Genesis (the sources later known as P and E). These two, with the Yahwist (J) and Deuteronomic (D) sources, made up the four main sources ever since widely recognized in the documentary analysis of the Pentateuch.

To the purely literary analysis a new generation of critics (outstandingly J. Wellhausen, 1876–7) added a new criterion. The documentary sources were correlated with the religious history of Israel in so persuasive a manner that for long the Wellhausenist construction commanded the allegiance of a majority of OT scholars. Vastly augmented knowledge of Near Eastern religious and literary history, especially for the period 2000–800 BC, has now increasingly exposed the weaknesses of Wellhausenism, but of the rival constructions that have been propounded none has received anything like the acceptance which Wellhausenism once enjoyed. Interest has shifted from distinct literary sources to the continuous history of growing tradition in the life of Israel.

As for the NT, a dominant critical problem in Gospel study has been the interrelation of the Synoptic Gospels. The most notable step forward here was taken when C. Lachmann (1835) argued that Mark was the earliest of the Synoptics and was drawn upon by the other two. Source criticism in the Fourth Gospel (*cf.* R. Bultmann, E.T. 1971) has never proved convincing; criticism of this Gospel has centred round its historical character, purpose, date and authorship (*GOSPELS; *JOHN, GOSPEL OF).

The Tübingen school of F. C. Baur (1831) and his colleagues correlated the Pauline Epistles with the early history of the church, interpreted along lines similar to those laid down in Hegel's philosophy of history. Paul (of whose Epistles only Romans, 1 and 2 Corinthians and Galatians were held to be genuine) stood in sharp antithesis to the Judaizing Petrine party with regard to the way of salvation; later NT writings (notably Acts) reflect a synthesis of the two opposing positions. Even more radical was the criticism of W. C. van Manen (1890), who treated *all* the Pauline Epistles as pseudepigrapha. His position was generally rejected; the Tübingen position has been subjected to severe criticism (in England notably by J. B. Lightfoot, B. F. Westcott and W. Sanday) and wholesale modification, but its influence can be traced in NT study to the present day.

III. Form and tradition criticism

While the main schools of biblical source criticism have been predominantly literary in their interest, others have insisted on the importance of determining the oral prehistory of the written sources, and of classifying the source material into its appropriate 'forms' or categories of narrative, utterance, *etc.*

In the OT this approach has proved specially fruitful in the study of the *Psalms; their classification according to their principal types (*Gattungen*), especially by H. Gunkel (1904), where each type is related to a characteristic life-setting, has done more for the understanding of the Psalter than anything else in the 20th century.

From Scandinavia in recent times has come a more radical challenge to the basic principles of classical OT criticism in the 'traditio-historical method' of I. Engnell and the 'Uppsala school'. This method makes much more room for oral transmission alongside documentary sources, and emphasizes the great reliability of material orally transmitted.

In the NT form criticism has been intensively applied to the Gospels from 1919 onwards. By the classification of the Gospel material according to 'form' an attempt has been made to get behind the postulated documentary sources so as to envisage the state of the tradition in the pre-literary stage. Both narrative and sayings have been classified according to 'form'; but such classification throws little light on the historicity of any particular incident or utterance. The common association of form criticism with a very sceptical estimate of the historical trustworthiness of the Gospels is mostly due not to form criticism itself but to the theological outlook of many form critics. Much form criticism has endeavoured to establish the life-setting of the various units of the Gospel tradition, and this life-setting is usually discovered in the worship and witness of the early church. But a life-setting of one kind in the early church does not necessarily exclude an original life-setting in the ministry of Jesus. The form criticism of the Gospels reminds us of the inadequacy of literary analysis alone to account for their composition, and it underlines the fact that no stratum of gospel tradition, however far back we press our investigation, portrays any other Jesus than the divinely-commissioned Messiah, the Son of God.

A major task today is to establish by critical means, if possible, the continuity between the earliest attainable form of the tradition and the historical Jesus.

IV. Redaction criticism

The author of a biblical book may have received material handed down by tradition, but he did not reproduce it exactly as he received it. He was not a mere transmitter; he was an author with his own life-setting and point of view, and he shaped his material accordingly. The study of his own contribution to his work is the business of redaction criticism.

For example, the books of Joshua, Judges, Samuel and Kings contain much ancient material, some of it practically contemporary with the events which it records. But these books as they stand constitute a continuous historical corpus, compiled under the influence of Josiah's reformation and completed *c.* 562 BC. Again, much of the tradition received by the Chronicler has been preserved to us in separate form in Samuel and Kings; he may also have drawn on other sources no longer accessible to us. But on all his material he has left the impress of his characteristic outlook. Similarly, in the Gospels we can distinguish between the tradition which the Evangelists received (much of it common to two or more of them) and the distinctive work of each of the four. If tradition criticism of the Gospels is largely a matter of 'rediscovering the teaching of Jesus', redaction criticism is concerned with 'rediscovering the teaching of the Evangelists'.

BIBLIOGRAPHY. W. R. Smith, *The Old Testament in the Jewish Church*², 1892; T. K. Cheyne, *Founders of Old Testament Criticism*, 1893; C. H. Dodd, *New Testament Studies*, 1953; *idem*, *More New Testament Studies*, 1968; J. Knox, *Criticism and Faith*, 1953; P. E. Kahle, *The Cairo Geniza*², 1959; I. Engnell, 'Methodological Aspects of Old Testament Study', *VT Suppl.* 7, 1959, pp. 13ff.; R. Bultmann, *The Formation of the Gospel Tradition*, E.T. 1963; G. E. Ladd, *The New Testament and Criticism*, 1967; N. Perrin, *Rediscovering the Teaching of Jesus*, 1967; *idem*, *What is Redaction Criticism?*, 1970; J. Rohde, *Rediscovering the Teaching of the Evangelists*, E.T. 1968; K. Koch, *The Growth of the Biblical Tradition*, E.T. 1969; W. G. Kümmel, *The New Testament: The History of Interpretation of its Problems*, E.T. 1972; H. Harris, *The Tübingen School*, 1975; G. W. Anderson (ed.), *Tradition and Interpretation*, 1979; I. H. Marshall (ed.), *New Testament Interpretation*, 1977. F.F.B.

BILHAH (Heb. *bilḥâh*). **1.** A servant-girl in Laban's household, given to Rachel on her marriage; in her mistress' place she bore Dan and Naphtali to Jacob (Gn. 29:29ff.). Theories which start from the assumption that the 'sons of Israel' never actually existed as one family must suppose 'sons of Bilhah' to have a special meaning; *e.g.* Steuernagel (followed by Burney, *Judges*, pp. cvif., cx n.) equates them with 'Canaanite tribes which amalgamated with Rachel tribes'; but there is no common factor in the records concerning Dan and Naphtali which would support such a hypothesis. **2.** A Simeonite settlement, 1 Ch. 4:29, spelt *bālâh* in Jos. 19:3, *baʿalâh* in Jos. 15:29; site unknown. J.P.U.L.

BINDING AND LOOSING (Aram. *ʾasar* and *šᵉrāʾ*; Gk. *deō*, *lyō*). Rabbinic terms used in Mt. 16:19 of Peter's doctrinal authority to declare things forbidden or permitted; and in Mt. 18:18 of the disciples' disciplinary authority to condemn or absolve. The disciplinary authority differs from personal rabbinic power in being inseparable from the gospel proclaimed; so in Mt. 10:12–15 the preaching disciples pronounce no human judgment; and in Mt. 13:30; 22:13, the 'binding' symbolism signifies divine judgment. The doctrinal authority is exercised through the apostolic teaching (Acts 2:42) and a teaching ministry (2 Tim. 2:24–26), not indiscriminately.

deō (alone) is used symbolically of marriage (1 Cor. 7:29), legal ties (Rom. 7:2), and Paul's service (Acts 20:22). *lyō* (alone) is used of laws relaxed (Mt. 5:19), sins forgiven (Rev. 1:5), and (*cf. deō*) of deliverance (Lk. 13:16).

BIBLIOGRAPHY. *IDB*, 1, p. 438; R. Bultmann, *The History of the Synoptic Tradition*², 1968; *JewE*, 3, p. 215; O. Cullmann, *Peter: Disciple–Apostle–Martyr*, 1953, pp. 204–206. D.H.T.

BIRTHDAY. The day of birth and its anniversaries were usually a day of rejoicing and often of feasting. Only two such anniversaries are recorded in Scripture, that of Joseph's pharaoh (Gn. 40:20) and that of Herod Antipas (Mt. 14:6; Mk. 6:21). In Egypt, celebration of birthdays is mentioned at least as early as the 13th century BC, and probably goes back much earlier (Helck and Otto, *Kleines Wörterbuch der Ägyptologie*, 1956, p. 115, with textual references). Pharaoh's accession was likewise kept as a feast-day, as is indicated by a text of Amenophis II, *c.* 1440 BC (Helck, *JNES* 14, 1955, pp. 22–31); observation of the royal birthday is attested under Ptolemy V (*c.* 205–182 BC; Budge, *The Rosetta Stone*, 1951, p. 8). An amnesty on a royal birthday is mentioned in a wisdom-papyrus of the 4th/5th century BC (S. R. K. Glanville, *The Instructions of 'Onchsheshonqy*, 1, 1955, p. 13). The birthday celebrations of the Herods were well known in Rome; see H. Hoehner, *Herod Antipas*, 1972, pp. 160–161, n. 5. K.A.K.

BISHOP.

I. Application of the term

In classical Greek, both gods and men can be described as *episkopoi* or 'overseers' in a general and non-technical sense; inscriptions and papyri of wide distribution use the word to denote magistrates, who sometimes appear to have adminis-

BIBLICAL ETHICS
See Ethics, biblical, Part 1.

BIBLICAL INTERPRETATION
See Interpretation, biblical, Part 2.

BILEAM
See Ibleam, Part 2.

BILQIS
See Sheba, queen of, Part 3.

BIRDS
See Animals, Part 1.

■ **BITTER HERBS**
See Herbs, Part 2.

■ **BITTERN**
See Animals, Part 1.

■ **BLACK RAT**
See Animals, Part 1.

tered the revenues of heathen temples; Plutarch (*Numa* 9) calls the Roman pontifex *episkopos* of the Vestal Virgins; and the word can apply also to philosophers, especially Cynics, when acting as spiritual directors. The LXX employs the same term to describe taskmasters or officers (Ne. 11:9; Is. 60:17), and *episkopē* in reference to a visitation of God (Gn. 50:24; *cf.* Lk. 19:44). In the NT the name is applied pre-eminently to Christ (1 Pet. 2:25), next to the apostolic office (Acts 1:20, quoting Ps. 109:8), and finally to the leaders of a local congregation (Phil. 1:1).

II. Qualifications and function

It is improbable that the Christian use of the term was directly copied from either pagan or Jewish sources; taken over as a generic description of responsible office, its meaning was defined in accordance with the qualifications demanded by the church. These are listed in 1 Tim. 3:1ff. and Tit. 1:7ff.: blameless moral character, teaching ability, a hospitable nature, patience, experience, sobriety, leadership and complete integrity, or in other words, the qualities required in a good teacher, pastor and administrator. It appears to be virtually certain that the terms 'bishop' and *'presbyter' are synonymous in the NT. In Acts 20:17, 28 Paul describes the presbyters of Ephesus as *episkopoi*; he says that the Holy Spirit has made them overseers of the flock, and this might be thought to imply that only now in his absence are they to succeed to the episcopal duties which he himself has previously performed; but the usage elsewhere current is against this interpretation. Thus, in Tit. 1:5 Titus is enjoined to ordain elders, and immediately afterwards (v. 7), in obvious reference to the same persons, the qualifications of a bishop are described; again, the verb *episkopein* is used to describe the elders' function in 1 Pet. 5:2; and while 1 Tim. 3 confines itself to bishops and deacons, the mention of elders in 5:17 suggests that the eldership is another name for the episcopate. There was a plurality of bishops in the single congregation at Philippi (Phil. 1:1), from which we may conclude that they acted corporately as its governing body.

III. The rise of monarchical episcopacy

There is no trace in the NT of government by a single bishop; the position of James at Jerusalem (Acts 15:13; 21:18; Gal. 2:9, 12) was quite exceptional, and the result of his personal relationship to Christ; but influence is a different thing from office. Among the Apostolic Fathers, Ignatius is the only one who insists on monarchical episcopacy, and even he never states that this is of divine institution—an argument which would have been decisive, if it had been available for him to use. Jerome, commenting on Tit. 1:5, remarks that the supremacy of a single bishop arose 'by custom rather than by the Lord's actual appointment', as a means of preventing schisms in the church (*cf. Ep.* 146). It seems most probable that monarchical episcopacy appeared in the local congregations when some gifted individual acquired a permanent chairmanship of the board of presbyter-bishops, or when the church expanded, and the presbyters were scattered to outlying congregations, leaving only one of their number in the mother church. Harnack thought that the elders were the ruling body, while the bishops and deacons were the liturgical leaders and administrators employed by them. Others have seen the origins of the later episcopate in the position held by Paul's lieutenants Timothy and Titus; but these men are never called bishops, and we meet them in letters of recall, which make no clear provision for the appointment of personal successors. Whatever may have been the reason for the rise of the monarchical episcopate, its effect was to divide up the tasks and attributes of the presbyter-bishop, some of them adhering to the bishop and some to the presbyter.

We do not know how bishops were at first instituted to their office; but the emphasis on popular election in Acts 6, Clement of Rome and the *Didache* suggests that this was an early practice; and it was doubtless followed by prayer and imposition of hands (*CHURCH GOVERNMENT).

BIBLIOGRAPHY. See under *MINISTRY and *PRESBYTER. G.S.M.W.
R.T.B.

BITHYNIA. A territory on the Asiatic side of the Bosporus, bequeathed by its last king to the Romans in 74 BC and subsequently administered with Pontus as a single province. The area was partitioned between a number of flourishing Greek republics. It early attracted the attention of Paul (Acts 16:7), though he apparently never fulfilled his ambition of preaching there. Others did so, however (1 Pet. 1:1), and by AD 111 there was a thoroughly well-established church, even extending to rural areas, which had excited a good deal of local opposition (Pliny, *Ep.* 10. 96). E.A.J.

BITUMEN. In the EVV of the OT the Hebrew words *kōp̄er* (Gn. 6:14) and *zep̄eṯ* (Ex. 2:3; Is. 34:9) are rendered 'pitch', and *ḥēmār* (Gn. 11:3; 14:10; Ex. 2:3) 'bitumen' (AV 'slime'). It would seem better, however, to render all three terms by 'bitumen', since, while pitch is strictly the product of a distillation process, bitumen, a natural derivative of crude petroleum, is found ready to hand in Mesopotamia and Palestine, and is therefore more probably the material referred to. The word *kōp̄er* is derived from Akkadian *kupru* (from *kapāru*, 'to smear'), an outside origin for *zep̄eṯ* is suggested by its W and S Semitic cognates, while *ḥēmār* may be a native Hebrew word from the verb *ḥāmar*, 'to ferment, boil up'. In view of the diverse origins of the three terms, it seems probable that they all meant the same thing and that no scientific distinctions are to be observed. (*ARK.)

BIBLIOGRAPHY. R. J. Forbes, *Studies in Ancient Technology*, 1, 1955, pp. 1–120; *KB*³, p. 471.
T.C.M.

BLASPHEMY.

I. In the Old Testament

Here the root meaning of the word is an act of effrontery in which the honour of God is insulted by man. The proper object of the verb is the name of God, which is cursed or reviled instead of being honoured. (Compare the common biblical and rabbinical phrase, 'Blessed art thou, O Lord.') The penalty of the outrage of blasphemy is death by stoning (Lv. 24:10–23; 1 Ki. 21:9ff.; Acts 6:11; 7:58). In the first reference it is a half-caste Israelite who sins in this way; and, generally speaking, blasphemy is committed by pagans (2 Ki. 19:6, 22 = Is. 37:6, 23; Pss. 44:16; 74:10, 18; Is. 52:5), sometimes incited to it by the bad example and moral lapses of the Lord's people (2 Sa. 12:14). It follows also that when God's people

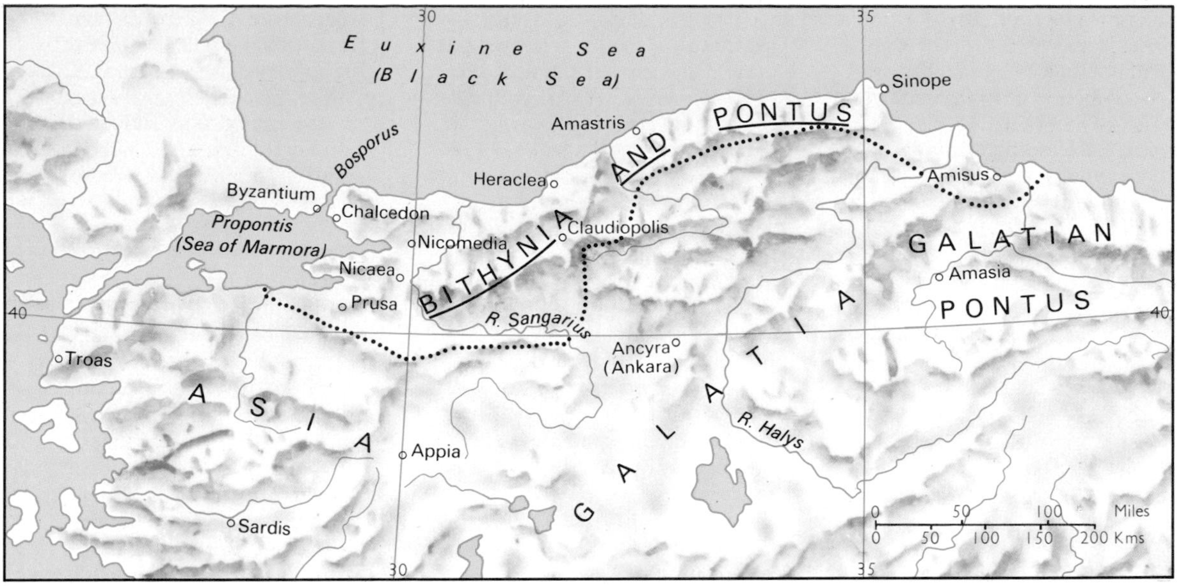

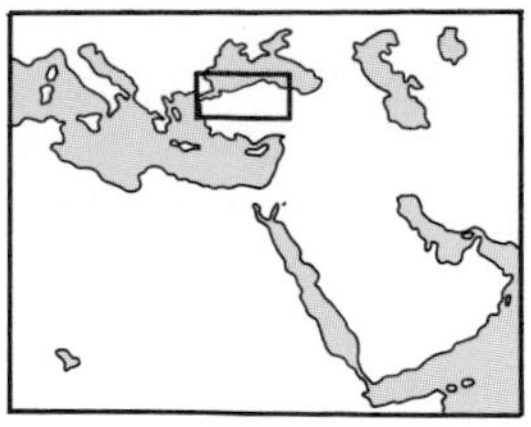

Bithynia; administered by the Romans as a single province with neighbouring Pontus.

fall into idolatry they are regarded as committing the blasphemy of the heathen (Is. 65:7; Ezk. 20:27). The name of Yahweh which it is Israel's peculiar destiny to hallow (see G. F. Moore, *Judaism*, 2, 1927–30, p. 103) is profaned by the faithless and disobedient people.

II. In the New Testament

Here there is an extension of the meaning. God is blasphemed also in his representatives. So the word is used of Moses (Acts 6:11); Paul (Rom. 3:8; 1 Cor. 4:12; 10:30); and especially the Lord Jesus, in his ministry of forgiveness (Mk. 2:7 and parallels), at his *trial (Mk. 14:61–64), and at Calvary (Mt. 27:39; Lk. 23:39). Because these representatives embody the truth of God himself (and our Lord in a unique way), an insulting word spoken against them and their teaching is really directed against the God in whose name they speak (so Mt. 10:40; Lk. 10:16). Saul of Tarsus fulminated against the early followers of Jesus and tried to compel them to blaspheme, *i.e.* to curse the saving name (Acts 24:11), and thereby to renounce their baptismal vow in which they confessed that 'Jesus is Lord' (*cf.* 1 Cor. 12:3; Jas. 2:7). His misdirected zeal, however, was not simply against the church, but against the Lord himself (1 Tim. 1:13; *cf.* Acts 9:4).

The term is also used, in a weaker sense, of slanderous language addressed to men (*e.g.* Mk. 3:28; 7:22; Eph. 4:31; Col. 3:8; Tit. 3:2). Here the best translation is 'slander, abuse'. These verses condemn a prevalent vice; but their warning may be grounded in a theological as well as an ethical context if we remember Jas. 3:9. Men are not to be cursed because on them, as men, the 'formal' image of God is stamped and the human person is, in some sense, God's representative on earth (*cf.* Gn. 9:6).

There are two problem texts. 2 Pet. 2:10–11 speaks of blasphemy against 'the glorious ones' whom angels dare not revile. These are probably evil angelic powers against whom false teachers presumed to direct their insults (*cf.* Jude 8). The blasphemy against the Holy Spirit (Mt. 12:32; Mk. 3:29) carries with it the awful pronouncement that the sinner is 'guilty of an eternal sin' which cannot be forgiven. The verse is a solemn warning against persistent, deliberate rejection of the Spirit's call to salvation in Christ. Human unresponsiveness inevitably leads to a state of moral insensibility and to a confusion of moral issues wherein evil is embraced as though it were good ('Evil, be thou my Good'; *cf.* Is. 5:18–20; Jn. 3:19). The example of this attitude is that of the Pharisees, who attributed Jesus' works of mercy to Satan. In such a frame of mind repentance is not possible to the hardened heart because the recognition of sin is no longer possible, and God's offer of mercy is in effect peremptorily refused. To be in this perilous condition is to cut oneself off from the source of forgiveness. Hebert adds a helpful pastoral note: 'People who are distressed in their souls for fear that they have committed the sin against the Holy Ghost should in most cases be told that their distress is proof that they have not committed that sin' (*TWBR*, p. 32).

BIBLIOGRAPHY. *HDB*, 1, p. 109; H. W. Beyer, *TDNT* 1, pp. 621–625; H. Währisch, C. Brown, W. Mundle in *NIDNTT* 3, pp. 340–347.

R.P.M.

BLESSED. The most frequent OT word is *bārûḵ*. When applied to God it has the sense of praise (Gn. 9:26; 1 Ki. 1:48; Ps. 28:6, *etc.*), and when used of man denotes a state of happiness (1 Sa. 26:25; 1 Ki. 2:45). *'ašᵉrê* ('how happy!', Ps. 1:1) is always used of man and has for its NT equivalent *makarios*. The latter is used in pagan Greek literature to describe the state of happiness and well-being such as the gods enjoy. In the NT it is given a strong spiritual content, as revealed in the Beatitudes (Mt. 5:3–11) and elsewhere (Lk. 1:45; Jn. 20:29; Acts 20:35; Jas. 1:12). The word seems also to contain a congratulatory element, as a note in *Weymouth's New Testament* suggests: 'People who are blessed may outwardly be much to be pitied, but from the higher and therefore truer standpoint they are to be envied, congratulated, and imitated.' *eulogētos* is used only of Christ and God (Rom. 9:5; Eph. 1:3).

BIBLIOGRAPHY. J. Pedersen, *Israel: Its Life and Culture*, 1926; *TDOT* 1, pp. 445–448; *TDNT* 4, pp. 362–370; *NIDNTT* 1, pp. 215–217.

W.W.W.

BLESSING. The OT word is *bᵉrāḵâ*, and generally denotes a

BLOOD, AVENGER OF
See Avenger of blood, Part 1.

BLOOD, FIELD OF
See Akeldama, Part 1.

BLUE
See Colours, Part 1.

BLUE ROCK THRUSH
See Animals, Part 1.

BOAR
See Animals, Part 1.

BOASTING
See Pride, Part 3.

BOAT
See Ships, Part 3.

bestowal of good, usually conceived of as material (Dt. 11:26; Pr. 10:22; 28:20; Is. 19:24, *etc*.). Often it is contrasted with the curse (Gn. 27:12; Dt. 11:26–29; 23:5; 28:2; 33:23), and sometimes is used of the formula of words which constitute a 'blessing' (Gn. 27:36, 38, 41; Dt. 33:1). The NT word *eulogia* is used also in the latter sense (Jas. 3:10), but in addition denotes both the spiritual good brought by the gospel (Rom. 15:29 mg.; Eph. 1:3) and material blessings generally (Heb. 6:7; 12:17; 2 Cor. 9:5, 'gift').

BIBLIOGRAPHY. H. W. Beyer, *TDNT* 2, pp. 754–764; H.-G. Link, U. Becker, *NIDNTT* 1, pp. 206–218.

W.W.W.

BLOOD. The point chiefly to be determined is whether 'blood' in biblical usage points basically to life or to death. There are those who hold that in the sacrificial system of the OT 'blood' represents life liberated from the limitations of the body and set free for other purposes. The ceremonial manipulation of blood on this view represents the solemn presentation to God of life, life surrendered, dedicated, transformed. The death occupies a subordinate place or even no place at all. On this view 'the blood of Christ' would mean little more than 'the life of Christ'. The evidence, however, does not seem to support it.

In the first place there is the statistical evidence. Of the 362 passages in which the Hebrew word *dam* occurs in the OT, 203 refer to death with violence. Only six passages connect life and blood (17 refer to the eating of meat with blood). From this it is clear enough that death is the association most likely to be conjured up by the use of the term.

Then there is the lack of evidence adduced in support of the life theory. Exponents of this view regard it as self-evident from passages such as Lv. 17:11, 'the life of the flesh is in the blood'. But the scriptural passages can just as well be interpreted of life yielded up in death, as of life set free.

It is undeniable that in some places atonement is said to have been secured by death, *e.g*. Nu. 35:33, 'for blood pollutes the land, and no expiation can be made for the land (lit. for the land it will not be atoned) for the blood that is shed in it, except by the blood of him who shed it'. See Ex. 29:33; Lv. 10:17.

The OT, then, affords no grounds for the far-reaching statements that are sometimes made. *Atonement is secured by the death of a victim rather than by its life. This carries over into the NT. There, as in the OT, blood is more often used in the sense of death by violence than in any other sense. When we come to the blood of Christ there are some passages which indicate in the plainest possible fashion that death is meant. Such are the references to being 'justified by his blood' (Rom. 5:9; parallel to 'reconciled . . . by the death of his Son' in v. 10), 'the blood of his cross' (Col. 1:20), the reference to coming 'by water and blood' (1 Jn. 5:6), and others.

Sometimes the death of Christ is thought of as a sacrifice (*e.g*. the blood of the covenant). But a close examination of all these passages indicates that the term is used in the same way as in the OT. That is to say, the sacrifices are still understood to be efficacious by virtue of the death of the victim. 'The blood of Christ' accordingly is to be understood of the atoning death of the Saviour.

BIBLIOGRAPHY. *TDNT* 1, pp. 172–177; S. C. Gayford, *Sacrifice and Priesthood*^{2}, 1953; L. Morris, *The Apostolic Preaching of the Cross*^{3}, 1965; F. J. Taylor, in *TWBR*; H. C. Trumbull, *The Blood Covenant*, 1887; A. M. Stibbs, *The Meaning of the Word 'Blood' in Scripture*, 1947.

L.M.

BOANERGES. The name given by Jesus to the sons of Zebedee and recorded only in Mk. 3:17. Its derivation is uncertain, but it is most likely to be the equivalent of the Heb. *b*^{e}*nê regeš* ('sons of confusion or thunder') but might be from *b*^{e}*nê r*^{e}*ḡaz* ('sons of wrath'; *cf*. Jb. 37:2). It is strange that *b*^{e}*nê* should be transliterated by *boanē-* in Gk.; a dialect pronunciation is probably indicated.

The title seems not to have been greatly used. It is variously seen to be appropriate in their fiery temper (Lk. 9:54–56), which may have caused James' death (Acts 12:2), and in the heavenly resonance of the Johannine writings.

R.E.N.

BOAZ. The hero of the book of *Ruth, a wealthy landowner of Bethlehem, a benevolent farmer who had a concern for his workers' welfare and a sense of family responsibility. This led him to redeem Ruth, the widow of a distant relative, in place of her next-of-kin, under the levirate marriage law. He thus became the great-grandfather of David (Ru. 4:17–22; *cf*. Mt. 1:5).

M.B.

BODY. The principal Hebrew words translated 'body' are *g*^{e}*wiyyâ*, used primarily of a 'corpse', though also of the living human body (Gn. 47:18), and *bāśār*, which means *'flesh'. Contrary to Greek philosophy and much modern thought, the emphasis in Hebrew is not on the body as distinct from the soul or spirit. J. A. T. Robinson (*The Body*, 1952) maintains that the Hebrews did not rigidly differentiate (*i*) form and matter, (*ii*) the whole and its parts, (*iii*) body and soul, or (*iv*) the body from the next self or object. 'The flesh-body was not what partitioned a man off from his neighbour, it was rather what bound him in the bundle of life with all men and nature.' In Aramaic sections of Daniel, often regarded as late and influenced by Greek thought, there may be more of a distinction between body and spirit (7:15), where the word (*niḏneh*) translated 'within me' is probably a loan-word, from Persian, meaning 'sheath'.

The common Hebrew word for flesh (*bāśār*) comes near to presenting a distinction from spirit (Is. 31:3), and may have influenced Paul in his theological use of the term. The usage of the term for *'heart' in Heb. could perhaps be said to approach what we would mean by spirit (Ps. 84:2), but it is significant that it is at the same time a physical organ. It is noteworthy that much modern psychology is realizing the essential unity of the whole man.

On the other hand, in Hebrew thought there were no clearly defined physiologically unifying concepts, such as the nervous or circulatory systems, and the various organs are sometimes spoken of as having a seeming independence of action (Mt. 5:29, 30) (*EYE, *HAND, *LIP, *etc*.), though this is obviously synecdoche in certain passages, *e.g*. Dt. 28:4, *beṭen* = 'belly', translated 'body' in RSV. Likewise La. 4:7, *'eṣem* = 'bone'.

The NT usage of *sōma*, 'body', keeps close to the Hebrew and avoids the thought of Greek philosophy, which tends to castigate the body as evil, the prison of the soul or reason, which was seen as good. Paul however does use 'body of sin' as a theological term parallel to 'flesh' indicating the locality of operation of sin. There is, however, a clearer distinction in the NT between body and soul or spirit (Mt. 10:28; 1 Thes. 5:23; Jas. 2:26).

But it may be doubted whether the Bible gives us a view of man as existing apart from the body, even in the future life after death. The clearly-enunciated belief in a physical resurrection found in the NT (1 Cor. 15:42–52; 1 Thes. 4:13–18), foreshadowed in the OT (Dn. 12:2), militates against any idea of man enduring apart from some bodily manifestation or form of expression, though this does not imply the regrouping of the self-same material atoms (1 Cor. 15:44). A passage which at first sight seems to suggest separation from the body (2 Cor. 5:1–8) is perhaps best explained by J. A. T. Robinson (*In the End God*, 1950) as referring not to death, but the parousia, thus not to the distinction between soul or spirit and body, but between the future resurrection body and the present mortal body. Yet it is at least arguable that Lk. 23:43; Phil. 1:23; Heb. 12:23; Rev. 6:9–11, *cf.* 20:4–6 teach that departed Christians are in conscious joy with Christ, prior to resurrection.

The form of the resurrection body—the 'spiritual body' of 1 Cor. 15—can only be glimpsed from what we know of Christ's risen body, which left no corpse in the tomb, and, it seems, passed through the graveclothes (Lk. 24:12, 31). His bodily ascension does not necessarily suppose movement to a certain locality known as heaven, but suggests the emergence of his body into a larger life transcending the space-time limitations which bind us.

The metaphor of the church as the * Body of Christ (1 Cor. 12:12ff., *etc.*) develops the idea of the body as the essential form and means of expression of the person.

BIBLIOGRAPHY. E. C. Rust, *Nature and Man in Biblical Thought*, 1953; A. R. Johnson, *The Vitality of the Individual in the Thought of Ancient Israel*, 1949; J. A. T. Robinson, *The Body*, 1952; H. G. Schütz, S. Wibbing, J. A. Motyer, *NIDNTT* 1, pp. 229–242.

B.O.B.

BODY OF CHRIST. This phrase has a threefold use in the NT.

1. The human body of Jesus Christ, insisted on by the NT writers in the face of docetism as real (denial that Jesus Christ came in the flesh is 'of antichrist', 1 Jn. 4:2–3). The reality of Christ's body is the proof of his true manhood. That the Son should take a human body is thus a fact essential for salvation (*cf.* Heb. 2:14ff.) and specifically for atonement (Heb. 10:20). The transformation (not relinquishment) of it at the resurrection is a guarantee and prototype of the resurrection body for believers (1 Cor. 15; Phil. 3:21).

2. The bread at the Last Supper over which Christ spoke the words 'This is my body' (recorded in Mt. 26; Mk. 14; Lk. 22; 1 Cor. 11, *cf.* 1 Cor. 10:16). The words have been interpreted historically as meaning both 'This represents my sacrifice' and also 'This is myself'. Interpretation must be controlled by reference to the person of Christ, to his sacrifice, and to the church, in that order.

3. The exact phrase is used by Paul in 1 Cor. 10:16; 12:27 as a description of a group of believers—*cf.* 'one body in Christ' (Rom. 12:5) and 'body' in verses referring to a local church, or to the universal church, *i.e.* 1 Cor. 10:17; 12:12; Eph. 1:23 (but see C. F. D. Moule, *Colossians*, p. 168); 2:16; 4:4, 12, 16; 5:23; Col. 1:18, 24; 2:19; 3:15. It should be noted that the phrase is 'body of Christ', not 'of Christians', and that it has visible, congregational and also eschatological significance. In Rom. and 1 Cor. it defines the unity existing between members of each local congregation; in Col. and Eph. the whole church is in view, with Christ as the head.

The origin of Paul's image has been sought in the OT idea that as each part receives its function from the whole so the whole is weakened when any part fails; also in Gk. Stoic ideas; or, more likely, through Acts 9, it expresses the conviction that Christ is totally identified with all Christians.

The exegetical problem is to establish the amount of metaphor in the phrase. If it is literal, the church is viewed as the extension of the incarnation. Paul's diverse usage on the one hand, and the probable OT background on the other, point rather to its being a metaphor instructing church members that their existence and unity depend on Christ, and that each member has power to promote or to imperil unity.

BIBLIOGRAPHY. Arndt; J. A. T. Robinson, *The Body*, 1952; E. Best, *One Body in Christ*, 1955; E. Schweizer, *TDNT* 7, pp. 1067–1094; H. G. Schütz, S. Wibbing, J. A. Motyer, in *NIDNTT* 1, pp. 229–242.

M.R.W.F.

BONES (Heb. *'eṣem*, common in the OT; Gk. *osteon*, in the NT only 5 times). As the basic and most durable part of the human body, the bones are used to describe the deepest feelings, affections and affiliations (Gn. 29:14; Jdg. 9:2; Jb. 2:5; 30:30; Ps. 22:17) often with 'flesh' as a parallel. The decent burial of the bones, or corpse, was regarded as an important matter (Gn. 50:25; Ezk. 39:15; Heb. 11:22 RSVmg.). Contact with them caused defilement (Nu. 19:16); to burn men's bones on altars was a most effective way of deconsecrating the altars (2 Ki. 23:20).

The bones preserved some of the vitality of the individual (2 Ki. 13:21), but dry bones less so (Ezk. 37:1–2, and figuratively v. 11). To break or scatter the bones was utterly to defeat an enemy (Ps. 53:5; Is. 38:13) but to burn his bones was wrong (Am. 2:1). B.O.B.

BOOK OF LIFE (Heb. *sēper ḥayyîm*; Gk. *biblos* or *biblion zōēs*, 'the roll of the living').

1. It is used of natural life, Ps. 69:28, where 'let them be blotted out of the book of the living' means 'let them die'. *Cf.* Ex. 32:32f., where Moses prays to be blotted out of God's book if Israel is to be destroyed; Ps. 139:16 ('in thy book were written . . . the days that were formed for me'); Dn. 12:1, where all the righteous who 'shall be found written in the book' will survive the eschatological tribulation.

2. In later Judaism and the NT it is used of the life of the age to come. Thus Is. 4:3, where 'every one who has been enrolled for life in Jerusalem' refers to natural life, is re-interpreted in the Targum as speaking of 'eternal life'. So in the NT the book of life is the roster of believers, *e.g.* Phil. 4:3; Rev. 3:5; 22:19, *etc.* At the last judgment everyone not enrolled in the book of life is consigned to the fiery lake (Rev. 20:12, 15); this is the book of life of the slaughtered Lamb (Rev. 13:8; 21:27), in which the names of

BODYGUARD
See Guard, Part 2.

BOETHUSIANS
See Herodians, Part 2.

BOOK
See Writing, Part 3.

the elect have been inscribed 'from the foundation of the world' (17:8). The same idea is expressed in Lk. 10:20, 'your names are written in heaven'; Acts 13:48, 'as many as were ordained (*i.e.* inscribed) to eternal life believed'. F.F.B.

BOOTH. A word sometimes used in the EVV to translate the Hebrew term *sukkâ*, a booth or rude temporary shelter made of woven boughs (Ne. 8:14–17). This type of structure figured particularly in the annual Feast of *Tabernacles (Lv. 23:34; Dt. 16:13, AV, RV 'tabernacles'), but was also used by armies in the field (*PAVILION, *TENT), and in agriculture as a shelter from the sun (see Jb. 27:18; Jon. 4:5); or for cattle (Gn. 33:17; *SUCCOTH). T.C.M.

BOOTHS, FEAST OF
See Tabernacles, feast of, Part 3.

BOTCH
See Health, Part 2.

BOW AND ARROW
See Armour, Part 1.

BOX TREE
See Trees, Part 3.

BOZEZ
See Seneh, Part 3.

BOWELS (Heb. *mēʿîm*; Gk. *splanchna*). The Hebrews had no clear idea of the physiology of the internal organs. RSV translates *mēʿîm* and *splanchna* variously by 'belly', Jon. 1:17; *'body', 2 Sa. 7:12; *'breast', Ps. 22:14; *'heart', Jb. 30:27; 1 Jn. 3:17; *'soul', Is. 16:11; *'stomach', Ezk. 3:3; *'womb', Ps. 71:6; and only by 'bowels' where the reference is clearly to 'intestines', usually as visible by reason of death or an abdominal wound, 2 Sa. 20:10; Acts 1:18.

The translation is also sometimes figurative, 'anguish' (Je. 4:19); especially in NT, 'affections' (2 Cor. 6:12). Gk. has a cognate verb *splanchnizomai* (Lk. 10:33), 'to feel compassion'. B.O.B.

BOX. 1. Heb. *paḵ*, 'flask', used as an oil container by Samuel when anointing Saul (1 Sa. 10:1, AV 'vial') and by one of the sons of the prophets when anointing Jehu (2 Ki. 9:1, 3). Narrow-necked juglets found on Iron Age sites may have been called *paḵ*, but the LXX *phakos*, lentil-shaped, suggests a lentoid flask with two handles, of similar date. (*ARK OF THE COVENANT.)

2. Gk. *alabastron*, a perfume bottle, not necessarily of alabaster. The woman at Simon the leper's house may have broken off the narrow neck (Mt. 26:7; Mk. 14:3; *cf.* Lk. 7:37). A.R.M.

BOZRAH. 1. A city of Edom whose early king was Jobab (Gn. 36:33; 1 Ch. 1:44). Its later overthrow was predicted by Amos (1:12) and taken as symbolic of the defeat of powerful Edom and of God's avenging all his enemies (Is. 34:6; 63:1). Bozrah is usually identified with modern Buseirah, a fortified city of 19 acres atop a crag at

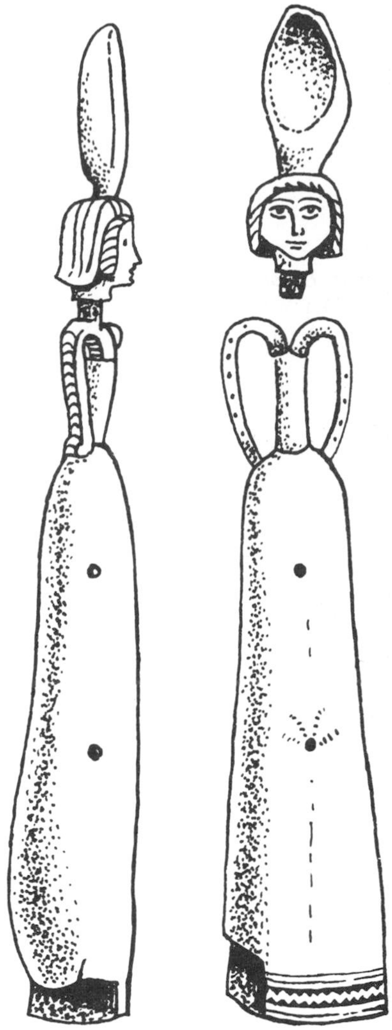

Ivory unguent vase with stopper pierced to enable contents to flow into a bowl. Lachish. 14th cent. BC.

Native booth erected by man who is guarding a field against intruders. (ZR)

the head of Wadi Hamayideh, *c.* 60 km N of Petra and *c.* 40 km SSE of the Dead Sea, controlling the *King's Highway from Elath and thus able to deny passage to the Israelites (Nu. 20:17). Excavations at Buseirah 1971–6 have uncovered three principal levels of occupation in the 8th century BC and later, though not as yet earlier (C. Bennett, *Levant* 5, 1973, pp. 1–11; 6, 1974, pp. 1–24).

2. A city of Moab (Je. 48:24; LXX Bosor), perhaps to be identified with Bezer, a town rebuilt by king *Mesha *c.* 830 BC, possibly Umm al-'Amad, NE of Medeba, used as a levitical city of refuge.

3. A town of SE Hauran, *c.* 120 km S of Damascus at the head of the King's Highway, captured by Judas Maccabeus (165–160 BC; 1 Macc. 5:26–28; Jos., *Ant.* 12. 336). Bozrah (mod. Busra eski-Sham, and probably the Busruna [Bozrah] of the 14th century BC *Amarna texts) became the most N provincial capital of Roman Arabia in NT times. D.J.W.

BRANCH. 1. The word represents various Heb. and Gk. words meaning shoot, twig, bough, palm-branch, *etc.* It occurs frequently in passages where Israel is spoken of under the figure of a tree, *e.g.* a vine (Ps. 80:11; Ezk. 17:6; Na. 2:2; *cf.* Jn. 15:1ff.) or a cedar (Ezk. 17:23) or an olive (Ho. 14:6; *cf.* Rom. 11:16ff.). Branches of trees, palm, myrtle and willow were used ceremonially at the Feast of Tabernacles for making *booths (*sukkôṯ*) (Lv. 23:40; Ne. 8:15), and for carrying in procession with cries of *Hosanna (Ps. 118:27; Mishnah, *Sukkah* 4). *Cf.* Jesus' triumphal entry into Jerusalem (Mt. 21:8–9; Mk. 11:8–10; Jn. 12:13).

2. Of special interest is the Messianic use of the word (Heb. *ṣemaḥ*) for the scion of the family of David who would come to rule Israel in righteousness. Explicitly prophesied in Je. 23:5; 33:15, the expression looks back to Is. 4:2 (*cf.* Is. 11:1, Heb. *nēṣer*). Zc. 3:8; 6:12 show that the title 'branch' was a recognized Messianic term after the Exile, used to incorporate the idea of priest-king.

3. In Ex. 25:31ff.; 37:17ff. the word is used of the golden lampstand in the tabernacle, which is traditionally depicted with a central stem and three branches on either side. The Heb. *qāneh* 'reed' may have been misunderstood here, for the seven-branched candlestick is not known earlier than the 1st century BC.

BIBLIOGRAPHY. J. G. Baldwin, '*Ṣemaḥ* as a Technical Term in the Prophets', *VT* 14, 1964, pp. 93–97; R. North, 'Zechariah's Seven-Spout Lampstand', *Biblica* 51, 1970, pp. 183ff. J.G.B.

BREAD. Bread was the all-important commodity of the ancient Near East, and the price of grain is an infallible index to economic conditions at any given time. In early Babylonia the grain of corn provided the basic unit for

BRACELET
See Ornaments, Part 2.

BRAMBLE
See Plants (Thorns), Part 3.

BRAZEN SERPENT
See Serpent, bronze, Part 3.

Pottery figure kneading dough, from Buqbaq cemetery, ez-Zib (Achzib). Iron Age II, 9th–early 6th cent. BC. (ZR)

BREAKFAST
See Meals, Part 2.

BREAKING OF BREAD
See Lord's Supper, Part 2.

Baking bread. One servant is kneading dough while the other tends the fire. Egyptian model from Asyut. Middle Kingdom, c. 1900 BC. (BM)

the system of weights, and cereal took the place of money in commerce. Hosea paid part of the price of his wife in grain.

While we possess much information about the price of grain, references to the price of bread are extremely rare because it was usually made by each housewife. One reference from the Hammurapi period (18th century BC) gives 10 *še* (about a twentieth of a shekel) as the price of about 2½ litres (4 *sila*) of bread, and half this amount was a man's daily ration. (B. Meissner, *Warenpreise in Babylonien*, p. 7.) In 2 Ki. 7:1 the price quoted for cereal seems abnormally high, but it was doubtless considerably lower than in the preceding famine. In Rev. 6:6 the prices describe graphically the grim conditions of famine.

Barley bread was probably the most widely used. The fact that barley was also fed to horses (1 Ki. 4:28) does not necessarily imply that it was considered inferior, any more than is oats in our day. Wheat bread was more highly prized and was probably fairly common. Spelt was also used, but rye does not seem to have been cultivated. On occasions various cereals may have been mixed together and, as Ezk. 4:9 shows, even lentil and bean meal were added.

The general term for grain was *dāḡān*. After threshing and winnowing, the grain was either crushed in a *mortar with a pestle or was ground in a *mill by rubbing the upper stone to and fro on the nether millstone. The term for flour or meal in general was *qemaḥ*, and when necessary this was qualified by the addition of the name of the cereal (Nu. 5:15). What was probably a finer quality was called *sōleṯ* (*cf.* 1 Ki. 4:22), but some scholars take this word to mean 'groats'. This was the meal used in the offerings (Ex. 29:40; Lv. 2:5, *etc.*).

The word *qālî'*, often translated 'parched corn', was probably roasted grains, which were eaten without further preparation.

The flour, mixed with water and seasoned with salt, was kneaded in a special trough. To this, leaven in the form of a small quantity of old fermented dough was added until the whole was leavened. Unleavened bread also was baked. Leaven was not used in the offerings made by fire (Lv. 2:11, *etc.*), and its use was forbidden during Passover week. The baking was done either over a fire on heated stones or on a griddle, or in an oven. Leavened bread was usually in the form of round, flat loaves, and unleavened in the form of thin cakes. The form called *'uḡâ* was probably the griddle cake, since it required turning (Ho. 7:8).

When bread was kept too long it became dry and crumbly (Jos. 9:5 and 12). In Gilgamesh 11. 225–229, there is an interesting account of the deterioration of bread (*ANET*, p. 95). (*FOOD.)

That so vital a commodity should leave its mark on language and symbolism is not surprising. From earliest times the word 'bread' was used for food in general (Gn. 3:19 and Pr. 6:8, where Heb. has 'bread'). Since it was the staple article of diet, it was called 'staff' of bread (Lv. 26:26), which is probably the origin of our phrase 'staff of life'. Those who were responsible for bread were important officials, as in Egypt (Gn. 40:1), and in Assyria a chief baker is honoured with an eponymy. Bread was early used in sacred meals (Gn. 14:18), and loaves were included in certain offerings (Lv. 21:6, *etc.*). Above all, it had a special place in the sanctuary as the 'bread of the Presence'. The manna was later referred to as 'heavenly bread' (see Ps. 105:40). Our Lord referred to himself as the 'bread of God' and as the 'bread of life' (Jn. 6:33, 35), and he chose the bread of the Passover to be the symbolic memorial of his broken body. W.J.M.

BREAST. Four uses of the word may be distinguished. **1.** Heb. *daḏ* or *šaḏ* (Jb. 3:12; Ezk. 23:21, *etc.*); Gk. *mastos*, with reference to sucking, *etc.*, as of a woman, or an animal (La. 4:3; Lk. 11:27). **2.** The same used figuratively (Is. 60:16; 66:11), symbolic of riches. **3.** Heb. *ḥāzeh* (Ex. 29:26; Lv. 8:29, *etc.*), the breast portion of an animal, often offered as a wave-offering. **4.** Aram. *ḥ^a^ḏî* (Dn. 2:32), the chest, equivalent to the Gk. *stēthos* in the NT, where smiting upon the breast is a sign of anguish (Lk. 18:13), and leaning upon the breast a sign of affection (Jn. 13:23, 25). The word 'bosom', Heb. *ḥêq* (Mi. 7:5), presents a close parallel in this sense. Ho. 13:8 RSV, 'tear open their breast', Heb. *lēḇ* 'their *heart*'. B.O.B.

BREASTPIECE OF THE HIGH PRIEST. Heb. *ḥōšen*, interpretatively translated 'breastplate', 'breastpiece' (Ex. 28:4, 15–30; 39:8–21; *cf.* LXX, *peristēthion*, Ex. 28:4), is, however, etymologically obscure. The former relation to Arab. cognates with the sense 'beauty' is not now usually given credence and no other cognate attracts confidence. Most commentators tend towards the contextual translation 'pouch'. Made of the same materials as the ephod (Ex. 28:15), the breastpiece was a square pouch (v. 16), with gold rings at the 4 corners (vv. 23, 26). The lower rings were fastened by blue laces to rings above the girdle of the ephod (v. 28). On the breastpiece were set 12 gems engraved with the names of the tribes (vv. 17–21), and gold cords fastened the upper rings to the two similarly engraved gems on the shoulders of the ephod (vv. 9–12, 22–25). Thus, symbolically, on the one hand the nation, in God's sight, rested on a high-priestly person and work; on the other hand, the priest carried continually into God's presence the people, as a loved responsibility (v. 29); and equally, as containing the oracular *Urim and Thummim (v. 30)—hencc the title 'breastpiece of judgment' (v. 15; *cf.* the customary LXX, *logion tēs kriseōs*, 'oracle of judgment')—the breastpiece symbolizes the priest as the announcer of God's will to man (*cf.* Mal. 2:6–7).

BIBLIOGRAPHY. Josephus, *Ant.* 3. 162; B. S. Childs, *Exodus*, 1974, p. 526; U. Cassuto, *A Commentary on the Book of Exodus*, 1967, p. 375. J.A.M.

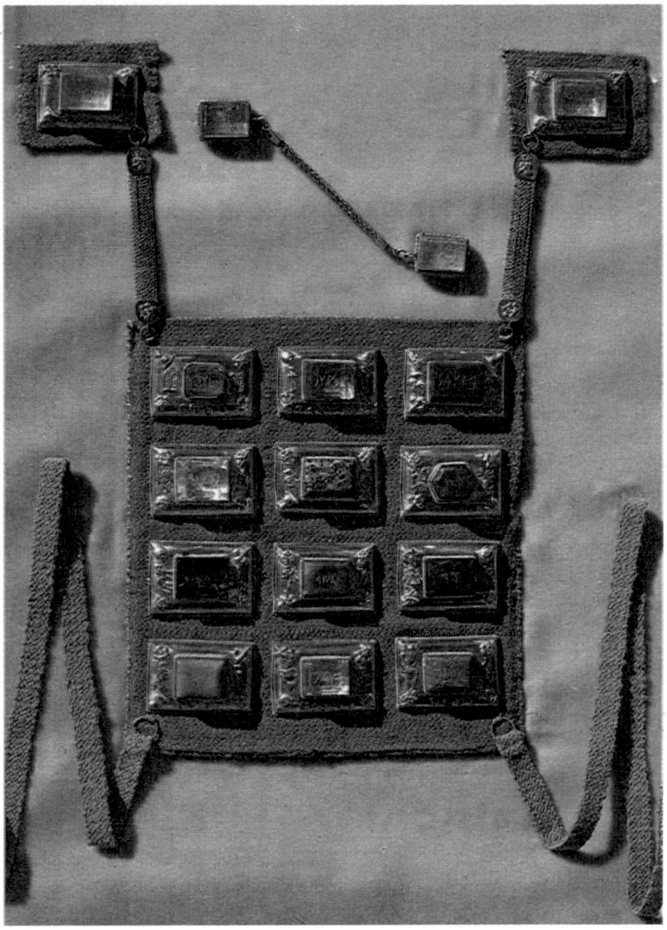

Modern replica of Aaron's breastpiece, showing the stones with the symbol employed for each of the twelve tribes. (GLCW)

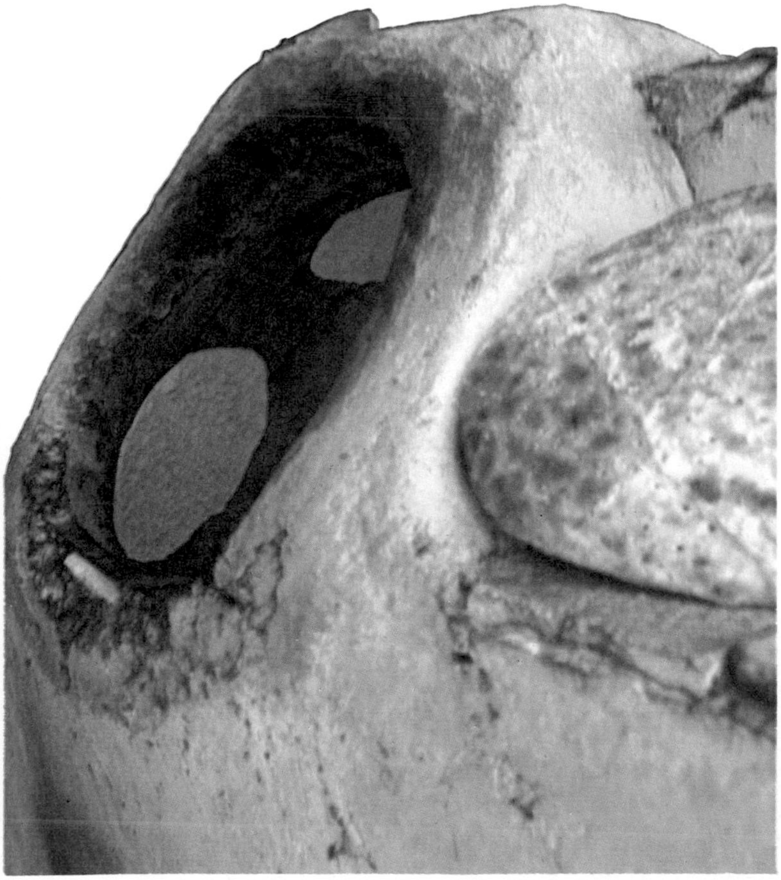

Flat dough placed on the wall of a heated oven. Iran. (RH)

BRETHREN OF THE LORD. Four men are described in the Gospels as 'brothers' of Jesus, *viz.* James, Joses, Simon and Judas (Mt. 13:55; Mk. 6:3). The native townsmen of Jesus expressed amazement that a brother of these men should possess such wisdom and such power (Mk. 6:2–3). On the other hand, Jesus contrasted his brothers and his mother, who were bound to him by physical ties, with his disciples, who in virtue of their obedience to the will of his Father were regarded by him as his spiritual 'brothers' and 'mother' (Mt. 12:46–50). Three views have been held as to the nature of the relationship between these men and Jesus.

a. The 'brothers' were the younger children of Joseph and Mary. This view is supported by the *prima facie* meaning of 'firstborn' in Lk. 2:7, and by the natural inference from Mt. 1:25 that after the birth of Jesus normal marital relations between Joseph and Mary followed. It was strongly advocated by Helvidius in the 4th century, but came to be regarded as heretical in the light of the doctrine, in-

BREASTPLATE See Breastpiece, Part 1.

Brick made of sun-dried Nile clay mixed with chopped straw, stamped with the name and titles of Rameses II. c. 1290 BC. (DJW)

creasingly attractive as the ascetic movement developed, that Mary was always virgin. Since the Reformation it has been the view most commonly held by Protestants.

b. The 'brothers' were the children of Joseph by a former wife. This view, first promulgated in the 3rd century and defended by Epiphanius in the 4th, became the accepted doctrine of the Eastern Orthodox Church. It has no direct support from the NT. Its advocates have usually supposed, however, that the opposition of the brothers to Jesus during his earthly life was largely due to jealousy of the achievements of their younger half-brother.

c. The 'brothers' were the cousins of Jesus. This view, put forward by Jerome in defence of the doctrine of the perpetual virginity of the mother of Jesus, has remained the official teaching of the Roman Catholic Church. It is based on the following series of arbitrary assumptions: (i) that the correct interpretation of Jn. 19:25 is that there were three, not four, women standing near the cross, *viz.* Mary the mother of Jesus, her sister identified with 'Mary of Clopas', and Mary of Magdala; (ii) that the second Mary in the Johannine passage is identical with the Mary described in Mk. 15:40 as 'the mother of James the less and of Joses'; (iii) that this 'James the less' is the apostle called in Mk. 3:18 'the son of Alphaeus'; (iv) that the second Mary in Jn. 19:25 was married to Alphaeus. Why she should be described as 'of Clopas', which presumably means 'the wife of Clopas', Jerome admitted that he was ignorant. The theory would seem to demand either that Clopas is another name for Alphaeus, or that this Mary was married twice. By this ingenious but unconvincing exegesis Jerome reduced the number of men called James in the NT to two—the son of Zebedee, and James the Lord's brother, who was also an apostle and known as 'the less' to distinguish him from the son of Zebedee! It is probable that 'my brethren' in Mt. 28:10 refers to a wider group than 'the brothers' already mentioned.

BIBLIOGRAPHY. See the excursus by J. B. Lightfoot 'The Brethren of the Lord' in *Saint Paul's Epistle to the Galatians*[2], 1866, pp. 247–282; J. J. Gunther, 'The Family of Jesus', *EQ* 46, 1974, pp. 25ff.; J. W. Wenham, 'The Relatives of Jesus', *EQ* 47, 1975, pp. 6ff.; and the introductions to the commentaries mentioned under *JAMES, EPISTLE OF.

R.V.G.T.

BRIBE

See Gift, Part 1.

BRICK. A lump of mud or clay, usually rectangular, sun-dried or kiln-baked ('burnt'); the commonest building material of the ancient biblical world. At first moulded by hand, bricks early began to be made ('struck') with open, rectangular, wooden moulds. The mud was mixed with sand, chopped straw, *etc.*, the bricks struck off in long rows, and left to dry out; see Petrie, *Egyptian Architecture*, 1938, pp. 3–13; Lucas, *Ancient Egyptian Materials and Industries*[4], 1962, pp. 48–50. Bricks often bore stamped impressions: in Egypt, the name of the pharaoh or of the building they were used in; in Babylonia, also the king's name and dedication; *e.g.* Nebuchadrezzar, of whom five different stamps are known. For these and Nebuchadrezzar's brick-making techniques, see R. Koldewey, *Excavations at Babylon*, 1914, pp. 75–82 and figures.

Sun-dried brick was the universal building material of Mesopotamia, where kiln-baked bricks were often used for facings and pavements (*cf.* also Gn. 11:3). In Egypt sun-dried brick was usual for all but the most important and permanent buildings (*i.e.* stone temples and tombs); kiln-baked bricks are almost unknown before Roman times. Various forms of bonding were practised.

Ex. 5:6–19 accurately reflects brick-making usage in ancient Egypt; straw or stubble was regularly used in the 19th and 20th Dynasties (13th–12th centuries BC), as bricks so made proved much stronger. In contemporary papyri one official reports of his workmen, 'they are making their quota of bricks daily', while another complains, '. . . at Qenqenento, . . . there are neither men to make bricks nor straw in the neighbourhood'; *cf.* R. A. Caminos, *Late-Egyptian Miscellanies*, 1954, pp. 106, 185. The straw itself is not so much a binding-agent, but its chemical decay in the clay released an acid which (like glutamic or gallotannic acid) gave the clay greater plasticity for brick-making. This effect (but not, of course, the chemistry) was evidently a well-known one. See A. A. McRae in *Modern Science and Christian Faith*, 1948, pp. 215–219, after E. G. Acheson, *Transactions of the American Ceramic Society* 6, 1904, p. 31; further comment and references in Lucas, *op. cit.*, p. 49; and *cf.* also C. F. Nims, *BA* 13, 1950, pp. 21–28.

In Palestine sun-dried brick was also the norm; city and house walls

Brickmakers, including Syrian slaves, working under an Egyptian task-master. Tomb of Rekh-mi-Rē', Thebes. c. 1450 BC. (LD)

were often of brick upon a stone foundation.

For 'burning incense upon bricks' (Is. 65:3), *cf.* mud-brick altars from a very early period at Megiddo, *ANEP*, p. 229, fig. 729. (*ARCHITECTURE, *WALLS.)

BIBLIOGRAPHY: K. A. Kitchen, 'From the Brickfields of Egypt', *TynB* 27, 1976, pp. 137–147.

K.A.K.

BRICK-KILN. Oven for baking mud bricks. In the biblical East sun-dried mud bricks were always the cheapest and commonest building material, but were not specially durable (*e.g.* in rainy weather). Burnt *bricks were almost indestructible. They were used in Mesopotamia for facings, pavements, *etc.*, in important buildings from very early times, but are hardly known in Palestine or Egypt before Roman times. Hence brick-kilns are regularly found in Mesopotamia but not by the Nile or Jordan. In the AV of 2 Sa. 12:31; Je. 43:9; Na. 3:14 the term *malbēn* is rendered 'brickkiln', but this seems to be incorrect. The *malbēn* is the rectangular, hollow wooden brick-mould for making ordinary sun-dried bricks in 2 Sa. and Na., and is used figuratively to describe the rectangular brick pavement in Tahpanhes in Jeremiah. In 2 Sa. 12:31 the meaning is that David put the Ammonites to hard labour (in the verb, reading *d* for *r*, very similar letters in Heb.), with saws, harrows, axes and brick-moulds (*malkēn* is probably for *malbēn*, *MT* margin/*Qᵉrê*).

The 'fiery furnace' into which Daniel's three friends were cast as punishment (Dn. 3:6, 11, 15, 19–23) was very likely a brick-kiln, one of those that must have supplied burnt bricks to Nebuchadrezzar's Babylon. The word used, *'attûn*, 'furnace', is probably identical with the Assyro-Babylonian word *utūnum*, 'furnace, kiln'. Outside of Daniel, Nebuchadrezzar's cruel punishment is attested not only in Je. 29:22 but also by actual inscriptions: in a Babylonian letter of *c.* 1800 BC and in an Assyrian court regulation of *c.* 1130 BC people were (or might be) thrown into a furnace as a punishment; see G. R. Driver, *AfO* 18, 1957, p. 129, and E. F. Weidner, *AfO* 17, 1956, pp. 285–286. The practice is used as a comparison in Ps. 21:9. On the 'fiery furnace' being a brick-kiln, compare the reference to the flames of similar modern brick-kilns lighting up the sky near Babylon by R. Koldewey, *The Excavations at Babylon*, 1914, pp. 81–82. The brick-kilns of ancient Babylonia may have looked like the large pottery-kiln excavated in Nippur and pictured in B. Meissner, *Babylonien und Assyrien*, 1, 1920, p. 234 and figs. 55–56.

K.A.K.

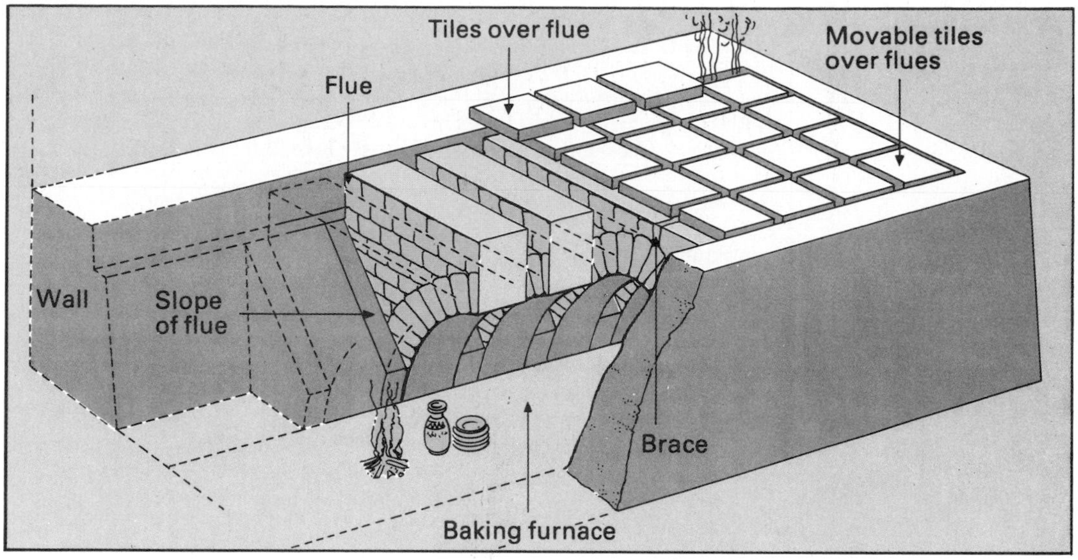

A pottery kiln, excavated at Nippur.

BRIDE, BRIDEGROOM. These two words are quite naturally complementary to each other (Jn. 3:29a) and are found side by side in Is. 62:5; Je. 7:34; 16:9; 25:10; 33:11; Rev. 18:23. 'The voice of the bridegroom and the voice of the bride' in these references is parallel with 'the voice of mirth and gladness', and illustrates the rich concept of marital joy of which the Bible often speaks (*e.g.* Ps. 128; Pr. and Ct.). Is. 42:5 extends this significance to include a comparison between human relationships and God's joy in his people Israel, who are regarded as his bride (*cf.* Is. 54:6; Je. 2:2; 3:20; Ezk. 16:8; 23:4; Ho. 2:16). This metaphor prepares the way for the NT allusions to the church as the bride of Christ, especially in the Epistles (2 Cor. 11:2; Eph. 5:25–27, 31f.; *cf.* Rev. 19:7; 21:2; 22:17). According to this picture the Lord is the divine Bridegroom who seeks his bride in love and enters into covenant relations with her.

Whether this allegory of Christ and the church is derived from the teaching of Jesus or not is a debatable point. Some deny the allegorical interpretation of Mt. 25:1–12 on the ground that the Messiah is not represented in the OT and in the rabbinical literature as a Bridegroom (so J. Jeremias, *TDNT* 4, pp. 1099–1106, and *The Parables of Jesus*, E.T. 1954, p. 46). But, on the other hand, there is the witness of Mk. 2:19–20 (*cf.* Mt. 9:15; Lk. 5:34–35), which shows that the term Bridegroom was used by the Lord as a Messianic designation and corresponds to his use of the third person in speaking of himself as 'the Son of man' (so V. Taylor, *The Gospel according to St Mark*, 1952, *ad loc.*). This is further confirmed if the variant reading of Mt. 25:1, 'to meet the bridegroom and the bride', is accepted; and there is early and important attestation of it (see A. H. McNeile, *The Gospel according to St Matthew*, 1915, *ad loc.*; F. C. Burkitt, *JTS* 30, 1929, pp. 267–270; T. W. Manson, *The Sayings of Jesus*, 1949, pp. 243f., who makes an interesting and plausible suggestion to explain the identity of the bride). See also Jn. 3:29b for John the Baptist as 'the friend of the bridegroom', *i.e.* the groomsman (Heb. *šôšᵉḇîn*), who acted as 'best man' (*cf.* 1 Macc. 9:39). He was the agent for the bridegroom in arranging the marriage and played an important part in the wedding festivities, as did also the bridegroom's attendants, who are referred to in Mk. 2:19 (AV) as 'the sons of the bridechamber'.

BIBLIOGRAPHY. For a full study of 'the bridal dignity of the church', see C. Chavasse, *The Bride of Christ*, 1939. See also A. Isaksson, *Marriage and Ministry in the New Temple*, 1965; J. P. Sampley, *And the Two Shall Become One Flesh*, 1971.

R.P.M.

BRICKS, COLOURED GLAZE
See Ornaments, Part 2.

BRIDECHAMBER
See Marriage, Part 2.

BRIDESMAIDS
See Marriage, Part 2.

BRIDLE
See Metheg-ammah, Part 2.

BRIER
See Plants (Thorns), Part 3.

BRIMSTONE (Heb. *goprîṯ*, Gk. *theion*, 'sulphur'), a yellow crystalline solid, with medicinal and fumigating properties, which occurs in the natural state in regions of volcanic activity such as the valley of the Dead Sea (*cf.* Gn. 19:24). The element burns readily in air, and is consequently associated in the Bible with fire (*e.g.* Gn. 19:24; Ps. 11:6; Ezk. 38:22; Lk. 17:29; Rev. 9:17–18; 14:10; 19:20; 20:10; 21:8), and appears in figures of the burning wrath of God (Is. 30:33; 34:9; Rev. 14:10). The usual environment of its natural occurrence also led to the use of the word to indicate barrenness of land (Dt. 29:23; Jb. 18:15). That the substance was well known in the ancient world is suggested by the occurrence of cognates to *goprîṯ* in Akkadian, Aramaic and Arabic. *theion* occurs already in Homer, and is regularly used in the LXX to translate *goprîṯ*. 'Brimstone' was the form current in 1611 of a Middle English word, meaning 'burn(ing)-stone', which had appeared, for instance, in Wyclif's Bible as (among other spellings) 'brunston'. The word, though archaic in modern extra-biblical usage, has been retained by the RV and RSV.

BIBLIOGRAPHY. R. Campbell Thompson, *A Dictionary of Assyrian Chemistry and Geology*, 1936, pp. 38–39; *KB*³, p. 193.

T.C.M.

BRONZE SERPENT
See Serpent, bronze, Part 3.

BROOCH
See Ornaments, Part 2.

BROOK. The word *naḥal* is used variously of a perennial stream, the flow of water and the dried course of a river-bed. Apart from the Jordan itself, nearly all the perennial streams are left-bank tributaries of the Jordan fed by springs. Such is the Kishon (1 Ki. 18:40), the second largest river by volume, and the Jabbok, modern Zerka (Gn. 32:22–23). The brook in full spate is used metaphorically (*e.g.* Am. 5:24), while the ephemeral nature of the dried-up brook is also used (Jb. 6:15). A severe drought will terminate the flow even of spring-fed brooks (*e.g.* 1 Ki. 17:2–7). Sometimes the stream-bed has a mantle of vegetation owing to the shallow water-table. Thus 'the brook of the willows' (Is. 15:7) may describe the cover of oleander bushes and other vegetation. In poetry *mayim*, 'water', is frequently used of the channel bed (Jb. 12:15; Ps. 42:1; Is. 8:7; Joel 1:20). (*EGYPT, RIVER OF.) J.M.H.

BROTHERLY LOVE. Gk. *philadelphia* (Rom. 12:10; 1 Thes. 4:9; Heb. 13:1; 1 Pet. 1:22; 2 Pet. 1:7) means, not figurative brother-*like* love, but the love of those united in the Christian brotherhood (*adelphotēs*, 1 Pet. 2:17; 5:9; *cf.* the adjective *philadelphos*, 1 Pet. 3:8). Outside Christian writings (*e.g.* 1 Macc. 12:10, 17) *philadelphia* is used only of men of common descent. In the OT, 'brother', like 'neighbour', meant 'fellow Israelite' (Lv. 19:17f.; *cf.* Acts 13:26). Jesus widened the scope of love for fellow men (Mt. 5:43–48; Lk. 10:27–37), but also, by calling his followers his own (Mk. 3:33ff.; Mt. 28:10; Jn. 20:17) and one another's (Mt. 23:8; Lk. 22:32) brethren, and by the Johannine command to love one another (Jn. 13:34; 15:12, 17), established the special love of fellow Christians which *philadelphia* describes (*cf.* Rom. 8:29).

This is shown in the common life of the church (*cf. homothymadon*, 'with one accord, together', Acts 1:14; 2:46; 4:24; 5:12; 15:25). It is an outworking of Christ's love (Eph. 5:1f.) which it is natural to find among Christians (1 Thes. 4:9f.), but which must be increased (1 Thes. 4:10) and deepened (Rom. 12:10) so as to be lasting (Heb. 13:1), genuine (*anypokritos*, 1 Pet. 1:22; *cf.* Rom. 12:9), and earnest (*ektenēs*, 1 Pet. 1:22; *cf.* 4:8). It is shown in a common way of thinking (*to auto phronein*, Rom. 12:16; 15:5; 2 Cor. 13:11; Phil. 4:2; *cf.* Gal. 5:10; Phil. 2:2, 5; 3:15) and living (*tō autō stoichein*, Phil. 3:16), especially in hospitality (Heb. 13:1f.; 1 Pet. 4:8f.) and help to needy Christians (Rom. 12:9–13). It proves, to Christians themselves (1 Jn. 3:14) and to the world (Jn. 13:35), the genuineness of their faith (1 Jn. 2:9–11; 3:10; 4:7, 11, 20; 5:1.)

philadelphia cannot by definition be realized outside the 'household of faith', but it is associated with honouring (1 Pet. 2:17) and doing good to (Gal. 6:10) all. Its converse is not exclusiveness or indifference to those outside (*hoi exō*, Mk. 4:11; 1 Cor. 5:12f.; Col. 4:5; 1 Thes.

Female mourners, from the tomb of Ramose at Thebes. c. 1400 BC. (PAC)

4:12), but the constraining, dividing and still unconsummated love of Christ (2 Cor. 5:14; *cf.* Lk. 12:50–53). (*LOVE, *FAMILY, *NEIGHBOUR.)

BIBLIOGRAPHY. A. Nygren, *Agape and Eros*², 1953, pp. 153–155; *TDNT* 1, pp. 144–146; *NIDNTT* 1, pp. 254–260; 2, pp. 547–550. P.E.

BURDEN. A noun used about 80 times to translate several Heb. and Gk. words. **1.** Heb. *maśśā'*, 'thing lifted up', and other cognate words from the root *nāśā'*, 'he lifted up'. This word occurs most frequently, notably of prophetic utterances. (*ORACLE.) **2.** Heb. *sāḇal*, 'to bear a load' (in various derivative forms). **3.** Heb. *yāhaḇ*, 'to give' (Ps. 55:22 only). **4.** Heb. *ᵃḡuddâ*, 'bundle' (Is. 58:6, AV, only). **5.** Gk. *baros*, 'something heavy'. **6.** Gk. *phortion*, 'something to be borne'. **7.** Gk. *gomos*, 'the freight' of a ship (Acts 21:3, AV).

Those terms which occur more than once vary little in meaning, and seem at times to be interchangeable. A burden is whatever renders body or mind uneasy (*e.g.* Zp. 3:18); as much as one can bear (2 Ki. 5:17); government in church or state (Nu. 11:17); prediction of heavy judgment (Is. 13); labour, bondage, affliction, fear (Ps. 81:6; Ec. 12:5; Mt. 20:12); Christ's laws (Mt. 11:30; Rev. 2:24); God's ceremonial law and men's superstitious ceremonies (Mt. 23:4; Acts 15:28); men's infirmities (Gal. 6:2). J.D.D.

BURIAL AND MOURNING.

I. In the Old Testament

a. The times of the Patriarchs

It was customary for successive generations to be buried in the family tomb (cave or rock-cut); thus Sarah (Gn. 23:19), Abraham (Gn. 25:9), Isaac and Rebekah, Leah (Gn. 49:31) and Jacob (Gn. 50:13) were all buried in the cave of Machpelah, E of Hebron. Individual burial was sometimes necessitated by death at a distance from the family tomb; so Deborah near Bethel (Gn. 35:8) and Rachel on the road to Ephrath (Gn. 35:19–20), their tombs being marked by an oak and a pillar respectively. Besides weeping, mourning already included rending one's garments and donning sackcloth (Gn. 37:34–35), and might last for as long as 7 days (Gn. 50:10). The embalming of Jacob and Joseph and the use of a coffin for Joseph in Egyptian fashion was exceptional (Gn. 50:2–3, 26). Mummification required removal of the viscera for separate preservation, and desiccation of the body by packing in salt (not brine); thereafter the body was packed with impregnated linen and entirely wrapped in linen. Embalming and mourning usually took 70 days, but the period for embalming could be shorter, as for Jacob.

b. The Pentateuchal legislation

Prompt burial, including that of the bodies of hung criminals, was the norm (Dt. 21:22–23). Contact with the dead and formal mourning brought ceremonial defilement. Mourning by weeping, rending the garments and unbinding the hair was permitted to the Aaronic priests (Lv. 21:1–4), but not to the high priest (Lv. 21:10–11) or the Nazirite under vow (Nu. 6:7). Expressly forbidden to priests (Lv. 21:5) and people (Lv. 19:27–28; Dt. 14:1) were laceration ('cuttings in the flesh'), cutting the corners of the beard, baldness between the eyes and 'rounding' (mutilation?) of the corner(s) of the head. Eating of tithes in mourning or offering them to the dead (Dt. 26:14) was also forbidden. These were heathen, Canaanite practices. Women captured in war might mourn their parents for one month before marrying their captors (Dt. 21:11–13). The national leaders Aaron (Nu. 20:28–29; Dt. 10:6) and Moses (Dt. 34:5–8) were each accorded 30 days' national mourning after burial.

c. Israel in Palestine

(i) *Burial.* When possible, people were buried in the ancestral inheritance in a family tomb: so Gideon and Samson (Jdg. 8:32; 16:31), Asahel and Ahithophel (2 Sa. 2:32; 17:23), and eventually Saul (2 Sa. 21:12–14). Burial in one's 'house', as of Samuel (1 Sa. 25:1, *cf.* 28:3) and Joab (1 Ki. 2:34), may merely mean the same, unless it was more literally under the house or yard floor. The body was borne to rest on a bier (2 Sa. 3:31). Lack of proper burial was a great misfortune (1 Ki. 13:22; Je. 16:6). Tombs were usually outside the town; there is limited archaeological evidence for family tombs having an irregular rock-cut chamber (or chambers) with benches, reached by a short, sloping shaft blocked by a stone cut to fit over the entrance. The upstart treasurer *Shebna drew Isaiah's condemnation in hewing himself an ostentatious rock-tomb (Is. 22:15–16). Pottery and other objects left with the dead became a pure formality during the Israelite period, by contrast with elaborate Canaanite funerary provision. Memorial pillars were sometimes erected in Israel as elsewhere in antiquity; 2 Sa. 18:18 is an anticipatory example. Outside Jerusalem was a tract of land set aside for 'the graves of the common people' (2 Ki. 23:6; Je. 26:23). This, doubtless, was for simple interments, and was paralleled by similar cemeteries at other towns.

The grave of an executed criminal or foe was sometimes marked by a heap of stones. Examples are the sinner Achan (Jos. 7:26), rebellious Absalom (2 Sa. 18:17), the king of Ai, and the five Canaanite kings (Jos. 8:29; 10:27). Cremation was not a Hebrew practice, but in difficult circumstances a corpse might be burnt and the remains buried pending proper burial in the ancestral tomb, as with Saul (1 Sa. 31:12–13) and probably envisaged in Am. 6:10. For royal burials, *SEPULCHRE OF THE KINGS.

(ii) *Mourning.* In Palestine in the 2nd and 1st millennia this included: (1) baldness of head and cutting the beard; (2) lacerating the body; (3) rending garments and wearing sackcloth; (4) scattering dust on the head and wallowing in ashes; and (5) weeping and lamentation. Not all of these were favoured by the law. (See section *b*, above.) For Hebrew mourning, see the action of David (2 Sa. 1:11–12; 13:31), the woman of Tekoah (2 Sa. 14:2), and note the allusions in the prophets (Is. 3:24; 22:12; Je. 7:29; Ezk. 7:18; Joel 1:8; Am. 8:10; Mi. 1:16). For Tyrian seafarers, Philistia and Moab, see Ezk. 27:30, 32; Je. 47:5; Is. 15:2–3 and Je. 48:37.

Notable deaths sometimes occasioned poetic laments. So David lamented over Saul and Jonathan (2 Sa. 1:17–27) and Jeremiah and others over Josiah (2 Ch. 35:25). For professional mourners, *cf.* Je. 9:17–18; Am. 5:16. After a funeral a breaking-fast meal was possibly given to mourners (Je. 16:7; *cf.* Ho. 9:4). A 'great burning' sometimes marked the funeral of Judaean kings (2 Ch. 16:14; 21:19–20; Je. 34:5).

d. Non-funereal mourning

Mourning was associated with

BROW
See Forehead, Part 1.

BROWN BEAR
See Animals, Part 1.

BUBAL HARTEBEEST
See Animals, Part 1.

BUCKLE
See Ornaments, Part 2.

BUCKLER
See Armour, Part 1.

BUILDER
See Arts and Crafts, Part 1.

BUL
See Calendar, Part 1.

repentance or contrition (*e.g.* Ex. 33:4; Joel 1:13; 2:12–13; Ezr. 9: 3, 5) or took place because of misfortune (*e.g.* 2 Sa. 13:19; 15:32; Jb. 2:12–13). There are also references to laceration, weeping, *etc.*, in pagan-(izing) cult-practices. *Cf.* the actions of Baal's prophets on Mt Carmel (1 Ki. 18:28), and those of the men of Israel who came with oblations for God (Je. 41:5). Ezekiel saw in a vision the women of Jerusalem weeping for the god Tammuz (Ezk. 8:14); and Isaiah depicts pagan observances at graves being performed by the rebellious Israelites (Is. 65:4).

BIBLIOGRAPHY. For Canaanite tombs analogous to those used by the Patriarchs, see K. M. Kenyon, *Digging up Jericho*, 1957, pp. 233–255. For laceration in Ugaritic (N Canaanite) epics, see *DOTT*, 1958, p. 130; see also J. A. Callaway, 'Burial in Ancient Palestine from the Stone Age to Abraham', *BA* 26, 1963, pp. 74–91; E. M. Myers, 'Secondary Burials in Palestine', *BA* 33, 1970, pp. 2–29. K.A.K.

II. In the New Testament

The corpse. Tabitha was washed and displayed in an upstairs room (Acts 9:39). The arms and legs of Lazarus and Jesus were bound in linen bands (*keiriai, othonia*) impregnated with aromatic perfumes, and a piece of linen was wrapped around their heads (Jn. 11:44; 20:6–7). That Palestinian Jews borrowed Lat. *sudarium* (handkerchief, napkin) to describe a 'turban' is evident from this Johannine usage and from Mishnaic *ṣûdārîn*, which Jastrow (*Lexicon*, p. 962) defines as 'a scarf wound around the head and hanging down over the neck'. One must presume also that the body itself was clothed; perhaps the sing. *sindōn* (Mk. 15:46 and par.) indicates a linen shift (contrast *Apoc. Moses* 40:1–7 in 1st century AD: plur. *sindones* = winding-bands). If *M.Shabbath* 23. 5 reflects normal 1st century practice the corpse was anointed immediately, and its chin bound 'not to raise it, but so that it does not sink lower'; similarly *Semahoth* 1. 2 describes an immediate binding of the jaws, indicating the function of the *sudarium.* Jesus recognized an anticipation of normal burial-customs among the Jews when his feet or head were anointed at Bethany (Mk. 14:3–9; Jn. 11:2; 12:7); but the preparations of the women to anoint him were thwarted (Mk. 16:1; Lk. 23:56). The Mishnaic plural *taḵrîḵîn* confirms the sense 'bindings', 'wrappings' for Johannine *keiriai, othonia* (S. Safrai, *The Jewish People in the First Century*, 1974, 1. 2, p. 777, *e.g. M.Kilaim* 9. 4, *Maaser Sheni* 5. 12); and the corresponding verb is even more explicit at *Semahoth* 12. 10: 'A man may wrap (*m^eḵārēḵ*) and bind (the corpse of) a man, but not (the corpse of) a woman . . .' However, at *M.Sanhedrin* 6. 5 H. Danby (*Mishnah*, 1933) translated 'garments'; and D. Zlotnik (*Tractate Mourning*, 1966, p. 22) assumes a 'linen garment' at the death of Gamaliel II *c.* AD 130. Perhaps too one should note R. Nathan (late 2nd century AD): 'In the same clothes (*k^eṣût*) which go with him to Sheol will a man appear in the age to come.' All of this seems to suggest both wrappings and garments.

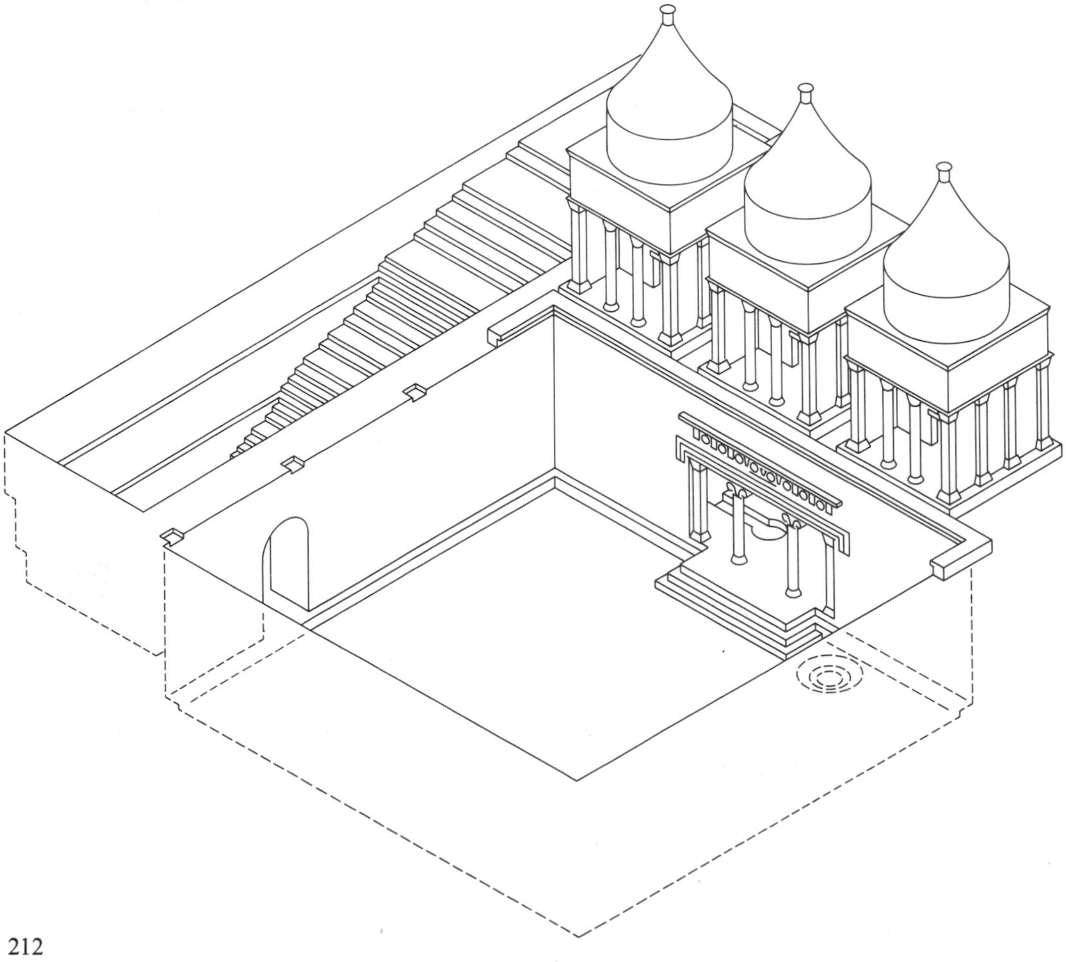

Reconstruction by Vincent of the 'pyramids' or 'monuments' at the tomb of Queen Helena of the Adiabēnians, erected between AD 46/7 and 55: popularly called the 'Tombs of the Kings'. This is the most elaborate of all known tombs at Jerusalem in the period 40 BC–AD 70. (HV)

Burial and mourning. Those who mourned at the house of Jairus 'wept and lamented' (Mk. 5:38), forming a large throng (Mt. 9:23) and making a great disturbance; presumably they beat their breasts in grief (as Lk. 18:13; 23:48). Similarly when Stephen was buried there was 'great lamentation' (Acts 8:2). One is reminded of the 2nd century BC Wisdom of Jesus ben Sirach (Ecclus.) 38:16–18:

'My son, shed tears over a dead man,
and intone the lament to show your own deep grief;
bury his body with due ceremonial,
and do not neglect to honour his grave.
Weep bitterly, wail most fervently;
observe the mourning the dead man deserves' (JB).

Jairus hired pipers for the mourning (Mt. 9:23), presumably to accompany a formal dirge both at the house and during the procession; for Josephus indicates that in AD 67 in Jerusalem (when the Jewish revolt in Galilee had failed), '. . . many hired pipers who accompanied their dirges' (*BJ* 3. 435–437). Later rabbinic law exacted special obligations from a husband to his dead wife; R. Judah (late 2nd century AD) said: 'Even the poorest in Israel should hire not less than two flutes and one wailing woman' (*M.Ketuboth* 4. 4). That no corpse was permitted to stay overnight within the walls of Jerusalem was a rabbinic *dictum* rather than normal practice (A. Guttmann, *HUCA* 60, 1969–70, pp. 251–275); nevertheless many texts indicate burial the same day. Jn. 11:39 expects the stench of decomposition within 4 days (probably earlier). At Nain Jesus met a procession on its way to the tomb including the mother and many townspeople. The body was on a bier (*soros*) carried by bearers. *Semahoth* 4. 6 refers to the use of the bier at Jerusalem, and to a eulogist who preceded it and spoke the praises of the dead. Similarly *M.Berakoth* 3. 1 mentions those who carried the *miṭṭah* (bier), those who relieved them, those who went before and those who went behind. One may contrast with this the funeral of King Herod (4 BC), whose body was displayed on a golden couch (*klinē*) studded with precious stones and wore the royal purple and a golden crown (*Ant.* 17. 196–199; *BJ* 1. 670–673). His son Archelaus gave a sumptuous funerary banquet to the people, as was the custom of the more well-to-do, whose pious generosity 'impoverished' them (*BJ* 2. 1). King Herod himself had spent lavishly on the funeral of Antigonus (whom he murdered)—on the furnishing of the burial-vault, costly spices burnt as incense, the personal adornment (*kosmos*) of the corpse (*Ant.* 15. 57–61). But Josephus was aware that expense was not the point:

Jerusalemite sarcophagus in a style marked by the spacing and plasticity of Greek feeling. Sarcophagi are not common at Jerusalem in this period. This one comes from a tomb W of the Old City commonly identified with 'Herod's monument(s)'. 40 BC–AD 135. (JPK)

*Burial-chamber N of the Old City of Jerusalem, showing a vaulted burial recess (bench-*arcosolium) *together with the much commoner burial-tunnel cut beneath it. The chamber is within tomb no. 7 of a monumental rock-cut group which includes the so-called 'tomb of the Sanhedrin'.* (JPK)

> The pious rites which the Law provides for the dead do not consist of costly obsequies or the erection of notable monuments. The funeral ceremony is undertaken by the nearest kin, and all who pass while burial is in progress must join the procession and mourn with the family. After the funeral the house and its inhabitants must be purified (*Contra Apionem* 2. 205).

Mourning continued after the funeral. In the 2nd century BC its rules and sanctions held for 7 days (Ecclus. 22:12); at the end of the 1st century BC Archelaus mourned 7 days for Herod (*BJ* 2. 1), and in the 1st century AD this remained the norm (*Ant.* 17. 200). In the 2nd century AD the rabbis still refer to *šib̲ʿāh* or 'the seven days of mourning' (*Semahoth* 7). A longer period of 30 days was exceptional (*BJ* 3. 435–437).

Tombs. Ancient rock-cut tombs of the period *c.* 40 BC–AD 135 surround the walls of Jerusalem on three sides (but not on the W, from where the prevailing winds blew), including those of more well-to-do families at Sanhedriyya (*PEQ* 84, 1952, pp. 23–38; *ibid.* 86, 1954, pp. 16–22; *Atiqot* 3, 1961, pp. 93–120), and the poorer tombs, rich in finds, at '*Dominus flevit*' on the Mt of Olives. Most magnificent of all is the tomb of queen Helena of Adiabene. A few stone sarcophagi are found, but mostly the dead were laid in *kok̲in*, sometimes on bench-*arcosolia*; a rock-cut sarcophagus beneath an *arcosolium* (recessed archway in tomb-wall) is extremely rare, the only well-known example being in tomb 7 at Sanhedriyya in Jerusalem. The *kok̲* is the only type of burial-place referred to in the Mishnah (*M.Baba Bathra* 6. 8); the ideal rabbinic arrangement—two *kôk̲îm* opposite the tomb-entry and three in either side-wall—is rarely found. A *kôk̲* was a burial-tunnel cut vertically into the wall of the chamber like a deep oven, set back over projecting rock-ledges around the chamber-walls (interrupted only by the the entry-step), which left an oblong pit at the centre of the chamber to give a standing man head-room. The sarcophagus (rare), projecting continuous ledge and *kôk̲* are the only possible resting-places for a body in the smaller and less pretentious rock-cut tombs. These consisted of one or more chambers with a low square entry, such that one had to crawl through it. The closing-stone was either like an enormous cork, slotting into a rebate round the small entry as into the neck of a bottle; or it was a rough boulder. For this type of tomb see *AJA* 51, 1947, pp. 351–365, *Atiqot* (English) 3, 1961, pp. 108–116 (many in Heb. journals). It is clear that such a tomb—which one stooped to enter, which was closed by a stone that had to be rolled aside, and in which the body might have been placed initially on the projecting ledge—would match the Gospel descriptions of the place where Joseph put the body of Jesus. More elaborate tombs are much rarer, but combined the 'pit-ledge-*kôk̲*' arrangement with one or more bench-*arcosolia* (*Bankbogengräber*), where the body was visible on a flat ledge cut lengthwise into the wall of the burial chamber—*i.e. along* the wall, not deep into it—making a space *c.* 2 m long beneath an archway along the whole length of the wall. Such tombs usually consist of several chambers, not one, and often had an entry-vestibule with a wide, tall entry, giving access to the usual small square entry into the burial-chamber(s). Often too there was an ornamented façade, even a pediment, frieze, cornice, distyle in-antis colonnade or separate monument. Beyond this the tomb of Helena had an elaborate system of chambers with both *kôk̲îm* and bench-*arcosolia.* This tomb and the royal Herodian tomb are the only ones of this period (up to AD 135) to have a closing-stone like a large round cheese or a millstone.

All undisturbed tombs of this period also contain ossuaries, small limestone chests in which the bones were gathered up and reburied. *M.Sanhedrin* 6. 5b refers to this custom in the case of criminals, first buried in two special cemeteries by the Sanhedrin of Jerusalem (after the death penalty), then formally reburied in the family tomb. The bones of a crucified man have been found in his family tomb (*IEJ* 21, 1970, pp. 18–59). More general discussion of the 'gathering of bones' (*ossilegium*) in early rabbinic documents is particularly detailed in *Semahoth* 12–13, and involves the rabbis of *c.* AD 120 and later. Possibly it was the elder Eleazar bar Zadok whose father—before AD 70—urged that his bones must be gathered and reburied in a *d*ᵉ*lôṣqōmā'* (ossuary), as his own father's bones had been buried. The archaeological evidence from Jerusalem dates the use of ossuaries from *c.* 30 BC to AD 135, succeeding the large Hasmonaean bone-chambers (*IEJ* 8, 1958, pp. 101–105; 17, 1967, pp. 61–113). In the Tomb of Helena bones were also put into small box-like compartments near the *kok̲im.* E. M. Meyers has tried to prove continuous secondary burial from a very ancient period (*Jewish Ossuaries: Reburial and Rebirth*, 1971); see the important review by L. Y. Rahmani, *IEJ* 23, 1973, pp. 121–126, rejecting the identity of the Jerusalemite ossuary-burial with earlier practices.

Holy Sepulchre, *Garden tomb*, *Turin shroud.* Of these three the *Holy Sepulchre* has by far the greatest claim to authenticity—see especially articles by C. W. Wilson in *PEQ*, 1902–04. It is extremely unlikely that the site of 'Skull Place' (Golgotha) was lost before AD 135. Moreover in the early 4th century AD Eusebius was confident that the tomb of Jesus had been buried beneath a Roman temple dedicated to Aphrodite (*Life of Constantine* 3. 26), perhaps a Temple of Venus built by Hadrian (*PEQ* 1903, pp. 51–56, 63–65). The Christian pilgrim Arculf (AD 670) visited the Holy Sepulchre, and describes the burial-place in detail; unfortunately it has since been covered by marble panels. The description of Arculf indicates either a regular trough-arcosolium (impossible to date before the 2nd century AD) or perhaps the type shown here. This latter is extremely rare before AD 135 and therefore unlikely *c.* AD 30 (but not impossible; perhaps the last Jewish monumental tombs at Jerusalem date before the revolts of AD 66–70 and 132–5, and even before the unrest of the 50s and early 60s). Other tombs very close to the traditional one (and still within the Holy Sepulchre) are of the regular 1st-century type (see R. H. Smith, *BA* 30, 1967, pp. 74–90, especially pp. 83–85, and the articles by C. Clermont-Ganneau, C. W. Wilson and C. R. Conder, *PEQ* 1877, pp. 76–84, 128–134).

The Garden tomb was first said to be the tomb of Jesus in the 19th century, and has been an attractive site for evangelical devotions ever since. It has the merit of displaying a simple rock-cut tomb in a garden, a setting obviously similar to that described in the Gospels. But it has no claim to authenticity, and was

Rock-cut tomb (Doric style) in the Kedron valley at Jerusalem. An inscription (early to mid 1st cent. BC*) states that two generations of priests of the line of Hezir (1 Ch. 24:15) were buried in the tomb. The solid rock-cut pyramid may possibly be associated with the tomb as its monument. Late 2nd–early 1st cent.* BC. (JPK)

'identified' on the basis of generalities. The burial-forms—single troughs cut round 3 sides of a chamber into which they project (*i.e.* they are not beneath *arcosolia*) —are unknown in Jerusalem in the NT period. Current Israeli research suggests an Iron Age date.

The Turin shroud, a piece of linen *c.* 3 m × 1 m, has on it a painting or impression of a human corpse, said to be the body of Jesus. The fact that natural facial highlights are reversed on film has been interpreted in two quite different ways —either that paint was used and has deteriorated (details: H. Thurston, *Catholic Encyclopaedia*, 13, 1912, p. 763), or that chemical emanations were produced by human agony (argued by Vignon in 1902; see A. J. Otterbein, *New Catholic Encyclopaedia*, 13, 1967, p. 187). The shroud is certainly the one which was displayed at Lirey in France in the 14th century, perhaps also at Constantinople from the 12th century. But NT and other early texts do not indicate the use of a shroud in the 1st century; rather winding-bands for the head and limbs and a linen shift or other garments for the body. The suggestion of Thurston that the shroud of Turin had the corpse of Jesus painted on it to be displayed at a liturgical Easter drama seems most reasonable (other 'shrouds' were certainly used in this way). J.P.K.

BURNING BUSH. The call of Moses to be Israel's deliverer took place when he turned to see the marvel of the bush which burned and yet was not consumed (Ex. 3:3). Like all such manifestations which the Bible records—*e.g.* the smoking-flashing oven (Gn. 15:17) and the cloudy-fiery pillar (Ex. 13:21)—the burning bush is a self-revelation of God, and not, as some hold, of Israel in the furnace of affliction. The story commences by saying that 'the *angel of the Lord appeared to him' (Ex. 3:2); the Hebrew translated 'in a flame' more aptly signifies 'as' or 'in the mode of' a flame (v. 2); Moses (v. 6) 'was afraid to look at God'; Dt. 33:16 speaks of 'him that dwelt in the bush'. The revelation thus conveyed may be summarized in the three words 'living', 'holy' and 'indwelling'. The bush is not consumed because the flame is self-sufficient, self-perpetuating. Equally, and by a consistent symbolism (*e.g.* Gn. 3:24; Ex. 19:18), the flame is the unapproachable holiness of God (v. 5), being, indeed, the first overt expression of the divine holiness in Scripture Thirdly, so as to reveal the sovereign grace of God who, though self-sufficient, freely chooses and empowers instruments of service, the flame in the bush declares that the living, holy God is the Indweller. Thus the revelation at the bush is the background of the promise of the divine presence to Moses (v. 12), of the implementation of the covenant with the fathers (Ex. 2:24; 3:6; 6:5), of the divine name (v. 14), and of the holy law of Sinai.

BIBLIOGRAPHY. U. Cassuto, *A Commentary on the Book of Exodus*, 1967; B. S. Childs, *Exodus*, 1974. J.A.M.

BUZI. The father of Ezekiel (Ezk. 1:3). The Jewish tradition that he was Jeremiah must be firmly rejected, being based on an unwarranted supposition and fanciful etymology. He was a priest, probably a Zadokite and most likely of a more important priestly family, since his son was carried into captivity with Jehoiachin (2 Ki. 24:14–16). H.L.E.

CABUL. The name of a border city in the tribal location of Asher (Jos. 19:27), situated 16 km NE of Carmel. The ironic use in 1 Ki. 9:13 probably rests on a popular etymology signifying 'as nothing' (Heb. *k*ᵉ*ḇal*), but possibly Cabul (mod. Kabul) was the chief town of the area, or the border post between Tyrian and Israelite territory.

BIBLIOGRAPHY. G. W. van Beek, 'Cabul' in *IDB*; *LOB*, pp. 275, 277 n. 51. J.A.M.

BURNT-OFFERING
See Sacrifice, Part 3.

BUSTARD
See Animals, Part 1.

BUTTERFLY
See Animals, Part 1.

BYWORD
See Proverb, Part 3.

CAB
See Weights and measures, Part 3.

Simplified family tree of the Julio-Claudians.

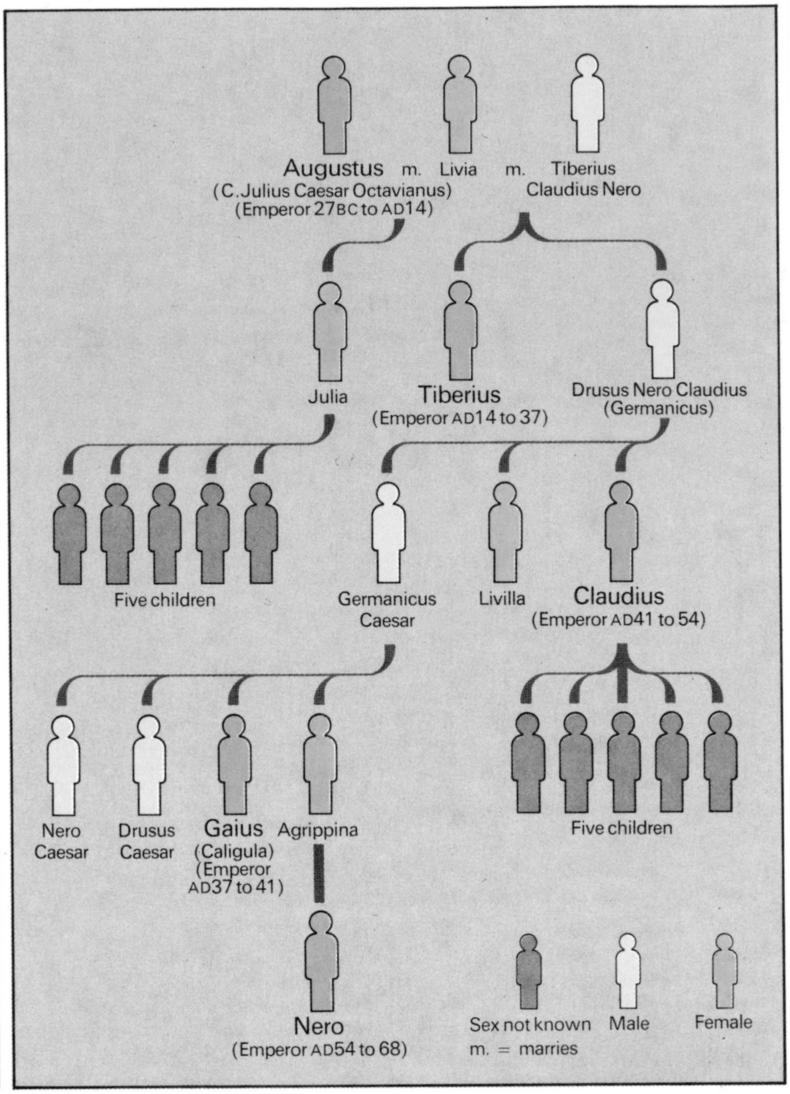

CAESAR

CAESAR. The name of a branch of the aristocratic family of the Julii which established an ascendancy over the Roman republic in the triumph of Augustus (31 BC) and kept it till Nero's death (AD 68). This hegemony (at it is nicely called in Lk. 3:1, Gk.; RSV 'reign' is too precise a term) was an unsystematic compound of legal and social powers, novel to Roman tradition in its monopoly of leadership rather than its form or theory. It was not technically a monarchy. Its success produced so thorough a re-orientation of government, however, that, on the elimination of the Caesarian family, their position was institutionalized and their name assumed by its incumbents.

Gold aureus with bust of Augustus Caesar. 27 BC–AD 14. (RG)

One of the bases of a Caesar's power was his extended tenure of a provincial command embracing most of Rome's frontier forces. Judaea always fell within this area, hence Paul's appeal (Acts 25:10–11) against the procurator, which would not have been possible where the governor was a fully competent proconsul and thus Caesar's equal. Hence also the Jewish custom of referring to Caesar as a king (Jn. 19:12, 15). The dynastic family was from their point of view monarchical. Even where the technical powers were not in Caesarian hands, however, the same terminology occurs (Acts 17:7; 1 Pet. 2:13, 17). The force of Hellenistic traditions of royal suzerainty over the republics, re-directed through the universal oath of personal allegiance to the Caesarian house and their association in the imperial cult, nullified the strict Roman view of the Caesar's position. His quasi-monarchical role in any case simplified Rome's imperial task. But the cult of the Caesar came to pose an agonizing problem for Christians (Pliny, *Ep.* 10. 96–97 and perhaps Rev. 13).

The Roman Empire at the beginning of the reign of Tiberius Caesar in AD 14. The gradual extension of direct Roman rule in the E led to a somewhat changed provincial organization, especially in Asia Minor, by the time of Paul.

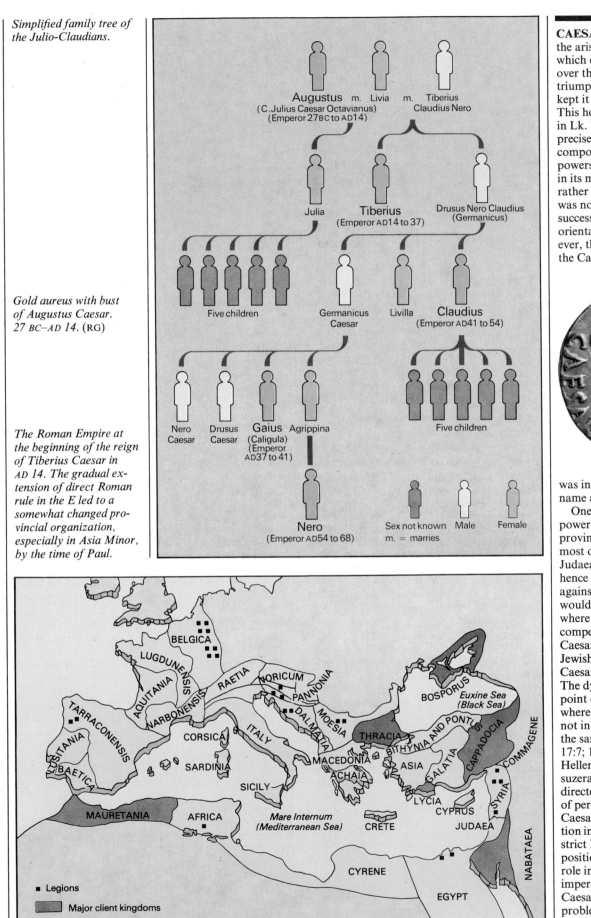

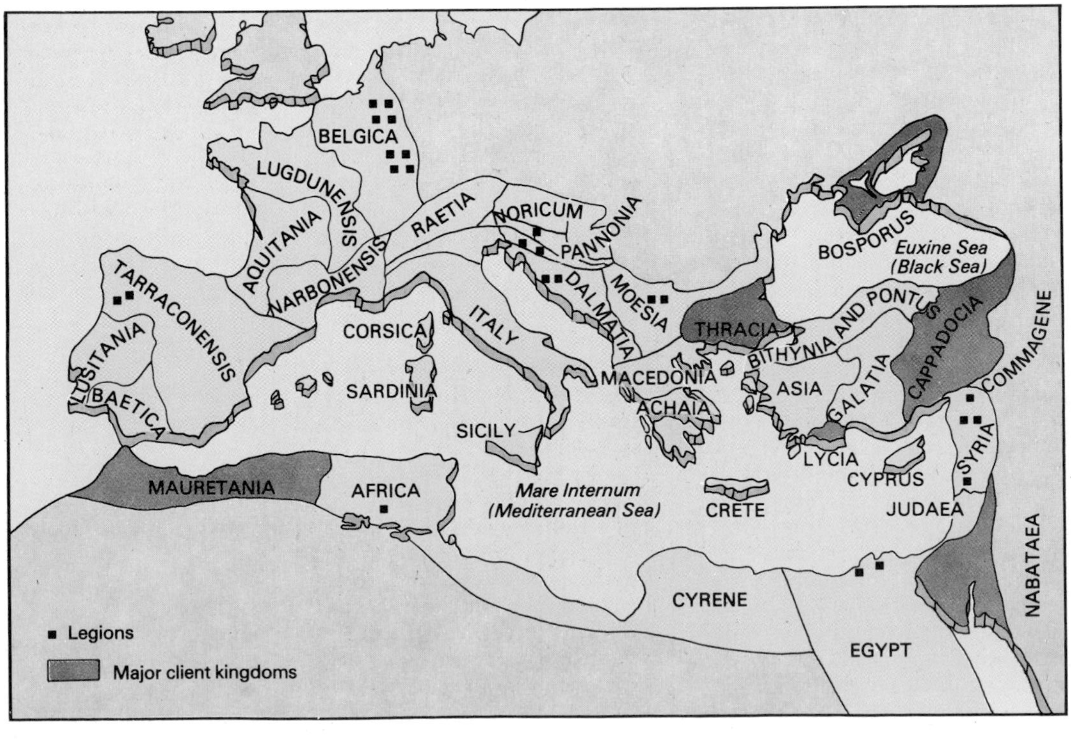

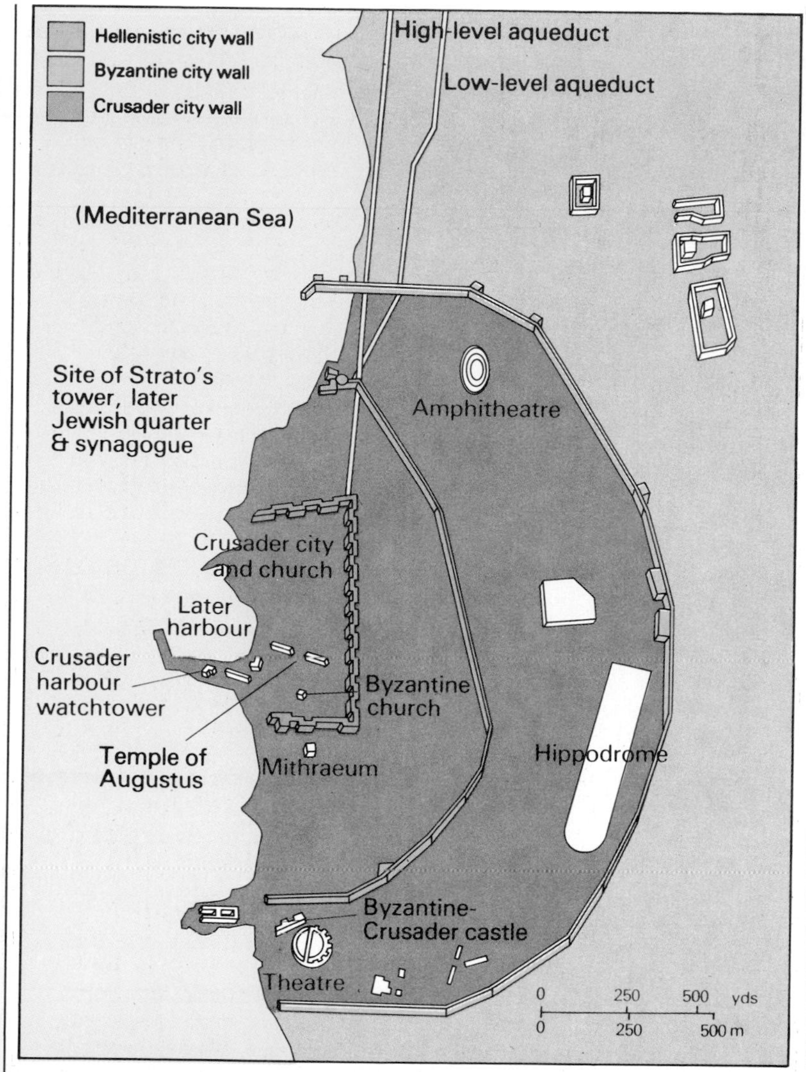

Caesarea; plan of the ancient city.

The Caesars referred to in the NT are, in the Gospels, Augustus (Lk. 2:1), and elsewhere Tiberius, and in the Acts, Claudius (Acts 11:28; 17:7; 18:2), and elsewhere Nero.

BIBLIOGRAPHY. Suetonius, *Lives of the Caesars*; Tacitus, *Annals*; *CAH*, 10–11; F. Millar, *The Emperor in the Roman World*, 1977.

E.A.J.

CAESAREA. This magnificent city, built by Herod the Great on the site of Strato's Tower, stood on the Mediterranean shore 37 km S of Mt Carmel and about 100 km NW of Jerusalem. Named in honour of the Roman emperor Caesar Augustus, it was the Roman metropolis of Judaea and the official residence both of the Herodian kings and the Roman procurators. It stood on the great caravan route between Tyre and Egypt, and was thus a busy commercial centre for inland trade. But Caesarea was also a celebrated maritime trading-centre, due largely to the construction of elaborate stone breakwaters N and S of the harbour. A vault discovered in the Caesarea harbour complex has yielded late 3rd century AD Mithraic material. An aqueduct section uncovered in 1974 revealed another legionary inscription, adding to two others previously known. The Caesarea Porphyry statue is thought to

Section of the high-level aqueduct at Caesarea Maritima, built by King Herod. This city on the Mediterranean coast at the site of an earlier Phoenician foundation (Strato's Tower) was created by King Herod between 22 and 10 BC. (JPK)

Harbour at Caesarea. (SH)

Top right: *Coin of Caesarea depicting goddess of the city enthroned in a temple. AD 98–117.* (RG)

represent Hadrian. The city was lavishly adorned with palaces, public buildings and an enormous amphitheatre. One outstanding architectural feature was a huge temple dedicated to Caesar and Rome, and containing vast statues of the emperor. Traces of this ruin can still be seen S of the site of Kaisarieh on the Plain of Sharon.

Like other NT Mediterranean communities, Caesarea had a mixed population, making for inevitable clashes between Jews and Gentiles. When Pilate was procurator of Judaea he occupied the governor's residence in Caesarea. Philip, the evangelist and deacon, brought Christianity to his home city, and subsequently entertained Paul and his companions (Acts 21:8). Paul departed from Caesarea on his way to Tarsus, having escaped his Jewish enemies in Damascus (Acts 9:30). Caesarea was the abode of the centurion Cornelius and the locale of his conversion (Acts 10:1, 24; 11:11). At Caesarea Peter gained greater insight into the nature of the divine kingdom by realizing that God had disrupted the barriers between Gentile and Jewish believers (Acts 10:35), and had dispensed with such classifications as 'clean' and 'unclean'.

Paul landed at Caesarea when returning from his second and third missionary journeys (Acts 18:22; 21:8). Paul's fateful decision to visit Jerusalem was made here also (Acts 21:13), and it was to Caesarea that he was sent for trial by Felix (Acts 23:23–33) before being imprisoned for 2 years. Paul made his defence before Festus and Agrippa in Caesarea, and sailed from there in chains when sent by Festus to Rome on his own appeal (Acts 25:11).

Bibliography. A. Negev, *IEJ* 22, 1972, pp. 52f., pl. 8; L. I. Levine, *Caesarea under Roman Rule*, 1975; *idem*, *Roman Caesarea: An Archaeological-Topographical Study*, 1975; C. T. Fritsch (ed.), *Studies in the History of Caesarea Maritima*, 1, 1975. R.K.H.

CAESAREA PHILIPPI. A beautiful locality at the foot of Mt Hermon, on the main source of the river Jordan, famed as the place of Peter's confession (Mt. 16:13ff.). It may be the OT Baal-gad. Baal was the deity worshipped there in OT times; the Greeks later substituted their god Pan, and the town took the name Paneas, the shrine

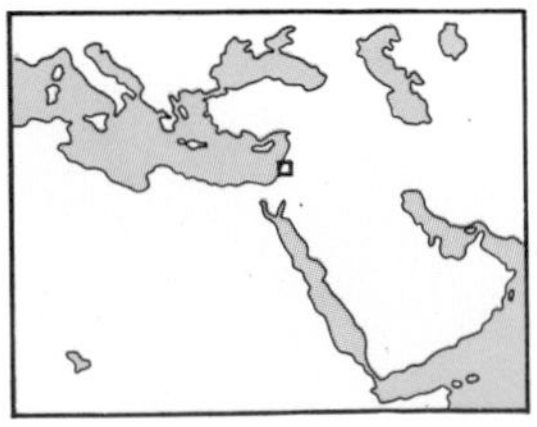

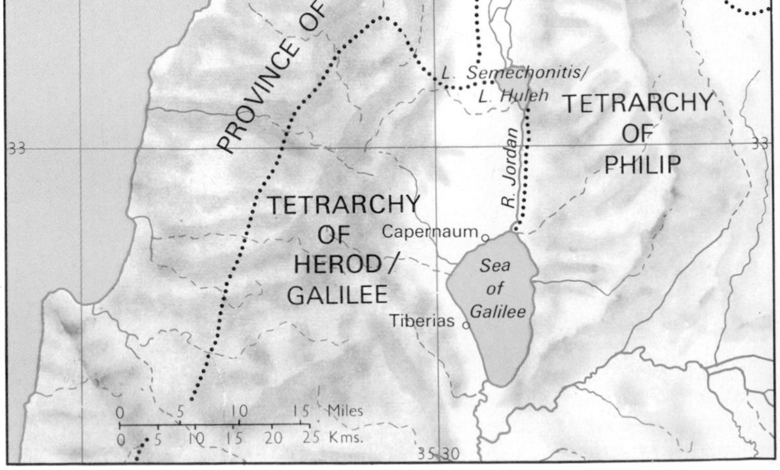

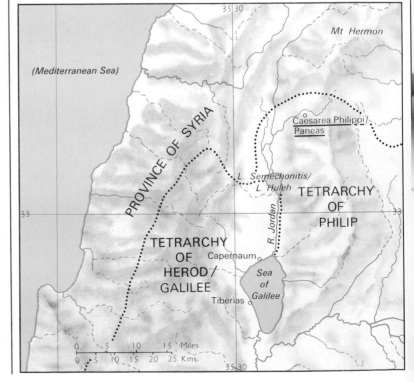

Caesarea Philippi, on the main source of the river Jordan. The town was named after Augustus Caesar and Philip the tetrarch.

itself being called Panion. When the Seleucid ruler Antiochus III wrested Palestine (together with the whole of Coelesyria) from the Ptolemies, Paneas was the scene of one of the decisive battles (200 BC). Herod the Great built a marble temple to Augustus Caesar, who had given him the town; and Philip the tetrarch later in the same emperor's reign further adorned the town, renaming it Caesarea in the emperor's honour. The addition 'Philippi'—*i.e.* of Philip—was to distinguish it from the coastal *Caesarea (*cf.* Acts 8:40). Agrippa II then rebuilt the town in Nero's reign, and gave it another name, Neronias; but this name was soon forgotten. The town had a considerable history in Crusader times. Its ancient name persists as Banias today. There is a shrine there to the Muslim al-Khidr, equated with St George. D.F.P.

CAESAR'S HOUSEHOLD. A Roman aristocrat's household (Gk. *oikia*, Lat. *familia*) was his staff of servants, primarily those held in slavery, but probably also including those manumitted and retaining obligations of clientship as his freedmen. Their duties were extremely specialized, and covered the full range of domestic service, professional duties (medicine, education, *etc.*), and business, literary and secretarial assistance. In the case of the Caesars, their permanent political leadership made their household the equivalent of a modern civil service, providing the experts in most fields of state. Its servile origins, and the eastern responsibilities of the Caesars, made it largely Greek and oriental in its composition. It is not therefore surprising to find it well represented amongst the believers in Rome (Phil. 4:22).

BIBLIOGRAPHY. J. B. Lightfoot, *Philippians*[7], 1883, pp. 171–178; P. R. C. Weaver, *Familia Caesaris*, 1972. E.A.J.

CAIAPHAS (Mt. 26:57; Jn. 11:49; Acts 4:6). Joseph, called Caiaphas, was high priest from AD 18 to 36, when he was deposed by Vitellius, governor of Syria. He was son-in-law to Annas (Jn. 18:13), and seems to have worked in close co-operation with him. He was high priest at the trial of Jesus and during the persecutions described in the early chapters of Acts. D.R.H.

CAIN (Heb. *qayin*). **1.** The eldest son of Adam and Eve (Gn. 4:1), at whose birth Eve said, 'I have gotten (*qānîṯî*) a man' (AV). Since this account is unlikely to have been originally couched in Heb., no judgment can be made on the validity of the pun, and nothing can be concluded from apparent etymologies of the name. He was an agriculturalist (Gn. 4:2), unlike *Abel, who was a shepherd, and being 'of the evil one' (*ek tou ponērou*, 1 Jn. 3:12) and out of harmony with God (Heb. 11:4), his offering (*minḥâ*) was rejected (Gn. 4:3–7) and he subsequently killed his brother (Gn. 4:8). God punished him by sending him to become a wanderer, perhaps a nomad, in the land of *Nod (Gn. 4:9–16), and to protect him from being slain himself God set a 'mark' (*'ôṯ*, 'sign, token', *cf.* Gn. 9:12–13) 'for' (*l*ᵉ) him. The nature of the 'mark' is unknown. Cain was the father of *Enoch. Parallels to the conflict between Cain and Abel have been drawn from Sumerian literature, where disputations concerning the relative merits of agriculture and herding are found, but in none of those known does the farmer kill the herdsman, and such a conflict probably only reflects the historical situation in Mesopotamia from late prehistoric times onwards. (*NOMADS.)

BIBLIOGRAPHY. S. N. Kramer, 'Sumerian Literature and the Bible', in *Analecta Biblica* 12, 1959, p. 192; *History Begins at Sumer*, 1958, pp. 164–166, 185–192; C. J. Gadd, *Teachers and Students in the Oldest Schools*, 1956, pp. 39ff.; S. H. Hooke, 'Cain and Abel', in *The Siege Perilous*, 1956, pp. 66ff.

2. The name of a town, written with the article (*haqqayin*), in the S of the territory allotted to Judah (Jos. 15:57), and probably to be identified with modern Khirbet Yaqin to the SE of Hebron. See A. Alt, *Palästina-jahrhbuch* 22, 1926, pp. 76–77. T.C.M.

CALAH. A city founded by Asshur, a follower of Nimrod, moving from *Shinar (Gn. 10:11). The Assyr. *Kalḫu* (mod. Nimrud)

Head of a woman carved in ivory, originally covered with gold leaf. Probably part of the decoration of palace furniture. Known as the 'Mona Lisa' of ancient Iraq. Calah. c. 8th cent. BC. (SI)

lies 40 km S of Nineveh on the E bank of the river Tigris. The principal excavations there by Sir Henry Layard in 1845–8, the British School of Archaeology in Iraq 1949–63 and the Iraqi government and Polish expeditions 1970–6 have traced the city's history from prehistoric to Hellenistic times. Soundings show early influences from the S before the main citadel (550 × 370 m) was rebuilt by Shalmaneser I (*c.* 1250 BC) and again by Ashurnasirpal II in 879 BC. The city then covered an area of 40 square km and had a population of about 60,000. It was from Calah that *Shalmaneser III attacked Syria, and his Black Obelisk recording the submission of Jehu and stelae mentioning Ahab were originally set up in the main square. Inscriptions of Tiglath-pileser III and Sargon II mention their attacks on Israel and Judah launched from this Assyrian military capital. A list of personal names written in Aramaic may attest the presence of captives settled here. Sargon II, conqueror of Samaria, stored his booty here. Esarhaddon subsequently built himself a palace here and recorded his treaties with conquered peoples on tablets set up in the Temple of Nabu. Many of the discoveries of sculptures, ivories, metal objects and weapons, found in the citadel

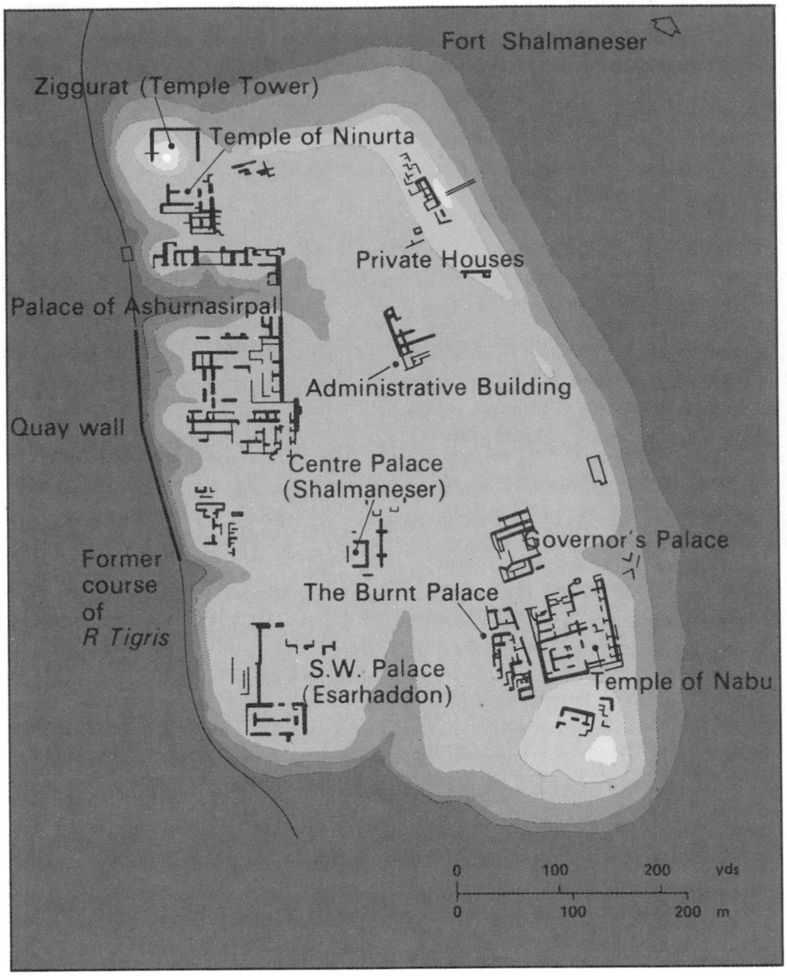

Plan of the citadel at Calah.

View of the excavations in progress at Calah, showing the ziggurat terrace and the palace of Ashurnasirpal II. (DJW)

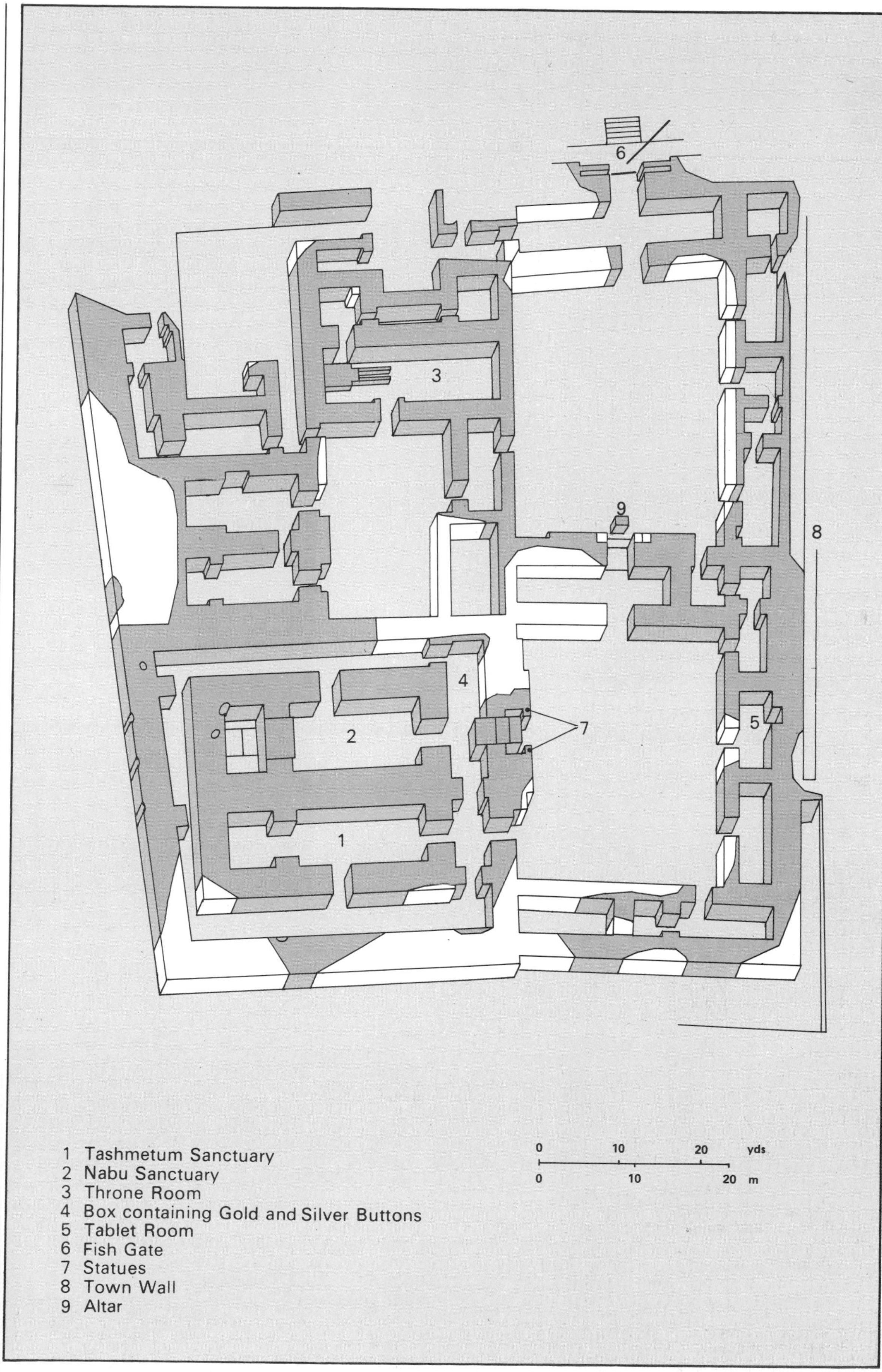

Plan of the temple of Nabu at Calah.

Stele of King Ashur-nasirpal II, recording his military exploits, building achievements and the 10-day feast given to 59,654 people to celebrate the opening of his new citadel and palaces at Calah (Nimrud). c. 876 BC. (BSAI)

The remains of the temple-tower (ziggurat) at Calah. (DJW)

CALEBITES
See Eshtaol, Part 1.

and barracks of 'Fort Shalmaneser' in the outer town, illustrate the splendour of the booty taken from Syria and Palestine and the might of the Assyrian army. Calah fell to the Medes and Babylonians in 612 BC.

BIBLIOGRAPHY. M. E. L. Mallowan, *Nimrud and its Remains*, 1965; *Iraq* 13–27, 1952–65; 36–38, 1974–7. D.J.W.

CALEB (Heb. *kālēḇ*). **1.** Third son of Hezron son of Pharez: Jerahmeel's youngest brother; 'Chelubai' (1 Ch. 2:9). From him, through Ephrathah, lines of descent are given in 1 Ch. 2:18ff. to Bezalel, Moses' chief craftsman; in 2:24, to the settlers of Tekoa; in 2:50ff., to the settlers of Kiriath-jearim, Bethlehem, Netophah, Zorah, Eshtaol, Beth-geder and others (the Kenite families named in 2:55 may be loosely connected).

2. 'Brother of Jerahmeel' (1 Ch. 2:42), possibly the same as **1**, from whom descent was traced in the towns of Ziph, Maon and Beth-zur (the names Hebron and Tappuach also occur). This list may refer in part to Caleb **3**, father of Achsah (v. 49).

3. Caleb ben Jephunneh, an outstanding leader of Judah, whose faithfulness in the mutiny at Kadesh won him exemption from the curse pronounced there (Nu. 14:24). He directed the invasion of Judaea and settled at Hebron (Jos. 1; 15). From Jos. 14:6, *etc.*; 1 Ch. 4:14–15, we learn that he was a *Kenizzite. *Nabal was his descendant.

4. 'Brother of Shuhah', spelt 'Chelub' in 1 Ch. 4:11. J.P.U.L.

CALENDAR.

I. In the Old Testament

There is no precise Heb. equivalent of the Lat. *calendarium*, the passage of the year being generally marked by reference to the months, agricultural seasons or the principal festivals.

a. The year (Heb. *šānâ*—so named from the change or succession of the seasons) was at first reckoned to begin with the autumn (seventh) month of Tishri (Ex. 23:16; 34:22), the time also of the commencement of the sabbatical year (Lv. 25:8–10). While in Egypt the Hebrews may have conformed to the solar year of 12 months, each of 30 days + 5 additional days, *i.e.* 365 days (Herodotus, 2. 4), but if so a change was made thereafter and the 'beginning of months' or first month of the year was fixed in the spring (Ex. 12:2; 13:3–4; 23:15; Dt. 16:1, 6). Thereafter the Hebrew year followed the W Semitic Calendar with a year of 12 lunar months (1 Ki. 4:7; 1 Ch. 27:1–15). It is not certain whether the commencement of the year in spring (Nisan) was for use only in the ritual, since there is some evidence for the year for civil purposes being sometimes reckoned from the autumn month of Tishri (*CHRONOLOGY OF THE OLD TESTAMENT).

b. The month (see table). The Hebrew calendar year was composed of lunar months, which began when the thin crescent of the new moon was first visible at sunset. The day of the new moon thus beginning was considered holy. The month (Heb. *yeraḥ*, *'moon') was reckoned to consist of 29/30 days and, since the lunar year was about 11 days less than the solar year, it was periodically necessary to intercalate a thirteenth month in order that new year's day should not fall before the spring of the year (March–April). No precise details are known of the method used by the Hebrews to accommodate the agricultural with the lunar calendar. They may have interposed a second Adar (twelfth month) or second Elul (sixth month) within the lunar cycle of 3, 6, 11, 14, 17 or 19 years. There is some evidence for the Hebrew use of intercalated months after Adar (Nu. 9:11; 2 Ch. 30:2–3; *cf.* 1 Ki. 12:32–33), though possibly sometimes after Nisan (*cf.* 2 Ch. 30:2ff.) as was done in Mesopotamia. A strictly solar calendar was used in the book of *Jubilees* (*c.* 105 BC); *cf. 1 Enoch* 72–82.

The observation of the autumnal equinox, *i.e.* 'the going out of the year' (see Ex. 23:16), and of the spring or vernal equinox, called 'the return of the year' (1 Ki. 20:26; 2 Ch. 36:10, AV), was important for controlling the calendar and consequently the festivals. Thus the year began with the new moon nearest to the vernal equinox when the sun was in Aries (Jos., *Ant.* 3. 201), and the Passover on the fourteenth day of Nisan coincided with the first full moon (Ex. 12:2–6).

The early month names were probably local Palestinian references to the seasons, and differ from the designation of the months named in texts from Syria (Ras-Shamra, Alalaḫ, Mari). Some are known from Phoenician also. *Abib*, 'ripening of corn' (Ex. 13:4); *Ziw* (AV Zif; 1 Ki. 6:1, 37); *Ethanim* (1 Ki. 8:2) and *Bul* (1 Ki. 6:38) of

Representation of the Hebrew calendar, showing seasons and festivals with modern equivalents.

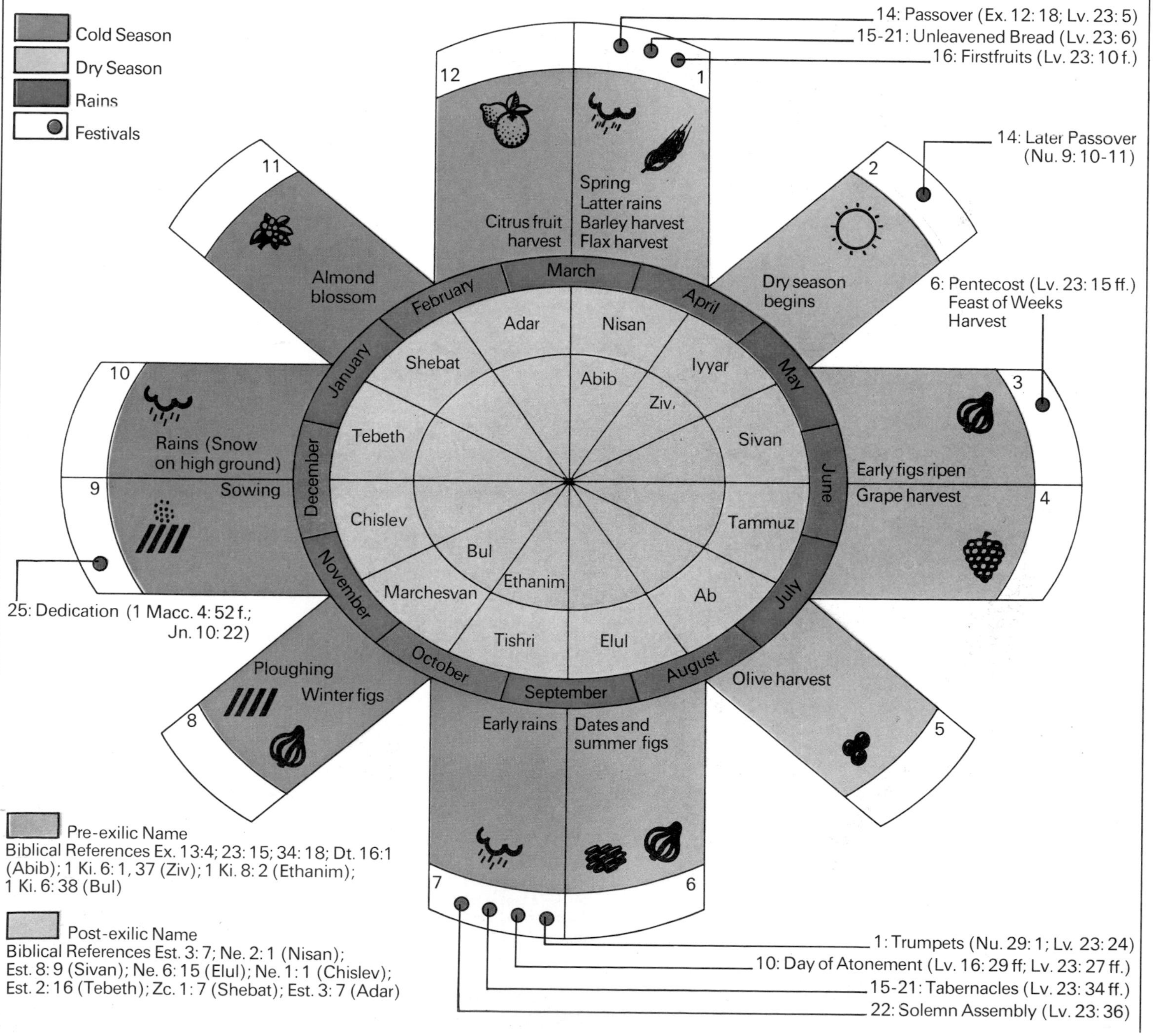

Hebrew calendar which lists the various agricultural tasks for the year. From Gezer. Height 11 cm. 10th cent. BC. (PEF)

uncertain meaning, are the only names extant from this period. At all periods the months were usually designated numerically; first, Ex. 12:2; second, Gn. 7:11; third, Ex. 19:1; fourth, 2 Ki. 25:3; fifth, Nu. 33:38; sixth, 1 Ch. 27:9; seventh, Gn. 8:4; eighth, Zc. 1:1; ninth, Ezr. 10:9; tenth, Gn. 8:5; eleventh, Dt. 1:3; twelfth, Est. 3:7. In post-exilic times the month-names of the Babylonian calendar were followed (see table).

c. The seasons—the agricultural calendar. Although the Hebrews adopted a calendar based on lunar months, they also, as agriculturalists, commonly indicated time of year by the season rather than by the names or numeration of the months. Thus, the year which in Palestine divided approximately into the dry season (April–September) and the rainy season (October–March) could be again subdivided generally into seed-time' (November–December) and 'harvest' (April–June; Gn. 8:22). More specific designations would indicate to the local inhabitants actual months, *e.g.* wheat (Gn. 30:14; Jdg. 15:1) or barley harvest (2 Sa. 21:9; Ru. 1:22) denotes March–April; the 'earing time' (Ex. 34:21) would be March; and 'the first ripe grapes' (Nu. 13: 20) the month *Tammuz* (June–July). 'The first rains' (based on the old civil calendar beginning in *Tishri*) fell in September–October, and the 'latter rains' in March–April. The 'summer-fruit' (*qāyiṣ*) of August–September gave its name to the 'summer', also called the 'heat'. The months *Ṭebet* and *Šebaṭ* were the 'cold' months (see table under heading 'Seasons').

With the above OT references may be compared the agricultural calendar roughly written on stone, perhaps a palimpsest inscribed by a schoolboy in the 10th century BC, found at Gezer in 1908. The translation is uncertain, but it lists the agricultural operations for the 12 months of the year beginning with the autumn: 'Two months of storage. Two months of sowing. Two months of spring growth. Month of pulling flax. Month of barley harvest. Month when everything (else) is harvested. Two months of pruning (vines). Month of summer fruit' (*cf. DOTT*, pp. 201–203).

d. Other ways of accounting times and seasons are covered by general words for a specified 'time' or festival (*'iddān*, Dn. 7:25; *mō'ēḏ*, Dn. 12:7; *z^{e}mān*, Ec. 3:1; Ne. 2:6), *cf.* Ps. 104:27. Historical events are normally dated by the regnal years of rulers or by synchronism with some memorable national event, *e.g.* the Exodus; the sojourn in Egypt (Ex. 12:40); the construction of the first Temple (1 Ki. 6:1); or the 70-year Exile in Babylon (Ezk. 33:21); or the earthquake in the reign of Uzziah (Am. 1:1; Zc. 14:5).

BIBLIOGRAPHY. J. Finegan, *Handbook of Biblical Chronology*, 1964; J. B. Segal, *VT* 7, 1957, pp. 250–307; *JSS* 7, 1962, pp. 212–221.

D.J.W.

II. Between the Testaments

The 'year of the kingdom of the Greeks' (1 Macc. 1:10) is the Seleucid era, dating officially from the first day of the Macedonian month Dios (September/October) in 312 BC. This era is followed in 1 Macc., though in some of the sources used in that book (under the influence of the Babylonian reckoning of the beginning of the year from Nisan) the era is dated from March/April, 311 BC.

III. In the New Testament

Dates in the NT are occasionally reckoned by reference to Gentile rulers. The most elaborate example is in Lk. 3:1f., where the beginning of the ministry of John the Baptist is dated not only 'in the fifteenth year of the reign of Tiberius Caesar' (*i.e.* AD 27–28, according to the reckoning retained in the former Seleucid realm, where a new regnal year was held to start in September/October), but also by reference to rulers then in office, whether secular or sacerdotal, in Judaea and the neighbouring territories. *Cf.* datings by reference to the emperors Augustus (Lk. 2:1) and Claudius (Acts 11:28), the provincial governors Quirinius (Lk. 2:2) and Gallio (Acts 18:12), and Herod, king of the Jews (Mt. 2:1; Lk. 1:5).

For the most part, however, the

NT writers measure time in terms of the current Jewish calendar (or calendars). The record is punctuated by reference to Jewish festivals and other sacred occasions. This is especially so in the Fourth Gospel; *cf.* Jn. 2:13, 23 (Passover); 5:1 (perhaps the New Year); 6:4 (Passover); 7:2 (Tabernacles; in v. 37 'the last day, that great day of the feast' is the eighth day; *cf.* Lv. 23:36; Nu. 29:35; Ne. 8:18); 10:22 (Dedication, on 25th Kislew; *cf.* 1 Macc. 4:59); 11:55ff. (Passover). *Cf.* also Mt. 26:2; Mk. 14:1; Lk. 22:1 (Passover and Unleavened Bread); Acts 2:1 (Pentecost); 12:3f. (Passover and Unleavened Bread); 18:21, AV (perhaps Passover); 20:6 (Unleavened Bread); 20:16 (Pentecost); 27:9 (where 'the fast' is the Day of Atonement, about which time sailing in the Mediterranean came to an end for the winter); 1 Cor. 16:8 (Pentecost).

Among days of the week, the sabbath is frequently mentioned. The 'second first sabbath' (Lk. 6:1 mg.) is probably a technical term whose meaning can no longer be determined with certainty. Friday is 'the day of Preparation (Gk. *paraskeuē*), that is, the day before the sabbath (Gk. *prosabbaton*)' (Mk. 15:42; *cf.* Jn. 19:31); 'the day of Preparation of the Passover' (Jn. 19:14) means 'Friday of Passover week' (Gk. *paraskeuē tou pascha*). The 'first day of the week' (Gk. *mia sabbatou* or *mia tōn sabbatōn*, *i.e.* one day after the sabbath) receives a new significance from its being the resurrection day; *cf.* (in addition to the resurrection narratives in the Gospels) Acts 20:7; 1 Cor. 16:2; also 'the *Lord's day' (Gk. *kyriakē hēmera*) in Rev. 1:10.

In general, the Jewish calendar in NT times (at least before AD 70) followed the Sadducean reckoning, since it was by that reckoning that the Temple services were regulated. Thus the day of Pentecost was reckoned as the fiftieth day after the presentation of the first harvested sheaf of barley, *i.e.* the fiftieth day (inclusive) from the first Sunday after Passover (*cf.* Lv. 23:15f.); hence it always fell on a Sunday, as it does in the Christian calendar. The Pharisaic reckoning, which became standard after AD 70, interpreted 'sabbath' in Lv. 23:15 as the festival day of Unleavened Bread and not the weekly sabbath; in that case Pentecost always fell on the same day of the month (an important consideration for those in whose eyes it marked the anniversary of the law-giving) but not on the same day of the week.

Even more important than the minor calendrical differences between Sadducees and Pharisees was the cleavage between the Sadducees and Pharisees, on the one hand, and those, on the other hand, who followed the 'sectarian' calendar known from the book of *Jubilees* and now also from the Qumran literature. If Jesus and his disciples followed this 'sectarian' calendar, that might explain how they kept the Passover before his arrest, while the chief priests and their associates did not keep it until after his crucifixion (Jn. 18:28).

BIBLIOGRAPHY. J. C. Dancy, *Commentary on I Maccabees*, 1954, pp. 48ff.; N. Geldenhuys, *Commentary on Luke*, 1950, pp. 649ff.; A. Jaubert, *La Date de la Cène*, 1957, and 'Jésus et le calendrier de Qumrân', *NTS* 7, 1960–1, pp. 1ff.; J. van Goudoever, *Biblical Calendars*, 1959; J. B. Segal, *The Hebrew Passover from the Earliest Times to AD 70*, 1963; J. Finegan, *Handbook of Bible Chronology*, 1963; E. J. Bickerman, *Chronology of the Ancient World*, 1968; E. J. Wiesenberg and others, 'Calendar' in *EJ*; W. M. O'Neil, *Time and the Calendars*, 1975. F.F.B.

CALF
See Cattle, Part 1.

CALF, GOLDEN. 1. The golden image made after the Exodus by Aaron and the Israelites at Sinai while Moses was in the mountain. On finding that they were idolatrously worshipping it as God with sacrifices, feasting and revelry, Moses destroyed it (Ex. 32:4–8, 18–25, 35; Dt. 9:16, 21; Ne. 9:18; Ps. 106:19–20; Acts 7:41). This idol is

The Egyptian god Apis, the bull-calf of Memphis. Bronze. Length 15 cm. 4th cent. BC. (BM)

sometimes thought to be the Egyptian Apis-bull of Memphis (see *IBA*, p. 39, fig. 33) or the Mnevis bull of Heliopolis, but these are too far away from Goshen to have been really familiar to the Hebrews. In fact, there were several not dissimilar bull-cults in the E Delta, much closer to the Hebrews in Goshen, which they could have aped later at Sinai. To the SW of *Goshen (Tumilat-area), in the 10th Lower Egyptian nome or province, called 'the Black Bull', there was an amalgam of Horus-worship and bull- or calf-cult; farther N and extending along the NW of Goshen itself, the 11th Lower Egyptian nome also possessed a bull-cult linked with Horus-worship; other traces are known. (See E. Otto, *Beiträge zur Geschichte der Stierkulte in Aegypten*, 1938, pp. 6–8, 32–33.) In Egypt, the bull or calf was a symbol of fertility in nature, and of physical strength (*cf.* Otto, *op. cit.*, pp. 1–2, 24f., and *passim*), and, as elsewhere in the Near East, could even perhaps have had links with the worship of the host of heaven. (*Cf.* Wainwright, *JEA* 19, 1933, pp. 42–52, especially pp. 44–46. For certain reserves, see Otto, *op. cit.*, p. 7, n. 4. Perhaps *cf.* also Acts 7:41–42 in conjunction?)

In nearby Canaan, however, the bull or calf was the animal of Baal or Hadad, god(s) of storm, fertility and vegetation, and, as in Egypt, symbolized fertility and strength. Bearing in mind the close links between Canaan and the Egyptian E Delta (*EGYPT, *MOSES) and the presence of many Semites in the Delta besides the Israelites, it is possible to view the idolatry at Sinai as a blending of contemporary, popular bull- and calf-cults, Egyptian and Canaanite alike, with their emphasis on natural strength and fertility. In any case, it represented a reduction of the God of Israel (*cf.* 'feast to the Lord', Ex. 32:5) to the status of an amoral (tending to immoral) nature-god like those of the surrounding nations, and meant that he could then all too easily be identified with the Baals. This God rejected, refusing to be identified with the god of the calf, hence condemning it as the worship of an 'other' god, and therefore idolatry (Ex. 32:8).

2. At the division of the Hebrew kingdom, Israel's first king, Jeroboam I, wishing to counteract the great attraction of the Temple at Jerusalem in Judah, set up two golden calves, in Bethel and Dan, to be centres of Israel's worship of Yahweh (1 Ki. 12:28–33; 2 Ki. 17:16; 2 Ch. 11:14–15; 13:8). In Syria-Palestine the gods Baal or Hadad were commonly thought of (and shown) as standing upon a bull or calf, emblem of their powers of fertility and strength (see *ANEP*, pp. 170, 179, figs. 500, 501, 531), and Jeroboam's action had the same disastrous implications as Aaron's golden calf: the reduction of Yahweh to a nature-god, and his subsequent identification with the Baals of Canaan. With this would go a shift in emphasis from righteousness, justice and an exemplary moral standard to purely physical and material considerations, sliding easily into immorality with a religious backing, with social disintegration, and total loss of any sense of the divinely appointed mission of the chosen people in a darkened world. All this was bound up in the idolatry that was 'the sin of Jeroboam, son of Nebat'.

Jehu (2 Ki. 10:29) removed the more obvious and explicit Baal-worship in Israel, but not the calves of a Baalized Yahweh. Hosea (8:5–6; 13:2) prophesied the coming end of such 'worship'. K.A.K.

CALL, CALLING. In OT and NT there are some 700 occurrences of the word as verb, noun or adjective. The principal Heb. root is *qr'*; in Gk. *kalein* (with its compounds, and derivatives *klētos*, 'called', and *klēsis*, 'calling'), *legein* and *phōnein* are used. In both languages other verbs are occasionally rendered by parts of 'to call', *e.g. 'mr* in Is. 5:20, and *chrēmatizein* in Rom. 7:3.

I. In the Old Testament

a. 'Call to', hence 'invite or summon (by name)' (Gn. 3:9, *etc.*); 'summon an assembly' (La. 1:15). 'Call upon the name' is found from Gn. 4:26 onwards ('men began to call upon the name of the Lord'), and denotes the claiming of God's protection either by summoning assistance from one whose name (*i.e.* character) was known, or by calling oneself by the name of the Lord (*cf.* Gn. 4:26 AVmg.; Dt. 28:10; Is. 43:7).

b. 'Give a name to' is found in such verses as Gn. 1:5 ('God called the light Day'). Those verses where God is the subject indicate the underlying unity of the two senses of *qr'*, thereby revealing its theological meaning. The first sense implies a call to serve God in some capacity and for some particular purpose (1 Sa. 3:4; Is. 49:1). The meaning of the sense is not simply to identify; it is both to describe (Gn. 16:11; *cf.* Mt. 1:21) and to indicate a relationship between God the nominator and his nominee, especially Israel. Is. 43:1 epitomizes God's call and naming of Israel to be his, separated from other nations, granted the work of bearing witness, and the privilege of the protection afforded by his name. God alone initiates this call, and only a minority (remnant) respond (*e.g.* Joel 2:32).

II. In the New Testament

Here the same usages are found, and the call of God is now 'in Christ Jesus' (Phil. 3:14). It is a summons to bear the name of Christian (1 Pet. 4:16; Jas. 2:7; Acts 5:41; Mt. 28:19) and to belong to God in Christ (1 Pet. 2:9). 'Call to' is found in, *e.g.*, Mk. 2:17 and 'give a name to' in Lk. 1:59. The present passive participle is in frequent use, as in Lk. 7:11. Jesus called disciples and they followed him (Mk. 1:20). The Epistles, especially Paul's, make clear the theological meaning of Christ's call. It comes from God, through the gospel for salvation through sanctification and belief (2 Thes. 2:14) to God's kingdom (1 Thes. 2:12), for fellowship (1 Cor. 1:9) and service (Gal 1:15). Other writers impart this full meaning to God's call through Jesus (*cf.* Heb. 3:1; 9:15; 1 Pet. 2:21; 1 Jn. 3:1 especially—'. . . that we should be called children of God; and so we are'). Those who respond are 'called' (1 Cor. 1:24; Lightfoot translates as 'believers'). Paul equates call and response (Rom. 8:28ff.) to emphasize God's unchanging purpose (Rom. 9:11), *i.e.*, Paul sees the call as effective. The saying of Jesus in Mt. 22:14 distinguishes 'the called', those who hear, from 'the chosen', those who respond and become 'choice'.

Many commentators interpret 'calling' in 1 Cor. 7:20ff. as a particular occupation. Rather *klēsis* here means the divine calling of each man as a concrete historical event, *i.e.* as including in itself the outward circumstances in which it was received. Slavery as such is not incompatible with faith in Christ.

BIBLIOGRAPHY. Arndt, pp. 399f.; K. L. Schmidt, *TDNT* 3, pp. 487–536; *TWBR*; L. Coenen, *NIDNTT* 1, pp. 271–276; J.-J. von Allmen, *Vocabulary of the Bible*, 1958.

M.R.W.F.

CALNEH, CALNO. 1. Calneh. The name of a city founded by Nimrod in the land of *Shinar (Gn. 10:10, AV). Since no city of this name is known in Babylonia, some scholars propose to point the Heb. *kullānâ*, 'all of them', as in Gn. 42:36; 1 Ki. 7:37. This would then be a comprehensive clause to cover such ancient cities as Ur and Nippur (identified with Calneh in TB). Those who locate Shinar in N Mesopotamia equate this city with **2** and also with *CANNEH.

2. Calno (Kalno), Is. 10:9; Kalneh, Am. 6:2 (LXX *pantes*, 'all', see **1**). A town Kullania mentioned in Assyr. tribute lists. Associated with Arpad. Modern Kullan Köy 16 km SE of Arpad (*AJSL* 51, 1935, pp. 189–191).

BIBLIOGRAPHY. *JNES* 3, 1944, p. 254. D.J.W.

CALVARY. The name occurs once only in the AV, in Lk. 23:33, and not at all in most EVV. The word comes from the Vulgate, where the Lat. *calvaria* translates the Gk. *kranion*; both words translate Aramaic *gulgoltâ*, the 'Golgotha' of Mt. 27:33, meaning 'skull'. Three possible reasons for such a name have been propounded: because skulls were found there; because it was a place of execution; or because the site in some way resembled a skull. All we know of

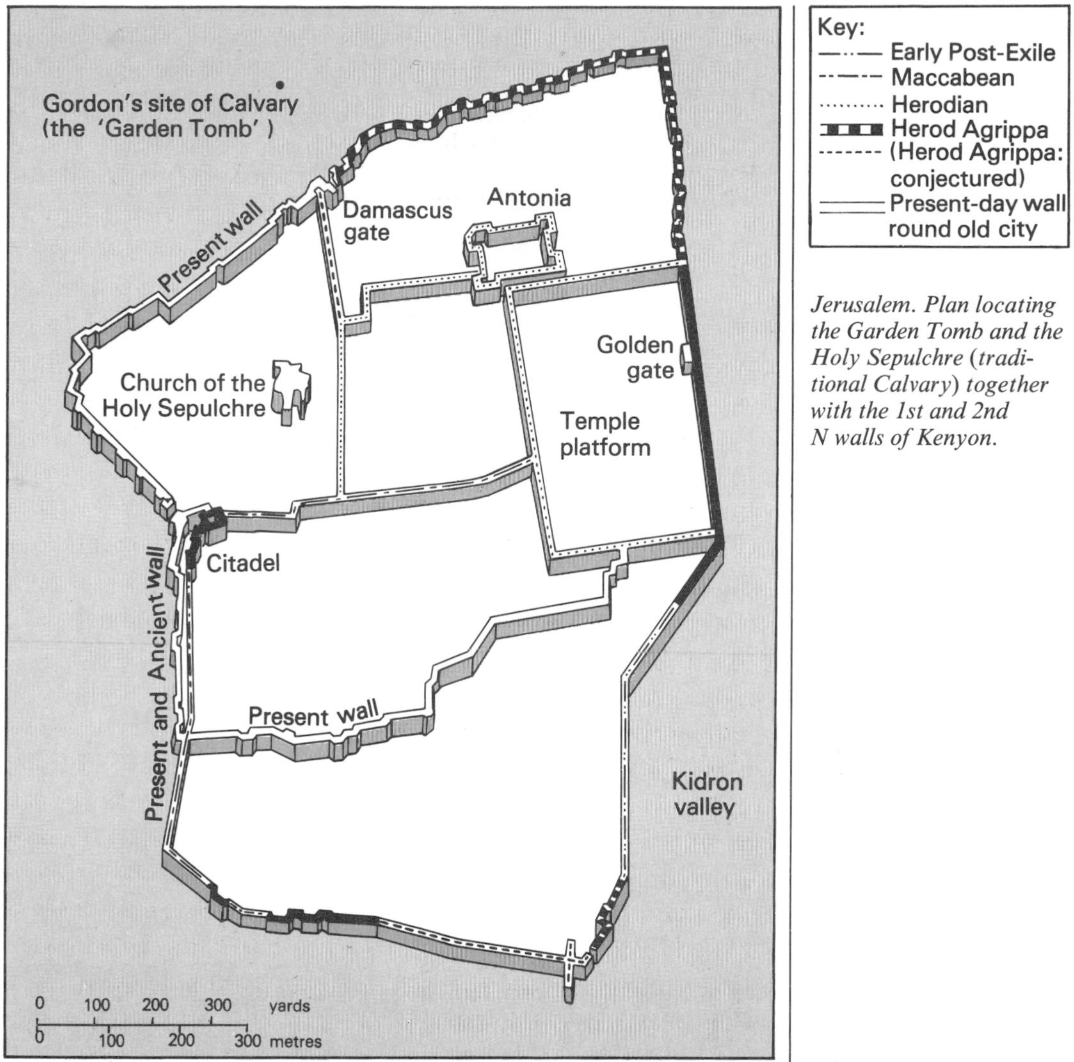

Jerusalem. Plan locating the Garden Tomb and the Holy Sepulchre (traditional Calvary) together with the 1st and 2nd N walls of Kenyon.

The traditional site of Calvary (Golgotha) outside the 2nd wall of Jerusalem. Part of a model of Herodian Jerusalem incorporating a theory of the area embraced by the 2nd and 3rd N walls, based on the work of Avi-Yonah which differs from that proposed by Kenyon, though both place the site outside the 2nd N wall. (JPK) (HC)

This rock-formation near the 'Garden Tomb' resembles a skull, which has led to its popular identification as Golgotha (Calvary), the 'Place of a skull' (Jn. 19:17). (DJW)

the site from Scripture is that it was outside Jerusalem, fairly conspicuous, probably not far from a city gate and a highway, and that a garden containing a tomb lay near by.

Two Jerusalem localities are today pointed out as the site of the Lord's cross and tomb; the one is the Church of the Holy Sepulchre, the other Gordon's Calvary, commonly known as the Garden Tomb. Unfortunately it has always proved difficult to debate the question objectively; in some quarters the identification one accepts is almost the touchstone of one's orthodoxy. The Church of the Holy Sepulchre marks the site of a temple to Venus which the emperor Constantine removed, understanding that it stood over the sacred site. The tradition thus goes back at least to the 4th century. But in view of the operations and activities of Titus in the 1st century and Hadrian in the 2nd, the identification must still be viewed as precarious. It has at least been clarified by recent excavations that the traditional site lay outside the city walls in the time of Christ. On the other hand, the evidence of the church itself may indicate a tomb of slightly too late a date to be authentic: see *BURIAL AND MOURNING (NT).

The Garden Tomb was first pointed out in 1849; a rock formation there resembles a skull; and admittedly the site accords with the biblical data. But there is no tradition nor anything else to support its claim. The more ancient site is much more likely; but any identification must remain conjectural.

BIBLIOGRAPHY. L. E. Cox Evans, *PEQ* 1968, pp. 112–136; K. M. Kenyon, *Digging up Jerusalem*, 1974; and other bibliography under *JERUSALEM. D.F.P.

CAMEL (Heb. *gāmāl*; Gk. *kamēlos*). A desert quadruped, famous for its ability to cross desert regions through being able to carry within itself several days' water-supply. The Heb. term (like the popular use of the word 'camel' in English) does *not* distinguish between the two characteristic kinds of camel: the one-humped animal (*Camelus dromedarius*) or 'dromedary' of Arabia, and the two-humped beast (*Camelus bactrianus*) or Bactrian camel from NE of Iran (Bactria, now in Turkmen and NW Afghanistan). In antiquity, both kinds are represented on the monuments.

In Scripture, camels are first mentioned in the days of the Patriarchs (*c.* 1900–1700 BC). They formed part of the livestock wealth of Abraham and Jacob (Gn. 12:16; 24:35; 30:43; 32:7, 15) and also of Job (1:3, 17; 42:12). On only two notable occasions are the Patriarchs actually shown using camels for transport: when Abraham's servant went to Mesopotamia to obtain a wife for Isaac (Gn. 24:10ff.), and when Jacob fled from Laban (Gn. 31:17, 34)—neither an everyday event. Otherwise, camels are attributed only to the Ishmaelites/Midianites, desert traders, at this time (Gn. 37:25). This very modest utilization of camels in the patriarchal age corresponds well with the known rather limited use of camels in the early 2nd millennium BC (see below).

In the 13th century BC the Egyptian beasts of burden smitten with disease included horses (the most valuable), asses (the most usual) and camels (a rarity), besides others (Ex. 9:3); and in the law camels were forbidden as food (Lv. 11:4; Dt. 14:7).

The mention of camels in the Pentateuch, especially in Genesis, has been often and persistently dismissed as anachronistic by some but stoutly defended by others. The truth appears to be as follows. From the 12th century BC the camel (and camel-nomadism) becomes a regular feature in the biblical world (other than Egypt, where it remains rare). Before this date, definite but very limited use was made of the camel. Though limited and imperfect, the extant evidence clearly indicates that the domesticated camel was known by 3000 BC, and continued in limited use as a slow-moving burden-carrier down through the 2nd millennium BC, the ass being the main beast of burden. (*ANIMALS OF THE BIBLE.)

Archaeological evidence. From the evidence available, only a few items bearing on Genesis and Exodus can be cited here. First and foremost, a mention of the (domesticated) camel occurs in a cuneiform tablet from Alalaḫ in N Syria (18th century BC) as GAM.MAL; see Wiseman, *JCS* 13, 1959, p. 29 and Goetze, *ibid.*, p. 37, on text 269, line 59. Lambert (*BASOR* 160, 1960, pp. 42–43), however, disputes the Alalaḫ camel-reference, and instead produces evidence for knowledge of the camel in the Old Babylonian period (*c.* 19th century BC) in a text from Ugarit. Then there is the kneeling camel-figure from Byblos of similar date (Montet, *Byblos et l'Égypte*, 1928, p. 91 and plate 52, No. 179). Albright's objection (*JBL* 64, 1945, p. 288) that it has no hump (hence not a camel) is ruled out because the figure is incomplete and has a socket by which a separately-fashioned hump and load were once fixed (this is also noted by R. de Vaux, *RB* 56, 1949, p. 9, nn. 4–5). A camel's jaw was found in a Middle Bronze Age tomb at Tell el-Fara' by Nablus (*c.* 1900–1550 BC) (de Vaux, *op. cit.*, p. 9, n. 8). Nor

Single-humped camels (dromedaries) being brought as tribute to King Tiglath-pileser III by an Arab queen. Relief from Calah (Nimrud). 744–727 BC. (BM)

Bactrian camels among the tribute brought to King Shalmaneser III. From the Black Obelisk. Calah (Nimrud). c. 830 BC. (BM)

CAMPHIRE See Herbs (Henna), Part 2.

does this exhaust the evidence for the patriarchal period.

In the Egyptian Fayum province was found a camel-skull dated to the 'Pottery A' stage, *i.e.* within the period *c.* 2000–1400 BC, the period from the Patriarchs practically to Moses; see O. H. Little, *Bulletin de l'Institut d'Égypte* 18, 1935–6, p. 215. From the Memphis region comes a figure of a camel with two water-jars (clear evidence of its domestication in Egypt) datable by associated archaeological material to about the 13th century BC (Petrie, *Gizeh and Rifeh*, 1907, p. 23 and plate 27). Albright (*JBL* 64, 1945, pp. 287–288) wished to lower the date of this example; but as he fails to offer specific evidence of any kind in support of his contention, it must be dismissed. Palestine also affords some evidence of camels at this general period. Hence the references in Exodus, Leviticus and Deuteronomy are no more objectionable than those in Genesis.

In the Judges' period Israel was troubled by camel-riding Midianites (repelled by Gideon, Jdg. 6–8) and others, *e.g.* the Hagarites (1 Ch. 5:21); likewise Saul and David fought camel-using Amalekites (1 Sa. 15:3; 27:9; 30:17). The Arabians made particular use of camels in peace and war—so did the Queen of Sheba (1 Ki. 10:2; 2 Ch. 9:1) and the people of Kedar and 'Hazor' (Je. 49:29, 32). Hazael the Aramaean brought 40 camel-loads of gifts from king Ben-hadad to Elisha (2 Ki. 8:9). *Cf.* the pictures of Assyrian, Arabian and Aramaean camels cited at the end of this article. The Jews who returned to Judaea with Zerubbabel after the Exile had 435 camels (Ezr. 2:67; Ne. 7:69). In NT times camel's hair furnished clothing for John the Baptist (Mt. 3:4; Mk. 1:6), while the camel featured in two of Christ's most striking word-pictures (Mt. 19:24 = Lk. 18:25; Mt. 23:24).

BIBLIOGRAPHY. For one-humped camels, see *ANEP*, p. 20, fig. 63, p. 52, fig. 170, p. 58, fig. 187, p. 132, fig. 375 (Assyrian and Arabian ones), p. 59, fig. 188 (Aramaean). For two-humped camels, see *ANEP*, p. 122, fig. 355 = *IBA*, p. 57, fig. 51, for Assyrian times, and H. Frankfort, *Art and Architecture of the Ancient Orient*, 1954, plate 184B of Persian period.

Specially valuable for the camel in antiquity are the richly-documented studies by R. Walz, in *Zeitschrift der Deutschen Morgenländischen Gesellschaft* 101, n.s. 26, 1951, pp. 29–51; *ibid*, 104, n.s. 29, 1954, pp. 45–87; and in *Actes du IVᵉ Congrès Internationale des Sciences Anthropologiques et Ethnologiques*, 3, Vienna, 1956, pp. 190–204. More recent are: F. S. Bodenheimer, *Animal and Man in Bible Lands*, 1960, under 'camelides', and W. Dostal in F. Gabrieli, W. Dostal, G. Dossin, *etc.*, *L'antica società beduina*, ed. Gabrieli, 1959; G. S. Cansdale, *Animals of Bible Lands*, 1970. K.A.K.

CANA (Gk. *kana*, probably from Heb. *qānâ*, 'place of reeds'). A Galilean village in the uplands W of the lake, mentioned in John's Gospel only. It was the scene of Jesus' first miracle (Jn. 2:1, 11), the place where with a word he healed the nobleman's son who lay sick at Capernaum (4:46, 50), and the home of Nathanael (21:2). Not definitely located, it has been identified by some with Kefr Kenna, about 6 km NNE of Nazareth on the road to Tiberias. This site, where excavations have been made, is a likely place for the events of Jn. 2:1–11, having ample water springs, and providing such shady fig trees as that suggested in Jn. 1:48. Many modern scholars, however, prefer an identification with Khirbet Kănā, a ruined site 14 km N of Nazareth, which local Arabs still call Cana of Galilee. J.D.D.

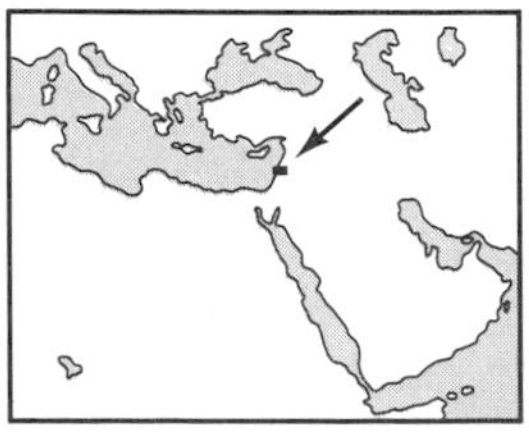

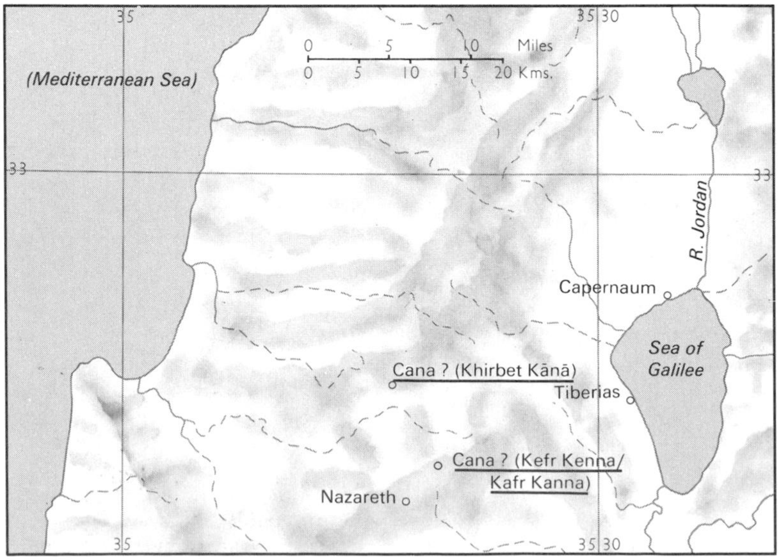

Sites suggested as ancient Cana.

CANAAN. Son of Ham, grandson of Noah, who laid a curse upon him (Gn. 9:18, 22–27). In Gn. 10:15–19 eleven groups who historically inhabited Phoenicia in particular and Syria–Palestine in general are listed as his descendants. See also the following article. K.A.K.

CANAAN, CANAANITES. A Semitic-speaking people and their territory, principally in Phoenicia. Their racial affinities are at present uncertain.

I. The name

The name Canaan (Heb. *kᵉna'an*) of people and land derives from that of their forebear Canaan or Kna' (see previous article) according to both Gn. 10:15–18 and native Canaanite–Phoenician tradition as transmitted by Sanchuniathon and preserved by Philo of Byblos. *Kna'(an)* is the native name of the Canaanites–Phoenicians applied to them both in Greek sources and by the Phoenicians themselves (*e.g.* on coins; see W. F. Albright, p. 1, n. 1, in his paper, 'The Rôle of the Canaanites in the History of Civilization', in *The Bible and the Ancient Near East, Essays for W. F. Albright*, 1961, pp. 328–362; cited hereafter as *BANE* Vol.). The meaning of *Kn'(n)* is unknown. Outside the Bible, the name occurs both with and without the final *n*. This *n* could be either a final *n* of a common Semitic type, or else a Hurrian suffix (Albright, *op. cit.*, p. 25, n. 50). Formerly, some linked *kn'(n)* with words for 'purple dye', esp. in Hurrian (with Speiser, *Language* 12, 1936, p. 124), but this was disproved by Landsberger (*JCS* 21, 1967, p. 106f.).

II. Extent of Canaan

'Canaan' in both Scripture and

external sources has threefold reference. **1.** Fundamentally it indicates the land and inhabitants of the Syro-Palestinian coastland, especially Phoenicia proper. This is indicated within Gn. 10:15–19 by its detailed enumeration of Sidon 'the first-born', the *Arkite, the Sinite, the Zemarite and Hamath in the Orontes valley. More specifically Nu. 13:29; Jos. 5:1; 11:3; Jdg. 1:27ff. put the Canaanites on the coastlands, in the valleys and plains, and the Jordan valley, with Amorites and others in the hills. Notably the inscription of Idrimi, king of Alalaḫ in the 15th century BC, mentions his flight to Ammia in coastal Canaan (S. Smith, *The Statue of Idrimi*, 1949, pp. 72–73; *ANET*³, pp. 557–558).

2. 'Canaan(ite)' can also cover, by extension, the hinterland and so Syria–Palestine in general. Thus, Gn. 10:15–19 includes also the Hittite, Jebusite, Amorite, Hivite and Girgashite, explaining that 'the families of the Canaanite spread abroad' (v. 18); this wider area is defined as extending coastally from Sidon to Gaza, inland to the Dead Sea cities Sodom and Gomorrah and apparently back up N to *Lasha (location uncertain). See also Gn. 12:5; 13:12; or Nu. 13:17–21; 34:1–2, with the following delimitation of W Palestinian boundaries; Jdg. 4:2, 23–24 calls Jabin (II) of Hazor titular 'king of Canaan'. This wider use is also encountered in early external sources. In their Amarna letters (14th century BC) kings of Babylon and elsewhere sometimes use 'Canaan' for Egypt's Syro-Palestinian territories generally. And the Egyptian Papyrus Anastasi IIIA (lines 5–6) and IV (16: line 4) of 13th century BC mention 'Canaanite slaves from Huru' (= Syria–Palestine generally) (R. A. Caminos, *Late-Egyptian Miscellanies*, 1954, pp. 117, 200).

3. The term 'Canaanite' can bear the more restricted meaning of 'merchant, trafficker', trading being a most characteristic Canaanite occupation. In Scripture this meaning may be found in Jb. 41:6; Is. 23:8; Ezk. 17:4; Zp. 1:11; the word *kn't* in Je. 10:17 is even used for 'wares, merchandise'. A stele of the pharaoh Amenophis II (*c.* 1440 BC) lists among his Syrian captives '550 *maryannu* (= noble chariot-warriors), 240 of their wives, 640 *Kn'nw*, 232 sons of princes, 323 daughters of princes', among others (*ANET*, p. 246). From this, Maisler (*BASOR* 102, 1946, p. 9) infers that the 640 *Kn'nw* (Canaaneans) found in such exalted company are of the merchant 'plutocracy of the coastal and the trading centres of Syria and Palestine'; but this is uncertain.

III. Canaanites and Amorites

Alongside the specific, wider and restricted uses of 'Canaan(ite)' noted above, *'Amorite(s)' also has both a specific and a wider reference. Specifically, the Amorites in Scripture are part of the hill-country population of Palestine (Nu. 13:29; Jos. 5:1; 11:3). But in its wider use 'Amorite' tends to overlap directly the term 'Canaanite'. 'Amorite' comes in under 'Canaan' in Gn. 10:15–16 for a start. Then, Israel is to conquer Canaan (= Palestine) in Nu. 13:17–21, *etc.*, and duly comes to dwell in the land of the Amorites, overcoming 'all the people' there, namely Amorites (Jos. 24:15, 18). Abraham reaches, and is promised, Canaan (Gn. 12:5, 7; 15:7, 18), but occupation is delayed as 'the iniquity of the Amorites is not yet complete' (Gn. 15:16). Shechem is a Canaanite principality under a Hivite ruler (Gn. 12:5–6; 34:2, 30), but can be called 'Amorite' (Gn. 48:22).

The documentary theory of literary criticism has frequently assayed to use these overlapping or double designations, Canaanites and Amorites (and other 'pairs'), as marks of different authorship (see, *e.g.*, S. R. Driver, *Introduction to the Literature of the Old Testament*⁹, 1913, p. 119, or O. Eissfeldt, *The Old Testament, an Introduction*, 1965, p. 183). But any such use of these terms does not accord with the external records which have no underlying 'hands', and it must therefore be questioned.

In the 18th century BC Amurru is part of Syria in the Alalaḫ tablets, while Amorite princes are mentioned in a Mari document in relation to Hazor in Palestine itself (*cf.* J.-R. Kupper, *Les Nomades en Mésopotamie au temps des Rois de Mari*, 1957, pp. 179–180). As Hazor is the Canaanite city *par excellence* of N Palestine, the mingling of people and terms is already attested in Abraham's day. In the 14th/13th centuries BC the specific kingdom of Amurru of Abdi-aširta, Aziru, and their successors in the Lebanon mountain region secured a firm hold on a section of the Phoenician

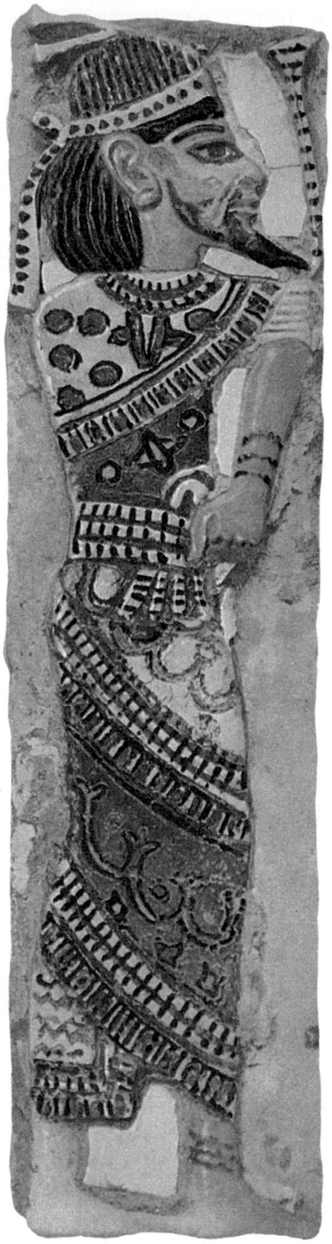

Elaborately-dressed Canaanite prisoner from Syria, depicted on an Egyptian faience tile. Height 25·5 cm. 1195–1164 BC (Rameses III). (OIUC)

coast and its Canaanite seaports by conquest and alliance 'from Byblos to Ugarit' (Amarna Letter No. 98). This *Amorite control in coastal Canaan is further attested by the Battle of Qadesh inscriptions of Rameses II (13th century BC) mentioning the timely arrival inland of a battle force from a 'port in the land of Amurru' (see Gardiner, *Ancient Egyptian Onomastica* I, 1947, pp. 188*–189*, and Gardiner, *The Kadesh Inscriptions of Ramesses II*, 1960, on this incident). This is independent evidence for a contiguous use of Amor(ites) and Canaan(ites) in Moses' time. The use of these terms as the distinguishing marks of different literary hands is thus erroneous. In any case the situation reflected in

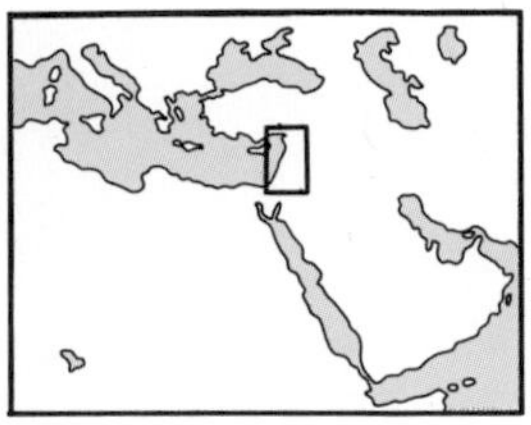

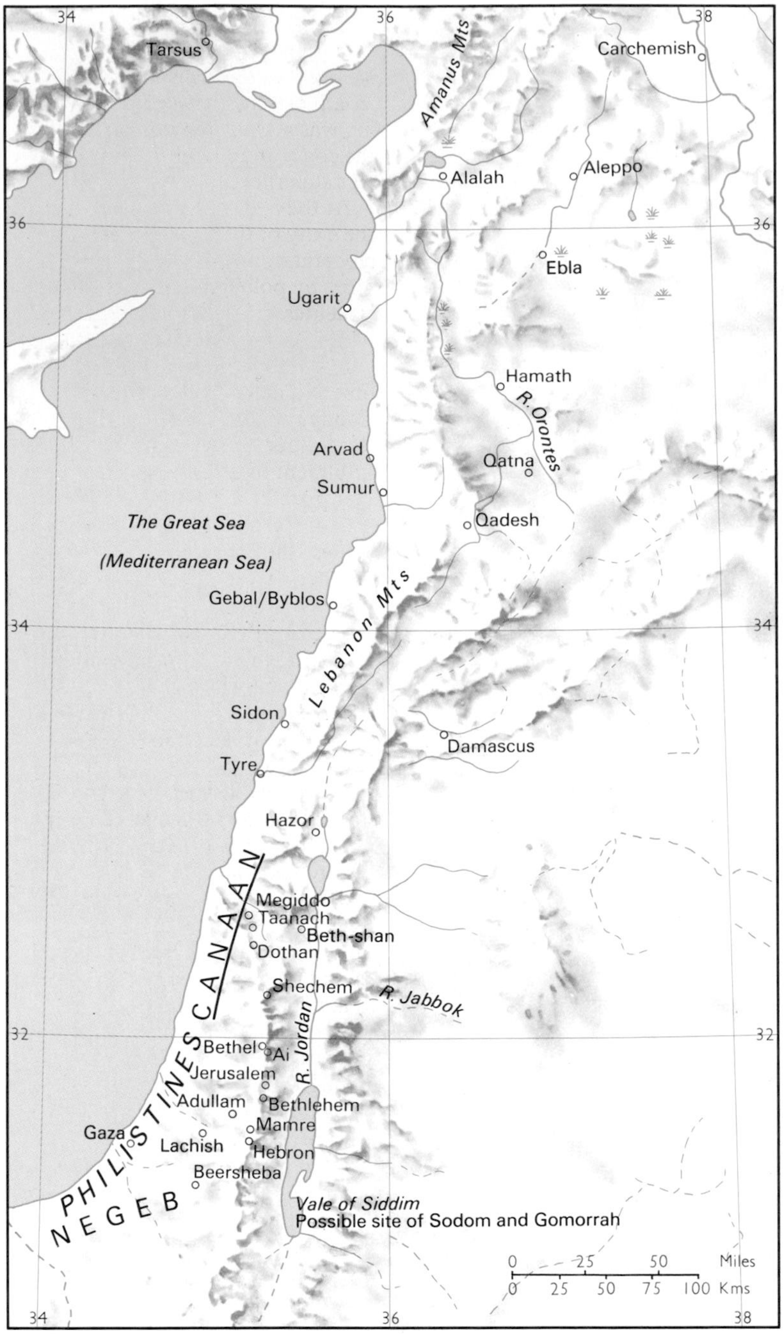

Canaan and its neighbours.

the Pentateuch and Joshua by this usage was radically changed by the impact of the sea peoples at the end of the 13th century BC, after which date the emergence of that usage would be inexplicable.

IV. The language

The definition of what is or is not 'Canaanite' is much controverted. Within the general group of the NW Semitic languages and dialects, biblical Hebrew (*cf.* Is. 19:18) and the W Semitic glosses and terms in the Amarna tablets can correctly be termed 'S Canaanite' along with Moabite and Phoenician. Separate but related are Aramaic and Ya'udic. Between these two groups comes Ugaritic. Some hold this latter to be a separate NW Semitic language, others that it is Canaanite to be classed with Hebrew, *etc.* Ugaritic itself betrays historical development linguistically, and thus the Ugaritic of the 14th/13th centuries BC is closer to Hebrew than is the archaic language of the great epics (Albright, *BASOR* 150, 1958, pp. 36–38). Hence it is provisionally possible to view NW Semitic as including S Canaanite (Hebrew, *etc.*), N Canaanite (Ugaritic) and Aramaic. *Cf.* S. Moscati (*The Semites in Ancient History*, 1959, pp. 97–100), who (rather radically) would abolish 'Canaanite'; and J. Friedrich (*Scientia* 84, 1949, pp. 220–223), on this question. The distinction between 'Canaanite' and 'Amorite' is almost illusory, and little more than dialectal. On NW Semitic *ā* versus Canaanite *ō*, *cf.* Gelb, *JCS* 15, 1961, pp. 42f. They differ in little more than the sibilants. Texts from the N Syrian city of * Ebla are written in a dialect that appears to be W Semitic and to show affinities with S Canaanite, according to the decipherer, G. Pettinato, who calls it 'Palaeo-Canaanite' (*Orientalia* n.s. 44, 1975, pp. 361–374, esp. 376ff.). (* LANGUAGE OF THE OLD TESTAMENT.)

V. Canaanite history

The presence of Semitic-speaking people in Palestine in the 3rd millennium BC is so far explicitly attested only by two Semitic placenames in a text of that age: *Ndi'* which contains the element *'il(u)*, god', and *n..k..* which begins with *ain*, 'spring, well', both these names occurring in an Egyptian tombscene of 5th/6th Dynasty, *c.* 2400 BC.

However, the question as to whether these indicate the presence of Canaanites, and just when Canaanites appeared in Palestine, is a matter of dispute. It is certain that Canaaanites and Amorites were well established in Syria-Palestine by 2000 BC, and a NW-Semitic-speaking element at Ebla in N Syria by *c.* 2300 BC.

Throughout the 2nd millennium BC, Syria–Palestine was divided among a varying number of Canaanite/Amorite city-states. For the 19th/18th century BC, many names of places and rulers are recorded in the Egyptian Execration Texts. On the organization of some of the separate states in Palestine in this, the patriarchal period, see also A. van Selms, *Oudtestamentische Studiën* 12, 1958 (*Studies on the Book of Genesis*), pp. 192–197.

During the period roughly 1500–1380 BC, these petty states were part of Egypt's Asiatic empire; in the 14th century BC the N ones passed under Hittite suzerainty, while the S ones remained nominally Egyptian. Early in the 13th century BC Egypt regained effectual control in Palestine and coastal Syria (the Hittites retaining N and inner Syria), but this control evaporated as time passed (*cf.* H. Klengel, *Geschichte Syriens*, 1–3, 1965–70). Thus Israel in the late

13th century met Canaanite/Amorite, but not specifically Egyptian, opposition (except for Merenptah's abortive raid). The 'conquest' by Rameses III, *c.* 1180 BC, was a sweeping raid, mainly *via* the coast and principal routes, and was superficial.

At the end of the 13th century BC the sway of the Canaanite/Amorite city-states, now decadent, was shattered by political upheavals. The Israelites, under Joshua, entered W Palestine from across the Jordan, gaining control of the hill-country first and defeating a series of Canaanite kings. For the Hebrews, the conquest of Canaan was the fulfilment of an ancient promise to their forefathers (Gn. 17:8; 28:4, 13–14; Ex. 6:2–8). They were to dispossess the peoples of the land as expelled by God, and to destroy those who remained (*cf.* Dt. 7:1, 2ff.); this was in consequence of divine judgment on long centuries of persistent wickedness by these peoples (Dt. 9:5, *cf.* Gn. 15:16), and not from any merit on Israel's part.

Meantime, the sea-peoples of the Egyptian records (including Philistines) had destroyed the Hittite empire and swept through Syria and Palestine to be halted on the Egyptian border by Rameses III; some, especially *Philistines, establishing themselves on the Palestinian coast. Finally, Aramaean penetration of inland Syria swiftly increased in the century or so following. The result was that the Canaanites now ruled only in Phoenicia proper with its ports and in isolated principalities elsewhere. From the 12th century BC onwards, the former Bronze Age Canaanites in their new, restricted circumstances emerged as the more-than-ever maritime *Phoenicians of the 1st millennium BC, centred on the famous kingdom of *Tyre and *Sidon. On the history of the Canaanites, especially as continuing as Phoenicians, see Albright, *BANE* Vol., pp. 328–362.

VI. Canaanite culture

Our knowledge of this is derived from two main sources: first, literary, from the N Canaanite and Babylonian texts discovered at *Ugarit (Ras Shamra, on the Syrian coast) with odd fragments elsewhere; and second, archaeological, in the sense of being derived from the excavated objects and remains from and of towns and cemeteries in Syria and Palestine.

Bronze Canaanite god from Ugarit with gold-plated head-dress and silver overlay on body. Height 17·9 cm. 15th–14th cent. BC. (MC)

CANAL
See River, Part 3.

a. Canaanite society

Most of the Canaanite city-states were monarchies. The king had extensive powers of military appointment and conscription, of requisitioning lands and leasing them in return for services, of taxation, including tithes, customs-dues, real-estate tax, *etc.*, and of corvée to requisition the labour of his subjects for state purposes. This is directly reflected in Samuel's denunciation of a kingship like that of the nations round about (1 Sa. 8, *c.* 1050 BC), and clearly evident in the tablets from Alalaḫ (18th–15th centuries BC) and Ugarit (14th–13th centuries BC) (see I. Mendelsohn, *BASOR* 143, 1956, pp. 17–22). Military, religious and economic matters were under the king's direct oversight; the queen was an important personage sometimes appealed to by high officials; the court was elaborately organized in larger states like Ugarit (for the latter, *cf.* A. F. Rainey, *The Social Stratification of Ugarit*, 1962).

The basic unit of society was the family. For the period of the 19th–15th centuries BC, the great N Canaanite epics from Ugarit (see *Literature*, below) betray the main features of family life (see A. van Selms, *Marriage and Family Life in Ugaritic Literature*, 1954). Further information is afforded by legal documents for the 14th/13th centuries BC. Among larger social units, besides the obvious ones of towns with their associated villages (in Ugarit state, see Virolleaud, *Syria* 21, 1940, pp. 123–151, and *cf.* briefly, C. H. Gordon, *Ugaritic Literature*, p. 124), for which compare the assignment of towns with their villages ('suburbs') in Jos. 13ff., one may note the widespread organization of guilds. These include primary producers (herdsmen, fowlers, butchers and bakers), artisans (smiths, working in copper (or bronze) and silver, potters, sculptors, and house-, boat- and chariot-builders), and traders, both local and long-distance. Priests and other cult-personnel (see below), also musicians, had guilds or groups; and there were several special classes of warriors. Several inscribed javelin- or spear-heads found in Palestine perhaps belonged to late-Canaanite mercenary troops of the 12/11th centuries BC, the sort of people commanded by a Sisera or Jabin (Jdg. 4, *etc.*); these also illustrate the free use of early W Semitic alphabetic script in the Palestine of the Judges. It has been suggested that in Canaanite society in 13th-century BC Palestine there was a sharp class distinction between upper-class patricians and lower-class, half-free serfs, the contrast with the relatively humble and homogeneous Israelites possibly being reflected in the excavated archaeological sites.

b. Literature

This is principally represented by N Canaanite texts from *Ugarit. These include long, but disordered and fragmentary, sections of the Baal Epic (deeds and fortunes of Baal or Hadad), which goes back linguistically to perhaps *c.* 2000 BC; the legend of Aqhat (vicissitudes of the only son of good king Dan'el) perhaps from *c.* 1800 BC; the story of King Keret (bereft of family, he gains a new wife virtually by conquest, and also incurs the wrath of the gods) perhaps about 16th century BC; and other fragments. All extant copies date from the 14th/13th centuries BC. The high-flown poetry of the early epics has clearly demonstrated the archaic flavour of much Hebrew OT poetry in its vocabulary and turns of speech. For full translations of the epics, so important for early Canaanite religions, see C. H. Gordon, *Ugaritic Literature*, 1949; G. R. Driver, *Canaanite Myths and Legends*, 1956; A. Caquot, M. Sznycer, A. Herdner, *Textes Ougaritiques* I, 1974. Selections are given in *ANET*, pp. 129–155, and in *DOTT.*

c. Religion

The Canaanites had an extensive pantheon, headed by El. More prominent in practice were *Baal (lord'), *i.e.* Hadad the storm-god, and *Dagon, with temples in Ugarit and elsewhere. The goddesses *Asherah, Astarte (*Ashtaroth) and Anath—like Baal—had multi-coloured personalities and violent characters; they were goddesses of sex and war. Kothar-and-Hasis was artificer-god (*cf.* Vulcan), and other and lesser deities abounded.

Actual temples in Palestine include remains at Beth-shan, Megiddo, Lachish, Shechem and especially Hazor (which had at least three), besides those in Syria at Qatna, Alalaḫ or Ugarit. The Ugaritic texts mention a variety of animals sacrificed to the gods: cattle, sheep (rams and lambs) and birds (including doves)—plus, of course, libations. Animal bones excavated in several Palestinian sites support this picture.

The title of high priest (*rb khnm*) is attested for Canaanite religion at Ugarit. That the *qdšm* of the Ugaritic texts were cult prostitutes is very possible; at any rate, the *qdšm* were as much an integral part of Canaanite religion there as they were forbidden to Israel (Dt. 23:17–18, *etc.*). Human sacrifice in 2nd-millennium Canaanite religion has not yet been isolated archaeologically with any certainty, but there are indications that it was customary. That Canaanite religion appealed to the bestial and material in human nature is clearly evidenced by the Ugaritic texts and in Egyptian texts of Semitic origin or inspiration; *cf.* Albright, *Archaeology and Religion of Israel*[3], 1953, pp. 75–77, 158–159, 197, n. 39; see also *CALF, GOLDEN. When the full import of this is realized it will be the more evident that physically and spiritually the sophisticated crudities of decaying Canaanite culture and emergent Israel with a unique mission could not coexist.

BIBLIOGRAPHY. A. R. Millard, 'The Canaanites', in *POTT*, pp. 29–52. For discoveries at Ugarit, see Schaeffer's reports in *Syria* since 1929, and the fully documented series of volumes, *Mission de Ras Shamra* by Schaeffer, Virolleaud and Nougayrol.

K.A.K.

CANANAEAN (Gk. *Kananaios*, from Heb. and Aram. *qannā'* or Aram. *qan'ān*, 'zealot', 'zealous'). In Mt. 10:4; Mk. 3:18 (RV and RSV rightly for AV 'Canaanite'), the surname of Simon, one of the Twelve. In Lk. 6:15; Acts 1:13 he is called by the equivalent Greek term *Zēlōtēs*, 'zealot'. The presence of a *Zealot (or past Zealot) among the apostles gives rise to interesting speculation; he may not, of course, have been a Zealot proper, but received the designation from Jesus or his fellow apostles because of his temperament. The fact that Mark, followed by Matthew, used the Semitic form suggests, however, the more technical sense.

F.F.B.

CANDACE. The name or, more properly, title of the Ethiopian queen whose minister was converted under the ministry of Philip (Acts 8:27). For the extent of her kingdom, which probably centred in the region of Upper Nubia

(Meroë) rather than in modern-day Ethiopia, see *ETHIOPIA. Women rulers, probably queen mothers, bearing this title during the Hellenistic period, are well attested in ancient literature, *e.g.* Pseudo-Callisthenes (3. 18), Strabo (17. 820), Pliny (*NH* 6. 186).

BIBLIOGRAPHY. Arndt; E. Ullendorff in *NTS* 2, 1955–6, pp. 53–56.

D.A.H.

CANNEH. The name of a settlement or town mentioned, with *Haran and *Eden, as trading with Tyre (Ezk. 27:23). The site is unknown, but the above association suggests the area of the middle Euphrates, and this has support from Assyr. documents of the 7th century BC.

T.C.M.

CANON OF THE OLD TESTAMENT.

I. The term 'Canon'

The term 'Canon' is borrowed from Greek, in which *kanōn* means a rule. Since the 4th century *kanōn* has been used by Christians to denote an authoritative list of the books belonging to the OT or NT. There has long been some difference of opinion about the books which should be included in the OT. Indeed, even in pre-Christian times, the Samaritans rejected all its books except the Pentateuch; while, from about the 2nd century BC onwards, pseudonymous works, usually of an apocalyptic character, challenged for themselves the status of inspired writings and found credence in certain circles. In the rabbinical literature it is related that in the first few centuries of the Christian era certain sages disputed, on internal evidence, the canonicity of five OT books (Ezekiel, Proverbs, Song of Songs, Ecclesiastes, Esther). In the patristic period there was uncertainty among Christians whether the Apocrypha of the Greek and Latin Bible were to be regarded as inspired or not. Difference on the last point came to a head at the Reformation, when the church of Rome insisted that the Apocrypha were part of the OT, on an equal footing with the rest, while the Protestant churches denied this. Though some of the Protestant churches regarded the Apocrypha as edifying reading (the Church of England, for example, continuing to include them in its lectionary 'for example of life but not to establish any doctrine'), they were all agreed that, properly speaking, the OT Canon consists only of the books of the Hebrew Bible—the books acknowledged by the Jews and endorsed in the teaching of the NT. The Eastern Orthodox Church was for a time divided on this issue, but is latterly tending more and more to come down on the Protestant side.

What qualifies a book for a place in the Canon of the OT or NT is not just that it is ancient, informative and helpful, and has long been read and valued by God's people, but that it has God's authority for what it says. God spoke through its human author, to teach his people what to believe and how to behave. It is not just a record of revelation, but the permanent written form of revelation. This is what we mean when we say that the Bible is 'inspired' (*INSPIRATION), and it makes the books of the Bible in this respect different from all other books.

II. The first emergence of the Canon

The doctrine of biblical inspiration is fully developed only in the pages of the NT. But far back in Israel's history we already find certain writings being recognized as having divine authority, and serving as a written rule of faith and practice for God's people. This is seen in the people's response when Moses reads to them the book of the covenant (Ex. 24:7), or when the book of the Law found by Hilkiah is read, first to the king and then to the congregation (2 Ki. 22–23; 2 Ch. 34), or when the book of the Law is read to the people by Ezra (Ne. 8:9, 14–17; 10:28–39; 13:1–3). The writings in question are a part or the whole of the Pentateuch—in the first case quite a small part of Exodus, probably chapters 20–23. The Pentateuch is treated with the same reverence in Jos. 1:7f.; 8:31; 23:6–8; 1 Ki. 2:3; 2 Ki. 14:6; 17:37; Ho. 8:12; Dn. 9:11, 13; Ezr. 3:2, 4; 1 Ch. 16:40; 2 Ch. 17:9; 23:18; 30:5, 18; 31:3; 35:26.

The Pentateuch presents itself to us as basically the work of Moses, one of the earliest, and certainly the greatest, of the OT prophets (Nu. 12:6–8; Dt. 34:10–12). God often spoke through Moses orally, as he did through later prophets too, but Moses' activity as a writer is also frequently mentioned (Ex. 17:14; 24:4, 7; 34:27; Nu. 33:2; Dt. 28:58, 61; 29:20f., 27; 30:10; 31:9–13, 19, 22, 24–26). There were other prophets in Moses' lifetime and more were expected to follow (Ex. 15:20; Nu. 12:6; Dt. 18:15–22; 34:10), as they did (Jdg. 4:4; 6:8), though the great outburst of prophetic activity began with Samuel. The literary work of these prophets started, as far as we know, with Samuel (1 Sa. 10:25; 1 Ch. 29:29), and the earliest kind of writing in which they seem to have engaged extensively was history, which afterwards became the basis of the books of Chronicles (1 Ch. 29:29; 2 Ch. 9:29; 12:15; 13:22; 20:34; 26:22; 32:32; 33:18f.), and probably of Samuel and Kings too, which have so much material in common with Chronicles. Whether Joshua and Judges likewise were based on prophetic histories of this kind we do not know, but it is quite possible. That the prophets on occasion wrote down oracles also is clear from Is. 30:8; Je. 25:13; 29:1; 30:2; 36:1–32; 51:60–64; Ezk. 43:11; Hab. 2:2; Dn. 7:1; 2 Ch. 21:12. Of course, to say all this is to accept the *prima facie* evidence of the OT books as historical: for discussions of other views, see *PENTATEUCH, *DEUTERONOMY, *CHRONICLES, *etc.*

The reason why Moses and the prophets wrote down God's message, and did not content themselves with delivering it orally, was sometimes to send it to another place (Je. 29:1; 36:1–8; 51:60f.; 2 Ch. 21:12); but quite as often to preserve it for the future, as a memorial (Ex. 17:14), or a witness (Dt. 31:24–26), that it might be for the time to come for ever and ever (Is. 30:8). The unreliability of oral tradition was well known to the OT writers. An object-lesson here was the loss of the book of the Law during the wicked reigns of Manasseh and Amon: when it was rediscovered by Hilkiah its teaching came as a great shock, for it had been forgotten (2 Ki. 22–23; 2 Ch. 34). The permanent and abiding form of God's message was therefore not its spoken but its written form, and this explains the rise of the OT Canon.

How long the *Pentateuch took to reach its final shape we cannot be sure. However, we saw in the case of the book of the covenant, referred to in Ex. 24, that it was possible for a short document like Ex. 20–23 to become canonical before it had grown to anything like the length of the book which now embodies it. The book of

CANDLESTICK. See Lamp, Part 2.

CANE, SWEET See Herbs, Part 2.

Genesis also embodies earlier documents (Gn. 5:1), Numbers includes an item from an ancient collection of poems (Nu. 21:14f.), and the main part of the book of Deuteronomy was laid up as canonical beside the ark in Moses' lifetime (Dt. 31:24–26), before the account of his death can have been added. The analogy between the *covenants of Ex. 24; Dt. 29–30 and the ancient Near Eastern treaties is suggestive, since the treaty documents were often laid in a sacred place, like the tables of the Ten Commandments and the book of Deuteronomy; and this was done when the treaty was made. The appropriate time for the covenants between God and Israel to be made was undoubtedly the time when the Pentateuch says they were made, at the Exodus, when God formed Israel into a nation; so it is in that period that the laying up of the Decalogue and Deuteronomy in the sanctuary should be dated, in accordance with the Pentateuchal account, and this means that the recognition of their canonicity should also be dated as from then.

While there was a succession of prophets, it was of course possible for earlier sacred writings to be added to and edited in the manner indicated above, without committing the sacrilege about which warnings are given in Dt. 4:2; 12:32; Pr. 30:6. The same applies to other parts of the OT. Joshua embodies the covenant of its last chapter, vv. 1–25, originally written by Joshua himself (v. 26). Samuel embodies the document on the manner of the kingdom (1 Sa. 8:11–18), originally written by Samuel (1 Sa. 10:25). Both these documents were canonical from the outset, the former having been written in the very book of the Law at the sanctuary of Shechem, and the latter having been laid up before the Lord at Mizpeh. There are signs of the growth of the books of Psalms and Proverbs in Ps. 72:20 and Pr. 25:1. Items from an ancient collection of poems are included in Joshua (10:12f.), Samuel (2 Sa. 1:17–27) and Kings (1 Ki. 8:53, LXX). Kings names as its sources the *Book of the Acts of Solomon*, the *Book of the Chronicles of the Kings of Israel* and the *Book of the Chronicles of the Kings of Judah* (1 Ki. 11:41; 14:19, 29, *etc.*; 2 Ki. 1:18; 8:23, *etc.*). The latter two works, combined together, are probably the same as the *Book of the Kings of Israel and Judah*, often named as a source by the canonical books of Chronicles (2 Ch. 16:11; 25:26; 27:7; 28:26; 35:27; 36:8; and, in abbreviated form, 1 Ch. 9:1; 2 Ch. 24:27). This source book seems to have incorporated many of the prophetic histories which are also named as sources in Chronicles (2 Ch. 20:34; 32:32).

Not all the writers of the OT books were prophets, in the narrow sense of the word; some of them were kings and wise men. But their experience of inspiration led to their writings also finding a place in the Canon. The inspiration of psalmists is spoken of in 2 Sa. 23:1–3; 1 Ch. 25:1, and of wise men in Ec. 12:11f. Note also the revelations made by God in Job (38:1; 40:6), and the implication of Pr. 8:1–9:6 that the book of Proverbs is the work of the divine Wisdom.

III. The closing of the first section (the Law)

The references to the Pentateuch (in whole or part) as canonical, which we saw in the other books of the OT, and which continue in the intertestamental literature, are remarkably numerous. This is doubtless due in part to its fundamental importance. References to other books as inspired or canonical are, within the OT, largely confined to their authors: the chief exceptions are probably Is. 34:16; Ps. 149:9; Dn. 9:2. Another reason for this frequency of reference to the Pentateuch may, however, be that it was the first section of the OT to be written and recognized as canonical. The likelihood that this was so arises from the fact that it was basically the work of a single prophet of very early date, which was edited after his death but was not open to continual addition, whereas the other sections of the OT were produced by authors of later date, whose number was not complete until after the return from the Exile. No-one doubts that the Pentateuch was both complete and canonical by the time Ezra and Nehemiah, in the 5th century BC, and it may have been so considerably earlier. In the 3rd century BC it was translated into Greek, thus becoming the first part of the LXX. In the mid-2nd century BC we have evidence of all 5 books, including Genesis, being attributed to Moses (see Aristobulus, as cited by Eusebius, *Preparation for the Gospel* 13. 12). Later in the same century the breach between Jews and Samaritans seems to have become complete, and the preservation of the Hebrew Pentateuch by both parties since proves that it was already their common property. All this is evidence that the first section of the Canon was now closed, consisting of the 5 familiar books, neither more nor less, with only minor textual variations persisting.

IV. The evolution of the second and third sections (the Prophets and Hagiographa)

The rest of the Hebrew Bible has a different structure from the English. It is divided into two sections: the Prophets, and the Hagiographa or (other) Scriptures. The Prophets comprise 8 books: the historical books Joshua, Judges, Samuel and Kings, and the oracular books Jeremiah, Ezekiel, Isaiah and the Twelve (the Minor Prophets). The Hagiographa comprise 11 books: the lyrical and wisdom books, Psalms, Job, Proverbs, Ecclesiastes, Song of Songs and Lamentations; and the historical books, Daniel (see below), Esther, Ezra–Nehemiah and Chronicles. This is the traditional order, according to which the remaining book of the Hagiographa, Ruth, is prefaced to Psalms, as ending with the genealogy of the psalmist David, though in the Middle Ages it was moved to a later position, alongside the other 4 books of similar brevity (Song of Songs, Ecclesiastes, Lamentations and Esther). It is noteworthy that in Jewish tradition Samuel, Kings, the Minor Prophets, Ezra–Nehemiah and Chronicles are each reckoned as a single book. This may indicate the capacity of an average Hebrew leather scroll at the period when the canonical books were first listed and counted.

Doubt has sometimes been thrown, for inadequate reasons, on the antiquity of this way of grouping the OT books. More commonly, but with equally little real reason, it has been assumed that it reflects the gradual development of the OT Canon, the grouping having been a historical accident, and the Canon of the Prophets having been closed about the 3rd century BC, before a history like Chronicles and a prophecy like Daniel (which, it is alleged, naturally belong there) had been recognized as inspired or perhaps even written. The Canon of the Hagiographa, according to this popular hypothesis, was not closed until the Jewish synod of Jamnia or Jabneh about AD 90, after an open

OT Canon had already been taken over by the Christian church. Moreover, a broader Canon, containing many of the Apocrypha, had been accepted by the Greek-speaking Jews of Alexandria, and was embodied in the LXX; and the LXX was the OT of the early Christian church. These two facts, perhaps together with the Essene fondness for the pseudonymous apocalypses, are responsible for the fluidity of the OT Canon in patristic Christianity. Such is the theory.

The reality is rather different. The grouping of the books is not arbitrary, but according to literary character. Daniel is half narrative, and in the Hagiographa, as the traditional order arranges them, it seems to be placed with the histories. There are histories in the Law (covering the period from the creation to Moses) and in the Prophets (covering the period from Joshua to the end of the Monarchy), so why should there not be histories in the Hagiographa also, dealing with the third period, that of the Exile and return? Chronicles is put last among the histories, as a summary of the whole biblical narrative, from Adam to the return. It is clear that the Canon of the Prophets was *not* completely closed when Chronicles was written, for the sources it quotes are not Samuel and Kings but the fuller prophetic histories which seem to have served as sources for Samuel and Kings as well. The earliest elements in the Prophets, incorporated in books such as Joshua and Samuel, are certainly very old, but so are the earliest elements in the Hagiographa, incorporated in books such as Psalms, Proverbs and Chronicles. These elements may have been recognized as canonical before the final completion of even the first section of the Canon. The latest elements in the Hagiographa, such as Daniel, Esther and Ezra–Nehemiah, belong to the end of OT history. But the same is true of the latest elements in the Prophets, such as Ezekiel, Haggai, Zechariah and Malachi. Even though the books of the Hagiographa do tend to be later than the Prophets, it is only a tendency, and the overlap is considerable. Indeed, the very assumption that the Hagiographa are a late collection may have led to their individual books being dated later than they otherwise would have been.

Since the books in both these sections are by a variety of authors and are usually independent of one another, it may well be that they were recognized as canonical individually, at different dates, and at first formed a single miscellaneous collection. Then, when the prophetic gift had been for some while withdrawn, and their number was seen to be complete, they were more carefully classified, and were divided into two distinct sections. 'The books', spoken of in Dn. 9:2, may have been one growing body of literature, loosely organized, and containing not only works by prophets like Jeremiah, but also works by psalmists like David. The tradition in 2 Macc. 2:13 about Nehemiah's library reflects such a mixed collection: 'he, founding a library, gathered together the books about the kings and prophets, and the books of David, and letters of kings about sacred gifts'. The antiquity of this tradition is shown not only by the likelihood that some such action would be necessary after the calamity of the Exile, but also by the fact that the 'letters of kings about sacred gifts' are simply being preserved because of their importance, and have not yet been embodied in the book of Ezra (6:3–12; 7:12–26). Time had to be given after this for books like Ezra to be completed, for the recognition of the latest books as canonical, and for the realization that the prophetic gift had ceased, and only when these things had happened could the firm division between Prophets and Hagiographa and the careful arrangement of their contents be made. The division had already been made towards the end of the 2nd century BC, when the prologue to the Greek translation of Ecclesiasticus was composed, for this prologue repeatedly refers to the three sections of the Canon. But it seems likely that the division had not long been made, for the third section of the Canon had not yet been given a name: the writer calls the first section 'the Law', and the second section (because of its contents) 'the Prophets' or 'the Prophecies', but the third section he simply describes. It is 'the others that have followed in their steps', 'the other ancestral books', 'the rest of the books'. This language implies a fixed and complete group of books, but one less old and well-established than the books it contains. The three sections are also referred to, in the first century AD, by Philo (*De Vita Contemplativa* 25) and by Christ (Lk. 24:44), both of whom give the third section its earliest name of 'the Psalms'.

V. The closing of the second and third sections

The date when the Prophets and Hagiographa were organized in their separate sections was probably about 165 BC. For the 2 Maccabees tradition just quoted continues by speaking of the second great crisis in the history of the Canon: 'And in the same way Judas (Maccabaeus) collected all the books that had been lost on account of the war which had come upon us, and they are still in our possession' (2 Macc. 2:14). The 'war' in question is the Maccabean war of liberation from the Syrian persecutor Antiochus Epiphanes. The hostility of Antiochus against the Scriptures is on record (1 Macc. 1:56f.), and it is indeed probable that Judas would have needed to gather copies of them together when the persecution was over. Judas knew that the prophetic gift had ceased a long time before (1 Macc. 9:27), so what is more likely than that, in gathering together the scattered scriptures, he arranged and listed the now complete collection in the way which from that time became traditional? Since the books were as yet in separate scrolls, which had to be 'collected', what he would have produced would not have been a volume but a collection, and a list of the books in the collection, divided into three.

In drawing up his list, Judas probably established not only the firm division into Prophets and Hagiographa, but also the traditional order and number of the books within them. A list of books has to have an order and number, and the traditional order, recorded as a *baraita* from an older source in the Babylonian Talmud (*Baba Bathra* 14b–15a), is the one given earlier in this article, making Chronicles the last of the Hagiographa. This position for Chronicles can be traced back to the 1st century AD, since it is reflected in a saying of Christ's in Mt. 23:35 and Lk. 11:51, where the phrase 'from the blood of Abel to the blood of Zechariah' probably means all the martyred prophets from one end of the Canon to the other, from Gn. 4:3–15 to 2 Ch. 24:19–22. The traditional number of the canonical books is 24 (the 5 books of the

Law, together with 8 books of the Prophets and the 11 books of the Hagiographa listed above), or 22 (Ruth being in that case appended to Judges, and Lamentations to Jeremiah, in order to conform the count to the number of letters in the Hebrew alphabet). The number 24 is first recorded in 2 Esdras 14:44–48, about AD 100, but may also be alluded to in Rev. 4:4, 10, *etc.*, for the *baraita* in *Baba Bathra* seems to imply that the authors of the OT books, as well as the books themselves, were 24 in number, like the elders of Revelation. The number 22 is first recorded in Josephus (*Contra Apion* 1.8), just before AD 100, but also, probably, in the fragments of the Greek translation of the book of *Jubilees* (1st century BC?). If the number 22 goes back to the 1st century BC, so does the number 24, for the former is an adaptation of the latter to the number of letters in the alphabet. And since the number 24, which combines some of the smaller books into single units but not others, seems to have been influenced in this by the traditional order, the order too must be equally old. There is no doubt about the identity of the 24 or 22 books—they are the books of the Hebrew Bible. Josephus says that they have all been accepted as canonical from time immemorial. Individual attestation can be provided for the canonicity of nearly all of them from writings of the 1st century AD or earlier. This is true even of 4 out of 5 disputed by certain of the rabbis: only the Song of Songs, perhaps because of its shortness, remains without individual attestation.

Such evidence implies that by the beginning of the Christian era the identity of all the canonical books was well known and generally accepted. How, then, has it come to be thought that the third section of the Canon was not closed until the synod of Jamnia, some decades after the birth of the Christian church? The main reasons are that the rabbinical literature records disputes about 5 of the books, some of which were settled at the Jamnia discussion; that many of the LXX MSS mix apocryphal books among the canonical, thus prompting the theory of a wider Alexandrine Canon; and that the Qumran discoveries show the apocalyptic pseudepigrapha to have been cherished, and perhaps reckoned canonical, by the Essenes. But the rabbinical literature records similar, though more readily answered, academic objections to many other canonical books, so it must have been a question of removing books from the list (had this been possible), not adding them. Moreover, one of the 5 disputed books (Ezekiel) belongs to the second section of the Canon, which is admitted to have been closed long before the Christian era. As to the Alexandrian Canon, Philo of Alexandria's writings show it to have been the same as the Palestinian. He refers to the 3 familiar sections, and he ascribes inspiration to many books in all 3, but never to any of the Apocrypha. In the LXX MSS, the Prophets and Hagiographa have been rearranged by Christian hands in a non-Jewish manner, and the intermingling of Apocrypha there is a Christian phenomenon, not a Jewish. At Qumran the pseudonymous apocalypses were more likely viewed as an Essene appendix to the standard Jewish Canon than as an integral part of it. There are allusions to this appendix in Philo's account of the Therapeutae (*De Vita Contemplativa* 25) and in 2 Esdras 14:44–48. An equally significant fact discovered at Qumran is that the Essenes, though at rivalry with mainstream Judaism since the 2nd century BC, reckoned as canonical some at least of the Hagiographa, and had presumably done so since before rivalry began.

VI. From Jewish Canon to Christian

The LXX MSS are paralleled by the writings of the early Christian Fathers, who (at any rate outside Palestine and Syria) normally used the LXX or the derived Old Latin version. In their writings, there is both a wide and a narrow Canon. The former comprises those books from before the time of Christ which were generally read and esteemed in the church (including the Apocrypha), but the latter is confined to the books of the Jewish Bible, which scholars like Melito, Origen, Epiphanius and Jerome take the trouble to distinguish from the rest as alone inspired. The Apocrypha were known in the church from the start, but the further back one goes, the more rarely are they treated as inspired. In the NT itself, one finds Christ acknowledging the Jewish Scriptures, by various of their current titles, and accepting the three sections of the Jewish Canon and the traditional order of its books; one finds Revelation perhaps alluding to their number, and most of the books being referred to individually as having divine authority; but none of the Apocrypha. The only apparent exception is the reference to *1 Enoch* in Jude 14f., which may be just an *argumentum ad hominem* to converts from the apocalyptic school of thought, who seem to have been numerous.

What evidently happened in the early centuries of Christianity was this. Christ passed on to his followers, as Holy Scripture, the Bible which he had received, containing the same books as the Hebrew Bible today. The first Christians shared with their Jewish contemporaries a full knowledge of the identity of the canonical books. However, the Bible was not yet between two covers: it was a memorized list of scrolls. The breach with Jewish oral tradition (in some matters a very necessary breach), the alienation between Jew and Christian, and the general ignorance of Semitic languages in the church outside Palestine and Syria, led to increasing doubt on the Canon among Christians, which was accentuated by the drawing up of new lists of the biblical books, arranged on other principles, and the introduction of new lectionaries. Such doubt about the Canon could only be resolved, and can only be resolved today, in the way it was resolved at the Reformation—by returning to the teaching of the NT, and the Jewish background against which it is to be understood.

BIBLIOGRAPHY. S. Z. Leiman, *The Canonization of Hebrew Scripture*, 1976; A. C. Sundberg, *The OT of the Early Church*, 1964; J. P. Lewis, *Journal of Bible and Religion* 32, 1964, pp. 125–132; M. G. Kline, *The Structure of Biblical Authority*, 1972; J. D. Purvis, *The Samaritan Pentateuch and the Origin of the Samaritan Sect*, 1968; B. F. Westcott, *The Bible in the Church*, 1864; W. H. Green, *General Introduction to the OT: the Canon*, 1899; H. E. Ryle, *The Canon of the OT*, 1895; M. L. Margolis, *The Hebrew Scriptures in the Making*, 1922; S. Zeitlin, *A Historical Study of the Canonization of the Hebrew Scriptures*, 1933; R. L. Harris, *Inspiration and Canonicity of the Bible*, 1957. R.T.B.

The Old Testament Canon: grouping of the books

Hebrew Bible		Christian Bible
I The Law (Pentateuch)	Genesis	Genesis
	Exodus	Exodus
	Leviticus	Leviticus
	Numbers	Numbers
	Deuteronomy	Deuteronomy
II The Prophets	Joshua	Joshua
	Judges	Judges
	Samuel	Ruth
	Kings	Samuel (1 and 2)
	Isaiah	Kings (1 and 2)
	Jeremiah	Chronicles (1 and 2)
	Ezekiel	Ezra
	Hosea	Nehemiah
	Joel	Esther
	Amos	Job
	Obadiah	Psalms
	Jonah	Proverbs
	Micah	Ecclesiastes
	Nahum	Song of Solomon
	Habakkuk	Isaiah
	Zephaniah	Jeremiah
	Haggai	Lamentations
	Zechariah	Ezekiel
	Malachi	Daniel
III The Writings (Hagiographa)	Psalms	Hosea
	Proverbs	Joel
	Job	Amos
	Song of Solomon	Obadiah
	Ruth	Jonah
	Lamentations	Micah
	Ecclesiastes	Nahum
	Esther	Habakkuk
	Daniel	Zephaniah
	Ezra	Haggai
	Nehemiah	Zechariah
	Chronicles	Malachi

- The Law
- Prophets
- Wisdom Writings
- Historical

*See also article on Apocrypha

The canonical arrangement of the books of the OT according to Christian tradition, compared with the original order in Hebrew.

Opposite page: Some of the main stages in the acceptance of the Canon of the New Testament in the West.

CANON OF THE NEW TESTAMENT.

I. The earliest period

Biblical theology demands as its presupposition a fixed extent of biblical literature: this extent is traditionally fixed, since the era of the great theological controversies, in the Canon of the NT. 'Canon' is here the latinization of the Gk. *kanōn*, 'a reed', which, from the various uses of that plant for measuring and ruling, comes to mean a ruler, the line ruled, the column bounded by the line, and hence, the list written in the column. Canon is the list of books which the church uses in public worship. *kanōn* also means rule or standard: hence a secondary meaning of Canon is the list of books which the church acknowledges as inspired Scripture, normative for faith and practice. Our understanding of inspiration requires, then, not only that we fix the text of Scripture and analyse the internal history of scriptural books, but also that we trace as accurately as possible the growth of the concept of a canon and of the Canon itself.

In this investigation, especially of the earliest period, three matters must be distinguished clearly: the knowledge of a book evinced by a particular Father or source; the attitude towards such a book as an inspired Scripture on the part of the Father or source (which may be shown by introductory formulae such as 'It is written' or 'As the scripture says'); and the existence of the concept of a list or canon in which the quoted work figures (which will be shown, not only by actual lists but also by reference to 'the books' or 'the apostles', where a literary corpus is intended). This distinction has not always been made, with resultant confusion. Quotations, even in the earliest period, may be discovered; but whether quotation implies status as inspired Scripture is a further question for which precise criteria are frequently lacking. This being so, it is not surprising that a decision about the existence of any canonical list or concept of a canon often fails to find any direct evidence at all, and depends entirely upon inference.

The earliest point at which we can take up the investigation is in the data provided by the NT itself. The apostolic church was not without Scripture—it looked for its doctrine to the OT, usually in a Gk. dress, though some writers appear to have used the Heb. text. Apocrypha such as *1 Enoch* were also used in some circles. Whether the term 'canonical' should be applied here is debatable, as the Jewish Canon was not yet fixed, at least *de jure*, and when it was it was moulded by anti-Christian controversy, in addition to other factors. In worship, the church already used some of its own peculiar traditions: in the Lord's Supper the Lord's death was 'proclaimed' (1 Cor. 11:26) probably in word (*sc.* the earliest Passion narrative) as well as in the symbols of the ordinance. The account of the Lord's Supper itself is regarded as derived 'from the Lord', a closely guarded tradition: we find this terminology too in places where ethical conduct is based on dominical utterance (*cf.* 1 Cor. 7:10, 12, 25; Acts 20:35). This is in the main oral material, a phrase which, as form criticism has shown, is by no means intended to suggest imprecision of outline or content. Written repositories of Christian tradition are at best hypothetical in the earliest apostolic age; for although it has been proposed to find in the phrase 'according to the scriptures' (1 Cor. 15:3–4) a reference to documents at this early date, this has met with but little favour. In this material, then, whether oral or written, we find at the earliest stage a church consciously preserving its traditions of the passion, resurrection, life (*cf.* Acts 10:36–40) and teaching of Jesus. Quite evidently, however, whatever was known and preserved by anyone did not exclude in his view the validity and value of traditions elsewhere preserved. The preservation is to a large extent unselfconscious in this 'prehistoric' stage of the development of Christian Scripture. It continues in the making of the Gospels, where two main streams are developed in independence of each other. It would appear that little escaped inclusion in these.

The epistolary material in the NT also possesses from the beginning a certain claim, if not to inspiration, at least to be an authoritative and adequate teaching on points of doctrine and conduct; yet it is as clear that no letter is written for other than specific recipients in a specific historical situation. The collection of a corpus of letters evidently post-dates the death of Paul: the Pauline corpus is textually homogeneous and there is more weighty evidence for the suggestion, most thoroughly developed by E. J. Goodspeed, that its collection was a single act at a specific date (probably about AD 80–85), than for the earlier view of Harnack that the corpus grew slowly. The corpus from the start would enjoy high status as a body of authoritative Christian literature. Its impact upon the church in the late 1st and early 2nd centuries is plain from the doctrine, language and literary form of the literature of the period. There is no corresponding evidence for any such corpora of non-Pauline writings at so early a date; nor does the Acts seem to have been produced primarily as a teaching document. The Revelation of John, on the contrary, makes the clearest claim to direct inspiration of any NT document, and is the sole example in this literature of the utterances and visions of the prophets of the NT church. Thus we have, in the NT itself, several clear instances of Christian material, even at the oral stage, viewed as authoritative and in some sense sacred: yet in no case does any writing explicitly claim that it alone preserves tradition. There is no sense, at this stage, of a Canon of Scripture, a closed list to which addition may not be made. This would appear to be due to two factors: the existence of an oral tradition and the presence of apostles, apostolic disciples, and prophets, who were the foci and the interpreters of the dominical traditions.

II. The Apostolic Fathers

The same factors are present in the age of the so-called Apostolic Fathers and are reflected in the data provided by them for Canon studies. As regards the Gospels, Clement (*First Epistle*, *c.* AD 90) quotes material akin to the Synoptics yet in a form not strictly identical with any particular Gospel; nor does he introduce the words with any formula of scriptural citation. John is unknown to him. Ignatius of Antioch (martyred *c.* AD 115) speaks frequently of 'the gospel': yet in all cases his words are patient of the interpretation that it is the message, not a document, of which he speaks. The frequent affinities with Matthew may indicate that this source was utilized, but other elucidations are possible. Whether John was known to him remains a matter of debate, in which the strongest case appears

Some of the main stages in the acceptance of the Canon of the New Testament in the West

	Irenaeus of Lyons c. AD 130-200	Muratorian Canon AD 170-210	Eusebius' EH 3.25 c. AD 260-340	Athanasius' 39th Paschal letter AD 367	Present Order
Matthew					Matthew
Mark					Mark
Luke					Luke
John					John
Acts					Acts
Romans					Romans
1 Corinthians					1 Corinthians
2 Corinthians					2 Corinthians
Galatians					Galatians
Ephesians					Ephesians
Philippians					Philippians
Colossians					Colossians
1 Thessalonians					1 Thessalonians
2 Thessalonians					2 Thessalonians
1 Timothy					1 Timothy
2 Timothy					2 Timothy
Titus					Titus
Philemon					Philemon
Hebrews					Hebrews
James			D		James
1 Peter					1 Peter
2 Peter			D		2 Peter
1 John					1 John
2 John			D		2 John
3 John			D		3 John
Jude			D		Jude
Revelation					Revelation

	Irenaeus of Lyons	Muratorian Canon	Eusebius' EH 3.25	Athanasius' 39th Paschal letter	
Wisdom of Solomon					
Apocalypse of Peter			S		
Shepherd of Hermas		**	S	*	
Acts of Paul			S		
Epistle of Barnabas			S		
The Didache			S	*	
Gospel according to the Hebrews			S		

Gospels

Pauline Epistles, probably collected into a corpus c. AD 80-85

'Catholic' Epistles

D Disputed

Apocryphal (selected works)

S Spurious

* Permitted reading

** Permitted reading but not for public worship

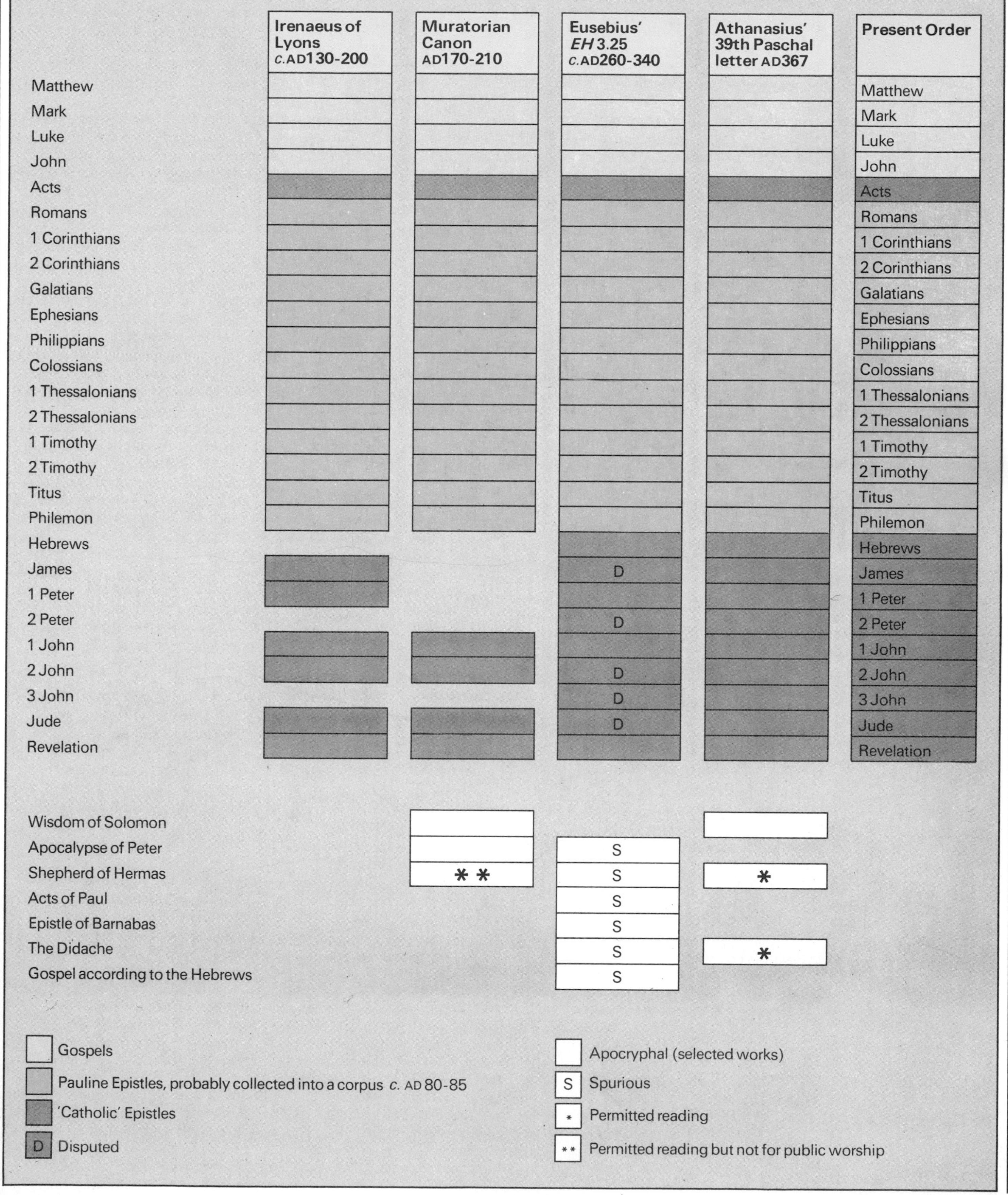

to be that it was not. Papias, fragmentarily preserved in Eusebius and elsewhere, gives us information on the Gospels, the precise import of which remains uncertain or controversial: he specifically asseverates his preference for the 'living and abiding voice', contrasted with the teaching of books. Polycarp of Smyrna's letter to the Philippians shows clear knowledge of Matthew and Luke. He is then the earliest unambiguous evidence for their use, but if, as is most likely, his letter is in fact the combination of two written at different times (*viz.* chs. 13–14 *c.* AD 115; the rest *c.* AD 135), this will not be so early as once was thought. The so-called *2 Clement* and the *Epistle of Barnabas* both date about AD 130. Both use much oral material, but attest the use of the Synoptics too; and each introduces one phrase from the Gospels with a formula of scriptural citation.

There is considerable and wide knowledge of the Pauline Corpus in the Apostolic Fathers: their language is strongly influenced by the apostle's words. Yet, highly valued as his letters evidently were, there is little introduction of quotations as scriptural. A number of passages suggest that a distinction was made in all Christian circles between the OT and writings of Christian provenance. The Philadelphians judged the 'gospel' by the 'archives' (Ignatius, *Philad.* 8. 2): *2 Clement* speaks of 'the books (*biblia*) and the apostles' (14. 2), a contrast which is probably equivalent to 'Old and New Testaments'. Even where the gospel was highly prized (*e.g.* Ignatius or Papias), it is apparently in an oral rather than a written form. Barnabas is chiefly concerned to expound the OT; the *Didache*, didactic and ethical material common to Jew and Christian. Along with material from the canonical Gospels or parallel to them, most of the Apostolic Fathers utilize what we anachronistically term 'apocryphal' or 'extra-canonical' material: it was evidently not so to them. We are still in a period when the NT writings are not clearly demarcated from other edifying material. This situation in fact continues yet further into the 2nd century, and may be seen in Justin Martyr and Tatian. Justin records that the 'memoirs of the apostles' called Gospels were read at Christian worship: his quotations and allusions, however, afford evidence that the extent of these was not identical with the four, but contained 'apocryphal' material. This same material was used by Tatian in his harmony of the Gospels known as the *Diatessaron*, or, as in one source, perhaps more accurately, as *Diapente*.

III. Influence of Marcion

It was towards the close of the 2nd century that awareness of the concept of a canon and scriptural status begins to reveal itself in the thought and activity of Christians. The challenge of heretical teachers was largely instrumental in stimulating this. One such was Marcion of Sinope who broke with the church in Rome in about AD 150, but was probably active in Asia Minor for some years previously. Believing himself the interpreter of Paul, he preached a doctrine of two Gods: the OT was the work of the Just God, the Creator, harsh judge of men: Jesus was the emissary of the Good (or Kind) God, higher than the Just, sent to free men from that God's bondage: crucified through malice of the Just God, he passed on his gospel, first to the Twelve, who failed to keep it from corruption, and then to Paul, the sole preacher of it. Since Marcion rejected the OT, according to this scheme, he felt the need of a distinctively Christian Scripture, and created a definite Canon of Scripture: *one* Gospel, which stood in some relation or other to our present Luke, and the ten Epistles of Paul (omitting Hebrews and the Pastorals), which constituted the *Apostolos*.

Certain features of the growth of the Catholic Canon, which supervenes upon the age of Justin and Tatian, appear due to the challenge which the Marcionite scriptures presented to the church, especially the dominant place occupied by Paul, in spite of his relative neglect in the mid-2nd century. Former generations, guided by the theories of Harnack, have seen this factor present also in two documentary sources, namely, a series of prologues to the Pauline Epistles in some Latin manuscripts, which de Bruyne considered to show signs of Marcion's tendentious teaching, thus termed 'Marcionite prologues', and certain prologues to the Gospels of Mark, Luke and John (extant chiefly in Latin), which have been termed 'anti-Marcionite', on the assumption that they were prefaced to the components of the fourfold Gospel at the time of its creation as a unity. Lately, however, these hypotheses, which have often been received as facts, have been trenchantly criticized and no longer appear certainly acceptable.

The other main heretical teaching against which the emergent concept of the Canon was used was that of the various Gnostics. From the Nag-Hammadi (*CHENOBOSKION) discoveries we can now know these better than did previous generations. It seems clear that the majority of the books which later constituted the NT were known in Gnostic circles. For instance, some moving passages in the so-called *Gospel of Truth* draw upon Revelation, Hebrews, Acts and the Gospels. Again, the *Gospel of Thomas* contains much material akin to the Synoptics, either derived from these or from a parallel oral tradition. But what is significant is that the latter mingles these sayings common to the Synoptic tradition with others of which canonical Scripture bears no trace; while the title of the former shows how the doctrine of a Gnostic teacher is presented as on a par with other Gospel documents. The emergence is a crystallization of the awareness that there was a clear distinction between teaching transmitted in documents of known antiquity as of apostolic origin, and recent teaching which could not be thus validated even if it claimed esoteric tradition or revelation as its source.

IV. Irenaeus to Eusebius

In the second half of the 2nd century, as has been intimated, clear evidence of the concept of a canon appears, although not all the books now included in the Canon are decided upon in any one church. Irenaeus of Lyons, in his work *Against the Heresies*, gives plain evidence that by his time the fourfold Gospel was axiomatic, comparable with the four corners of the earth and the four winds of heaven. Acts is quoted by him, sometimes explicitly, as Scripture. The Pauline Epistles, the Revelation and some Catholic Epistles are regarded, although not often explicitly as Scripture, yet (especially in the two former cases) sufficiently highly to indicate that here is a primary source of doctrine and authority to which reference must be made in the context of controversy. Against the so-called esoteric knowledge of his opponents, Irenaeus stresses the traditions of the church as apostolically derived. In these traditions, the Scriptures of the NT have their place. We know, however, that he definitely rejected Hebrews as non-Pauline.

Hippolytus of Rome, contemporary of Irenaeus, is known to us through writings only partially extant. He cites most NT books, speaking explicitly of two testaments and of a fourfold Gospel. Many critics are willing to ascribe to him the fragmentary list of canonical Scriptures preserved in Latin in a MS at Milan, known as the Muratorian Canon (after its first editor Ludovico Muratori). This ascription should not be taken as proved, however: the Latin is not necessarily a translation. A reference to the recent origin of the *Shepherd* of Hermas places it within the approximate dates AD 170–210. The extant part of the document gives a list of NT writings with some account of their origin and scope. Here again we meet a fourfold Gospel, acknowledgment of the Pauline Epistles, knowledge of some Catholic Epistles, the Acts of the Apostles and the Revelation of John; also included as canonical are the *Apocalypse of Peter* (there is no reference to any Petrine Epistle) and, rather surprisingly, the *Wisdom of Solomon*. The *Shepherd* is mentioned, but is not regarded as fit for use in public worship. The date of this document makes it highly significant, not only as witness to the existence at that time of a wide-embracing concept of the Canon but also of the marginal uncertainties, the omissions and the inclusion of writings later rejected as apocryphal.

The state of affairs shown in these sources was widespread and continued into the 3rd century. Tertullian, Clement of Alexandria and Origen all make wide use of the NT Scriptures, either in controversy, in doctrinal discussion or in actual commentary upon the component books. The majority of books in the present Canon are known to them and given canonical status; but uncertainty remains in the case of Hebrews, some of the Catholic Epistles and the Revelation of John. Uncanonical Gospels are cited, *agrapha* quoted as authentic words of the Lord, and some works of the Apostolic Fathers such as the *Epistle of Barnabas*, the *Shepherd* and the *First Epistle of Clement* are cited as canonical or scriptural. We find great codices even of the 4th and 5th centuries which contain some of these latter: the Codex Sinaiticus includes Barnabas and Hermas; the Codex Alexandrinus includes the *First* and *Second Epistles of Clement*. Claromontanus contains a catalogue of canonical writings in which Hebrews is absent, and *Barnabas*, the *Shepherd*, the *Acts of Paul* and the *Apocalypse of Peter* are included. In brief, the idea of a definite canon is fully established, and its main outline firmly fixed: the issue now is which books out of a certain number of marginal cases belong to it. The position in the church in the 3rd century is well summarized by Eusebius (*EH* 3. 25). He distinguishes between acknowledged books (*homologoumena*), disputed books (*antilegomena*) and spurious books (*notha*). In the first class are placed the four Gospels, the Acts, the Epistles of Paul, 1 Peter, 1 John and (according to some) the Revelation of John; in the second class he places (as 'disputed, nevertheless known to most') James, Jude, 2 Peter, 2 and 3 John; in the third class the *Acts of Paul*, the *Shepherd*, the *Apocalypse of Peter*, the *Epistle of Barnabas*, the *Didache*, the *Gospel according to the Hebrews* and (according to others) the Revelation of John. These latter, Eusebius suggests, might well be in the second class were it not for the necessity of guarding against deliberate forgeries of Gospels and Acts under the name of apostles, made in a strictly heretical interest. As examples of these he names the *Gospels* of *Thomas*, *Peter* and *Matthias*, and the *Acts of Andrew* and *John*. These 'ought to be reckoned not even among the spurious books but shunned as altogether wicked and impious'.

V. Fixation of the Canon

The 4th century saw the fixation of the Canon within the limits to which we are accustomed, both in the W and E sectors of Christendom. In the E the definitive point is the Thirty-ninth Paschal Letter of Athanasius in AD 367. Here we find for the first time a NT of exact bounds as known to us. A clear line is drawn between works in the Canon which are described as the sole sources of religious instruction, and others which it is permitted to read, namely, the *Didache* and the *Shepherd*. Heretical apocrypha are said to be intentional forgeries for the purposes of deceit. In the W the Canon was fixed by conciliar decision at Carthage in 397, when a like list to that of Athanasius was agreed upon. About the same period a number of Latin authors showed interest in the bounds of the NT Canon: Priscillian in Spain, Rufinus of Aquileia in Gaul, Augustine in N Africa (whose views contributed to the decisions at Carthage), Innocent I, bishop of Rome, and the author of the pseudo-Gelasian Decree. All hold the same views.

VI. The Syriac Canon

The development of the Canon in the Syriac-speaking churches was strikingly different. It is probable that the first Scripture known in these circles was, in addition to the OT, the apocryphal *Gospel according to the Hebrews* which left its mark upon the *Diatessaron* when that took its place as the Gospel of Syriac Christianity. It is likely that Tatian introduced also the Pauline Epistles and perhaps even the Acts: these three are named as the Scriptures of the primitive Syriac church by the *Doctrine of Addai*, a 5th-century document which in its account of the beginnings of Christianity in Edessa mingles legend with trustworthy tradition. The next stage in the closer alignment of the Syriac Canon with the Greek was the production of the 'separated gospels' (*Evangelion da-Mepharreshe*) to take the place of the *Diatessaron*. This was by no means easily accomplished. The Peshitta (textually a partially corrected form of the *Evangelion da-Mepharreshe*) was produced at some time in the 4th century; it contains, in addition to the fourfold Gospel, the Paulines and the Acts, the Epistles of James, 1 Peter and 1 John, *i.e.* the equivalent of the basic Canon accepted in the Greek churches about a century before. Two versions of the remaining books of the eventually accepted Canon were produced among the Syriac Monophysites: that of Philoxenos is probably extant in the so-called Pococke Epistles' and 'Crawford Apocalypse', while the later version of Thomas of Harkel also contains 2 Peter, 2 and 3 John, and Jude, and the version of Revelation published by de Dieu is almost certainly from this translation. Both show in their slavish imitation of Greek text and language, as well as in the mere fact of their production, the ever-increasing assimilation of Syriac Christianity to a Greek mode.

VII. Recapitulation

We may recapitulate by tracing the canonical fortunes of the individual books of the NT. The four Gospels circulated in relative independence until the formation of the fourfold Canon. Mark was apparently eclipsed by its two 'expansions', but not submerged. Luke, in spite of Marcion's patronage, does not seem to have encountered opposition. Matthew very early achieved that predominant place which it occupied till the modern era of scholarship. John was in rather different case, since in the late 2nd century there was considerable opposition to it, of which the so-called Alogoi and the Roman presbyter Gaius may serve as examples; this was no doubt due to some of the obscurities which still surround some aspects of its background, origin and earliest circulation. Once accepted, its prestige continued to grow, and it proved of the highest value in the great doctrinal controversies and definitions. The Acts of the Apostles did not lend itself to liturgical or controversial use; it makes little appearance until after the time of Irenaeus; from then on it is firmly fixed as part of the Scriptures. The Pauline Corpus was securely established as Scripture from the earliest times. Marcion apparently rejected the Pastorals; otherwise we have no record of doubts concerning them, and already Polycarp holds them as authoritative. Hebrews, on the other hand, remained in dispute for several centuries. In the E, Pantaenus and Clement of Alexandria are known to have discussed the critical problems of its authorship; Origen solved the question by assuming that Pauline thought was here expressed by an anonymous author; Eusebius and some others report the doubts of the W, but after Origen the letter was accepted in the E. It is noteworthy that the letter takes pride of place after Romans in the 3rd-century Chester Beatty papyrus (p^{46}). In the W doubts persisted from the earliest days: Irenaeus did not accept it as Pauline, Tertullian and other African sources pay it little regard, 'Ambrosiaster' wrote no commentary upon it, and in this was followed by Pelagius. The councils of Hippo and Carthage separate Hebrews from the rest of the Pauline Epistles in their canonical enumerations, and Jerome reported that in his day the opinion in Rome was still against authenticity. The matter was not considered settled until a century or so later. The corpus of the Catholic Epistles is evidently a late creation, post-dating the establishment of the essential structure of the Canon at the end of the 2nd century. Its exact constitution varies from church to church, and Father to Father. The First Epistle of John has a certain place from the time of Irenaeus: the Second and Third are but little quoted, and sometimes (as in the Muratorian Canon) we are uncertain whether both are being referred to. This may, of course, be due to their slenderness or apparent lack of theological import. The First Epistle of Peter, too, has a place only less secure (note, however, the ambiguities of the Muratorian Canon); the Second is still among the 'disputed books' in Eusebius' day. The status of James and Jude fluctuates according to church, age and individual judgment. (We may note here how Jude and 2 Peter are grouped with a veritable pot-pourri of religious literature as one volume in a papyrus in the Bodmer collection.) For inclusion in this corpus there appear to have competed with all these such works as the *Shepherd, Barnabas*, the *Didache*, the Clementine 'correspondence', all of which seem to have been sporadically recognized and utilized as scriptural. The Revelation of John was twice opposed: once in the 2nd century because of its apparent support of the claims of Montanus to prophetic inspiration, once in the late 3rd century on critical grounds, by comparison with the Gospel of John, in the controversy of the Dionysii of Rome and Alexandria. Both kinds of doubt contributed to the continued mistrust with which it was viewed by the Gk. churches, and its very late acceptance in the Syriac and Armenian churches. In the W, on the contrary, it was very early accorded a high place; it was translated into Latin on at least three different occasions, and numerous commentaries were dedicated to it from the time of Victorinus of Pettau (martyred 304) onwards.

VIII. The present position

So the Canon of the NT grew and became fixed in that form in which we now know it. In the 16th century both Roman and Protestant Christianity, after debate, reaffirmed their adherence to the traditions, and the Roman church has yet more recently emphasized its continued adherence. Conservative Protestantism, too, continues to use the Canon received by tradition, and even the representatives of liberal theology generally abide by it. Doubtless, in the face of modern biblical research and the new acknowledgment of non-apostolic authorship which some scholars, at least, feel obliged to make concerning some of the NT documents, we need to understand afresh the factors and motives which underlie the historical processes here outlined. The inclusion of documents in the Canon is the Christian church's recognition of the authority of these documents. There is no Canon in the earliest times because of the presence of apostles or their disciples, and because of the living oral traditions. In the mid-2nd century, the apostles are dead, but their memoirs and other monuments attest their message: at the same time heresy has arisen, and by its appeal either to theological theory or to new inspiration has necessitated a fresh appeal to orthodoxy's authority, and a closer definition of authoritative books. Thus the fourfold Gospel and the Pauline Corpus, already widely used, are declared to be scriptural, together with some other works with claims to apostolic authorship. Both doctrinal and scholarly discussion and development continue the process of recognition until, in the great era of the intellectual and ecclesiastical crystallization of Christianity, the Canon is completed. Three criteria were utilized, whether in the 2nd or the 4th century, to establish that the written documents are the true record of the voice and message of apostolic witness. First, attribution to apostles: this does not meet all cases; such Gospels as Mark and Luke were accepted as the works of close associates of the apostles. Secondly, ecclesiastical usage: that is, recognition by a leading church or by a majority of churches. By this were rejected many apocrypha, some perhaps innocuous and even containing authentic traditions of the words of Jesus, many more mere fabrications, but none known to be acknowledged by the majority of churches. Thirdly, congruence with the standards of sound doctrine: on this ground the Fourth Gospel is at first in doubt and at length accepted; or, to give a contrary case, the *Gospel of Peter* is banned by Serapion of Antioch because of its docetic tendencies in spite of its claim to apostolic title. Thus the history of the canonical development of the NT Scripture shows it to be a collection attributed to apostles or their disciples which in the view of the church in the first four Christian centuries was justly thus attributed because it adequately declared and defined apostolic doctrine, and so its components had been or were considered to be fit for public reading at divine worship. When this is understood, with the gradual growth and variegated nature of the Canon, we can see why there were, and still are, problems and doubts about particular works there included. But taking these three criteria as adequate, orthodox Protestant Christianity today finds no reasons to reject the decisions of earlier generations and accepts the NT as a full and authoritative record of divine revelation as declared from of old by men chosen, dedicated and inspired.

BIBLIOGRAPHY. Th. Zahn, *Geschichte des neutestamentlichen Kanons*, 1888–92; M.-J. Lagrange, *Histoire ancienne du Canon du Nouveau Testament*, 1933; A. Souter, *The Text and Canon of the New Testament*[2], 1954; J. Knox, *Marcion and the New Testament*, 1942; E. C. Blackman, *Marcion and His Influence*, 1948; *The New Testament in the Apostolic Fathers*, 1905; J. N. Sanders, *The Fourth Gospel in the Early Church*, 1943; J. Hoh, *Die Lehre des heiligen Irenaeus ueber das Neue Testament*, 1919; W. Bauer, *Der Apostolos der Syrer*, 1903; *idem*, *Rechtgläubigkeit und Ketzerei im ältesten Christentum*, 1934 (²rev., 1964; E.T. 1971); R. P. C. Hanson, *Tradition in the Early Church*, 1962; J. Regul, *Die antimarcionitischen Evangelienprologe*, 1969; R. M. Grant, 'The New Testament Canon' (*Cambridge History of the Bible*, Vol. 1, 1970, ch. 10, pp. 284–308 and 593f.); H. von Campenhausen, *The Formation of the Christian Bible*, 1972. J.N.B.

CAPERNAUM.

I. Name

NT manuscripts mostly read *Kapharnaoum*, though *Kapernaoum* appears in minuscules dependent on Codex Alexandrinus. Clearly Kapharnaoum is the original form, directly transcribing Semitic *kᵉp̄ar naḥûm*, 'village of Nahum'. This Semitic form is found at *Qohelet Rabbah* 1. 8 and 7. 26. Josephus (*BJ* 3. 517) refers to the spring *Kapharnaoum*, equivalent to Semitic *'en-kᵉp̄ar-naḥûm*. His *Vita* 403 should probably be read *Kepharnakōn* (original of the MSS PRA, favoured by Thackeray). This is the same word with *nûn*-ized ending and *k* for *ḥ*.

II. Location

Evidence from the NT, Josephus, Christian pilgrim-texts, mediaeval Jewish itineraries, extant monumental remains and current excavations indicates that Capernaum was undoubtedly located at *Tell Hum*, and was inhabited continuously from the 1st century BC to the 7th century AD. The Gospels are almost sufficient in themselves to fix the site, indicating that Capernaum was (*a*) by the lake-side (Mt. 4:13); (*b*) near a political border, so that a customs-post (Mk. 2:14) and military detachment were necessary (Mt. 8:5–13; Lk. 7:1–10); (*c*) near Gennesaret (Mk. 6:53; Jn. 6:22, 59), which is an area of highly productive land at the NW of the Lake. In short Capernaum was the nearest village to the river Jordan on the NW shores of the Sea of Galilee, a position occupied in fact by the ruins of *Tell Hum*. This is confirmed by Josephus *Vita* 403, which indicates a village close to Julias (*et-Tell*) in the direction of Magdala/Tarichaeae (*Mejdel*).

Capernaum was also near a most copious spring which watered Gen-

Remains of insula *2 at Capernaum, showing walls, window-frames and a court in the foreground. Built of local black volcanic basalt. Continuously occupied from the 1st cent. BC to the 7th cent. AD.* (JPK)

nesaret (*BJ* 3. 519) and can only be the site *et-Tabgha*. But Arabic *et-Tabgha* is also undoubtedly a corruption of Gk. *Heptapēgōn* (place of seven springs). This 'Seven Springs' is mentioned by Egeria *c.* AD 383 (Lat. *septem fontes*), and by Theodosius (AD 530). Theodosius provides us with our only detailed early itinerary round the NW shores of the Sea of Galilee, moving N from Tiberias in Roman miles: 2 m Magdala, 2 m Heptapēgōn, 2 m Capernaum, 6 m Bethsaida. Thus Capernaum was 2 miles (3½ km) N of Tabgha, which exactly locates *Tell Hum*. The name *Seven* Springs indicates a Semitic original denoting copious waters, but it was the Greek term that survived. In Arabic the succession is *Mejdel*, *et-Tabgha*, *Tell Hum*. The first two names correspond to the list of Theodosius, but *Hum* can hardly be a reduction of *Nahum*—which begins with a long syllable—nor is there in fact a *tell* (mound) at this site, but merely a *khirbe* or *rujm* (ruin or tumble of stones). Mediaeval Jewish itineraries provide the answer. The tomb of Rabbi Tanhum was thought to be here; by a natural progression the itineraries refer to the place baldly as 'Tanhum'. Degeneration from Tanhum to *tell hum* (dark mound) is readily comprehensible. The list of Theodosius locates Capernaum to the N of *et-Tabgha*. Note that the old rival site to *Tell Hum*, *Khirbet Munja* or *Minyeh*, is S of *et-Tabgha*. Its name has long been thought to be a survival of the *Munyat Hisham* or *el-Munya* of Arab sources. Excavation has now confirmed this by uncovering an Ummayad chateau, not a Jewish village (*IEJ* 10, 1960, pp. 240–243).

Monuments are also important in confirming the site of Capernaum. Egeria saw a synagogue there of fine ashlars, approached 'by many steps'. It is in fact an unusual feature of the synagogue remains at *Tell Hum* that they are set up on a high platform, and have a balcony at the front which is reached by high flights of steps from the sides. Egeria was also shown a church (*ecclesia*) when she came to Capernaum (*c.* AD 383). She says that it had been made from the house of the apostle Peter, and the walls of this house were incorporated into it, still standing in their original form (*ita stant sicut fuerunt*). The pilgrim from Piacenza (AD 570) tells us that he entered Peter's house in Capernaum, but it had been replaced by a basilica.

III. History

Until the conversion of Constantine the Great (AD 306–337) Jewish communities flourished in Galilee under their rabbis and Patriarchs. About AD 335 Constantine was informed by a Jew of Tiberias, the Christian convert Joseph, that Tiberias, Sepphoris, Nazareth and Capernaum were entirely inhabited by those of Jewish race, who rigorously excluded Gentiles from their settlements. Joseph secured ready permission from the emperor to build 'churches for Christ' (*ekklēsiai*) in these places (Epiphanius, *Haer*. 30. 4. 1 = *PG* 41. 425), and managed to convert a derelict temple of Hadrian at Tiberias and erect a small church at Sepphoris. Yet it was not perhaps until the 5th century AD that Gentile Christians fully established themselves in this Jewish 'ghetto'. How far through all this time the 'Judeo-Christian' sect was established at Capernaum and elsewhere in Galilee is difficult to say. From stories in the rabbis one learns of *minîm* (heretics) at Tiberias, Sepphoris and Capernaum (2nd/3rd centuries AD). Only one tale is told about Capernaum, that R. Hananya was persuaded by *minîm* to break the sabbath-rule by riding a donkey (*c.* AD 110). These Jewish Christians held to the Law, attended synagogue and avoided contact with Gentiles; but they healed and spoke in the name of Jesus. Jerome says that the Pharisees called them 'Nazaraeans'; that they still flourished in his day (late 4th/early 5th centuries AD) 'in the synagogues of the East'; and that they were neither faithful Jews nor genuine Christians.

IV. Excavations

Excavations by the Franciscan *Custodia di Terra Santa*, directed by V. Corbo, began at Capernaum (*Tell Hum*) in 1968 and are still in progress. The synagogue had long before (1905) been cleared by Kohl and Watzinger to its flagstone pavement, and dated by comparison with Severan monuments in Syria to the late 2nd or early 3rd centuries AD. The plan which the Germans exposed was of a long, colonnaded assembly-hall divided into a central nave and side-aisles; this hall faced S and was connected on its E side to an impressive annexe, a colonnaded courtyard. Both the hall and annexe were raised up on a high platform (*podium*), and had a balcony in front of them reached by imposing flights of steps on either side. One would certainly suppose that this was the synagogue seen by Egeria (*c.* AD 383) at Capernaum, reached by an ascent of 'many steps'.

But if the dates argued for Egeria's pilgrimage by Devos and accepted by Wilkinson (AD 381–384) are correct, she must have seen the synagogue while it was being constructed. Eighteen trenches in and around the synagogue have yielded pottery (carefully studied by S. Loffreda) and coins establishing that work was begun *c.* AD 350 and completed *c.* AD 450. The rubble fill (stratum B) of the *podium* rests on destroyed houses (stratum A); it is sealed from above by a thick and unbroken mortar (stratum C) in which the flagstones of the hall and annexe were set. Excavations in the synagogue have not yet been completed and will be published in a separate volume when they are; the definitive publications so far are *Caf. 1* and *Stud. Hier*. (see bibliography). A further trench across the entire E/W width of the hall is planned (*Stud. Hier*., p. 176). According to the material published so far, the earliest possible date for the pavement of the hall and its E colonnade is AD 383, since the latest coins from the sealed fill beneath the mortar are AD 352–360 (*Caf. 1*, pp. 121, 163) and AD 383–408 (*Stud. Hier*., p. 164, under the stylobate for the E colonnade). The latest coin embedded within the thick mortar before it had set (trench 2, stratum C) is also from AD 383 (*LA* 22, 1972, pp. 15–16). These late dates for the synagogue were totally unexpected and have aroused great controversy (*IEJ* 21, 1971, pp. 207–211; 23, 1973, pp. 37–45, 184; *Ariel* 32, 1973, pp. 29–43).

Two successive shrines, totally different from each other, were excavated on the same site only one block of houses distant from the synagogue. The later shrine is the *basilica* seen by the Piacenza pilgrim: a small memorial completed by *c.* AD 450 in the unusual form of a double octagon. Its central ring is sited exactly over the main room of a house built in the 1st century BC. The basilica replaced a shrine of the early 4th century AD, possibly built by Joseph of Tiberias, which encapsulated the same early house, leaving its original walls standing,

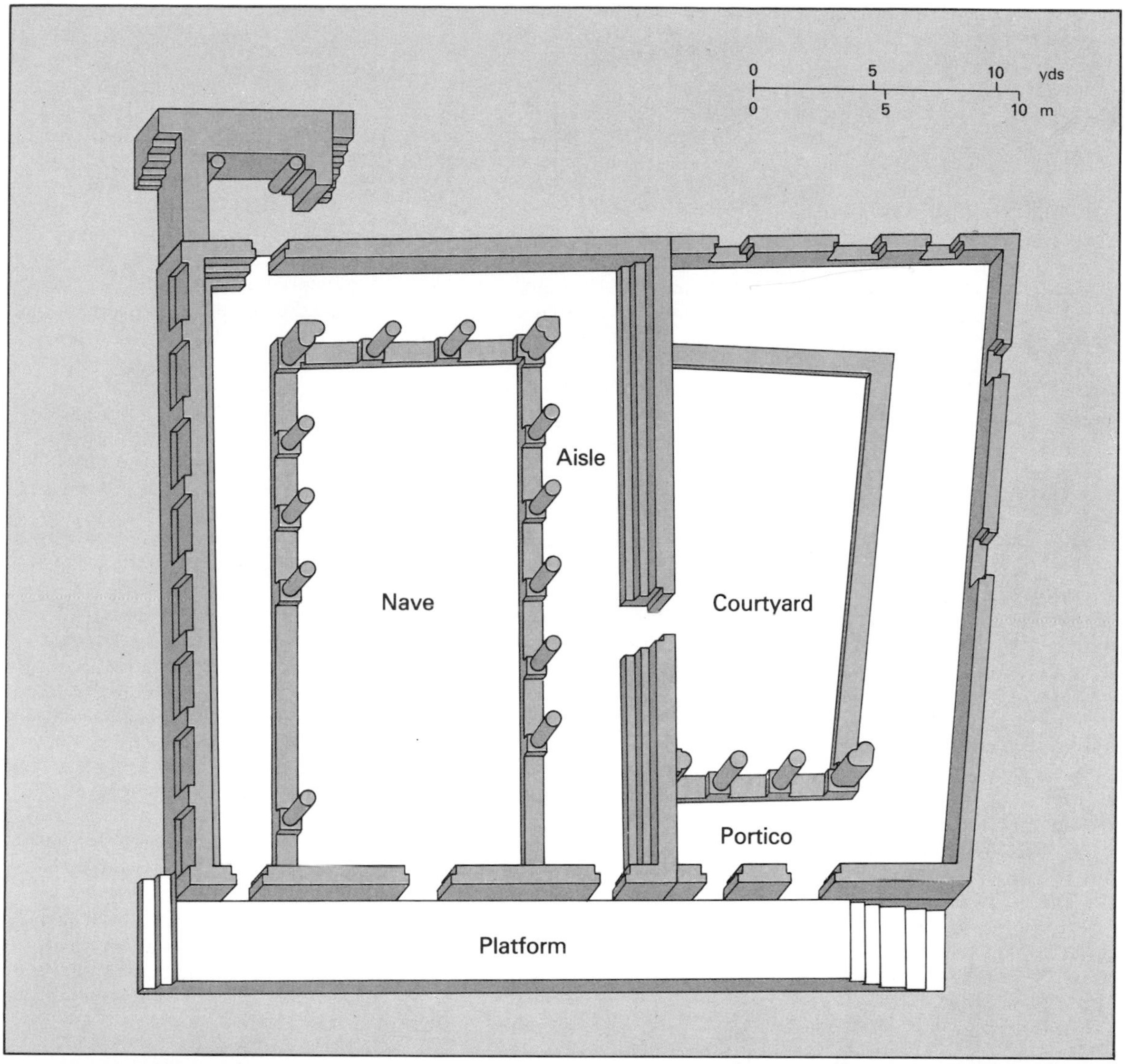

Ground plan of the Capernaum synagogue. Alongside the roofed prayer-hall was a colonnaded courtyard or annexe, both being raised on a high podium mounted by steps. Late 4th/early 5th cent. AD.

The reconstructed synagogue at Tell Hum (Capernaum), now redated to the late 4th/early 5th cent. AD. The best preserved of all the Galilean synagogues, only the lowest three to four courses of the walls, the column bases and the floor-paving remained in situ *before the Franciscan reconstructions.* (RP)

as Egeria was shown. The main room of this house had once again been marked out. In particular its walls were plastered and enlivened by painted designs in bold colours. On fallen pieces of plaster *graffiti* in Greek (a few Semitic) were found, including the words *amen*, *Lord* and *Jesus*. Clearly this was the traditional house of Peter, visited by pilgrims.

Excavation of these monuments and of five blocks (*insulae*) of houses indicates that Capernaum was inhabited continuously between the early 1st century BC and the 7th century AD. The houses are part of a village which was *c.* 800 by 250 m in extent, as sherds and remains indicate. Of the excavated area, *insulae* 1–3 are the older ones, begun in the 1st century BC; *insulae* 4–5 developed from the 4th century AD. The traditional house of Peter (*insula* 1) and the block between this and the synagogue (*insula* 2) are most fully studied by the excavators, and are reproduced as isometric drawings (*Caf. 1*, pl. X, XV). Corbo estimates that *insula* 2 could have housed fifteen families, about 130/150 people. It has only a few entries into the roads outside, and consists of small rooms opening on to a number of internal courtyards. Steps survive, and must have led up to terrace-roofs of earth and straw (as Mk. 2:4: healing of the paralytic), since the walls of basalt fieldstones and earth-mortar could not have supported an upper storey. The floors are of basalt cobbles covered by earth. *Insula* 2 was occupied from the beginning of the 1st century AD to the 7th century AD without a break; its original walls remained in use unchanged. A succession of floors provides sherds and coins for dating.

BIBLIOGRAPHY. E. W. G. Masterman, *PEQ* 1907, pp. 220–229; *idem*, *Studies in Galilee*, 1909; F.-M. Abel, *Capharnaum*, in *DBS*, 1, 1928; V. Corbo, *The House of St Peter at Capharnaum*, 1969; *idem*, *Cafarnao 1: Gli edifici della città*, 1975; *idem*, *Studia Hierosolymitana in honore di P. Bellarmino Bagatti*, 1, 1976, pp. 159–176; S. Loffreda, *Cafarnao 2: La Ceramica*, 1974; A. Spijkerman, *Cafarnao 3: Catalogo delle monete della città*, 1975; E. Testa, *Cafarnao 4: I graffiti della casa di S. Pietro*, 1972; R. North, *Bib* 58, 1977, pp. 424–431; *EAEHL*, 1, pp. 286–290. J.P.K.

CAPHTOR (*kap̄tôr*). The home of the *kap̄tōrîm* (Dt. 2:23), one of the peoples listed in the Table of *Nations as descended, with Casluhim, whence went forth the *Philistines, from Mizraim (Gn. 10:14; 1 Ch. 1:12). Caphtor was the land from which the Philistines came (Je. 47:4; Am. 9:7), and it is presumably the Philistines, as erstwhile sojourners in Caphtor, who are referred to as Caphtorim in Dt. 2:23. It is probable that the biblical name is to be identified with Ugaritic *kptr*, and *kap-ta-ra* in a school text from Assur which may well be a copy of one of 2nd-millennium date. It is likewise held by many scholars that Egyp. *kftyw* is also to be connected with this group, all of which refer in all probability to *Crete. At its height in the 2nd millennium, Minoan Crete controlled much of the Aegean area, and this would accord with the biblical description of Caphtor as an *'î*, a term which can mean both 'island' and 'coastland'. W Asia was influenced in art and other ways by the Aegean, and this may explain the occurrence in the Bible of the term *kap̄tôr* as applying to an architectural feature, evidently a column capital, rendered in the AV by 'knop' (Ex. 25:31–36; 37:17–22) and 'lintel' (Am. 9:1; Zp. 2:14).

BIBLIOGRAPHY. A. H. Gardiner, *Ancient Egyptian Onomastica*, Text, I, 1947, pp. 201*–203*; R. W. Hutchinson, *Prehistoric Crete*, 1962, pp. 106–112; T. C. Mitchell in *AOTS*, pp. 408, 413; K. A. Kitchen in *POTT*, p. 54. T.C.M.

CAPITAL. 1. Heb. *kap̄tôr* (*a*) ornamental top of pillars, Am. 9:1; Zp. 2:14 (AV 'lintel'); (*b*) ornamental round protrusion (LXX *sphairōtēr*) in the *lampstand, Ex. 25:31–36; 37:17–22 (AV 'knop', whereas in

The throne-room of the Bronze Age Minoan palace at Knossos, Crete (probably biblical Caphtor). Largely reconstructed. c. 1450–1400 BC (late Minoan II). (PAC)

Capital from the Apadana (audience-hall) of the palace at Susa (Shushan), Persia, showing a double-headed bull surmounting volutes. Height 6 m. 4th cent. BC. (MC)

1 Ki. 6:18; 7:24 AV 'knop' represents p^{e}*qā'îm* = RSV 'gourds', Targ. 'eggs').

2. Heb. *kôṯereṯ* (*a*) spherical capital 5 cubits high on each of the pillars, *Jachin and Boaz, in Solomon's *Temple, 1 Ki. 7:16–42; 2 Ch. 4:12; Je. 52:22 (AV 'chapiter'); (*b*) a circular lip projecting upwards round the edge of the hole in the top of the stand in which was placed the basin of each mobile laver, 1 Ki. 7:31 (RSV 'crown', AV 'chapiter').

3. Heb. *ṣep̄eṯ*, 2 Ch. 3:15, same as **1.** (*b*) (AV 'chapiter').

4. Heb. *rô'š* (literally, 'head'), term used for the capitals (AV 'chapiters') on pillars in the tabernacle, Ex. 36:38; 38:17.

D.W.G.

Superimposed Ionic capitals surmounted by a palmette (ornament of radiating petals). From Babylon. 7th–6th cent. BC. (SMB) (AMM)

Ionic capital, believed to come from the façade of the upper gallery of the Stoa at Athens. (RP)

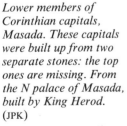

Lower members of Corinthian capitals, Masada. These capitals were built up from two separate stones: the top ones are missing. From the N palace of Masada, built by King Herod. (JPK)

Corinthian capital in a provincial heterodox style from Nabataean Syria (Suweda, Jebel Druze). 1st cent. AD. (JPK)

CAPPADOCIA. A highland province, much of it around 900 m, in the E of Asia Minor, bounded on the S by the chain of Mt Taurus, E by the Euphrates and N by Pontus, but its actual limits are vague. It was constituted a Roman province by Tiberius, AD 17, on the death of Archelaus. In AD 70 Vespasian united it with Armenia Minor as one of the great frontier bulwarks of the empire. Under later emperors, especially Trajan, the size and importance of the province greatly increased. It produced large numbers of sheep and horses. The trade route between Central Asia and the Black Sea ports passed through it, and it was easily accessible from Tarsus through the Cilician Gates. Jews from it were present at Jerusalem on the day of *Pentecost (Acts 2:9). Some of the Dispersion to whom Peter wrote lived in Cappadocia (1 Pet. 1:1).

J.W.M.

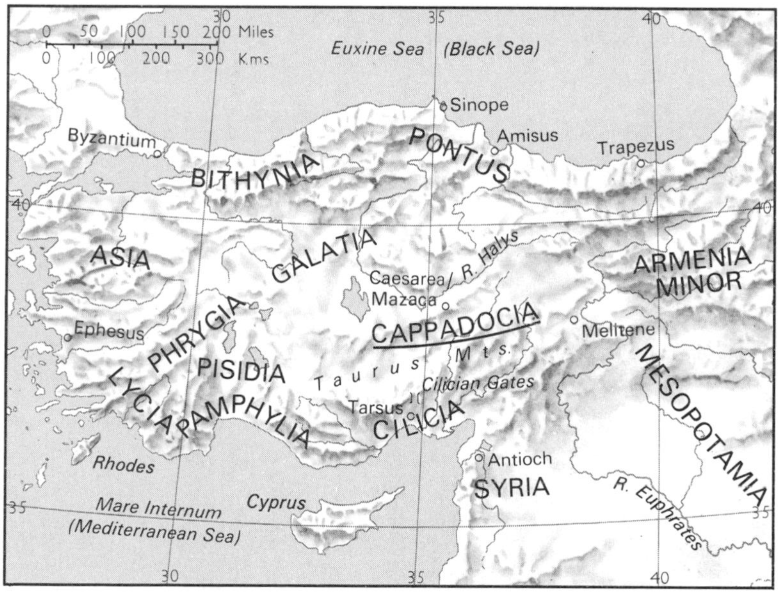

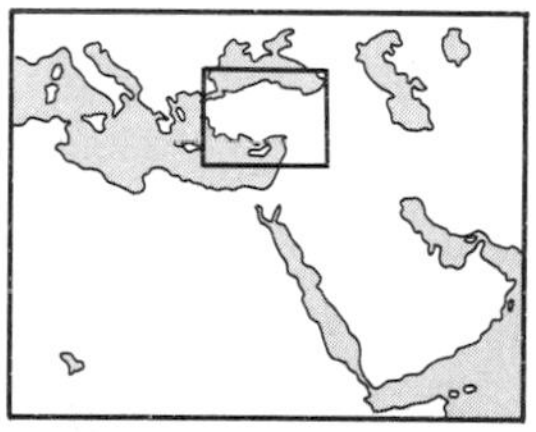

Cappadocia, a province of the Roman empire in E Asia Minor.

CAPTAIN. The nearest Hebrew equivalent is *śar*, which can denote a leader of thousands, hundreds or fifties (Ex. 18:25; 1 Sa. 8:12). *rô'š* ('head') may occasionally be translated 'captain' as in Nu. 14:4. In Saul's reign the Israelite military machine was not yet at the peak of its efficiency, but the basis of organization had been established; the army consisted of companies headed by 'captains of thousands' (1 Sa. 17:18). David's standing army was led by 'The Thirty', commanders who had won their spurs while David was a fugitive from Saul. David also organized a militia and 1 Ch. 27:1–15 shows how it was divided into 12 battalions, each of which served for a month per year under the direction of its captain. 'Captain' is also used in connection with the chariot force of the N kingdom in the 9th century (1 Ki. 16:9, 'captain [*śar*] of half his chariots'). In the NT *chiliarchos*, lit. 'commander of a thousand men', is translated 'captain' at Jn. 18:12. It is also the term used for the Roman military tribune in Acts 21:31–33, 37, and can be used of any military officer (Mk. 6:21). *stratēgos*, originally referring to an army commander, is Luke's word for the captains of the Temple who would have been of

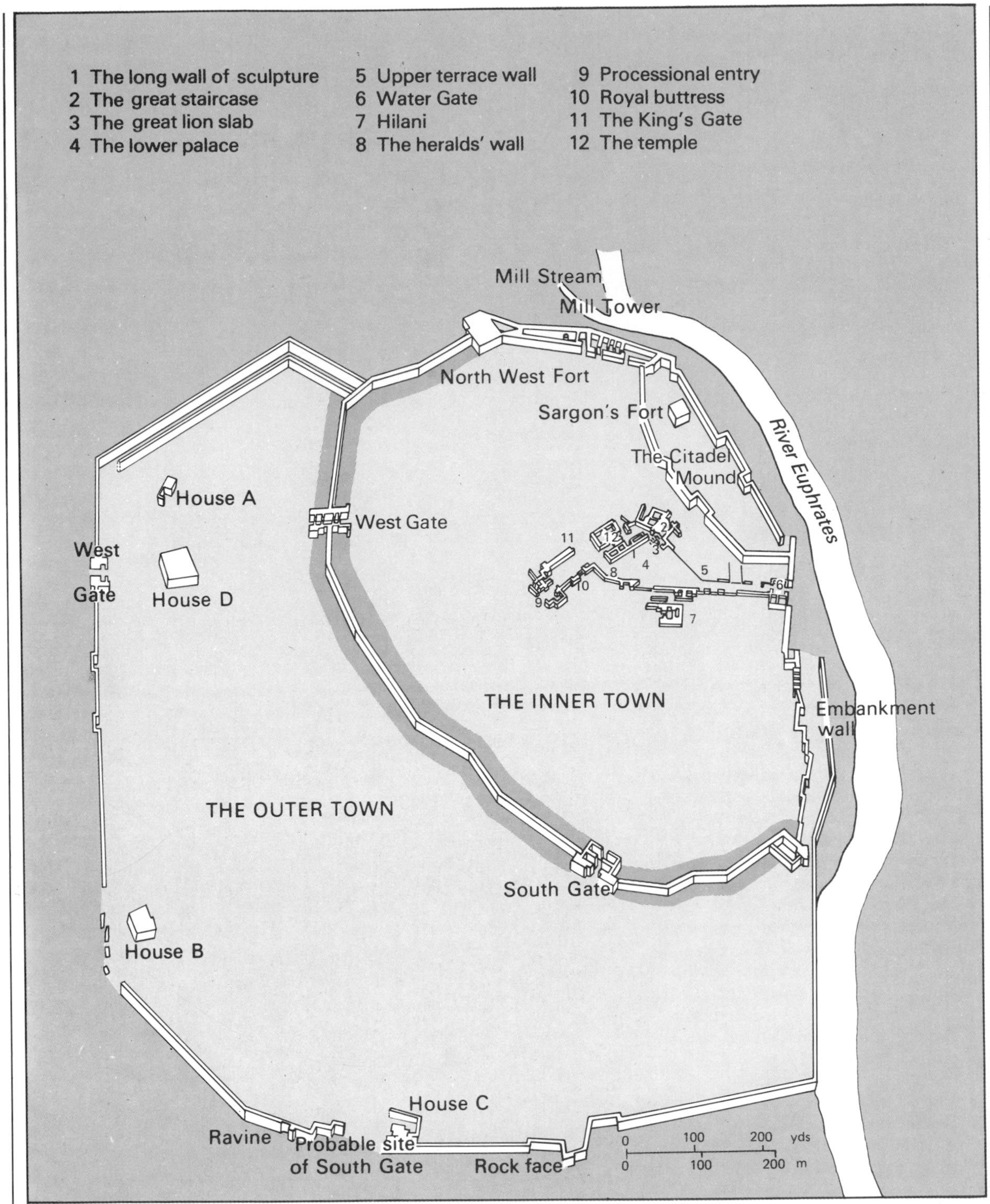

Plan of the site of Carchemish, showing areas of excavations.

CARBUNCLE See Jewels, Part 2.

levitical or priestly stock (Lk. 22:4, 52; Acts 4:1, *etc.*). *archēgos*, translated 'captain' in AV of Heb. 2:10, is better rendered 'pioneer' with RSV. *stratopedarchos* in some MSS of Acts 28:16 is translated 'captain of the guard' in AV; the operative clause is treated as secondary and therefore omitted by RSV. R.P.G.

CARCHEMISH. A city (mod. Jerablus) which guarded the main ford across the river Euphrates *c.* 100 km NE of Aleppo. It is first mentioned in a text of the 18th century BC as an independent trade-centre (Mari, Alalaḫ). As a Syrian city-state it had treaties with Ugarit and other states (Mitanni) during the 2nd millennium BC and continued as a neo-Hittite state after Inī-Teṣub (*c.* 1100) until Pisiris was defeated by Sargon II in 717 BC. Thereafter Carchemish was incorporated as an Assyr. province. The event is noted in Is. 10:9. In 609 BC Neco II of Egypt moved *via* Megiddo to recapture the city (2 Ch. 35:20), which was made a base from which his army harassed the Babylonians. However, in May–June 605 BC Nebuchadrezzar II led the Babylonian forces who entered the city by surprise. The Egyptians were utterly defeated in hand-to-hand fighting in and around the city (Je. 46:2) and pursued to Hamath. Details of this battle, which resulted in the Babylonian control of the W, are given in the Babylonian Chronicle.

Excavations in 1912 and 1914 uncovered Hittite sculptures, a lower palace area with an open palace (*bît-ḫilani*), and evidence of the battle and later Babylonian occupation.

BIBLIOGRAPHY. C. L. Woolley, *Carchemish*, 1–3, 1914–52; D. J. Wiseman, *Chronicles of Chaldaean Kings*, 1956, pp. 20–27, 68–69; J. D. Hawkins, *Iraq* 36, 1974, pp. 67–73; W. W. Hallo in C. F. Pfeiffer, *The Biblical World*, 1966, pp. 65–69.

D.J.W.

CARMEL (Heb. *karmel*, 'garden-land', 'fruitful land'). The word is used as a common noun in Hebrew with this meaning; examples are Is. 16:10; Je. 4:26; 2 Ki. 19:23; 2 Ch. 26:10. It can even be used of fresh ears of grain, as in Lv. 2:14; 23:14. Thus, the limestone Carmel hills probably got their name from the luxuriant scrub and woodland that covered them. In the OT two places bear this name.

1. A range of hills, *c.* 50 km long, extending from NW to SE, from Mediterranean (S shore of Bay of Acre) to the plain of Dothan. Strictly, Mt Carmel is the main ridge (maximum height *c.* 530 m) at the NW end, running *c.* 19 km inland from the sea, forming a border of Asher (Jos. 19:26). This densely vegetated and little-inhabited region was a barrier pierced by two main passes, emerging at Jokneam and Megiddo, and a lesser one emerging at Taanach; between the first two, the hills are lower and more barren but have steep scarps. The main N–S road, however, passes by Carmel's hills through the plain of Dothan on the E. Carmel's luxuriant growth is reflected in Am. 1:2; 9:3; Mi. 7:14; Na. 1:4; also in Ct. 7:5 in an apt simile for thick, bushy hair. The forbidding figure of Nebuchadrezzar of Babylon marching against Egypt is once compared with the rocky eminences of Carmel and Tabor (Je. 46:18).

Joshua's vanquished foes included 'the king of Jokneam in Carmel' (Jos. 12:22). It was here that Elijah in the name of his God challenged the prophets of Baal and Asherah, the deities promoted by Jezebel, and won a notable victory against them (1 Ki. 18; 19:1–2). The text makes it obvious that it was Jezebel's gods that were thus discredited; as she came from Tyre, the Baal was almost certainly Baal-melqart the chief god there. This god also penetrated Aram; see *Ben-hadad for a stele to this deity. *Baal was still worshipped on Carmel as 'Zeus Heliopolitēs Carmel' in AD 200 (Ap-Thomas, *PEQ* 92, 1960, p. 146). Alt considered this Baal as purely local, a view refuted by the biblical text, and Eissfeldt preferred Baal-shamêm who is less appropriate than Baal-melqart (latter also advocated by de Vaux).

2. A town in Judah (Jos. 15:55), at present-day Khirbet el-Karmil (var. Kermel or Kurmul), some 12 km SSE of Hebron, in a rolling, pastoral region (Baly, p. 164) ideal for the flocks that Nabal grazed there in David's time (1 Sa. 25). His wife Abigail was a Carmelitess, and Hezro, one of David's warriors (2 Sa. 23:35; 1 Ch. 11:37) probably hailed from there. Saul passed that way on his return from the slaughter of the Amalekites (1 Sa. 15:12).

BIBLIOGRAPHY. D. Baly, *Geography of the Bible*, 1974, pp. 149 (map 51), 172f.

K.A.K.

CART, WAGON (Heb. *ʿᵃgālâ*, from the 'rolling' of wheels). Originally in Babylonia (Early Dynastic period) sledges were devised for carrying light loads, and these were soon adopted in Egypt and other flat countries. With the advent of the wheel, and the consequent increased mobility, carts early came into common use throughout Babylonia (*ṣumbu*), Egypt (Gn. 45:19–21; 46:5), and Palestine, as a 2- or 4-wheeled vehicle used principally in the S and low-lying Shephelah. However, in the hills their use was restricted to the main tracks (1 Sa. 6:12), and they were not commonly used for long distances (Gn. 45). They could carry one or two drivers with a light load,

CARIANS
See Cherethites, Part 1.

CARNELIAN
See Jewels, Part 2.

CAROB
See Plants (Nuts, Pods), Part 3.

CARPET VIPER
See Animals, Part 1.

Wooded hills of the Carmel range. (FNH)

Wagon drawn by two oxen, carrying prisoners into captivity. Detail of relief from palace of Ashurbanipal at Nineveh. 7th cent. BC. (MC)

CARVINGS
See Art, Part 1.

CASTANETS
See Music, Part 2.

CASTOR-OIL
See Plants, Part 3.

CAT
See Animals, Part 1.

CATERPILLAR
See Animals, Part 1.

despite a general instability (1 Ch. 13:7–9). The main use was transporting the more bulky harvest in country districts (Am. 2:13).

Such carts were made by carpenters of wood (1 Sa. 6:7), and could therefore be dismantled and burnt (v. 14; Ps. 46:9, see below). Some were covered wagons (Nu. 7:3). The two wheels, either solid or spoked, were sometimes equipped with a heavy metal tread (see Is. 28:27–28). Wagons were usually drawn by two oxen or milch-cows (Nu. 7:3–8; 2 Sa. 6:3–7) and are represented on Assyr. sculptures showing the fall of Lachish in 701 BC (British Museum). The 'covered wagon' of Nu. 7:3 may be a *chariot (as RSV; *cf.* Idrimi statue, Alalaḫ, *ANET*, p. 557), though wagons were also used for military transport (Ps. 46:9, RSV chariot'). The wheeled vehicle may have preceded the threshing-sledge in Is. 28:27–28. The figurative reference to a cart-rope in Is. 5:18 is now obscure. D.J.W.

CASTLE. Five Hebrew words and one Greek word were thus translated in the AV. All have been differently translated in the RSV with the exception of *'armôn*. This appears as 'castle' (Pr. 18:19), but also as 'citadel' (1 Ki. 16:18) and 'tower' (Ps. 122:7), since it may be applied to any building of eminence.

G.W.G.

CASTOR AND POLLUX (Gk. *dioskouroi*, lit. 'sons of Zeus'). The sign of the Alexandrian ship in which Paul sailed from Malta to Puteoli on his way to Rome (Acts 28:11, AV). RV and RSV render 'The Twin Brothers'. According to Gk. mythology they were the sons of Leda. They were worshipped especially at Sparta and were regarded as the special protectors of sailors. Their images were probably fastened one on either side of the bow of the vessel. J.W.M.

CATHOLIC EPISTLES. During the course of the formation of the *Canon of the NT the Epistles of James, 1 and 2 Peter, 1, 2 and 3 John and Jude came to be grouped together and known as 'Catholic' (AV General'), because, with the exception of 2 and 3 John, they were addressed to a wider audience than a local church or individual. Clement of Alexandria speaks of the epistle sent out by the Council at Jerusalem (Acts 15:23) as 'the catholic epistle of all the Apostles'; and Origen applies the term to the *Epistle of Barnabas*, as well as to the Epistles of John, Peter and Jude. Later the word 'Catholic' was applied to Epistles which were accepted by the universal church and were orthodox in doctrine; so it became synonymous with 'genuine' or 'canonical'. Thus with regard to other documents put forward in the name of Peter, Eusebius says 'we know nothing of them being handed down as catholic writings' (*EH* 3. 3).

R.V.G.T.

CATTLE. Nomads and agriculturists alike counted their wealth and regulated their sacrificial worship by possessions in cattle. Heb. *b^ehēmâ*, *beast (sing. or collective), denotes the larger domestic animals—*cf.* Gk. *ktēnos*. The Gk. term frequently, the Heb. occasionally (Ne. 2:12, 14) indicates a mount. The plural may (Jb. 40:15), but need not (*cf.* Ps. 49:12, 20) describe the hippopotamus. *šôr* is an ox or cow—the stalled or fattened ox was a symbol of luxury (Pr. 15:17).

ʾalāpîm (plural only) is used for cattle in general. b^eʿîr has a normal, though not exclusive, reference to beasts of burden. *bāqār* is a generic word incapable of pluralization denoting 'cattlehood', frequently accompanied by a defining word. *ʿēḡel* is commonly used for calf or heifer. *par* is a bull, fem. *pārâ*. The latter is used for the spectacular red heifer ceremonial of Nu. 19. In Lk. 17:7; Jn. 4:12, Gk. suggests sheep or goats, rather than AV 'cattle'. Heb. *miqneh* (*e.g.* Gn. 13:2) means primarily wealth or possessions, derivatively cattle, the significant form of ancient E wealth, *cf.* Arab. *m'āl*, also Heb. *m*^{e}*lā'ḵâ*. *'anšê miqneh* are herdsmen or nomads. (*ANIMALS OF THE BIBLE.)

BIBLIOGRAPHY. W. Bauder, C. Brown, *NIDNTT* 1, pp. 113–119; J. Gess, R. Tuente, *NIDNTT* 2, pp. 410–414; G. S. Cansdale, *Animals of Bible Lands*, 1970. R.A.S.

CAUDA, modern Gavdho (Gozzo), is an island off the S of Crete. Some ancient authorities call it Claude (as in AV). Paul's ship was in the vicinity of Cape Matala when the wind changed from S to a strong ENE, and drove it some 40 km before it came under the lee of Cauda, where the crew were at last able to make preparations to face the storm (Acts 27:16; *SHIPS AND BOATS). K.L.McK.

CAVE. Except in Jb. 30:6, where *ḥôr*, 'hole', is used, the Heb. word usually rendered 'cave' is *m*^{e}*ʿārâ*. Natural caves are no rarity in Palestine, as nearly all the hill-country of Palestine W of the Jordan (except a basalt outcrop in S Galilee) is of limestone and chalk. Such caves were used as dwellings, hiding-places and tombs from the earliest times.

a. Use as dwellings

Remarkable cave-dwellings of 34th/33rd centuries BC have been excavated at Tell Abu Matar, just S of Beersheba. Great caverns had been hollowed out as homes of several chambers linked by galleries for a prosperous community of cultivators and copper-workers. In much later days (early 2nd millennium BC), Lot and his two daughters lodged in a cave after the fall of Sodom and Gomorrah (Gn. 19:30),

Bulls made from carved shell set in bitumen. Part of a frieze from the temple of Ninhursag, al 'Ubaid (near Ur, Iraq). Height 22 cm. Length 115 cm. c. 2900 BC. (BM)

Egyptians herding cattle. Painting from the tomb of Nebamun, Thebes. c. 1400 BC. (BM)

and David and his band frequented the great cave at Adullam (1 Sa. 22:1; 24), and Elisha stayed in one at Horeb (1 Ki. 19:9–13).

b. Use as refuges

Joshua cornered 5 Canaanite kings who hid thus at Makkedah (Jos. 10:16ff.). Israelites also hid in this way from Midianite (Jdg. 6:2) and Philistine (1 Sa. 13:6) invaders. Elijah's friend Obadiah hid 100 prophets in caves 'by fifties' from the sword of Jezebel (1 Ki. 18:4, 13); *cf.* Is. 2:19; Heb. 11:38. Evidence of their use as refuges through the ages has been recovered from caves in the Jordan Valley and by the Dead Sea.

c. Use as tombs

This was a very common practice from prehistoric times onwards (*BURIAL AND MOURNING). Famous instances in Scripture are the cave at Machpelah used by Abraham and his family (Gn. 23, *etc.*), and that whence Jesus summoned Lazarus from the dead (Jn. 11:38).

BIBLIOGRAPHY. For the use of caves as dwellings, see K. M. Kenyon, *Archaeology in the Holy Land*, 1960, pp. 77–80, fig. 10; T. Abu Matar, *cf.* E. K. Vogel, *Bibliography of Holy Land Sites*, 1974, p. 15; *EAEHL*, 1, pp. 152–159; as refuges, see P. W. and N. Lapp, *Discoveries in the Wadi ed-Daliyeh*, *AASOR* 41, 1976; P. Benoit, J. T. Milik, R. de Vaux, *Les Grottes de Murabba'at, Discoveries in the Judaean Desert*, 2, 1961; Y. Yadin, *The Finds from the Bar Kokhba Period in the 'Cave of Letters'*, 1963. K.A.K.

Sandstone cliffs beside the Dead Sea. Qumran cave 4 is in the foreground. (ARM)

CENCHREAE, the modern Kichries, a town near Corinth which served as outport for the city, handling its traffic with the Aegean and the Levant. Cenchreae had a church in which Phoebe served (Rom. 16:1–2); this was perhaps a fruit of Paul's long stay in Corinth. Here the apostle shaved his head, in observance of a vow he had taken (Acts 18:18), prior to leaving for Ephesus. J.H.P.

CENSER. In many rituals an *altar was specifically devoted to the burning of incense. Its form was usually either a bowl mounted on a pedestal, often conical in shape, *i.e.* 'incense-altar' (Heb. *miqṭereṯ*, LXX *thymiatērion*, 2 Ch. 26:19; Ezk. 8:11); so translate for censer (AV) in Heb. 9:4 (B. F. Westcott, *The Epistle to the Hebrews*, 1903, pp. 248–250). *libanotos* is used in Rev. 8:3, 5. On the altar perfumes such as frankincense or cedar-pine were piled or thrown to create a sweet-smelling smoke (*BASOR* 132, 1953, p. 46). Small stone incense-altars with concave bowls on legs are commonly found, or depicted in ancient art, *e.g.* the horned altar from Megiddo. For illustrations, see *ANEP*, pp. 575–581, 626.

Some censers were portable and made of bronze (*maḥtâ*, Lv. 10:1; 16:12; Nu. 16:6) or gold (1 Ki. 7:50), and used for carrying a few burning coals (so NIV; AV 'censer'; RSV 'firepan'). The 'censer' of Ezr. 1:9 (RSV, *maḥlāp̄*) may denote some other vessel (NIV 'silver dishes'; NEB 'of various kinds'; AV 'knife').

D.W.G.
D.J.W.

CENSUS (Lat. *census*, 'assessment', appearing as a loan-word in Gk. *kēnsos*, 'tribute money', in Mt. 17:25; 22:17, 19; Mk. 12:14).

I. In the Old Testament

The outstanding censuses in OT are those from which the book of Numbers receives its name, at the beginning (Nu. 1) and end (Nu. 26) of the wilderness wanderings; and that held by David (2 Sa. 24:1–9; 1 Ch. 21:1–6). In all these it was men of military age who were numbered. Two different sets of totals for David's census have been preserved—in 2 Sa., 800,000 men of Israel and 500,000 men of Judah; in 1 Ch., 1,100,000 men of Israel and

470,000 men of Judah. The plague which followed the census is recorded in both accounts as a divine judgment for David's sin in numbering the people. The censuses of Numbers have been regarded, especially by W. F. Albright ('The Administrative Divisions of Israel and Judah', *JPOS* 5, 1925, pp. 20ff.; *From the Stone Age to Christianity*, 1940, pp. 192, 222), as other variant accounts of David's census, but their totals are considerably less than those of 2 Sa. and 1 Ch. Nevertheless, the transmitted totals

of the wilderness censuses—603,550 in Nu. 1 and 601,730 in Nu. 26—call for some interpretation. One suggestion is that *'elep̄* in the enumeration originally meant something like 'tent-group' rather than 'thousand', so that the figure of 'forty-six thousand five hundred' given for Reuben in Nu. 1:21 meant 46 tent-groups, amounting in all to 500 men (W. M. F. Petrie, *Egypt and Israel*, 1911, pp. 40ff.) (* NUMBER, **2**).

A census of the Judaeans in Nehemiah's time (445–433 BC) is reproduced in Ezr. 2:1–65; Ne. 7:6–67. The total is given as 42,360, together with 7,582 servants and singers.

II. In the New Testament

Two Roman censuses are mentioned in NT, each being denoted by Gk. *apographē*, translated 'enrolment' in Lk. 2:2 and 'census' in Acts 5:37.

The census of Acts 5:37, which was marked by the insurrection led by * Judas of Galilee, was held in AD 6. In that year Judaea was incorporated into the Roman provincial system, and a census was held in order to assess the amount of tribute which the new province should pay to the imperial exchequer. The census was conducted by P. Sulpicius Quirinius, at that time imperial legate of Syria. The suggestion that Israel should pay tribute to a pagan overlord was deemed intolerable by Judas, and by the party of the * Zealots, whose formation has been dated from this time.

The census of Lk. 2:1ff., in the course of which Christ was born in Bethlehem, raises a number of problems. It is, however, widely agreed: (i) that such a census as Luke describes could have taken place in Judaea towards the end of Herod's reign (37–4 BC); (ii) that it could have formed part of an empire-wide enrolment, as Lk. 2:1 indicates; (iii) that it could have involved the return of each householder to his domicile of origin, as Lk. 2:3 states. (i) In Herod's later years Augustus treated him as a subject; all Judaea had to take an oath of loyalty to Augustus as well as to Herod (Jos., *Ant.* 16. 290; 17. 42). Compare the census imposed in AD 36 in the client-kingdom of Archelaus (Tacitus, *Annals* 6. 41). (ii) There is evidence of census activity in various parts of the Roman empire between 11 and 8 BC; that for a census in Egypt in 10–9 BC (first of a series held every 14 years) is specially persuasive. (iii) The custom described in Lk. 2:3 (evidently as something familiar) is attested from Egypt in AD 104. On the relation of Quirinius to this earlier census, * QUIRINIUS.

BIBLIOGRAPHY. W. M. Ramsay, 'The Augustan Census-System', in *BRD*, pp. 255ff.; F. F. Bruce, 'Census Papyri', *Documents of New Testament Times*, forthcoming.

F.F.B.

CHALDEA, CHALDEANS. The name of a land, and its inhabitants, in S Babylonia, later used to denote Babylonia as a whole, especially during the last dynasty of Babylonia (626–539 BC); a semi-nomadic tribe occupying the deserts between N Arabia and the Persian Gulf (*cf.* Jb. 1:17) who early settled in this area occupying Ur 'of the Chaldees' (Gn. 11:28; Acts 7:4) and are distinct from the Aramaeans. The proposed derivation from Chesed (Gn. 22:22) is unsubstantiated but the Heb. *Kaśdîm* may reflect an earlier form of the name than the Assyr. From at least the 10th century BC

CEPHAS
See Peter, Part 3.

CEREAL
See Grain, Part 2.

CEREMONIAL DEFILEMENT
See Clean, Part 1.

CHAFF
See Fuel, Part 1.

CHALCEDONY
See Jewels, Part 2.

Incense-stand, the upper bowl heaped with incense. It stood alongside an altar used by King Ashurbanipal. Nineveh. c. 650 BC. (BM)

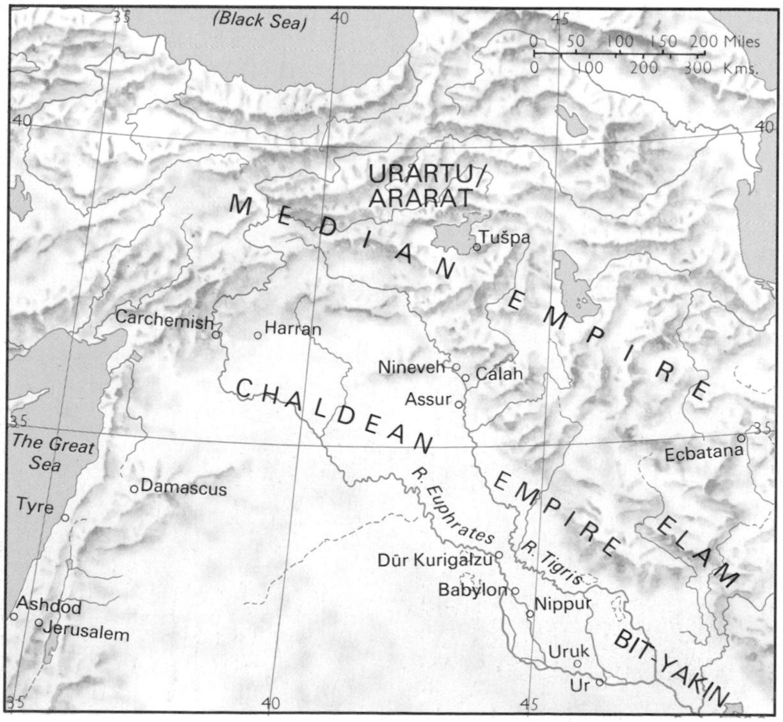

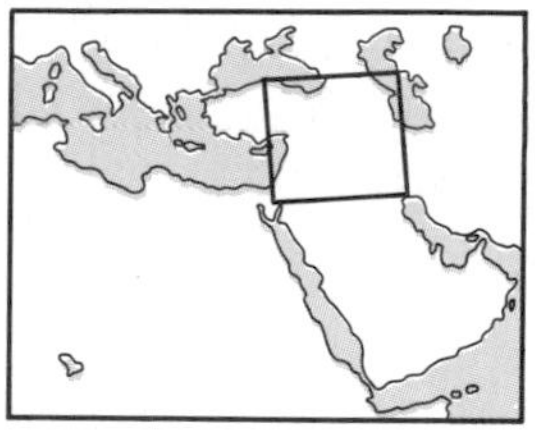

Chaldea: a name for part of Babylonia taken over for the whole land in 8th and 7th cents. BC.

Fugitives, probably Chaldeans, hiding from Assyrian troops in the marshlands of S Babylonia. Sennacherib's palace, Nineveh. c. 690 BC. (BM)

the land of *Kaldu* is named in the Assyr. annals to designate the 'Sea-land' of the earlier inscriptions. Ashurnasirpal II (883–859 BC) distinguished its peoples from the more northerly Babylonians, and Adad-nirari III (*c.* 810 BC) names several chiefs of the Chaldeans among his vassals. When Marduk-apla-iddina II (* MERODACH-BALADAN), the chief of the Chaldean district of Bit-Yakin, seized the throne of Babylon in 721–710 and 703–702 BC he sought help from the W against Assyria (Is. 39). The prophet Isaiah warned of the danger to Judah of supporting the Chaldean rebels (Is. 23:13) and foresaw their defeat (43:14), perhaps after the initial invasion by Sargon in 710 BC. Since Babylon was at this time under a Chaldean king, 'Chaldean' is used as a synonym for Babylonian (Is. 13:19; 47:1, 5; 48:14, 20), a use later extended by Ezekiel to cover all the Babylonian dominions (23:23).

When Nabopolassar, a native Chaldean governor, came to the Babylonian throne in 626 BC, he inaugurated a dynasty which made the name of Chaldean famous. Among his successors were Nebuchadrezzar, Amēl-Marduk (* EVIL-MERODACH), Nabonidus and Belshazzar, 'king of the Chaldeans' (Dn. 5:30). The sturdy southerners provided strong contingents for the Babylonian army attacking Judah (2 Ki. 24–25).

In the time of Daniel the name was again used of Babylonia as a whole (Dn. 3:8), and Darius the Mede ruled the kingdom of the 'Chaldeans' (Dn. 9:1). The 'tongue of the Chaldeans' (Dn. 1:4) was, perhaps, a semitic Babylonian dialect, the name 'Chaldee' being, rarely in modern times, wrongly applied to Aramaic (* TARGUMS). The prominence of the classes of priests who, at Babylon and other centres, maintained the ancient traditions of astrology and philosophy in the classical Babylonian languages led to the designation 'Chaldean' being applied alike to priests (Dn. 3:8), astrologers and educated persons (Dn. 2:10; 4:7; 5:7, 11).

BIBLIOGRAPHY. D. J. Wiseman, *Chronicles of Chaldaean Kings*, 1956; A. R. Millard, *EQ* 49, 1977, pp. 69–71, on the use of the name and its origin. D.J.W.

CHALKSTONES. An expression which is used once in the OT (Is. 27:9) as a figure of what must be done to idolatrous altars if forgiveness and restoration are to come. They are to be 'pulverized' as if they were made of gypsum or limestone. T.C.M.

CHAMBERLAIN. The English word denotes the guardian of the (royal) chamber; in E antiquity men who performed this function were regularly eunuchs, and therefore words for 'chamberlain' and * 'eunuch' are to a large extent interchangeable. This is true of Heb. *sārîs* and Gk. *eunouchos* (it is from the latter word, literally meaning 'bed-keeper', that 'eunuch' is derived).

In Acts 12:20 'the king's chamberlain' represents Gk. *ton epi tou koitōnos tou basileōs*, literally, 'him who was over the king's bedchamber'. In Rom. 16:23 * Erastus, 'the chamberlain of the city' (AV), is 'the city treasurer' (Gk. *oikonomos tēs poleōs*, *cf.* RV, RSV); a Corinthian inscription mentions a man of that name as 'aedile'. F.F.B.

CHAMBERS OF THE SOUTH
See Stars, Part 3.

CHAMOIS
See Animals, Part 1.

CHANCE
See Providence, Part 3.

CHANGE OF NAME
See Name, Part 2.

CHANGES OF RAIMENT. The Heb. *ḥ^a^lîpôt*, translated 'changes' in AV, suggests the meaning 'new clothes', particularly festival attire (RSV 'festal garments'). Such clothes were greatly prized, and were used as tangible evidence of royal wealth, both Egyptian and Syrian. When presented as gifts, the number of garments indicated the giver's status and generosity, while the recipient was honoured with special favour (Gn. 45:22; 2 Ki. 5:5, 22–23). The enormous amount (30) involved in Samson's wager reflects either their lower value in the Judges period or, more probably, Samson's overwhelming confidence (Jdg. 14:12–13). Clothes were used as a means of payment at *Alalaḫ, and it may be that the 'festal garments' of the OT had a similar function.

BIBLIOGRAPHY. D. J. Wiseman, *AOTS*, pp. 128–129, 134.

M.J.S.

CHARIOT.

I. In the ancient Near East

Heavy wheeled vehicles drawn by asses were used for war and ceremonial in S Mesopotamia in the 3rd millennium BC, as is shown by discoveries from Ur, Kish and Tell Agrab. The true chariot, however, which was of light construction and was drawn by the swifter horse, did not appear until the 2nd millennium. It is probable that the horse (*ANIMALS OF THE BIBLE) was introduced by the peoples of the S Russian steppe who precipitated many folk movements in the 2nd millennium, and the likelihood that the word for horse in many ancient Near Eastern languages, including Heb. (*sûs*), was derived from an Indo-European original suggests that these people played an important part in its introduction. In the cuneiform inscriptions, 'horse' is commonly written with a logogram which signifies 'foreign ass', but the phonetic writing (*sisû*), which also occurs, is first found, significantly enough, in the 19th-century tablets from Kültepe in Asia Minor, indicating perhaps the linguistic influence of the forerunners of the N nomads, who not long after entered the Near East in large numbers. Perhaps as a result of these early contacts, the northerners developed the light horse-drawn war-chariot, and when in the first half of the 2nd millennium new peoples entered the ancient world, Hittites in Anatolia, Kassites in Mesopotamia and Hyksos in Syro-Palestine and Egypt, they brought the chariot with them.

The foreign character of the chariot is emphasized by the fact that in many of the Semitic languages of the ancient world the word for chariot was formed from the root *rkb*, 'to ride', resulting, for instance, in Akkad. *narkabtu*, Ugaritic *mrkbt*, Heb. *merkāḇâ*, and the form was even adopted in New Kingdom Egypt (*mrkb.t*). In the second half of the millennium, a class of society whose members were known as *mariannu* is attested at Alalaḫ, Ugarit, in the Amarna letters, and in New Kingdom Egypt. This indicated an individual of esteemed rank characterized particularly by the ownership of a chariot or wagon, and in many instances the best translation seems to be 'chariot warrior'. The word is

CHAOS
See Rahab, Part 3.

CHAPITER
See Capital, Part 1.

CHAPLET
See Ornaments, Part 2.

CHARACTER
See Inner man, Part 2.

A gift of cloth or clothing is brought as tribute. Bas-relief, N staircase of the Apadarna, Persepolis. Achaemenid, reign of Xerxes, 485–465 BC. (RH)

An archer riding in a chariot drawn by two horses. Imprint from a Neo-Assyrian cylinder seal. 9th–7th cent. BC. (MC)

usually considered of Indo-European origin (though some favour a Hurrian derivation), which would further illustrate the milieu of its introduction in the Near East. This is again emphasized by the treatise on horse-training by one Kikkuli of Mitanni, which was found in the cuneiform archives at Boghaz-Koi (* HITTITES). This work, written in Hurrian, contains a number of technical terms which are evidently Indo-European, the language-group of the rulers of Mitanni, who were among the newcomers with horses and chariots in the 2nd millennium.

By the second half of the 2nd millennium the two great powers, the Hittites and the Egyptians, were equipped with horse-drawn chariots, as indeed were many of the small Aramaean and Canaanite city states of Syro-Palestine, and it was in this milieu that the Israelites found themselves on their conquest of Palestine. In the 1st millennium the Assyrians developed this engine as the basis of one of their principal arms, and indeed it became an essential element in plains warfare.

In general, the chariot was of very light construction, wood and leather being extensively employed, and only the necessary fittings being of bronze or iron. The car was usually open at the back, and fitments for shields and receptacles for spears and archers' equipment were disposed on the outside of the front or side panels. The wheels were generally 6-spoked, but occasionally there were 4, and some of the later Assyrian ones had 8. While the wheels usually stood about waist-high, a bas-relief of Ashurbanipal shows an 8-spoked one as high as a man, with a nail-studded tyre, probably of iron. The practice of fixing scythes to the wheels was probably not introduced until Persian times. There were usually two horses—though in the time of Ashurnasirpal II the Assyrians had a third, running at the side as a reserve, a practice subsequently abandoned—and these were yoked on either side of the pole, which curved upwards from the floor level of the car. The yoke, which had been developed for harnessing oxen, was unsuitable for horses, but the more practical horse-collar did not come into use until well into the Christian era.

The crew consisted of from two to four men. The Egyptians favoured two, a driver and a warrior, but the Assyrians added a third, the *šalšu rakbu*, 'third rider', who manipulated a shield to protect the others. This was the most usual number, and was also employed by the Hittites, but in the time of Ashurbanipal a fourth man was sometimes placed in the Assyrian vehicles.

The chariot was obviously of main service in campaigns on flat country, and could be a handicap in irregular terrain, as is shown on the Bronze Gates of Shalmaneser III, which depict the difficulties encountered in a campaign to the source of the Tigris.

King Tutankhamun in his chariot, hunting lions in the desert. Left side of lid of painted wooden casket found in the king's tomb. c. 1350 BC. (PAC)

II. In the Old Testament

In company with the other Semitic-speaking peoples of antiquity, the Hebrews chiefly described the chariot by derivatives of *rkb*. The commonest form, used over 100 times, is *reke̱ḇ*; *merkāḇâ* is used some 44 times; and *riḵbâ* (Ezk. 27:20) and *r*ᵉ*ḵûḇ* (Ps. 104:3) once each. The word *merkāḇ*, while used of chariot in 1 Ki. 4:26, seems to have more the meaning of 'riding-seat' in Lv. 15:9 (AV 'saddle') and Ct. 3:10 (AV 'covering'). Also from *rkb* is formed *rakkāḇ*, 'charioteer', as used in 1 Ki. 22:34; 2 Ki. 9:17 (EVV 'horseman' on account of 'horse' in vv. 18–19, but he could be a 'charioteer' on horseback); and 2 Ch. 18:33. Of the terms not formed from *rkb*, the commonest, *ᵃgālâ*, probably usually signifies wagon or *cart, though in a poetic phrase in Ps. 46:9 it seems to mean chariot. In Ezk. 23:24 it is said of a warlike invasion that 'they shall come against thee with *hōṣen reḵeḇ* . . .' where *hōṣen* is a *hapax legomenon* of uncertain meaning. AV translates these terms as 'chariots, wagons', RV as 'weapons, chariots' and RSV as 'from the north with chariots'. The rendering of *reḵeḇ* as chariots rather than wagons is preferable. One other *hapax legomenon, 'appiryôn* in Ct. 3:9, is rendered 'chariot' by AV, but it is possible that this may mean 'palanquin' or 'litter', perhaps being an Iranian loan-word.

As one would expect, all the references to chariots in the Pentateuch concern the Egyptians. Joseph in his success came to own one (Gn. 41:43; 46:29; 50:9), and the fleeing Israelites were pursued by them (Ex. 14; *cf.* Ex. 15:4, 19; Dt. 11:4). The only exception is Dt. 20:1, and this looks forward to the things to be encountered during the conquest. While from the military point of view chariots were of little use in the hill country, and the Israelites who were without chariots seem to have taken this part of the land first, the 'chariots of iron' (*i.e.* with iron fittings) of the Canaanites of the plains (Jos. 17:16; Jdg. 1:19) and of the Philistines of the coast (1 Sa. 13:5) were a more formidable weapon. The excavations at Hazor have shown what a large number of chariots could have been accommodated in a city at this period (see Jos. 11 and Jdg. 4–5). Chariots were looked upon as symbols of the worldly splendour of a king (*cf.* 1 Sa. 8:11), but though David kept 100 captured chariot-horses after one battle (2 Sa. 8:4; *cf.* also 2 Sa. 15:1), it was not till the time of Solomon that they were incorporated into the Israelite forces as a main arm. At this time the best horses were bred in Cilicia and the best chariots manufactured in Egypt, and Solomon established himself as a middleman in trading these (1 Ki. 10:28–29). For his own army he established 'chariot cities' at *Hazor, *Megiddo, *Gezer and Jerusalem and reorganized his army to include 1,400 chariots (1 Ki. 9:15–19; 10:26). The Israelite chariot carried three men, the third man, like his Assyrian counterpart, the *šalšu rakbu*, being called the *šālîš* (*e.g.* 1 Ki. 9:22; AV renders variously as 'captain', 'lord', 'prince'). The division of the kingdom at Solomon's death was such that Israel kept most of the chariot forces, since Hazor, Megiddo and Gezer were all in its territory, and most of the territory of Judah was hill country where chariots were of less use. In Israel Ahab had a large chariot force, as is shown by the statement of Shalmaneser III that he brought 2,000 (read more probably '200') chariots to the battle of Qarqar (853 BC; Kurkh Stele 2. 91), and it is probable that the stables uncovered at *Megiddo, which have hitherto been ascribed to Solomon, are really due to him, Solomon's perhaps still lying buried in the mound. This large force was reduced by the setbacks suffered in the Aramaean wars, and indeed it is stated that Jehoahaz was left with no more than 10 chariots

Assyrian chariot drawn by a single horse. Wall-painting from the palace at Til Barsip, Syria. 8th cent. BC. (AP)

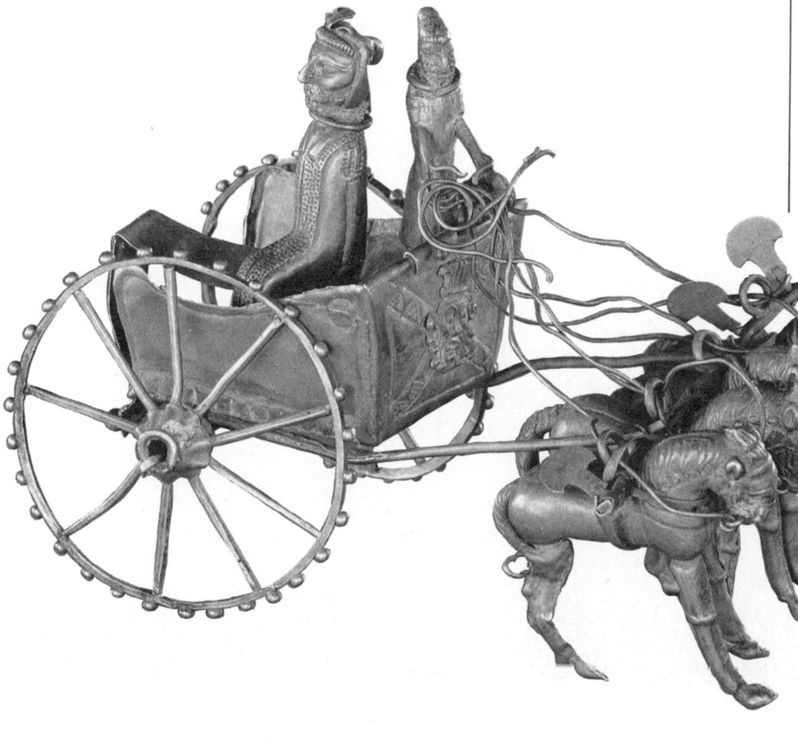

Golden chariot from the Oxus treasure. Drawn by four horses, it contains the driver and a passenger, and is unusual in having two yoke-poles rather than one. 5th cent. BC. (BM)

(2 Ki. 13:7). Samaria, as the capital, housed a chariot force, and it is illuminating that when the city fell to Sargon he took only 50 chariots (*Annals* 15), a clue to the declining forces of Israel. Judah was, of course, not entirely without chariots, as is shown by the fact that Josiah evidently had two personal ones at the battle of Megiddo (2 Ch. 35:24), but they may have been limited to those of high rank.

III. In the New Testament

Chariots do not figure greatly in the NT, the best-known reference being to that in which the Ethiopian eunuch was evangelized by Philip (Acts 8). The Gk. word used here, *harma*, the common word for 'chariot' in Homer, occurs in the LXX usually for *reḵeḇ*. In the Apocalypse chariots are twice referred to, Rev. 9:9 (*harma*); 18:13 (*rheda*).

BIBLIOGRAPHY. I. V. G. Childe, in Singer, Holmyard and Hall (eds.), *A History of Technology*, 1954, pp. 724–728; S. Piggott, *Prehistoric India*, 1950, pp. 266–267, 273–281; Lefèvre des Noëttes, *L'Attelage, le Cheval de Selle à travers les ages*, 1931; O. R. Gurney, *The Hittites*, 1952, pp. 104–106, 124–125; T. G. E. Powell in *Culture and Environment. Essays in Honour of Sir Cyril Fox*, 1963, pp. 153–169; C. J. Gadd, *The Assyrian Sculptures*, 1934, pp. 27–28, 30–35; A. Salonen, *Die Landfahrzeuge des Alten Mesopotamien*, 1951; *Hippologica Accadica*, 1955, pp. 11–44.

II. R. de Vaux, *Ancient Israel*, 1961, pp. 222–225, 535; Y. Yadin, *The Art of Warfare in Biblical Lands*, 1963, pp. 4–5, 37–40, 74–75, 113, 284–287, 297–302; N. Na'aman, *Tel Aviv* 3, 1976, pp. 97–102 (Ahab's chariots). T.C.M.

CHARIOTEER
See Armour, Part 1.

CHARISMATA
See Spiritual gifts, Part 3.

CHASTISEMENT
See Suffering, Part 3.

CHEETAH
See Animals, Part 1.

CHELUB(AI)
See Caleb, Part 1.

CHEBAR. The name of a river in Babylonia, by which Jewish exiles were settled; the site of Ezekiel's visions (1:1, 3; 3:15, 23; 10:15, 20, 22; 43:3). The location is unknown, though Hilprecht proposed an identification with the *nāri kabari* ('great canal'), a name used in a Babylonian text from Nippur for the Shaṭṭ-en-Nil canal running E of that city.

BIBLIOGRAPHY. E. Vogt, *Biblica* 39, 1958, pp. 211–216. D.J.W.

CHEDORLAOMER (Heb. *keḏorlā'ōmer*; Gk. *Chodolla(o)gomor*). The king of Elam, leader of a coalition with *Amraphel, *Arioch and *Tidal, who marched against Sodom and Gomorrah, which had rebelled against him after 12 years as his vassals (Gn. 14:1–17). He was pursued by Abraham who slew him near Damascus (v. 15).

This ruler has not been certainly identified, but the name is unquestionably Elamite *kutir/kudur*, 'servant', usually followed by a divine name, *e.g.* Lagamar (used in Old Bab. names from Mari). Albright identifies Chedorlaomer with King Kitir-Nahhunti I, *c.* 1625 BC (*BASOR* 88, 1942, pp. 33ff.) but the equation of Nahhundi with La'omer is unproven as is the complex view, based on the so-called 'Chedorlaomer' tablets in the British Museum (7th century BC) in which Astour identifies KU.KU. KU.MAL as a king of Elam and representing the 'East', taking Gn. 14 as a late Midrash (in *Biblical Motifs*, 1966, pp. 65–112 (ed. A. Altmann)). The *Ebla texts, however, imply a possibility of early contact between Syria and Elam. D.J.W.

CHEEK (Heb. *leḥî*, of cheek or jaw of man or animal, also of jawbone (Jdg. 15:15); Gk. *siagōn*). A blow on the cheek is indicative of ignominy or defeat (Jb. 16:10; Mt. 5:39), plucking or shaving off the beard more so (Is. 50:6; 1 Ch. 19:4). B.O.B.

CHEMOSH (Heb. *kemôš*), the god of the Moabites, the people of Chemosh (Nu. 21:29; Je. 48:46). The sacrifice of children as a burnt-offering was part of his worship (2 Ki. 3:27). Solomon erected a high place for Chemosh in Jerusalem (1 Ki. 11:7), but Josiah destroyed this (2 Ki. 23:13). (*MOAB, *MOABITE STONE.) J.A.T.

CHENOBOSKION (lit. 'goose-pasture'; Coptic *Sheneset*), an ancient town in Egypt, E of the Nile, *c.* 48 km N of Luxor. Here one of the earliest Christian monasteries was founded by Pachomius, *c.* AD 320. Chenoboskion has acquired new fame because of the discovery at Jabal al-Ṭārif, in its vicinity, *c.* 1945, of a library of Gnostic literature (mainly Coptic translations from Gk.)—49 documents in 13 papyrus codices. They are commonly referred to as the Nag Hammadi documents, presumably because it was in Nag Hammadi, W of the river (the nearest modern town to the scene of the discovery), that the discovery was first reported. One of the codices was acquired by the Jung Institute in Zürich, whence it is called the Jung Codex; the others are the property of the Coptic Museum in Cairo. The two best-known of these documents are *The Gospel of Truth*, contained in the Jung Codex, and *The Gospel of Thomas*, contained in one of the codices at

Tiglath-pileser III of Assyria in his chariot. Relief from Calah (Nimrud). 745–727 BC. (BM)

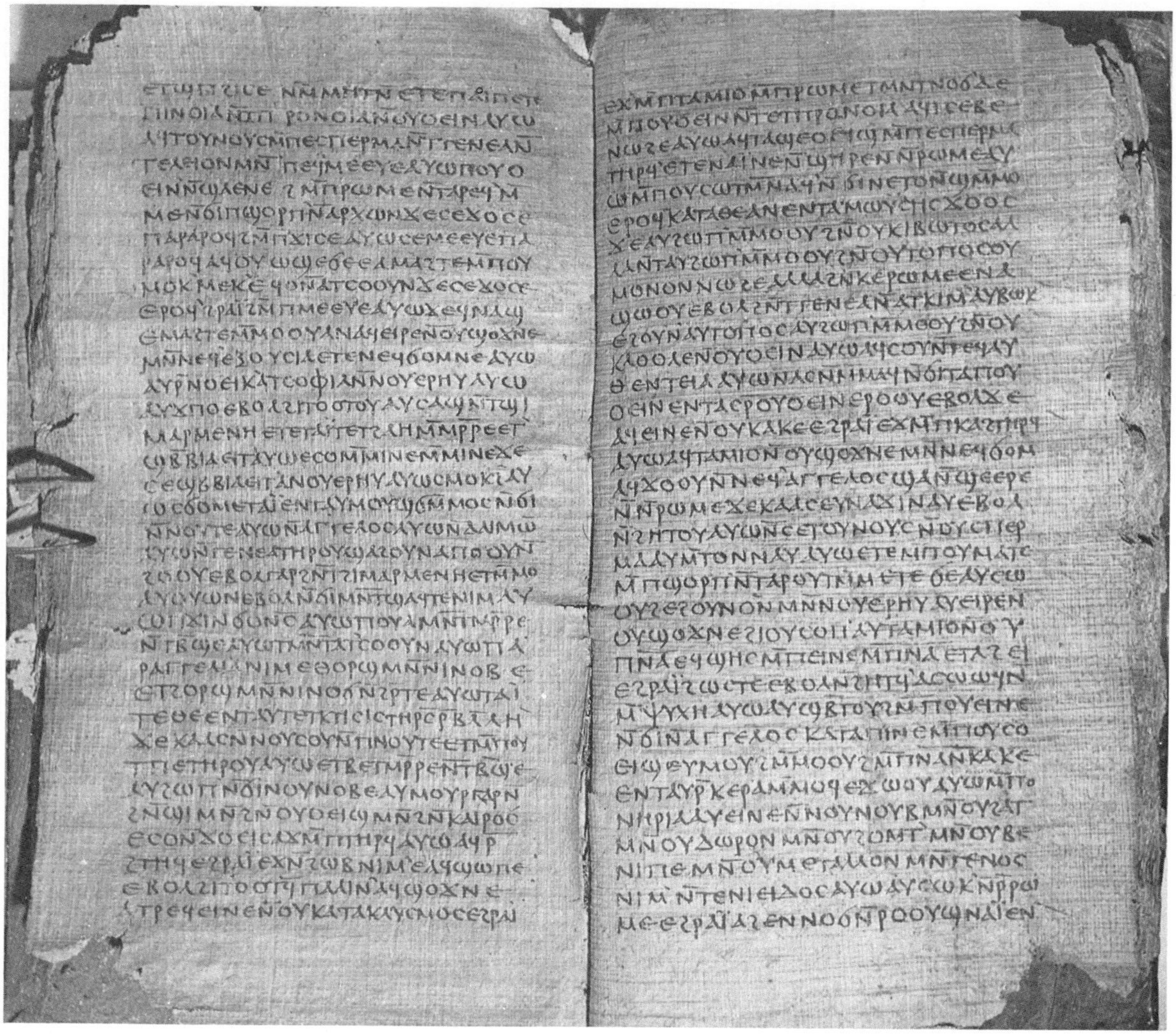

Codex 2, containing The Secret Book of John *and* The Sacred Book of the Invisible Great Spirit (*or* Gospel of the Egyptians) *from the Gnostic library found near Chenoboskion* (*open at pp. 28–29*). (CGS)

Cairo. *The Gospel of Truth* is a speculative meditation on the Christian message, coming from the Valentinian school of Gnosticism, and quite probably the work of Valentinus himself (*c*. AD 150). *The Gospel of Thomas* is a collection of 114 sayings ascribed to Jesus, 2nd-century fragments of which (in Gk.) were found at Oxyrhynchus at the end of the 19th century and beginning of the 20th. The whole collection is in course of publication and will make an invaluable contribution to our knowledge of * Gnosticism.

BIBLIOGRAPHY. F. L. Cross (ed.), *The Jung Codex*, 1955; K. Grobel, *The Gospel of Truth*, 1960; R. M. Grant and D. N. Freedman, *The Secret Sayings of Jesus*, 1960; W. C. van Unnik, *Newly Discovered Gnostic Writings*, 1960; J. Doresse, *The Secret Books of the Egyptian Gnostics*, 1960; R. McL. Wilson, *Studies in the Gospel of Thomas*, 1960, *The Gospel of Philip*, 1962; B. Gärtner, *The Theology of the Gospel of Thomas*, 1961; M. L. Peel, *The Epistle to Rheginos*, 1969; M. Krause in W. Foerster (ed.), *Gnosticism*, 2, 1974, pp. 3–120; D. M. Scholer, *NagHammadi Bibliography 1948–1969*, 1971, updated annually in *NovT*; J. M. Robinson (ed.) *The Facsimile Edition of the Nag Hammadi Codices*, 1972ff.; *The Coptic Gnostic Library*, 1975ff.; *The Nag Hammadi Library in English*, 1977.

F.F.B.

CHEPHIRAH (Heb. *kᵉpîrâh*). A Hivite fortress on a spur 8 km W of Gibeon, Jos. 9:17. Modern Khirbet Kefireh, dominating the Wadi Qatneh, which leads down to Aijalon. It became Benjaminite territory, Jos. 18:26. The Gola-list (Ezr. 2:25; Ne. 7:29) associates it with * Kiriath-jearim. See J. Garstang, *Joshua-Judges*, 1931, pp. 166, 369.

J.P.U.L.

CHERETHITES (Heb. *kᵉrēṯî*). A people who were settled alongside the Philistines in S Palestine (1 Sa. 30:14; Ezk. 25:16; Zp.2:5). In the reign of David they formed, with the Pelethites, his private bodyguard under the command of Benaiah the son of Jehoiada (2 Sa. 8:18; 20:23; 1 Ch. 18:17). They remained loyal to him through the rebellions of Absalom (2 Sa. 15:18) and Sheba (2 Sa. 20:7), and were present when Solomon was anointed for kingship (1 Ki. 1:38, 44), though the fact that they are never again mentioned after this suggests that their loyalty to David depended on the personal factor which ended with his death.

It seems reasonable to suppose that the Cherethites were Cretans and the Pelethites * Philistines, the latter name being perhaps an analogic adaptation of *pᵉlištî* on the basis of *kᵉrēṯî*, together with assimilation of *š* to following *ṯ*, to form the easy phrase *hakkᵉrēṯî wᵉhappᵉlēṯî*, 'the Cherethites and the Pelethites'. This being so, the distinction between them was that though they both came from Crete, the Cherethites were native Cretans,

CHESNUT, CHESTNUT
See Trees (Plane), Part 3.

CHIEF SEATS
See Synagogue, Part 3.

CHILDLESS MARRIAGE
See Nuzi, Part 2.

CHILDREN OF EDEN
See Telassar, Part 3.

CHILDREN OF GOD
See Sons of God, Part 3.

CHILDREN OF THE EAST
See East, children of the, Part 1.

CHINESE CITRON
See Trees (Apple), Part 3.

whereas the Pelethites had only passed through the island in their travels from some other original homeland.

It seems that mercenaries from the Aegean were now, as in later times, not uncommon, for though Jehoiada no longer employed the Cherethites and Pelethites, he did have Carian troops (2 Ki. 11:4, 19; *kārî*, translated 'captains' in AV).

BIBLIOGRAPHY. A. H. Gardiner, *Ancient Egyptian Onomastica*, Text, I, 1947, p. 202*; J. A. Montgomery, *The Books of Kings*, *ICC*, 1951, pp. 85–86; R. de Vaux, *Ancient Israel*, 1961, pp. 123, 219–221. T.C.M.

CHERITH. A tributary of the river Jordan beside which Elijah was fed when he hid from Ahab at God's command (1 Ki. 17:3, 5). Locations S of Gilgal or E of the Jordan have been proposed. D.W.B.

CHERUBIM (Heb. *k^erûḇîm*). The plural of 'cherub', represented in the OT as symbolic and celestial beings. In the book of Genesis they were assigned to guard the tree of life in Eden (Gn. 3:24). A similar symbolic function was credited to the golden cherubim, which were placed at either end of the cover ('mercy seat') of the ark of the covenant (Ex. 25:18–22; *cf.* Heb. 9:5), for they were thought of as protecting the sacred objects which the ark housed, and as providing, with their outstretched wings, a visible pedestal for the invisible throne of God (*cf.* 1 Sa. 4:4; 2 Sa. 6:2; 2 Ki. 19:15; Pss. 80:1; 99:1, *etc.*). In Ezk. 10 the chariot-throne of God, still upborne by cherubim, becomes mobile. Representations of those winged creatures were also embroidered on the curtains and veil of the tabernacle and on the walls of the Temple (Ex. 26:31; 2 Ch. 3:7).

Figures of cherubim formed part of the lavish decorations of Solomon's Temple (1 Ki. 6:26ff.). Two of these, carved in olivewood and overlaid with gold, dominated the inner sanctuary. They stood about 5 m in height, with a total wing-spread of similar dimensions, and when placed together they covered one entire wall. Cherubim were also carved in the form of a frieze around the wall of Solomon's Temple, and they appeared together with animal representations on decorative panels forming part of the base of the huge brass basin ('molten sea') which contained the water for ritual ablutions.

In other OT allusions, especially in the poetical books, they are symbolical representations of the storm-winds of heaven; thus in 2 Sa. 22:11 (Ps. 18:10) God was spoken of as riding upon a cherub (an expression which has as its parallel clause, 'he was seen upon the wings of the wind').

The OT does not describe the appearance and general nature of cherubim clearly. They were generally represented as winged creatures having feet and hands. In Ezekiel's vision of the restored Jerusalem the carved likenesses of cherubim had two faces, one of a man and the other of a young lion (Ezk. 41:18f.), whereas in those seen in his vision of the divine glory, each of the cherubim had 4 faces and 4 wings (Ezk. 10:21). To what extent they were thought to be possessed of moral and ethical qualities is unknown. They were invariably in close association with God, and were accorded an elevated, ethereal position.

Archaeological discoveries have brought to light some ancient representations of creatures which may be cherubim. At Samaria ivory panels depicted a composite figure with a human face, an animal body with 4 legs, and 2 elaborate and conspicuous wings. Excavations at the ancient Phoenician city of Gebal (the Gk. Byblos) have revealed a carved representation of two similar cherubim supporting the throne of Hiram king of Gebal, who reigned *c.* 1000 BC.

Symbolic winged creatures were a prominent feature alike of ancient Near Eastern mythology and architecture. Representations of this kind were a common feature of Egyptian animism, while in Mesopotamia, winged lions and bulls guarded buildings of importance. The Hittites popularized the griffin, a highly composite creature consisting of the body of a lion with the head and wings of an eagle, and in general appearance resembling a sphinx.

BIBLIOGRAPHY. *ICC*, *Genesis*, pp. 89f., *Ezekiel*, pp. 112–114, *Revelation*, 1, pp. 118–127; art. 'Cherub' in *JewE*; art. 'Cherubim' in *HDB* and *DAC*; H. Heppe, *Reformed Dogmatics*, E.T. 1950. R.K.H.

Winged sphinxes (cherubim). Phoenician style ivory carving, from Calah (Nimrud). Height 8·2 cm. 9th–8th cent. BC. (BM)

CHESULLOTH (Heb. *k^esullôṯ*), Jos. 19:18; Chisloth-tabor, Jos. 19:12. A town of Issachar in the plain W of Tabor; Zebulun occupied the hills to the NW. Modern Iksal preserves the name. J.P.U.L.

CHINNERETH. A fortified city, Jos. 19:35 (probably mod. Khirbet el-Oreimah), also spelt Chinneroth (Jos. 11:2), which gave its name to the sea of Chinnereth (Nu. 34:11), known in NT as the lake of Gennesaret (Lk. 5:1), Sea of Galilee or Sea of Tiberías. Josephus uses the term Gennesar (*War* 2.573). The name could be derived from *kinnôr*, harp, from the shape of the lake N.H.

CHIOS. One of the larger Aegean islands off the W coast of Asia Minor, this was a free city-state under the Roman empire until Vespasian's day. Paul's ship on

The plain of Chinnereth. (RP)

the way from Troas to Patara anchored for a night near the island (Acts 20:15). J.D.D.

CHLOE. Greek female name, signifying 'verdant', especially appropriated to Demeter.

'Chloe's people' told Paul of the Corinthians' schisms (1 Cor. 1:11) and perhaps other items in 1 Cor. 1–6. That the tactful Paul names his informants suggests they were not Corinthian. Possibly they were Christian slaves of an Ephesian lady visiting Corinth. Whether Chloe was herself a Christian is unknown.

F. R. M. Hitchcock (*JTS* 25, 1924, pp. 163ff.) argues that a pagan body, associated with the Demeter-cult, is intended. A.F.W.

CHISLEV
See Calendar (Kislew), Part 1.

CHOIR
See Music, Part 2.

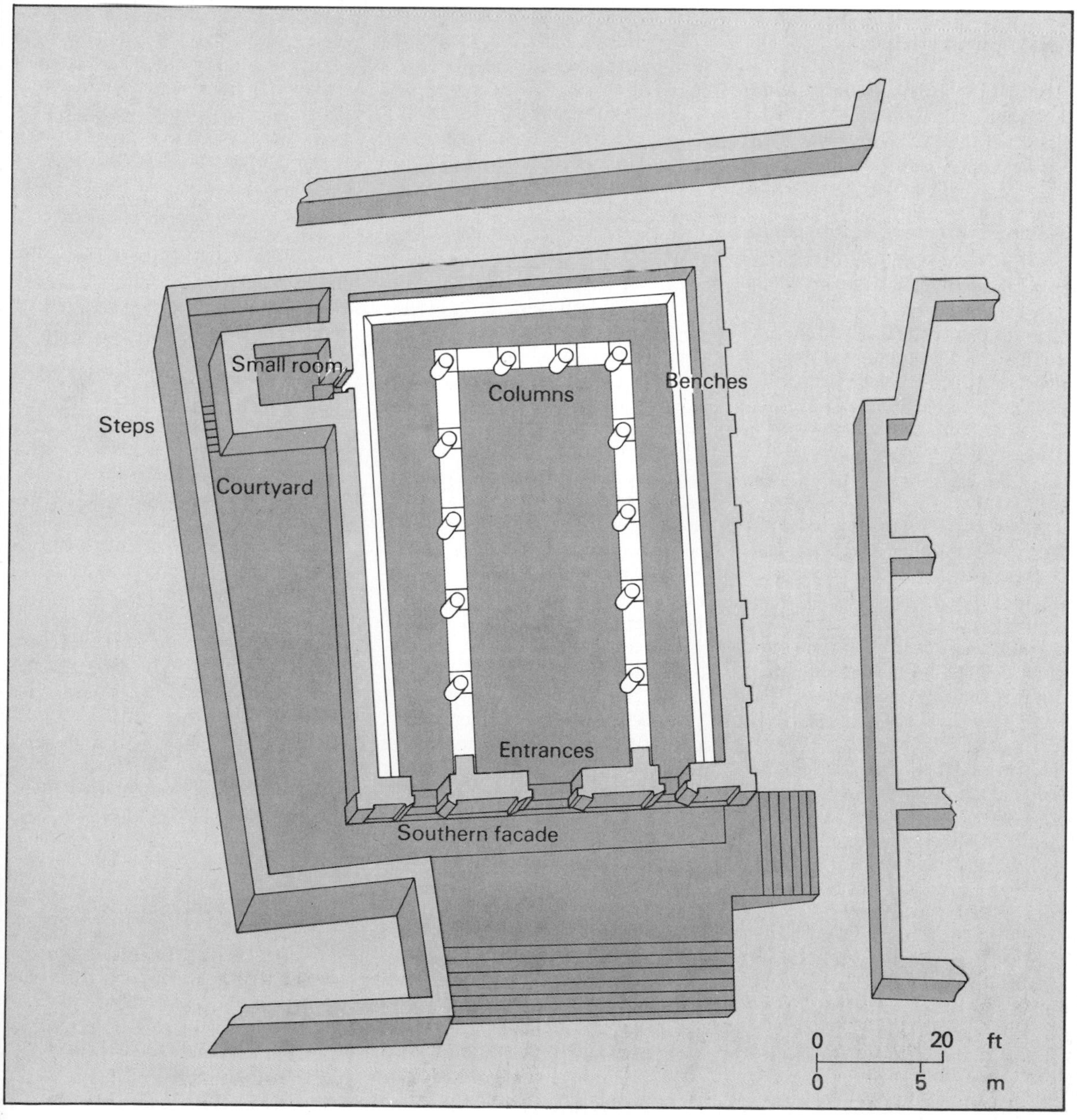

Ground plan of the Chorazin synagogue.

Remains of the synagogue at Chorazin. Date uncertain. (JPK)

CHORAZIN. A town on the Sea of Galilee associated with the Lord's preaching and miracles, but which he denounced because it did not repent (Mt. 11:21; Lk.10:13). Now identified with Kerazeh, 4 km N of Capernaum (Tell Hum?), the black basalt ruins of its synagogue can still be seen. J.W.M.

CHRIST See Jesus Christ, Part 2.

CHRISTIAN. The 3 occurrences (Acts. 11:26; 26:28; 1 Pet. 4:16) all imply that it was a generally recognized title in the NT period, though it is evident that there were other names which Christians themselves used, and perhaps preferred (*cf.* H. J. Cadbury, *BC*, 5, 1933, pp. 375ff.).

a. Origin of the name

The formation seems to be Latin, where plural nouns ending in *-iani* may denote the soldiers of a particular general (*e.g. Galbiani*, Galba's men, Tacitus, *Hist.* 1. 51), and hence partisans of an individual. Both elements are combined in the quasi-military *Augustiani* (see below). In the late 1st century AD at least, *Caesariani* was used of Caesar's slaves and clients, and in the Gospels we meet the *Herodianoi*, who may have been partisans or clients of Herod (*HERODIANS).

Christian(o)i, therefore, may have originally been thought of as 'soldiers of Christus' (Souter), or 'the household of Christus' (Bickerman), or 'the partisans of Christus' (Peterson). H. B. Mattingly has recently given an ingenious turn to the latter interpretation by suggesting that *Christiani*, by an Antiochene joke, was modelled on *Augustiani*, the organized brigade of chanting devotees who led the public adulation of Nero Augustus; both the enthusiasm of the believers and the ludicrous homage of the imperial cheer-leaders being satirized by the implicit comparison with each other. But the name 'Christian' may well be older than the institution of the *Augustiani.*

b. Place and period of origin

Luke, who clearly knew the church there well, places the first use of the name at Syrian Antioch (Acts 11:26). The Latinizing form is no obstacle to this. The context describes events of the 40s of the 1st century AD, and Peterson has argued that the contemporary persecution by Herod Agrippa I (Acts 12:1) evoked the name *Christian(o)i* as a parallel to their foes, the *Herodian(o)i.* If *Augustiani* be the model, the title cannot have been coined before AD 59, and Acts 11:26 cannot be taken as implying any date for the title. There is, however, good reason to associate the occasion with what precedes, for Luke has just shown Antioch as the first church with a significant pure-Gentile, ex-pagan element: that is, the first place where pagans would see Christianity as something other than a Jewish sect. Appropriate names for the converts would not be long in coming.

At any rate, 'Christian' was well established in the 60s. The 'smart' Herod Agrippa II (Acts 26:28) uses it, doubtless satirically, to Paul (Mattingly: 'In a moment you'll be persuading me to enroll as a *Christianus*'). Peter, probably from Rome just before the Neronian persecution, warns 'the elect' in parts of Asia Minor that no-one should be ashamed if called on to suffer as a Christian (1 Pet. 4:16—this need not imply a formal charge in a lawcourt); and Nero, according to Tacitus (*Annals* 15. 44), trumped up a charge against a sect 'whom the common people *were calling* (*appellabat*—the tense is significant) Christians'.

c. The source of the name

The verb *chrēmatisai* (RSV 'were called') in Acts 11:26 is variously interpreted. Bickerman, translating it 'styled themselves', holds that 'Christian' was a name invented in the Antiochene church. His translation is possible, but not necessary, and it is more likely that Antiochene pagans coined the word. Certainly elsewhere, it is non-Christians who use the title—Agrippa, the accusers in 1 Peter, the 'common people' in Tacitus. The verb is frequently translated 'were publicly called' (*cf.* Rom. 7:3), referring to official action in registering the new sect under the name 'Christians'. (Registration would easily account for a Latin title.) But the verb could be used more loosely, and perhaps Luke means no more than that the name came into popular use in the first city where a distinctive name became necessary. From this it might early and easily pass into official and universal use.

d. Subsequent use

If 'Christian' was originally a nickname, it was, like 'Methodist' later on, adopted by the recipients. Increasingly, believers would have to answer the question 'Are you a Christian?', and there was no shame in accepting what was intended as a term of opprobrium when it contained the very name of the Redeemer (1 Pet. 4:16). And it had a certain appropriateness: it concentrated attention on the fact that the distinctive element in this new religion was that it was centred in the Person, Christ; and if the name *Christos* was unintelligible to most pagans, and they sometimes confused it with the common name *Chrēstos*, meaning 'good, kind', it was a *paronomasia* which could be turned to good effect. And so, in the earliest 2nd-century literature, the name is employed without question by the Christian bishop Ignatius (in Antioch) and the pagan governor Pliny (in the area addressed in 1 Peter).

BIBLIOGRAPHY. T. Zahn, *INT*, 2, 1909, pp. 191ff.; E. Peterson, *Frühkirche, Judentum und Gnosis*,

1959, pp. 64–87; E. J. Bickerman, *HTR* 42, 1949, pp. 109ff.; H. B. Mattingly, *JTS* n.s. 9, 1958, pp. 26ff. A.F.W.

CHRONICLES, BOOKS OF.

I. Outline of contents

Chronicles tells the story of Israel up to the return from exile, concentrating on matters of importance concerning her religious life.

a. Introduction (1 Ch. 1–9): genealogies tracing the line of descent from Adam through the patriarch (1) to the tribe of Judah (with its royal line) (2:1–4:23) and the other tribes (4:24–8:40), and on to those who returned from exile (9).

b. The acts of David (1 Ch. 10–29): his coming to power (10–12), his bringing the ark to Jerusalem and plans for a permanent Temple (13–17), his military victories (18–20) and his arrangements for the building of the Temple (21–29).

c. The acts of Solomon (2 Ch. 1–9): his building and dedication of the Temple and his other achievements.

d. The history of Judah from the rebellion of the N tribes to the exile (2 Ch. 10–36): the account of the S kingdom proceeds reign by reign, with special attention being paid to the religious reforms of Hezekiah and Josiah. The conclusion (36:22–23) introduces the return from exile.

II. Origin

The Talmud (*Baba Bathra* 15a) attributes Chronicles to Ezra. Like most OT books, however, Chronicles is of anonymous authorship, and no conclusions are possible as to who wrote it. Its interest in the Levites has been taken to indicate an origin among this group, but this is not a necessary inference. Little more precision is possible concerning its date. The last event alluded to is the return from exile (2 Ch. 36:22–23), and Chronicles could have been written soon after this in the Jerusalem community. On the other hand, the list of descendants of Jehoiachin (Jeconiah) (1 Ch. 3:17–24) seems to cover six generations from the exile, which takes us down to *c.* 400 BC as the earliest the book could have been finished. It could be, however, that the genealogies were supplemented later, and the main body of the work could still belong to a period soon after the exile. There is no certain reflection of the Greek period, and the beginning and end of the Persian empire (537–331 BC) thus probably mark the limits within which Chronicles must have been written.

The story of Chronicles is continued in Ezra, and the former's final verses are almost identical with the latter's opening. This has commonly been taken to suggest that at least Ezr. 1–6 is the original continuation of Chronicles. Alternatively, it may indicate that a later writer wanted to provide such a link (so H. G. M. Williamson, *Israel in the Books of Chronicles*, 1977).

III. Literary characteristics

The main bulk of the work, 1 Ch. 10–2 Ch. 36, parallels 1 Sa. 31–2 Ki. 25, and is frequently verbally identical with these earlier books. Although this might indicate that Chronicles and Samuel–Kings were independently utilizing material from an earlier work which is now lost, it seems more likely that Samuel–Kings itself is Chronicles' major source. Chronicles may thus be seen as essentially a revised edition of the earlier work, related to it rather in the way that (according to the usual theory) Matthew and Luke are to Mark's Gospel. (The 'Chronicles' to which Kings refers—*e.g.* 2 Ki. 20:20—are earlier royal annals and not the biblical books of Chronicles.)

Chronicles seems to have used a different edition of Samuel–Kings from the one which appears in the Hebrew Bible, and this makes it difficult with certainty to identify points at which it introduced changes to Samuel–Kings (see W. E. Lemke in *HTR* 58, 1965, pp. 349–363). But apparently earlier material was sometimes taken over virtually as it stood (*e.g.* 1 Ch. 19), or modified (*e.g.* 1 Ch. 21), or replaced by an alternative version (*e.g.* 2 Ch. 24). Sometimes extensive sections were omitted (*e.g.* those concerning the N kingdom) and other material inserted (*e.g.* concerning David's arrangements for the Temple). Old and new material is moulded into longer sections which offer a theological/historical exposition of a particular period (*e.g.* the reign of Hezekiah), and the various parts then take their place in the Chronicler's new total framework of a history of God's dealings with his people from creation to the return from exile.

The author's method suggests on the one hand that he regarded Samuel–Kings as an authoritative religious text, which he wished to apply to his own age. In this connection he has been described as an exegete of the earlier work (P. R. Ackroyd, 'The Chronicler as Exegete', *JSOT* 2, 1977), or his work has been spoken of as interpretative midrash (M. D. Goulder, *Midrash and Lection in Matthew*, 1974: with chapter on Chronicles). On the other hand, he did wish to bring a specific message from God applied to the people of his own day, and it is this that leads him to his extensive reworking of his text, omitting what was now irrelevant, adding material that was now newly relevant, changing what was now misleading, and so on.

Chronicles has been regarded as poorer history than Samuel–Kings, though for questionable reasons. Its greater concentration on ecclesiastical rather than political affairs has made it seem further from a modern historian's ideal than Samuel–Kings is. Some of its alterations to Samuel–Kings raise historical problems: notably, many of the financial and military figures are vastly increased. This may be the ancient equivalent to allowing for inflation, though textual corruption or misunderstanding has often been suspected (see R. K. Harrison, *IOT*, 1970, pp. 1163–1165). Religious practices (*e.g.* the offering of sacrifice) are made to conform clearly to the Pentateuchal law and the practice of the writer's own day—here the author perhaps resembles an artist painting the figures of the past in the dress of his own age. Such characteristics have led to the questioning of the extra material Chronicles includes which does not appear in Samuel–Kings. But where this material can be checked (for instance, by archaeological discoveries) it has seemed to be of historical value (see J. M. Myers, *I Chronicles*, *AB*, 1965, p. lxiii and *passim* in Myers' two commentaries).

IV. Emphases

In its choice and treatment of its material, Chronicles manifests certain characteristic emphases, a concern with faithful worship, purity and trusting obedience (see J. E. Goldingay, *Biblical Theology Bulletin* 5, 1975, pp. 99–126).

a. Faithful worship. A comparison of the accounts of the reigns of David and Solomon in Samuel–Kings and in Chronicles

CHRISTOLOGY
See Jesus Christ, titles of, Part 2.

soon reveals that Chronicles is not very interested in their political or military achievement. They appear as the founders of the worship of the Temple, which is 'the hub of the Lord's kingdom on earth' (Myers, p. lxviii). Similarly, the ministry of the prophets whom Chronicles portrays centres on their concern for right worship and their involvement with the Temple, and the ministry of the Levites is the great privilege of leading the joyful worship of the Temple. Naturally the priests fulfil their sacrificial role in the Temple, too, and Chronicles often notes how the law was properly kept as regards the conducting of worship according to God's will.

b. Purity. A second reason for Chronicles' emphasis on David is that it supports his belief that David's tribe, Judah, is the true Israel. God chose Judah as leader of the tribes (as is reflected in its prominence in the genealogies) and out of Judah chose David to be king over Israel for ever. It was in Judah's capital that the Temple was located and the worship of Yahweh rightly offered. By their rebellion, the N tribes have cut themselves off from the sphere of God's grace and action. The Lord is not with them and Judah should dissociate herself from them—but only in as far as they persist in rebellion. The door is always open for them to return, and they still appear in the genealogies' roll-call of 'the complete kingdom of God' (M. D. Johnson, *The Purpose of the Biblical Genealogies*, 1969, p. 57).

c. Trusting obedience. Many of the stories the author adds to the Samuel–Kings framework emphasize the power of God, which his people are challenged to trust in the crises that confront them. Many of his other modifications to Samuel–Kings are designed to make even clearer than the earlier books do that God's justice, too, is at work in his people's history, so that men who are faithful to God (or who repent of their sin) find blessing, while trouble comes when men turn away from him (*cf.* the versions of the stories of Rehoboam, Joash, Manasseh and Josiah).

V. Context and implications of its thought

Chronicles is one of the later OT books, and it shows a knowledge of many parts of the OT. Its genealogies are dependent on Genesis, Joshua, *etc.*, and the main narratives, as we have noted, are substantially derived from Samuel–Kings. Chronicles also reflects the style and way of thinking of Deuteronomy as well as the emphases of the 'priestly' laws in Leviticus. It quotes extensively from Psalms which appear in the Psalter, and the homilies it includes often take up phrases in particular from the prophets (see G. von Rad, 'The Levitical sermon in *I* and *II Chronicles*', in *The Problem of the Hexateuch and other Essays*, 1966).

It represents an important stream of post-exilic thinking; but not, of course, the only such stream. Its outlook deserves to be compared with others, such as the wisdom tradition with its profound questionings and the prophetic/apocalyptic perspective with its eschatological orientation. The tension with these should not be exaggerated, but they do manifest differences in emphasis. Chronicles' contribution is to affirm that all is not an enigma (as Job and Ecclesiastes indicate some were inclined to believe); nor (as apocalyptic thinking might imply) has God absented himself from history until some hoped-for moment when he will break into it again. He can be known in the Temple and its worship, and he is to be trusted and obeyed in everyday life in the confident hope that his gracious lordship will be known in the community's experience. Again, if there were other circles that were either too inclined to assimilate to paganism around, or alternatively too ready to cut themselves off from anyone who was not of the purest Judaean blood, Chronicles urges a firm stand for the ways of Yahweh, but implies an openness to all who are prepared to share that commitment.

BIBLIOGRAPHY. In addition to works quoted above, P. R. Ackroyd, *I and II Chronicles, Ezra, Nehemiah, TBC*, 1973; J. M. Myers, *Int* 20, 1966, pp. 259–273; D. N. Freedman, *CBQ* 23, 1961, pp. 436–442; extensive further bibliography in H. G. M. Williamson, *Israel in the Books of Chronicles*, 1977. J.E.G.

CHRONOLOGY OF THE OLD TESTAMENT.

CHRONOLOGY OF THE OLD TESTAMENT. The aim of such a chronology is to determine the correct dates of events and persons in the OT as precisely as possible, that we may better understand their significance.

I. Sources and methods of chronology

a. Older method

Until about a century ago OT dates were calculated almost entirely from the biblical statements (so Ussher). Two difficulties beset this approach. First, the OT does not provide all the details needed for this task, and some sequences of events may be concurrent rather than consecutive. Secondly, the ancient versions, *e.g.* the LXX, sometimes offer variant figures. Hence schemes of this kind are subject to much uncertainty.

b. Present methods

Modern scholars try to correlate data culled both from the Bible and from archaeological sources, in order to obtain absolute dates for the Hebrews and for their neighbours. From *c.* 620 BC, a framework is provided by the Canon of Ptolemy and other classical sources (*e.g.* Manetho, Berossus) which can be completed and corrected in detail from contemporary Babylonian tablets and Egyptian papyri, *etc.*, for the two great riverine states. The margin of error almost never exceeds a year, and in some cases is reduced to a week within a month, or even to nil.

Good dates from *c.* 1400 BC onwards are available, based on Mesopotamian data. The Assyrians each year appointed an official to be *limmu* or eponym, his name being given to his year of office. They kept lists of these names and often noted down events under each year, *e.g.* a king's accession or a campaign abroad. Thus, if any one year can be dated by our reckoning, the whole series is fixed. An eclipse of the sun in the year of the eponym Bur-Sagale is that of 15 June 763 BC, thus fixing a whole series of years and events from 892 to 648 BC, with material reaching back to 911 BC. Alongside these *limmu*-lists, king-lists giving names and reigns take Assyrian history back to nearly 2000 BC, with a maximum error of about a century then, which narrows to about a decade from *c.* 1400 BC until *c.* 1100 BC. Babylonian king-lists and 'synchronous histories' narrating contacts between Assyrian and Babylonian kings help to establish the history of the two kingdoms between *c.* 1400 BC and *c.* 800 BC. Finally, the scattered information from contemporary tablets and annals of various reigns provides first-hand evidence for some periods.

Good dates from *c.* 1200 BC back to *c.* 2100 BC can be obtained from Egyptian sources. These include king-lists, year-dates on contemporary monuments, cross-checks with Mesopotamia and elsewhere, and a few astronomical phenomena dated exactly in certain reigns. By this means, the 11th and 12th Dynasties can be dated to *c.* 2134–1786 BC, and the 18th to 20th Dynasties to *c.* 1552–1070 BC, each within a maximum error of some 10 years; the 13th to 17th Dynasties fit in between these two groups with a maximum error of about 15 or 20 years in their middle. Mesopotamian dates during 2000–1500 BC depend largely on the date assignable to Hammurapi of Babylon: at present it varies within the period 1850–1700 BC, the date 1792–1750 BC (S. Smith) being as good as any.

Between 3000 and 2000 BC all Near Eastern dates are subject to greater uncertainty, of up to two centuries, largely because they are inadequately linked to later dates. Before 3000 BC, all dates are reasoned estimates only, and are subject to several centuries' margin of error, increasing with distance in time. The 'Carbon-14' method of computing the dates of organic matter from antiquity is of most service for the period before 3000 BC, and such dates carry a margin of error of ± 250 years. Hence this method is of little use to biblical chronology; the possible sources of error in the method require that 'Carbon-14' dates must still be treated with reserve.

Such a framework for Mesopotamia and Egypt helps to fix the dates of Palestinian discoveries and of events and people in the Bible; thus the story of the Heb. kingdoms affords cross-links with Assyria and Babylonia. The successive levels of human occupation discerned by archaeologists in the town-mounds ('tells') of ancient Palestine often contain datable objects which link a series of such levels to corresponding dates in Egyptian history down to the 12th century BC. Thereafter, the changes of occupation can sometimes be linked directly with Israelite history, as at *Samaria, *Hazor and *Lachish. Israelite dates can be fixed within a margin of error of about 10 years in Solomon's day, narrowing to almost nil by the time of the fall of Jerusalem in 587 BC.

The margins of error alluded to arise from slight differences in names or figures in parallel king-lists, actual breakage in such lists, reigns of yet unknown duration and the limitations of certain astronomical data. They can be eliminated only by future discovery of more detailed data.

Further complications in chronology stem from the different modes of calendaric reckoning used by the ancients in counting the regnal years of their monarchs. By the accession-year system, that part of a civil year elapsing between a king's accession and the next New Year's day was reckoned not as his first year, but as an 'accession-year' (that year being credited to the previous ruler), and his first regnal year was counted from the first New Year's day. But by the non-accession-year system of reckoning, that part of the civil year between a king's accession and the next New Year's day was credited to him as his first regnal 'year', his second being counted from the first New Year's day. The type of reckoning used, by whom, of whom, and when, is especially important for right understanding of the chronological data in Kings and Chronicles.

II. Primeval antiquity before Abraham

The creation is sufficiently dated by that immortal phrase, 'in the beginning . . .', so distant is it. The period from Adam to Abraham is spanned by genealogies in the midst of which occurs the Flood. However, attempts to use this information to obtain dates for the period from Adam to Abraham are hindered by lack of certainty over the right interpretation. A literal Western interpretation of the figures as they stand yields too low a date for events recorded, *e.g.* the Flood. Thus, if, for example, Abraham's birth is set at about 2000 BC (the earliest likely period), the figures in Gn. 11:10–26 would then yield a date for the Flood just after 2300 BC—a date so late that it would fall some centuries *after* Sir Leonard Woolley's flood-level at Ur, itself of too late a date to be the flood of either the Heb. or Bab. records. Similar difficulties arise if Adam's date be further calculated in this way from Gn. 5 on the same basis.

Hence an attempted interpretation must be sought along other lines. Ancient Near Eastern documents must be understood in the first place as their writers and readers understood them. In the case of genealogies, this involves the possibility of abbreviation by omission of some names in a series. The main object of the genealogies in Gn. 5 and 11 is apparently not so much to provide a full chronology as to supply a link from earliest man to the great crisis of the Flood and then from the Flood down through the line of Shem to Abraham, forefather of the Hebrew nation. The abbreviation of a *genealogy by omission does not affect its value ideologically as a link, as could be readily demonstrated from analogous ancient Near Eastern sources. Hence genealogies, including those of Gn. 5 and 11, must always be used with great restraint whenever it appears that they are open to more than one interpretation.

III. Dates before the monarchy

a. The Patriarchs

Three lines of approach can be used for dating the Patriarchs: mention of external events in their time, statements of time elapsed between their day and some later point in history, and the evidence of period discernible in the social conditions in which they lived.

The only two striking external events recorded are the raid of the four kings against five in Gn. 14 (*AMRAPHEL, *ARIOCH, *CHEDORLAOMER) and the destruction of the cities of the plain in Gn. 19 (*PLAIN, CITIES OF THE), both falling in Abraham's lifetime.

None of the kings in Gn. 14 has yet been safely identified with a particular individual in the 2nd millennium BC, but the names can be identified with known names of that general period, especially 1900 to 1500 BC. Power-alliances formed by rival groups of kings in Mesopotamia and Syria are particularly typical of the period 2000–1700 BC: a famous letter from Mari on the middle Euphrates says of this period, 'there is no king who of himself is the strongest: ten or fifteen kings follow Hammurapi of Babylon, the same number follow Rim-Sin of Larsa, the same number follow Ibal-pi-El of Eshnunna, the same number follow Amut-pi-El of Qatna, and twenty kings follow Yarim-Lim of Yamkhad.' In this period also, Elam was one of several prominent kingdoms.

Glueck has endeavoured to date the campaign of Gn. 14 from its supposed archaeological results: he claims that the line of city-settlements along the later 'King's Highway' was clearly occupied at the start of the 2nd millennium (until the 19th century BC, on modern dating), but that soon thereafter the area suddenly ceased to be occupied, except for roving nomads, until about 1300 BC, when the Iron Age kingdoms of Edom, Moab and Ammon were effectually founded.

Similar reasoning has been applied to the date of the fall of the cities of the plain, although their actual remains appear now to be beyond recovery (probably being under the Dead Sea).

This picture of an occupational gap between the 19th and 13th centuries BC has been criticized by Lankester Harding in the light of certain recent finds in Transjordan, including Middle Bronze tombs and an important Middle and Late Bronze temple. However, the views of neither Glueck nor Harding need be pressed to extremes; in all probability the view of a reduced density of population between the 19th and 13th centuries is true in general and of the Highway cities in particular, while at certain isolated points occupation may have been continuous.

Two main statements link the day of the Patriarchs with later times. In Gn. 15:13–16 Abraham is forewarned that his descendants will dwell in a land not theirs for some four centuries. The 'fourth generation' of v. 16 is difficult; if a 'generation' be equated with a century (*cf.* Ex. 6:16–20), this usage would be unusual. A possible but dubious alternative is to see in v. 16 a prophetic allusion to Joseph's journey to Canaan to bury Jacob (Joseph being in the 'fourth generation' if Abraham is the first). The entry of Jacob into Egypt (Gn. 46:6–7) was the starting-point of the general four centuries of Gn. 15:13 as well as of the more specific 430 years of Ex. 12:40. The Hebrew *MT* form of Ex. 12:40, giving Israel 430 years in Egypt, is to be preferred to the LXX variant, which makes 430 years cover the sojournings in both Canaan and Egypt, because Ex. 12:41 clearly implies that 'on that very day', after 430 years, on which Israel went forth from Egypt was the anniversary of that distant day when the Patriarch Israel and his family had entered Egypt. Hence an interval of 430 years from Jacob's entry till Moses and Israel's departure seems assured. The genealogy of Ex. 6:16–20, which can hardly cover the 430 years if taken 'literally' Western-wise, is open to the same possibility of selectivity as those of Gn. 5 and 11, and so need raise no essential difficulty. Three points are worthy of reflection. First, although Moses is apparently in the fourth generation from the Patriarch Jacob through Levi, Kohath and Amram (Ex. 6:20; 1 Ch. 6:1–3), yet Moses' contemporary Bezalel is in the seventh generation from Jacob through Judah, Perez, Hezron, Caleb, Hur and Uri (1 Ch. 2:18–20), and his younger contemporary Joshua is in the twelfth generation from Jacob through Joseph, Ephraim, Beriah, Rephah, Resheph, Telah, Tahan, Laadan, Ammihud, Elishama and Nun (1 Ch. 7:23–27). Hence there is a possibility that Moses' genealogy is abbreviated by comparison with those of Joshua and even Bezalel. Secondly, Moses' 'father' Amram and his brothers gave rise to the clans of Amramites, Izharites, *etc.*, who already numbered 8,600 male members alone within a year of the Exodus (Nu. 3:27–28), an unlikely situation unless Amram and his brothers themselves flourished distinctly earlier than Moses. Thirdly, the wording that by Amram Jochebed 'bore' Moses, Aaron and Miriam (Ex. 6:20; Nu. 26:59), like 'became the father', AV 'begat', in Gn. 5 and 11, need not imply immediate parenthood but also simply descent. Compare Gn. 46:18, where the preceding verses show that great-grandsons of Zilpah are included among 'these she bore to Jacob'. On these three points, see also *WDB*, p.153. For the date of the Exodus occurring on independent grounds 430 years after a late-18th-century date for Jacob, see below.

The social conditions reflected in the patriarchal narratives afford no close dating, but fit in with the general date obtainable from Gn. 14 and 19 and from the use of the 430-year figure to the Exodus. Thus the social customs of adoption and inheritance in Gn. 15–16; 21; *etc.*, show close affinity with those observable in cuneiform documents from Ur, *etc.*, ranging in date from the 18th to 15th centuries BC.

The great freedom to travel long distances—witness Abraham's path including Ur and Egypt—is prominent in this general age: compare envoys from Babylon passing Mari to and from Hazor in Palestine. For power-alliances at this time, see above. In the 20th and 19th centuries BC in particular, the Negeb ('the South') of the later Judaea supported seasonal occupation, as illustrated by Abraham's periodic journeys into 'the South'. The general results, bearing in mind the traditional figures for the lives, births and deaths of the Patriarchs, is to put Abraham at about 2000–1850, Isaac about 1900–1750, Jacob about 1800–1700 and Joseph about 1750–1650; these dates are deliberately given as round figures to allow for any later adjustment. They suit the limited but suggestive archaeological evidence, as well as a plausible interpretation of the biblical data.

A date for the entry of Jacob and his family into Egypt at roughly 1700 BC would put this event and *Joseph's ministry in the Hyksos period of Egyptian history, during which rulers of Semitic stock posed as pharaohs of Egypt; the peculiar blend of Egyptian and Semitic elements in Gn. 37:1 would agree with this.

b. The Exodus and Conquest

(For alternative Egyptian dates in this section, see the Chronological Tables.) The next contact between Israel and her neighbours occurs in Ex. 1:11, when the Hebrews were building the cities Pithom and Ra'amses in Moses' time. Ra'amses was Egypt's Delta capital named after, and largely built by, Rameses II (*c.* 1290–1224 BC) superseding the work of his father Sethos I (*c.* 1304–1290 BC); this is true of Qantir, the likeliest site for Ra'amses. Rameses I (*c.* 1305–1304 BC) reigned for just over a year, and so does not come into consideration. Before Sethos I and Rameses II, no pharaoh had built a Delta capital since the Hyksos period (Joseph's day); the city Ra'amses is thus truly an original work of these two kings, and not merely renamed or appropriated by them from some earlier ruler, as is sometimes suggested. Hence, on this bit of evidence, the Exodus must fall after 1300 BC and preferably after 1290 BC (accession of Rameses II). A lower limit for the date of the Exodus is probably indicated by the so-called Israel Stele, a triumphal inscription of Merenptah dated to his fifth year (*c.* 1220 BC), which mentions the defeat of various cities and peoples in Palestine, including Israel. Some deny that Merenptah ever invaded Palestine; for Drioton, *La Bible et l'Orient*,

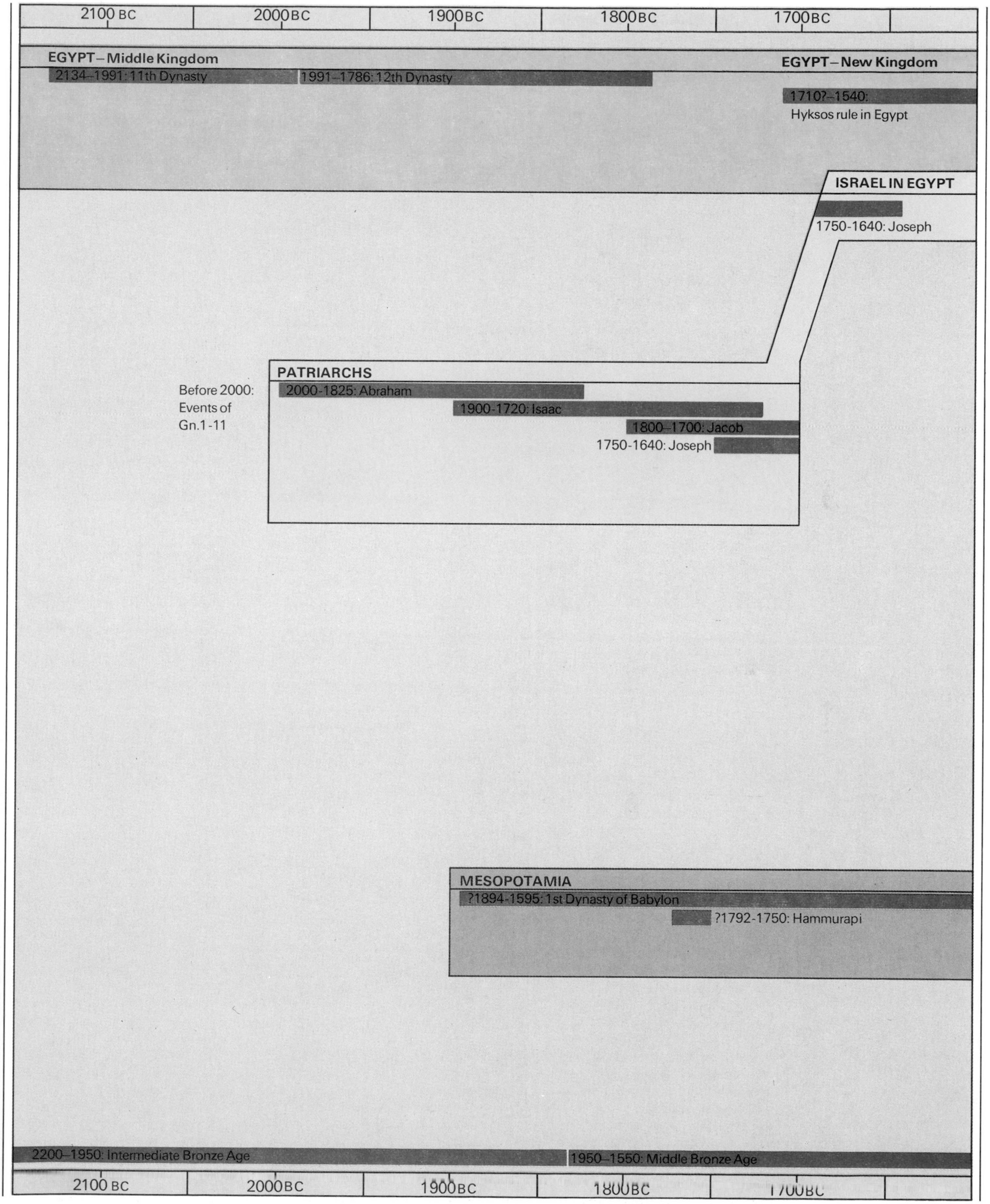
2100 BC
2000 BC
1900 BC
1800 BC
1700 BC
EGYPT – Middle Kingdom
2134–1991: 11th Dynasty
1991–1786: 12th Dynasty
EGYPT – New Kingdom
1710?–1540:
Hyksos rule in Egypt
ISRAEL IN EGYPT
1750-1640: Joseph
PATRIARCHS
Before 2000:
Events of
Gn.1-11
2000-1825: Abraham
1900-1720: Isaac
1800–1700: Jacob
1750-1640: Joseph
MESOPOTAMIA
?1894-1595: 1st Dynasty of Babylon
?1792-1750: Hammurapi
2200–1950: Intermediate Bronze Age
1950–1550: Middle Bronze Age
2100 BC
2000 BC
1900 BC
1800 BC
1700 BC

	1500BC	1400BC	1300BC	1200BC	1100BC

EGYPT—New Kingdom

1552-1305 (or –1294);18th Dynasty,incl.:
1490-1437: Tuthmosis III (or 1479-1426)
1390-1353: Amenophis III (or 1394-1357)
1361-1345: Amenophis IV/Akhenaten (or 1365-1349)
1304-1290: Sethos I (or 1293-1279)

1305-1198 (or 1294-1187):
19th Dynasty, incl.:
1305-1304: Rameses I
(or 1294-1293)
1290-1224: Rameses II (or 1279-1213)
1224-1214: Merenptah (or 1213-1203)

1198-1069: 20th Dynasty, *i.e.*
Setnakht and Rameses III-XI
(or 1187-1069)

ISRAEL IN EGYPT

1280/60 (approx.): The Exodus ●
? 1350-1230 Moses
? 1300-1190 Joshua
1220: 'Israel Stele' (or 1209)

JUDGES 1220-1050

●1240/20 (approx.): Israel crosses the Jordan
1220/00?-1050/45?: Period of the judges
1125?: Deborah and Barak ●
1115?-1075?: Eli's judgeship
1075?-1035?: Samuel, judge and prophet
? 1350-1230 Moses
? 1300-1190 Joshua

MESOPOTAMIA

(Kassite Dynasty)
●1500: Burnaburiash I
1350: Kurigalzu I ●
1345-1329: Kurigalzu II

ASSYRIA

1274-1245: Shalmaneser I
1244-1208: Tukulti-Ninurta I
1224-1219: Adad-shuma-iddina
1124-1103: Nebuchadrezzar I (Babylonia)
1115-1077: Tiglath-pileser I

1550-1400: Late Bronze Age I
1400-1300: Late Bronze Age IIa
1300-1200: Late Bronze Age IIb
1200-1000: Iron Age I

	1500BC	1400BC	1300BC	1200BC	1100BC

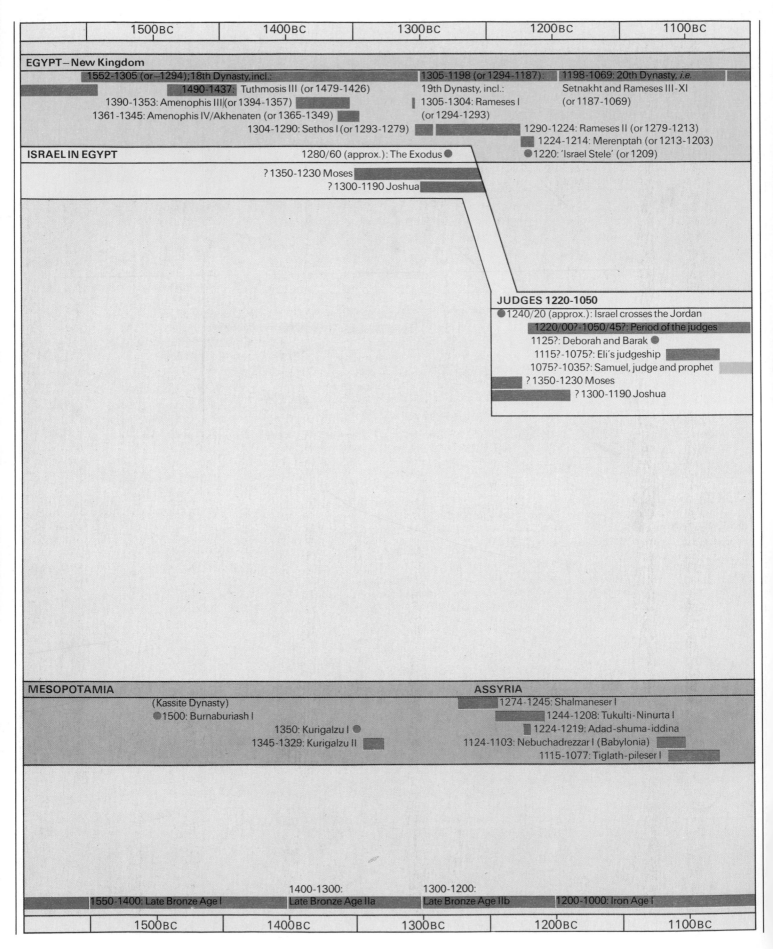

1000 BC | 900 BC | 800 BC | 700 BC | 600 BC

EGYPT – Late Period

1069-945: 21st Dynasty, incl.: Psusennes I, Amenemope, Siamūn, Psusennes II

945-715: 22nd Dynasty, incl.:
945-924: Sheshonq I (Shishak)
924-889: Osorkon I
889-874: Takeloth I
874-850: Osorkon II
767-730: Sheshonq V
730-715: Osorkon IV

716-664: 25th Dynasty
716-702: Shabako ('Shabaka')
702-690: Shebitku ('Shabataka')
690-664: Taharqa ('Tirhakah')
664-656: Tanwetamani ('Tanutamen')

664-525: 26th Dynasty
664-610: Psammetichus I
610-595: Neco II
595-589: Psammetichus II
589-570: Apries (Hophra)
570-526: Amasis (Ahmose II)
526-525: Psammetichus III

UNITED MONARCHY

1050-930
1050/45?-1011/10: Saul
1011/10-971/70: David
971/70-931/30: Solomon

JUDAH

931/30-913: Rehoboam
925: Sheshonq I's (Shishak) invasion of Palestine
913-911/10: Abijam
911/10-870/69: Asa
870/69-848: Jehoshaphat (Co-regent from 873/2)
848-841: Jehoram (Co-regent from 853)
841: Ahaziah
841-835: Athaliah
835-796: Joash
796-767: Amaziah
c. 810-750: Joel
767-740/39: Azariah (Uzziah) (Co-regent from 791/90)
c. 742-687: Micah
c. 740-700: Isaiah
740/39-732/31: Jotham (Co-regent from 750)
732/31-716/15: Ahaz (Co-regent from 744/43; senior partner from 735)
716/15-687/86: Hezekiah (Co-regent from 729)
687/86-642/41: Manasseh (Co-regent from 696/95)
642/41-640/39: Amon
640/39-609: Josiah
609: Jehoahaz
c. 664-612: Nahum
c. 640: Zephaniah
c. 621-580: Jeremiah
c. 605: Habakkuk
c. 587: Obadiah

THE EXILE UNDER BABYLON 720-539

605: Daniel taken
597
597
Many

609-597: Jehoiakim
Battle of Carchemish: and his friends are to Babylon
:Jehoiachin
: 2 Adar (15/16 March), Jerusalem taken by Nebuchadrezzar II. Jews exiled, including Jehoiachin and Ezekiel
597-587: Zedekiah
587: Fall of Jerusalem. More Jews into exile

THE JEWS

c. 520: Haggai
c. 520: Zechariah
538: Zerubbabel, Sheshbazzar and others return to Jerusalem
537: Rebuilding of the Temple begun
520: Temple-building resumed
516: Temple completed, 3 Adar (10 March)

THE DIVIDED KINGDOMS 930-720

ISRAEL

931/30-910/09: Jeroboam I
910/09-909/08: Nadab
909/08-886/85: Baasha
886/85-885/84: Elah
885/84: Zimri
885/84: Tibni
885/84-874/73: Omri
874/73-853: Ahab
853-852: Ahaziah
852-841: Joram
841-814/13: Jehu
814/13-798: Jehoahaz
798-782/81: Jehoash
782/81-753: Jeroboam II (Co-regent from 793/92)
c. 760: Amos
c. 760: Jonah
753-752: Zechariah
752: Shallum
752-742/41: Menahem
742/41-740/39: Pekahiah
740/39-732/31: Pekah
732/31-723/22: Hoshea
c. 755-722: Hosea
722: Fall of Samaria

ARAM (AND PHOENICIA)

?990-965: Hadad/r-ezer of Zobah.
c. 980: Toi of Hamath
(979/78-945/44: Hiram I of Tyre)

DAMASCUS (AND TYRE)

?955-925: Rezon
?925-915: Hezion
?915-900: Tabrimmon
?900-860?: Ben-hadad I, son of Tabrimmon
Either ?860-843: Ben-hadad II, Assyrian Hadadidri, contemporary of Ahab
or: ?900-843: Ben-hadad I, son of Tabrimmon, Assyrian Hadadidri, contemporary of Ahab
898/97-866/65: Ethbaal I of Tyre
843-796: Hazael
796-770: Ben-hadad III/II
?770-750: Dominance of Jeroboam II of Israel
?750-732: Rezin
732: Fall of Damascus to Tiglath-pileser III

ASSYRIA

933: Ashur-dan II
883-859: Ashurnasirpal II
859-824: Shalmaneser III
853: Battle of Qarqar
745-727: Tiglath-pileser III
727-722: Shalmaneser V
722-705: Sargon II
c. 760: Jonah
705-681: Sennacherib
681-669: Esarhaddon
669-627: Ashurbanipal
612: Fall of Nineveh
609/08: End of Assyria

EXILE

BABYLONIA

2nd Dynasty of Isin
5th Dynasty (Sealand)
8th Dynasty (Elamite)

BABYLON

626-605: Nabopolassar
c. 604-535: Daniel
605-562: Nebuchadrezzar II
595-570: Ration-tablets of Jehoiachin at Babylon, 10th to 35th years of Nebuchadrezzar II
c. 593-570: Ezekiel
562-560: Amēl-Marduk (Evil-merodach)
562: Captive Jehoiachin favoured by Amēl-Marduk
560-556: Neriglissar
556: Labashi-Marduk
556-539: Nabonidus. (Belshazzar usually acting in Babylon)
539: Fall of Babylon

PERSIA

539-530: Cyrus
530-522: Cambyses
522-486: Darius I

1000-580: Iron Age II

1000 BC | 900 BC | 800 BC | 700 BC | 600 BC

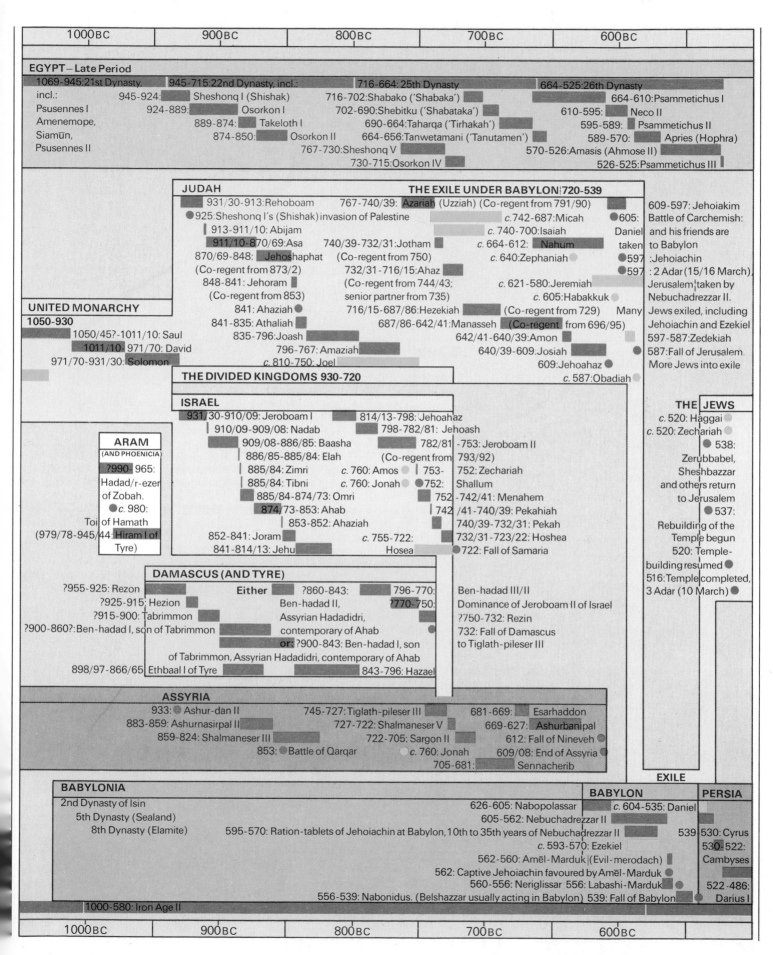

| | 400 BC | 300 BC | 200 BC | 100 BC | |

EGYPT

323/05-282: Ptolemy I Soter
● 320: Judaea annexed by Ptolemy I
285/2-246: Ptolemy II Philadelphus
246-222: Ptolemy III Euergetes
222-205: Ptolemy IV Philopator
204-180: Ptolemy V Epiphanes
198: Palestine passes from Egyptian to Syrian rule till 63 BC

THE INTER-TESTAMENTAL PERIOD

| THE EXILE UNDER PERSIA 539-331 | MACEDONIAN RULE 331-320 EGYPTIAN RULE 320-198 | SELEUCID RULE AND THE MACCABEES 198-63 | ROMAN RULE 63- |

THE JEWS

● c. 460: Malachi
● 458: Ezra goes to Jerusalem
445-433: Nehemiah at Jerusalem

JUDAEA

167-40: Maccabees / Hasmoneans in Judaea
● 167: Mattathias inspires revolt at Modin
166-161: Judas Maccabaeus
160-143: Jonathan Maccabaeus
143-135: Simon Maccabaeus
135-104: John Hyrcanus I
104/03: Aristobulus I
103-76: Alexander Jannaeus
76-67: Queen Salome Alexandra and Hyrcanus II
67-40: Hyrcanus II and Aristobulus II
63: Pompey establishes Roman protectorate ●
40: Herod appointed king of Judaea by Rome ●
37-4: Herod the Great

c. 7 ● Birth of John the Baptist
c. 7 ● Birth of Jesus Christ

150 BC-AD 70: General period of the Dead Sea scrolls

SYRIA

312-281: Seleucus I Nicator
281-261: Antiochus I Soter
261-246: Antiochus II Theos
246-226/25: Seleucus II
226/25-223: Seleucus III Soter
223-187: Antiochus III the Great
187-175: Seleucus IV
175-163: Antiochus IV Epiphanes
163-162: Antiochus V
162-150: Demetrius I
139/38-129: Antiochus VII Sidetes

CHRONOLOGICAL OUTLINE: OLD TESTAMENT

Special note. All dates are best taken as 'about' BC, as the possible variation can run to a century or more in 2000 BC, down to a decade by 1000 BC. Most of the dates for the Hebrew monarchies are quoted in double form, *e.g.* Asa, 911/10-870/69 BC, and Baasha, 909/8-886/5 BC, because the Hebrew year does not coincide with the January to December of our civil year. Apparent variations from biblical lengths of reign are not real but stem from the kinds of regnal-year reckoning then in use.

For other Near Eastern rulers, space and scope forbid any attempt to set forth here the vast amount of documentation and reasoning which underlie the dates given in the preceding tables. From *c.* 900 BC onward, Assyrian, Babylonian and Persian dates are nearly all very closely fixed. Dates for Aramaean kings, *e.g.* of Zobah and Damascus, are approximations based on the OT and Assyr. references and rare inscriptions from Syria itself. Dates for the Phoenicians Hiram I and Ethbaal I (father of Jezebel) are based on synchronisms and regnal years derived from the OT references and Josephus, *Against Apion* 1. 116-126.

The two sets of dates given for later 18th and 19th Dynasties of Egypt depend on the two possible dates offered by lunar data for the accession of Rameses II, *i.e.* 1290 and 1297 BC. At present neither Egyptian nor related Near Eastern data are sufficiently free of gaps and uncertainties to enable a final choice to be made between these two dates; *cf.* M. L. Bierbrier, *The Late New Kingdom in Egypt*, 1975, pp. viii-xi, 109ff.

PERSIAN EMPIRE

486-465/64: Xerxes I (Ahasuerus)
464-423: Artaxerxes I
423-404: Darius II Nothus
404-359: Artaxerxes II Mnemon
359/58-338/37: Artaxerxes III Ochus
338/37-336/35: Arses
336/35-331: Darius III Codomanus
331-323: Alexander of Macedon
580-330: Iron Age III

| | 400 BC | 300 BC | 200 BC | 100 BC | |

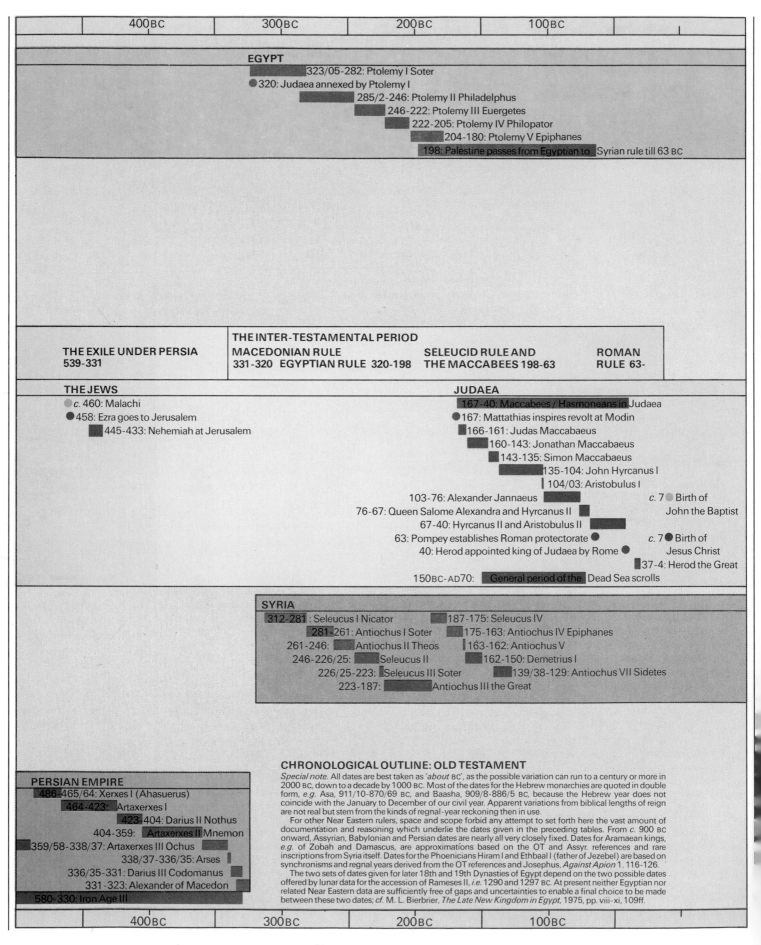

1955, pp. 43–46, the Palestinian peoples were merely overawed by Merenptah's great victory in Libya, which his stele principally commemorates; and the mention of Israel would be an allusion to the Hebrews disappearing into the wilderness to, as the Egyptians would think, certain death. See further, C. de Wit, *The Date and Route of the Exodus*, 1960. The Exodus would then fall in the first five years of Merenptah (*c.* 1224–1220 BC). However, this view is open to certain objections. An inscription of Merenptah in a temple at Amada in Nubia in strictly parallel clauses names him as 'Binder of Gezer' and 'Seizer of Libya'. 'Seizer of Libya' refers beyond all doubt to Merenptah's great Libyan victory in his 5th year, recounted at length in the Israel Stele. Hence the very specific, strictly parallel, title 'Binder of Gezer' must refer to successful intervention by Merenptah in Palestine, even if of limited scope. With this would agree the plain meaning of the Israel Stele's references to Ascalon, Gezer, Yenoam, Israel and Khuru as 'conquered', 'bound', 'annihilated', 'her crops are not' and 'widowed' respectively. Then, the reference to 'Israel, her crops (= lit. 'seed') are not' may reflect the Egyptians' practice of sometimes burning the growing crops of their foes—applicable to Israel beginning to settle in Palestine, but *not* to Israel going forth into the wilderness. Hence, on the likelier interpretation of the Israel Stele here upheld, Israel must have entered Palestine before 1220 BC, and the Exodus 40 years earlier would therefore fall before 1260 BC. The probable date of the Exodus is thus narrowed down to the period 1290–1260 BC. A good average date for the Exodus and wanderings would thus be roughly the period 1280–1240 BC. For views which postulate more than one Exodus, or that some tribes never entered Egypt, there is not a scrap of objective external evidence, and the biblical traditions are clearly against such suggestions.

The figure of 40 years for the wilderness travels of the Hebrews is often too easily dismissed as a round figure which might mean anything. This particular 40-year period is to be taken seriously as it stands, on the following evidence. Israel took a year and a fraction in going from Ra'amses to Kadesh-barnea (they left Ra'amses on the fifteenth day of the 'first month', Nu. 33:3) leaving Mt Sinai on the twentieth day of the second month of the second year, Nu. 10:11. To this period, add at least: 3 days, Nu. 10:33; perhaps a further month, Nu. 11:21; and 7 days, Nu. 12:15; total 1 year and 2½ months' travel; then the subsequent 38 years from Kadesh-barnea to crossing the brook Zered (Dt. 2:14 and Nu. 21:12), Moses addressing Israel in the plains of Moab in the eleventh month of the fortieth year (Dt. 1:3). The function of the 40 years in replacing one generation (rebellious) by another is clearly stated in Dt. 2:14.

The statement that Hebron was founded 7 years before Zoan in Egypt (Nu. 13:22) is sometimes linked with the contemporary Era of Pi-Ramesse in Egypt, covering 400 years from approximately 1720/1700 to about 1320/1300 BC. This Era would then run parallel to the 430 years of Hebrew tradition. This idea, however, is interesting rather than convincing.

The Palestinian evidence agrees in general terms with the Egyptian data. Even allowing for some settlements flourishing earlier (*e.g.* Lankester Harding's temple site at Amman), intensive occupation of the Iron Age kingdoms of Edom and Moab ringed by powerful border forts or blockhouses dates principally from about 1300 BC onwards. Hence these kingdoms could hardly have effectively opposed Israel (as in Nu. 20) before *c.* 1300 BC. Thus again the Exodus is better dated after 1300 BC than before it.

Various Palestinian city-sites show evidence of clear destruction in the second half of the 13th century BC, which would agree with the onset of the Israelites placed at roughly 1240 BC onward. Such sites are Tell Beit Mirsim (possibly biblical Debir/Kiriath-sepher), Lachish, Bethel and Hazor. Two sites only have given rise to controversy: Jericho and Ai.

At Jericho the broad truth seems to be that Joshua and Israel did their work so well that Jericho's ruins lay open to the ravages of nature and of man for five centuries until Ahab's day (*cf.* 1 Ki. 16:34), so that the Late Bronze Age levels, lying uppermost, were almost entirely denuded, even earlier levels being distinctly affected. Thus on some parts of the mound the uppermost levels that remain date as far back as the Early Bronze Age (3rd millennium BC), but the evidence from other parts and the tombs demonstrates clearly the existence of a large Middle Bronze Age settlement subsequently much denuded by erosion. The exceedingly scanty relics of Late Bronze Age Jericho (*i.e.* of Joshua's age) are so few simply because they were exposed to erosion for an even longer period, from Joshua until Ahab's reign; and any areas not occupied by the Iron Age settlement of Ahab's time and after have been subject to erosion right down to the present day. Hence the nearly total loss of Late Bronze Jericho of the 14th century BC and the likelihood of the total loss of any settlement of the 13th century BC.

The walls attributed to the Late Bronze Age by Garstang prove, on fuller examination, to belong to the Early Bronze Age, *c.* 2300 BC, and so cease to be relevant to Joshua's victory. The apparent cessation of Egyptian kings' scarabs at Jericho with those of Amenophis III (died *c.* 1353 BC) does not of itself prove that Jericho fell then, but merely witnesses to the temporary eclipse of direct Egyptian influence in Palestine in the time of that king and his immediate successors, known also from other sources. Of Mycenaean pottery (commonly imported into Syria–Palestine in the 14th and 13 centuries BC), a paucity at Jericho likewise does not prove that Jericho fell earlier in the 14th century rather than well on in the 13th. The fact has been overlooked hitherto that these imported vessels are sometimes very rare on inland Syro-Palestinian sites at the same time as they are common in other settlements at, or readily accessible from, the coast. Thus the equally inland town of Hama in Syria is known to have been occupied during the 13th century BC, but it yielded only two late Mycenaean potsherds—which is less than even the few from Jericho; for Hama, see G. Hanfmann, review of P. J. Riis, 'Hama II', pt. 3, in *JNES* 12, 1953, pp. 206–207. The net result of all this is that a 13th-century Israelite conquest of *Jericho cannot be formally proven on the present archaeological evidence, but neither is it precluded thereby.

*Ai presents a problem demanding further field-research; the parts of the mound of Et-Tell so far excavated ceased to be occupied about 2300 BC. The answer may be that a Late Bronze settlement is still to be located in the neighbourhood, but certainty is at present unattainable.

The Habiru/Apiru, known from the Tell el-Amarna tablets to have been active in Palestine about 1350 BC, are sometimes equated with the invading Israelites ('Hebrews') under Joshua. But 1350 BC is too early a date for the conquest, as already shown above. Further, the term Habiru/Apiru is applied to many other people besides the biblical Hebrews in documents ranging in date from 1800 to 1150 BC and in space as far afield as Mesopotamia, Egypt, Syria and Asia Minor. The Israelites may well have been reckoned as Habiru/Apiru, but obviously they cannot be identified with any given group of these without additional evidence.

(For a new statement of the archaeological and other evidence for a 15th-century-BC date for the Exodus and the Conquest, see J. J. Bimson, *Redating the Exodus and Conquest*, 1978.)

c. From Joshua until David's accession

This period presents a problem in detail which cannot be finally solved without more information. If the 40 years of the Exodus journeyings, the 40 years of David's reign and the first 3 of Solomon's be subtracted from the total of 480 years from the Exodus to Solomon's 4th year (1 Ki. 6:1) a figure of about 397 years is obtained for Joshua, the elders, the judges and Saul. The archaeological evidence indicates roughly 1240 BC for the start of the conquest (see above), giving only some 230 years to 1010 BC, the probable date of David's accession. However, the actual total of recorded periods in Joshua, Judges and Samuel amounts neither to 397 nor to 230 years, but to $470 + x + y + z$ years, where x stands for the time of Joshua and the elders, y for the number of years beyond 20 that Samuel was judge and z for the reign of Saul, all unknown figures. But the main outline of the problem need not be difficult to handle in principle, if viewed against the background of normal ancient oriental modes of reckoning, which alone are relevant. It is nowhere explicitly stated that either the 397 years obtained from using 1 Ki. 6:1 or the 470 plus unknown years of Joshua–Samuel must all be reckoned consecutively, nor need this be assumed. Certain groups of judges and oppressions are clearly stated to be successive ('and after him . . .'), but this is not said of all: at least three main groups can be partly contemporary. So between the evidently consecutive 230 years obtained archaeologically and the possibly partly-concurrent 470-plus-unknown years recorded, the difference of some 240-plus-unknown years can readily be absorbed. The 397 years in turn would then be simply a selection on some principle not yet clear (such as omission of oppressions or something similar) from the greater number of the 470-plus-unknown total years available.

In Near Eastern works involving chronology, it is important to realize that ancient scribes did not draw up synchronistic lists as is done today. They simply listed each series of rulers and reigns separately, in succession on the papyrus or tablet. Synchronisms were to be derived from special historiographical works, not the king-lists or narratives serving other purposes. An excellent example of this is the Turin Papyrus of Kings from Egypt. It lists at great length all five Dynasties 13 to 17 in successive groups, totalling originally over 150 rulers and their reigns accounting for at least 450 years. However, it is known from other sources that all five Dynasties, the 150-odd rulers and 450-odd regnal years alike, must all fit inside the 234 years from *c.* 1786 to *c.* 1552 BC: rarely less than two series, and sometimes three series, of rulers are known to have reigned contemporaneously. The lack of cross-references between contemporaries (*e.g.* among the judges) is paralleled by similar lack of such references for most of the period of Egyptian history just cited.

A similar situation can be discerned in the king-lists and history of the Sumerian and Old Babylonian city-states of Mesopotamia. Hence, there is no reason why such methods should not apply in a work like the book of Judges. It must be stressed that in no case, biblical or extra-biblical, is it a question of inaccuracy, but of the methods current in antiquity. All the figures may be correct in themselves—it is their interpretation which needs care. Selective use of data by omission, as suggested above for the origin of the 397 (of 480) years, is known from both Egyptian lists and Mesopotamian annals, as well as elsewhere. The biblical figures and archaeological data together begin to make sense when the relevant ancient practices are borne in mind; any final solution in detail requires much fuller information.

IV. The Hebrew monarchies

a. The United Monarchy

That David's reign actually lasted 40 years is shown by its being a compound figure: 7 years at Hebron, 33 at Jerusalem (1 Ki. 2:11). Solomon's reign of 40 years began with a brief co-regency with his father of perhaps only a few months; *cf.* 1 Ki. 1:37–2:11; 1 Ch. 28:5; 29:20–23, 26–28. As Solomon's reign appears to have ended *c.* 931/30 BC, he acceded *c.* 971/70 BC, and David at *c.* 1011/10 BC.

The reign of Saul can only be estimated, as something has happened in the Hebrew text of 1 Sa. 13:1; but the 40 years of Acts 13:21 must be about right, because Saul's fourth son, Ishbosheth, was not less than 35 years old at Saul's death (dying at 42, not more than 7 years later, 2 Sa. 2:10). Hence if Jonathan the eldest was about 40 at death, Saul could not be much less than 60 at death. If he became king shortly after being anointed as a 'young man' (1 Sa. 9:2; 10:1, 17ff.), he probably would not be younger than 20 or much older than 30, so practically guaranteeing him a reign of 30 or 40 years. Thus if taken at a middle figure of about 25 years old at accession with a reign of at least 35 years, the biological data suit, and likewise Acts 13:21 as a figure either round or exact. Saul's accession is thus perhaps not far removed from about 1045 or 1050 BC.

b. The Divided Monarchy

(i) *To the fall of Samaria.* From comparison of the Assyrian *limmu* or eponym lists, king-lists and historical texts, the date 853 BC can be fixed for the battle of Qarqar, the death of Ahab and accession of Ahaziah in Israel; and likewise Jehu's accession at Joram's death in 841 BC. The intervening reigns of Ahaziah and Joram exactly fill this interval if reckoned according to the customary methods of regnal counting. Similar careful reckoning by ancient methods gives complete harmony of figures for the reigns of both kingdoms back to the accessions of Rehoboam in Judah and Jeroboam in Israel in the year 931/930 BC. Hence the dates given above for the United Monarchy.

Likewise the dates of both sets of kings can be worked out down to the fall of Samaria not later than 720 BC. This has been clearly shown by E. R. Thiele, *Mysterious Numbers of the Hebrew Kings*[2], 1965. It is possible to demonstrate, as he has done, co-regencies between Asa and Jehoshaphat, Jehoshaphat and Jehoram, Amaziah and Azariah (Uzziah), Azariah and Jotham, and Jotham and Ahaz. However, Thiele's objections to the synchronisms of 2 Ki. 17:1 (12th year of Ahaz equated with accession of Hoshea in Israel), 2 Ki. 18:1 (3rd year of Hoshea with accession of Hezekiah of Judah) and 2 Ki. 18:9–10 (equating Hezekiah's 4th and 6th years with Hoshea's 7th and 9th) are invalid. Thiele took these for years of sole reign, 12/13 years in error. However, the truth appears to be that in fact these four references simply continue the system of co-regencies: Ahaz was co-regent with Jotham 12 years, and Hezekiah with Ahaz. This practice of co-regencies in Judah must have contributed notably to the stability of that kingdom; David and Solomon had thus set a valuable precedent.

(ii) *Judah to the fall of Jerusalem.* From Hezekiah's reign until that of Jehoiachin, dates can still be worked out to the year, culminating in that of the Babylonian capture of Jerusalem in 597 BC, precisely dated to 15/16 March (2nd of Adar) 597 by the Babylonian Chronicle tablets covering this period. But from this point to the final fall of Jerusalem, some uncertainty reigns over the precise mode of reckoning of the Hebrew civil year and of the various regnal years of Zedekiah and Nebuchadrezzar in 2 Kings and Jeremiah. Consequently two different dates are current for the fall of Jerusalem: 587 and 586 BC. The date 587 is here preferred, with Wiseman and Albright (against Thiele for 586).

V. The Exile and after

Most of the dates in the reigns of Babylonian and Persian kings mentioned in biblical passages dealing with this period can be determined accurately. For over half a century, opinions have been divided over the relative order of Ezra and Nehemiah at Jerusalem. The biblical order of events which makes *Ezra reach Jerusalem in 458 BC and *Nehemiah arrive there in 445 is perfectly consistent under close scrutiny (*cf.* J. S. Wright).

The intertestamental period is reasonably clear; for the main dates, see the chronological table.

BIBLIOGRAPHY. *Near Eastern chronology:* W. C. Hayes, M. B. Rowton, F. Stubbings, *CAH*[3], 1970, ch. VI: Chronology; T. Jacobsen, *The Sumerian King List*, 1939—deals with the early Mesopotamian rulers; R. A. Parker and W. H. Dubberstein, *Babylonian Chronology 626 BC–AD 75*, 1956—full dates for Babylonian, Persian and later kings for 626 BC–AD 75, with tables; A. Parrot, *Archéologie Mésopotamienne*, II, 1953—Pt. Two: II deals with Hammurapi and related problems, and discusses the Assyrian king-lists; S. Smith, *Alalakh and Chronology*, 1940—deals with Hammurapi and critical use of Assyro-Babylonian king-lists; E. R. Thiele, *Mysterious Numbers of the Hebrew Kings*[2], 1965. A. Jepsen and A. Hanhart, *Untersuchungen zur Israelitisch-Jüdischen Chronologie*, 1964; J. Finegan, *Handbook of Biblical Chronology*, 1964; V. Pavlovsky, E. Vogt, *Bib.* 45, 1964, pp. 321–347, 348–354. A. Ungnad, *Eponymen*, in E. Ebeling and B. Meissner, *Reallexikon der Assyriologie*, 2, 1938, pp. 412–457—full statement and texts of the Assyrian eponym-lists.

Egypt: É. Drioton and J. Vandier, *L'Égypte* (Coll. *Clio*, I: 2), 1962—standard source of reference for Egyptian history and chronology; Sir A. H. Gardiner, in *JEA* 31, 1945, pp. 11–28—Egyptian regnal and civil years; R. A. Parker, *The Calendars of Ancient Egypt*, 1950—standard work; R. A. Parker in *JNES* 16, 1957, pp. 39–43—on dates of Tuthmosis III, Dynasty 18 and Rameses II, Dynasty 19; W. G. Waddell, *Manetho*, 1948—standard work; R. J. Williams, in *DOTT*, pp. 137–141—gives the Israel Stele.

Palestine: W. F. Albright, *Archaeology of Palestine*, 1956—a very convenient outline of its subject; N. Glueck, *Rivers in the Desert*, 1959—a popular summary of his work on 20th century BC seasonal occupation of the Negeb, continuing his reports in *BASOR*, Nos. 131, 137, 138, 142, 145, 149, 150, 152 and 155; N. Glueck, *The Other Side of the Jordan*, 1940, [2]1970—on the question of Middle Bronze and Iron Age settlements in Transjordan, concerning the dates of Abraham and the Exodus; G. L. Harding in *PEQ* 90, 1958, pp. 10–12—against Glueck on Transjordanian settlement; H. H. Rowley, 'The Chronological Order of Ezra and Nehemiah', in *The Servant of the Lord and Other Essays on the Old Testament*, 1952, pp. 129ff.; J. S. Wright, *The Building of the Second Temple*, 1958—for the post-exilic dates; *idem, The Date of Ezra's Coming to Jerusalem*[2], 1958.

The fall of Judah: D. J. Wiseman, *Chronicles of Chaldaean Kings (626–556 BC)*, 1956—fundamental for its period; compare the following: W. F. Albright in *BASOR* 143, 1956, pp. 28–33; E. R. Thiele, *ibid.*, pp. 22–27; H. Tadmor, in *JNES* 15, 1956, pp. 226–230; D. J. A. Clines, 'Regnal Year Reckoning in the Last Years of the Kingdom of Judah', *AJBA* 2, 1972, pp. 9–34.

K.A.K.
T.C.M.

CHRONOLOGY OF THE NEW TESTAMENT. The early Christians were little interested in chronology, and the scantiness of data in the NT writings and uncertainties as to the interpretation of most of the data which they do provide make NT chronology a thorny subject. It is, moreover, an unfinished subject, since light may yet arise from unexpected quarters. At present we can at most points merely weigh probabilities and say on which side the balance seems to be inclined.

1. Chronology of the life of Jesus

a. His birth

The birth of Jesus took place before the death of Herod the Great (Mt. 2:1; Lk. 1:5), therefore not later than 4 BC (Jos., *Ant.* 17. 191; 14. 389, 487).

According to Lk. 2:1–7, Jesus was born at the time of an enrolment made when Quirinius was governor of Syria. Now Quirinius cannot have governed Syria until after his consulship in 12 BC, and there is no record in Josephus or the Roman historians of his having done so in the interval 11–4 BC. But he was governor of Syria in AD 6/7 and made then the enrolment of Judaea which occasioned the revolt of Judas the Galilean (Jos., *Ant.* 18. 1ff.) This had led some to think that in Lk. 2:2 the enrolment made at Jesus' birth has been confused with this later and better known enrolment. It is possible, however, that *Quirinius governed Syria from 11 BC to the coming of Titius as its governor in 9 BC (so, *e.g.*, Marsh, *Founding of the Roman*

Empire, p. 246, n. 1), and that Augustus decided to make an enrolment after consultation with Herod when the latter visited him in 12 BC. Jesus' birth may thus have taken place in 11 BC. Attempts to determine its month and day have had no real results.

Halley's comet seen in 12 BC was a brilliant spectacle well fitted to be the harbinger of him who was to be the Light of the world. But in antiquity comets were usually regarded as portents of evil. The Italian astronomer Argentieri's conclusion that this comet was the star of the Magi rests on two questionable assumptions, that Jesus was born on a Sunday and that he was born on 25 December.

Recognizing that the word translated 'star' in Mt. 2 denotes only a single star, adherents of the well-known Saturn–Jupiter conjunction theory of the star of the Magi have separated into two schools, the one maintaining that *the* star of Israel was Saturn (so Gerhardt, *Das Stern des Messias*) and the other that it was Jupiter (so Voigt, *Die Geschichte Jesu und die Astrologie*). But it seems unlikely that a conjunction of these two planets would have signified to E astrologers the birth of a king.

b. The commencement of his ministry

Between the birth of Jesus and the commencement of his ministry there was a period of 'about thirty years' (Lk. 3:23). But the commencement referred to there may not be that of the ministry, and it is not known what amplitude the 'about' allows. The assertion, 'You are not yet fifty years old' (Jn. 8:57), suggests that in the course of his ministry Jesus was in his forties, and according to Irenaeus there was a tradition to that effect among the Asian elders. But the Jews' remark may allude to the levitical age of retirement (Nu. 4:3). They are saying to Jesus, 'If you are still, as you claim, in God's service, you cannot be even as much as 50 years old.'

Jesus began his ministry after John the Baptist had begun his, therefore not earlier than the fifteenth year of the reign of Tiberius (Lk. 3:1). For sound reasons the view that this year is reckoned from the time when Tiberius became coregent with Augustus is now generally abandoned. Since Augustus died on 19 August 14, the second year of Tiberius' reign began on 1 October 14 in the Syrian calendar, on 1 Nisan 15 in the Jewish calendar. Consequently in Lk. 3:1 the fifteenth year of his reign means either 27 (1 Oct.)–28, or 28 (1 Nisan)–29. The latter is the more likely, for here Luke appears to use a source derived from a Baptist circle, and in many early writings, pagan, Jewish and Christian, Tiberius' fifteenth year comprises part of 29.

Lk. 3:21 indicates that there was some time between the call of the Baptist and the baptism of Jesus, but its length cannot be determined. The baptism of Jesus was followed by the 40 days in the wilderness, the call of the first disciples, the marriage in Cana and a brief stay in Capernaum. After these happenings, which occupied at least 2 months, Jesus went to Jerusalem for the first Passover of his ministry (Jn. 2:13). Its date may appear to be given by the statement of the Jews, 'It has taken forty-six years to build this temple' (Jn. 2:20), with the remark in Jos., *Ant.* 15. 380, that Herod in the eighteenth year of his reign (20/19 BC) 'undertook to build' this Temple. But he assembled much material before building commenced, and the time thus spent may not be included in the 46 years. Moreover, the statement of the Jews perhaps implies that the building had already been completed some time before this Passover.

c. The end of his ministry

Jesus was crucified when Pontius Pilate was procurator of Judaea (all four Gospels, Tacitus, *Ann.* 15. 44, and possibly Jos., *Ant.* 18. 63f.), therefore in one of the years 26–36. Various attempts have been made to determine which of these is the most likely.

(i) From Lk. 13:1 and 23:12 it may be inferred that Pilate had already been procurator for some time before the crucifixion, and therefore that it can hardly have taken place so early as 26 or 27.

(ii) In many early authorities the crucifixion is assigned to the consulship of the Gemini, *i.e.* to 29. But this dating was by no means accepted everywhere throughout the early church; and there is no proof that, as some think, it embodies a reliable tradition. The writers who give it, of whom Tertullian (*c.* AD 200) is the earliest, belong mainly to the Latin West. The 25th of March, the month-date of the crucifixion given by Hippolytus, Tertullian and many others, was a Friday in 29; but the crucifixion took place at the time of the Paschal full moon, and in 29 that moon was almost certainly in April.

(iii) When Pilate was procurator he offended the Jews by setting up votive shields in the palace at Jerusalem. Herod Antipas took a leading part in furthering a request to Tiberius for its removal. This, some scholars maintain, explains the enmity referred to in Lk. 23:12. Tiberius granted the request; and this, the same scholars maintain, he cannot have done so long as he was under the influence of his confidant Sejanus, an arch-enemy of the Jews. The crucifixion, it is concluded, must have taken place after the death of Sejanus in October 31, therefore not earlier than 32. But the enmity may equally well have been occasioned by the slaughter mentioned in Lk. 13:1 or by some dispute about which history is silent.

(iv) Keim, in his *Jesus of Nazareth*, 2, pp. 379ff., determines 'the great year in the world's history' in dependence on the statement of Josephus (*Ant.* 18. 116) that the defeat of Antipas by Aretas in 36 was considered by some to have come 'from God, and that very justly, as a punishment of what he did against John, that was called the Baptist'. The execution of John, Keim concludes, must have taken place but 2 years previously, in 34, and the crucifixion in 35. But punishment does not always follow hard on the heels of crime; and while the origin of the hostility between Antipas and Aretas may well have been the divorce by the former of the daughter of the latter, there are indications in Josephus that there was an interval between the divorce and the war of 36.

(v) Of attempts to determine the year of the crucifixion the most fruitful is that made with the help of astronomy. According to all four Gospels, the crucifixion took place on a Friday; but whereas in the Synoptics that Friday is 15 Nisan, in John it is 14 Nisan. The problem then that has to be solved with the help of astronomy is that of determining in which of the years 26–36 the 14th and 15th Nisan fell on a Friday. But since in NT times the Jewish month was lunar and the time of its commencement was determined by observation of the new moon, this problem is basically that of determining when the new moon became visible. Studying this problem, Fotheringham and Schoch have each arrived at a formula by applying which they find that 15 Nisan was a Friday only in 27 and 14 Nisan a Friday only in 30 and 33. Since as the year of the crucifixion 27 is out of the question, the choice lies between 30 (7 April) and 33 (3 April).

In the Synoptic chronology of passion week events are assigned to 15 Nisan which are unlikely on that day of holy convocation. The Johannine chronology of that week certainly seems to be in itself the more probable, and until at least the beginning of the 3rd century it appears to have been the more generally accepted throughout the church. Attempts to reconcile the Gospels on this matter have not secured general consent, and discussion of the problem continues. But it is noteworthy that the calculations of the astronomers do not point to a year for the crucifixion that can on other grounds be accepted in which 14 Nisan was a Thursday.

d. The length of his ministry

To know the length of Jesus' ministry is more important than to know when it began or ended. There are three principal theories as to its length.

(i) *The 1-year theory.* Its first supporters considered it a strong confirmation of it that Jesus had applied to himself the Isaianic passage which foretells 'the acceptable year of the Lord' (Is. 61:2; Lk. 4:19). The theory was widely accepted in the ante-Nicene period. Renewed interest in it dates from the 17th century. Among challenging presentations of it are those of van Bebber, *Zur Chronologie des Lebens Jesu*, 1898, and Belser in *Biblische Zeitschrift* 1, 1903; 2, 1904.

(ii) *The 2-year theory.* Its supporters, of whom one of the earliest was Apollinaris of Laodicea, maintain that in the interval from Jesus' baptism to his crucifixion the only Passovers were the three explicitly mentioned in Jn. (2:13; 6:4; 11:55). Little, if at all, in favour in the Middle Ages, this theory now commands a large following.

(iii) *The 3-year theory.* Its earliest known supporter was Melito of Sardis. But its wide acceptance in post-Nicene times and throughout the Middle Ages must be put down mainly to the influence of Eusebius. He rejected the literal interpretation of the word 'year' in the phrase 'the acceptable year of the Lord' and showed convincingly that only a ministry of fully 3 years satisfied the requirements of the Fourth Gospel. In our time also this theory commands a large following.

Because of the Passover of Jn. 6:4, a verse that has excellent manuscript authority, the 1-year theory must be rejected. That a decision may be made between the 2- and the 3-year theories, the interval between the Passovers of Jn. 2:13 and 6:4 must be carefully examined.

Since ordinarily there were 6 months between seedtime and harvest, the words 'There are yet four months, then comes the harvest' (Jn. 4:35) cannot be a proverbial saying, but must relate to the circumstances obtaining at the time when they were spoken. Jesus' return to Galilee mentioned in Jn. 4:43 must then have taken place in winter. That the unnamed feast of Jn. 5:1 was Purim, as, following Kepler, many supporters of the 2-year theory have maintained, is unlikely. Purim was observed in February/March, therefore soon after Jesus' return. But the words 'after this' (Jn. 5:1) indicate that there was a considerable interval between his return and his next visit to Jerusalem. The unnamed feast is more likely to have been the following Passover in March/April or the following Pentecost or Tabernacles. Certain supporters of the 2-year theory, while agreeing that it was the following Passover, identify the latter with the Passover of Jn. 6:4, some maintaining that in Jn. 6:4 'at hand' means 'just past' and others that Jn. 6 should be read immediately before Jn. 5. But 'at hand' in Jn. 6:4 cannot mean 'just past', since, as is clear from the words 'after this' in Jn. 6:1, there was a considerable interval between the events of Jn. 5 and those of Jn. 6. There is, moreover, no textual evidence in support of the proposed rearrangement of chapters. It would appear, therefore, that there was a Passover between those of Jn. 2:13 and 6:4 and consequently that the duration of Jesus' ministry was fully 3 years.

According to the first of the above-mentioned theories, the first and last Passovers of Jesus' ministry were those of 29 and 30, according to the second those of 28 and 30, according to the third those of 30 and 33.

II. The chronology of the apostolic age

a. From Pentecost to the conversion of Paul

When, 3 years after his conversion (Gal. 1:18), Paul escaped from Damascus, an official there, 'the ethnarch of king Aretas', 'guarded the city of the Damascenes' to seize him (2 Cor. 11:32f.). According to some, this official was the sheikh of a band of Arabs, subjects of Aretas, encamped outside the city walls. But Paul's reference to him suggests an official who acted within the city. According to others, Damascus was under direct Roman administration, and this official was the representative of the Arab community resident within it (*cf.* the ethnarch of the Jews in Alexandria, Jos., *Ant.* 14. 117). But this representative would not have had power to guard the city. At this time, then, Aretas apparently possessed Damascus, and this official was his viceroy there. Coins show that Damascus was in Roman hands until 33. When in 37 Vitellius the governor of Syria marched against Aretas, he proceeded not to Damascus but S towards Petra. That he would not have done unless Damascus had still been in Roman hands. Aretas, who died in 40, must then have taken over Damascus between 37 and 40, and Paul's conversion must be dated between 34 and 37.

There are no clear indications that the interval under consideration was long. The stoning of Stephen was, some have urged, an illegal act on which the Jews would not have ventured during Pilate's procuratorship, and consequently must be dated not earlier than 36. But no-one can say when such an outburst of fanaticism may not take place. Others have noted that before Paul's conversion Christianity had spread to Damascus. But as yet there were apparently no organized Christian communities outside Jerusalem. Rapid advance in those early pentecostal days is likely; and while a tradition preserved in Irenaeus and in the *Ascension of Isaiah* that this interval was one of 18 months may be of doubtful value, Paul's conversion seems more likely in 34 or 35 than in 36 or 37.

b. From Paul's first post-conversion visit to Jerusalem to the famine-relief visit

In 37 or 38 Paul visited Jerusalem

40 BC	30 BC	20 BC	10 BC		AD 10	AD 20	

ROMAN RULERS

- 27 BC–AD 14: Caesar Augustus
- AD 14–37: Tiberius

PALESTINIAN RULERS

- 37–4 BC: Herod the Great, king of Judaea
- 4 BC–AD 6: Archelaus, Ethnarch of Judaea
- 4 BC–AD 39: Herod Antipas, Tetrarch of Galilee
- 4 BC–AD 34: Herod Philip, Tetrarch of Ituraea
- AD 26–36: Pontius Pilate, Roman Procurator

THE LIFE OF CHRIST

- 8/7 BC?: Birth of John the Baptist
- 8/7 BC?: Birth of Jesus
- AD 29?: Baptism of Jesus
- AD 29?: Death of John the Baptist

THE ACTS OF THE APOSTLES AND THE EARLY CHURCH

40 BC	30 BC	20 BC	10 BC		AD 10	AD 20	

	AD 40	AD 50	AD 60	AD 70	AD 80	AD 90	AD 100

ROMAN RULERS

AD 14–37: Tiberius

AD 37–41: Caligula

AD 41–54: Claudius

AD 54–68: Nero

AD 68–69: Galba

● AD 69: Otho

● AD 69: Vitellius

AD 69–79: Vespasian

AD 79–81: Titus

AD 81–96: Domitian

PALESTINIAN RULERS

4 BC–AD 39: Herod Antipas, Tetrarch of Galilee

4 BC–AD 34: Herod Philip, Tetrarch of Ituraea

AD 26–36: Pontius Pilate, Roman Procurator

AD 41–44: Herod Agrippa I, king of Judaea

AD 50–c. 93: Herod Agrippa II, Tetrarch of Northern Territory

AD c. 52–c. 60: Felix, Roman Procurator

AD c. 60–62: Festus, Roman Procurator

THE LIFE OF CHRIST

● AD 30: (Passover) Jesus in Jerusalem (Jn. 2:13)

AD 30/31 (December/January): Jesus in Samaria (Jn. 4:35)

● AD 31 (Feast of Tabernacles): Jesus in Jerusalem (Jn. 5:1)

● AD 32 (Passover): Feeding of the Five Thousand (Jn. 6:4) (Feast of Tabernacles): Jesus in Jerusalem (Jn. 7:2)

AD 32 (Feast of Dedication): Jesus in Jerusalem (Jn. 10:22)

● AD 33 (Passover): Crucifixion and Resurrection

THE ACTS OF THE APOSTLES AND THE EARLY CHURCH

● AD 33 Pentecost

● AD 34 or 35: Paul's conversion

● AD 37 or 38: Paul's first visit to Jerusalem

AD 46–47: First Missionary Journey

● AD 48: Apostolic Council in Jerusalem

AD 48–51: Second Missionary Journey AD 50: Paul reaches Corinth

● AD 53: Third Missionary Journey begins

AD 54–57: Paul's stay in Ephesus AD 57: Departure for Troas

AD 58: Meeting with Titus in Europe AD 58–59: Paul in Macedonia and Achaia (and Illyria?)

● AD 59: Paul returns to Jerusalem

AD 59–61: Imprisonment in Caesarea AD 61: Appeal to Caesar and departure for Rome

AD 62: Arrival in Rome AD 62–64: Imprisonment in Rome

AD 62?: Martyrdom of James, the Lord's brother ● ● AD 70: Fall of Jerusalem AD c. 100: Death of John ●

AD 81–96: Persecutions under Domitian

AD 40	AD 50	AD 60	AD 70	AD 80	AD 90	AD 100

for the first time since his conversion, stayed 15 days and then, departing for Syria and Cilicia, remained there until called by Barnabas to assist him in Antioch. A year later the two paid the famine-relief visit to Jerusalem of Acts 11:29f. and 12:25.

Since in Acts 12:1–24 Luke breaks away from his account of this visit that he may bring his history of the church in Jerusalem up to the time of it, it follows that he dates it after the death of Agrippa I. Particulars given in Josephus indicate that he died in 44, perhaps before 1 Nisan. His persecution of the church, which took place at a Passover season, may then be dated 43, but perhaps not earlier, there having apparently been no long time between it and his death.

The famine predicted by Agabus befell Judaea when Tiberius Alexander was procurator (46–48). Conditions were at their worst in the year following the one in which the harvest had failed and immediately before the new harvest was cut. Just then Helena, queen of Adiabene, came to Jerusalem and fetched its inhabitants corn from Egypt. As papyri show, famine conditions obtained in Egypt in the second half of 45. Helena's servants are not then likely to have found corn there until, at the earliest, after the harvest there of 46. The bad harvest in Palestine must then have been that of 46 or that of 47. The collection made in Antioch is likely to have been forwarded only when the Judaean Christians began to feel the need of it, therefore towards the end of 45 or 46. The earlier of these dates makes slightly more room for subsequent events, and is to be preferred.

c. The first missionary journey

Returning to Antioch, Paul and Barnabas soon afterwards, probably early in 46, began the first missionary journey. Sailing to Salamis in Cyprus, they crossed the island to Paphos, where they met Sergius Paulus the proconsul. That he is the Sergius Paulus whom Pliny names in his *Historia Naturalis* as one of his authorities, is uncertain. An inscription in Rome mentions one L. Sergius Paullus as a curator of the Tiber in the reign of Claudius, but that he subsequently governed Cyprus is not known. An inscription found at Soloi in Cyprus ends with the date 'year 13, month Demarchousios 25', but has as postscript the statement, 'He [the Apollonius of the inscription] also revised the senate when Paulus was proconsul.' This Paulus may possibly be the Paulus of the Acts. But Apollonius may not have revised the senate in year 13; moreover, what 'year 13' itself means is also uncertain. Whilst another inscription shows that the year of Paulus' proconsulship was neither 51 nor 52, it is not possible with the information which inscriptions at present provide to determine that year precisely.

In advancing W from Salamis the missionaries are likely to have preached in the towns to which they came. They may then have reached Paphos by autumn and, crossing to Perga, have begun their mission in Pisidia and Lycaonia before winter set in. Since 12 months seem sufficient time for that mission, their return to Antioch may be put in autumn 47.

d. The Apostolic Council

Early in 48, 14 years after his conversion, Paul with Barnabas attended the Apostolic Council of Acts 15.

Some identify this Council with the conference of Gal. 2:1–10, feeling that the objection that in Galatians Paul cannot have left the Jerusalem visit of Acts 11:30 unmentioned is not valid, since he adduces the visit of Gal. 1:18 for one reason and that of Gal. 2:1 for another. To show that he was 'an apostle, not from men nor through man', he states that he had no contact with the apostles until 3 years after his conversion. His purpose in mentioning a later visit to Jerusalem is to assure the Galatians that his apostleship to the Gentiles was then recognized by the leaders of the church. (*COUNCIL, JERUSALEM and *GALATIANS, EPISTLE TO THE.)

Some put the visit of Acts 11:30 before Agrippa's persecution of the church and maintain that the Council of Acts 15 (= Gal. 2:1–10) took place then. But that is chronologically difficult, since Paul's conversion must then be dated not later than 30. Others hold that the Council took place after the first missionary journey, but that it was then, and not earlier, that the famine-relief collection made in Antioch was carried to Jerusalem. Luke, it is assumed, had two accounts of this visit, one originating in Antioch and one in Jerusalem, and wrongly thought that they referred to different visits. J. Knox, in his *Chapters in a Life of Paul* (1954), not only condensed Paul's evangelistic activity into one period (40–51), but placed the Apostolic Council after it. His radical revision of Paul's chronology has not, however, commanded support.

e. The second missionary journey

Paul began his second journey apparently late in spring 48. After visiting the churches in Syria and Cilicia and those already founded in Asia Minor, he entered a new field, 'the region of Phrygia and Galatia' (Acts 16:6). No account is given of his missionary work there. But it must have included the founding of the churches to which the Epistle to the Galatians was later addressed, if (according to the view everywhere entertained until the 19th century) these churches were in Galatia in the ethnographical sense. The founding of them may have occupied Paul until early in 49. The mission which followed in Macedonia and Achaia ended shortly after the Gallio episode (Acts 18:12–17), the time of which can with the help of an inscription be set within narrow limits. In this inscription, a rescript of Claudius to the Delphians dated to his '26th imperatorial acclamation', Gallio is mentioned as proconsul. Now inscriptions (*CIL*, 3. 476 and 6. 1256) show that Claudius was acclaimed for the 23rd time on a date later than 25 January 51 and for the 27th time before 1 August 52. This makes it very probable that he was acclaimed for the 26th time, and consequently that the rescript was written, in the first half of 52. But before then Gallio had investigated the boundary question with which it is concerned and had corresponded with Claudius about it. The rescript must then belong to the second half of Gallio's year as proconsul, and that year must have begun in summer 51. Acts 18:12 indicates that Gallio had been in office for some time before the Jews acted. But they are not likely to have waited for more than, say, a couple of months. Since Paul had been in Corinth for 18 months before this episode, he must have arrived there early in 50; and since after it he tarried in Corinth 'many days longer' (Acts 18:18), an expression which here cannot denote more than 1 or 2 months, he may have returned to Syria before winter 51/52.

On arrival in Corinth Paul found Aquila and Priscilla lately come from Rome because Claudius had ordered all Jews to leave the city. Orosius puts this expulsion order in Claudius' ninth year, 49 (25 January)–50. While there is uncertainty as to where Orosius found this date, it may rest on good authority. It accords well with the conclusion that Paul reached Corinth early in 50.

f. From the beginning of Paul's third missionary journey to his arrival in Rome

Paul's third journey can hardly have begun earlier than 52; and since it included a 3-years' stay in Ephesus (Acts 20:31) and 3 months spent in Greece (Acts 20:3), its end must be dated 55 at the earliest. The coming of Festus as procurator in place of Felix 2 years later (Acts 24:27) must then be dated 57 at the earliest. Since Festus' successor was in Palestine by Tabernacles 62 (Jos., *BJ* 6. 300ff.), Festus, who died in office, must have arrived by 61 at the latest. Of these possible years 57–61, most scholars reject 57 and 58 as too early and, adopting 59 or 60, put Paul's arrival in Rome in 60 or 61.

But, when procurator, Festus permitted an embassy to carry a request to Rome, and there it was granted them 'to gratify Poppaea, Nero's wife' (Jos., *Ant.* 20. 195). Since Nero married Poppaea in May 62, Festus may still have been alive in April. A new provincial coinage introduced in Judaea in AD 59 (the last before the revolt of 66) may point to his entering office in that year.

Paul's return from Corinth to Syria was perhaps occasioned by sickness, and he may not have commenced his third journey until 53. Returning to the region of Phrygia and Galatia, he entered it this time by way of Galatia (Acts 18:23) and, after what from Acts 19:1 appears to have been a considerable mission in central Asia Minor, came to Ephesus, probably in autumn 54. In 57, after the riot there, he left for Troas. Crossing to Europe early in 58, he met Titus, who relieved him of anxiety about the Corinthian church. He then laboured in Macedonia and Achaia and possibly in Illyria (Rom. 15:19) and returned to Jerusalem in 59. In 61, after 2 years' imprisonment in Caesarea, he appealed to Caesar and in the autumn (Acts 27:9) sailed for Rome, arriving there in 62.

Noting that, according to Josephus, Felix on returning to Rome escaped punishment for his misdoings in Palestine thanks to the intervention of his brother Pallas, 'who was then had in the greatest honour by him (Nero)' and that, according to Tacitus, Nero removed Pallas from office soon after his accession, noting also that in the *Chronicle* of Eusebius (Hieronymian version) the coming of Festus as procurator is put in Nero's second year, and regarding the period of 2 years of Acts 24:27 as that of Felix's procuratorship, certain scholars maintain that Festus succeeded Felix in 55 or 56. Objections to this 'ante-dated' chronology are that it allows scant room for the happenings of Paul's third journey, that it assumes the less natural interpretation of Acts 24:27, and that Josephus himself puts the events of Felix's procuratorship in Nero's reign.

g. From Paul's arrival in Rome to the end of the apostolic age

For at least 2 years, *i.e.* until 64, the year of the Neronian persecution, Paul remained a prisoner in Rome. As to what befell him then nothing is known with certainty.

Peter was miraculously delivered out of the hands of Agrippa (Acts 12:3ff.). Later he attended the Apostolic Council and later still visited Antioch (Gal. 2:11ff.). Reference to a Cephas party in Corinth (1 Cor. 1:12) affords no absolute proof that Peter came there. There is sufficient evidence that eventually he came to Rome, but of his association with that city only his martyrdom is reasonably certain.

James the Lord's brother was stoned to death in 62, according to Jos., *Ant.* 20. 200, which passage may, however, be an interpolation. Shortly before the Jewish War (66–70) the Jerusalem Christians fled to Pella. What persecutions of Christians there were in Domitian's reign (81–96) were due apparently to personal enmity or popular fury and not to state action. There is but little evidence that the apostle John suffered martyrdom along with his brother James (Acts 12:2). That, as Irenaeus (*Adv. Haer.* 2. 22. 5) records, he lived on to the time of Trajan, is much more likely. His death (*c.* 100) marks the end of the apostolic age.

For dating of NT books, see articles on individual books.

BIBLIOGRAPHY. Ginzel, *Handbuch der mathematischen und technischen Chronologie*, 1906–14; Cavaignac, *Chronologie*, 1925; J. Finegan, *Handbook of Biblical Chronology*, 1964; U. Holzmeister, *Chronologia Vitae Christi*, 1933; J. K. Fotheringham, 'The Evidence of Astronomy and Technical Chronology for the Date of the Crucifixion' in *JTS*, 35, 1934, 146ff.; E. F. Sutcliffe, *A Two Year Public Ministry*, 1938; G. Ogg, *The Chronology of the Public Ministry of Jesus*, 1940; *The Chronology of the Life of Paul*, 1968; L. Girard, *Le Cadre chronologique du Ministère de Jésus*, 1953; A. Jaubert, *La Date de la Cène*, 1957; D. Plooij, *De Chronologie van het Leven van Paulus*, 1918; U. Holzmeister, *Historia Aetatis Novi Testamenti*, 1938; J. Dupont, *Les Problèmes du Livre des Actes*, 1950; G. B. Caird, *The Apostolic Age*, 1955, Appendix A; J. J. Gunther, *Paul, Messenger and Exile: A Study in the Chronology of his Life and Letters*, 1972; J. A. T. Robinson, *Redating the New Testament*, 1976.

G.O.

CHURCH.

I. Meaning

The English word 'church' is derived from the Gk. adjective *kyriakos* as used in some such phrase as *kyriakon dōma* or *kyriakē oikia*, meaning 'the Lord's house', *i.e.* a Christian place of worship. 'Church' in the NT, however, renders Gk. *ekklēsia*, which mostly designates a local congregation of Christians and never a building. Although we often speak of these congregations collectively as the NT church or the early church, no NT writer uses *ekklēsia* in this collective way. An *ekklēsia* was a meeting or assembly. Its commonest use was for the public assembly of citizens duly summoned, which was a feature of all the cities outside Judaea where the gospel was planted (*e.g.* Acts 19:39); *ekklēsia* was also used among the Jews (LXX) for the *'congregation' of Israel which was constituted at Sinai and assembled before the Lord at the annual feasts in the persons of its representative males (Acts 7:38).

In Acts, James, 3 John, Revelation and the earlier Pauline letters, 'church' is always a particular local congregation. 'The church through-

CHRYSOLITE

See Jewels, Part 2.

CHRYSOPRASE

See Jewels, Part 2.

out all Judea and Galilee and Samaria' (Acts 9:31) may look like an exception, but the singular could be distributive (*cf.* Gal. 1:22) or, more likely, is due to the fact that the verse concludes a section about how 'the church in Jerusalem' (Acts 8:1) was persecuted and its members scattered. Although every local congregation is 'the church of God' (1 Cor. 1:2), Paul makes no use of the term in connection with his doctrine of justification and salvation, and it is conspicuously absent from his discussion of Israel and the Gentiles in Rom. 9–11. But in the later Colossians and Ephesians Paul generalizes his use of 'church' to indicate, not an ecumenical church, but the spiritual and heavenly significance of each and every local 'body' which has Christ as its 'head', and by which God demonstrates his manifold wisdom through the creation of 'one new man' out of all races and classes. In God's purpose there is only one church, one gathering of all under the headship of Christ. But on earth it is pluriform, seen wherever two or three gather in his name. There is no need to explain the relation between the one and the many. Like the believer, the church is both local and 'in heaven'. Heb. 12:23 also has a picture of a heavenly 'assembly' (*ekklēsia*), but this is based on the model of the 'congregation of Israel' at Sinai, and it is uncertain whether the 'first-born' who comprise it are human or heavenly beings. Likewise, Jesus' 'church' of Mt. 16:18 may not be identical with what Paul means by 'church'. Jesus may mean the gathering of his apostles to form, under him, the restored house of David (*cf.* Mt. 19:28; Acts 15:16), by means of which salvation would come to the Gentiles (Rom. 15:12). (In Mt. 18:17, 'the church' refers to the synagogue.) Paul likens the local church to a *body whose members are mutually dependent (1 Cor. 12:12ff.), and to a building being erected, especially a *temple for God's Spirit (1 Cor. 3:10ff.). Metaphors of growth are used, and also the image of a flock being fed (Acts 20:28; 1 Pet. 5:2). 'Church' is not a synonym for 'people of God'; it is rather an *activity* of the 'people of God'. Images such as 'aliens and exiles' (1 Pet. 2:11) apply to the people of God in the world, but do not describe the church, *i.e.* the people assembled with Christ in the midst (Mt. 18:20; Heb. 2:12).

II. The church at Jerusalem

The church in the Christian sense appeared first in Jerusalem after the ascension of Jesus. It was made up of the predominantly Galilean band of Jesus' disciples together with those who responded to the preaching of the apostles in Jerusalem. Its members saw themselves as the elect remnant of Israel destined to find salvation in Zion (Joel 2:32; Acts 2:17ff.) and as the restored tabernacle of David which Jesus himself had promised to build (Acts 15:16; Mt. 16:18). Jerusalem was thus the divinely-appointed locale for those who awaited the final fulfilment of all God's promises (Acts 3:21). Externally, the group of baptized believers had the character of a sect within Judaism. It was called 'the sect of the Nazarenes' by a professional orator (Acts 24:5, 14; *cf.* 28:22), while its own adherents called their distinctive faith 'the *Way'. It was more or less tolerated by Judaism throughout the 30-odd years of its life in Judaea, except when the Jewish authorities were disturbed by its fraternization with Gentile churches abroad. But the essentially Jewish character of the Jerusalem church should be noted. Its members accepted the obligations of the law and the worship of the Temple. Their distinctive belief was that Jesus of Nazareth was Israel's Messiah, that God himself had vindicated this by raising him from the dead after he had suffered for Israel's redemption, and that the 'great and manifest day' of the Lord was even now upon them and would culminate in a final appearance of Messiah in judgment and glory.

Their distinctive practices included a baptism in the name of Jesus, regular attendance at instruction given by the apostles, and *'fellowship' on a household basis, which Luke described as being 'the breaking of bread and the prayers' (Acts 2:41–46). The first leadership of the church was by the twelve (Galilean) apostles, especially *Peter and *John, but soon gave way to that of *elders in the regular Jewish manner, with *James the brother of Jesus as president (Gal. 2:9; Acts 15:6ff.). The latter's presidency extended through most of the life of the Jerusalem church, possibly from as early as the thirties (Gal. 1:19; *cf.* Acts 12:17) until his execution *c.* AD 62. It may well have been associated with the church's Messianic conceptions. 'The *throne of David' was a much more literal hope among believing Jews than we commonly realize, and James was also 'of the house and lineage of David'. Was he thought of as a legitimate Protector, or Prince Regent, pending the return of Messiah in person? Eusebius reports that a cousin of Jesus, Simeon son of Clopas, succeeded James as president, and that Vespasian, after the capture of Jerusalem in AD 70, is said to have ordered a search to be made for all who were of the family of David, that there might be left among the Jews no-one of the royal family (*EH* 3. 11-12).

The church became large (Acts 21:20) and included even priests and Pharisees in its membership (6:7; 15:5). At the outset it included also many *Hellenists, Greek-speaking Jews of the Dispersion who came as pilgrims to feasts or for various reasons were staying in Jerusalem. Such Jews were often more wealthy than those of Jerusalem, and displayed piety by bringing 'alms to their nation' (*cf.* Acts 24:17). When the church adopted the practice of mutual support, a typical benefactor was the Cypriot *Barnabas (Acts 4:34–37), and when a committee was needed to administer the relief the Seven appointed were, to judge by their names, Hellenists (6:5). It was apparently through this Hellenist element that the gospel overflowed the narrow limits of Judaistic Christianity and created fresh streams in alien territories. *Stephen, one of the Seven, came into debate in a Hellenist synagogue in Jerusalem (of which Saul of Tarsus was possibly a member) and was charged before the Sanhedrin with blaspheming the Temple and the Mosaic law. His defence certainly shows a liberal attitude towards the inviolability of the Temple, and the persecution which followed his death may have been directed against this sort of tendency among Hellenist believers rather than against the law-abiding Christianity of the apostles who remained in Jerusalem when others were 'scattered'. *Philip, another of the Seven, took the gospel to Samaria and, after baptizing a foreign eunuch near the old Philistine city of Gaza, went preaching up the coast till he came to the largely pagan Caesarea, where soon afterwards Peter found himself admitting uncircumcised Gentiles to baptism.

Significantly it was Hellenists who went from Jerusalem to Antioch and there preached to Gentiles without any stipulation about the Mosaic law. After Stephen, the Hellenistic element in the Jerusalem church seemed to disappear and its Judaic character to prevail. Some of its members disapproved of the gospel's being offered to Gentiles without obligation to keep the law and went off to press their point of view in the new churches (Acts 15:1; Gal. 2:12; 6:12f.). Officially, however, the Jerusalem church gave its approval not only to Philip's mission in Samaria and the baptism of Cornelius at Caesarea, but to the policy of the new church at Antioch and its missionaries. In *c.* AD 49 a *council of the Jerusalem church was formally asked what should be demanded of 'those of the Gentiles who turn to God'. It was determined that, while Jewish believers would, of course, continue to circumcise their children and keep the whole law, these requirements should not be laid on Gentile believers, although the latter should be asked to make certain concessions to Jewish scruples which would make table-fellowship between the two groups easier, and to keep the law concerning sexual purity (Acts 15:20, 29; 21:21–25). The proceedings reflect the primacy of Jerusalem in matters of faith and morals. Indeed, throughout the first generation it was 'the church' *par excellence* (see Acts 18:22, where the Jerusalem church is meant). This is noticeable in the attitude of Paul (Gal. 1:13; Phil. 3:6), who impressed it on his churches (Rom. 15:27). His final visit to Jerusalem *c.* AD 57 was in recognition of this spiritual primacy. He was greeted by 'James and all the elders' and reminded that the many members of the church were 'all zealous for the law'. Its scrupulosity, however, did not save it from suspicion of disloyalty to Jewish national hopes. James 'the Just' was judicially murdered at the instigation of the high priest *c.* AD 62.

When the war with Rome broke out in AD 66 the church came to an end. Its members betook themselves, says Eusebius, to Pella in Transjordan (*EH* 3. 5). Thereafter they divided into two groups: the Nazarenes, who keeping the law themselves, had a tolerant attitude towards their Gentile fellow-believers, and the Ebionites, who inherited the Judaizing view of obligation to the law. Later Christians listed the Ebionites among the heretics.

III. The church at Antioch

The Jerusalem believers had no exclusive claim on the term *ekklēsia*, despite its OT associations, and the mixed assemblage of Jewish and Gentile believers which was formed at Antioch on the Orontes was without ceremony also called 'the church' there (Acts 11:26; 13:1). Moreover *Antioch, not Jerusalem, was the model of the 'new church' which was to appear all over the world. It was founded by Hellenist Jews. Here believers were first dubbed *Christians, or 'Christites', by their Gentile neighbours (Acts 11:26). Antioch became the springboard for the expansion of the gospel throughout the Levant. The key figure at first was *Barnabas, himself perhaps a Hellenist but enjoying the full confidence of the Jerusalem leaders who sent him to investigate. He is first named among the 'prophets and teachers', who are the only functionaries we know to have been in this church. He brought Saul the converted Pharisee from Tarsus—an interesting solvent for the ferment! Barnabas also led two missionary expeditions to his own country of *Cyprus, and with Paul made the first incursions into Asia Minor. There were important links between Antioch and Jerusalem. Prophets from Jerusalem came up and ministered (Acts 11:27), as did Peter himself and delegates from James (Gal. 2:11–12), not to mention the Pharisaic visitors of Acts 15:1. In return, Antioch expressed its fellowship with Jerusalem by sending relief in time of famine (Acts 11:29) and later looked to the Jerusalem church to provide a solution to the legal controversy. The prophetic leadership of the church included an African called Symeon, Lucius of Cyrene and a member of Herod Antipas's entourage. The author of Acts has been claimed as a native of Antioch (Anti-Marcionite Prologues). But the greatest fame of the church at Antioch was that it 'commended' Barnabas and Saul 'to the grace of God for the work which they . . . fulfilled' (Acts 14:26).

IV. Pauline churches

While *Paul and Barnabas were clearly not the only missionaries of the first generation, we know next to nothing about the labours of others, including the twelve apostles themselves. Paul, however, claimed to have preached the gospel 'from Jerusalem and as far round as Illyricum' (Rom. 15:19), and we know that he founded churches on the Antiochene pattern in the S provinces of Asia Minor, in Macedonia and Greece, in W Asia where he made *Ephesus his base, and, by inference from the Epistle to *Titus, in *Crete. Whether he founded churches in *Spain (Rom. 15:24) is unknown. Everywhere he made cities his centre, whence he (or his associates) reached other cities of the province (Acts 19:10; Col. 1:7). Where possible, the Jewish *synagogue was the jumping-off point, Paul preaching there as a rabbi as long as he was given opportunity. In time, however, a separate *ekklēsia*—the word must sometimes have had the flavour of *synagōgē* (*cf.* Jas. 2:2, RV)—of Jewish and Gentile converts came into being, each with its own elders appointed by the apostle or his delegate from among the responsible senior believers. The *family played an important role in the development of these churches. The OT in Greek was the sacred Scripture of all these churches, and the key to its interpretation was indicated in certain selected passages together with a clearly defined summary of the gospel itself (1 Cor. 15:1–4). Other 'traditions' concerning Jesus' ministry and teaching were laid on every church (1 Cor. 11:2, 23–25; 7:17; 11:16; 2 Thes. 2:15), with fixed patterns of ethical instruction in regard to social and political obligation. It is unknown who regularly administered *baptism or presided at the *Lord's Supper, though both ordinances are mentioned. How frequently or on what days the church assembled is also unknown. The meeting at Troas 'on the Saturday night' (Acts 20:7, NEB) may be a model, and if so would support the view that the use of 'the first day of the week' (or 'the first day after the sabbath') for Christian assembly began simply by using the night hours which followed the close of the sabbath (see H. Riesenfeld, 'The Sabbath and the Lord's Day in Judaism, the Preaching of Jesus and Early Christianity', *The Gospel Tradition*, 1970).

But it is not clear that there was a church at Troas; the occasion may merely have marked the parting of Paul's travelling companions, the time being dictated by travelling arrangements. The first day could not have been observed as a sabbath, however, since it was not a holiday for Gentiles, and Paul would have no binding rules about keeping days unto the Lord (Rom. 14:5). Jewish members must have observed many customs not joined in by their Gentile brethren. The fullest evidence for what took place when a church actually assembled is 1 Cor. 11–14. There was no organizational link between Paul's churches, though there were natural affinities between churches in the same province (Col. 4:15–16; 1 Thes. 4:10). All were expected to submit to Paul's authority in matters of the faith—hence the role of Paul's letters and of the visits of *Timothy—but this authority was spiritual and admonitory, not coercive (2 Cor. 10:8; 13:10). Local administration and discipline were autonomous (2 Cor. 2:5–10). No church had superiority over any other, though all acknowledged Jerusalem as the source of 'spiritual blessings' (Rom. 15:27), and the collection for the saints there was a token of this acknowledgment.

V. Other churches

The origin of the other churches mentioned in the NT is a matter of inference. There were Jewish and Gentile believers in Rome by *c.* AD 56 when Paul wrote his Epistle to them. 'Visitors from Rome, both Jews and proselytes' were present at Pentecost (Acts 2:10), and among greetings in Rom. 16 is one to two 'of note among the apostles', *Andronicus and Junias, kinsmen of Paul's who were converted before him. Is this a complimentary reference to their having brought the gospel to Rome? 'Brethren' came to meet Paul and his party when they went to *Rome, but our knowledge of the church there, its composition and its status, is problematical.

The address of *1 Peter shows that there was a group of churches scattered along the S coast of the Black Sea and its hinterland ('Pontus, Galatia, Cappadocia, Asia, and Bithynia') of either Jewish or Jewish–Gentile membership. These are the parts which Paul was prevented from entering (Acts 16:6–7), which may imply that they were the scene of another man's foundation, perhaps the work of Peter himself. But we learn nothing distinctive of these churches from the Epistle. Oversight and responsibility for 'feeding the flock' in each place was exercised by elders (1 Pet. 5:1–2).

This exhausts our knowledge of the founding of particular churches in NT times. A little more about the W Asian churches emerges from the Apocalypse. It is thought that churches must surely have been founded at least in Alexandria and in Mesopotamia, if not farther E, within the 1st century, but of this there is no certain evidence.

Of the life and organization of the churches generally, we know very little, except for Jerusalem, which was not typical. Yet what we know makes us confident that their unity lay in the gospel itself, acceptance of the OT Scriptures and acknowledgment of Jesus as 'Lord and Christ'. Differences of *church government, forms of *ministry, moulds of thought and levels of moral and spiritual achievement were probably greater than we commonly realize. No one NT church, nor all the churches together—though they formed no visible unity—exercises any authority over our faith today. This divine *authority belongs only to the apostolic gospel as contained in the whole of the Scriptures. (*POWER OF THE KEYS; *PETER, **IV**.)

BIBLIOGRAPHY. F. J. A. Hort, *The Christian Ecclesia*, 1897; R. Newton Flew, *Jesus and His Church*, 1938; K. L. Schmidt, *TDNT* 3, pp. 501–536; *BC*; Hans Lietzmann, *The Beginnings of the Christian Church*, 1937; F. F. Bruce, *The Spreading Flame*, 1958; Gregory Dix, *Jew and Greek*, 1953; E. Schweizer, *Church Order in the New Testament*, 1961; A. Cole, *The Body of Christ*, 1964. D.W.B.R.

CHURCH GOVERNMENT. The NT provides no detailed code of regulations for the government of the church, and the very idea of such a code might seem repugnant to the liberty of the gospel dispensation; but Christ left behind him a body of leaders in the apostles whom he himself had chosen, and he also gave them a few general principles for the exercise of their ruling function.

I. The Twelve and Paul

The Twelve were chosen that they might be with Christ (Mk. 3:14), and this personal association qualified them to act as his witnesses (Acts 1:8); they were from the first endowed with power over unclean spirits and diseases (Mt. 10:1), and this power was renewed and increased, in a more general form, when the promise of the Father (Lk. 24:49) came upon them in the gift of the Holy Spirit (Acts 1:8); on their first mission they were sent forth to preach (Mk. 3:14), and in the great commission they were instructed to teach all nations (Mt. 28:19). They thus received Christ's authority to evangelize at large.

But they were also promised a more specific function as judges and rulers of God's people (Mt. 19:28; Lk. 22:29–30), with power to bind and to loose (Mt. 18:18), to remit and to retain sins (Jn. 20:23). Such language gave rise to the conception of the keys, traditionally defined in both mediaeval and Reformed theology as: (*a*) the key of doctrine, to teach what conduct is forbidden and what permitted (this is the technical meaning of binding and loosing in Jewish legal phraseology), and (*b*) the key of discipline, to exclude and excommunicate the unworthy, and to admit and reconcile the contrite, by declaring or praying for God's forgiveness, through the remission of sins in Christ alone.

Peter received these powers first (Mt. 16:18–19), as he also received the pastoral commission to feed Christ's flock (Jn. 21:15), but he did so in a representative, rather than in a personal, capacity; for when the commission is repeated in Mt. 18:18, authority to exercise the ministry of reconciliation is vested in the body of disciples as a whole, and it is the faithful congregation, rather than any individual, which acts in Christ's name to open the kingdom to believers and to close it against unbelief. None the less, this authoritative function is primarily exercised by preachers of the word, and the process of sifting, of conversion and rejection, is seen at work from Peter's first sermon onwards (Acts 2:37–41). When Peter confessed Christ, his faith was typical of the rock-like foundation on which the church is built (Mt. 16:18), but in fact the foundations of the heavenly Jerusalem contain the names of all of the apostles (Rev. 21:14; *cf.* Eph. 2:20); these acted as a body in the early days of the church, and, despite Peter's continued eminence (Acts 15:7; 1 Cor. 9:5; Gal. 1:18; 2:7–9), the idea that Peter exercised any constant primacy among them is

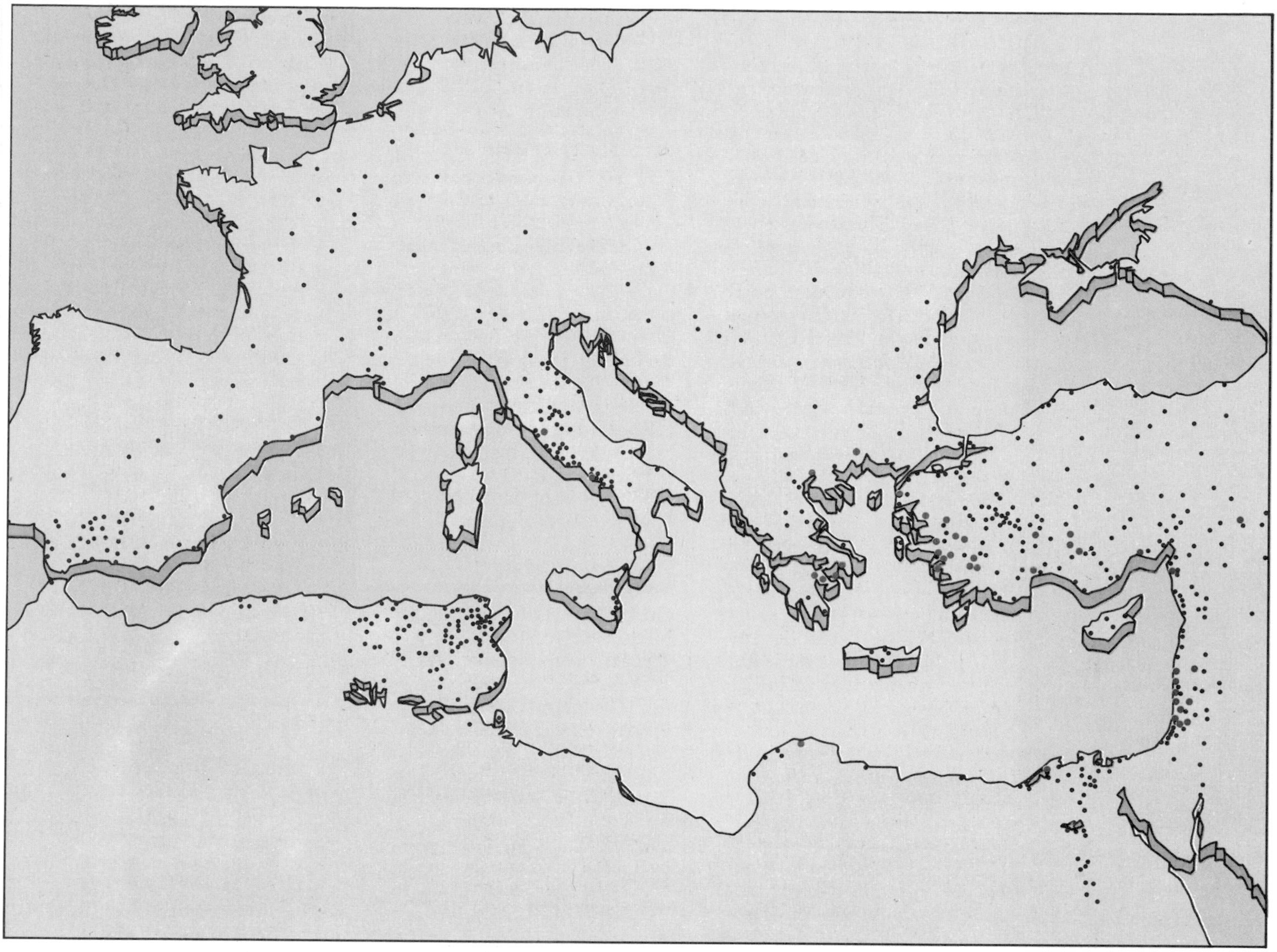

Christian congregations of the 1st cent. AD *(shown in red) and churches founded before Diocletian's persecution of* AD *304 (black).*

refuted, partly by the leading position occupied by James in the Jerusalem *Council (Acts 15:13, 19), and partly by the fact that Paul withstood Peter to the face (Gal. 2:11). It was in a corporate capacity that the apostles provided leadership for the primitive church; and that leadership was effective both in mercy (Acts 2:42) and in judgment (Acts 5:1–11). They exercised a general authority over every congregation, sending two of their number to supervise new developments in Samaria (Acts 8:14), and deciding with the elders on a common policy for the admission of Gentiles (Acts 15), while Paul's 'care of all the churches' (2 Cor. 11:28) is illustrated both by the number of his missionary journeys and by the extent of his correspondence.

II. After the ascension

Their first step, immediately after Christ's ascension, was to fill the vacancy left by the defection of Judas, and this they did by means of a direct appeal to God (Acts 1:24–26). Others were later reckoned in the number of apostles (1 Cor. 9:5–6; Gal. 1:19), but the qualifications of being an eye-witness of the resurrection (Acts 1:22), and of having been in some way personally commissioned by Christ (Rom. 1:1, 5), were not such as could be extended indefinitely. When the pressure of work increased, they appointed seven assistants (Acts 6:1–6), elected by the people and ordained by the apostles, to administer the church's charity; these seven have been regarded as deacons from the time of Irenaeus onwards, but Philip, the only one whose later history is clearly known to us, became an evangelist (Acts 21:8) with an unrestricted mission to preach the gospel, and Stephen's activities were not dissimilar. Church-officers with a distinctive name are first found in the elders of Jerusalem, who received gifts (Acts 11:30) and took part in Council (Acts 15:6). This office (*PRESBYTER) was probably copied from the eldership of the Jewish synagogue; the church is itself called a synagogue in Jas. 2:2, and Jewish elders, who seem to have been ordained by imposition of hands, were responsible for maintaining the observance of God's law, with power to excommunicate law-breakers. But the Christian eldership, as a gospel ministry, acquired added pastoral (Jas. 5:14; 1 Pet. 5:1–3) and preaching (1 Tim. 5:17) duties. Elders were ordained for all the Asian churches by Paul and Barnabas (Acts 14:23), while Titus was enjoined to do the same for Crete (Tit. 1:5); and although the disturbances at Corinth may suggest that a more complete democracy prevailed in that congregation (*cf.* 1 Cor. 14:26), the general pattern of church government in the apostolic age would seem to be a board of elders or pastors, possibly augmented by prophets and teachers, ruling each of the local congregations, with deacons to help, and with a general superintendence of the entire church provided by apostles and evangelists. There is nothing in this system which corresponds exactly to the modern diocesan episcopate; *bishops, when they are mentioned (Phil. 1:1), form a board of local congregational officers, and the position occupied by Timothy and Titus is that of Paul's personal lieutenants in his missionary work. It seems most likely that one elder acquired a permanent chairmanship of the board, and that he was then specially designated with the title of bishop; but even when the monarchical bishop appears in the letters of Ignatius, he is still the pastor of a single congregation. NT terminology is much more fluid; instead of anything resembling a hierarchy, we meet with such vague descriptions as 'he who rules', those who 'are over you in the Lord' (*proïstamenoi*, 'presidents'; Rom. 12:8; 1 Thes. 5:12) or 'those who have the rule over you' or 'your leaders' (*hēgoumenoi*, 'guides'; Heb. 13:7, 17, 24). The *angels of the churches in Rev. 2:3 have sometimes been regarded as actual bishops, but they are more probably personifications of their respective communities. Those in responsible positions are entitled to honour (1 Thes. 5:12–13; 1 Tim. 5:17), maintenance (1 Cor. 9:14; Gal. 6:6) and freedom from trifling accusations (1 Tim. 5:19).

III. General principles

Five general principles can be deducted from the NT teaching as a whole: (*a*) all authority is derived from Christ and exercised in his name and Spirit; (*b*) Christ's humility provides the pattern for Christian service (Mt. 20:26–28); (*c*) government is collegiate rather than hierarchical (Mt. 18:19; 23:8; Acts 15:28); (*d*) teaching and ruling are closely associated functions (1 Thes. 5:12); (*e*) administrative assistants may be required to help the preachers of the word (Acts 6:2–3). See also *MINISTRY and bibliography there cited.

G.S.M.W.

CHUZA
See Joanna, Part 2.

CIRCLE OF JORDAN
See Plain, cities of the, Part 3.

Cilicia, a Roman province important in the vital trade route between Syria and Asia Minor, which ran through the Cilician Gates.

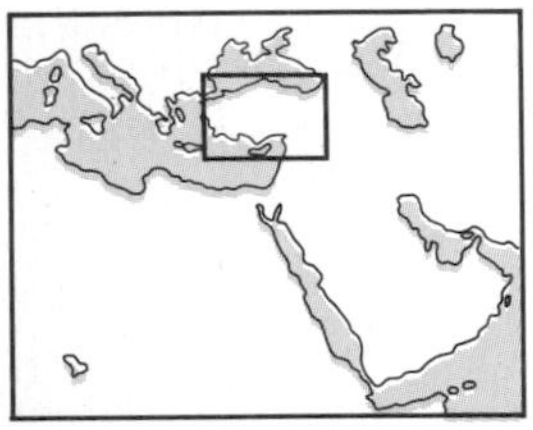

CILICIA. A region in SE Asia Minor. The W part, known as Tracheia, was a wild plateau of the Taurus range, the home of pirates and robbers from prehistoric to Roman times. The E part, known as Cilicia Pedias, was a fertile plain between Mt Amanus in the S, Mt Taurus in the N and the sea; and the vital trade route between Syria and Asia Minor lay through its twin majestic passes, the Syrian Gates and the Cilician Gates. Cilicia was officially made a province before 100 BC, but effective rule began only after Pompey's pirate drive in 67 BC. Cicero was governor here in 51 BC. The province apparently disappeared under the Early Empire, Augustus ceding Tracheia partly to the native dynasty and partly to the adjacent client kingdoms of Galatia and Cappadocia. Pedias, which consists of 16 semi-autonomous cities, of which Tarsus was the most outstanding, was administered by Syria until after Tracheia was taken from Antiochus IV of Commagene in AD 72. Then Vespasian re-combined both regions into the single province of Cilicia (Suetonius, *Vespasian* 8). Thus Paul, its most distinguished citizen, and Luke, both writing accurately of the earlier period, are strictly correct in combining Cilicia (*i.e.* Pedias) in one unit with Syria (Gal. 1:21 variant; Acts 15:23, 41; see E. M. B. Green, Syria and Cilicia', *ExpT* 71, 1959–60, pp. 50–53, and authorities quoted there).

E.M.B.G.
C.J.H.

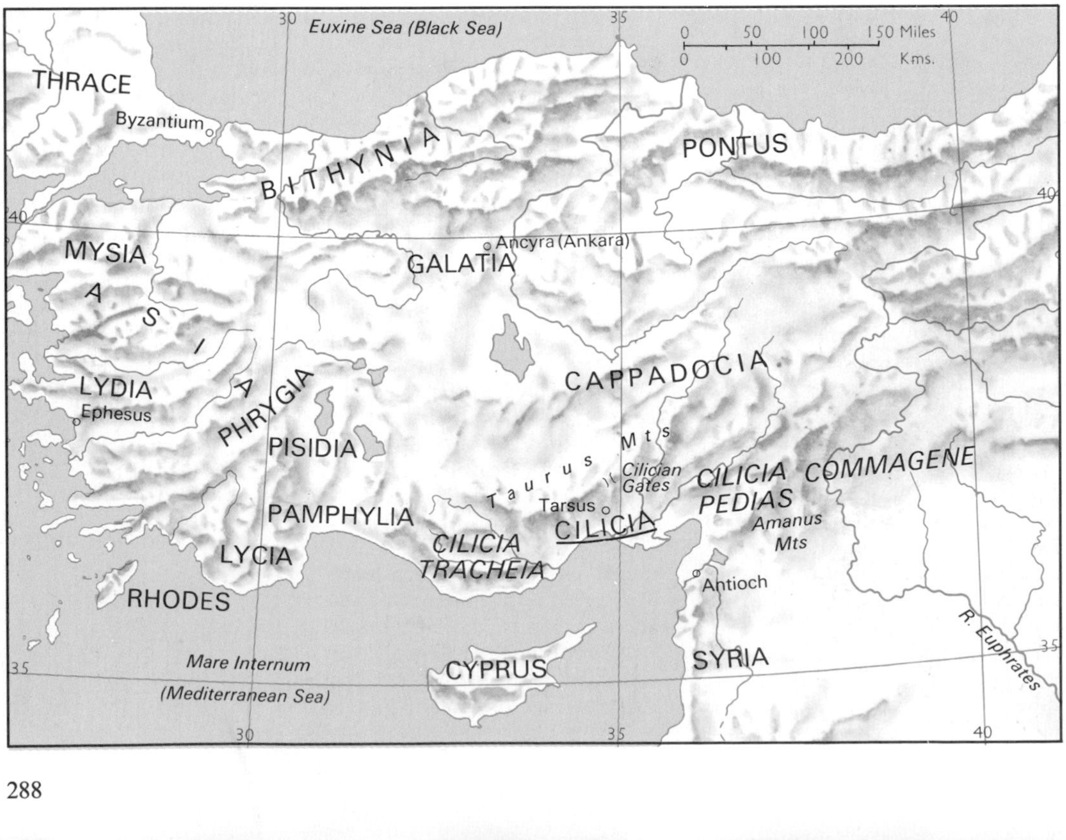

CIRCUMCISION.

I. In the Old Testament

The OT gives a coherent account of the origin and practice of circumcision in Israel.

a. Origin and occurrence

It is alleged that Ex. 4:24ff. and Jos. 5:2ff., along with Gn. 17, offer three different accounts of the origin of the rite, but, in fact, Ex. 4:24ff. can hardly be explained unless infant or child circumcision was already an established practice, and Jos. 5:2ff. states that those who left Egypt were circumcised. Gn. 17 remains as the sole biblical account of the origin of Israelite circumcision. It was integrated into the Mosaic system in connection with the Passover (Ex. 12:44), and apparently continued throughout the OT (*e.g.* Je. 9:25–26). It is a foundation feature of NT Judaism, and occasioned the Judaistic controversies of the apostolic period. The Jews in the NT had so associated circumcision with Moses that they had virtually forgotten its more fundamental association with Abraham (Acts 15:1, 5; 21:21; Gal. 5:2–3). Our Lord had to remind them that it antedated Moses (Jn. 7:22); Paul is emphatic that it was the current understanding of the Mosaic connection which was obnoxious to Christianity (Gal.

5:2–3, 11, *etc.*), and constantly brings his readers back to Abraham (Rom. 4:11; 15:8, *etc.*).

b. Significance of the practice

In Gn. 17 the divine covenant is set out first as a series of promises, personal (vv. 4b–5: Abram becomes the new man with new powers), national (v. 6, the predicted rise of monarchic nationhood), spiritual (v. 7, the pledged relationship of God with Abraham and his descendants). When the covenant is, secondly, expressed in a sign, circumcision (vv. 9–14), it is this totality of divine promise which is symbolized and applied to the divinely nominated recipients. This relationship of circumcision to foregoing promise shows that the rite signifies the gracious movement of God to man, and only derivatively, as we shall see, the consecration of man to God. This truth underlies Jos. 5:2ff.: while the nation walked in the wilderness under God's displeasure (*cf.* Nu. 14:34), the covenant was, as it were, in suspended animation, and circumcision lapsed. Or again, when Moses spoke of possessing 'uncircumcised lips' (Ex. 6:12, 30; *cf.* Je. 6:10), only the gift of God's word could remedy it. Further, the NT speaks of circumcision as a 'seal' (Rom. 4:11) upon God's gift of righteousness. Circumcision, therefore, is the token of that work of grace whereby God chooses out and marks men for his own.

The covenant of circumcision operates on the principle of the spiritual union of the household in its head. The covenant is 'between me and you and your descendants after you' (Gn. 17:7), and vv. 26–27 notably express the same truth: 'Abraham . . . Ishmael . . . and all the men of his house . . . were circumcised with him.' Thus, from its inception, infant circumcision was the distinctive Israelite custom, not derived from Egyptian or other practice, and contrasting sharply with the puberty rites of other nations: the latter point to social acknowledgment of adult status, the former to a status before God and a prevenience of divine grace.

Those who thus became members of the covenant were expected to show it outwardly by obedience to God's law, expressed to Abram in its most general form, 'Walk before me, and be blameless' (Gn. 17:1). The relation between circumcision and obedience remains a biblical constant (Je. 4:4; Rom. 2:25–29; *cf.* Acts 15:5; Gal. 5:3). In this respect, circumcision involves the idea of consecration to God, but not as its essence. Circumcision embodies and applies covenant promises and summons to a life of covenant obedience. The blood which is shed in circumcision does not express the desperate lengths to which a man must go in self-consecration, but the costly demand which God makes of those whom he calls to himself and marks with the sign of his covenant.

This response of obedience was not always forthcoming, and, though sign and thing signified are identified in Gn. 17:10, 13–14, the Bible candidly allows that it is possible to possess the sign and nothing more, in which case it is spiritually defunct and, indeed, condemnatory (Rom. 2:27). The OT plainly teaches this, as it calls for the reality appropriate to the sign (Dt. 10:16; Je. 4:4), warns that in the absence of the reality the sign is nothing (Je. 9:25), and foresees the circumcising of the heart by God (Dt. 30:6).

II. In the New Testament

The NT is unequivocal: without obedience, circumcision becomes uncircumcision (Rom. 2:25–29); the outward sign fades into insignificance when compared with the realities of keeping the commandments (1 Cor. 7:18–19), faith working by love (Gal. 5:6) and a new creation (Gal. 6:15). Nevertheless, the Christian is not at liberty to scorn the sign. Although, in so far as it expressed salvation by works of law, the Christian must shun it (Gal. 5:2ff.), yet in its inner meaning he needs it (Col. 2:13; *cf.* Is. 52:1). Consequently, there is a 'circumcision of Christ', the 'putting off (of) the body (and not only part) of the . . . flesh', a spiritual transaction not made with hands, a relation to Christ in his death and resurrection, sealed by the initiatory ordinance of the new covenant (Col. 2:11–12).

In Phil. 3:2 Paul uses the deliberately offensive word *katatomē*, 'those who mutilate the flesh' (RSV), 'the concision' (AV). He is not defaming circumcision on Christians (*cf.* Gal. 5:12). The cognate verb (*katatemnō*) is used (Lv. 21:5, LXX) of forbidden heathen mutilations. To Christians, who are 'the circumcision' (Phil. 3:3), the enforcement of the outmoded sign is tantamount to a heathenish gashing of the body.

BIBLIOGRAPHY. L. Koehler, *Hebrew Man*, 1956, pp. 37ff.; G. A. F. Knight, *A Christian Theology of the Old Testament*, 1959, pp. 238f.; G. R. Beasley-Murray, *Baptism in the New Testament*, 1962; P. Marcel, *The Biblical Doctrine of Infant Baptism*, 1953, pp. 82ff.; J. P. Hyatt, 'Circumcision', *IDB*; J. Sasson, *JBL* 85, 1966, pp. 473ff.; H. C. Hahn, 'Circumcision', *NIDNTT* 1, pp. 307–312. J.A.M.

CISTERN (Heb. *bôr* or *bō'r*, from *bā'ar*, 'to dig or bore'), a subterranean reservoir for storing water which was collected from rainfall or from a spring. In contrast, the cylindrical well (b^e*'ēr*) received water from percolation through its walls. However, the term *bôr* is translated *'well' or *'pit' many times and 'cistern' only 5 times

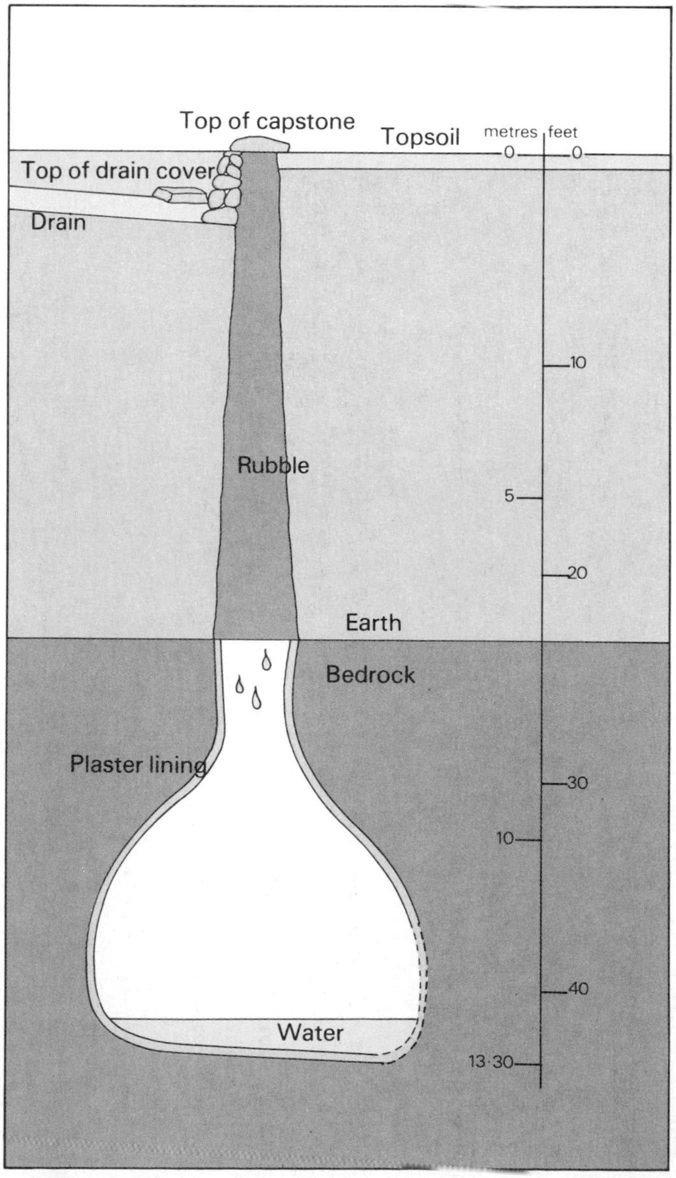

Sectional drawing of a cistern, fed by underground drain, excavated at Tell Ta'annek. Water would be drawn by using a bucket.

in AV and 14 times in RSV. Many cisterns are found in Palestine, where rainfall is scarce from May to September. They are usually pear-shaped with a small opening at the top which can be sealed to prevent accidents (Ex. 21:33–34) and unauthorized use. Both Joseph (Gn. 37:22) and Jeremiah (Je. 38:6) nearly perished in such pits (*cf.* Zc. 9:11). Most homes in Jerusalem had private cisterns (2 Ki. 18:31; *cf.* Pr. 5:15); but there were also huge public cisterns, one in the Temple area having a capacity of over 2 million gallons. By *c.* 1500 BC cisterns were cemented (P. W. Lapp, *BASOR* 195, 1969, pp. 2–49), thus permitting large settlements in the barren Negeb region (*cf.* 2 Ch. 26:10), especially in Nabataean and Byzantine times. *Cf.* N. Glueck, *Rivers in the Desert*, 1959, p. 94; S. M. Paul and W. G. Dever, *Biblical Archaeology*, 1974, pp. 127–162; *EJ*, 5, pp. 578f. J.C.W.

Cistern with layer of plaster as waterproofing. Masada. (RP)

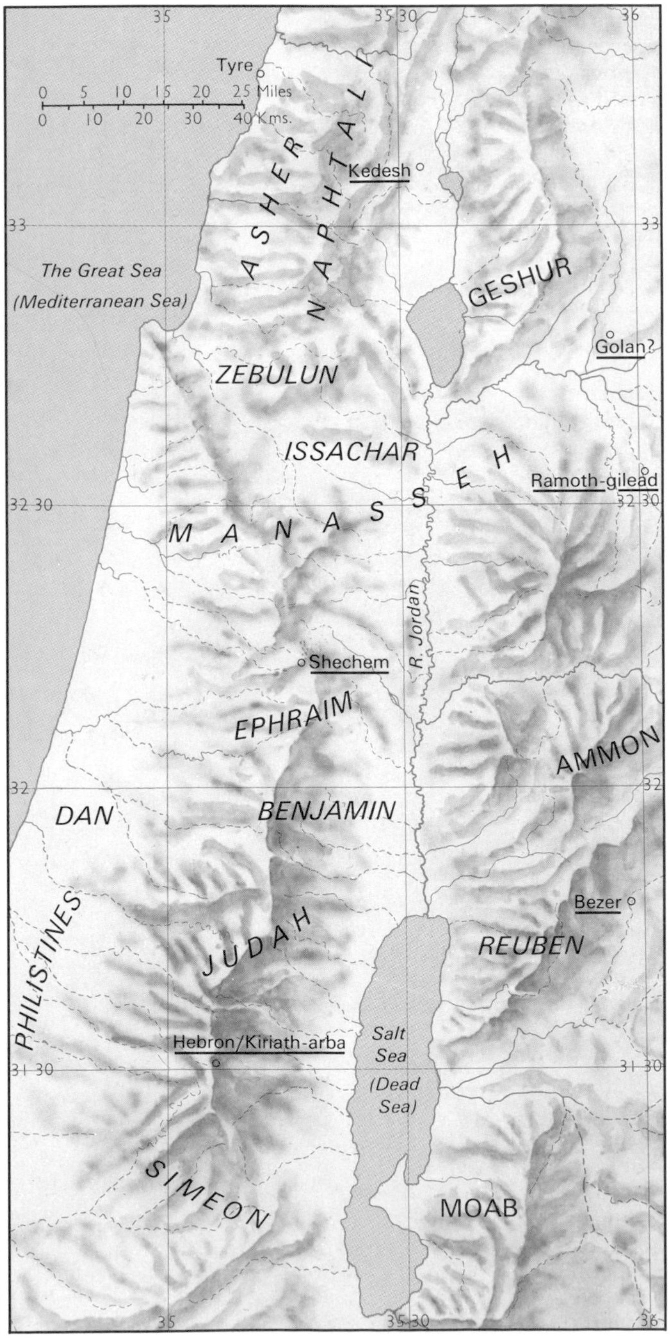

The cities of refuge (Jos. 20).

CITIES OF REFUGE. These were places of asylum mentioned principally in Nu. 35:9–34 and Jos. 20:1–9 (where they are named). They are also mentioned in Nu. 35:6; Jos. 21:13, 21, 27, 32, 38; 1 Ch. 6:57, 67. From these it appears that they were among the cities of the Levites. Dt. 4:41–43; 19:1–13 deal with the institution indicated by this name (*cf.* Ex. 21:12–14).

In Israel's public life the law of retribution was to be applied, and is, moreover, specified in the *lex talionis* (see Ex. 21:23–25, *etc.*) which particularly applied in cases of bloodshed (see Gn. 9:5f.; Ex. 21:12; Lv. 24:17, *etc.*; *cf.* also Dt. 21:1–9). In ancient Israel at least, the duty of punishing the slayer rested upon the *gō'ēl*, the nearest male relative (*AVENGER OF BLOOD). A distinction was made between slaying a man purposely or unawares. The wilful murderer was to be killed, while the unintentional murderer could find asylum in one of the cities of refuge. It may be said that the institution of the cities of refuge mainly served to prevent excesses which might develop from the execution of what is usually called the 'blood-feud'.

In 'the book of the covenant', Israel's oldest collection of laws, there is already a stipulation concerning this matter (Ex. 21:12–14). Perhaps the tendency of this regulation can be described as follows. Israel knew the ancient practice, which also prevailed among other nations, of regarding the altar or the sanctuary as an asylum. Here it is stipulated that the wilful slayer shall not find a refuge near the altar, though the unintentional slayer may do so. But the altar may be at a great distance, and, moreover, he cannot stay permanently near the altar, in the sanctuary. So the Lord announces that he will make further provisions for this matter. The curious expression 'God let him fall into his hand' has been interpreted in the sense that the unintentional murderer is an instrument of God, and accordingly it is only natural that God should look after his protection. Examples of the altar as an asylum in Israel occur in 1 Ki. 1:50–53; 2:28–34, while expressions such as those used in Pss. 27:4–6; 61:4; Ob. 17 show that this practice was well known in Israel.

There are characteristic differences between the two principal groups of regulations concerning the cities of refuge, Nu. 35:9ff.; Dt. 19:1ff. (*cf.* Dt. 4:41–43). As to the regulations of Nu. 35, which were also given in the plains of Moab (v. 1), we should note the following. The term 'cities of refuge, cities where a person is received (?)' is used. In due course Israel is to appoint three cities on the E side of Jordan, and three cities on the W side (vv. 13ff.), which cities are to be among the cities of the Levites (v. 6). The 'congregation' is to pronounce the final judgment (vv. 12, 24). (During the wanderings through the desert this body made decisions in such cases. Here no further stipulation is made as to what body is to act in a similar capacity once Israel had settled in Canaan.) In vv. 16–23 criteria are given to define accurately whether one has to do with intentional or unintentional murder. The unintentional slayer is to remain in the city until the death of the high priest (vv. 25, 28, 32). In this connection the stay receives the character of an exile, of penance (vv. 28, 32). Note also the stipulations of vv. 30–32, with the important motivation, given in vv. 33f.

Dt. 4:41–43 narrates how 'Moses set apart three cities in the east beyond the Jordan'. Dt. 19:1ff. stipulates that, after the conquest of Canaan, three cities of refuge shall be appointed on the W side of Jordan, and another three in case of a further extension of Israel's territory (the last regulation was apparently never carried out). It is emphasized that the Israelites should take care that a slayer who killed ignorantly was within easy reach of a city of refuge (vv. 3, 6ff.). To indicate the difference between a wilful and unintentional murder, an example is given in v. 5. The elders of the slayer's dwelling-place are to make the final decision (v. 12).

According to Jos. 20, the following cities of refuge were appointed during Joshua's lifetime: Kedesh, Shechem, Kiriath-arba (= Hebron), Bezer, Ramoth and Golan. Jos. 20 assumes as known both the regulations of Nu. 35 and of Dt. 19. A new feature here is that the elders of the cities of refuge also have a responsibility (vv. 4–5).

Nothing is known about the putting into practice of the right of asylum. Except for 1 Ki. 1:50–53; 2:28–34, it is not mentioned, which *per se* need not surprise us. It is possible that, as the central authority established itself more firmly, the right of asylum decreased in significance.

Concerning the dating of these passages and the historicity of the facts they contain, Wellhausen and the scholars who follow him hold them to be the result of a development, as follows. Originally the sanctuary was the asylum. In the 7th century BC the authors of Deuteronomy aimed at the centralization of the cult. In this connection they secularized the right of asylum, and replaced the sanctuaries by a few cities and superseded the priests by the elders. Nu. 35 contains a project dating from the exilic or post-exilic time which was never carried out. Jos. 20 dates from an even later period. Nowadays many scholars are of the opinion that this institution dates from a much older time, *e.g.* from the time of David (Albright and others).

There seems to be no reason why we should not accept that the regulations in question date, at least in essence, from Moses' time. It is obvious that this cannot be discussed as an isolated question, for it is closely connected with the dating of sources. Suffice it to say here that only in ancient times did these six cities belong to Israel's territory, Golan already being lost shortly after Solomon's death, and Bezer about 850 BC (according to the *MOABITE STONE).

Two questions remain for discussion. First, why was the unintentional slayer to remain in the city of refuge till the death of the high priest? One answer given is that his guilt devolved upon the high priest and was atoned for by the (untimely) death of the high priest. A similar view occurs already in the Talmud (*Makkoth* 2b) and is still defended, among others by Nicolsky and Greenberg. This view has something attractive about it (*cf.* Ex. 28:36–38), but is still questionable. It is better to take the view that by the death of the high priest a definite period was concluded. Perhaps it is allowed, with van Oeveren, to work out this view in the following way: the cities of refuge were among the cities of the Levites; so the unintentional slayer, dwelling in a city of refuge, was linked up with the tribe of Levi; the death of the high priest, the chief of the tribe of Levi, unfastened this link.

Secondly, can it be stated with regard to the unintentional slayer that justice gave way to mercy? Probably the best thing to say is that the question cannot be answered, because the OT does not distinguish between mercy and justice in the way we do. But the pronouncement that the decrees which the Lord gave to Israel were good and just (Dt. 4:6ff., *etc.*) certainly applies to the regulations concerning the cities of refuge.

The answer to these two questions affects the extent to which we are to regard the regulations about the cities of refuge as Christological. It is undoubtedly legitimate to call Christ our Refuge. But to work out the parallel between Christ and the cities of refuge in further details is precarious.

For the opinions of later Judaism on these regulations, see the Mishnah tractate *Makkoth* 2, and the tractate in the Talmud associated with it (*cf.* also Löhr, p. 34).

BIBLIOGRAPHY. N. M. Nicolsky, 'Das Asylrecht in Israel', *ZAW* 48, 1930, pp. 146–175; M. Löhr, *Das Asylwesen im Alten Testament*, 1930; C. L. Feinberg, 'The Cities of Refuge', *BS* 103, 1946, pp. 411–416; 104, 1947, pp. 35–48; W. F. Albright, *Archaeology and the Religion of Israel*, 1956, pp. 120–125; R. de Vaux, *Ancient Israel*, 1961, pp. 160–163; M. Greenberg, 'The Biblical Conception of Asylum', *JBL* 78, 1959, pp. 125–132; B. van Oeveren, *De Vrijsteden in het Oude Testament*, 1968 (with a summary in German, pp. 257–260, and with an extensive bibliography). N.H.R.

CITRON
See Trees (Thyine), Part 3.

CITY.

I. In the Old Testament

The word *îr* occurs 1,090 times in the OT and describes a wide variety of permanent settlements. It does not appear to have regard to size or rights (*cf.* Gn. 4:17; 19:29; 24:10; Ex. 1:11; Lv. 25:29, 31; 1 Sa. 15:5; 20:6; 2 Ki. 17:6; Je. 51:42–43, 58; Jon. 3:3; Na. 3:1).

There are other words used in the Bible for city. Of the Hebrew words we note *qiryâ* (Ezr. 4:10), *qiryā'* (Ezr. 4:15, *etc.*), *qereṯ* (Jb. 29:7; Pr. 8:3; 9:3, *etc.*), *ša'ar*, literally 'gate', but used frequently for city or town in Deuteronomy (5:14; 12:15; 14:27–28).

A city was either walled or unwalled. The spies that Moses sent to Canaan were told to report on this point (Nu. 13:19, 28). In their report they spoke of cities which were 'walled and very great' (*cf.* Dt. 1:28, 'walled up to heaven'). Many of the Canaanite cities which the Israelites encountered at the time of the Conquest were, in fact, walled. Modern excavation of several ancient cities gives information about the precise nature of the walls and the area enclosed. Excavation reports for specific cities should be consulted in each case.

The word *ḥāṣēr* seems to be used specifically for the open village in distinction from *îr*, which was often walled. In order to be specific, a city defended by solid structures was called *'îr mibṣar*, a fortified city (Je. 34:7).

In the normal city there was a central area where commerce and law were transacted, and round about were the 'suburbs' (*migrāš*, 'pasture grounds'), where farming was carried on (Nu. 35:2; Jos. 14:4; 1 Ch. 5:16; 6:55; Ezk. 48:15, 17). There seem to have been villages as well in the general neighbourhood of the bigger towns, which were described as 'daughters', *bānôṯ*, and which were probably unwalled (Nu. 21:25; 32:42; 2 Ch. 28:18; Ne. 11:25–31). Where the central city was walled it was the place of shelter for the entire surrounding population in times of danger (*FORTIFICATION AND SIEGECRAFT). In pre-Israelite times many of these areas with their walled city were small city-states ruled by a 'king', *meleḵ*, and owing allegiance to some great power such as Egypt.

There are numerous references to non-Israelite cities in the OT, among the most famous being Pithom and Ra'amses, the store-cities of the pharaoh (Ex. 1:11), the cities of the Philistines, which were really city-states of the Greek type (1 Sa. 6:17–18), Damascus, the Syrian capital, *Nineveh, 'an exceedingly great city, three days' journey in breadth' (Jon. 3:3), *Babylon the great (Dn. 4:30; Je. 51:37, 43, 58), *Susa (Shushan), the capital of Persia (Est. 1:2). Excavation and general archaeological research have given us much significant information about some of these cities. Thus Nineveh was surrounded by walls of nearly 16 km circumference. In the neighbourhood were two other Assyrian cities, Khorsabad and Nimrud (*CALAH), both of some size. In addition, there were numerous villages in the area. The extent of the city that was in the mind of the writer of Jonah may not be quite clear today, but there is good reason to think of 'an exceedingly great city'. Again Babylon was a remarkable city with great fortifications and palaces.

Inside the walls of any of these ancient cities would be found the houses of the citizens, possibly the large houses of the nobles, and even a *palace. Excavations in Palestine have given a good idea of the lay-out of these cities. The gates of the city, of which many have now been excavated (*e.g.* Megiddo, Hazor, Gezer, Tell Sheba) were the place of commerce and law, and here the judges sat to give their decisions (Gn. 19:1; 2 Sa. 15:2–6; 1 Ki. 22:10; Am. 5:10, 12, 15). The number of gates varied. In Jericho there seems to have been only one gate, but in other cities there may have been several. The ideal city of Ezekiel had 12 gates (Ezk. 48:30–35; *cf.* Rev. 21:12–13). The area behind the walls was normally carefully planned with a ring-road all around the city and houses behind it, and other roads farther inside. Houses, public buildings, shrines or temples, and open spaces can be discerned on the excavators' plans.

Sometimes cities had a specific purpose. The Egyptian cities of Pithom and Ra'amses were store cities (Ex. 1:11) or 'treasure' cities.

Solomon had cities for 'chariots and for horsemen' (1 Ki. 4:26; 9:19) as well as cities for stores. We judge that these were for defence and for grain storage. Excavations at Megiddo were particularly instructive in this regard, for they revealed that this town had at one time a huge grain storage-bin of some 500,000 litres capacity. A common picture brought to light by excavation is of a city gate with storehouses not far from the gate (*e.g.* Tell Sheba).

At times cities were used in bargaining between states, and when treaties were drawn up and boundaries were adjusted there was often a transfer of cities from one state to another (1 Ki. 9:10–14; 20:34). At times, also, cities formed part of a marriage dowry (1 Ki. 9:16). Again, people of neighbouring states were always anxious to gain access to the markets of their neighbours and to 'make streets' in their cities (1 Ki. 20:34), where trade could be carried on.

In any discussion of the term 'city' in reference to the Bible *Jerusalem should receive a special place, for among the cities of Israel Jerusalem predominated as the seat of the house of David and the centre of the religious life of the nation. It is termed the 'city of David' and the 'city of God', terms which have a close association with the pre-exilic worship of Israel and her king and which are reflected in many of the psalms. The character of Jerusalem in the last days of the kings has been greatly illuminated by the work of Kathleen Kenyon, whose excavations on the E slopes of the ancient city, where it overlooked the Kedron, showed terraces all along the slope which supported rows of houses. There was a massive collapse in the attack of Nebuchadrezzar. The W wall of the city of those days has recently been discovered.

Jerusalem lay in ruins for nearly a century before the new city was built. It was unwalled at first, but under Nehemiah was once again protected by a wall, traces of which are still to be seen.

When the OT was translated into Greek the Hebrew *'îr* became *polis* in the LXX. But whereas the Greek *polis* had political overtones and meant 'state' or 'body politic' rather than merely 'city', the term in its Hebrew setting was apolitical. Only Philo among the later Jewish writers used the term *polis* in a political sense.

BIBLIOGRAPHY. 'Cities' in S. M. Paul and W. G. Dever, *Biblical Archaeology*, 1973, pp. 3–26.

J.A.T.

II. In the New Testament

In the NT *polis* is frequently found. In the Gospels it bears the extended and non-political sense of village,

Model of the lower city of Jerusalem. The raised Temple area is in the background. AD 66. (JPK) (HC)

Model of the city of Megiddo in the 1st millennium BC, *showing storehouses, administrative buildings and gateway.* (SH)

etc., which is germane to the Jewish background of Jesus' ministry. In Acts it is used of various Hellenistic cities of Asia Minor and Europe but bears no reference to their political structure. In Rom. 16:23 we find the Corinth treasurer or steward (the term is known from inscriptions) in fellowship with the Christian church: apart from Paul's boast in Acts 21:39, this is practically the only place in the NT where we find even the most distant allusion to the political structure of the city. It may be tempting, however, to see in the words of Acts 15:28 *edoxen tō pneumati tō hagiō kai hēmin*, a phrase framed upon the civic formulary *edoxen tē boulē kai tō dēmō*. Even so, however attractive and suggestive the idea that here the Holy Spirit takes the place of the council and the apostles the assembly of citizens, it is quite clear that neither the apostles nor Luke are concerned to press the analogy. It may also be significant to note that the word *parrēsia* (the Christian's 'boldness' or 'freedom of speech') earlier has the specifically political connotation of the citizen's right to free speech in the assembly.

The verb *politeuomai* means in the NT simply 'to live one's life, to conduct oneself' (Acts 23:1; Phil. 1:27). The noun *politeia*, 'commonwealth' or 'body politic', is used with reference to the rights and privileges of Israel (Eph. 2:12). *politeuma* is used in Phil. 3:20, where some seek to find in it the technical use as 'colony', and to translate the verse 'we are a colony of heaven' (so appropriate to Philippi). To render it thus, however, involves turning the sentence about, and the suggestion must be rejected. We find here either the less specific 'citizenship' (*cf.* Philo, *Concerning the Confusion of Tongues* 78; *Epistle to Diognetus* 5. 9) or the very general 'way of life' (as AV 'conversation'), in which case *cf.* 2 Cor. 4:18.

Jerusalem still possesses for the NT writers the title 'holy city' and ranks high in the esteem of Jesus as the city of the great King (Mt. 5:35). It remained until AD 70 a centre of Christian influence and a focus of esteem. Yet it is spoken of also as a city of sinful men who have persecuted and slain the prophets, over which Jesus weeps as he sees the approach of its doom. This spiritual ambivalence strikes us in Revelation. Jerusalem is the beloved city (20:9), object of God's promises, centre of the millennial reign; but in ch. 11 the holy city is Sodom and Egypt where the Lord was crucified, and even the great city, a term normally reserved for the adversary of God (see chs. 16–18), of which Jerusalem in that hour was the locus and type. We may compare Paul's contrast of two Jerusalems in Gal. 4:24–26.

For the writer to the Hebrews and his addressees (whoever and however Hebrew either were), the emphasis lies upon the heavenly

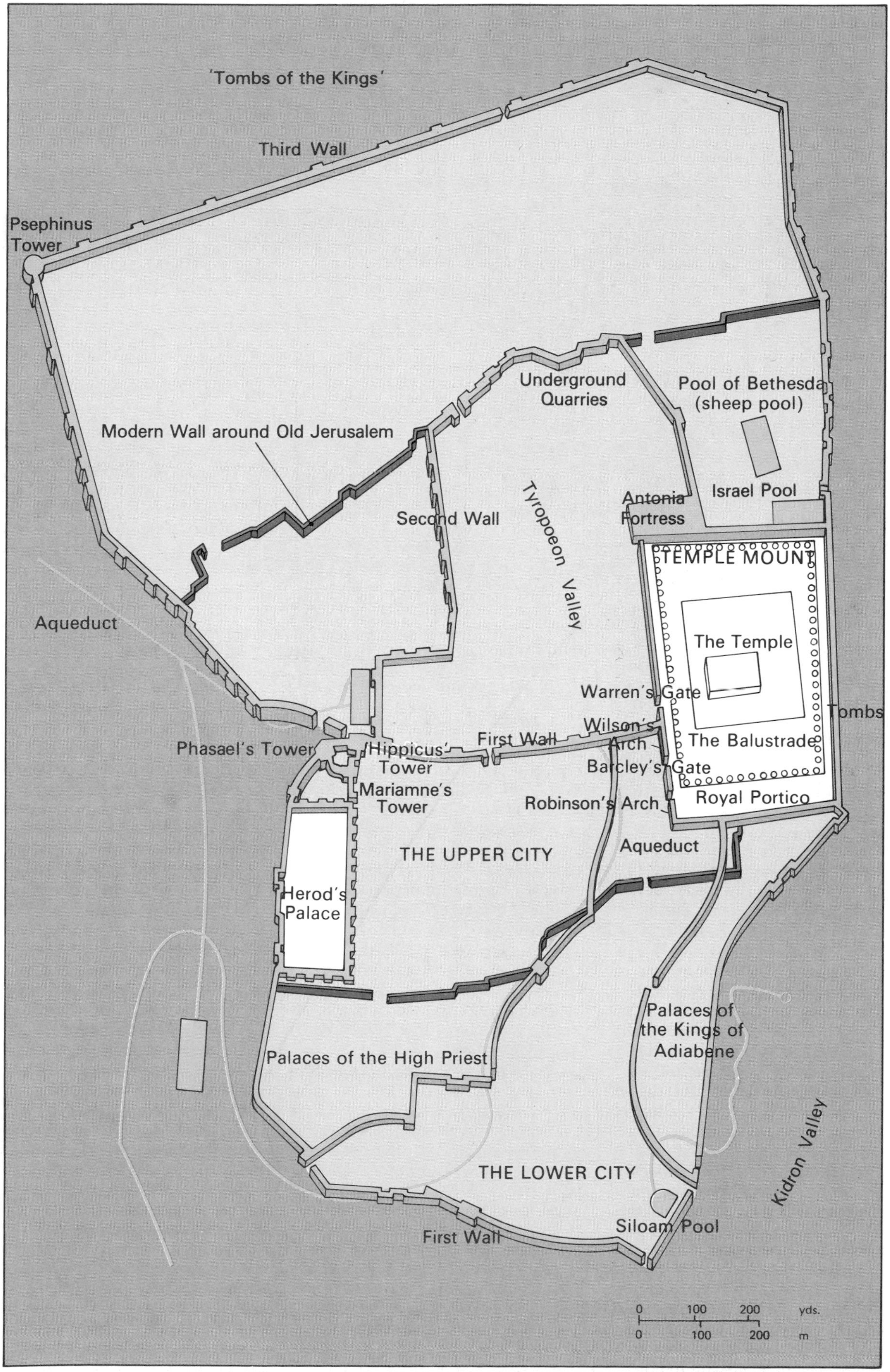
'Tombs of the Kings'
Third Wall
Psephinus Tower
Modern Wall around Old Jerusalem
Underground Quarries
Pool of Bethesda (sheep pool)
Israel Pool
Antonia Fortress
Second Wall
Tyropoeon Valley
TEMPLE MOUNT
The Temple
Aqueduct
Warren's Gate
Wilson's Arch
Tombs
The Balustrade
Barcley's Gate
Phasael's Tower
'Hippicus' Tower
First Wall
Mariamne's Tower
Robinson's Arch
Royal Portico
THE UPPER CITY
Aqueduct
Herod's Palace
Palaces of the Kings of Adiabene
Palaces of the High Priest
Kidron Valley
THE LOWER CITY
Siloam Pool
First Wall
0 100 200 yds.
0 100 200 m

The Herodian city of Jerusalem.

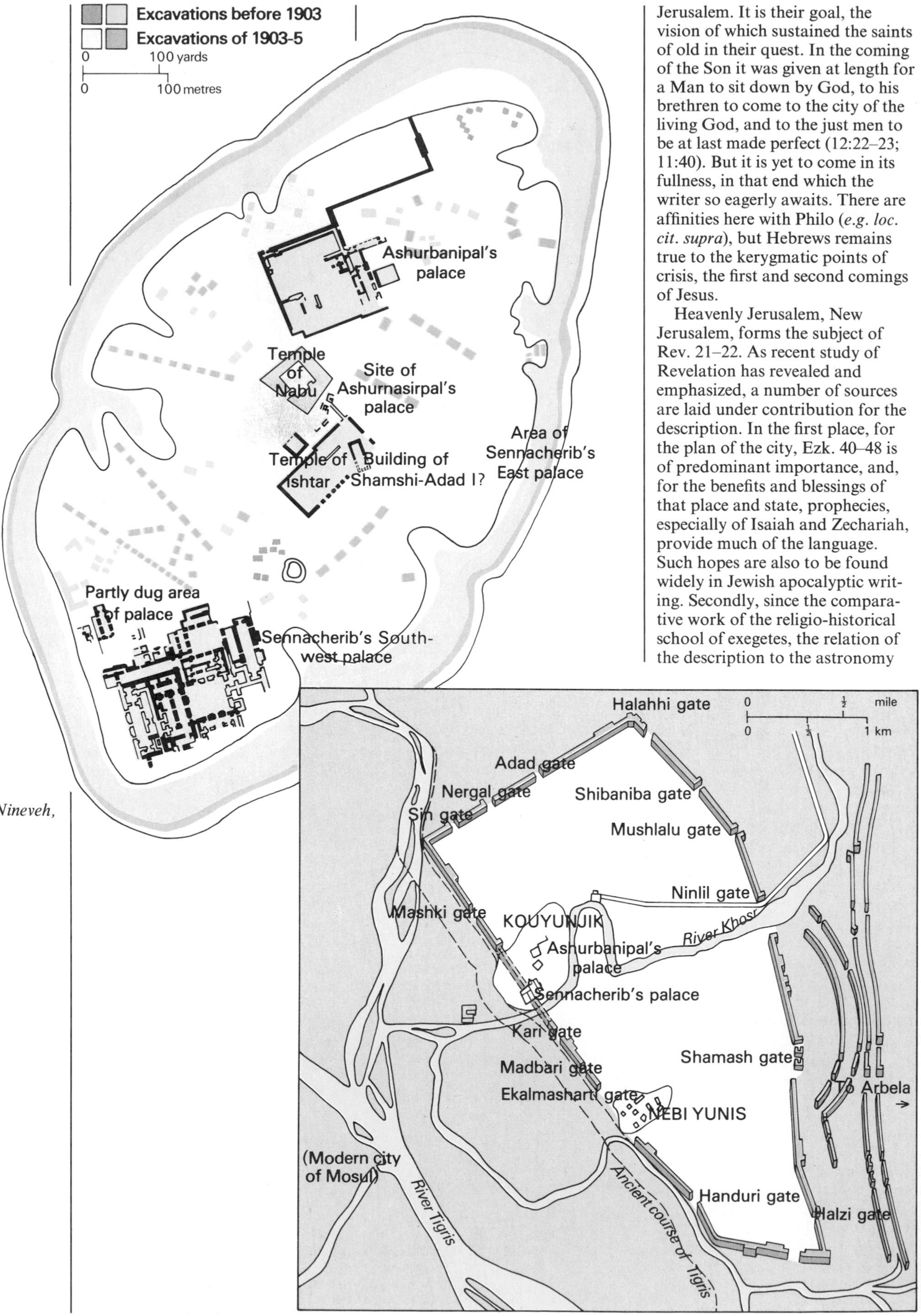

The layout of the Assyrian city of Nineveh, c. 650 BC.

Jerusalem. It is their goal, the vision of which sustained the saints of old in their quest. In the coming of the Son it was given at length for a Man to sit down by God, to his brethren to come to the city of the living God, and to the just men to be at last made perfect (12:22–23; 11:40). But it is yet to come in its fullness, in that end which the writer so eagerly awaits. There are affinities here with Philo (*e.g. loc. cit. supra*), but Hebrews remains true to the kerygmatic points of crisis, the first and second comings of Jesus.

Heavenly Jerusalem, New Jerusalem, forms the subject of Rev. 21–22. As recent study of Revelation has revealed and emphasized, a number of sources are laid under contribution for the description. In the first place, for the plan of the city, Ezk. 40–48 is of predominant importance, and, for the benefits and blessings of that place and state, prophecies, especially of Isaiah and Zechariah, provide much of the language. Such hopes are also to be found widely in Jewish apocalyptic writing. Secondly, since the comparative work of the religio-historical school of exegetes, the relation of the description to the astronomy

The lofty bronze and wood gates of Shalmaneser III's temple at Balawat near Nineveh. In this British Museum reconstruction winged lions which guarded the gates of Ashurnasirpal's palace are also shown. Assyrian. c. 850 BC. (BM)

and astrology of antiquity has tended to be stressed. The twelve precious stones of the foundation are well-known counterparts of the twelve Zodiacal signs: the intermingled stones and pearls reflect the starry heavens above, and both street and stream the Milky Way: the cubic dimensions of the city and its vast size are patterned on the vastness of space. Even the heavenly wall has its origin in the pillars of the sky. Thirdly, numerous parallels may also be drawn between this description and that of Hellenistic cities (and Babylon, their possible pattern) in Greek geographers and orators. In these sources we find a tetragonal plan, a central street, praise of a river flanked by avenues or dotted with wooded islets, visions of cities adorned with fine trees and rendered salubrious by natural situation and flora. Yet there is one marked contrast. There were many temples in Hellenistic cities; there is none, nor any need of one, in the new Jerusalem. No one source necessarily excludes the others; the recognition of all brings out the spiritual meaning of this vision. In the appointed end, when God is All in all, we find the fulfilment of Israel's hopes, the realization of God's promises to her; the manifestation, in a city which has the glory of God, of the reality already declared by the heavens and the

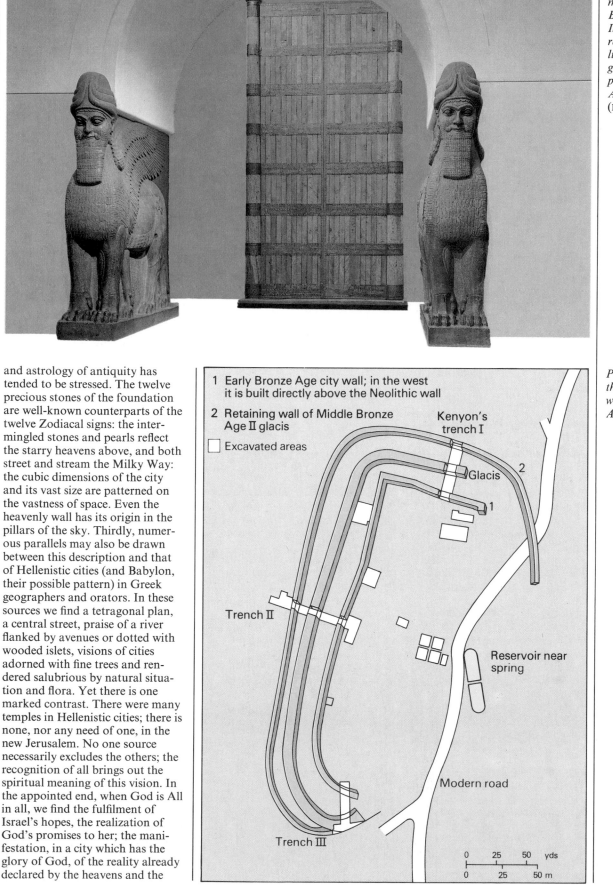

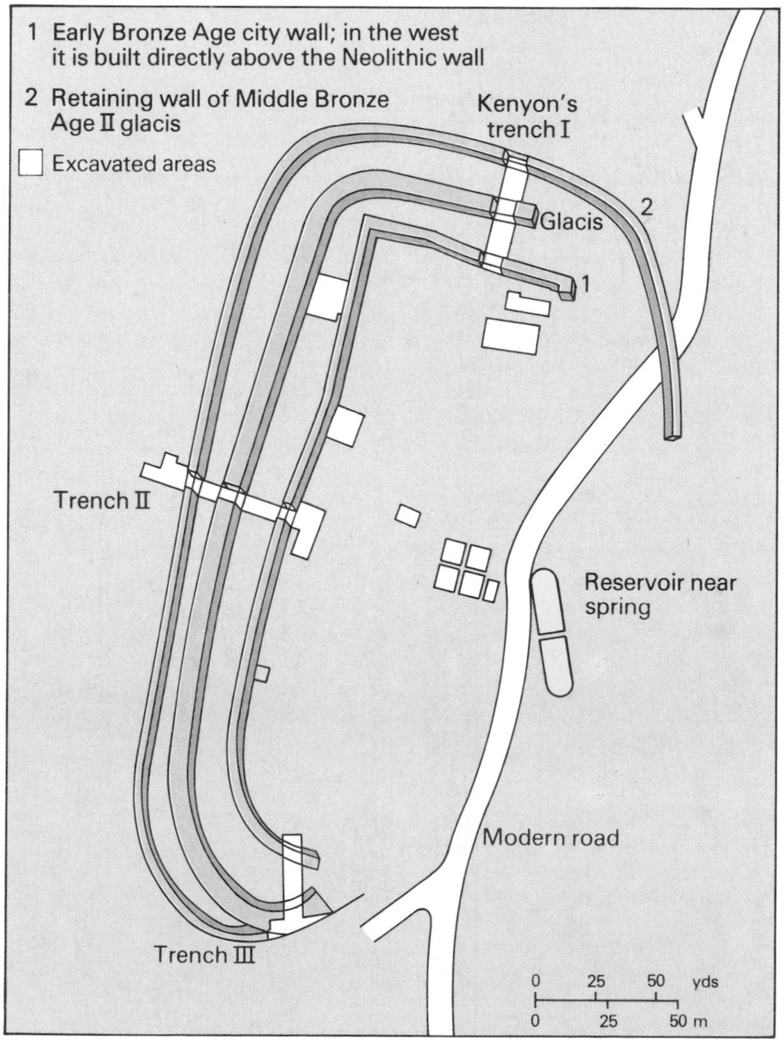

Plan showing the lines of the Early Bronze Age wall and Middle Bronze Age glacis at Jericho.

firmament; and the answer to all aesthetic yearnings and national aspirations in the place to which the kings of the earth bring their glory. Of this city the reborn are citizens, and to it all pilgrims of faith tend. The city is also described as the Lamb's bride; it is in another aspect his church for which he died, the pattern and goal of all human society. In the last analysis this chief of scriptural cities is men, not walls: just men made perfect, the city of the living God.

BIBLIOGRAPHY. R. de Vaux, *Ancient Israel*, 1961, pp. 229–240; M. du Buit, *Géographie de la Terre Sainte*, 1958; R. S. Lamon and G. M. Shipton, *Megiddo I*, 1939; G. Loud, *Megiddo II*, 1948, pp. 46–57; R. de Vaux, articles on excavations at Tell el-Far'a in *Revue Biblique* 1947–52; *TWBR*, *s.v.*; W. M. Ramsay, *The Cities of St Paul*, 1907; E. M. Blaiklock, *Cities of the NT*, 1965; D. H. McQueen, *The Expositor* (Ninth Series) 2, 1924, pp. 221–226; R. Knopf, *Festschrift für G. Heinrici*, 1914, pp. 213–219; W. Bousset, R. H. Charles, G. B. Caird, G. R. Beasley-Murray, commentaries on *Revelation* on *loc. cit.*

J.N.B.

Marble head of Claudius Caesar, who is mentioned twice in the book of Acts (11:28 and 18:2). Height c. 21 cm. (RG)

CITY RULERS
See Authorities, city, Part 1.

CITY WALL
See Walls, Part 3.

CLAUDA
See Cauda, Part 1.

CLAUDIA. A Roman Christian, greeting Timothy (2 Tim. 4:21); in some imaginative reconstructions the wife of *Pudens, and even, on the bad authority of *Apostolic Constitutions* 7. 2. 6, mother of *Linus. Alford, *in loc.*, identifies Timothy's friend with the British Claudia, whose marriage with one Pudens is celebrated by Martial (*cf. Epig.* 4. 13 with 11. 53), and with the hypothetical Claudia of a putative Pudens in a Chichester inscription (*CIL* 7. 11). Martial, however, came to Rome only in AD 66, and implies scarcely Christian proclivities of his Pudens. Another Pudens and Claudia appear in *CIL* 6. 15066; but Claudia is a very common contemporary name.

BIBLIOGRAPHY. J. B. Lightfoot, *Clement*, I, pp. 76ff.; G. Edmundson, *The Church in Rome*, 1913, pp. 244ff.

A.F.W.

CLAUDIUS. Roman Caesar from AD 41 to 54. He is supposed, on inconclusive grounds in each case, to have taken 3 different measures to deal with Christianity. (*a*) He expelled Jews from Rome for rioting at the instigation of Chrestus (Suetonius, *Claudius* 25). This is presumably the incident referred to in Acts 18:2. Chrestus is either a personal name or a variant of Christus. Suetonius assumes the former, and was, moreover, capable of recognizing Christianity. Even if he was wrong, it need not refer to *Christian* Messianism. Neither Paul's welcome in Rome nor the Epistle to the Romans suggests any history of conflict between Jews and Christians there. (*b*) Claudius reprimanded Jewish agitators imported into Alexandria from Syria (H. I. Bell, *Jews and Christians in Egypt*, 1924). Apollos's defective knowledge of Christianity, however, suggests that these were not Christians. (*c*) A Caesarian decree (*JRS* 22, 1932, pp. 184ff.), perhaps of Claudius, punished tomb robbery and was apparently published in Galilee. Whether or not this refers to the resurrection is likely to remain a moot point.

BIBLIOGRAPHY. A. Momigliano, *Claudius*², 1961.

E.A.J.

Gold aureus of Claudius, Roman Emperor, AD 41–54. (BM)

CLAUDIUS LYSIAS. In Acts 21:31ff. the military tribune (Gk. *chiliarchos*, 'captain of a thousand'; AV, RV 'chief captain'; RSV 'tribune of the cohort') in command of the Roman garrison of the Antonia Fortress in Jerusalem, who took Paul into custody. He had acquired his Roman citizenship by purchase (Acts 22:28); his *nomen* Claudius suggests that he had bought it in the principate of Claudius, when Roman citizenship became increasingly available for cash down. His *cognomen* Lysias implies that he was of Greek birth. His letter to Felix about Paul (Acts 23:26–30) subtly rearranges the facts so as to place his own behaviour in the most favourable light.

F.F.B.

CLEAN AND UNCLEAN. The Heb. *ṭum'â* ('uncleanness') occurs 26 times, whereas the adjective *ṭāmē'* ('unclean') is found 72 times. Other words appear less frequently. The Gk. *akatharsia* ('uncleanness') and *akathartos* ('unclean') occur 41 times. Other terms are found less often. The concept of cleanness is conveyed by the Heb. *ṭāhōr*, *bārār* and synonyms; the NT employs *katharos* almost exclusively. In the biblical words for 'clean', the physical, ritual and ethical usages overlap.

I. Cleanliness highly regarded

Bodily cleanliness was esteemed highly and practised in Bible lands. Herodotus (2. 27) stated that Egyptian priests bathed twice each day and twice each night. In Israel physical cleanness rendered a man ready to approach God, if his motive was proper. As early as the age of Noah the distinction between clean and unclean obtained. Gn. 7:2 records: 'Take with you seven pairs of all clean animals, the male and his mate; and a pair of the animals that are not clean, the male and his mate.' The early references in Genesis to clean and unclean *animals appear to have in mind the question of whether these animals were intended for sacrifice or not. Gn. 9:3 is explicit that 'every moving thing that lives shall be food for you'. The regulations in Lv. 11 and Dt. 14 make the distinction as a basis for food laws. It is stated: 'This is the law pertaining to beast and bird and every living creature that moves through the waters, and every creature that swarms upon the earth: to make a distinction between the unclean and the clean, and between the living creature that may be eaten and the living creature that may not be eaten' (Lv. 11:46–47).

II. In earliest times

In patriarchal times and in the era of the Monarchy in Israel the differentiation is found. Compare Gn. 31:35 (the case of Rachel with the household gods of her father, Laban) and 1 Sa. 20:26 (the incident of David's absence from the table of King Saul). Unfortunately, some writers have largely misunderstood the important distinctions here, because they have related all OT regulations of this character to alleged originally superstitious taboos. (*Cf.* A. S. Peake, *HDB*, 4, pp. 825ff.).

III. Under the prophets

The prophets, whose high ethical standards have been acclaimed on every hand, spoke of uncleanness also. Isaiah, envisioning the future age of righteousness, predicted that the way of holiness would not be traversed by the unclean (35:8); again, he called upon Jerusalem to gird on her strength, for the uncircumcised and the unclean would no longer trouble her in the hour of her glory (52:1). The plea is further made by the evangelical prophet for those in holy service to avoid any unclean thing, and to be clean in the handling of the sacred vessels of the Lord (52:11). Hosea, the prophet of the heart-broken love of God, warned his people that the N kingdom would not only return to Egypt, but would eat the unclean in Assyria (9:3). Amos, the unparalleled champion of the righteousness of God, in response to coercion which would muzzle his prophetic testimony, foretold that Amaziah of Bethel would experience the hand of God heavily upon him in his immediate family, and would himself die in an unclean land (7:17). The priestly Ezekiel expressed in various ways the loathing he felt for the pollution of his people, and his own abhorrence for the manner in which he was called upon to portray it dramatically before them (4:14).

IV. The Mosaic law

The law of Moses made clear distinctions between clean and unclean, the holy and unholy (Lv. 10:10). Uncleanness was primarily ceremonial defilement, not moral, unless done wilfully. It kept a man from the service of the sanctuary and from fellowship with his co-religionists. Ceremonial defilement was contracted in several ways, and provision was made for cleansing.

a. Contact with a dead body rendered the individual unclean (Nu. 19:11–22). The human corpse was the most defiling, according to OT regulations. In all probability it epitomized for the people of God the full gravity and ultimate consequences of sin.

b. Leprosy, whether in a person, clothing or a house, was polluting (Lv. 13–14).

c. Natural (those connected with the functions of reproduction) and unnatural issues were defiling to the observant Israelite (Lv. 12; 15).

d. Eating the flesh of an unclean bird, fish or animal made one unclean. Lv. 11 and Dt. 14 contain extended lists of the clean and unclean. Beasts of prey were considered unclean, because they consumed the blood and flesh of their victims. Unclean birds for the most part were birds of prey or those which fed on carrion. Fish without fins and scales were unclean. Some have thought that their serpent-like appearance accounts for the prohibition against them, but we now know that the prohibition of this group was wise on hygienic grounds. Both shellfish and crustaceans can easily cause food-poisoning and may also carry disease (G. S. Cansdale, *Animals of Bible Lands*, 1970, p. 213). Eating of flesh of animals torn to pieces or

Model of the fortress of Antonia, Jerusalem. Claudius Lysias was commander of the Roman garrison here c. AD 59. (HC)

violently slain was a source of uncleanness (Ex. 22:31; Lv. 17:15; Acts 15:20, 29). Eating of blood was forbidden from earliest times (Gn. 9:4).

e. Physical impairments were considered like uncleanness in their power to exclude from approach to the altar. The regulations are given explicitly for the sons of Aaron, the ministering priests in the sanctuary (Lv. 21:16–24). Finally, unpunished murder (Dt. 21:1–9) and especially idolatry (Ho. 6:10) rendered the land unclean. The former struck at the image of God (Gn. 9:6), whereas the latter was a violation of the spiritual worship due to God (Ex. 20:4).

V. In post-exilic times

The scribes of post-exilic times and the Pharisees of the NT period enlarged artificially the distinction between clean and unclean (Mk. 7:2, 4). An elaborate and burdensome system developed therefrom. For example, a canonical book rendered the hands unclean; a non-canonical book did not. The largest of the six divisions of the Mishnah deals with the subject of purifications. The multiplied regulations give validity to the observation of our Lord: 'You have a fine way of rejecting the commandment of God, in order to keep your tradition!' (Mk. 7:9).

VI. The necessity and form of purification

Israel was to be holy (Lv. 11:44–45) and separate from all uncleanness. Ceremonial uncleanness spoke of sin. Bodily cleanliness was required in their society. Laws of cleanliness were followed by the observant in their approach to God. The clean person is the one who can approach God in worship. See Ex. 19:10f.; 30:18–21; Jos. 3:5. In religious usage the clean denoted that which did not defile ceremonially. The term was employed of beasts (Gn. 7:2), places (Lv. 4:12), objects (Is. 66:20) or persons who were not ceremonially (ritually) defiled (1 Sa. 20:26; Ezk. 36:25). Ethical cleanness or purity is in view in Pss. 19:9; 51:7, 10. A rare usage in the sense of 'blameless' or 'guiltless' is found in Acts 18:6.

The usual mode of purification was bathing of the body and washing of the clothes (Lv. 15:8, 10–11). Cleansing from an issue called for a special cleansing (Lv. 15:19), also childbirth (Lv. 12:2, 8; Lk. 2:24), leprosy (Lv. 14), contact with a corpse (Nu. 19; for a Nazirite, Nu. 6:9–12). Cleansing may be physical (Je. 4:11; Mt. 8:3); ritual, by a sin-offering (Ex. 29:36), to expiate sin (Nu. 35:33), to remove ceremonial defilement (Lv. 12:7; Mk. 1:44); ethical, either by man's removal of the uncleanness or sin (Ps. 119:9; Jas. 4:8), or by God's removal of the guilt (Ezk. 24:13; Jn. 15:2). Ritual cleansing was effected by water, fire or the ashes of a red heifer. Ps. 51:7 is a good example of the ceremonial as a figure of the ethical or spiritual. David prayed: 'Purge me with hyssop, and I shall be clean; wash me, and I shall be whiter than snow.'

VII. The New Testament view

In his teachings Christ emphasized moral, rather than ceremonial, purity (Mk. 7:1–23). His strongest denunciations were against those who elevated the ritual and external over the moral and ethical. What is important is not ceremonial, but moral, defilement. A careful reading of certain NT texts will give indications of the customs of the Jews regarding cleanness and defilement. Mk. 7:3–4 is a concise statement of the regulations concerning washing of hands, defilement contracted in the market-place and cleansing of utensils. Jn. 2:6 touches upon the method of purifying upon entering a household, and Jn. 3:25 indicates that the matter of cleansing was a ready subject for disputation. Strict regulations governed purification for the Feast of the Passover; these are alluded to in Jn. 11:55 and 18:28. The leper once cleansed was enjoined to offer for his cleansing what the law of Moses required (Mk. 1:44). In order to allay the opposition against him and procure for himself a readier acceptance in his message, Paul underwent the rite of purification in the Temple in Jerusalem (Acts 21:26). This puzzling behaviour must be evaluated in the light of his policy to be 'all things to all men'—*inter alia*, to live as a Jew when among Jews—'for the sake of the gospel' (1 Cor. 9:22 f.). It does not detract from the truth that Christ repealed all the levitical regulations on unclean meats and practices (Mt. 15:1–20 and Mk. 7:6–23), in the light of which Peter was commanded to act (Acts 10:13ff.), and Paul promulgated his precepts for Christian conduct (Rom. 14:14, 20; 1 Cor. 6:13; Col. 2:16, 20–22; Tit. 1:15). It is emphasized in Heb. 9:13f. that the only pollution that matters *religiously* is that of the conscience, from which the sacrifice of Christ, offered in the spiritual realm, alone can cleanse.

As is to be expected, the Gospels have most to say of the distinction between clean and unclean. Purification is treated in the Gospels under several categories. It is seen in relation to leprosy (Mt. 8:2; Mk. 1:44; Lk. 5:14; 17:11–19). The word used in this connection is *katharizein*, but in Lk. 17:15 (the case of the ten lepers) *iasthai* ('to heal') is employed. The cleansing of the leper had two parts: (*a*) the ritual with the two birds (Lv. 14); and (*b*) the ceremony 8 days later. In regard to food there was the ritualistic washing of the hands (Mt. 15:1–20; Mk. 7:1–23; Jn. 2:6; 3:25). As already indicated, there was a purification in connection with the Passover (Jn. 11:55; 18:28). There had to be a thoroughgoing removal of all leaven from the home (Ex. 12:15, 19–20; 13:7). Finally, following childbirth an offering was brought at the termination of the period of uncleanness, that is, 40 days for a male child and 80 for a girl (Lk. 2:22).

VIII. Conclusion

Some have supposed that the laws regulating clean and unclean not only had the effect of hindering social and religious intercourse with the heathen, especially in the matter of eating, but were originally given to accomplish this purpose. Moore feels there is neither internal nor external evidence to support this position (*Judaism*, 1, 1927, p. 21). He reasons thus: 'They were ancient customs, the origin and reason of which had long since been forgotten. Some of them are found among other Semites, or more widely; some were, so far as we know, peculiar to Israel; but as a whole, or we may say, as a system, they were the distinctive customs which the Jews had inherited from their ancestors with a religious sanction in the two categories of holy and polluted. Other peoples had their own, some of them for all classes, some, as among the Jews, specifically for the priests, and these systems also were distinctive' (*op. cit.*, pp. 21–22).

In the discussion of the far-reaching rules which differentiate between clean and unclean among animals, fowl and fish, various reasons have been given for these laws. The traditional and most obvious reason is the religious or spiritual: 'You shall be men consecrated to me' (Ex. 22:31). Another explanation is the hygienic. It was espoused by Maimonides, the great Jewish philosopher of the Middle Ages in Spain, and other notable scholars. The argument, now supported by modern research, was that scaleless fish and the swine tend to produce diseases (Cansdale, *op. cit.*, p. 99). Still another interpretation was the psychological. The forbidden animals appeared either loathsome or begat a spirit of cruelty in those who ate them. A fourth reason is the dualistic. The Israelites, like the Persians, are said to have assigned all unclean animals to an evil power. Another explanation is the national, which holds that the Israelites were surrounded with such prohibitions in order to keep them separate from all other nations. Opponents of this view have pointed out that the animals forbidden in the law of Moses are practically the same as those proscribed in the Hindu, Babylonian and Egyptian religions.

The most popular theory in critical circles is that advanced by W. Robertson Smith (*The Religion of the Semites*, p. 270). Köhler states it succinctly, 'In view of the fact that almost every primitive tribe holds certain animals to be tabooed, the contention is that the forbidden or tabooed animal was originally regarded and worshipped as the totem of the clan; but the facts adduced do not sufficiently support the theory, especially in regard to the Semites, to allow it to be more than an ingenious conjecture . . .' (*JewE*, 4, p. 599). If the scriptural data are allowed their normal force, the spiritual and hygienic explanations are the correct ones.

BIBLIOGRAPHY. A. C. Zenos, 'Pure, Purity, Purification', *Standard Bible Dictionary*, pp. 719–721; G. A. Simcox, 'Clean and Unclean, Holy and Profane', *EBi*, 1, pp. 836–848; J. Hastings, 'Clean', *HDB*, 1, p. 448; R. Bruce Taylor, 'Purification', *DCG*, 2, pp. 457–458; P. W. Crannell, 'Clean' and 'Cleanse', *ISBE*, 1, pp. 667–668; Uncleanness', *WDB*, p. 617; A. S. Peake, 'Unclean, Uncleanness', *HDB*, 4, pp. 825–834; Charles B. Williams, 'Uncleanness', *ISBE*, 5, pp. 3035–3037; *JewE*, 4, pp. 110–113 and 596–600; George F. Moore, *Judaism*, 1–2, 1927; M. Douglas, *Purity and Danger*, 1966; G. S. Cansdale, *Animals of Bible Lands*, 1970, pp. 99, 213. C.L.F.

CLEMENT. A Philippian Christian mentioned in Phil. 4:3. It is uncertain whether the reference means that the 'true yokefellow' addressed by Paul is asked to assist Clement as well as Euodia and Syntyche; or that Clement as well as Euodia and Syntyche laboured with Paul in the work of the gospel. AV appears to adopt the former interpretation and RSV the latter. Some of the early Fathers identified him with Clement, the bishop of Rome at the close of the 1st century; but as the date of Clement of Rome's death is uncertain, and the name was a common one, this also must be regarded as uncertain. R.V.G.T.

CLEOPAS (a contracted form of *Cleopatros*). One of the two disciples accosted by the risen Jesus on the afternoon of the first Easter Day as they were returning to their home at Emmaus (Lk. 24:18). (*CLOPAS.) R.V.G.T.

CLOPAS ('Cleophas', AV) is mentioned in Jn. 19:25, where one of the women who stood near the cross is said to have been Mary *hē tou Klōpa*, an expression which could mean daughter, wife or mother of Clopas. The view that Clopas was the father of the apostle described in the lists of the apostles as 'James, the son of Alphaeus' rests on the assumption that Clopas and Alphaeus are renderings of the same Hebrew word—pronounced differently. In the early Latin and Syriac versions the Cleopas of Lk. 24:18 was confused with the Clopas of Jn. 19:25, but it is probable that they were two different people with two distinct names, as *eo* was usually contracted into *ou* and not into *ō*. R.V.G.T.

CLOUD. The regularity of the seasons in the Mediterranean area gives climatic significance to the appearance of clouds. But apart from the direction of wind influencing the weather and the colour of the evening sky, there is little evidence that the Hebrews understood the meteorological signs.

Clouds were well recognized as an indication of moisture. During the rainy season in the winter half-year, air-streams bringing rainfall are associated with cumulus clouds rising from the Mediterranean sea—'a cloud rising in the west' (Lk. 12:54). Hence Elijah's servant looked seawards for the first indication that the spell of drought was to be broken (1 Ki. 18:44). Towards the end of the rainy season in April–May 'clouds that bring the spring rain' (Pr. 16:15) describe the king's favour, since they provide the necessary moisture to swell the ripening ears of grain. Contrasted are the high cirrus rainless clouds (Jude 12), which draw in desert air from the SE and E, called Sirocco or Khamsīn, in association with depressions. The clouds and wind without rain (Pr. 25:14), the 'heat by the shade of a cloud' (Is. 25:5) and subsequently the 'sky of brass' (Dt. 28:23) vividly describe these dust-storms.

Clouds brought by sea-breezes readily dissolve as the hot, dry air of the interior is encountered. Thus the 'morning cloud' (Ho. 6:4) is symbolic of transitory things, of human prosperity (Jb. 30:15) and of human life (Jb. 7:9). It is also a text on the reality of divine forgiveness (Is. 44:22).

The usual luminosity of the Palestinian sky emphasizes that clouds cover and obscure (Ezk 32:7), and the joy of 'a cloudless morning' (2 Sa. 23:4) is vividly described. Like the cloud which hides the sun, divine favour or a supplication may be intercepted (La. 2:1; 3:44). Job prays that clouds may cover up the day of his birth (Jb. 3:5).

The cloud frequently means the whole circle of the sky; *cf.* 'the bow in the clouds' (Gn. 9:14). It represents the sphere of partial knowledge and hidden glory where God has a mysterious purpose in their motions (Jb. 36:29; 37:16; 38:37; Ps. 78:23). Thus too a cloud closes the scene of the incarnation (Acts 1:9), the transfiguration (Mt. 17:5; Mk. 9:7; Lk. 9:34), and clouds herald the second advent (Rev. 1:7). To the Israelites the cloud of God's presence was intimately related to their religious symbolism (Ex. 13:21; 40:34; 1 Ki. 8:10).

The clouds of Mk. 14:62, *etc.*, may refer to the ascension rather than the parousia. J.M.H.

CNIDUS. A city of Caria in SW Asia Minor, where Paul's ship changed course on its way to Rome (Acts 27:7). Cnidus had Jewish inhabitants as early as the 2nd century BC (1 Macc. 15:23), and had the status of free city. J.D.D.

CLEOPHAS
See Clopas, Part 1.

CLIMATE OF PALESTINE
See Palestine, Part 2.

CLOTHES MOTH
See Animals, Part 1.

COASTLANDS
See Island, Part 2.

COAT OF MAIL
See Armour, Part 1.

COAT OF MANY COLOURS
See Joseph, Part 2.

COBRA
See Animals, Part 1.

COCK
See Animals, Part 1.

COCKATRICE
See Animals, Part 1.

COCKLE
See Plants, Part 3.

COAL. In the OT (*MT*) there are 5 Heb. words rendered 'coal'. **1.** *gaḥeleṯ* (*e.g.* Pr. 26:21) means burning, as opposed to unlit, fuel; it is metaphorically employed in 2 Sa. 14:7; 22:9, 13. **2.** *peḥām* (*e.g.* Pr. 26:21; Is. 44:12) is used indifferently of unlit and burning fuel. **3.** *riṣpâ* (*e.g.* Is. 6:6; 1 Ki. 19:6) means a flat stone girdle (*cf.* Arab. *raḍf*, *raḍafa*). **4.** *rešep̄* (*e.g.* Ct. 8:6) means 'burning coals'; it should perhaps be rendered 'fiery pestilence' in Hab. 3:5. **5.** *šᵉḥôr* (*e.g.* La. 4:8) is literally 'blackness'.

In the NT the Gk. word *anthrax*, 'coal', occurs once (Rom. 12:20) as a metaphor for feelings of shame, but elsewhere *anthrakia*, 'a heap of burning *fuel', is used. R.J.W.

COELESYRIA (Gk. *koilē syria*, 'hollow Syria'), 1 Esdras 2:17, *etc.*; 2 Macc. 3:5, *etc.*, the valley lying between the Lebanon and Anti-lebanon ranges, modern El-Biqa' (*cf. biq'aṯ 'āwen*, 'the Valley of Aven', Am. 1:5). As a political region under the Ptolemaic and Seleucid empires it frequently embraces a wider area, sometimes stretching to Damascus in the N and including Phoenicia to the W or Judaea to the S. From 312 to 198 BC it formed part of the Ptolemaic empire, but fell to the Seleucids in consequence of the battle of Panion in the latter year. Coelesyria was an administrative division of the province of Syria after the Roman occupation (64 BC). Herod was appointed military prefect of Coelesyria by Sextus Caesar in 47 BC and again by Cassius in 43 BC. F.F.B.

COLLECTION (PAULINE CHURCHES). The collection (Gk. *logeia*) which Paul organized in his Gentile churches for the relief of the poverty of the Jerusalem church. In the 2 years preceding his last visit to Jerusalem (AD 57) it engaged his attention increasingly; it would, indeed, be difficult to exaggerate the important part which it played in his apostolic strategy.

I. Background

At the conference in Jerusalem (*c.* AD 46) at which it was agreed that he and Barnabas should continue to prosecute the work of Gentile evangelization, while the leaders of the Jerusalem church would concentrate on the Jewish mission (Gal. 2:1–10), the Jerusalem leaders added a special request that Barnabas and Paul should continue to remember 'the poor'—a request which is best understood against the background of the famine relief which the church of Antioch had sent to the Jerusalem believers by the hand of Barnabas and Paul (Acts 11:30). In reporting this request Paul adds that this was a matter to which he himself paid special attention. It was in his mind throughout his evangelization of the provinces to E and W of the Aegean, and in the closing years of that period he applied himself energetically to the organizing of a relief fund for Jerusalem in the churches of Galatia, Asia, Macedonia and Achaia.

II. Evidence from Corinthian correspondence

We first learn about this fund from the instructions given to the Corinthian Christians in 1 Cor. 16:1–4; they had been told about it and wanted to know more. From what he says to them we learn that he had already given similar instructions to the churches of Galatia—presumably in the late summer of AD 52, when he passed through 'the Galatic region and Phrygia' on his way from Judaea and Syria to Ephesus (Acts 18:22f.). Thanks to Paul's Corinthian correspondence, more details are known about the organizing of the fund in Corinth than in any of the other contributing churches.

If Paul's instructions to his converts in Corinth had been carried out, then each householder among them would have set aside a proportion of his income week by week for some 12 months, so that the church's contribution would have been ready to be taken to Jerusalem in the spring of the following year by the delegates appointed by the church for that purpose. The tension which developed soon afterwards between many of the Corinthian Christians and Paul perhaps occasioned a falling off in their enthusiasm for this good cause. Next time Paul wrote to them about it (in the aftermath of the reconciliation resulting from the severe letter which he sent to them by Titus) he expressed the assumption that they had been setting money aside for the fund systematically ever since they received his instructions, and told them how he had been holding up their promptness as an example to the Macedonian churches. But when one reads between the lines, it is plain that he had private misgivings on this score; hence he sent Titus back to Corinth with two companions to help the church to complete the gathering together of its contributions (2 Cor. 8:16–24). Some members of the church probably felt that this was a subtle way of putting irresistible pressure on them: he was 'crafty', they said, and got the better of them 'by guile' (2 Cor. 12:16).

At the time when Paul sent Titus and his companions to Corinth to see about this matter, he himself was in Macedonia, helping the churches of that province to complete their share in it. Those churches had been passing through a period of unspecified trouble as a result of which they were living at bare subsistence level, if that; and Paul felt that he could hardly ask them to contribute to the relief of fellow-Christians who were no worse off than themselves. But they insisted on making a contribution, and Paul was greatly moved by this token of divine grace in their lives (2 Cor. 8:1–5). He pays them a warm tribute in writing to the Corinthians in order to encourage the latter to give as generously from their comparative affluence as the Macedonians gave from their destitution.

III. Evidence from Roman correspondence

Paul makes one further reference to this relief fund in his extant letters, and this reference is particularly informative, because it comes in a letter to a church which was not of Paul's planting and which therefore was not involved in the scheme and indeed had no prior knowledge of it. Writing to the Roman Christians to prepare them for his intended visit to their city on the way to Spain, he tells them that the business of this relief fund must be completed before he can set out on his W journey (Rom. 15:25–28). From this reference we acquire some further insight into the motives behind the collection. The strengthening of fellowship between the church of Jerusalem and the Gentile mission was a major concern of Paul's, and his organization of the relief fund was in large measure designed to promote this end. He knew that many members of the Jerusalem church looked with great suspicion on the independent direction taken by his

Gentile mission: indeed, his mission-field was repeatedly invaded by men from Judaea who tried in one way or another to undermine his authority and impose the authority of Jerusalem. But in denouncing them Paul was careful not to give the impression that he was criticizing the church of Jerusalem or its leaders. On the other hand, many of his Gentile converts would be impatient of the idea that they were in any way indebted to the church of Jerusalem. Paul was anxious that they should recognize their substantial indebtedness to Jerusalem. He himself had never been a member of the Jerusalem church and denied emphatically that he derived his gospel or his commission from that church; yet in his eyes that church, as the mother-church of the people of God, occupied a unique place in the Christian order. If he himself were cut off from fellowship with the Jerusalem church, his apostolic activity, he felt, would be futile.

What could be better calculated to allay the suspicions entertained in the Jerusalem church about Paul and his Gentile mission than the manifest evidence of God's blessing on that mission with which Paul planned to confront the Jerusalem believers—not only the monetary gift which would betoken the Gentile churches' practical interest in Jerusalem but living representatives of those churches, deputed to convey their contributions? Writing to his friends in Corinth Paul holds out to them the prospect that their Jerusalem fellow-Christians will be moved to a deep feeling of brotherly affection for them 'because of the surpassing grace of God in you' (2 Cor. 9:14). That all suspicions would in fact be allayed was not a foregone conclusion—Paul asks the Roman Christians to join him in prayers that his 'service for Jerusalem may be acceptable to the saints' there (Rom. 15:31)—but if this would not allay them, nothing would.

Paul may have envisaged this appearance of Gentile believers with their gifts in Jerusalem as at least a token fulfilment of those Hebrew prophecies which spoke of the 'wealth of the nations' as coming to Jerusalem and of the brethren of its citizens as being brought 'from all the nations as an offering to the Lord' on his 'holy mountain' (Is. 60:5; 66:20). But if Paul had those prophecies in mind, perhaps the Jerusalem leaders had them in mind also, and drew different conclusions from them. In the original context, the wealth of the nations is a tribute which the Gentiles bring to Jerusalem in acknowledgment of her supremacy. In Paul's eyes the contributions made by his converts to the Jerusalem relief fund constituted a voluntary gift, an expression of Christian grace and gratitude, but it is conceivable that the recipients looked on them rather as a tribute due from the Gentile subjects of the Son of David.

Even the 'unbelievers in Judea', from whom Paul expected some opposition (Rom. 15:31), might nevertheless be impressed by the visible testimony of so many representative believers from the Gentile lands in their midst. We know that at the very time when Paul was preparing to sail for Judaea with his converts and their gifts, he was pondering the relation, in the divine programme, between his Gentile mission and the ultimate salvation of Israel: this also is a subject on which he lays bare his thought in his letter to the Romans. In this letter, indeed, he sets the collection for Jerusalem, with the problem of Jerusalem itself, in the context to which, in his judgment, they properly belong—the context of God's saving purpose for all mankind.

IV. Reticence of Acts

The delegates of the contributing churches probably included all those fellow-voyagers with Paul from Corinth or Philippi to Judaea who are named in Acts 20:4: Sopater of Beroea, Aristarchus and Secundus from Thessalonica, Gaius of Derbe and Timothy (originally from Lystra), and Tychicus and Trophimus from the province of Asia (the latter of whom we know from Acts 21:29 to have been a Gentile Christian from Ephesus). It would be unwise to attach sinister importance to the absence of a Corinthian name from Luke's list. The list may not be exhaustive; it may be confined to those who had travelled to Corinth from other places to join Paul. Paul had been spending several weeks with Gaius, his host, and other Corinthian friends; moreover, he had just told the Roman Christians how Macedonia and Achaia had resolved to contribute to the Jerusalem relief fund. Achaia, for Paul, meant Corinth and the places around it, and there is no breath of a suggestion in his letter to the Romans that 'Achaia' had not carried out its resolve. We should, indeed, consider the possibility that (in spite of some grumblings over Paul's 'craftiness' in sending Titus to help with the organizing of their contribution) the Corinthian church asked Titus to convey their gift to Jerusalem; if so, the omission of the name of Titus here is of a piece with its omission throughout the whole narrative of Acts. No delegate from the church of Philippi is listed; the narrator himself may have served in that capacity.

When Paul and his companions reached Jerusalem, they were received by James and the other elders of the mother-church, who welcomed them and presumably accepted gratefully the gifts which they brought. The saving adverb 'presumably' is necessary because the record of Acts is completely silent about the collection, except where Paul says, in his defence before Felix, that he had come to Jerusalem 'to bring to my nation alms and offerings' (Acts 24:17).

Luke's almost total silence on the subject may have been apologetically motivated. Apart from the insistence that no evidence was forthcoming to substantiate the allegation that he had violated the sanctity of the Temple, the contents of Paul's defence before Felix would have a greater relevance to his later appearance before the emperor's tribunal in Rome than to his appearance before the procurator of Judaea, and this might well be true of the allusion to 'alms and offerings'. If it can no longer be held that Acts was written to brief counsel for Paul's defence before Caesar, or otherwise to serve as a document in the case, the possibility remains that some material of this kind was used by Luke as source-material. The charge, expressed or implied, that Paul had diverted to a sectarian interest money which ought to have gone to the maintenance of the Temple or to the relief of the Judaeans as a whole, like the charge that, as 'a ringleader of the Nazarenes', he was stirring up subversion in Jewish communities throughout the Roman world, would have been more relevant to a trial before Caesar than to a case falling within the jurisdiction of Felix. A misrepresentation of the nature and purpose of the collection was probably included in the indictment

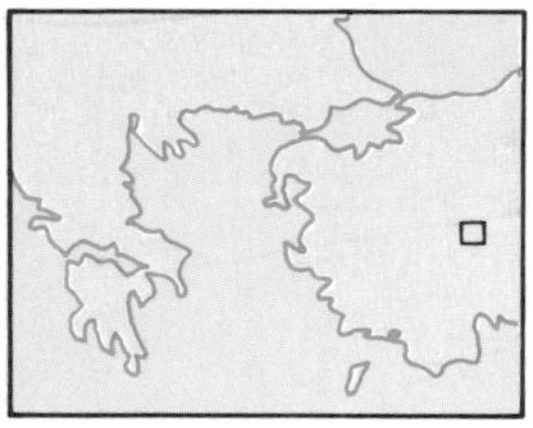

prepared by Paul's prosecutors against the time when his appeal to Caesar came up for hearing; if so, this could account for Luke's reticence.

Bibliography. C. H. Buck, 'The Collection for the Saints', *HTR* 43, 1950, pp. 1ff.; D. Georgi, *Die Geschichte der Kollekte des Paulus für Jerusalem*, 1965; K. Holl, 'Der Kirchenbegriff des Paulus in seinem Verhältnis zu dem der Urgemeinde', *Gesammelte Aufsätze zur Kirchengeschichte* 2, 1928, pp. 44ff.; A. J. Mattill, 'The Purpose of Acts: Schneckenburger Reconsidered', in *Apostolic History and the Gospel*, ed. W. W. Gasque and R. P. Martin, 1970, pp. 108ff.; K. F. Nickle, *The Collection: A Study in Paul's Strategy*, 1966.

F.F.B.

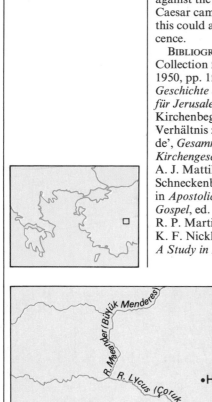

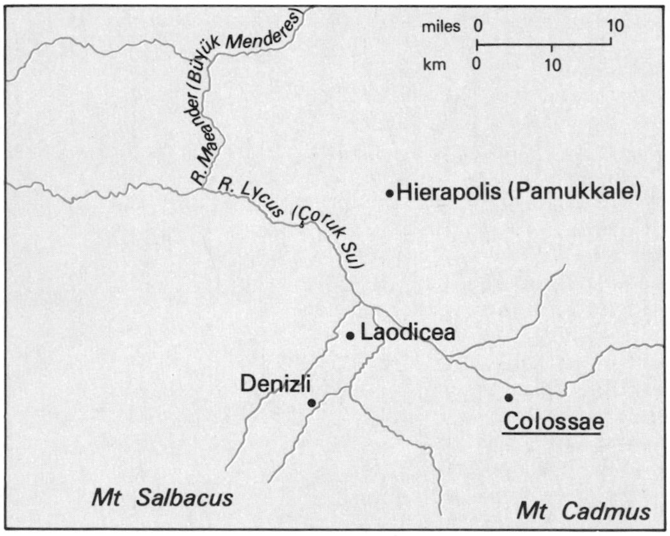

Colossae in the Roman province of Asia.

COLONY. A corporation of Roman citizens settled in foreign parts and enjoying local self-government. The objective was sometimes strategic, more often the rehabilitation of veterans or the unemployed, probably never economic or cultural romanization. In the E colonies were rare, and often composed of Gk.-speaking citizens in any case. The practice even grew up of conferring colonial status on Gk. republics for honorific reasons. The self-conscious Romanism at Philippi (Acts 16:12) was probably therefore exceptional, and none of the other colonies mentioned in the NT is noticed as such (Corinth, Syracuse, Troas, Pisidian Antioch, Lystra, Ptolemais and possibly Iconium). Prominent in the affairs of most foreign states, however, was an association (*conventus*) of resident Roman citizens. The 'visitors from Rome' at Jerusalem (Acts 2:10) are an example of this.

Bibliography. A. H. M. Jones, *The Greek City from Alexander to Justinian*, 1940, pp. 61–84; A. N. Sherwin-White, *The Roman Citizenship*², 1973; B. Levick, *Roman Colonies in Southern Asia Minor*, 1967. E.A.J.

COLOSSAE. A city in the Roman province of Asia, in the W of what is now Asiatic Turkey. It was situated about 15 km up the Lycus valley from *Laodicea, on the main road to the E. It was originally the point at which the great routes from Sardis and Ephesus joined, and at a defensible place with an abundant water-supply. It was an important city in the Lydian and Persian periods, but later it declined when the road through Sardis to Pergamum was resited farther W at the prosperous new foundation of Laodicea. The site is now uninhabited; it lies near Honaz, 16 km E of the town of Denizli.

The gospel probably reached the district while Paul was living at Ephesus (Acts 19:10), perhaps through Epaphras, who was a Colossian (Col. 1:7; 4:12–13). Paul had apparently not visited Colossae when he wrote his letter (Col. 2:1), though his desire to do so (Phm. 22) may have been met at a later date. Philemon (Phm. 1) and his slave Onesimus (Col. 4:9; Phm. 10) were members of the early Colossian church. The mixture of Jewish, Greek and Phrygian elements in the population of the city was probably found also in the church: it would have been fertile ground for the type of speculative heresy which Paul's letter was designed to counter.

The neighbourhood was devastated by an earthquake, dated by Tacitus (*Ann.* 14. 27) to AD 60. There is no hint of this in the Epistle, which we must suppose was written before news of the disaster had reached Rome. E.M.B.G.
C.J.H.

COLOSSIANS, EPISTLE TO THE.

I. Outline of contents

a. 1:1–2. Address.

b. 1:3–8. Thanksgiving for the faith and love of the Colossian Christians, and for the fruit of preaching the gospel among them.

c. 1:9–12. Prayer for their growth in understanding, and consequently in good works.

d. 1:13–23. The glory and greatness of Christ, the Image of God, his Agent in the creation of all things, the Head of the church, the One who by his cross reconciled all things to himself.

e. 1:24–2:3. Paul's labours and sufferings in making known the mystery of Christ, and in seeking to present every man perfect in Christ.

f. 2:4–3:4. The specific warning against false teaching, and the apostle's answer to it.

g. 3:5–17. The sins of the old life to be put off, and the virtues of the new to be put on with Christ.

h. 3:18–4:1. Instructions concerning conduct, to wives and husbands, children and parents, servants and masters.

i. 4:2–6. Exhortation to prayer and wisdom of speech.

j. 4:7–18. Personal messages.

II. Authorship

Doubts about the genuineness of Colossians were expressed first in the 19th century; in particular the Tübingen school rejected the Pauline authorship of this and other letters on the basis of 2nd-century Gnostic ideas supposed to be present in them. More seriously regarded today are arguments based on the vocabulary, style and doctrine of this letter as compared with other Pauline letters, but these are not sufficiently strong to have led many scholars to reject the Pauline authorship. The marked similarity to *Ephesians has led a few to argue for the genuineness of that letter and against that of Colossians (*e.g.* F. C. Synge, *Philippians and Colossians*, 1951), but the evidence has nearly always been taken overwhelmingly to indicate the priority of Colossians. A few scholars, like H. J. Holtzmann and C. Masson, have argued for a more complex relationship between the two letters.

The connection of Colossians with the little letter of *Philemon and the nature of that letter are such that it stands virtually as Paul's 'signature' to Colossians. The letter to Philemon concerns the runaway slave, Onesimus, who was returning to his master; this letter (4:9) says that along with Tychicus this Onesimus was being sent back to Colossae. Archippus is named as of the household of Philemon in that letter (v. 2); in this (4:17) there is a special message for the same man. There are greetings from Epaphras, Mark, Aristarchus, Demas and Luke in Philemon (vv. 23f.); the same people are specially mentioned in this letter (in 4:10–14). It is hard to imagine either or both of these references to particular people as inauthentic and fictitious. The only alternative is to see them as linking together the letters to Philemon and to the Colossians as having the same author and being written at the same time. As C. F. D. Moule puts it (*CGT*, p. 13), 'It seems . . . impossible to doubt that Philemon was written by St Paul, or to doubt the close connection between Philemon and Colossians.'

III. Destination of the Epistle

*Colossae was a city of Phrygia in the Roman province of Asia, situated, like Hierapolis and Laodicea, in the valley of the river Lycus. Its former importance was diminished by NT times, and was further reduced by a disastrous earthquake in the year AD 60. Paul did not found the church there, nor had he visited it when he wrote this letter (1:4, 7–9; 2:1). On his second missionary journey he passed to the N of the Lycus valley (Acts 16:6–8). On his third missionary journey Ephesus was for 3 years the centre of his labours (Acts 19:1–20; 20:31), and it is most likely that at this time the gospel reached Colossae through the agency of the Colossian Epaphras (1:7; 4:12). Most of the Christians there were Gentiles (1:27; 2:13), but from the time of Antiochus the Great there had been considerable and influential settlements of Jews in the neighbourhood.

IV. Time and place of writing

That Colossians was written from prison is clear from the words of 4:3, 10 and 18. Serious consideration has been given to three places as possible sites of Paul's imprisonment when the letter was penned. **1.** Ephesus. The most specific argument in favour of this is the statement of the 2nd-century Marcionite prologue to Colossians. If, however, Colossians and *Ephesians were written at the same time (as indicated by 4:7f. and Eph. 6:21f.), this possibility is ruled out decisively. **2.** Caesarea. A number of arguments have been given in favour of Caesarea. Bo Reicke argues this way on the basis of the destructive earthquake referred to above, but the beginning of Paul's Roman imprisonment was probably earlier than the year that the earthquake took its toll in the Lycus valley. It is not likely that all of those named in ch. 4 were with the apostle when he was in prison in Caesarea. **3.** Rome. There is no difficulty urged against the Roman origin of the letter that has not been adequately met. There is no place more likely than Rome to which the fugitive Onesimus would go, and the contents and personal references of the letter would seem to be more suited to Paul's Roman imprisonment than to any other. A date of AD 60 therefore seems likely.

V. Reason for the Epistle

Two matters brought the church in Colossae especially before Paul and occasioned the writing of this letter. First, he was writing to Philemon in Colossae sending back his runaway, but now converted, slave, Onesimus (Phm. 7–21). He could also take the opportunity of writing to the whole Colossian church. Secondly, Epaphras had brought to Paul a report of that church, which included many encouraging things (1:4–8), but apparently also disquieting news of the false teaching that threatened to lead its members away from the truth of Christ. This news pressed the apostle to write as he did.

VI. The false teaching

In his characteristic manner Paul meets the challenge confronting the Colossian church by positive teaching rather than point-by-point refutation. Thus we do not know fully what it involved, but we may infer three things:

1. It gave an important place to the powers of the spirit world to the detriment of the place given to Christ. In 2:18 he speaks of 'worship of angels', and other references to the relation of the spiritual creation to Christ (1:16, 20; 2:15) appear to have similar significance.

2. Great importance was attached to outward observances, such as feasts and fasts, new moons and sabbaths (2:16f.), and probably also circumcision (2:11). These were presented proudly as the true way of self-discipline and the subjection of the flesh (2:20ff.).

3. The teachers boasted that they possessed a higher philosophy. This is clear from 2:4, 8, 18; and we may assume also that Paul, in his frequent use of the terms 'knowledge' (*gnōsis* and *epignōsis*), 'wisdom' (*sophia*), 'understanding' (*synesis*) and 'mystery' (*mystērion*), was countering such a view.

Some (*e.g.* Hort and Peake) have maintained that Jewish teaching could sufficiently account for all these different elements. Lightfoot argued that the false teaching was that of the Essenes, and we now have considerable knowledge of the Essene-like sect of the Dead Sea Scrolls, though we do not know of the presence of such a sect in the Lycus valley in the 1st century AD. Others have identified the Colossian heresy with one of the Gnostic schools known to us from 2nd-century writers. We may not label it precisely. Syncretism in religion and philosophy prevailed in those days. We would probably be near to the truth in calling the teaching a Judaistic form of Gnosticism.

Paul deals with its three errors as follows:

1. It is a misguided humility, he tells the Colossians, that exalts angels, and emphasizes the functions of the spirit powers of good and the fear of the principalities of evil. Christ is the Creator and Lord of all things in heaven and on earth, and the Vanquisher of all evil powers (1:15ff.; 2:9ff.). All the fullness (*plērōma*) of the Godhead is in Christ. (Here too Paul was probably taking and putting to a Christian use one of the key words of the false teaching.)

2. The way of holiness is not by an asceticism that promotes only spiritual pride, nor by self-centred efforts to control the passions, but by putting on Christ, setting one's affections on him, and so stripping off all that is contrary to his will (2:20ff.; 3:1ff.).

3. The true wisdom is not a man-made philosophy (2:8), but the *'mystery' (revealed secret) of God in Christ, who indwells those who receive him (1:27), without distinction of persons (3:10f.).

BIBLIOGRAPHY. J. B. Lightfoot, *Saint Paul's Epistles to the Colossians and to Philemon*, 1875; T. K. Abbott, *The Epistles to the Ephesians and to the Colossians*, *ICC*, 1897; C. F. D. Moule, *The Epistles of Paul the Apostle to the Colossians and to Philemon*, *CGT*, 1957; F. F. Bruce in *The Epistles of Paul to the Ephesians and to the Colossians*, *NLC*, 1957; H. M. Carson, *The Epistles of Paul to the Colossians and Philemon*, *TNTC*, 1960; R. P. Martin, *Colossians and Philemon*, *NCB*, 1974; the series of

Chart showing colours referred to in the Bible, with a selection of Hebrew and Greek terms and examples of their use. Biblical languages had relatively few words for different colours.

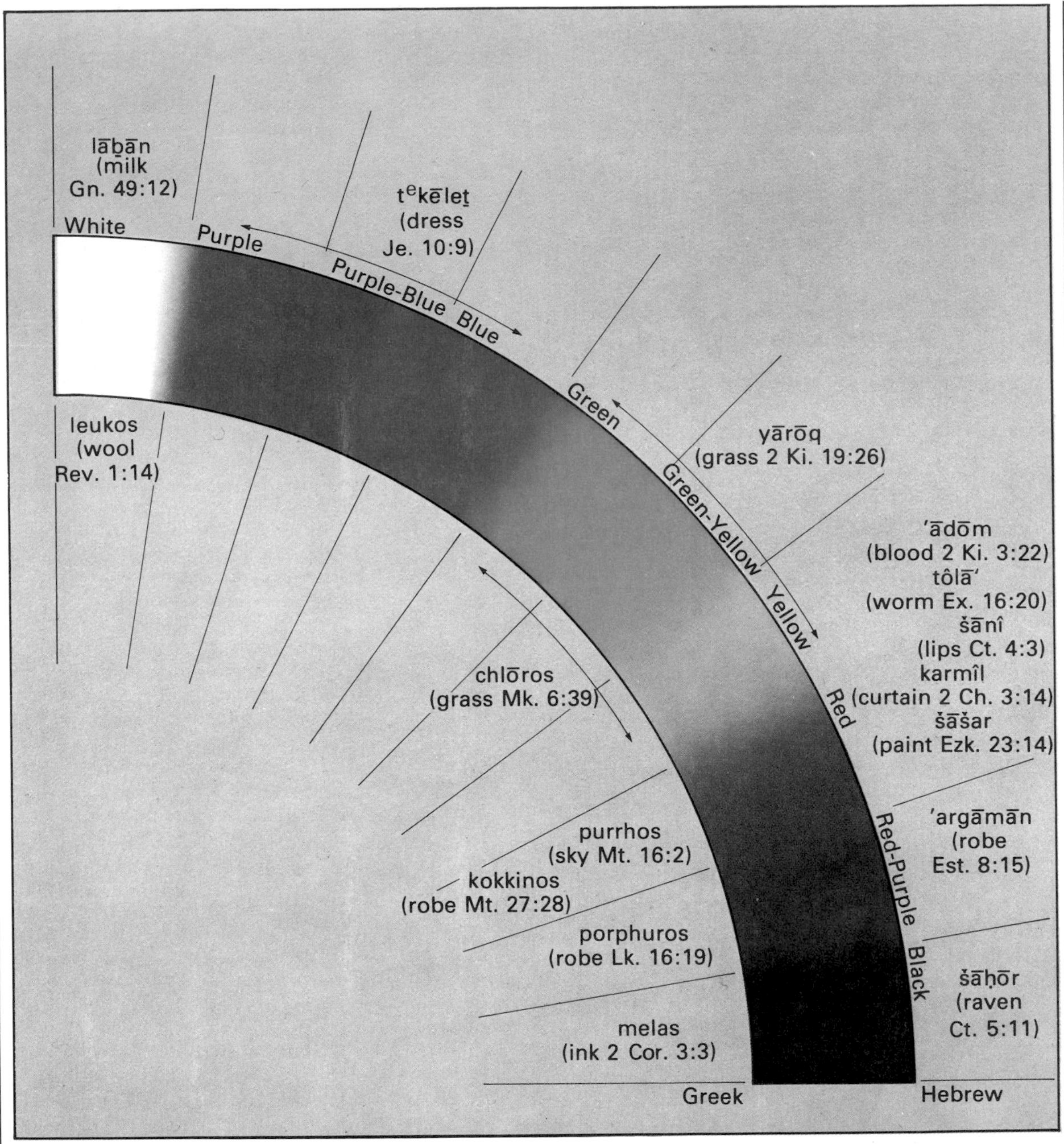

articles on Col. by Bo Reicke, E. Schweizer, G. R. Beasley-Murray, C. F. D. Moule, G. E. Ladd and others in *Review and Expositor* 70, 1973, pp. 429ff.

F.F.

COLOURS. Colour-adjectives appear but sparsely in OT and NT alike, for a variety of reasons. The first reason is specific: the Bible, being the account of God's dealings with a nation, and not the subjective record of a nation's aesthetic experience, is sparing in descriptive writing of the kind that involves extensive and precise use of adjectives of colour. Even where nature, animate or inanimate, is described in the OT (as frequently in the Pentateuch, Job and Pss.), it is in its more awe-inspiring aspects, as fitting reflection of its Creator.

The second reason is more general and linguistic: biblical Hebrew did not possess a complex and highly-developed colour vocabulary, such as exists in most modern Indo-European languages today. Thus, close definition of colour would have been difficult if not impossible, unless by the use of simile or metaphor. But this reason, which seems at first sight to be purely linguistic, turns out to be psychological, after all; for it is an axiom of linguistics that any culture, no matter how primitive, develops that vocabulary which is perfectly adequate to express its thought and desires. This linguistic paucity, then, corresponds to a lack of interest in colour as an aesthetic experience on the part of the Hebrew people; their practical concern was more with the nature of the material of which the article was made, by virtue of which it was a particular colour. Indeed, many of their colour-words were descriptive of origin rather than shade; *'argāmān*, for instance, generally translated 'purple' (*e.g.* Ex. 25:4), is reddish-purple cloth, usually woollen. It is a borrowed word, and probably means 'tribute'. Other similar words (*šānî, karmîl, tôlā'*) either contain a reference to the *murex*, the shellfish from whose juice the costly dye was obtained, or to the cochineal insect or shield-louse, which yielded a rich red. In consequence, one clothed in purple is not to the Hebrew primarily a beautiful object. He is a king, or wealthy man; just as one in sack-cloth is not primarily an ugly object, but a beggar or a mourner. This approach makes easy the symbolic use of colour, which appears spasmodically in the OT and fully developed in the Apocalypse. However, even the RSV appears to have itself used 'crimson' and 'scarlet' quite indiscriminately, so little stress should be laid on the exact colour. *šāšar*, 'vermilion' (Je. 22:14 and Ezk. 23:14) is an exception: it was a lead or iron oxide, yielding a bright red pigment suitable for wall-painting, not for the dyeing of clothing.

The NT writers were, of course, fully equipped with the extensive and flexible Gk. colour-vocabulary; but they were, by virtue of their subject, concerned with colour as such even less than the writers of the OT. In any case, fixity of shade, and therefore exact precision of terminology, had to wait until the advent of purely chemical dyes, which are easier to control, and the consequent development of colour-charts. In common with other ancient peoples, the Greeks were much more impressed by the contrast between light and shade than that between different colours. In other words, they tended to see and describe all colours as graduations between black and white. To compensate, they had a remarkably rich vocabulary to describe degrees of refracted light. When this is realized, many imagined Bible problems disappear; the fields of Jn. 4:35, are not 'already white for harvest' but 'gleaming'; Ex. 25:4 groups 'blue and purple and scarlet' together, not only as all alike being symbols of richness, but because to the writer they were akin, perhaps scarcely differentiated, as being 'dark', not 'light', colours, similarly produced, and all alike being colours of textiles, *i.e.* artefacts and not natural objects. For Joseph's coat, see *JOSEPH.

BIBLIOGRAPHY. Platt, *CQ* 1935; A. E. Kober, *The Use of Color Terms in the Greek Poets*, 1932; F. E. Wallace, *Colour in Homer and in Ancient Art*, 1927; I. Meyerson (ed.), *Problèmes de la Couleur*, 1957; G. T. D. Angel, *NIDNTT* 1, pp. 203–206; and see Index in *NIDNTT* 3. A.C.

COMMUNION. In the NT the basic term, translated variously as 'communion', 'fellowship', 'communicate', 'partake', 'contribution', 'common' (in the sense of the Latin *communis*), stems from the Greek root *koin-*. There are two adjectives, *koinōnos* (found 10 times) and *synkoinōnos* (found 4 times), which are used as nouns also; and two verbs *koinōneō* (8 times) and *synkoinōneō* (3 times); and the noun *koinōnia* (20 times).

The fundamental connotation of the root *koin-* is that of sharing in something (genitive) with someone (dative); or the simple cases may be replaced by a prepositional phrase. In both constructions nouns may be replaced by prepositions. Very rarely it may mean 'to give a share in' something; the most characteristic NT usage is that which employs *koin-* with the genitive of the thing (or person) shared. There is also another NT use in which the term is found actively of a 'willingness to give a share'; hence the meaning 'generosity'. A third meaning emerges from the first use, with the sense of 'sharing' or 'fellowship' (which arises out of a common sharing of something). The results of the recent linguistic researches of such scholars as H. Seesemann and A. R. George may be stated in the latter's words: 'The important thing is that these words (belonging to the *koin-* family) refer primarily, though not invariably, to participation in something rather than to association with others: and there is often a genitive to indicate that in which one participates or shares' (A. R. George, *Communion with God in the New Testament*, p. 133). From this ground-plan of the word, the NT passages may be divided into three classes, according to whether the predominant idea is (*a*) having a share; (*b*) giving a share; or (*c*) sharing.

a. 'Having a share'

Under this heading we may classify, first of all, the adjectives which are used to describe partners in some common enterprise, *e.g.* Christian work (2 Cor. 8:23), or secular business (Lk. 5:10); also those who share in a common experience (*e.g.* persecution, Heb. 10:33; Rev. 1:9; suffering, 2 Cor. 1:7; worship, 1 Cor. 10:18; murder, Mt. 23:30; the compact with demons in pagan cult worship, 1 Cor. 10:20). Then it is used similarly of those who enjoy certain privileges in common, *e.g.* Rom. 11:17; 1 Cor. 9:23. References to a common sharing in direct spiritual realities are Phil. 1:7; 1 Pet. 5:1; and 2 Pet. 1:4, although in the first text the 'grace' in question may be that of apostleship in which both the apostle and church share, and of which Paul writes in Rom. 1:5; Eph. 3:2, 8.

The verb *koinōneō* and its cognate form, which adds the prefix *syn* meaning 'together with', occur in 11 passages in the NT; but some of these will fall more naturally under section *b*, *i.e.* they will lend themselves best to the translation 'generosity'. But under this heading we may note Rom. 15:27; Eph. 5:11; 1 Tim. 5:22; 2 Jn. 11; Rev. 18:4; Phil. 4:14; Heb. 2:14.

The noun is found to denote the corporate Christian life with the thought that believers share together in certain objective realities (*cf.* E. Lohmeyer, *Der Brief an die Philipper*, 1956, p. 17, who denies that it is ever found in Paul's writing in the sense of a bond joining Christians together, but always with the meaning of participation in an object outside the believer's subjective experience). These references are most notably: **1.** 1 Cor. 10:16 ('participation in the blood and body of Christ'); **2.** 1 Cor. 1:9, where Anderson Scott's view aims at seeing *koinōnia* as a designation of the church; but his interpretation here and elsewhere is being increasingly abandoned in favour of the objective sense of the genitive (or, with Deissmann, the 'mystical genitive' or 'genitive of fellowship'). So the best translation of a difficult verse is 'fellowship with his Son, Jesus Christ our Lord' whether in the sense of 'sharing in' or 'sharing with' him; **3.** Phil. 2:1, where the issue is to decide between a subjective genitive ('any fellowship wrought by the Spirit': so Anderson Scott, *Christianity According to St Paul*, 1927, pp. 160ff.), or an objective genitive ('fellowship with the Spirit', 'participation in the Spirit': so convincingly Seesemann); **4.** 2 Cor. 13:14, where again the choice is between *koinōnia* as fellowship which is created by the Holy Spirit and fellowship as participation in the Holy Spirit, a translation (*cf.* RSVmg.) which is much in favour since Seesemann's discussion in 1933; **5.** 2 Cor. 8:4, 'taking part in the relief of the saints'; and **6.** Phil. 3:10, where the genitive is clearly objective, meaning that Paul's 'own actual

COLT
See Animals, Part 1.

COMMANDER
See Governor, Part 2.

COMMITMENT
See Name, Part 2.

COMMON LAND
See Suburb, Part 3.

COMMON LIFE
See Brotherly love, Part 1.

sufferings are a real participation in Christ's sufferings, suffered by virtue of his communion with Christ' (A. R. George, *op. cit.*, p. 184; *cf.* R. P. Martin, *Philippians*, *TNTC*, pp. 49–50; and *Philippians*, *NCB*, 1976, pp. 133ff. [biblio.]).

b. 'Giving a share'

The main texts which support the interpretation of *koinōnia* as 'giving a share' are 2 Cor. 9:13, 'the generosity of your contribution for them and for all others'. 'Your contribution' represents the Greek *tēs koinōnias*, for which Seesemann proposes the translation *Mitteilsamkeit*, *i.e.*, in this context, generosity. This same rendering may be suggested also for Phil. 1:5 in which case the object of Paul's gratitude to God is the generosity of the Philippian Christians in their support of the apostolic ministry for the progress of the gospel. Similarly, the same translation clarifies Phm. 6.

Another reference under this heading is Rom. 15:26, which indicates that *koinōnia* can take on a concrete form as a generosity which clothes itself in practical action, and is so applied to the collection for the saints of the Jerusalem church in their poverty-stricken condition (*cf.* 2 Cor. 8:4). In this light we may consider, finally, Acts 2:42, although A. R. George rules out the meaning of 'almsgiving', 'generosity'. Other views which have been offered to explain this reference are an allusion to the *Lord's Supper (*cf.* C. H. Dodd, *The Johannine Epistles*, 1946, p. 7); a technical expression for having a community of goods as in Acts 2:44; 4:32, as C. E. B. Cranfield takes it in *TWBR*, p. 82; Anderson Scott's view that the term *hē koinōnia* = the fellowship) is the translation of a special Heb. word *ḥ[a]ḇûrâ* meaning a religious society within Judaism; a recent proposal of J. Jeremias that Acts 2:42 lists, in its four notes of the church's corporate life, the liturgical sequence of early Christian worship, in which case *koinōnia* may be an allusion to the offering (*The Eucharistic Words of Jesus*, E.T. 1955, p. 83, n. 3, but in [2]E.T. 1966, pp. 118–121 this view is withdrawn); and the view that *koinōnia* describes the inward spiritual bond which joined the early Jerusalem brotherhood and which expresses itself in the outward acts of a pooling of material resources (*cf.* L. S. Thornton, *The Common Life in the Body of Christ*, 1942, p. 451). See, further, R. N. Flew, *Jesus and His Church*[2], 1943, pp. 109–110.

c. 'Sharing'

Under this heading there are only three possible occurrences where *koinōnia* is used absolutely or with the preposition *meta* (with). These are Acts 2:42; Gal. 2:9 and 1 Jn. 1:3ff.

BIBLIOGRAPHY. The most important treatment of the *koin-* group of words in the NT is that by H. Seesemann, *Der Begriff KOINŌNIA im Neuen Testament*, *ZNW*, Beiheft 14, 1933. His conclusions are utilized by most subsequent writers on this theme, especially A. R. George, *Communion with God in the New Testament*, 1953, who provides a full discussion of most of the controverted passages to which allusion has been made above. He gives also a complete bibliography, to which may be added the most recent contribution to the subject, M. McDermott, 'The Biblical Doctrine of KOINONIA', *BZ* 19. 1–2, 1975, pp. 64–77, 219–233. See too J. Eichler, J. Schattenmann, *NIDNTT* 1, pp. 635–644.

(*LORD'S SUPPER.) R.P.M.

COMPASSION. In the Bible it is a divine as well as a human quality. In RSV the word is often used to translate Heb. *ḥāmal* and *raḥ[a]mîm*, which are, however, in AV more frequently rendered by 'pity' or 'spare' and 'mercy' or 'tender mercies' respectively. Thus compassion, pity and mercy can be regarded as synonyms. In the NT the most frequent words are *eleeō* (and cognate forms), translated by 'have compassion', 'have mercy' and 'have pity', and *eleos*, which is always translated 'mercy'. *oikteirō* is found twice and translated 'have compassion' and *oiktirmōn* three times with the meaning 'merciful' and 'of tender mercy'.

The prophets and other men of God were deeply aware of the wonder of God's *mercy to sinful men. They taught that anyone who had experienced this would feel it his duty to have compassion on his fellows, especially 'the fatherless, the widow, and the foreigner' (frequently named together as in Dt. 10:18; 14:29; 16:11; 24:19; Je. 22:3, *etc.*) and also on those in *poverty and the afflicted (Ps. 146:9; Jb. 6:14; Pr. 19:17; Zc. 7:9–10; Mi. 6:8). There is no doubt from the frequent references in Deuteronomy that God expected his people to show compassion not only to each other but to foreigners who lived among them. Through the teaching of our Lord Jesus Christ, especially in the parable of the good Samaritan (Lk. 10), it is clear that compassion is to be shown by his disciples to anyone who needs their help. It is to be like his, not only in being without respect of persons, but also in that it is expressed in deeds (1 Jn. 3:17) which may involve personal sacrifice. J.W.M.

COMPENSATION
See Crime, Part 1.

CONCISION
See Circumcision, Part 1.

CONCUBINE. The practice of concubinage was widespread in the biblical world. In Mesopotamia the husband was free to have legal sexual relations with slaves. In Assyria the husband was able to take several free-born concubines as well as his 'veiled' wife, although the 'concubine' was subject to the wife's authority. Her sons were entitled to share the inheritance. Concubines who bore children and who behaved arrogantly could be treated as slaves but not sold (*cf.* *Laws of Hammurapi* 146–147; 170–171). In Cappadocia (19th century BC) and Alalaḫ where a wife failed to produce a son within a specified time (3 or 7 years respectively) the husband was entitled to marry a second wife. In Ugarit a man who possessed a concubine was called a *b'l ššlmt*, 'the possessor of a female who completes (the family)'. Sarah provided a slave concubine for Abraham (Gn. 16:2–3) and handmaidens given as a marriage gift to Leah and Rachel became Jacob's concubines (Gn. 29:24, Zilpah; Gn. 29:29, Bilhah). Concubines were protected under Mosaic law (Ex. 21:7–11; Dt. 21:10–14), although they were distinguished from wives (Jdg. 8:31; 2 Sa. 5:13; 1 Ki. 11:3; 2 Ch. 11:21) and were more easily divorced (Gn. 21:10–14). Kings such as Solomon went to excess in a plurality of wives and concubines. To lie with a monarch's concubine was tantamount to usurpation of the throne (2 Sa. 3:7; 16:21–22; 1 Ki. 2:21–24). Two terms are used in the OT, *pîlegeš*, a term of non-Semitic origin, and the Aram. *l[e]ḥēnâ* (Dn. 5:2–3, 23), a 'temple servant'. The former term is used in the times of the Patriarchs, the Conquest and the early kingdom, with the most frequent use in the days of the Judges. The practice created tension with wives in all periods and later prophets encouraged monogamy (Mal. 2:14ff.). The ideal woman of Pr. 31 belonged to a monogamous society.

In the NT monogamy was enjoined by Jesus (Mt. 5:32; 19:3–12, *etc.*), and by NT writers (1 Tim. 3:2, 12). The contemporary Greek and Roman world still practised concubinage. Among the Greeks, *pallakai*, 'concubines', were regularly maintained for sexual pleasure and children born from such unions, although free, were bastards. It was the wives (*gynaikes*) who bore legitimate children. In the Roman world the state of *concubinatus*, or 'lying together', involved informal but more or less permanent unions without a marriage ceremony. Children of such unions took the legal status of their mother and were deprived of the status of citizens. Against such a background monogamy was the only form of marriage for Christians. Unmarried men who had a concubine were obliged to marry or be refused baptism; the believing woman could be baptized.

BIBLIOGRAPHY. A. F. Rainey, *EJ*, 5, col. 862f.; R. de Vaux, *Ancient Israel*, 1962, pp. 24–25, 29, 53–54, 83, 86, 115–117; 'Marriage', *Dictionary of Biblical Archaeology*, ed. E. M. Blaiklock (forthcoming).

J.A.T.

CONFESSION. The word to 'confess' in both the Heb. and the Gk. (*yādâ* and *homologein*) has, as in English, a twofold reference. There is confession of faith and confession of sin. On the one hand, confession means to declare publicly a personal relationship with and allegiance to God. It is an act of open joyful commitment made to God in the presence of the world, by which a congregation or individuals bind themselves in loyalty to God or Jesus Christ. It is an avowal of faith which can have eternal eschatological consequences. On the other hand, it means to acknowledge sin and guilt in the light of God's revelation, and is thus generally an outward sign of repentance and faith. It may or may not be followed by forgiveness (Jos. 7:19; Lv. 26:40; Ps. 32:5; Mt. 27:4; 1 Jn. 1:9).

The biblical use of the word appears to reflect the language of ancient treaties where a vassal agrees to the terms of the *covenant made by his suzerain, and binds himself by an oath to be loyal. Likewise from the legal context of confession of guilt in a court of law, the term is transferred to the confession of sin to God.

I. In the Old Testament

In the OT confession frequently has the character of praise, where the believer in gratitude declares what God has done redemptively for Israel or his own soul. The noun (*tôḏâ*) may thus mean confession, thanksgiving, praise, or even be used for a company of people singing songs of praise. Such acknowledgment of God's mighty acts of mercy and deliverance is consequently closely related to the confession of sin. Both aspects of confession form an integral part of prayer and true worship (Gn. 32:9–11; 1 Ki. 8:35; 2 Ch. 6:26; Ne. 1:4–11; 9; Jb. 33:26–28; Pss. 22; 32; 51; 116; Dn. 9). Confession can lead the believer to pledge himself anew to God, to sing hymns of praise, to offer joyful sacrifice, and can give him a desire to tell others of God's mercy and to identify himself with the worshipping congregation in the house of God at Jerusalem.

Confession is not only personal and individual; it has a liturggical connotation where, as on the Day of *Atonement in the context of expiation and intercession, the high priest vicariously confesses the sins of the people, laying his hands on the head of a live goat which symbolically carries sin away from the covenant community (Lv. 16:21). In similar fashion Moses vicariously pleads for Israel (Ex. 32:32; *cf.* Ne. 1:6; Jb. 1:5; Dn. 9:4ff.).

Confession in the sense of joyful acknowledgment is prominent in the Qumran texts where frequently the psalms begin, 'I thank thee, Lord, because . . .', in a way similar to our Lord's prayer in Mt. 11:25 (1QH 2. 20, 31, *etc.*).

II. In the New Testament

In the NT the Gk. word to 'confess' has the generic meaning of acknowledging something to be the case in agreement with others; it is primarily used with reference to faith in Christ. It gathers up the OT aspects of thanksgiving and joyful praise, as well as of willing submission, as in Mt. 11:25; Rom. 15:9; Heb. 13:15. In this it follows the LXX usage of the word, as in Pss. 42:6; 43:4–5; Gn. 29:34. It means, however, more than mental assent. It implies a decision to pledge oneself in loyalty to Jesus Christ as Lord in response to the work of the Holy Spirit.

To confess Jesus Christ is to acknowledge him as the Messiah (Mt. 16:16; Mk. 4:29; Jn. 1:41; 9:22), as the Son of God (Mt. 8:29; Jn. 1:34, 49; 1 Jn. 4:15), that he came in the flesh (1 Jn. 4:2; 2 Jn. 7), and that he is Lord, primarily on the ground of the resurrection and ascension (Rom. 10:9; 1 Cor. 12:3; Phil. 2:11).

Confession of Jesus Christ is linked intimately with the confession of sins. To confess Christ is to confess that he 'died for our sins', and conversely to confess one's sins in real repentance is to look to Christ for forgiveness (1 Jn. 1:5–10). In preparation for the coming of Christ, John the Baptist summoned people to confess their sins, and confession was a constant element in the ministry both of our Lord and of the apostles (Mt. 3:6; 6:12; Lk. 5:8; 15:21; 18:13; 19:8; Jn. 20:23; Jas. 5:16).

Although addressed to God, confession of faith in Jesus Christ should be made openly 'before men' (Mt. 10:32; Lk. 12:8; 1 Tim. 6:12), by word of mouth (Rom. 10:9; Phil. 2:11), and may be costly (Mt. 10:32–39; Jn. 9:22; 12:42). It is the opposite of 'denying' the Lord. Confession of sin is likewise primarily addressed to God, but may also be made before men, for example, in corporate confession by a congregation or its representative in public prayer. Where the confession is for the benefit of the church or of others, an individual may openly confess sins in the presence of the church or of other believers (Acts 19:18; Jas. 5:16), but this should never be unedifying (Eph. 5:12). True repentance may require an acknowledgment of guilt to a brother (Mt. 5:23–24), but there is no suggestion that confession of private sin must be made to an individual presbyter.

Confession of Jesus Christ is the work of the Holy Spirit, and as such is the mark of the true church, the Body of Christ (Mt. 10:20; 16:16–19; 1 Cor. 12:3). For this reason it accompanies baptism (Acts 8:37; 10:44–48), out of which practice emerged some of the earliest creeds and confessions of the church, which acquired added significance with the rise of error and false doctrine (1 Jn. 4:2; 2 Jn. 7).

The perfect pattern of confession is given to us in Jesus Christ himself, who witnessed a good confession before Pontius Pilate (1 Tim. 6:12–13). He confessed that he is

CONEY
See Animals, Part 1.

CONFECTIONARIES
See Cosmetics, Part 1.

the Christ (Mk. 14:62) and that he is a King (Jn. 18:36). His confession was before men, over against the false witness of his enemies (Mk. 14:56) and the denial of a disciple (Mk. 14:68), and was infinitely costly, with eternal consequences for all men. The church in her confession identifies herself 'before many witnesses' with the 'good confession' of her crucified and risen Saviour. Her confession (of faith and of sin) is a sign that the old man is 'dead with Christ' and that she is possessed by her Lord, whom she is commissioned to serve. In her confession she is called to participate through the Spirit in the vicarious intercessions of Christ, 'the apostle and high priest of our confession' (Heb. 3:1), who has already confessed our sins on the cross and given praise to God (Heb. 2:12; Rom. 15:9, quoting Pss. 18:49; 22:22).

Confession in the NT (like denial of Christ) has an eschatological perspective, leading to either judgment or salvation, because it is the outward manifestation of faith or lack of it. Christ will one day confess before the Father those who confess him today, and deny those who deny him (Mt. 10:32–33; Lk. 12:8; 2 Tim. 2:11–13). Confession with the mouth is made to salvation (Rom. 10:9–10, 13; 2 Cor. 4:13–14), and our confessions today are a foretaste of the church's confessions of the last day, when every tongue shall confess that Jesus Christ is Lord (Rom. 14:11–12; Phil. 2:11; Rev. 4:11; 5:12; 7:10).

Bibliography. O. Cullmann, *The Earliest Christian Confessions*, 1949; J. N. D. Kelly, *Early Christian Creeds*, 1950; H. N. Ridderbos, in R. Banks (ed.), *Reconciliation and Hope* (Leon Morris Festschrift), 1974; R. P. Martin, *An Early Christian Confession: Philippians 2:5–11 in Recent Interpretation*, 1960.

J.B.T.

CONIAH
See Jehoiachin, Part 2.

CONFIRMATION. 1. Gk. *bebaiōsis* (Phil. 1:7; Heb. 6:16) is thus rendered, meaning 'a making firm' and 'a valid ratification', respectively. In the OT seven Heb. roots are translated by 'affirm', 'make firm', 'reaffirm', 'confirm' (*e.g.* Is. 35:3; Est. 9:32). In the NT four Gk. verbs are similarly used. 1. *bebaioun*; *e.g.* Rom. 15:8, 'confirm the promises'. 2. *kyroun*, used of a covenant (Gal. 3:15, 'ratified'), and of a personal attitude (2 Cor. 2:8—AV 'confirm your love'; RSV 'reaffirm your love'). 3. *mesiteuein*, *e.g.* Heb. 6:17 (AV 'confirm', RV, RSV 'interpose with an oath') where the meaning is that a promise is guaranteed because God is acting as Mediator. 4. *epistērizein* is Luke's word in Acts for the strengthening effect of an apostolic mission on fellow-Christians (11:2, Western Text), on the souls of the disciples (14:22), on the churches (15:41) and brethren (15:32).

2. The ecclesiastical rite known as 'confirmation', or 'laying on of hands', is not traced to these verses, where Luke speaks only of the consolidating effect on faith of the apostolic presence and preaching, but, presumably, to such passages as Acts 8:14–17; 19:1–6, where laying on of hands precedes a spectacular descent of the Holy Spirit upon previously baptized persons. Two observations may be made. In the first place, in these verses in Acts the gift of the Spirit is associated primarily with baptism, not with a subsequent and separate rite of 'laying on of hands' (*cf.* Heb. 6:2). Secondly, Acts shows no constant sequence. Thus, laying on of hands may precede baptism, and be performed by one not an apostle (9:17ff.); in Acts 6:6; 13:3 it is associated, not with baptism, but with special tasks to be done (*cf.* Nu. 27:18, 20, 23) in connection with the missionary activity of the church.

Bibliography. G. W. H. Lampe, *The Seal of the Spirit*, 1951; H. Schönweiss *et al.*, *NIDNTT* 1, pp. 658–664; H. Schlier, *TDNT* 1, pp. 600–603; for the rite of 'confirmation', see *ODCC*. M.R.W.F.

CONGREGATION, SOLEMN ASSEMBLY. The noun 'congregation' is used to render several Heb. words, one of which is also translated 'assembly'.

1. *mô'ēḏ* and *'ēḏâ* come from the root *yā'aḏ*, 'to appoint, assign, designate'. *mô'ēḏ* means an appointed time or place, or meeting, and occurs 223 times (*e.g.* Gn. 18:14; Ho. 9:5, 'appointed festival'). In its most frequent use *'ōhel mô'ēḏ* means the 'tent of meeting', AV 'tabernacle of the congregation'—a translation which fails to convey the sense of 'due appointment' (*e.g.* Ex. 27:21). In Is. 14:13 *mô'ēḏ* is used for 'mount of the congregation'. See *BDB*. *'ēḏâ* occurs 149 times (not in Dt.), and means a company of people assembled together by appointment (*e.g.* Ex. 16:1–2, where the congregation of Israel are assembled by God for the purpose of journeying from Egypt to Canaan).

2. *qāhāl* occurs 123 times, and comes from a root meaning 'assemble together', whether for war (*e.g.* 2 Sa. 20:14), rebellion (Nu. 16:3) or a religious purpose (*e.g.* Nu. 10:7). It is used in Dt. 5:22, where all Israel is assembled to hear the words of God, and in Dt. 23:3, where solemn statements of excommunication are being made. On the distinction between *'ēḏâ* and *qāhāl*, see *HDB*, *TWBR* and especially *TDNT* 3, pp. 487–536 (*ekklēsia*). It appears that *'ēḏâ*, the older word, is in frequent use in Ex. and Nu., and bears an almost technical sense of 'those gathered together' (for a specific purpose), but that *qāhāl*, preferred by Deuteronomy and later writers, came to mean 'all Israel gathered together by God as a theocratic state'.

3. The rare word *'ᵃṣereṯ*, from a root meaning 'restrain' or 'confine', is rendered 'solemn assembly' (*e.g.* Is. 1:13; Ne. 8:18; Am. 5:21) in connection with high festivals, *e.g.* Unleavened Bread, Tabernacles (Dt. 16:8; Lv. 23:36). This word, translated into Gk. as *panēgyris*, lies behind 'festal gathering and assembly' in Heb. 12:23, RSVmg.

4. In the LXX *ekklēsia* was usually employed to translate *qāhāl*, sometimes for *'ēḏâ*, for which *synagōgē* was also used. In the NT *ekklēsia* is normally rendered *'church', though Luke uses it in its classical sense in Acts 19:39, 41 of a summoned political assembly. In Acts 13:43 *synagōgē* is rendered 'congregation' by the AV (RV and RSV correctly 'synagogue'); its use in Jas. 2:2 indicates a Jewish–Christian meeting. Since *synagōgē*, like 'church' in Eng., had come to mean both the gathering and the building, and since the Christians no longer met in synagogues, they chose *ekklēsia* to describe themselves.

Bibliography. K. L. Schmidt, *TDNT* 3, pp. 501–536; L. Coenen, *NIDNTT* 1, pp. 291–307.

M.R.W.F.

CONSCIENCE.

I. Background

The OT has no word for 'conscience', and the Gk. term *syneidēsis* is virtually absent from the LXX. If the concept which it denotes is not to be regarded as an innovation by the NT writers, its origin must therefore be sought in a world of Gk. rather than Heb. ideas. Many scholars opt in fact for a Stoic origin of the term, including C. H. Dodd (*Romans* in *MNTC*, pp. 35–37), C. K. Barrett (*Romans* in *BNTC*, p. 53) and J. Moffatt (on 1 Cor. 8:7ff. in *MNTC*). But C. A. Pierce (*Conscience in the New Testament*, 1955, pp. 13ff.) suggests instead that the background to the word in the NT is to be found in non-philosophical, popular Gk. thought (see also J. Dupont, *Gnosis*, 1949, p. 267). Pierce further believes that the term came into the NT as a result of the troubles at Corinth, in which appeals to 'conscience' were being made in order to justify controversial actions, notably the eating of food offered to idols (Pierce, pp. 60ff.; *cf.* 1 Cor. 8:7–13). This would explain the absence of the term from the OT and Gospels, and its prevalence in Paul—especially in the Corinthian letters.

II. Meaning

The foundation-word of the group to which *syneidēsis* belongs is *synoida*, which occurs rarely in the NT and means 'I know in common with' (Acts 5:2; *cf.* the strict etymology of *conscientia*, the Lat. equivalent of *syneidēsis*), or—as it is used in the particular construction *hautō syneidenai*—something akin to the faculty of 'self-knowledge' (1 Cor. 4:4, which NEB translates as 'I have nothing on my conscience'). The chief meaning of *syneidēsis* in the NT is an extension of this idea, and implies more than simply 'consciousness', since it includes moral judgment on the quality (right or wrong) of a conscious act. To some extent the way for this meaning had already been prepared in Judaism.

In the OT, as in Gk. philosophy, the judgment of actions was normally referred to the state or to the law. But in 1 Sa. 24:5 'heart' (Heb. *lēḇ*), in the phrase 'David's heart smote him', plays the part of conscience, and conforms to the usual meaning of 'conscience' in popular Gk. as the pain suffered by man as man when by his actions begun or completed he 'transgresses the moral limits of his nature' (Pierce, p. 54; the effect of a 'bad conscience' in this sense is illustrated, although the term is not used, by the action of Adam and Eve in Gn. 3:8). The one occurrence of *syneidēsis* as such in the LXX (outside the Apocrypha) is Ec. 10:20, where RSV translates *en syneidēsei sou* as '(even) in your *thought* (the Heb. is literally "knowledge"), do not curse the king'. This obviously does not follow the pattern just noted, however; and it is only at Wisdom 17:11, the single certain Apocryphal appearance of the term (NEB, 'wickedness proves a cowardly thing when condemned by an inner witness, and in the grip of conscience gives way to forebodings of disaster') that we find a clear anticipation of the NT use and meaning of *syneidēsis*. (But *cf.* Jb. 27:6; also Ecclus. 14:2, and the variant reading at 42:18.)

III. New Testament usage

The NT use of 'conscience' must be considered against the background of 'the idea of God, holy and righteous, creator and judge, as well as redeemer and quickener' (Pierce, p. 106). The truth of this remark is evident from the fact that the NT writers see man's conscience negatively as the instrument of judgment, and positively as the means of guidance.

The term *syneidēsis* often occurs in the Pauline letters, as well as in Heb., 1 Pet. and two (Pauline) speeches in Acts (23:1; 24:16). In its Pauline setting the word describes first of all the pain suffered by man when he has done wrong (see Rom. 13:5, where Paul urges 'subjection' for the sake of *syneidēsis* as well as *orgē*—the personal and social manifestations of God's judgment). From this man is delivered by dying to sin through incorporation into Christ (*cf.* Rom. 7:15; 8:2). However, it is possible for man's conscience—the faculty by which he apprehends the moral demands of God, and which causes him pain when he falls short of those demands—to be inadequately disciplined (1 Cor. 8:7), to become weakened (v. 12) and even defiled (v. 7; *cf.* Tit. 1:15), and to grow seared and ultimately insensible (*cf.* 1 Tim. 4:2). Thus it is essential for the conscience to be properly educated, and indeed *informed*, by the Holy Spirit. That is why 'conscience' and 'faith' cannot be separated. By repentance and faith man is delivered from conscience as 'pain'; but faith is also the means whereby his conscience is quickened and instructed. To walk in 'newness of life' (Rom. 6:4) implies a living, growing faith, through which the Christian is open to the influence of the Spirit (Rom. 8:14); and this in turn is the guarantee of a 'good' or 'clear' conscience (1 Pet. 3:16; *cf.* Acts 23:1).

An important and developed use of *syneidēsis* in Paul occurs in Rom. 2:14f. The implication of this passage is that God's general revelation of himself as good and demanding goodness faces all men with moral responsibility. For the Jews the divine demands were made explicit in the Sinaitic Code, while the Gentiles perform 'by nature' what the law requires. But the recognition of holy obligations, whether by Jew or Gentile, is something individually apprehended (the law is 'written on their hearts', v. 15) and, according to personal response, morally judged (for 'their conscience also bears witness' with the understanding of their heart, *ibid.*). Thus 'conscience' belongs to all men, and through it God's character and will are actively appreciated. At the same time it may be regarded as a power 'apart' from man himself (*cf.* Rom. 9:1; and the echo of the Pauline doctrine of 'conscience' in Rom. at Jn. 8:9, in the phrase 'convicted by their own conscience'—although this is rejected as a gloss by RSV and NEB, and the whole *pericope de adultera* is omitted by the best MSS).

Like Paul, the writer of Heb. uses the term *syneidēsis* with both a negative and a positive reference. Under the terms of the old covenant, man's guilty conscience in relation to God could not be perfected (Heb. 9:9); but deliverance has been made possible by the work of Christ under the terms of the new covenant (9:14), and by the appropriation of the benefits of the death of Jesus through Christian initiation (10:22; *cf.* 1 Pet. 3:21). In terms of spiritual growth, therefore, a worshipper's conscience may be described as 'good' (Heb. 13:18).

To summarize, the NT significance of 'conscience' is twofold: it is the means of moral judgment, painful and absolute because the judgment is divine, upon the actions of an individual completed or begun; and it also acts as a witness and guide in all aspects of the believer's sanctification.

BIBLIOGRAPHY. J. Dupont, *Gnosis*, 1949; and *Studia Hellenistica*, pp. 119–153; O. Hallesby, *Conscience*, 1950; C. A. Pierce, *Conscience in the New Testament*, 1955; W. D. Stacey, *The Pauline View of Man*, 1956, pp. 206–210; J. N. Sevenster, *Paul and Seneca*, 1961, esp. pp. 84–102; R. Schnack-

■ **CONSERVATION OF SOIL**
See Agriculture, Part 1.

■ **CONSTELLATIONS**
See Stars, Part 3.

■ **CONTAINERS**
See Vessels, Part 3.

enburg, *The Moral Teaching of the New Testament*, 1965, pp. 287–296; M. E. Thrall, *NTS* 14, 1967–8, pp. 118–125 (against Pierce); C. Brown in *NIDNTT* 1, pp. 348–353.

S.S.S.

CONTENTMENT. The noun 'contentment' occurs only once in RSV (1 Tim. 6:6), but its Gk. equivalent *autarkeia* appears also in 2 Cor. 9:8 as 'enough'; the adjective *autarkēs* in Phil. 4:11 and the verb *arkeō* in Lk. 3:14; 1 Tim. 6:8; Heb. 13:5; 3 Jn. 10; see also 2 Cor. 12:9, 'is sufficient'. *autarkeia* denotes freedom from reliance upon others, whether other persons or other things; hence the satisfaction of one's needs (2 Cor. 9:8) or the control of one's desires (1 Tim. 6:6, 8). It is not a passive acceptance of the *status quo*, but the positive assurance that God has supplied one's needs, and the consequent release from unnecessary desire. The Christian can be 'self-contained' because he has been satisfied by the grace of God (2 Cor. 12:9). The Christian spirit of contentment follows the fundamental commandment of Ex. 20:17 against covetousness, the precept of Pr. 15:17; 17:1, the exhortations of the prophets against avarice (*e.g.* Mi. 2:2) and supremely the example and teaching of Jesus, who rebuked the discontent which grasps at material possessions to the neglect of God (Lk. 12:13–21) and who commended such confidence in our Father in heaven as will dispel all anxiety concerning physical supplies (Mt. 6:25–32). In the OT the phrase 'be content' (from Heb. *yā'al*) indicates pleasure or willingness to do a certain action, usually one which has been requested by another person, *e.g.* Ex. 2:21; Jdg. 17:11; 2 Ki. 5:23, AV.

J.C.C.

CONVERSION.

1. Meaning of the word

A turning, or returning, to God. The chief words for expressing this idea are, in the OT, *šûḇ* (translated in EVV 'turn' or 'return'), and, in the NT, *strephomai* (Mt. 18:3; Jn. 12:40: the middle voice expresses the reflexive quality of the action, *cf.* the French 'se convertir'); *epistrephō* (regularly used in LXX to render *šûḇ*) and (in Acts 15:3 only) the cognate noun *epistrophē*. Despite the AV of Mt. 13:15; 18:3; Mk. 4:12; Lk. 22:32; Jn. 12:40; Acts 3:19; 28:27 (all changed to 'turn' or 'turn again' in RSV), *epistrephō* is not used in the NT in the passive voice. *šûḇ* and *epistrephō* can be used transitively as well as intransitively: in the OT God is said to turn men to himself (15 times); in the NT preachers are spoken of as turning men to God (Lk. 1:16f., echoing Mal. 4:5–6; Jas. 5:19f.; probably Acts 26:18). The basic meaning which the *strephō* word-group, like *šûḇ*, expresses is to turn *back* (*re*turn: so Lk. 2:39; Acts 7:39) or turn *round* (*about* turn: so Rev. 1:12). The theological meaning of these terms represents a transference of this idea into the realm of man's relationship with God.

II. Old Testament usage

The OT speaks mostly of national conversions, once of a pagan community (Nineveh: Jon. 3:7–10), otherwise of Israel; though there are also a few references to, and examples of, individual conversions (*cf.* Ps. 51:13, and the accounts of Naaman, 2 Ki. 5; Josiah, 2 Ki. 23:25; Manasseh, 2 Ch. 33:12f.), together with prophecies of worldwide conversions (*cf.* Ps. 22:27). Conversion in the OT means, simply, turning to Yahweh, Israel's covenant God. For Israelites, members of the covenant community by right of birth, conversion meant turning to 'Yahweh *your God*' (Dt. 4:30; 30:2, 10) in whole-hearted sincerity after a period of disloyalty to the terms of the covenant. Conversion in Israel was thus essentially the returning of backsliders to God. The reason why individuals, or the community, needed to '(re)turn to the Lord' was that they had turned away from him and strayed out of his paths. Hence national acts of returning to God were frequently marked by leader and people 'making a *covenant', *i.e.* making together a fresh solemn profession that henceforth they would be wholly loyal to God's covenant, to which they had sat loose in the past (so under Joshua, Jos. 24:25; Jehoiada, 2 Ki. 11:17; Asa, 2 Ch. 15:12; Hezekiah, 2 Ch. 29:10; Josiah, 2 Ch. 34:31). The theological basis for these public professions of conversion lay in the doctrine of the covenant. God's covenant with Israel was an abiding relationship; lapses into idolatry and sin exposed Israel to covenant chastisement (*cf.* Am. 3:2), but could not destroy the covenant; and if Israel turned again to Yahweh, he would return to them in blessing (*cf.* Zc. 1:3) and the nation would be restored and healed (Dt. 4:23–31; 29:1–30:10; Is. 6:10).

The OT stresses, however, that there is more to conversion than outward signs of sorrow and reformation of manners. A true turning to God under any circumstances will involve inward self-humbling, a real change of heart and a sincere seeking after the Lord (Dt. 4:29f.; 30:2, 10; Is. 6:9f.; Je. 24:7), and will be accompanied by a new clarity of knowledge of his being and his ways (Je. 24:7; *cf.* 2 Ki. 5:15; 2 Ch. 33:13).

III. New Testament usage

In the NT, *epistrephō* is only once used of the return to Christ of a Christian who has lapsed into sin (Peter: Lk. 22:32). Elsewhere, backsliders are exhorted, not to conversion, but to repentance (Rev. 2:5, 16, 21f.; 3:3, 19), and the conversion-words refer only to that decisive turning to God whereby, through faith in Christ, a sinner, Jew or Gentile, secures present entry into the eschatological kingdom of God and receives the eschatological blessing of forgiveness of sins (Mt. 18:3; Acts 3:19; 26:18). This conversion secures the salvation which Christ has brought. It is a once-for-all, unrepeatable event, as the habitual use of the aorist in the oblique moods of the verbs indicates. It is described as a turning from the darkness of idolatry, sin and the rule of Satan, to worship and serve the true God (Acts 14:15; 26:18; 1 Thes. 1:9) and his Son Jesus Christ (1 Pet. 2:25). It consists of an exercise of *repentance and *faith, which Christ and Paul link together as summing up between them the moral demand of the gospel (Mk. 1:15; Acts 20:21). Repentance means a change of mind and heart towards God; faith means belief of his word and trust in his Christ; conversion covers both. Thus we find both repentance and faith linked with conversion, as the narrower with the wider concept (repentance and conversion, Acts 3:19; 26:20; faith and conversion, Acts 11:21).

Though the NT records a number of conversion experiences, some more violent and dramatic (*e.g.* that of Paul, Acts 9:5ff.; of Cornelius, Acts 10:44ff.; *cf.* 15:7ff.; of the Philippian jailer, Acts 16:29ff.), some more quiet and unspectacular (*e.g.* that of the eunuch,

Acts 8:30ff.; of Lydia, Acts 16:14), the writers show no interest in the psychology of conversion as such. Luke makes space for three accounts of the conversions of Paul and of Cornelius (Acts 10:5ff.; 22:6ff.; 26:12ff.; and 10:44ff.; 11:15ff.; 15:7ff.) because of the supreme significance of these events in early church history, not for any separate interest in the manifestations that accompanied them. The writers think of conversion dynamically—not as an experience, something one feels, but as an action, something one does—and they interpret it theologically, in terms of the gospel to which the convert assents and responds. Theologically, conversion means committing oneself to that union with Christ which baptism symbolizes: union with him in death, which brings freedom from the penalty and dominion of sin, and union with him in resurrection from death, to live to God through him and walk with him in newness of life through the power of the indwelling Holy Spirit. Christian conversion is commitment to Jesus Christ as divine Lord and Saviour, and this commitment means reckoning union with Christ to be a fact and living accordingly. (See Rom. 6:1–14; Col. 2:10–12, 20ff.; 3:1ff.)

IV. General conclusion

Turning to God under any circumstances is, psychologically regarded, man's own act, deliberately considered, freely chosen and spontaneously performed. Yet the Bible makes it clear that it is also, in a more fundamental sense, God's work in him. The OT says that sinners turn to God only when themselves turned by God (Je. 31:18f.; La. 5:21). The NT teaches that when men will and work for the furthering of God's will in regard to their salvation, it is God's working in them that makes them do so (Phil. 2:12f.). Also, it describes the initial conversion of unbelievers to God as the result of a divine work in them in which, by its very nature, they could play no part, since it is essentially a curing of the spiritual impotence which has precluded their turning to God hitherto: a raising from death (Eph. 2:1ff.), a new birth (Jn. 3:1ff.), an opening of the heart (Acts 16:14), an opening and enlightening of blinded eyes (2 Cor. 4:4–6), and the giving of an understanding (1 Jn. 5:20). Man responds to the gospel only because God has first worked in him in this way. Furthermore, the accounts of Paul's conversion and various references to the power and conviction imparted by the Spirit to the converting word (*cf.* Jn. 16:8; 1 Cor. 2:4f.; 1 Thes. 1:5) show that God draws men to himself under a strong, indeed overwhelming, sense of divine constraint. Thus, the AV's habit of rendering the active verb 'turn' by the interpretative passive, 'be converted', though bad translation, is good biblical theology. (*REGENERATION.)

BIBLIOGRAPHY. G. Bertram, *TDNT* 7, pp. 722–729; F. Laubach, J. Goetzmann, U. Becker, *NIDNTT* 1, pp. 354–362. J.I.P.

CORD, ROPE. A number of Heb. words and one Gk. word are thus rendered in the RSV. **1.** *ḥeḇel* is the most common and it is the usual word for rope, being translated 'rope' in Jos. 2:15, *etc.*, 'line' in Mi. 2:5, *etc.*, 'cord' in Est. 1:6, and 'tackle' in Is. 33:23. Some consider it is related etymologically to the English 'cable'. **2.** *'aḇōṯ*, lit. 'something intertwined', is also common and is rendered 'rope' in Jb. 39:10, *etc.*, 'branch' in Ps. 118:27, *etc.*, and 'cart rope' in Is. 5:18. **3.** *yeṯer*, the third general word, is variously rendered in Jdg. 16:7; Jb. 30:11 and Ps. 11:2. Rope was normally made of twisted hair or strips of skin. **4.** *mêṯār* (Ex. 35:18, *etc.*) is a tent-cord. **5.** *ḥûṭ* (Ec. 4:12) is thread.

6. The only word employed in the NT is *schoinion*, 'bulrush rope', which is rendered 'cord' in Jn. 2:15 and 'ropes' in Acts 27:32. G.W.G.

CORINTH. A city of Greece at the W end of the isthmus between central Greece and the Peloponnesus, in control of trade routes between N Greece and the Peloponnese and across the isthmus. The latter was particularly important because much trade was taken across the isthmus rather than round the stormy S promontories of the Peloponnese. There were two harbours, Lechaeum 2·5 km W on the Corinthian Gulf, connected with the city by long walls; and Cenchreae 14 km E on the Saronic Gulf. Corinth thus became a flourishing centre of trade, as well as of industry, particularly ceramics. The town is dominated by the Acrocorinth (566 m), a steep, flat-topped rock surmounted by the acropolis, which in ancient times contained, *inter alia*, a temple of Aphrodite, goddess of love, whose service gave rise to the city's proverbial immorality, notorious already by the time of Aristophanes (Strabo, 378; Athenaeus, 573).

Egyptian papyrus rope from Saqqara. Probably Ptolemaic period. (FNH)

From the late 4th century until 196 BC Corinth was held mainly by the Macedonians; but in that year it was liberated, with the rest of Greece, by T. Quinctius Flamininus, and joined the Achaean League. After a period of opposition to Rome, and social revolution under the dictator Critolaus, the city was, in 146 BC, razed to the ground by the consul L. Mummius, and its inhabitants sold into slavery.

In 46 BC Corinth was rebuilt by Caesar and began to recover its prosperity. Augustus made it the capital of the new province of Achaea, now detached from Macedonia and ruled by a separate proconsular governor.

Paul's 18-months' stay in Corinth in his second missionary journey (Acts 18:1–18) has been dated by an inscription from Delphi which shows that Gallio came to Corinth as proconsul in AD 51 or 52 (Acts 18:12–17; *PAUL, section II). His *bēma*, or judgment seat (Acts 18:12), has also been identified, as has the *macellum* or meat-market (1 Cor. 10:25). An inscription near the theatre men-

COPPER SCROLL
See Dead Sea scrolls, Part 1.

COR
See Weights and measures, Part 3.

CORAL
See Jewels, Part 2.

CORE
See Korah, Part 2.

CORIANDER
See Herbs, Part 2.

tions an aedile *Erastus, who possibly is the treasurer of Rom. 16:23.

BIBLIOGRAPHY. Strabo, 378–382; Pausanias, 2. 1–4; Athenaeus, 573; *Corinth I–VIII* (Princeton University Press), 1951 onwards; *EBr*, *s.v.* 'Corinth' (with older bibliography); Excavation reports annually from 1896 to *AJA*, *JHS*, *Hesperia*; J. G. O'Neill, *Ancient Corinth*, 1930; H. G. Payne, *Necrocorinthia*, 1931; H. J. Cadbury, *JBL* 53, 1934, pp. 134ff.; O. Broneer, *BA* 14, 1951, pp. 78ff. Fine plates may be seen in A. A. M. van der Heyden and H. H. Scullard, *Atlas of the Classical World*, 1959, pp. 43f. J.H.H.

CORINTHIANS, EPISTLES TO THE.

I. Outline of contents

1 Corinthians

a. Greetings, and prayer for the recipients (1:1–9).

b. Christian wisdom and the unity of the church (1:10–4:21):

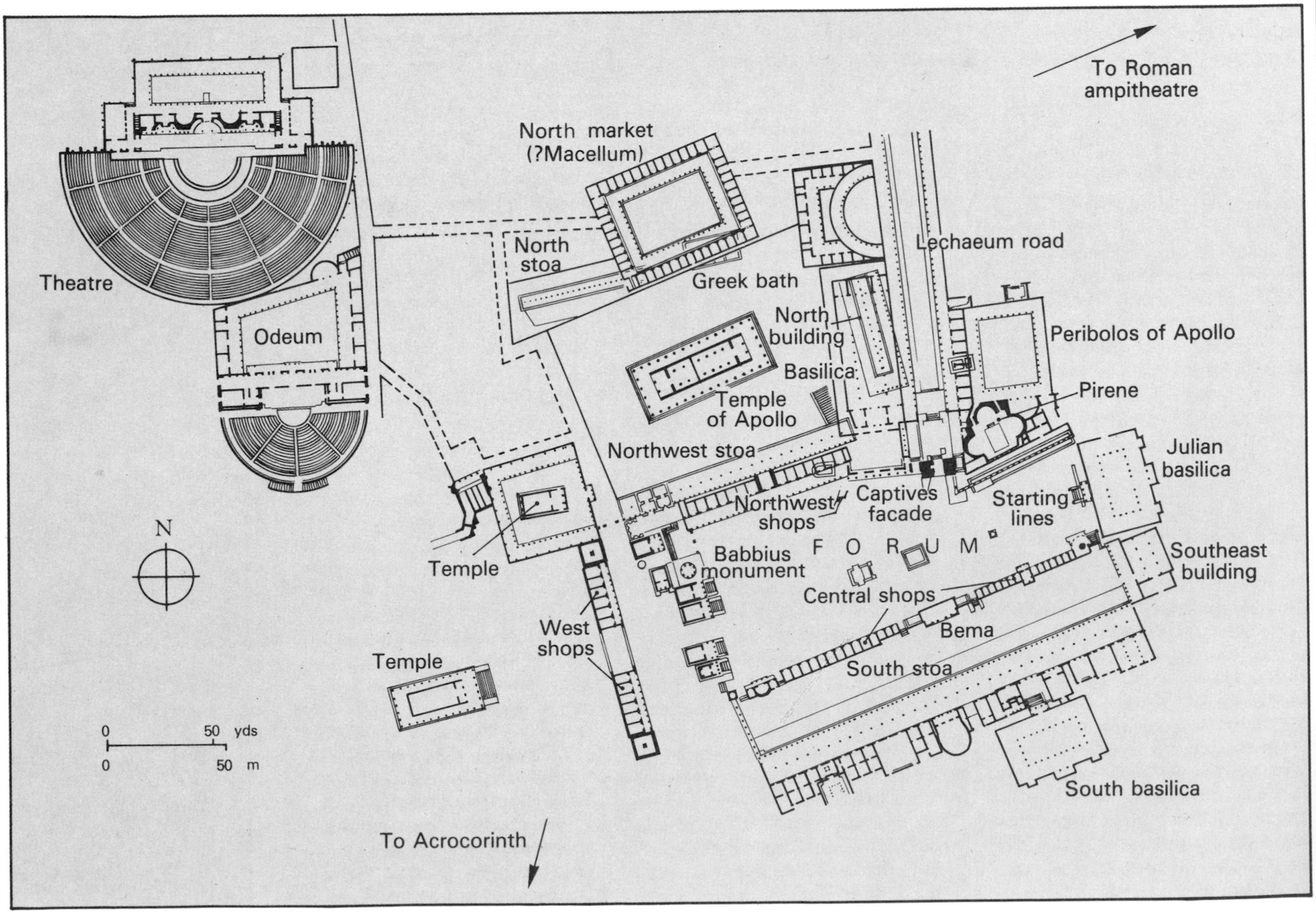

(i) The statement of the problem (1:10–16): the Corinthians are putting the unity of the church at risk by following a variety of leaders.

(ii) 'Wisdom' and the gospel (1:17–2:5): the world's wisdom is folly to God; the Corinthians were not chosen by God for their wisdom; Paul preached not wisdom but Christ crucified, in demonstration of the Spirit and of power.

(iii) True wisdom (2:6–13): God's true wisdom is imparted only to those in whom his Spirit works: they understand God's plans (2:9) and gifts (2:12).

(iv) The status of the Corinthians (2:14–3:4): But the Spirit is not being allowed to work in this way in the Corinthian church because of their unspiritual attitudes.

(v) The apostles and the church (3:5–4:5): Paul explains how the Corinthians ought to regard their apostles, and warns them to build aright on the foundation which he laid.

(vi) Conclusions (4:6–21): They must realize that they do not yet reign in the kingdom of the New Age, and learn humility.

c. Problems in Corinthian church life (5:1–6:20):

(i) A man and his father's wife (5:1–13): the church is conniving at a heinous sin, perhaps even boasting in this expression of 'Christian freedom'.

(ii) Lawsuits (6:1–11): Perhaps a comment on a *cause célèbre*.

(iii) Prostitution (6:12–20).

d. Answers to questions (7:1–14:40):

(i) Is celibacy the Christian ideal? (7:1–40): Paul's principles (7:1–7, 17–24); application to various cases (7:8–16, 25–40).

(ii) Meat offered to idols (8:1–11:1): the principles involved (8:1–13); the conflict with Christian liberty (9:1–27); an awesome example from Israel's history (10:1–13), and conclusions (10:14–11:1).

(iii) Behaviour in the Christian assembly (11:2–14:40): marital authority (11:2–16); attitudes to one another at the common meal (11:17–34); the principles governing the gifts of the Spirit: they do not contradict the gospel (12:1–3); they are all equally important (12:4–30); the most important thing is not which gift is possessed but whether it is used in love (12:31–13:13); practical considerations governing the use of these gifts: they should help the whole church (14:1–25); conclusions (14:26–40).

e. A fundamental problem tackled (15:1–58):

(i) The resurrection of Jesus an essential part of the gospel (15:1–11).

(ii) The implications of this: we too shall rise when the 'last enemy' is finally destroyed (15:12–34).

(iii) The relationship between the natural realm and the spiritual (15:35–50): there are different sorts of bodies (15:35–41); the resurrected body is very different from the present one (15:42–50).

(iv) The essence of *eschatology (15:51–58): we must yet 'put on' this new body (either through death and resurrection, or exceptionally through change) before we inherit the kingdom (*cf.* 4:8).

f. The collection, and closing remarks (16:1–24).

2 Corinthians

a. Greetings and prayer of thanksgiving (1:1–7).

b. Explanations for Paul's apparently inconsistent behaviour (1:8–2:13): Paul gives an account of what he has experienced of suffering and the accompanying comfort of God (1:8–11); and explains that his changes of plan were made in good faith and for the benefit of the Corinthians themselves (1:12–2:13).

c. Not our glory, but God's (2:14–4:12):

(i) A paean of praise for victory in Christ (2:14–17).

(ii) The glory of the new covenant (3:1–4:6): Paul is commending not himself (3:1–6) but the glorious covenant of the Spirit (3:7–11) which enables him boldly but in transparent honesty to proclaim the gospel (3:12–4:6).

(iii) A comparison between the treasure of the gospel and the vessel in which it is carried (4:7–12).

d. The basis of Paul's confidence (4:13–5:10): Paul's confidence is in the God who can raise the dead, so that even the prospect of death cannot diminish this confidence.

e. The motivation of the apostle (5:11–21):

(i) The love of Christ (5:11–15).

(ii) The good news of reconciliation (5:16–21).

f. An appeal for a response (6:1–7:4):

(i) For a positive response to Paul himself (6:1–13; 7:2–4).

(ii) For purity in the life of the church (6:14–7:1).

g. Paul's joy and confidence in his Corinthian church (7:5–16): his letter has had its effect (7:5–13) and Paul's trust in the church has been vindicated (7:14–16).

h. The collection (8:1–9:15):

(i) A tactful reminder that the Corinthians have not yet fulfilled their original offer of financial aid (8:1–7).

(ii) The basis of Christian giving (8:8–15).

(iii) Titus' zeal in this service (8:16–24).

(iv) Encouragement to the Corinthians to vindicate Paul's boast (9:1–15).

i. Warning against false apostles (10:1–13:10):

(i) An appeal for complete obedience (10:1–6).

(ii) Paul's challenge to the troublemakers (10:7–18): he does not really need to defend his authority in Corinth, since he was the first to bring the gospel there; but these men are boasting 'in other men's labours' (10:15).

(iii) Paul's own credentials (11:1–12:13): if the Corinthians are determined to have them, Paul's credentials are as good as any other man's (11:1–29); but he would rather boast in his weakness, not his strengths (11:30–12:10). Yet this is all folly; the only fact of any significance is that the church experienced the true signs of an apostle (12:11–13).

(iv) Paul's defence against the charge of defrauding the church (12:14–18): perhaps in the face of an accusation that the moneys for the collection had found their way into Paul's own pocket.

(v) Paul's ultimate concern (12:19–13:10): not that his own name might be cleared, but that his beloved church might improve and be built up.

j. Closing greetings (13:11–14).

II. The church at Corinth

a. Its milieu

The *Corinth which Paul evangelized *c.* AD 50 was a relatively new city. In ancient literature Corinth has a reputation for vice of every kind; but this was a reputation foisted upon Old Corinth by her trading-rival Athens. It is thus irrelevant for our understanding of the situation at the time of Paul. So also is the groundless tradition that the city was a centre of cult prostitution in honour of the god-

Opposite page: Ruins of Corinth. The acropolis dominates the city in the plain below. View along Lechaeum road towards the city centre. (ARM)

Opposite page: Plan of the centre of Corinth, refounded as a Roman colony in 44 BC, incorporating the remains of the Greek city dating from c. 540 BC.

dess Aphrodite. The morals of secular Corinth are likely to have been no better or worse than those of any other Mediterranean port. That there was a Jewish community in the city is attested by Acts 18:4. In 1898 a door-lintel from a synagogue (probably slightly later than the time of Paul) was excavated at Corinth.

b. Its foundation

Paul says little about the founding of the church, but a brief account will be found in Acts 18. Paul stayed with the Jewish couple *Aquila and Prisca, probably already Christians, and recently expelled from Rome. As was his custom, Paul preached in the synagogue and persuaded 'Jews and Greeks' (Acts 18:4); that is, Jews and proselytes or 'God-fearers' (a phrase which includes Jews, proselytes and Gentiles who had adopted most of the Jewish religion without taking the final step of circumcision). Perhaps as a result of the arrival of two more members of this unorthodox sect of the Nazarene (Acts 18:5), the Jewish authorities began to oppose Paul's use of the synagogue for his preaching. Paul withdrew, taking with him a number of Jewish converts, notably the ruler of the synagogue, and moved next door into the house of a (converted?) 'God-fearer', Titius *Justus. This group formed the nucleus of the Corinthian church, which grew rapidly (Acts 18:8, 10). The relationships between these two groups of neighbours must have remained tense, and the Jews took advantage of a change of proconsulship (*GALLIO) to make an attack upon Paul in the courts; but this was unsuccessful and the result was that the church was able to grow unmolested while Paul stayed the (for him) unusually long time of 18 months before sailing for Syria with Aquila and Prisca.

c. Its composition

As well as the Jews and proselytes who accompanied Paul on his move from the synagogue, the church consisted of subsequent converts, probably from both Jewish and pagan backgrounds. The debate still proceeds as to whether the church was predominantly Jewish-Christian or predominantly pagan-convert in constitution: there are no cogent reasons for it to have been either.

Socially the church embraced a wide range, including under its aegis the wealthy city-treasurer *Erastus; an erstwhile president of the synagogue; the refugee Jewish saddler Aquila, and the domestic slaves (if so they were) of *Chloe. Although not in the main of high birth or education (1 Cor. 1:26), the church probably affected an air of intellectual pretension (*cf.* E. A. Judge, *The Social Pattern of Christian Groups in the First Century*, 1960, pp. 59–61).

d. Its intellectual background

To account for the surprisingly rapid development of so many errors so soon in a church where Paul had taught for so long, many scholars have suggested that we should look for one underlying cause, and a wide range of possible background influences have been suggested, from a predominantly Jewish situation (so J. M. Ford, 'The First Epistle to the Corinthians or the First Epistle to the Hebrews?', *CBQ* 28, 1966, pp. 402–416) to an influx of all-but full-blown *Gnosticism (so W. Schmithals, *Gnosticism in Corinth*, 1971). Before this question is discussed, a few comments about the thought-world of the time may be relevant.

There was certainly a significant Jewish group in the church. The Judaism of the *Dispersion was strongly influenced by many other currents of thought, including those from the Greek philosophical schools, and esoteric, 'proto-Gnostic' ideas; but still, of course, basing itself on the Torah, at least in so far as this was practicable. While sacrifice could be offered only in Jerusalem (involving a pilgrimage far beyond the means of most), Diaspora Jews were renowned in the Greek world for their adherence to circumcision and the sabbath, and for their refusal to eat swine's flesh. In many circles, however, the Torah was interpreted allegorically rather than literally (*PHILO). Jews often, though by no means exclusively, lived together in a 'Jewish quarter', and had certain civil rights, such as their own law-courts.

Gentile converts may have already been proselytes or 'God-fearers', or may have come directly from paganism. These latter would have been familiar with the usual Hellenistic pantheon and forms of worship, possibly including cult-prostitution. Ecstasy, including speaking in *tongues, was a common phenomenon in Graeco-Oriental religions, and this may help to account for the Corinthians' misuse of Christian *spiritual gifts, and possibly for the ecstatically-produced blasphemy of 1 Cor. 12:2f.

The pagan temples played a significant part in religious, and hence daily, life: they functioned as restaurants and social centres, as well as being significant (but not the only) sources of the butchers' meat-supply (*IDOLS, MEATS OFFERED TO; *MEAT MARKET).

As well as the emotional and cultic elements, Hellenistic religions also appealed to the intellect, and *Gnosticism found a fertile seed-bed here. Many of these religions developed a strongly dualist outlook, for which matter was illusory and evil, whereas only the objects of thought, in the realm of the soul, were concrete and good. This easily led to a premium on knowledge; to a belief (also found in Hellenistic Judaism) in the immortality of the soul rather than the resurrection of the body; and, perhaps rather strangely, to both asceticism (in which the 'evil' world is simply rejected) and libertinism (in which the 'good' soul is held to be undefiled, no matter what the illusory body may do).

All of these factors no doubt contributed to the particular problems which arose in the church.

e. The source(s) of its problems

Several single factors have been suggested as the underlying cause for the Corinthians' errors:

(i) **Gnosticism.* Schmithals' suggestion that this is the source of the Corinthians' problems has already been noted. It suffers, however, from grave drawbacks, not least because there is no evidence that Gnosticism as a system can be dated so early. Also, Schmithals is forced to assume that Paul misunderstood the situation, since he does not effectively answer Gnostic teachings (see C. K. Barrett, 'Christianity at Corinth', *BJRL* 46, 1963–4, pp. 269–297).

(ii) *A change in Paul's own teaching*. J. C. Hurd, *The Origin of 1 Corinthians*, 1965, has developed the elaborate thesis that Paul was obliged in the face of the Jerusalem Council (Acts 15) to change his message radically, to the puzzlement of the Corinthians who remained faithful to his original preaching of freedom, *wisdom and enthusiasm. It is impossible to deal adequately with Hurd's thesis here, but three points are noteworthy. Hurd's reconstruction of events forces him to treat the chronology and history of the book of Acts in a cavalier fashion, and to postulate that within 2 years Paul preached at Corinth, underwent his *volte-face*, and then developed the 'mature' position expressed in 1 Cor. This seems far too short a time for such a development. Second, it is remarkable that Paul does not mention the Apostolic Decree, if he is now concerned to commend it to his churches. Third, Hurd's thesis fails to provide a satisfactory exegesis of the letter. For a more detailed critique, see J. W. Drane, *Paul: Libertine or Legalist?*, 1975, pp. 97f.

(iii) *An un-Pauline development of Paul's preaching*. A. C. Thiselton ('Realized Eschatology at Corinth', *NTS* 24, 1977–8, pp. 510–526) has recently suggested that the Corinthians developed Paul's own *eschatology far beyond his own position, and believed themselves to be already reigning in the kingdom of the New Age in which 'all things are lawful' (1 Cor. 4:8; 6:12; 10:23). Thiselton believes that he can interpret most of the letter on the basis of this view, though it makes heavy weather of some problems such as the lawsuits of ch. 6.

Other scholars have looked for the answer in a combination of factors: Drane (*op. cit.*), for instance, suggests that the Corinthians may have been influenced by gnostic ideas, if not by fully-developed Gnosticism, and by a misinterpretation of Paul's own letter to the *Galatians. This position is not incompatible with that of Thiselton, and some combination of these factors perhaps provides the best basis for an interpretation of the letter.

In 2 Cor. the problem seems to be rather different: here Paul is facing a personal attack on himself (2 Cor. 10:10) mounted by some people whom he in turn styles 'false apostles, deceitful workmen, servants of Satan and only disguised as apostles' (2 Cor. 11:13–15). Paul's stress on his own lack of oratorical ability, his refusal to assert his apostolic authority, and his weakness (11:6–7, 30), lead us to suppose that these people placed stress on their own great rhetoric, spiritual authority and strength. They are Hebrews (11:22) and presumably claim authority from the mother-church in Jerusalem. Indeed, it has been suggested on the basis of the phrase 'superlative apostles' (11:5; 12:11) that these men are none other than the Jerusalem apostles themselves, and that we have here a development of the split Paul mentions in Gal. 2:11f. But Paul would not be likely to compare himself on equal terms with men he regards as satanic, so it seems most reasonable to regard the 'superlative apostles' as a group distinct from the 'false apostles'. We then appear to be dealing with three groups:

(i) The 'superlative apostles' at Jerusalem, whose authority is being invoked over against Paul's, but to whom Paul regards himself as equal, not inferior.

(ii) The 'false apostles', perhaps sent by the Jerusalem apostles, but going beyond the bounds of the agreement of Gal. 2:9; and perhaps wilfully ignoring the wishes of the Jerusalem apostles.

(iii) The Corinthians themselves, in danger of being misled, but not as yet opposed to Paul (see C. K. Barrett, 'Paul's Opponents in II Corinthians', *NTS* 17, 1970–1, pp. 233–254).

III. The integrity of the letters

It is virtually certain that Paul had a greater correspondence with the Corinthian church than is preserved in Scripture. 1 Cor. 5:9–13 probably (though the verb in 5:9 could be translated 'I am writing') refers to a previous letter warning the church to separate from the immoral (that is, immoral Christians, but this was misinterpreted). We shall style this letter 'Cor. A'.

2 Cor. 2:3–11; 7:8–13a also refer to a previous letter. It is doubtful that this is 1 Cor., for the following reasons:

(i) the tone of this letter (see 2 Cor. 2:4; 7:8) is hardly the tone in which 1 Cor. is written.

(ii) this letter followed a 'painful visit' (2 Cor. 2:1–3; 12:14; 13:1–3), which does not seem to be true for 1 Cor.

(iii) despite the superficial similarity, 2 Cor. 2:5ff. does not seem to be referring to the same situation as 1 Cor. 5:5, since in 2 Cor. the wrongdoer appears to have offended against Paul personally.

So if we call our 1 Cor. 'Cor. B', there appears to have been a 'Cor. C' (*i.e.* the letter referred to in 2 Cor.) before our 2 Cor. ('Cor. D'). Hence there appear to have been at least four epistles of Paul to the Corinthians. What happened to the others? There are two possibilities: either they have perished, or they survive as fragments in our 1 and 2 Cor. This second possibility is not just suggested on the assumption that we *must* possess all that Paul ever wrote: there is some evidence in the letters themselves that they may be composite.

(i) 2 Cor. 10–13 looks like 'Cor. E'. Even before anyone suggested that 2 Cor. may be composite, people had noted the sharp change of tone at ch. 10; and the contents also fit (see Barrett for details). It is further argued that these chapters are better understood as having been written *before* 1–11: *cf.* the references to Paul's visit in 10:6; 13:2 and 10 with those in 1:23; 2:3 and 9; or the references to boasting in 10:7f.; 11:18 and 12:1 with those in 3:1 and 5:12.

(ii) 2 Cor. 6:14–7:1 looks like 'Cor. A'. Again the contents fit, and if this section is removed from 2 Cor., the 'edges' match up quite remarkably.

(iii) It is also argued that 1 Cor. 8–10 is easier to understand as two (or even more) letters. Perhaps the most thorough attempt to analyse the Corinthian correspondence into several parts is that of W. Schmithals, 'Die Korintherbriefe als Briefsammlung', *ZNW* 64, 1973, pp. 263–288, where no fewer than nine separate letters are postulated. On this whole exercise, *cf.* C. K. Barrett, *1 Corinthians*, pp. 12–17 and *2 Corinthians*, pp. 11–21.

But at the very best partition-theories are counsels of despair: they raise as many problems as they solve, especially about the workings of the mind of the final editor. If it is possible to make sense of the letters as they stand, such theories should be rejected.

IV. Paul's dealings with the Corinthian church

The following attempts to present a reasonable reconstruction of the probable events in the history of the Corinthian church of which we have any knowledge.

a. Immediately after Paul's departure

Other preachers and teachers had come and gone: notably Apollos (Acts 19:1) and quite possibly Peter, or perhaps some emissaries from him (*cf.* 1 Cor. 1:12). Even at this stage there appears to have been something wrong, and Paul must have received reports of immorality, either actual or threatened, in the church.

b. 'Cor. A'

Paul responded to this problem with a letter warning the church to have nothing to do with the immoral (*cf.* 1 Cor. 5:9). We cannot say more about the letter than that, except that it may have been written in ignorance of the true gravity of the situation, and appears to have been misunderstood.

c. Corinthian news reaches Paul

Paul had news from three sources before writing 1 Cor.:

(i) *Chloe's people visited Paul, reporting that the church had split under various leaders. These may have simply been rallying-points for groups with basically the same beliefs, or have represented real differences of belief (though Paul gives no indication in his letter that he is addressing deeply divided groups). The splits may even, if Chloe's people brought the Corinthians' letter, have been caused by the writing of the letter itself, with the different groups wanting to send it to different authorities.

(ii) Stephanas, Fortunatus and Achaicus (1 Cor. 16:17) probably reported the situations which prompted Paul to write chs. 5 and 6 of his letter.

(iii) The Corinthians had also written a letter to Paul, raising a variety of questions, which he answers in 1 Cor. 7:1–16:4. In his reply Paul several times quotes from their letter to him; *cf.* 'It is good for a man not to touch a woman' (7:1); 'All of us possess knowledge' (8:1) and 'All things are lawful' (10:23). The letter appears to have asked, among other things, 'Is celibacy the Christian ideal?' (discussed in ch. 7 of Paul's reply); 'Why should Christians not feel free to join in idol sacrifices and eat sacrificed meat, since we know that the idols are nothing?' (discussed in chs. 8–10); 'Are our practices (presumably they described them in some detail) in our times of worship correct?' (discussed in chs. 11–14); 'Have we not already experienced the only *"resurrection" we are going to, in our new life in Christ?' (discussed in ch. 15); and 'What about the collection?' (discussed in ch. 16).

d. Paul replies: 'Cor. B'

Paul's response is our 1 Cor. Its length, and the emotion engendered by the issues raised, are more than adequate to account for the occasionally disjointed form of the letter. However, the letter appears to have failed in its intention: we read in 2 Cor. 2:1 and 13:2 of the necessity for further action.

e. The 'painful visit'

That further action took the form of another visit to Corinth, but this visit appears also to have been a failure: the church is still strife-torn, and Paul is rebuffed by one individual who personally offends him.

f. 'Cor. C'

Paul again attempts to achieve by letter what he was unable to achieve in the flesh: he delivers a stinging rebuke to his flock. This letter was delivered by Titus (2 Cor. 7:5–8) and is not now extant. Having written it, Paul went through agonies of regret, and was so upset that he could not complete his work, despite the opportunities: he finally left his work to go to meet Titus and learn how the letter had been received (2 Cor. 2:12f.). When he met Titus, however, he was overjoyed to learn that his letter had been just what was needed; the Corinthians had repented and were now solidly behind Paul, and Titus' report was thoroughly encouraging.

g. 'Cor. D'

Delighted with the restoration of good relationships between himself and his church, Paul immediately wrote again, this time a letter of praise and joy (our 2 Cor. 1–9).

h. Further news arrives

Before Paul had sent off his letter (or perhaps even immediately after) news appears to have arrived to the effect that this victory in Corinth had not after all been complete. Either Titus had been over-optimistic or else there had been a radical change: some outsiders, styling themselves 'apostles' and with the highest of credentials, were challenging Paul's *authority and beginning to lead his flock astray.

Alternatively, we may assume that Paul knew of the existence of this 'pocket of resistance' all along, but reserved his strictures until the end. This view, however, makes heavier weather of the change in tone, and does not account for the fact that Paul gives no indication that he has moved on from addressing the whole church to addressing a minority within it.

i. 'Cor. E'

Paul responded with a blistering attack on these 'false apostles', and re-asserted his own authority in another letter or an appendix to 'Cor. D'. This is our 2 Cor. 10–13. Was this successful? We can only surmise. No further correspondence from Paul to the church survives, though in about AD 96 Clement, bishop of Rome, found it necessary to take up the cudgels once again against this wayward church. The church was again split, this time because some of the younger men had ousted their presbyters. Clement saw the problem as one of pride (an issue not wholly absent from Paul's letters), and the quarrel as more personal than doctrinal. So perhaps on the major issues Paul won the day, though the victory may not have been as complete as he would have liked.

V. Authenticity and dates

Whatever is made of their integrity, there can be no doubt as to the authenticity of these two epistles: they have always been regarded as part of the undisputed Pauline Corpus. For the dating of the letters we may begin at the fixed point provided by the proconsulship of *Gallio which enables us to date the event of Acts 18:12 in the middle of AD 51 or 52 (proconsuls took up their posts in July). After this Paul stayed 'many days' (Acts 18:18), leaving perhaps towards the end of that same year. Acts 19 records his subsequent activities: a brief visit to Ephesus, then to Jerusalem and back to Ephesus where he stayed for over 2 years. Here it is most reasonable to place the writing of 1 Cor., so it may be dated somewhere in AD 53 or 54. 2 Cor. would have been written not long after this, at the latest in AD 55.

BIBLIOGRAPHY. *Commentaries:* Perhaps the best commentaries on the two letters are those of C. K. Barrett in the *Black* series (1968 and 1973). Others include: *On 1 Cor.:* Calvin; F. Godet, 1886; A. Robertson and A. Plummer, *ICC*, 1911 (Gk. text); L. Morris, *TNTC*, 1958; J. Héring, 1962 (Fr. ed. 1948); H. Conzelmann, *Hermeneia*, 1975.

On 2 Cor.: Calvin; A. Plummer, *ICC*, 1915 (Gk. text); R. V. G. Tasker, *TNTC*, 1958; P. E. Hughes, 1962.

Other studies: F. F. Bruce, *Paul: Apostle of the Free Spirit*, 1977, chs.

23 and 24; D. Georgi, *Die Gegner des Paulus im 2. Korintherbrief*, 1964. D.R. de L.

CORNELIUS. In Acts 10:1ff. a Roman centurion of Caesarea in Palestine, one of the class of Gentiles known as 'God-fearers' because of their attachment to Jewish religious practices, such as almsgiving and prayer, for which Cornelius receives special mention. Cornelius was a common *nomen* in the Roman world ever since Publius Cornelius Sulla in 82 BC emancipated 10,000 slaves and enrolled them in his own *gens Cornelia.* The Cornelius of Acts is specially notable as the first Gentile convert to Christianity. As he and his household and friends listened to Peter's preaching, they believed and received the Holy Spirit, whereupon they were baptized at Peter's command. The importance of this occasion in Luke's eyes is emphasized by repetition (*cf.* Acts 11:1–18; 15:7, 14). The 'Italian Cohort' to which Cornelius belonged was an auxiliary cohort of Roman citizens, whose presence in Syria in the 1st century AD is inscriptionally attested. F.F.B.

CORNERSTONE. The NT references draw their meaning from three passages in the OT. The first is Ps. 118:22 where the stone rejected by the builders has become 'the head of the corner' (Heb. *rô'š pinnâ*, LXX *kephalē gōnias*). In its original context this reflected the Psalmist's own jubilation at his vindication over the enemies who had rejected him, but in its liturgical setting in the Feast of Tabernacles the psalm came to refer more to national than to personal deliverance. In rabbinical exegesis it was accorded a Messianic interpretation and this prepared the way for its use by Christ of himself in Mt. 21:42; Mk. 12:10; Lk. 20:17. Peter also used the text in Acts 4:11 and 1 Pet. 2:7 to explain Christ's rejection by the Jews and his exaltation by God to be head of the church. The phrase 'head of the corner' can indicate one of the large stones near the foundations of a building which by their sheer size bind together two or more rows of stones, but it is more likely to refer to the final stone which completes an arch or is laid at the top corner of a building (so Jeremias). This idea underlies Eph. 2:20 (Gk. *akrogōniaios, sc. lithos*), where Paul pictures the stones of the new temple as joined together by Christ who as the cornerstone gives the building completeness and unity. Christ is elsewhere described as the church's *foundation, but Eph. 2:20 reverses the figure and regards the first-generation apostles and prophets as the foundation, with Christ as the summit and consummation.

The second passage (Is. 28:16) probably referred originally to the massive stonework of the Temple, symbolizing the Lord's abiding presence among his people, a feature which was firm, unshakeable, reliable. The juxtaposition in Isaiah of the words 'foundation' and 'cornerstone' suggests either identity or similarity of meaning, but the NT blending of this with the third passage (Is. 8:14) in Rom. 9:33 and in 1 Pet. 2:6 has effectively weakened the link and left the emphasis on Christ as a *stumbling-block to those without faith, but as security to those who believe.

BIBLIOGRAPHY. S. H. Hooke, 'The Corner-Stone of Scripture', in *The Siege Perilous*, 1956, pp. 235–249; F. F. Bruce, 'The Corner Stone', *ExpT* 84, 1972–3, pp. 231–235. J.B.Tr.

SE corner of the Temple area wall at Jerusalem. The lower courses are Herodian masonry. (RP)

CORRUPTION (Gk. *phthora, diaphthora*) in EVV, and especially AV, usually connotes the transience of the present world order. In Rom. 8:21 it is used of the liability of the material universe to change and decay; contrast the 'imperishable' (Gk. *aphthartos*) inheritance reserved for believers (1 Pet. 1:4). In 1 Cor. 15:42ff. it denotes the liability of the 'natural' body to *death and dissolution; 'perishable' (Gk. *phthartos*) is practically equivalent to 'mortal' (Gk. *thnētos*), as 'imperishable' (Gk. *aphtharsia*), predicated of the 'spiritual' body, is a synonym of 'immortality' (Gk. *athanasia*). In Acts 2:27ff.; 13:35ff. 'corruption' (in the sense of decomposition) is

CORMORANT
See Animals, Part 1.

CORNELIAN
See Jewels, Part 2.

CORNET
See Music, Part 2.

CORPORATE PERSONALITY
See Servant of the Lord, Part 3.

the rendering of Gk. *diaphthora*, quoted from Ps. 16:10, LXX, for *MT* *šaḥaṯ* (RSV 'the * Pit'), parallel to Sheol. As a Messianic 'testimony' Ps. 16:10 in LXX lends itself even better than *MT* to the case of Jesus, whose body, being raised from death, 'saw no corruption' (Acts 13:37). (* HELL, * ESCHATOLOGY.)

BIBLIOGRAPHY. E. F. Sutcliffe, *The Old Testament and the Future Life*, 1946, pp. 76–81; J. Jeremias, 'Flesh and Blood cannot inherit the Kingdom of God', *NTS* 1, 1955–6, pp. 155ff. F.F.B.

CORUNDUM
See Jewels, Part 2.

COS (Acts 21:1). A massive and mountainous island, one of the Sporades group, off the SW coast of Asia Minor, near Halicarnassus. It was colonized at an early period by Dorian Greeks, and achieved fame as the site of the medical school founded in the 5th century BC by Hippocrates, and again as a literary centre, the home of Philetas and Theocritus, in the 3rd century BC. It was also noted for fine weaving.

The Romans made Cos a free state in the province of Asia, and the emperor Claudius, influenced by his Coan physician, conferred on it immunity from taxes. Herod the Great was a benefactor of the people of Cos. K.L.McK.

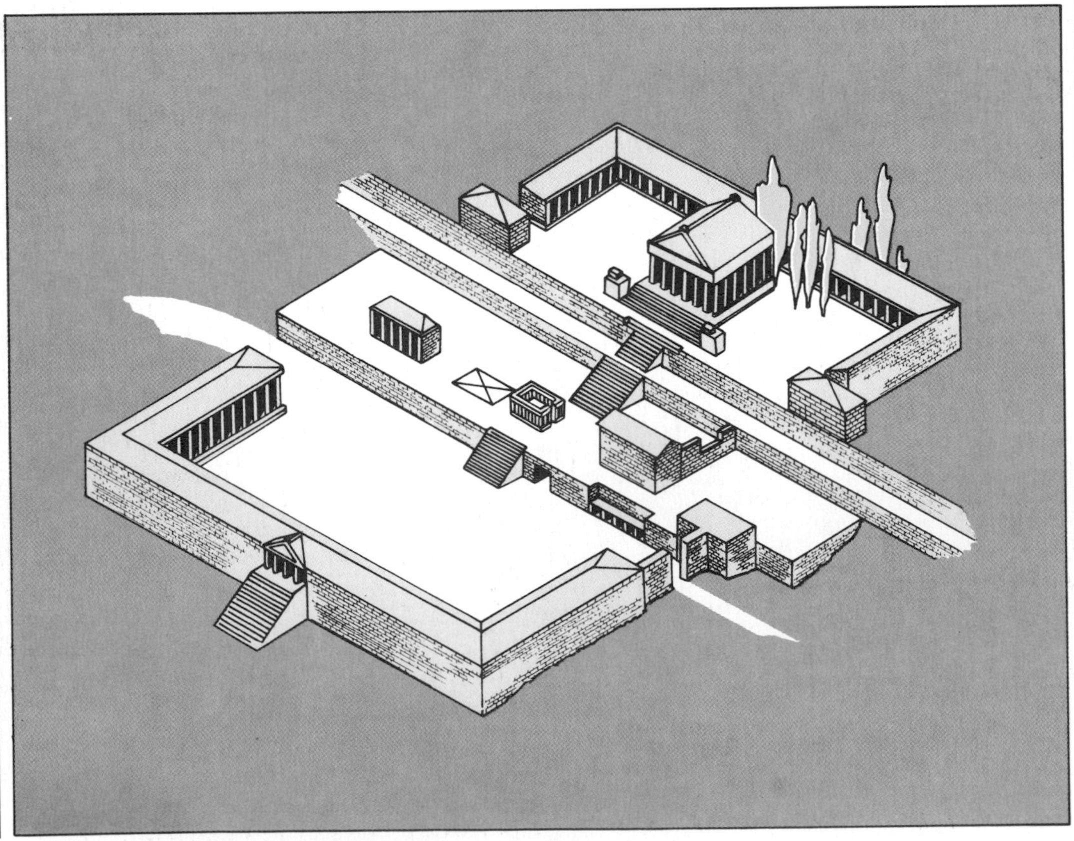

The Asclepieum, the main sanctuary on the island of Cos, dedicated to the healing god Asclepius. 4th cent. BC–AD 554.

COSMETICS AND PERFUMERY.

I. Introductory

a. Scope

By cosmetics is here understood that wide range of concoctions from pulverized minerals, vegetable oils and extracts, and animal fats which has been used from earliest times to beautify, improve or restore personal appearance ('visual' cosmetics) or to produce pleasing fragrances ('odoriferous' cosmetics).

b. Cosmetic vessels and appliances

In Scripture, little is said of the boxes, phials, flasks, spoons and other cosmetic trinkets known from archaeology. Besides the 'perfume boxes' of Is. 3:20, a rendering the accuracy of which has been questioned, there is the well-known flask of precious ointment or spikenard with which the repentant woman anointed Christ's head (Lk. 7:37; *cf.* Mt. 26:7; Mk. 14:3). But Israelite town-sites in Palestine have produced many little patterned cosmetic-bowls; at most periods the tiny-handled pottery vessels probably served for scent-bottles, while from 14th/13th-century BC Lachish comes a superb ivory ointment-flask. Egyptian ladies of rank favoured elaborate ivory cosmetic-spoons featuring lotuses, maidens, ducks, *etc.*, in shape, and these were sometimes used in Palestine too. For eye-paint there were many little boxes and tubes, and the paint was commonly applied with a little stick (*spatula*) of wood or bronze. Egypt has yielded scores of such pots and spatulae. (* MIRROR.)

c. Hygiene

Throughout the biblical East, oil to anoint the body, with the object of soothing the sun-dried skin, was almost as essential as food and drink. This use of oil was customary except in mourning; see Dt. 28:40 (its loss, a curse); Ru. 3:3; 2 Sa. 12:20 (*cf.* Mt. 6:17). A striking example is the clothing, feeding and anointing of the repatriated troops of King Ahaz (*c.* 730 BC), described in 2 Ch. 28:15. Those with a passion for luxury, however, made free with expensive ointments (Am. 6:6), a sure way to empty one's purse (Pr. 21:17).

External sources corroborate the biblical picture. In Ramesside Egypt (13th century BC) one papyrus mentions 600 *hin* of 'anointing-oil' for a gang of workmen; other workmen are given 'ointment to anoint them, three times in the month', or 'their corn-ration and their ointment' (see R. A. Caminos, *Late Egyptian Miscellanies*, 1954, pp. 307–308, 312, 470). The same situation held true in Mesopotamia from at least the 18th century BC onwards. Oriental cosmetics, it must be remembered, were as much used for utilitarian as for decorative purposes. (See the oil-distribution texts from Mari, J. Bottéro, *Archives Royales de Mari*, 7, texts 5–85.)

II. Perfumers and perfume-making

In 1 Sa. 8:13 Samuel pictures a typical king 'like all the nations round about' as requiring the services of 'perfumers and cooks and bakers'. Three aspects of this passage find illumination in external sources: the existence of palace perfumeries, the association of cosmetics-manufacture and cooking, and the basic (Heb.) term *rqḥ*.

a. Royal perfumeries

The great palace at Mari on the middle Euphrates (18th century BC) had its own perfumery, the *bīt-raqqi*, which had to supply large quantities of various ointments for the king's dignitaries and soldiers, and the perfumes which were required for bodily use, for ritual, festivals and royal banquets. See J. Bottéro, *Archives Royales de Mari*, 7, 1957, *Textes Économiques et Administratifs*, pp. 3–27 (texts 5–85), 176–183 (the various oils), 183–184 (large quantities), 274, n. 2, and p. 360 (*bīt-raqqi*).

b. Methods of manufacture associated with cooking

The implication of 1 Sa. 8:13, which groups together perfumers (AV 'confectionaries'), cooks and bakers, also corresponds to ancient usage. The techniques of the perfumer were closely related to cooking. The perfume of flowers, *etc.*, could be extracted and 'fixed' by three processes. First is *enfleurage*: steeping the flowers in fat and continually changing them. Second is *maceration*: dipping the flowers, *etc.*, into hot fats or oils at 65° C (150° F). This was most widespread and closest to cooking. Third is *expressing*: squeezing out the scent-bearing juices by compressing flowers, *etc.*, in a bag. Oil of myrrh and other gum-resins were obtained by heating the substance concerned in a greasy-type 'fixative' oil/fat (plus water to avoid scent-evaporation); the perfume-essence of the myrrh or other 'resin' was thereby transferred to the greasy oil/fat which could then be strained off as liquid perfume. For these processes, see R. J. Forbes, *Studies in Ancient Technology*, 3, 1955, pp. 9–10, and references, and A. Lucas, *JEA* 23, 1937, pp. 29–30, 32–33. The N Canaanite texts of Ugarit mention 'oil of the perfumer' (*šmn rqḥ*; see Gordon, *Ugaritic Literature*, 1949, p. 130) and items such as '10 logs of oil', '3 logs of perfume' (*tlṯ lg rqḥ*; see Gordon, *Ugaritic Textbook*, 3, 1965, p. 427, No. 1354—14th/13th century BC; the same measure (log) is used in Lv. 14:10, 12, 15, 21, 24) (* WEIGHTS AND MEASURES).

These processes, so akin to cooking with fats, *etc.*, are sometimes pictured in Egyptian tomb-paintings of the 15th century BC, showing people pouring and stirring the mixture in heated pans, or moulding incense into fancy shapes. Typical examples will be found in Davies, *JEA* 26, 1940, plate 22 with p. 133, and Forbes, *op. cit.*, p. 13 and fig. 1. The cookery aspect of perfumery is also directly reflected in an Egyptian term for 'perfumer', *ps-sgnn*, lit. 'cooker of ointment', and by the use of fire in the elaborate cosmetics-recipes from Assyria (on which see E. Ebeling, *Parfümrezepte und Kultische Texte aus Assur*, 1950).

c. The rqḥ terminology

The ordinary participle *roqaḥ* is used for 'perfumer' in Ex. 30:25, 35 (AV 'compound', 'confection'); 37:29, and also in 1 Ch. 9:30, where it refers to priests commissioned by David and Saul to make perfumes for the tabernacle. It also occurs in Ec. 10:1, where it is identical with Ugaritic *šmn rqḥ* quoted above. *raqqāḥ*, fem. *raqqāḥâ*, is the noun-form for 'professional perfumer'; the latter is found in 1 Sa. 8:13 (AV 'confectionaries'), the former occurs in Ne. 3:8, 'Hananiah, a member (lit. 'son') of the perfumers' (guild)'. (*Cf.* Mendelsohn, *BASOR* 80, 1940, p. 18.) Of words for 'perfume' itself, *rōqaḥ* occurs in Ex. 30:25, 35; *riqqûaḥ*, 'unguents', in Is. 57:9; *reqaḥ*, of spiced wine in Ct. 8:2 (* FOOD); *merqaḥ*, 'perfume' or 'fragrance' (RSV), in Ct. 5:13; *m^eruqqāḥîm* is verbal passive in 'compounded with the perfumery of the artificer' in 2 Ch. 16:14; *mirqaḥaṯ* is 'ointment, perfumery' in 'makers of ointment', 1 Ch. 9:30, and in 'an ointment, a perfume of the perfumer's art', Ex. 30:25; finally, *merqāḥâ*, '(pot of) ointment' in Jb. 41:31, and perhaps in an imperative, 'spice the spicery', in a cooking context (?spiced meat), in Ezk. 24:10 (difficult).

Egyptian wooden toilet-box decorated with veneers of ebony and inlays of ivory and blue glazed composition. Thebes. 18th Dynasty. c. 1400 BC. (BM)

III. 'Visual' cosmetics

a. 'Painting' of face and body

From the earliest times, ancient Oriental womenfolk used to paint round their eyes and darken their eyebrows with mineral pastes which were usually black. At first this was largely medicinal in aim (to protect the eyes from strong sun-glare), but it speedily became principally a feminine fashion, giving an enlarged and intense appearance to the eyes. This is attested in Egypt, Palestine and Mesopotamia.

In 841 BC Queen Jezebel is said to have used such cosmetics. 2 Ki.

A wall-painting in the tomb of User-het showing an Egyptian barber dressing the hair of a recruit of Amenhotep II, 1447–1421 BC. (PAC)

Israelite ivory cosmetic-spoon. The handle is decorated with the inverted 'palmette' that may represent a stylized tree of life. Hazor. Period of Jeroboam II, c. 750 BC. (YY)

9:30 indicates that she 'treated her eyes with eye-paint (*pûḵ*) and adorned her head' before going to the window whence she was thrown to her death at Jehu's word. Over two centuries later two Hebrew prophets pictured their idolatrous nation, faithless to God, as a woman made up for illegitimate lovers. Jeremiah (4:30) says 'you enlarge your eyes with eye-paint (*pûḵ*)', while Ezekiel (23:40) alleges 'you painted (*kāḥal*) your eyes . . .'. Note also Keren-happuch, the name of Job's third daughter (42:14), 'horn of eye-paint'—*i.e.* source of beauty. Such eye-paint was prepared by grinding the mineral concerned to a fine powder and mixing it with water or gum to form a paste that could be kept in a receptacle and applied to the face with the finger or a spatula (see **I.***b*, above).

The minerals used require some comment. In Roman times an antimony compound was used in eye-preparations; the Lat. for antimony sulphide and then antimony itself is *stibium*. Unfortunately this has led to ancient Oriental eye-paints being generally dubbed antimony or stibium—in large measure, wrongly so. In Egypt green malachite was quickly superseded by black eye-paint (Egyp. *msdmt*). Analysis of many excavated samples has shown that this consisted principally of *galena* (lead sulphide), never of antimony except as an accidental impurity. (See A. Lucas, *Ancient Egyptian Materials and Industries*[4], 1962, pp. 80–84 and *cf.* pp. 195–199.) In Mesopotamia the Babylonians called their black eye-paint *guḫlu*, alleged to be either galena or antimony/stibium. (For the former, see Forbes, *Studies in Ancient Technology*, 3, p. 18, who adduces no evidence for his case; for the latter, see R. C. Thompson, *Dictionary of Assyrian Chemistry and Geology*, 1936, pp. 49–51, where the evidence produced is irrelevant—but his 'needles of "lead"' would suit galena better than antimony.) *guḫlu* is same as Heb. *kāḥal*, 'to paint (eyes)', and passed into Arabic as *kohl*, 'eye-paint'. Modern Arab. *kohl* is often just moistened soot; it can include galena but not antimony (*cf.* Lucas, *op. cit.*, p. 101). Hence Heb. *pûḵ*, 'eye-paint', was very likely galena rather than antimony. Thus, the *'aḇnê pûḵ* in the Temple treasures (1 Ch. 29:2) would be 'lumps of galena'. The use of *pûḵ* in Is. 54:11 (AV 'fair colours', RSV 'antimony') may presuppose the employment of (powdered) galena as part of an (dark-tinted) adhesive (*e.g.* resin) for setting gem-stones. For resin plus powdered minerals in tinted adhesives for setting jewellery, *etc.*, see Lucas, *op. cit.*, pp. 12–13.

In Egypt red ochre (red oxide of iron), often found in tombs, may have served as a rouge for colouring the cheeks (Lucas, *op. cit.*, p. 104). Egyptian ladies also used powder-puffs (Forbes, *op. cit.*, p. 20 and fig. 4) and lipstick (see the lively picture reproduced in *ANEP*, p. 23, fig. 78). In antiquity the leaves of the fragrant henna-plant (see **IV**, below) were crushed to provide a red dye for feet, hands, nails and hair (Lucas, *op. cit.*, p. 107). In Mesopotamia the Sumerians used for face-powder yellow ochre, quaintly called 'golden clay' or 'face bloom'; the Babylonians commonly used red ochre (Forbes, *op. cit.*, p. 20). Similar fads doubtless pleased coquettish Hebrew ladies like those of Is. 3:18–26.

b. Hairdressing and restoratives

Hair-styles were part of ancient Near Eastern fashions. In Egypt skilled hairdressers attended to the coiffure (and wigs) of the great. For reproductions of these hairdressers and details of the hair-styles and the hair-pins used, see *ANEP*, p. 23, figs. 76–77, and refs. on p. 259, and also E. Riefstahl, *JNES* 15, 1956, pp. 10–17 with plates 8–14. Mesopotamia also had its fashions in hairdressing (*cf.* B. Meissner, *Babylonien und Assyrien*, 1, 1920, pp. 410–411; *RA* 48, 1954, pp. 113–129, 169–177; 49, pp. 9ff.). Canaan and Israel, too, provide examples of a variety of coiffures with curls long or short (see G. E. Wright, *Biblical Archaeology*, 1957, p. 191 and figs. 136–137, 72). In this connection notice Isaiah's jibe (3:24) and Jezebel's adorning her head (2 Ki. 9:30). Ornate combs were popular (see, *e.g.*, *ANEP*, p. 21, fig. 67). Men in the Semitic world (in contrast to Egypt) rejoiced in fine beards and took care over their hair—witness Samson's seven locks (Jdg. 16:13, 19). Barbers and razors are well known in the OT (*e.g.* Ezk. 5:1, *etc.*) and in the ancient Orient alike (*ANEP*, p. 24, figs. 80–83). Restoratives to repair the ravages of age were eagerly sought. Recipes found in the Egyptian medical papyri include one hopefully entitled 'Book of Transforming an Old Man into a Youth'; several were devoted to improving the complexion (see the renderings in Forbes, *op. cit.*, pp. 15–17).

IV. 'Odoriferous' cosmetics in personal use

a. Perfumery in the Song of Songs

'Ointment' is simply *šemen* (*ṭôḇ*) (1:3; 4:10); *rēaḥ*, 'fragrance', applies to man-made ointments (1:3) and nature's scents (2:13) alike. Spikenard or nard (1:12; 4:13–14) is here very likely to be the same as the *lardu* of Assyro-Babylonian inscriptions, the root of the ginger-grass *Cymbopogon schoenanthus* imported perhaps from Arabia (see R. C. Thompson, *Dictionary of Assyrian Botany*, 1949, p. 17). But the NT *nardos pistikē*, 'precious (spike)nard' (Mk. 14:3; Jn. 12:3), is probably the *Nardostachys jatamansi* of India (Himalayas), a very expensive import for Roman Palestine. 'Bether' (Ct. 2:17, AV) is either a place-name or 'cleft mountains', rather than a spice. For myrrh (1:13; 3:6; 4:6; 5:1) and liquid myrrh, *mōr ʿōḇēr* (5:5, 13), see **V.***a*, below; for frankincense, see **V.***b*, below. The expressions 'mountain(s), hill, of myrrh, frankincense, spices' (4:6; 8:14) may perhaps allude to the terraces (mentioned also by Egyptian texts) on which the producing trees grew.

In 1:14; 4:13 *kōp̄er* may be the henna-plant with fragrant flowers whose leaves when crushed yield a red dye; see on henna, Lucas, *op. cit.*, pp. 107, 355–357. 'Perfumed' in 3:6 is *meqat̩t̩eret̩*, same root as *qet̩ōret̩*, 'incense'; as for 'powders of the merchant', see the powder-puff reference at the end of **III.***a*, above. In 4:14 *karkōm* is usually rendered as saffron; it could be either or both of saffron-crocus and turmeric, which yield a yellow dye (Thompson, *op. cit.*, pp. 160–161, and refs. on Assyr. *azupiranu* and *kurkanu* for these). For calamus and cinnamon, see **V.***a*, below; on aloes, see *Herbs. The verses 5:13; 6:2 allude to beds of spices, *bōśem*, perhaps here specifically balm of Gilead, as opposed to its more general meaning of spices. For mandrakes (7:13), see *Plants. 'Spiced wine' (8:2) is known elsewhere in the ancient East (*FOOD).

b. Other references

bōśem, 'perfume', in Is. 3:24 is a general term in Scripture for spices; *cf.* the gifts of the Queen of Sheba (1 Ki. 10:2, 10), the treasures of Hezekiah (2 Ki. 20:13) and the references in the Song of Solomon (4:10, 14, 16; 8:14). Cleansing and beautifying of the body are apparently implied in the term *tamruq* used in Est. 2:3 (AV, RV 'purifications'; RSV 'ointments'), when Esther and others were preparing for King Ahasuerus. The perfume' of Pr. 27:9 is *qᵉṭōreṯ* ('incense'). The 'precious ointment' of Ec. 7:1 (as of Ct. 1:3) is *šemen ṭôḇ*, exactly the term *šamnu ṭâbu* already used by a dignitary in a Mari tablet of the 18th century BC who requests it to rub himself with (C. F. Jean, *Archiv Orientální* 17:1, 1949, p. 329, A179, l. 6). Perfumes were put on clothes (Ps. 45:8), sprinkled on couches (Pr. 7:17), and precious oil (*šemen ṭôḇ* again) was poured upon the head, as in Aaron's anointing (Ps. 133). Perfumes or spices were burnt at the funerals of the great (2 Ch. 16:14).

For Gn. 37:25, see 'Myrrh', 'Balm', 'Spices', in *Herbs, and *Joseph.

V. Sacred perfumery

a. The holy anointing oil

For anointing the tabernacle and its furnishings, and the Aaronic priests at induction, not for profane use (Ex. 30:22–33). Several of its constituents can be identified. Myrrh, Heb. *mōr*, is a fragrant gum-resin of the tree-species *balsamo-dendron* and *commiphora* of S Arabia and Somaliland. Its fragrance resides in the 7–8% content of volatile oil. It is this essence that could be incorporated into a liquid perfume by heating with fixative oil/fat and straining off (see **II.***b*, above). Besides the 'liquid myrrh' of Ct. 5:5, 13, this liquid myrrh-perfume may be what is meant by 'flowing' or 'liquid myrrh' (*mor-dᵉrôr*) in Ex. 30:23, and is probably the *šmn mr* of 14th/13th-century BC Canaanite texts from Ugarit (Gordon, *Ugaritic Literature*, 1949, p. 130: texts 12 + 97, lines 2, 8, 15 and 120, line 15) and of the contemporary Amarna Letter No. 25, IV:51 (*šaman murri*); the Heb. word *mōr* is therefore early, not 'late' as is wrongly stated in *BDB*, p. 600b. Egyptian *'ntyw*, 'myrrh', was also used in this liquid form, for anointing and medicine (refs. Erman and Grapow, *Wörterbuch der Aegyptischen Sprache*, 1, p. 206: 7). It is this kind of liquid myrrh that is the true *stacte* (Lucas, *JEA* 23, 1937, pp. 29–33; Thompson, *Dictionary of Assyrian Botany*, p. 340).

The precise identity of the 'sweet cinnamon', *qinnmon bešem* (Ex. 30:23; *cf.* Pr. 7:17; Ct. 4:14) is uncertain. There is no formal evidence that this term represents the *Cinnamomum zeylanicum*, native to Ceylon; other plants with aromatic bark or wood in this cinnamon/cassia group are possible (*cf.* Thompson, *op. cit.*, pp. 189–190). That the Egyp. *ti-šps*-wood is cinnamon (Forbes, *Studies in Ancient Technology*, 3, p. 8, Table II, and Lucas, *op. cit.*, p. 354, by implication) is wholly uncertain. See also cassia, below. For fragrant cosmetic woods in Egypt (samples), see Lucas, p. 119; Shamshi-Adad I of Assyria also sought them (G. Dossin, *Archives Royales de Mari*, 1, No. 88, ll. 27–30—*iṣu riqu*).

The 'sweet calamus' (Ex. 30:23, AV, RV) or 'aromatic cane' (RSV) is Heb. *qᵉnēh-bōśem*, and its identity with the 'sweet cane from a far country' (Je. 6:20, and also the 'calamus' of Ezk. 27:19), *qāneh haṭṭôḇ*, is not certain. The latter, however, is very likely the *qanu ṭâbu* of Assyro-Babylonian texts, from 18th century BC onwards (for that of Mari, see C. F. Jean, *Archiv Orientální* 17: 1, 1949, p. 328). And this is probably the *Acorus calamus* having an aromatic rhizome or stem-root; see Thompson, *op. cit.*, pp. 20–21. In New Kingdom Egypt, 15th–12th centuries BC, the scented *ḳnn*-plant is identified as *Acorus calamus* (G. Jéquier, *Bulletin de l'Institut Français d'Archéologie Orientale* 19, 1922, pp. 44–45, 259 and n. 3; Caminos, *Late-Egyptian Miscellanies*, 1954, p. 209—*ḳnni*-oil). Actual plant stalks in a pot labelled 'perfume' or similar were found in Tutankhamūn's tomb, *c.* 1340 BC (Lucas, p. 119). The '50 talents of reeds' in an Ugarit tablet (Gordon, *Ugaritic Literature*, p. 130, text 120: 9–10) among other aromatics might be sweet cane, but hardly cinnamon (Sukenik, *Tarbiz* 18, 1947, p. 126; see Gordon, *Ugaritic Textbook*, 3, 1965, p. 479, No. 2244).

Finally, there is cassia, which translates Heb. *qiddâ* in Ex. 30:24 and Ezk. 27:19. Whatever the real identity of this might be, it is very possible that *qiddâ* is the same as Egyp. *ḳdt* in Papyrus Harris I of *c.* 1160 BC (so Forbes, *op. cit.*, p. 8, Table II). The other Heb. term often rendered 'cassia'—*qᵉṣî'āh*—is obscurer still. However, if in meaning this term is parallel to Arab. *salīḫāh*, 'peeled', and this in turn to Assyro-Bab. *kasi ṣîri* (as Thompson, *op. cit.*, p. 191, would suggest), then it might well be Assyr. *qulqullânu*, modern Arab. *qulqul*, the *Cassia tora* (Thompson, *op. cit.*, pp. 188–192). *Cf.* name of Job's second daughter (Jb. 42:14). (*HERBS, Cassia.)

b. The sacred incense

For the significance of incense, see *Incense. Only its make-up is dealt with here. The general Heb. word for incense (which also appears as 'smoke', and 'perfume' at times) is *qᵉṭoreṯ*, known as a loan-word in Egyp. from the 12th century BC (Erman and Grapow, *Wörterbuch d. Aeg. Sprache*, 5, p. 82: 3); other forms from the root *qṭr* occur. In the sacred incense of Ex. 30:34–38 the last two constituents are easiest to identify. One of these, Heb. *ḥelbᵉnāh*, is pretty certainly galbanum, *Ferula galbaniflua* Boiss., growing in Persia and known in Mesopotamia (Bab. *buluḫḫum*) from the 3rd millennium BC onwards. (See Thompson, *op. cit.*, pp. 342–344; W. von Soden, *Akkadisches Handwörterbuch*, Lieferung 2, 1959, p. 101 and refs.)

Frankincense, Heb. *lᵉḇônāh* ('white'), is named from its appearance as whitest of the gum-resins used for incense; it comes from the genus of trees *Boswellia* of S Arabia and Somaliland, and is the classical olibanum. The Egyptian

Ivory double comb decorated with a lion and trees. Combs of this type were in common use throughout the ancient Near East. Canaanite, from Megiddo. 7·4 cm × 10·2 cm. 1350–1150 BC. (OIUC)

queen Hatshepsut apparently had such trees brought to Egypt *c.* 1490 BC, and small balls of frankincense were found in Tutankhamūn's tomb (*c.* 1340 BC). See Lucas, *op. cit.*, pp. 111–113. *naṭap̄*, 'drops', is given as *stacte* in LXX, but for true *stacte* see **V.*a*** above on myrrh. The name suggests a natural exudation and suitable for incense—perhaps a storax (*cf.* on these, Lucas, *op. cit.*, p. 116; Thompson, *op. cit.*, pp. 340–342) or else balm of Gilead, *opobalsamum*, *etc.*, on which see Thompson, pp. 363–364. The last term, *šᵉḥēleṯ*, is quite uncertain; LXX renders as *onyx*, hence EVV onycha—part of a mollusc giving an odour when burnt (Black and Cheyne, *EBi*, under Onycha). But it might just conceivably be a plant-product, *šiḫiltu* in Assyr. medicine (Aram. *šiḫlâ*), Thompson, *Dictionary of Assyrian Chemistry*, 1936, p. 73 and n. 1; but hardly Assyr. *saḫlê*, 'cress' (for which see Thompson, *Dictionary of Assyrian Botany*, 1949, pp. 55–61). But *šḫlt* in Ugarit-text 12 + 97 among aromatics and foodstuff (Gordon, *Ugaritic Literature*, p. 130, 1. 4; *Ugaritic Textbook*, 3, p. 488, No. 2397) could very well be Heb. *šᵉḥēleṯ* and even Assyr. *šiḫiltu* and Aram. *šiḫlâ* already mentioned. None of these is Assyr. *saḫullatu*, because this latter must be read as *ḫullatu* (Thompson, *op. cit.*, p. 69). To attempt any closer solution would be too hazardous at present.

For an attempt to reconstitute the sacred incense of Ex. 30, see *Progress*, Vol. 47, No. 264, 1959–60, pp. 203–209 with specimen.

K.A.K.

COUNCIL. In the OT (AV) the word appears once only, as a translation of Heb. *rigmâ* (Ps. 68:27) in referring to 'the princes of Judah and their council', a general word which could be rendered 'company' (so AVmg.) or 'throng' (RSV). The similar word 'counsel' is used in Je. 23:18, 22, AV (RV, RSV 'council'), of the privy council (Heb. *sôḏ*) of Yahweh (*cf.* 1 Ki. 22:19ff.; Jb. 1:6ff.; 2:1ff.), where his decrees are announced; true prophets have access to this council and so have foreknowledge of those decrees.

In the NT two Gk. words are used. *symboulion* denotes a consultation of people (Mt. 12:14), or the provincial governor's advisory board (Acts 25:12). *synedrion*, a 'sitting together', is used most frequently with reference to the *Sanhedrin, the supreme court of the Jews, but sometimes also to lesser courts (*e.g.* Mt. 10:17; Mk. 13:9), of which Jerusalem had two and each Palestinian town one. J.D.D.

COUNCIL, JERUSALEM. The Council of Jerusalem is the name commonly given to the meeting convened between delegates from the church of Antioch (led by Paul and Barnabas) and the apostles and elders of the church of Jerusalem, to discuss problems arising from the large influx of Gentile converts into the church (Acts 15:2–29). Many commentators identify this meeting with the one described in Gal. 2:1–10; the view taken here, however, is that in Gal. 2:1–10 Paul refers to an earlier conference which he and Barnabas had with James the Just, Peter and John, at which the Jerusalem leaders recognized the vocation and status of Paul and Barnabas as apostles to the Gentiles. (For the view that one and the same occasion is referred to, see *CHRONOLOGY OF THE NEW TESTAMENT, section **II.*d*.**)

I. The occasion

The rapid progress of the gospel among Gentiles in Antioch (Acts 11:19ff.) and in Cyprus and Asia Minor (Acts 13:4–14:26) presented the conservative Jewish believers in Judaea with a serious problem. The apostles had acquiesced in Peter's evangelization of the household in Caesarea because it was attended by evident marks of divine approval (Acts 10:1–11:18), but if the spread of the gospel among Gentiles continued on the present scale there would soon be more Gentiles than Jews in the church, with a consequent threat to the maintenance of Christian moral standards. To this problem many Jewish Christians had a simple solution. Let the Gentile converts be admitted to the church in the same way as Gentile proselytes were admitted into the commonwealth of Israel: let them be circumcised and accept the obligation to keep the Jewish law.

Thus far these conditions had not been imposed on Gentile converts. No word appears to have been said about circumcision to Cornelius and his household, and when Titus, a Gentile Christian, visited Jerusalem with Paul and Barnabas on the earlier occasion the question of circumcising him was not even aired (Gal. 2:3). Now, however, some zealots for the law in the Jerusalem church decided to press upon the Gentile Christians of Antioch and her daughter-churches the necessity of taking on themselves the yoke of the law. Their pressure proved so persuasive in the recently-founded churches of Galatia that Paul had to send these churches the urgent protest which we know as his Epistle to the *Galatians. In Antioch itself they caused such controversy that the leaders of the church there decided to have the whole question ventilated and settled at the highest level. Accordingly, the Council of Jerusalem was convened (*c.* AD 48).

II. The main question settled

The debate was opened by the Pharisaic party in the Jerusalem church, who insisted that the Gentile converts must be circumcised and required to keep the law. After much disputing, Peter reminded the Council that God had already shown his will in the matter by giving the Holy Spirit to Cornelius and his household on the ground of their faith alone. Paul and Barnabas supported Peter's argument by telling how God had similarly blessed large numbers of believing Gentiles through their ministry. Then James the Just, leader of the Jerusalem church, summed up the debate and expressed his judgment that no conditions should be imposed on the Gentile converts beyond the condition of faith in Christ with which God had clearly shown himself to be satisfied. The Gentile cities, he said, had no lack of witnesses to the Mosaic law; but the entry of Gentiles into the church of the Messiah was the fulfilment of the promise that David's fallen tent would be set up again and his sovereignty be re-established over Gentile nations (Am. 9:11f.).

III. A practical issue decided

Once the main question of principle was settled in a way which must have given complete satisfaction to the Antiochene delegation, a practical matter remained to be dealt with, affecting the day-to-day fellowship between Jewish and Gentile converts where there were mixed communities. It would be a sign of grace and courtesy if Gentile Christians respected certain Jewish scruples. Hence, at James's suggestion, the letter in which the Jerusalem leaders conveyed their findings to the Gentile churches of Syria and Cilicia (including that of Antioch) ended with an admonition to them to abstain from certain kinds of food which their brethren of Jewish stock would find offensive, and to conform to the Jewish code of relations between the sexes. Without such concessions from Gentile Christians, there would have been grave practical difficulties in the way of their enjoying unrestrained table-fellowship with Jewish Christians (When it is remembered that in those days the Lord's Supper was regularly taken in the course of a general fellowship meal, the importance of this consideration will be realized.) There is no real substance in the objection that Paul would not have agreed to communicate these conditions to his Gentile converts (as he is said to have done in Acts 16:4). Where basic principles were not compromised, Paul was the most conciliatory of men, and he repeatedly urges on Christians this very duty of respecting the scruples of others in such matters (*cf.* Rom. 14:1ff.; 1 Cor. 8:1ff.). Nevertheless, when the Corinthians asked Paul for a ruling on food offered to idols he appealed to first principles and not to the Jerusalem decree.

After a generation or two, the situation which called forth the Jerusalem Council and the apostolic letter of Acts 15:23–29 disappeared, and the Western Text of Acts adapts the letter to a new situation by altering its requirements in a more purely ethical direction—requiring abstention from idolatry, bloodshed and fornication. But the requirements in their original form were observed by Christians in Gaul and N Africa late in the 2nd century, and were incorporated by Alfred the Great in his English law-code towards the end of the 9th century.

BIBLIOGRAPHY. W. L. Knox, *The Acts of the Apostles*, 1948, pp. 40ff.; C. S. C. Williams, *The Acts of the Apostles*, 1957, pp. 177ff.; E. Haenchen, *The Acts of the Apostles*, 1971, pp. 440ff.

F.F.B.

COUNSELLOR (Heb. *yô'ēṣ*, 'one who gives advice or counsel'). The basic idea appears in Pr. 24:6b. The word is used as a designation of the Messiah in Is. 9:6, where in respect to the giving of counsel he is said to be a wonder (*pele'*). RSV uses 'Counsellor' to translate *paraklētos* in Jn. but has 'advocate' in 1 Jn. 2:1.

The word *paraklētos* derived from the verb *parakaleō*, literally 'to call beside', has been interpreted both actively and passively; actively as meaning one who stands by and exhorts or encourages, whence the AV 'Comforter' in Jn. 14:16, 26; 15:26; 16:7; passively as meaning one called to stand by someone, particularly in a lawcourt (though as a friend of the accused rather than a professional pleader), whence 'advocate' in 1 Jn. 2:1. Many versions simply transliterate the Greek; hence the name 'Paraclete' for the Holy Spirit.

parakaleō is frequently used in the NT to mean 'exhort', 'encourage', and Acts 9:31 speaks expressly of the *paraklēsis* of the Holy Spirit, which probably means the 'exhortation' or 'encouragement' of the Spirit (though it may mean the invocation of the Spirit's aid).

There is little evidence for an active use of *paraklētos* outside the NT or the patristic commentators on the Gospel passages, who seem to derive the sense 'consoler' or 'encourager' simply from the general context, which speaks of the disciples' sense of desolation at Jesus' departure and of their need to be taught more about him. In Gk. translation of Jb. 16:2, Aquila and Theodotion used *paraklētoi* where LXX has *paraklētores*, the regular active noun for 'comforters'.

On the other hand, the help of the Spirit promised in Mt. 10:19–20; Mk. 13:11; Lk. 12:11–12 is precisely that of an advocate before the Jewish and secular authorities. Even Jn. 16:8–11 has a forensic tone, though admittedly rather of prosecution than defence. The translation 'advocate' is more appropriate in 1 Jn. 2:1, where the sinner is thought of as arraigned before God's justice. Even here, however, the more general sense is not impossible.

The evidence is nicely balanced, and since so many words in the fourth Gospel seem intended to suggest more than one meaning, an ambiguous rendering such as RSV 'Counsellor' is probably to be preferred.

Critics have argued that the application of the word *paraklētos* in the Gospel to the Spirit and in the Epistle to Jesus Christ indicates the different authorship of the two works. But: (i) the Spirit's *paraklēsis* is amid earthly dangers and difficulties: Jesus appears for us in heaven; (ii) these different but parallel offices are reflected also in Rom. 8:26, 34: the Spirit makes intercession in us and the risen Christ for us in heaven; (iii) the words *allos paraklētos* used in Jn. 14:16, though Greek usage permits the translation 'another, a Paraclete', may mean simply 'another Paraclete', implying that Jesus himself is a Paraclete. (* SPIRIT, HOLY.)

BIBLIOGRAPHY. C. K. Barrett, *JTS* n.s. 1, 1950, pp. 7–15; G. Johnston, *The Spirit-Paraclete in the Gospel of John*, 1970, pp. 80–118.

M.H.C.

COURAGE. The Heb. word *ḥāzaq* means literally 'to show oneself strong'. Other words, *e.g. rûaḥ*, 'spirit' (Jos. 2:11), *lēḇāḇ*, 'heart' (Dn. 11:25) and *'āmaṣ*, 'to be quick' or 'alert', exhibit the basic attitude from which courage flows. Courage is, therefore, a quality of the mind, and, as such, finds a place among the cardinal virtues (Wisdom 8:7). Its opposite, cowardice, is found among the mortal sins (Ecclus. 2:12–13). The quality can be seen only in its manifestations and especially, in the OT, on the battlefield (Judges, Samuel, Chronicles). The moral idea is not entirely absent. Those who are objects of God's special care are to 'fear not' (Is. 41:13–14; Je. 1:8; Ezk. 2:6).

The absence of the word from the NT is striking. The noun *tharsos* occurs only once (Acts 28:15). The ideal for the Christian is not the Stoic *aretē* (virtue), but a quality of life based on faith in the present Christ. Here is no 'grin and bear it' attitude, but a more than natural one which sees an occasion for victory in every opposition (*cf.* 1 Cor. 16:9).

The verb *tharreō*, a form current from the time of Plato with the sense of 'to be confident, hopeful, of good courage', is found in Heb. 13:6; and in 2 Cor. 5:6, 8 ('good courage'); 7:16 ('perfect confidence'); 10:1–2 ('boldness'). The cognate term *tharseō* appears with more emotional overtones and is rendered 'take heart' in Mt. 9:2, 22; Mk. 10:49, but as 'take courage' in Acts 23:11. Courage is a Christian duty but also a constant possibility for one who places himself in the almighty hands of God. It shows itself in patient endurance, moral steadfastness and spiritual fidelity.

H.D.McD.

Model of the outer court of the Temple, Jerusalem, showing its surrounding colonnade of porches. Gentiles were permitted to enter this court. (JPK) (HC)

COURTYARD See House, Part 2.

COURT. 1. Heb. *ḥāṣēr* (*ḥāṣîr*, Is. 34:13, AV), 'an enclosure or court', as found in a private house (2 Sa. 17:18, AV) or a palace (1 Ki. 7:8), or in a garden (Est. 1:5). It is very commonly used of the court of the *tabernacle (*e.g.* Ex. 27; 35; 38); of the inner court (*heḥāṣēr happ^enîmîṯ*, *e.g.* 1 Ki. 6:36) and the outer court (*heḥāṣēr haḥîsōnâ*, *e.g.* Ezk. 10:5) of the Temple of Solomon; and the courts of the *Temple in the vision of Ezekiel (Ezk. 40–46). See **4**, below.

2. *^azārâ*, a word of rare occurrence, and therefore uncertain meaning, but evidently used in the sense of 'court' and so translated in 2 Ch. 4:9; 6:13. **3.** *bayiṯ*, 'house', rendered '(king's) court' in AV of Am. 7:13 (*bêṯ mamlāḵâ*), but RV and RSV give variant translations. **4.** *'îr*, 'city' in 2 Ki. 20:4, and so translated in RV, but AV and RSV follow some MSS, the *Q^erē*, and the ancient VSS in reading (*ḥa*)*ṣer*, 'court' (see **1**, above). **5.** Gk. *aulē*, an open enclosure, once (Rev. 11:2) translated 'court' (*PALACE).

In Herod's *Temple, which is not systematically described in the Bible, there were four courts, those of the Gentiles, the Women, the Men (Israel) and the Priests, in ascending order of exclusiveness (*ARCHITECTURE). T.C.M.

COUSIN. The AV rendering in Lk. 1:36 and 1:58 (plural) of Gk. *syngenēs*, 'one of the same family'. Because of the modern restricted use of the Eng. word 'cousin', a more accurate translation would be 'kinswoman' (so RV, RSV). (*KIN.) In Col. 4:10 *anepsios* ('sister's son' in AV) means 'cousin' (so RV, RSV). J.D.D.

COVENANT, ALLIANCE.

I. Terminology

The two key-words in the Bible for covenant or alliance are Heb. *b^erîṯ* and Gk. *diathēkē*. *b^erîṯ* usually refers to the act or rite of the making of a covenant and also to the standing contract between two partners. *diathēkē* is the Gk. translation (LXX) of the word *b^erîṯ* which is taken over in the NT. Its meaning is 'testament'. Along with *b^erîṯ* various other terms are used in a covenantal context. The most important are *'āhēḇ* 'to love', *ḥesed* 'covenant love' or 'covenant solidarity', *tôḇâ* 'goodness' or 'friendship', *šālôm* 'covenantal peace' or 'covenantal prosperity' and *yāda'* 'to serve faithfully in accordance with the covenant'. With the exception of *ḥesed* all the other terms can be somehow connected to terminology in ancient Near Eastern treaties.

Various verbs are used in connection with *b^erîṯ*. The technical term is *kāraṯ b^erîṯ*, lit. 'to cut a covenant', which points to the ancient rite of cutting an animal with the forming of a treaty or covenant. When the verb *kāraṯ* is used with the prepositions *l^e* or *'im*, it points in the direction of a covenant contracted by a superior. Many verbs are used in place of *kāraṯ*, *e.g.* *hēqîm*, 'to establish', *nāṯan* 'to give', *higgîḏ* 'to declare', *nišba'* 'to swear', *he'^emîḏ* 'to confirm', *ṣiwwâ* 'to command' and *śām* 'to make'. Various verbs are also used to denote the participation of the people in the covenant, *e.g.* *bô'* 'to come into a covenant relationship with the Lord' (2 Ch. 15:12), *āḇar* 'to enter into such a relationship' (Dt. 29:12) and *āmaḏ* 'to stand in a covenant relationship'. Two verbs are used for keeping the covenant, *viz.* *nāṣar* and *šāmar*. A whole cluster of verbs are used for breaking the covenant: in the first place *lō'* with *nāṣar* and *šāmar*, then *e.g.* *šāḵaḥ* 'to forget', *āḇar* 'to transgress', *mā'as* 'to despise', *pārar* 'to break', *šāqar* 'to be false to', *ḥillēl* 'to profane' and *šāḥaṯ* 'to corrupt'.

II. Covenantal rites

We are not well informed on covenantal rites, because of lack of material. There are, however, a few vestiges of these rites left in available material. The slaughtering of an animal (sheep, donkey, bull, *etc.*) is described in the Mari texts, the Alalaḫ tablets and in the OT. It was the custom to cut the animal in two or three parts (so lately advocated by Cazelles). Part of it was burnt in honour of the god and part of it was eaten at a covenantal meal. In Gn. 15 such a rite is described. In Ex. 24 the same rite is mentioned. In this case the sacrifice and the covenantal meal are clearly described. In certain ancient Near Eastern vassal treaties it is stated that the vassal is compelled to visit the great king annually to renew the treaty. Although the OT is not clear on this point, it is not unlikely that the same custom existed in Israel. It is possible that the Israelites gathered with a certain festival (New Year's festival) to renew the covenant.

III. Alliance or treaty

(*i*) *In the ancient Near East.* The idea of making a treaty pervades almost the whole history of the ancient Near East. It is only by chance that we are well informed on certain Near Eastern treaties, *e.g.* the Hittite treaties, the treaties of Esarhaddon and the Aramaean treaty of Sefire. A close study of, *e.g.*, the Mari tablets and those of Amarna shows that a treaty background existed between various of the nations and groups mentioned. The usage of, *e.g.*, father-son, or lord-servant (*abdu*) shows that in a friendly relationship the great king

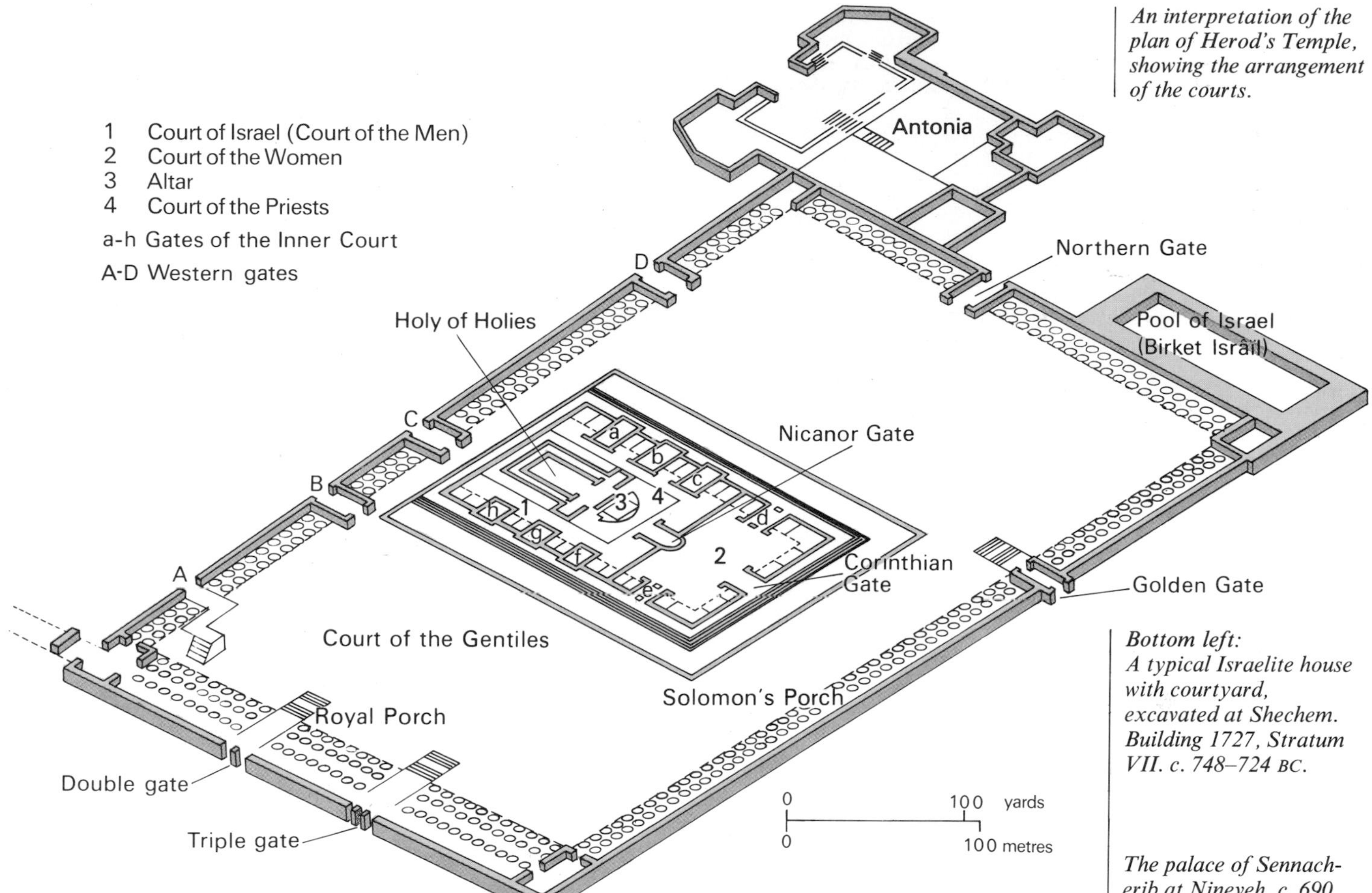

An interpretation of the plan of Herod's Temple, showing the arrangement of the courts.

Bottom left: A typical Israelite house with courtyard, excavated at Shechem. Building 1727, Stratum VII. c. 748–724 BC.

The palace of Sennacherib at Nineveh, c. 690 BC, showing the courtyard arrangement common in Assyrian royal architecture.

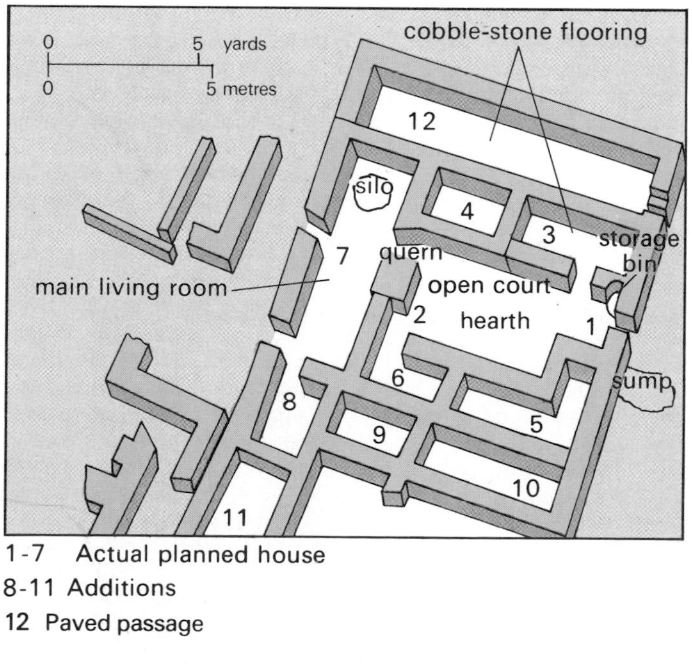

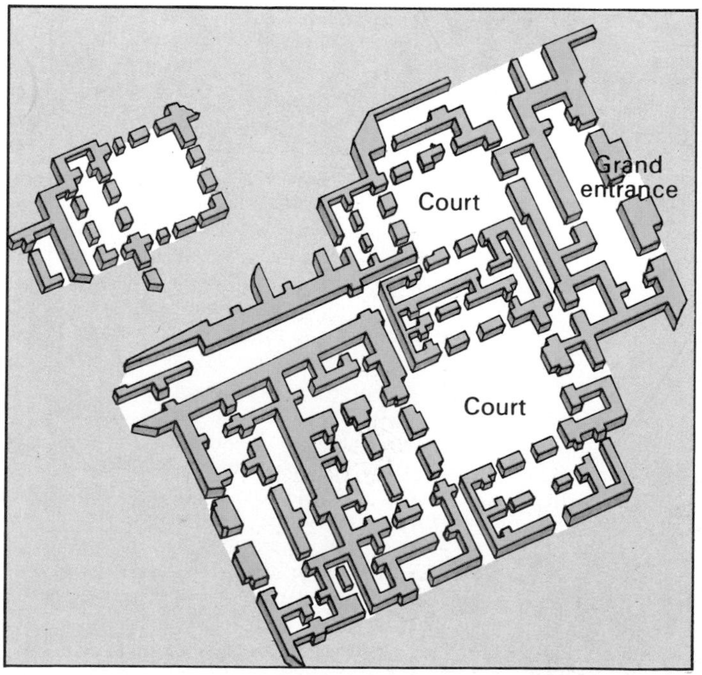

is usually called 'father' and the vassal king 'son', and in a more stern relationship the great king is called 'lord' and his vassal 'servant'. Two main types of treaties occurred: (1) a treaty of equals in which the two partners are called 'brothers', *e.g.* the treaty between Hattusilis III and Rameses II. The stipulations in this kind of treaty are restricted mainly to acknowledgment of borders and the return of runaway slaves. (2) a vassal-treaty was contracted between a great king (conqueror) and a minor king. These treaties were built up more or less around the following scheme: preamble or introduction, in which the great king is introduced with all his titles and attributes; the historical prologue, in which the history of the relationship between the great king and the vassal's forefathers and the vassal himself is sketched. It is not a stereotyped history, but actual historical occurrences which are described with strong emphasis on the benevolent deeds of the great king to the vassal and his country. Then the stipulations of the treaty are given. These consist, *e.g.*, of the following: prohibition of any relationship with a country outside the Hittite sphere; prohibition of hostility to other Hittite vassals; immediate help to the great king in times of war; the vassal must not listen to any slandering of the great king but immediately report it to the king; the vassal must not hide deserting slaves or refugees; the vassal must appear once a year before the king to pay his taxes and to renew the treaty. The stipulations are followed by the compulsion on the vassal to deposit the written treaty in the temple and to read it occasionally. This is followed by a list of gods as witnesses, in which the gods of the great king are prominently placed. Even certain natural phenomena such as heaven and earth, mountains, sea, rivers, *etc.*, are called in as witnesses. The vassal treaty is concluded by curses and blessings. Certain curses will come into effect when the treaty is broken. These curses are of a wide variety and it is clear that certain of them are reserved for the divine sphere and others could be executed by the army of the great king. When the treaty is kept, certain blessings will accrue to the vassal, *e.g.* the eternal reign of his descendants. Variations on this theme occur in later vassal treaties, *e.g.* in the vassal treaties of Esarhaddon heavy emphasis is laid on the curse motif. In the Sefire treaty the curse is illustrated by the melting of a wax figure, *etc.*, a kind of magic act.

(*ii*) *In the OT.* It is clear from the OT that the treaty relationship with foreign nations was not unknown to the Israelites. Both types of treaties, those between equals and vassal treaties, occur in the OT. Vestiges of a parity treaty between the Israelites and the Midianites (Ex. 18) are discernible, although many unsolved problems existed, *e.g.* the relationship between Midianites and Kenites and the later hostility between Midianites and Israelites. The best example of a parity treaty, however, is the one between the Israelites and the Phoenicians. It started probably between David and Hiram (note the word *'ōhēḇ*, 'loved', in expressing the relationship between David and Hiram, 1 Ki. 5:1) and was renewed on a more elaborate scale between Solomon and Hiram. They are called brothers, and one of their transactions, *viz.* the exchange of certain cities for timber, *etc.*, can be paralleled by the same kind of transaction in the Alalaḫ tablets, also in the treaty sphere. This treaty relationship is later inherited by N Israel after the division of the Israelite kingdom. The good relations between the Omrides and the Phoenicians were built on this treaty. We know, *e.g.*, that the parity treaty between Hattusilis III and Rameses II was concluded with a marriage between the daughter of Hattusilis and Rameses. The marriage between Jezebel and Ahab must be understood as a partial fulfilment of the conditions of the treaty.

The best example of a vassal treaty in the OT is the one contracted between the Israelites and Gibeonites (Jos. 9–10). The vassal character of the treaty is evident in the terminology. The Gibeonites came to the Israelites and told them that they wanted to become their slaves. The expression 'we are your slaves' (*ᵃḇāḏeḵâ ᵃnāḥnû*) is definitely referring to vassalage. The treaty was contracted and then a covenantal peace (*šālôm*) between the two parties existed. Although most modern scholars regard Jos. 10 as a later addition, it is to be observed that the military assistance of the Israelites to the Gibeonites after the forming of the treaty was a well-known treaty obligation on the major partner (*e.g.* clearly stated in the vassal treaties discovered at Ugarit). It is thus abundantly clear that the Israelites were well aware of various forms of treaties as they were applied elsewhere in the ancient Near East.

IV. Biblical covenants

(*i*) *The covenant with the Lord.* The idea of a covenant relationship between a god and a king or his people is well attested through the history of the ancient Near East. It occurs in various forms with a great diversity of material. This is not always expressly stated, but can be deduced from terminology used. The idea of such a covenant was thus not at all foreign to the Israelites. At the same time the treaty relationship was well known to them, as we have seen above. It is thus not surprising that the Lord used this form of relationship to give expression to his relation with his people. This could have started early, because such an idea was well known in the ancient Near East from well back in the 3rd millennium BC.

(*ii*) *Early covenants.* Biblical tradition mentions two covenants contracted between God and Noah (Gn. 6:18; Gn. 9:8–17). It is clearly called a covenant, with a certain obligation on Noah and certain promises from the Lord. This is a prelude to biblical covenants where the promise plays an important role.

(*iii*) *The patriarchal covenant.* This is transmitted to us in two traditions, *viz.* Gn. 15 and 17. The Lord has contracted this covenant with Abraham with strong emphasis on the promise (especially in Gn. 17). Two promises were made, *viz.* the multiplication of Abraham's offspring and the inheritance of the *Promised Land. It is obvious, *e.g.* from the book of Exodus, that the promise of a large offspring is regarded as fulfilled (*cf.* Ex. 1:7–22). The description of the conquering of the Promised Land in Joshua points to the fulfilment of the promise of inheritance. The patriarchal covenant is thus mainly promissory. In this it is closely related to the Davidic covenant. The author of Exodus, although describing the forming of the new Sinaitic covenant, still emphasizes the importance of the patriarchal covenant. With the breaking of the Sinai covenant (Ex. 32) this author demonstrates that the patriarchal covenant was still in force (Ex. 33:1). It is thus to be noted that the

One of nine copies of the treaty or covenant terms imposed by Esarhaddon, king of Assyria, on his vassals in May 672 BC. It bears the seals of the god of Assyria and of the ruling dynasty. The reverse lists the curses which would befall anyone who disregarded the stipulations. Nimrud. (BSAI)

Sinai covenant did not replace the patriarchal covenant, but co-existed with it.

(*iv*) *The Sinai covenant*. According to biblical tradition, this covenant was formed with Moses as mediator at Sinai after the Israelites were wonderfully saved by the Lord from their Egyptian bondage. In Ex. 24 the actual rite of the covenant-forming is described. This description has an ancient flavour. A sacrifice was made to the Lord. The blood of the sacrificial animals was divided in two parts, one of which was poured out against the altar. Mention is also made of the book of the covenant. Nothing is said of the contents of this book. Some scholars hold that this refers to the Decalogue and others that it refers to the preceding Covenant Code. We have here a new covenant in which the law is read, followed by the response of the people, sacrifice, sealing by oath and finally the covenant meal. It is clear that the author of Exodus has combined the covenant-forming with the stipulations of the Covenant Code. In Ex. 19 the theophany of the Lord is described; in Ex. 20 the policy of the Lord for his people is sketched (the Decalogue); in Ex. 21–23 the stipulations are given and in Ex. 24 the actual rite of the covenant is described. It is important to note that this covenant has a detailed description of stipulations. As we have seen from the Hittite vassal treaties, stipulations are part and parcel of the treaty form. But we must bear in mind that this is an Israelite covenant which could follow in certain aspects well-known treaty or covenant forms, but could deviate in other aspects from the restricted number of forms we know from the ancient Near East. The stipulations of the Covenant Code are totally different in content from what we know of treaty stipulations. Special circumstances and the different religious background should account for this. At the end of the Covenant Code as a kind of epilogue the promissory character is discernible. Here the reference to the Promised Land is again taken up.

(*v*) *The Davidic covenant*. This covenant is mainly promissory. We agree with various scholars who hold that this covenant is closely connected to the Sinai covenant. It is not to be regarded as a new covenant, but as a further extension of the Sinai covenant. The Davidic covenant became necessary with the development of a new historical situation. The Israelite king was now the mediator between the Lord and his people. A covenant with this king thus became a necessity. The latest research has shown that a close link also exists between the patriarchal and Davidic covenants. Both covenants are of the promissory type. The patriarchal promises were fulfilled with the growing of the Israelite population and with the inheritance of Palestine. It was thus necessary to make new promises in the new situation which developed. With the new promise to David of an eternal reign by his descendants, the patriarchal covenant was in a certain sense superseded by the new covenant. In 2 Sa. 7 the covenant is embedded in a narrative form, but certain terminology clearly points to the covenant background, *e.g.* God will be a father for David's son and the king will be a son for God. The eternal throne of David's descendants can be paralleled to the promise in the form of a blessing in the Hittite vassal treaties, *viz.* that the faithful vassal's sons would reign eternally on his throne. The Davidic covenant, as it is clear from Pss. 2 and 110, had profound influence on later expectations in the OT and even in the NT.

(*vi*) *Covenant in the NT*. In *c.* 600 BC a great upsurge of interest in the covenant occurred (*e.g.* in Jeremiah). The influence of the covenant idea was also strongly felt during the intertestamental period, as K. Baltzer and A. Jaubert have shown. The sect of Qumran can be regarded as a covenant community. It is to be expected that this would also be true in the NT. In the NT the word 'covenant' (*diathēkē* as a Gk. translation of *b^e^rîṯ*) is used in close connection with the * Lord's Supper (*cf.* Mk 14:22–25; 1 Cor. 11:23–25). With the institution of the Holy Communion Jesus refers to his body as the bread and his blood as the wine. This is obviously a reference to Jesus as the paschal lamb which must be slaughtered with Passover and be eaten by his disciples. The paschal lamb became the covenant animal and the Holy Communion a covenant meal. Interesting is Christ's reference to the new testament of his blood. Note the prominent role of blood in the covenant-forming at Sinai (Ex. 24:8). The killing of Jesus as the paschal lamb will take place at Golgotha the next day. Christ's sacrifice on the cross is the most important part of the forming of a new covenant. Paul correctly interpreted Christ's crucifixion as taking on him the curses of the law in order to redeem mankind (Gal. 3:13). With the new covenant the curse of the old Sinaitic covenant is removed by Christ. He became the new Davidic King on the eternal throne. At once two old covenants were superseded: the curses of the Sinai covenant were removed and the promise of the Davidic covenant fulfilled.

(*vii*) *Renewal and ratification of the covenant*. The renewal of the covenant means that the covenant is broken and must be renewed to come into force again. The best example of this is in Ex. 32–34, where the Sinai covenant is broken by Aaron and the Israelites by making a golden bull for worship. When Moses came back, the curses of breaking the covenant were applied by killing a number of Israelites (Ex. 32:26–28). Moses acted as mediator to renew the broken covenant. He went back on the mountain to receive once more the stipulations for the renewed covenant (Ex. 34). Jeremiah regarded the covenant as so totally broken that it could be replaced only by a new covenant (Je. 31:31).

The ratification of the covenant is when a covenant is renewed without necessarily being broken. The best example of this is in Jos. 23–24. In Jos. 23 a description is given of Joshua's final commandments to the Israelites in which they are requested to keep the covenant. According to Jos. 24, with a strong covenant background, the Israelites were gathered at Shechem to renew the covenant with the Lord. Some scholars think that the covenant communion was for the first time formed at Shechem because of the ancient tradition of covenant-forming at this place. We are following the biblical tradition and regard the meeting at Shechem as a ratification of the covenant.

V. The covenant and the prophets

The view of Wellhausen, still followed by many scholars, is that the covenant idea is foreign to the earlier prophets. The idea is only developed from the time of the Deuteronomist onwards (*cf.*, *e.g.*, the views of Kutsch and Perlitt). This view is mainly built on the assumption that nothing can be discovered of the covenant idea in the earlier prophets and that the usage of *b^e^rîṯ* is almost non-existent. It is true that *b^e^rîṯ* is scarce in these writings, but it is a question whether we could ascribe the scarcity of a term to the non-existence of an institution or not. There might have been a reason for the avoidance of *b^e^rîṯ*, *e.g.* a wrong conception could have existed amongst the readers and listeners of the real meaning of the term. Recent research has shown that the covenant idea pervades most of the writings of the prophets, if we use a wider approach and look for the different elements in the covenant, *e.g.* the curse and blessing and the breaking of the covenant by contravening the stipulations. What will happen when the stipulations are broken? Then a covenant lawsuit will follow. The connection between the prophetic office and law is clear from a close study of the prophetic writings. There is no difference in approach to the law between prophets like Hosea, Amos, Isaiah and Jeremiah. Why should Jeremiah be singled out as a protagonist of the covenant just because he has used *b^e^rîṯ* and the others not?

One of the main problems of the prophetic writings is the origin of the prophetic threat. Another problem is the combination of prophetic threat and blessing. A close study of the threats shows that many of them can be closely linked to roughly contemporary curses in vassal treaties, *e.g.* those of Esarhaddon and Sefire. The curse was, however, not only restricted to treaties, but used for a variety of purposes in the ancient Near East. It is to be observed that the treaty curse has certain characteristics which occur also in the prophetic threat. This makes it probable that the prophets regarded the covenant as broken and that as a result of this, certain curses would come into effect. This implies that the prophets were familiar with the covenant form. The fact that they have pronounced threats when the law (of the covenant) is broken, but blessing and prosperity when the law (of the covenant) is kept, shows their special knowledge of the covenant form. The whole problem of threat and blessing beside each other can then be explained by the breaking or the keeping of the covenant.

The covenant lawsuit, which is well attested in the ancient Near East, as Harvey has shown, can be traced from an early source like Dt. 32 to the early and later prophets, *e.g.* Is. 1:2–3, 10–20; Je. 2:4–13; Mi. 6:1–8. In the lawsuit the Israelites are accused of idolatry. It means that they have violated one of the conditions of the covenant, *viz.* not to worship any other god. On this, judgment is pronounced in the form of threats or curses. It is striking that in certain lawsuits heaven and earth are called in as witnesses. The parallel with the much earlier Hittite vassal treaties, where heaven and earth are also regarded as witnesses, is most illuminating. This points to a close link with the treaty or covenant form.

VI. The covenant and theology

Eichrodt in his *Theology of the Old Testament* takes covenant as the central idea of the OT. Israelite religious thought was built up around this concept. From the discussion above it is clear how pervading and important the covenant idea was for the Israelites. It does not, however, exclude other modes of expressing relationship between the Lord and his people. The covenant with its stipulations opens up the possibility of transgression and sin, with the consequence of judgment and punishment. This is one of the main themes of the OT. Another important feature of the covenant is promise and expectation. The Davidic covenant with the promise of an eternal throne gave rise to the expectation of the glorious coming of the Messiah, Son of David. This forms the important link between OT and NT. The covenant is thus the most important link between the Testaments. With the new covenant of the NT a fresh expectation is given of the *parousia* of the Messiah. This shows that the covenant and the expectations which it creates, are also responsible for the main theme of eschatological expectation.

BIBLIOGRAPHY. For a good bibliography up to 1977, *cf.* D. J. McCarthy, *Old Testament Covenant*², 1978. The following is a selection from a vast literature: K. Baltzer, *The Covenant Formulary*, 1971; W. Beyerlin, *Origins and History of the Oldest Sinaitic Traditions*, 1965; P. J. Calderone, *Dynastic Oracle and Suzerainty Treaty*, 1966; H. Cazelles, *DBS*, 7, 1964, pp. 736–858; R. E. Clements, *Abraham and David*, 1967; F. C. Fensham, 'Covenant, Promise and Expectation', *TZ* 23, 1967, pp. 305–322; *idem*, 'Common Trends in Curses of the Near Eastern Treaties and *Kudurru*-inscriptions compared with Maledictions of Amos and Isaiah', *ZAW* 75, 1963, pp. 155–175; *idem*, 'The Treaty between the Israelites and the Tyrians', *VT Supp* 17, 1969, pp. 78ff.; G. Fohrer, 'AT-Amphiktyonie und Bund', *ThL* 91, 1966, pp. 802–816, 893–904; J. Harvey, *Le plaidoyer prophétique contre Israël après la rupture de l'alliance*, 1967; D. R. Hillers, *Treaty-curses and the Old Testament Prophets*, 1964; *idem*, *Covenant: The History of a Biblical Idea*, 1968; H. B. Huffmon, 'The Covenant Lawsuit and the Prophets', *JBL* 78, 1959, pp. 286–295; A. Jaubert, *La notion d'alliance dans le judaïsme aux abords de l'ère chrétienne*, 1963; K. A. Kitchen, 'Egypt, Ugarit, Qatna and Covenant', *Festschrift für C. F. A. Schaeffer*, 1980; M. G. Kline, *Treaty of the Great King*, 1963; E. Kutsch, *Verheissung und Gesetz*, 1973; J. L'Hour, *La morale de l'alliance*, 1966; N. Lohfink, *Die Landverheissung als Eid*, 1967; D. J. McCarthy, *Treaty and Covenant*, 1963; G. E. Mendenhall, *Law and Covenant in Israel and the Ancient Near East*, 1955; J. Muilenburg, 'The Form and Structure of the Covenantal Formulations', *VT* 9, 1959, pp. 74–79; M. Noth, *Das System der zwölf Stämme Israels*, 1930; L. Perlitt, *Bundestheologie im Alten Testament*, 1969; A. Phillips, *Ancient Israel's Criminal Law*, 1970; H. Graf Reventlow, *Gebot und Predigt im Dekalog*, 1962; L. Rost, 'Sinaibund und Davidsbund', *ThL* 72, 1947, pp. 129–134; W. Schottroff, *Der Altisraelitische Fluchspruch*, 1969; R. Smend, *Die Bundesformel*, 1963; G. E. Wright, 'The Lawsuit of God: A Form-Critical Study of Deut. 32', *In Honour of J. Muilenburg*, 1962, pp. 26–27; W. Zimmerli, *The Law and the Prophets*, 1965.

F.C.F.

COVENANT, BOOK OF THE. In Ex. 24:7 'the book of the covenant' (*sēp̄er habbᵉrîṯ*) is read by Moses as the basis of Yahweh's covenant with Israel, at its ratification at the foot of Sinai. Probably this 'book' was the Decalogue of Ex. 20:2–17. It has, however, become customary to give the designation 'The Book of the Covenant' to Ex. 20:22–23:33 (which may at one time have occupied a later position in the record). In 2 Ki. 23:2, 21; 2 Ch. 34:30 'the book of the covenant' is the Deuteronomic law. (*DEUTERONOMY.)

Here we are concerned with Ex. 20:22–23:33, conventionally called 'The Book of the Covenant' and in any case the oldest extant codification of Israelite law. It comprises 'judgments' (*mišpāṭîm*, 'precedents') and 'statutes' (*dᵉḇārîm*, lit. 'words'). The 'judgments' take the form of case-laws: 'If a man do so-and-so, he shall pay so much.' The 'statutes' take the categorical or 'apodictic' form: 'You shall (not) do so-and-so.' Intermediate between those types are the participial laws (so called because they are expressed by means of the Hebrew participle), of the type: 'He that does so-and-so shall surely be put to death.' This type frequently replaces the 'If a man . . .' type when the death penalty is prescribed.

The principle on which the laws in this code are arranged does not lie on the surface, but it has been persuasively argued that each section falls within the scope of one of the Ten Commandments: the code could thus be described as 'a running midrash to the decalogue' (E. Robertson, *The Old Testament Problem*, 1950, p. 95; *cf.* A. E. Guilding, 'Notes on the Hebrew Law Codes', *JTS* 49, 1948, pp. 43ff.).

I. Cultic regulations

The code begins with two cultic regulations: the making of gods of silver or gold is forbidden (Ex. 20:22f.) and an 'altar of earth' is prescribed (20:24–26), neither manufactured of hewn stones nor approached by steps, like the more elaborate altars of Israel's neighbours.

II. Judgments

There follows a series of case-laws (21:1–22:17). These cover such civil and criminal cases as the treatment of Hebrew slaves (21:2–6), the sale of one's daughter into slavery (21:7–11), murder and manslaughter (21:12–14), injury to parents (21:15, 17), kidnapping (21:16), assault and battery (21:18–27, incorporating the *lex talionis*, 21:23–25), a goring ox (21:28–32), accidents to animals (21:33f.), killing of one ox by another (21:35f.), theft (22:1–4), damage to crops (22:5f.), deposits and loans (22:7–15), seduction (22:16f.).

It is this section of the code that presents affinities with the other ancient law-codes of the Near East—those of Ur-nammu of Ur, Lipitishtar of Isin, Bilalama (?) of Eshnunna and Hammurapi of Babylon, for example. These are constructed on the same general lines as the Israelite case-law. The Hittite code, too, in several points of detail and arrangement, shows resemblances to these Israelite laws, although the general outlook of the Hittite code differs from that of other Near Eastern codes, reflecting the Indo-European principle of compensation for injury done rather than the Semitic insistence on *talio* (retaliatory punishment).

While the Israelite case-laws are comparable to these other codes, they reflect a simpler way of life. A settled agricultural community is presumed, and people live in houses, but there is nothing of the rather elaborate urban organization or social stratification of Hammurapi's code. Full-grown men in the Israelite community are either citizens or serfs, whereas in Hammurapi's code the punishment for physical injury, for example, is graduated according as the injured person is a superior, an equal, a 'vassal' or a serf.

A life-setting in the early days of agricultural settlement in Israel suggests itself, and we may recall that such settlement began before the crossing of the Jordan—if not at Kadesh-barnea, then certainly in Transjordan, where the conquered kingdoms of Sihon and Og, with their cities, were occupied by Israelites (Nu. 21:25, 35).

In Ex. 18 we have a picture of

COVERING
See Vesture, Part 3.

COW
See Cattle, Part 1.

CRAFTS
See Arts and crafts, Part 1.

CRAFTSMAN
See Arts and crafts, Part 1.

CRANE
See Animals, Part 1.

Israelite case-law in formation; Moses and his assistants adjudicate on cases which are submitted to them. With this we may associate the alternative name of Kadesh given in Gn. 14:7, En-mishpat, *i.e.* the spring where judgment is given.

III. Statutes

The 'apodictic' laws which constitute the remaining part of the code have the form of directions (*tôrâ*) given by God through one of his spokesmen (*cf.* the function of the priest in Mal. 2:7), preferably at a sanctuary—in the first instance, through Moses at Sinai or Kadesh. They have no parallel in the ancient law-codes of W Asia, but it has been pointed out that they have close stylistic affinities with ancient Near Eastern treaties, especially treaties in which a superior imposes conditions on a vassal. The Decalogue, which is also couched in this apodictic style, is the constitution of the covenant established by Yahweh with Israel; the other apodictic laws are corollaries to the basic covenant-law. Many of the statutes of Ex. 22:18–23:33 are concerned with what we should call religious practice, *e.g.* the offering of firstfruits (22:29f.; 23:19a), sabbatical years and days (23:10–12), the three pilgrimage festivals (23:14–17). In 23:15 we find the beginning of a reinterpretation of these festivals to commemorate events in Israel's redemptive history. Ex. 23:10–19 has been regarded as a self-contained ritual code (compare the so-called 'Kenite' code of 34:17–26). But the statutes also include ethical and humanitarian injunctions, protecting those who have no natural protector (22:21–24), forbidding excessive severity to debtors (22: 25–27), insisting on judicial impartiality, especially where one of the litigants is an alien who might feel himself at a disadvantage (23: 6–9). We should remember that the Israelites knew no such clear-cut distinction between civil and religious law as we take for granted today.

IV. Conclusion

The code ends with Yahweh's assurance of success and prosperity to Israel if his covenant-law is obeyed, accompanied by a solemn warning against fraternization with the Canaanites.

While the 'statutes' take the form of direct utterances of God, the 'judgments' also derive their authority from him (Ex. 18:19; 21:1).

BIBLIOGRAPHY. H. Cazelles, *Études sur le Code de l'Alliance*, 1946; G. E. Mendenhall, *Law and Covenant in Israel and the Ancient Near East*, 1955; A. Alt, 'The Origins of Israelite Law', *Essays on OT History and Religion*, E.T. 1966; K. Baltzer, *The Covenant Formulary*, 1971; B. S. Childs, *Exodus*, 1974, pp. 440–496. F.F.B.

COVETOUSNESS. The Hebrews visualized the soul as full of vigorous desires which urged it to extend its influence over other persons and things. There was *ḥāmaḏ*, to desire a neighbour's possessions (Dt. 5:21; Mi. 2:2), *beṣa'*, the desire for dishonest gain (Pr. 28:16; Je. 6:13) and *'āwâ*, selfish desire (Pr. 21:26). These are all rendered in AV by 'covetousness'. The OT places covetousness under a ban (Ex. 20:17), and Achan is stoned for the crime in Jos. 7:16–26.

Gk. *epithymia* expresses any intense desire, which if misdirected may be concentrated on money, as in Acts 20:33; 1 Tim. 6:9; Rom. 7:7. Gk. *pleonexia* generally expresses ruthless self-assertion, 2 Cor. 2:11; 7:2, which is applied to possessions in Lk. 12:15, and repudiated by Christ in Mk. 7:22. The word is often associated with immorality in lists of vices (Eph. 4:19; *cf.* Philo), and, being in essence the worship of self, is characterized as the ultimate idolatry in Eph. 5:5 and Col. 3:5. It can be rendered 'avarice' in 2 Cor. 9:5 and 2 Pet. 2:3. Gk. *zēlos* is used to inculcate an intense desire for spiritual gifts in 1 Cor. 12:31; but it describes a very sordid carnal strife in Jas. 4:2. D.H.T.

CREATION.

I. The biblical doctrine

This must not be confused or identified with any scientific theory of origins. The purpose of the biblical doctrine, in contrast to that of scientific investigation, is ethical and religious. Reference to the doctrine is widespread in both the OT and the NT, and is not confined to the opening chapters of Genesis. The following references may be noted: in the prophets, Is. 40:26, 28; 42:5; 45:18; Je. 10:12–16; Am. 4:13; in the Psalms, 33:6, 9; 90:2; 102:25; also Jb. 38:4ff.; Ne. 9:6; and in the NT, Jn. 1:1ff.; Acts 17:24; Rom. 1:20, 25; 11:36; Col. 1:16; Heb. 1:2; 11:3; Rev. 4:11; 10:6.

A necessary starting-point for any consideration of the doctrine is Heb. 11:3, 'By faith we understand that the world was created by the word of God.' This means that the biblical doctrine of creation is based on divine revelation and understood only from the standpoint of faith. It is this that sharply distinguishes the biblical approach from the scientific. The work of creation, no less than the mystery of redemption, is hidden from man and can be perceived only by faith.

The work of creation is variously attributed to all three persons of the Trinity: to the Father, as in Gn. 1:1; Is. 44:24; 45:12; Ps. 33:6; to the Son, as in Jn. 1:3, 10; Col. 1:16; to the Holy Spirit, as in Gn. 1:2; Jb. 26:13. This is not to be taken to mean that different parts of creation are attributed to different persons within the Trinity, but rather that the whole is the work of the triune God.

The words in Heb. 11:3, 'what is seen was made out of things which do not appear', taken with Gn. 1:1, 'in the beginning God created the heavens and the earth', indicate that the worlds were not made out of any pre-existent material, but out of nothing by the divine Word, in the sense that prior to the divine creative fiat there was no other kind of existence. This *creatio ex nihilo* has important theological implications, for among other things it precludes the idea that matter is eternal (Gn. 1:1 indicates that it had a beginning) or that there can be any kind of dualism in the universe in which another kind of existence or power stands over against God and outside his control. Likewise it indicates that God is distinct from his creation, and it is not, as pantheism maintains, a phenomenal, or external, manifestation of the Absolute.

At the same time, however, it is clear that the idea of primary creation contained in the formula *creatio ex nihilo* does not exhaust the biblical teaching on the subject. Man was not created *ex nihilo*, but out of the dust of the ground (Gn. 2:7) and the beasts of the field and the fowls of the air were formed out of the ground (Gn. 2:19). This has been called secondary creation, a creative activity making use of already created materials, and stands alongside primary creation as part of the biblical testimony.

Statements such as Eph. 4:6, 'One God . . . above all, and

through all, and in all' indicate that God stands in a relationship of both transcendence and immanence to the created order. In that he is 'above all' and 'over all' (Rom. 9:5), he is the transcendent God, and independent of his creation, self-existent and self-sufficient. Thus creation must be understood as a free act of God determined only by his sovereign will, and in no way a necessary act. He did not need to create the universe (see Acts 17:25). He chose to do so. It is necessary to make this distinction, for only thus can he be God the Lord, the unconditioned, transcendent one. On the other hand, in that he is 'through all, and in all', he is immanent in his creation (though distinct from it), and it is entirely dependent on his power for its continued existence. 'In him [*en autō*] all things hold together' (Col. 1:17) and 'in him we live and move and have our being' (Acts 17:28).

The words 'by thy will they existed and were created' (Rev. 4:11), *cf.* 'created through him, and for him' (Col. 1:16), indicate the purpose and goal of creation. God created the world 'for the manifestation of the glory of his eternal power, wisdom and goodness' (*Westminster Confession*). Creation, in other words, is theocentric, and intended to display the glory of God; to be, as Calvin says, 'the theatre of his glory'. J.P.

II. The Genesis account

The basic Genesis account of creation is Gn. 1:1–2:4a. It is a lofty, dignified statement devoid of those coarser elements that are to be found in the non-biblical creation stories (see section **III**, below). This chapter makes a series of assertions about how the visible world came into being. Its form is that of a simple eyewitness account and no attempt is made to introduce subtleties of a kind which would be appreciated by modern scientific knowledge. Even granting the fact of revelation, a simple phenomenological creation story would describe the origin of only those elements in the world around that were visible to the naked eye. To the degree that Gn. 1 deals with simple observable phenomena, it is parallel to many other creation stories, for all such stories will have to deal with the earth, sea, sky, sun, moon and stars, animals and man.

The fact of inspiration preserved the writer of Gn. 1 from the language and crudities of contemporary polytheism, but the writer remained an ordinary man who used his eyes to good advantage as he sought to describe the way in which God brought this world into being. Comparison of the biblical creation story with the Babylonian story does give a number of parallels, but the external relationship between the two is not clear. It cannot, however, be one of simple borrowing, for there is a depth and dignity in Gn. 1 that is not to be found in the Babylonian story. A. Heidel, *The Babylonian Genesis*, ch. 3, gives a full discussion of the relation between the two stories.

a. Things created

Taking Gn. 1 as a simple phenomenological account, then, the first item concerns the creation of light. It must be one of the simplest of all human observations, that day and night occur in regular sequence, and that light is an indispensable necessity for all life and growth. 'Who caused this to be so?' asks the author of Gn. 1. The answer is, God did (vv. 3–5). A second simple observation is that not merely are there waters below, which form the seas and the underground springs, but there are waters above which provide the source of rain. Between the two is the firmament (*rāqîa'*, something beaten out). Who caused this to be so? God did (vv. 6–8). Again, it is a matter of common experience that seas and land-masses are distributed in specific areas of the earth's surface (vv. 9–10). That too is God's doing. Then, the earth has produced vegetation of many kinds (vv. 11–13). That too is God's handiwork. There are no subtleties of botanical distinction, but the writer knows only three broad groupings of plant life, grass (*deše'*, young, new, vegetation), herb (*'ēśeḇ*, plants) yielding seed after its kind, and trees (*'ēṣ*) yielding fruit whose seed is in itself. Presumably the writer felt that this simple classification covered all cases. The next observation is that heavenly bodies are set in the firmament, sun, moon, stars (vv. 14–19). It was God who placed them there to mark off times and seasons. It would be altogether too subtle to expect the writer to distinguish meteors, planets, nebulae, *etc.* Turning to the spheres in which living creatures are to be found, the writer observes that the waters brought forth 'the moving creature that hath life' (v. 20, *šereṣ*, swarming things, small animals to be found in large numbers, *cf.* RSV 'swarms of living creatures'), and great whales (sea monsters) and every living creature that moves (v. 21, *tannîn*, sea monster, serpent). There is no attempt to make fine distinctions between the various species of sea animals in the zoological sense. It suffices to say that God made the animals of the sea, both small and great. God also made the birds that fly in the firmament (vv. 20–22, *'ôp̄*). The term *'ôp̄* covers all varieties of birds. Whence came the multitudes of creatures that people the earth? God made these too. Then again, the earth brought forth living creatures (vv. 24–25, *nep̄eš ḥayyâ*), which are classified by the writer as cattle (*bᵉhēmâ*, animals), creeping things (vv. 24–25, *remeś*) and beasts of the earth (vv. 24–25, *ḥayyâ*). Zoological distinctions are not to be found here either. The writer was evidently persuaded that his simple classification covered all the main types of terrestrial life sufficiently for his purpose. Finally, God made man (vv. 26–27, *'āḏām*) in his own image and likeness, a phrase that is immediately defined as having dominion over the denizens of earth, sea and firmament (vv. 26, 28). And God created (*bārā'*) man composite, male and female (v. 27, *zāḵār* and *nᵉqēḇâ*).

b. Chronology of events

Close examination of this chapter will reveal a schematic presentation in which the creative acts are compressed into a pattern of 6 days, there being 8 creative acts introduced by the words *And God said.*

If we insist on a strict chronology of events here, we become troubled by the appearance of the luminaries on the fourth day. This problem is avoided if we treat Gn. 1 like some other passages in the Bible which are concerned with great facts but not the chronology (*cf.* the temptation narratives in Mt. 4 and Lk. 4 which stress the *fact* of the temptations but give different orders; see also Ps. 78:13, 15, 24, which stress the *fact* of God's care for the liberated people of Israel, but place the manna incident after the smiting of the rock, contrary to Exodus). If the writer of Gn. 1 is concerned to stress the *fact* of creation and is not particularly concerned with the chronological sequence of events, we avoid a number of difficulties.

There is a reasonably consistent

scheme in the arrangement of the material. The first 3 days are preparatory. The giving of light and the preparation of firmament, seas, land and vegetation are preliminary to the setting of inhabitants in a prepared home. Birds occupy the firmament, fishes the seas, animals and man the land. Days 1 and 4 do not quite follow the scheme, but there is some sort of correlation. Days 3 and 6 each have two creative acts. The seventh day lies outside the scheme and tells of God's rest of enjoyment when his work was completed, the pattern for rest for his creation, one day in seven.

Something is lost if in interpreting this chapter we press the exegesis to unnecessary limits. The whole is poetic and does not yield to close scientific correlations.

The emphasis in the chapter is on what God said (vv. 3, 6, 9, 11, 14, 20, 24, 26). It is the divine creative word that brings order out of chaos, light out of darkness, life out of death. More weight should be given to the word 'said' (*'āmar*), than to the words 'create' or 'make', for creation is asserted to be the product of God's personal will. It is true that the word 'create' (*bārā'*) is used of the heavens and the earth (v. 1), of the great sea monsters and living creatures (v. 21) and of man (v. 27), and that this verb is used exclusively elsewhere in the OT for divine activity. But in Gn. 1 other words are used as well. Thus 'made' (*'āśâ*) is used of the firmament (v. 7), the luminaries (v. 16), the beasts, cattle and creeping things (v. 25), and of man (v. 26). Again, the divine activity is described under the jussive form of the verb in several places: 'let . . . be' (vv. 3, 6, 14–15), 'let . . . be gathered' (v. 9), 'let . . . bring forth' (vv. 11, 20, 24). In the interests of variety the writer has gathered a range of verbs which together stress the divine activity. But the essential activity springs from the Word of God ('God said').

c. The meaning of 'day'

Again, the word 'day' has occasioned difficulty. In the Bible this word has several meanings. In its simplest form it means a day of 24 hours. But it is used of a time of divine judgment ('day of the Lord', Is. 2:12f.), an indefinite period of time ('day of temptation', Ps. 95:8), a long period of (say) 1,000 years (Ps. 90:4). On the view that a day is 24 hours, some have insisted that the creation was carried out in 6 days literally. This does not agree with the facts of geology, nor does it allow for the use of poetic, symbolic or schematic arrangements, in biblical literature. Others have argued that a day represents a long period, and have sought to find a correlation with the geological records, a view which is tied too closely to the current scientific theories, and these are notoriously prone to change. If we allow that Gn. 1 has an artificial literary structure and is not concerned to provide a picture of chronological sequence but only to assert the fact that God made everything, we avoid these speculations and hypotheses.

A related problem is how to interpret the phrase 'evening and morning'. It is possible that we do not know what the writer meant. Among suggestions offered are the following: it refers to the Jewish system of reckoning the day from sunset to sunset, that is from evening, *via* morning, to the next evening; or, '*evening*' marks the completion of a period whose *terminus a quo* was the morning which dawned with the creation of light, while the 'morning' that follows marks the beginning of the new day and the end of the night section of the old day. These views are the exact opposite of each other, and suggest that the meaning is not clear.

Some writers have sought to overcome the difficulty of the 6 days by suggesting that creation was revealed to the writer in 6 days, rather than carried out in 6 days. Six visions of the divine activity were granted to the author, in each of which one aspect of God's creative work was dealt with. Each of the visions was cast into precisely the same form commencing with the words 'And God said . . .' and concluding with 'And the evening and the morning were the . . . day'.

It is argued that the six blocks of material may have been written down on six similar tablets with a similar structure and a similar colophon to conclude each (P. J. Wiseman, see Bibliography). The view is an interesting one, but is really a variant of the idea that in Gn. 1 we have to do with a literary composition arranged in an artificial way in order to teach the lesson that it was God who made all things. No comment is made about the divine method of working.

d. Genesis 1 and science

Questions of the relation of Gn. 1 to the geological and biological sciences have been approached in many ways. The Concordist view has sought to find a more or less exact correlation between science and the Bible. Parallels have been drawn between the geological strata and statements in Genesis in a chronological sequence. Some have insisted that the phrase 'after its kind' is a complete refutation of the theory of evolution. It is not, however, at all clear what the Hebrew word 'kind' (*mîn*) means, except as a general observation that God so made creatures that they reproduced in their families. But if the Hebrew word is not understood, it is also true to say that the biological groupings are not at all finally decided. Let it be agreed that the Bible is asserting that, however life came into being, God lay behind the process, then the chapter neither affirms nor denies the theory of evolution, or any theory for that matter.

Gn. 1:2 has been made the ground for the theory of a gap in the world's history. It is asserted that the translation should be: 'and the earth *became* without form and void'. That is, it was created perfect, something happened, and it became disordered. Subsequently God re-created it by refashioning the chaos. The gap in time allows, in this view, for the long geological ages before the calamity. The original creative act is said to belong to the dateless past and to give scope for the geological eras. It should be said that there is neither geological evidence for this, nor is this translation at all likely. This phrase in Hebrew normally means 'and it was', not 'and it became'.

Many writers have sought to find a second creation story in Gn. 2 which is said to have a different chronological order from that in Gn. 1. Such a view is not necessary if we regard Gn. 2 as part of the fuller narrative Gn. 2 and 3, in which Gn. 2 merely forms an introduction to the temptation story, and provides the setting without any attempt to give a creation story, and certainly not to give a chronological sequence of events.

It ought to be asserted finally, that while there is still a good deal of discussion about the exact significance of Gn. 1, all must agree that the one central assertion of the chapter is that God made all that constitutes this universe in which we live. If we assert this on the simple observational level, the nature of the passage is such as to enable an easy extension to those areas which cannot be seen by the naked eye. J.A.T.

III. Ancient Near Eastern theories

No myth has yet been found which explicitly refers to the creation of the universe, and those concerned with the organization of the universe and its cultural processes, the creation of man and the establishment of civilization are marked by polytheism and the struggles of deities for supremacy in marked contrast to the Heb. monotheism of Gn. 1–2. Most of these tales form part of other texts and the views of these early people have to be gleaned from religious writings which, though dated to the first part of the 2nd millennium BC, may well go back to earlier sources, as now evidenced by a creation story from *Ebla dated 2350 BC.

a. Sumer and Babylonia

There are a number of creation stories linked with the supremacy ascribed to various ancient cities and the deity conceived to have first dwelt there. Thus Nippur was thought to have been inhabited only by gods prior to the creation of mankind. Enki, the god of the deep and of wisdom, chose Sumer and then set about founding neighbouring territories, including the paradise Dilmun. He first appointed the rivers, marshes and fishes, and then the sea and the rain. Next, earth's cultural requirements are met by the provision of grain and green growth, the pickaxe and the brick-mould. The high hills are covered with vegetation and cattle and sheep fill the folds.

Another myth tells of the paradise Dilmun in which the mother-goddess Ninhursag produces offspring without pain or travail, though Enki, after eating plants, is cursed and falls sick until cured by a specially created goddess *Nin.ti*, whose name means 'the lady of the rib' and 'the lady who makes live', both reflecting the name of *Eve.

'Enki and Ninhursag' concerns the creation of man from clay. This followed a battle in which Enki led the host of the good against Nammu, the primeval sea. Then with the aid of Nin-mah, the earth-mother-goddess, he creates frail man.

The best known of the Babylonian creation-myths is the adaptation of the Sumerian cosmogony called *enuma eliš* from its initial words, 'When on high the heavens were not named and earth below had not been called by name.' Tiamat (*cf.* Heb. *t*^{e}*hōm*, the deep) and Apsu (the sweet-water) existed, but after other gods were born Apsu tried to do away with them because of their noise. One of the gods, Ea, the Sumerian Enki, killed Apsu; then Tiamat, bent on revenge, was herself killed by Ea's son Marduk, the god of Babylon in whose honour the poem was composed. Marduk used the two halves of Tiamat to create the firmament of heaven and earth. He then set in order the stars, sun and moon, and lastly, to free the gods from menial tasks, Marduk, with the help of Ea, created mankind from the clay mingled with the blood of Kingu, the rebel god who had led Tiamat's forces. The only similarities between these and Gn. 1–2 is the mention of the deep (*t*^{e}*hōm* in 1:2 is not necessarily a mythological personification), the divine rest after creation and the subdivision of the record into six (W. G. Lambert, *JTS* 16, 1965, pp. 287–300, and P. J. Wiseman, *Clues to Creation in Genesis*, 1977).

Other creation epics differ in detail. One tells how, when 'all lands were sea', the gods were created and the city of Babylon built. Marduk therefore made a reed mat over the waters on which he and the mother-goddess Aruru created man. There followed the creation of beasts, rivers, green herbs, lands and domesticated animals. Yet another myth ascribes the creation of the heavens to Anu and of the earth to Ea. Here again, when the land, and the gods thought necessary to its order, had provided a temple and its supplies of offerings, man was created to serve the gods, as in the *Atra-hasīs* and earlier epics.

b. Egypt

Among a number of allusions to creation, one, dated *c.* 2350 BC, describes the act of the god Atum who brought forth gods on a primeval hill above the waters of Chaos. Atum 'who came into being by himself' next brought the world into order and out of the dark deep assigned places and functions to the other deities, including Osiris. The theologians of Memphis, as of Thebes, had their way of justifying the emergence of their city and god.

Babylonian cuneiform tablet containing the first part of the Epic of Atra-hasīs *describing the creation of man (to relieve the gods of the work of cultivating the land). Copied c. 1635 BC. Height 25 cm.* (BM)

For them it was the god Ptah who conceived the creation and brought it into being by his commanding word, an early reflection, found also in the Sumerian texts, of the *Logos* doctrine. Another myth ascribes to the sun-god Rē‘ the victory over the underworld Apophis. According to this version, mankind was created from Rē‘'s tears, all men being created equal in opportunity to enjoy the basic necessities of life.

It will be seen that throughout the ancient Near East there was a conception of a primary watery emptiness (rather than chaos) and darkness; that creation was a divine act *ex nihilo* and that man was made by direct divine intervention for the service of the gods. The Hebrew account, with its clarity and monotheism, stands out unique; there are no struggles between deities or attempts to exalt any special city or race. D.J.W.

c. Ancient Greece

To the Greeks in general the gods they worshipped were not responsible for the creation of the world, but rather were beings created, or begotten, by vaguely conceived deities or forces which they replaced. Hesiod, in his *Theogony*, says that first of all Chaos came into being, then Earth, who, impregnated by Heaven, became the great mother of all. In fact, rather than creation there is an automatic development, mainly by procreation, from undefined beginnings. There are many variations in detail, and the philosophers rationalized them in various ways. The *Epicureans attributed all to chance combinations of atoms, and the pantheistic *Stoics conceived of a **logos*, or impersonal world-principle.

Of particular interest is the Orphic myth, although it was probably accepted by comparatively few, for some have seen in Orphism significant parallels with Christianity. In this the great creator is Phanes, who emerged from an egg, and after creating the universe and the men of the Golden Age retired into obscurity until his great-grandson Zeus swallowed him and all his creation and subsequently re-created the existing world. The men of the present race arose from the blasted remains of the Titans who had killed and eaten Dionysus son of Zeus, and so have in them elements both of evil and of the divine. Dionysus was restored to life by Zeus, and was often identified with Phanes. K.L.McK.

BIBLIOGRAPHY. *The biblical doctrine:* C. Hodge, *Systematic Theology*, 1, 1878, pp. 553ff.; S. Harris, *God the Creator and Lord of All*, 1, 1897, pp. 463–518; J.-J. von Allmen, *Vocabulary of the Bible*, 1957 (*s.v.* 'Creation'). *The Genesis account:* F. Delitzsch, *Commentary on Genesis*, E.T. 1888; P. J. Wiseman, *Clues to Creation in Genesis*, 1977; A. Heidel, *The Babylonian Genesis*, 1950, pp. 82–140; W. J. Beasley, *Creation's Amazing Architect*, 1953, for a typical Concordist treatment; N. H. Ridderbos, *Is There a Conflict between Genesis 1 and Natural Science?*, 1957. *Non-biblical views:* see *ANET*, pp. 1–9; S. N. Kramer, *Mythologies of the Ancient World*, 1961, for details of Sumerian and other traditions; and A. Heidel, *op. cit.*, for a discussion of their relation to Genesis. See also W. K. C. Guthrie, *Orpheus and Greek Religion*, 1935, pp. 79ff; H. H. Esser, I. H. Marshall, in *NIDNTT* 1, pp. 376–389.

CREATURES. Tr. of *ḥayyâ* and *nep̄eš ḥayyâ* in OT, *zōon*, *ktisma* and sometimes *ktisis* in NT, emphasizing mainly the aspect of being alive rather than createdness.

The term embraces 'all flesh that is upon the earth' (Gn. 9:16) which is under the all-seeing eye of God (Heb. 4:13) and within the scope of the gospel (Col. 1:23). Elsewhere man is distinguished from other creatures as having responsibility for them (Gn. 2:19), but abusing his position by idolatry (Rom. 1:25), yet in Christ being reborn as God intended him to be—'a kind of first fruits of his creatures' (Jas. 1:18).

The term also includes celestial beings (Ezk. 1; Rev. 5, *et passim*) where earthly imagery is taken up into the vision of the worship of heaven. P.A.B.

CREED. It is clear that a full-scale creed in the sense in which J. N. D. Kelly defines it ('a fixed formula summarizing the essential articles of the Christian religion and enjoying the sanction of ecclesiastical authority', *Early Christian Creeds*[3], 1972, p. 1) is not found in the NT. The so-called 'Apostles' Creed' does not go back to apostolic times. Yet recent investigation in the field of symbolic theology will not postpone the church's creed-making to the 2nd and subsequent centuries. There are clear indications that what appear as credal fragments, set in the context of the church's missionary preaching, cultic worship and defence against paganism, are already detectable in the NT. We shall examine some representative examples of these confessional forms. (A more extended discussion will be seen in V. H. Neufeld, *The Earliest Christian Confessions*, 1963, and R. P. Martin, *Worship in the Early Church*, 1974, ch. 5.)

a. Missionary preaching

There is evidence that in the primitive church there was a corpus of distinctive Christian teaching held as a sacred deposit from God (see Acts 2:42; Rom. 6:17; Eph. 4:5; Phil. 2:16; Col. 2:7; 2 Thes. 2:15; and especially in the Pastoral Epistles, 1 Tim. 4:6; 6:20; 2 Tim. 1:13–14; 4:3; Tit. 1:9). This body of doctrinal and catechetical instruction, variously known as 'the apostles' teaching', 'the word of life', 'the pattern of doctrine', the apostolic 'traditions', 'the deposit', the 'sound words', formed the basis of Christian ministry, and was to be held firm (Jude 3; and especially in Heb. 3:1; 4:14; 10:23), handed on to other believers as the apostolic men themselves had received it (see 1 Cor. 11:23ff.; 15:3, where the verbs, 'received', 'delivered', are technical terms for the transmission of authoritative teaching; *cf.* B. Gerhardsson, *Memory and Manuscript*, 1961), and utilized in the public proclamation of the gospel. In fact, the term 'gospel' designates the same web of truth, the *Heilsgeschichte*, which proclaims God's redeeming mercy in Christ to men (Rom. 2:16; 16:25; 1 Cor. 15:1ff.).

b. Cultic worship

Under this heading the cultic and liturgical acts of the church as a worshipping community may be shown to reveal credal elements, *e.g.* in baptism (Acts 8:37 according to the Western Text; Rom. 9:9: see J. Crehan, *Early Christian Baptism and the Creed*, 1950); in the worshipping life of the church, especially in the eucharist, with which are associated ceremonial declarations of faith, hymnic compositions, liturgical prayers and devotional exclamations (as in 1 Cor. 12:3; 16:22, which is probably the earliest example of corporate prayer, *Marānā thā*, 'Our Lord, come!' and Phil. 2:5–11, on which *cf.* R. P. Martin, *Carmen Christi: Philippians ii. 5–11 in Recent Interpretation and in the Setting of Early Christian Worship*, *NTS* Monograph series 4, 1967); and in exorcism for which formulae used in the casting out of evil spirits (*e.g.* Acts 16:18; 19:13) came into prominence, as in the Jewish practice.

c. Cullmann's theory of formulation

O. Cullmann, *The Earliest Christian Confessions*, E.T. 1949, pp. 25ff., has set forth the theory that the formulation of early creeds was controlled partly by the polemical needs of the church in the pagan world. When arraigned before the magistrates and required to attest their allegiance, the Christians' reply would be 'Jesus Christ is Lord'; and thus a credal form was shaped and systematized.

The NT 'creeds' range in scope from the simple confession, 'Jesus is Lord', to implicit Trinitarian formulations, as in the apostolic benediction of 2 Cor. 13:14 and such references as Mt. 28:19 (on which, see Martin, *Worship in the Early Church*, ch. 8; A. W. Wainwright, *The Trinity in the New Testament*, 1962); 1 Cor. 12:4ff.; 2 Cor. 1:21ff.; 1 Pet. 1:2; but excepting the interpolated 1 Jn. 5:7f. There are binitarian creeds which associate the Father and the Son, as in 1 Cor. 8:6 (which may be a Christianized version of the Jewish credo known as the *Shema'*, based on Dt. 6:4ff.); 1 Tim. 2:5f.; 6:13f.;

2 Tim. 4:1. The main type, however, is the Christological formula with such detailed summaries as in 1 Cor. 15:3ff.; Rom. 1:3; 8:34; Phil. 2:5–11; 2 Tim. 2:8; 1 Tim. 3:16 (on which, see R. H. Gundry in *Apostolic History and the Gospel*, ed. W. W. Gasque and R. P. Martin, 1970, pp. 203–222) and 1 Pet. 3:18ff. (on which, see R. Bultmann, *Coniectanea Neotestamentica* 11, 1949, pp. 1–14). R.P.M.

CRESCENS. Companion of Paul (2 Tim. 4:10) on service in 'Galatia'. Elsewhere Paul uses this term of Anatolian Galatia, but here it could equally designate European Gaul, as most ancient commentators and some MSS interpret it. If so, with the contiguous references to Titus's Dalmatian mission, it may point to a concerted penetration of the W by associates of the imprisoned Paul. The name is Lat., and infrequent in Gk.

BIBLIOGRAPHY. Zahn, *INT*, 2, pp. 25f. A.F.W.

CRETE. A mainly mountainous island in the Mediterranean lying across the S end of the Aegean. It is about 250 km long, and its breadth varies from 56 km to 11 km. It is not mentioned by name in the OT, but it is probable that the *Cherethites, who formed part of David's bodyguard, came from it, and the place-name *Caphtor probably referred to the island and the adjacent coastlands which fell within its dominion during the 2nd millennium BC. In the NT Cretans (*Krētes*) are mentioned among those present at Pentecost (Acts 2:11), and later the island (*Krētē*) is named in the account of Paul's journey to Rome (Acts 27:7–13, 21). His ship sailed past Salmone at the E end and put into a port called Fair Havens near Lasea in the centre of the S coast, and Paul advised wintering there. He was overruled, however. The ship set out to coast round to a better wintering-berth at Phoenix in the SW, but a strong wind sprang up, driving them out to sea, and finally to Malta. After his imprisonment at Rome, Paul evidently revisited Crete, for he left *Titus there to carry on the work. The unflattering description of the Cretans in Tit. 1:12 is a quotation from Epimenides of Crete (quoted also in Acts 17:28a).

Our knowledge of the island's

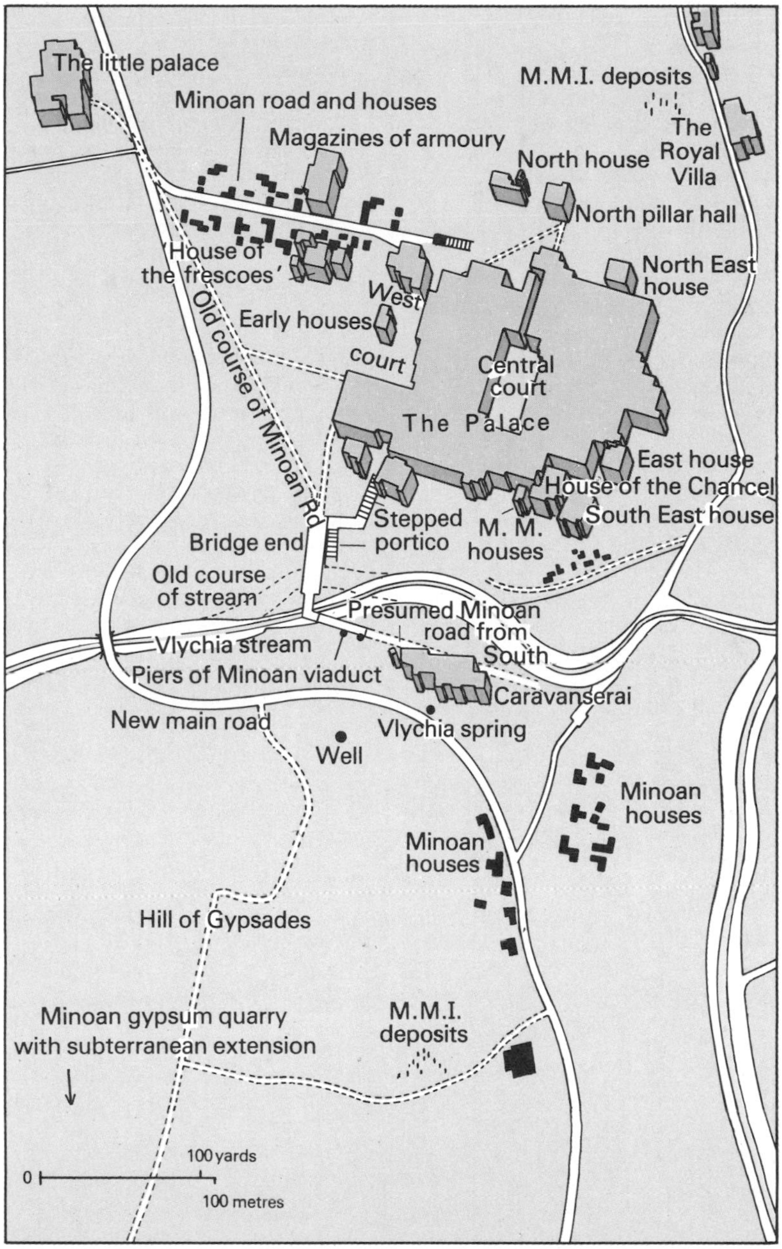

Plan of the palace of Minos at Knossos and its surroundings.

CREEPING THING
See Animals, Part 1.

CRESCENT
See Ornaments, Part 2.

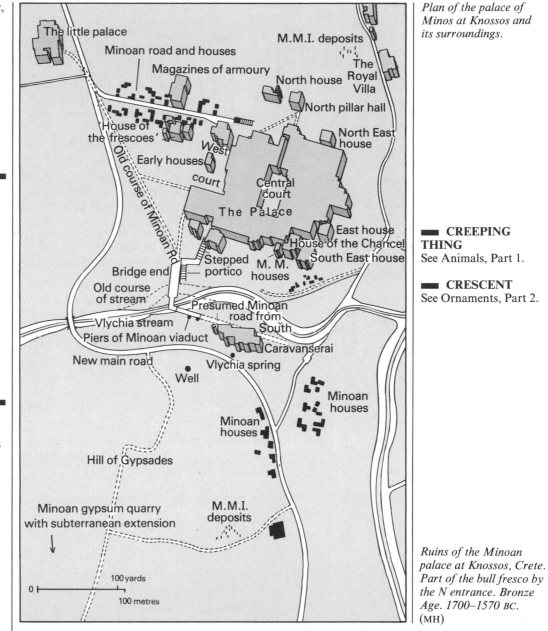

Ruins of the Minoan palace at Knossos, Crete. Part of the bull fresco by the N entrance. Bronze Age. 1700–1570 BC. (MH)

history is derived chiefly from archaeology. There were neolithic settlements on it in the 4th and 3rd millennia BC, but it was in the Bronze Age that a powerful civilization was achieved. This was centred upon Knossos, a site excavated over many years by Sir Arthur Evans. The Early Bronze Age (Early Minoan I–III, *c.* 2600–2000 BC) was a period of gradual commercial expansion, which was continued during the Middle Bronze Age (Middle Minoan I–III, *c.* 2000–1600 BC). In this latter period writing (on clay and copper tablets) was in use, first of all in the form of a pictographic script (*c.* 2000–1650 BC) and then in a simplified form, known as Linear A (*c.* 1750–1450 BC). Neither of these scripts has been positively deciphered (C. H. Gordon's suggestion that Linear A was used to write Akkadian has not been widely accepted).

The peak of Cretan civilization was reached in the early part of the Late Bronze Age (Late Minoan I(–II), *c.* 1600–1400 BC). The Linear A script continued in use during part of this period, but a third script, Linear B, appeared at Knossos (Late Minoan II, known only from Knossos). This was finally deciphered in 1953 by M. Ventris, and found to be couched in an archaic form of Gk. (Mycenaean), suggesting that the Late Minoan II period at Knossos was due to an enclave of Gk.-speaking invaders. Similar tablets have also been found at Mycenae and Pylos on the mainland of Greece, where the script continued to be used after the decline of Minoan civilization, a decline which was accelerated by the violent destruction, perhaps by pirates, of most of the towns in Crete, around 1400 BC. This decline continued through the last phases of the Bronze Age (Late Minoan III, *c.* 1400–1125 BC). Towards the end of this period Dorian Greeks came to the island and ushered in the Iron Age.

Discoveries in Egypt, and at such sites as Ras Shamra (*cf.* the name of king *krt* in the cuneiform tablets), Byblos and Atchana (Alalaḫ) in Syria, show that Cretan commerce had extended to W Asia by the Middle Minoan II period (1st quarter of the 2nd millennium), and from this time on the folk-movements, in which the *Philistines played a part and which culminated in the invasion of the 'Sea Peoples' in the 14th century, were taking place. Throughout the Iron Age the island was divided among a number of feuding city–states, until

Crete and the E Mediterranean in OT times.

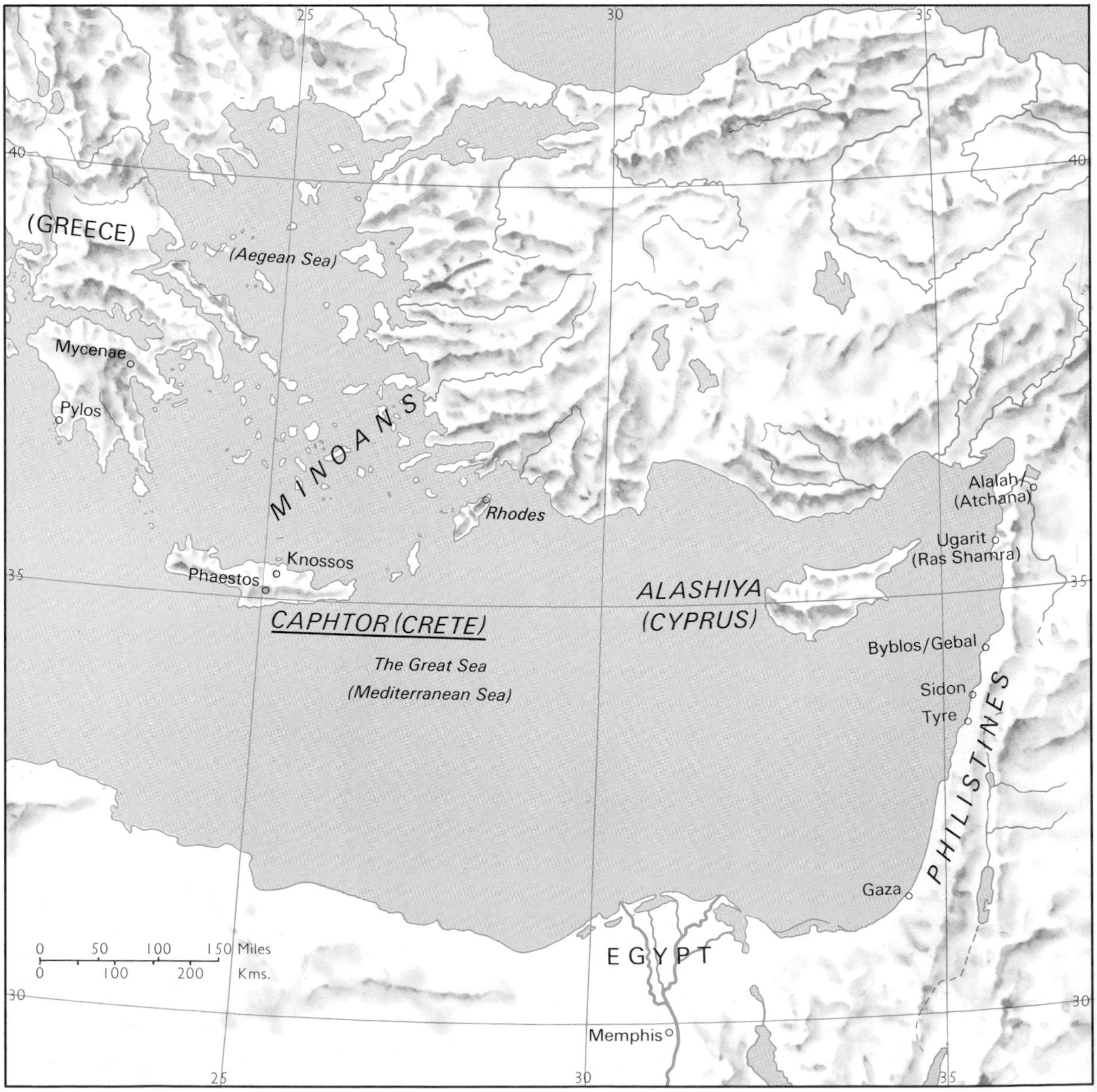

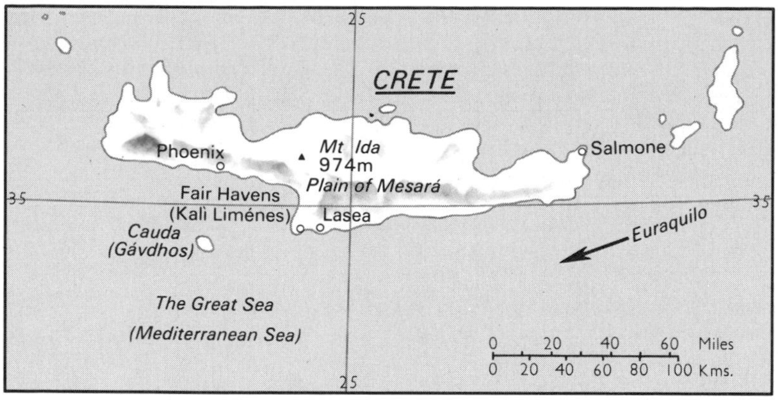

The island of Crete in NT times, showing the direction of the wind Euraquilo.

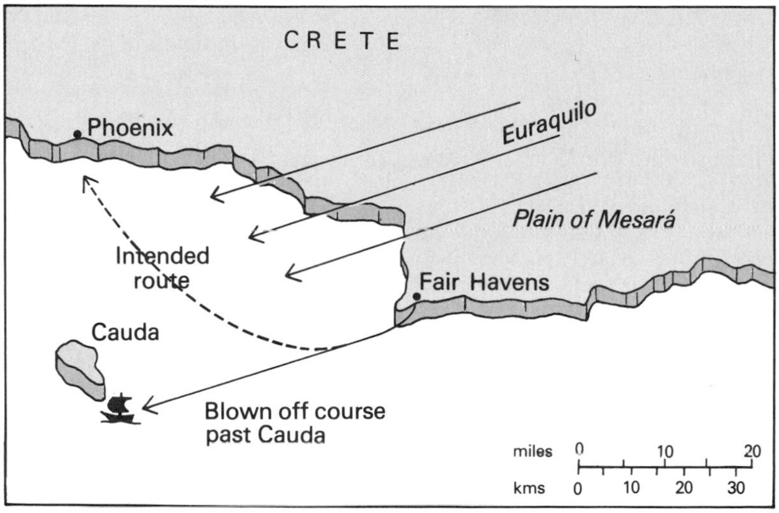

A diagrammatic representation of how Paul, sailing from Fair Havens, was blown off course past Cauda.

it was subdued by Rome in 67 BC.

BIBLIOGRAPHY. J. D. S. Pendlebury, *The Archaeology of Crete*, 1939; R. W. Hutchinson, *Prehistoric Crete*, 1962; H. J. Kantor, *The Aegean and the Orient in the Second Millennium BC*, 1947; J. Chadwick, *The Decipherment of Linear B*, 1958; A. Hopkins, *Crete: Its Past, Present and People*, 1978; C. H. Gordon, *HUCA* 26, 1955, pp. 43–108; *JNES* 17, 1958, pp. 245–255. T.C.M.

CRIME AND PUNISHMENT. Crime and punishment can be taken either in the juridical or in the religious sense, the latter in one way closely related to the former. We have thus to investigate the meaning of both to get a clear conception of our subject. The combination of crime and punishment in a strictly legal sense raises questions. The clear-cut distinction between criminal and civil offences of modern times is not present in OT and Near Eastern jurisprudence. Every offence was committed, in the first place, against a certain person or community, and the only way to put the wrong right was to compensate the injured or wronged person.

Jurisprudence was also connected all over the Near East with the divine. The god sanctioned the laws of a community. This is evident, *e.g.*, from the prologue of the laws of Ur-Nammu, where Nanna, the Sumerian moon god, is mentioned; there is the famous law code of Hammurapi with the well-known stele presenting the god Shamash and Hammurapi in front of him receiving the symbols of authority and justice. In a very special sense this is also true of the OT. The promulgation of laws is closely connected with the forming of the *covenant. This can now be paralleled by certain treaties like the treaty between Ir-IM of Tunip and Niqmepa of Alalaḫ, where a covenant is made, with certain mutual obligations couched in the typical form of Near Eastern jurisprudence. This is, however, only a formal parallel. The OT tradition takes the promulgation back to the covenant's origin at Sinai, giving every law the sanction of the Lord.

For our purpose it is preferable to sketch the meaning and background of crime and punishment separately.

I. Crime

a. Etymology

There is a close affinity between crime, guilt and punishment. This is evident from the Heb. word *'āwōn*, translated 55 times as 'offence' or 'crime', 159 times as 'guilt' and 7 times as 'punishment'. The basic meaning of crime is to act in a consciously crooked or wrong way. The word *reša'* means guilt and crime, and refers to the way of life of an irreligious person. The Heb. word in verb form, *šāgâ*, gives the meaning to act wrongly in ignorance. Another Heb. word, *peša'*, has the emphatic meaning rebellion or revolt. The common word for an offence, crime or sin is the verb *ḥāṭā'*, and noun *ḥēṭ'*. It has the double connotation of an offence against human beings (*e.g.* Gn. 41:9); and sin against God (*e.g.* Dt. 19:15). The basic meaning of the word was presumably 'to miss something', 'to err'; and this meaning was carried over to the sphere of offences against humanity and the deity. The whole idea of sin in OT and NT (Gk. *hamartia* is a direct translation of *ḥēṭ'*) is built up around this word.

In the Gk. NT the most important words connected with crime are *hamartia, hamartēma, asebeia, adikia, parakoē, anomia, paranomia, paraptōma. hamartia* and *hamartēma* mean to 'miss a mark', thus closely bound in meaning to the Heb. *ḥēṭ'*, denoting sin. *asebeia* and *adikia* mean to be actively irreligious and to be deliberately against God, a type of conduct usually regarded in the OT as the impious way of living, and described by *rāšā'*. *parakoē* means to be actively disobedient; the OT calls disobedience a refusing to hear (*lō' šāma'*, *e.g.* in Je. 9:13; 35:17). It denotes an action against the law, like *paranomia*. The nearest parallel in the OT is *'āwōn*. It is interesting to note that no technical terminology was used in biblical times to describe a transgression of law. Near Eastern jurisprudence has not developed a theoretical legal terminology. *parabasis* literally means to transgress, to transgress the existing laws with individual acts, *e.g.* Rom. 4:15. *paraptōma* is a less rigorous word than all those already discussed. It has the meaning of sin not of the worst enormity. 'Fault' comes nearest to the meaning, *e.g.* Gal. 6:1.

b. The treatment of offences

Legal decisions in Near Eastern

CRIB
See Manger, Part 2.

CRICKET
See Animals, Part 1.

Rebel Judaeans, probably leading citizens, being flayed alive by their Assyrian captors after the siege of Lachish. Relief from the SW palace of Sennacherib at Kuyunjik (Nineveh). 704–681 BC. (BM)

civil and criminal law were made to protect individuals and the community against injustice. It is obvious from the general casuistic style of Near Eastern jurisprudence that the codified laws as found in the laws of Ur-Nammu, of the city of Eshnunna, of Hammurapi, of the Middle Assyrian times, as well as of certain laws from the Covenant Code and other parts of the Pentateuch, must be regarded as decisions by famous kings, officials, elders or heads of families, and not as a theoretical legal system built up by judges and sages. Every stipulation in the casuistic legal material is made to protect certain rights and to restore by compensation the damage done. For example, negligence in not properly looking after a goring ox was regarded as a crime when that ox gored a man, a slave or someone else's ox, *e.g.* Ex. 21:28–32, 35–36; Laws of Eshnunna §§53–55. According to Exodus, when negligence causes the death of a free person, the negligent person is punished by death. In all other cases fixed compensation in kind or in shekels must be paid. Even in criminal offences, such as rape or theft, the guilty person must compensate the victim. For the rape of a young girl, the OT prescribes fixed compensation to the amount of the normal bride-price. This shows that the value of the girl is diminished in a way which makes it impossible for her father, who has the legal right over her, to give her to another person for the usual bride-price. The guilty person, then, has to compensate the father for his loss, *e.g.* Ex. 22:16–17. This is true of all codified laws of the Near East, where in some cases further stipulations are inserted to cover various situations, *e.g.* in a special sense in the Middle Assyrian laws.

There is, however, one type of law, which A. Alt in 1934 considered as quite foreign to anything discovered outside the Israelite world, namely apodictic law, which is now called prohibitives and vetitives. The publication in 1958, however, of 'covenant' forms using a similar apodictic method in Assyr. times may show that such legal phraseology in the second person was not unknown elsewhere in the ancient Near East. What is unique in the OT legislation is that the laws in apodictic style are direct commands from the Lord to his people. The Ten Commandments, for example, are typical of this kind of law. 'You shall not kill' (Ex. 20:13) is given as a direct command by God to his people at Sinai, according to the reliable OT tradition. These laws originated in the sacred sphere of the Lord, and came as part of the Israelite religion right at the beginning of their nationhood when the covenant between God and his people was made. From the OT tradition it is also obvious that the casuistic laws were regarded as laws sanctioned by God. The whole corpus of legal material is immediately regarded as divinely inspired. These laws, promulgated with the covenant at Sinai, were there to bind the people to God and to unite the various tribes and individuals. Any transgression against a fellow-Israelite is a transgression against God.

c. Types of offences in Hebrew law

The more important types of offences are murder, assault, theft, negligence and transgressions of a moral and religious nature. In case of murder a distinction is made between an intentional act and unintentional manslaughter (*e.g.* Ex. 21:12–14). Murder was regarded all over the ancient Near East as a grave offence and, with a few exceptions, was punished by the death of the murderer. In the Bible human life, created by God, is regarded as precious. Assault which damaged the human body is also severely punished, but almost always with fixed compensation. Hebrew law is unique against Near Eastern legal practices in that a bodily injury inflicted by a master on his slave is punished by the release of the slave. Theft and negligence are usually punished by restitution or fixed compensation.

d. A distinction made

The OT as well as the NT makes a distinction between a mere transgression and a crooked and sinful life. The way of life was regarded as very important, especially in the Wisdom literature. The existence of the wicked is described in detail, *e.g.* in Ps. 1, which is closely connected with the Wisdom material of the OT. This psalm gives expression to wickedness and crime as the way of life of the ungodly, the sinners and the scornful. The life of these groups is a denial of the law of God. This kind of ungodly life means rebellion against God, and this is closely linked with all kinds of unrighteous deeds against other people. The clearest representation of this attitude is present in the writings of the prophets around 600 BC, and is especially stressed by Jeremiah. Crime against fellow-men is always regarded as crime against the Lord. A deep religious interpretation is thus attached to crime and transgression.

e. The New Testament interpretation

It is precisely this religious interpretation which predominates in the NT. Every transgression is taken as an offence against God. Paul's conception in Rom. 7 is that the law brings knowledge of sin, but cannot take it away; it even quickens the consciousness of sin and makes transgressions abound (7:7–11). Law is, however, not sin, but is intended to restrain transgression by ordaining penalties. By knowing the law, our sinful nature (*hamartia*) is provoked and entices us to individual sinful acts (*parabasis*). The sinful nature, the sinful way of life, is expressed by Paul in terms of the flesh (*sarx*); to describe the life saved by Christ, the word 'spiritual' (*pneuma*) is used. Every life which is not saved by Christ is sinful in nature, and thus culpable, and has to be punished by God.

II. Punishment

a. Etymology

Among the more important biblical words connected with punishment, the stem *šlm* has the meaning 'to compensate', or 'to restore the balance'. This word has a specific legal connotation, as is also evident from certain Amarna Letters. The stem *ykḥ* has a legal meaning 'to punish', *e.g.* in Gn. 31:37; Jb. 9:33; 16:21, but in numerous other places has the more usual meaning 'to reprove'. The stem *ysr* is more widely used in the sense of punishment. It is interesting to note that in Ugaritic (Canaanite cuneiform) this word is present in the sense of instruction, as also in Heb. The noun *mûsār* is also used; this stem is thus linked up with an education background and not primarily with legal punishment. It is corrective punishment, as is the punishment inflicted by a father on his son. A strong word, used with the Lord as subject, is the stem *nqm*. Mendenhall pointed out that this, in the light of cuneiform material from Mari, means to vindicate. Vindication in the sense of punishment inflicted by God on the wicked is present, for example, in Nahum.

It is an interesting feature that in the NT, where the concept of divine punishment is fully realized, words with this connotation are used in only seven places. It is evident that *dikē*, the common word for judgment, may also have the secondary meaning 'punishment', much the same as the Heb. *mišpāṭ*. The only words with the clear meaning of punishment are *timōria* and *kolasis*. In classical Gk. the former has a vindicative character, very much like *nqm* in Heb. But in *koinē* and in NT Gk. this meaning is hardly found. The term became synonymous with *kolasis*, the ordinary word for punishment, *e.g.* Mt. 25:46; Acts 4:21; 22:5; 26:11; Heb. 10:29; 2 Pet. 2:9; 1 Jn. 4:18. In Matthew *kolasis* is used for the final punishment in contrast to eternal life. The same meaning for the final judgment is present in 2 Peter, where the punishment is connected with the eschatological day of judgment, a later development from the OT conception of the Day of the Lord.

b. The practice of blood revenge

Every crime or transgression must be punished, according to the common legal principles of the Near East. Primarily, this punishment was inflicted in the more primitive nomadic or semi-nomadic society by the victim or his relations, *e.g.* a common Semitic legal procedure is that a murderer must be punished by death by the dead person's nearest relations (*AVENGER OF BLOOD). This is still Islamic law. We have numerous examples of blood revenge in the OT, *e.g.* Ex. 21:23–25; 22:2–3. This is called *ius talionis*. The common formula of the *ius talionis* can not only be traced back to the Old Babylonian Code of Hammurapi but is also present in a much later votive tablet discovered at Marseilles. It is the very basis of the Islamic law of 'deliberate homicide'.

c. The dispensing of justice

Decisions on various cases were made by judges or elders or the head of a family, usually in the city gate. Their activity is not to be confused with the modern conception of judge. These judges were arbitrators between two parties (the Heb. word *šāpaṭ* sometimes means 'to decide between two parties'). This role of arbitration was not only played by elders and officials but also by the king himself, *cf.*, *e.g.*, the decision made by David in favour of the woman of Tekoa (2 Sa. 14) and the wise decision of Solomon (1 Ki. 3:16ff.). But it is also clear that in nomadic and semi-nomadic society retribution was in some cases inflicted without the help of an arbitrator, *e.g.* in case of murder, where the common law of blood revenge took place. On the other hand, in modern bedouin society people travel long distances to a famous judge to get his decision on a case.

Both in civil and criminal offences the judge gave decisions designed to maintain 'social equilibrium'. When a bodily injury was inflicted, or damage done to a neighbour's property (which was taken in a much broader sense than our modern one, so that his wife, children and slaves, for example, were also included), the loss was restored by fixed compensation. It is, however, incorrect to suggest that in all cases only the value of the damage was paid; *e.g.* a thief had to compensate for stolen property such as cattle and sheep with five times its value in the former, and four times in the latter, case (*cf.* Ex. 22:1). This was probably used as a kind of deterrent against theft.

d. God as Judge

It is a fact that God is regarded in the Bible as the supreme Judge. This conception is not alien to the ancient Near East, *e.g.* in a very important cuneiform tablet of Mari, the god Shamash is described as judge of gods and men. Very early in the history of Israel God was regarded as Creator of all things. This makes him the Possessor of his creation. Any damage done to his creation is a direct act of rebellion against himself.

From a legal standpoint this gives him the right to punish. On the other hand, laws were made and sanctioned by God to protect his creation. His own commands put him under the compulsion to punish any transgression of them. Some places in the OT give the impression that the punishment decided on by the elders or officials was sufficient. On the other hand, it is evident that people who get away without human punishment are punished by God, some of them by a violent death, others by great damage (*cf.* Nu. 16). The idea shifted from punishment during a man's lifetime to the *Day of the Lord, with a final judgment where everybody shall be judged according to his deeds. The idea of a judgment after death is present also in the Egyptian conception of death. A deceased person is weighed over against the goddess Maat and receives his due according to his weight. The biblical conception does not only refer to judgment after death but also to a final judgment at the eschatological end of days. This idea is fully developed in the NT in the eschatological parts of the Gospels, in parts of Paul's Epistles, in 2 Peter and in Revelation (*e.g.* Mt. 24–25; Mk. 13; Lk. 21; 1 Thes. 5; 2 Thes. 2; 2 Pet. 3; Rev. 20–22). (*ESCHATOLOGY.)

III. Conclusion

It is evident that crime and punishment were not only bound up with ordinary jurisprudence but also with the divine. A crime against a human being or his property is a crime against God, and must be punished either by the authorities or by God. A transgression of religious stipulations must likewise be punished by God. A wicked way of life is rejected by God and punished.

BIBLIOGRAPHY. A. Alt, *Die Ursprünge des israelitischen Rechts*, 1934; G. Mendenhall, *Law and Covenant in Israel and the Ancient Near East*, 1955; H. Cazelles, *Études sur le code de l'alliance*, 1946; M. Noth, *Die Gesetze im Pentateuch*, 1940; R. C. Trench, *The Synonyms of the New Testament*, 1901; D. J. Wiseman, 'The Laws of Hammurabi again', *JSS* 7, 1962, pp. 161–168; W. Eichrodt,

Ashurbanipal's soldiers beating defeated rebel Elamites after the battle of the River Ulai in 653 BC. (BM)

CRIMSON
See Colours, Part 1.

CRITICISM, BIBLICAL
See Biblical criticism, Part 1.

CROCUS
See Plants, Part 3.

CROPS
See Agriculture, Part 1.

Rameses II holding prisoners, perhaps threatening them with decapitation. (PP)

Theologie des Alten Testaments, 1948; F. C. Fensham, *The mišpāṭîm in the Covenant Code* (typed dissertation), 1958; *idem*, 'Transgression and Penalty in the Book of the Covenant', *JNSL* 5, 1977, pp. 23–41; E. Gerstenberger, *Wesen und Herkunft des 'apodiktischen Rechts'*, 1965; G. Liedke, *Gestalt und Bezeichnung alttestamentlicher Rechtssätze*, 1971; H. J. Boecker, *Redeformen des Rechtsleben im Alten Testament*, 1964; *idem*, *Recht und Gesetz im Alten Testament und im Alten Orient*, 1976; A. Phillips, *Ancient Israel's Criminal Law*, 1970; B. S. Jackson, *Theft in Early Jewish Law*, 1972. F.C.F.

CRISPUS. He was *archisynagōgos* (*SYNAGOGUE) at Corinth. His conversion, with his family, was significant, most Corinthian Jews being bitterly hostile (Acts 18:5–8); hence, perhaps, his baptism by Paul himself (1 Cor. 1:14). *Acts of Pilate* 2. 4 probably intends him.

The name (meaning 'curly') is Lat., but is used elsewhere by Jews (*cf.* TJ *Yebhamoth* 2. 3; 12. 2; Lightfoot, *HHT* in 1 Cor. 1:14). Pesh., Goth. (*v.l.*) read 'Crispus' for 'Crescens' in 2 Tim. 4:10. A.F.W.

CROSS, CRUCIFIXION. The Gk. word for 'cross' (*stauros*; verb *stauroō*; Lat. *crux*, *crucifigo*, 'I fasten to a cross') means primarily an upright stake or beam, and secondarily a stake used as an instrument for punishment and execution. It is used in this latter sense in the NT. The noun occurs 28 times and the verb 46. The crucifixion of live criminals did not occur in the OT (*stauroō* in the LXX of Est. 7:10 is the Heb. *tālâ*, meaning 'to hang'). Execution was by stoning. However, dead bodies were occasionally hung on a tree as a warning (Dt. 21:22–23; Jos. 10:26). Such a body was regarded as accursed (hence Gal. 3:13) and had to be removed and buried before night came (*cf.* Jn. 19:31). This practice accounts for the NT reference to Christ's cross as a 'tree' (Acts 5:30; 10:39; 13:29; 1 Pet. 2:24), a symbol of humiliation.

Crucifixion was practised by the Phoenicians and Carthaginians and later used extensively by the Romans. Only slaves, provincials and the lowest types of criminals were crucified, but rarely Roman citizens. Thus tradition, which says

Scenes of torture by Assyrian forces, involving loss of limbs and impalement, after the capture of the city of Kulisi. From the bronze gates of Balawat. Shalmaneser III, 858–824 BC. (BM)

that Peter, like Jesus, was crucified, but Paul beheaded, is in line with ancient practice.

Apart from the single upright post (*crux simplex*) on which the victim was tied or impaled, there were three types of cross. The *crux commissa* (St Anthony's cross) was shaped like a capital T, thought by some to be derived from the symbol of the god Tammuz, the letter *tau*; the *crux decussata* (St Andrew's cross) was shaped like the letter X; the *crux immissa* was the familiar two beams †, held by tradition to be the shape of the cross on which our Lord died (Irenaeus, *Haer*. 2. 24. 4). This is strengthened by the references in the four Gospels (Mt. 27:37; Mk. 15:26; Lk. 23:38; Jn. 19:19–22) to the title nailed to the cross of Christ over his head.

After a criminal's condemnation, it was the custom for a victim to be scourged with the *flagellum*, a whip with leather thongs, which in our Lord's case doubtless greatly weakened him and hastened eventual death. He was then made to carry the cross-beam (*patibulum*) like a slave to the scene of his torture and death, always outside the city, while a herald carried in front of him the 'title', the written accusation. It was this *patibulum*, not the whole cross, which Jesus was too weak to carry, and which was borne by Simon the Cyrenian. The condemned man was stripped naked, laid on the ground with the cross-beam under his shoulders, and his arms or his hands tied or nailed (Jn. 20:25) to it. This cross-bar was then lifted and secured to the upright post, so that the victim's feet, which were then tied or nailed, were just clear of the ground, not high up as so often depicted. The main weight of the body was usually borne by a projecting peg (*sedile*), astride which the victim sat. There the condemned man was left to die of hunger and exhaustion. Death was sometimes hastened by the *crurifragium*, breaking of the legs, as in the case of the two thieves, but not done in our Lord's case, because he was already dead. However, a spear was thrust into his side to make sure of death, so that the body could be removed, as the Jews demanded, before the sabbath (Jn. 19:31ff.).

The method of crucifixion seems to have varied in different parts of the Roman empire. Secular writers of the time shrink from giving detailed accounts of this most cruel and degrading of all forms of punishment. But new light has been thrown on the subject by archaeological work in Judaea. In the summer of 1968 a team of archaeologists under V. Tzaferis discovered four Jewish tombs at Giv'at ha-Mivtar (Ras el-Masaref), Ammunition Hill, near Jerusalem, where there was an ossuary containing the only extant bones of a (young) crucified man, dating from probably between AD 7 and AD 66, judging from Herodian pottery found there. The name Jehoḥanan is incised. Thorough research has been made into the causes and nature of his death and may throw considerable light on our Lord's form of death.

The young man's arms (not his hands) were nailed to the *patibulum*, the cross-beam, which might indicate that Lk. 24:39; Jn. 20:20, 25, 27 should be translated 'arms'. The weight of the body was probably borne by a plank (*sedecula*) nailed to the *simplex*, the upright beam, as a support for the buttocks. The legs had been bent at the knees and twisted back so that the calves were parallel to the *patibulum* or cross-bar, with the ankles under the buttocks. One iron nail (still *in situ*) had been driven through both his heels together, with his right foot above the left. A fragment shows that the cross was of olive wood. His legs had both been broken, presumably by a forcible blow, like those of Jesus' two companions in Jn. 19:32.

If Jesus died in similar fashion, then his legs were not fully extended as in traditional Christian art. His contorted leg muscles would then have probably caused severe pain with spasmodic contractions and rigid cramps. This could have contributed to the shortened time of his death in 6 hours, hastened doubtless by the earlier scourging.

Drawing showing the position of the body during crucifixion, based on a skeleton found near Jerusalem. (PS)

Top right: Skeletal remains of a man who had been crucified, found in a tomb, Jerusalem. Shown here are the two ankle-bones pierced by a nail. 1st cent. AD. (JLH)

Contemporary writers describe it as a most painful form of death. The Gospels, however, give no detailed description of our Lord's physical sufferings, but simply and reverently say 'they crucifed him'. According to Mt. 27:34, our Lord refused any form of alleviation for his sufferings, doubtless that he might preserve clarity of mind to the end, in doing his Father's will. Hence the fact that he was able to comfort the dying thief, and pronounce the rest of the seven wonderful words from the cross.

The NT writers' interest in the cross is neither archaeological nor historical, but Christological. They are concerned with the eternal, cosmic, soteriological significance of what happened once for all in the death of Jesus Christ, the Son of God, on the cross. Theologically, the word 'cross' was used as a summary description of the gospel of salvation, that Jesus Christ 'died for our sins'. So the 'preaching of the gospel' is 'the word of the cross', 'the preaching of Christ crucified' (1 Cor. 1:17ff.). So the apostle glories 'in the cross of our Lord Jesus Christ', and speaks of suffering persecution 'for the cross of Christ'. Clearly the word 'cross' here stands for the whole glad announcement of our redemption through the atoning death of Jesus Christ.

'The word of the cross' is also 'the word of reconciliation' (2 Cor. 5:19). This theme emerges clearly in the Epistles to the Ephesians and Colossians. It is 'through the cross' that God has reconciled Jews and Gentiles, abolishing the middle wall of partition, the law of commandments (Eph. 2:14–16). It is 'by the blood of his cross' that God has made peace, in reconciling 'all things to himself' (Col. 1:20ff.). This reconciliation is at once personal and cosmic. It comes because Christ has set aside the bond which stood against us with its legal demands, 'nailing it to the cross' (Col. 2:14).

The cross, in the NT, is a symbol of shame and humiliation, as well as of God's wisdom and glory revealed through it. Rome used it not only as an instrument of torture and execution but also as a shameful pillory reserved for the worst and lowest. To the Jews it was a sign of being accursed (Dt. 21:23; Gal. 3:13). This was the death Jesus died, and for which the crowd clamoured. He 'endured the cross, despising the shame' (Heb. 12:2). The lowest rung in the ladder of our Lord's humiliation was that he endured 'even death on a cross' (Phil. 2:8). For this reason it was a 'stumbling block' to the Jews (1 Cor. 1:23; *cf.* Gal. 5:11). The shameful spectacle of a victim carrying a *patibulum* was so familiar to his hearers that Jesus three times spoke of the road of discipleship as that of cross-bearing (Mt. 10:38; Mk. 8:34; Lk. 14:27).

Further, the cross is the symbol of our union with Christ, not simply in virtue of our following his example, but in virtue of what he has done for us and in us. In his substitutionary death for us on the cross, we died 'in him' (*cf.* 2 Cor. 5:14), and 'our old man is crucified with him', that by his indwelling Spirit we might walk in newness of life (Rom. 6:4ff.; Gal. 2:20; 5:24ff.; 6:14), abiding 'in him'.

BIBLIOGRAPHY. M. Hengel, *Crucifixion*, 1977; J. H. Charlesworth, *ExpT* 84, 1972–3, pp. 147–150; V. Tzaferis, *IEJ* 20, 1970, pp. 18–32; J. Wilkinson, *ExpT* 83, 1971–2, pp. 104–107; W. Barclay, *Crucified and Crowned*, 1961; B. Siede, E. Brandenburger, C. Brown, in *NIDNTT* 1, pp. 389–405; J. Schneider, *TDNT* 7, p. 572; R. de Vaux, *Ancient Israel*, 1961, p. 159.

J.B.T.

CROW
See Animals, Part 1.

Opposite page: Crown as worn by King Marduk-nādin-ahhe of Babylonia. Boundary stone relating to a grant of land. 1116–1101 BC. (BM)

CROWN. A distinctive head-dress, often ornate, worn by kings and other exalted persons.

I. In the Old Testament

The high priest's crown was a gold plate inscribed 'Holy to the Lord', fastened to his mitre or turban by blue cord, this being an emblem of consecration (Ex. 29:6; 39:30; Lv. 8:9; 21:12). After the Exile, in 520 BC, Zechariah (6:11–14) was commanded by God to make gold and silver crowns and to place them on the head of Joshua the high priest, these being (later) laid up in the

Temple as emblems of God's favour. They may have been combined in one double crown, uniting priestly and regal offices in one person.

Among royal crowns, David's gold crown was an emblem of his God-given kingship (Ps. 21:3; *cf.* 132:18; withdrawal of God's gift—and crown—*cf.* Ps. 89:39; Ezk. 21:25–26). Joash's actual coronation is recorded (2 Ki. 11:12; 2 Ch. 23:11). David captured the gold, stone-inset crown of the king (or god Milcom) of Ammon, which weighed a talent (2 Sa. 12:30; 1 Ch. 20:2). Ammonite statues show kings or gods wearing large high crowns (see F. F. Bruce, *Israel and the Nations*, 1969, pl. I). For crown set with stones, *cf.* Zc. 9:16. The great royal crown of Vashti, Ahasuerus' queen (Est. 1:11), came to Esther's head (2:17), and the royal apparel with which Mordecai eventually was honoured included a gold crown (Est. 6:8; 8:15).

Besides being the mark of royalty (Pr. 27:24), a crown became metaphorical of glory (Jb. 19:9; Is. 28:5; 62:3; Je. 13:18; La. 5:16; Pr. 4:9; 12:4; 14:24; 16:31; 17:6), and sometimes, less happily, of pride (Jb. 31:36; Is. 28:1, 3).

The Bible world offers many examples of a variety of crowns. In Egypt the king and the gods wore a variety of tall and elaborate crowns of varying significance as well as a simple gold circlet or diadem. Most characteristic is the great Double Crown of Upper and Lower Egypt combined, incorporating the red crown of Lower Egypt (flat cap, with spiral at front and tall projection at rear) and above it the white crown of Upper Egypt (tall and conical with a knob at the top). Pharaoh's diadems were always fronted by the *uraeus* or royal cobra. In Mesopotamia the Assyr. kings wore a truncated conical cap adorned with bands of coloured embroidery or precious stones, or a simple diadem. The kings of Babylon wore a curving mitre ending in a point; see H. Frankfort, *Art and Architecture of the Ancient Orient*, 1954, plates 87–89, 95, 109–110, 114, 116, 120.

Palestinian excavations have yielded a series of circlets or diadems; for one of strip gold patterned with dots, see W. M. F. Petrie, *Ancient Gaza III*, 1933, plates 14: 6, 15. See also for further examples, K. Galling, *Biblisches Reallexikon*, 1937, cols. 125–128 and figures. K.A.K.

Rameses III's crown, an unusual combination of the lower Egyptian red crown with twin plumes. Tomb of Amenhirkhopshef, Valley of Queens. c. 1170 BC. (PAC)

Bottom right: Crowns from the Egyptian relief in the temple of Seti, Abydos. c. 1300 BC. (PAC)

Ashurbanipal, king of Assyria (669–c. 627 BC), wearing the royal embroidered headdress, possibly a type of turban wound round a cap (fez). (BM)

II. In the New Testament

There are two words to be considered. The more important is *stephanos*, which denotes properly a chaplet or a circlet. It is used of Christ's crown of thorns. 'Thorns' are no more specific in Gk. than in English, so that it is impossible to be sure just what plant was used. What is clear is that this 'crown' was a mocking symbol of royalty, perhaps also of divinity (see H. St J. Hart, *JTS* n.s. 3, pp. 66–75). But though the *stephanos* might denote a crown of royalty (Rev. 6:2, *etc.*), its more usual use was for the laurel wreath awarded to the victor at the Games or for a festive garland used on occasions of rejoicing. These uses underlie most of the NT references. Thus Paul reminds the Corinthians that athletes strive 'to receive a perishable wreath' and he adds, 'but we an imperishable' (1 Cor. 9:25). It is important that the seeker after the crown 'competes according to the rules' (2 Tim. 2:5). Sometimes the Christian's crown is here and now, as when Paul thinks of his converts as his crown (Phil. 4:1; 1 Thes. 2:19). More usually it is in the hereafter, as the 'crown of righteousness, which the Lord, the righteous judge, will award to me on that Day' (2 Tim. 4:8). There are references also to a 'crown of life' (Jas. 1:12; Rev. 2:10), and to 'an unfading crown of glory' (1 Pet. 5:4). The crown may be lost, for Christians are exhorted to hold fast lest it be taken from them (Rev. 3:11). God has crowned man 'with glory and honour' (Heb. 2:7), and Jesus was crowned likewise, 'so that by the grace of God he might taste death for every one' (Heb. 2:9).

diadēma is not frequent (Rev. 12:3; 13:1; 19:12). In the NT it is always a symbol of royalty or honour. L.M.

CUP. The ancient cup was a bowl, wider and shallower than the normal teacup. While usually made of pottery, it was sometimes of metal (Je. 51:7).

1. Heb. *kôs*, commonly used for a drinking-vessel, whether the pharaoh's (Gn. 40:11) or a poor man's (2 Sa. 12:3). This could be of a size to hold in the hand or might be larger (Ezk. 23:32), with a rim (1 Ki. 7:26). In Solomon's court they were made of gold. **2.** Heb. *gāḇîa'*. This is the name given to Joseph's silver divining cup (Gn. 44:2ff.) and to the bowls of the

King Darius I of Persia (521–486 BC) wearing a crown. Relief at Bisitun, Iran.

golden candlestick in the tabernacle, which were formed like almond blossom (Ex. 25:31ff.). In Je. 35:5 (AV 'pots') it is used for a pitcher. It may have been named as flower- or goblet-shaped. **3.** Heb. *sap̄*. At the Passover the blood was held in this bowl (Ex. 12:22, AV 'bason'). It was also a household vessel, appearing among equipment given to David (possibly of metal, contrasted with earthenware, 2 Sa. 17:28) and as a large wine bowl (Zc. 12:2). **4.** Heb. *qubba'aṯ* (Is. 51:17, 22) was evidently a large wine vessel, explained as *kôs*. **5.** Heb. *'aggān*. This was the common name for a large bowl in the ancient Semitic world used in sacred rites (Ex. 24:6) or for serving wine at a banquet (Ct. 7:2). With the storage jar, it could be hung from a peg (Is. 22:24). (* VESSELS.)

In the NT Gk. *potērion* denotes a drinking-vessel of any sort. Pottery continued in common use (Mk.

CROWN OF THORNS
See Thorns, crown of, Part 3.

CRUCIFIXION
See Cross, Part 1.

CUBIT
See Weights and measures, Part 3.

CUCUMBER
See Vegetables, Part 3.

CULT OF THE DEAD
See Ancestor worship, Part 1.

CULT PROSTITUTES
See Prostitution, Part 3.

CUMMIN
See Herbs, Part 2.

CUNNING
See Sleight, Part 3.

King Ashurnasirpal II of Assyria holds a drinking vessel, probably containing wine. Stone relief from the NW palace at Calah (Nimrud). 883–859 BC. (BM)

■ **CURIOUS ARTS**
See Magic, Part 2.

■ **CURRENCY**
See Money, Part 2.

King Ur-Nanshe of Lagash drinking from a cup. Behind him is the smaller figure of the cup-bearer, Anita. Tello. White limestone. c. 15 cm × 12 cm. Mid-3rd millennium BC. (MC)

7:4), but the rich were now able to possess glass as well as metal cups, which were normally goblet-shaped, *cf.* the chalice depicted on coins of the first revolt (see *IBA*, p. 89). The cup used at the Last Supper was probably an earthenware bowl, sufficiently large for all to share (Mt. 26:27).

Throughout the Bible, cup is used figuratively as containing the share of blessings or disasters allotted to a man or nation or his divinely appointed fate (Pss. 16:5; 116:13; Is. 51:17; Mt. 26:39ff.; Jn. 18:11). (*LORD'S SUPPER.) A.R.M.

CUPBEARER (Heb. *mašqeh*, 'one giving to drink'). The 'butler' of Joseph's pharaoh (Gn. 40:1ff.) both in Heb. and by function was the king's cupbearer. His office as depicted in Gn. 40 corresponds in part to the (wider) Egyp. *wdpw* of early times and especially the Middle Kingdom period (broadly, *c.* 2000–1600 BC; *cf.* Joseph *c.* 1700 BC), and exactly to the later term *wb'*, 'cupbearer', of New Kingdom times (*c.* 1600–1100 BC), which includes Moses' day. See A. H. Gardiner, *Ancient Egyptian Onomastica*, 1, 1947, pp. 43*, 44* on No. 122 (*wb'*), and J. Vergote, *Joseph en Égypte*, 1959, pp. 35–40 (esp. p. 36). The Egyptian cupbearers, *wb'*, were often called *w'b-'wy*, 'pure of hands', and in the 13th century BC one such cupbearer is actually entitled *wb' dp irp*, 'cupbearer (or, butler) who tastes the wine' (R. A. Caminos, *Late-Egyptian Miscellanies*, 1954, p. 498). These officials (often foreigners) became in many cases confidants and favourites of the king and wielded political influence; this is very evident in 20th-Dynasty Egypt (12th century BC), and *cf.* Nehemiah. The (lesser) cupbearers of high Egyptian dignitaries are sometimes shown serving wine in the tomb-paintings.

Cupbearers were part of Solomon's glittering court that so impressed the queen of Sheba (1 Ki. 10:5; 2 Ch. 9:4); for a somewhat earlier cupbearer at a Palestinian court (Canaanite), see left end of the Megiddo ivory illustrated in E. W. Heaton, *Everyday Life in Old Testament Times*, 1956, p. 164, fig. 80, or W. F. Albright, *Archaeology of Palestine*, 1960, p. 123, fig. 31.

Nehemiah (1:11) was cupbearer to Artaxerxes I of Persia (*c.* 464–423 BC) and, like his earlier colleagues in Egypt, enjoyed royal trust and favour, and had access to the royal ear. For a picture of an Assyr. cupbearer, see H. Frankfort, *Art and Architecture of the Ancient Orient*, 1954, plate 89. K.A.K.

CURSE. The main biblical vocabulary of the curse consists of the Heb. synonyms *'ārar*, *qālal* and *'ālâ*, corresponding to the Gk. *kataraomai*, *katara* and *epikataratos*; and the Heb. *heḥ^{e}rîm* and *ḥērem*, corresponding to the Gk. *anathematizō* and *anathema*.

The basic meaning of the first group is malediction. A man may utter a curse, desiring another's hurt (Jb. 31:30; Gn. 12:3); or in confirmation of his own promise (Gn. 24:41; 26:28; Ne. 10:29); or as a pledge of the truth of his testimony in law (1 Ki. 8:31; *cf.* Ex. 22:11). When God pronounces a curse, it is, *a.*, a denunciation of sin (Nu. 5:21, 23; Dt. 29:19–20), *b.*, his judgment on sin (Nu. 5:22, 24, 27; Is. 24:6), and *c.*, the person who is suffering the consequences of sin by the judgment of God is called a curse (Nu. 5:21, 27; Je. 29:18).

However, for the Hebrew, just as a word was not a mere sound on the lips but an agent sent forth, so the spoken curse was an active agent for hurt. Behind the word stands the soul that created it. Thus, a word which is backed by no spiritual capacity of accomplishment is a mere 'word of the lip' (2 Ki. 18:20 RVmg.), but when the soul is powerful the word is clothed in that power (Ec. 8:4; 1 Ch. 21:4). The potency of the word is seen in some of our Lord's healing miracles (Mt. 8:8, 16; *cf.* Ps. 107:20), and in his cursing of the barren fig-tree (Mk. 11:14, 20–21). In Zc. 5:1–4 the curse, representing the law of God, itself flies through the land, discerns sinners and purges them out. A curse is as substantial a danger to the deaf man as is a stumbling-block to the blind, for he cannot take 'evasive action' by appeal to the more potent 'blessing' of Yahweh (Lv. 19:14; Ps. 109:28; contrast Rom. 12:14). The rehearsing of the blessings and curses on Mts Gerizim and Ebal (Dt. 27:11ff.; Jos. 8:33) reveals the same dynamic view of the curse. On the borders of Canaan, Moses set before the people 'life and death, the blessing and the curse' (see Dt. 30:19). The first national act on entering the land is to activate both: the blessing which will overtake' the obedient, and the curse which will 'overtake' the disobedient (Dt. 28:2, 15). Between these two poles the national life moves.

It is because of the relation between obedience and blessing, disobedience and cursing (Dt. 11:26–28; Is. 1:19–20) that Dt. 29:12, for example, can speak of God's covenant as his 'curse', and Zc. 5:3 can call the Decalogue the 'curse'. The word of God's grace and the word of God's wrath are the same word: the word which promises life is but a savour of death and judgment to the rebel, and therefore a curse. When God's curse falls on his disobedient people, it is not the abrogation but rather the implementation of his covenant (Lv. 25:14–45). Paul uses this truth to expound the doctrine of redemption. The law is a curse to those who fail to obey it (Gal. 3:10), but Christ redeemed us by becoming a curse for us (Gal. 3:13), and the very means of his death itself proves that he took our place, for 'cursed be every one that hangs on a tree'. This quotation from Dt. 21:23, where 'accursed of God' means 'under God's curse', displays the curse of God against sin falling on the Lord Jesus Christ, who thus became a curse for us.

The Heb. root *ḥāram* means 'to seclude from society' (Koehler, *Lexicon*, *s.v.*). This is borne out by OT usage. In general, the word applies to things open to human use but deliberately rendered unavailable to man. (*a*) Lv. 27:29 ('devoted') likely refers to capital punishment: the death penalty cannot be evaded. (*b*) In Ezk. 44:29; Nu. 18:14 offerings to God are called *ḥērem*, set apart for exclusively religious purposes. Lv. 27:21ff. parallels *ḥērem* with *qōḏeš* ('holiness') in order to express two sides of the same transaction: man sets something utterly apart for God (*ḥērem*), God accepts it and marks it as his own (*qōḏeš*), whereupon it becomes irredeemable by man. (*c*) Characteristically, the word is used of 'utter destruction'. Sometimes the implied reason is the wrath of God (*e.g.* Is. 34:5), but more often it is in order to remove a potential contagion for Israel's sake (Dt. 7:26; 20:17). Any contact with such a 'devoted thing' involved implication in its contagion, and share in its fate (Jos. 6:18; 7:1, 12; 22:20; 1 Sa. 15:23; 1 Ki. 20:42). However, while Achan involved himself and his house in the destruction of Jericho, Rahab, by identifying herself with Israel, escaped the curse and saved her house also (Jos. 6:21–24; 8:26–27; Jdg. 21:11). (*d*) Spiritually, *ḥērem* is the judgment of God against impenitent sinners (Mal. 4:6), and it is here that the impossibility of redeeming the *ḥērem* is clearly seen, *cf.* the NT, **anathema*, Gal. 1:8–9; 1 Cor. 16:22; Rom. 9:3.

BIBLIOGRAPHY. J. Pedersen, *Israel*, 1–2, 1926; 3–4, 1940, *passim*; D. Aust *et al.*, 'Curse', *NIDNTT* 1, pp. 413–418; H. C. Berichts, *JBL* 13, 1963; J. B. Payne, *The Theology of the Older Testament*, 1962, pp. 201ff., *etc.*; J. B. Lightfoot, *Galatians*, 1880, on 3:10, 13, and pp. 152–154. J.A.M.

CUSH. 1. Classed under Ham, and father of the hunter Nimrod (Gn. 10:6–8; 1 Ch. 1:8–10).

2. A region encompassed by the river Gihon (Gn. 2:13); probably in W Asia and unrelated to **4** below; see E. A. Speiser in *Festschrift Johannes Friedrich*, 1959, pp. 473–485.

3. A Benjaminite, some utterance of whom occasioned a psalm (7) of David seeking deliverance and justice.

4. The region S of Egypt, *i.e.* Nubia or N Sudan, the 'Ethiopia' of classical writers (not modern Abyssinia). The name Cush in both Heb. and Assyr. derives from Egyp. *Kš* (earlier *K's, K'š*), 'Kush'. Originally the name of a district somewhere between the second and third cataracts of the Nile *c.* 2000 BC, 'Kush' became also a general term for Nubia among the Egyptians, which wider use Hebrews, Assyrians and others took over (G. Posener, in *Kush* 6, 1958, pp. 39–68).

In 2 Ch. 21:16 Arabians are 'near' the Ethiopians —*i.e.* just across the Red Sea from them; *Syene or Seveneh (mod. Aswan) was the frontier of Egypt and Ethiopia in the 1st millennium BC (Ezk. 29:10). The far-removed location of Cush/Ethiopia gives point to Pss. 68:31; 87:4; Ezk. 29:10; Zp. 2:12; 3:10; and perhaps Am. 9:7; it is one limit of Ahasuerus' (Xerxes) vast Persian empire (Est. 1:1; 8:9 and texts of Xerxes' time). Ethiopian contingents featured in the armies

Faience tile showing a negro (Cushite) prisoner. Height 25 cm. From the temple of Rameses III at Medinet Habu, W Thebes, c. 1170 BC. (OIUC)

CURTAINS
See Tabernacle, Part 3.

CUSTODIAN
See Schoolmaster, Part 3.

CUTWORM
See Animals, Part 1.

CYMBALS
See Music, Part 2.

of * Shishak against Rehoboam (2 Ch. 12:3) and of * Zerah against Asa (2 Ch. 14:9, 12–13; 16:8). Later, throughout Isaiah (11:11; 18:1ff. [preceding Egypt, 19:1ff.]; 20:3–5; and 43:3; 45:14), Egypt and Ethiopia are closely linked—for in the prophet Isaiah's time the 'Ethiopian' 25th Dynasty ruled over both; so, *e.g.*, King * Tirhakah, Is. 37:9 (= 2 Ki. 19:9), *cf.* 36:6, *etc.* Na. 3:9 also reflects this. But later still, from *c.* 660 BC onwards, the fortunes (and thrones) of Egypt and Ethiopia became separate again, and Ezekiel (30:4–5, 9) proclaims Egypt's impending fate as a warning to Ethiopia; in Je. 46:9, likewise, Ethiopians are merely mercenaries in the Egyptian forces again as in the days of Shishak. The 'topaz' came from this land (Jb. 28:19) of unchangeably dark skins (Je. 13:23), as did Ebed-melech at the Judaean court (Je. 38:7ff.; 39:15ff.), and Queen Candace's minister (Acts 8:27). The runner who bore news of Absalom's death to David was a 'Cushite' (2 Sa. 18:21, 23, 31–32). Ethiopia recurs in the prophecies of Ezk. 38:5 and Dn. 11:43. On Nu. 12:1, see * ETHIOPIAN WOMAN.
K.A.K.

CUSHAN-RISHATHAIM. The king of Aram-Naharaim (E Syria–N Mesopotamia) who subjugated Israel for 8 years until their deliverance by Othniel (Jdg. 3:8–10). Both Heb. and Gk. versions take it as an unfamiliar composite personal name, otherwise unknown. Various attempts have been made to identify this name, which may be related to Cushan, an archaic term for the Midianites (Hab. 3:7) who, as nomads, reached Syria (* ARAM), where there is a place *Qsnrm* (Kushan-rōm). Some have tried to identify him with the Syrian Irsu, who ruled Egypt for 8 years about 1200 BC (*JNES* 13, 1954, pp. 231–242). An ancient interpretation of the name as 'Cushan of double wickedness' underlies the *MT* vocalization 'rishathaim'; *cf.* also the Kassite name Kašša-rišat, or the Ethiopian * Cush.
D.J.W.

CUSHION. The only use of the word (Gk. *proskephalaion*) is in Mk. 4:38, where it refers to a pillow perhaps kept for the seat of honour in the stern of a boat. Cranfield defends the use of the Gk. *epi* (on, against), employed here with the 'accusative of place where'. Its rarity suggests the possibility that it is a graphic detail of eyewitness evidence.
J.B.J.

CUTH, CUTHAH. An ancient city in Babylonia (Akkad. *kûtu* from Sumer. *gu-du-a*), the seat of the god Nergal, whose inhabitants were deported by Sargon to repopulate Samaria (2 Ki. 17:24, 30). The site, represented today by the mound called Tell Ibrahīm, was briefly excavated in 1881–2 by Hormuzd Rassam, who noted that it had at one time been a very extensive city.

BIBLIOGRAPHY. H. Rassam, *Asshur and the Land of Nimrod*, 1897, pp. 396, 409–411.
T.C.M.

CYPRUS. The island of Cyprus, some 225 km long, and 100 km wide at its broadest, lies in the E Mediterranean some 100 km W of the coast of Syria and about the same distance from the Turkish coast.

Cyprus is not mentioned by that name in the OT, where it is probably referred to as * Elishah; the people called * Kittim in Gn. 10 may also have settled there at a later period. In the NT the island is named *Kypros* in Acts. Barnabas was a native of it (4:36), as were some of the other early disciples, and the church in the island was further augmented by refugees from the first persecution (Acts 11:19–20; 21:16). Paul and Barnabas travelled across the island from Salamis to Paphos at the beginning of their first missionary journey (Acts 13:4–13). It was at Paphos that they encountered * Bar-jesus, the sorcerer, and the proconsul (*anthypatos*) Sergius Paulus. Paul did not visit the island on his second missionary journey, but Barnabas went there separately with Mark (Acts 15:39). When returning from his third journey, Paul's ship passed it to the SW (Acts 21:3), and on the voyage to Rome contrary winds prevented him from landing (Acts 27:4). There is no other mention of the island in the Bible, but the church there continued to flourish, sending three bishops to the Council of Nicaea in AD 325.

There are traces of neolithic settlement on the island, and its Bronze Age culture shows evidence of contacts with Asia Minor and Syria. In the 15th century BC the Minoan civilization of * Crete extended to Cyprus, and in the following century there is evidence of colonization by the Mycenaeans, who were succeeding to the Cretan power on the Greek mainland. It was probably in this century that the copper mines, which in Roman times became famous enough for the metal to be named after the island (Lat. *cyprium*), first came into extensive use, and as a result of this Cyprus appears frequently in the records of the surrounding nations (* ELISHAH) at this period. In spite of outside influence, the basic Minoan–Mycenaean culture remained dominant, being evidenced particularly by the so-called Cypro-Minoan inscriptions (two early collections 15th and 12th centuries BC), which show close affinities with the Cretan Linear scripts. This script was still found in use in the late 1st millennium, together with the dialect of Gk. most closely related to that in the Minoan Linear B Tablets, Arcadian, which had presumably been superseded in S Greece and Crete by Doric.

Cyprus lay in the path of the 'Sea Peoples', and excavations at Enkomi and Sinda have revealed a late type of Mycenaean pottery from which the so-called * 'Philistine' pottery of Palestine was clearly a development. In the 9th or 8th century BC Phoenicians settled on the island and later a number of bilingual inscriptions occur (*c.* 600–200 BC), of Phoenician and Greek severally with the Cypro-Minoan, now called classical Cypriot, script which was still in use at this time. That the Phoenicians did not gain much power is shown by an account of tribute to Esarhaddon in 672 BC, when only one Phoenician, as opposed to nine Greek kings, is mentioned (tribute had also been paid to Sargon in 709). In the 6th century Egypt dominated the island until it became part of the Persian empire under Cambyses in 525. In 333 BC it submitted to Alexander, and after a brief period under Antigonus it passed to the Ptolemies. It was made a Roman province in 58 BC, and after various changes it became a Senatorial province in 27 BC, from which time it was governed by a proconsul (Gk. *anthypatos*; *cf.* Acts 13:7).

BIBLIOGRAPHY. Sir G. F. Hill, *A History of Cyprus*, 1940; E. Gjerstad, *The Swedish Cyprus Expedition* 4, 2, 1948 (Geometric,

Bronze statue of a horned god from Enkomi, Cyprus. 12th cent. BC. (SH)

Top left:
Gold pectoral of the Mycenaean–Canaanite period from Enkomi. c. 1400–1200 BC. (MH)

Bottom left:
Prehistoric bronze jug from Enkomi. c. 1400–1200 BC. (MH)

The island of Cyprus in OT times.

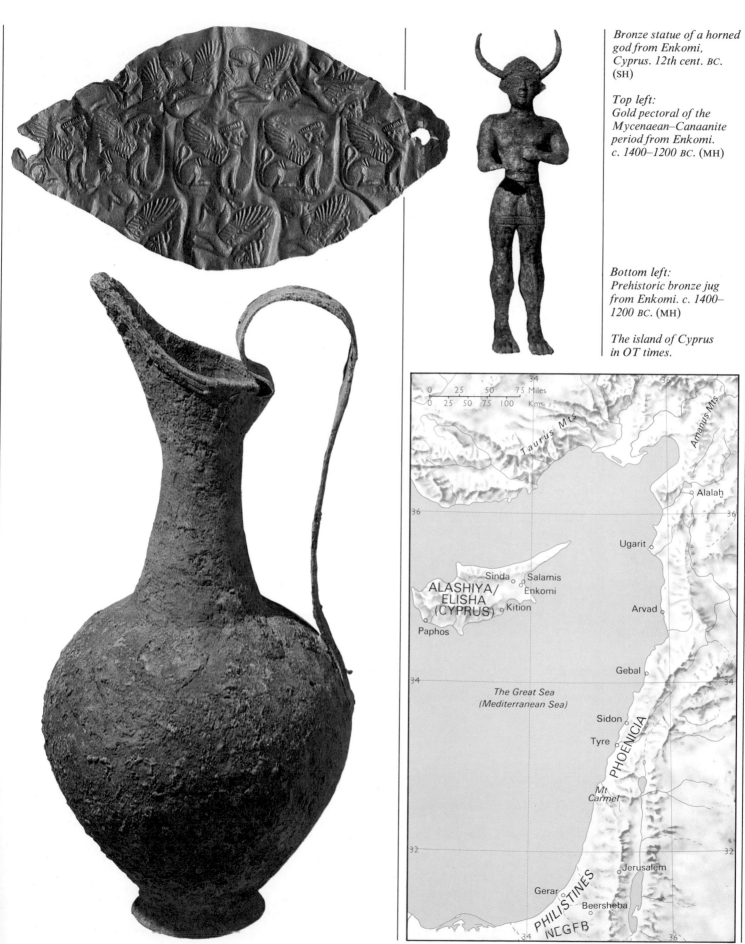

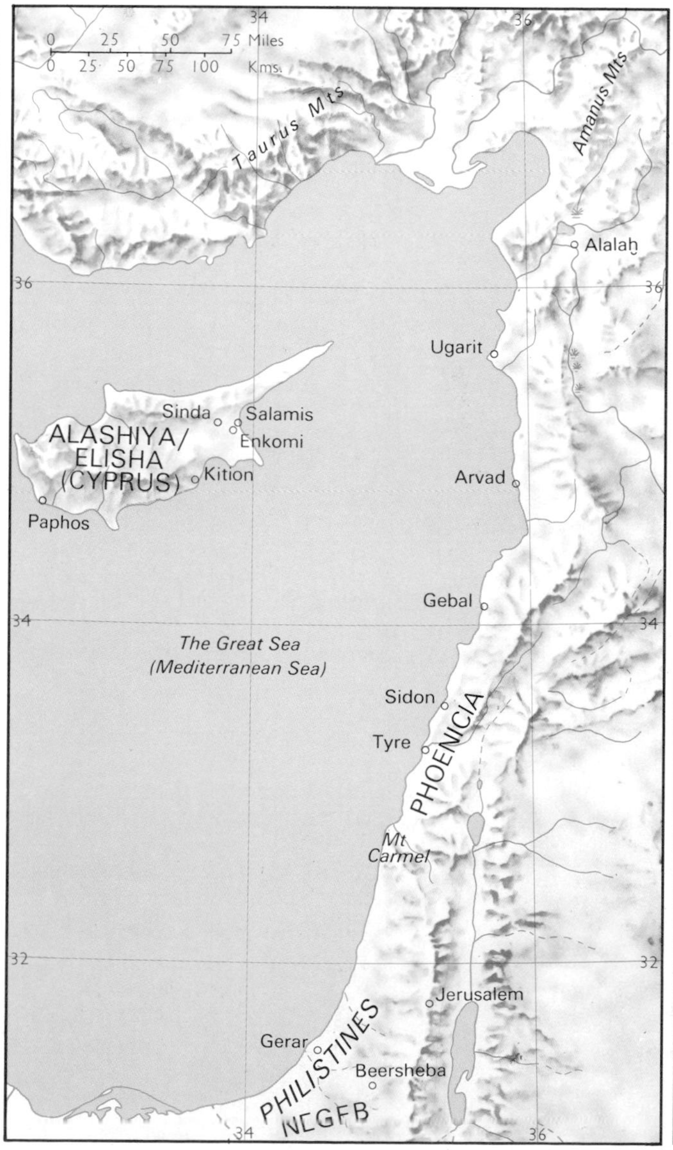

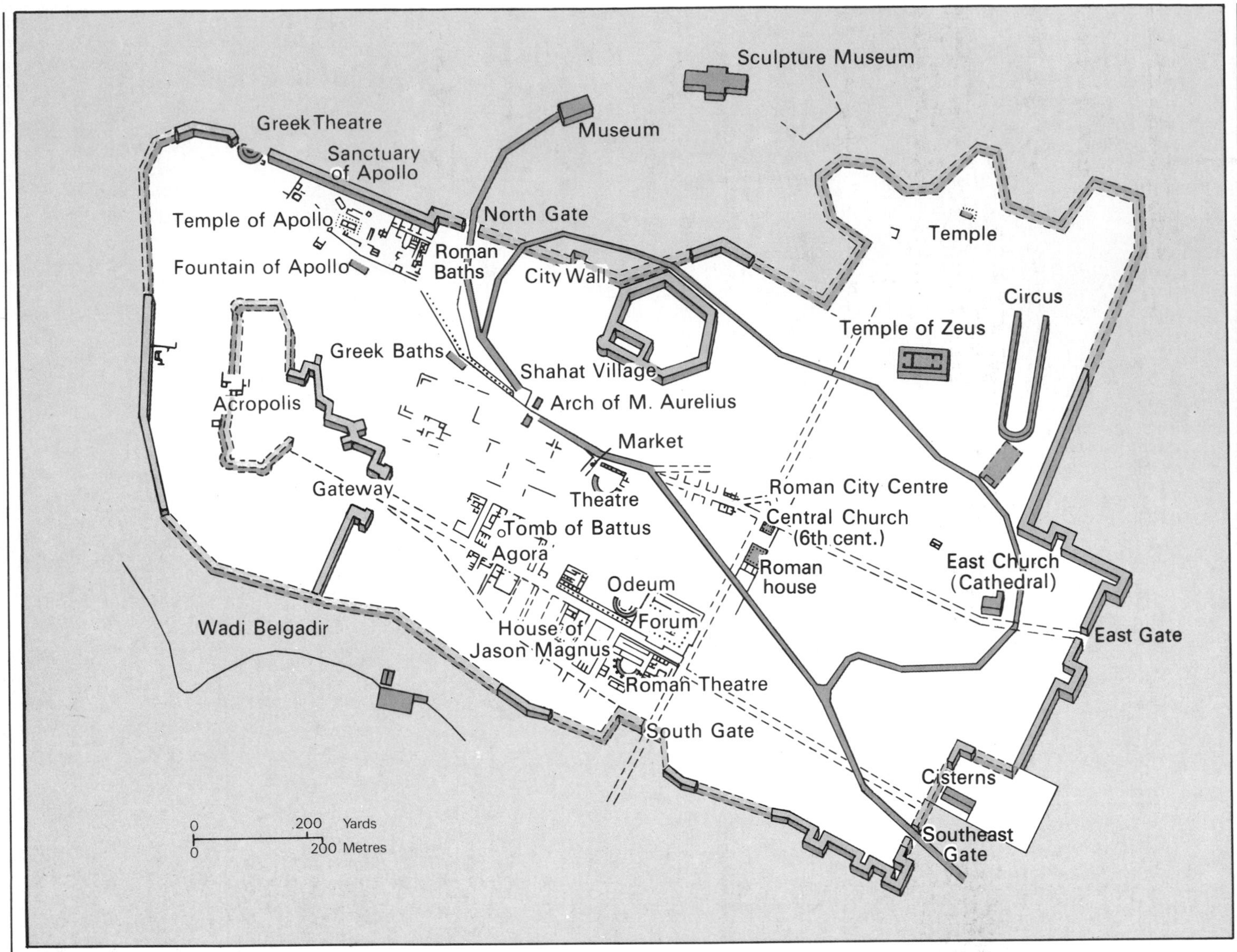

Plan of Cyrene, N Africa, founded by Greek emigrants c. 631 BC. *Monuments from ancient to modern times.*

Archaic and Classical periods); 4, 3, 1956 (Hellenistic and Roman periods); V. Karageorghis, *The Ancient Civilization of Cyprus*, 1969. T.C.M.

CYRENE. A port in N Africa, of Dorian foundation, rich in corn, silphium, wool and dates. It became part of the Ptolemaic empire in the 3rd century BC, and was bequeathed to Rome in 96 BC, becoming a province in 74 BC. Josephus quotes Strabo as stating that Cyrene encouraged Jewish settlement, and that Jews formed one of the four recognized classes of the state (*Ant.* 14. 114). Josephus mentions also a Jewish rising there in Sulla's time, and Dio Cassius (68) another in Trajan's. To this Jewish community belonged Simon the cross-bearer (Mk. 15:21 and parallels), some of the missionaries to Antioch (Acts 11:20) and the Antiochene teacher * Lucius. It was also represented in the Pentecost crowd (Acts 2:10) and evidently had its own (or a shared) synagogue in Jerusalem (Acts 6:9).

BIBLIOGRAPHY. P. Romanelli, *La Cirenaica Romana*, 1943; A. Rowe, D. Buttle and J. Gray, *Cyrenaican Expeditions of the University of Manchester*, 1956; J. Reynolds, *JTS* n.s. 11, 1960, pp. 284ff.

J.H.H.

CYRENIUS
See Quirinius, Part 3.

CYRUS (Heb./Aram. *kôreš*; Elam/Old Persian *kūruš*; Bab. *kuraš*). Persian king of the Achaemenid dynasty. Cyrus may have been an early dynastic name. Cyrus I was a contemporary of Ashurbanipal of Assyria, *c.* 668 BC, and therefore possibly known to Isaiah, who foresaw the restoration of the Jerusalem Temple through this new power which would free Jews from exile (Is. 44:28). Cyrus would be God's 'Messiah'-deliverer and an instrument of the divine plan (Is. 45:1).

Cyrus II (the Great), grandson of Cyrus I, came to the throne *c.* 559 BC. In 549 he conquered his mother's father, Astyages, the Median king, his overlord, founding the Persian (Achaemenid) empire. He took the titles 'king of the Medes' and 'king of Elam' (A. K. Grayson, *Babylonian Historical-Literary Texts*, 1975, p. 31). He conquered Croesus, and his kingdom of Lydia, and in 547 marched through Assyria. A few years later he was already threatening Babylonia, but it was not until 16 October 539 that the Persians with Gobryas entered Babylon, having diverted the river and thus been able to penetrate the city along the dried-up river bed to effect a surprise

Reputed tomb of Cyrus II, king of Persia c. 559–529 BC. The tomb is built of limestone blocks tied together with iron cramps. Pasargadae. Base 14·6 m × 13·4m. (MEPHA)

(Bab. Chronicle, *ANET*, p. 366; *DOTT*, p. 82; Herodotus, 1. 189–191; *cf.* Dn. 5:30). 17 days later Cyrus himself entered the city amid scenes of jubilation.

Cyrus' own inscriptions bear out the OT view of a sympathetic ruler. In his first year he issued a decree by which he 'gathered together all the inhabitants (who were exiles) and returned them to their homes' and in the same decree restored deities to their renovated temples (see Cyrus Cylinder, *ANET*, p. 316; *DOTT*, pp. 92–94; Ezr. 6:1ff.). The Jews, having no images, were allowed to restore their Temple and its fittings (Ezr. 6:3). During the first 3 years of the rule of Cyrus in Babylonia Daniel prospered (Dn. 1:21; 6:28; 10:1), but then, according to Josephus (*Ant.* 10. 249), was removed to Media or more probably to Susa the Persian capital (Dn. 8:2). For the theory that Cyrus might also have been called 'Darius the Mede', see *DARIUS. In Babylonia Cyrus was succeeded in 530 BC by his son Cambyses (II) who had been also for a while his co-regent.

BIBLIOGRAPHY. *Acta Iranica*, 1st Series, 1974, 1–3.

D.J.W.

DABERATH. A levitical city of Issachar (1 Ch. 6:72; Jos. 21:28, where AV has 'Dabareh'), probably on the border of Zebulun (Jos. 19:12). It is usually identified with the ruins near the modern village of Debûriyeh, at the W foot of Mt Tabor. (*DEBORAH.)

J.D.D.

DAGON. In the OT Dagon is a principal deity of the Philistines worshipped in Samson's time at Gaza (Jdg. 16:21–23), at Ashdod (to Maccabean days, 1 Macc. 10:83–85; 11:4) and at Beth-shan in the days of Saul and David (1 Sa. 5:2–7; 1 Ch. 10:10 with 1 Sa. 31:10). The true origin of this god's name is lost in antiquity, and even his precise nature is uncertain. The common idea that he was a fish-deity appears to have no foundation in fact, being adumbrated in Jerome (*BDB*, p. 1121) and first clearly expressed by Kimhi in the

DAGGER
See Armour, Part 1.

The Cyrus Cylinder, which tells how he captured Babylon without a battle and remedied the evil done by his predecessors by sending prisoners from Babylonia back to their own lands, aiding the restoration of temples and returning their gods. This edict would have included the Jews. Baked clay. Length 25 cm. Babylon. 536 BC. (BM)

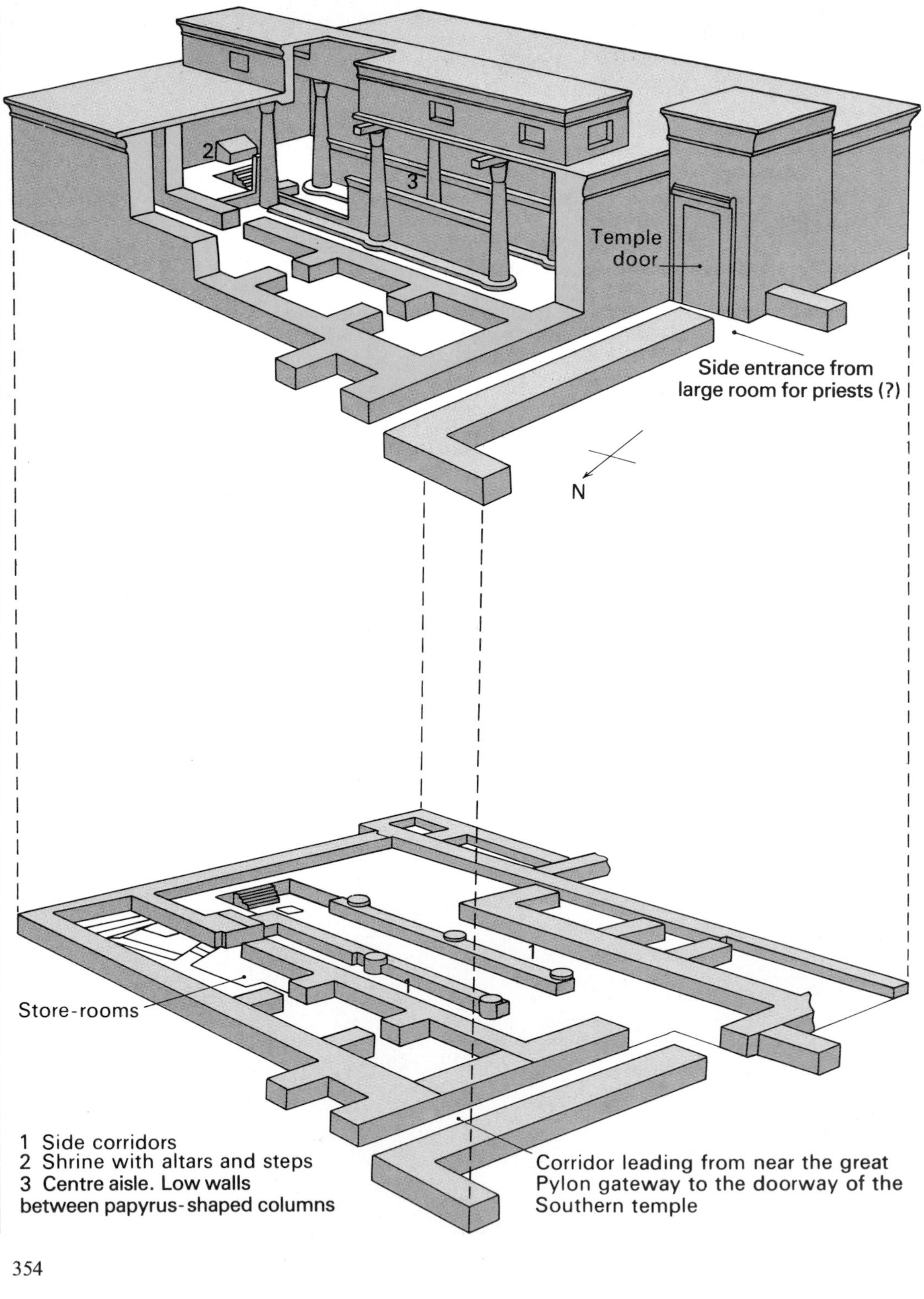

Plan and suggested reconstruction of the Canaanite temple of Dagan, built for Rameses III at Beth-shean, possibly where the Philistines fastened Saul's head (1 Ch. 10 : 10). 12th cent. BC.

13th century AD (Schmökel), influenced solely by the outward similarity between 'Dagon' and Heb. *dāḡ*, 'fish'. The fish-tailed divinity on coins from Arvad and Ascalon is linked with Atargatis and has no stated connection with Dagon (Dhorme and Dussaud). The common Heb. word *dāḡān*, 'grain, corn' (*BDB*, p. 186) may be derived from the name of the god Dagon or Dagan or be its origin; it is thus possible that he was a vegetation or grain god (*cf.* W. F. Albright, *Archaeology and the Religion of Israel*[3], 1953, pp. 74 and 220, n. 15).

From at least 2500 BC onwards, Dagon received worship throughout Mesopotamia, especially in the Middle-Euphrates region, in which, at Mari, he had a temple (18th century BC) adorned with bronze lions (see illustration in A. Champdor, *Babylon*, 1959). Many personal names were compounded with Dagon.

In the 14th century BC and earlier, Dagon had a temple at Ugarit in N Phoenicia, identified by two stelae in it dedicated to his name; these are pictured in *Syria* 16, 1935, plate 31: 1–2, opposite p. 156, and translated by Albright, *op. cit.*, p. 203, n. 30. This temple had a forecourt (?), an antechamber, and probably a tower (plan in C. F. A. Schaeffer, *The Cuneiform Texts of Ras Shamra-Ugarit*, 1939, plate 39), the whole probably taking the form of the ancient model illustrated by C. L. Woolley (*A Forgotten Kingdom*, 1953, p. 57, fig. 9). In the Ugaritic (N Canaanite) texts Dagon is father of Baal. At Beth-shan, one temple discovered may be that of 1 Ch. 10:10 (see A. Rowe, *Four Canaanite Temples of Beth Shan*, 1, 1940, pp. 22–24). That Dagon had other shrines in Palestine is indicated by two settlements each called Beth-dagon (Jos. 15:41; 19:27) in the territories of Judah and Asher. Rameses II mentions a B(e)th-D(a)g(o)n in his Palestinian lists (*c.* 1270 BC), and Sennacherib a Bit-Dagannu in 701 BC.

BIBLIOGRAPHY. H. Schmökel, *Der Gott Dagan*, 1928, and in Ebeling and Meissner (eds.), *Reallexikon der Assyriologie*, 2, 1938, pp. 99–101; E. Dhorme and R. Dussaud, *Les Religions de Babylonie et d'Assyrie . . . des Hittites . . . Phéniciens, etc.*, 1949, pp. 165–167, 173, 364f., 371, 395f.; M. Dahood, in S. Moscati (ed.), *Le antiche divinità semitiche*, 1958, pp. 77–80; M. Pope, in W. Haussing (ed.), *Wörterbuch der Mythologie*, 1, 1965, pp. 276–278. For Mari material, see J. R. Kupper, *Les Nomades en Mésopotamie au temps des Rois de Mari*, 1957, pp. 69–71.

K.A.K.

DALMANUTHA. In Mk. 8:10 a district on the coast of the Lake of Galilee, to which Jesus and his disciples crossed after the feeding of the four thousand. It has never been satisfactorily identified. (Magadan in the parallel passage, Mt. 15:39, is equally unknown.) Various emendations have been proposed (including F. C. Burkitt's suggestion that it represents a corruption of Tiberias combined with its earlier name Amathus), but it is best to keep the attested reading and await further light. F.F.B.

DALMATIA. A Roman province in the mountainous region on the E of the Adriatic, formed by the emperor Tiberius. Its name was derived from an Illyrian tribe that inhabited it. It was bounded on the E by Moesia and the N by Pannonia. It is mentioned in 2 Tim. 4:10, and is identical with *Illyricum (Rom. 15:19). B.F.C.A.

DAMASCUS.

a. Location

The capital city of Syria (Is. 7:8) situated E of the Anti-Lebanon Mts and overshadowed in the SW by Mt Hermon (Ct. 7:4). It lies in the NW of the Ghuta plain 700 m above sea-level and W of the Syrian–Arabian desert. The district is famous for its orchards and gardens, being irrigated by the clear Abana (mod. Barada) and adjacent Pharpar rivers, which compared favourably with the slower, muddy Jordan (2 Ki. 5:12) and Euphrates rivers (Is. 8:5–8). It is a natural communications centre, linking the caravan route to the Mediterranean coast (*c.* 100 km to the W) through Tyre (Ezk. 27:18) to Egypt with the tracks E across the desert to Assyria and Babylonia, S to Arabia, and N to Aleppo. The city was of special importance as head of an *Aramaean state in the 10th–8th centuries BC.

The centre of the modern city lies beside the Barada river, part of it occupying the area of the old walled city. Some streets follow the lines of Roman times, including Straight Street (*Darb al-mustaqim*) or Long Street (*Sūq al-Tawilēh*) as in Acts 9:11. The great mosque built in the 8th century AD is said to cover the site of the temple of *Rimmon (2 Ki. 5:18).

b. Name

The meaning of Damascus (Gk. *Damaskos*; Heb. *Dammeśeq*; Aram. *Darmeśeq*; 1 Ch. 18:5; 2 Ch. 28:5) is unknown. The *ʾ^{a}ram darmeśeq* of 1 Ch. 18:6 corresponds to the modern (*Dimašk-*)*eš-šām* as 'Damascus of the North (Syria)'. The name is found in Egyp. *Tjmšqw* (Tuthmosis III) and Amarna Letters (14th century) and cuneiform inscriptions as *Dimašqi*. Other names in the latter texts are *ša imerišu* (perhaps 'caravan city') and *Bīt-Haza'-ili* ('House of Hazael') in the 8th century BC (*DOTT*, p. 57). See *ANET*, p. 278, n. 8.

c. History

Damascus appears to have been occupied from prehistoric times. In

Bronze lions guarding the entrance to the temple of Dagan (Dagon) at Mari, Syria. Length c. 70 cm. Babylonia. 18th cent. BC. (MC)

DAILY LIFE
See Patriarchal age, Part 3.

DAILY WAGE
See Money, Part 2.

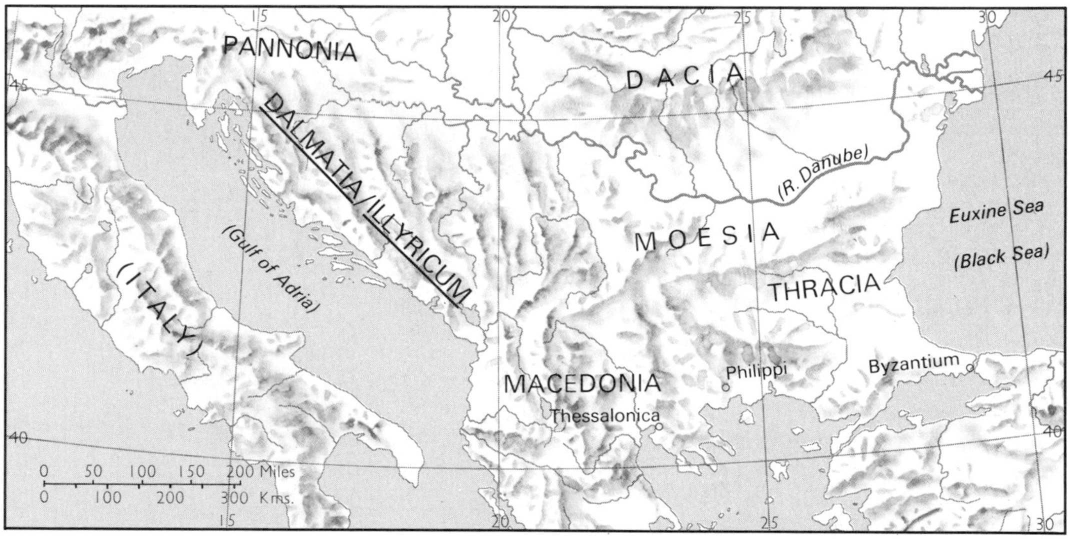

The Roman province of Dalmatia.

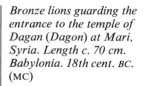

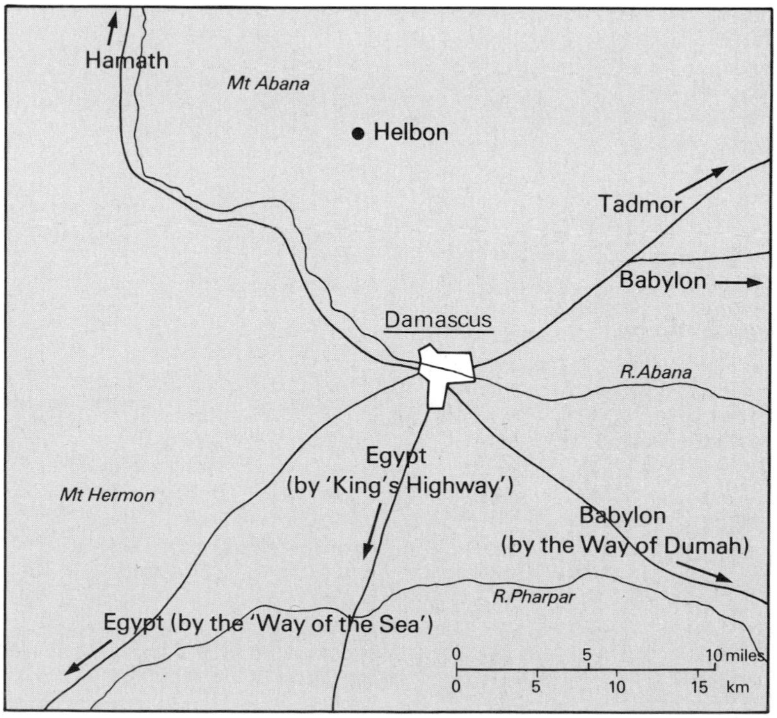

Damascus.

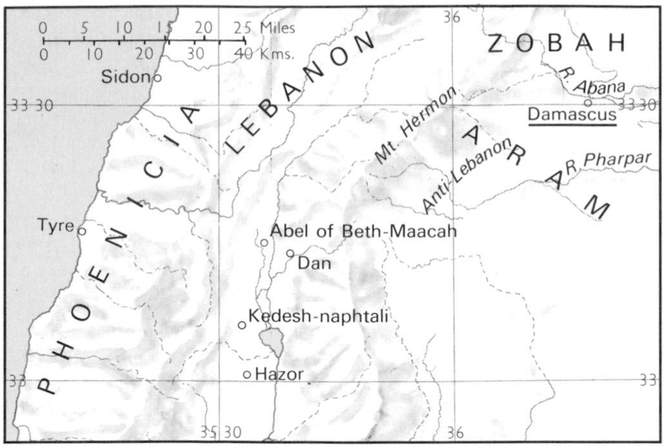

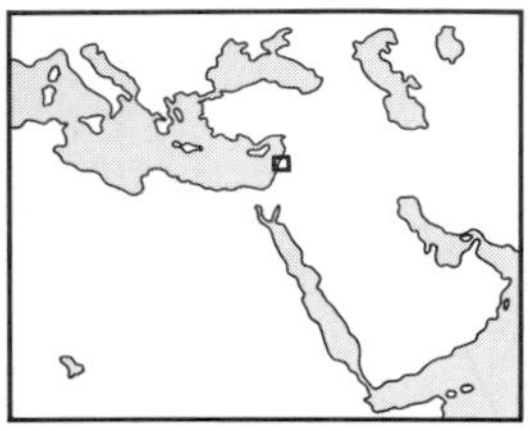

The location of OT Damascus, capital of Syria.

Top right:
Part of Straight Street (al-Salheya), Damascus, Syria. (RH)

A typical house-construction on the ancient wall of Damascus. From such a place Paul would have escaped from the city. (DJW)

the 2nd millennium BC it was a well-known city near which Abraham defeated a coalition of kings (Gn. 14:15). It is possible that his servant Eliezer was from this city (Gn. 15:2; Syr. and vss). David captured and garrisoned Damascus after his defeat of the troops it had contributed in support of Hadad-ezer of Zobah (2 Sa. 8:5f.; 1 Ch. 18:5). Rezon of Zobah, who escaped from this battle, later entered the city which was made the capital of a newly formed Aramaean city-state of *Aram (Syria; 1 Ki. 11:24). The city increased its influence under Rezon's successors Hezion and his son Tabrimmon. By the time of the accession of the latter's son Ben-hadad I (*c.* 900–860 BC) Damascus was the dominant partner in the treaty made by Asa of Judah to offset the pressure brought against him by Baasha of Israel (2 Ch. 16:2). The same king (if not Ben-hadad II—see *CHRONOLOGY OF THE OLD TESTAMENT) made the provision of merchants' quarters in Damascus a term of a treaty made with Ahab (1 Ki. 20:34). The aim of this treaty was to gain the support of Israel for the coalition of city-states to oppose the Assyrians. Ben-hadad (Assyr. Adad-idri) of Damascus provided the largest contingent of 20,000 men at the indecisive battle of Qarqar in 853 BC. Ben-hadad may be the unnamed 'king of Aram', in fighting whom Ahab met his death (see 1 Ki. 22:29–36).

In the plain near Damascus the prophet Elijah anointed Hazael, a Damascene noble, as the future king of Syria (1 Ki. 19:15), and Elisha, who had healed the general Naaman of Damascus, was invited there by Hazael to advise on Ben-hadad's health (2 Ki. 8:7). In 841 BC Hazael had to face renewed attacks by the Assyrians under Shalmaneser III. For a time he held the pass leading through the Lebanon Mts, but having lost 16,000 men, 1,121 chariots and 470 cavalry was forced to retreat within Damascus, where he successfully withstood a siege. The Assyrians fired orchards and plantations round the city before they withdrew (*DOTT*, p. 48; *ANET*, p. 280). In 805–803 BC Adad-nirari III led fresh Assyrian attacks on Hazael and Damascus. A further campaign in 797 BC by Adad-nirari so weakened Damascus that J(eh)oash of Israel was able to recover towns on his N border previously lost to Hazael (2 Ki. 13:25).

Under Rezin (Assyr. *Raḫianu*)

Aram again oppressed Judah (2 Ki. 16:6), and in 738 was, with Menahem of Israel, a vassal of Tiglath-pileser III of Assyria. Soon thereafter Rezin revolted, captured Elath and took many Judaeans captive to Damascus (2 Ch. 28:5). Ahaz of Judah thereupon appealed for help to Assyria who responded by launching a series of punitive raids in 734–732 BC, which culminated in the capture of Damascus, as prophesied by Isaiah (17:1) and Amos (1:4–5), and the death of Rezin. The spoiling of the city (Is. 8:4), the deportation of its inhabitants to Kir (2 Ki. 16:9), and its destruction were cited as an object-lesson to Judah (Is. 10:9f.). In return for this assistance Ahaz was summoned to pay tribute to the Assyrian king at Damascus, where he saw and copied the altar (2 Ki. 16:10–12) which led to the worship of Syrian deities within the Temple at Jerusalem (2 Ch. 28:23). Damascus was reduced to a subsidiary city within the Assyrian province of Hamath and henceforth lost its political, but not completely its economic, influence (*cf.* Ezk. 27:18). Judaean merchants continued to reside in the city, and the border of Damascus was considered the boundary of the ideal Jewish state (Ezk. 47:16–18; 48:1; Zc. 9:1).

In the Seleucid period Damascus lost its position as capital, and thus much trade, to Antioch, though it was restored as capital of Coele-syria under Antiochus IX in 111 BC. The Nabataean Aretas won the city in 85 BC, but lost control to Tigranes of Armenia. Damascus was a Roman city from 64 BC to AD 33.

By the time of Paul's conversion Aretas IV (9 BC–AD 40), who had defeated his son-in-law Herod Antipas, had an ethnarch in the city (2 Cor. 11: 32–33). The city had many synagogues (Acts 9:2; Jos., *BJ* 2. 20) and in these, after being led to the house of Judas in Straight Street (9:10–12) where he was visited by Ananias, Paul first preached. Opposition forced Paul to escape over the city wall (9:19–27) but he returned to the city after a period spent in nearby Arabia (Gal. 1:17). Damascus continued to be subsidiary to Antioch, both politically and economically, until its supremacy was restored by the Arab conquest of AD 634.

BIBILIOGRAPHY. M. F. Unger, *Israel and the Aramaeans of Damascus*, 1957; A. Jepsen, *AfO* 14, 1942, pp. 153–172. D.J.W.

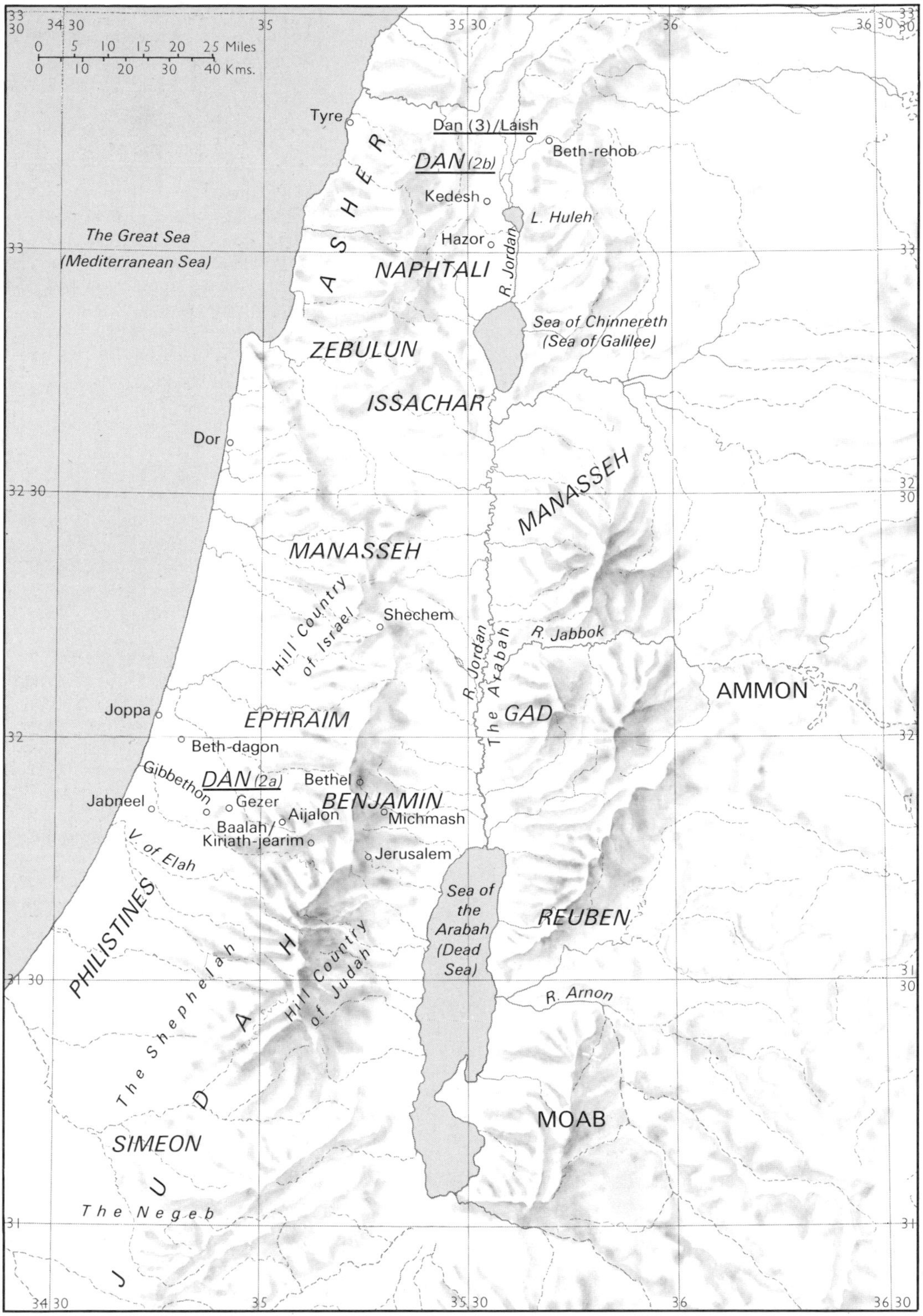

The two areas of settlement of the tribe of Dan and the city of Dan.

DAN (Heb. *dān*, commonly treated as active participle of *dîn*, 'to judge'). **1.** One of the 12 sons of Jacob, the elder of the two sons borne to him by Rachel's maid-servant Bilhah (Gn. 30:1–6), eponymous ancestor of the tribe of Dan.

2. One of the 12 tribes of Israel. Its first settlement lay between the territories of Ephraim, Benjamin and Judah (Jos. 19:40ff.). Pressed back into the hill-country by the Amorites, who themselves were being pressed from the W by the Philistines and other sea peoples who had occupied the Mediterranean seaboard, the majority of the Danites migrated N to find a new home near the source of the Jordan (Jos. 19:47; Jdg. 1:34;

18:1ff.). Some members of the tribe, however, remained in their earlier settlement, with the Philistines as their W neighbours; it is in this region that the stories of Samson, a Danite hero, have their setting (Jdg. 13:1ff.). It is possibly the remnant of the tribe that stayed in its first home that is described in Deborah's song (Jdg. 5:17) as remaining 'with the ships'—however we are to understand the 'ships' (various uncertain emendations have been proposed). M. Noth, on the other hand, suggests that Dan had to 'buy its settlement' in the N 'by accepting a certain amount of compulsory labour service in S Phoenician seaports' (*The History of Israel*, p. 80). The S remnant appears to have been absorbed ultimately in Judah; the N Danites were deported by Tiglath-pileser III in 732 BC (2 Ki. 15:29). The aggressive qualities of the Danites are celebrated in the benedictions of Gn. 49:16f. and Dt. 33:22.

Dan is missing from the list of tribes in Rev. 7:5–8, either intentionally or by a primitive corruption. Irenaeus (*Adv. Haer.* 5. 30. 2) explains the omission by saying that antichrist is to come from the tribe of Dan—a belief which he bases on Je. 8:16, LXX ('from Dan shall we hear the noise of his swift horses').

3. A city in the N Danite territory, mod. Tell el-Qadi or Tell Dan, near one of the sources of Jordan. Its earlier name was Laish (Jdg. 18:29; called Leshem in Jos. 19:47), appearing as Lus(i) in Egyptian texts of *c.* 1850–1825 BC. It was the most N Israelite city, hence the phrase 'from Dan to Beersheba' (*e.g.* Jdg. 20:1). The shrine established here under the priesthood of Moses' grandson Jonathan and his descendants (Jdg. 18:30) was elevated (along with Bethel) to the status of a national sanctuary by Jeroboam I (1 Ki. 12:29f.), and so remained until 'the captivity of the land' under Tiglath-pileser III.

BIBLIOGRAPHY. H. H. Rowley, 'The Danite Migration to Laish',

Egyptian girls engaged in various forms of dancing and games. Tomb of Mereru-ka, Saqqara. Limestone. Reign of Teti, 6th Dynasty, 2350–2200 BC. (OIUC)

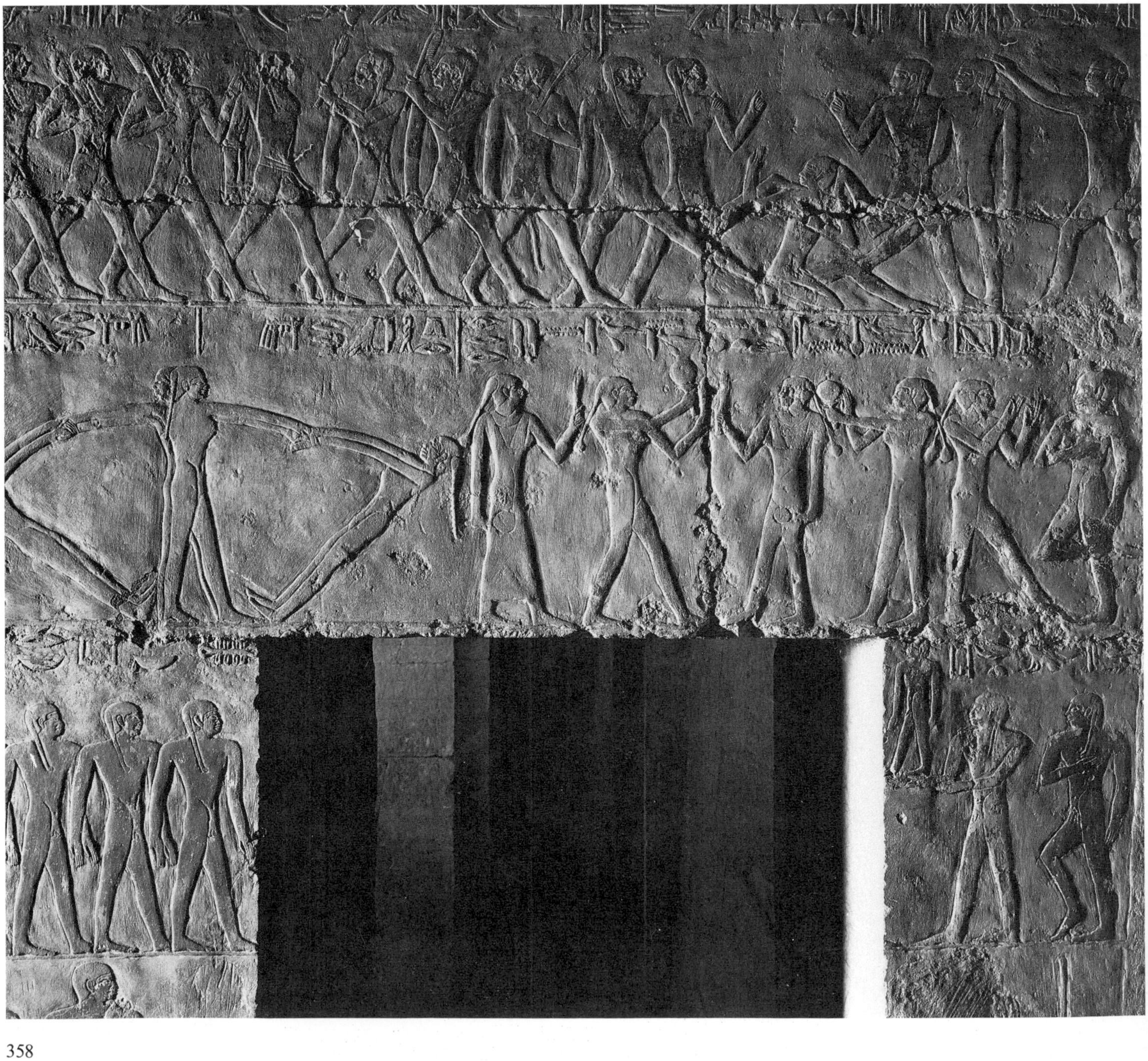

Top left:
Spring at Dan. (RS)

Bronze figure of a dancing girl. Etruscan. c. 460 BC. (BM)

Part of a wall-painting from a tomb at Thebes, showing two girls dancing to music. Height 30 cm. Thutmose IV or Amenhotep III. 1421–1377 BC. (BM)

ExpT 51, 1939–40, pp. 466–471; M. Noth, *The History of Israel*, 1960, pp. 67ff. *et passim*; J. Gray, *Joshua, Judges and Ruth*, *NCB*, 1967, pp. 287f. F.F.B.

DANCE. The OT makes occasional reference to dancing as a source of amusement only (*e.g.* Ex. 32:19; Ec. 3:4), but usually behind the activity is some form of religious significance. Groups of women engaged in it on occasions of national celebration, such as after the crossing of the Red Sea (Ex. 15:20) after military victories (1 Sa. 18:6) and at religious festivals (Jdg. 21:19–21). Less frequently, men also are recorded as having danced (*e.g.* 2 Sa. 6:14).

In NT times the Greek custom of employing professional women dancers was followed in the case of Salome at Herod's birthday feast (Mk. 6:21–22); there was dancing at the prodigal son's homecoming festivities (Lk. 15:25); and it was such a common part of daily life that it entered into children's games (Mt. 11:17; Lk. 7:32; *cf.* Jb. 21:11).

For a comprehensive treatment, see the corresponding article in *EBi*. J.D.D.

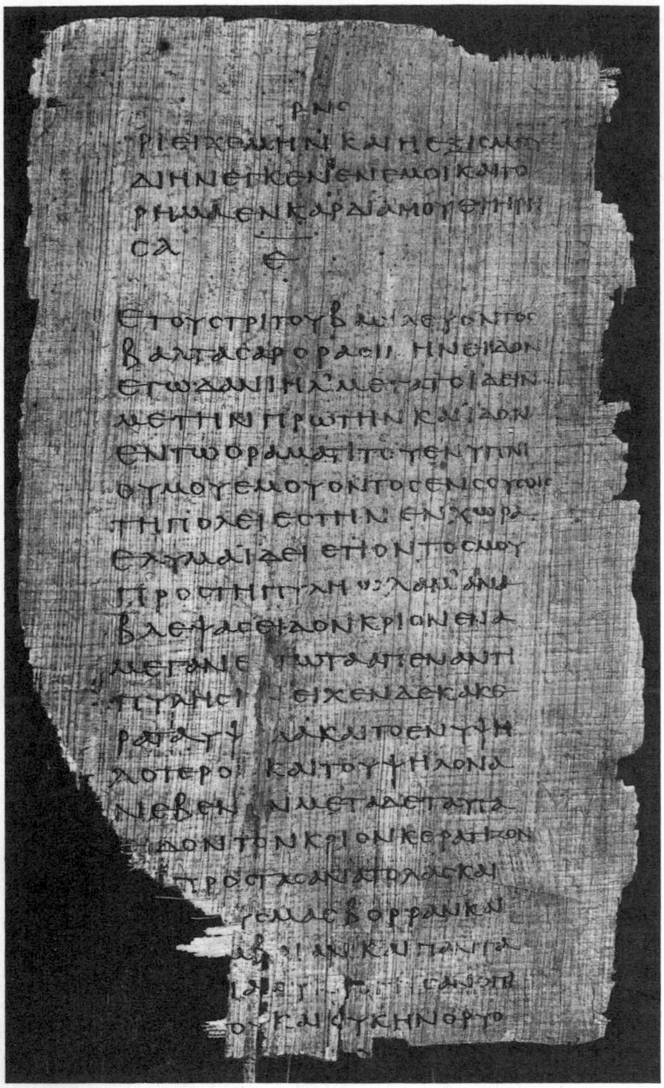

Part of the book of Daniel (7:28–8:48) from a Greek papyrus MS *of c.* AD *250, originally containing Ezekiel, Daniel and Esther in the Septuagint translation. One of eleven books from a Christian library found N of Memphis, Egypt.* (CBL)

DANIEL (Heb. *dāniyyē'l, dāni'ēl,* 'God is my judge'). **1.** Second son of David (1 Ch. 3:1) and Abigail, called also 'Chileab' (AVmg.). Although older than his brothers Absalom and Adonijah, nothing more is recorded of him, suggesting that he died young. **2.** A descendant of Ithamar, who accompanied Ezra (8:2) and was a signatory to the covenant (Ne. 10:1, 6). **3.** A man of extraordinary wisdom and righteousness whose name is coupled with Noah and Job (Ezk. 14:14, 20), and who is mentioned again in 28:3. Ezekiel need not be referring to the Ugaritic mythological *Dan'el* (*cf. ANET*³, pp. 149–155) even though his spelling (*Dāni'ēl*) is slightly different from that of his contemporary (*Dānîy'ēl*), for in personal names the vowel letters were in free variation with one another, just as *Dō'ēg* the Edomite (1 Sa. 21:7; 22:9) is spelt *Dôyēg* in 1 Sa. 22:18, 22. Furthermore, Daniel's wisdom had become proverbial as early as 603 BC (Dn. 2:1), a number of years before Ezekiel spoke of it (Ezk. 28:3). Thus, he may be the same as the following.

4. The fourth of the so-called 'greater' prophets, of whose early career nothing is known except for what we are told in the book which bears his name. An Israelite of royal or noble descent (*cf.* Jos., *Ant.* 10. 188), he was carried captive to Babylon by Nebuchadrezzar in the third year of Jehoiakim, and with various companions trained for the king's service (Dn. 1:1–6). Following a custom of the time, he was given (v. 7) the Babylonian name of *Belteshazzar. He gained a reputation first as an interpreter of other men's visions (ch. 2–5), then of his own, in which he predicted the future triumph of the Messianic kingdom (ch. 7–12).

Renowned for sagacity, he successfully occupied leading governmental posts under Nebuchadrezzar, Belshazzar and Darius. His last recorded vision was on the banks of the Tigris in the third year of Cyrus.

There is a brief reference to 'the prophet Daniel' in Mt. 24:15 (= Mk. 13:14). (*DANIEL, BOOK OF.)

J.D.D.
J.C.W.

DANIEL, BOOK OF.

I. Outline of contents

Chs. 1–6 are largely historical in content, with Daniel speaking of himself in the third person. Ch. 1 records his being carried away captive from Judah to Babylon and his subsequent rise to power. In the next five chapters he is seen serving as chief minister and interpreter of dreams to a number of Gentile kings. The visions of chs. 2, 4 and 5 are given to the Babylonian kings Nebuchadrezzar and Belshazzar, and reveal the destiny of Gentile kings and kingdoms. At the end of ch. 5 the capture of Babylon by Darius the Mede is briefly mentioned. This is followed by an account of Daniel's continued influence and the plot against his life. This historical section ends with his miraculous deliverance and a brief note to the effect that he 'prospered during the reign of Darius and the reign of Cyrus the Persian'.

In chs. 7–12 the historical background almost fades from sight as Daniel himself, speaking now in the first person, becomes the recipient of visions which emphasize the destiny of Israel in relation to Gentile kingdoms.

II. Authorship and date

Modern critical scholarship is practically unanimous in its rejection of the book as a 6th-century BC document written by Daniel, in spite of the testimony of the book itself and the statement of our Lord that the 'desolating sacrilege' was 'spoken of by the prophet Daniel' (Mt. 24:15). Critics claim that the book was compiled by an unknown author about 165 BC, because it contains prophecies of post-Babylonian kings and wars which supposedly become increasingly accurate as they approach that date (11:2–35). It is further claimed that the book was written to encourage faithful Jews in their conflict with Antiochus Epiphanes (*cf.* 1 Macc. 2:59–60) and that it was enthusiastically received by them as being genuine and authentic and was immediately placed in the Hebrew Canon.

In addition to its doubtful implications with regard to predictive prophecy, this critical view must be rejected for the following reasons.

1. The assumption that the author placed Darius I before Cyrus and made Xerxes the father of Darius I (*cf.* 6:28; 9:1) ignores the fact that Daniel is speaking of Darius the Mede, a governor under Cyrus whose father had the same name as the later Persian king. Critics do not question the fact that the author was an extremely brilliant Jew (*cf.* R. H. Pfeiffer, *IOT*, 1948, p. 776). But no intelligent Jew of the 2nd century BC could have committed such historical blunders as the critics suppose, with Ezra 4:5–6 before him, especially since he puts Xerxes as the fourth king after Cyrus in Daniel 11:2 (*cf.* A. A. Bevan, *A Short Commentary on the Book of Daniel*, 1892, p. 109).

2. If the book were as full of serious historical blunders as the critics claim (*cf.* H. H. Rowley, *Darius the Mede and the Four World Empires of the Book of Daniel*, 1935, pp. 54–60), Jews of the Maccabean period would never have accepted it as canonical. Educated Palestinians of that era had access to the writings of Herodotus, Ctesias, Berossus, Menander and other ancient historians whose works have long since been lost to us, and they were well acquainted with the names of

Cyrus and his successors on the throne of Persia—yet they saw no historical blunders in the book of Daniel, while rejecting such works as 1 Maccabees as being unworthy of the Canon (*cf.* R. D. Wilson, *Studies in the Book of Daniel*, 1917, p. 149).

3. The discovery of manuscript fragments of the book of Daniel in Cave 1 and Cave 4 of Wadi Qumran showing the Hebrew–Aramaic and Aramaic–Hebrew transition points in the text has called into serious question the need for positing a Maccabean date for the book (*cf.* W. S. LaSor, *Amazing Dead Sea Scrolls*, 1956, pp. 42–44).

4. The author gives evidence of having a more accurate knowledge of Neo-Babylonian and early Achaemenid Persian history than any known historian since the 6th century BC. Regarding Dn. 4, Robert H. Pfeiffer wrote: 'We shall presumably never know how our author learned that the new Babylon was the creation of Nebuchadnezzar (4:30), as the excavations have proved' (*op. cit.*, p. 758). Regarding Dn. 5, the portrayal of Belshazzar as co-king of Babylon under Nabonidus has been brilliantly vindicated by archaeological discoveries (*cf.* R. P. Dougherty, *Nabonidus and Belshazzar*, 1929; and J. Finegan, *Light From the Ancient Past*², 1959, p. 228). Regarding Dn. 6, recent studies have shown that Darius the Mede corresponds remarkably well with what is known from the Nabonidus Chronicle and numerous other contemporary cuneiform documents of Gubaru, whom Cyrus appointed as 'the Governor of Babylon and the Region beyond the River'. It is no longer possible to attribute to the author the false concept of an independent Median kingdom between the fall of Babylon and the rise of Cyrus (*cf.* J. C. Whitcomb, *Darius the Mede*, 1959. For an alternative view, see also *DARIUS). Again, the author knew enough of 6th-century BC customs to represent Nebuchadrezzar as being able to make and alter the laws of Babylon with absolute sovereignty (Dn. 2:12–13, 46), while depicting Darius the Mede as being helpless to change the laws of the Medes and Persians (6:8–9). Also, he accurately represented the change from punishment by fire under the Babylonians (Dn. 3) to punishment by the lions' den under the Persians (Dn. 6), since fire was sacred to the Zoroastrians (*cf.* A. T. Olmstead, *The History of the Persian Empire*, 1948, p. 473).

On the basis of a careful comparison of the cuneiform evidence concerning Belshazzar with the statements of Dn. 5, R. P. Dougherty concluded that 'the view that the fifth chapter of Daniel originated in the Maccabean age is discredited' (*op. cit.*, p. 200). But the same conclusion must be reached concerning the fourth and sixth chapters of Daniel as well, as we have pointed out above. Therefore, since the critics are almost unanimous in their admission that the book of Daniel is the product of one author (*cf.* R. H. Pfeiffer, *op. cit.*, pp. 761–762), we may safely assert that the book could not possibly have been written as late as the Maccabean age.

Finally, it must be stated that the classic arguments for a 2nd-century BC date for the book are untenable. The fact that the book was placed in the third part of the Heb. Canon (the Writings) rather than in the second (the Prophets) in the 4th century AD in the Bab. Talmud is not determinative; for over 200 years earlier Josephus placed Daniel among the prophets (*Against Apion* 1. 8). R. L. Harris further demonstrates that the popular three-stage canonization theory 'can no longer be held' (*Inspiration and Canonicity of the Bible*, 1969, p. 148).

Again, the failure of Ben-Sira, the author of Ecclesiasticus (180 BC), to mention Daniel among the famous men of the past certainly does not prove that he knew nothing of Daniel. This is evident from the fact that he also failed to mention Job, all the judges (except Samuel), Asa, Jehoshaphat, Mordecai and even Ezra (Ecclus. 44–49).

The presence of the three Gk. names for musical instruments (translated 'lyre', 'trigon' and 'harp' in 3:5, 10), another of the arguments for a late date, no longer constitutes a serious problem, for it has become increasingly clear that Gk. culture penetrated the Near East long before the time of Nebuchadrezzar (*cf.* W. F. Albright, *From Stone Age to Christianity*², 1957, p. 337; E. M. Yamauchi in J. B. Payne (ed.), *New Perspectives in the OT*, 1970, pp. 170–200). Persian loan-words for technical terms are likewise consistent with an early date. The Aramaic of Daniel (2:4b–7:28) closely resembles that of Ezra (4:7–6:18; 7:12–26) and the 5th-century BC Elephantine papyri (*cf.* G. L. Archer in J. B. Payne (ed.), *New Perspectives in the OT*, 1970, pp. 160–169), while the Hebrew of Daniel resembles that of Ezekiel, Haggai, Ezra and Chronicles more than that of Ecclesiasticus (180 BC; *cf.* G. L. Archer in J. H. Skilton (ed.), *The Law and the Prophets*, 1974, pp. 470–481).

III. The prophecies of Daniel

This important apocalyptic book provides the basic framework for Jewish and Gentile history from the time of Nebuchadrezzar to the second advent of Christ. An understanding of its prophecies is essential to the proper interpretation of the Olivet discourse of Christ (Mt. 24–25; Lk. 21), Paul's doctrine of the man of sin (2 Thes. 2), and the book of Revelation. The book of Daniel is also of great importance theologically for its doctrines of angels and the resurrection.

Among those who take the conservative view of the date and authorship of the book, there are two main schools of thought today concerning the interpretation of the prophecies it contains. On the one hand, some commentators interpret Daniel's prophecies of the great image (2:31–49), the four beasts (7:2–27) and the seventy weeks (9:24–27) as culminating in the first coming of Christ and related events, for they find in the church, the new Israel, the fulfilment of God's promises to the Jews, the old Israel. Thus, the stone which strikes the image (2:34–35) points to the first coming of Christ and the subsequent growth of the church. The ten horns of the fourth beast (7:24) are not necessarily contemporary kings; the little horn (7:24) does not necessarily represent a human being; and the phrase 'a time, two times, and half a time' (7:25) is to be interpreted symbolically. Likewise, the 'seventy weeks of years' (9:24) are symbolical; and this symbolical period ends with the ascension of Christ with all six of the goals (9:24) accomplished by that time. It is the death of the Messiah that causes the Jewish sacrifice and oblation to cease, and the 'desolator' (9:27) refers to the subsequent destruction of Jerusalem by Titus.

Other commentators, however (including the author), interpret these prophecies as culminating in the second advent of Christ, with the nation of Israel prominent once again in God's dealings with the human race. Accordingly, the great image of Dn. 2 represents the Satan-dominated 'kingdom of the world' (Rev. 11:15) in the form of Babylon, Medo-Persia, Greece and Rome, with Rome continuing in some form to the end of this age. This godless empire finally culminates in ten contemporaneous kings (2:41–44; *cf.* 7:24; Rev. 17:12) who are destroyed by Christ at his second coming (2:45). Christ then establishes his kingdom on earth (*cf.* Mt. 6:10; Rev. 20:1–6), which becomes 'a great mountain' and fills 'the whole earth' (2:35).

Dan-jaan, sometimes identified with the town of Dan, but more probably a N town in the district of Dan: perhaps Ijon.

Dn. 7 depicts the same four monarchies as wild beasts, the fourth (Rome) producing ten horns which correspond to the toes of the image (7:7). There is an advance over the second chapter, however, in that the antichrist is now introduced as an eleventh horn who plucks up three of the others and persecutes the saints for 'a time, two times, and half a time' (7:25). That this phrase means three and a half years may be seen by a comparison of Rev. 12:14 with 12:6 and 13:5. The destruction of the antichrist, in whom the power of the four monarchies and the ten kings is finally concentrated (Rev. 13:1–2; 17:7–17; *cf.* Dn. 2:35) is accomplished by 'one like a son of man' (Dn. 7:13) who comes 'on the clouds of heaven' (*cf.* Mt. 26:64; Rev. 19:11ff.).

The 'little horn' of Dn. 8:9ff. is not to be identified with that of 7:24ff. (the antichrist), for he does not emerge from the fourth monarchy but from a division of the third. Historically, the little horn of Dn. 8 was Antiochus Epiphanes, the Seleucid persecutor of Israel (8:9–14). Prophetically, in the author's personal view, this little horn represents the eschatological king of the N who opposes the antichrist (8:17–26; *cf.* 11:40–45).

The prophecy of the 70 weeks (9:24–27) is felt to be of crucial importance for biblical eschatology. The writer believes that the 70 weeks of years are to be reckoned from the decree of Artaxerxes I to rebuild Jerusalem in 445 BC (Ne. 2:1–8) and terminate with the establishment of the millennial kingdom (9:24). It seems clear that a gap or hiatus separates the end of the 69th week from the beginning of the 70th (9:26), for Christ placed the desolating sacrilege at the very end of the present age (Mt. 24:15 in context; *cf.* Dn. 9:27). Such prophetic gaps are not uncommon in the OT (*e.g.* Is. 61:2; *cf.* Lk. 4:16–21). Thus, the 70th week, according to dispensationalist premillennialists, is a 7-year period immediately preceding the second advent of Christ, during which time antichrist rises to world dominion and persecutes the saints.

Dn. 11:2ff. foretells the rise of four Persian kings (the fourth being Xerxes); Alexander the Great; and various Seleucid and Ptolemaic kings, culminating in Antiochus Epiphanes (11:21–32), whose atrocities provoked the Maccabean wars (11:32b–35). Verse 35b is regarded as providing the transition to eschatological times. First the antichrist comes into view (11:36–39); and then the final king of the N, who, according to some premillennial scholars, will crush temporarily both the antichrist and the king of the S before being destroyed supernaturally on the mountains of Israel (11:40–45; *cf.* Joel 2:20; Ezk. 39:4, 17). In the meantime, antichrist will have recovered from his fatal blow to begin his period of world dominion (Dn. 11:44; *cf.* Rev. 13:3; 17:8).

The great tribulation, which lasts

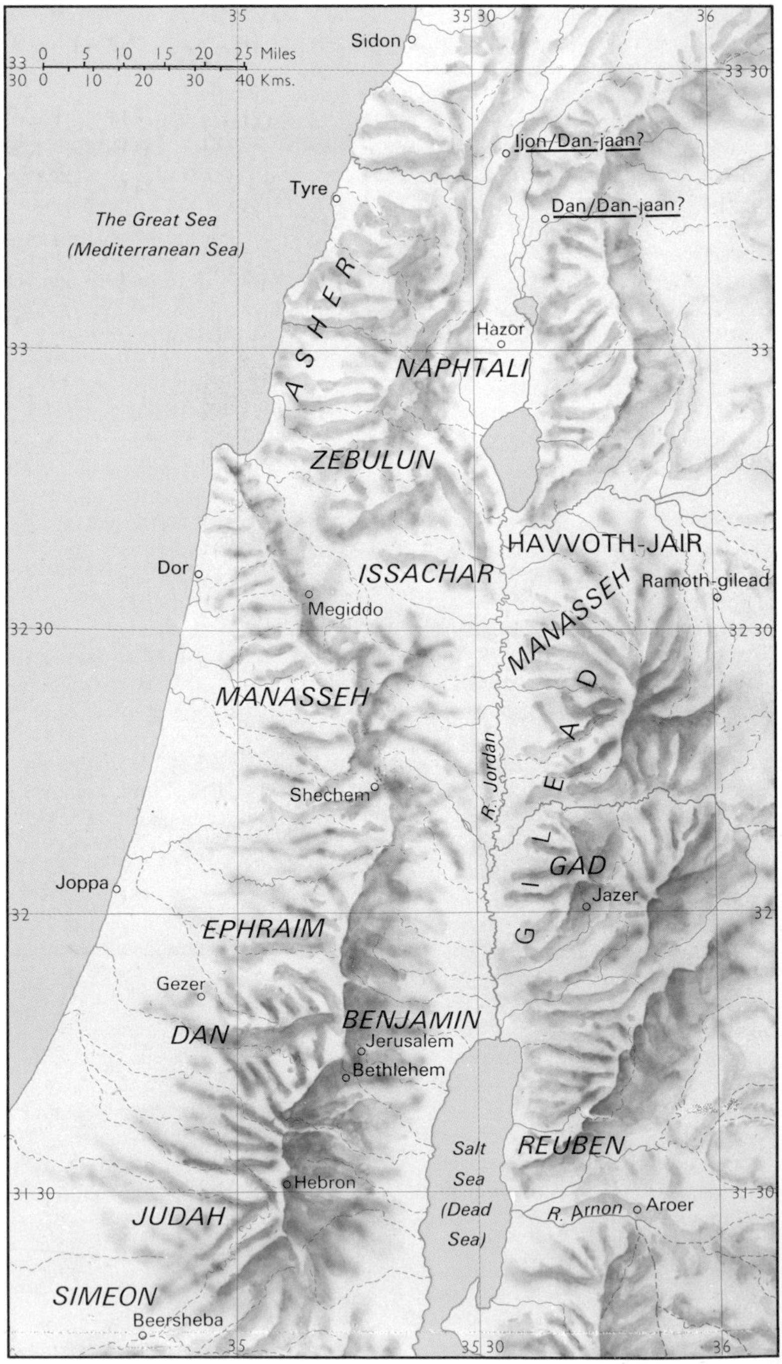

3½ years (Dn. 7:25; *cf.* Mt. 24:21), begins with the victory of the archangel Michael over Satan's heavenly armies (Dn. 12:1; *cf.* Rev. 12:7ff.), and ends with the bodily resurrection of tribulation saints (Dn. 12:2–3; *cf.* Rev. 7:9–14). Although the tribulation period lasts only 1,260 days (Rev. 12:6), an additional 30 days seem to be required for the cleansing and restoration of the Temple (Dn. 12:11), and yet another 45 days before the full blessedness of the millennial kingdom is experienced (12:12).

BIBLIOGRAPHY. R. D. Wilson, *Studies in the Book of Daniel,* 1, 1917; 2, 1938; J. A. Montgomery, *The Book of Daniel, ICC*, 1927; R. P. Dougherty, *Nabonidus and Belshazzar*, 1929; H. H. Rowley, *Darius the Mede and the Four World Empires in the Book of Daniel*, 1935; C. Lattey, *The Book of Daniel*, 1948; E. J. Young, *The Prophecy of Daniel*, 1949, and *The Messianic Prophecies of Daniel*, 1954; H. C. Leupold, *Exposition of Daniel*, 1949; R. D. Culver, *Daniel and the Latter Days*, 1954; J. C. Whitcomb Jr, *Darius the Mede*, 1959; D. J. Wiseman, *Notes on Some Problems in the Book of Daniel*, 1965; J. Walvoord, *Daniel*, 1971; Leon Wood, *A Commentary on Daniel*, 1973; J. G. Baldwin, *Daniel*, *TOTC*, 1978. J.C.W.

DAN-JAAN. Joab and his companions came to Dan-jaan in compiling the census ordered by David (2 Sa. 24:6–9). Starting from *Aroer, E of the Dead Sea, they camped S of the city in the valley of the Gadites (the Arnon basin), then went N to Jazer, through Gilead and other territory to Dan-jaan and its environs, and to Sidon (probably the territorial boundary is meant). Thence they moved S, past a Tyrian outpost, ending in Beersheba. As Beersheba is also mentioned in David's instructions along with Dan (v. 2), some scholars identify Dan-jaan with the well-known Dan. More probably it was a N town in the district of Dan, perhaps *Ijon of 1 Ki. 15:20 (*LOB*, p. 264). Among readings given by LXX is Dan-jaar, perhaps 'Dan of the Woods'. Another LXX reading, 'and from Dan they turned round to Sidon' seems indefensible. Jaan might be a personal name (*cf.* 1 Ch. 5:12 for a possible cognate); a place name *y'ny* is known in Ugaritic. W.J.M. A.R.M.

Darius I (521–486 BC), holding a sceptre, sits enthroned to receive the submission of vassals. Persepolis treasury. Limestone. Height c. 2·5 m. (OIUC)

DARIUS (Heb. *Dārᵉyāweš*; Akkad. Elamite, *Dariawuš*; Old Persian, *Darayavauš*; Gk. *Dareios*).

1. Darius the Mede, the son of Ahasuerus (Xerxes; Dn. 9:1), received the government on the death of Belshazzar (5:30–31), being made king of the Chaldeans (9:1) at the age of 62 (5:31). He bore the title of 'king' (6:6, 9, 25) and the years were marked by his reign (11:1). He appointed 120 subordinate governors under three presidents, of whom one was Daniel (6:2), who prospered in his reign (6:28). According to Jos. (*Ant.* 10. 249), Daniel was removed by Darius to Media.

Since Darius the Mede is not mentioned by name outside the book of Daniel, and the contemporary cuneiform inscriptions reckon no king of Babylon between Nabonidus (and Belshazzar) and the accession of Cyrus, his historicity has been denied and the OT account of this reign considered a conflation of confused traditions (H. H. Rowley, *Darius the Mede*, 1935). On the other hand, the narrative has all the appearance of

DARIC
See Money, Part 2.

Rock-cut monument of Darius I showing rebels submitting to the king. The inscription in Old Persian, Elamite and Babylonian helped in the decipherment of cuneiform script. Bisitun, near Khermanshah, Iran. 521–486 BC. (RH)

Cylinder seal and impression, showing Darius I hunting. The inscription gives his name and title ('The Great King') in Old Persian, Elamite and Babylonian cuneiform. Agate. Height 4·5 cm. Thebes, Egypt. 521–486 BC. (BM)

genuine historical writing, and in the absence of many historical records of this period there is no reason why the history should not be accepted.

There have been many attempts to identify Darius with persons mentioned in the Babylonian texts. The two most reasonable hypotheses identify Darius with (*a*) Gubaru, (*b*) *Cyrus. Gubaru was governor of Babylon and of the region beyond the river (Euphrates). There is, however, no specific evidence that he was a Mede, called king, named Darius, a son of Ahasuerus, or aged about 60. Cyrus, who was related to the Medes, was called 'king of the Medes' and is known to have been about 62 years old on becoming king of Babylon. According to the inscriptions, he appointed many subordinate officials, and documents were dated by his regnal years. This theory requires that Dn. 6:28 be translated '. . . in the reign of Darius, *even* in the reign of Cyrus the Persian' as an explanation by the writer of the use of sources using two names for the one person. The weakness of this theory lies in the fact that Cyrus is nowhere named son of Ahasuerus (but this might be a term used only of royal persons) or as 'of the seed of a Mede'.

2. Darius I, son of Hystaspes, who was king of Persia and of Babylon, where he succeeded Cambyses (after two usurpers had been displaced), and ruled 521–486 BC. He enabled the returned Jews to rebuild the Temple at Jerusalem with Jeshua and Zerubbabel (Ezr. 4:5; Hg. 1:1; Zc. 1:1).

3. Darius II (Nothus), who ruled Persia and Babylon (423–408 BC), called 'Darius the Persian' in Ne. 12:22, perhaps to distinguish him from 'Darius the Mede'. Since the father of Jaddua the high priest is mentioned in an Elephantine papyrus *c.* 400 BC, there is no need to assume that this Jaddua was the high priest who met Alexander in 332 BC and that the Darius here meant is Darius III (Codomanus), who reigned *c.* 336–331 BC.

BIBLIOGRAPHY. J. C. Whitcomb, *Darius the Mede*, 1959; D. J. Wiseman, *Notes on some Problems in the Book of Daniel*, 1970, pp. 9–16.

D.J.W.

DATES
See Chronology, Part 1.

DAUGHTER OF SIDON
See Tyre, Part 3.

DATHAN (Heb. *dāṯān*, 'fount'?). A Reubenite, son of Eliab. Nu. 16:1–35 tells how, with his brother, Abiram, and *Korah, a Levite, he rebelled against Moses. J.D.D.

DAVID (Heb. *dāwiḏ*, sometimes *dāwîḏ*; root and meaning doubtful, but see *BDB in loc.*; the equation with a supposed Old Bab. (Mari) *dawîdum*, 'chief', is now discounted (*JNES* 17, 1958, p. 130; *VT Supp* 7, 1960, pp. 165ff.); *cf.* Laesoe, *Shemsharah Tablets*, p. 56). The youngest son of Jesse, of the tribe of Judah, and second king of Israel. In Scripture the name is his alone, typifying the unique place he has as ancestor, forerunner and foreshadower of the Lord Jesus Christ—'great David's greater son'. There are 58 NT references to David, including the oft-repeated title given to Jesus—'Son of David'. Paul states that Jesus is 'descended from David according to the flesh' (Rom. 1:3), while Jesus himself is recorded by John as saying 'I am

A large golden bowl with flutes and bosses inscribed in Persian cuneiform with the name of Darius. Diameter 21 cm. Hamadan. 5th cent. BC. (Met NY)

the root and the offspring of David' (Rev. 22:16).

When we return to the OT to find who this is who occupies a position of such prominence in the lineage of our Lord and the purposes of God, the material is abundant and rich. The story of David is found between 1 Sa. 16 and 1 Ki. 2, with much of the material paralleled in 1 Ch. 2–29.

I. Family background

Great-grandson of Ruth and Boaz, David was the youngest of eight brothers (1 Sa. 17:12ff.) and was brought up to be a shepherd. In this occupation he learnt the courage which was later to be evidenced in battle (1 Sa. 17:34–35) and the tenderness and care for his flock which he was later to sing of as the attributes of his God. Like Joseph, he suffered from the ill-will and jealousy of his older brothers, perhaps because of the talents with which God had endowed him (1 Sa. 18:28). Modest about his ancestry (1 Sa. 18:18), David was to father a line of notable descendants, as the genealogy of our Lord in Matthew's Gospel shows (Mt. 1:1–17).

II. Anointing and friendship with Saul

When God rejected Saul from the kingship of Israel, David was revealed to Samuel as his successor, who anointed him, without any ostentation, at Bethlehem (1 Sa. 16:1–13). One of the results of Saul's rejection was the departure of the Spirit of God from him, with a consequent depression of his own spirit, which at times seems to have approached madness. There is an awesome revelation of divine purpose in the providence by which David, who is to replace Saul in the favour and plan of God, is selected to minister to the fallen king's melancholy (1 Sa. 16:17–21). So the lives of these two were brought together, the stricken giant and the rising stripling. At first all went well. Saul was pleased with the youth, whose musical skill was to give us part of our richest devotional heritage, appointed him his armour-bearer. Then the well-known incident involving Goliath, the Philistine champion, changed everything (1 Sa. 17). David's agility and skill with the sling outdid the strength of the ponderous giant, whose slaughter was the signal for an Israelite repulsion of the Philistine force. The way was clear for David to reap the reward promised by Saul—the hand of the king's daughter in marriage, and freedom for his father's family from taxation; but a new factor changed the course of events—the king's jealousy of the new champion of Israel. As David returned from the slaying of Goliath, the women of Israel greeted him, singing, 'Saul has slain his thousands, and David his ten thousands'. Saul, unlike his son *Jonathan in a similar situation, resented this and, we are told, 'eyed David from that day on' (1 Sa. 18:7, 9).

III. The hostility of Saul

Saul's dealings with David declined progressively in amity, and we find the young national hero escaping a savage attack on his life by the king, reduced in military honour, cheated of his promised bride and married to Saul's other daughter, Michal, after a marriage settlement which was meant to cause David's death (1 Sa. 18:25). It would appear from 1 Sa. 24:9 that there was a group at Saul's court which deliberately fomented trouble between Saul and David, and the situation deteriorated steadily. Another abortive attempt by Saul at slaying David with his spear was followed by an attempted arrest, foiled only by a stratagem of Michal, David's wife (1 Sa. 19:8–17). A marked feature of this period in David's life is the way in which Saul's two children, Jonathan and Michal, allied themselves with David and against their own father.

IV. Flight from Saul

The next stages in the story of David are marked by a constant flight from the relentless pursuit of Saul. No resting-place is safe for long; prophet, priest, national enemy—none can give him shelter, and those who help him are cruelly punished by the rage-maddened king (1 Sa. 22:6–19). After a narrow escape from destruction by the Philistine war-lords, David eventually established the Adullam band, at first a heterogeneous collection of fugitives, but later an armed task-force which harried the foreign invaders, protected the crops and flocks of outlying Israelite communities, and lived off the generosity of the latter. The churlish refusal of one of these wealthy sheep-farmers, Nabal, to recognize any indebtedness to David is recorded in 1 Sa. 25, and is interesting in introducing Abigail, later to become one of David's wives. Chs. 24 and 26 of the same book record two instances when David spared the life of Saul, out of mingled piety and magnanimity. Eventually David, quite unable to curb the hostility of Saul, came to terms with the Philistine king, Achish of Gath, and was granted the frontier town of Ziklag in return for the occasional use of his warrior band. When the Philistines went out in force against Saul, however, the war-lords demurred at David's presence in their ranks, fearing a last-minute change of loyalty, so he was spared the tragedy of Gilboa, which he later mourned in one of the loveliest elegies extant (2 Sa. 1:19–27).

V. King in Hebron

Once Saul was dead, David sought the will of God and was guided to return to Judah, his own tribal region. Here his fellow-tribesmen anointed him king, and he took up royal residence in Hebron. He was then 30 years old, and he reigned in

Hebron for 7½ years. The first 2 years of this period were occupied by civil war between the supporters of David and the old courtiers of Saul, who had set up Saul's son Eshbaal (Ishbosheth) as king in Mahanaim. It may be doubted whether Eshbaal was more than a puppet, manipulated by Saul's faithful captain, Abner. With the death of these two by assassination, organized opposition to David came to an end, and he was anointed king over the 12 tribes of Israel in Hebron, from which he was soon to transfer his capital to Jerusalem (2 Sa. 3–5).

VI. King in Jerusalem

Now began the most successful period in David's long reign, which was to last for another 33 years. By a happy combination of personal bravery and skilled generalship he led the Israelites in such a systematic and decisive subjugation of their enemies—Philistines, Canaanites, Moabites, Ammonites, Aramaeans, Edomites and Amalekites—that his name would have been recorded in history quite apart from his significance in the divine plan of redemption. The contemporary weakness of the powers in the Nile and Euphrates valleys enabled him, by conquest and alliance, to extend his sphere of influence from the Egyptian frontier and the Gulf of Aqabah to the upper Euphrates. Conquering the supposedly impregnable Jebusite citadel of Jerusalem, he made it his capital, whence he bestrode the two major divisions of his kingdom, later to become the divided kingdoms of Judah and Israel. A palace was built, highways opened, trade routes restored, and the material prosperity of the kingdom secured. This, however, could never be the sole, nor yet the main, ambition of 'a man after Yahweh's own heart', and we soon see evidence of David's religious zeal. He brought back the ark of the covenant from Kiriath-jearim and placed it in a special tabernacle prepared for it in Jerusalem. It was during the return of the ark that the incident occurred which led to the death of Uzzah (2 Sa. 6:6–8). Much of the religious organization which was to enrich the later Temple worship owes its origin to the arrangements for the service of the tabernacle made by David at this time. In addition to its strategic and political importance, Jerusalem thus acquired the even greater religious significance, with which its name has been associated ever since.

It is all the more to be wondered at and remembered in godly fear, that it was in this period of outward prosperity and apparent religious fervour that David committed the sin referred to in Scripture as 'the matter of Uriah the Hittite' (2 Sa. 11). The significance and importance of this sin, both for its intrinsic heinousness and for its consequences in the whole ensuing history of Israel, cannot be overestimated. David repented deeply, but the deed was done, and stands as a demonstration of how sin spoils God's purpose for his children. The poignant cry of anguish with which he greeted the news of the death of *Absalom was only a feeble echo of the heart's agony which knew that death, and many more, to be but part of the reaping of the harvest of lust and deceit sown by him so many years before.

Absalom's rebellion, in which the N kingdom remained loyal to David, was soon followed by a revolt on the part of the N kingdom, led by Sheba, a Benjaminite. This revolt, like Absalom's, was crushed by Joab. David's dying days were marred by the scheming of Adonijah and Solomon for his throne, and by the realization that the legacy of internecine bloodshed foretold by *Nathan had still to be spent.

In addition to David's standing army, led by his kinsman Joab, he

The kingdom of David.

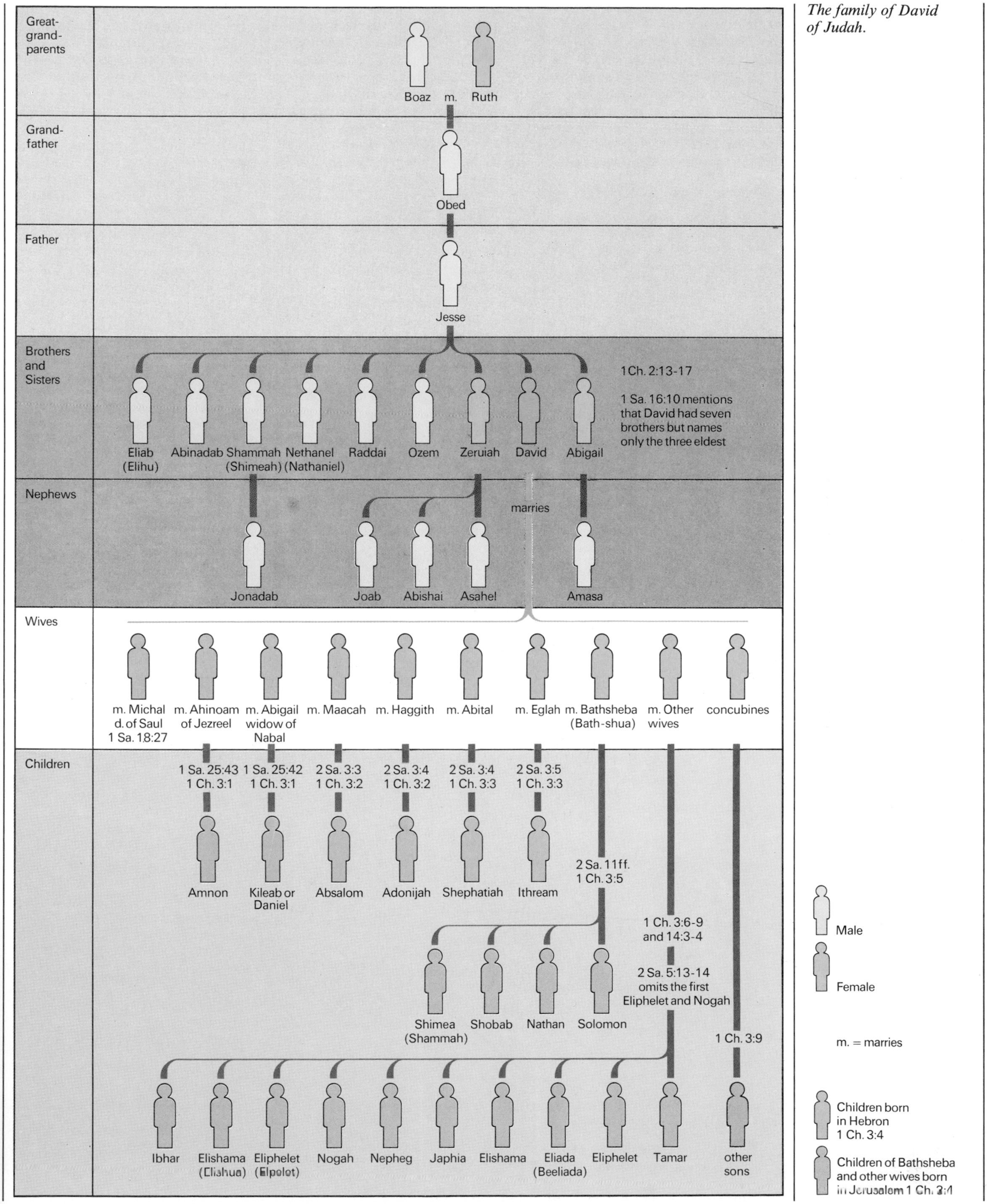

Great-grand-parents
Boaz m. Ruth
Grand-father
Obed
Father
Jesse
Brothers and Sisters
Eliab (Elihu)
Abinadab
Shammah (Shimeah)
Nethanel (Nathaniel)
Raddai
Ozem
Zeruiah
David
Abigail
1 Ch. 2:13-17
1 Sa. 16:10 mentions that David had seven brothers but names only the three eldest
Nephews
marries
Jonadab
Joab
Abishai
Asahel
Amasa
Wives
m. Michal d. of Saul 1 Sa. 18:27
m. Ahinoam of Jezreel
m. Abigail widow of Nabal
m. Maacah
m. Haggith
m. Abital
m. Eglah
m. Bathsheba (Bath-shua)
m. Other wives
concubines
Children
1 Sa. 25:43 1 Ch. 3:1
1 Sa. 25:42 1 Ch. 3:1
2 Sa. 3:3 1 Ch. 3:2
2 Sa. 3:4 1 Ch. 3:2
2 Sa. 3:4 1 Ch. 3:3
2 Sa. 3:5 1 Ch. 3:3
Amnon
Kileab or Daniel
Absalom
Adonijah
Shephatiah
Ithream
2 Sa. 11ff. 1 Ch. 3:5
1 Ch. 3:6-9 and 14:3-4
2 Sa. 5:13-14 omits the first Eliphelet and Nogah
Shimea (Shammah)
Shobab
Nathan
Solomon
1 Ch. 3:9
Ibhar
Elishama (Elishua)
Eliphelet (Elpelet)
Nogah
Nepheg
Japhia
Elishama
Eliada (Beeliada)
Eliphelet
Tamar
other sons
Male
Female
m. = marries
Children born in Hebron 1 Ch. 3:4
Children of Bathsheba and other wives born in Jerusalem 1 Ch. 3:4

The family of David of Judah.

had a personal bodyguard recruited mainly from warriors of Philistine stock, whose loyalty to him never wavered. There is abundant evidence in the historical writings to which reference has already been made of David's skill in composing odes and elegies (see 2 Sa. 1:19–27; 3:33–34; 22; 23:1–7). An early tradition describes him as 'the sweet psalmist of Israel' (2 Sa. 23:1), while later OT writings refer to his direction of the musical worship of Israel, his invention of and skill in playing musical instruments, and his composition (Ne. 12:24, 36, 45–46; Am. 6:5). Seventy-three of the psalms in the Bible are recorded as 'David's', some of them in ways which clearly imply authorship. Most convincingly of all, our Lord himself spoke of David's authorship of at least one psalm (Lk. 20:42), using a quotation from it to make plain the nature of his Messiahship.

VII. Character

The Bible nowhere glosses over the sins or character defects of the

The wars of David.

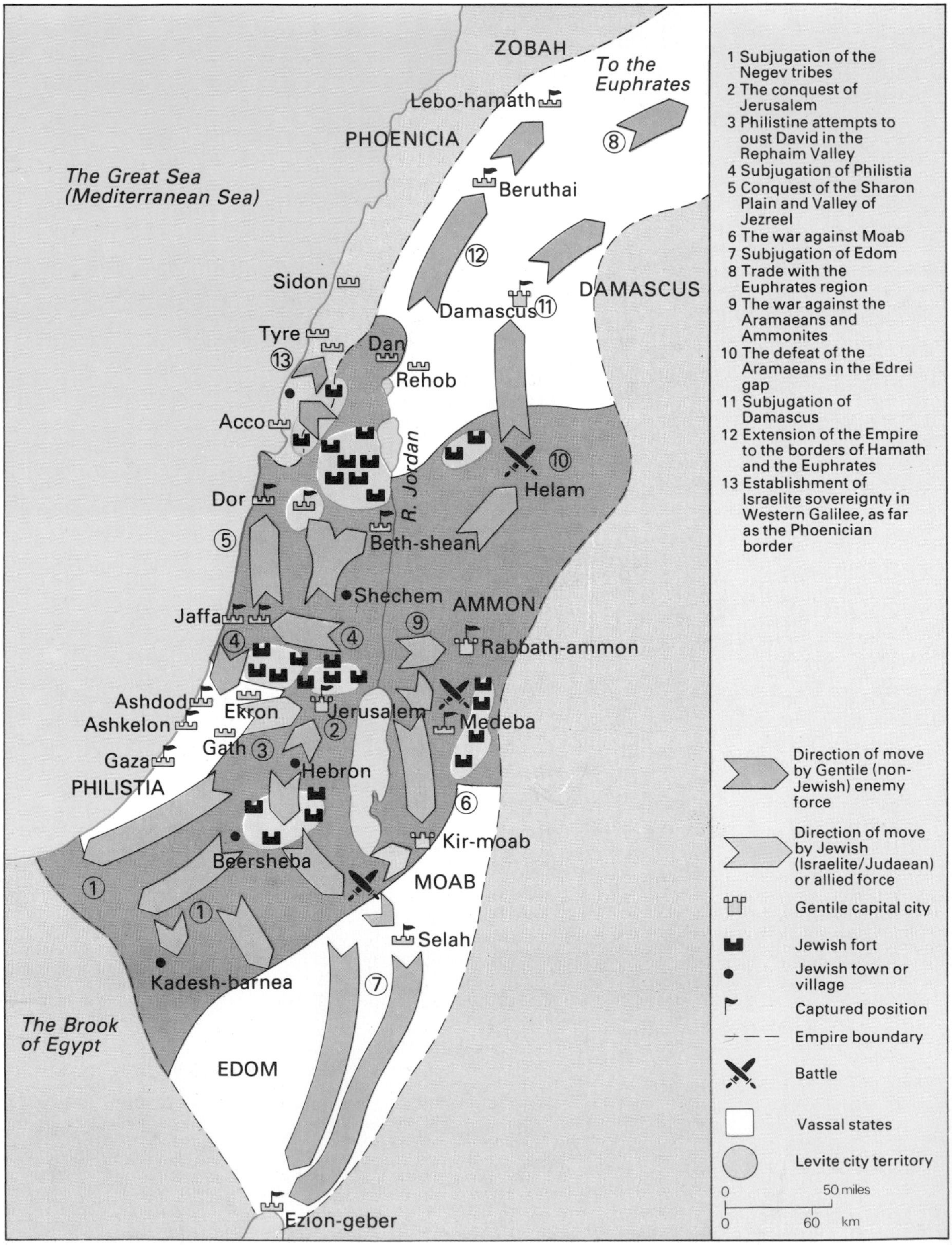

children of God. 'Whatever was written in former days was written for our instruction' (Rom. 15:4). It is part of the task of Scripture to warn by example, as well as to encourage. The sin of David in the matter of Uriah the Hittite is a cardinal instance of this. Let this blot be seen for what it is – a stain on a character otherwise fair and wondrously to the glory of God. It is true that there are elements in the experience of David which seem foreign and even repugnant to the child of the new covenant. Yet 'he . . . served the counsel of God in his own generation' (Acts 13:36), and in that generation he stood out as a bright and shining light for the God of Israel. His accomplishments were many and varied; man of action, poet, tender lover, generous foe, stern dispenser of justice, loyal friend, he was all that men find wholesome and admirable in man, and this by the will of God, who made him and shaped him for his destiny. It is to David, not to Saul, that the Jews look back with pride and affection as the establisher of their kingdom, and it is in David that the more far-sighted of them saw the kingly ideal beyond which their minds could not reach, in the image of which they looked for a coming Messiah, who should deliver his people and sit upon the throne of David for ever. That this was not idealistic nonsense, still less idolatry, is indicated by the NT endorsement of the excellences of David, of whose seed Messiah indeed came, after the flesh.

BIBLIOGRAPHY. G. de S. Barrow, *David: Shepherd, Poet, Warrior, King*, 1946; A. C. Welch, *Kings and Prophets of Israel*, 1952, pp. 80ff.; D. F. Payne, *David: King in Israel*, forthcoming. For a concise estimate of the 'Davidic' psalms, see N. H. Snaith, *The Psalms, A Short Introduction*, 1945, where Ewald's rearrangement is cited with approval. For an important and interesting appraisal of David's official role as divine representative and the significance of Jerusalem in the religious life of the monarchy, see A. R. Johnson, *Sacral Kingship in Ancient Israel*, 1955. T.H.J.

DAY OF THE LORD. This expression forms part of the *eschatology of the Bible. It has various equivalents, such as 'the day', 'in that day'.

In this article we consider the uses of the actual phrase. Am. 5:18–20, the earliest use, shows that the phrase was already a standard one in popular phraseology. To the people it meant the day when Yahweh would intervene to put Israel at the head of the nations, irrespective of Israel's faithfulness to him. Amos declares that the Day means judgment for Israel. So also in Is. 2:12f.; Ezk. 13:5; Joel 1:15; 2:1, 11; Zp. 1:7, 14; Zc. 14:1.

Other prophets, conscious of the sins of other nations as well as of Israel, declare that the Day will come on individual nations as a punishment for their brutalities, *e.g.* Babylon, Is. 13:6, 9; Egypt, Je. 46:10; Edom, Ob. 15; many nations, Joel 2:31; 3:14; Ob. 15.

The Day of the Lord is thus the occasion when Yahweh actively intervenes to punish sin that has come to a climax. This punishment may come through an invasion (Am. 5–6; Is. 13; Ezk. 13:5), or through some natural disaster, such as a locust invasion (Joel 1–2). All lesser interventions come to a head in the actual coming of the Lord himself. At this Day there are truly repentant believers who are saved (Joel 2:28–32), while those who remain enemies of the Lord, whether Jews or Gentiles, are punished. There are also physical effects on the world of nature (Is. 2).

In the NT the Day of the Lord (as in 2 Thes. 2:2) is the second coming of Christ, and the phrase 'the day of Jesus Christ', or an equivalent, occurs in 1 Cor. 1:8; 5:5; Phil. 1:6. 10; 2:16; 2 Thes. 2:2 (AV). The coming is unexpected (1 Thes. 5:2; 2 Pet. 3:10), yet certain signs must occur first, and these should be discerned by Christians (2 Thes. 2:2f.). Physical effects on the world of nature accompany the Day (2 Pet. 3:12f.). J.S.W.

DAY'S JOURNEY (Nu. 11:31; 1 Ki. 19:4; Jon. 3:4; Lk. 2:44). In the E distances were commonly considered in terms of hours and days. Thus a day's journey might be reckoned as 7–8 hours (perhaps 30–50 km), but it was a somewhat indefinite expression appropriate to a country where roads and other factors vary greatly. It should not be confused with a sabbath day's journey, for which see *WEIGHTS AND MEASURES. J.D.D.

DAYSPRING (Heb. *šaḥar*, 'dawn'; Gk. *anatolē*, 'uprising', elsewhere in AV 'east'). The 'place' of the dayspring (Jb. 38:12, RSV 'dawn') is the daily-changing point of the horizon at which the sun comes up. The Gk. (Lk. 1:78) presents difficulties of interpretation, but could intend a comparison of the Messiah with the rising of the sun. See A. R. C. Leaney, *The Gospel according to St Luke*, 1958, pp. 90–91. J.D.D.

DEACON. RSV renders 'deacon' only at Phil. 1:1 and 4 times in 1 Tim. 3; but the Gk. word thus represented, *diakonos* (generally in AV 'minister' or 'servant'), occurs some 30 times in NT, and the cognates *diakoneō* (to 'minister') and *diakonia* ('ministry') occur between them a further 70 times. In the majority of the 100 occurrences of the words there is no trace of a technical meaning relating to specialized functions in the church; in a few it is necessary to consider how far *diakonos* and its cognates have acquired such a connotation.

I. Derivation

Basically, *diakonos* is a servant, and often a table-servant, or waiter. In Hellenistic times it came also to represent certain cult and temple officials (see examples in *MM*), foreshadowing the Christian technical use. The more general sense is common in NT, whether for royal servants (Mt. 22:13) or for a servant of God (1 Thes. 3:2, TR). In a single passage Paul describes Epaphras as a 'deacon' of Christ and himself as a 'deacon' of the gospel and of the church (Col. 1:7, 23, 25). Others exercise a *diakonia* towards Paul (Acts 19:22; *cf.* Phm. 13 and perhaps Col. 4:7; Eph. 6:21), the context showing that they are his assistants in evangelistic work. To find here the origin of the later idea of the bishop with his deacon is straining language. In other words, *diakonia* is here being applied especially to preaching and pastoral work.

In NT, however, the word never quite loses its connection with the supply of material needs and service (*cf.*, *e.g.*, Rom. 15:25 in context; 2 Cor. 8:4). A waiter is a *diakonos* still (Jn. 2:5, 9); the table-waiting of Martha (Lk. 10:40) and of Peter's mother-in-law (Mk. 1:31) is *diakonia*. It is in this light that we are to see Christ's insistence that his coming was in order to minister (Mk. 10:45): significantly this claim is set in Lk. 22:26f. in the context of table-service. The

DAVID, CITY OF
See Jerusalem, Part 2.

DAVID, NAME OF
See Goliath, Part 2.

DAVID, SEPULCHRE OF
See Sepulchre of kings, Part 3.

DAY
See Calendar, Part 1.

DAY OF ATONEMENT
See Atonement, Day of, Part 1.

DAY OF MORDECAI
See Mordecai, Part 2.

DAY OF WRATH
See Wrath, Part 3.

DAY OF YAHWEH
See Salvation, Part 3.

DAYSMAN
See Mediator, Part 2.

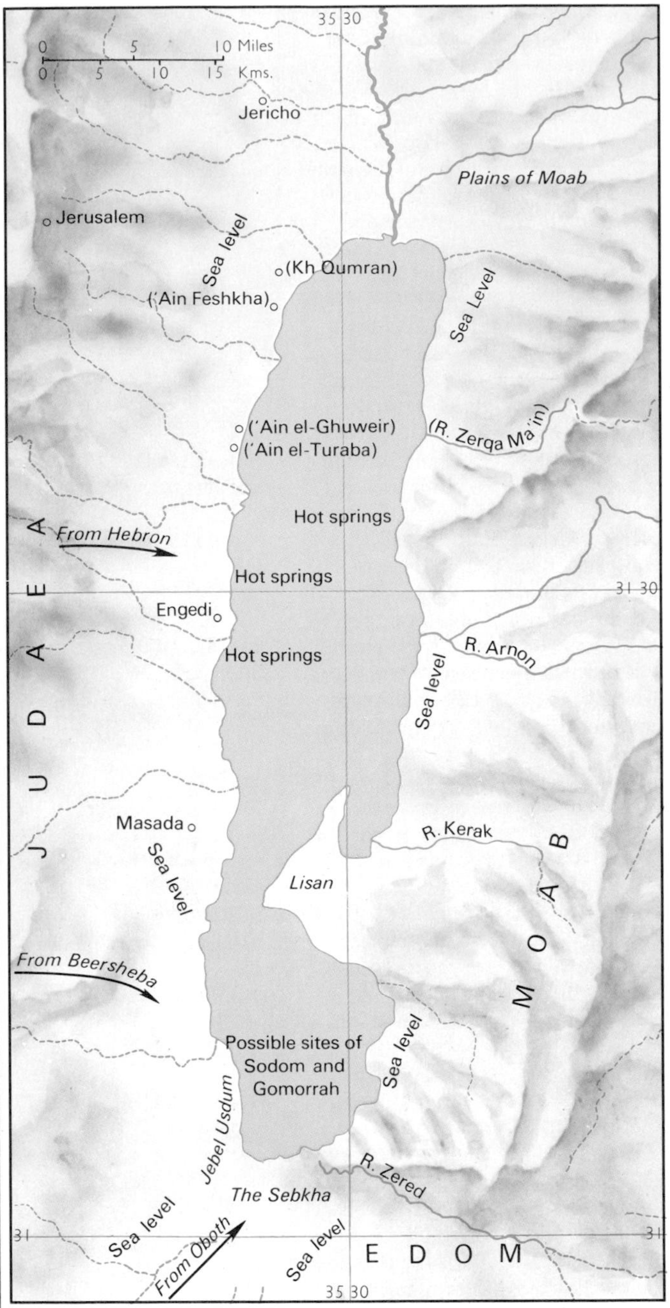

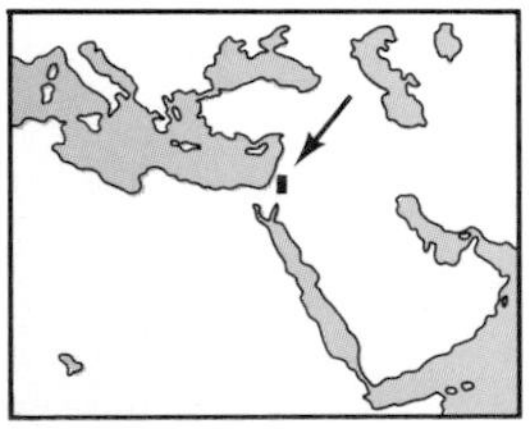

The Dead Sea, also called the Salt Sea or Sea of the Arabah.

Top right: Sections through the Dead Sea at the N basin and at the Lisan peninsula in the S.

Lord is the Deacon *par excellence*, the table-waiter of his people. And, as these passages show, 'deaconship' in this sense is a mark of his whole church.

II. The New Testament diaconate

As we have seen, there was contemporary analogy for 'deacons' as cult officials. When, therefore, we find the church greeted 'with the bishops and deacons' (Phil. 1:1) it is natural to see a reference to two particular classes within the church. It is true that Hort can see rather the 'ruling' and the 'serving' elements together making up the church, but it is doubtful if this could be applied to 1 Tim. 3, where

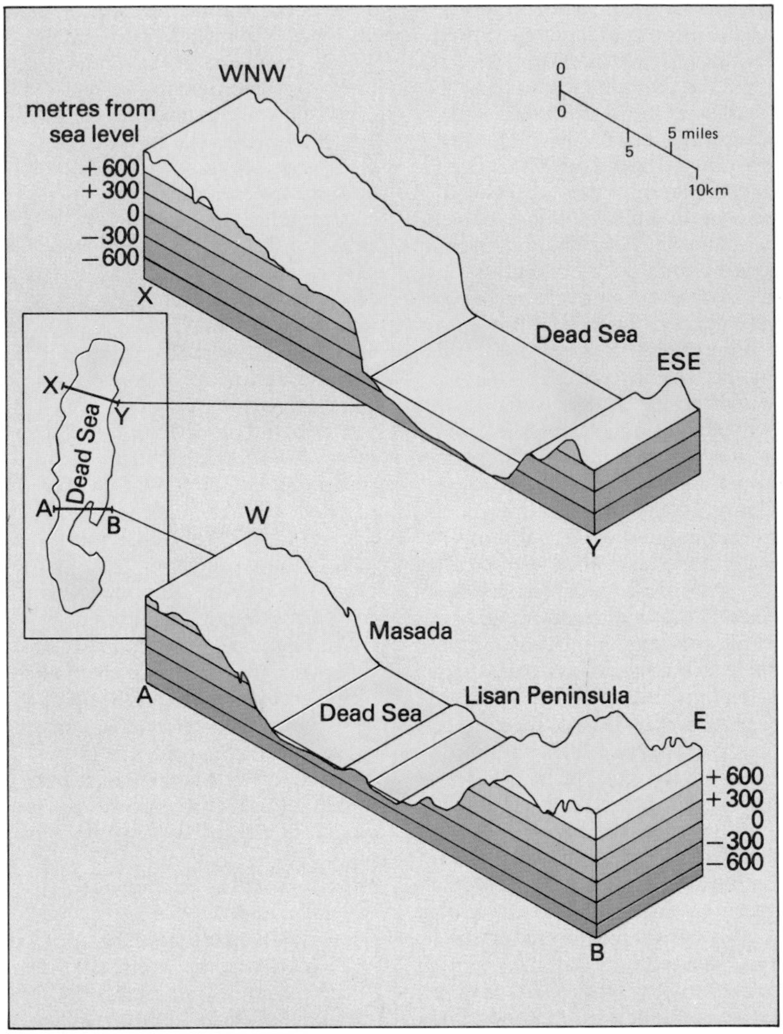

a list of qualifications for bishops is immediately followed by a parallel list for deacons: sobriety, straightforwardness, freedom from excess and greed, probity. These would be particularly appropriate for those with responsibilities in finance and administration, and the prominence of social service in the early church would make *diakonos* an especially suitable word for such people—the more so since the love feast, involving literal table-service, was a regular agency of charity. While *diakonia* is a mark of the whole church, it is also a special gift—parallel with prophecy and government, but distinct from generous giving—to be exercised by those who possess it (Rom. 12:7; 1 Pet. 4:11). And while any servant of Christ is rightly called a 'deacon', the term may be particularly applied to those who minister, like Phoebe (Rom. 16:1), in the ways mentioned. But whether the diaconate existed universally under this name, or whether, for instance, the 'helps' at Corinth (1 Cor. 12:28) were equivalent to the 'deacons' at Philippi, remains uncertain. There is little to suggest that in NT times the term 'deacon' is ever more than semi-technical, or that it has any connection with the Jewish *ḥazzān* (*SYNAGOGUE). Significantly, immediately after listing the qualifications for deacons, Paul returns to the general sense of the word in exhorting Timothy himself (1 Tim. 4:6. *Cf.* also 1 Pet. 4:10 with 4:11).

The account in Acts 6 of the appointment by the Jerusalem church of seven approved men to supervise the administration of the widows' fund is commonly taken as the formal institution of the diaconate. It is doubtful if this has much basis in language. Leaving aside unprovable theories which see the Seven as but the Hellenistic counterpart of the Twelve, we may note, first, that the Seven are never called 'deacons', and secondly, that while the cognate words are used they apply equally to the *diakonia* of the Word exercised by the Twelve (v. 4) and to that of the tables (whether for meals or money) exercised by the Seven (v. 2). Laying on of hands is too common in Acts to be seen as a special milestone here (*ORDINATION), and the careers of Stephen and Philip show that the Seven were not confined to table-service.

There is, however, weight in Lightfoot's argument that the position Luke gives to the incident reflects his view of its high significance. It is 'one of those representative facts of which the earlier part of his narrative is almost wholly made up' (*Philippians*[5], p. 188). The significance lies, however, not in the institution of an order in the ministerial hierarchy, but as the first example of that delegation of administrative and social responsibilities to those of appropriate character and gifts, which was to become typical of the Gentile churches, and the recognition of such duties as part of the ministry of Christ.

Ecclesiastical usage institutionalized and narrowed the NT conception. Early non-canonical literature recognizes a class of deacons without specifying their functions (*cf.* *1 Clement* 42; Ignatius, *Magnesians* 2. 1; *Trallians* 2. 3; 7. 3). Later literature shows the deacons undertaking functions such as attending the sick, which must have been part of Christian *diakonia* in apostolic times; but their duties in the Eucharist (*via* table-service at the communal meal?), and personal relationship with the monarchical bishop, become increasingly prominent. The occasional limitation of the diaconate to seven is probably due to deliberate archaizing.

BIBLIOGRAPHY. H. W. Beyer, *TDNT* 2, pp. 81–93; J. B. Lightfoot, *The Christian Ministry* (= *Philippians*[5], pp. 181ff.); F. J. A. Hort, *The Christian Ecclesia*, 1897, pp. 198ff.; A. M. Farrer in *The Apostolic Ministry*, ed. K. E. Kirk, 1946, especially pp. 142ff.; B. Reicke, *Diakonie, Festfreude und Zelos*, 1951, pp. 9ff.; K. Hess, *NIDNTT* 3, pp. 544–553. A.F.W.

DEACONESS. *Phoebe was *diakonos* of the church at Cenchreae (Rom. 16:1): a title rendered by AV 'servant', but by RSV, with greater probability, 'deaconess'.

Greek Fathers regularly read 1 Tim. 3:11 as 'Even so must *women* be grave, *etc.*' (similarly RSV), taking the qualities which follow as the requirements for women deacons rather than for deacon's wives. This gives a better sequence than AV ('Even so must their wives be grave', *etc.*), and perhaps more appropriateness: Theodore of Mopsuestia tellingly interprets 'not slanderers' as 'not babbling confidences received in their ministry' (ed. Swete, 2, p. 128).

About AD 111 Pliny, governor of Bithynia, reports that he has questioned under torture two maidservants who were called deaconesses (*ministrae*) concerning Christian rites (*Epistolae* 10. 96). 'Maidservant' here may denote their secular position, or their function in the Christian community: Pliny was doubtless looking for evidence of cannibalism.

Thereafter there seems no clear literary notice of deaconesses before the 3rd century *Didascalia*. Some have therefore doubted the existence of such an office in NT times. But, meticulous as early Christians were in observing the proprieties, many functions allotted to deaconesses in later literature (*e.g.* visiting women in pagan households) would also apply in apostolic times. The appointment of deaconesses, then, is *a priori* likely: and Lk. 8:2f. may be deeply significant. Their duties would be precisely analogous to those of deacons: they were, as our two NT passages suggest, simply 'female deacons'. (The later special word *diakonissa* would develop as the deacon's distinctive functions became liturgical.)

BIBLIOGRAPHY. Essays by C. H. Turner and W. Collins in *The Ministry of Women*, 1919; J. G. Davies, *JEH* 14, 1962, pp. 1ff.

A.F.W.

DEAD SEA. OT: 'Salt Sea' (Gn. 14:3), 'Eastern Sea' (Ezk. 47:18), 'Sea of the Arabah' (Dt. 4:49); classical: *Asphaltites*, later 'Dead Sea'; Arabic: 'Sea of Lot'.

The great rift valley reaches its deepest point at the Dead Sea basin. The surface of the water is on average 427 m below sea-level, and the deepest point of the bed some 433 m lower still. The Sea is about 77 km long and stretches from the sheer cliffs of Moab some 10 or 14 km across to the hills of Judah. On this W side is a narrow shore bounded by many terraces, the remains of earlier beaches. Except for a few springs (*e.g.* 'Ain Feshkha and Engedi, *cf.* Ct. 1:14), the Judaean coast is arid and bare. Four main streams feed the Sea from the E: the Mojin (Arnon), Zerqa Ma'in, Kerak and the Zered. The rate of evaporation is so great (temperature reaches 43°C in summer) that the inflow of these waters and the Jordan serves only to keep the sea-level constant. The annual rainfall is about 5 cm. Luxuriant vegetation is to be found where the rivers flow in or where

Opposite page: The salt-encrusted shore of the Dead Sea. (JLH)

there are fresh-water springs. The oases around the Kerak and the Zered delta show how fertile this basin could be (*cf.* Gn. 13:10), as Ezekiel saw in his vision of a river of pure water flowing from Jerusalem to sweeten the Salt Sea (Ezk. 47:8–12).

Until the mid-19th century it was possible to ford the sea from Lisan ('tongue'), a peninsula which projects from beside the Kerak to within 3 km of the opposite shore. Traces of a Roman road remain. Masada, an almost impregnable fortress built by the Maccabees and by Herod, guarded this road on the edge of Judaea. S of the Lisan, the sea is very shallow, gradually disappearing into the salty marsh (Zp. 2:9) called the Sebkha.

The concentrated chemical deposits (salt, potash, magnesium, and calcium chlorides and bromide, 25% of the water), which give the Dead Sea its buoyancy and its fatal effects on fish, may well have been ignited during an earthquake and caused the rain of brimstone and fire destroying Sodom and Gomorrah. Lot's wife, stopping to look back, was overwhelmed by the falling salt, while her family, hastening on, escaped (Gn. 19:15–28). Archaeological evidence suggests a break of several centuries in the sedentary occupation from early in the 2nd millennium BC. A hill of salt (*Jebel Usdum*, Mt Sodom) at the SW corner is eroded into strange forms, including pillars which are known as 'Lot's Wife' by local Arabs (*cf.* Wisdom 10:7). Salt was obtained from the shore (Ezk. 47:11), and the Nabataeans traded in the bitumen which floats on the surface (see P. C. Hammond, *BA* 22, 1959, pp. 40–48). Throughout the OT period the sea acted as a barrier between Judah and Moab and Edom (*cf.* 2 Ch. 20:1–30), although it may have been used by small trading boats, as it was in Roman times. (*PLAIN, CITIES OF THE; *PATRIARCHAL AGE; *ARCHAEOLOGY; *JORDAN; *ARABAH; *DEAD SEA SCROLLS.)

BIBLIOGRAPHY. G. A. Smith, *Historical Geography of the Holy Land*, 1931, pp. 499–516; D. Baly, *The Geography of the Bible*, 1974.

A.R.M.

DEAD SEA SCROLLS. A popular name given to collections of MS material found in a number of regions W of the Dead Sea in 1947 and the years following. They fall for the most part into three groups which have no relation one with another.

I. Qumran texts

Most important of the Dead Sea Scrolls are those which have been discovered since 1947 in 11 caves in and around the Wadi Qumran, NW of the Dead Sea. The MS contents of these caves are, in the main, all that remain of the library of a Jewish community which had its headquarters in the neighbouring building complex now called Khirbet Qumran. The community appears to have occupied this place during the two centuries preceding AD 70 (with a break of 30 years between *c.* 34 and 4 BC).

This community, in all probability a branch of the *Essenes, arose among the pious Jews (*ḥᵃsîḏîm*) who maintained their covenant-loyalty unblemished under the persecution in the days of Antiochus Epiphanes (175–164 BC). They could not accept as the will of God the ensuing settlement which gave the high priesthood as well as the chief civil and military power to the Hasmonean dynasty. Under the leadership of one whom they called the 'Teacher of Righteousness' they withdrew to the wilderness of Judaea, where they organized themselves as the righteous remnant of Israel, 'a people prepared for the Lord'. They expected the early arrival of the new age which would bring the present 'epoch of wickedness' to an end. They endeavoured, by diligent study and practice of the law, to win divine favour for themselves and expiate the errors of their misguided fellow Israelites; they also expected to be the executors of divine judgment on the ungodly at the end-time.

The end-time, they believed, would be marked by the rise of three figures foretold in OT prophecy—the prophet like Moses of Dt. 18:15ff., the Davidic Messiah and a great priest of Aaron's line. This priest would be head of state in the new age, taking precedence even over the Davidic Messiah. The Davidic Messiah would be a warrior-prince, leading the faithful hosts of Israel to annihilating victory over the 'sons of darkness' (chief among whom were the Gentile forces of the Kittim, probably the Romans). The prophet would communicate the will of God to his people at the end of the age, as Moses had done at the beginning of their history.

The men of Qumran refused to acknowledge the high priests of Jerusalem during the 'epoch of wickedness', partly because they did not belong to the legitimate house of Zadok (deposed under Antiochus Epiphanes) and partly because they were morally unfit for their sacred office. One of them, evidently a Hasmonean priest-king, and perhaps to be identified with Jonathan, brother and successor of Judas Maccabaeus, is described as the 'Wicked Priest' *par excellence*, because of the violent hostility which he showed to the Teacher of Righteousness and his followers. The community preserved in its own ranks the framework of Zadokite priests and Levites, ready to restore a worthy sacrificial worship in the purified Temple of the new Jerusalem (which was no heavenly city, but the old Jerusalem renewed). But until that time of restoration, the community constituted a living temple, the general membership being the holy place and the inner council the holy of holies, with praising lips and obedient lives as acceptable sacrifices.

The community library, of which some 500 documents have been identified (the great majority in a sadly fragmentary condition), comprised biblical and non-biblical writings. About 100 scrolls are books of the OT in Heb.; among these all the OT books are represented (some of them several times over), with the exception of Esther. Whether this exception is significant or accidental is difficult to say. These biblical MSS date from the last few centuries BC and the earlier part of the 1st century AD. They exhibit at least three distinct text-types of Hebrew Scripture—the proto-Massoretic type (probably of Babylonian provenance) from which the received Hebrew text is descended; the text underlying the LXX (probably of Egyptian provenance); and a text (probably of Palestinian provenance) closely related to the Samaritan Pentateuch. Some exhibit a mixed type of text; *e.g.* Cave 4 has yielded a MS of Numbers (4Q Num.[b]) whose text is midway between the Samaritan and LXX types, and one of Samuel (4Q Sam.[b]) which has been thought to exhibit a text superior to *MT* and LXX alike. Another MS of Samuel from the same cave (4Q Sam.[a]) is of special interest; it exhibits a text not only close to that underlying LXX but also standing closer than *MT* does to the text of Samuel used by the Chronicler. The discovery of these biblical MSS has reduced by 1,000 years and more the gap separating the time of writing from the oldest surviving copies, and has made immense contributions to the textual history of the OT. (*TEXTS AND VERSIONS, **1. III**).

Some LXX fragments have also been found in the Qumran caves, and some targumic literature—notably an Aramaic targum of Job from Cave 11. A few books of the Apocrypha have also been identified, including Tobit (in Aramaic and Heb.), Ecclesiasticus (in Heb.), the *Epistle of Jeremiah* (in Gk.), *1 Enoch* (in Aramaic) and *Jubilees* (in Heb.).

The non-biblical scrolls, taken in conjunction with the evidence provided by the excavation of Khirbet Qumran and a subsidiary building near 'Ain Feshkha, 3 km to the S, give us welcome information about the beliefs and practices of the community. We must bear in mind, of course, that not every book in a community's library reflects the community's ideas and behaviour. But much of the Qumran literature presents a self-consistent picture on which we can reasonably rely for some conception of life at Qumran.

The Qumran community practised rigorous self-discipline. Entrance into the community was hedged about by strict conditions, including a testing novitiate. Their interpretation of the law was severe, more so than that of the severest Pharisaic school. Indeed, it is probably the Pharisees who are referred to in the Qumran literature as 'seekers after smooth things' (*cf.* Is. 30:10). The men of Qumran had regular ceremonial ablutions, they held fellowship meals, admission to which was closely guarded, they followed a calendar similar to that prescribed in the book of *Jubilees*. They interpreted the hope of Israel in apocalyptic terms, and believed that they themselves had an important part to play in the realization of that hope. They interpreted prophetic Scripture as referring to persons and events of their own days and the days which lay immediately ahead. This interpretation finds clearest expression in the biblical commentaries (*pᵉšārîm*), several of which have been recovered from the Qumran caves. According to the Qumran exegetes, the prophets knew by revelation what God was going to do at the end-time, but they did not know when the end-time would come. This additional revelation was given by God to the Teacher of Righteousness, who communicated it to his disciples. They had accordingly an insight into the meaning of the prophetical oracles which was denied to other Jews, and they were conscious of the favour which God had bestowed on them by initiating them into the mysteries of his purpose and the time and manner of its fulfilment.

The expectations of the Qumran community, however, were not fulfilled in the way for which they had looked. They appear to have abandoned their headquarters during the war of AD 66–73; it was probably at that time that their books were stored for safety in the surrounding caves. What happened to the survivors of the community is obscure, but it seems likely that some at least of them made common cause with the refugee church of Jerusalem.

Resemblances have been traced between the Qumran community and the early church in regard to their eschatological outlook, remnant consciousness, biblical exegesis and religious practices. But there are important differences to set against these resemblances. Their ceremonial ablutions and fellowship meals did not have the sacramental significance of Christian baptism and the Eucharist. The early Christians, like Jesus himself, mixed freely with their fellows in the common ways of life, instead of forming ascetic communities in the wilderness. The NT presents Jesus as Prophet, Priest and Prince of the house of David in his single person, instead of distributing these offices among three distinct figures, as was done in Qumran eschatology. And indeed it is Jesus in every respect who gives Christianity its uniqueness. The Teacher of Righteousness was a great leader and teacher, but he was no Messiah or Saviour, not even in his followers' eyes. Jesus was to the early Christians all that the Teacher of Righteousness was to the Qumran community, and much more—Messiah and Saviour, Servant of the Lord and Son of man. When the Teacher of Righteousness died (or, in Qumran idiom, 'was gathered in'—an expression which suggests natural death), his followers *may* have expected him to rise from the dead before the general resurrection of the end-time (though this is very doubtful); certainly none of them ever claimed that he did so.

The copper scroll from Cave 3 has probably nothing to do with the Qumran community. It is more likely that it belonged to a Zealot band which was based on Qumran during the war of AD 66–73; it appears to contain (in code) an inventory of temple treasure, divided into 61 *caches* in Jerusalem and the district to the E and S.

II. Texts of the Bar-kokhba war

In caves in the Wadi Murabba'at, about 18 km S of Qumran, a quantity of MS material was found around 1952. Most of this belonged to the period when these caves were occupied by an outpost of the army of Bar-kokhba, leader of the second Jewish revolt against Rome (AD 132–5). The documents included letters written to Bar-kokhba, and two letters written by him, from which it appeared that his proper patronymic was Ben-Kosebah; he calls himself 'Simeon Ben-Kosebah, prince of Israel'. (The title Bar-kokhba, 'son of the star', was due to Rabbi Akiba's hailing him as the 'star' of Nu. 24:17, in other words the Davidic Messiah.) Many fragmentary biblical MSS of this period were found in the caves, all of them exhibiting a 'proto-Massoretic' type of text.

About the same time as the Murabba'at caves were explored, further MSS of the Bar-kokhba period were discovered in the Naḥal Ḥever, S of En-gedi. These included fragments of Heb. Scripture and a fragmentary copy of a Gk. version of the Minor Prophets, showing a text similar to that used by Justin Martyr (*c.* AD 150). This version has been tentatively identified by D. Barthélemy with Origen's *Quinta*.

Similar discoveries were subsequently made in three other wadis in the same area. Here too were caves which were used as headquarters by contingents of Bar-kokhba's guerrilla forces. The documents found in them included two scroll fragments inscribed with Ex. 13:1–16 and a small fragment containing parts of seven lines of Ps. 15.

III. Khirbet Mird

From the ruined site of Khirbet Mird (formerly a Christian monastery), N of the Kidron valley, MSS of great interest were unearthed about 1950 by members of the Ta'amire tribe of bedouin (the same tribe as was responsible for

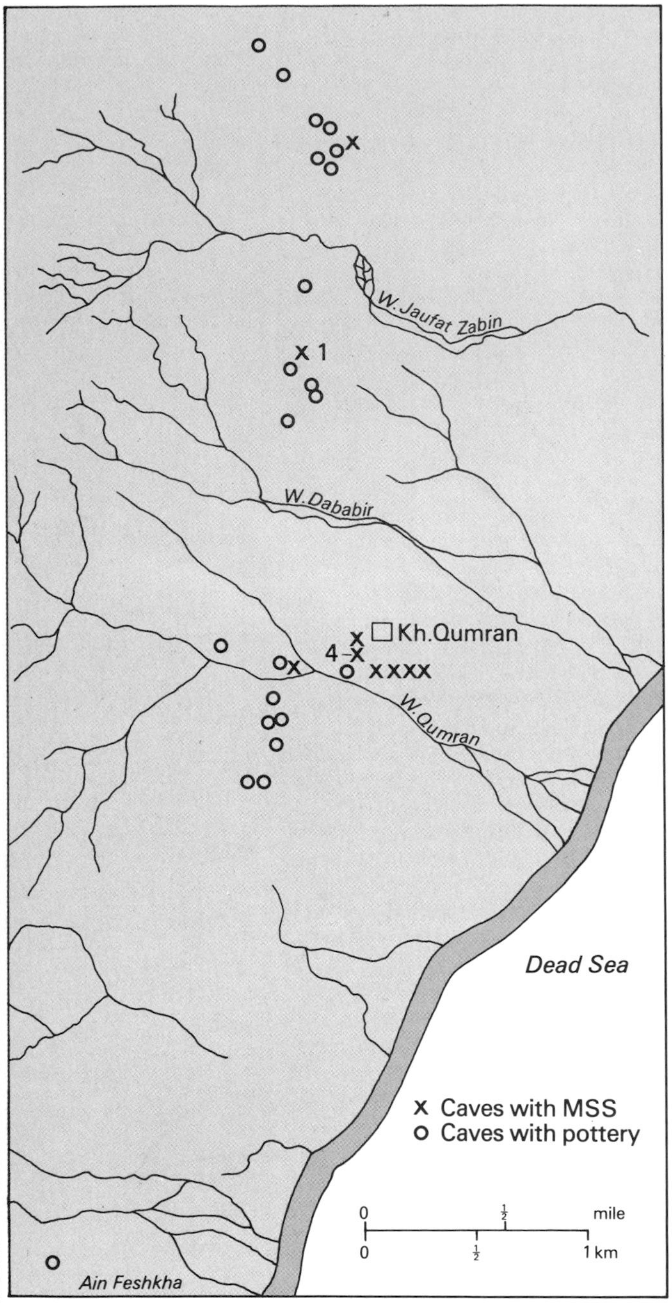

The Qumran area, showing location of the caves in which pottery and manuscripts have been found.

■ **DEAL**
See Weights and measures, Part 3.

the earliest Qumran discoveries). These were of much later date than the MSS found at Qumran and Murabba'at. They include papyrus fragments of private letters in Arabic from the 7th and 8th centuries, a Syr. letter on papyrus written by a Christian monk, a fragment of the *Andromache* of Euripides and a number of biblical texts in Gk. and Palestinian Syriac. The Gk. biblical texts included fragments of uncial codices of Wisdom, Mark, John and Acts, to be dated between the 5th and 8th centuries; those in Palestinian Syriac (many of which were palimpsests) included fragments of Joshua, Luke, John, Acts and Colossians.

BIBLIOGRAPHY. M. Burrows, *The Dead Sea Scrolls*, 1955, and *More Light on the Dead Sea Scrolls*, 1958; F. M. Cross, *The Ancient Library of Qumran and Modern Biblical Studies*, 1958; J. T. Milik, *Ten Years of Discovery in the Wilderness of Judaea*, 1959; F. F. Bruce, *Second Thoughts on the Dead Sea Scrolls*³, 1966; *The Teacher of Righteousness in the Qumran Texts*, 1957, and *Biblical Exegesis in the Qumran Texts*, 1960; A. Dupont-Sommer, *The Essene Writings from Qumran*, 1961; G. Vermes, *The Dead Sea Scrolls in English*, 1962; E. Lohse, *Die Texte aus Qumran: Hebräisch und Deutsch*, 1964; A. R. C. Leaney, *The Rule of Qumran and its Meaning*, 1966; R. de Vaux, *Archaeology and the Dead Sea Scrolls*, 1973; J. A. Sanders, 'The Dead Sea Scrolls—A Quarter Century of Study', *BA* 36, 1973, pp. 110ff.; G. Vermes, *The Dead Sea Scrolls: Qumran in Perspective*, 1977; D. Barthélemy and J. T. Milik (ed.), *Discoveries in the Judaean Desert*, 1955ff.; J. Carmignac (ed.), *Revue de Qumran*, 1958ff.

F.F.B.

DEATH. From one point of view death is the most natural of things: 'it is appointed for men to die once' (Heb. 9:27). It may be accepted without rebellion: 'Let us also go, that we may die with him' (Jn. 11:16). From another, it is the most unnatural of things. It is the penalty for sin (Rom. 6:23), and it is to be feared as such. Both points of view are to be found in the Bible, and neither should be overlooked. Death is a biological necessity, but men do not die simply as the animals die.

I. Physical death

Death seems to be necessary for bodies constituted as ours are. Physical decay and ultimate dissolution are inescapable. Yet the Bible speaks of death as the result of sin. God said to Adam, 'in the day that you eat of it you will die' (Gn. 2:17). Paul tells us that 'sin came into the world through one man and death through sin' (Rom. 5:12), and again that 'the wages of sin is death' (Rom. 6:23). Yet when we look more closely into the matter we see that Adam did not die physically on the day that he disobeyed God. And in Rom. 5 and 6 Paul is contrasting the death that came about through Adam's sin with the life that Christ brings men. Now the possession of eternal life does not cancel out physical death. It is opposed to a spiritual state, not to a physical event. The inference that we draw from all this is that that death which is the result of sin is more than bodily death.

But with this we must take the other thought that the scriptural passages which connect sin and death do not qualify death. We would not understand from them that something other than the usual meaning attached to the word. Perhaps we should understand that mortality was the result of Adam's sin, and that the penalty includes both physical and spiritual aspects. But we do not know enough about Adam's pre-fallen condition to say anything about it. If his body was like ours, then it was mortal. If it was not, we have no means of knowing what it was like, and whether it was mortal or not.

It seems better to understand death as something that involves the whole man. Man does not die as a body. He dies as a man, in the totality of his being. He dies as a spiritual and physical being. And the Bible does not put a sharp line of demarcation between the two aspects. Physical death, then, is a fit symbol of, and expression of, and unity with, the deeper death that sin inevitably brings.

II. Spiritual death

That death is a divine penalty. We have already noticed that Rom. 6:23 regards death as 'the wages' of sin, *i.e.* as the due reward for sin. Paul can speak of certain sinners who know 'God's decree that those who do such things deserve to die' (Rom. 1:32). It is the thought of God's decree that underlies John's reference to the 'mortal sin' (1 Jn. 5:16). This is a very important truth. It enables us to see the full horror of death. And at the same time, paradoxically, it gives us hope. Men are not caught up in a web woven by blind fate, so that, once having sinned, nothing can ever be done about it. God is over the whole process, and if he has decreed that death is the penalty of sin, he has also determined to give life eternal to sinful men.

Sometimes the NT emphasizes the serious consequences of sin by referring to 'the second death' (Jude 12; Rev. 2:11, *etc.*). This is a rabbinic expression which signifies eternal perdition. It is to be understood along with passages wherein our Lord spoke of 'eternal fire pre-

pared for the devil and his angels' (Mt. 25:41), 'eternal punishment' (set in contrast to 'eternal life', Mt. 25:46), and the like. The final state of impenitent man is variously described as death, punishment, being lost, *etc*. Obviously it would be unwise to equate it with any one of them. But equally obviously on the Bible view it is a state to be regarded with horror.

Sometimes the objection is made that this is inconsistent with the view of God as a loving God. There is a profound mystery here, but at least it can be said that the objection, as commonly stated, overlooks the fact that death is a state as well as an event. 'To set the mind on the flesh is death,' writes Paul (Rom. 8:6). He does not say that the mind of the flesh will cause death. He says that it *is* death. He adds that it 'is hostile to God; it does not submit to God's law, indeed it cannot'. The same truth is put in a different way when John says, 'He who does not love abides in death' (1 Jn. 3:14). When we have grasped the truth that death is a state, we see the impossibility of the impenitent being saved. Salva-

The oldest manuscript of a complete book of the OT, the scroll of Isaiah (1Q Is[a]) found in cave 1 at Qumran, by the Dead Sea, 1947. Is. 38:8–40:28 is shown. Leather scroll, 27 cm × 7·26 m. Qumran. c. 100 BC. (JCT)

Two parts of a copper sheet, c. 2·5 m long, found hidden in a cave (no. 3) at Khirbet Qumran. The inscription engraved on it lists the hiding-places of gold and silver vessels and incense. Late 1st cent. AD. (JCT)

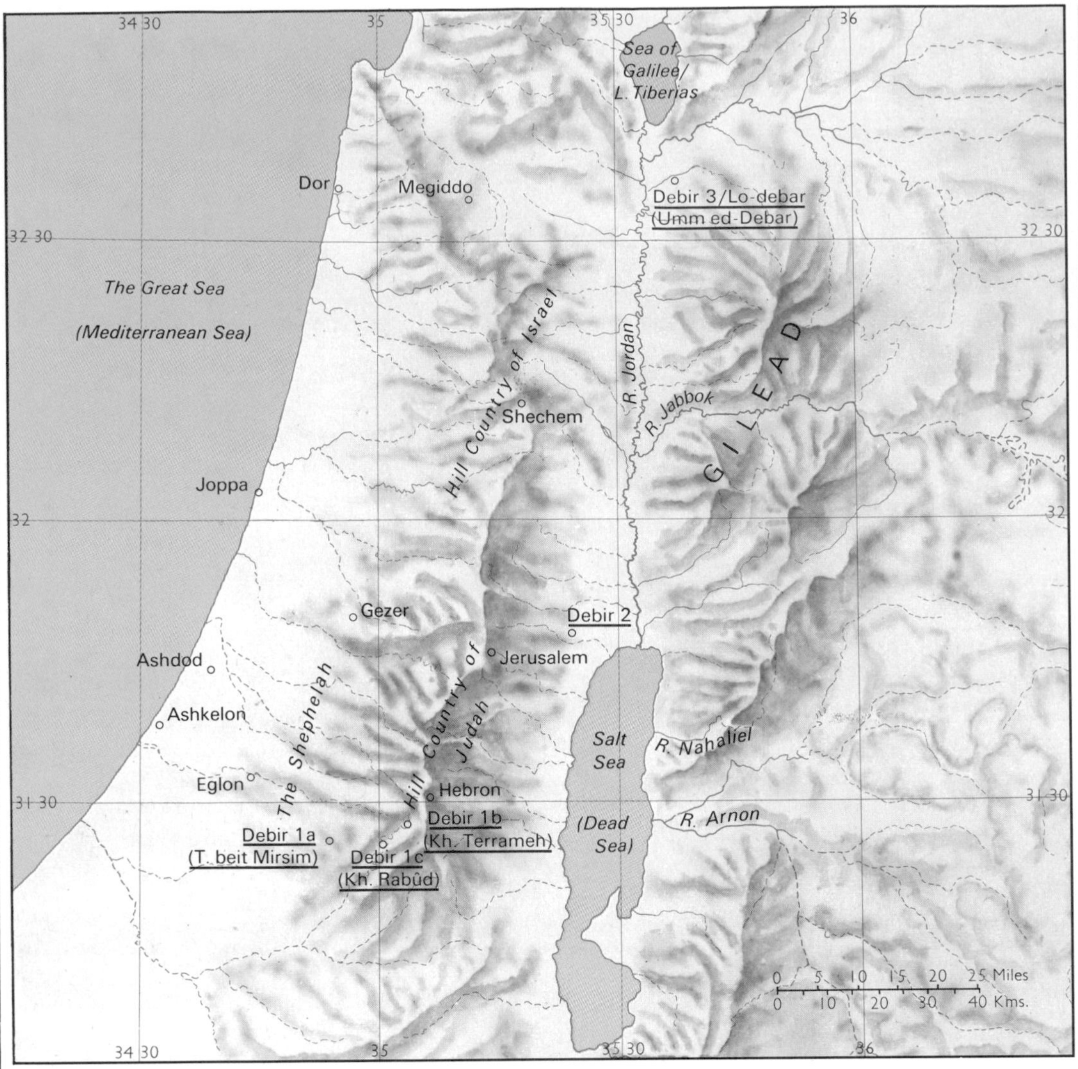

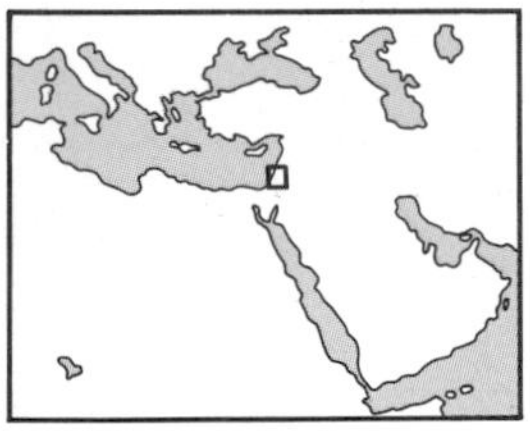

Debir: possible locations.

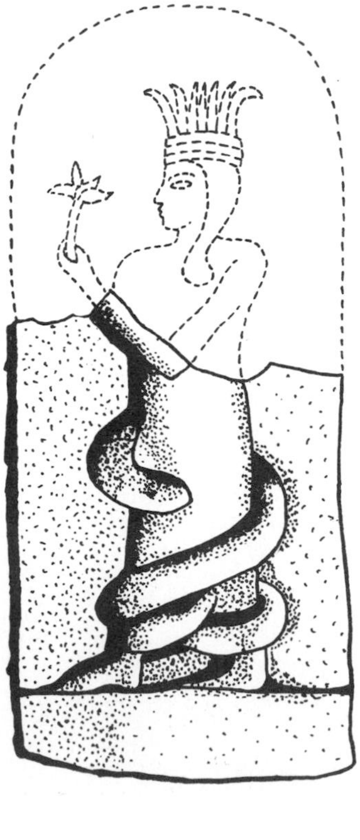

A reconstruction of a stele, showing a serpent goddess, found at Tell beit Mirsim, one of the locations proposed for Debir.

tion for such is a contradiction in terms. For salvation a man must pass from death into life (Jn. 5:24).

III. Victory over death

An interesting feature of NT teaching on death is that the emphasis is on life. If we look up a concordance we find that in most places *nekros* ('dead') is used of resurrection from the dead or the like. The Scripture faces death, as it faces all reality. But its interest is in life, and death is treated more or less incidentally as that from which men are saved. Christ took upon him our nature, 'that through death he might destroy him who has the power of death, that is, the devil' (Heb. 2:14). The devil's power is always regarded as subject to God's overruling (Jb. 2:6; Lk. 12:5, *etc.*). He is no absolute disposer of death. Nevertheless death, the negation of life, is his proper sphere. And Christ came to put an end to death. It was through death, as the Hebrews passage indicates, that he defeated Satan. It was through death that he put away our sin. 'The death he died he died to sin, once for all' (Rom. 6:10). Apart from Christ, death is the supreme enemy, the symbol of our alienation from God, the ultimate horror. But Christ has used death to deliver men from death. He died that men may live. It is significant that the NT can speak of believers as 'sleeping' rather that as 'dying' (*e.g.* 1 Thes. 4:14). Jesus bore the full horror of death. Therefore for those who are 'in Christ' death has been transformed so that it is no more than sleep.

The extent of the victory over death that Christ won is indicated by his resurrection. 'Christ being raised from the dead will never die again; death no longer has dominion over him' (Rom. 6:9). The resurrection is the great triumphal event, and the whole of the NT note of victory originates here. Christ is 'the Author of life' (Acts 3:15), 'Lord both of the dead and of the living' (Rom. 14:9), 'the Word of life' (1 Jn. 1:1). His victory over death is complete. And his victory is made available to his people. Death's destruction is certain (1 Cor. 15:26, 54ff.; Rev. 21:4). The second death has no power over the believer (Rev. 2:11; 20:6). In keeping with this the NT understands eternal life not as the immortality of the soul, but in terms of the resurrection of the body. Nothing could more graphically illustrate the finality and the completeness of death's defeat.

Not only is there a glorious future, there is a glorious present. The believer has already passed out of death and into life (Jn. 5:24; 1 Jn. 3:14). He is 'free from the law of sin and death' (Rom. 8:2). Death cannot separate him from God (Rom. 8:38f.). Jesus said, 'If any one keeps my word, he will never see death' (Jn. 8:51). Such words do not deny the reality of biological death. Rather they point us to the truth that the death of Jesus means that the believer has passed altogether out of the state which is death. He is brought into a new state, which is aptly characterized as life. He will in due course pass through the gateway we call death. But the sting has been drawn. The death of Jesus means victory over death for his followers.

BIBLIOGRAPHY. C. S. Lewis,

Miracles, 1947, pp. 150ff.; J. Pelikan, *The Shape of Death*, 1962; K. Rahner, *On the Theology of Death*, 1961; Leon Morris, *The Wages of Sin*, 1955; M. Paternoster, *Thou Art There Also: God, Death, and Hell*, 1967. L.M.

DEBIR (Heb. d^{e}*ḇîr*). **1.** A city on the S side of the Judaean hills, held by Anakim before the Israelite invasion, then by Kenizzites (Jos. 10:38; 11:21; 15:15 = Jdg. 1:11). A levitical town (Jos. 21:15). In Jos. 15:49 it is equated with Kiriath-sanna; since the Achsah story recalls Kiriath-sepher as the Canaanite name, it has been argued that *sanna* is a mis-spelling or 'Debir' is an incorrect gloss (M. Noth, *Josua*[2], *ad loc.*, and *JPOS* 15, 1935, pp. 44–47; H. M. Orlinsky, *JBL* 58, 1939, p. 255). The leading identifications are: (*a*) Tell beit Mirsim, 20 km WSW of Hebron (W. F. Albright, *BASOR* 15, 1924; 47, 1932; *AASOR* 17, 21); a commanding site, but facing N rather than S; occupied from the Hyksos period to the end of the Monarchy, but authorities differ as to the duration and significance of breaks (S. Yeivin, *Israelite Conquest of Canaan*, 1971, p. 47; K. M. Kenyon, *Archaeology in the Holy Land*[3], 1970, pp. 214, 308; *LOB*, p. 199). (*b*) Kh. Terrameh, 8 km SW of Hebron (M. Noth, *JPOS* 15, 1935, pp. 48ff.), is a feasible location but rather near Hebron; it lacks archaeological proof. (*c*) Kh. Rabbud, 13 km SW of Hebron (K. Galling, *ZDPV* 70, 1954, pp. 135ff.); excavated by M. Kochavi in 1969; occupied from Late Bronze Age to 586 BC (*Tel Aviv* 1, 1974, pp. 2–33).

2. On the N border of Judah (Jos. 15:7); probably above the Wadi Debr, which is the lower part of the Wadi Mukallik, or near Tughret ed-Debr, S of the Ascent of *Adummim. See *GTT*, p. 137.

3. In the N of Gad (Jos. 13:26) (*MT Lidebir*); probably Umm ed-Debar, 16 km S of Lake Tiberias; *LOB*, p. 232.

4. The Canaanite king of *Eglon who fought against Joshua (Jos. 10:3). The kings are named only in that text; there is no reason to see in it any evidence that the city of Debir was involved in the alliance. J.P.U.L.

DEBORAH (Heb. d^{e}*ḇôrâ*, 'bee'). **1.** Rebekah's nurse, whose death at Bethel is recorded in Gn. 35:8;

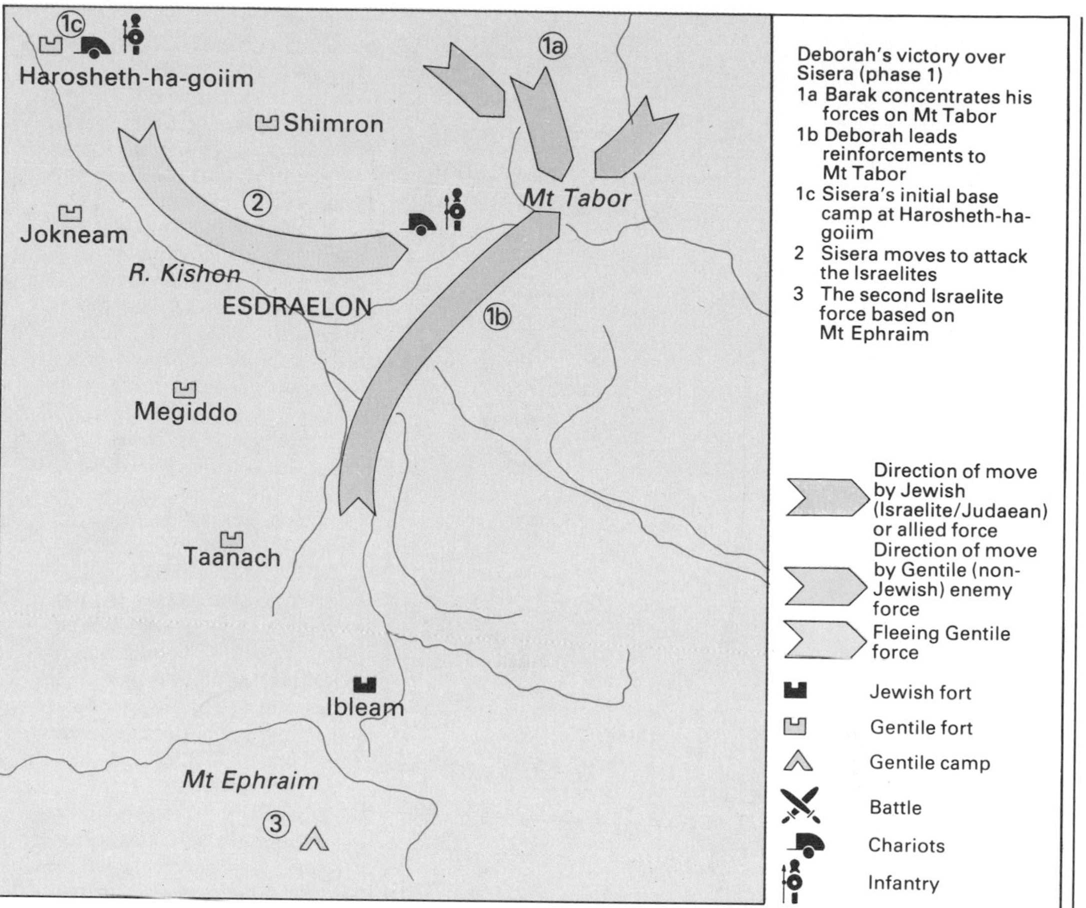

Deborah's victory over Sisera (phase 1)
1a Barak concentrates his forces on Mt Tabor
1b Deborah leads reinforcements to Mt Tabor
1c Sisera's initial base camp at Harosheth-ha-goiim
2 Sisera moves to attack the Israelites
3 The second Israelite force based on Mt Ephraim

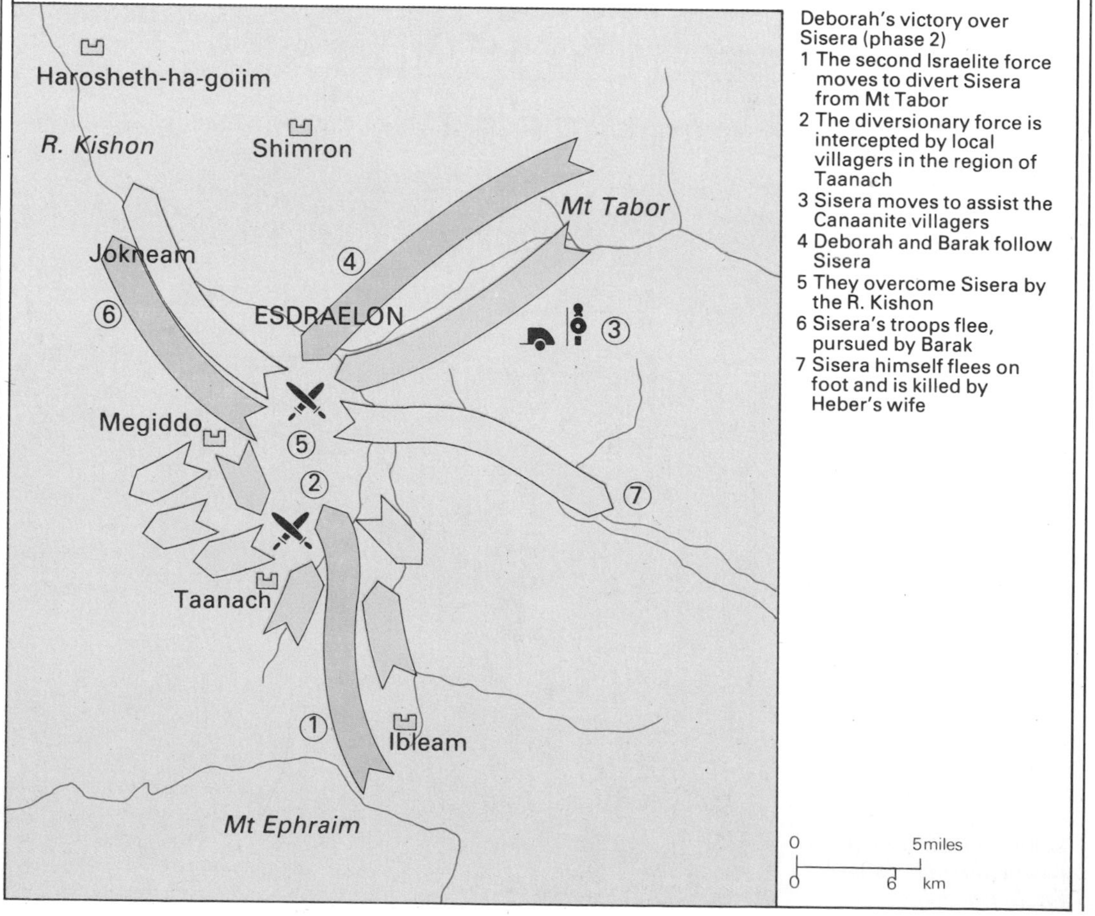

Deborah's victory over Sisera (phase 2)
1 The second Israelite force moves to divert Sisera from Mt Tabor
2 The diversionary force is intercepted by local villagers in the region of Taanach
3 Sisera moves to assist the Canaanite villagers
4 Deborah and Barak follow Sisera
5 They overcome Sisera by the R. Kishon
6 Sisera's troops flee, pursued by Barak
7 Sisera himself flees on foot and is killed by Heber's wife

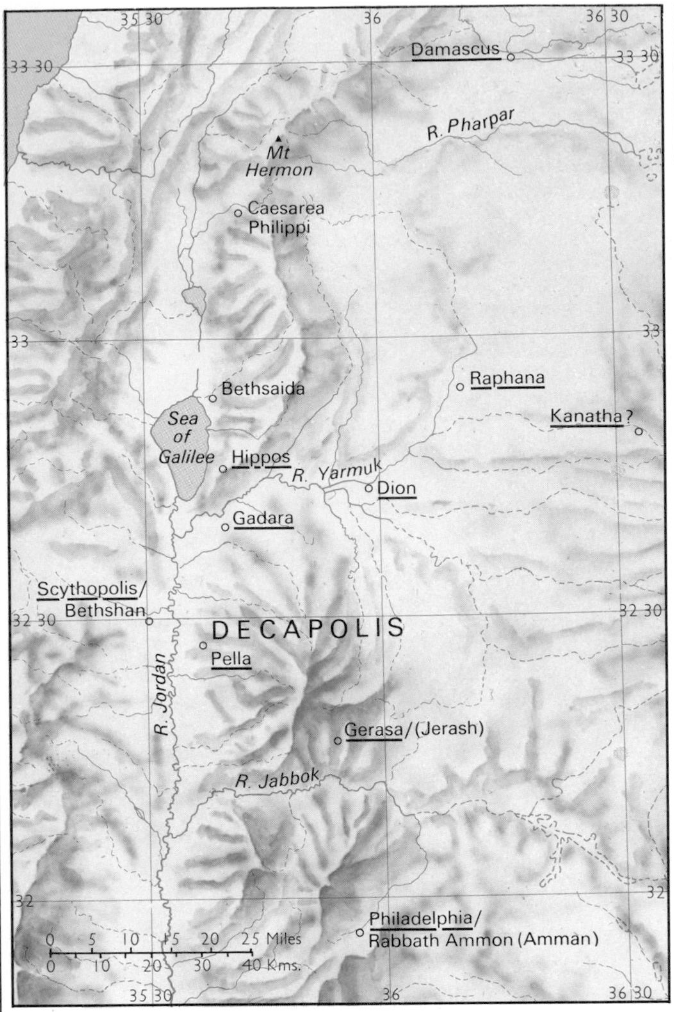

the tree beneath which she was buried was known as Allon-bacuth, 'the oak (or terebinth) of weeping'.

2. A prophetess who appears in the list of judges of Israel (*c.* 1125 BC). According to Jdg. 4:4ff., she had her headquarters under 'the palm tree of Deborah' between Ramah and Bethel, and was consulted there by Israelites from various tribes who wished to have their disputes settled—either disputes which proved too intractable for their local judges or intertribal disputes. She was thus a judge in the ordinary, non-military sense of the word, and it was probably because of her judicial and charismatic renown that the Israelites had recourse to her in the straits to which they were reduced under Sisera's oppression. She commanded * Barak to take the field as Israelite commander-in-chief against Sisera, and consented to accompany him at his insistence; the result was the crushing defeat of Sisera at the battle of Kishon (Jdg. 4:15; 5:19ff.).

She is called (Jdg. 4:4) the wife of Lappidoth (lit. 'torches'), and she is described (Jdg. 5:7) as 'a mother in Israel'. It has been argued that this last phrase means 'a metropolis in Israel' (*cf.* 2 Sa. 20:19), and that the reference is to the city of Daberath (Jos. 21:28; 1 Ch. 6:72), modern Debûriyeh at the W foot of Mt Tabor; but there is nothing in the narrative or in the poem to prepare us for the prominence which would thus suddenly be given to such an obscure place.

The song of Deborah (Jdg. 5:2–31a) has been preserved from the 12th century BC with its language practically unmodernized, and is thus one of the most archaic passages in the OT. It was evidently composed on the morrow of the victory which it celebrates, and is an important source of information on tribal relations in Israel at the time. It may be divided into eight sections: an exordium of praise (vv. 2–3); the invocation of Yahweh (4–5); the desolation under the oppressors (6–8); the mustering of the tribes (9–18); the battle of Kishon (19–23); the death of Sisera (24–27); the description of Sisera's mother awaiting his return (28–30); and the epilogue (31a). It is from the song, rather than from the prose narrative of ch. 4, that we learn what precisely brought about Sisera's defeat: a cloudburst flooded the watercourse of Kishon and swept away the Canaanite chariotry (21), throwing the army into confusion and making it an easy prey for Barak's men.

The vivid and moving description of Sisera's mother (28ff.) has been felt to confirm the feminine authorship of the song; if it betrays

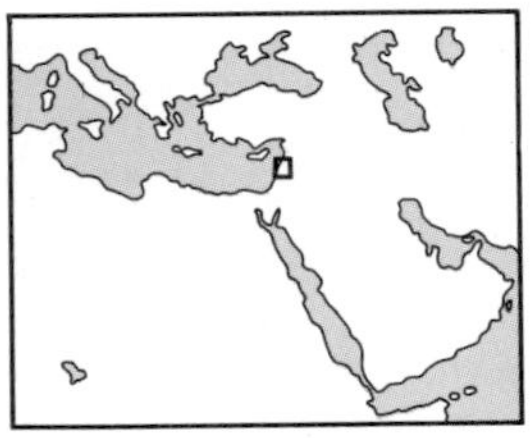

Decapolis, the Greek name for the league of ten Hellenized cities and their territories. Cities underlined are the ten named by Pliny.

Hippos, one of the ten cities (Decapolis) around the Sea of Galilee. (RP)

sympathy of a sort, it is not a compassionate sympathy.

Deborah is apostrophized in the song not only in v. 12 but probably also in v. 7, where the repeated Heb. *qamtî* may be understood not as the normal first person singular ('I arose') but as an archaic second person singular ('thou didst arise'); *cf.* RSV.

BIBLIOGRAPHY. A. D. H. Mayes, *Israel in the Period of the Judges*, 1974. F.F.B.

DEBT, DEBTOR.

a. Lending, loan

Loans in Israel were not commercial but charitable, granted not to enable a trader to set up or expand a business but to tide a peasant farmer over a period of poverty. Since the economy remained predominantly agricultural up to the end of the Monarchy, there developed no counterpart to the commercial loan system already existing in Babylonia in 2000 BC. Hence the legislation contains not mercantile regulations but exhortations to neighbourliness. The same outlook persists in Ecclus. 29. The background changes in the NT. The debtors in the parable of the unjust steward (Lk. 16:1–8) are either tenants who pay rent in kind or merchants who have goods on credit. The description of sins as debts (Mt. 6:12) is a Jewish commonplace which Jesus employs, not to characterize the relationship between God and man as one between creditor and debtor, but to proclaim the grace and enjoin the duty of forgiveness (Lk. 7:41f.; Mt. 18:21–27).

b. Interest, usury

The word 'usury' in the AV has not the modern sense of exorbitant interest. The complaint in the OT is not that interest is excessive but that it is charged at all. All three Codes (Ex. 22:25, JE; Dt. 23:19f., D; Lv. 25:35ff., H) forbid it as an unbrotherly exploitation of a fellow-Israelite's misfortune. Dt. 23:20 (*cf.* 15:1–8) allows that a foreigner may be charged. Interest is mentioned as an established practice in the Code of Hammurapi and earlier Babylonian laws. The word *nešeḵ* (lit. 'something bitten off') probably denotes simply rapacious exaction from a debtor, though the play on the word *nôšᵉḵîm* in Hab. 2:7 RVmg. (meaning both 'payers of interest' and 'biters') may imply a sum which eats away the savings set aside for repayment. The synonym *tarbîṯ* ('increase') and the Gk. *tokos* ('offspring') take the more modern view of interest as a growth upon principal. In keeping with a changed economy, Jesus approves of investment to earn income (Mt. 25:27; Lk. 19:23) but retains the traditional distrust of any charge on a private loan (Lk. 6:31ff.).

c. Pledge, surety

Security took the form of a pledge of some personal effect for a small temporary loan (Dt. 24:10; Jb. 24:3), the mortgage of real estate (Ne. 5) or the surety of a guarantor (Pr. 6:1–5; Ecclus. 8:13; 29:14–20). Where there was no security to forfeit debtors could be sold into slavery (Ex. 22:3; 2 Ki. 4:1; Am. 2:6; 8:6, *etc.*). The laws are framed to mitigate the severity of custom. Restrictions are laid on the range of pledgeable items and conditions of borrowing (Dt. 24). By a sort of 'Statute of Limitations' all debts were to be cancelled every seventh year (Dt. 15:1ff., only Dt. mentions debts in connection with the year of Jubilee), and Israelites giving service in discharge of debts to be released (Lv. 25:39–55). This legislation seems not to have been observed historically. Elisha helps the widow in 2 Ki. 4:1–7 not by invoking the law but by working a miracle. Ne. 5 makes no appeal to Dt. 15 (though *cf.* Ne. 10:31 and Je. 34:13f.). In the Judaistic period Hillel invented a system for legal evasion of Dt.15, the purpose of which was not to frustrate or circumvent the law but to adapt it to a commercial economy.

BIBLIOGRAPHY. R. de Vaux, *Ancient Israel*, 1961; J. D. M. Derrett, *Law in the New Testament*, 1970. A.E.W.

DECAPOLIS. A large territory S of the Sea of Galilee, mainly to the E of Jordan, but including Bethshean to the W. The Greeks had occupied towns like Gadara and Philadelphia as early as 200 BC. In 63 BC Pompey liberated Hippos, Scythopolis and Pella from the Jews. He annexed the cities to the province of Syria, but gave them municipal freedom. About AD 1 they formed a league for trade and mutual defence against Semitic tribes. Pliny named the ten original members as Scythopolis, Pella, Dion, Gerasa, Philadelphia, Gadara, Raphana, Kanatha, Hippos and Damascus. Ptolemy included other towns S of Damascus in a list of 18 cities in the 2nd century AD.

Inhabitants of Decapolis joined the great crowds which followed Christ in Mt. 4:25. He landed in the territory at Gerasa (Mk. 5:1; Origen reads Gergesa, a site on the cliff). The presence of so many swine suggests a predominantly Gentile population who, on suffering economic loss through the miracle, requested Christ's departure, despite the demoniac's testimony. Christ revisited Decapolis when making an unusual detour through the Hippos area on a journey from Sidon to the E shore of Galilee (Mk. 7:31). The Jewish church retired to Pella before the war of AD 70.

BIBLIOGRAPHY. *DCG*; G. A. Smith, *Historical Geography of the Holy Land*, 1931, pp. 595–608; H. Bietenhard, 'Die Dekapolis von Pompeius bis Traian', *ZDPV* 79, 1963, pp. 24–58; Pliny, *NH* 5. 18. 74. D.H.T.

DECEIT. From Heb. root *rāmâ*, meaning treachery or guile (Ps. 34:13). It is used of a witness, of balances and of a bow (Ps. 78:57). It is expressed by several Gk. words, *e.g. planē*, 'error' (Eph. 4:14); *dolos*, 'cunning', 'treachery' (Rom. 1:29; Mk. 7:22); *apatē*, 'beguiling pleasure' (Mt. 13:22; Heb. 3:13; Col. 2:8). Since the devil is the archdeceiver (Rev. 20:10) his children are described as 'full of deceit', *e.g.* Elymas (Acts 13:10). Conversely, in Christ's mouth there is no deceit (1 Pet. 2:22) and in the true Israelite Nathanael no guile (Jn. 1:47).

BIBLIOGRAPHY. Arndt; *MM*; *HDB*; W. Günther, *NIDNTT* 2, pp. 457–461. D.H.T.

DECISION, VALLEY OF. Mentioned in Joel 3:14 as the place of God's judgment on the nations, the 'valley of decision' is also called (vv. 2, 12) 'the valley of Jehoshaphat'. V. 16 suggests proximity to Zion, but, as Am. 1:2 shows, this wording may be a prophetic formula rather than an indication of location. 'Jehoshaphat', meaning 'Yahweh judges', may be symbolic rather than topographic. 2 Ch. 20 would explain the symbolism: in the valley of Beracah, 24 km S of Jerusalem, King Jehoshaphat observed Yahweh's victory over

DECALOGUE See Ten Commandments, Part 3.

heathen nations, a microcosm of the Day of Yahweh. However, from the 4th century AD onwards the name 'valley of Jehoshaphat' has been given to the valley between the Temple Hill and the Mount of Olives. J.A.M.

DECREE. In the AV the term occurs frequently in Esther, Ezra and Daniel as a translation of various Heb. and Aram. words for royal decrees. RSV often differentiates between them, using 'interdict' in Dn. 6:8, 'sentence' (RV 'law') in Dn. 2:9 and 'decree' in Ezr. 5:13. God, as King of the earth, is said in the OT to make decrees (Dn. 4:24; Ps. 2:7), and the world is controlled by them: there is one for the rain, Jb. 28:26, and one for the sea, Pr. 8:29 (RSV 'command'), where we should speak of laws of nature. The Heb. *ḥōq*, 'statute' (Ps. 119:5, 8, 12, *etc.*), is the nearest biblical approach to the 'decrees of God' spoken of by theologians.

In the NT the Gk. *dogma* describes special decrees of the Roman emperor in Lk. 2:1 and Acts 17:7 (*cf.* E. A. Judge, 'The Decrees of Caesar at Thessalonica', *RTR* 30, 1971, pp.1–7). In Acts 16:4 it is used of the findings of the Jerusalem Council: *cf.* Gk. usage for authoritative decisions of groups of philosophers. In Eph. 2:15 and Col. 2:14, 20 it refers to Jewish enactments.

BIBLIOGRAPHY. Arndt; *HDB*; *MM*. D.H.T.

DECORATION
See Art, Part 1.

DEEP
See Sheol, Part 3.

DEER
See Animals, Part 1.

DEFEAT
See Foot, Part 1.

DEFENCE
See Fortification and siegecraft, Part 1.

DEFILEMENT
See Clean, Part 1.

DEISM
See Providence, Part 3.

DEITY OF JESUS
See Incarnation, Part 2.

DELPHIC ORACLE
See Python, Part 3.

DELUGE
See Flood, Part 1.

DEDAN. A city and people of NW *Arabia, famous for its role in the caravan trade (Is. 21:13; Ezk. 27:20—the reference in *MT* of v. 20 is probably due to a textual error—*cf.* RSV), since it lay on the well-known 'incense route' from S Arabia to Syria and the Mediterranean. It is mentioned in close association with Sheba in the Table of *Nations (Gn. 10:7—*cf.* 1 Ch. 1:9) and elsewhere (Gn. 25:3; 1 Ch. 1:32; Ezk. 38:13), and probably played a part in the trading relations established by Solomon with the queen of Sheba (1 Ki. 10). But it only comes into prominence in OT texts in the 7th century BC (Je. 25:23; 49:8; Ezk. 25:13; 27:20), when it may have been a Sabaean trading colony (von Wissman); this would help to explain why, in the biblical genealogies, it is associated with both N and S Arabian peoples. It is mentioned by Nabonidus in one of his inscriptions (*ANET*, p. 562), and seems to have been at least temporarily conquered by him (mid-6th century BC): some Arabian inscriptions found near Taima', which mention Dedan, may refer to his wars (*POTT*, p. 293). The site of the city of Dedan is that now known as al-'Ula, some 110 km SW of Taima'. A number of Dedanite inscriptions are known, and give the names of one king and several gods of the Dedanites (*POTT*, p. 294). Subsequently the kingdom seems to have fallen into Persian hands, and later still (3rd–2nd centuries BC?) came under Lihyanite rule. With the arrival of the Nabataeans Dedan gave place to the neighbouring city of Hegra (Medain Salih) as the main centre in the area.

BIBLIOGRAPHY. *POTT*, pp. 287–311, esp. 293–296, with bibliography, to which add W. F. Albright, *Geschichte und Altes Testament* (*Festschrift* A. Alt), 1953, pp. 1–12; H. von Wissmann, *RE* Supp. Bd. 12, cols. 947–969; M. C. Astour, *IDBS*, p. 222.
G.I.D.

DEDICATION. The term is used in the OT almost exclusively of the consecration of things, *e.g.* the altar (Nu. 7:10), silver and gold (2 Sa. 8:11). Three Heb. words are used: *ḥᵃnukkâ*, 'consecration'; *qōḏeš*, 'a thing separated, hallowed'; *ḥērem*, 'a thing devoted to God'. (*CURSE, *BAN.) D.G.S.

DEDICATION, FEAST OF (Gk. *ho enkainismos tou thysiastēriou*, 1 Macc. 4:47–59; *ta enkainia*, Jn. 10:22, rendering Heb. *ḥᵃnukkâ*, from *ḥānaḵ*, 'dedicate'). Held on 25 Kislew, and lasting 8 days, it originally celebrated the winter solstice, but later commemorated the cleansing of the Temple and altar by Judas Maccabaeus in 164 BC, 3 years to the day after their defilement by Antiochus Epiphanes. Its resemblance in mode of celebration to the Feast of Tabernacles (2 Macc. 10:6) was deliberate, though, unlike the great feasts, it might be celebrated outside Jerusalem. The prominent feature of illuminations gave it the name Feast of Lights (Jn. 9:5; Jos., *Ant.* 12. 325). The sole NT reference (Jn. 10:22) indicates the season of the year.

BIBLIOGRAPHY. O. S. Rankin, *The Origins of the Festival of Hanukkah*, 1930. T.H.J.

DEHAVITES, DEHAITES. A name occurring in an Aramaic list (Ezr. 4:9, AV) prepared for Artaxerxes, which enumerates the various peoples who had been settled in Samaria by *Ashurbanipal. The name (*Kᵉṯîḇ*: *dehāwē'*; *Qᵉrē*: *dehāyē'*) falls in the list between the 'Susanchites' and the Elamites, and from the facts that *Susa was in Elam, and that no satisfactory identification for *dehāwē'* has been found in extra-biblical sources, it has been plausibly suggested that it be read *dēhû* (for *dî-hû'*), 'that is' (with Codex Vaticanus *hoi eisin*), which would result in the rendering, 'the Susians, that is the Elamites' (so RSV).

BIBLIOGRAPHY. G. Hoffmann, *ZA* 2, 1887, p. 54; F. Rosenthal, *A Grammar of Biblical Aramaic*, 1961, §35. T.C.M.

DEMAS. A co-worker with Paul in the first imprisonment, sending greetings in Phm. 24 and Col. 4:14. In the latter he alone is mentioned without commendation. There follows the pathetic notice of his desertion in the second imprisonment (2 Tim. 4:10; Parry neatly renders 'left me in the lurch'). Paul's words, 'in love with (*agapēsas*) this present world', suggest that personal interest, not cowardice, took Demas to Thessalonica: perhaps he was a Thessalonian. The name is not uncommon; it may be a pet-form of Demetrius. John Chapman (*JTS* 5, 1904, pp. 364ff.) argued that Demas, restored, is the Demetrius of 3 Jn. 12; but this is as conjectural as is the ugly portrait of Demas in the *Acts of Paul and Thecla*. A.F.W.

DEMETRIUS was a common Gk. name, and two people bearing it are mentioned in the NT.

1. A Christian whose witness is commended in 3 Jn. 12.

2. The silversmith of Ephesus, who stirred up a riot against Paul (Acts 19:24, 38).

Conjectures have been made identifying the two (J. V. Bartlet, *JTS* 6, 1905, pp. 208f., 215), while J. Chapman (*JTS* 5, 1904, pp. 364ff.) would identify **1** above with Demas, the companion of Paul (Col. 4:14; Phm. 24; 2 Tim. 4:10).

The name also occurs in the Apocrypha, where it refers to three kings of the Seleucid dynasty. Demetrius I Soter was king of Syria 162–150 BC. Son of Seleucus IV, he obtained the throne on the death of his uncle *Antiochus Epiphanes IV by killing Antiochus' son, Eupator, and his general Lysias. He continued his predecessor's persecution of the Maccabees, and was killed by Alexander Balas (1 Macc. 10:50). His son, Demetrius II Nicator, avenged his father's death by overcoming Balas in 145 BC and, after a reign characterized by intrigue and duplicity, he was taken captive in 138 BC by Mithradates I of Persia. Demetrius III Eucaerus, the son of Antiochus Grypos, appears briefly on the stage of history in 88 BC to aid in the defeat of Jannaeus, but quickly fell from favour. See R. H. Pfeiffer, *History of New Testament Times*, 1949. D.H.W.

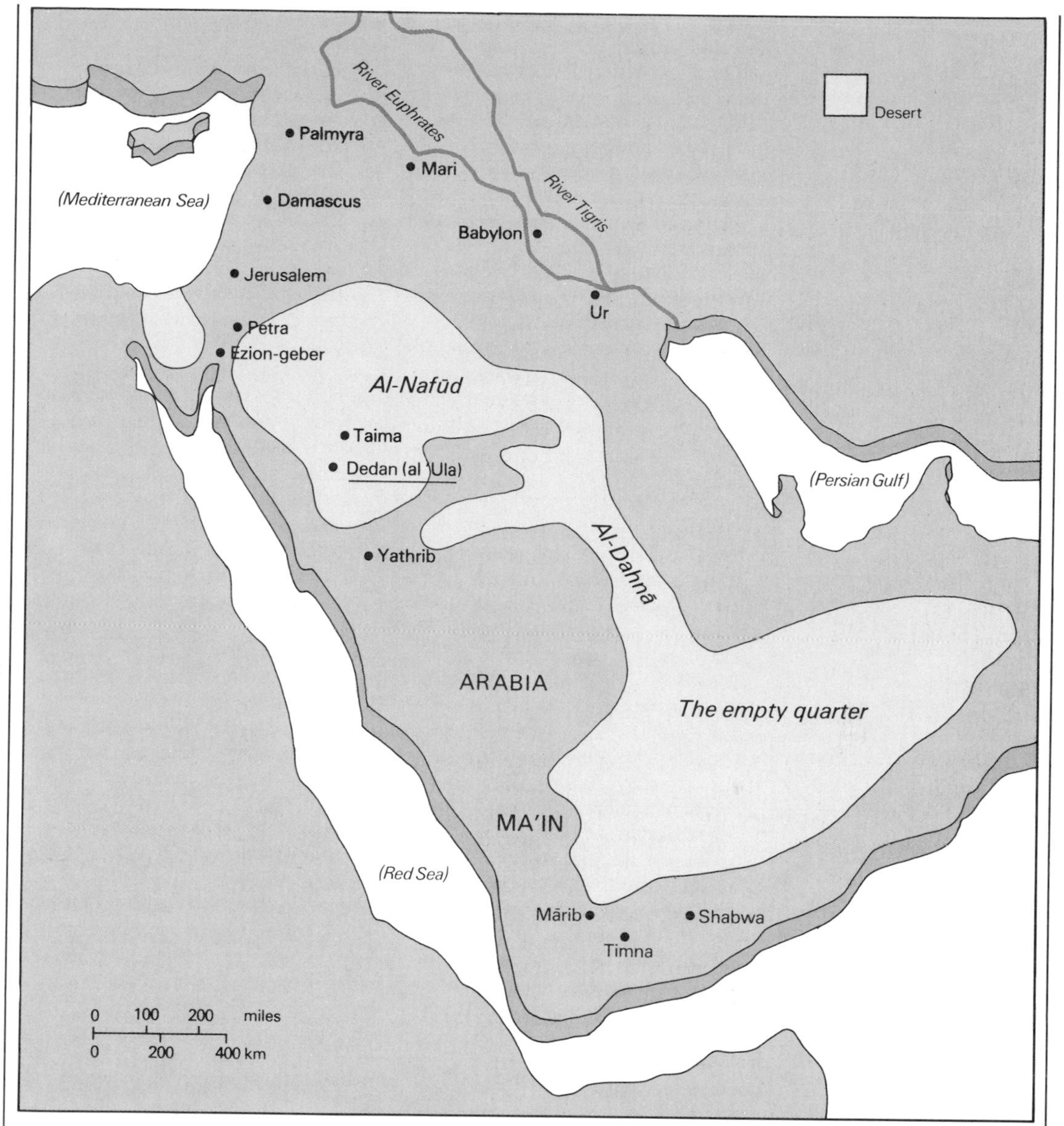

The site of the city of Dedan, now known as al-'Ula, in NW Arabia.

DEMON.

I. In the Old Testament

In the OT there are references to demons under the names *śā'îr* (RSV 'satyrs', Lv. 17:7; 2 Ch. 11:15) and *šēḏ* (Dt. 32:17; Ps. 106:37). The former term means 'hairy one', and points to the demon as a satyr. The latter is of uncertain meaning, though it is evidently connected with a similar Assyr. word. In such passages there is the thought that the deities who were served from time to time by Israel are no true gods, but are really demons (*cf.* 1 Cor. 10:19f.). But the subject is not one of great interest in the OT, and the relevant passages are few.

II. In the Gospels

It is otherwise when we turn to the Gospels. There are many references there to demons. The usual designation is *daimonion*, a diminutive of *daimōn*, which is found in Mt. 8:31, but apparently with no difference of meaning (the parallel accounts use *daimonion*). In the classics *daimōn* is frequently used in a good sense, of a god or of the divine power. But in the NT *daimōn* and *daimonion* always refer to spiritual beings hostile to God and men. Beelzebul (*BAAL-ZEBUB) is their 'prince' (Mk. 3:22), so that they may be regarded as his agents. This is the sting behind the accusation that Jesus had 'a demon' (Jn. 7:20; 10:20). Those who opposed his ministry tried to link him with the very forces of evil, instead of recognizing his divine origin.

In the Gospels there are many references to people possessed by demons. A variety of effects results, such as dumbness (Lk. 11:14), epilepsy (Mk. 9:17f.), a refusal to wear clothing and a living among the tombs (Lk. 8:27). It is often said in modern times that demon-possession was simply the way people had in the 1st century of referring to conditions that we today would call sickness or madness. The Gospel accounts, however, distinguish between sickness and possession by demons. For example, in Mt. 4:24 we read of 'the sick, those afflicted with various diseases and pains, demoniacs, epileptics (*selēniazomenous*, which may mean 'lunatics' as AV), and paralytics'. None of these classes appears to be identical with the others.

Neither in the OT nor in the Acts and Epistles do we find many references to demon-possession. (The incident of Acts 19:13ff. is exceptional.) Apparently it was a phenomenon especially associated with the earthly ministry of our Lord. It should surely be interpreted as an outburst of demoniacal opposition to the work of Jesus.

The Gospels picture Jesus as in continual conflict with *evil spirits. To cast out such beings from men was not easy. His opponents recognized both that he did this, and also that it required a power greater than human. Therefore they attributed his success to the indwelling of *Satan (Lk. 11:15), exposing themselves to the counter that this would spell ruin in the kingdom of the evil one (Lk. 11:17f.). Jesus' power was that of 'the Spirit of God' (Mt. 12:28) or, as Luke expresses it, 'if it is by the finger of God that I cast out demons . . .' (Lk. 11:20).

The victory that Jesus won over demons he shared with his followers. When he sent out the Twelve he 'gave them power and authority over all demons and to cure diseases' (Lk. 9:1). Again, the seventy could report when they returned from their mission, 'Lord, even the demons are subject to us in your name' (Lk. 10:17). Others than Jesus' immediate disciples might use his name to cast out demons, a fact which caused perturbation to some of the inner circle, but not to the Master (Mk. 9:38f.).

DEMYTHOLOGIZING
See Myth, Part 2.

DENY
See Confession, Part 1.

DEODORANT
See Herbs, Part 2.

DEPOSIT
See Earnest, Part 1.

III. Other New Testament references

After the Gospels there are few references to demons. In 1 Cor. 10:20f. Paul is concerned with idol worship, and regards idols as in reality demons, a use we see again in Rev. 9:20. There is an interesting passage in Jas. 2:19, 'the demons believe—and shudder'. It reminds us of Gospel passages in which the demons recognized Jesus for what he was (Mk. 1:24; 3:11, *etc.*).

There seems no reason *a priori* why we should reject the whole concept of *demon-possession. When the Gospels give us good evidence that it did take place it is best to accept this.

BIBLIOGRAPHY. N. Geldenhuys, *Commentary on Luke's Gospel*, pp. 174f.; J. M. Ross, *ExpT* 66, 1954–5, pp. 58–61; E. Langton, *Essentials of Demonology*, 1949. L.M.

DEMON-POSSESSION. Apparent possession by spirits is a world-wide phenomenon. It may be sought deliberately, as by the shaman and witch-doctor among primitive peoples, and by the medium among both primitive and civilized men and women. It may come upon individuals suddenly, as with watchers at the Voodoo rites, or in the form of what is generally known as demon-possession. In each case the possessed person behaves in a way that is not normal for him or her, speaks in a voice totally different from normal, and often shows powers of telepathy and clairvoyance.

In the Bible the pagan prophets probably sought possession. The prophets of Baal in 1 Ki. 18 would come in this category. Mediums, who were banned in Israel, must have deliberately cultivated possession, since the law regards them as guilty people, not as sick (*e.g.* Lv. 20:6, 27). In the OT *Saul is an outstanding example of unsought possession. The Spirit of the Lord leaves him, and 'an evil spirit from the Lord tormented him' (1 Sa. 16:14; 19:9). We may fairly interpret this by saying that, if a person has been powerfully open to the Holy Spirit in a charismatic way, disobedience is liable to be followed by the entry into his life of an evil spirit allowed by God. On the other hand, we may simply say that 'evil' has no moral connotation here, but signifies depression. The spirit is driven away by David's playing: since playing was normally accompanied by singing, it was probably David's psalm-singing that drove away the spirit, as Robert Browning implies in his poem *Saul*.

The NT records many cases of possession. It is as though Satan had concentrated his forces in a special way to challenge Christ and his followers. The Gospel records show that Christ distinguished between ordinary illness and those that accompanied demon-possession. The former were healed by laying on of hands or anointing, the latter by commanding the demon to depart (*e.g.* Mt. 10:8; Mk. 6:13; Lk. 13:32; also Acts 8:7; 19:12). Possession was apparently not always continuous, but when it came it produced effects that were often violent (Mk. 9:18). Blindness and dumbness, when caused by possession, would presumably have been persistent (*e.g.* Mt. 9:32–33; 12:22).

Most psychologists dismiss the idea of demon-possession. A good representative writer is T. K. Oesterreich, whose German work is published in English as *Possession, Demoniacal and Other, among Primitive Races, in Antiquity, the Middle Ages, and Modern Times*, 1930. He maintains that the equivalents of possession today are 'a particularly extensive complex of compulsive phenomena'. So also W. Sargant in *Battle for the Mind* (1957) and *The Mind Possessed* (1973). On the other hand, there is the classic by J. L. Nevius, a missionary doctor in China, *Demon Possession and Allied Themes*, 1892. This book takes demon-possession as a genuine phenomenon, and most missionaries would probably agree.

It is possible to take an intermediate position, and to hold that a demon can seize on a repressed facet of the personality, and from this centre influence a person's actions. The demon may produce hysterical blindness or dumbness, or symptoms of other illnesses, such as epilepsy. Among many peoples an epileptic fit has been regarded as a sign of possession by a spirit or a god, and indeed epileptics are often psychically sensitive. The Bible does not link epilepsy with demon-possession, and even the description of the fits of the possessed boy in Mt. 17:14f.; Mk. 9:14f.; Lk. 9:37f., seem to indicate something more than mere epilepsy. The nature of epilepsy is still unknown, but it can be artificially induced in apparently normal people (W. G. Walter, *The Living Brain*, 1953, pp. 60f.). Students of personality disorders know that it is often impossible to say just how these are triggered off. We are not saying that all, or even the majority, are due to demon-possession, but some may be.

The Bible does not say what conditions predispose to demon-possession, though Christ's words in Mt. 12:44–45 indicate that an 'empty house' can be reoccupied. The early church cast out demons in the name of Jesus Christ (Acts 16:18), but it would seem that there were also non-Christian exorcists who met with some success (Lk. 11:19; though note Acts 19:13–16).

The command to 'try the spirits' in 1 Jn. 4:1–3 shows that there were false prophets in the church who spoke under possession. Since the spiritualists make much of this verse, it should be noted that the Bible never speaks of possession by any good departed spirit or by an angel. The alternatives are either the Holy Spirit or an evil spirit. See also 1 Cor. 12:1–3.

BIBLIOGRAPHY. W. M. Alexander, *Demonic Possession*, 1902; M. F. Unger, *Demons in the World today*, 1971; V. White, *God and the Unconscious*, 1952, chapter 10; J. S. Wright, *Mind, Man, and the Spirits* (formerly *What is Man?*), 1972, pp. 108ff.; J. Richards, *But deliver us from evil*, 1974. J.S.W.

DEPUTY. In the OT, two words are used: Heb. *niṣṣāḇ*, 'one set up', used in 1 Ki. 22:47 of the viceroy or regent who administered Edom when it was tributary to Judah in Jehoshaphat's reign; and Heb. *peḥâ*, in Est. 8:9; 9:3 (AV; RSV *'governor').

In the NT, AV rendering of Gk.

Opposite page: Bronze figure of a dagger-bearing Babylonian demon with an incantation inscribed over his tunic. (BM)

anthypatos (Acts 13:7–8, 12; 19:38) and *anthypateuō* ('was the deputy', Acts 18:12), RSV *proconsul'.
F.F.B.

DERBE (Lycaonian *delbeia*, 'juniper'). In Acts 14:6ff. a city of Lycaonia, the most easterly place visited by Paul and Barnabas when they founded the churches of S Galatia. Paul and Silas visited it on their westward journey through Asia Minor (Acts 16:1). Paul's fellow-traveller Gaius came from Derbe (Acts 20:4; the Western Text brings him from Doberus in Macedonia). The site of Derbe was identified in 1956 by M. Ballance at Kerti Hüyük, 21 km NNE of Karaman (Laranda), some 100 km from Lystra (whence Acts 14:20b must evidently be translated: 'and on the morrow he set out with Barnabas for Derbe'). In 1964 M. Ballance attempted to identify the site even more precisely at Devri Şehri, 4 km SSE of Kerti Hüyük. It may have lain beyond the E frontier of Roman Galatia, in the client kingdom of Commagene.

BIBLIOGRAPHY. M. Ballance, 'The Site of Derbe: A New Inscription', *AS* 7, 1957, pp. 147ff.; and 'Derbe and Faustinopolis', *AS* 14, 1964, pp. 139ff.; B. Van Elderen, 'Some Archaeological Observations on Paul's First Missionary Journey', in W. W. Gasque and R. P. Martin (eds.), *Apostolic History and the Gospel*, 1970, pp. 156ff. F.F.B.

DESCENT INTO HADES. Although the doctrine of the descent of Christ into hell is firmly embedded in the early Christian creeds (it first appears in 4th-century Arian formularies), its place in Scripture is in fact circumferential. It receives explicit mention possibly twice (1 Pet. 3:19; 4:6), and is indirectly referred to in only two other places (Acts 2:27 and Rom. 10:7), where it is hinted at by the reinterpretation of OT passages—Ps. 16 in the case of Acts, and Dt. 30. It is doubtful whether we are right to press for a reference to the *descensus ad inferos* in Eph. 4:9f., since the comprehensive movement in these verses is best understood as forming a parallel to that in the 'kenotic' passage Phil. 2:5–11.

The references in the two Petrine passages are more direct, but by no means clear. The context of the first (1 Pet. 3:19) is the congruent suffering of Christ (the climax of which was his death) and of the Christian. It was after his passion and 'in the spirit' (*pneumati*) that the Lord 'preached' (the technical term *ekēryxen*) to the *'spirits in prison'. As victor, and no longer victim, Christ proclaimed his triumph (*kēryssein* is to be distinguished from *euangelizein*, 4:6) inclusively.

In 1 Pet. 4:6 the thought of preaching the good news to the 'dead' arises from a consideration of the painfulness as well as the glory of being dead to sin. This, says Peter, may well involve suffering for Christ's sake, as Christ suffered for ours (4:1f.). It was this gospel that judged the 'dead', and gave them the opportunity of sharing God's eternal life (v. 6). This may well refer to Christians who have heard the gospel while alive, and died before the Lord's return (so Selwyn, Stibbs and Dalton). Others interpret 'the dead' as meaning those who are spiritually dead; and a third view connects this verse with 3:19, and sees in it a further reference to the 'spirits in prison'. In this case the thought of judgment (= death, here) is subordinate to that of life (the fullness of God's life, denoted by *zōsi*, as opposed to the transitoriness of man's life, implied in 4:2 by the verb *bioō*, similarly translated).

The interval between the death and the resurrection of Jesus cannot be regarded as without significance. But the event claimed by Christians as taking place then, whether or not Peter has it in mind in these two passages, is more a matter of theology than chronology. Then the *meaning* becomes more important than the manner, and we can understand the *descensus* as a part of the triumphant activity of Christ, who is Lord of hell as well as of heaven (*cf.* Rev. 1:18 and Phil. 2:10), and who thus completes his involvement in every conceivable area of experience.

BIBLIOGRAPHY. See the commentaries on 1 Pet., esp. those by E. G. Selwyn, 1946; A. M. Stibbs, 1959; J. N. D. Kelly, 1969; E. Best, 1971. See also C. E. B. Cranfield, *ExpT* 69, 1957–8, pp. 369–372; W. J. Dalton, *Christ's Proclamation to the Spirits*, 1965. S.S.S.

DESIRE. In their numerous references to 'desire' the OT and NT provide many acute and incisive psychological insights. Indeed both

DESERT
See Wilderness, Part 3.

by the diversity of the vocabulary of 'desire', and the manner of handling it, the Bible makes plain an important part of its doctrine of man.

In the OT 'desire' means much more than merely 'to long for', 'to ask for' or 'to demand'. In Heb. psychology the whole personality was involved in desire. Hence 'desire' could easily become 'covetousness', leading to 'envy' and 'jealousy', *etc.* Among the Hebrews 'desire' was the request which the *nepeš* (the 'soul' or 'self') made of the personality (Dt. 14:26, RV). 'Desire' was the inclination of the *nepeš* (2 Sa. 3:21). And when the whole 'soul' lay behind an inclination or desire that was sinful then the soul, it was said, 'lusted a lust' (see Nu. 11:4, 6). It was against this kind of covetousness that the tenth commandment was directed (Ex. 20:17), because when such sinful desire was given free rein the well-being of the whole community was endangered (Je. 6:13–15).

In the NT sinful desire is stimulated by the will to get rich (1 Tim. 6:9); so much so that it is equated with 'the love of money' (v. 10). But it may also manifest itself in illicit sexual desire (Mt. 5:28), or in what Paul describes as 'the desires of the flesh and of the thoughts' (Eph. 2:3, RVmg.). The NT testifies also to what is an observable fact in human experience: that if these sinful desires are gratified instead of crucified they become a consuming fire (Col. 3:5f.). On the other hand, where God is the object of the soul's desire (Rom. 10:2a), and his best gifts (1 Cor. 12:31), the body becomes the instrument of righteousness (Rom. 6:12f.).

J.G.S.S.T.

Fragment of a leather scroll containing Dt. 32:41–43 in a Hebrew text (4Q DT^q) found in cave 4 at Qumran. 1st cent. BC. (RM)

DESOLATING SACRILEGE (abomination of desolation', AV). The phrase (Heb. *šiqqûṣ šōmēm*) occurs first in Dn. 12:11, with variants in Dn. 9:27; 11:31. *šiqqûṣ* = an offensive object, due to uncleanness, then an idol as offensive to God; *šiqqûṣ šomēm* probably represents a contemptuous equivalent for *Baal šamēm*, 'lord of heaven': the 'lord' is a mere 'idol', and he is not 'of heaven' (*šamēm*) but he 'desolates' (*šomēm*). The name appears to have in view the action of Antiochus Epiphanes, who placed on the altar in the Jerusalem Temple a small idolatrous altar, described in 1 Macc. 1:54ff. as the 'desolating sacrilege' (Gk. *bdelygma erēmōseōs*). With it, according to Jewish tradition, went an image—almost certainly of Zeus, the lord of heaven, bearing the emperor's likeness. This sacrilege created 'desolation', *i.e.* not destruction, but desolating horror (or possibly making the Temple to be 'desolate', emptied of God and his true worshippers). In Mk. 13:14; Mt. 24:15 a related sacrilege may well be in view; it is a sign of the impending destruction of the Temple (not the destruction itself). The sacrilege has been interpreted as the appearance of the Antichrist (*cf.* 2 Thes. 2:3f., and note that in Mark 'standing' is masculine in gender), or of the sacrilegious Roman army (*cf.* Lk. 21:20). Possibly it is linked with the standards of the Romans, which had images of the emperor attached for worship; to bring these within the Temple area (the Roman garrison was adjacent to the Temple) would have been a 'sacrilege creating desolation', leading to war and the destruction of both Temple and city. Luke's version is best viewed as a translation for Gentile readers, to whom the biblical phrase would be largely incomprehensible.

BIBLIOGRAPHY. G. Kittel, *TDNT* 2, p. 660; G. R. Beasley-Murray, *A Commentary on Mark 13*, 1957, pp. 54–72; W. G. Kummel, *Prophecy and Fulfilment*, 1957, pp. 95–103; A. L. Moore, *The Parousia in the New Testament*, 1966; L. Hartmann, *Prophecy Interpreted*, 1966; C. H. Dodd, *More New Testament Studies*, 1968; R. T. France, *Jesus and the Old Testament*, 1971.

G.R.B.-M.

DETERMINISM
See Providence, Part 3.

DEUTERO-ISAIAH
See Isaiah, book of, Part 2.

DEUTERONOMY, BOOK OF. The name Deuteronomy derives from the LXX rendering of a phrase in 17:18. The king was to prepare 'a copy of this law'. The phrase is rendered in Greek as *to deuteronomion touto*, *lit.* this second law. Subsequently the Vulgate rendered the Greek as *deuteronomium*. The contents of the book were regarded as a second law, the first having been given on Mt Horeb (Sinai) and the second (repetition) on the plains of Moab.

I. Outline of contents

The book falls naturally into three sections.

a. 1:1–4:43. First address of Moses. A historical retrospect describing God's mighty acts between Horeb and Beth-peor (1:6–3:29) is followed by an appeal to Israel to hearken and obey as God's chosen people.

b. 4:44–28:68. Moses' second address. The section is lengthy. The nature of the covenant faith with its fundamental demand for total allegiance to Yahweh is presented to Israel (5:1–11:32). Lessons are drawn from the past (8:1–10:11) and Israel is called to commitment (10:12–11:32). In 12:1–26:19 the law of God with its detailed covenant stipulations is presented. The section deals with aspects of worship (12:1–16:17), the character of Israel's leaders (16:18–18:22), criminal law (19:1–21), the Holy War (20:1–20), a range of miscellaneous laws (21:1–25:19) and two rituals (26:1–19). The need to undertake a covenant renewal in the land, and to respond to the covenant challenge is given in 27:1–26. Finally, the *covenant sanctions, that is, the curses and blessings of the covenant, are set out in 28:1–68.

c. 29:1–30:20. Moses' third address. A recapitulation of the covenant demand including, among other things, a historical review (29:1–9), an exhortation to commitment (29:10–15), a warning of punishment for disobedience (29:16–28) and a solemn appeal to choose life (30:11–20).

Finally, the last acts of Moses, his parting words and his call for a covenant-renewal ceremony every seventh year (31:1–13). Moses' charge to Joshua (31:14–23), his song of witness (31:30–32:47), final blessing and his death (32:48–34:12) bring the book to a close.

II. A covenant manifesto

Probably no book in the OT gives such profound and continuous expression to the covenant idea. Yahweh, the Lord of the Covenant, who performed unprecedented saving acts to redeem his people Israel, made a covenant with them (4:23, 31; 5:2–3; 9:9; 29:1, 12) which he would remember and keep (7:9, 12) and display 'covenant faithfulness' or 'steadfast loyalty' (*ḥeseḏ*, 5:10; 7:9, 12) towards them. For their part, loyalty to Yahweh and to his covenant would find expression in their obedience to the covenant stipulations, the 'law' (*tôrâ*). Reference is made to 'this book of the law' (28:61; 29:21; 30:10; 31:26) and 'this law' (1:5; 4:18; 17:18–19; 27:3, 8, 26). More precisely the law is defined as 'testimonies' (*'eḏûṯ*), 'statutes' (*mišpaṭîm*) and 'ordinances' (*ḥuqqîm*). Sometimes only two of these terms appear, 'testimonies and statutes' (6:17), or 'statutes and judgments' (AV)/'statutes and ordinances' (RSV) (4:1; 12:1). All these constituted a body of teaching which provided Israel with guidance for living in fellowship with Yahweh and with one another. Such a life would enable Israel to enjoy to the full all the blessings of the covenant. To live any other life was tantamount to a rejection of Yahweh's gracious intention for his people.

III. The theology of Deuteronomy

Both the literary shape of Deuteronomy and its underlying central concept provide clues to the basic theology of the book. In summary the book expounds:

a. Yahweh, as the Lord of the covenant, Israel's sovereign Lord, King, Judge and Warrior who undertook mighty saving acts for

A diagram showing the changes in form and contents of law codes, treaties and covenants in OT times.

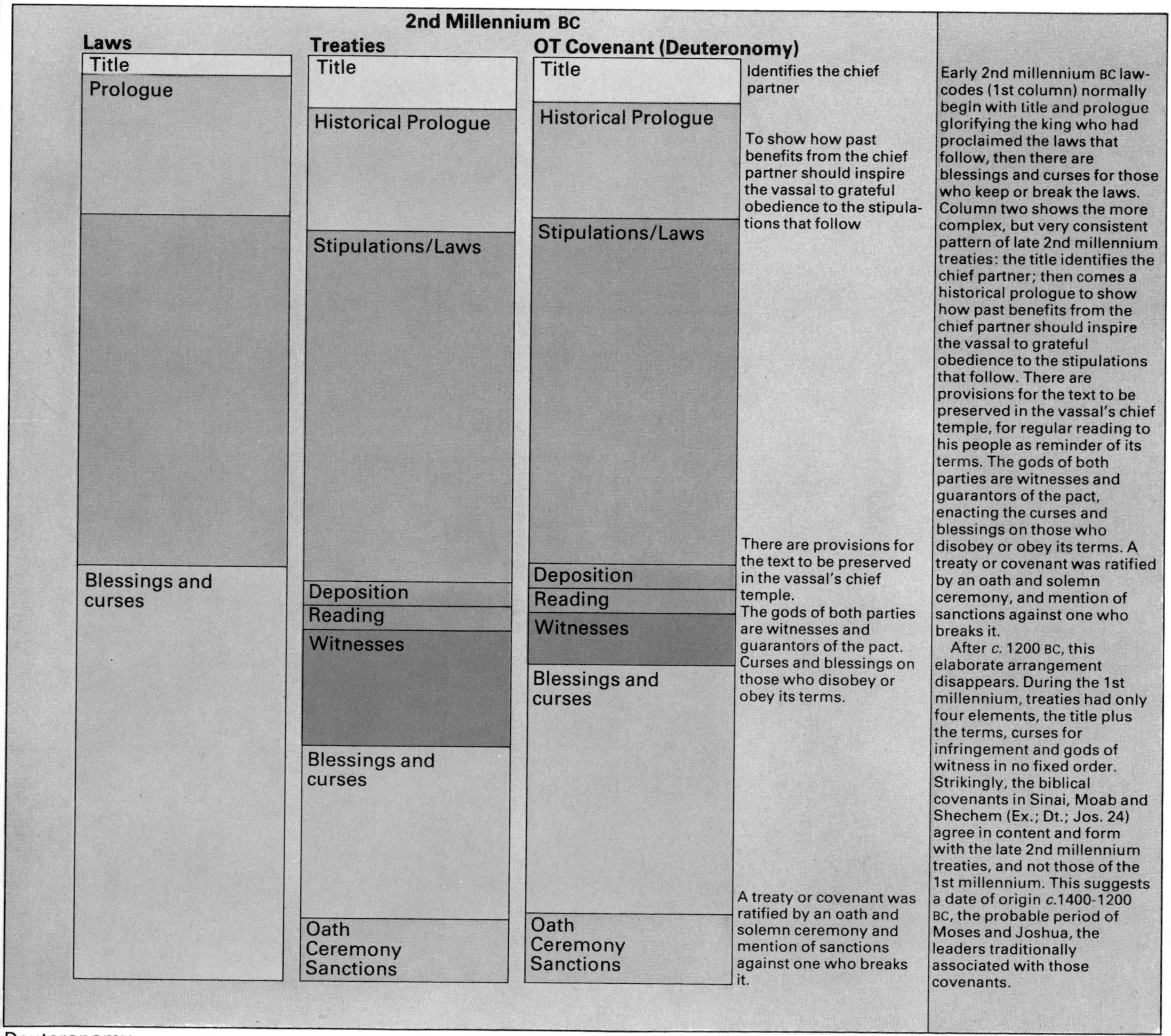
2nd Millennium BC
Laws
Title
Prologue
Blessings and curses
Treaties
Title
Historical Prologue
Stipulations/Laws
Deposition
Reading
Witnesses
Blessings and curses
Oath Ceremony Sanctions
OT Covenant (Deuteronomy)
Title
Historical Prologue
Stipulations/Laws
Deposition
Reading
Witnesses
Blessings and curses
Oath Ceremony Sanctions
Identifies the chief partner
To show how past benefits from the chief partner should inspire the vassal to grateful obedience to the stipulations that follow
There are provisions for the text to be preserved in the vassal's chief temple.
The gods of both parties are witnesses and guarantors of the pact.
Curses and blessings on those who disobey or obey its terms.
A treaty or covenant was ratified by an oath and solemn ceremony and mention of sanctions against one who breaks it.
Early 2nd millennium BC law-codes (1st column) normally begin with title and prologue glorifying the king who had proclaimed the laws that follow, then there are blessings and curses for those who keep or break the laws. Column two shows the more complex, but very consistent pattern of late 2nd millennium treaties: the title identifies the chief partner; then comes a historical prologue to show how past benefits from the chief partner should inspire the vassal to grateful obedience to the stipulations that follow. There are provisions for the text to be preserved in the vassal's chief temple, for regular reading to his people as reminder of its terms. The gods of both parties are witnesses and guarantors of the pact, enacting the curses and blessings on those who disobey or obey its terms. A treaty or covenant was ratified by an oath and solemn ceremony, and mention of sanctions against one who breaks it.
After c. 1200 BC, this elaborate arrangement disappears. During the 1st millennium, treaties had only four elements, the title plus the terms, curses for infringement and gods of witness in no fixed order. Strikingly, the biblical covenants in Sinai, Moab and Shechem (Ex.; Dt.; Jos. 24) agree in content and form with the late 2nd millennium treaties, and not those of the 1st millennium. This suggests a date of origin c.1400-1200 BC, the probable period of Moses and Joshua, the leaders traditionally associated with those covenants.
Deuteronomy

Israel and demanded their obedience.

b. Yahweh, as the God of history, able to perform saving acts in Egypt, in the wilderness, in Canaan, the leader of Israel's armies, able to fulfil his purposes for Israel in the face of every enemy.

c. Israel, as the people of the covenant, obligated to love, to obey, to worship and to serve Yahweh exclusively. That way lay peace (*šālôm*) and life (*ḥayyîm*).

d. The worship of the God of the covenant, based on love and gratitude and finding expression both in personal devotion and in a carefully defined range of festivals and rituals.

IV. The structure of Deuteronomy

Even a cursory reading of the book suggests that a more complex plan lies behind the book. Several attempts have been made to define the structure. M. Noth, 1948, proposed that chs. 1–4 were the introduction to a great historical work stretching from Joshua to 2 Kings, while the rest of Deuteronomy was a great prologue to this history. G. von Rad, 1932, regarded the book as a cultic celebration, perhaps a feast of covenant-renewal, arranged in four segments, (1) Historical (1–11), (2) The Law (12:1–26:15), (3) The Sealing of the Covenant (26:16–19), (4) The Blessings and Curses (27f.).

When G. E. Mendenhall, 1955, drew attention to the many parallels between the Hittite treaties of the 2nd millennium and the *covenant of Yahweh with Israel, a new turn was given to the study of the structure of Deuteronomy. The Hittite treaties comprised (1) a preamble; (2) a historical prologue; (3) the treaty stipulations: (*a*) general, (*b*) specific; (4) the treaty sanctions, curses and blessings; (5) the witnesses, plus clauses requiring the treaty document to be deposited in the Temple and the periodic public reading of the treaty.

M. G. Kline, 1963, proposed that Deuteronomy was a unity, and held it to be an authentic Mosaic document cast in the form of the ancient Near Eastern treaty, as follows: (1) preamble (1:1–5); (2) historical prologue (1:6–4:45); (3) the covenant stipulations (5:1–26:19); (4) the covenant sanctions and oath (27:1–30:20); (5) dynastic disposition, covenant continuity (31:1–34:12).

D. J. McCarthy, 1963, accepted the view that the basic structure of Deuteronomy was that of an ancient Near Eastern treaty, but argued that chs. 1–3 should be set apart as a piece of historical writing, chs. 4, 29 and 30 should be seen as formal units in themselves comprising all the elements of the covenant scheme. He held that chs. 5–28 comprised the kernel framed between two speeches in covenant form.

G. J. Wenham, 1970, has argued that Deuteronomy constitutes a distinctive OT covenant form resembling both the Law Codes and the Near Eastern treaties, but assuming a shape somewhere between them as follows: (1) historical prologue (1:6–3:29); (2a) basic stipulations (4:1–40; 5:1–11:32); (2b) detailed stipulations (12:1–26:19); (3) document clause requiring the recording and renewal of the covenant (27:1–26); (4) blessings (28:1–14); (5) curses (28:15–68); (6) recapitulation (29:1–30:20), concluding with an appeal. The later chs. 31–34 do not belong to the covenant form but represent a covenant-renewal.

M. Weinfeld, 1972, allows that Deuteronomy follows a literary tradition of covenant writing rather than imitating a periodic cultic ceremony (von Rad). But while the book preserves the motifs of the old covenant tradition, he argues that these were re-worked and adapted to the covenant literary pattern by scribes/wise men of the Hezekiah–Josiah period under the strong influence of Assyrian treaty models.

It seems beyond question that the structure of Deuteronomy is related in some way to the political treaties of the ancient Near East, although it appears to be a particular adaptation of the model in a form that was distinctive for Israel.

V. The basic social and religious background of Deuteronomy

It is widely recognized today that a great deal of Deuteronomy is ancient, although the exact age of such parts is not easy to define. It is almost a refrain in the commentary of G. von Rad, 1966, that such and such a law is 'early' or 'earlier'. In his view Deuteronomy is firmly rooted in the sacred and cultic traditions of the old Israelite tribal system of the pre-monarchical period, even though its present form may represent a modification to suit a later stage in Israel's history.

A. C. Welch, 1924, considered that the cultic laws of chs. 12, 14, 16 and 27 all point to the primitive conditions of the age of settlement probably about the 10th century. E. Robertson, 1949, 1950, argued strenuously that Deuteronomy was drawn up under the guidance of Samuel as the standard law book, both civil and religious, for the emerging monarchy and therefore represents a period of about the 11th century.

Certainly the society portrayed in Deuteronomy is an early one. Israel's neighbours are Canaanites (7:1–5; 20:16f.), Amalekites (25:17–19), Ammonites and Edomites (23:3–6). There are laws about the discharge of the Holy War (20:1–20; 21:10–14; 23:10–14; 25:17–19). There is no Temple. The only reference to a king (17:14–20) is to the king that shall arise. Many of the laws have close parallels to the Laws of Hammurapi. Some reflect a background of Canaanite religion (14:21b); others reflect an agricultural society of a simple kind and deal with such items as standing crops (23:24–25), millstones (24:6), oxen treading corn (25:4), landmarks (19:14), *etc.* Although some of these features were applicable over a long period, there are good grounds for arguing that behind the present Deuteronomy lies an ancient and authentic period of national existence which pre-dated the Monarchy. It has been argued that there is a deliberate 'archaizing' on the part of the writer. But archaizing is based on a knowledge of the past and much in Deuteronomy would have been quite meaningful in a simple rural economy in pre-monarchical times in Israel.

VI. Deuteronomy and the central sanctuary

The central sanctuary plays an important part in Deuteronomy. There is a 'place which the Lord your God shall choose' (12:5, 11, 18; 18:6–8; 31:10–13, *etc.*). There is no indication that this place is specifically Jerusalem, although it became so eventually. The central sanctuary seems to have moved from place to place in earlier years. Thus the Ark rested at Gilgal (Jos. 4:19; 5:9; 9:6), Shechem (Jos. 8:33), Bethel (Jdg. 20:18, 26–28; 21:2), Shiloh (Jos. 18:1; Jdg. 18:31; 1 Sa. 1:7, 24; 4:3, *etc.*). It is extremely difficult to decide whether the relevant texts specify one particular place at a particular time, a permanent place for all time or even a variety of places at a particular time, each of which was approved. Certainly the books of Kings and excavations at Arad, Dan and Beersheba suggest that, in practice, several places existed. The reforming kings of later centuries like Asa, Hezekiah and Josiah sought to regularize the 'high places' where there were irregular practices, or even to centralize worship in Jerusalem.

What seems evident is that Deuteronomy presents the ideal, feasible and capable of operation in the days of Moses, impossible to maintain from the days of the Conquest onwards though not forgotten by reformers, but never realized till post-exilic times. There was a central sanctuary in Moses' day in the first half of the 13th century BC. The ideal place it was intended to occupy in Israel's national and religious life is set out in Deuteronomy.

VII. The date and authorship of Deuteronomy

Few questions have proved more difficult to answer than this. On the surface the NT seems to imply Mosaic authorship of the Pentateuch and hence of Deuteronomy (Mt. 19:8; Mk. 12:26; Lk. 24:27, 44; Jn. 7:19, 23; Acts 13:39; 15:5; 1 Cor. 9:9; 2 Cor. 3:15; Heb. 9:19; 10:28). The difficulty with all these references is that the exact meaning of the term *Moses* is not clear. It may refer simply to the Pentateuch scroll and not to authorship. Deuteronomy itself refers to Moses speaking (1:6, 9; 5:1; 27:1, 9; 29:2; 31:1, 30; 33:1, *etc.*) and to writing (31:9, 24).

But none of these statements permits the conclusion that Deuteronomy as we have it today came completely, or even in large measure, from Moses himself. One has to allow for editorial activity and adaptations of original Mosaic material to a later age. Even if it could be shown that much of the geography, the legal background and the society would suit a generally Mosaic age, this falls short of a complete Mosaic authorship. Four main views have been proposed about the authorship and date of the book:

a. A substantially Mosaic date and authorship with a certain amount of post-Mosaic material;

b. A date in the period Samuel–Solomon. Much of the material is held to go back to the time of Moses, but the book as we have it was compiled 300–400 years after Moses' death.

c. A date in the Hezekiah–Josiah period during the 7th century BC. It is not denied that there may well be a considerable stratum of Mosaic material and that Mosaic principles underlie much of the work. But the book represents a gathering together of ancient material preserved in religious and prophetic circles in a time of profound apostasy when the nation needed to be recalled to its ancient covenant obligations. These were set out in terms of addresses given by Moses at the time of Israel's entry into the land. The publication of this collection of material lent support to Josiah in his reform.

d. A post-exilic date and authorship. The book was not a programme of reform but the wishful thinking of unrealistic post-exilic dreamers.

Increasingly scholars are recognizing that although any investigation of the origin of Deuteronomy will lead ultimately to the figure of Moses himself, it is quite impossible to decide on the date at which Deuteronomy reached its final form. There are two aspects to the problem: (1) the age of the original data, and (2) the period at which those data were drawn together. There are grounds for thinking that much in Deuteronomy goes back to Moses' time and much to be said for the view that Moses himself provided Israel with the heart of Deuteronomy. However, it became necessary in new situations to re-present the words of Moses and to show their relevance for a new day. There are several key points in Israel's history when this might have happened—in the days when the kingdom was newly established under Saul, or David, or Solomon; in the critical period following the break-up of the kingdom on Solomon's death; or again at a number of critical points in the centuries that followed. We have to allow both for the powerful influence of Moses and for editorial processes which brought the book to its present shape. While there seems little reason to deny that a substantial part of Deuteronomy was in existence some centuries before the 7th century BC, it is not possible to say how much of it comprises the *ipsissima verba* of Moses himself.

BIBLIOGRAPHY. P. Buis and J. Leclerq, *Le Deutéronome*, 1963; R. E. Clements, *God's Chosen People*, 1968; P. C. Craigie, *Deuteronomy*, 1977; S. R. Driver, *Deuteronomy*, *ICC*, 1902; G. H. Davies, 'Deuteronomy', in *Peake's Commentary on the Bible*, rev. 1962; C. F. Keil and F. Delitzsch, *Biblical Commentary on the Old Testament*, 3, 1864; M. G. Kline, *Treaty of the Great King*, 1963; G. T. Manley, *The Book of the Law*, 1957; D. J. McCarthy, *Treaty and Covenant*, 1963; G. E. Mendenhall, *Law and Covenant in Israel and the Ancient Near East*, 1955; E. W. Nicholson, *Deuteronomy and Tradition*, 1967; E. Robertson, *The Old Testament Problem*, 1950; G. von Rad, *Deuteronomy*, 1966; *idem*, *Studies in Deuteronomy*, 1953; G. A. Smith, *The Book of Deuteronomy*, 1918; J. A. Thompson, *Deuteronomy*, *TOTC*, 1974; *idem*, *The Ancient Near Eastern Treaties and the Old Testament*, 1964; M. Weinfeld, *Deuteronomy and the Deuteronomic School*, 1972; A. C. Welch, *The Code of Deuteronomy*, 1924; *idem*, *Deuteronomy and the Framework to the Code*, 1932; G. J. Wenham, *The Structure and Date of Deuteronomy* (unpublished Ph.D. thesis, London, 1970); *idem*, 'Deuteronomy and the Central Sanctuary', *TynB* 22, 1971, pp.103–118; G. E. Wright, 'Deuteronomy', in *IB*, 2; *idem*, *The Old Testament and Theology*, 1965.

J.A.T.

DEW. The Heb. *ṭal*, 'sprinkled moisture', is referred to indiscriminately for dew and night mist. As the effects upon plants of dew (*i.e.* condensation of water vapour on a cooled surface), and of mist (*i.e.* condensation in the air), are not yet understood, the difference is perhaps irrelevant. Moist air drawn in from the sea is largely responsible for dew-fall in W Palestine, especially in the districts near the coast and on the W slopes of the mountains, though it does not occur in summer in the Jordan valley S of Beisan and on the W uplands of Transjordan. According to Ashbel, the number of yearly dew-nights varies from 250 on the sandy soil of Gaza and the high slopes of Mt Carmel to 100–150 days in the Judaean Highlands, dropping rapidly E in the Jordan trough. The maximum dew occurs in the beneficial summer months when the plants need moisture most. Duvdevani has experimented with two types of condensation. 'Downward dew' is characteristic of summer in areas of

DEVELOPMENT OF RELIGION
See Ancestor worship, Part 1.

loose soil, *i.e.* with good soil-cooling conditions. 'Upward dew' results from the condensation of water vapour from damp soil, and is therefore more frequent in the winter season. This may be the explanation of Gideon's signs (Jdg. 6:36–40). In his first experience so heavy was the night mist or dew, that he wrung out from the fleece a bowl full of water, while the hard-baked earth of the threshing-floor was dry. In the second experience the fleece was dry, while the earth, perhaps the disturbed soil in the edge of the threshing-floor, produced conditions for 'upward dew' from the soil, inadequate to moisten the fleece.

Scriptural references show that, though dew-fall is mysterious, its incidence is well known. 'Who has begotten the drops of dew?' says the Lord as he answers Job (38:28), and its origin is considered heavenly (Gn. 27:28; Dt. 33:28; Hg. 1:10; Zc. 8:12). It falls suddenly (2 Sa. 17:12), gently (Dt. 32:2), lies all night (Jb. 29:19), and exposure to it is discomforting (Ct. 5:2; Dn. 4:15, 23, 25, 33), but it quickly evaporates in the morning (Jb. 7:9; Ho. 6:4). Dew is to be expected in the hot summer weather of harvest (Is. 18:4; *cf.* Ho. 14:5; Mi. 5:7).

Dew is beneficial to summer crops. This has been proved conclusively by agronomical field-studies made since 1937. The ancients therefore were not exaggerating it as a source of blessing. Dew is sufficiently copious to permit dry-farming in the absence of rain (Ecclus. 18:16; 43:22). It allows geophytes to be cultivated in the Negeb and aids the vine harvest; hence the prayer, 'May God give you of the dew of heaven, and of the fatness of the earth, and plenty of grain and wine' (Gn. 27:28; *cf.* Dt. 33:28). The absence of dew was therefore a cause of severe plight (Hg. 1:10; *cf.* Jb. 29:19; Zc. 8:12), intensifying the drought in the absence of rain (1 Ki. 17:1; *cf.* 2 Sa. 1:21). Its preciousness is therefore taken up as an emblem of resurrection; 'thy dew is a dew of light, and on the land of the shades thou wilt let it fall' (Is. 26:19). From this prophecy was based the talmudic phrase 'the dew of resurrection'.

The passage in Ps. 133:3 appears to state that the dew of Hermon comes down on the mountain of Zion. This is incapable of a geographical interpretation. It may be a proverbial expression for plentiful dew, since Hermon receives a maximum amount. In consequence of the heavy dew on Hermon and Mt Carmel, the soft, friable limestone rapidly disintegrates and the soil is frequently replenished. Thus, these mountains have been symbolic of fertility.

BIBLIOGRAPHY. D. Ashbel, *Bioclimatic Atlas of Israel*, 1950, pp. 51–55; S. Duvdevani, 'Dew observations and their significances', *Proc. United Nations Scientific Conference in the Conservation and Utilization of Resources*, 1949, 4.

J.M.H.

DIADEM
See Crown, Part 1.

DIAL
See Steps, Part 3.

DIAMOND
See Jewels, Part 2.

DIANA
See Artemis, Part 1.

DIASPORA
See Dispersion, Part 1.

DIDRACHMON
See Money, Part 2.

DIDYMUS
See Thomas, Part 3.

DILL
See Herbs, Part 2.

DIBLATH, DIBLAH. Occurring only in Ezk. 6:14, no place of this name has been identified, and it is probably an ancient scribal error for *Riblah as RSV text; LXX already read Diblah. J.D.D.

DIBON. 1. A town in Judah, occupied after the Exile (Ne. 11:25) but not identifiable today.

2. Dibon (Heb. *dîḇôn*) of Moab, marked by the modern village of Dhiban, to the E of the Dead Sea and 6 km N of the river Arnon. The city is mentioned by Ramesses II, who claimed its capture (K. A. Kitchen, *JEA* 50, 1964, pp. 63–70). Originally it belonged to Moab, but it was captured by Sihon, king of the Amorites, in pre-Israelite times (Nu. 21:26). The Israelites took it at the time of the Exodus (Nu. 21:30), and it was given to the tribes of Reuben and Gad (Nu. 32:2–3). Gad built Dibon, however (Nu. 32:34), and hence it is called Dibon-gad (Nu. 33:45), although in Jos. 13:15ff. it is reckoned to Reuben. It is probably one of the halting-places on the Exodus journey and is referred to in Nu. 33:45–46. Israel lost it later, it was regained by Omri and lost again to Mesha, king of Moab, who speaks of it on the *Moabite Stone, lines 21 and 28. Isaiah and Jeremiah knew it as a Moabite town (Is. 15:2; Je. 48:18, 22).

Archaeological excavations were carried out by the American Schools of Oriental Research in 1950–5 in the SE, NW and NE corners of the mound. There is some evidence for Early Bronze Age occupation, some levels at bedrock, a wall and pottery from Early Bronze III. The Moabite occupation proper dates from Iron I and is represented by several large buildings. In the SE corner the remains are from Iron II extending from the mid-9th century to the destruction by Nebuchadrezzar in 582 BC. Here lay a royal quarter, possibly built by Mesha. Later remains come from the Nabataean, Byzantine and Arab periods.

BIBLIOGRAPHY. F. M. Abel, *Géographie de la Palestine*, 2, 1937, pp. 304–305; N. Glueck, *Exploration in Eastern Palestine*, 3, *AASOR* 18–19, 1937–8, pp. 115, 224ff.; W. H. Morton, *BASOR* 140, 1955, pp. 5 ff.; R. E. Murphy, *BASOR* 125, 1952, pp. 20–23; W. L. Reid, *BASOR* 146, 1957, pp. 6–10; A. D. Tushingham, *BASOR* 133, 1954, pp. 6–26; 138, 1955, pp. 29–34; *AASOR* 40, 1972; F. V. Winnett, *BASOR* 125, 1952; *idem*, and W. L. Reid, *AASOR* 36–37, 1961.

J.A.T.

DINAH (Heb. *dînâ*, 'judgment' or 'judged'). Daughter of Jacob by Leah (Gn. 30:21; 46:15). While Jacob was encamped near Shechem, Dinah went out to visit the local womenfolk (Gn. 34); however, Shechem, son of Hamor, Hivite prince of Shechem, was attracted to her, apparently forced himself upon her, and then sought her in marriage from Jacob. But Jacob's sons were indignant; they stipulated circumcision of the Shechemites before any marriage could be agreed to. Then Simeon and Levi (obviously with their retainers) caught the Shechemites off guard and slaughtered them treacherously. This deed was disapproved of (Gn. 34:30) and denounced (Gn. 49:5–7) by Jacob. The recording of sad incidents of this kind involving womenfolk is noted as a mark of early (pre-Solomonic) date for such narratives by C. H. Gordon, *HUCA* 26, 1955, p. 80. K.A.K.

DIONYSIUS THE AREOPAGITE. A member of the aristocratic council of Athens (*AREOPAGUS); one of Paul's few Athenian converts (Acts 17:34). A 2nd-century tradition (Dionysius of Corinth in Eusebius, *EH* 3. 4; 4. 23), that he was the first bishop of Athens may rest only on this passage. A body of much later mystical writings was long accepted as his and exercised a very strong influence in the Middle Ages (see partial English tr. by C. E. Rolt; R. Roques, 'Dionysius Areopagitica' in *RAC* for recent study). Other speculations about Dionysius, possibly related to the pagan Dionysos cult, are traced by Rendel Harris, *Annotators of the Codex Bezae*, 1901, pp. 76ff. A.F.W.

DIOTREPHES. A refractory person of overweening ambition who would not recognize John the Elder, publicly attacked him, forbade the reception of his adherents, and, whether by formal excommunication or physical violence, excluded those who did receive them. Though the Elder's personal intervention would eventually be decisive, the effect of his letters could be annulled by the present influence of Diotrephes (3 Jn. 9–10). It is not clear whether this was in virtue of a regular office (*e.g.* as an early monarchical bishop—*cf.* T. Zahn, *INT*, 3, pp. 374ff.) or by dominance of personality among his peers (*cf.* J. V. Bartlet, *JTS* 6, 1905, pp. 204ff.). For other imaginative reconstructions, *cf.* J. Chapman, *JTS* 5, 1904, pp. 357ff., 517ff.; B. H. Streeter, *The Primitive Church*, 1929, pp. 83ff.; C. H. Dodd, *The Johannine Epistles*, 1945, pp. 161ff. A.F.W.

DISCIPLE. A disciple (from Lat. *discipulus*, 'pupil, learner', corresponding to Gk. *mathētēs*, from *manthanō*, 'to learn') is basically the pupil of a teacher. The corresponding Heb. term *limmûḏ* is somewhat rare in the OT (Is. 8:16; 50:4; 54:13; *cf.* Je. 13:23), but in the rabbinical writings the *talmîḏ* (*cf.* 1 Ch. 25:8) is a familiar figure as the pupil of a rabbi from whom he learned traditional lore. In the Gk. world philosophers were likewise surrounded by their pupils. Since pupils often adopted the distinctive teaching of their masters, the word came to signify the adherent of a particular outlook in religion or philosophy.

Jewish usage is seen in the NT references to the disciples of the Pharisees (Mk. 2:18). The Jews considered themselves to be ultimately disciples of Moses (Jn. 9:28), since his teaching formed the basis of rabbinic instruction. The followers of John the Baptist were known as his disciples (Mk. 2:18; Jn. 1:35). The term was probably applied to his close associates. They practised prayer and fasting in accordance with his instructions (Mk. 2:18; Lk. 11:1), and some of them cared for him in prison and saw to his burial (Mt. 11:2–7; Mk. 6:29).

Although Jesus (like John) was not an officially recognized teacher (Jn. 7:14f.), he was popularly known as a teacher or rabbi (Mk. 9:5; 11:21; Jn. 3:2), and his associates were known as disciples. The word can be used of all who responded to his message (Mt. 5:1; Lk. 6:17; 19:37), but it can also refer more narrowly to those who accompanied him on his travels (Mk. 6:45; Lk. 8:2f.; 10:1), and especially to the twelve apostles (Mk. 3:14). Discipleship was based on a call by Jesus (Mk. 1:16–20; 2:13f.; Lk. 9:59–62; even Lk. 9:57f. presupposes Jesus' invitation in general terms). It involved personal allegiance to him, expressed in following him and giving him an exclusive loyalty (Mk. 8:34–38; Lk. 14:26–33). In at least some cases it meant literal abandonment of home, business ties and possessions (Mk. 10:21, 28), but in every case readiness to put the claims of Jesus first, whatever the cost, was demanded. Such an attitude went well beyond the normal pupil–teacher relationship and gave the word 'disciple' a new sense. Faith in Jesus and allegiance to him are what determine the fate of men at the last judgment (Lk. 12:8f.).

Those who became disciples were taught by Jesus and appointed as his representatives to preach his message, cast out demons and heal the sick (Mk. 3:14f.); although these responsibilities were primarily delegated to the Twelve, they were not confined to them (Mk. 5:19; 9:38–41; Lk. 10:1–16).

According to Luke, the members of the early church were known as disciples (Acts 6:1f., and frequently thereafter). This makes it clear that the earthly disciples of Jesus formed the nucleus of the church and that the pattern of the relationship between Jesus and his earthly disciples was constitutive for the relationship between the risen Lord and the members of his church. The word, however, is not found outside the Gospels and Acts, and other NT writers used a variety of terms (believers, saints, brothers) to express more fully the characteristics of discipleship after Easter.

BIBLIOGRAPHY. K. H. Rengstorf, *TDNT* 4, pp. 415–460; E. Schweizer, *Lordship and Discipleship*, 1960; M. Hengel, *Nachfolge und Charisma*, Berlin, 1968; *NIDNTT* 1, pp. 480–494. I.H.M.

DISPERSION. The term 'Dispersion' (Gk. *diaspora*) can denote either Jews scattered in the non-Jewish world (as in Jn. 7:35; 1 Pet. 1:1) or the places in which they reside (as in Jas. 1:1; Judith 5:19).

I. Origins

It is difficult to know how early the voluntary dispersion of Israel began; there are hints of an early 'colony' in Damascus (1 Ki. 20:34), and Solomon's expansionist policies may well have led to earlier commercial outposts. But the conquering kings of Assyria and Babylonia introduced a new factor, the compulsory transplantation of sections of the population to other parts of their empire (2 Ki. 15:29; 17:6; 24:14ff.; 25:11ff.). Involved in this policy was the removal of the classes providing the natural leadership and the skilled craftsmen. Many of these transplanted groups, especially from the N kingdom, probably lost their national and religious identity, but the Judaean community in Babylon had a rich prophetic ministry, learnt to retain the worship of the God of Israel without Temple or sacrifice, and produced the purposeful men who returned to rebuild Jerusalem. Only a portion, however, returned under Cyrus; a sizeable and intensely self-conscious Jewish community remained in mediaeval times, with its own recension of the Talmud.

II. Extent

The Israelites abroad were not forgotten at home, and prophetic pictures of God's gracious intervention in the last times include the happy restoration of 'the dispersed of Israel' (*e.g.* Is. 11:12; Zp. 3:10; *cf.* also Ps. 147:2, where LXX significantly renders 'the *diasporai* of Israel'). The area of the prophets' visions is often much wider than the Assyrian and Babylonian empires. In other words, another dispersion—probably originally voluntary, but reinforced, as Je. 43:7; 44:1 show, by refugees—had already begun. Jews were settling in Egypt and beyond, and in less-known areas. Some rather lurid light is cast on what the communities in Egypt could be like by the Aramaic papyri found at Elephantine (*PAPYRI, *SEVENEH) as distant as the First Cataract, from a Jewish trading-community with its own altar and idiosyncrasies.

With Alexander the Great's con-

DISEASE
See Health, Part 2.

DISINFECTANT
See Herbs, Part 2.

DISOBEDIENCE
See Obedience, Part 2.

A Babylonian model of a sheep's liver made of clay, marked off into fifty sections, inscribed with omens and magical formulae for the use of diviners. 13·3 cm × 8·3 cm. 1830–1530 BC. (BM)

quests a new era of the Dispersion begins: a steadily increasing stream of Jewish immigrants is noticed in the most diverse places. In the 1st century AD Philo numbered the Jews in Egypt at a million (*In Flaccum* 43). Strabo the geographer, somewhat earlier, notes the number and status of the Jews in Cyrene, adding: 'This people has already made its way into every city, and it is not easy to find any place in the habitable world which has not received this nation, and in which it has not made its power felt' (quoted by Jos., *Ant.* 14. 115, Loeb edition).

Of the general truth of Strabo's estimate there is abundant evidence. Syria had large Jewish 'colonies'. Juster (1914) listed 71 cities in Asia Minor which the Dispersion affected: the list could doubtless be augmented today. Roman writers such as Horace testify in no friendly fashion to the presence and habits of Jews in the capital. As early as 139 BC there was an expulsion of the Jews from Rome: the edict mentioned in Acts 18:2 had several precedents. But somehow the Jews always came back. For all their unpopularity—barely concealed in the speeches of the governors Pilate and Gallio, quite evident in the mob-cries of Philippi (Acts 16:20) and Ephesus (Acts 19:34)—the Jews established themselves as a kind of universal exception. Their social exclusiveness, their incomprehensible taboos and their uncompromising religion were all tolerated. They alone might be exempted from 'official' sacrifices, and (since they would not march on the sabbath) from military service. Under Seleucids, Ptolemies and Romans alike, the Dispersion, with much patent dislike to face, and occasionally outbreaks of savage violence, enjoyed, in the main, peace and prosperity.

The spread of the Dispersion was not confined to the Roman empire: it was prominent in the Persian sphere of influence too, as the account of the Pentecost crowd illustrates (Acts 2:9–11). Josephus has revealing stories of Jewish freebooters of Fra Diavolo stature in Parthia (*Ant.* 18. 310ff.), and of the conversion and circumcision of the king of the buffer state of Adiabene (*Ant.* 20. 17ff.).

III. Characteristics

The oddities of Elephantine are not typical of later Dispersion Judaism. The life of most of these communities lay in the law and the synagogue, though it may be noted that the refugee Zadokite high priest Onias set up a temple at Leontopolis in Egypt, in the 2nd century BC, on the basis of Is. 19:18ff., and said that most of the Egyptian Jews had temples 'contrary to what is proper' (*Ant.* 13. 66). But in the nature of things they could not live exactly as the Jews in Palestine. The westward Dispersion had to live in the Greek world, and it had to speak Greek. One major result of this was the translation of the sacred books into Greek, the Septuagint (*TEXTS AND VERSIONS). The legends about its origin at least bear witness to the missionary spirit of Hellenistic Judaism. Although it may be misleading to generalize from Alexandria, we can see there a prosperous and educated Jewish community seeking to make intellectual contact with an established Greek culture. The 'de-Messianized' but otherwise orthodox Judaism of the book of Wisdom and of Philo are characteristic products. There is evidence also of Jewish missionary apologetic directed to pagans of Greek education, and of codes of instruction for pagan converts. There is perhaps a slightly satirical commentary on Diaspora Judaism's understanding of its mission in Rom. 2:17–24.

Hellenistic Jewish culture was faithful to law and nation (*cf.* Phil. 3:5–6—the confession of a Jew of the Dispersion). The communities paid the half-shekel Temple tax, and maintained contact with each other and with Jerusalen (*cf.* Acts 28:21f.). The devout visited Jerusalem for the great feasts when possible (Acts 2:5ff.; 8:27) and often had closer ties with the mother-country. But so different had the cultural atmosphere become that the Dispersion communities had their own synagogues there (*cf.* Acts 6:9). It is possible that Stephen learnt some of his radicalism about the Temple from Diaspora Judaism in pre-conversion days.

Notwithstanding Jewish unpopularity, it is clear that Judaism strongly attracted many Gentiles. The simple but majestic worship of one God, the lofty ethics, the generally high standards of family life, brought many, including people of rank, to the synagogues. The necessity of circumcision probably held back many men from becoming full *proselytes, but numbers remained in attendance as 'God-fearers'. Thus we regularly find Gentiles in the synagogues during Paul's missionary journeys (*cf.* Acts 13:43ff.; 14:1; 17:4; 18:4ff.).

A less happy aspect of the attraction of Judaism was the widespread belief, to which many sources testify, that Jews possessed special magical powers and that their sacred words were particularly efficacious in incantations. Undoubtedly unscrupulous Jews traded on this reputation, and we meet one such in Acts 13:6ff. It is likely, too, that there was a fringe of Jewish syncretistic and sectarian teaching which dealt in the mystery and occult so fascinating to the Hellenistic world. Some pagan cults—such as the Sabazios cult in Phrygia—eagerly scattered Judaic ingredients into their exotically flavoured religious pot-pourri; but, however important these may be for the history of Christian heresy (*GNOSTICISM), there is little evidence that they were in themselves representative of and significant for Dispersion Judaism as a whole. As might be expected, archaeological study reveals considerable formal differences, and differing degrees of cultural exclusiveness, at various times and places; but nothing indicates that there was any major indecision in Diaspora Judaism as to the uniqueness of Israel's God, his revelation in the Torah, and his people.

IV. Relation to Christianity

The influence of the Dispersion in preparing the way for the gospel is beyond doubt. The synagogues stretched over the greater part of the known world were the stepping-stones of the early missionaries. Acts shows Paul, the self-confessed apostle to the Gentiles, regularly opening his evangelistic work by synagogue preaching. Almost as regularly a division follows, the majority of Israelites by birth refusing the proffered Messiah, the Gentiles (*i.e.* the proselytes and God-fearers) receiving him joyfully. Representative converts, such as Cornelius and the Ethiopian eunuch, had first been proselytes or God-fearers. Clearly the God-fearers—children of the Dispersion—are a vital factor in early church history. They came to faith with some previous knowledge of God and the Scriptures, and already watchful of idolatry and immorality.

The LXX also performed a missionary service beyond its effect on those Gentiles in contact with synagogues; and more than one Christian Father testifies that the reading of the LXX played a vital part in his conversion.

An apparent confusion in some pagan writers makes it difficult to tell whether Judaism or Christianity is alluded to. This may be due to the fact that so often a Christian community arose within the bosom of Diaspora Judaism: and to an ignorant or indifferent pagan, even if he believed the horror stories about Christian arson and cannibalism, the attitude of converts towards many traditional practices might seem to be Jewish. On the other hand, Jewish influence on many leading converts helps to explain why 'Judaizing' was such a peril in the apostolic church.

It is interesting that Peter and James, both Palestinian Jews, address Christians as 'the Dispersion' (Jas. 1:1; 1 Pet. 1:1). Like the members of the old dispersion, they are 'sojourners' where they live; they enjoy a solidarity unknown to the heathen; and they owe a transcendent loyalty to the Jerusalem which is above.

BIBLIOGRAPHY. J. Juster, *Les Juifs dans l'Empire Romain*, 1914; A. Causse, *Les Dispersés d'Israel*, 1929; E. Schürer, *History of the Jewish People*, 2, 1978; *BC*, 1, pp. 137ff.; E. R. Goodenough, *Jewish Symbols in the Greco-Roman period*, 1953–68 (relation to pagan symbolism); R. McL. Wilson, *The Gnostic Problem*, 1958; V. Tcherikover, *Hellenistic Civilization and the Jews*, 1959; H. J. Leon, *The Jews of Ancient Rome*, 1960; M. Grant, *The Jews in the Roman World*, 1973; E. M. Smallwood, *The Jews under Roman Rule*, 1977.

A.F.W.

DIVINATION. The usual Heb. word translated 'divination' and 'diviner' is the root *qsm*. The root *nḥš* is used in Gn. 44:5, 15, and elsewhere this is translated 'enchanter', 'enchantment', 'use enchantments'. The root *'nn* is sometimes coupled with the former words, and is translated 'observe times' (RV 'practise augury'), and twice 'soothsayings'.

Divination is roughly the attempt to discern events that are distant in time or space, and that consequently cannot be perceived by normal means. A similar definition could be given for the seership aspect of prophecy, as exercised in, *e.g.*, 1 Sa. 9:6–10. Hence the term could be used occasionally in a good sense, as we might speak of a prophet having clairvoyant gifts without thereby approving all forms of clairvoyance. Thus Balaam is a diviner as well as being inspired of God (Nu. 22:7; 24:1). The divination condemned in Ezk. 13:6–7 is specified as 'lying'. In Mi. 3:6–7, 11, divining is a function of the prophets, though here also they have prostituted their gift; *cf.* Zc. 10:2. In Pr. 16:10 *qesem* ('inspired decisions') is used of the divine guidance given through the king.

Apart from these general uses, divination is condemned, except for two passages noted below. God's people are forbidden to use divination and enchantments as the pagan world did (Lv. 19:26; Dt. 18:9–14), and 2 Ki. 17:17; 21:6 record their disobedience. Pagan diviners are mentioned in 1 Sa. 6:2; Is. 44:25; Ezk. 21:22.

Divination may take many forms. One can make two broad divisions, namely, internal and mechanical: the former is either the trance inspiration of the shaman type, or direct second sight; the latter makes use of technical means, such as sand, entrails of a sacrifice, or in modern times tea-leaves. These divisions cannot be pressed, since the objects may release the clairvoyant faculty, as with crystal-gazing. Balaam may have released his powers in this way (Nu. 24:1).

The following forms are mentioned in the Bible.

a. Rhabdomancy. Ezk. 21:21. Sticks or arrows were thrown into the air, and omens were deduced from their position when they fell. Ho. 4:12 could also be a reference to this.

b. Hepatoscopy. Ezk. 21:21. Examination of the liver or other entrails of a sacrifice was supposed to give guidance. Probably shapes and markings were classified, and the priest interpreted them.

c. **Teraphim.* Associated with divination in 1 Sa. 15:23 ('idolatry', RSV); Ezk. 21:21; Zc. 10:2. If the teraphim were images of dead ancestors, the divination was probably a form of spiritualism.

DISQUALIFICATION
See Reprobate, Part 3.

DISTAFF
See Spinning, Part 3.

DIVES
See Lazarus, Part 2.

DIVINERS' OAK
See Meonenim, oak of, Part 2.

DOG-STAR
See Stars, Part 3.

DONKEY
See Animals, Part 1.

DOVE
See Animals, Part 1.

DOWRY
See Marriage, Part 2.

DOXOLOGY
See Lord's Prayer, Part 2.

DRACHMON, DRACHMA
See Money, Part 2.

d. Necromancy, or the consultation of the departed. This is associated with divination in Dt. 18:11; 1 Sa. 28:8; 2 Ki. 21:6, and is condemned in the Law (Lv. 19:31; 20:6), the Prophets (Is. 8:19–20) and the historical books (1 Ch. 10:13). The medium was spoken of as having an *'ôḇ*, translated 'a familiar spirit', or in modern terms 'a control'. An associated term, translated 'wizard', is *yid'ônî*, probably from the root *yāḏa'*, 'know', and presumably refers to the supernatural knowledge claimed by the spirit and in a secondary sense by its owner.

e. Astrology draws conclusions from the position of the sun, moon and planets in relation to the zodiac and to one another. While not condemned, astrology is belittled in Is. 47:13 and Je. 10:2. The wise men (* MAGI) who came to the infant Jesus (Mt. 2:9) were probably trained in Bab. tradition which mixed astronomy with astrology.

f. Hydromancy, or divination through water. Here forms and pictures appear in the water in a bowl, as also in crystal-gazing. The gleam of the water induces a state of light trance, and the visions are subjective. The only reference to this in the Bible is Gn. 44:5, 15, where it might appear that Joseph used his silver cup for this purpose. But one cannot say how much credence to give to a statement that comes in a section where Joseph and his steward are deliberately deceiving his brothers.

g. Lots. In the OT the lot was cast to discover God's will for the allocation of territory (Jos. 18–19, *etc.*), the choice of the goat to be sacrificed on the Day of Atonement (Lv. 16), the detection of a guilty person (Jos. 7:14; Jon. 1:7), the allocation of Temple duties (1 Ch. 24:5), the discovery of a lucky day by Haman (Est. 3:7). In the NT Christ's clothes were allocated by lot (Mt. 27:35). The last occasion in the Bible on which the lot is used to divine the will of God is in the choice of Matthias (Acts 1:15–26), and there may be a significance in that this is before Pentecost. (See also * URIM AND THUMMIM.)

h. * *Dreams* are often counted as a means of divination, but in the Bible there is no instance of a person's deliberately asking for guidance or supernatural knowledge through dreams, except perhaps the false prophets in Je. 23:25–27. The spontaneous dream, however, is often a means of divine guidance.

In Acts 16:16 a girl has a spirit of divination. The Gk. here is *pythōn*. The famous Delphic oracle was in the district of Pytho, and the term evidently was used loosely for anyone supernaturally inspired, as was the priestess at Delphi. (* MAGIC AND SORCERY.)

BIBLIOGRAPHY. C. Brown, J. S. Wright, *NIDNTT* 2, pp. 552–562.

J.S.W.

DIZAHAB. One of the places named in Dt. 1:1 to define the site of the speeches which follow. It has often been identified with Ḏahab on the E coast of the Sinai peninsula (*e.g.* Rothenberg and Aharoni), but this is not easily reconciled with the other data given (*cf.* v. 5). A location in N Moab is required, and eḏ-Ḏheibe (30 km E of Ḥesbân/Heshbon) seems the most probable suggestion so far.

BIBLIOGRAPHY. F. M. Abel, *Géographie de la Palestine*, 2, 1937, p. 307 and map 4; B. Rothenberg and Y. Aharoni, *God's Wilderness*, 1961, pp. 144, 161.

G.I.D.

DOCTRINE. In the OT the word occurs chiefly as a translation of *leqaḥ*, meaning 'what is received' (Dt. 32:2; Jb. 11:4; Pr. 4:2; Is. 29:24). The idea of a body of revealed teaching is chiefly expressed by *tôrâ*, which occurs 216 times and is rendered as 'law'.

In the NT two words are used. *didaskalia* means both the act and the content of teaching. It is used of the Pharisees' teaching (Mt. 15:9; Mk. 7:7). Apart from one instance in Colossians and one in Ephesians, it is otherwise confined to the Pastoral Epistles (and seems to refer often to some body of teaching used as a standard of orthodoxy). *didachē* is used in more parts of the NT. It too can mean either the act or the content of teaching. It occurs of the teaching of Jesus (Mt. 7:28, *etc.*) which he claimed to be divine (Jn. 7:16–17). After Pentecost Christian doctrine began to be formulated (Acts 2:42) as the instruction given to those who had responded to the *kērygma* (Rom. 6:17). There were some in the church whose official function was to teach this to new converts (*e.g.* 1 Cor. 12:28–29). For the content of the *didachē*, see E. G. Selwyn, *The First Epistle of St Peter*, 1946, Essay II.

R.E.N.

DODANIM. The name of a people descended from Javan, son of Japheth, mentioned twice in the OT (Gn. 10:4: Heb. *dōḏānîm*, LXX *Rhodioi*; 1 Ch. 1:7: Heb. *rôḏānîm*, LXX *Rhodioi*). The Genesis reference is probably to be read (with the Samaritan Pentateuch) *rôḏānîm* (*d* and *r* are readily confused in both the old and the 'square' Heb. scripts), referring to the inhabitants of the island of Rhodes. See E. Dhorme, *Syria* 13, 1932, pp. 48–49.

T.C.M.

DOOR-POST, GATE-POST, POST. 1. Heb. *mᵉzûzôṯ* were the wooden planks which framed a doorway and which supported the lintel, *mašqôp̄*, and on which an * amulet was later fixed. Blood was sprinkled on them at the first Passover (Ex. 12:7, 22–23), a slave's ear was pierced against one when he chose to remain with his master (Ex. 21:6), and the posts were to be written upon (Dt. 6:9; 11:20). The term is also used of temples (1 Sa. 1:9; 1 Ki. 6:33; Ezk. 41:21) and gates (Jdg. 16:3).

2. *'ayil*. Used mainly of Ezekiel's temple (40:9–10, *etc.*) where it is translated 'post' AV and 'jamb' RSV. It is thought to be a projection from the wall, such as a pilaster.

3. *sap̄*, 'post' AV, see * THRESHOLD.

C.J.D.

DOR. A city on the Mediterranean coast of Palestine, just S of Carmel. Its king joined with Jabin, king of Hazor, in his fight against Israel and shared in his defeat (Jos. 11:1–2; 12:23). Though on the borders of Asher, it was given to Manasseh, who failed to drive out the Canaanite inhabitants (Jdg. 1:27). See also 1 Ki. 4:11; 1 Ch. 7:29. It is associated with, but distinguished from, En-dor (Jos. 17:11). It is mentioned as 'a town of the Tjeker' in the Wen-Amon story, 11th century BC (*ANET*, p. 26). In Graeco-Roman times it was called Dora (neuter plural); *cf.* Josephus, *Ant.* 5. 87; 8. 35; *Ap.* 2. 114, 116; *Vita* 31.

G.T.M.

DORCAS, or Tabitha ('gazelle'), was renowned for charity in the church at Joppa (Acts 9:36). When she died they sent two members to Lydda for the apostle Peter. He came immediately, and following Jesus' example, excluded the mourners. Then he knelt and prayed, and fulfilled his divine commission (Mt. 10:8). She is the only woman disciple so called (*mathētria*) in the NT. M.B.

DOTHAN. The fertile plain of Dothan separates the hills of Samaria from the Carmel range. It provides an easy pass for travellers from Bethshan and Gilead on their way to Egypt. This was the route of the Ishmaelites who carried Joseph into Egypt. The good pasturage had attracted Jacob's sons from Shechem, 32 km to the S. Near the town (now *tell dōṯā*) are rectangular cisterns about 3 m deep similar to the pit into which Joseph was put (Gn. 37:17ff.). Elisha led the Syrian force, which had been sent to capture him, along the hill road to Samaria, 16 km S. His servant was encouraged by a vision of heavenly forces arrayed on the hill to the E of the town (2 Ki. 6:13–23).

Excavations (1953–60) revealed a walled city of the Early and Middle Bronze Ages, and a Late Bronze Age settlement apparently using the older city wall. Thothmes III lists Dothan among his conquests (*c.* 1480 BC). It was probably one of the towns which was absorbed by the Israelites, but not actually conquered (*cf.* Jdg. 1:27). Areas of the Iron Age town which have been cleared show the narrow streets and small houses with storage-pits and bread-ovens of Elisha's day. Among the finds are fifteen pieces of silver in a pottery box representing an individual's savings. There was also settlement in the Assyrian and Hellenistic periods (*cf.* Judith 4:6; 7:3).

BIBLIOGRAPHY. Excavation reports by J. P. Free, *BA* 19, 1956, pp. 43–48, 1953–5 seasons; *BASOR* 131, 1953, pp. 16–29; 135, 1954, pp. 14–20; 139, 1955, pp. 3–9; 143, 1956, pp. 11–17; 147, 1957, pp. 36–37; 152, 1958, pp. 10–18; 156, 1959, pp. 22–29; 160, 1960, pp. 6–15; *EAEHL* 1, pp. 337–339.

A.R.M.

DRAGON. In the OT two Heb. words are so translated by the AV.

1. *tan*, 'jackal' (so RSV). It always occurs in the plural, usually masculine (*tannîm*: Jb. 30:29; Ps. 44:19; Is. 13:22; 34:13; 35:7; 43:20; Je. 9:11; 10:22; 14:6; 49:33; 51:37; Ezk. 29:3; Mi. 1:8), but once in the feminine (*tannôṯ*: Mal. 1:3). In La. 4:3 the form *tannîn* occurs, but this is probably *tan* with the rare plural ending *-în* (nunation, as found in the Moabite Stone), and not a member of **2** below.

2. *tannîn*. A word of uncertain meaning, probably unrelated to *tan*. It is translated in AV 'dragon', 'whale' (Gn. 1:21; Jb. 7:12; RSV 'sea monster') and 'serpent' (Ex. 7:9–10, 12), the last being a satisfactory rendering in the Exodus passage, and it also seems to be the sense in Dt. 32:33 and Ps. 91:13; and possibly in Ne. 2:13. The other occurrences are less easy to define. In Gn. 1:21 evidently large sea-

This composite creature (mushruššu), *with a serpent's head, a lion's body and hind claws of an eagle, formed part of a frieze of similar symbolic figures (including bulls and serpent dragons) on the Ishtar Gate, Babylon. c. 600* BC. (SAOB)

Cylinder seal. The scene is generally interpreted as the slaughter of the dragon Tiamat ('the sea') by the god Marduk who is armed with a thunderbolt and other weapons. If this is so, it illustrates one version of the Babylonian epic of creation. (BM)

DREAD
See Fear, Part 1.

DREAMER
See Nehelam, Part 2.

DREGS
See Lees, Part 2.

creatures such as the whale are intended, and this may be the meaning of Jb. 7:12 and Ps. 148:7, though, on the basis of an Arabic cognate, 'water spout' is suggested by some (*e.g.* RVmg. for the latter). In Ps. 74:13; Is. 27:1 and 51:9, the crocodile may be intended, and the association with Egypt suggests the same possibility in Ezk. 29:3; 32:2, and even Je. 51:34. None of these meanings can be certain, and the term may in some contexts refer to an apocalyptic creature of some kind, as in NT *drakōn*, 'dragon', used figuratively of Satan in Rev. 12–13; 16 and 20. The word occurs in the LXX chiefly for *tannîn*.

BIBLIOGRAPHY. G. R. Driver in Z. V. Togan (ed.), *Proceedings of the Twenty-Second Congress of Orientalists . . . Istanbul . . ., 1951*, 2, 1957, pp. 114–115; A. Heidel, *The Babylonian Genesis*[2], 1951, pp. 102–105.

T.C.M.

DREAM. If comparing the 'dream' literature of the Babylonians and the Egyptians with the references to dreams in the OT, one is impressed by the Hebrews' lack of preoccupation with this phenomenon. Nor is the religious significance of the dreams that are recorded in the OT at all prominent. Indeed, dreams are said to derive from the activities in which the dreamer has been immersed during the day (Ec. 5:3). However, the OT recognizes that, whatever the origin of a dream, it may become a means by which God communicates with men, be they Israelites (1 Ki. 3:5) or non-Israelites (Gn. 20:3ff.).

Dreams recorded in Scripture are of two kinds. First, there are those consisting of the ordinary dream phenomena in which the sleeper 'sees' a connected series of images which correspond to events in everyday life (Gn. 40:9–17; 41:1–7). Secondly, there are dreams which communicate to the sleeper a message from God (Gn. 20:3–7; 1 Ki. 3:5–15; Mt. 1:20–24). On occasions there is virtually no distinction between a dream and a *vision during the night (Jb. 4:12f.; Acts 16:9; 18:9f.)

In interpreting dreams the Bible distinguishes between the dream-phenomena reported by non-Israelites and by Israelites. Gentiles such as pharaoh (Gn. 41:15ff.) and his high-ranking officers (40:12f., 18f.) require Joseph to explain their dreams, and Nebuchadrezzar needs Daniel (Dn. 2:17ff.). On occasion God himself speaks and so renders human intervention unnecessary (Gn. 20:3ff.; 31:24; Mt. 2:12). But when the members of the covenant community dream, the interpretation accompanies the dream (Gn. 37:5–10; Acts 16:9f.).

This subject is important for the OT view of prophecy. Among the Hebrews there was a close association between dreams and the function of the prophet. The *locus classicus* is Dt. 13:1–5, where the prophet is mentioned along with the dreamer without betraying any sense of incongruity. The close connection in Heb. thought between dreaming and prophesying is again revealed in Je. 23:25–32. It is also clear that in the days of Samuel and Saul it was commonly believed that the Lord spoke through dreams as well as by Urim and prophets (1 Sa. 28:6). Joel 2:28 (quoted Acts 2:17) links prophecy, dreams and visions with the outpouring of the Spirit.

Moses is described as the only prophet to whom the Lord spoke 'mouth to mouth, clearly, and not in dark speech' (Nu. 12:6–8; *cf.* Dt. 34:10), but the context shows that vision and dream are equally valid means of prophetic revelation (Nu. 12:6). Jeremiah censures the false prophets for treating the dreams of their own subconscious as revelations from God (Je. 23:16, 25–27, 32), but he admits that a true prophet can have a genuine prophetic dream (v. 28), the proof being the hammerlike message it contained (v. 29). Jeremiah himself certainly knew the dream form of prophetic inspiration (31:26).

In the NT Matthew records five dreams in connection with the birth and infancy of Jesus, in three of which an angel appeared with God's message (Mt. 1:20; 2:12–13, 19, 22). Later he records the troubled dream of Pilate's wife (27:19). Other passages speak of *visions rather than dreams, but the borderline is thin.

BIBLIOGRAPHY. *EBT*, 1, pp. 214ff.; P. J. Budd, *NIDNTT* 1, pp. 511–513; *ZPEB*, 2, p. 162; E. D. Ehrlich, *Der Traum im Alten Testament*, *BZAW* 73, 1953; A. L. Oppenheim, *The Interpretation of Dreams in the Ancient Near East*, 1956.

J.G.S.S.T.
J.S.W.

DRESS. The OT does not give us a detailed description of the various kinds of dress which were worn in Palestine. However, the Egyp., Bab. and Hittite monuments enable us to get a good idea of the general dress. In the tomb of Khnumhotep at Beni-hasan (Egypt) we find a procession of Asiatics who arrive in Egypt with eyepaint (*ANEP*, fig. 3). They are all dressed in vividly coloured garments, and this gives a clue as to how Abraham and other nomads were clad in about the 12th Egyptian Dynasty.

According to Gn. 3:7, 21 the origin of dress is associated with the sense of shame. It is a shame to be naked (Gn. 9:22–23) and this is especially the fate of prisoners and fugitives (Is. 20:4; Am. 2:16; Mk. 14:52). Children, however, used to run naked up to puberty.

The most important garments seem to have been a kind of loin- or waist-cloth, a long or short shirt or robe, an upper garment and a cloak, not to speak of the belt, headdress, veil and sandals.

a. Men's dress

We find but few mentions of a loin- or waist-cloth (*'ēzôr*) reaching from the waist to the knee. This was a common dress during the Bronze II and III ages, but it disappears as a civilian dress during Bronze III, although remaining as a military dress (Ezk. 23:15; Is. 5:27). Almost as primitive is an animal skin and the hairy cloak or mantle (Zc. 13:4; 2 Ki. 1:8; Mt. 3:4), which was worn only by prophets and poor people (Ecclus. 40:4) or for penitence. Covering of the hips and thighs was required only of priests (Ex. 28:42; 39:28). Otherwise these breeches were unknown in the OT and in the ancient Near East, except among the Persians, who knew the *šalwâr*, probably the *sarbâl* of Dn. 3:21, 27.

The ordinary shirt, which becomes predominant in Bronze III and is the normal dress in the Iron Age, is mentioned in the Bible as *kuttōneṯ* (Gk. *chitôn*), which seems to have been made of linen or wool. It is worn next to the skin and reaches down to the knees or to the ankles. It is made with or without sleeves, short or long (see Benzinger, *Hebr. Arch.*, figs. 59–60; Marston, *The Bible Comes Alive*, plate 15, bottom). For work or while running, this shirt was pulled up (Ex. 12:11; 2 Ki. 4:29). The Bible also mentions a *kuttōneṯ passîm*, which was a special kind of garment (Gn. 37:3, 23, 32), and was worn also by princes (2 Sa. 13:18–19). It was possibly a highly

Fine linen robe, gold collar and diadem worn by Queen Ahmose-Nefertari (c. 1550 BC). Wall-painting from Thebes. c. 1150 BC. (BM)

Top left: Royal kilt and fine linen robe worn by King Amenhotep I (c. 1540 BC). He carries a crook, insignia of kingship. Wall-painting from Thebes. c. 1150 BC. (BM)

Semi-nomadic 'Asiatic' smiths from Palestine. The multi-coloured garments of the smiths contrast with the plain white Egyptian dress. Tomb of Khnumhotep III. c. 1890 BC. (PAC)

coloured garment, a kind of plaid twisted round the body, as is shown by the Syrian ambassadors to Tutankhamūn (*ANEP*, fig. 52). The shirt, presumably worn underneath it, is possibly the *sāḏin* (Jdg. 14:12; Pr. 31:24; Is. 3:23; LXX *sindōn*), but might include in this class of garments the *m*e*'îl*, regularly torn as a sign of mourning (Ezr. 9:3; Jb. 1:20; 2:12), and worn by men of importance, *e.g.* Jonathan (1 Sa. 18:4), Samuel (1 Sa. 2:19; 15:27; 28:14), Saul (1 Sa. 24:4, 11), Job and his friends (Jb. 1:20; 2:12) and Ezra (Ezr. 9:3).

The ordinary mantle is generally called *śimlâ*. It can be identified with the *'abâye* of the modern *fellahin* (Benzinger, *Hebr. Arch.*, fig. 73). This is a more or less square piece of cloth, which is sometimes thrown over one shoulder or, as now, over both shoulders. There are openings for the arms at the sides. This cloak, which everybody possessed, could not be given in loan, as it was used at night as a covering (Ex. 22:25–26; Dt. 24:13). It was generally taken off for work (Mt. 24:18; Mk. 10:50). It was also used to carry all kinds of objects (see Ex. 12:34; Jdg. 8:25; 2 Ki. 4:39; Hg. 2:12).

Another cloak was called *'adderet*, which it is not easy to describe. It was sometimes made of a costly material (Jos. 7:21, 24) and was worn by the king (Jon. 3:6) and by prophets (1 Ki. 19:13, 19; 2 Ki. 2:13–14), where it was possibly made from animal's skin. It was

Syrian tribute-bearers wearing a shirt-like garment (Heb. kᵉṯoneṯ*) which came down to the ankles. A roll of cloth, wrapped round, formed an outer garment (Heb.* simlah*). 1·32 m × 1·12 m. Thebes. Reign of Thutmose IV, 1421–1413 BC.* (BM)

not in general use, and the word does not appear in late Hebrew.

For a head-covering Israelites probably wore a folded square of cloth as a veil for protection against the sun, or wrapped it as a turban around the head. RSV translates *miḡbā‘ôṯ* as ‘caps’ (Ex. 28:40; Lv. 8:13) and *p*^{e}*’ēr* as ‘headdress’ (Is. 3:20) and ‘linen turbans’ (Ezk. 44:18); AV ‘bonnet’. Notable men and women wore in later times the *ṣānîp̱* (Is. 3:23; 62:3), which was a piece of cloth twisted round the head.

The poor people generally went about barefoot, but the sandal was known (Dt. 25:10; Am. 2:6; 8:6). The soles (*n*^{e}*‘ālîm*) were of leather or wood and tied with thongs (*ś*^{e}*rôḵ*) (Gn. 14:23; Is. 5:27; Mk. 1:7; Lk. 3:16, AV ‘latchet’). These were not worn inside the house.

b. Women’s dress

The dress of women was very much the same as that for men. But the difference must have been sufficiently noticeable, because it was forbidden for men to wear women’s clothes, and vice versa (Dt. 22:5). The difference has to be sought in finer material, more colours and the use of a veil and a kind of headcloth (*miṭpaḥaṯ*: Is. 3:22, AV ‘wimple’; translated ‘mantle’ in Ru. 3:15), which could be used to carry loads (Benzinger, *Hebr. Arch.*, fig. 59; Marston, *loc. cit.*). The most common dresses for the Israelite women are the *kuttōneṯ* and the *śimlâ*. The fine underwear *saḏîn* is also worn by women (Pr. 31:24; Is. 3:23). For feasts, women wore a more costly attire (1 Tim. 2:9). Hip and thigh clothing was not worn. A long train or veil was used by ladies of rank (Is. 47:2; Na. 3:5). Articles mentioned in the catalogue of Is. 3:18ff. cannot now be more particularly identified.

c. Dress for special occasions

Festive attire was distinctive from ordinary dress only in that the material was more costly (Gn. 27:15; Mt. 22:11–12; Lk. 15:22). The colour was preferably white (Ec. 9:8; Mk. 9:3; Rev. 3:4). Tissues of byssus, scarlet and purple were much appreciated (Pr. 31:22; Ecclus. 6:30; Je. 4:30). Women liked to adorn their clothes with gold and silver (2 Sa. 1:24; Ps. 45:9, 14–15; Ezk. 16:10, 13; 27:7).

Dress for mourning and penitence (*śaq*) was probably some kind of haircloth similar to the mantle of the prophets. This was worn with a belt and sometimes on the naked body (Gn. 37:34; 2 Sa. 3:31; 1 Ki. 21:27; 2 Ki. 6:30).

d. Dress of priests

The oldest sacred dress seems to have been the *’ēpôḏ baḏ*, probably a simple loin-cloth (2 Sa. 6:14, 20). The priests of Nob were known as men who wore the ‘linen ephod’ (1 Sa. 22:18). Samuel (1 Sa. 2:18) and David (2 Sa. 6:14) wore a simple linen ephod. This ordinary ephod has to be distinguished from the ephod of the high priest made of costly material (byssus = *šēš*), worked with gold, purple, scarlet or the like. This part of the dress reached from the breast down to the hips. It was held in place by two shoulder-bands and was tied round the waist (Ex. 39:1–26). There is also mention of an ephod which was used for the oracles. This was hung in the Temple (1 Sa. 21:9). The ordinary priests wore during the liturgical service a cloth which covered the hips and thighs (Ex. 28:42–43; Lv. 16:4) and a long embroidered linen tunic with sleeves (Ex. 28:40; 39:27), also an elaborately worked belt of twined linen, blue, purple and scarlet stuff (Ex. 28:40; 39:29) (Nötscher, *Bibl. Alterumskunde*, 1940). They had

Similarly Judaeans, depicted on Shalmaneser III’s Black Obelisk, wear a k^{e}ṯoneṯ *with fringed hem, over which is draped a* simlah *with the tasselled end thrown over the left shoulder. Pointed caps and sandals were worn for travel.* (BM)

DROMEDARY
See Animals, Part 1.

DROSS
See Reprobate, Part 3.

DRUM
See Music, Part 2.

DRUNKENNESS
See Wine, Part 3.

DUGONG
See Animals, Part 1.

DULCIMER
See Music, Part 2.

also a kind of turban called *miṣnep̄eṯ* (Ex. 28:4, 37, 39; 29:6; 39:28). As in Egypt and Babylon, it was forbidden for priests to wear woollen clothes (Ezk. 44:17). They were not allowed to wear sandals in the Temple (Ex. 3:5; 29:20).

BIBLIOGRAPHY. In general: M. G. Houston, *Ancient Egyptian and Persian Costume and Decoration*², 1954; *ANEP*, figs. 1–66 and *passim*; H. F. Lutz, *Textiles and Customs among the People of the Ancient Near East*, 1923. Near East with special reference to the OT: I. Benzinger, *Hebräische Archäologie*³, 1927, pp. 72–89. Egyptian material in A. Erman, *Life in Ancient Egypt*, 1894 (old but useful), pp. 200–233; *BA* 24, 1961, pp. 119–128 (for tasselled garments). All these works are profusely illustrated. C.D.W.

DRUSILLA. Born in AD 38 (Jos., *Ant*. 19. 354), the youngest daughter of *Herod Agrippa I, and sister of Agrippa II, who gave her in marriage to a Syrian petty king, Azizus of Emesa. The procurator *Felix, abetted by the Cypriot magician Atomos (whom some, following an inferior text of Josephus (*Ant*. 20. 142), connect with the 'Elymas' of Acts 13:8), persuaded her to desert Azizus and to marry him.

The Western Text records that it was Drusilla, not her husband, who wanted to meet Paul (AD 57), but it seems doubtful whether in this sophisticated Jewish teenager the apostle would find a receptive listener to his discourse on 'justice and self-control and future judgment' (Acts 24:24–25). J.D.D.

DUALISM. Several characteristic themes of biblical doctrine can be better understood if considered against their background of dualistic thought. The word 'dualism' has been variously used in the history of theology and philosophy, but the basic conception is that of a distinction between two principles as independent of one another and in some instances opposed to one another. Thus in theology God is set over against some spiritual principle of evil or the material world, in philosophy spirit over against matter, in psychology soul or mind over against body.

I. God and the powers of evil

The first use of the term 'dualism' was in Hyde's *Historia Religionis Veterum Persarum*, published in 1700. Although it is a matter for dispute among experts whether Persian religion as a whole should be described as dualistic, it is clear that at some periods of Mazdaeism there existed a belief in a being evil by his own nature and the author of evil, who does not owe his origin to the creator of good but exists independently of him. This being brought into existence creatures opposed to those created by the good spirit.

With these views the Israelites certainly came in contact through Persian influences on them, but any such belief in the existence of evil from eternity and its creative power, even if modified by a belief in the ultimate victory of good, was unacceptable to the biblical writers. Satan and all the powers of evil are subordinated to God, not only in his final victory but also in their present activity and in their very being as fallen creatures of his (*cf.* especially Jb. 1–2; Col. 1:16–17).

II. God and the world

Many ancient cosmogonies picture God or the gods as imposing order and form on a formless but pre-existent matter. However malleable to the divine hand, matter which is not itself created by God necessarily imposes a limit on the divine operation, assimilating it to the creative activity of man, who always has to deal with a given material.

In the biblical conception of creation, although God and the world are kept very clearly distinct and Pantheism is rigorously avoided, the world is regarded as owing not only its form but also its very being to God (Heb. 11:3; *cf.* 2 Macc. 7:28).

III. Spirit and matter

Dualism finds more philosophical expression in the making of an absolute distinction between spirit and matter, coupled with a considerable tendency to regard spirit as good and matter as positively evil or at best an encumbrance to spirit.

This moral depreciation of matter as contrasted with spirit is contrary to the Christian doctrine of creation and the biblical understanding of sin. The situation is both better and worse than dualism portrays it. On the one hand, matter is not inherently evil; the Creator saw all that he had made as good (Gn. 1:31); on the other hand, the evil consequences of rebellion against God affect not only the material but also the spiritual realm. There are spiritual hosts of wickedness in the heavenly places (Eph. 6:12) and the most heinous sins are spiritual. Nor does the Bible altogether accept the metaphysical distinction of spirit and matter. Hebrew dynamism sees the world less in terms of static substance than of a constant activity of divine providence which as readily uses material agencies as it does purely spiritual powers. Thus modern scientific concepts of the inter-relation of energy and matter are more akin to the biblical outlook than is a Platonist or idealist dualism. 'God is spirit' (Jn. 4:24); but 'the Word became flesh' (Jn. 1:14).

IV. Soul and body

A particular instance of the Heb. avoidance of dualism is the biblical doctrine of man. Greek thought, and in consequence many Hellenizing Jewish and Christian sages, regarded the body as a prison-house of the soul: *sōma sēma*, 'the body is a tomb'. The aim of the sage was to achieve deliverance from all that is bodily and thus liberate the soul. But to the Bible man is not a soul in a body but a body/soul unity; so true is this that even in the resurrection, although flesh and blood cannot inherit the kingdom of God, we shall still have bodies (1 Cor. 15:35ff.). M.H.C.

DUKE (Heb. *'allûp̄*, ? leader of an *'elep̄*, 'thousand'). AV title (RSV 'chief') of the sons of Seir the Horite (Gn. 36:20–30), of Esau's grandsons by Adah and Basemath and his sons by Aholibamah (Gn. 36:1–19), and of Esau's later(?) descendants (Gn. 36:40–43; 1 Ch. 1:51–54). Characteristic title of tribal chiefs of Edom down to Moses' time (Ex. 15:15), and known also in Ugaritic about then. In Jos. 13:21, 'dukes' of AV represents Heb. *nāsîḵ*, *i.e.* 'princes' of Sihon. K.A.K.

DUMAH. 1. Son of Ishmael and founder of an Arab community (Gn. 25:14; 1 Ch. 1:30). These descendants gave their name to Dumah, capital of a district known as the Jawf, about halfway across N Arabia between Palestine and

Dress of Assyrian king (Sargon II) and attendants. Reconstruction. Khorsabad. Height of central figure 3 m. 721–705 BC. (AP)

Top left:
Dress of an Egyptian prince (on left), Rameses III, 1195–1164 BC. (PAC)

Bottom left:
Judaeans, women and children, wearing a long garment or wimple. Sculpture of Sennacherib's capture of Lachish. Nineveh. Early 7th cent. BC. (MH)

Sumerian woman at worship. She wears a kilt-type garment, a kaunakes, *made of strips of cloth or wool, almost certainly a conventional representation of the sheep's fleece. The typical style leaves the right shoulder bare. Mari. c. 2900–2460 BC.* (SI)

An Elamite archer of the Persian guard wearing ceremonial robe. Glazed brick. Height 1·85 m. Susa. 5th cent. BC. (SMB)

Richly embroidered clothes worn by King Marduk-nādin-ahhe of Babylonia. Depicted on a boundary stone. 1116–1101 BC. (BM)

Bottom left:
Roman citizen wearing a toga over his tunica. c. 1st cent. AD. (RS)

The Emperor Nerva in full Roman military dress. (RS)

Typical bow-legged dwarf figure as frequently shown on Old Babylonian cylinder seals. Enlarged impression. 18th cent. BC. (DJW)

S Babylonia. Dumah is modern Arabic Dûmat-al-Jandal, and the Adummatu of Assyrian and Babylonian royal inscriptions in the 7th to 6th centuries BC (references in Ebeling and Meissner, *Reallexikon der Assyriologie*, 1, 1932, pp. 39–40).

2. The name is apparently used figuratively of that nearer semi-desert land, Edom (Seir), in a brief oracle of Isaiah (21:11–12).

3. A township in Judah (Jos. 15:52), usually identified with the present ed-Dômeh or ed-Dûmah, *c.* 18 km SW of Hebron. The name Rumah in 2 Ki. 23:36 might conceivably be for Dumah in Judah; see *GTT*, § 963, p. 368. K.A.K.

DUNG. The word is used in the AV to translate various Heb. terms. Heb. *'aśpōṯ*, usually rendered 'dunghill', is probably a refuse-tip, rubbish-dump or ash-heap, and is used as a simile to convey the haunt of the destitute (1 Sa. 2:8; Ps. 113:7; La. 4:5); *cf.* also Lk. 14:35. Jerusalem's Dung Gate (the same word) in Ne. 2:13; 3:13–14; 12:31, may be the gate by which refuse was taken out of the city. A grimmer comparison was of unburied corpses (perishing) as dung (*dōmen*) in the fields (2 Ki. 9:37, Jezebel; Je. 8:2; 9:22; 16:4; 25:33; *cf.* Jb. 20:7; Zp. 1:17). Disobedient priests are once threatened that the dung of their sacrifices (*i.e.* that which is unclean, *cf.* Ex. 29:14; Lv. 4:11; 8:17, *etc.*) will be spread upon their faces and they removed with it (Mal. 2:3). Jehu turned a temple of Baal into a latrine (2 Ki. 10:27). Utter privation under siege was pictured as eating dung (2 Ki. 18:27). The 'dunghills' (*neWālî/û*) of Ezr. 6:11; Dn. 2:5; 3:29, should probably be 'ruin-heaps'.

Animal-dung had of old two main uses: for fuel and for manure. As fuel, it would often be mixed with straw (*cf.* Is. 25:10) and dried; it was then suitable for heating the simple 'bread ovens' of clay or stones used in Palestine, human dung being so used only exceptionally (Ezk. 4:12–15) and often burnt up (*cf.* the simile of 1 Ki. 14:10). When Ben-hadad II closely besieged Samaria, poor food and fuel (doves' dung) sold at inflated prices (2 Ki. 6:25). For dung as fuel into modern times, see Doughty, *Travels in Arabia Deserta.*

Ps. 83:10 may refer to manuring the ground, while Lk. 13:8 with reference to the fig-tree certainly does. In a powerful metaphor Paul counted all things as dung (AV) or refuse, in comparison with the 'surpassing worth' of knowing Christ (Phil. 3:8). K.A.K.

DURA (Aram. *Dûrā'*; LXX *Deeira*). The place in the administrative district of Babylon where King Nebuchadrezzar set up an image for all to worship (Dn. 3:1). Possibly Tell Dēr (27 km SW of Baghdad), though there are several Bab. places named Dūru. Oppert reported structures SSE of Babylon at 'Doura' (*Expédition scientifique en Mésopotamie*, 1, 1862, pp. 238–240). Pinches (*ISBE*) proposed the general interpretation of the plain of the 'Wall' (Bab. *dūru*), part of the outer defences of the city. For the name Dura, *cf.* Dura (Europos); Old Bab. *Da-mara* (*Orientalia* 21, 1952, p. 275, n. 1). D.J.W.

DUST. Heb. *'āḇāq*, *'āpār*, dust of the earth, is used literally and in similes to express: multitude (Gn. 13:16; Is. 29:5); smallness (Dt. 9:21; 2 Ki. 13:7); poverty (1 Sa. 2:8); abasement (Gn. 18:27) (*ASHES); dust on the head as a sign of sorrow (Jb. 2:12; Rev. 18:19); contrition (Jos. 7:6).

Man's lowliness is emphasized by his being taken from the dust (Gn. 2:7; Jb. 4:19; Ps. 103:14) and by his ultimate return to dust (Gn. 3:19; Jb. 17:16). Paul distinguishes the present mortal body as 'the image of the man of dust', inherited from Adam, from the immortal or 'spiritual' body to be put on at the resurrection, as 'the image of the man of heaven' (1 Cor. 15:44–49). The serpent is sentenced to 'eat dust' (Gn. 3:14) and warning of judgment is conveyed by shaking the dust off the feet (Mt. 10:14–15; Acts 13:51). P.A.B. F.F.B.

DWARF (Heb. *daq*, 'thin', 'small'). Used to denote one of the physical disabilities which precluded a man from officiating as a priest (Lv. 21:20), the exact meaning of the Heb. word is not clear. The same word is used of the lean kine and blasted ears in Pharaoh's dream (Gn. 41:3, 23), and the reference may simply be to a withered person. Dwarfs in the ancient Near East were always thought to be possessed of special (frequently magical) powers. See *IEJ* 4, 1954, pp. 1ff.; *HUCA* 26, 1955, p. 96. J.D.D.

EAR. 1. In the OT Heb. *'ōzen*, possibly derived from a root meaning 'pointed', is used of the ears of animals (Am. 3:12), and more frequently of man. There are parallels to this word in other Near Eastern languages. The denominative verb *'āzan* (in the Hiph'îl) means 'to give ear', 'to hear'. In the NT Gk. *ous* is commonly used. Occasionally (*e.g.* Acts 17:20) *akoē*, from *akouō*, 'to hear', is also found. In the incident of the cutting off of the ear (Mt. 26:51) the word is *ōtion*, meaning particularly the external lobe.

While NT concepts envisage the interdependence of the members of the *body (1 Cor. 12:16), the OT views them more as semi-independent organs. This is clear in the case of the ear, which God planted (Ps. 94:9), or dug (Ps. 40:6 mg.), and which not only hears but attends (Ne. 1:6), tests words (Jb. 34:3), and can be stopped from hearing (Is. 33:15) or made heavy, rendering hearing difficult (Is. 6:10). God is spoken of also as having ears in the same way (Is. 59:1), different from the unhearing ears of the idols (Ps. 135:17). The ears must be used aright to get the true meaning of words (Mt. 11:15).

There are two OT customs which focus attention especially on the ear. The one was the rite of confirming a Hebrew slave in perpetual, voluntary service, by nailing his ear to his master's door (Ex. 21:6). The other was the putting of the blood of the sacrifice upon the right ear, thumb and toe of the priest (Lv. 8:23–24). Both probably have reference to securing obedience. To 'open the ear' is used in Heb. as a figurative expression for revealing (*e.g.* Is. 50:5).

2. An ear of grain. This would be of barley in the OT, of corn in the NT (Ex. 9:31; Mk. 4:28). The Heb. word *'āḇîḇ* gives rise to the name for the first month, the month of the Passover, at the time of the barley harvest (Ex. 23:15). B.O.B.

EARNEST (Gk. *arrabōn*, a Semitic loan-word; Heb. *'ērāḇôn*; Lat. *arrha*, *arr(h)abo*). AV translation of a commercial term, probably brought W by Phoenician traders. It means, strictly, the first instalment of a gift or payment, put down as a pledge that the rest will follow later (*cf.* the down-payment in modern hire-purchase). Paying the earnest makes obligatory payment of the remainder.

In this sense Paul calls the gift of the Spirit an earnest of the Christian's inheritance (Eph. 1:14; 2 Cor. 1:22; 5:5)—a guarantee (RSV), foretaste and first instalment of coming glory.

More generally, an *arrabōn* is any pledge or deposit, of whatever sort, given in token that a larger payment will later be made; so in LXX, Gn. 38:17–18, 20, rendering *'ērāḇôn*.

BIBLIOGRAPHY. O. Becker, *NIDNTT* 2, pp. 39f.; J. Behm, *TDNT* 1, p. 475. J.I.P.

EARTH. 1. The physical *world in which man lives, as opposed to the heavens, *e.g.* Gn. 1:1; Dt. 31:28; Ps. 68:8; Dn. 6:27, *etc.* (Heb. *'ereṣ* or Aram. *'ᵃra'*). This word is ambiguous in so far as it sometimes expresses this wider meaning of 'earth' (*i.e.* so far as the Hebrews knew it) and sometimes only 'land', a more restricted area. In the accounts of the Flood (Gn. 6–9) and of the division of speech (Gn. 11:1) each meaning has its advocates. This ambivalence is not peculiar to Hebrew; suffice it to mention the Egyptian word *ta'*, which likewise means land (as in 'conqueror of all lands') and earth ('you who are upon earth', *i.e.* the living).

2. Dry land as opposed to the sea, Gn. 1:10, *etc.* (Heb. *'ereṣ*; also *yabbešeṯ*, 'dry land' in Dn. 2:10). Phrases such as 'pillars of the earth', 'foundation of the earth' (1 Sa. 2:8; Jb. 9:6; Ps. 102:25; Is. 48:13) are simply poetic expressions from early Semitic which do not imply a doctrine of a table-like surface upon supports. The 'water under the earth' (Ex. 20:4) probably refers to subterranean springs and pools which, as the main source of water in Palestine, are referred to in poetic passages such as Pss. 24:2; 136:6; *cf.* Gn. 8:2.

3. The ground-surface, the soil which supports vegetation and so all life, *e.g.* Gn. 1:11–12; Dt. 26:2 (both *'ereṣ* and *'ᵃḏāmâ* are so used). Soil served for temporary altars (Ex. 20:24); the Aramaean Naaman took Israelite soil on which to worship Israel's God (2 Ki. 5:17). Torn clothes and the placing of earth on the head were tokens of mourning (2 Sa. 1:2; 15:32).

4. In passages such as Gn. 11:1; Ps. 98:9; La. 2:15, the word comes to mean, by transference, the inhabitants of the earth or part of it. In the NT Gk. *gē* is variously translated, generally 'earth', and appears with all these four meanings. For **1** see, *e.g.*, Mt. 6:10 and note the restricted use in Jn. 3:22, 'land of Judea'; for **2** see Acts 4:24 and *cf.* Mk. 4:1; for **3** see Mt. 25:18, 25 and *cf.* Mt. 10:29; for **4** see Rev. 13:3 (AV 'world'). K.A.K.

EARTHQUAKE. Earthquakes have been the *alter ego* of *Palestine consequent on its geological structure. In the biblical record earthquakes or their associated phenomena are recorded at various periods and attested in some excavations (*e.g.* Y. Yadin, *Hazor*, 1975, pp.150–151), at Mt Sinai on the giving of the law (Ex. 19:18), in the days of Saul (1 Sa. 14:15), Elijah (1 Ki. 19:11), Uzziah (Am. 1:1; Zc. 14:5) and Paul and Silas (Acts 16:26). An earthquake associated with crustal fissures destroyed Korah and his companions (Nu. 16:31), and a similar event may have been associated with the destruction of Sodom and Gomorrah (see Am. 4:11). The earthquake at the crucifixion is described in Mt. 27:51f. with miraculous manifestations.

There are many references to this terrible form of natural calamity: Jdg. 5:4; Pss. 18:7; 29:6; 97:4; 114:4; Joel 2:10; 3:16; Am. 8:8; Na. 1:5; Hab. 3:6; Zc. 14:4; Rev. 6:12; 8:5; 11:13; 16:18. The earthquake was

DWELLING
See Tent, Part 3.

DYEING
See Arts and crafts, Part 1.

EAGLE
See Animals, Part 1.

EAR, PIERCED
See Symbol, Part 3.

EARRING
See Ornaments, Part 2.

EASTERN SEA
See Dead Sea, Part 1.

EATING
See Meals, Part 2.

figurative of divine judgment (Is. 29:6; Ezk. 38:19ff.). Earthquakes (*rîbu*) are also attested in Assyr. texts (*Iraq* 4, 1927, pp. 186–189).

BIBLIOGRAPHY. For a list of earthquakes in the Christian era, see E. Hull, art. 'Earthquake' in *HDB*, 1, p. 634. J.M.H. D.J.W.

EAST. A bearing indicated in the OT by the phrase *mizraḥ-šemeš*, 'rising of the sun' (*e.g.* Nu. 21:11; Jdg. 11:18), or more frequently by *mizrāḥ*, 'rising', alone (*e.g.* Jos. 4:19), and once (Ps. 75:6) by *môṣā'*, 'going forth', alone. In the NT the same usage is found with *anatolē*, 'rising' (*e.g.* in Mt. 2:1). The rising of the luminaries gave the ancient peoples their standard of direction, so the term *qeḏem*, 'front', or some variation of the root *qdm*, was thus frequently employed to designate the E. The word *qdm* is attested from *c.* 2000 BC as a loan-word in the Egyptian 'Story of Sinuhe' and from the 14th century in the Ugaritic texts. The wisdom of the East (probably *Babylonia rather than Moab, 1 Ki. 4:30; *cf.* Mt. 2:1–12) was proverbial, and comparable to that of *Egypt. T.C.M.

EAST, CHILDREN OF THE (Heb. *bᵉnê-qeḏem*). A general term applied to various peoples living to the E (and NE, Gn. 29:1) of Canaan, and used in association with such neighbours as the Midianites, Amalekites (Jdg. 6:3), Moabites, Ammonites (Ezk. 25:10) and Kedarites (Je. 49:28). Sometimes *nomads are indicated (Ezk. 25:4), but the term could evidently also apply to the inhabitants of Mesopotamia (1 Ki. 4:30), and the patriarch Job is described (1:3) as one of the *bᵉnê-qeḏem*. (*EAST, *KADMONITES.)

BIBLIOGRAPHY. A. Musil, *Arabia Deserta*, 1927, pp. 494ff.; P. K. Hitti, *History of the Arabs*, 1956, p. 43. T.C.M.

EASTER, a word used in the Germanic languages to denote the festival of the vernal equinox, and subsequently, with the coming of Christianity, to denote the anniversary of the resurrection of Christ (which in Gk. and Romance tongues is denoted by *pascha*, 'Passover', and its derivatives). Tyndale, Coverdale and others give 'Easter' as a rendering of *pascha*, and one example survives in AV, at Acts 12:4 ('after Easter', where RV and RSV have 'after the Passover'; similarly NEB).

In the 2nd century AD and later there was considerable diversity and debate over the dating of the Christian Easter; the churches of Asia Minor for long followed the 'quartodeciman' reckoning, by which it was observed regularly on the 14th of Nisan, while those of Rome and elsewhere followed a calendar which commemorated the passion year by year on a Friday and the resurrection on a Sunday. The latter mode prevailed. F.F.B.

EBAL (OBAL). 1. A 'son' of *Joktan (Gn. 10:28; 1 Ch. 1:22); one of the Semitic families which inhabited S Arabia. **2.** A descendant of Esau (Gn. 36:23).

BIBLIOGRAPHY. *IDB*, 3, p. 579 (art. 'Obal'). J.D.D.

EBAL, MOUNT. The northern, and higher, of two mountains which overshadowed Shechem, the modern Nablus. It lies N of the Vale of Shechem, 427 m above the valley and 938 m above sea-level. The space between Ebal and its neighbour Gerizim, S of the vale, provides a natural amphitheatre with wonderful acoustic properties. At the close of his discourse in Dt. 5–11 Moses points to the two mountains on the W horizon beyond Gilgal and Moreh (Shechem) and announces that when they have entered the land a blessing shall be set on Gerizim and a curse on Ebal.

After the laws of Dt. 12–26 the narrative is resumed, and Moses gives detailed instructions. First, great stones were to be set up on Mt Ebal, covered with cement, and the law inscribed on them. The practice of writing on plaster laid on stones, previously known from Egypt, is now attested in Palestine itself, in the 8th century BC wall-inscriptions from Tell Deir Alla (J. Hoftijzer, *BA* 39, 1976, p. 11; for the date, *cf.* p. 87). After this an altar of unhewn stones was to be erected and sacrifices offered (Dt. 27:1–8). The Samaritan Pentateuch (*TEXTS AND VERSIONS, **1. V**) reads 'Gerizim' for 'Ebal' in v. 4; the textual variation seems to be connected in some way with the existence of a Samaritan temple on Mt Gerizim, but it is not certain which reading is the more original. Another possibility is that the Samaritan reading is due to the uneasiness felt in a late period at sacrifice (vv. 6–7) being offered on 'the mountain of the curse' (*cf.* 11:29).

In a further address (Dt. 27:9–28:68) Moses ordered that six tribes should stand on Gerizim to pronounce blessing on obedience and six should stand on Ebal to lay curses on disobedience (27:9–13). Following upon this, the Levites shall call down curses on the tribes for sins against God or man, many of which could be done in secret (27:15–26). By their response of 'Amen' the people are to condemn such practices openly. After victories in the centre of Palestine, Joshua gathered the people at Shechem, where these ceremonies were duly performed (Jos. 8:30–35).

The rituals described have been seen as evidence for regarding Deuteronomy as a document in treaty-form (M. G. Kline, *The Treaty of the Great King*, 1963, ch. 2, esp. pp. 33–34) and for supposing that in early times there was a recurring festival for the renewal of the covenant at Shechem (G. von Rad, *The Problem of the Hexateuch and Other Essays*, E.T. 1966, pp. 37–38). Whatever the merits of these particular theories, Dt. 27 certainly contains early material of great importance for the early history of Israelite religion.

BIBLIOGRAPHY. G. Adam Smith, *The Historical Geography of the Holy Land*[25], 1931, ch. 6 ('The View from Mt Ebal'); R. J. Coggins, *Samaritans and Jews*, 1975, pp. 73, 155. G.T.M. G.I.D.

EBED-MELECH (Heb. *eḇed-meleḵ*, a common name = 'servant of the king'). Ethiopian servant of Zedekiah who rescued Jeremiah from a dungeon (Je. 38:7–13), and for this his life was to be spared at the sack of Jerusalem (Je. 39:15–18). D.J.W.

EBENEZER (Heb. *'eḇen 'ēzer*, 'stone of help').

1. The site of the dual defeat of Israel at the hands of the Philistines near Aphek in the N of Sharon. The sons of Eli were slain, the ark taken (1 Sa. 4:1–22), and a period of Philistine overlordship begun which continued until the days of national reinvigoration under the Monarchy.

2. The name of the stone which Samuel erected between Mizpah and Shen some years after this battle, to commemorate his victory over the Philistines (1 Sa. 7:12). The stone was probably given the same name as the site of Israel's earlier defeat in order to encourage the impression that that defeat had now been reversed. The exact site of the stone is unknown. R.J.W.

EBER. 1. The son of Salah or Shelah (1 Ch. 1:18–19, 25) and great-grandson of Shem who, when aged 34, became father of Peleg (Gn. 11:16) and later of other sons and daughters, one of whom was Joktan (Gn. 10:21, 25). He lived 464 years according to Gn. 11:16–17. Some identify him with Ebru(m), king of *Ebla, Syria, *c.* 2300 BC.

Eber (Heb. *'ēḇer*), meaning 'one who emigrates', is the same as the name Hebrew (Ḫabiru). His sons lived at a time when there was a 'division' as at *Babel, perhaps between those who were 'Arabs' (probably by metathesis the same as, or a dialectal variant for, *'ēḇer*) under *Joktan and those who lived semi-sedentary lives on irrigated land (Akkad. *palgu*) under *Peleg. The name Eber appears to be used as a poetic description of Israel in Nu. 24:24.

2. A Gadite family (1 Ch. 5:13). **3.** Two Benjaminites (1 Ch. 8:12, 22). **4.** The head of a priestly family of Amok who returned to Jerusalem from Babylonia with Zerubbabel (Ne. 12:20). D.J.W.

EBLA. Capital of a city-state, 70 km S of Aleppo, Syria, mod. Tell Mardiḫ, excavated by the Italian archaeological mission to Syria since 1964. The discovery of an archive of 18,000 texts dated *c.* 2300 BC is of importance for the history of the region and background to the Gn. narratives.

The city was occupied during the Proto-Syrian I (*c.* 3000–2400 BC) and II (*c.* 2400–2000 BC) periods; from the latter period texts have been found both in the royal palace and on the acropolis. The city was destroyed either by Sargon or by Naram-Sin of Akkad. As a commercial centre it was ruled by kings including Eb(e)rum, variously compared with *Eber (Gn. 10:24) or *'iḇrî* ('Hebrew-Hapiru'). Ebla attacked *Mari *c.* 2350 and Ebrum made a treaty with Dudya of Ashur, hitherto known only from king lists as the first of 'the seventeen kings who lived in tents' and considered by some as a fictional eponymous ancestor. Ebla is later named in texts from *Ur, *Alalaḫ, Kanish in Anatolia and *Egypt, and thrived till *c.* 1450 BC.

The texts are written in Sumerian and an early NW Semitic dialect (called initially 'Paleo-Canaanite' or 'Eblaic/Eblaite'). These show the Semitic influence in the area from an early period. The literary types follow the contemporary Mesopotamian styles (Fara, Abū Salabikh) and the school tradition which survived into the Akkadian texts of *Ugarit. They include accounts of creation and a flood, mythologies, incantations, hymns and proverbs. Historical and legal texts, royal edicts, letters and possibly some laws show the great potential of this site. Lexical texts include thirty-two bilinguals (Sumerian-Eblaite) and many duplicates. These with many administrative and economic texts show the activity of a commercial centre with a quarter of a million inhabitants trading with Cyprus, Palestine and the major capitals in grain, textiles, wood and wine. The royal family held much power but employed 'elders' (*abū*) and 'gover-

Some of 15,000 inscribed cuneiform tablets as found, fallen from their shelves in the archive room (L. 2769) of the royal palace of Ebla (Tell Mardiḫ). c. 2300 BC. (PM)

Ecbatana, capital of Media to Achaemenid times.

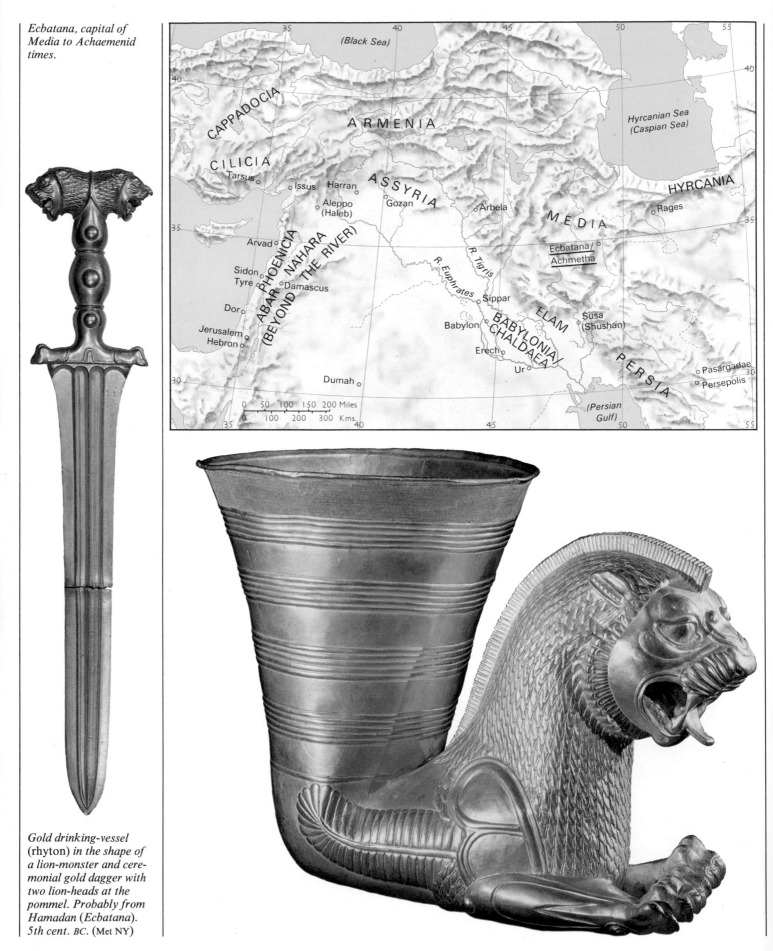

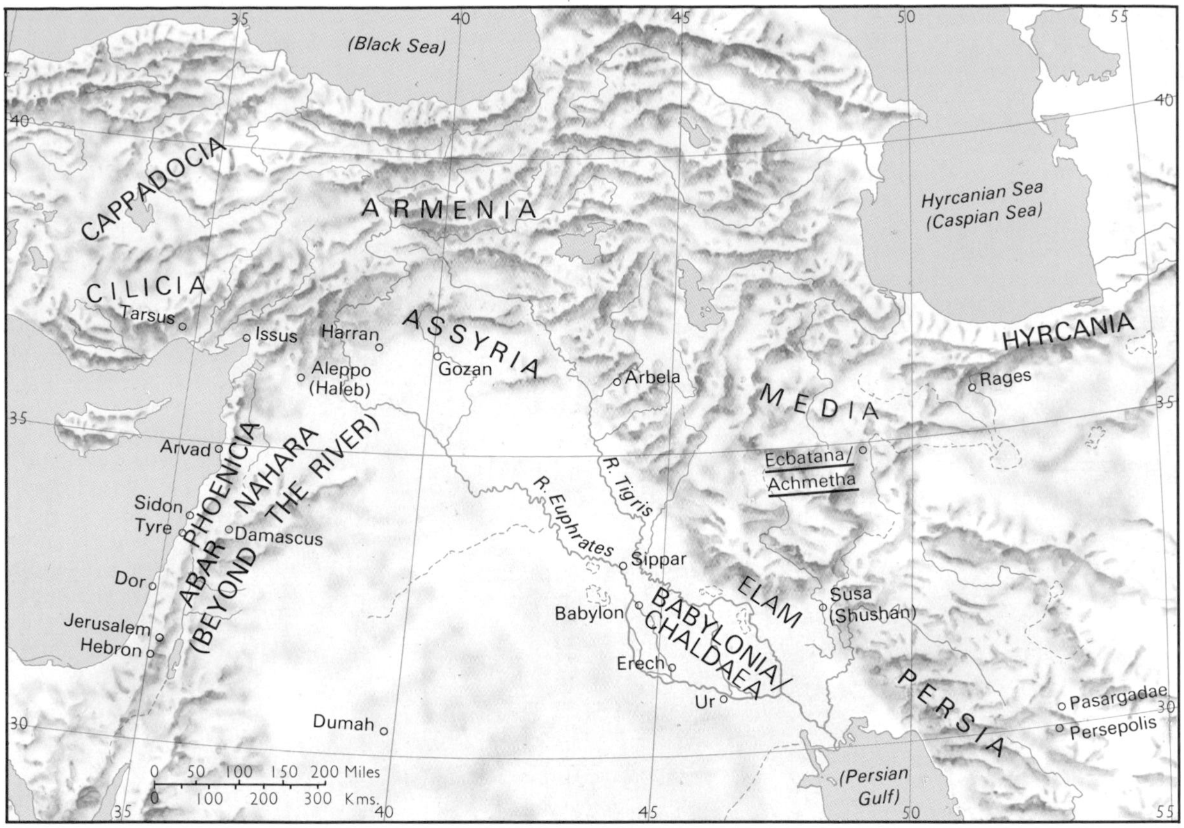

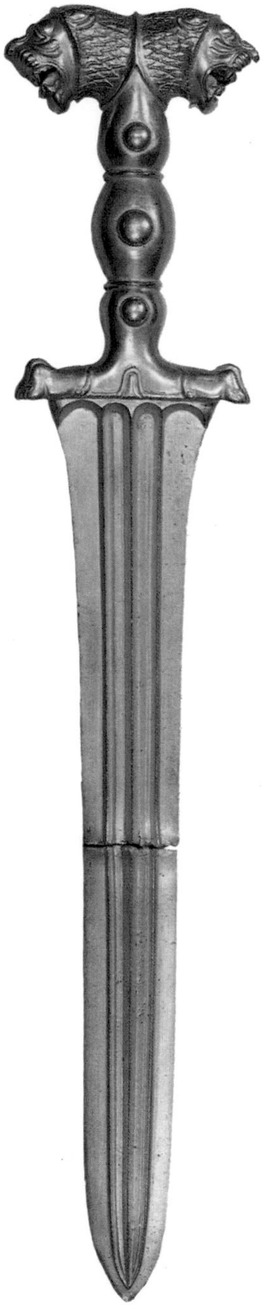

Gold drinking-vessel (rhyton) *in the shape of a lion-monster and ceremonial gold dagger with two lion-heads at the pommel. Probably from Hamadan (Ecbatana). 5th cent. BC.* (Met NY)

View of a room at the royal palace at Ebla in which more than 1,000 written documents were stored. c. 2300 BC. (PM)

EBRON
See Abdon, Part 1.

nors' (*šāpiṭum*) whose role was similar to the later biblical judges.

Lexical texts cover the usual school lists of animals, fish, birds, professions and objects (for these with proverbs, see 1 Ki. 4:32–33). More than 500 place-names listed are said to include Hazor, Lachish, Gezer, Dor, Megiddo, Ashtaroth, Jerusalem, Joppa and Sinai. Personal names so far cited include Išra'el, Isma'el, Abarama, Mika'el, Mikaya, but there is as yet no evidence that these are to be identified with similar biblical names or that the names ending hypocoristic *-ya* refer to an early use of the divine name Yah(weh).

It is anticipated that these texts, like the later ones from Syria (*MARI, *ALALAH) will be of importance for our understanding of the patriarchal age and provide new details of the language, life and literature of early Semitic peoples. They are generally too early to have direct bearing on the OT other than the tradition of early writing and literature. Decisive comment must await full publication.

BIBLIOGRAPHY. *BA* 39, 1976, pp. 44–52, and articles by P. Mattiae and G. Pettinato in journals (*Orientalia* 44, 1975, pp. 367f., *etc.*).

D.J.W.

ECBATANA (AV **ACHMETHA**), mod. Hamadan. The former capital of the Median empire, it became the summer residence of the Persian kings after *Cyrus had founded the *Persian empire (*c.* 540 BC). Herodotus (1. 98) and Judith 1:1–4 describe the magnificence of the city. The decree of Cyrus (Ezr. 6:3–5), authorizing the rebuilding of the Temple under *Zerubbabel (Ezr. 1:2; 3:8–13), was filed here in the royal archives, and re-issued with additions by *Darius (Ezr. 6:6–12).

D.J.A.C.

ECCLESIASTES, BOOK OF. The writer calls himself *qōheleṯ*. The fem. ending probably denotes an office that is held, in this instance the office of a caller of assemblies. Hence 'Preacher' or 'Teacher' is a reasonable translation.

I. Outline of contents

The theme of the book is a search for the key to the meaning of life. The Preacher examines life from all angles to see where satisfaction can be found. He finds that God alone holds the key, and he must be trusted. Meanwhile we are to take life day by day from his hand, and glorify him in the ordinary things.

Within this general framework Ecclesiastes falls into two main divisions of thought, (*a*) 'the futility of life', and (*b*) 'the answer of practical faith'. These run concurrently through its chapters. In the outline below, those passages belonging to the first category are printed in roman type, and those belonging to the second in italic.

1:1–2. The theme stated.

1:3–11. Nature is a closed system, and history a mere succession of events.

1:12–18. Wisdom discourages man.

2:1–11. Pleasure leaves him unsatisfied.

2:12–23. Wisdom is to be rated above such things, but death defeats the wise and foolish alike.

2:24–26. *Take life day by day from God, and glorify him in ordinary things.*

3:1–15. *Live step by step and remember that God alone knows the whole plan.*

3:16. The problem of injustice.

3:17. *God will judge all.*

3:18–21. Man dies like the beasts.

3:22. *God must therefore be glorified in this life.*

4:1–5. The problems of oppression and envy.

ECONOMIC CONDITIONS
See Bread, Part 1.

EDEN, CHILDREN OF
See Telassar, Part 3.

4:6. *Quietness of spirit is therefore to be sought.*
4:7–8. The lonely miser.
4:9–12. *The blessing of friendship.*
4:13–16. The failure of kings.
5:1–7. *The nature of the true worshipper.*
5:8–9. Oppressive officialdom.
5:10–17; 6:1–12. Money brings many evils.
5:18–20. *Be content with what God gives.*
7:1–29. *Practical wisdom, involving the fear of God, is a guide for life.*
8:1–7. *Man must submit to God's commands even though the future is hidden.*
8:8–9:3. The problem of death, which comes to good and bad alike.
9:4–10. *Since death is universal, use life energetically while its powers remain.*
9:11–12. *But do not be proud of natural talents.*
9:13–10:20. *More proverbs for practical living.*
11:1–8. *Since the future cannot be known, man must co-operate sensibly with the natural laws that are known.*
11:9–12:8. *Remember God in youth, for old age weakens the faculties.*
12:9–12. *Listen to wise words.*

To summarize its contents, the book constitutes an exhortation to live a God-fearing life, realizing that one day account must be rendered to him.

II. Authorship and date

Although the writer says that he was king over Israel (1:12), and speaks as though he were Solomon, he nowhere says that he is Solomon. The style of the Heb. is later than Solomon's time. If Solomon was the author, the book underwent a later modernization of language. Otherwise a later writer may have taken up a comment on life that had been made by Solomon, 'Vanity of vanities, all is vanity,' and used this as a text to show why even a wise and wealthy king should say such a thing. We cannot tell at what date the book received its present form, since there are no clear historical allusions in it. About 200 BC is commonly suggested.

III. Interpretation

(See the outline of contents above.) The interpretation is partially bound up with the question of the unity of the book. Those who reject the unity hold that there is an original nucleus by a sceptical writer who queried God's hand in the world. This was worked over by one or more writers, one at least trying to redress the balance on the side of orthodoxy (*e.g.* 2:26; 3:14, *etc.*), and another possibly inserting the Epicurean passages (*e.g.* 2:24–26; 3:12–15, *etc.*). It would, however, be strange if an orthodox writer thought it worth while to salvage what was fundamentally a book of scepticism. Moreover, why should a sceptic be commended as wise (12:9)?

If the book is a unity, some take it as the musings of the natural man. The Preacher gives up the problems of God and man, but holds that it is best to live a quiet and normal life, avoiding dangerous extremes (*e.g.* A. Bentzen, *IOT*, 2, p. 191). The closing summary in 12:13–14 suggests that the book is not primarily sceptical, and that the so-called Epicurean passages are not intended in the Epicurean sense. Life is a riddle, for which the Preacher tries to find the key. The meaning of life is not to be found in the acquisition of knowledge, money, sensual pleasures, oppression, religious profession or folly. Either these things prove empty or something happens against which they are helpless. Even God's hand at times is inscrutable. Man is so made that he must always try to make sense of the universe, since God has set eternity in his heart; yet God alone knows the whole pattern (3:11, RVmg.).

Therefore the plan for man is to take his life each day from the hand of God, and enjoy it from him and for him. This theme should be compared with what Paul says about the vanity of the world in Rom. 8:20–25, 28.

BIBLIOGRAPHY. C. H. H. Wright, *The Book of Koheleth*, 1883; H. Ranston, *Ecclesiastes and the Early Greek Wisdom Literature*, 1925; G. S. Hendry, 'Ecclesiastes' in *NBCR*; J. Paterson, *The Book that is Alive*, 1954, pp. 129–150; F. D. Kidner, *A Time to Mourn, and a Time to Dance: Ecclesiastes and the Way of the World*, 1976.

J.S.W.

ED. It is related in Jos. 22 that when the two and a half tribes left Shiloh to take up their possessions E of Jordan, they set up 'an altar of great size' (v. 10) on the banks of the river, not for sacrifice, but as a 'witness' (Heb. *'ēḏ*). Fearing a schism, their brethren sent Phinehas and ten princes to protest (vv. 13–14), but they were satisfied that, on the contrary, it was to bear witness to their loyalty to Yahweh (v. 28). In v. 34 *MT* the word *'ēḏ* occurs only once, in the phrase 'it is a witness', but its earlier occurrence after 'they called the altar' is presupposed by AV, RV (*'Ed'*), and RSV, NEB ('Witness'). G.T.M.

F.F.B.

EDEN. 1. The name of the Levite(s) who shared in Hezekiah's reforms (2 Ch. 29:12; 31:15).

2. A place that traded with Tyre, associated with Harran and Canneh (Ezk. 27:23). This Eden and its people are identical with the Beth-eden (House of Eden) of Am. 1:5 and the 'children' of Eden of 2 Ki. 19:12; Is. 37:12—and these comprise the Assyrian province (and former kingdom) of Bit-Adini between Harran and the Euphrates at Carchemish. See further on *TELASSAR, *EDEN, HOUSE OF, and literature there cited. K.A.K.

EDEN, GARDEN OF. The place which God made for Adam to live in, and from which Adam and Eve were driven after the Fall.

I. The name

The *MT* states that God planted a garden in Eden (*gan-b^e'ēḏen*; Gn. 2:8), which indicates that the garden was not co-extensive with Eden, but must have been an enclosed area within it. The LXX and Vulg. and subsequent commentators have noted that to a Hebrew-speaker the name *'ēḏen* would suggest the homophonous root meaning 'delight'; but many scholars now hold that Eden is not a proper name, but a common noun from the Sumerian *edin*, 'plain, steppe', borrowed either direct from Sumerian, or *via* Akkadian (*edinu*), the garden thus being situated in a plain, or flat region. From its situation in Eden the garden came to be called the 'garden of Eden' (*gan-'ēḏen*; Gn. 2:15; 3:23–24; Ezk. 36:35; Joel 2:3), but it was also referred to as the 'garden of God' (*gan-'^{e}lōhîm*, Ezk. 28:13; 31:9) and the 'garden of the Lord' (*gan-YHWH*, Is. 51:3). In Gn. 2:8ff. the word *gan*, 'garden', and in Is. 51:3

'ēden itself, is rendered *paradeisos* by the LXX, this being a loan-word from Old Persian (Avestan) *pairidaēza*, 'enclosure', which came to mean 'park, pleasure ground', and from this usage came English *'paradise' for the garden of Eden.

II. The rivers

A river came from Eden, or the plain, and watered the garden, and from thence it was parted and became four heads (*rā'šîm*, Gn. 2:10). The word *rō'š*, 'head, top, beginning', is interpreted variously by scholars to mean either the beginning of a branch, as in a delta, going downstream, or the beginning or junction of a tributary, going upstream. Either interpretation is possible, though the latter is perhaps the more probable. The names of the four tributaries or mouths, which were evidently outside the garden, are given as *pîšôn* (Gn. 2:11), *gîḥôn* (2:13), *ḥiddeqel* (2:14) and *p^erāṯ* (2:14). The last two are identified, without dissent, with the *Tigris and *Euphrates respectively, but the identifications for the Pishon and Gihon are almost as diverse as they are numerous, ranging from the Nile and Indus to tributaries of the Tigris in Mesopotamia. Sufficient data are not available to make it possible to identify either of these two rivers with certainty.

Gn. 2:6 states that 'a mist (*'ēḏ*) went up from the earth, and watered the whole face of the ground'. It is possible that *'ēḏ* corresponds to Akkad. *edû*, itself a loan-word from Sumerian *id*, 'river', indicating that a river went up or overflowed upon the ground and provided natural irrigation. It seems reasonable to understand this as relating to the inside of the garden.

III. The contents of the garden

If the statement in Gn. 2:5–6 may be taken to indicate what did subsequently take place within the garden, an area of arable land (*śāḏeh*, AV 'field') to be tilled by Adam may be postulated. On this were to grow plants (*śî^aḥ*) and herbs (*'ēśeḇ*), perhaps to be understood as shrubs and cereals respectively. There were also trees of every kind, both beautiful and fruit-bearing (Gn. 2:9), and two in particular in the middle of the garden, the tree of life, to eat from which would make a man live for ever (Gn. 3:22), and the tree of knowledge of good and evil, from which man was specifically forbidden to eat (Gn. 2:17; 3:3). Many views of the meaning of 'the knowledge of good and evil' in this context have been put forward. One of the most common would see it as the knowledge of right and wrong, but it is difficult to suppose that Adam did not already possess this, and that, if he did not, he was forbidden to acquire it. Others would connect it with the worldly knowledge that comes to man with maturity, and which can be put to either a good or bad use. Another view would take the expression 'good and evil' as an example of a figure of speech whereby an autonymic pair signifies totality, meaning therefore 'everything' and in the context universal knowledge. Against this is the fact that Adam, having eaten of the tree, did not gain universal knowledge. Yet another view would see this as a quite ordinary tree, which was selected by God to provide an ethical test for the man, who 'would acquire an experiential knowledge of good or evil according as he was stedfast in obedience or fell away into disobedience' (*NBC*, pp. 78f.). (*FALL, *TEMPTATION.) There were also animals in the garden, cattle (*b^ehēmâ*, *BEAST), and beasts of the field (Gn. 2:19–20), by which may perhaps be understood those animals which were suitable for domestication. There were also birds.

IV. The neighbouring territories

Three territories are named in connection with the rivers. The Tigris is said to have gone 'east of Assyria' (*qiḏmaṯ 'aššûr*, literally 'in front of *'aššûr*'; Gn. 2:14), an expression which could also mean 'between *'aššûr* and the spectator'. The name *'aššûr* could refer either to the state of Assyria, which first began to emerge in the early 2nd millennium BC, or the city of Assur, mod. Qal'at Sharqât on the W bank of the Tigris, the earliest capital of Assyria, which was flourishing, as excavations have shown, in the early 3rd millennium BC. Since even at its smallest extent Assyria probably lay on both sides of the Tigris, it is probable that the city is meant and that the phrase correctly states that the Tigris ran to the E of Assur. Secondly, the river Gihon is described as winding through (*sāḇaḇ*) 'the whole land of Cush' (*kûš*, Gn. 2:13). *Cush in the Bible usually signifies Ethiopia, and has commonly been taken in this passage (*e.g.* AV) to have that meaning; but there was also a region to the E of the Tigris, from which the Kassites descended in the 2nd millennium, which had this name, and this may be the meaning in this passage. Thirdly, the Pishon is described as winding through the whole land of *Havilah (Gn. 2:11). Various products of this place are named: gold, *bdellium and *šōham*-stone (Gn. 2:11–12), the latter being translated 'onyx' in the EVV, but being of uncertain meaning. Since bdellium is usually taken to indicate an aromatic gum, a characteristic product of Arabia, and the two other biblical usages of the name Havilah also refer to parts of Arabia, it is most often taken in this context to refer to some part of that peninsula.

V. The location of the garden of Eden

Theories as to the location of the garden of Eden are numerous. That most commonly held, by Calvin, for instance, and in more recent times by F. Delitzsch and others, is the view that the garden lay somewhere in S Mesopotamia, the Pishon and Gihon being either canals connecting the Tigris and Euphrates, tributaries joining these, or in one theory the Pishon being the body of water from the Persian Gulf to the Red Sea, compassing the Arabian peninsula. These theories assume that the four 'heads' (AV) of Gn. 2:10 are tributaries which unite in one main stream, which then joins the Persian Gulf; but another group of theories takes 'heads' to refer to branches spreading out from a supposed original common source, and seeks to locate the garden in the region of Armenia, where both the Tigris and Euphrates take their rise. The Pishon and Gihon are then identified with various smaller rivers of Armenia and Trans-Caucasia, and in some theories by extension, assuming an ignorance of true geography in the author, with such other rivers as the Indus and even Ganges.

The expression 'in Eden, in the east' (Gn. 2:8), literally 'in Eden from in front', could mean either that the garden was in the E part of Eden or that Eden was in the E from the narrator's point of view, and some commentators have taken it as 'in Eden in old times', but in either case, in the absence of certainty as to the meaning of the other indications of locality, this information cannot narrow it down further.

In view of the possibility that, if the Deluge was as universal as the Bible account suggests, the geographical features which would assist in an identification of the site of Eden would have been altered, the site of Eden remains unknown.

VI. Dilmun

Among the Sumerian literary texts discovered early this century at Nippur in S Babylonia, one was discovered which described a place called Dilmun, a pleasant place, in which neither sickness nor death were known. At first it had no fresh water, but Enki the water-god ordered the sun-god to remedy this, and, this being done, various other events took place, in the course of which the goddess Ninti (*EVE) is mentioned. In later times the Babylonians adopted the name and idea of Dilmun and called it the 'land of the living', the home of their immortals. Certain similarities between this Sumerian notion of an earthly paradise and the biblical Eden emerge, and some scholars therefore conclude that the Genesis account is dependent upon the Sumerian. But an equally possible explanation is that both accounts refer to a real place, the Sumerian version having collected mythological accretions in the course of transmission.

BIBLIOGRAPHY. S. R. Driver, *The Book of Genesis*[8], 1911, pp. 57–60; J. Skinner, *Genesis*[2], *ICC*, 1930, pp. 62–66; W. F. Albright, 'The Location of the Garden of Eden', *AJSL* 39, 1922, pp. 15–31; E. A. Speiser, 'The Rivers of Paradise', *Festschrift Johannes Friedrich*, 1959, pp. 473–485; M. G. Kline, 'Because It Had Not Rained', *WTJ* 20, 1957–8, pp. 146ff. On **VI**, S. N. Kramer, *History Begins at Sumer*, 1956, pp. 193–199; N. M. Sarna, *Understanding Genesis*, 1966, pp. 23–28.

T.C.M.

EDEN, HOUSE OF (Heb. *bêṯ 'eḏen*, Am. 1:5; sometimes written *b[e]nê 'eḏen*, 2 Ki. 19:12; Is. 37:12, which may be a contraction of *b[e]nê bêṯ 'eḏen*, 'children of the house of Eden'). It is probably referred to in Ezk. 27:23 as one of the places trading with Tyre, and its association with Gozan and Harran suggests a location on the middle Euphrates.

It is very probably to be identified with the Aramaean state of Bît-Adini which lay between the river Baliḫ and the Euphrates, and blocked the path of the Assyrian expansion to N Syria. Under these circumstances it could not last long, and its main city Til Barsip, modern Tell Aḥmar, on the E bank of the Euphrates, was taken by Shalmaneser III, and in 855 BC the state became an Assyrian province. It is presumably to this conquest that both Amos and Rabshakeh referred over a century later (*BASOR* 129, 1953, p. 25).

BIBLIOGRAPHY. Honigmann, *Reallexikon der Assyriologie*, 2, 1933–8, pp. 33–34; E. Forrer, *Die Provinzeinteilung des assyrischen Reiches*, 1920, pp. 12f., 25f.; F. Thureau Dangin and M. Dunand, *Til Barsib*, 1936; W. W. Hallo, *BA* 23, 1960, pp. 38–39.

T.C.M.

EDER, EDAR (Heb. *'ēḏer*, 'flock'). **1.** The place of Israel's encampment between Bethlehem and Hebron (Gn. 35:21). In Mi. 4:8 'tower of the flock' (RVmg. 'of Eder') was probably the site of a watch-tower erected against sheep thieves. **2.** A town to the S of Judah near to the Edomite border; perhaps mod. Khirbet el-'Adar 8 km S of Gaza (Jos. 15:21). Y. Aharoni proposed to emend this name to *Arad (*LOB*, pp. 105, 298). **3.** A Levite of David's time. A member of the house of Merari and a son of Muhi (1 Ch. 23:23; 24:30). **4.** A Benjaminite, and son of Beriah (1 Ch. 8:15).

R.J.W.

EDOM, EDOMITES.

I. Biblical

The term Edom (*'eḏôm*) denotes either the name of Esau, given in memory of the red pottage for which he exchanged his birthright (Gn. 25:30; 36:1, 8, 19), or the Edomites collectively (Nu. 20:18, 20–21; Am. 1:6, 11; 9:12; Mal. 1:4), or the land occupied by Esau's descendants, formerly the land of Seir (Gn. 32:3; 36:20–21, 30; Nu. 24:18). It stretched from the Wadi Zered to the Gulf of Aqabah for *c.* 160 km, and extended to both sides of the

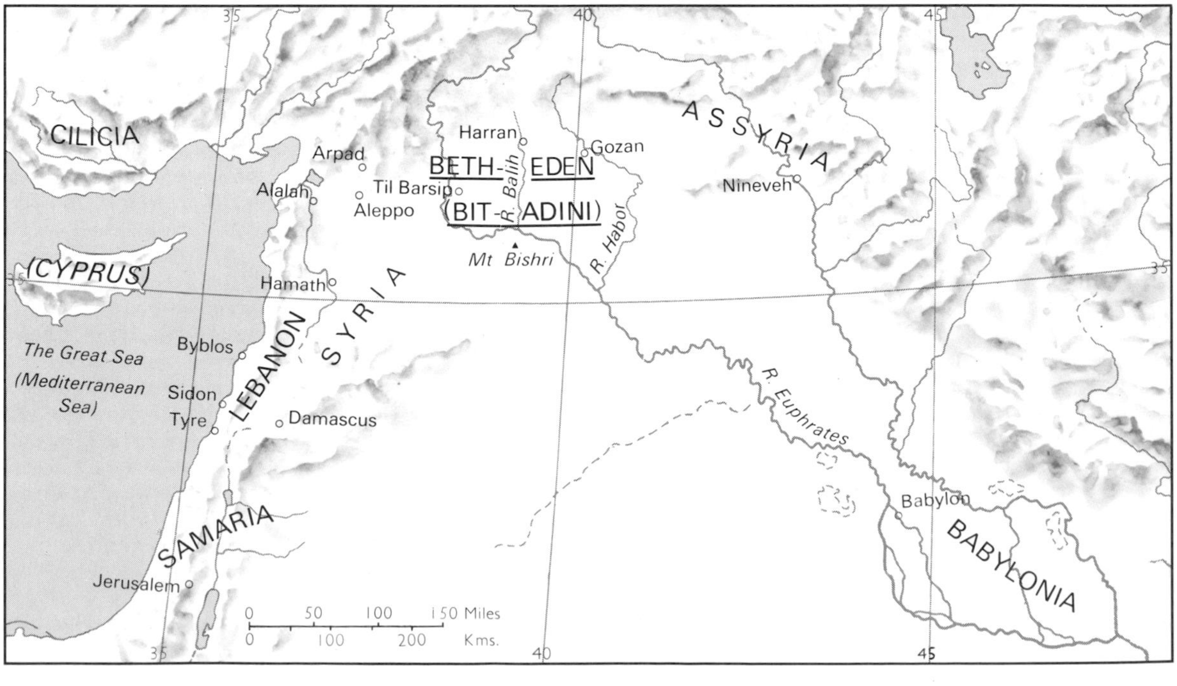

Beth-Eden ('the house of Eden'), probably the Aramaean state of Bît-Adini.

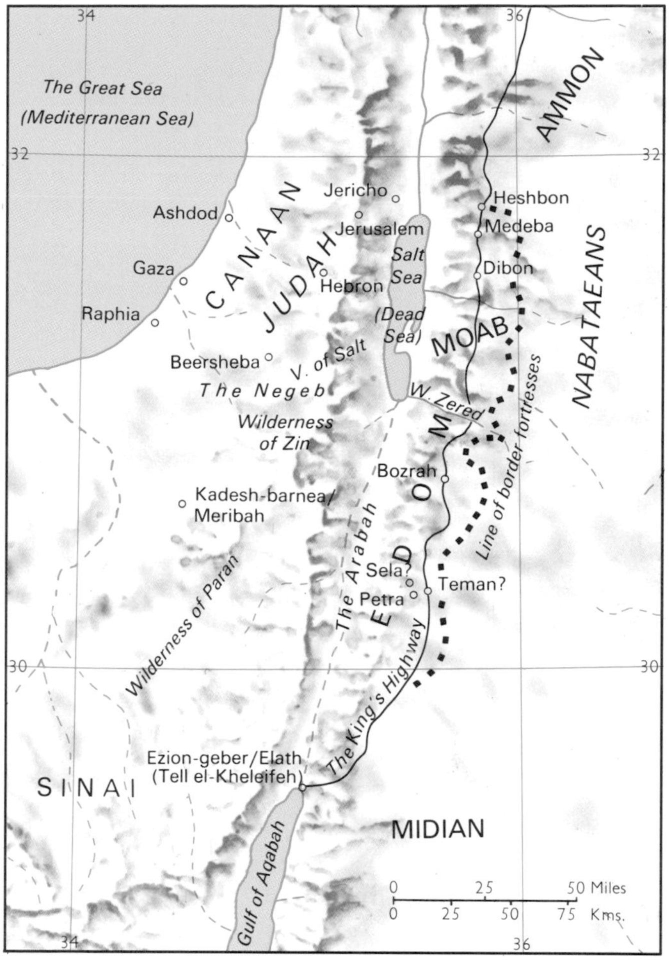

Arabah or wilderness of Edom (2 Ki. 3:8, 20), the great depression connecting the Dead Sea to the Red Sea (Gn. 14:6; Dt. 2:1, 12; Jos. 15:1; Jdg. 11:17–18; 1 Ki. 9:26, *etc.*). It is a rugged, mountainous area, with peaks rising to 1,067 m. While not a fertile land, there are good cultivable areas (Nu. 20:17, 19). In Bible times the king's highway passed along the E plateau (Nu. 20:14–18). The capital, *Sela, lay on a small plateau behind Petra. Other important towns were Bozrah and Teman.

The Edomites (*’ᵉḏôm*, *’ᵃḏômîm*) were descendants of Edom (Esau, Gn. 36:1–17). Modern archaeology has shown that the land was occupied before Esau's time. We conclude that Esau's descendants migrated to that land and in time became the dominant group incorporating the original Horites (Gn. 14:6) and others into their number. After *c.* 1850 BC there was a break in the culture of Edom till just before *c.* 1300 BC and the land was occupied by nomads.

Esau had already occupied Edom when Jacob returned from Harran (Gn. 32:3; 36:6–8; Dt. 2:4–5; Jos. 24:4). Tribal chiefs (AV 'dukes') emerged here quite early (Gn. 36:15–19, 40–43; 1 Ch. 1:51–54), and the Edomites had kings 'before any king reigned over the Israelites' (Gn. 36:31–39; 1 Ch. 1:43–51).

At the time of the Exodus, Israel sought permission to travel by the king's highway, but the request was refused (Nu. 20:14–21; 21:4; Jdg. 11:17–18). Notwithstanding this discourtesy, Israel was forbidden to abhor his Edomite brother (Dt. 23:7–8). In those days Balaam predicted the conquest of Edom (Nu. 24:18).

Joshua allotted the territory of Judah up to the borders of Edom (Jos. 15:1, 21), but did not encroach on their lands. Two centuries later King Saul was fighting the Edomites (1 Sa. 14:47) although some of them were in his service (1 Sa. 21:7; 22:9, 18). David conquered Edom and put garrisons throughout the land (2 Sa. 8:13–14. Emend *’ᵃrām* in v. 13 to *’ᵉḏôm* because of a scribal confusion of *resh* 'r' and *daleth* 'd'. *Cf.* 1 Ch. 18:13). There was considerable slaughter of the Edomites at this time (2 Sa. 8:13), and 1 Ki. 11:15–16 speaks of Joab, David's commander, remaining in Edom for six months 'until he had cut off every male in Edom'. Some must have escaped, for Hadad, a royal prince, fled to Egypt and later became a trouble to Solomon (1 Ki. 11:14–22). This conquest of Edom enabled Solomon to build a port at Ezion-geber, and to exploit the copper-mines in the region, as excavation shows (1 Ki. 9:26–28).

In Jehoshaphat's time the Edomites joined the Ammonites and Moabites in a raid on Judah (2 Ch. 20:1), but the allies fell to fighting one another (vv. 22–23). Jehoshaphat endeavoured to use the port at Ezion-geber, but his ships were wrecked (1 Ki. 22:48). At this time Edom was ruled by a deputy, who acted as king (1 Ki. 22:47). This 'king' acknowledged the supremacy of Judah and joined the Judah–Israel coalition in an attack on Mesha, king of Moab (2 Ki. 3:4–27).

Under Joram (Jehoram), Edom rebelled, but, although Joram defeated them in battle, he could not reduce them to subjection (2 Ki. 8:20–22; 2 Ch. 21:8–10), and Edom had a respite of some 40 years.

Amaziah later invaded Edom, slew 10,000 Edomites in the Valley of Salt, captured Sela their capital and sent 10,000 more to their death by casting them from the top of Sela (2 Ki. 14:7; 2 Ch. 25:11–12). Uzziah, his successor, restored the port at Elath (2 Ki. 14:22), but under Ahaz, when Judah was being attacked by Pekah and Rezin, the Edomites invaded Judah and carried off captives (2 Ch. 28:17). The port of Elath was lost once again. (Read 'Edom' for 'Aram' in 2 Ki. 16:6, as RSV.) Judah never again recovered Edom. Assyr. inscriptions show that Edom became a vassal-state of Assyria after *c.* 736 BC.

After the fall of Judah, Edom rejoiced (Ps. 137:7). The prophets foretold judgment on Edom for her bitter hatred (Je. 49:7–22; La. 4:21–22; Ezk. 25:12–14; 35:15; Joel 3:19; Am. 9:12; Ob. 10ff.). Some Edomites pressed into S Judah and settled to the S of Hebron (*IDUMAEA). Edom proper fell into Arab hands during the 5th century BC, and in the 3rd century BC was overrun by the Nabataeans. Through these centuries yet other Edomites fled to Judah. Judas Maccabaeus later subdued them (1 Macc. 5:65), and

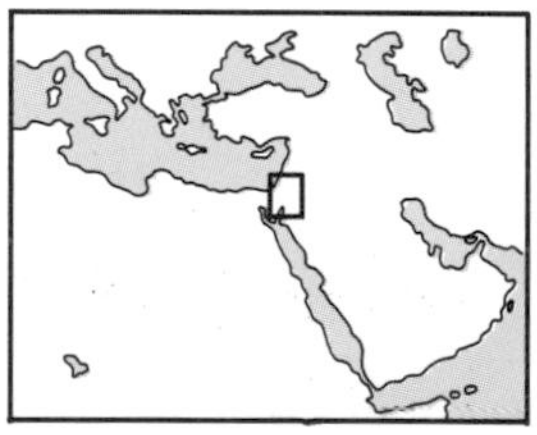

The land of the Edomites between the Dead Sea and the Gulf of Aqabah.

Top left:
The mountains of Edom, near Petra. (ARM)

Impression of the king of Edom's seal, from Umm el-Biyāra. Size 2 cm. 7th cent. BC. (BIAAH)

John Hyrcanus compelled them to be circumcised and incorporated into the Jewish people. The Herods were of general Edomite stock.

II. Archaeological

If we date the emergence of the Edomites proper from the end of the Late Bronze Age and the beginning of the Iron Age, there is a limited range of archaeological evidence throughout the centuries until Roman times. A few important sites have been excavated—Tawilân was occupied from the 8th to the 6th centuries BC. Tell el-Kheleifeh on the Gulf of Aqabah was occupied throughout the period of Israel's kings, and later. Umm el-Biyāra (behind Petra) has been investigated. A variety of small Iron Age fortresses on the borders of Edom is known. Important data are preserved on

Scribes recording the booty taken by Sennacherib, king of Assyria (704–681 BC). They use the cuneiform script on a clay tablet or writing-board and Aramaic on a papyrus and leather roll. Width 70 cm. Nineveh. (BM)

Wooden writing-tablet, coated with wax, used as a school exercise book. The top two lines are carefully written, probably by the schoolmaster. These have been copied twice below, between ruled lines, in a student's rougher hand. This follows a practice typical of schools in NT times and earlier. 26 cm × 18 cm. 2nd cent. AD. (BL)

Bottom right: The Hebrew alphabet written on a potsherd, possibly by a student copyist at Qumran, Dead Sea. c. 1st cent. BC. (RM)

Assyrian records from about 733 BC to the end of the Assyrian empire in 612 BC. Some aspects of the general culture are beginning to emerge, *e.g.* several important seals and ostraca reveal names and deities and throw light on commercial transactions. The name of the deity *Qaus* appears in personal names. But, in general, the archaeological information is comparatively sparse at present.

BIBLIOGRAPHY. F. M. Abel, *Géographie de la Palestine*, 2, 1937, pp. 281–285; D. Baly, *The Geography of the Bible*, 1974; C. M. Bennett, *RB* 73, 1966, pp. 372ff.; 76, 1969, pp. 386ff.; Nelson Glueck, *The Other Side of Jordan*, 1940; *AASOR* 15, 18–19; various articles in *BASOR* 71–72, 75–76, 79–80, 82, 84–85; *BA* 28, 1965, pp. 70ff.; J. Lindsay, *Tyndale Paper* 21, 3, 1976, Melbourne; B. Rothenberg, *PEQ* 94, 1962, pp. 5ff.; J. R. Bartlett in *POTT*, pp. 229–258; *LOB*.

J.A.T.

EDREI (Heb. *'eḏre'î*). **1.** A chief city of the Amorite kingdom of Og, where Israel defeated the Amorites in a pitched battle (Nu. 21:33; Dt. 1:4; 3:1; Jos. 12:4; 13:12, 31). Probably modern Der'a, 24 km ENE of Irbid (so Eusebius); this occupies a key point for communications in the Bashan area, and has remains dating from the Early Bronze Age. See F. M. Abel, *Géographie de la Palestine*, 2, 1937, p. 310; R. Hill, *VT* 16, 1966, pp. 412ff.

2. A town in Naphtali (Jos. 19:37); named next to Abel-beth-maacah in the list of Tuthmosis III.

J.P.U.L.

EDUCATION. The child has always been of paramount importance in Judaism, as the Mishnah and Talmud clearly show in several passages. For that matter, Jesus certainly taught the value of children, in his kindly treatment of them as well as in his instruction regarding them. Because of this, there are a number of source-books for the study of education in the biblical period to be found in the OT, the Apocrypha and the Mishnah; *viz.* Proverbs, Ecclesiasticus, Wisdom of Solomon and *Pirqe Aboth*, quite apart from useful allusions in other books. On the other hand, actual details of schooling are few; the word 'school' occurs but once in AV, and then refers merely to a lecture-room borrowed by Paul (Acts 19:9), not to any Jewish or Christian school.

I. Early links with religion

Three events stand out in the history of Jewish education. They centre on three persons, Ezra, Simon ben-Shetaḥ and Joshua ben-Gamala. It was Ezra who established Scripture (such as it was at the time) as the basis for schooling; and his successors went on to make the synagogue a place of instruction as well as a place of worship. Simon ben-Shetaḥ enacted, about 75 BC, that elementary schooling should be compulsory. Joshua ben-Gamala improved existing organization, appointing teachers in every province and town, a century later. But otherwise it is not easy to date innovations. Even the origins of the synagogue are obscure, though the Exile is a likely time for their rise. Schürer doubts the historicity of Simon ben-Shetaḥ's enactment, though most scholars accept it. In any case, Simon did not institute the elementary school, but merely extended its use. Simon and Joshua in no way interfered with existing trends and methods, and indeed Ezra only made more definite the previous linking of religion with everyday life. So it will prove better to divide the topic by subject rather than date, since none of the three men made sweeping changes.

II. The development of schools

The place of learning was exclusively the home in the earliest period, and the tutors were the parents; and teaching in the home continued to play an important part in the whole of the biblical period. As it developed, the synagogue became the place of instruction. Indeed, the NT and Philo support Schürer's view that the synagogue's purpose was primarily instructional, and only then devotional; the synagogue ministry of Jesus consisted in 'teaching' (*cf.* Mt. 4:23). The young were trained in either the synagogue itself or an adjoining building. At a later stage the teacher sometimes taught in his own house, as is evidenced by the Aramaic phrase for 'school', *bêṯ sāp̄ᵉrâ*, literally 'teacher's house'. The Temple porticoes, too, proved very useful for rabbis, and Jesus did much of his teaching there (*cf.* Mt. 26:55). By Mishnaic times, eminent rabbis had their own schools for higher learning. This feature probably started in the time of Hillel and Shammai, the famed 1st-century BC rabbis. An elementary school was called *bêṯ has-sēp̄er*, 'house of the book', while a college for higher education was known as *bêṯ miḏrāš*, 'house of study'.

III. Teaching as a profession

The first tutors were the parents, as we have seen, except in the case of royal children (*cf.* 2 Ki. 10:1). The importance of this role is stressed here and there in the Pentateuch, *e.g.* Dt. 4:9. Even as late as the Talmud, it was still the parent's responsibility to inculcate the law, to teach a trade and to get his son married. After the period of Ezra, there arose a new profession, that of the scribe (*sōp̄ēr*), the teacher in

Wooden writing-board from an Egyptian school. Lists, in this case probably Cretan names, were written on these tablets as textbooks. c. 1000 BC. (BM)

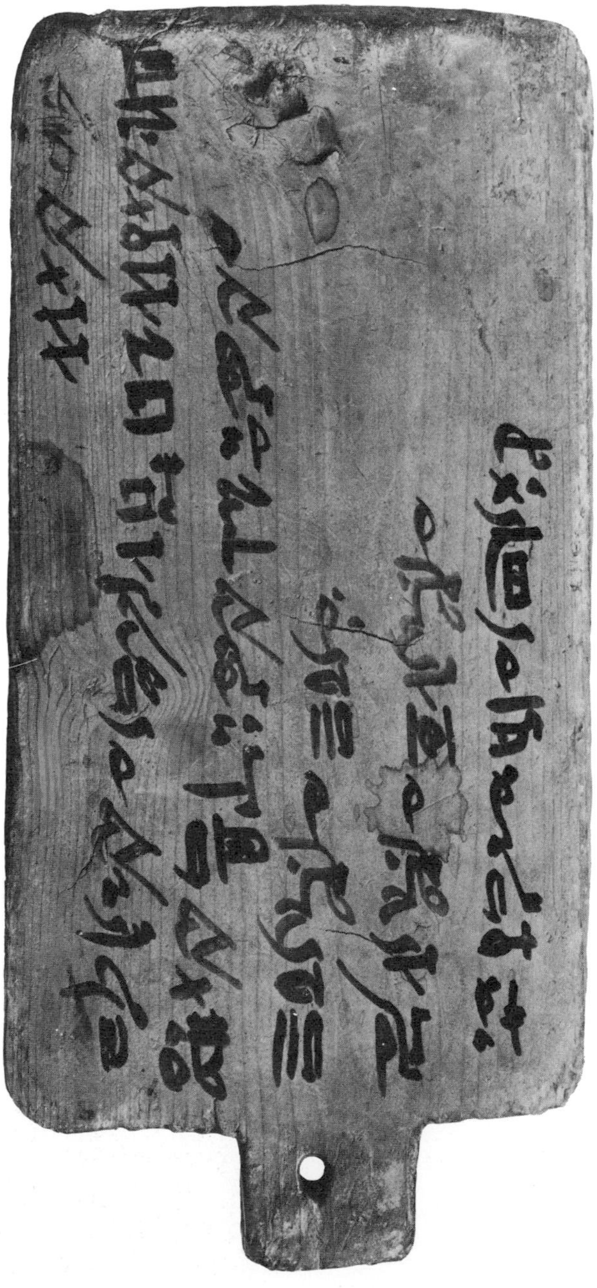

the synagogue. The scribes were to change their character by NT times, however. The 'wise', or 'sages', seem to have been a different guild from the scribes, but their exact nature and function are obscure. The 'sage' (*ḥāḵām*) is, of course, frequently mentioned in Proverbs and later wisdom literature. By the NT period, there were three grades of teacher, the *ḥāḵām*, the *sōp̄ēr* and the *ḥazzān* ('officer'), in descending order. Nicodemus was presumably of the highest grade, the 'teachers of the law' (Lk. 5:17, where the Gk. term is *nomodidaskalos*) of the lowest. The generic term 'teacher' (Heb. *m*ᵉ*lammēḏ*; Aram. *sāp̄*ᵉ*râ*) was usually applied to the lowest grade. But the honorific titles given to teachers (rabbi, *etc.*) indicate the respect in which they were held. Ideally, they were not to be paid for teaching, but frequently a polite fiction granted them remuneration for time spent instead of services rendered. Ecclus. 38:24f. considers manual labour beneath a teacher's dignity; besides, leisure is a necessary adjunct to his task. But later on there were many rabbis who learnt a trade. Paul's views can be seen in 1 Cor. 9:3ff. The Talmud gives stringent rulings about the qualifications of teachers; it is interesting that none of them is academic—they are all moral, except those that prescribe that he must be male and married.

IV. The scope of education

This was not wide in the early period. The child would learn ordinary moral instruction from his mother, and a trade, usually agricultural, plus some religious and ritual knowledge, from his father. The interplay of religion and agricultural life would have been self-evident at every festival (*cf.* Lv. 23, *passim*). The festivals also taught religious history (*cf.* Ex. 13:8). So even at the earliest period everyday life and religious belief and practice were inseparable. This was the more so in the synagogue, where Scripture became the sole authority for both belief and daily conduct. Life, indeed, was itself considered a 'discipline' (Heb. *mûsār*, a frequent word in Proverbs). Education, then, was and remained religious and ethical, with Pr. 1:7 its motto. To read was essential for the study of Scripture; writing was perhaps less important, although it was known as early as Jdg. 8:14. Basic arithmetic was taught. Languages were not taught *per se*, but note that, as Aramaic became the vernacular, study of the Heb. Scriptures became a linguistic exercise.

Girls' education was wholly in their mothers' hands. They learnt the domestic arts, simple moral and ethical instruction, and they were taught to read in order to become acquainted with the law. Their education was considered important, however, and they were even encouraged to learn a foreign language. King Lemuel's mother apparently proved an able teacher to him (Pr. 31:1); this chapter also shows the character of the ideal woman.

V. Methods and aims

Methods of instruction were largely by repetition; the Heb. verb *šānâ*, 'repeat', came to mean both 'learn' and 'teach'. Mnemonic devices such as acrostics were therefore employed. Scripture was the textbook, but that other books were not unknown is evidenced by Ec. 12:12. The value of rebuke was known (Pr. 17:10), but an emphasis on corporal chastisement is to be found in Proverbs and Ecclesiasticus. But discipline was much milder in Mishnaic times.

Until comparatively late times, it was customary for the pupil to sit on the ground at his teacher's feet, as did Paul at Gamaliel's (Acts 22:3). The bench (*sap̄sāl*) was a later invention.

Jewish education's whole function was to make the Jew holy, and separate from his neighbours, and to transform the religious into the practical. Such, then, was normal Jewish education; but undoubtedly there were schools after a Gk. pattern, especially in the closing centuries BC, and indeed Ecclesiasticus may have been written to combat deficiencies in such non-Jewish instruction. Hellenistic schools were found even in Palestine, but of course more frequently among Jewish communities elsewhere, notably in Alexandria.

In the infant church child and parent were told how to behave towards one another (Eph. 6:1, 4). Church officers had to know how to rule their own children. There were no Christian schools in early days; for one thing, the church was too poor to finance them. But the children were included in the church fellowship, and doubtless received their training there as well as in the home.

BIBLIOGRAPHY. W. Barclay, *Educational Ideals in the Ancient World*, 1959, chs. I, VI; F. H. Swift, *Education in Ancient Israel*, 1919; E. B. Castle, *Ancient Education and Today*, 1961, ch. V; *TDNT* 5, pp. 596–625; entries *s.v.* 'Education' in *IDB* and *EJ*. (*WISDOM; *WISDOM LITERATURE; *WRITING.) D.F.P.

EGLON (Heb. *'eglôn*). **1.** A city near Lachish, in the S confederacy against Joshua; eventually occupied by Judah (Jos. 10:3; 15:39). W. F. Albright's identification with Tell el-Hesi (*BASOR* 17, 1925, p. 7) has been widely accepted (J. Simons, *GTT*, p. 147; *LOB*, p. 199) and is not inconsistent with the sequence in Jos. 10:34; the position and stratigraphy present problems, however, and M. Noth's choice of Tell Eitun (20 km ESE, near the hills) may yet prove correct. See G. E. Wright, *BA* 34, 1971, pp. 76–88; S. Yeivin, *Israelite Conquest of Canaan*, 1971, pp. 52, 81 (n. 100).

2. The king of Moab who occupied territory W of the Jordan early in the period of the Judges, and was assassinated by Ehud (Jdg. 3:12ff.). J.P.U.L.

EGYPT. The ancient kingdom and modern republic in the NE corner of Africa and linked with W Asia by the Sinai isthmus.

I. Name

a. Egypt

The word 'Egypt' derives from the Gk. *Aigyptos*, Lat. *Aegyptus*. This term itself is probably a transcript of the Egyp. *Ḥ(wt)-k'-Pt(ḥ)*, pronounced roughly Ha-ku-ptah, as is shown by the cuneiform transcript *Ḫikuptaḫ* in the Amarna letters, *c.* 1360 BC. 'Hakuptah' is one of the names of Memphis, the old Egyptian capital on the W bank of the Nile just above Cairo (which eventually replaced it). If this explanation is correct, then the name of the city must have been used *pars pro toto* for Egypt generally besides Memphis by the Greeks, rather as today Cairo and Egypt are both *Miṣr* in Arabic.

b. Mizraim

The regular Heb. (and common Sem.) word for Egypt is *miṣrayim*. The word first occurs in external sources in the 14th century BC: as *mṣrm* in the Ugaritic (N Canaanite) texts and as *miṣri* in the Amarna letters. In the 1st millennium BC, the Assyr.-Bab. texts refer to *Muṣur* or *Muṣri*; unfortunately they use this term ambiguously: for Egypt on the one hand, for a region in N Syria/S Asia Minor on the other, and (very doubtfully) for part of N Arabia (see literature cited by Oppenheim in *ANET*, p. 279, n. 9). For the doubtful possibility of the N Syrian *Muṣri* being intended in 1 Ki. 10:28, see *MIZRAIM. The term *Muṣri* is thought to mean 'march(es)', borderlands, and so to be applicable to any fringe-land (Egyptian, Syrian or Arabian; *cf.* Oppenheim, *loc. cit.*). However true from an Assyr. military point of view, this explanation is hardly adequate to account for the Heb./Canaanite form *miṣrayim*/*mṣrm* of the 2nd millennium, or for its use. That *miṣrayim* is a dual form reflecting the duality of Egypt (see **II**, below) is possible but quite uncertain. Spiegelberg, in *Recueil de Travaux* 21, 1899, pp. 39–41, sought to derive *mṣr* from Egyp. (*ỉ*)*mḏr*, '(fortification-) walls', referring to the guard-forts on Egypt's Asiatic frontier from *c.* 2000 BC onwards, the first feature of the country to be encountered by visiting Semites from that time. The fact that the term might be assimilated to Semitic *māṣôr*, 'fortress', adds weight to this. However, a final and complete explanation of *miṣrayim* cannot be offered at present.

II. Natural features and geography

a. General

The present political unit 'Egypt' is roughly a square, extending from the Mediterranean coast of Africa in the N to the line of 22° N latitude (1100 km from N to S), and from the Red Sea in the E across to the line of 25° E longitude in the W, with a total surface-area of roughly 1,000,250 sq. km. However, of this whole area, 96% is desert and only 4% usable land; and 99% of Egypt's population live in that 4% of viable land.

The real Egypt is the land reached by the Nile, being Herodotus' oft-quoted 'gift of the Nile'. Egypt is in a 'temperate zone' desert-belt having a warm, rainless climate: in a year Alexandria has barely 19 cm of rain, Cairo 3 cm and Aswan virtually nil. For life-giving water, Egypt depends wholly on the Nile.

b. The two Egypts

Historically ancient Egypt consists of the long, narrow Nile valley from the first cataract at Aswan

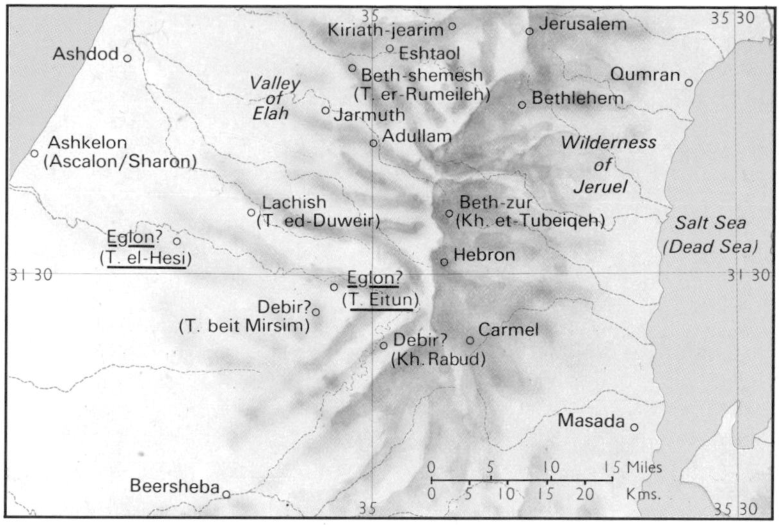

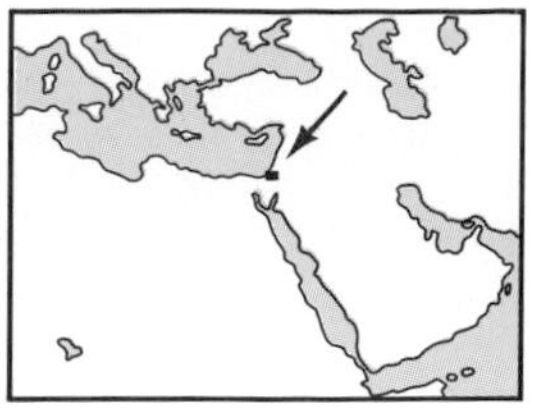

Two possible locations for Eglon: Tell el-Hesi or Tell Eitun.

(not from the second, as today) to the Memphis/Cairo district, plus the broad, flat triangle (hence its name) of the Delta from Cairo to the sea. The contrast of valley and delta enforce a dual nature upon Egypt.

(i) *Upper Egypt.* Bounded on either side by cliffs (limestone to the N and sandstone to the S of Esna some 530 km S of Cairo), the valley is never more than *c.* 19 km wide and sometimes narrows to a few hundred metres (as at Gebel Silsileh). At its annual inundation the *Nile deposited fresh silt upon the land beyond its banks each year until the Aswan barrages halted deposition in modern times. As far as the waters reach, green plants can grow; immediately beyond, all is desert up to the cliffs.

(ii) *Lower Egypt.* Some 20 km N of Cairo, the Nile divides into two main branches. The N branch reaches the sea at Rosetta, and the E at Damietta about 145 km away; from Cairo to the sea is roughly 160 km. Between the two great arms of the Nile, and over a con-

King Akhenaten (1380–1362 BC*) and Queen Nefert-iti standing with offerings for the sun-god Aton. Height 43 cm. Tell el-Amarna.* (PAC)

The colossal (c. 20 m high) statue of King Rameses II at his temple at Abu Simbel, lower Egypt. 1301–1234 BC. (KAK)

siderable area beyond them to the E and W, stretches the flat, swampy Delta-land, entirely composed of river-borne alluvium and intersected by canals and drainage-channels. Lower Egypt has, from antiquity, always included the northernmost part of the Nile valley from just S of Memphis/Cairo, in addition to the Delta proper. In ancient times tradition held that the Nile had seven mouths on the Delta coast (Herodotus), but only three are recognized as important in ancient Egyptian sources.

c. The Egypt of antiquity

To the W of the Nile valley stretches the Sahara, a flat, rocky desert of drifted sand, and parallel with the valley a series of oases—great natural depressions, where cultivation and habitation are made possible by a supply of artesian water. Between the Nile valley and Red Sea on the E is the Arabian desert, a mountainous terrain with some mineral wealth: gold, ornamental stone, including alabaster, breccia and diorite. Across the Gulf of Suez is the rocky peninsula of Sinai.

Egypt was thus sufficiently isolated between her deserts to develop her own individual culture; but, at the same time, access from the E by either the Sinai isthmus or Red Sea and Wadi Hammamat, and from

Judgment scene from the Papyrus of Ani, a royal scribe and governor of the granaries. The heart is weighed against a feather in the presence of Osiris. Height 38 cm. Total length c. 23 m. Thebes. c. 1300 BC. (BM)

the N and S by way of the Nile was direct enough for her to receive (and give) external stimulus.

The ancient geography of pharaonic Egypt is a subject of considerable complexity. The historic nomes or provinces first clearly emerge in the Old Kingdom (4th Dynasty) in the 3rd millennium BC, but some probably originated earlier as territories of what were originally separate little communities in prehistory. There were reckoned 22 of these nomes for Upper Egypt and 20 for Lower Egypt in the enumeration that was traditional by Graeco-Roman times, when geographical records are fullest.

III. People and language

a. People

The earliest evidences of human activity in Egypt are flint tools of the Palaeolithic age from the Nile terraces. But the first real Egyptians who settled as agriculturists in the Nile valley (and of whom physical remains survive) are those labelled as Taso-Badarians, the first predynastic (prehistoric) culture. They appear to be of African origin, together with the two successive prehistoric culture-phases, best called Naqada I and II, ending about 3000 BC or shortly thereafter. Modern Egyptians are in direct descent from the people of ancient Egypt.

b. Language

The ancient Egyptian language is of mixed origin and has had a very long history. It is usually called 'Hamito-Semitic', and was basically a Hamitic tongue (*i.e.* related to the Libyco-Berber languages of N Africa) swamped at an early epoch (in prehistory) by a Semitic language. Much Egyptian vocabulary is directly cognate with Semitic, and there are analogies in syntax. Lack of early written matter hinders proper comparison with Hamitic. On the affinities of the Egyptian language, see A. H. Gardiner, *Egyptian Grammar*, § 3, and (in more detail) G. Lefebvre, *Chronique d'Égypte*, 11, No. 22, 1936, pp. 266–292.

In the history of the Egyptian language, five main stages may conveniently be distinguished in the written documents. *Old Egyptian* was an archaic and terse form, used in the 3rd millennium BC. *Middle Egyptian* was perhaps the vernacular of Dynasties 9–11 (2200–2000 BC) and was used universally for

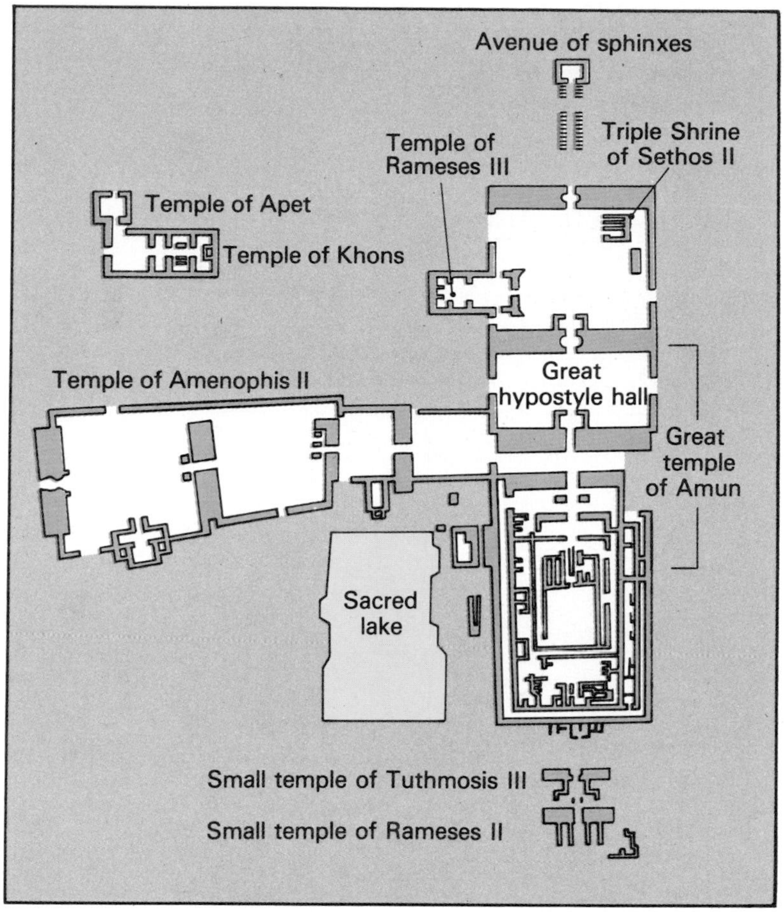

Plan of temple at Karnak, including the Great Hypostyle Hall built by Sethos I and Rameses II, c. 1300–1220 BC. They also built the Delta capital named after the latter ('Ra'amses', Ex. 1:11).

List of Palestinian and Syrian towns captured by Sheshonq I ('Shishak', 945–924 BC) on the S wall of the Amon temple at Karnak. The names are important for the light which they shed on the Egyptian invasion of Palestine (1 Ki. 14:25–26; 2 Ch. 12:2–4). (KAK)

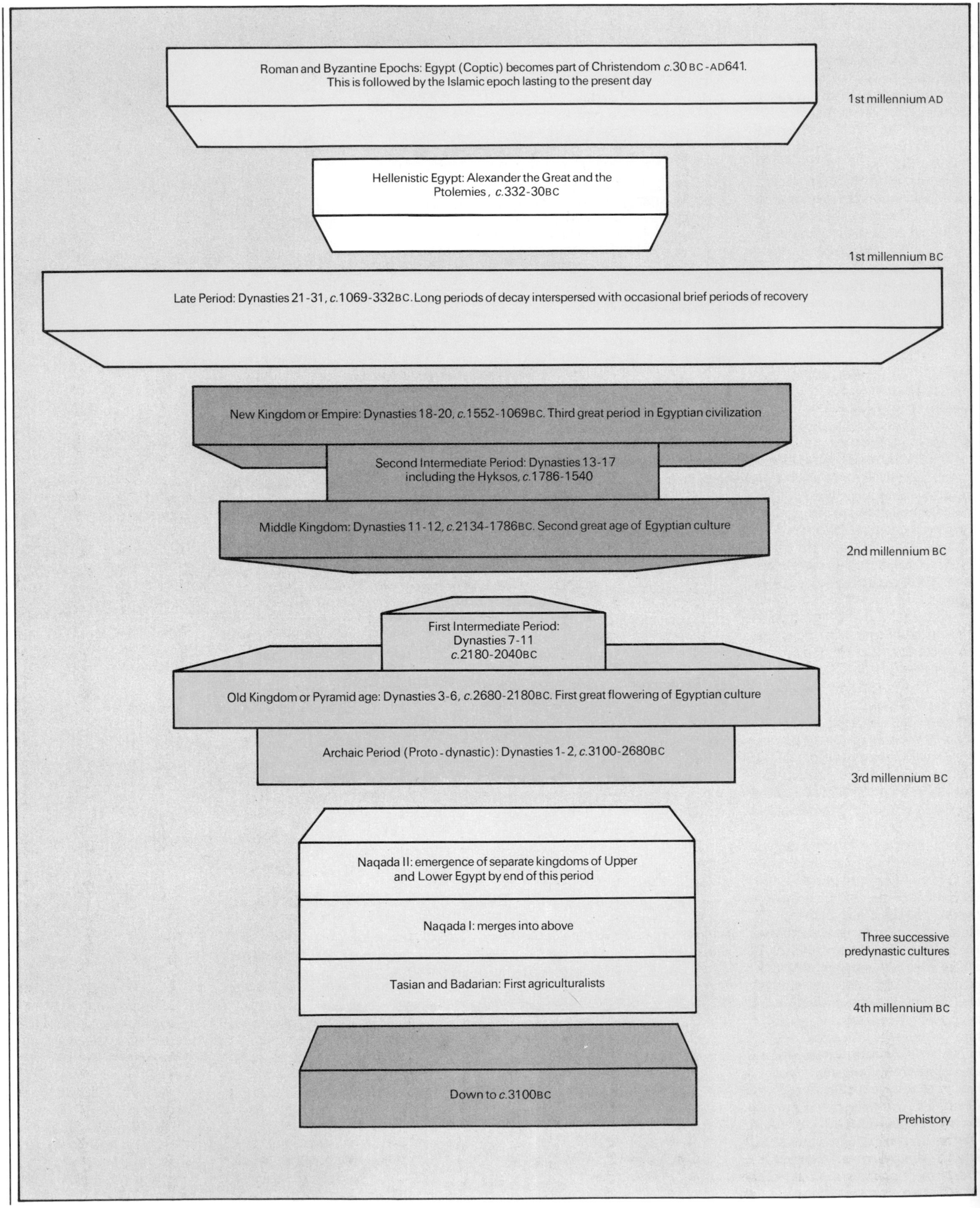

Roman and Byzantine Epochs: Egypt (Coptic) becomes part of Christendom c.30 BC-AD641. This is followed by the Islamic epoch lasting to the present day
1st millennium AD
Hellenistic Egypt: Alexander the Great and the Ptolemies, c.332-30BC
1st millennium BC
Late Period: Dynasties 21-31, c.1069-332BC. Long periods of decay interspersed with occasional brief periods of recovery
New Kingdom or Empire: Dynasties 18-20, c.1552-1069BC. Third great period in Egyptian civilization
Second Intermediate Period: Dynasties 13-17 including the Hyksos, c.1786-1540
Middle Kingdom: Dynasties 11-12, c.2134-1786BC. Second great age of Egyptian culture
2nd millennium BC
First Intermediate Period: Dynasties 7-11 c.2180-2040BC
Old Kingdom or Pyramid age: Dynasties 3-6, c.2680-2180BC. First great flowering of Egyptian culture
Archaic Period (Proto-dynastic): Dynasties 1-2, c.3100-2680BC
3rd millennium BC
Naqada II: emergence of separate kingdoms of Upper and Lower Egypt by end of this period
Naqada I: merges into above
Tasian and Badarian: First agriculturalists
Three successive predynastic cultures
4th millennium BC
Down to c.3100BC
Prehistory

written records during the Middle Kingdom and early New Kingdom (to *c.* 1300 BC), and continued in use in official texts, in a slightly modified form, as late as Graeco-Roman days. *Late Egyptian* was the popular speech of the New Kingdom and after (16th–8th centuries BC), but was already coming into popular use two centuries before this time (1800–1600). It is also the language of documents and New Kingdom literature and official texts from Dynasty 19 onwards. Old, Middle and Late Egyptian were written in hieroglyphic and hieratic scripts (*WRITING). *Demotic* is really the name of a script, applied to the still more evolved form of Egyptian current in documents dating from the 8th century BC to Roman times. *Coptic*, the last stage of Egyptian, and the native language of Roman-Byzantine Egypt, has several dialect forms and was turned into a literary medium by Egyptian Christians or Copts. It was written, not in Egyptian script, but in the Coptic alphabet, which is composed of the Greek alphabet plus seven extra characters taken over from the old Demotic script. Coptic has survived as the purely liturgical language of the Coptic (Egyptian) Church down to modern times, its use being equivalent to that of Latin in the Roman Catholic Church.

IV. History

Of Egypt's long history only the salient features and those periods of direct relevance to biblical studies are discussed below. For further detail, see the classified Bibliography at the end of the article.

a. Egypt before 2000 BC

(i) *Predynastic Egypt.* During the three successive phases of predynastic settlement the foundations for historic Egypt were laid. Communities grew up having villages, local shrines and belief in an after-life (evidenced by burial-customs). Late in the final prehistoric phase (Naqada II) definite contact with Sumerian Mesopotamia existed, and Mesopotamian influences and ideas were so strong as to leave their mark on formative Egyptian culture (*cf.* H. Frankfort, *Birth of Civilisation in the Near East*, 1951, pp. 100–111). It is at his point that hieroglyphic writing appears, Egyptian art assumes its characteristic forms and monumental architecture begins.

(ii) *Archaic Egypt.* The first pharaoh of all Egypt was apparently Narmer of Upper Egypt, who conquered the rival Delta kingdom; he was perhaps the Menes of later tradition, and certainly the founder of Dynasty 1. Egyptian culture advanced and matured rapidly during the first two Dynasties.

(iii) *Old Kingdom.* In Dynasties 3–6, Egypt reached a peak of prosperity, splendour and cultural achievement. King Djoser's step-pyramid and its attendant buildings is the first major structure of cut stone in history (*c.* 2650 BC). In Dynasty 4 the pharaoh was absolute master, not in theory only (as was always the case) but also in fact, as never occurred before or after. Next in authority to the divine king stood the vizier, and beneath him the heads of the various branches of administration. At first members of the royal family held such offices. During this period material culture reached high levels in architecture (culminating in the Great Pyramid of Kheops, Dynasty 4), sculpture and painted relief, as well as in furnishings and jewellery. In Dynasty 5 the power of the kings weakened economically, and the priesthood of the sun-god Rēʿ stood behind the throne. In Dynasty 6 the Egyptians were actively exploring and trading in Nubia (later Cush). Meanwhile the decline in the king's power continued. This situation reached its climax late in the 94 years' reign of Pepi II. The literature of the time included several wisdom-books: those of Imhotep, Hardidief, (?Kairos) to Kagemni, and, of especial note, that of Ptah-hotep.

(iv) *First Intermediate Period.* In the Delta, where the established order was overthrown, this was a time of social upheaval (revolution) and of Asiatic infiltration. New kings in Middle-Egypt (Dynasties 9 and 10) then took over and sought to restore order in the Delta. But eventually they quarrelled with the princes of Thebes in Upper Egypt, and these then declared their independence (Dynasty 11) and eventually vanquished their northern rivals, reuniting Egypt under one strong sceptre (that of the Intef and Mentuhotep kings). The disturbances of this troubled epoch shattered the bland self-confidence of Old Kingdom Egypt and called forth a series of pessimistic writings that are among the finest and the most remarkable in Egyptian literature.

b. The Middle Kingdom and Second Intermediate Period

(i) *Middle Kingdom.* Eventually the 11th Dynasty was followed by Amenemhat I, founder of Dynasty 12, the strong man of his time. He and his Dynasty (*c.* 1991 BC) were alike remarkable. Elected to an unstable throne by fellow-nobles jealous for their local autonomy, Amenemhat I sought to rehabilitate the kingship by a programme of material reform announced and justified in literary works produced as royal propaganda (see G. Posener, *Littérature et Politique dans l'Égypte de la XIIᵉ Dynastie*, 1956). He therein proclaimed himself the (political) saviour of Egypt. He accordingly rebuilt the administration, promoted agricultural prosperity and secured the frontiers, placing a series of forts on the Asiatic border. The administration was no longer at 11th-Dynasty Thebes, which was too far S, but moved back to the strategically far superior area of Memphis, to Ithet-Tawy, a centre specifically built for the purpose. Sesostris III raided into Palestine, as far as Shechem ('Sekmem'). The extent of Egyptian influence in Palestine, Phoenicia and S Syria in Dynasty 12 is indicated by the execration texts (19th century BC) which record the names for magical cursing of possibly-hostile Semitic princes and their districts, besides Nubians and Egyptians. (See W. F. Albright, *JPOS* 8, 1928, pp. 223–256; *BASOR* 81, 1941, pp. 16–21 and *BASOR* 83, 1941, pp. 30–36.)

This was the golden age of Egypt's classical literature, especially short stories. This well-organized 12th-Dynasty Egypt, careful of its Asiatic frontier, was in all probability the Egypt of Abraham. The charge which pharaoh gave to his men concerning Abraham (Gn. 12:20) when he left Egypt is exactly paralleled (in reverse) by that given with regard to the returning Egyptian exile Sinuhe (*ANET*, p. 21, lines 240–250) and, pictorially, by the group of 37 Asiatics visiting Egypt, shown in a famous tomb-scene at Beni-hasan (see, *e.g.*, *IBA*, fig. 25, pp. 28–29). Amūn of Thebes, fused with the sun-god as Amen-Rēʿ, had become chief national god; but in Osiris resided most of the Egyptians' hopes of the after-life.

(ii) *Second Intermediate Period and Hyksos.* For barely a century after 1786 BC, a new line of kings,

Opposite page: Chart outlining the principal periods in the chronology of Egypt from prehistoric times until AD 641.

Head from a massive statue of Amenophis (Amenhotep III), king of Egypt c. 1400 BC, *once thought to be the pharaoh at the time of the Israelite Exodus. W Thebes. Height c. 1·2 m. 18th Dynasty.* (BM)

A Syrian warrior with his Egyptian wife. He drinks through a reed from a large two-handled jar. Tell el-Amarna. Reign of Akhenaten, 1380–1362 BC. (SMB)

the 13th Dynasty, held sway over most of Egypt, still ruling from Ithet-Tawy. Their reigns were mostly brief so that a vizier might thus serve several kings. Deprived of settled, firm, personal royal control, the machinery of state inevitably began to run down. At this time many Semitic slaves were to be found in Egypt, even as far as Thebes (*JOSEPH), and eventually Semitic chiefs (Egyp. 'chiefs of foreign lands' *ḥḳ'w-ẖ'swt* = Hyksos) gained prominence in Lower Egypt and then (perhaps by a swift *coup d'état*) took over the kingship of Egypt at Ithet-Tawy itself (forming the 15th–16th 'Hyksos' Dynasties), where they ruled for about 100 years. They established also an E Delta capital, Avaris (on S of modern Qantir). These Semitic pharaohs assumed the full rank and style of traditional royalty. The Hyksos at first took over the Egyptian state administration as a going concern, but as time passed, Semitic officials were appointed to high office; of these the chancellor Ḥūr is the best-known.

Into this background, Joseph (Gn. 37–50) fits perfectly. Like so many others, he was a Semitic servant in the household of an important Egyptian. The royal court is punctiliously Egyptian in etiquette (Gn. 41:14; 43:32; *JOSEPH), yet the Semite Joseph is readily appointed to high office (as in the case of Ḥūr, perhaps, a little later). The peculiar and ready blend of Egyptian and Semitic elements mirrored in the Joseph-narrative (independent of its being a Heb. story set in Egypt) fits the Hyksos period perfectly. Furthermore, the E Delta is prominent under the Hyksos (Avaris), but not again in Egyptian history until Moses' day (*i.e.* the 19th Dynasty, or, at the earliest, the very end of the 18th).

Eventually princes at Thebes clashed with the Hyksos in the N; King Kamose took all Egypt from Apopi III ('Awoserrē) except for Avaris in NE Delta, according to his recently discovered historical stele (see L. Habachi, *The Second Stela of Kamose*, 1972). Finally, Kamose's successor Ahmose I (founder of the 18th Dynasty and the New Kingdom) expelled the Hyksos regime and its immediate adherents (Egyp. as well as Asiatic) from Egypt and worsted them in Palestine. An outline of this period's culture (illustrated) is in W. C. Hayes, *Scepter of Egypt*, 2, 1959, pp. 3–41.

Painting from the tomb of Khnum-hotep III at Beni-Hassan. Ibsha, a foreign ruler, arrives in Egypt with thirty-seven 'Asiatics' (Semites), possibly travelling smiths. The scene recalls the visit to Egypt of Abraham and Sarah or of Jacob's sons (cf. Gn. 43:11). Height of figures c. 50 cm. c. 1890 BC. (PAC)

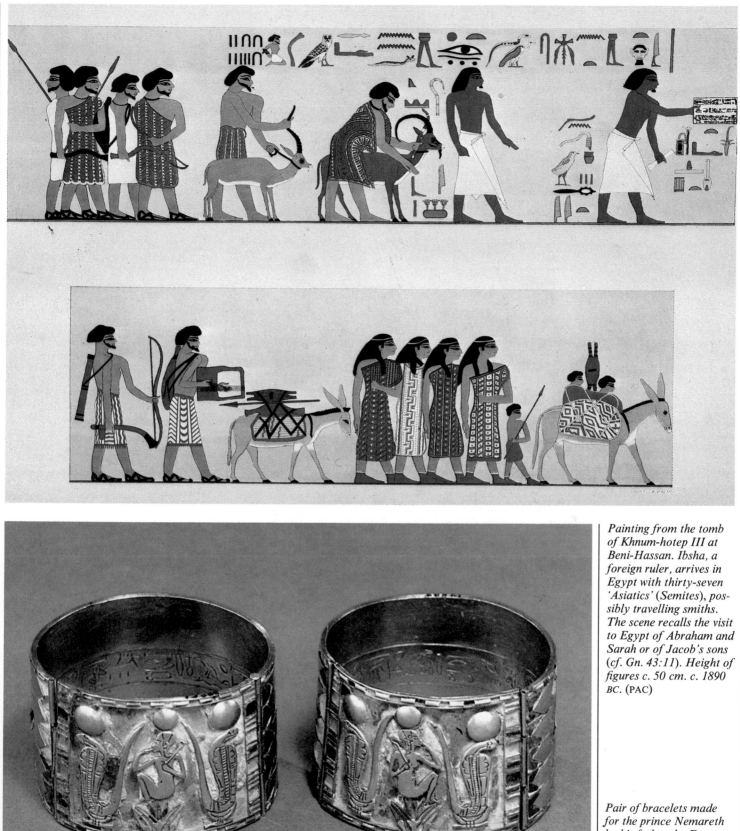

Pair of bracelets made for the prince Nemareth by his father the Egyptian king Sheshonq I (the Shishak who raided Jerusalem, 1 Ki. 14:25). Height c. 7 cm. Gold and lapis lazuli. c. 940 BC. (BM)

The pyramids of Giza built during the 4th Dynasty of the Old Kingdom. c. 2680–2565 BC. (MH)

The Giza pyramids were constructed with massive granite blocks which were originally covered with limestone slabs. (KAK)

c. New Kingdom—the Empire

The next five centuries, from *c.* 1552 to *c.* 1069 BC, witnessed the pinnacle of Egypt's political power and influence and the age of her greatest outward grandeur and luxury, but also, by their end, the breakdown of the old Egyptian spirit and eventual dissolution of Egyptian life and civilization which came about during the Late Period.

(i) *Dynasty 18*. The first kings of this line (except Tuthmosis I) were apparently content to expel the Hyksos and to rule Egypt and Nubia in the old 12th-Dynasty tradition. But the energetic Tuthmosis III took up the embryo policy of his grandfather Tuthmosis I, aiming to conquer Palestine–Syria and set the national boundary as far from Egypt proper as possible, in order to avoid any repetition of the Hyksos dominion. The princes of the Canaanite/Amorite city-states were reduced to tribute-paying vassals. This structure lasted almost a century till late into the reign of Amenophis III (*c.* 1360 BC); for this brief spell, Egypt was the paramount power in the ancient Near East.

Thebes was not sole capital at this time: Memphis in the N was more convenient administratively (especially for Asia). Amenophis III showed particular predilection for Aten, the sun-god manifest in the solar disc, while seeking to curb priestly ambition and still officially honouring Amūn. But his son Amenophis IV broke completely with Amūn and then with almost all the old gods, proscribing their worship and excising their very names from the monuments. Amenophis IV proclaimed the sole worship of Aten, changed his own name to Akhenaten and moved to his own newly-created capital-city in Middle Egypt (Akhet-Aten, the modern Tell el-Amarna). Only he and the royal family worshipped Aten directly; ordinary men worshipped Aten in the person of the divine pharaoh Akhenaten himself.

Meantime, Egypt's hold on Syria–Palestine slackened somewhat. The petty princes there were free to fight each other in pursuit of personal ambition, denouncing each other to the pharaoh and seeking military aid from him to further their own designs. This information comes from the famous Amarna Letters. At home, Akhenaten eventually had to compromise with the opposing forces, and within 2 or 3 years of his death Amūn's worship, wealth and renown were fully restored.

General Haremhab now assumed control and began to set the affairs of Egypt to rights again. At his death the throne passed to his colleague Paramessu, who, as Rameses I, founded Dynasty 19 and reigned for 1 year.

(ii) *Dynasty 19.* Roughly 1300–1200 BC. Following Haremhab's internal restoration of Egypt, Sethos I (son of Rameses I) felt able to reassert Egyptian authority in Syria. His clash with the Hittites was not unsuccessful and the two powers made a treaty. Sethos began a large building programme in the NE Delta (the first since Hyksos times) and had a residence there. He may have founded the Delta capital so largely built by his son Rameses II, who named it after himself, 'Pi-Ramessē', 'House of Rameses' (the Raamses of Ex. 1:11). Rameses II posed as the imperial pharaoh *par excellence*, dazzling later generations to such an extent that nine later kings took his name (Rameses III–XI). Besides the Delta residence, this king undertook extensive building throughout all Egypt and Nubia during his long reign of 66 years. In Syria he campaigned (usually against the Hittites) for 20 years (including the battle of Qadesh) until, wearied of the struggle, and with other foes to face, he and his Hittite contemporary Hattusil III finally signed a treaty of lasting peace between them. His successor Merenptah made one brief raid into Palestine (his capture of Gezer is attested by an inscription at Amada independent of the famous Israel Stele), apparently brushing with a few Israelites among others, and had to beat off a dangerous invasion (that of the 'Sea Peoples') from Libya; his successors were ineffective.

The first half of Dynasty 19 apparently witnessed the Israelite oppression and Exodus (*CHRONOLOGY OF THE OLD TESTAMENT). The restoration of firm order under Haremhab and the great impetus given to building activity in the E Delta by both Sethos I and Rameses II, with the consequent need of a large and economic labour-force, set the background for the Heb. oppression which culminated in the work on Pithom and Ra'amses described in Ex. 1:8–11. *Ra'amses was the great Delta-residence of the pharaoh, and *Pithom a township in the Wadi Tumilat. Ex. 1:12–22 gives some details of the conditions of this slavery, and for background to the Hebrews' brick-making, see *BRICK; *MOSES.

As for the early life of Moses, there is nothing either exceptional or incredible in a W Semite's being brought up in Egyptian court circles, perhaps in a *harim* in a Delta pleasure-residence, the pharaohs having several such scattered *harims* (*cf.* J. Yoyotte in G. Posener, *Dictionary of Egyptian Civilization*, 1962). At least from the reign of Rameses II onwards, Asiatics were brought up in royal *harims*, with the purpose of holding office (see S. Sauneron and J. Yoyotte, *Revue d'Égyptologie* 7, 1950, pp. 67–70). The thoroughly Semitic Ben-'Ozen from Ṣûr-Bāšān ('Rock of Bashan') was royal cupbearer (*wb'-nsw*) to Merenptah (J. M. A. Janssen, *Chronique d'Égypte* 26, No. 51, 1951, pp. 54–57 and fig. 11), and another Semitic cupbearer of his was called Pen-Ḥaṣu[ri], ('he of Hazor') (*cf.* Sauneron and Yoyotte, *op. cit.*, p. 68, n. 6). On a lower level, an Egyptian of *c.* 1170 BC scolds his son for joining in blood-brotherhood with Asiatics in the Delta (J. Černý, *JNES* 14, 1955, pp. 161ff.). Hence the Egyptian training and upbringing of Moses in Ex. 2 is entirely credible; the onus of proof lies upon any who would discredit the account. A further implication is that Moses would have an Egyptian education, one of the best available in his day. See further *MOSES. For the magicians, *MAGIC AND SORCERY; and for the plagues, *PLAGUES OF EGYPT. For the flight of fugitives (comparable to that of Moses in Ex. 2:15), *cf.* the flight of two runaway slaves in Papyrus Anastasi V (*ANET*, p. 259) and clauses on the extradition of fugitives in the treaty between Rameses II and the Hittites (*ANET*, pp. 200–203). For movements of peoples or large groups, see the Hittite example quoted in the article *EXODUS, and for the number of Israelites at the Exodus, *WILDERNESS OF WANDERING. Between Egypt and Canaan at this period there was constant coming and going (*cf.* the frontier-reports in *ANET*, pp. 258–259). The age of the 19th Dynasty was the most cosmopolitan in Egyptian history. More than in Dynasty 18, Hebrew–Canaanitic loan-words penetrated Egyptian language and literature by the score, and Egyptian officials proudly showed off their knowledge of the Canaanite tongue (Papyrus Anastasi I, see *ANET*, p. 477b). Semitic deities (Baal, Anath, Resheph, Astarte or Ashtaroth) were accepted in Egypt and even had temples there. Thus the Hebrews could hardly fail to hear something of the land of Canaan, and Canaanites with their customs were before their eyes, before they had even stirred from Egypt; the knowledge of such matters displayed in the Pentateuch does not imply a date of writing after the Israelite invasion of Canaan, as is so often erroneously surmised.

(iii) *Dynasty 20.* In due course, a prince Setnakht restored order. His son Rameses III was Egypt's last great imperial pharaoh. In the first decade of his reign (*c.* 1190–1180 BC) great folk-movements in the E Mediterranean basin swept away the Hittite empire in Asia Minor, entirely disrupted the traditional Canaanite–Amorite city-states of Syria–Palestine and threatened Egypt with invasion from both Libya and Palestine. These attacks Rameses III beat off in three desperate campaigns, and he even briefly carried Egyptian arms into Palestine. Since his successors Rameses IV–XI were for the most part ineffective personally, the machinery of state became increasingly inefficient and corrupt, and chronic inflation upset the economy, causing great hardship for the common people. The famous robberies of the royal tombs at Thebes reached their peak at this time.

d. Late-Period Egypt and Israelite History

From now on, Egypt's story is one of a decline, halted at intervals, but then only briefly, by occasional kings of outstanding character. But the memory of Egypt's past greatness lingered on far beyond her own borders, and served Israel and Judah ill when they were foolish enough to depend on the 'bruised reed'.

(i) *Dynasty 21 and the united monarchy.* Late in the reign of Rameses XI the general Herihor (now also high priest of Amūn) ruled Upper Egypt and the prince Nesubanebded I (Smendes) ruled Lower Egypt; this was styled, politically, as a 'renaissance' (*wḥm-mswt*). At the death of Rameses XI (*c.* 1069 BC), Smendes at Tanis became pharaoh, the succession being secured for his descendants (Dynasty 21), while, in return, Herihor's successors at Thebes were confirmed in the hereditary high-priesthood of Amūn, and in the rule of Upper Egypt under the Tanite pharaohs. So in Dynasty 21, one half of Egypt ruled the whole only by gracious permission of the other half!

These peculiar circumstances help to explain the modest foreign policy of this Dynasty in Asia: a policy of friendship and alliance with neighbouring Palestinian states, military action being restricted to 'police' action to safeguard the frontier in the SW corner of Palestine nearest the Egyptian border. Commercial motives would also be strong, as Tanis was a great port. All this links up with contemporary OT references.

When King David conquered Edom, Hadad the infant Edomite heir was taken to Egypt for safety. There he found a welcome so favourable that, when he was grown up, he gained a royal wife (1 Ki. 11:18–22). A clear example of 21st Dynasty foreign policy occurs early in Solomon's reign. A *pharaoh 'smote Gezer' and gave it as dowry with his daughter's hand in marriage-alliance with Solomon (1 Ki. 9:16; *cf.* 3:1; 7:8; 9:24; 11:1). The combination of 'police' action in SW Palestine (Gezer) and alliance with the powerful Israelite state gave Egypt security on her Asiatic frontier and doubtless brought economic gain to both states. At Tanis was found a damaged triumphal relief-scene of the pharaoh Siamūn smiting a foreigner—apparently a Philistine, to judge by the Aegean-type axe in his hand. This very specific detail strongly suggests that it was Siamūn who conducted a 'police' action in Philistia (reaching Canaanite Gezer) and became Solomon's ally. (For this scene, see P. Montet, *L'Égypte et la Bible*, 1959, p. 40, fig. 5.)

(ii) *The Libyan Dynasties and the divided monarchy*. 1. *Shishak. When the last Tanite king died in 945 BC a powerful Libyan tribal chief (? of Bubastis/Pi-beseth) acceded to the throne peacefully as Sheshonq I (biblical Shishak), thereby founding Dynasty 22. While consolidating Egypt internally under his rule, Sheshonq I began a new and aggressive Asiatic foreign policy. He viewed Solomon's Israel not as an ally but as a political and commercial rival on his NE frontier, and therefore worked for the break-up of the Hebrew kingdom. While Solomon lived, Sheshonq shrewdly took no action apart from harbouring political refugees, notably Jeroboam son of Nebat (1 Ki. 11:29–40). At Solomon's death Jeroboam's return to Palestine precipitated the division of the kingdom into the two lesser realms of Rehoboam and Jeroboam. Soon after, in Rehoboam's 'fifth year', 925 BC (1 Ki. 14:25–26; 2 Ch. 12:2–12), and apparently on pretext of a bedouin border incident (stele-fragment, Grdseloff, *Revue de l'Histoire Juive en Égypte*, 1, 1947, pp. 95–97), Shishak invaded Palestine, subduing Israel as well as Judah, as is shown by the discovery of a stele of his at Megiddo (C. S. Fisher, *The Excavation of Armageddon*, 1929, p. 13 and fig.). Many biblical place-names occur in the list attached to the triumphal relief subsequently sculptured by Shishak on the temple of Amūn (Karnak) in Thebes (see *ANEP*, p. 118 and fig. 349). (See also *SUKKIIM.) Sheshonq's purpose was limited and definite: to gain political and commercial security by subduing his immediate neighbour. He made no attempt to revive the empire of Tuthmosis or Rameses.

2. *Zerah. It would appear from 2 Ch. 14:9–15; 16:8, that Sheshonq's successor Osorkon I sought to emulate his father's Palestinian success but was too lazy to go himself. Instead, he apparently sent as general Zerah the Ethiopian, who was soundly defeated by Asa of Judah *c.* 897 BC. This defeat spelt the end of Egypt's aggressive policy in Asia. However, again like Sheshonq I, Osorkon I maintained relations with Byblos in Phoenicia, where statues of both pharaohs were found (*Syria* 5, 1924, pp. 145–147 and plate 42; *Syria* 6, 1925, pp. 101–117 and plate 25).

3. Egypt and Ahab's dynasty. Osorkon I's successor, Takeloth I, was apparently a nonentity who allowed the royal power to slip through his incompetent fingers. Thus the next king, Osorkon II, inherited an Egypt whose unity was already menaced: the local Libyan provincial governors were becoming increasingly independent, and separatist tendencies appeared in Thebes. Hence, he apparently returned to the old 'modest' foreign policy of (similarly-weak) Dynasty 21, that of alliance with his Palestinian neighbours. This is hinted at by the discovery, in Omri and Ahab's palace at Samaria, of an alabaster vase of Osorkon II, such as the pharaohs included in their diplomatic presents to fellow-rulers (illustrated in Reisner, *etc.*, *Harvard Excavations at Samaria*, 1, 1924, fig. on p. 247). This suggests that Omri or Ahab had links with Egypt as well as Tyre (*cf.* Ahab's marriage with Jezebel). Osorkon II also presented a statue at Byblos (M. Dunand, *Fouilles de Byblos*, 1, pp. 115–116 and plate 43).

4. Hoshea and 'So king of Egypt'. The 'modest' policy revived by Osorkon II was doubtless continued by his ever-weaker successors, under whom Egypt progressively fell apart into its constituent local provinces with kings reigning elsewhere (Dynasty 23) alongside the main, parent 22nd Dynasty at Tanis/Zoan. Prior to a dual rule (perhaps mutually agreed), the Egyptian state was rocked by bitter civil wars centred on Thebes (*cf.* R. A. Caminos, *The Chronicle of Prince Osorkon*, 1958), and could hardly have supported any different external policy.

All this indicates why Israel's last king, Hoshea, turned so readily for help against Assyria to *So king of Egypt' in 725/4 BC (2 Ki. 17:4), and how very misplaced was his trust in an Egypt so weak and divided. No help came to save Samaria from its fall. The identity of 'So' has long been obscure. He is probably Osorkon IV, last pharaoh of Dynasty 22, *c.* 730–715 BC. The real power in Lower Egypt was wielded by Tafnekht and his successor Bekenrenef (Dynasty 24) from Sais in the W Delta; so powerless was Osorkon IV that in 716 BC he bought off Sargon of Assyria at the borders of Egypt with a gift of twelve horses (H. Tadmor, *JCS* 12, 1958, pp. 77–78).

(iii) *Ethiopia—the 'bruised reed'*. In Nubia (Cush) there had meantime arisen a kingdom ruled by princes who were thoroughly Egyptian in culture. Of these, Kashta and Piankhy laid claim to a protectorate over Upper Egypt, being worshippers of Amūn of Thebes. In one campaign, Piankhy subdued Tafnekht of Lower Egypt to keep Thebes safe, but promptly returned to Nubia.

However, his successor Shabaka (*c.* 716–702 BC) promptly reconquered Egypt, eliminating Bekenrenef by 715 BC. Shabaka was a friendly neutral towards Assyria;

in 712 he extradited a fugitive at Sargon II's request, and sealings of Shabaka (possibly from diplomatic documents) were found at Nineveh. Doubtless, Shabaka had enough to do inside Egypt without meddling abroad; but unfortunately his successors in this Dynasty (the 25th) were less wise. When *Sennacherib of Assyria attacked Hezekiah of Judah in 701 BC the rash new Ethiopian pharaoh Shebitku sent his equally young and inexperienced brother *Tirhakah to oppose Assyria (2 Ki. 19:9; Is. 37:9), resulting in dire defeat for Egypt. The Ethiopian pharaohs had no appreciation of Assyria's superior strength—after this setback, Tirhakah was defeated twice more by Assyria (*c.* 671 and 666/5, as king) and Tanutamen once—and their incompetent interference in Palestinian affairs was disastrous for Egypt and Palestine alike. They were most certainly the 'bruised reed' of the Assyrian king's jibe (2 Ki. 18:21; Is. 36:6). Exasperated by this stubborn meddling, Ashurbanipal in 664/3 BC finally sacked the ancient holy city Thebes, pillaging fourteen centuries of temple treasures. No more vivid comparison than the downfall of this city could the prophet Nahum find (3:8–10) when proclaiming the oncoming ruin of Nineveh in its turn. However, Assyria could not occupy Egypt, and left only key garrisons.

(iv) *Egypt, Judah and Babylon.* In a now disorganized Egypt, the astute local prince of Sais (W Delta) managed with great skill to unite all Egypt under his sceptre. This was Psammetichus I, who thereby established the 26th (or Saite) Dynasty. He and his successors restored Egypt's internal unity and prosperity. They built up an effective army round a hard core of Greek mercenaries, greatly enhanced trade by encouraging Greek merchants and founded strong fleets on the Mediterranean and Red Seas. But, as if in compensation for the lack of real, inner vitality, inspiration was sought in Egypt's past glories; ancient art was copied and archaic titles were artificially brought back into fashion.

Externally, this dynasty (except for the headstrong Hophra) practised as far as possible a policy of the balance of powers in W Asia. Thus, Psammetichus I did not attack Assyria but remained her ally against the reviving power of Babylon. So, too, Neco II (610–595 BC) was marching to help a reduced Assyria (2 Ki. 23:29) against Babylon, when Josiah of Judah sealed Assyria's fate by delaying Neco at Megiddo at the cost of her own life. Egypt considered herself heir to Assyria's Palestinian possessions, but her forces were signally defeated at Carchemish in 605 BC so that all Syria–Palestine fell to Babylon (Je. 46:2). Jehoiakim of Judah thus exchanged Egyp. for Bab. vassalage for 3 years. But as the Bab. chronicle-tablets reveal, Egypt and Babylon clashed in open conflict in 601 BC with heavy losses on both sides; Nebuchadrezzar then remained 18 months in Babylonia to refit his army. At this point Jehoiakim of Judah rebelled (2 Ki. 24:1f.), doubtless hoping for Egyptian aid. None came; Neco now wisely kept neutral. So Nebuchadrezzar was not molested in his capture of Jerusalem in 597 BC. Psammetichus II maintained the peace; his state visit to Byblos was linked rather with Egypt's acknowledged commercial than other interests in Phoenicia. He fought only in Nubia. But Hophra (589–570 BC; the Apries of the Greeks) foolishly cast dynastic restraint aside, and marched to support Zedekiah in his revolt against Babylon (Ezk. 17:11–21; Je. 37:5), but returned in haste to Egypt when Nebuchadrezzar temporarily raised his (second) siege of Jerusalem to repulse him—leaving Jerusalem to perish at the Babylonian's hand in 587 BC. After other disasters, *Hophra was finally supplanted in 570 BC by Ahmose II (Amasis, 570–526 BC). As earlier prophesied by Jeremiah (46:13 ff.), Nebuchadrezzar now marched against Egypt (as referred to in a damaged Bab. tablet), doubtless to prevent any recurrence of interference from that direction. He and Ahmose must have reached some understanding, for henceforth, till both were swallowed up by Medo-Persia, Egypt and Babylon were allies against the growing menace of Media. But in 525 BC Egypt followed her allies into Persian dominion, under Cambyses. On this period, see further, *BABYLONIA and *PERSIA.

(v) *The base kingdom.* At first Persian rule in Egypt (Darius I) was fair and firm; but repeated Egyptian rebellions brought about a harshening of Persian policy. The Egyptians manufactured anti-Persian propaganda that went down well in Greece (*cf.* Herodotus); they shared a common foe. Briefly, during *c.* 400–341 BC, Egypt's last native pharaohs (Dynasties 28–30) regained a precarious independence until they were overwhelmed by Persia to whom they remained subject for just 9 years, until Alexander entered Egypt as 'liberator' in 332 BC. (See F. K. Kienitz, in Bibliography, and G. Posener, *La Première Domination Perse en Égypte*, 1936). Thereafter, Egypt was first a Hellenistic monarchy under the *Ptolemies and then fell under the heel of Rome and Byzantium. From the 3rd century AD, Egypt was a predominantly Christian land with its own, eventually schismatic (Coptic) church. In AD 641/2 the Islamic conquest heralded the mediaeval and modern epochs.

V. Literature

a. Scope of Egyptian literature

(i) *3rd millennium BC.* Religious and wisdom-literature are the best-known products of the Old Kingdom and 1st Intermediate Period. The great sages Imhotep, Hardidief [?Kairos] to Kagemni, and Ptahhotep produced 'Instructions' or 'Teachings' (Egyp. *sb'yt*), written collections of shrewd maxims for wise conduct of everyday life, especially for young men hopeful of high office, so beginning a very long tradition in Egypt. The best-preserved is that of Ptahhotep; see Z. Žába, *Les Maximes de Ptahhotep*, 1956. For the Pyramid Texts and Memphite Theology, see **VI**, below.

In the 1st Intermediate Period, the collapse of Egyptian society and the old order may be pictured in the *Admonitions of Ipuwer*, while the *Dispute of a Man Tired of Life with his Soul* reflects the agony of this period in terms of a personal conflict which brings man to the brink of suicide. The *Instruction for King Merikarē* shows remarkable regard for right dealing in matters of state, while the *Eloquent Peasant*'s nine rhetorical speeches within a narrative prose prologue and epilogue (*cf.* Job) call for social justice.

(ii) *Early 2nd millennium BC.* In the Middle Kingdom, stories and propaganda-works are outstanding. Finest of the narratives is the *Biography of Sinuhē*, an Egyptian who spent long years of exile in Palestine. The *Shipwrecked Sailor* is a nautical fantasy. Among the propaganda, the *Prophecy of Neferty* ('*Neferrohu*' of older books) is a pseudo-prophecy to announce Amenemhat I as saviour of Egypt. On prediction in Egypt, see Kitchen, *Tyndale House Bulletin* 5/6, 1960, pp. 6–7 and refs. Two loyalist 'Instructions', *Sehetepibrē* and *A Man to his Son*, were intended to identify the good life with loyalty to the throne in the minds of the ruling and labouring classes respectively. The poetry of the *Hymns to Sesostris III* apparently also expresses that loyalty. For administrators in training, the *Instruction of Khety son of Duauf* or *Satire of the Trades* points out the advantages of the scribal profession over all other (manual) occupations by painting these in dark colours. For tales of magicians, *MAGIC AND SORCERY (Egyptian).

(iii) *Late 2nd millennium BC.* During this period the Empire produced further stories, including delightful fairy-tales (*e.g. The Foredoomed Prince*; *Tale of the Two Brothers*), historical adventure (*The Capture of Joppa*, a precursor of *Alibaba and the Forty Thieves*) and biographical reports such as the *Misadventures of Wenamūn*, who was sent to Lebanon for cedarwood in the ill-starred days of Rameses XI. Poetry excelled in three forms: lyric, royal and religious. Under the first head come some charming love-poems, in general style heralding the tender cadences of the Song of Songs. The Empire pharaohs commemorated their victories with triumph-hymns, the finest being those of Tuthmosis III, Amenophis III, Rameses II and Merenptah (Israel Stele). Though less prominent, wisdom is still well represented; beside the 'Instructions' of Ani and Amennakhte, there is a remarkable ode on the Immortality of Writing. For Amenemope's wisdom see *b.* (i) 2, below.

(iv) *1st millennium BC.* Less new literature is known from this epoch so far. In Demotic the 'Instruction' of 'Onchsheshonqy dates to the last centuries BC, and the *Stories of the High Priests of Memphis* (magicians) to the 1st centuries AD. Most Coptic (Christian) literature is translated from Gk. church literature, Shenoute being the only outstanding native Christian writer.

b. Egyptian literature and the OT

The very incomplete survey given above will serve to emphasize the quantity, richness and variety of early Egyptian literature; besides the additional matter under Religion below, there is a whole body of historical, business and formal texts. Egypt is but one of the Bible lands; the neighbouring countries, too, offer a wealth of writings (*ASSYRIA; *CANAAN; *HITTITES.) The relevance of such literatures is twofold: firstly, with regard to questions of direct contact with the Heb. writings; and secondly, in so far as they provide dated, first-hand comparative and contemporary material for objective control of OT literary forms and types of literary criticism.

(i) *Questions of direct contact.* 1. Gn. 39; Ps. 104. In times past the incident of Potiphar's unfaithful wife in Gn. 39 has occasionally been stated to be based on a similar incident in the mythical *Tale of Two Brothers*. But an unfaithful wife is the only common point; the *Tale* is designedly a work of pure fantasy (the hero is changed into a bull, a persea-tree, *etc.*), whereas the Joseph-narrative is biography, touching actuality at every point. Unfortunately, unfaithful wives are not mere myth, either in Egypt or elsewhere (see an incidental Egyptian instance in *JNES* 14, 1955, p. 163).

Egyptologists today do not usually consider that Akhenaten's 'Hymn to Aten' inspired parts of Ps. 104 as Breasted once thought (*cf.* J. H. Breasted, *Dawn of Conscience*, 1933, pp. 366–370). The same universalism and adoration of the deity as creator and sustainer occur in hymns to Amūn both before and after the Aten hymn in date, which could carry these concepts down to the age of Heb. psalmody (so, *e.g.*, J. A. Wilson, *Burden of Egypt/Culture of Ancient Egypt*, pp. 224–229). But even this tenuous link-up can carry no weight, for the same universalism occurs just as early in W Asia (*cf.* the examples given in W. F. Albright, *From Stone Age to Christianity*, 1957 ed., pp. 12–13, 213–223) and is therefore too generally diffused to allow of its being made a criterion to prove direct relationship. The same point might be made with regard to the so-called penitential psalms of the Theban necropolis-workers of Dynasty 19. A sense of shortcoming or sin is not peculiar to Egypt (and is even, in fact, quite atypical there); and the Egyp. psalms should be compared with the confession of man's sinfulness made by the Hittite king, Mursil II (*ANET*, p. 395b) and with the Babylonian penitential odes. The latter again show the wide diffusion of a general concept (although it may have different local emphases); and they cannot be used to establish direct relationship (*cf.* G. R. Driver, *The Psalmists*, ed. D. C. Simpson, 1926, pp. 109–175, especially 171–175).

2. The Wisdom of Amenemope and Proverbs. Impressed by the close verbal resemblances between various passages in the Egyptian 'Instruction' of Amenemope (*c.* 1100 BC, see below) and the 'words of the wise' (Pr. 22:17–24:22) quoted by Solomon (equating the 'my knowledge' of 22:17 with that of Solomon from 10:1), many have assumed, following Erman, that Proverbs was debtor to Amenemope; only Kevin and McGlinchey ventured to take the opposite view. Others, with W. O. E. Oesterley, *Wisdom of Egypt and the Old Testament*, 1927, doubted the justice of a view at either extreme, considering that perhaps both Amenemope and Proverbs had drawn upon a common fund of Ancient Oriental proverbial lore, and specifically upon an older Heb. work. The alleged dependence of Proverbs upon Amenemope is still the common view (*e.g.* P. Montet, *L'Égypte et la Bible*, 1959, pp. 113, 127), but is undoubtedly too simple. By a thoroughgoing examination of both Amenemope and Proverbs against the entire realm of ancient Near Eastern Wisdom, recent research has shown that in fact there is *no* adequate basis for assuming a special relationship either way between Amenemope and Proverbs. Two other points require note. First, with regard to date, Plumley (*DOTT*, p. 173) mentions a Cairo ostracon of Amenemope that 'can be dated with some certainty to the latter half of the Twenty-first Dynasty'. Therefore the Egyp. Amenemope cannot be any later than 945 BC (= end of Dynasty 21), and Egyptologists now tend to favour a date in Dynasties 18–20. In any case, there is no objective reason why the Hebrew Words of the Wise should not be as old as Solomon's reign, *i.e.* the 10th century BC. The second point concerns the word *šilšôm*, found in Pr. 22:20, which Erman and others render as 'thirty', making Proverbs imitate the 'thirty chapters' of Amenemope. But Pr. 22:17–24:22 contains not 30 but 33 admonitions, and the simplest interpretation of *šlšwm* is to take it as elliptical for *'eṯmôl šilšôm*,

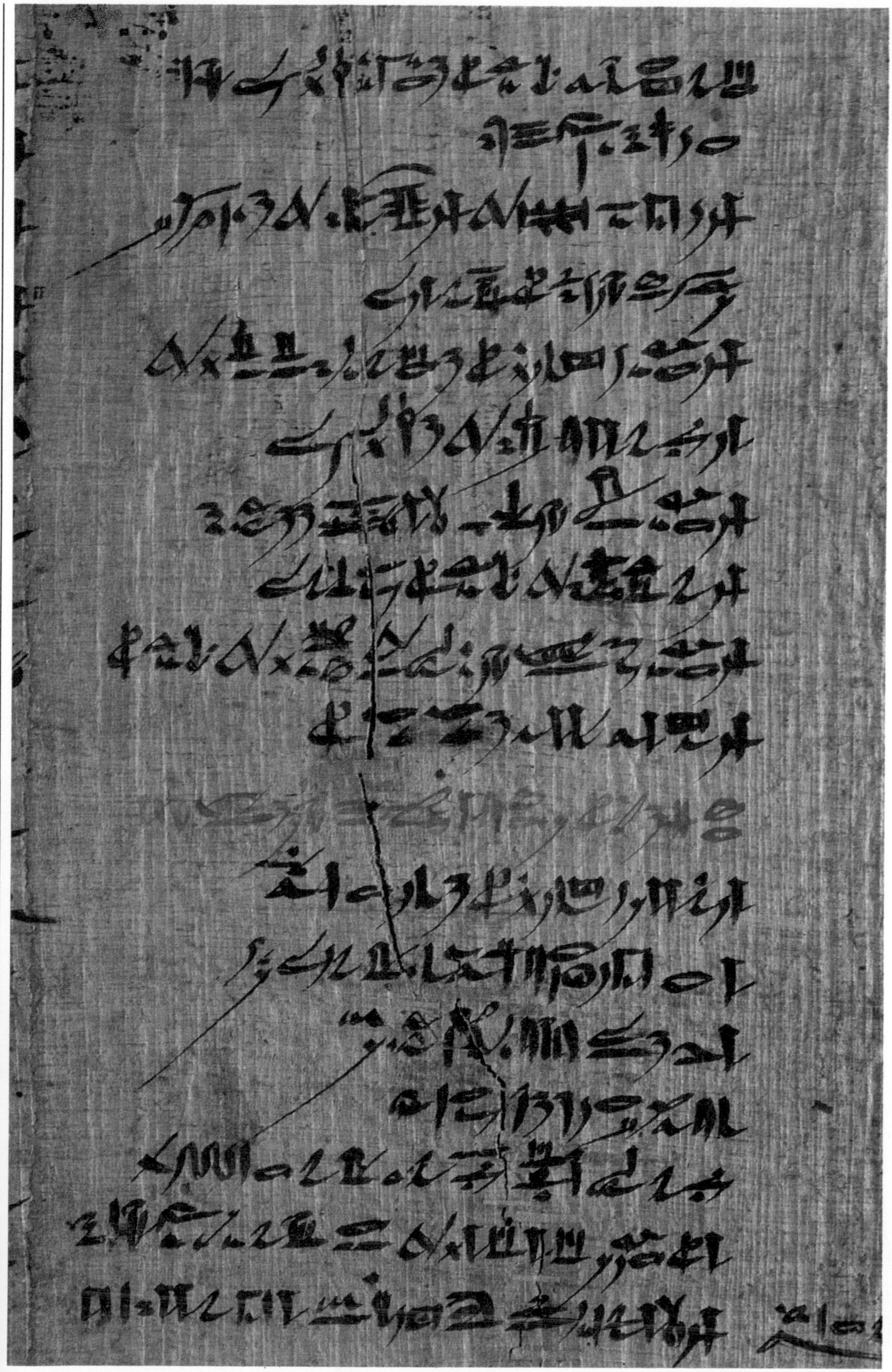

Papyrus (*c.* 1200 BC) *recording the Wisdom of Amenemope* (*c.* 1200 BC), *some of whose sayings are similar in content to those in the proverb collections of the OT and Mesopotamia.* (BM)

'formerly', 'already', and to render the clause simply as, 'Have I not written for thee, already, in/with counsels of knowledge?'

(ii) *Literary usage and OT criticism.* It is singularly unfortunate that the conventional methods of OT literary criticism (see also *BIBLICAL CRITICISM) have been formulated and developed, over the last century in particular, without any but the most superficial reference to the actual characteristics of the contemporary literature of the Bible world, alongside which the Hebrew writings came into existence and with the literary phenomena of which they present very considerable external, formal similarities. The application of such external and tangibly objective controls cannot fail to have drastic consequences for these methods of literary criticism. While Egyp. texts are a specially fruitful source of such external control-data, Mesopotamian, N Canaanite (Ugaritic), Hittite and other literatures provide valuable confirmation. See for preliminary survey, K. A. Kitchen, *Ancient Orient and Old Testament*, 1966, chs. 6–7.

VI. Religion

a. The gods and theology

Egyptian religion was never a unitary whole. There were always local gods up and down the land, among whom were Ptah, artificer-god of Memphis; Thoth, god of learning and the moon at Hermopolis; Amūn 'the hidden', god of Thebes, who overshadowed the war-god Mentu there and became state god of 2nd-millennium Egypt; Hathor, goddess of joy at Dendera; and many more. Then there were the cosmic gods: first and foremost Rēʿ or Atum the sun-god, whose daughter Maʿet personified Truth, Justice, Right and the cosmic order; then Nūt the sky-goddess and Shu, Geb and Nu, the gods of air, earth and the primordial waters respectively. The nearest thing to a truly national religion was the cult of Osiris and his cycle (with his wife, Isis, and son, Horus). The story of Osiris had great human appeal: the good king, murdered by his wicked brother Seth, becoming ruler of the realm of the dead and triumphing in the person of his posthumous son and avenger Horus, who, with the support of his mother Isis, gained his father's kingship on earth. The Egyptian could identify himself with Osiris the revivified in his kingdom of the hereafter; Osiris's other aspect, as a god of vegetation, linking with the annual rise of the Nile and consequent rebirth of life, combined powerfully with his funerary aspect in Egyptian aspirations.

b. Egyptian worship

Egyptian worship was a complete contrast to Hebrew worship in particular, and to Semitic in general. The temple was isolated within its own high-walled estate. Only the officiating priesthood worshipped in such temples; and it was only when the god went forth in glittering procession on great festivals that the populace actively shared in honouring the great gods. Apart from this, they sought their solace in household and lesser gods. The cult of the great gods followed one general pattern, the god being treated just like an earthly king. He was awakened from sleep each morning with a hymn, was washed and dressed (*i.e.* his image), and breakfasted (morning offering), did a morning's business, and had midday and evening meals (corresponding offerings) before retiring for the night. The contrast could hardly be greater between the ever-vigilant, self-sufficient God of Israel with his didactic sacrificial system, symbolizing the need and means of atonement to deal with human sin, and of peace-offerings in fellowship at tabernacle or Temple, and those earthly Egyp. deities of nature. For Egyp. temple-worship, *cf.* H. W. Fairman, *BJRL* 37, 1954, pp. 165–203.

c. Religious literature

To the 3rd millennium BC belong the Pyramid Texts (so-called from their being inscribed in 6th-Dynasty pyramids), a large body of 'spells', apparently forming incredibly intricate royal funerary rituals, and also the Memphite Theology, which glorifies the god Ptah as first cause, conceiving in the mind ('heart') and creating by the word of power ('tongue') (a distant herald of the *logos*-concept of John's Gospel (1:1ff.) transformed through Christ). At all times there are hymns and prayers to the gods, usually full of mythological allusions. In the Empire certain hymns to Amūn, and Akhenaten's famous Aten-hymn, remarkably illustrate the universalism of the day; see **V.** Literature, *b* (i) 1, above. Epics of the gods which at present remain to us exist only in excerpts. A ribald part of the Osiris-cycle survives in the *Contendings of Horus and Seth.* The Coffin Texts of the Middle Kingdom (usually painted inside coffins at that time) and the 'Book of the Dead' of the Empire and Late Period are nothing more than collections of magical spells to protect and benefit the deceased in the after-life; special guide-books to 'infernal' geography were inscribed on the tomb-walls of Empire pharaohs. On magical literature, *MAGIC AND SORCERY. See *ANET* for translations from religious texts.

d. Funerary beliefs

The Egyptians' elaborate beliefs about the after-life found expression in the concrete, material terms of a more-glorious, other-worldly Egypt ruled by Osiris. Alternative hereafters included accompanying the sun-god Rēʿ on his daily voyage across the sky and through the underworld, or dwelling with the stars. The body was a material attachment for the soul; mummification was simply an artificial means of preserving the body to this end, when tombs early became too elaborate for the sun's rays to desiccate the body naturally, as it did in prehistory's shallow graves. Objects in tombs left for the use of the dead usually attracted robbers. Egyptian concern over death was not morbid; this cheerful, pragmatic, materialistic people simply sought to take the good things of this world with them, using magical means so to do. The tomb was the deceased's eternal physical dwelling. The pyramids were simply royal tombs whose shape was modelled on that of the sacred stone of the sun-god Rēʿ at Heliopolis (see I. E. S. Edwards, *The Pyramids of Egypt*, 1961). The Empire pharaohs' secret rock-hewn tombs in the Valley of Kings at Thebes were planned to foil the robbers, but failed, like the pyramids they replaced.

BIBLIOGRAPHY. *General.* Popular introductions to ancient Egypt are: L. Cottrell, *The Lost Pharaohs*, 1950, and *Life under the Pharaohs*, 1955; P. Montet, *Everyday Life in Egypt in the Days of Ramesses the Great*, 1958. Very useful is S. R. K. Glanville (ed.), *The Legacy of Egypt*, 1942 (new edn., 1965); well illustrated is W. C. Hayes, *Sceptre of Egypt*, 1, 1953; 2, 1959. Likewise, G. Posener, S. Sauneron and J. Yoyotte, *Dictionary of Egyptian Civilization*, 1962. On Egypt and Asia, W. Helck, *Die Beziehungen*

Opposite page: Top left: Seated statuette of the goddess Isis suckling her son Horus. c. 7th cent. BC. (MH)

Opposite page: Top right: Gold pectoral with inlays showing the vulture-goddess Nekhbet clasping a symbol of eternity in her claws. From tomb-treasure of Tutankhamun. c. 1340 BC. (RH)

Opposite page: Bottom left: Gold and inlay pectoral, showing winged scarab (emblem of new life) upholding sun-barque, sacred eye and other symbols. From tomb-treasure of Tutankhamun. c. 1340 BC. (RH)

Opposite page: Bottom right: Wooden figure of Osiris, Egyptian god of the afterlife. He wears the Atef crown and holds the royal insignia (flail and crook). (MH)

Agyptens zum Vorderasien im 3. und 2. Jahrtausend v. Chr., 1962. A standard work is H. Kees, *Ägypten*, 1933, being part 1 of the *Kulturgeschichte des Alten Orients* in the *Handbuch der Altertumswissenschaft* series; also H. Kees, *Ancient Egypt, a Cultural Topography*, 1961, is useful and reliable. Full bibliography is obtainable from: I. A. Pratt, *Ancient Egypt*, 1925, and her *Ancient Egypt (1925–41)*, 1942, for nearly everything pre-war; W. Federn, eight lists in *Orientalia* 17, 1948; 18, 1949; and 19, 1950, for the years 1939–47; and J. M. A. Janssen, *Annual Egyptological Bibliography*, 1948ff., for 1947 onwards, plus B. J. Kemp, *Egyptology Titles*, annually. Also Porter-Moss, *Topographical Bibliography*, 7 vols.

Origin of name. Brugsch, *Geographische Inschriften*, 1, 1857, p. 83; A. H. Gardiner, *Ancient Egyptian Onomastica*, 2, 1947, pp. 124*, 211*.

Geography. Very valuable for the physical structure and geography of Egypt is J. Ball, *Contributions to the Geography of Egypt*, 1939. For modern statistics, see survey in *The Middle East, 1958*. Much information is contained in *Baedeker's Egypt*, 1929. The deserts find some description in A. E. P. Weigall, *Travels in the Upper Egyptian Deserts*, 1909. On the early state and settlement of the Nile valley, W. C. Hayes, 'Most Ancient Egypt' = *JNES* 22, 1964. For ancient Egyptian geography, a mine of information is (Sir) Alan Gardiner's *Ancient Egyptian Onomastica*, 3 vols., 1947, with good discussions and references to literature. See also *EGYPT, RIVER OF, *HANES, *MEMPHIS, *NAPHTUHIM, *NILE, *ON, *PATHROS, *PI-BESETH, *RA'AMSES, *THEBES, *ZOAN, *etc*.

Language. For details of, and bibliography on, the Egyp. language, see Sir A. H. Gardiner, *Egyptian Grammar*³, 1957. For Coptic, see W. C. Till, *Koptische Grammatik*, 1955, and A. Mallon, *Grammaire Copte*, 1956, for full bibliography; in English, *cf.* C. C. Walters, *An Elementary Coptic Grammar*, 1972.

History. The standard work is É. Drioton and J. Vandier, *L'Égypte* (Collection '*Clio*')⁴, 1962, with full discussions and bibliography. Valuable is J. A. Wilson, *The Burden of Egypt*, 1951, reprinted as a paperback, *The Culture of Ancient Egypt*, 1956. J. H. Breasted's *History of Egypt*, various dates, is now out of date, as is H. R. Hall's *Ancient History of the Near East*. See also A. H. Gardiner, *Egypt of the Pharaohs*, 1961; and esp. *CAH*³, Vols. 1 and 2, 1970ff.

On Egyp. historical writings, see L. Bull in R. C. Dentan (ed.), *The Idea of History in the Ancient Near East*, 1955, pp. 3–34; C. de Wit, *EQ* 28, 1956, pp. 158–169.

On rival Egyp. priesthoods, see H. Kees, *Das Priestertum im Ägyptischen Staat*, 1953, pp. 78–88 and 62–69, also *Nachträge*, 1958; see also J. A. Wilson, *Burden of Egypt/Culture of Ancient Egypt*, ch. ix. Late Period, see K. A. Kitchen, *The Third Intermediate Period in Egypt (1100–650 BC)*, 1972, esp. Part IV.

On Egypt under Persian dominion, see F. K. Kienitz, *Die Politische Geschichte Ägyptens, vom 7. bis zum 4. Jahrhundert vor der Zeitwende*, 1953. For the Babylonian chronicle-tablets, see D. J. Wiseman, *Chronicles of Chaldaean Kings*, 1956. For a small but very important correction of Egyptian 26th Dynasty dates, see R. A. Parker, *Mitteilungen des Deutschen Archäologischen Instituts, Kairo Abteilung*, 15, 1957, pp. 208–212.

For Graeco-Roman Egypt, see *CAH*, later volumes; Sir H. I. Bell, *Egypt from Alexander the Great to the Arab Conquest*, 1948, and his *Cults and Creeds in Graeco-Roman Egypt*, 1953 and later edns.; W. H. Worrell, *A Short Account of the Copts*, 1945.

Literature. For literary works, *cf.* W. K. Simpson (ed.), *The Literature of Ancient Egypt*, 1972, and M. Lichtheim, *Ancient Egyptian Literature*, 1–2, 1973–6; many historical texts in J. H. Breasted, *Ancient Records of Egypt*, 5 vols., 1906/7. Considerable but abbreviated selections appear in *ANET*. Brilliant work in listing, identifying and restoring Egyp. literature is Posener's *Recherches Littéraires*, 1–7, in the *Revue d'Égyptologie* 6–12 (1949–60). Still valuable in its field is T. E. Peet, *A Comparative Study of the Literatures of Egypt, Palestine and Mesopotamia*, 1931.

Religion. For Egyptian religion, a convenient outline in English is J. Černý, *Ancient Egyptian Religion*, 1952; fuller detail and bibliography in J. Vandier, *La Religion Égyptienne*, 1949; H. Kees, *Der Götterglaube im alten Ägypten*, 1956, is good; *cf.* also S. Morenz, *Egyptian Religion*, 1973. K.A.K.

EGYPT, RIVER OF. The correct identification of 'River of Egypt' is still uncertain; several distinct Heb. terms must be carefully distinguished. *y*ᵉ*'ôr miṣrayim*, 'river (= *Nile) of Egypt', refers exclusively to the Nile proper: its seasonal rise and fall being mentioned in Am. 8:8, and its upper Egyptian reaches in Is.7:18 (plural). The term *n*ᵉ*har miṣrayim*, '(flowing) river of Egypt', occurs once only (Gn. 15:18), where by general definition the promised land lies between the two great rivers, Nile and Euphrates. These two terms (*y*ᵉ*'ôr/n*ᵉ*har miṣrayim*) are wholly separate from, and irrelevant to, the so-called 'river of Egypt' proper, the *naḥal miṣrayim* or 'torrent-wadi of Egypt'. The identification of this term, however, is bound up with that of Shihor, as will be evident from what now follows.

In the OT it is clearly seen that Shihor is a part of the Nile; see the parallelism of Shihor and *y*ᵉ*'ôr* (Nile) in Is. 23:3, and Shihor as Egypt's Nile corresponding to Assyria's great river (Euphrates) in Je. 2:18. Shihor is the extreme SW limit of territory yet to be occupied in Jos. 13:3 and from which Israelites could come to welcome the ark into Jerusalem in 1 Ch. 13:5, and Jos 13:3 specifies it as east of Egypt'. Hence Shihor is the lowest reaches of the easternmost of the Nile's ancient branches (the Pelusiac), flowing into the Mediterranean just W of Pelusium (Tell Farameh). This term Shihor is by origin Egyp. *š-ḥr*, 'waters of Horus'; the Egyptian references agree with the biblical location in so far as they mention Shihor's producing salt and rushes for the not-distant Delta-capital Pi-Ramessē (Tanis or Qantir) and as the 'river' of the 14th Lower-Egyptian nome (province); see R. A. Caminos, *Late-Egyptian Miscellanies*, 1954, pp. 74, 78 (his Menzalah-identification is erroneous), and especially A. H. Gardiner, *JEA* 5, 1918, pp. 251–252.

The real question is whether or not the *naḥal miṣrayim*, 'river (torrent-wadi) of Egypt', is the same as the Shihor, easternmost branch of the Nile.

Against the identification stands the fact that elsewhere in Scripture the Nile is never referred to as a *naḥal*. The river of Is. 11:15 is often taken to be the Euphrates (note the Assyro-Egyp. context here, especially v. 16), and the threat to smite it into seven *nᵉḥālîm*, wadis traversable on foot, represents a transformation of (not the normal description for) the river concerned, whether Nile or Euphrates.

If the 'wadi of Egypt' is not the Nile, the best alternative is the Wadi el-'Arish, which runs N out of Sinai to the Mediterranean 145 km E of Egypt proper (Suez Canal) and 80 km W of Gaza in Palestine. In defence of this identification can be argued a perceptible change of terrain W and E from el-'Arish. Westward to Egypt there is only barren desert and slight scrub; eastward there are meadows and arable land (A. H. Gardiner, *JEA* 6, 1920, p. 115). Hence Wadi el-'Arish would be a practical boundary, including the usable land and excluding mere desert, in the specific delimitations of Nu. 34:5 and Jos. 15:4, 47 (*cf.* also Ezk. 47:19; 48:28). This is then simply echoed in 1 Ki. 8:65 (= 2 Ch. 7:8); 2 Ki. 24:7 and Is. 27:12. Jos. 13:3 and 1 Ch. 13:5 would then indicate the uttermost SW limit (Shihor) of Israelite activity (*cf.* above). Sargon II and Esarhaddon of Assyria also mention the Wadi or Brook of Egypt in their texts. In 716 BC Sargon reached the 'Brook (or Wadi) of Egypt' (*naḥal muṣur*), 'opened the sealed harbour of Egypt' mingling Assyrians and Egyptians for trade purposes, and mentioning 'the border of the City of the Brook of Egypt', where he appointed a governor. Alarmed by the Assyr. activity, the shadow-pharaoh Osorkon IV sent a diplomatic present of '12 big horses' to Sargon (H. Tadmor, *JCS* 12, 1958, pp. 34, 78).

All this fits well with *naḥal muṣur* being Wadi el-'Arish and the 'City' there being the settlement El-'Arish, Assyr. *Arzâ* (Tadmor, *art. cit.*, p. 78, note 194, with further bibliography on 'River of Egypt').

One or two points apparently favouring the alternative view, *viz.* that the 'Wadi of Egypt' is the Shihor/Pelusiac Nile-arm, must, however, not be overlooked. Many are inclined to equate precisely the terms of Jos. 13:3, Shihor, and Nu. 34:5, Jos. 15:4, 47 (likewise 1 Ki. 8:65 and 1 Ch. 13:5), *naḥal miṣrayim*, making Wadi of Egypt another name of the Shihor-Nile. But this would make no allowance for different nuances in the Scripture texts concerned as outlined above. Further, it is true that Sargon II could well have reached the Pelusiac (easternmost) arm of the Nile; his 'City' there would then be Pelusium—which would most decidedly alarm Osorkon IV. But the 'City' is certainly the Arza(ni) of Esarhaddon's inscriptions (*ANET*, pp. 290–292, *passim*) which corresponds well to 'Arish but not Pelusium (Egyp. *sỉnw, swn*). Finally, Egyptians and the 19th Dynasty evidently regarded the Pelusiac area as *de facto* the edge of Egypt proper: in Papyrus Anastasi III, 1: 10, Ḫuru (Palestine generally) extends 'from Silē to 'Upa (= Damascus)'; Silē ('Thel') is modern Qantara a few km S and E of the former Pelusiac Nile-arm (R. A. Caminos, *Late-Egyptian Miscellanies*, pp. 69, 73 and refs.). But this proves nothing about Israel's boundaries; as already mentioned, from Qantara to 'Arish is a desolate no-man's-land. In any case, 19th-Dynasty Egypt did assert authority and maintain wells across the entire coast-strip, Qantara–'Arish–Gaza (see A. H. Gardiner, *JEA* 6, 1920, pp. 99–116, on the military road here). The Shihor/Nile identification of the Wadi of Egypt has been advocated by H. Bar-Deroma, *PEQ* 92, 1960, pp. 37–56, but he takes no account of the contemporary Egyp. and Assyr. sources, the post-biblical matter cited being imprecise and of too late a date.

The subject is not closed, but Wadi el-'Arish is more likely to be the 'River (Wadi) of Egypt' than is the E Nile on present evidence.

K.A.K.

EGYPTIAN, THE. In Acts 21:38 an agitator for whom the Roman officer commanding the Antonia fortress mistook Paul when the latter was set upon in the Temple precincts. According to Josephus (*BJ* 2. 261–263; *Ant.* 20. 169–172), this Egyptian came to Jerusalem *c.* AD 54, claiming to be a prophet, and led a great multitude to the Mount of Olives, promising that, at his command, the city walls would

EGYPTIAN BACKGROUND
See Joseph, OT, Part 2.

EGYPTIAN PAPYRI
See Papyri, Part 2.

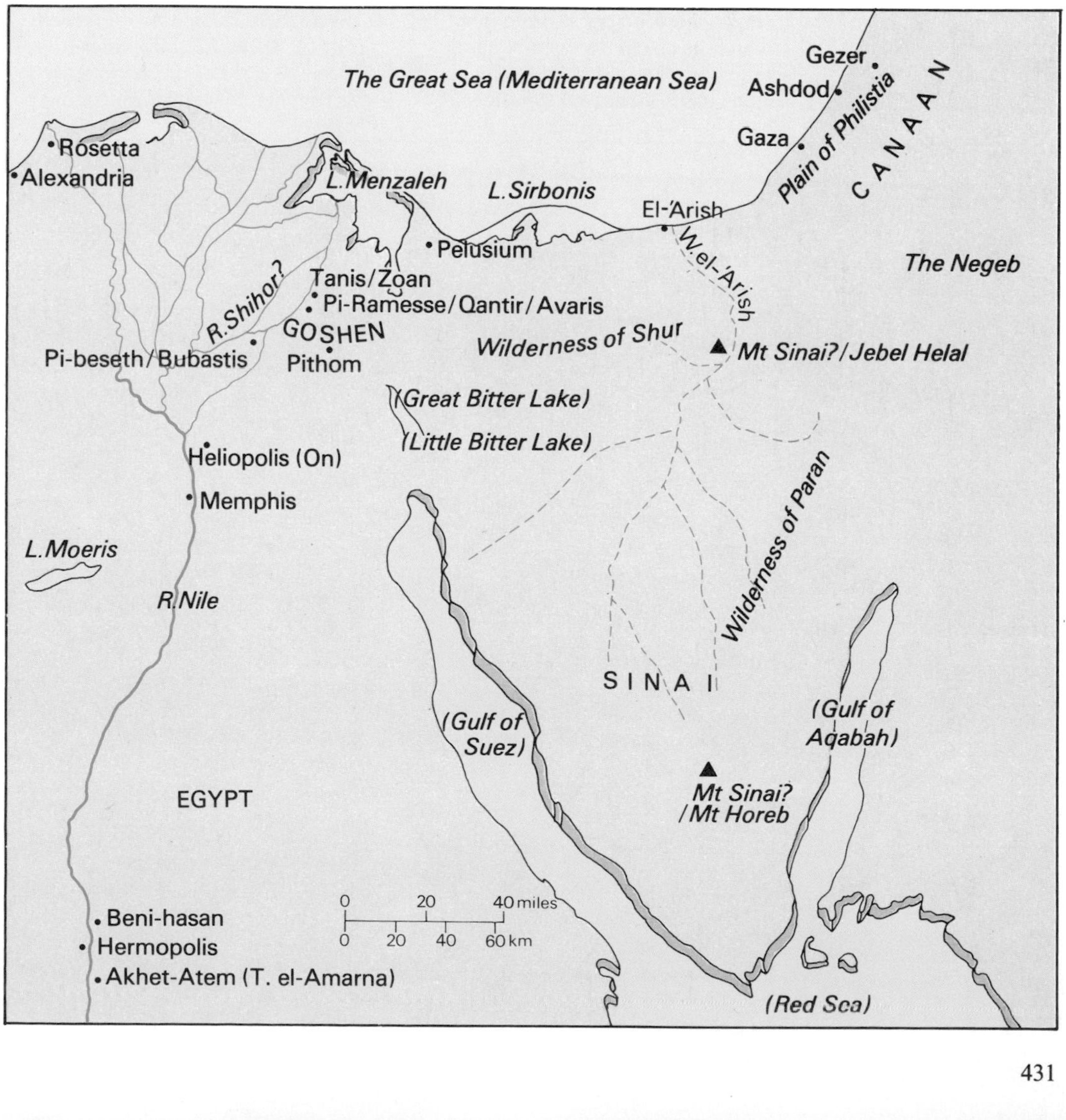

Egypt, showing the Wadi el-'Arish and the river Shihor, both possible identifications with the 'River of Egypt'.

EGYPTIAN TRAINING
See Moses, Part 2.

EGYPTIAN VERSION
See Texts and versions, Part 3.

EIGHT
See Number, Part 2.

EIGHTEEN BENEDICTIONS
See Synagogue, Part 3.

EL
See God, names of, Part 1.

Ekron, one of the five principal Philistine cities.

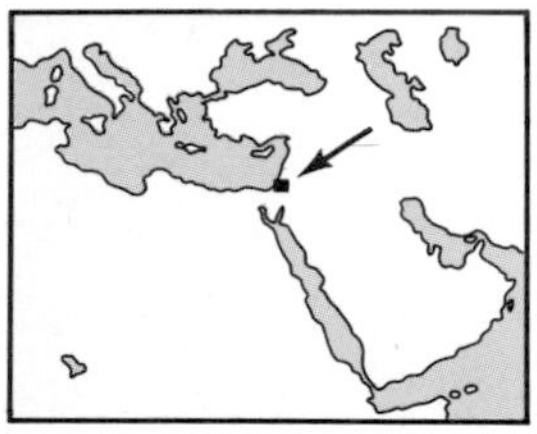

collapse before them. Soldiers sent by Felix dispersed his followers, with some bloodshed; the Egyptian escaped. (*ASSASSINS.)

F.F.B.

EHUD (Heb. *'ēhûḏ*). A Benjaminite name (1 Ch. 7:10; 8:6; Jdg. 3:15). Ehud, the son of Gera, led the revolt against the Moabite occupation of E Benjamin (Jdg. 3); gaining a private audience of King Eglon, he killed him in his own apartments, and rallied the Israelites to take advantage of the confusion into which the Moabites were thrown. His left-handedness was doubtless useful in taking Eglon unawares. The Heb. phrase 'deformed (lit. bound) in his right hand' is idiomatic; *cf.* Jdg. 20:16.

J.P.U.L.

EKRON. One of the five principal Philistine cities, and a place of importance, having villages dependent upon it (Jos. 15:45–46). Recent surveys suggest that it is to be identified with Khirbet al-Muqanna', which has hitherto been equated with * Eltekeh. Surface explorations in 1957 showed the site was occupied in the Early Bronze Age but evidently not again until the Early Iron Age. The peak period, when the walled city occupied an area of some 40 acres, making it in fact the largest Iron Age settlement yet found in Palestine, was characterized by typical Philistine pottery. The tell has a projection at the NE corner which perhaps represents the acropolis, and on the S slopes a double wall with gates and towers has been traced. In the allotment of territories Ekron was placed on the border between Judah and Dan (Jos. 15:11, 45–46; 19:43), but at the death of Joshua it remained to be possessed. It was finally taken by Judah (Jdg. 1:18), but must have been recaptured by the Philistines, for they took the ark there when it was removed from Gath (1 Sa. 5:10), and it was from there that it was despatched to Beth-shemesh on the cow-drawn cart (1 Sa. 6). It appears that Ekron was again temporarily in Israelite hands in the time of Samuel (1 Sa. 7:14), but the Philistines had retaken it by Saul's time (1 Sa. 17:52), and it was still held by them in the time of Amos (1:8). In 701 BC Padi the ruler of Ekron, a vassal of the Assyrians, was expelled by certain Ekronites and held captive by Hezekiah in Jerusalem, but Sennacherib, in his campaign of the year, retook Ekron (*am-qar-ru-na*) and restored Padi (*ANET*, pp. 287–288; *DOTT*, pp. 66–67). The city is mentioned in the Annals of Esarhaddon as tributary (*ANET*, p. 291; *DOTT*, p. 74), but was still at that time regarded as a Philistine city from the ethnic point of view (Je. 25:20; Zp. 2:4; Zc. 9:5, 7). The Bible is not concerned with the subsequent history of the city, though the name of the city god, * Baal-zebub (2 Ki. 1:2–3), is familiar from the NT.

BIBLIOGRAPHY. J. Naveh, *IEJ* 8, 1958, pp. 87–100, 165–170; Y. Aharoni, *PEQ* 90, 1958, pp. 27–31; Honigmann, *Reallexikon der Assyriologie*, 1, 1932, p. 99; T. C. Mitchell in *AOTS*, pp. 405–406.

T.C.M.

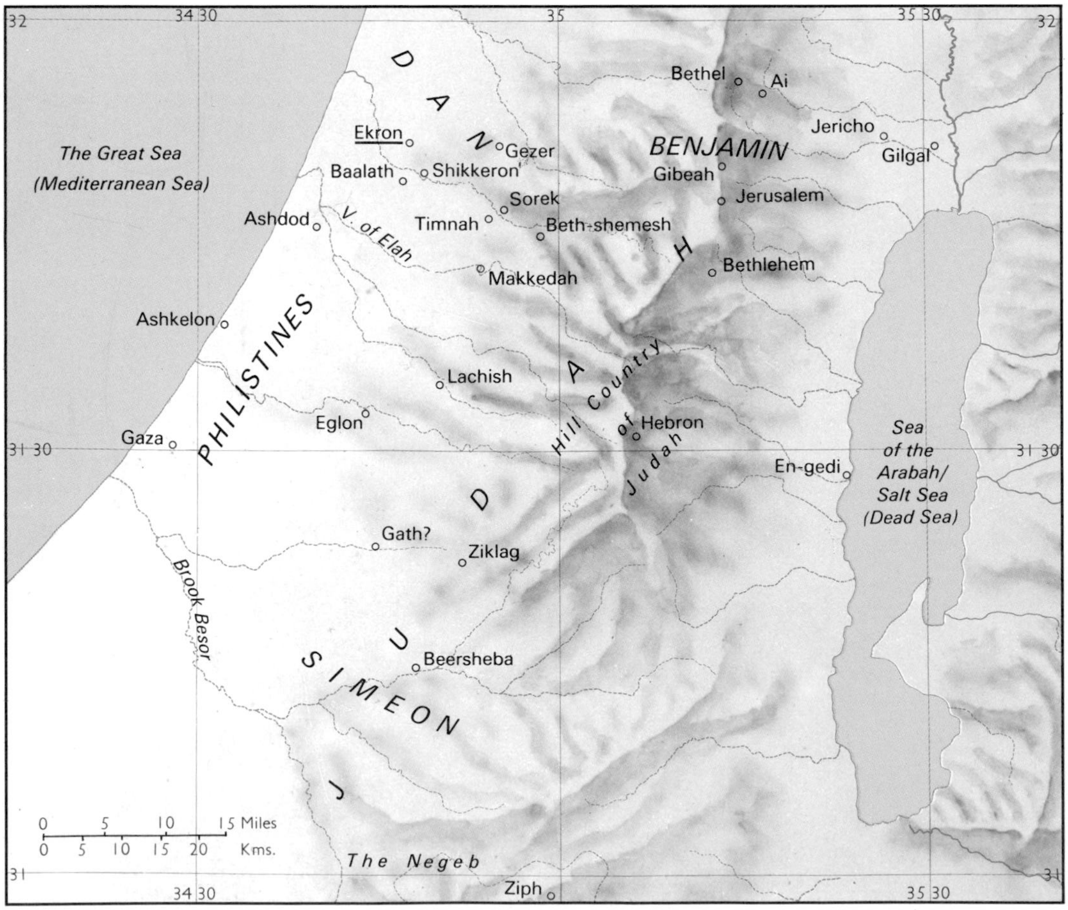

ELAH (Heb. *'ēlâ*, 'terebinth'). **1.** A tribal prince of Edom (Gn. 36:41; 1 Ch. 1:52), perhaps the chief of the district of Elah, possibly the seaport of * Elath. **2.** Son of Baasha, and king of Israel for 2 years until he was assassinated by Zimri during a drunken orgy in the house of Arza, his steward (1 Ki. 16:6–14). **3.** Father of Hoshea, the last king of Israel (2 Ki. 15:30; 17:1; 18:1, 9). **4.** Second son of Caleb, son of Jephunneh, Joshua's companion (1 Ch. 4:15). **5.** A Benjaminite who dwelt at Jerusalem after the Exile (1 Ch. 9:8). His name is one of those omitted in the parallel list in Ne. 11.

J.G.G.N.

ELAH (Heb. *'ēlâ*, 'terebinth'). A valley used by the Philistines to gain access to Central Palestine. It was the scene of David's victory over Goliath (1 Sa. 17:2; 21:9), and is generally identified with the modern Wadi es-Sant, 18 km SW of Jerusalem.

J.D.D.

ELAM, ELAMITES. The ancient name for the plain of Khuzistan, watered by the Kerkh river, which joins the Tigris just N of the Persian Gulf. Civilization in this area is as old as, and closely connected with, the cultures of lower Mesopotamia. A local pictographic script appeared very soon after the invention of * writing in Babylonia. The Elamites cannot be certainly linked with any other known race, although their language may be related to the Dravidian family. The reference to Elam as a son of Shem (Gn. 10:22) may well reflect the presence of early Semites in this area, and there is archaeological evidence in the time of Sargon I (*c.* 2350 BC) and his successors of their influence on the local culture. Rock sculptures depict typical Akkadian figures and bear Akkadian inscriptions, although carved for Elamite rulers. The mountainous region to the N and E was known as Anshan and, from an early period, formed a part of Elam. Sumerian and Semitic plainsmen looked upon these ranges as the abode of evil spirits, and early epics describe the terrors they held for those who crossed them in search of the mineral wealth of states beyond (see S. N. Kramer, *History Begins at Sumer*, 1958, pp. 57ff., 230ff.).

Its control of the trade routes to the Iranian plateau, and to the SE, made Elam the object of constant attacks from the plains of Mesopotamia. These in turn offered great wealth to any conqueror. A strong Elamite dynasty, a king being succeeded by his brother, then his son, arose about 2000 BC and gained control of several cities in Baby-

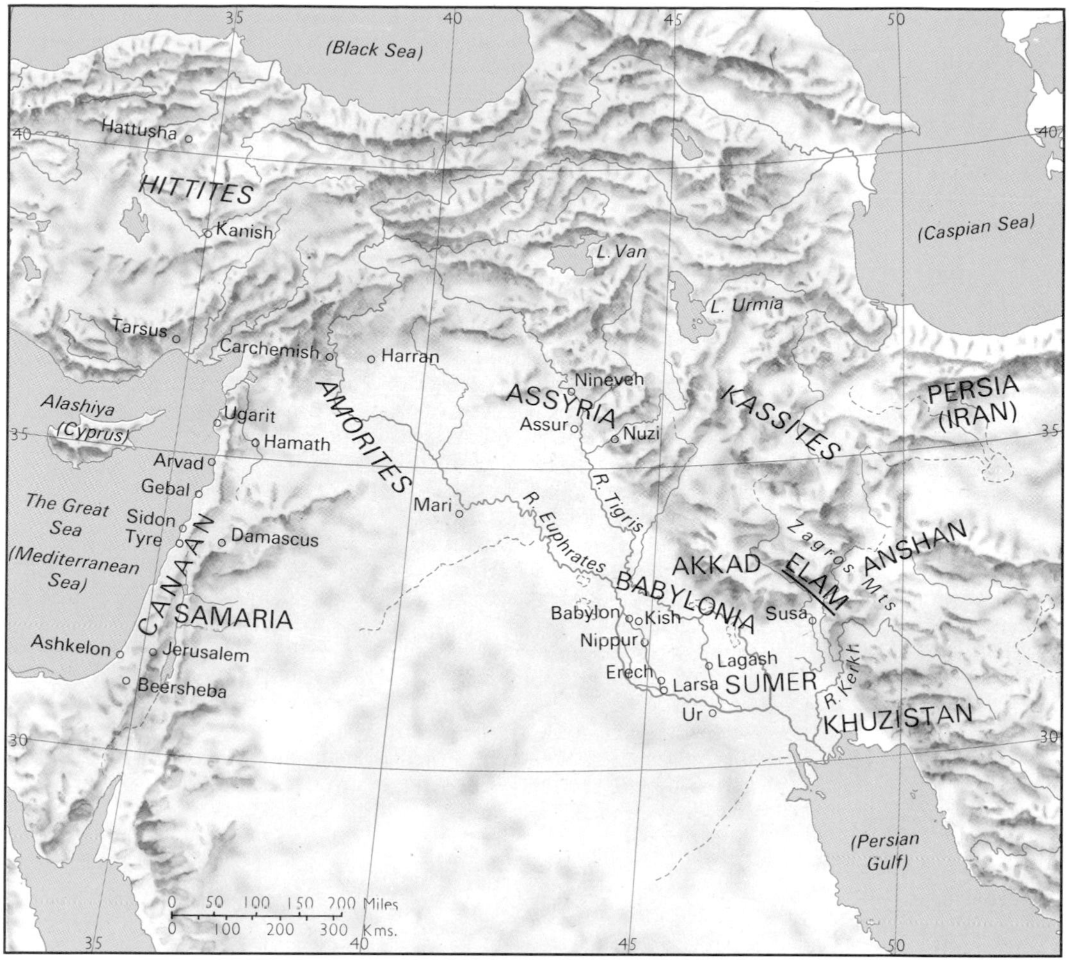

Elam, the ancient name for the plain of Khuzistan.

Bottom left:
Elamite statuette of a worshipper bearing a sacrificial offering, an ibex or a young goat. Part of a funerary deposit near the temple of Inshushinak at Susa. Height 6 cm. 13th–12th cent. BC. (MC)

The defeated king of Elam, Ummanaldash, being taken under escort to Ashurbanipal, king of Assyria. Nineveh. c. 640 BC. (BM)

EL-AMARNA
See Amarna, Part 1.

EL-BERITH
See Baal-berith, Part 1.

Sites of Elath/Ezion-geber settlements.

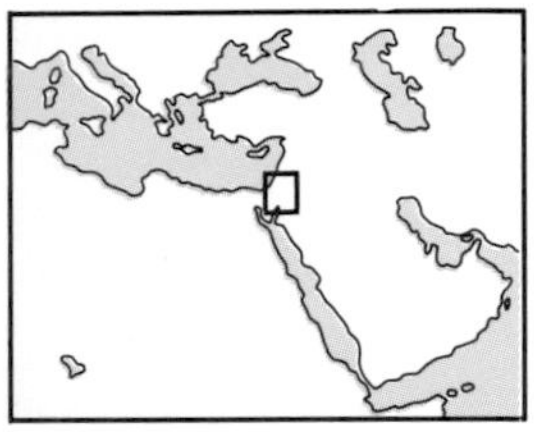

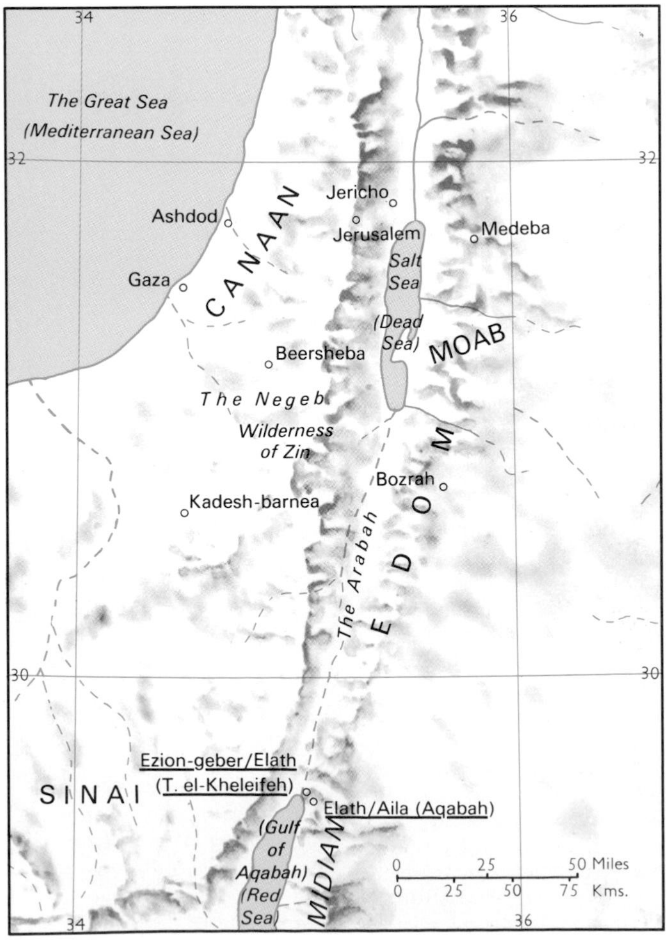

lonia, destroying the power of the Sumerian rulers of Ur and sacking it (see *ANET*, pp. 455ff., 480f.). To this period of Elamite supremacy should *Chedorlaomer probably be assigned (Gn. 14:1). Hammurapi of Babylon drove the Elamites out *c.* 1760 BC, but the 'Amorite' dynasty, to which he belonged, fell before Hittite and Elamite attacks *c.* 1595 BC. Invasions of Kassites coming from the central Zagros mountains (*BABYLONIA) drove the Elamites back to Susa, until a resurgence of power enabled them to conquer and rule Babylon for several centuries (*c.* 1300–1120 BC). Among trophies taken to Susa at this time was the famous Law stele of Hammurapi. Elamite history is obscure from *c.* 1000 BC until the campaigns of Sargon of Assyria (*c.* 721–705 BC). Sennacherib and Ashurbanipal subjected the Elamites and deported some of them to Samaria, taking Israelites to Elam (Ezr. 4:9; Is. 11:11).

After the collapse of *Assyria, Elam was annexed by the Indo-Europeans, who had gradually gained power in Iran following their invasions *c.* 1000 BC. Teispes (*c.* 675–640 BC), ancestor of Cyrus, bore the title 'king of Anshan' and Susa eventually became one of the three chief cities of the Medo-Persian empire.

Elam is called upon by Isaiah to crush Babylon (Is. 21:2) and this was carried out (*cf.* Dn. 8:2). Yet Elam will be crushed in turn, even the famous archers defeated (Je. 25:25; 49:34–39; *cf.* Is. 22:6; Ezk. 32:24). The crowd at Pentecost (Acts 2:9) contained men from as far away as Elam, presumably members of Jewish communities who had remained in exile in the semi-autonomous state of Elymais, though using Aramaic, the last flicker of Elamite independence. (*ARCHAEOLOGY, *MEDES, *PERSIA, *SUSA.)

BIBLIOGRAPHY. W. Hinz, *The Lost World of Elam*, 1972; E. Porada, *Ancient Iran*, 1965. A.R.M.

ELATH (ELOTH), EZION-GEBER. Settlement(s) at the N end of present-day Gulf of Aqabah. First mentioned as a stopping-place during Israel's wilderness journeyings (Nu. 33:35–36; Dt. 2:8) in the 13th century BC. Elath and/or Ezion-geber was then probably little more than wells and palm-groves near present-day Aqabah, which has always been the normal settlement-site in this district.

Solomon (*c.* 960 BC) developed copper- and iron-mining and smelting in the Arabah N of Ezion-geber, a new site (Tell el-Kheleifeh) 4 km W of Aqabah, old Elath. The view that Ezion-geber itself was a smeltery has now been abandoned (Rothenberg, *PEQ* 94, 1962, pp. 44–56; N. Glueck, *The Other Side of the Jordan*, 1970, pp. 113–115), but it may have been a depot. In phase I, Ezion-geber/Elath served also as the terminal port for Solomon's Red Sea trading-fleet to Ophir and Arabia (1 Ki. 9:26; 2 Ch. 8:17); some time after his reign, Ezion-geber was burnt down and eventually rebuilt (phase II) in the 9th century BC, probably by Jehoshaphat of Judah (*c.* 860 BC), whose fleet, doubtless imitating Solomon's, was wrecked (1 Ki. 22:48; 2 Ch. 20:36–37), probably on the rocks there, by the strong winds of this region. Under Jehoram of Judah (*c.* 848 BC), Edom revolted (2 Ki. 8:21–22), cutting off, burning and re-occupying Ezion-geber. Some 60 years later Uzziah (Azariah) of Judah (*c.* 780 BC) recovered Ezion-geber from the Edomites (2 Ki. 14:22; 2 Ch. 26:2), and rebuilt it as Elath (phase III). A seal of his successor Jotham was found in this rebuilt Elath. However, Rezin of Aram (Syria) took Elath from Ahaz of Judah (*c.* 730 BC), letting it revert to (? allied) Edomite control (2 Ki. 16:6; but in v. 6b, for 'the Syrians came . . . and dwelt', AV, RV, read 'the Edomites came', *etc.*, RSV, changing a single *r* to the very similar *d*).

During the 7th–4th centuries BC (phases IV and V), Elath remained Edomite; several 7th-century BC sealings of the obviously Edomite 'Qos'anal, servant of the king' (of Edom) were discovered in 'Edomized' Elath. Under Persian rule, trade through Elath to Arabia still flourished, as evidenced by the discovery of 5th- and 4th-century BC Aramaic ostraca (including wine receipts), and even fine Attic pottery in trans-shipment from Greece for Arabia. When the Nabataeans supplanted the Edomites, Elath was restricted to the site of present-day Aqabah, becoming known as Aila under the Nabataeans and Romans.

BIBLIOGRAPHY. For Nelson Glueck's excavations at Ezion-geber, see E. K. Vogel, *Bibliography of Holy Land Sites*, 1974, pp. 85–86; N. Glueck, *The Other Side of the Jordan*, 1970, pp. 103–137. Reconstruction of ancient Ezion-geber in N. Glueck, *The River Jordan*, 1946, p. 142, fig. 75. On state slavery at Ezion-geber, see I. Mendelsohn, *BASOR* 85, 1942, pp. 14–17.

K.A.K.

ELDAD (Heb. 'God has loved'). An Israelite elder, associated with Medad in Nu. 11:26–30; perhaps to be identified with Elidad (Nu. 34:21). He and Medad failed to appear at the tabernacle of the congregation when summoned there with the seventy elders by Moses. They nevertheless shared in the gift of prophecy which the elders received from the Lord. Far from forbidding this apparently irregular display of divine power, Moses rejoiced and wished that all the Lord's people might become prophets. Such ecstatic behaviour was a significant feature of early OT *prophecy. J.B.Tr.

ELDER. In most civilizations authority has been vested in those who by reason of age or experience have been thought best qualified to rule. It is not surprising therefore that the leaders in many ancient communities have borne a title derived from a root meaning 'old age'. In this respect the Heb. 'elder' (*zāqēn*) stands side by side with the Homeric *gerontes*, the Spartan *presbys*, the Roman *senatus* and the Arab *sheikh*.

In the Pentateuch elders are referred to among the Egyptians (Gn. 50:7) and the Moabites and Midianites (Nu. 22:7), as well as among the Israelites. In Ex. 3:16 the Israelites are represented as having had elders from the time of the Egyptian captivity, and it is with them that Moses is commanded to collaborate in his bid for freedom. They were probably the heads of families in the first instance, but Ex. 24:1 gives a fixed number of seventy. It was upon this inner circle of seventy elders that the Lord poured out the spirit in order that they should share the government of the people with Moses (Nu. 11:25).

After the wilderness period every city seems to have had its own ruling body of elders whose duties, according to Deuteronomic legislation, included acting as judges in apprehending murderers (Dt. 19:12), conducting inquests (Dt. 21:2) and settling matrimonial disputes (Dt. 22:15; 25:7). If theirs was a city of refuge they also heard pleas for asylum (Jos. 20:4; but see also Nu. 35:24). Their numbers varied, Succoth having seventy-seven (Jdg. 8:14), and they are associated with other civil officials, *e.g.* heads of tribes (Dt. 5:23; 29:10) and officers and judges (Jos. 8:33). Maybe the term 'elders' was a general word for the ruling body and included some of these officials.

The national body of elders of Israel' still exercised considerable influence under the Monarchy as the chieftains of the people, having first agitated for the appointment of a king (1 Sa. 8:4f.) and having finally accepted David (2 Sa. 5:3). Their position and influence were recognized by Solomon (1 Ki. 8:1, 3), Ahab (1 Ki. 20:7), Jezebel (1 Ki. 21:8), Jehu (2 Ki. 10:1), Hezekiah (2 Ki. 19:2) and Josiah (2 Ki. 23:1). Ezekiel in captivity dealt with them (Ezk. 8:1; 14:1; 20:1), and they appear also in Ezra's time and in the Gk. period. While their authority was originally civil, by NT times the 'elders of the people' (*presbyteroi tou laou*) shared with the chief priests the power of determining religious affairs and, if necessary, of expulsion from the *synagogue. See also *Sanhedrin and (for NT use) *Presbyter.

J.B.Tr.

ELEALEH (Heb. *'el'ālēh*, 'God is exalted'). A town E of Jordan always mentioned in conjunction with Heshbon. Conquered by Gad and Reuben (Nu. 32:3), rebuilt by the latter tribe (32:37), and later Moabite, it was the subject of prophetic warnings (Is. 15:4; 16:9; Je. 48:34). Identified with the modern el-'Al, 4 km NE of Heshbon.

J.D.D.

ELEAZAR. The name (meaning 'God has helped') of a number of OT figures. In all but a few cases (1 Sa. 7:1; 2 Sa. 23:9–10 [1 Ch. 11:12]; 1 Ch. 23:21–22; 24:28; Ezr. 8:33; 10:25; Ne. 12:42; Mt. 1:15) Eleazar the third son of Aaron, whom he succeeded as chief priest (Nu. 20:25–28; Dt. 10:6), is meant. Even before his father's death he is represented as having an important position in the priestly hierarchy (Nu. 3:32; 4:16; 16:37–40; 19:3–4), which resulted from the punishment of his elder brothers Nadab and Abihu (Lv. 10:1–2). As chief priest he is frequently mentioned alongside Moses or Joshua as a leader of the Israelites (*e.g.* Nu. 26:1; Jos. 14:1).

Almost all the OT references to Eleazar the son of Aaron derive from P or the Chronicler, so that the same critical questions arise as in the case of *Aaron. In post-exilic times 'the sons of Eleazar' formed one of the two main divisions of the full priesthood, 'the sons of Aaron' (1 Ch. 24:4–6; in Ezr. 8:2 his son Phinehas appears as the ancestor of the group). Since Zadok was at this time regarded as a descendant of Eleazar (1 Ch. 6:1–8, 50–53; 24:3), it appears that the high priesthood was held by members of this division. Ezra was an important member of it (Ezr. 7:5). It is widely thought that the tradition about Eleazar was developed in priestly circles to safeguard the exclusive privileges of this group, who have been the descendants of the priests who officiated in Jerusalem before the Exile (*cf.* Cody). If this is correct, it must affect the way in which the relevant texts are understood. But that Aaron did have a son Eleazar who followed him in his priestly office and had a son called Phinehas seems firmly established on the basis of older texts (Dt. 10:6; Jos. 24:33 and (?) Jdg. 20:28). According to Jos. 24:33 he was buried at Gibeah in the land of Ephraim.

BIBLIOGRAPHY. *IDB*, 2, pp. 75–76; A. Cody, *A History of Old Testament Priesthood*, 1969, pp. 171–174.

G.I.D.

ELECTION. The act of choice whereby God picks an individual or group out of a larger company for a purpose or destiny of his own appointment. The main OT word for this is the verb *bāḥar*, which expresses the idea of deliberately selecting someone or something after carefully considering the alternatives (*e.g.* sling-stones, 1 Sa. 17:40; a place of refuge, Dt. 23:16; a wife, Gn. 6:2; good rather than evil, Is. 7:15f.; life rather than death, Dt. 30:19f.; the service of God rather than of idols, Jos. 24:22). The word implies a decided preference for, sometimes positive pleasure in, the object chosen (*cf.*, *e.g.*, Is. 1:29). In LXX and the NT the corresponding verb is *eklegomai*. *eklegō* is commonly active in classical Gk., but the biblical writers always use it in the middle voice, with reflexive overtones: it thus means 'choose out for oneself'. *haireomai* is used synonymously of God's choice in 2 Thes. 2:13, as in Dt. 26:18, LXX. The cognate adjectives are Heb. *bāḥîr* and Gk. *eklektos*, translated 'elect' or 'chosen'; the NT also uses the noun *eklogē*, 'election'. The Heb. verb *yāḏa'*, 'know', which is used of various acts of knowing that, in idea at least, imply and express affection (*e.g.* relations between the sexes, and the believer's acknowledgment of God), is used to denote God's election (*i.e.* his taking cognizance of persons in love) in Gn. 18:19 (see RV); Am. 3:2; Ho. 13:5. The Gk. *proginōskō*, 'foreknow', is similarly used in Rom. 8:29; 11:2 to mean 'forelove' (*cf.* also the use of *ginōskō* in 1 Cor. 8:3 and Gal. 4:9).

I. Old Testament usage

Israelite faith was founded on the belief that Israel was God's chosen people. His choice of her had been made by means of two connected and complementary acts. (*a*) He chose Abraham and his seed, by taking Abraham out of Ur and bringing him to the promised land of Canaan, making there an everlasting covenant with him and his descendants, and promising him that his seed should be a blessing to all the earth (Gn. 11:31–12:7; 15; 17; 22:15–18; Ne. 9:7; Is. 41:8). (*b*) He chose Abraham's seed by redeeming them from slavery in Egypt, bringing them out of bondage under Moses, renewing the Abrahamic covenant with them in an amplified form at Sinai and setting them in the promised land as their national home (Ex. 3:6–10; Dt. 6:21–23; Ps. 105). Each of these acts of choice is also described as God's call, *i.e.* a sovereign utterance of words and disposal of events by which God summoned, in the one case, Abraham, and in the other, Abraham's seed, to acknowledge him as their God and live to him as his people (Is. 51:2; Ho. 11:1; *CALL). Israelite faith looked back to these two acts as having created the nation (*cf.* Is. 43:1; Acts 13:17).

The meaning of Israel's election appears from the following facts:

a. Its *source* was God's free omnipotent love. Moses' speeches in Deuteronomy stress this. When he chose Israel, God 'set his love on' Israel (Dt. 7:7; 23:5): why? Not because Israel first chose him, nor because Israel deserved his favour. Israel was in fact the reverse of attractive, being neither numerous nor righteous, but feeble, small and rebellious (Dt. 7:7; 9:4–6). God's love to Israel was spontaneous and free, exercised in defiance of demerit, having no cause save his own good pleasure. He made it his delight and satisfaction to do Israel good (Dt. 28:63; *cf.* 30:9) simply because he resolved to do so. It was true that in delivering Israel from Egypt he was keeping a promise made to the Patriarchs (Dt. 7:8), and there was a necessity of the divine character in that, for it is God's nature always to be faithful to his promises (*cf.* Nu. 23:19; 2 Tim. 2:13); but the making of this promise had itself been an act of free unmerited love, for the Patriarchs were themselves sinners (as Gn. is at pains to show), and God chose Abraham, the first recipient of the promise, out of idolatry (Jos. 24:2f.). Here too, therefore, the cause of election must be sought, not in man, but in God.

God is King in his world, and his love is omnipotent. Accordingly, he implemented his choice of Israel by means of a miraculous deliverance (by 'a mighty hand', Dt. 7:8, *etc.*) out of a state of helpless captivity. Ezk. 16:3–6 dwells on Israel's pitiable condition when God chose her; Ps. 135:4–12 extols his display of sovereignty in bringing his chosen people out of bondage into the promised land.

b. The *goal* of Israel's election was, proximately, the blessing and salvation of the people through God's separating them for himself (Ps. 33:12), and, ultimately, God's own glory through Israel's showing forth his praise to the world (Is. 43:20f.; *cf.* Pss. 79:13; 96:1–10), and bearing witness of the great things he had done (Is. 43:10–12; 44:8). Israel's election involved separation. By it, God made Israel a holy people, *i.e.* one set apart for himself (Dt. 7:6; Lv. 20:26b). He took them as his inheritance (Dt. 4:20; 32:9–12) and treasure (Ex. 19:5; Ps. 135:4), promising to protect and prosper them (Dt. 28:1–14), and to dwell with them (Lv. 26:11f.). Election made them his people, and him their God, in covenant together. It had in view living communion between them and him. Their destiny, as his chosen people, was to enjoy his manifested presence in their midst and to receive the multitude of good gifts which he promised to shower upon them. Their election was thus an act of blessing which was the fount of all other blessings. Hence the prophets express the hope that God would restore his people and presence to Jerusalem after the Exile, and re-establish conditions of blessing there, by saying that God will again 'choose' Israel and Jerusalem (Is. 14:1; Zc. 1:17; 2:12; *cf.* 3:2).

c. The *religious and ethical obligations* created by Israel's election were far-reaching. Election, and the covenant relationship based on it, which distinguished Israel from all other nations, was a motive to grateful praise (Ps. 147:19f.), loyal keeping of God's law (Lv. 18:4f.) and resolute non-conformity to the idolatry and wrongdoing of the unelected world (Lv. 18:2f.; 20:22f.; Dt. 14:1f.; Ezk. 20:5–7, *etc.*). Also, it gave Israel grounds for unfaltering hope and trust in God in times of distress and discouragement (*cf.* Is. 41:8–14; 44:1f.; Hg. 2:23; Ps. 106:4f.). Irreligious Israelites, however, were betrayed by the thought of the national election into complacently despising other nations, and assuming that they could always rely on God for protection and preferential treatment, no matter what their own lives were like (*cf.* Mi. 3:11; Je. 5:12). It was this delusion, and in particular the idea that Jerusalem, as the city of God, was inviolable, that the false prophets fostered in the days before the Exile (Je. 7:1–15; 23:9f.; Ezk. 13). In fact, however, as God had made plain from the first (Lv. 26:14ff.; Dt. 28:15ff.), national election implied a strict judgment of national sins (Am. 3:2). The Exile proved that God's threats had not been idle.

d. Within the chosen people, *God chose individuals for specific tasks* designed to further the purpose of the national election—*i.e.* Israel's own enjoyment of God's blessing, and, ultimately, the blessing of the world. God chose Moses (Ps. 106:23), Aaron (Ps. 105:26), the priests (Dt. 18:5), the prophets (*cf.* Je. 1:5), the kings (1 Sa. 10:24; 2 Sa. 6:21; 1 Ch. 28:5), and the Servant-Saviour of Isaiah's prophecy ('my elect', Is. 42:1; *cf.* 49:1, 5), who suffers persecution (Is. 50:5ff.), dies for sins (Is. 53) and brings the Gentiles light (Is. 42:1–7; 49:6). God's use of Assyria and 'my servant' Nebuchadrezzar as his scourges (Is. 7:18ff.; 10:5ff.; Je. 25:9; 27:6; 43:10), and of Cyrus, a man ignorant of God, as a benefactor to the chosen people (Is. 45:4), is termed by H. H. Rowley 'election without covenant' (*The Biblical Doctrine of Election*, 1950, ch. 5), but the phrase is improper; the Bible always reserves the vocabulary of election for the covenant people and covenant functionaries drawn from Israel's own ranks.

e. The promised blessings of election were *forfeited through unbelief and disobedience*. The prophets, facing widespread hypocrisy, insisted that God would reject the ungodly among his people (Je. 6:30; 7:29). Isaiah foretold that only a faithful remnant would live to enjoy the golden age that was to follow the inevitable judgment on Israel's sins (Is. 10:20–22; 4:3; 27:6; 37:31f.). Jeremiah and Ezekiel, living in the time of that judgment, looked for a day when God, as part of his work of restoration, would regenerate such of his people as he had spared, and ensure their covenant faithfulness for the future by giving each of them a new heart (Je. 31:31ff.; 32:39f.; Ezk. 11:19f.; 36:25ff.). These prophecies, with their focus on individual piety, pointed to an individualizing of the concept of election (*cf.* Ps. 65:4): they gave grounds for distinguishing between election to privilege and election to life, and for concluding that, while God had chosen the whole nation for the privilege of living under the covenant, he had chosen only some of them (those made faithful by regeneration) to inherit the riches of the relationship to himself which the covenant held out, while the rest forfeited those riches by their unbelief. The NT teaching about election assumes these distinctions; see especially Rom. 9.

II. New Testament usage

The NT announces the extension of God's covenant-promises to the Gentile world and the transference of covenant-privileges from the lineal seed of Abraham to a predominantly Gentile body (*cf.* Mt. 21:43) consisting of all who had become Abraham's true seed and God's true Israel through faith in Christ (Rom. 4:9–18; 9:6f.; Gal. 3:14ff., 29; 6:16; Eph. 2:11ff.; 3:6–8). The unbelieving natural branches were broken off from God's olive-tree (the elect community, sprung from the Patriarchs), and wild olive branches (believing Gentiles) were ingrafted in their place (Rom. 11:16–24). Faithless Israel was rejected and judged, and the international Christian church took Israel's place as God's chosen nation, living in the world as his people and worshipping and proclaiming him as their God.

The NT presents the idea of election in the following forms:

a. Jesus is hailed as God's elect one by the Father himself (Lk. 9:35, reading *eklelegmenos*, an echo of Is. 42:1), and probably by John the Baptist (Jn. 1:34, if *eklektos* is the right reading; see Barrett *ad loc.*). The sneer of Lk. 23:35 shows that 'the elect one' was used as a Messianic designation in Christ's day (as it is in the book of *Enoch*, 40:5; 45:3–5, *etc.*). In 1 Pet. 2:4, 6 Christ is called God's elect corner-stone; this echoes Is. 28:16, LXX. In reference to Christ, the designation 'points to the unique and distinctive office with which he is invested and to the peculiar delight which God the Father takes in him' (J. Murray in *Baker's Dictionary of Theology*, 1960, p. 179).

b. The adjective 'elect' denotes the Christian community in its character as the chosen people of God, in contrast with the rest of mankind. This usage simply echoes the OT. The church is 'an elect race' (1 Pet. 2:9, quoting Is. 43:20; *cf.* also 2 Jn. 1, 13), having the privileges of access to God and the responsibilities of praising and proclaiming him, and faithfully guarding his truth, which Israel had had before. As in the case of Israel, God had magnified his mercy by choosing poor and undistinguished persons for this momentous destiny (1 Cor. 1:27ff.; Jas. 2:5; *cf.* Dt. 7:7; 9:6); and, as before, God's gracious choice and call had created a people—his people—which had no existence as a people before (1 Pet. 2:10; Rom. 9:25f., citing Ho. 1:10; 2:23).

In the Synoptics Christ refers to the *eklektoi* (pl.) in various eschatological contexts. They are those whom God accepts, and will accept, because they have responded to the gospel invitation and come to the wedding-feast stripped of self-righteousness and clad in the wedding-garment provided by the host, *i.e.* trusting in God's mercy (Mt. 22:14). God will vindicate them (Lk. 18:7) and keep them through coming tribulation and peril (Mk. 13:20, 22), for they are the objects of his special care.

c. eklegomai is used of Christ's choice of his apostles (Lk. 6:13; *cf.* Acts 1:24; 9:15) and the church's choice of deacons (Acts 6:5) and delegates (Acts 15:22, 25). This is election to special service from among the ranks of the elect community, as in the OT. Christ's choosing of the Twelve for apostolic office involved the choosing of them out of the world to enjoy salvation (*cf.* Jn. 15:16, 19), except in the case of Judas (*cf.* Jn. 13:18).

III. Theological development in NT

The complete theological development of the idea of election is found in Paul's Epistles (see especially Rom. 8:28–11:36; Eph. 1:3–14; 1 Thes. 1:2–10; 2 Thes. 2:13–14; 2 Tim. 1:9–10). Paul presents divine election as a gracious, sovereign, eternal choice of individual sinners to be saved and glorified in and through Christ.

a. Election is a *gracious* choice. Election 'by grace' (Rom. 11:5; *cf.* 2 Tim. 1:9) is an act of undeserved favour freely shown towards members of a fallen race to which God owed nothing but wrath (Rom. 1:18ff.). And not only does God choose sinners to save (*cf.* Rom. 4:5; 5:6–8; Eph. 2:1–9); he chooses to save them in a way which exalts his grace by magnifying their sinfulness. He shuts up his elect, both Jew and Gentile, in a state of disobedience and unbelief, so that they display their true character as sinners, and stand out in history confessed as unbelievers, before he shows them his mercy (Rom. 11:30–32; the Gentiles, 9:30; 10:20; the Jews, 10:19, 21; 11:11, 25f. ['so' in v. 26 means 'through the coming in of the Gentiles']). Thus the outworking of election further exhibits the gratuitousness of grace.

b. Election is a *sovereign* choice, prompted by God's own good pleasure alone (Eph. 1:5, 9), and not by any works of man, accomplished or foreseen (Rom. 9:11), or any human efforts to win God's favour (Rom. 9:15–18). Such efforts would in any case be vain, for however high sinners aspire and however fast they run, they still in reality only sin (Rom. 8:7f.). God in sovereign freedom treats some sinners as they deserve, hardening (Rom. 9:18; 11:7–10, *cf.* 1:28; 1 Thes. 2:15f.) and destroying them (Rom. 9:21f.); but he selects others to be 'vessels of mercy', receiving 'the riches of his glory' (Rom. 9:23). This discrimination involves no injustice, for the Creator owes mercy to none, and has a right to do as he pleases with his rebellious creatures (Rom. 9:14–21). The wonder is not that he withholds mercy from some, but that he should be gracious to any. God's purpose of sovereign discrimination between sinner and sinner appeared as early as his limitation of the Abrahamic promise to Isaac's line and his setting of Jacob over Esau (Rom. 9:7–13). It was true from the first that not all who are descended from Israel belong to Israel' (Rom. 9:6), and that those Israelites who actually enjoyed the salvation promised to the chosen people were only 'a remnant, chosen by grace' (Rom. 11:5; 9:27–29). And it remains true, according to Paul, that it is God's sovereign election alone that explains why, when the gospel is preached, some do in fact respond to it. The unbelief of the rest requires no special explanation, for no sinner, left to himself, can believe (1 Cor. 2:14); but the phenomenon of faith needs explaining. Paul's explanation is that God by his Spirit causes the elect to believe, so that when men come to a true and active faith in Christ it proves their election to be a reality (1 Thes. 1:4ff.; Tit. 1:1; *cf.* Acts 13:48).

c. Election is an *eternal* choice. God chose us, says Paul, 'before the foundation of the world' (Eph. 1:4; 2 Thes. 2:13; 2 Tim. 1:9). This choice was an act of *predestination (Eph. 1:5, 11), a part of God's eternal purpose (Eph. 1:9), an exercise of loving foreknowledge whereby God determined to save

EL ELYON

See God, names of, Part 1.

those whom he foreknew (Rom. 8:29f.; *cf.* 1 Pet. 1:2). Whereas the OT, dealing with the national election to privilege, equates God's choosing with his calling, Paul, dealing with personal election to salvation, distinguishes the choice from the call, and speaks of God's calling (by which he means a summons to faith which effectively evokes a response) as a stage in the temporal execution of an eternal purpose of love (Rom. 8:30; 9:23f.; 2 Thes. 2:13f.; 2 Tim. 1:9). Paul stresses that election is eternal in order to assure his readers that it is immutable, and nothing that happens in time can shake God's resolve to save them.

d. Election is a choice of individual sinners to be saved *in and through Christ.* Election is 'in Christ' (see Eph. 1:4), the incarnate Son, whose historical appearing and mediation were themselves included in God's eternal plan (1 Pet. 1:20; Acts 2:23). Election in Christ means, first, that the goal of election is that God's chosen should bear Christ's image and share his glory (Rom. 8:29, *cf.* v. 17; 2 Thes. 2:14). They are chosen for holiness (which means Christlikeness in all their conduct) in this life (Eph. 1:4), and glorification (which means Christlikeness in all their being, *cf.* 2 Cor. 3:18; Phil. 3:21) in the life to come. Election in Christ means, second, that the elect are to be redeemed from the guilt and stain of sin by Christ, through his atoning death and the gift of his Spirit (Eph. 5:25–27; 2 Thes. 2:13; *cf.* 1 Pet. 1:2). As he himself said, the Father has given him a certain number of persons to save, and he has undertaken to do everything necessary to bring them all to eternal glory (Jn. 6:37–45; 10:14–16, 27–30; 17:2, 6, 9ff., 24). Election in Christ means, third, that the means whereby the blessings of election are brought to the elect is union with Christ—his union with them representatively, as the last Adam, and vitally, as the life-giver, indwelling them by his Spirit, and their union with him by faith.

IV. Significance of election for the believer

Paul finds in the believer's knowledge of his election a threefold religious significance.

a. It shows him that his salvation, first to last, is all of God, a fruit of sovereign discriminating mercy. The redemption which he finds in Christ alone and receives by faith alone has its source, not in any personal qualification, but in grace alone—the grace of election. Every spiritual blessing flows to him from God's electing decree (Eph. 1:3ff.). The knowledge of his election, therefore, should teach him to glory in God, and God only (1 Cor. 1:31), and to give him the praise that is his due (Rom. 11:36). The ultimate end of election is that God should be praised (Eph. 1:6, 12, 14), and the thought of election should drive ransomed sinners to incessant doxologies and thanksgivings, as it does Paul (Rom. 11:33f.; Eph. 1:3ff.; 1 Thes. 11:3ff.; 2 Thes. 2:13ff.). What God has revealed about election is to Paul a theme, not for argument, but for worship.

b. It assures the believer of his eternal security, and removes all grounds for fear and despondency. If he is in grace now he is in grace for ever. Nothing can affect his justified status (Rom. 8:33f.); nothing can cut him off from God's love in Christ (Rom. 8:35–39). He will never be safer than he is, for he is already as safe as he can be. This is precious knowledge; hence the desirability of making sure that one's election is a fact (*cf.* 2 Pet. 1:10).

c. It spurs the believer to ethical endeavour. So far from sanctioning licence (*cf.* Eph. 5:5f.) or presumption (*cf.* Rom. 11:19–22), the knowledge of one's election and the benefits that flow from it is the supreme incentive to humble, joyful, thankful love, the mainspring of sanctifying gratitude (Col. 3:12–17)

BIBLIOGRAPHY. Arndt; T. Nicol in *DAC*; J. Orr in *HDB* (1 vol.); C. Hodge, *Systematic Theology*, 2, pp. 331–353; H. H. Rowley, *The Biblical Doctrine of Election*, 1950; G. C. Berkouwer, *Divine Election*, 1960; *TDNT* 4, pp. 144–192; *NIDNTT* 1, pp. 533–543. J.I.P.

ELECT LADY. 2 John is addressed to 'the elect lady' (*eklektē kyria*). This may signify an individual, either unnamed, or named Electa, or Kyria, or Electa Kyria. There are fairly convincing objections to each of these suggestions. Further, the absence of personal allusions, the almost unvarying use of the plural, the contents of the letter and the concluding 'The children of your elect sister greet you' combine to make it likely that the Epistle is addressed to a church. No parallel is known, but this seems to be the least difficult explanation. L.M.

ELEMENTS. Gk. *stoicheia*, translated 'elements' in 2 Pet. 3:10, 12; 'elemental spirits' in Gal. 4:3, 9; Col. 2:8, 20 (AV 'rudiments'), is the neuter plural of the adjective *stoicheios*, which means 'standing in a row', 'an element in a series'. Hence *stoicheia* is used: **1.** for the letters of the alphabet when written out in series. From this use comes the meaning 'first principles', 'the ABC' of any subject, as in Heb. 5:12. **2.** It may also mean the component parts of physical bodies. In particular, the Stoics used the term for the four elements: earth, water, air, fire. **3.** There is evidence in Christian writers from the middle of the 2nd century AD for the use of *stoicheia* in an astronomical sense for the heavenly bodies (*cf.* Justin Martyr, *Apol.* 2. 5. 2). **4.** Evidence from the Orphic hymns and the *Hermetica*, coupled with modern Gk. usage, shows that *stoicheia* later came to mean 'angels', 'spirits' ('elemental spirits'). But it is not established that it was thus used as early as the 1st century AD; alleged early instances are either of doubtful meaning or of doubtful date. Jewish writers associate spirits or angels with various physical objects (*cf. 1 Enoch* 40:11–21; *Jubilees* 2:2) but do not call them *stoicheia* (of *2 Enoch* 16:7, sometimes cited for this, we do not have the Gk. text).

Critics have suggested all four senses for the Pauline passages. **2** agrees with the preoccupation with regulations about material things in Col. 2:21, and the reference to philosophy in 2:8. **3** agrees with the mention of calendar observances in Gal. 4:10. **4** agrees with the reference to false gods in Gal. 4:8 and to angels in Col. 2:18. Paul seems to apply his remarks equally to the Jewish and Gentile worlds, but this offers no criterion for his meaning. The Jews paid great attention to physical things and astronomy in the law and believed in the mediation of angels (*cf.* Gal. 3:19; 1:8); the Gentiles concerned themselves with the elements and with astronomy in their philosophy and worshipped false gods, whom Paul identifies with demons (1 Cor. 10:20). Perhaps the best interpretation on these lines combines senses **2** and **3** in the fashion of the *Sibylline Oracles* (2. 206; 8. 337). Sense **1**, 'the ABC of religion', accords well with the general context in Galatians, with its insistence that Paul's converts should not turn back to a system meant for the 'childhood' of religion, but this gives a strained sense to the genitive 'of the world', which must be taken to mean 'favoured by the world' or 'characteristic of the world'. The question has been in dispute since the Patristic period, and must be left open unless more evidence comes to light.

In 2 Pet. 3 the mention of *stoicheia* between 'heaven' and 'earth' in v. 10 strongly suggests sense **2**. Those who favour sense **4** in Paul have argued for it here also, pointing to the *Testament of Levi* 4:1; *1 Enoch* 68:2 for references to spirits being dissolved in fire.

BIBLIOGRAPHY. G. Delling, *TDNT* 7, pp. 670–687; E. Lohse, *Colossians and Philemon*, 1971, pp. 96–99. M.H.C.

ELHANAN. 1. In 2 Sa. 21:19, RV, RSV, we read that Elhanan the son of Jaare-oregim slew Goliath the Gittite. When this is compared with 1 Ch. 20:5, where we read, 'Elhanan the son of Jair slew Lahmi the brother of Goliath the Gittite', it is apparent from the setting and the names used that the two verses refer to the same event.

One solution is to conclude that in 2 Samuel we have an interesting example of how easily corruption may slip into the text. Jaare is the same as Jair with the two final Heb. letters reversed. The word *'ōrᵉgîm* is the Heb. for 'weavers' and has slipped in by careless copying, duplicating the place where EVV translate 'weavers'. The Heb. words for 'Bethlehemite' and 'Lahmi the brother' are so similar as to make it almost certain that one is the corruption of the other. We should therefore regard 1 Ch. 20:5 as the original and true reading. An alternative solution is to conclude that in 1 Ch. 20:5 we have a harmonistic midrash, designed to get rid of the apparent discrepancy between 2 Sa. 21:19 and 1 Sa. 17:12ff., where Goliath the Gittite is killed by David. But Elhanan may have been David's original name.

2. In 2 Sa. 23:24 and 1 Ch. 11:26 Elhanan, the son of Dodo, is named as one of David's mighty men. This is a different person.

BIBLIOGRAPHY. J. Weingreen, *From Bible to Mishna*, 1976, pp. 16f., 139. G.T.M.
F.F.B.

ELI. The story of Eli is told in 1 Sa. 1–4. He was 'the priest' in 'the house of the Lord' at Shiloh (1 Sa. 1:3, 7, 9). This 'house' must have been the inter-tribal sanctuary, incorporating the tabernacle (Jos. 18:1; Jdg. 18:31), with some additional structure; and here was the ark (1 Sa. 4:3). Eli's ancestry is not given, but by comparing 1 Ki. 2:27 with 1 Ch. 24:3 we deduce that Phinehas, his son, and therefore Eli himself, was a descendant of Ithamar, the youngest son of Aaron. We have no information as to how the priesthood passed from the line of Eleazar (1 Ch. 6:4–15); but the Samaritan tradition that it was seized from Uzzi when a child must be rejected as due to racial bias. (See E. Robertson, *The Old Testament Problem*, 1950, p. 176.)

From 1 Sa. 14:3 and 22:9ff. it appears that Eli's descendants, through Phinehas and his son Ahitub, continued to exercise the priesthood for a time at Nob.

Because of the scandalous conduct of Eli's sons, ineffectively rebuked by their father, a man of God came to pronounce a doom upon them and their descendants (1 Sa. 2:27–36). This was confirmed by a revelation to the child Samuel (1 Sa. 3:11–14). It was partially fulfilled in the death of Hophni and Phinehas (1 Sa. 4:11) and the ruthless murder of the priests in Nob (1 Sa. 22:9–20). But Abiathar escaped and shared with Zadok the priesthood under David (2 Sa. 19:11). But from this he was degraded by Solomon, in further fulfilment of the ancient prophecy (1 Ki. 2:26f.).

Eli 'had judged Israel forty years' (1 Sa. 4:18), a testimony to the service he rendered to his people. But it was marred by the sinful sacrilege of his sons, and by his failure to eject them from their sacred office. G.T.M.

ELIAB. 'God is father', a common OT name. **1.** A son of Helon, prince and representative of Zebulun (Nu. 1:9; 2:7, *etc.*). **2.** A Reubenite, the son of Pallu and father of Dathan, Abiram and Nemuel (Nu. 26:8–9). **3.** The eldest son of Jesse and brother of David (1 Sa. 16:5ff., *etc.*), father of Abihail (2 Ch. 11:18), and called 'Elihu' in 1 Ch. 27:18. **4.** A Gadite warrior and companion of David (1 Ch. 12:9). **5.** A levitical musician of the time of David (1 Ch. 15:18ff.). **6.** An ancestor of Samuel (1 Ch. 6:27), also called Eliel (1 Ch. 6:34) and Elihu (1 Sa. 1:1). G.W.G.

ELIAKIM (Heb. *'el-yāqîm*, 'God establishes'?; Gk. *Eliakeim*). The name of at least five different individuals. Two were ancestors of our Lord (Mt. 1:13; Lk. 3:30); one was a priest, a contemporary of Nehemiah (Ne. 12:41). Eliakim was also the one whom Pharaoh-neco made king after Josiah and whose name he changed to Jehoiakim (2 Ki. 23:34; 2 Ch. 36:4).

The most prominent individual to bear this name was the son of Hilkiah, who was appointed steward in place of the deposed Shebna (Is. 22: 20ff.). Since the time of Solomon (1 Ki. 4:6) this office had existed both in the N and S kingdoms (1 Ki. 16:9; 18:3; 2 Ki. 10:5), and was apparently even exercised

Seal inscribed 'belonging to Eliakim, assistant of Jehoiachin' (l'lyqm n'r ywkn). *Impressions of this seal have been found on jar-handles at Tell beit Mirsim, Beth-shemesh and Ramat Rahel. Perhaps this was the seal of Eliakim (6th cent.* BC*), but it may be of earlier date.*

by Jotham after Uzziah's leprosy (2 Ki. 15:5). When Sennacherib besieged Jerusalem Eliakim went to talk with the Rabshakeh (2 Ki. 18:18, 26–27; Is. 36:3, 11, 22), and Hezekiah then sent him to bear the news to Isaiah (2 Ki. 19:2; Is. 37:2). Eliakim appears also as 'servant of Jehoiachin' (*n'r ywkn*) on three seal-impressions of the 6th century BC. E.J.Y.

ELIAM
See Helam, Part 2.

ELIASHIB. There are several people with this name in the OT: a descendant of David (1 Ch. 3:24); a priest in the time of David (1 Ch. 24:12); a singer (Ezr. 10:24); a son of Zattu (Ezr. 10:27); a son of Bani (Ezr. 10:36). The name is also found on seals and ostraca at *Arad.

The most important was the high priest in the time of Nehemiah. He is first mentioned in Ezr. 10:6 as the father of Johanan, but is not called high priest at this time. Josephus says that Eliashib's father, Joiakim, was high priest when Ezra came to Jerusalem in 458 BC (*Ant.* 11. 154). When Nehemiah came in 445 BC Eliashib was high priest, and took part in the building of the city walls (Ne. 3:1, 20–21). Later he compromised, and formed a marriage

ELIEL
See Elihu, Part 1.

alliance with Tobiah (Ne. 13:4) and gave him a room in the Temple precincts (Ne. 13:5). One of his grandsons married Sanballat's daughter (Ne. 13:28). His genealogy is given in Ne. 12:10–11. J.S.W.

ELIEZER (Heb. *'ᵉlî'ezer*, 'God is [my?] help'). A name scattered right through biblical history.

1. Eliezer the Damascene, Abraham's chief servant, and his adopted heir before the birth of Ishmael and Isaac (Gn. 15:2–3). The custom whereby a childless couple could adopt someone from outside as an heir is very well attested during *c.* 2000–1500 BC; such an adoptive heir had to take second place to any subsequent first-born son. See also, D. J. Wiseman, *IBA*, 1959, pp. 25–26. For these customs in Ur, *c.* 1800 BC, see Wiseman, *JTVI* 88, 1956, p. 124. For similar customs in the *Nuzi tablets, see Speiser, *AASOR* 10, 1930, texts H 60, H 67, pp. 30, 32, *etc.*

2. Second son of Moses, named Eliezer in allusion to Moses' escaping the sword of Pharaoh (Ex. 18:4; 1 Ch. 23:15). Eliezer had only one son, Rehabiah, but the latter had many descendants, of whom one (Shelomith) became treasurer of David's dedicated things (1 Ch. 23:17–18; 26:25–26).

3. Grandson of Benjamin, and progenitor of a later Benjaminite clan (1 Ch. 7:8).

4. One of the seven priests who sounded the trumpets before the ark when David brought it into Jerusalem (1 Ch. 15:24). **5.** Eliezer son of Zichri, tribal ruler of Reuben under David (1 Ch. 27:16). **6.** The prophet who prophesied to King Jehoshaphat of Judah that his fleet of vessels at Ezion-geber would be wrecked in punishment for his alliance with the wicked King Ahaziah of Israel (2 Ch. 20:35–37).

7. One of eleven men commissioned by Ezra to seek out Levites for the return to Jerusalem in 458 BC (Ezr. 8:16ff.). **8–10.** Three men, including a priest and a Levite, who had taken alien wives (Ezr. 10:18, 23, 31). **11.** An Eliezer appears in Christ's earthly lineage as given by Luke (3:29). K.A.K.

ELIHU (Heb. *'ᵉlihû*, 'My God is he'). **1.** An Ephraimite, Samuel's paternal great-grandfather (1 Sa. 1:1), whose name seems to occur as Eliab in 1 Ch. 6:27 and as Eliel in 1 Ch. 6:34. **2.** One of the captains of Manasseh, who deserted to David just before the battle of Ziklag (1 Ch. 12:20). **3.** A Korahite, member of the gatekeepers, grandson of Obed-edom, and son of Shemaiah (1 Ch. 26:7). **4.** A chief officer of Judah, brother (or near relative) of David (1 Ch. 27:18), perhaps identical with Eliab (1 Sa. 16:6). **5.** Job's young friend, son of Barachel, a Buzite of the family of Ram (Jb. 32:2, 4–6; 34:1; 35:1; 36:1). His appearance at the end of the story is somewhat of a puzzle, since he was not included in the list of friends whose debate with *Job forms the bulk of the book. Elihu's speeches, with their strong stress on divine sovereignty, serve both to prepare for the revelation of God (Jb. 38) and to promote suspense by delaying it. D.A.H.

ELIJAH. The 9th-century prophet of Israel. His name appears in the Heb. OT as *'ēlîyyāhû* and *'ēlîyyâ*, in the Gk. OT as *Ēleiou*, and in the NT as *Ēleias*. The name means 'Yah is El' or 'Yahweh is God'.

Apart from the reference to Elijah in 1 Ki. 17:1 as 'the Tishbite, of Tishbe in Gilead', no information about his background is available. Even this reference is obscure. The *MT* suggests that while Elijah resided in Gilead (*mittōšāḇê gilᵉ'āḏ*) his birthplace was elsewhere (perhaps Tishbe of Naphtali). The LXX reads *ek thesbōn tēs galaad*, thus indicating a Tishbe of *Gilead. Josephus seems to concur (*Ant.* 8. 319). This has traditionally been identified with a site about 13 km N of the Jabbok.

Elijah's prophetic ministry is recorded in 1 Ki. 17–19; 21; 2 Ki. 1–2. These narratives are written in the purest classical Heb. 'of a type which can hardly be later than the 8th century' (W. F. Albright, *From the Stone Age to Christianity*, p. 307). They could not have enjoyed an existence for long in oral form. They describe his ministry to the N kingdom during the Omrid Dynasty (*OMRI). Elijah was contemporary with Ahab and Ahaziah, and from the position of the translation narrative (2 Ki. 2) and the answer to Jehoshaphat's question in 2 Ki. 3:11, we conclude that his translation probably occurred about the time of the accession to the throne of Jehoram of Israel. The difficulty presented to this conclusion by 2 Ch. 21:12–15 can possibly be resolved either by interpreting the much-controverted 2 Ki. 8:16 to teach a co-regency of Jehoshaphat and Jehoram, kings of Judah (*CHRONOLOGY OF THE OT) or by regarding the letter as a prophetic oracle written prior to his translation.

The Elijah cycle presents six episodes in the life of the prophet: his prediction of drought and his subsequent flight, the Mt Carmel contest, the flight to Horeb, the Naboth incident, the oracle about Ahaziah, and his translation. Except for the last, they are all basically concerned with the clash between the worship of Yahweh and *Baal. The Baal in these stories is Baal-melqart, the official protective deity of Tyre. Ahab fostered this Phoenician variant of the nature-religion of Canaan after his marriage with the Tyrian princess *Jezebel (1 Ki. 16:30–33), but it was Jezebel who was chiefly responsible for the systematic extermination of Yahweh worship and the propagation of the Baal cult in Israel (1 Ki. 18:4, 13, 19; 19:10, 14).

Elijah appears in the first episode (1 Ki. 17) without introduction, and after the delivery of the oracle to Ahab announcing a drought, he retires beyond Ahab's jurisdiction first to the wadi Cherith, E of Jordan, and then to Zarephath (modern Sarafend below Sidon still preserves the name and overlooks what remains of this ancient Mediterranean sea-port). Elijah was miraculously sustained in both places, and while at Zarephath he performed a miracle of healing (1 Ki. 17:17–24).

The second episode, 3 years later (1 Ki. 18:1; *cf.* Lk. 4:25; Jas. 5:17, which follow Jewish tradition), recounts the break in the drought following the overthrow of organized Baal worship on Mt Carmel. The drought imposed and withdrawn at Yahweh's word was a challenge to Baal's sovereignty over nature. 1 Ki. 17 had depicted Elijah in the very stronghold of Baal-melqart sustained by Yahweh while the country languishes (1 Ki. 17:12; *cf.* Jos., *Ant.* 8. 320–4). 1 Ki. 18 brings the challenge into the open, and Yahweh'ss supremacy is spectacularly demonstrated. That Baal worship in Israel was certainly not exterminated at Mt Carmel is seen from later references (*e.g.* 2 Ki. 10:18–21). For the presence of an altar of Yahweh on Mt Carmel, see *Altar. Keil suggests that this was probably built by pious Yahweh-worshippers after the division in the kingdom. Some commentators omit 1 Ki. 18:30b altogether, while others omit vv. 31–32a.

The third episode (1 Ki. 19) describing Elijah's flight to Horeb to avoid Jezebel's wrath is particularly significant. Horeb was the sacred mountain where the covenant God of Moses had made himself known, and Elijah's return to this place represents the return of a loyal but disheartened prophet to the very source of the faith for which he had contended. The closing commission in 1 Ki. 19:15–18 seems to have been only partially discharged by Elijah. The accession of Hazael and Jehu to the thrones of Syria and Israel respectively is recorded in the *Elisha cycle.

The Naboth incident (1 Ki. 21) illustrates and vindicates the principle embedded in the religious consciousness of Israel, that land owned by an Israelite family or clan was understood as a gift from Yahweh, and that failure to recognize this and respect the rights of the individual and family within the covenant community would issue in judgment. Elijah emerges as a champion of the strong ethical demands of the Mosaic faith so significantly lacking in the Baal cult.

The fifth episode in 2 Ki. 1 continues to illustrate the Yahweh–Baal clash. Ahaziah's dependence upon the life-god of Syria, Baalzebub (Baal-zebul of Ras Shamra texts, *cf.* Mt. 10:25 RVmg.; Baalzebub, meaning 'Lord of Flies', was probably a way of ridiculing the Syrian deity), evokes the judgment of God (2 Ki. 1:6, 16). A judgment of fire also falls on those who endeavoured to resist the word of Yahweh by harming his prophet (2 Ki. 1:9–15). The translation of Elijah in a whirlwind (*s^{e}ārâ*) brings to a dramatic close his spectacular prophetic career. The exclamation of Elisha (2 Ki. 2:12) is repeated in 2 Ki. 13:14 with reference to Elisha himself.

Two observations may be made about the importance of Elijah. First, he stands in the OT tradition of ecstatic prophecy coming through from the days of Samuel and he is also a forerunner of the 8th-century rhapsodists or writing *prophets. His link with the earlier tradition is seen in that he is first of all a man of action and his Spirit-determined movements defy human anticipation (1 Ki. 18:12). In the background of the Elijah pericope the prophetic schools of Samuel's day continue to exist (1 Ki. 18:4, 13; 2 Ki. 2:3, 5, 7). His link with the later prophets lies in his constant endeavour to recall his people to the religion of Moses, both in worshipping Yahweh alone as well as in proclaiming Mosaic standards of righteousness in the community. In both these respects he anticipates the more fully developed oracles of Amos and Hosea. This advocacy of the Mosaic faith by Elijah is supported by several details which suggest a parallel between Elijah and Moses. Elijah's return to Horeb is obvious enough, but there is also the fact that Elijah is accompanied and succeeded by Elisha as Moses was by Joshua. This parallel is quite striking. Not only has the death of Moses an air of mystery attaching to it (Dt. 34:6) but his successor secured the allegiance of Israel by participating in the same spirit as Moses and demonstrated his fitness for office by a miraculous river crossing (Dt. 34:9; Jos. 4:14). The translation narrative (2 Ki. 2) reproduces this pattern fairly precisely. The fact also that God answers Elijah by fire on two occasions (1 Ki. 18:38; 2 Ki. 1:10, 12) seems to look back to the exhibition of God's presence and judgment in fire in the Exodus narratives (*e.g.* Ex. 13:21; 19:18; 24:17; Nu. 11:1; 16:35). Little wonder that in Jewish Haggadic thought Elijah was viewed as the counterpart to Moses.

Second, his ministry is spoken of as being revived 'before the coming of the great and dreadful day of the Lord' (Mal. 4:5–6). This theme is a popular one in the Jewish Mishnah (*TALMUD AND MIDRASH), and was a common topic of discussion during the ministry of Jesus (Mk. 8:28). Jesus indicated that the Malachi prophecy had reference to the ministry of *John the Baptist (Mt. 11:14; 17:12f.). Elijah reappears in person on the mount of transfiguration (Mk. 9:4) and he is referred to elsewhere in the NT in Lk. 4:25–26; Rom. 11:2–4; Jas. 5:17–18.

Three other men of the same name appear in the OT, the first a Benjaminite priest (1 Ch. 8:27; Heb. *'ēlîyyâ*), and the second and third a priest and a layman respectively, who married foreign wives (Ezr. 10:21, 26; Heb. *'ēlîyyâ*).

BIBLIOGRAPHY. E. Fohrer, *Elia*², 1968; R. S. Wallace, *Elijah and Elisha*, 1957; H. H. Rowley, *Men of God*, 1963, ch. 2; J. Lindblom, *Prophecy in Ancient Israel*, 1963, ch. 2; commentaries on the books of Kings by J. A. Montgomery and H. S. Gehman, *ICC*, 1951, and J. Gray, *OTL*², 1970; F. James, *Personalities of the Old Testament*, 1939, ch. 9.

B.L.S.

ELIM (Heb. 'terebinths' or 'oaks'). Second stopping-place of the Israelites after their crossing of the Re(e)d Sea from Egypt. Beyond the wilderness of *Shur, E of the modern Suez canal, they first encamped at Marah in the wilderness of Etham not far away (because named after Etham in E Delta), and thence reached Elim with its twelve springs and seventy palmtrees. After this the Israelites went on 'and pitched by the Red Sea', before eventually reaching the wilderness of *Sin, Ex. 15:27; 16:1; Nu. 33:9–10.

By putting the stop at Elim shortly after the escape from Egypt and passage of its desert edge (Shur), and before a stop by the Red Sea prior to reaching the wilderness of Sin, the biblical references suggest that Elim is situated on the W side of the Sinai peninsula, facing on to the Gulf of Suez. Any closer location is still not certain, but a plausible suggestion of long standing is Wadi Gharandel (or, Ghurundel), a well-known watering-place with tamarisks and palms, *c.* 60 km SSE of Suez along the W side of *Sinai. (*WILDERNESS OF WANDERING.)

BIBLIOGRAPHY. E. Robinson, *Biblical Researches in Palestine*, 1, 1841, pp. 99–100, 105–106, and map at end; A. P. Stanley, *Sinai and Palestine*, 1887, pp. 37–38; Wright and Filson, *Westminster Historical Atlas to the Bible*, 1956, pp. 38–39 and plate V.

K.A.K.

ELISHA. The 9th-century prophet of Israel. His name appears in the Heb. OT as *'ᵉlîšā'*, in the Gk. OT as *Eleisaie*, in Josephus as *Elissaios* and in the NT as *Elisaios*. The name means 'God is salvation'. His father's name was Shaphat.

All that can be known about Elisha's background is found in 1 Ki. 19:16, 19–21. We are not told his age or his birthplace, but we may assume that he was a native of Abel-meholah (Tell Abū Sifri?) in the Jordan valley and was still only young when Elijah sought him out. That he was the son of a family of some means also seems clear.

ELIPHAZ
See Teman, Part 3.

His ministry, if we date it from his call, extended through the reigns of Ahab, Ahaziah, Jehoram, Jehu, Jehoahaz and Jehoash, a period of more than 50 years. The narratives of Elisha's ministry are recorded in 1 Ki. 19; 2 Ki. 2–9; 13, and comprise a series of some eighteen episodes. It is not possible to be certain of their chronological order throughout because of obvious breaks in the sequence of events (*e.g.*, *cf.* 2 Ki. 6:23 with 6:24; 5:27 with 8:4–5; 13:13 with 13:14ff.). These episodes do not betray the same tension between Yahweh and Baal worship as those of the *Elijah cycle. It is a ministry conducted at the head of the prophetic schools which consists of a display of signs and wonders both at a personal as well as a national level. Elisha emerges as a kind of seer in the tradition of Samuel to whom peasants and kings alike turn for help.

Examining these episodes in their biblical order, we make the following observations. (1) Elisha's call (1 Ki. 19:19–21) was not so much an anointing (*cf.* 1 Ki. 19:16) as an ordination by investiture with Elijah's prophetic mantle. Until Elijah's translation Elisha remained his servant (1 Ki. 19:21; 2 Ki. 3:11). (2) 2 Ki. 2:1–18 recounts Elisha's assumption of the role of his master. The double portion of the spirit upon Elisha recalls the language and thought of Dt. 21:17 while the whole episode is reminiscent of the replacement of Moses by Joshua as leader of Israel. (3) The healing of the injurious waters in 2 Ki. 2:19–22 also finds a parallel in the events of the Exodus (Ex. 15:22–25). (4) The incident in 2 Ki. 2:23–25 must be understood as a judgment upon the deliberate mockery of the new head of the school of Yahweh's prophets. Some scholars incline to the view that Elisha's baldness was a prophetic tonsure.

(5) The story of Elisha's part in the campaign of the three kings against *Moab (2 Ki. 3:1–27) records his request for music when receiving an oracle from Yahweh (v. 15). There is a strong suggestion of ecstatic prophecy here as in 1 Sa. 10:5–13 (*cf.* 1 Ch. 25:1). (6) 2 Ki. 4:1–7 is parallel to Elijah's miracle in 1 Ki. 17:8–16 and introduces (7) the longer story of Elisha's dealings with the Shunammite woman (2 Ki. 4:8–37), which has many points of similarity with 1 Ki. 17:8–24. (8) 2 Ki. 4:38–41 and (9) 4:42–44 occur at sessions with the fraternity of prophets at Gilgal, probably during the famine referred to in 2 Ki. 8:1. The second of these miracles anticipates the miracle of Jesus which is recorded in Mk. 6:35–44.

(10) The Naaman story (2 Ki. 5:1–27) cannot be dated with accuracy. It must have occurred during one of the temporary lulls in hostilities between Israel and Syria. The editorial comment in v. 1 ascribing the Syrian's victories to Yahweh should be compared with Am. 9:7. This cosmic view of Yahweh is recognized by Naaman (v. 15), and his request for Israelite soil (v. 17) need not necessarily be taken to imply that he believed Yahweh's influence to be confined to Israelite territory. Elisha makes no comment on this, but sends Naaman on his way (v. 19). Since most Israelites saw nothing wrong in including other gods in their debased worship of Yahweh, a Syrian who did not at once accept monotheism could hardly be blamed. (*RIMMON.)

(11) 2 Ki. 6:1–7 recounts a miraculous feat of Elisha and incidentally casts light on the size and habitations of prophetic fraternities (*cf.* 2 Ki. 4:38–44). (12) 2 Ki. 6:8–23 and (13) 6:24–7:20 depict Elisha as a counsellor of kings and a deliverer of the nation from national disaster (*cf.* 2 Ki. 3:1–27). The second of these episodes is said to involve *Ben-hadad of Aram and 'the king of Israel'. This is unfortunately obscure. (14) 2 Ki. 8:1–6 clearly belongs before 5:1–27. It is a continuation of the Shunammite story (2 Ki. 4:8–37).

(15) 2 Ki. 8:7–15, (16) 9:1–13, and (17) 13:14–19 all depict Elisha involved in affairs of state. The first of these describes the ascent of *Hazael to the throne of Damascus (*cf.* 1 Ki. 19:15). Elisha's reply (v. 10) may be understood to mean that the king would recover from his sickness but would die for other reasons, or it may have been the prophet's spontaneous reply that had to be corrected by a vision from Yahweh (*cf.* 2 Sa. 7:1–17; 2 Ki. 4:26–36). The anointing of Jehu discharged the last of the tasks committed to Elijah (1 Ki. 19:15–16) and precipitated the predicted overthrow of the Omrid Dynasty (1 Ki. 21:21–24). This prophetic-inspired revolt is in contrast to the corresponding priestly revolt in the S that removed Athaliah from the throne (2 Ki. 11). If he lived into the reign of Jehoash of Israel, he must have been about 80 years old at the time of his death. He appears as a favourite of the king, who realizes his political value (v. 14). Sympathetic or mimetic actions accompanying prophetic oracles are not uncommon in the OT.

Although Elisha is a prophet of the 9th century and belongs to the prophetic tradition which produced the 8th-century rhapsodists or writing prophets, he has more affinities with the ecstatic prophets of the 11th century. He is very like Samuel, with gifts of knowledge and foresight and a capacity to work miracles. He figures at the head of the prophetic schools and is in frequent demand because of his singular gifts. Although he is spoken of as having a home in Samaria (2 Ki. 6:32), he is, like Samuel, constantly moving about the land and enjoys an easy access into royal courts and peasant dwellings. While his relation to *Elijah is certainly suggestive of the relationship between Joshua and Moses, the fact that Elijah's ministry is reproduced in John the Baptist and Elisha's directly anticipates the miracle-aspect of the ministry of Jesus is even more significant. Elisha is referred to only once in the NT (Lk. 4:27).

BIBLIOGRAPHY. R. S. Wallace, *Elijah and Elisha*, 1957; J. A. Montgomery and H. S. Gehman, *The Books of Kings*, *ICC*, 1951; J. Gray, *1 and 2 Kings*, *OTL*, ²1970; F. James, *Personalities of the Old Testament*, 1939, ch. 10. B.L.S.

ELISHAH. The eldest son of *Javan (Gn. 10:4 = 1 Ch. 1:7), whose name was later applied to his descendants, who inhabited a maritime region (*'iyyê*, 'isles' or 'coastlands') which traded purple to Tyre (Ezk. 27:7). It is very probable that the biblical name *'ᵉlîšâ* (LXX *Elisa*) is to be equated with Alašia of the extra-biblical sources. This name occurs in the Egyptian and cuneiform (Boghaz-Koi, Alalaḫ, Ugarit) inscriptions, and it was the source of eight of the Amarna letters, in which it usually occurs in the form *a-la-ši-ia*. These texts indicate that Alašia was an exporter of copper, and it is possible, though not universally accepted, that it is to be identified with the site of Enkomi on the E coast of Cyprus, where excavations under C. F. A. Schaeffer have revealed an important trading-centre of the Late Bronze Age. The name Alašia would also apply to the area under the political domination of the city, and may at times have included outposts on the Phoenician coast.

Bibliography. R. Dussaud in C. F. A. Schaeffer, *Enkomi-Alasia*, 1952, pp. 1–10; *AS* 6, 1956, pp. 63–65; *KB*³, p. 55. T.C.M.

ELIZABETH (from Heb. *'ĕlîšeḇa'*, 'God is [my] oath'). The wife of Zechariah the priest, and mother of John the Baptist (Lk. 1:5ff.). Herself of priestly descent, Elizabeth is described in the AV as a 'cousin' (more accurately, 'kinswoman', RSV) of the Virgin Mary (Lk. 1:36), to whom she addressed the remarkable words of Lk. 1:42–45. J.D.D.

ELLASAR. The city or kingdom ruled by Arioch, an ally of *Chedorlaomer king of Elam, who attacked Sodom and captured Lot, Abraham's nephew (Gn. 14:1, 9). Identifications suggested depend on those proposed for the kings involved. These include: (*i*) *āl Aššur*—Ashur/Assyria (so Dhorme, Böhl, Dossin); (*ii*) Ilânsura—in the Mari texts, between Harran and Carchemish (Yeivin); (*iii*) Telassar—(2 Ki. 19:12; Is. 37:12) in N Mesopotamia as a parallel to * Shinar = Singara, but the name is to be read Til-Bašeri; (*iv*) Larsa—in S Babylonia. This depends on the outmoded equation *Amraphel = Hammurapi (of Babylon).

Bibliography. M. C. Astour in *Biblical Motifs*, ed. A. Altmann, 1966, pp. 77–78. D.J.W.

ELOI, ELOI, LAMA SABACHTHANI. Occurs in Mk. 15:34 and in a slightly different form in Mt. 27:46. It is one of the Lord's sayings on the cross, and is a quotation from Ps. 22:1. The form 'Eli' would be more likely to give rise to the confusion with Elijah, and the form in Matthew is thus more likely to be original. Our Lord uses the Aramaic, almost exactly the form of the Targum.

The difficulty of accounting for this saying is the strongest argument for its authenticity. Inadequate explanations are that it reflects the intensity of the Lord's human feeling, that it reveals the disappointment of his hope that in his extremity the Father would usher in the new age, or that he was merely reciting the Psalm as an act of devotion. It can be understood only in the light of the NT doctrine of the atonement, according to which Christ identified himself with sinful man and endured separation from God (*cf.* Phil. 2:8; 2 Cor. 5:21). It is a mystery we cannot fathom.

Bibliography. D. H. C. Read, 'The Cry of Dereliction', *ExpT* 68, 1956–7, pp. 260ff. A.G.

ELON (Heb. *'êlôn, 'êlôn*). **1.** A Hittite of Canaan (Gn. 26:34; 36:2). **2.** Head of a family in Zebulun (Gn. 46:14; Nu. 26:26) ('Helon', Nu. 1:9; 2:7 *etc.*). **3.** A Zebulunite judge of Israel (Jdg. 12:11–12). **4.** A S Danite town (Jos. 19:43); possibly Kh. W. Alin, 2 km E of Beth-shemesh (*GTT*, p. 349). Elon-beth-hanan (1 Ki. 4:9) may be this Elon (Mazar, *IEJ* 10, 1960, p. 67), or Aijalon (*LOB*, p. 278). The name,

ELOAH See God, names of, Part 1.

ELOHIM See God, names of, Part 1.

Places associated with Elijah and Elisha.

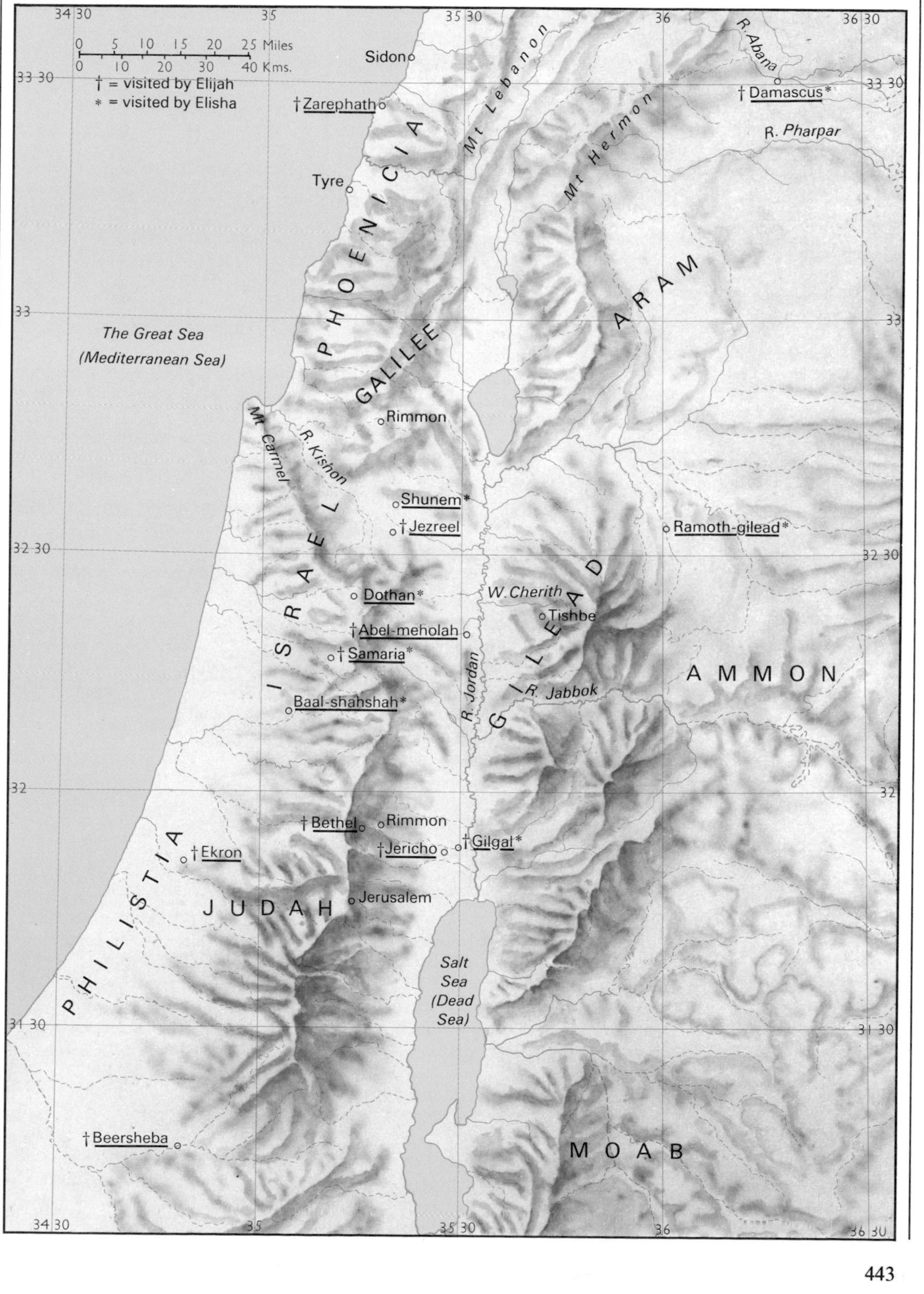

like * Elah, means 'terebinth' (RSV 'oak', Jos. 19:33). J.P.U.L.

Assyrian wall-painting from a provincial royal residence. The panels with geometrical designs are typical of the patterns used in embroidery at this period. Til Barsip. 8th cent. BC. (AP)

ELTEKEH. A city in Palestine allotted to the tribe of Dan (Jos. 19:44) and later made a levitical city (Elteke, Jos. 21:23). Sennacherib mentions it (Altakū) together with Timnā among his conquests in his annals for 701/700 BC (Chicago Cylinder 3. 6; Taylor Cylinder 2. 82–83). Some identify it with Khirbet el-Muqanna' *c.* 40 km W of Jerusalem (so Albright) but this may be * Ekron; Tell-esh-Shalaf, 16 km NNE of Ashdod, is an alternative (Mazar).

BIBLIOGRAPHY. D. D. Luckenbill, *The Annals of Sennacherib*, 1924, p. 32; W. F. Albright, *BASOR* 15, 1924, p. 8; B. Mazar, *IEJ* 10, 1960, pp. 72–77. T.C.M.

ELOTH
See Elath, Part 1.

EL-PARAN
See Paran, Part 3.

ELUL
See Calendar, Part 1.

ELYMAS
See Bar-Jesus, Part 1.

ELYON
See God, names of, Part 1.

ELZAPHAN (Heb. *'elṣāphān*, 'God has hidden'). **1.** Also called Elizaphan. A son of Uzziel, a Levite (Ex. 6:22) who, with his brother * Mishael, disposed of the bodies of Nadab and Abihu, who had been killed for desecrating the altar (Lv. 10:1–5). A leader of the Kohathites in the wilderness (Nu. 3:30), he also was the father of a house of priests (1 Ch. 15:8; 2 Ch. 29:13).

2. A son of Parosh who, representing the tribe of Zebulun, was to assist in the division of Canaan (Nu. 34:25). D.W.B.

EMBALMING
See Burial and mourning, Part 1.

EMBROIDERY. The ornamentation of cloth was of two main types: **1.** chequer work (*tašbēṣ*); **2.** coloured embroidery (*riqmâ*). RSV (Ex. 28:39) describes the former as weaving (*cf.* AV 'embroider'), the latter as needlework, though the methods used are not specified in the Hebrew (*cf.* NEB). Chequer work decorated the high priest's tunic (Ex. 28:4) and, worked in gold thread, a princess's wedding dress (Ps. 45:13). Such thread was cut from thin plates of beaten gold (Ex. 39:3). Some idea of the pattern produced is suggested by the use of the same term for the gold filigree work in which gems were set (Ex. 28:11).

Coloured embroidery decorated the high priest's girdle (Ex. 28:39), the screens for the tabernacle door (Ex. 26:36) and the gate of the court (Ex. 27:16). A distinction may be intended between this type of ornamentation and the equally

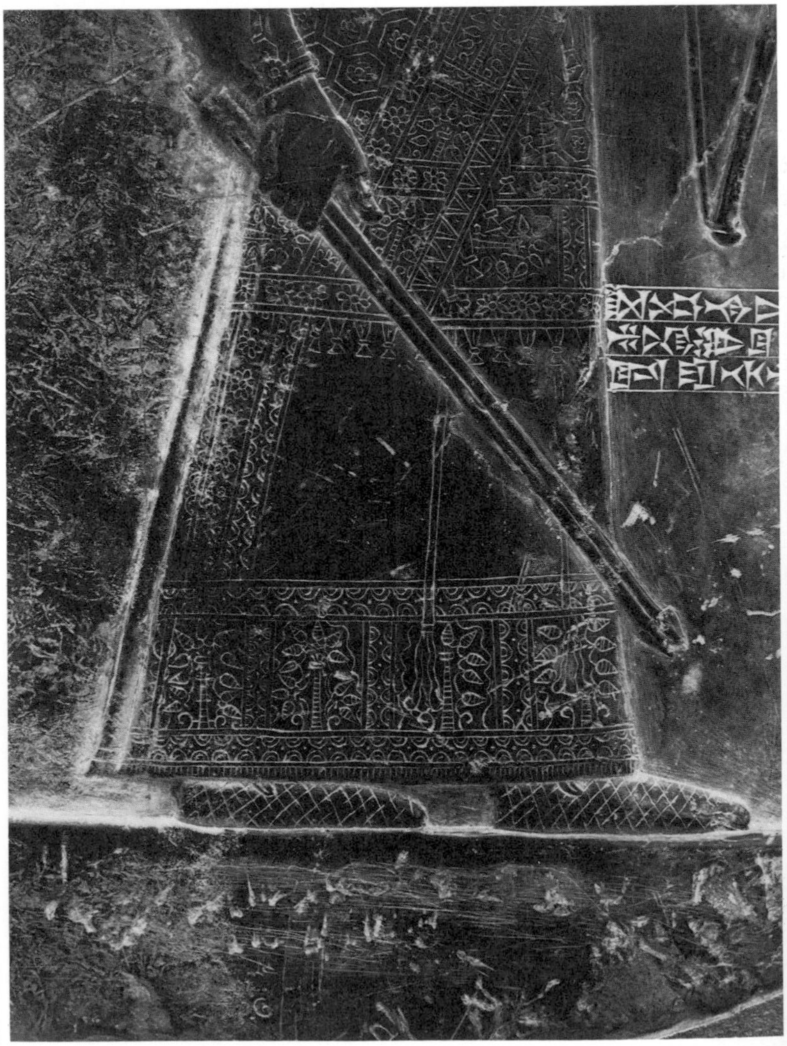

The richly embroidered hem of the material used for the royal robe of Marduk-nādin-ahhe, king of Babylonia, 1116–1101 BC. (BM)

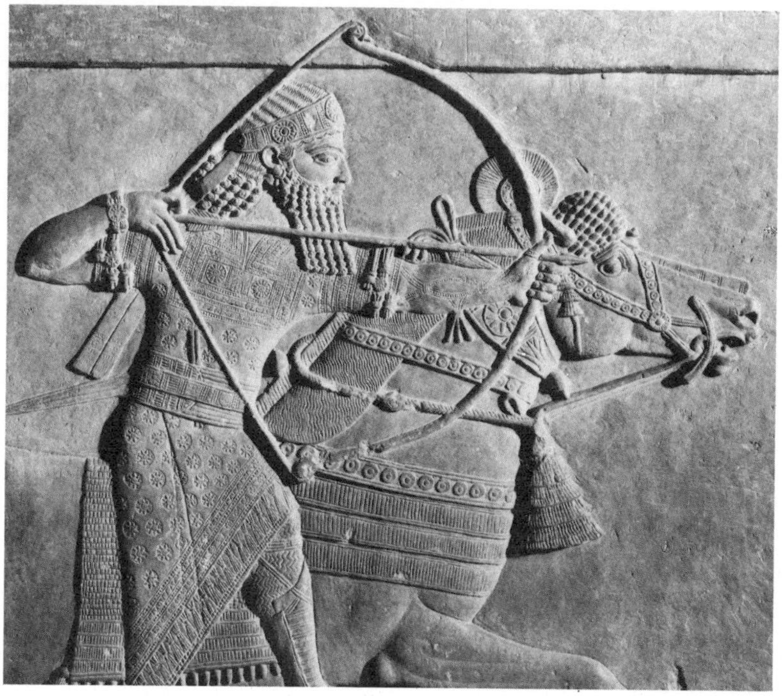

Embroidered tunic worn by Ashurbanipal, king of Assyria (668–c. 627 BC*). Relief of lion-hunt, Nineveh.* (BM)

EMERALD
See Jewels, Part 2.

EMERY
See Jewels, Part 2.

EMMANUEL
See Immanuel, Part 2.

EMPLOYER
See Wages, Part 3.

EMPTY TOMB
See Resurrection, Part 3.

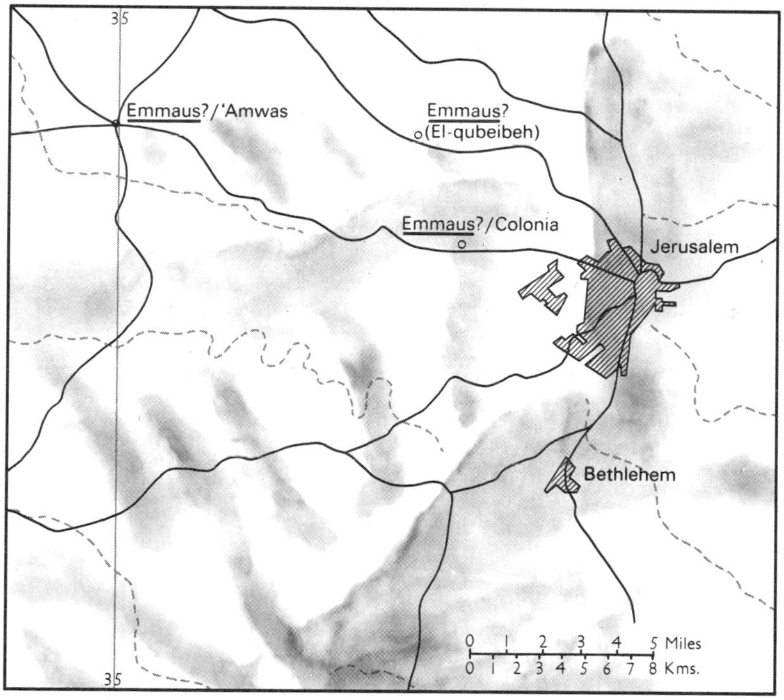

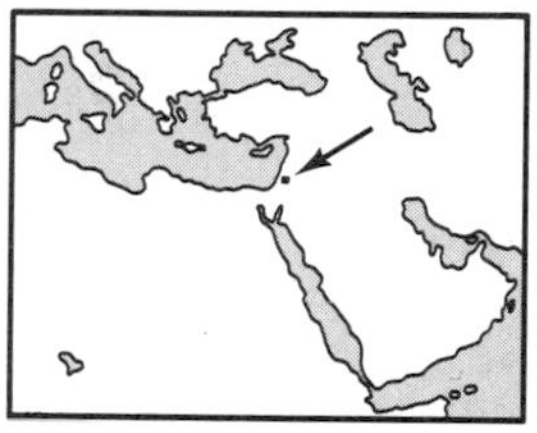

Three possible sites for the village of Emmaus, mentioned in Lk. 24:13.

intricate and richly coloured work of the ephod and breastpiece (Ex. 28:6, 15), the tabernacle curtains and veil (Ex. 26:1, 31), and the garments of those who ministered in the sanctuary (Ex. 39:1), since only the former is designated 'the work of the embroiderer' (*ma'ᵃśēh rōqēm*; Ex. 26:36).

Its value is evident from its importance for trade (Ezk. 27:16, 24) and as the spoils of war (Jdg. 5:30). It decorated not only clothing for men (Ezk. 16:18; 26:16) and women (Ezk. 16:10, 13; Ps. 45:14), but could be used for other ornamentation, *e.g.* a ship's sail (Ezk. 27:7). By an extended use the word is applied to the plumage of an eagle (Ezk. 17:3) and to the variegated stones prepared by David for the Temple (1 Ch. 29:2). Its intricacy made it a suitable figure to describe the human embryo (Ps. 139:15).

Appliqué work may have been used for the coloured pomegranates which, with golden bells, decorated the skirt of the high priest's robe (Ex. 28:33). (*ARTS AND CRAFTS.)

G.I.E.

EMIM. Early inhabitants of Moab, who were smitten in the plain of *Kiriathaim by Chedorlaomer in the time of Abraham (Gn. 14:5). They were described by Moses as a great and numerous people, to be compared in stature to the *Anakim (Dt. 2:10). They were evidently considered to belong to the peoples known as *Rephaim, but were called *'êmîm*, 'terrifying beings', by the Moabites who followed them in the area (Dt. 2:11). They are unknown outside the Bible. (*GIANT). T.C.M.

EMMAUS. A village, said to be 60 furlongs (11 km) from Jerusalem, to which *Cleopas and another disciple were journeying when Jesus appeared to them after his resurrection (Lk. 24:13). The site cannot be certainly identified. One possibility is the town still known as 'Amwas, 32 km WNW of Jerusalem, where Judas Maccabeus defeated Gorgias in 166 BC (1 Macc. 3:40, 57; 4:3). But this is at the wrong distance from Jerusalem, as given by Luke (unless the variant reading of 160 furlongs found in Codex Sinaiticus and other MSS preserves the original text); it also demands a long, though by no means impossible, walk by the travellers. Of places within about 11 km from Jerusalem two have been suggested. There was a village at El-qubeibeh in the 1st century, and Crusaders found a fort here named Castellum Emmaus; unfortunately the name cannot be traced back to the 1st century. Josephus (*BJ* 7. 217) refers to a military colony of Vespasian at Ammaous, some 6 km W of Jerusalem. This has been identified with Kaloniye (Lat. *colonia*) or with Kh. Beit Mizza (ancient Mozah); here again the distance is wrong, unless we suppose that Luke's 60 furlongs was meant as the total length of the outward and return journeys.

BIBLIOGRAPHY. J. Finegan, *The Archaeology of the New Testament*, 1969, pp. 177–180; *ZPEB*, 2, pp. 299f. I.H.M.

ENCAMPMENT BY THE SEA. The place where the Israelites camped by the sea and made the crossing (Ex. 13:18; 14:2) has been the subject of much controversy during the last 100 years. The question is inseparable from that of the location of such places as Baal-zephon, Etham, Migdol, Pihahiroth, Sea of Reeds and Succoth.

Two main traditions have grown up around the route of the Exodus out of Egypt: the 'Southern' theory favouring a route from the Wadi Tumilat region SE to the Suez area, and the 'Northern' theory advocating a crossing near Lake Menzaleh to S of Port Said.

The S theory was foreshadowed by Josephus (*Ant.* 2. 315), who considered the Israelites to have started from Latopolis (= Egyp. Babylon, Old Cairo) to a Baal-zephon on the Red Sea; Pierre Diacre and Antonin de Plaisance had a tradition of the Hebrews passing Clysma near the present-day Suez. Among moderns, Lepsius, Mallon, Bourdon (with a crossing at Clysma), Cazelles and Montet favoured this view.

The N route was championed by Brugsch, identifying the Sea of Reeds, *yam-sûp̄*, with Egyp. *p'-ṯwf* and placing it in Lake Serbonis on the Mediterranean shore with Baal-zephon at Ras Qasrun there. But this hardly agrees with the biblical account, in which God forbade Israel to go by 'the way of the land of the Philistines' (Ex. 13:17–18). Gardiner was the next to espouse the N route (*JEA* 5, 1918, pp. 261–269; *Recueil Champollion*, 1922, pp. 203–215), likewise O. Eissfeldt and N. Aimé-Giron, the former identifying Casios and Baal-zephon on the Mediterranean shore and the latter equating Baal-zephon with Tahpanhes (Phoenician papyrus). For Albright, see below.

H. Cazelles summed up the whole problem. He considers that later tradition from the LXX onward (note the LXX's *thalassa erythra*, 'Red Sea') speaks for a S route, but that study of the names in the Heb. text suggests that this latter indicates a N route by the Mediterranean; according to Cazelles, these N locations were due to an editor of J and E documents who (like Manetho and Josephus) associated the Hebrew Exodus with the expulsion of the Hyksos from Egypt. However, this is speculative.

Finally, there is an entirely different suggestion by W. F. Albright (*BASOR* 109, 1948, pp. 15–16). He placed Ra'amses at Tanis in the N, brought the Israelites SE past the places in the Wadi Tumilat (Pithom at Retabeh, Succoth at Tell el-Maskhutah) and then sharply back up N again (*cf.* 'that they turn back', Ex. 14:2) by the Bitter Lakes to the region of a Baal-zephon located at later Tahpanhes (Defneh); Migdol is then Tell el-Her just S of Pelusium, with the Sea of Reeds (*yam-sûp̄*) in this general area. Having thus left Egypt proper, the Israelites would then flee to the SE into the Sinai peninsula, so that Albright's route in its end-result becomes a 'southern' one (*i.e.* he does not take Israel by the forbidden way of the Philistines). Noth's reserves (*Festschrift Otto Eissfeldt*, 1947, pp. 181–190) are largely based on literary-critical considerations of doubtful relevance. As will be evident, the route of the Exodus is still a very live issue.

BIBLIOGRAPHY. N. Aimé-Giron, *Annales du Service des Antiquités de l'Égypte* 40, 1940–1, pp. 433–460; Bourdon, *RB* 41, 1932, pp. 370–382, 538–549; H. Cazelles, *RB* 62, 1955, pp. 321–364; O. Eissfeldt, *Baal-Zaphon, Zeus Casios und der Durchzug der Israeliten durch das Meer*, 1932; Lepsius, *Zeitschrift für Aegyptische Sprache* 21, 1883, pp. 41–53; Mallon, 'Les Hébreux en Égypte', *Orientalia* 3, 1921; Montet, *Géographie de l'Égypte Ancienne*, 1, 1957, pp. 218–219, and *L'Égypte et la Bible*, 1959, pp. 59–63; E. Uphill, *Pithom and Raamses*; *JNES* 27, 1968, pp. 291–316, and 28, 1969, pp. 15–39.

See also H. H. Rowley, *From Joseph to Joshua*, 1950, for much older bibliography, and C. de Wit, *The Date and Route of the Exodus*, 1960, for more specifically Egyptian aspects. M. Bietak, *Tell El-Dab'a II*, Vienna, 1975, is invaluable for E Delta topography and conditions. C.D.W.

ENDURANCE See Patience, Part 3.

ENDOR. Modern 'En-dûr, 6 km S of Mt Tabor. The town was assigned to Manasseh, but was never wrested from Canaanite possession (Jos. 17:11–12). The medium of Endor, of whom Saul inquired before his last battle (1 Sa. 28:7), was probably from this Canaanite stock, for an attempt had been made to do away with such practices among the Hebrews (1 Sa. 28:3). R.J.W.

EN-EGLAIM (Heb. *'ên-'eḡlayim*, 'spring of the two calves'). A place mentioned once only (Ezk. 47:10) as lying on the shore of the Dead Sea. Though the site is unknown, the reference to * En-gedi suggests a location somewhere in the NW sector. This site is distinct from Eglaim (*'eḡlayim*, Is. 15:8), a town in Moab.

BIBLIOGRAPHY. *GTT*, pp. 459–460; W. R. Farmer, *BA* 19, 1956, pp. 19–21. T.C.M.

EN-GANNIM (Heb. *'ên-gannîm*, 'spring of gardens'). **1.** A town in Judah's inheritance in the Shephelah (Jos. 15:34); perhaps modern Beit Jamal, 3 km S of Beth-shemesh.

2. A levitical city in Issachar's territory (Jos. 19:21; 21:29; called Anem, 1 Ch. 6:73). Variously identified with Jenin, Olam and Khirbet Beit Jann, SW of Tiberias. G.G.G.

EN-GEDI (Heb. *'ên-geḏî*, 'spring of the kid'). Important oasis and fresh water spring W of the Dead Sea, allotted to Judah at the conquest (Jos. 15:62). David hid there (1 Sa. 23:29; 24:1ff.), its rugged terrain and fertility making it an ideal refuge. Famous for aromatic plants and perfume (Ct. 1:14). Excavations 1949 and 1961–5 revealed several fortresses and a late synagogue. Hazazon-tamar = En-gedi (Gn. 14:7; 2 Ch. 20:2). See *EAEHL*, pp. 370ff. G.G.G.

ENGLISH VERSIONS OF THE BIBLE.

I. Anglo-Saxon versions

The history of versions of the Bible in English has its beginnings in challenging obscurity and uncertainty in the Anglo-Saxon period of the English language. The Venerable Bede has supplied a fascinating account (*Ecclesiastical History* 4, ch. 24) of a heavenly endowment granted to the herdsman Cædmon in the latter part of the 7th century AD, which enabled him to sing in English verse the substance and the themes of Scripture. Cædmon was followed, according to Bede's testimony, by others who endeavoured to write religious verse. Although Bede does not quote any of Cædmon's poetry verbatim, he gives us the sense of the initial verses attributed to him, verses of stirring freshness and exaltation. Surviving Anglo-Saxon metrical treatments or paraphrases of biblical materials, whether or not they are to be connected with Cædmon, witness to an important means of disseminating knowledge of the Scriptures in that period.

Part of a hoard of more than 100 bronzes found in the 'Cave of the treasure', Nahal Mishmar near En-gedi. Late 4th millennium BC. (RS)

To Bede himself has been attributed the translation of the Gospel according to John. His follower Cuthbert, in a letter on the death of his 'father and master', relates that Bede completed his translation of the Fourth Gospel on the day of his death at the virtual moment of his departure. If Bede did translate the entire Bible or the greater part of it into English, as certain evidence might indicate, his work has regrettably not survived.

Aldhelm (640–709) has been credited with a translation of the Psalms and indeed of much, if not all, of the Bible into English; but no extant MS can with certainty be said to represent his work. The Vespasian Psalter, the oldest surviving Latin text of the Psalms with a gloss or interlinear translation of the individual words into Anglo-Saxon, cannot with any assurance be held to contain Aldhelm's work. This MS of the Psalter was succeeded by a considerable number of others with Anglo-Saxon glosses.

King Alfred the Great (849–901) introduced his *Code of Saxon Laws* with an abbreviated and rearranged English rendering of the Ten Commandments and portions in English of Ex. 21–23 and Acts 15. William of Malmesbury says that Alfred was at work on an English translation of the Psalms at the time of his death. There has been disagreement as to whether Alfred's work is represented by the prose rendering in English of the first 50 psalms in the Paris Psalter. His translation of Gregory's *De cura pastorali* involved, of course, translation of the Scripture references in the text.

Ælfric, an abbot at about the beginning of the 11th century, made translations or paraphrases of extensive parts of the OT text.

Two MSS of the Gospels in Latin with an Anglo-Saxon gloss have survived. One of them is the famous Lindisfarne Gospels *c.* 700 with a gloss made *c.* 950. The other MS is the Rushworth Gospels, whose gloss is very much dependent on that of the Lindisfarne MS in Mark, Luke and John.

A noteworthy development in the Anglo-Saxon period was the competent translation of the four Gospels into a continuous English text, a text which is represented by six extant MSS.

II. Middle English versions

The development of a literature in Middle English begins in the closing part of the 12th century. About 1300 a metrical version of the Psalter appeared; it was followed by prose translations, one of which was the work of Richard Rolle of Hampole. Portions of the NT were also translated. The distinguishing achievement of the Middle English period, however, was the translation work associated with Wyclif (*c.* 1320–84) and the movement he represented. An earlier Wyclifite version was produced in the latter part of the 14th century *c.* 1380–3, a substantial portion of which was made by Nicholas of Hereford (from Genesis to Baruch 3:20) and the rest, including the NT, has been thought by some to have been made by Wyclif himself. Whatever may have been Wyclif's part in the actual work of translation, his zeal for the Scriptures and for making them accessible to the people in the English language must be credited with giving the impetus to this highly influential version. It was made from a Latin base and it clung to the original with some damage to English idiom and clarity, but it was a commendable new effort addressed to the needs of the present and facing towards the future. It was soon followed by a translation in smoother style which was quite probably made by John Purvey, a follower of Wyclif, with the assistance of others. The principles and procedures which were followed by Purvey were in many respects exemplary, and his revision was very influential. It was indeed finally superseded by the work of Tyndale and Coverdale in the 16th century, but its influence has been perpetuated through its successors.

III. William Tyndale

William Tyndale was the first to translate the NT directly from Greek into English. He received his MA degree at Oxford in 1515, the year before the appearance of Erasmus' Greek NT, the first printed NT in Greek actually to be published. Tyndale may have studied Greek at Cambridge. His zeal for making the Scriptures available in the vernacular is indicated in the story of his encounter with a 'learned man' who expressed the judgment that we might better be without the laws of God than without those of the Pope. To him Tyndale expressed defiance of the Pope and his laws and said that if God would spare his life he would cause a ploughboy to know more of the Scripture than his learned adversary did. Finding England uncongenial to his desire to lay the NT plainly before the eyes of the people in their native language, he went to Hamburg. He was never to return to the land which was to enter into his labours and to be enriched by his dedication.

In completing his translation of the NT, Tyndale made use of the 1519 and 1522 editions of Erasmus' Greek NT. He consulted also Erasmus' Latin translation, Luther's German text and the Latin Vulgate. The printing of his NT was begun in 1525 in Cologne,

CHRONOLOGICAL TABLE OF THE PRINCIPAL ENGLISH VERSIONS OF THE BIBLE

Date AD	Version (*italics*=Catholic version)	Translator
	ANGLO-SAXON VERSIONS	
Late 7th cent.	English verse (oral)	Caedmon
	John's Gospel, +?	Bede
	Psalms; entire Bible?	Aldhelm (640-709)
	Anglo-Saxon Psalter glosses	
Late 9th cent.	Ten Commandments	Alfred the Great (849-901)
	Ex. 21-23	
	Acts 15	
	Scripture refs. in Gregory's 'De Cura Pastorali'	
c.950	Anglo-Saxon gloss of the Lindisfarne Gospels	
	Anglo-Saxon gloss of the Rushworth Gospels	
11th cent.	Parts of the OT	Aelfric
	Four Gospels into continuous English text	
	MIDDLE ENGLISH VERSIONS	
c.1300	Metrical Psalter	
	Prose Psalter	Richard Rolle of Hampole
c.1380-1383	Wyclif Bible	Nicholas of Hereford and Wyclif (?)
	Revision of Wyclif's Bible	John Purvey
	SIXTEENTH-CENTURY VERSIONS	
1525/6	NT	William Tyndale
1530	Pentateuch	Tyndale
1531	Jonah	Tyndale
	Isaiah	George Joye
1534	OT selections	Tyndale
	NT revision	
	Psalms	Joye
	Lamentations	
	Jeremiah	
	Song of Moses at the Red Sea	
	Revision (unauthorized) of Tyndale's NT	
1535	NT revision	Tyndale
	First complete Bible in English	Miles Coverdale
1537	The Matthew Bible	John Rogers ? ('Thomas Matthew')
1538	Parallel English-Latin NT (Vulgate)	Coverdale
1539	Revision of the Matthew Bible	Richard Taverner
	The Great Bible	Coverdale, for Thomas Cromwell
1540	2nd edition of the Great Bible	Preface by Archbp. Cranmer
1545	Revised Primer ('Primer of Henry VIII')	
1557	Geneva NT	William Whittingham
1560	Geneva Bible	Various (including Whittingham)
1568	The Bishops' Bible	Matthew Parker and others
1572	Revised folio edition of the Bishops' Bible	
1582	*Rheims NT*	*Gregory Martin, William Allen and others*
	SEVENTEENTH-CENTURY VERSIONS	
1609-1610	*Douay OT*	*Gregory Martin and others*
1611	Authorized (King James) Version	Fifty-four translators
1613	Revision of AV	
1616-1623	Pentateuch	Henry Ainsworth
	Song of Solomon	
	Psalms	
	EIGHTEENTH-CENTURY VERSIONS	
1718-1719	*NT*	*Cornelius Nary*
1729	Greek and English NT	William Mace
1730	*NT*	*Robert Witham*
1738	*Fifth edition of Rheims NT*	
1745	The Primitive NT	William Whiston
1749-1772	*Two revisions of Douay OT, five revisions of Rheims NT*	*Richard Challoner*
1755	Revision of AV	John Wesley
1764	NT	Richard Wynne
	Bible	Anthony Purver
1768	Liberal translation of the NT	E. Harwood
1770	NT	John Worsley
1783-1810	*Revisions of Rheims and Douay texts*	*Bernard Mac Mahon*

	NINETEENTH-CENTURY VERSIONS	
1822	Paul's Epistles	Thomas Belsham (Unitarian)
1832	Paul's Epistles	Charles Eyre (Unitarian)
1833	NT	Rodolphus Dickinson
1840	NT	Samuel Sharpe (Unitarian)
1849-1860	*Annotated revision of Douay-Rheims text*	*Bishop Francis Patrick Kenrick*
1855	Gospels	Andrew Norton
1858	NT	Leicester Ambrose Sawyer
1862	OT & NT	Robert Young
1863	Gospels	G. W. Braineld
1869	NT	Henry Alford
	OT & NT	Robert Ainslie
1871	NT	J. N. Darby
1872	NT	J. B. Rotherham
1875	NT	Samuel Davidson
1881	Revised version of the AV NT	British & American companies
1882	Romans	Ferrar Fenton
1883	Paul's Epistles	Fenton
1885	RV complete Bible	British & American companies
1890	Bible	J. N. Darby
1895	Current English NT	Fenton
	TWENTIETH-CENTURY VERSIONS	
1898-1901	The Twentieth Century NT	Twenty lay scholars
1901	American Standard Edition (of RV)	American scholars
1903	Bible in Modern English	Fenton
	NT in Modern Speech	R. F. Weymouth
1913	NT	James Moffatt
1923	American translation of the NT	E. J. Goodspeed
	Riverside NT	W. G. Ballantine
1924	OT	Moffatt
	Centenary translation of the NT	Helen B. Montgomery
1927	American translation of the OT	A. R. Gordon, T. J. Meek, Leroy Waterman, J. M. Powis Smith
1935	*Westminster Version of the Sacred Scriptures, NT*	*Various Catholic scholars*
	Revision of Challoner's edition of the Rheims NT	*J. A. Carey*
1937	NT	C. B. Williams
	NT	*F. A. Spencer*
1941	The NT in Basic English	S. H. Hooke
	Revision of Challoner-Rheims NT	*Confraternity of Christian Doctrine*
1945	Berkeley Version of the NT	Gerrit Verkuyl
	NT (trans. from Vulgate)	*Monsignor R. A. Knox*
1946	Revision of American RV NT (RSV)	International Council of Religious Education
1947-1957	NT	J. B. Phillips
1948	The Letchworth Version (NT) in Modern English	T. F. & R. E. Ford
1949	Bible in Basic English	S. H. Hooke
	OT	*R. A. Knox*
1952	Entire RSV Bible	
	Plain English NT	C. K. Williams
1954	*NT*	*J. A. Kleist & J. L. Lilly*
1955	Authentic NT	H. J. Schonfield
	Revision of Knox's OT	
1956-1959	Expanded Translation of the Greek NT	K. S. Wuest
1958	The Amplified NT	Lockman Foundation
1959	The Berkeley Bible	Gerrit Verkuyl
1961	The New English Bible NT	Representatives of major British churches & Bible Societies
1962-1971	The Living Bible	K. N. Taylor
1963	The NT in the Language of Today	W. F. Beck
	New American Standard Bible (revision of the American RV)	Evangelical scholars
1965	*Catholic edition of RSV*	
1966	Today's English Version (Good News for Modern Man), NT	American Bible Society
	Jerusalem Bible	*Catholic scholars*
1968-9	New translation, NT	William Barclay
1969	The New Berkeley (Modern Language) Bible	Verkuyl
1970	The New English Bible OT	Representatives of major British churches, etc.
	The New American Bible	*Bishops' Committee of the Confraternity of Christian Doctrine*
1972	New International Version (NT)	Evangelical scholars
1973	The Translator's NT	British & Foreign Bible Society
1976	Complete Good News Bible	American Bible Society
1979	New International Version Holy Bible	Evangelical scholars

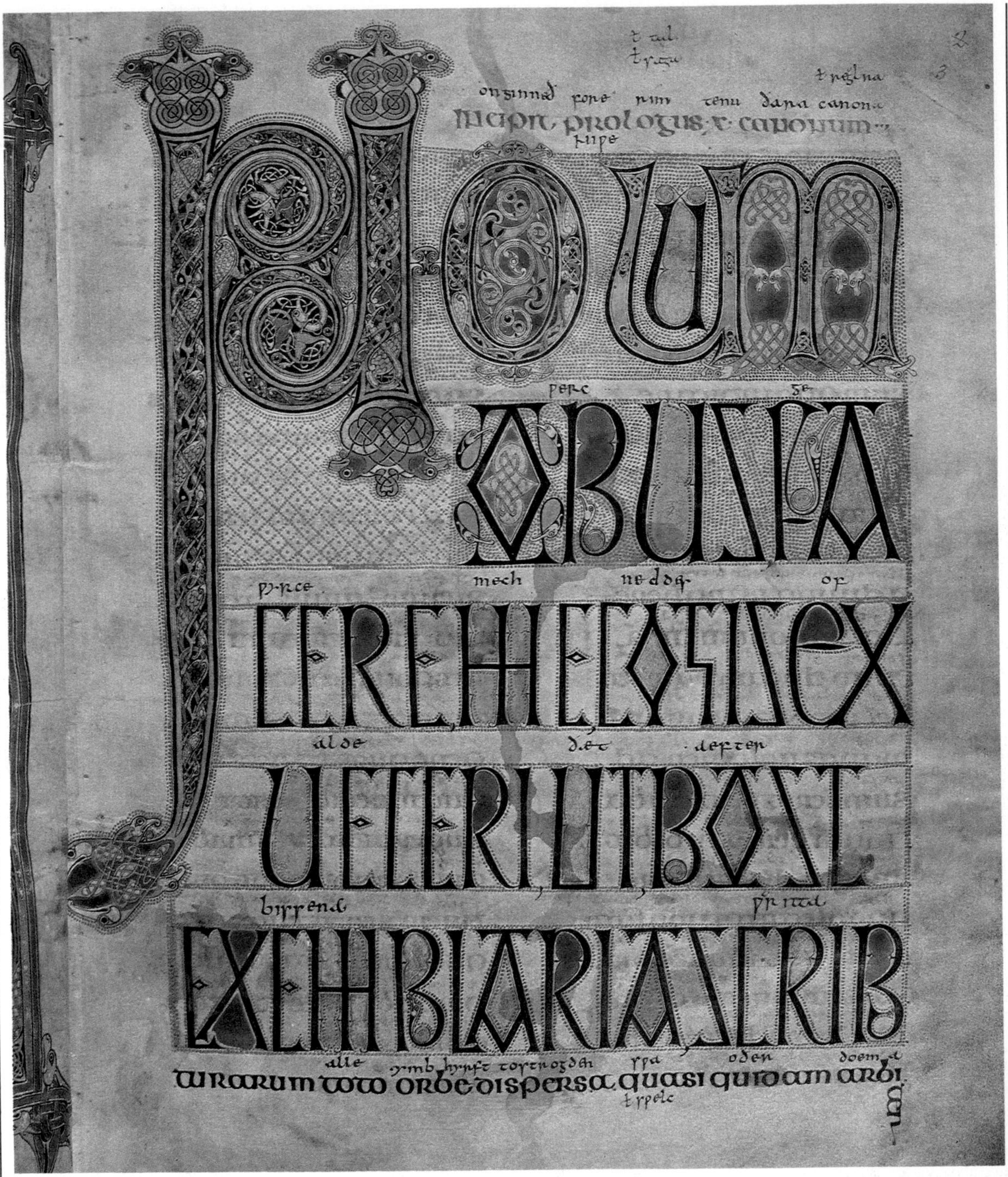

Ornamental letter page at the beginning of the prologue of the Lindisfarne Gospels. c. AD *700.* (BL)

but opposition forced him to flee to Worms with the sheets that had been printed. There before long (in 1525 or 1526) two editions were completed (one quarto, the other octavo) of 3,000 copies each. Virulent official opposition in England was so very successful in destroying copies of early issues of Tyndale's NT that there are only minimal remains today. Revised editions appeared in 1534 and 1535. Tyndale's NT, despite the opposition to it, could not be destroyed. The first printed English NT, the first made from the Greek, opened a new period in the history of the English Bible and made an ineradicable contribution to the English Bibles yet to come. The influence of the wording and structure of Tyndale's NT on the AV is immense, and the latter provides a continuing tribute to the simplicity, freshness, vitality and felicity of his work. Tyndale also published a translation of the Pentateuch in 1530, of Jonah in 1531 and of selections from the OT (published with his edition of the NT in 1534). An edition of the Pentateuch with a revised translation of Genesis was printed in 1534. There is good authority for believing that Tyndale translated an extensive additional section of the OT text, but before he could complete his translation of the Bible he suffered a martyr's death. In his OT work he used the Hebrew text. Among other works available to him were Luther's German translation, the Latin Vulgate and a Latin rendering by Pagninus. Like his version of the NT, Tyndale's faithful and vivid translation of books of the OT has been exceedingly influential. His dying prayer was that the Lord

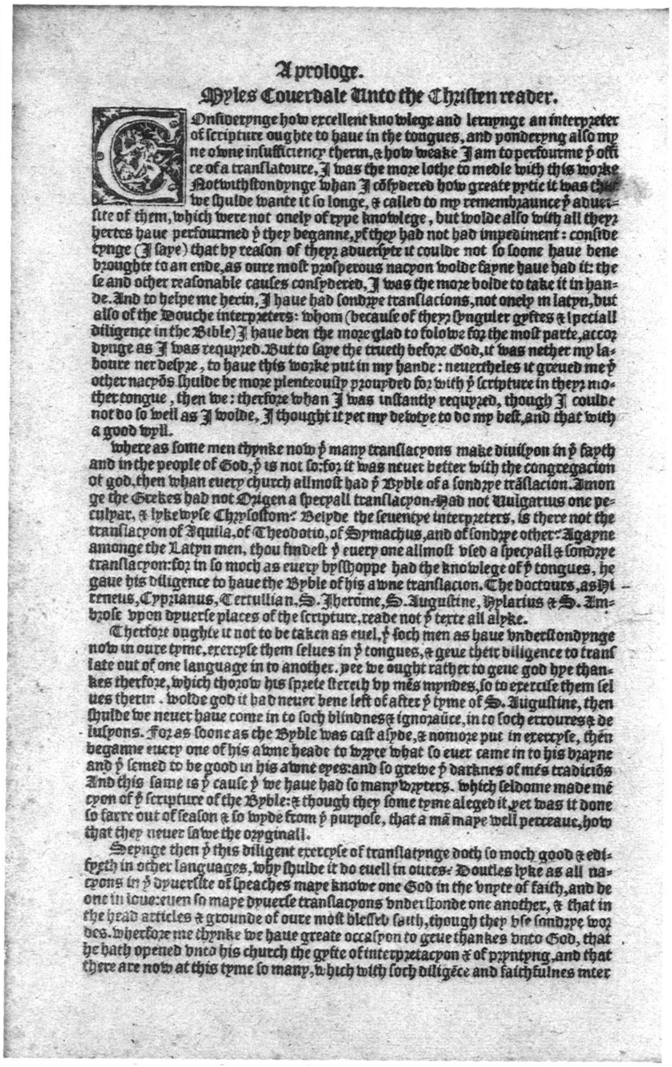

A prologe.

Myles Couerdale Unto the Christen reader.

Consyderynge how excellent knowlege and lernynge an interpreter of scripture oughte to haue in the tongues, and ponderyng also myne owne insufficiency therin, & how weake I am to perfourme ỷ office of a translatoure, I was the more lothe to medle with this worke. Notwithstondynge whan I cōsydered how greate pytie it was that we shulde wante it so longe, & called to my remembraunce ỷ aduersite of them, which were not onely of rype knowlege, but wolde also with all theyr hertes haue perfourmed ỷ they beganne, yf they had not had impediment: considerynge (I saye) that by reason of theyr aduersyte it coulde not so soone haue bene broughte to an ende, as oure most prosperous nacyon wolde fayne haue had it: these and other reasonable causes consydered, I was the more bolde to take it in hande. And to helpe me herin, I haue had sondrye translacions, not onely in latyn, but also of the Douche interpreters: whom (because of theyr synguler gyftes & speciall diligence in the Bible) I haue ben the more glad to folowe for the most parte, accordynge as I was requyred. But to saye the trueth before God, it was nether my laboure ner desyre, to haue this worke put in my hande: neuertheles it greued me ỷ other nacyōs shulde be more plenteously prouyded for with ỷ scripture in theyr mother tongue, then we: therfore whan I was instantly requyred, though I coulde not do so well as I wolde, I thought it yet my dewtye to do my best, and that with a good wyll.

Where as some men thynke now ỷ many translacyons make diuisyon in ỷ fayth and in the people of God, ỷ is not so: for it was neuer better with the congregacion of god, then whan euery church allmost had ỷ Byble of a sondrye trāslacion. Amonge the Grekes had not Origen a specyall translacyon? Had not Vulgarius one peculyar, & lykewyse Chrysostom? Beyde the seuentye interpreters, is there not the translacyon of Aquila, of Theodotio, of Symachus, and of sondrye other? Agayne amonge the Latyn men, thou findest ỷ euery one allmost vsed a specyall & sondrye translacyon: for in so moch as euery bysshoppe had the knowlege of ỷ tongues, he gaue his diligence to haue the Byble of his awne translacion. The doctours, as Hireneus, Cyprianus, Tertullian, S. Iherome, S. Augustine, Hylarius & S. Ambrose vpon dyuerse places of the scripture, reade not ỷ texte all alyke.

Therfore oughte it not to be taken as euel, ỷ soch men as haue vnderstondynge now in oure tyme, exercyse them selues in ỷ tongues, & geue their diligence to translate out of one language in to another. Yee we ought rather to geue god hye thankes therfore, which thorow his sprete stereth vp mēs myndes, so to exercise them selues therin. Wolde god it had neuer bene left of after ỷ tyme of S. Augustine, then shulde we neuer haue come in to soch blindnes & ignorāūce, in to soch erroures & delusyons. For as soone as the Byble was cast asyde, & nomore put in exercyse, then beganne euery one of his awne heade to wryte what so euer came in to his brayne and ỷ semed to be good in his awne eyes: and so grewe ỷ darknes of mēs tradiciōs And this same is ỷ cause ỷ we haue had so many wryters, which seldome made mēcyon of ỷ scripture of the Byble: & though they some tyme aleged it, yet was it done so farre out of season & so wyde from ỷ purpose, that a mā maye well perceaue, how that they neuer sawe the orygināll.

Seynge then ỷ this diligent exercyse of translatynge doth so moch good & edifyeth in other languages, why shulde it do euell in oures? Doutles lyke as all nacyons in ỷ dyuersite of speaches maye knowe one God in the vnyte of faith, and be one in loue: euen so maye dyuerse translacyons vnderstonde one another, & that in the head articles & grounde of oure most blessed faith, though they vse sondrye wordes. Wherfore me thynke we haue greate occasyon to geue thankes vnto God, that he hath opened vnto his church the gyfte of interpretacyon & of pryntyng, and that there are now at this tyme so many, which with soch diligēce and faithfulnes inter

would open the eyes of the king of England.

George Joye also had a significant part in the development of the English Bible in Tyndale's day. He graduated from Cambridge in 1513, was later influenced by Lutheran doctrine and found it necessary to seek refuge abroad *c.* 1527. He may have published a version of the Psalter in 1530, a version different from that which he published in 1534. He also published English translations of Isaiah (1531), of Jeremiah, Lamentations, and the Song of Moses at the Red Sea (1534), a revision of Tyndale's NT (1534) without Tyndale's authorization and with changes of which Tyndale did not approve. After Tyndale had issued his own revision of his NT in 1534, with selections from the OT, Joye published another edition of his NT, together with selections from the OT. He may also have published translations of Proverbs and Ecclesiastes. (See C. C. Butterworth, *The Literary Lineage of the King James Bible*, 1941, pp. 87ff.)

IV. Miles Coverdale

The first really notable name in the history of English Bible translation and revision in the period from Tyndale to the appearance of the AV is that of Miles Coverdale, whose work benefited from an altered royal and ecclesiastical attitude. In 1535 Coverdale published a translation (which he had prepared on the Continent) of the entire Bible, the first full Bible to be printed in English. This version was given a dedication to Henry VIII. It was made from German and Latin versions and with the aid of translations made by Tyndale. A folio edition and a quarto edition appeared in 1537. The quarto edition asserts on its title-page that it was set forth with the king's most gracious licence. In 1538 Coverdale published an edition of the Latin Vulgate NT with an English translation in parallel columns. His capacity for beautiful rhythm and phrasing have made an enduring contribution to the great tradition of English Bible translation.

V. The Matthew Bible

In 1537 there appeared a Bible whose title-page asserts that it was truly and purely translated into English by Thomas Matthew. This Bible has often been regarded as the work of one of Tyndale's followers, John Rogers, who regarded it as inexpedient to send it forth under his own name. It was virtually a compilation of Tyndale's and Coverdale's work with minor alterations. It was a fact of remarkable irony that a Bible which was substantially the work of Tyndale, who had been opposed by Henry VIII and the church, could now be dedicated to Henry and set forth with his most gracious licence! On the solicitation of Cranmer, the Archbishop of Canterbury, Thomas Cromwell secured Henry's authorization that this Bible would

The first page of the 'Prologue unto the Christian reader' from Miles Coverdale's Bible of 1535, the first full Bible to be printed in English. (BL)

Top left: Chapter 1 of the Acts of the Apostles from Wyclif's translation of the Bible. c. 1380. (BL)

be allowed by his authority to be bought and read within the realm.

VI. Taverner's Bible

Richard Taverner published in 1539 a revision of Matthew's Bible which introduced a number of improvements indicating some scholarly competence. It was not without influence on future versions, but has not generally been regarded as occupying a place in the main line of English versions of the Bible.

VII. The Great Bible

In 1539 there appeared a Bible which was to exercise enormous influence on England and on the subsequent history of the English Bible. It was prepared by Coverdale on the invitation of Thomas Cromwell, and has therefore been called Cromwell's Bible. Because of its large size it has also been called the Great Bible. The second edition of April 1540 and later editions had a preface by Archbishop Cranmer, and consequently the version has frequently been referred to as Cranmer's Bible. But regardless of its multiple designations, it is really a revision of Matthew's Bible. It was authorized for distribution among the people and for the use of every church. Copies were obtained for the churches; people collected around them, and even disturbed church services with their reading and discussions. Three editions appeared in 1540 and three more in 1541. The Psalter of the Great Bible has been perpetuated in the Book of Common Prayer.

VIII. The Geneva Bible

In the last years of Henry VIII no new editions of the English Bible were produced, and the official attitude towards the use of the Scriptures changed. The Great Bible was not banned, as were Tyndale's and Coverdale's Bibles, but its use was limited. The new attitude was carried over into the field of Primers, which contained selections from the Scriptures. In 1545 a revised Primer, frequently referred to as the Primer of Henry VIII, was published, and the use of any other was forbidden. In the reign of Edward VI the climate again became favourable to the development and use of the Bible in English. Many editions of the older translations were published, but practically no new work was done. Sir John Cheke did prepare an independent translation of Matthew and the beginning of Mark made from the Greek in a style designed to be intelligible to the less cultured, which tried to avoid words of non-English origin, but his work was not in fact published until 1843.

The reign of Mary Tudor was of a quite different character from that of Edward. Bibles were taken from churches, and many Protestants suffered martyrdom. Some fled to the Continent. A group of such men in Geneva was responsible for the production of the Geneva Bible. First, however, a Geneva NT was published in 1557, prepared chiefly, it would seem, by William Whittingham. This NT employed the verse divisions which Stephanus had introduced into the fourth edition of his Greek NT in 1551. Italics were used to distinguish words introduced by the translator to clarify the meaning. Whittingham seems to have used as the foundation text for his praiseworthy revision a recently published edition of Tyndale's NT.

In 1558 Elizabeth's reign began, and again the official attitude towards the use of the Bible and towards its translators changed. Whittingham and others nevertheless continued in Geneva until they had completed the version of the Bible on which they had been working. This Geneva Bible, dedicated to Elizabeth, was published in 1560. It made an enormous contribution to the Authorized Version, and achieved a dominant popularity in the period 1570–1620. A very scholarly work, it drew upon the unique competence and assistance of the great and devoted men who were in Geneva at the time, and upon works in different languages which were available there. The OT section was a painstaking revision of that of the Great Bible with careful attention to the Hebrew; and for the NT it drew upon the Whittingham 1557 edition. Because of its use of 'breeches' in Genesis 3:7 (a reading which, however, was not new), it became known as the 'Breeches Bible'. Verse divisions were employed throughout the entire Bible.

IX. The Bishops' Bible

The Geneva Bible was more accurate than the Great Bible, but official endorsement was not transferred to it. Instead, the Archbishop of Canterbury, Matthew Parker, promoted a revision of the Great Bible, with much of the work done by bishops. This revision, of varying merit, and at points considerably influenced by the Geneva Bible, was published in a folio edition in 1568. It came to be known as the Bishops' Bible, and received ecclesiastical authorization. A slightly revised quarto edition appeared in 1569. A folio edition with an extensive revision of the NT section was published in 1572. The Prayer Book version of the Psalms and the Bishops' Bible Psalter were printed in this edition in parallel columns. In following editions, except for that of 1585, only the Prayer Book Psalter was included. The 1572 revision had a substantial influence on the AV.

X. The Rheims–Douay Version

Roman Catholics, who during the reign of Elizabeth I had found refuge on the Continent, in 1582 brought forth in Rheims a NT which they hoped would counteract the influence of Protestant translations. This was the work of Gregory Martin, William Allen and others of the English College in Rheims. Their reason for addressing themselves to this task was not that which actuated Protestant translators (*i.e.*, a zealous desire to make the Word of God accessible to all men in the vernacular), for in their preface they held that, on the contrary, the translation of the Bible into the 'vulgar tongues' was not an absolute necessity, or even necessarily profitable. They based their translation on a Latin Vulgate basic text, but did give attention to the Greek, as is evidenced by their treatment of the definite article. They gave some attention also to previous works in English. Of set purpose they retained certain Latin words and followed their basic text closely, even, at times, to the point of sacrifice of intelligibility. For all this, they did provide a glossary to assist the English reader, and their work served to broaden the word-base on which the AV was constructed. The OT was not published until 1609–10 at Douai, which was too late to exert much, if any, influence on the AV. In style it was similar to the Rheims NT.

XI. The Authorized Version

At the Hampton Court Conference in 1604 a proposal was made by Dr John Reynolds, a Puritan and president of Corpus Christi College, Oxford, that a new translation of the Bible be made. This proposal, although not favoured by a majority of those present, did appeal to King James I, and resulted ultimately in the production of the AV. The king wished to have a uniform translation made by the finest scholars in the two English universities, a translation to be reviewed by the bishops and the most learned men in the church, afterwards presented to the Privy Council, and finally ratified by his authority.

James appointed fifty-four learned men for the work of translation, and the translators were divided into six companies. Among other things, the revisers were to follow the Bishops' Bible, and were to modify it as slightly as the 'truth of the original' or emphasis required; they were to retain the old ecclesiastical terms such as 'church', and marginal notes were to be avoided except for certain non-controversial uses.

Further information about the principles and practices which were followed by the revisers is furnished in the preface, 'The Translators to the Reader'. The Scriptures are there acknowledged to be high and divine, full and perfect; and their translation into the vernacular is shown to be necessary. The revisers appreciated the excellent translation work that had been done before. They never designed to make a new translation or to change a bad one into a good one, but their aim was 'to make a good one better, or out of many good ones, one principal good one, not justly to be excepted against'. They sought not praise, but the truth; their trust was in him who has the key of David.

They worked from the Hebrew text of the OT and from the Greek text of the NT. They did not labour with undue haste or hesitate to revise what they had done; but brought back to the anvil that which they had hammered. They consulted translators or commentators in various languages. When the text was not clear, they took account of diversity of signification and sense in the margin. They did not bind themselves to a uniformity of phrasing or an identity of words, but felt free to use synonyms. They avoided the obscurity of the Douay Bible with its Latinate element. Their desire was that the Bible speak like itself, that it be understood 'euen of the very vulgar'.

When the various companies had completed their work, twelve representatives chosen from among them revised the entire translation. After some further touching up the version was ready for publication. There is no record of official ecclesiastical or royal authorization, but the words 'appointed to be read in churches' appeared on the title-page of the first edition. Whether there was official formal authorization or not, the version immediately displaced the Bishops' Bible in the churches and in time gained a vic-

The Geneva Bible published in 1560. It became known as the 'Breeches Bible' because of the reference to 'breeches' in Gn. 3:7, shown here. (BL)

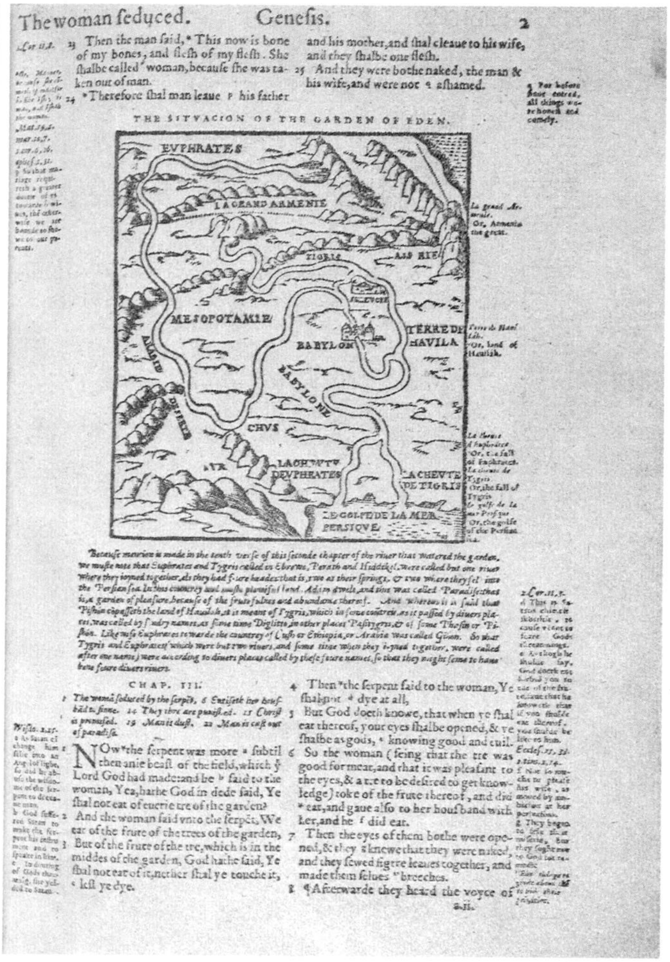
The woman ſeduced. Genesis. 2

23 Then the man ſaid, * This now is bone of my bones, and fleſh of my fleſh. She ſhalbe called woman, becauſe ſhe was taken out of man.
24 * Therefore ſhal man leaue his father and his mother, and ſhal cleaue to his wife, and they ſhalbe one fleſh.
25 And they were bothe naked, the man & his wife, and were not aſhamed.

THE SITVACION OF THE GARDEN OF EDEN.

Becauſe mencion is made in the tenth verſe of this ſeconde chapter of the riuer that watered the garden, we muſt note that Euphrates and Tygris called in Ebrewe, Perath and Hiddekel, were called but one riuer where they ioyned together, as they had foure heades: that is, two at their ſprings, & two where they fel into the Perſian ſea. In this countrey and moſt plentiful land, Adam dwelt, and this was called Paradiſe: that is, a garden of pleaſure because of the frutefulnes and abundance therof. And whereas it is ſaid that Piſhon compaſſeth the land of Hauilah, it is meant of Tygris, which in ſome countreis, as it paſſed by diuers places, was called by ſundry names, as ſome time Diglitto, in other places Paſitygris, & of ſome Theſin or Piſon. Likewiſe Euphrates towarde the countrey of Cuſh or Ethiopia, or Arabia was called Gihon. So that Tygris and Euphrates (which were but two riuers, and ſome time when they ioyned together, were called after one name) were according to diuers places called by theſe foure names, ſo that they might ſeme to haue bene foure diuers riuers.

CHAP. III.

1 The woma ſeduced by the ſerpēt, 6 Entiſeth her houſbād to ſinne. 14 They thre are puniſhed. 15 Christ is promiſed. 19 Man is duſt. 22 Man is caſt out of paradiſe.

1 NOw * the ſerpent was more ſubtil then anie beaſt of the field, which ẏ Lord God had made: and he ſaid to the woman, Yea, hathe God in dede ſaid, Ye ſhal not eat of euerie tre of the garden?
2 And the woman ſaid vnto the ſerpēt, We eat of the frute of the trees of the garden,
3 But of the frute of the tre, which is in the middes of the garden, God hathe ſaid, Ye ſhal not eat of it, nether ſhal ye touche it, leſt ye dye.
4 Then * the ſerpent ſaid to the woman, Ye ſhal not dye at all,
5 But God doeth knowe, that when ye ſhal eat thereof, your eyes ſhalbe opened, & ye ſhalbe as gods, knowing good and euil.
6 So the woman (ſeing that the tre was good for meat, and that it was pleaſant to the eyes, & a tre to be deſired to get knowledge) toke of the frute thereof, and did * eat, and gaue alſo to her houſband with her, and he did eat.
7 Then the eyes of them bothe were opened, & they knewe that they were naked, and they ſewed figge tre leaues together, and made them ſelues * breeches.
8 ¶Afterwarde they heard the voyce of

a.ii.

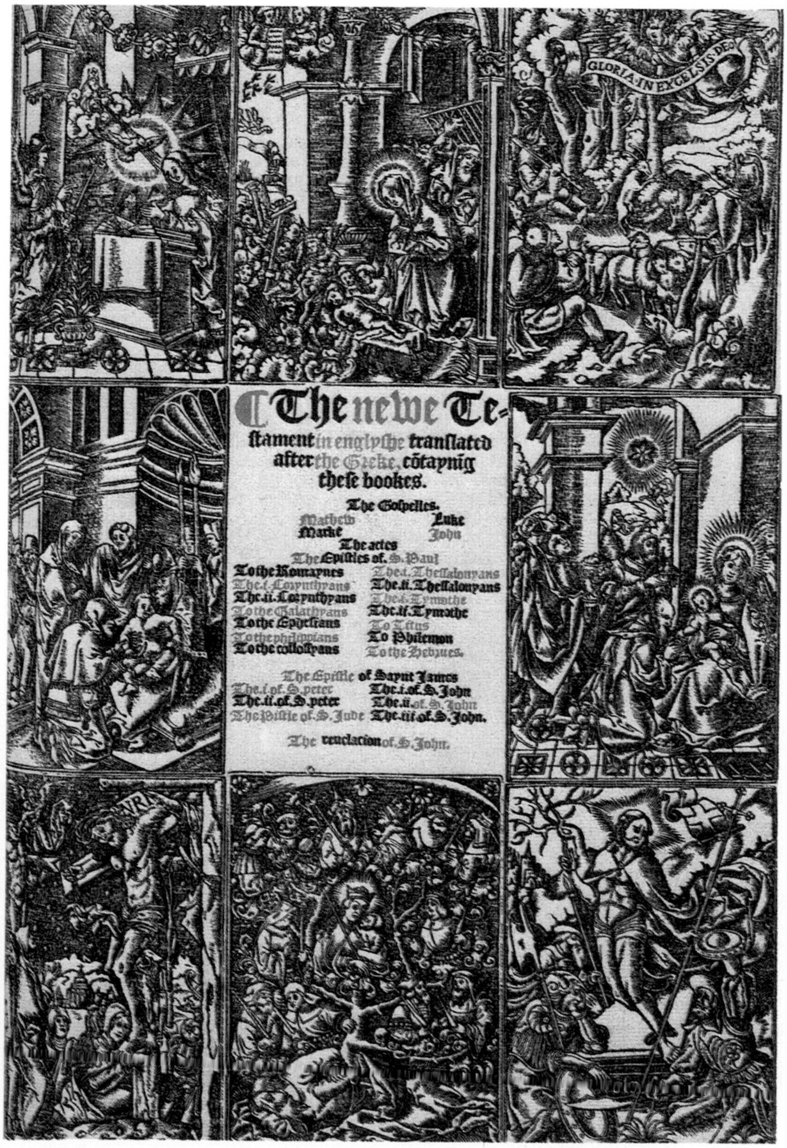

Bottom left: Frontispiece of the New Testament of the Great Bible published in 1539. (BL)

Of S. John, Ci.

The Reuelacion of sayncte John the deuine.

Happie are they that heare the worde of God and kepe it. He wryteth to the seuen congregacions in Asia/ seyth seuen candelstickes/ and in the myddes of them/ one lyke vnto the sonne of man.

The fyrst Chapter.

A The reuelacion of Jesus Christ/ which God gaue vnto him/ for to shewe vnto his seruauntes thyngs which must shortely come to passe. And he sent and shewed by hys angell vnto hys seruaunt John/ which bare recorde of the worde of God/ and of the testimony of Jesus Christ/ and of all thyngs that he sawe. Happy is he that redith/ & they that heare the wordes of the prophesy/ and kepe those thynges which are writtẽ therin. For the tyme is at hande.

The seuẽ churches in Asia. John to the .vij. cõgregacions in Asia. Grace be with you and peace/ from him which is and which was/ and which is to come/ & frõ the .vij. spretes which are present before hys trone/ and frõ Jesus Christ which is a faythfull wytnes/ & fyrst begotten of the deed: and Lorde ouer the kinges of the erth. Unto him that* loued vs/ and wesshed vs from synnes in his awne bloude/ and made vs kynges and prestes vnto God his father be glory & dominion for euermore. Amen.* Beholde he cometh with cloudes/ & all eyes shall se hym: & they also which peersed hym. And all kynredes of the erth shall wayle. Euen so: Amen. I am a* Alpha and Omega/ the begynnyng and the endynge/ sayth the Lorde almyghty/ which is & which was and which is to come.

C I John youre brother & companion in tribulaciõ/ & in the kyngdome & paciẽce which is in Jesu Christ/ was in the yle of Pathmos for the worde of God/ and for the wytnessing of Jesu Christ. I was in the sprete on a sondaye/ & herde behinde me a gret voyce/ as it had bene of a trompe sayinge: I am Alpha & Omega/ the fyrst and the laste. That thou seyst/ wryte in a boke/ & sende it vnto the congregaciõs which are in Asia/ vnto Ephesus/ and vnto Smyrna/ and vnto Pergamos/ & vnto Thiatira/ and vnto Sardis/ and vnto Philadelphia/ and vnto Laodicia.

The fyrste fygure.

And I turned backe to se the voyce that spake to me. And whẽ I was turned: I sawe seuen golden candelstickes/ & in the myddes of the candelstickes/ one lyke vnto the sonne of man/ clothed with a lynnẽ garment doune to the ground/ & gyrd about ẏ pappes wyth a golden gyrdle. His heed/ & his heares were whyte/ as whyte woll/ and as snowe: & hys eyes were as a flame of fyre: & hys fete lyke vnto brasse as though they brẽt in a fornace: & his voyce as ẏ sounde of many waters. And he had in his ryghte hande .vij. starres. And out of his mouthe went a sharpe two edged swearde. And his face shone euen as ẏ sonne in his strength.

And whẽ I saw him/ I fell at his fete/ euẽ as deed. And he layde his ryghte hande vpon me/ saying vnto me: feare not.* I am ẏ fyrst and the laste/ and am a lyue/ and was deed. And beholde I am a lyue for euermore/ and haue the keyes of hell and of deeth. Wryte therfore the thynges which thou hast sene/ and the thinges which are/ and the thinges which shalbe fulfylled here after: and the mistery of the .vij. starres which thou sawest in my ryght hande/ and the .vij. goldẽ candelstickes. The .vij. starres are the messengers

Seuen golden candelstickes. Seuen starres. Esaie .xliij. b. The starres are the preachers.

Marginal notes: Hebre. ix. d. i. Petri. ij. b. i. John. i. b. Math. xxiiij. c. Esaie. iij. c. a* Alpha and Omega are letters of the Greke crosserowe/ Alpha is the fyrst letter and Omega ẏ last.

N. v. of the

Part of Tyndale's New Testament, printed at Antwerp in 1535, showing how closely the AV *followed Tyndale at this point* (*Rev. 1*). (BL)

tory over the Geneva Bible in popular favour, although the latter continued in use privately for a long while. The AV gathered to itself the virtues of the long and brilliant royal line of English Bible translations; it united high scholarship with Christian devotion and piety. It came into being at a time when the English language was vigorous and young, and its scholars had a remarkable mastery of the instrument which Providence had prepared for them. Their version has justifiably been called 'the noblest monument of English prose'. The stylistic dependence of the AV on its predecessors has been sharply brought out by C. C. Butterworth in his work on *The Literary Lineage of the King James Bible*, 1941. Butterworth estimates in a study of selected passages that it is indebted to the earlier English translations of the Bible for about 60% of its text (pp. 230f.). The chief contributors were the Geneva Bible and the Geneva NT (about 19%), and Tyndale's translations, including the Matthew Bible (about 18%).

XII. From the Authorized to the Revised Version

It may be thought that with the appearance of the AV the high point in the history of the English Bible was attained and that all else is anti-climactic. But the story of the English Bible after 1611 must not be neglected. In the case of the AV itself, change and revision of an unofficial kind were introduced through the years. More than 300 changes are found in the 1613 edition. Very extensive modifications were introduced in editions published in the 18th century. Other English versions continued to be made. Henry Ainsworth from 1616 to 1623 published translations of the Pentateuch and the Song of Solomon, and his translation of these books and of the Psalms was published after his death. His work was animated by a desire for accurate rendering. Paraphrases became fairly numerous. Several significant contributions were made in the 18th century. William Mace published in 1729 a NT in Greek and English in which he attempted to take into account 'the most Authentic Manuscripts' and to use the accepted colloquial style of his day. Translations made in the 18th century by Philip Doddridge (*Family Expositor, or, a Paraphrase and Version of the New Testament*), George Campbell (*Translation of the Gospels*) and James Macknight (*A New Literal Translation of all the Apostolical Epistles*) were utilized in a NT published in 1818. In 1745 William Whiston published his *Primitive New Testament*, which uses the text of the AV, but modifies it in the interest of readings found in Codex Bezae, Codex Claromontanus and Codex Alexandrinus. John Wesley published in 1755 a revision of the AV.

Richard Wynne issued in 1764 *The New Testament, carefully collated with the Greek, corrected, divided and printed according to the subjects treated of.* Wynne sought to find a middle course between a literal rendering and loose paraphrase. Anthony Purver, a member of the Society of Friends, worked for 30 years on the translation of the Bible which he published in 1764. One of the most noteworthy of 18th-century efforts was that of E. Harwood, who published in 1768 his *Liberal Translation of the New Testament.* His use of an 'elegant', literary, paraphrastic 18th-century style dates his work.

John Worsley made an effort to translate the NT from the Greek into the 'Present Idiom of the English Tongue'. He wished to remove from the text obsolete and hardly intelligible words, and to bring the translation closer to the original. His translation was published posthumously in 1770. Other versions which were published (or printed) in the late 18th century were those of Gilbert Wakefield, W. H. Roberts, Thomas Haweis, William Newcome, who utilized Griesbach's Greek text of 1774–5, Nathaniel Scarlett, assisted by certain other 'men of piety and literature' (whose translation allows itself the freedom of arranging material in the form of a drama), and 'J. M. Ray'.

The 19th century brought forth translations of the Epistles of Paul by the Unitarians Thomas Belsham (1822) and Charles Eyre (1832), and of the entire NT by the Unitarian Samuel Sharpe (1840) from J. J. Griesbach's Greek text. In 1865 Sharpe published a revised text of the AV of the OT. Rodolphus Dickinson in 1833 with indifferent success published a NT in which he attempted to improve on the style of the AV. Among the literal translations of the 19th century, mention should be made of that of Robert Young in 1862. New textual information continued to be reflected in the English versions. 'Herman Heinfetter' made use of the Vatican MS; G. W. Braineld took into account the texts of Griesbach, Lachmann, Tischendorf, Alford and Tregelles in his translation of the Gospels (1863); Robert Ainslie used the AV in 1869, but modified it in the interest of readings favoured by Tischendorf; Samuel Davidson published in 1875 a translation of the NT from the text of Tischendorf; and J. B. Rotherham translated the NT from the text of Tregelles (1872).

Andrew Norton's new translation of the Gospels (1855) and Leicester Ambrose Sawyer's translation of the NT (1858) were efforts to use the style of their day. They have been credited with introducing the succession of the 'modern-speech' versions of the 20th century (H. Pope, *English Versions of the Bible*, pp. 546f.). Various private revisions of the AV were published in the 19th century.

XIII. Roman Catholic versions in the 18th and 19th centuries

In the 18th century a number of Roman Catholic efforts were made to provide an improved English version. Cornelius Nary published in 1718 and 1719 a NT translated from the Latin Vulgate with attention given to the Greek and Hebrew idiom, in which he attempted to use intelligible, idiomatic English. Robert Witham also desired to make the text of the English NT intelligible to the contemporary reader. His version, translated from the Latin Vulgate, was published in 1730. In 1738 the fifth and lightly revised edition of the Rhemish NT appeared, more than a century after the fourth edition (1633). Richard Challoner, who has been credited with some of the editorial work on this fifth edition, later published two revisions of the Douay OT and five of the NT (1749–72), and provided a simpler, more idiomatic type of text which continued in general use among English-speaking Roman Catholics until at least 1941. He was not averse to following the AV when he approved its readings. The revisions made by Bernard MacMahon 1783–1810 had a considerable influence, especially in Ireland. Bishop Francis Patrick Kenrick from 1849 to 1860 published a revised text of the Rheims–Douay version with annotations.

XIV. The Revised Version

Conviction that a revision of the AV had become necessary came to formal ecclesiastical expression in 1870, and a revision of the AV was undertaken by the Convocation of Canterbury of the Church of England. Distinguished scholars, not all of whom were members of the Church of England, participated in the project. (See B. F. Westcott, *A General View of the History of the English Bible*[3], 1927, pp. 324f.) Among the general principles adopted, it was agreed that as few changes as possible were to be made in the text of the AV consistent with faithfulness, and that such changes as were introduced should be expressed in the language of the AV and its predecessors.

The initial meeting of the NT Company was held on 22 June 1870, in the Jerusalem Chamber of Westminster Abbey. This opening session was preceded by a communion service conducted by the Dean of Westminster in the Henry VII Chapel. Among those who were admitted to the Lord's table was a Unitarian member of the company. Strong protest was naturally aroused. From this inauspicious beginning the company entered upon more than 10 years of labour. The assistance of American biblical scholars was sought; and two American companies, one for the OT and one for the NT, were formed. Exclusive copyright was given to the University Presses of Oxford and Cambridge; the American companies agreed not to publish an edition embodying their distinctive readings for 14 years after the publication of the English RV; the University Presses promised to publish during that period an appendix listing readings preferred by the American companies which had not been accepted by the British revisers. On 17 May 1881 the RV of the NT was published in England, and the whole Bible was published on 19 May 1885. The textual theories of Westcott and Hort were manifest in the NT; the OT characteristically followed the Massoretic Text, and much effort was made to represent the original faithfully and accurately even in details. Where possible the revisers attempted consistently to represent a given word in the original by a given English word. Because of its accuracy the RV has proved very valuable for study purposes. Its style, however, has not generally been approved by those who have been captivated by the rhythm and the music of the AV.

In 1901 the preferences of the American companies and other preferences of the surviving members of the committee were embodied in the text of an 'American Standard Edition' of the Revised Bible. Among the changes which were introduced the substitution of 'Jehovah' for 'LORD' and 'GOD' (in small capitals) was unwelcome to many. A note on a Gk. word for 'worship' was introduced in the NT, and at Jn. 9:38 it took a form which called forth most necessary objection.

XV. Since the Revised Version

The RV did not succeed in displacing the AV in the affections of the majority of Bible-readers, and they were furthermore unable to satisfy all of those who were persuaded of the need and desirability of revision. They did, however, break the way open to a remarkably prolific period of Bible translation work. Since 1881 there has been an unceasing flow of translations, or revisions of translations, of the NT, or the entire Bible, or of parts of the Bible. In the case of the NT new translations or revisions have been appearing on the average of more than one a year. Among them there has been a diversity in basic texts employed, in methods of translation, in language and style, and in theological viewpoint. The influence of the Greek text and of the principles of textual criticism advocated by Westcott and Hort has been strongly felt. The view that the Greek of the NT was in the main at least the popular, vernacular Greek of the 1st century and not the literary Greek of that time has encouraged translators to undertake versions in 'everyday English'. There has been a generally successful effort to achieve intelligibility and contemporaneity of expression. However, in the realm of felicity and grace of style the accomplishment has often been undistinguished. While devout and believing scholarship has been ably represented in this period, heterodoxy and rationalistic criticism have also been in evidence.

A number of the versions or revisions which have appeared since the time of the English RV might be given brief mention. Among the pioneers in the translation of the Scriptures into modern English was Ferrar Fenton, who published a translation of Romans 'direct from the original Greek into modern English' in 1882 and a translation of the Epistles of Paul in 1883. His NT translated into 'current English' appeared in 1895 and his *Bible in Modern English* in 1903. *The Twentieth Century New Testament*, the work of about twenty persons, was published from 1898 to 1901, and was subsequently issued in revised form. The *New Testament in Modern Speech*, R. F. Weymouth's much-used translation from the text of his *Resultant Greek Testament*, was posthumously published in 1903, with Ernest Hampden-Cook as editor. James Moffatt issued *The Historical New Testament* in 1901, in which he attempted to arrange the writings of the NT in a conjectured order of 'literary growth' and date of composition. In 1913 his new translation of the NT appeared. Its textual basis was mainly von Soden's Greek text. The clearly erroneous reading of the Sinaitic MS of the Old Syr. Version is followed at Mt. 1:16, and the reader is not assisted by any textual note (see J. G. Machen, *The Virgin Birth of Christ*, 1930, pp. 176ff.). Moffatt's translation of the OT was published in 1924. E. J. Goodspeed's 'American' translation of the NT, based on the Greek text of Westcott and Hort and intended to be expressed in popular American idiom, appeared in 1923, and the 'American' translation of the OT, prepared by A. R. Gordon, T. J. Meek, Leroy Waterman and J. M. Powis Smith, appeared in 1927. Attention should also be called to W. G. Ballantine's *Riverside New Testament* (1923); Helen B. Montgomery's *Centenary Translation of the New Testament* (1924); C. B. Williams' translation of the New Testament 'in the language of the people' (1937), a version which attempts a precise rendering of Gk. verb forms; *The New Testament in Basic English* (1941) and *The Bible in Basic English* (1949); Gerrit Verkuyl's *Berkeley Version of the New Testament* (1945), the Berkeley Version of the entire Bible (1959), the OT section of which was prepared by a sizeable staff of translators, with Gerrit Verkuyl as editor-in-chief, and the *New Berkeley* or *Modern Language Bible* (1969); J. B. Phillips' translation of the NT (1947–57; one-volume edition, 1958), at times quite free and paraphrastic; *The Letchworth Version* [of the NT] *in Modern English*, by T. F. Ford and R. E. Ford (1948), a remarkably successful light revision of the AV which conserves much of the stylistic beauty of its original; *The New World Translation of the Christian Greek Scriptures* (1950), a version prepared by the Jehovah's Witnesses; C. K. Williams' translation of the NT into a limited-vocabulary 'Plain English' (1952); H. J. Schonfield's *Authentic New Testament* (1955); Kenneth S. Wuest's *Expanded Translation of the Greek New Testament* (1956–9); the *Amplified New Testament* (1958); W. F. Beck's New Testament in the Language of Today (1963); William Barclay's *New Translation* of the New Testament (1968–9); and *The Translator's New Testament* (1973).

Several Roman Catholic translations of special interest have appeared. The NT section of *The Westminster Version of the Sacred Scriptures*, which was completed in 1935 (1913–35), was translated from the Greek by various men working on individual assignments under general editors. It employs a solemn or 'biblical' style with archaic forms. J. A. Carey issued a revision of the Challoner–Rheims NT in 1935. F. A. Spencer's translation of the NT from the Greek was published in 1937. In 1941 a revision of the Challoner–Rheims NT appeared in USA, prepared under the supervision of the Confraternity of Christian Doctrine by a large number of scholars. It was not bound by the official Clementine text of the Latin Vulgate, but its revisers were free to take account of critical editions. They succeeded in commendable measure in producing a version of clarity, simplicity and contemporary style.

Monsignor R. A. Knox published in 1945 a trial edition of a translation of the NT from the Vulgate and a slightly modified definitive edition in 1945, which was 'authorized by the Archbishops and Bishops of England and Wales'. It was accorded an official status along with the Rhemish version. Knox's translation of the OT from the Latin Vulgate was published in 1949 in two volumes 'for private use only'. A revision appeared in 1955 with hierarchical authorization. The translation of the NT by James A. Kleist and Joseph L. Lilly (1954) was made from the Greek. Kleist translated the Gospels from the text of Bover; Lilly translated the rest of the NT. The *Jerusalem Bible* (1966) is related to the French version *La Bible de Jérusalem*, though is not simply a translation of it. *The New American Bible* (1970), sponsored by the Bishops' Committee of the Confraternity of Christian Doctrine, represented a major translation effort. It was based on the original languages of Scripture or on what was held to be the oldest form of the text extant.

Several of the most widely used and most influential of recent versions remain to be mentioned. A committee-revision of the American RV, authorized by the International Council of Religious Education, was published in 1946 (NT; ^{2}1971), 1952 (entire Bible), 1965 (Catholic edition). This *Revised Standard Version* (RSV) differs considerably in important aspects from the AV and RV. It lacks their confidence in the Massoretic Hebrew text, and in places indulges in critical conjectures; it allows itself more freedom in rendering its text than did the AV and RV.

Another revision of the American RV, *The New American Standard Bible* (1963), prepared by evangelical scholars, is a close and faithful translation in a clear and readable style, which is admirable for study purposes. A further notable accomplishment by evangelicals is the NT in the *New International Version* (1974) (entire Bible 1978). It is a completely new translation into contemporary English, somewhat freer than is NASB. Very free in its rendering is the *New English Bible* (1961–1970), a version produced with the co-operation of representatives of the larger British churches (apart from the Roman Catholics), of the Oxford and Cambridge University Presses, and of the British and Foreign Bible Society and the National Bible Society of Scotland. Very extensively circulated have been the NT in *Today's English Version* or *Good News for Modern Man* (1966), followed by the complete *Good News Bible* (1976), prepared by the American Bible Society; and *The Living Bible* (1962–71), an exceedingly free paraphrase rather than a translation.

The history of the English versions of the Bible did not end with the AV. No version has, it is true, succeeded in superseding its excellence in style, but the efforts of many labourers since 1611 have not been without profit. The fruits of advancing knowledge and scholarship have been reflected in many translations which have been available for discriminating use alongside of the enduring embodiment of a great tradition, that 'noblest monument of English prose'.

BIBLIOGRAPHY. F. F. Bruce, *The Books and the Parchments*, 1950; *idem*, *The History of the Bible in English*[3], 1979; C. C. Butterworth, *The English Primers (1529–1545)*, 1953; *idem*, *The Literary Lineage of the King James Bible*, 1941; A. S. Herbert (ed.), *Historical Catalogue of Printed Editions of the English Bible*, 1968; S. L. Greenslade and G. W. H. Lampe (eds.), *The Cambridge History of the Bible*. vols. 2, 3 (1969, 1973); S. Kubo and W. Specht, *So Many Versions?*, 1975; J. I. Mombert, *A Hand-Book of the English Versions of the Bible* [*c*. 1883]; W. F. Moulton, *The History of the English Bible*[5], 1911; J. H. Penniman, *A Book about the English Bible*, 1919; A. W. Pollard, *Records of the English Bible*, 1911; H. Pope, *English Versions of the Bible*, revised and amplified by Sebastian Bullough, 1952; H. W. Robinson (ed.), *The Bible in its Ancient and English Versions*, 1940; P. M. Simms, *The Bible in America*, 1936; J. H. Skilton 'The Translation of the New Testament into English, 1881–1950: Studies in Language and Style' (doctoral dissertation, 1961); and B. F. Westcott, *A General View of the History of the English Bible*, third edition revised by W. A. Wright, 1927.

J.H.S.

Frontispiece of the Authorized Version or King James I's Bible, published in 1611. (BL)

ENGRAVING See Art, Part 1.

EN-HADDAH. 'Sharp spring', the name of a place which fell to the lot of Issachar (Jos. 19:21). Suggested identifications have been made (see *GTT*, p. 185), but the site has not been definitely identified. T.C.M.

EN-HAKKORE (Heb. *'ên-haqqôrē'*). The spring in Lehi from which Samson refreshed himself after slaughtering the Philistines with the jawbone of an ass (Jdg. 15:19). None of the places mentioned in the story has been identified. En-hakkore could mean 'the spring of the partridge' (*cf.* En-gedi, 'the spring of the goat'), but Jdg. 15 gives a coherent account of the origin of the name, indicating that it means 'the spring of him who called'. J.A.M.

EN-HAZOR. The name of a place which fell to the lot of Naphtali (Jos. 19:37). The site is unknown, though suggestions have been made (see *GTT*, p. 198). It is distinct from *Hazor. T.C.M.

ENOCH. 1. Son of Cain (Gn. 4:17) after whom a city was named.

2. Son of Jared and father of Methuselah (Gn. 5:18, 21). Enoch was a man of outstanding sanctity who enjoyed close fellowship with God (Gn. 5:22, 24: for the expression 'walked with God', *cf.* Gn. 6:9; Mi. 6:8; Mal. 2:6). Like Elijah (2 Ki. 2:11), he was received into the presence of God without dying (Gn. 5:24).

It is probable that the language of Pss. 49:15; 73:24 reflects the story of Enoch. In that case the example of Enoch's assumption played a part in the origin of Jewish hope for life with God beyond death. (In the Apocrypha, Wisdom 4:10–14 also treats Enoch as the outstanding example of the righteous man's hope of eternal life.)

In the NT, Heb. 11:5f. attributes Enoch's assumption to his faith; the expression 'pleased God' is the LXX translation of 'walked with God' (Gn. 5:24). Jude 14f. quotes a prophecy attributed to Enoch in *1 Enoch* 1:9.

In the intertestamental period Enoch became a popular figure: see Ecclus. 44:16; 49:14, 16 (Heb.); *Jubilees* 4:14–26; 10:17; and *1 Enoch*. Probably the legend of Enoch was elaborated in the Babylonian diaspora as a counterpart to the antediluvian sages of Mesopotamian legend. So Enoch became the initiator of the art of writing and the first wise man, who received heavenly revelations of the secrets of the universe and transmitted them in writing to later generations.

In the earlier tradition his scientific wisdom is prominent, acquired on journeys through the heavens with angelic guides, and including astronomical, cosmographical and meteorological lore, as well as the solar calendar used at Qumran. He was also God's prophet against the fallen angels. Later tradition (2nd century BC) emphasizes his ethical teaching and especially his apocalyptic revelations of the course of world history down to the last judgment. In the Similitudes (*1 Enoch* 37–71) he is identified with the Messianic Son of man (71:14–17), and some later Jewish traditions identified him with the nearly divine figure Metatron (*Targum of Pseudo-Jonathan*, Gn. 5:24; *3 Enoch*). Early Christian apocalyptic writings frequently expect his return to earth with Elijah before the End.

1 Enoch (*Ethiopic Enoch*) is among the most important intertestamental works. The complete text survives only in Ethiopic, but sections are extant in Greek and important fragments of the original Aramaic are now available from Qumran. *1 Enoch* comprises five books: the Book of Watchers (1–36), the Similitudes (37–71), the Astronomical Book (72–82), the Book of Dreams (83–90) and the Epistle of Enoch (91–105). The Qumran MSS include fragments of all these except the Similitudes, which are therefore now generally dated no earlier than the 1st century AD. Also from Qumran there are fragments of a hitherto almost unknown Book of Giants, which was probably the original fifth book of the Enoch Pentateuch, for which the Similitudes were later substituted.

The Qumran MSS help clarify the dates of these works. The oldest sections are the Astronomical Book and 6–19: these date from no later than the beginning of the 2nd century BC and may be as early as the 5th century. The Book of Watchers (incorporating 6–19) cannot be later than the mid-1st and is probably from the mid-3rd century BC. The Book of Dreams is from 165 or 164 BC. The Epistle of Enoch and Book of Giants may date from the end of the 2nd century BC.

Other works under the name of Enoch are from the Christian era. The Similitudes (*1 Enoch* 37–71) (important as perhaps illustrating the background to the use of 'Son of man' in the Gospels) seem to be a Jewish work, though some argue for Christian origin. *3 Enoch* (*Hebrew Enoch*) is a Jewish work of disputed date. *2 Enoch* (*Slavonic Enoch*) is a late Christian work which may incorporate Jewish material.

BIBLIOGRAPHY. R. H. Charles, *The Book of Enoch*, 1912; P. Grelot, *Recherches de Science Religieuse* 46, 1958, pp. 5–26, 181–210; J. T. Milik, *The Books of Enoch: Aramaic Fragments from Qumrân Cave 4*, 1976. R.J.B.

ENOSH. Son of Seth and father of Kenan (Gn. 4:26; 5:6–11; 1 Ch. 1:1; Lk. 3:38). His life-span is recorded as 905 years. In his time men began to call upon the covenant name of Yahweh. The Heb. word *'ᵉnôš*, 'man', occurs some 42 times in OT, and often suggests the aspect of frailty and mortality (Jb. 4:17); the corresponding verb *'ānaš* means 'to be weak' (*cf.* *ADAM). N.H.

EN-RIMMON (Heb. *'ên-rimmôn*, 'spring of the pomegranate'). A village in Judah reoccupied after the Exile (Ne. 11:29). Either it was formed by the coalescing of two separate villages Ain and Rimmon, or more probably, reading Jos. 15:32; 19:7; 1 Ch. 4:32 all as En-rimmon, it was always a single town, originally in Judah's inheritance (Jos. 15:32), but soon transferred to Simeon (Jos. 19:7). It has been identified with Umm er-Ramāmîn, 15 km N of Beersheba. M.A.M.

EN-ROGEL (Heb. *'ên-rōḡēl*, 'well of the fuller'). A water source just outside Jerusalem, some 200 m S of the confluence of the Valley of Hinnom and the Kidron valley. It is known today as Job's well. The well marked a point on the N boundary of Judah (Jos. 15:7) before David captured Jerusalem (2 Sa. 5:6ff.).

The narrative of Adonijah's abortive attempt to gain the throne in David's old age suggests the site had cultic associations (1 Ki. 1:9ff.). R.J.W.

EN-SHEMESH (Heb. *'ên-šemeš*, 'spring of the sun'). A point on the Judah–Benjamin border 4 km E of Jerusalem, below Olivet, and just S of the Jericho road, and now sometimes called the 'Spring of the Apostles'; modern 'Ain Haud.

J.D.D.

ENVY. A grudging regard for the advantages seen to be enjoyed by others—*cf.* Lat. *invidia* from *invideo*, 'to look closely at', then 'to look with malicious intent' (see 1 Sa. 18:9). The Heb. *qin'â* means originally a burning, then the colour produced in the face by a deep emotion, thus ardour, zeal, jealousy. RSV substitutes 'jealousy' for 'envy' in Jb. 5:2; Pr. 27:4; Acts 7:9; 1 Cor. 3:3, *etc.* But they are not synonymous. Jealousy makes us fear to lose what we possess; envy creates sorrow that others have what we have not. The word *qin'â* is used to express Rachel's envy for her sister (Gn. 30:1, *cf.* Gn. 37:11; Nu. 25:11, *etc.*). Its evils are depicted especially in the book of Proverbs: thus the question in 27:4: 'Who can stand before jealousy?' The NT *zēlos* is usually translated in a good sense as *'zeal' as well as in a bad sense as 'envy' (Jn. 2:17; *cf.* Col. 4:13 where it is translated 'worked hard' [AV 'great zeal']; note also its reference to God, 2 Ki. 19:31; Is. 9:7; 37:32, *etc.*). The word *phthonos* always appears in a bad sense except in the difficult verse Jas. 4:5, which should be translated as in RVmg. (A comparable sentiment is expressed in the Qumran *Manual of Discipline*, 4. 16–18.) *phthonos* is characteristic of the unredeemed life (Rom. 1:29; Gal. 5:21; 1 Tim. 6:4; Tit. 3:3). It was the spirit which crucified our Lord (Mt. 27:18; Mk. 15:10). Envy, *zēlos*, as inconsiderate zeal, is to be avoided by Christians (Rom. 13:13; 2 Cor. 12:20; Jas. 3:14, 16). See *NIDNTT* 1, pp. 557f.; *TDNT* 2, pp. 877–882.

H.D.McD.

EPAPHRAS. In Col. 1:7; 4:12; Phm. 23, one of Paul's friends and associates, called by him his 'fellow slave' and 'fellow prisoner'. The name is abbreviated from Epaphroditus, but Epaphras is probably not to be identified with the Epaphroditus of Phil. 2:25; 4:18 (as he is by T. R. Glover, *Paul of Tarsus*, 1925, p. 179). We gather that Epaphras evangelized the cities of the Lycus valley in Phrygia under Paul's direction during the latter's Ephesian ministry, and founded the churches of Colossae, Hierapolis and Laodicea. Later he visited Paul during his Roman captivity, and it was his news of conditions in the churches of the Lycus valley that moved Paul to write the Epistle to the Colossians.

BIBLIOGRAPHY. J. B. Lightfoot, *St Paul's Epistles to the Colossians and to Philemon*, 1879, pp. 29ff.

F.F.B.

EPAPHRODITUS. A Macedonian Christian from Philippi. There are no grounds for identifying him with Epaphras of Col. 1:7; 4:12, or Phm. 23. His name means 'comely' or 'charming'. Paul calls him 'your messenger' (*hymōn apostolon*, Phil. 2:25), where the word used is one more frequently translated elsewhere as 'apostle'. This does not mean that Epaphroditus held any office in the Philippian church; he was simply a messenger (*cf.* 2 Cor. 8:23) who brought the gift from the church to Paul in prison at Rome. He became seriously ill, possibly as a result of over-exerting himself in journeying from Philippi to Rome, or in serving Paul at Rome. The AV says 'he regarded not his life' (see Phil. 2:30), but RSV more correctly 'risking his life'. The word used is *paraboleusamenos*, 'having gambled with his life', from *paraboleuesthai* 'to throw down a stake, to make a venture'.

BIBLIOGRAPHY. J. Agar Beet, 'Epaphroditus and the gift from Philippi', *The Expositor*, 3rd Series, 9, 1889, pp. 64ff.; C. O. Buchanan, 'Epaphroditus' Sickness and the Letter to the Philippians', *EQ* 36, 1964, pp. 157ff.

D.O.S.

EPHESIANS, EPISTLE TO THE.

I. Outline of contents

This letter, in its form less restricted by particular controversial or pastoral needs than any other NT letter, stands as a wonderful declaration of the eternal purpose of God in Christ wrought out in his church (chs. 1–3), and of the practical consequences of that purpose (4–6).

a. God's eternal purposes for man in Christ, 1:1–3:21

1:1–2. Greeting.

1:3–14. Praise for all the spiritual blessings that come to men in Christ.

1:15–23. Thanksgiving for the readers' faith, and prayer for their experience of the wisdom and power of God.

2:1–10. God's purpose to raise men from the death of sin to new life in Christ.

2:11–22. His purpose to reconcile men not only to himself, but to one another—in particular to bring Jews and Gentiles together into the one people of God.

3:1–13. The privilege of the apostle's calling to preach the gospel to the Gentiles.

3:14–21. A second prayer, for the knowledge of the love of Christ, and his indwelling fullness; and a doxology.

b. Practical consequences, 4:1–6:24

4:1–16. Exhortation to walk worthily, and to work to build up the one body of Christ.

4:17–32. The old life of ignorance, lust and unrighteousness must be put off, and the new life of holiness put on.

5:1–21. A further call to live in love and purity, as children of light, full of praise and usefulness.

5:22–33. Instructions to wives and husbands, based on the analogy of the relationship between Christ and his church.

6:1–9. Instructions to children and parents, servants and masters.

6:10–20. Summons to Christian conflict in the armour of God and in his strength.

6:21–24. Concluding personal message.

II. Destination

Although the great majority of MSS and all the early VSS have the words 'at Ephesus' in 1:1, the 4th-century codices Vaticanus and Sinaiticus, the important corrector of the cursive 424, the cursive 1739, the papyrus 46 (dated AD 200) omit these words. Tertullian probably, Origen certainly, did not have them. Basil said they were lacking in the oldest MSS known to him. The heretic Marcion called this letter 'to the Laodiceans'. This small but very weighty evidence is supported by the evidence of the contents of the letter. It is difficult to explain such verses as 1:15; 3:2; 4:21, and the complete absence of personal greetings, if this were a letter addressed by Paul to Christians among whom he had laboured for 3 years (Acts 19:1–20 and 20:31). Yet it seems to have been addressed to a specific circle of Christians (1:15ff.; 6:21). The

ENSIGN
See Banner, Part 1.

ENVOY
See Ambassador, Part 1.

EPHAH
See Weights and measures, Part 3.

most likely interpretation of all the evidence is that the letter, if genuinely Paul's, was sent to a group of churches in Asia Minor (of which Ephesus was the greatest). Either one copy was sent to each in turn, the place-name being inserted in reading; or there may have been several copies with different addresses.

III. Authorship

There is abundant early evidence (perhaps going back to AD 95) of the use of this letter and from the end of the 2nd century we read of its unquestioned acceptance as the letter of Paul that it claims to be (1:1; 3:1). Since the end of the 18th century, however, the traditional authorship has been questioned. It is impossible here to do justice to the arguments for and against it. (They are set forward very fully, with opposite conclusions, in C. L. Mitton, *The Epistle to the Ephesians*, 1951, and A. van Roon, *The Authenticity of Ephesians*, 1974.) Very briefly the most important arguments against the genuineness of Ephesians are as follows:

1. Ephesians is not a real letter addressed to a particular situation like all the others we know as Paul's. It is more lyrical in style, full of participles and relatives, distinctive in its piling up of similar or related expressions. For the Pauline authorship it is argued that the absence of controversy accounts for the difference. We have here not the reasoned argument necessary in the other letters, but a 'prophetic declaration of incontrovertible, patent facts' (Dodd).

2. There are 42 words not otherwise used in the NT, and 44 more not used elsewhere by Paul. This argument can be assessed only by comparison with other Epistles, and by examining the words themselves. In the view of many the nature of the subject-matter sufficiently accounts for them.

3. It is urged that nowhere in Paul's writings have we such stress on the church and so little eschatology. Yet satisfying reasons can be given for the difference of emphasis, and in particular for the great exposition here of the part of the church in the eternal purpose of God.

4. Certain features and expressions are taken as indicative of a later date or another hand than that of the apostle, *e.g.* the reference to the 'holy apostles and prophets' (3:5; *cf.* 2:20), the treatment of the Gentile question and the self-abasement of 3:8. Each individual objection may be answered, though those who oppose the Pauline authorship urge the cumulative force of all the objections.

5. Other arguments are based on a comparison of Ephesians with other NT writings. This letter has more in common with non-Pauline writings (especially Luke and Acts, 1 Peter and the Johannine writings) than any other letter of the Pauline Corpus. Sometimes the resemblances in thought and expression are very striking, but rarely such as make literary dependence probable. They witness rather to a large common vocabulary, and perhaps also to a similar formalizing of teaching and belief in the early church in different places. (See E. G. Selwyn, *The First Epistle of St Peter*, 1946, pp. 363–466.) Most significant, however, is the extensive similarity in content, expression and even order of subject-matter between this letter and Colossians. It is almost universally accepted that Colossians is prior to Ephesians. Ephesians has the doctrine and exhortation of Colossians, only developed further. With the exception of 6:21f. and Col. 4:7f., there is no evidence of direct copying, but in Ephesians the same expressions are often used with a slightly different connotation; one passage in one letter resembles two in the other; one passage in Ephesians has a parallel in Colossians and also in another Pauline letter. To some these phenomena are the strongest arguments for the work of an imitator; in the view of others they make the apostolic authorship more sure.

IV. Purpose

Many scholars have opposed the Pauline authorship without giving any positive suggestion as to how the letter came to be written. Others have been more specific.

1. Some have seen it as 'an attempt to sum up and to recommend to a later generation the apostle's teaching' (M. Barth, *AB*, p. 57). E. J. Goodspeed, for example, sees it as written to introduce the collection of Paul's letters, the quintessence of Paul presented by one (Onesimus, he suggests) who was saturated in Paul's writings and Colossians most of all.

2. Others have seen a historical crisis in the life of the early church—the threat of Gnosticism, the threat to Christian unity, or the danger of a turning aside from the great Pauline doctrines—as calling forth this work, written in the name of the great apostle.

3. J. C. Kirby (*Ephesians: Baptism and Pentecost*, 1968) partly follows the views of others in drawing attention to a great deal of liturgical and didactic material in the Epistle, but goes further and gives reasons for thinking of Ephesians as the transformation into a letter of what basically was an annual covenant renewal service, held at the time of Pentecost, recalling to Christians the meaning of their baptism.

To many the arguments against the Pauline authorship appear strong. To some, one or another of the views of the suggested purposes seems attractive. Yet, as E. F. Scott puts it, the Epistle 'is everywhere marked by a grandeur and originality of thought which seems utterly beyond the reach of any mere imitator' (*MNTC*, p. 136). It is not easy to imagine a writer trying in Paul's name to present the essence of his theology and then turning to Colossians and quoting exactly the words of 4:7f. to give the impression that Ephesians was written at the same time as the letter to Colossae. It seems better to return to the Pauline authorship and reconstruct the situation that called forth Ephesians as follows.

Paul was a prisoner in Rome *c.* the year AD 61 (see *COLOSSIANS for other possibilities of the place of Paul's imprisonment at the time of writing). Onesimus, Philemon's runaway slave, had come to the apostle, been brought to faith in Christ and, with a letter from Paul, was being sent back to his master 'no longer as a slave, but more than a slave, as a beloved brother' (Phm. 16). At the same time the apostle had heard from Epaphras of the difficulties being faced, especially through false teaching, by the Colossian church. Thus when

Coin of Ephesus, Roman period, showing the statue of the goddess Diana (Artemis) enshrined within her temple there. c. AD 235. (BM)

Onesimus was returning to Colossae, Paul also sent Tychicus with a letter to that church, answering their problems and giving practical instructions concerning Christian living to Christians whom he had never met or taught personally. Writing thus to the Colossians, the apostle's mind was filled with the theme of the glory of Christ and his perfect provision for the life of men. Paul's thoughts turned to the other churches in the whole neighbourhood of Colossae, and, no longer having to deal with particular pastoral problems or doctrinal difficulties, he fulfilled his desire to express, in teaching and exhortation, in praise and prayer, the glory of the purpose of God in Christ and the responsibility of the church to make known that purpose by proclamation and by living in unity, love and purity. This letter was despatched with Philemon and Colossians, but sent to the various churches of the Roman province of Asia, of which Ephesus was one and indeed the most significant. In all probability this is the very letter that Paul in Col. 4:16 says that the Colossian Christians should receive 'from Laodicea'.

BIBLIOGRAPHY. T. K. Abbott, *The Epistles to the Ephesians and to the Colossians*, *ICC*, 1897; J. A. Robinson, *St Paul's Epistle to the Ephesians*, 1904; F. F. Bruce, *The Epistle to the Ephesians*, 1961; F. Foulkes, *The Epistle of Paul to the Ephesians*, *TNTC*, 1963; Markus Barth, *Ephesians*, *AB*, 1974.

F.F.

EPHESUS. The most important city in the Roman province of Asia, on the W coast of what is now Asiatic Turkey. It was situated at the mouth of the Caÿster River between the mountain range of Coressus and the sea. A magnificent road 11 m wide and lined with columns ran down through the city to the fine harbour, which served both as a great export centre at the end of the Asiatic caravan-route and also as a natural landing-point from Rome. The city, now uninhabited, has been undergoing excavation for many years, and is probably the most extensive and impressive ruined site of Asia Minor. The sea is now some 10 km away, owing to the silting process which has been at work for centuries. The harbour had to undergo extensive clearing operations at various times from the 2nd century BC; is that, perhaps, why Paul had to stop at Miletus (Acts 20:15–16)? The main part of the city, with its theatre, baths, library, agora and paved streets, lay between the Coressus ridge and the Caÿster, but the temple for which it was famed lay over 2 km to the NE. This site was originally sacred to the worship of the Anatolian fertility goddess, later identified with Greek Artemis and Latin Diana. Justinian built a church to St John on the hill nearby (hence the later name Ayasoluk—a corruption of *hagios theologos*), which was itself succeeded by a Seljuk mosque. The neighbouring settlement is now called Selçuk.

The original Anatolian settlement was augmented before the 10th century BC by Ionian colonists, and a joint city was set up. The goddess of Ephesus took a Greek name, but clearly retained her earlier characteristics, for she was repeatedly represented at later periods as a many-breasted figure. Ephesus was conquered by Croesus shortly after his accession in *c.* 560 BC, and owed some of its artistic glories to his munificence. After his fall in 546 it came under Persian rule. Croesus shifted the site of the archaic city to focus upon the temple of Artemis: Lysimachus, one of the successors of Alexander, forcibly replanted it about the harbour early in the 3rd century BC. Ephesus later formed part of the kingdom of Pergamum, which Attalus III bequeathed to Rome in 133 BC. It became the greatest commercial city of the Roman province of Asia. It then occupied a vast area, and its population may have numbered a third of a million. It is estimated that the great theatre built into Mt Pion in the centre of the city had a capacity of about 25,000.

Ephesus also maintained its religious importance under Roman rule. It became a centre of the emperor cult, and eventually possessed three official temples, thus qualifying thrice over for the proud title *neōkoros* ('temple-warden') of the emperors, as well as being *neōkoros* of Artemis (Acts 19:35). It is remarkable that Paul had friends among the *Asiarchs (*Asiarchai*, Acts 19:31), who were officers of the 'commune' of Asia, whose primary function was actually to foster the imperial cult.

The temple of Artemis itself had been rebuilt after a great fire in 356 BC, and ranked as one of the seven wonders of the world until its destruction by the Goths in AD 263. After years of patient search J. T. Wood in 1870 uncovered its remains in the marsh at the foot of Mt Ayasoluk. It had been the largest building in the Greek world. It contained an image of the goddess which, it was claimed, had fallen from heaven (*cf.* Acts 19:35). Indeed, it may well have been a meteorite originally. Silver coins from many places show the validity of the claim that the goddess of Ephesus was revered all over the world (Acts 19:27). They bear the inscription *Diana Ephesia* (*cf.* Acts 19:34).

There was a large colony of Jews at Ephesus, and they had long enjoyed a privileged position under Roman rule (Jos., *Ant.* 14. 225ff.; 14. 262ff.). The earliest reference to the coming of Christianity there is in *c.* AD 52, when Paul made a short visit and left Aquila and Priscilla there (Acts 18:18–21). Paul's third missionary journey had Ephesus as its goal, and he stayed there for over 2 years (Acts 19:8, 10), attracted, no doubt, by its strategic importance as a commercial, political and religious centre. His work was at first based on the synagogue: later he debated in the lecture-hall of Tyrannus, making of Ephesus a base for the evangelization of the whole province of Asia. The spread of Christianity, which refused syncretism, began to incur the hostility of vested religious interests. It affected not only the magic cults which flourished there (Acts 19:13ff.—one kind of magic formula was actually called *Ephesia grammata*) but also the worship of Artemis (Acts 19:27), causing damage to the trade in cult objects which was one source of the prosperity of Ephesus. There followed the celebrated riot described in Acts 19. Inscriptions show that the *grammateus* ('town clerk') who gained control of the assembly on this occasion was the leading civic official, directly responsible to the Romans for such breaches of the peace as illicit assembly (Acts 19:40). It has been suggested that his assertion 'there are proconsuls' (19:38), if it is not a generalizing plural, may fix the date with some precision. On Nero's accession in AD 54, M. Junius Silvanus, the proconsul of Asia, was poisoned by his subordinates Helius and Celer, who acted as proconsuls until the arrival of a regular successor.

Christianity evidently spread to

Ephesus, Turkey: the Arcadian Way leading to the theatre. This was constructed during the Hellenistic period (3rd–2nd cent. BC*), but altered in the reigns of Claudius (*AD *41–54), Nero (*AD *54–68) and Trajan (*AD *98–117). The auditorium seated 24,000 persons.* (SH)

Opposite page: Plan showing the main buildings of Ephesus so far recovered. The city was destroyed by the Goths in AD *263.*

*Colossae and the other cities of the Lycus valley at the period of Paul's stay in Ephesus (*cf.* Col. 1:6–7; 2:1). It was Paul's headquarters for most of the time of the Corinthian controversy and correspondence (1 Cor. 16:8), and the experience which he describes as 'fighting with wild beasts' happened there (1 Cor. 15:32). This seems to be a metaphorical allusion to something already known to the Corinthians, perhaps mob violence. (There was no amphitheatre at Ephesus, though the stadium was later adapted to accommodate beast-fighting.) G. S. Duncan (*St Paul's Ephesian Ministry*, 1929) has maintained that Paul was imprisoned two or three times at Ephesus, and that all the captivity Epistles were written from there and not from Rome. E. J. Goodspeed (*INT*, 1937), followed by C. L. Mitton and J. Knox, have located at Ephesus the collection of the Pauline Corpus of letters. There are difficulties in the hypothesis of an Ephesian imprisonment which suits the case, and although B. Reicke and J. A. T. Robinson have recently revived the idea that some or all of the captivity Epistles were written from Caesarea, it remains preferable to place them in Rome (see C. H. Dodd, *BJRL* 18, 1934, pp. 72–92).

After Paul's departure Timothy was left at Ephesus (1 Tim. 1:3). The Pastorals give a glimpse of the period of consolidation there. It is thought by many that Rom. 16 was originally addressed by Paul to Ephesus.

The city was later the headquarters of the John who had jurisdiction over the seven leading churches of Asia addressed in the Apocalypse. The church in Ephesus is addressed first of the seven (Rev. 2:1–7), as being the most important church in the *de facto* capital, and as being the landing-place for a messenger from Patmos and standing at the head of a circular road joining the seven cities in order. This church is flourishing, but is troubled by false teachers, and has lost its 'first love'. The false apostles (2:2) are most probably like the *Nicolaitans, who seem to have advocated compromise with the power of paganism for the Christian under pressure. The Ephesians were steadfast, but deficient in love. Ramsay characterized Ephesus as the 'city of change'. Its problems were the problems of a successful church coping with changing circumstances: the city too had had a long history of shifting sites (*cf.* 2:5b). The promise of eating of the tree of life is here probably set against the background of the sacred date-palm of Artemis, which figures on Ephesian coins.

According to Irenaeus and Eusebius, Ephesus became the home of John the apostle. A generation after his time Ignatius wrote of the continuing fame and faithfulness of the Ephesian church (*Ephesians* 8–9). The third General Council took place here in AD 431 to condemn Nestorian Christology, and sat in the double church of St Mary, the ruins of which are still to be seen. The city declined, and the progressive silting of its gulf finally severed it wholly from the sea.

BIBLIOGRAPHY. W. M. Ramsay, *The Letters to the Seven Churches*, 1904; J. T. Wood, *Modern Discoveries on the Site of Ancient Ephesus*, 1890; D. G. Hogarth, *Excavations at Ephesus: the Archaic Artemisia*, 1908; *RE*, *'Ephesos'*; G. E. Bean, *Aegean Turkey. An Archaeological Guide*, 1966; E. Akurgal, *The Ancient Ruins and Civilisations of Turkey*, 1973.

E.M.B.G.
C.J.H.

EPHPHATHA. The actual word addressed by Jesus to the deaf man (Mk. 7:34). It is probably an Aramaic imperative transliterated into Greek, and the Evangelist adds the translation (in Greek), 'be opened'. The Aramaic verb used is *p*^{e}*ṯaḥ*, 'to open'; it is not certain whether the simple passive (ethpeel) or intensive passive (ethpaal) was employed. The former form would be *'eṯp*^{e}*ṯaḥ*, the latter *'eṯpattaḥ*. It seems that in either case the *ṯ* was assimilated to the *p̄*; this is a regular feature of later Aramaic and its dialects (*e.g.* Syriac). An alternative possibility is that the word is Hebrew (niphal conjugation).

BIBLIOGRAPHY. S. Morag, *JSS* 17, 1972, pp. 198–202. D.F.P.

EPHRAIM. The second son of Joseph, born to him by Asenath, the daughter of Potipherah, before the years of famine came (Gn. 41:50–52). The sick Jacob acknowledged the two sons of Joseph (Gn. 48:5), blessing Ephraim with his right hand and Manasseh with his left (vv. 13–14), thus signifying that Ephraim would become the greater people (v. 19).

In the order of the tribes in the wilderness encampment the standard of Ephraim's camp was on the W side (Nu. 2:18). From the tribe of Ephraim Elishama was to stand with Moses (Nu. 1:10), and Joshua the son of Nun, one of the spies, was descended from Ephraim (Nu. 13:8). He was chosen with Eleazar the priest to divide the land (Nu. 34:17). Ephraim is also included in the blessing of Moses.

Under the valiant leadership of Joshua, Ephraim with the other tribes received its inheritance, which is described in Jos. 16. The territory may be roughly identified as follows. Proceeding W from Gilgal we come to Bethel, then to lower Beth-horon, W to Gezer, then N to Lod and W towards the sea, N to the Qanah river and then E to Tappuah, Janobah, Taanath-shiloh to Ataroth, then S to Nasrath and Gilgal.

From the beginning the tribe of Ephraim occupied a position of prestige and significance. It complained to Gideon that he had not called it to fight against the Midianites. His reply reveals the superior position of Ephraim. 'Is not the gleaning of the grapes of Ephraim better than the vintage of Abi-ezer?' (Jdg. 8:2). The men of Ephraim complained again in similar terms to Jephthah, and this led to war between the Ephraimites and the Gileadites.

The prestige of Ephraim kept it from looking with favour upon Judah. After the death of Saul, Abner, Saul's captain, made Eshbaal king over the N tribes, including Ephraim. Because of the Philistine domination, however, Eshbaal's authority was effectively limited to Transjordan. He reigned for 2 years, but Judah followed David (2 Sa. 2:8ff.). After Eshbaal's death the N tribes invited David to become their king.

Later David learnt that Israel followed after Absalom. The N tribes never did desire to yield to David's reign, but David grew continually greater and stronger. Under Solomon the S kingdom reached the pinnacle of splendour and prosperity. Nevertheless, even at this time, there was discontent in the N (1 Ki. 11:26ff.).

Rehoboam's folly provided the necessary pretext, and the N revolted, renouncing all claim to the promises made to David (1 Ki. 12:16). Nevertheless, God continued to send his prophets to the N kingdom, and one of the characteristics of the Messianic kingdom is to be the healing of the tragic schism introduced by Jeroboam the son of Nebat (*cf.* Ho. 1:11; Is. 11:13). Even when exile has overtaken the S as well as the N kingdom, Ephraim retains a special place: 'I am a father to Israel, and Ephraim is my first-born' (Je. 31:9).

E.J.Y.
F.F.B.

EPHRAIM (geographical). The boundaries of Ephraim are recorded in Jos. 16, and with Manasseh in Jos. 17. Only some of the main topographical features of these boundaries have so far been determined beyond dispute; most

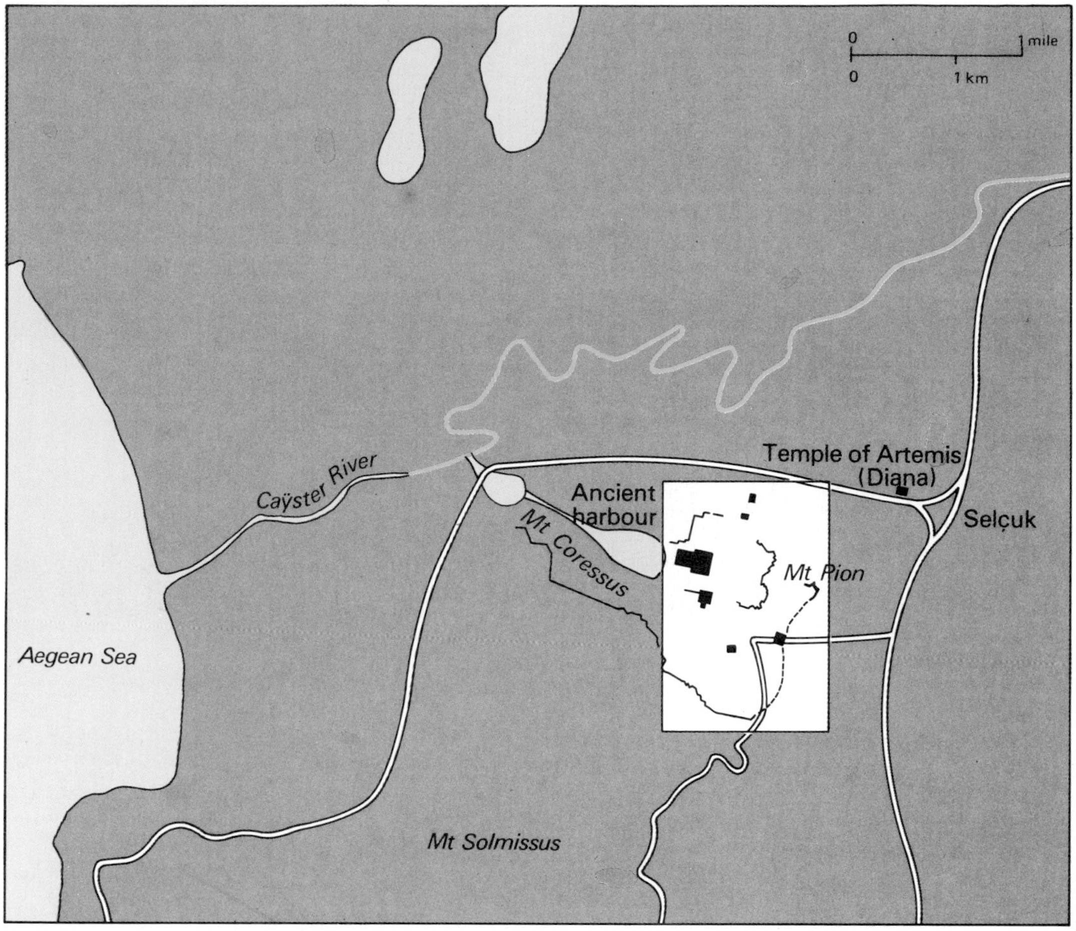

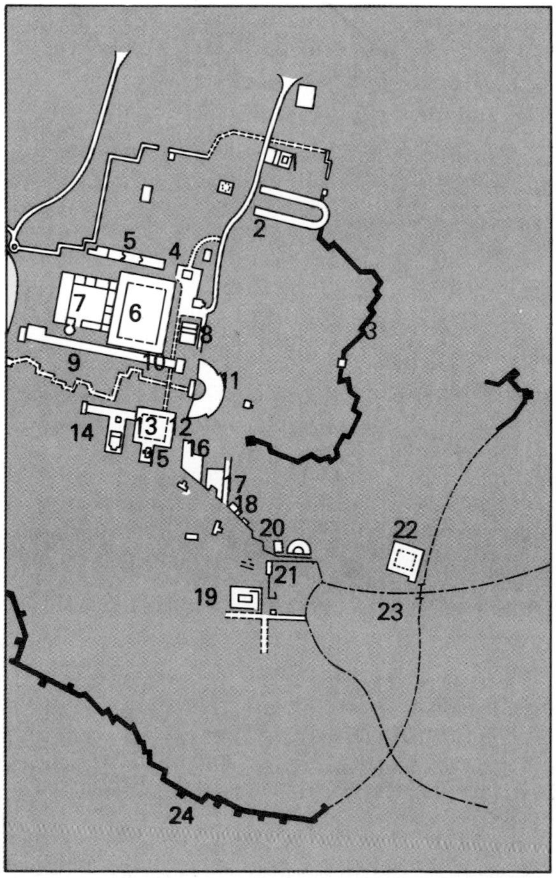
1 Vedius gymnasium
2 Stadium
3 City wall
4 Byzantine baths
5 Church of the Virgin Mary
6, 7 Harbour gymnasium and baths
8 Theatre gymnasium
9 Arkadiane
10 Fountain
11 Theatre
12 Marble road
13 Commercial agora (market place)
14 Temple of Serapis
15 Celsus library
16 Scholastika baths
17 Temple of Hadrian
18 Trajan's fountain
19 Temple of Domitian
20 Town hall and temple of Hestia Boulaia
21 North stoa of agora
22 East gymnasium
23 Magnesian gate
24 City wall

The mountains of Ephraim. (RS)

of the places mentioned cannot be precisely located at present.

The S boundary of Ephraim is most clearly expressed in Jos. 16:1–3, where, however, it is given as the (S) boundary of 'the children of Joseph', *i.e.* Ephraim-Manasseh. But as Manasseh was situated wholly to the N and NE of Ephraim, this boundary is, in practice, that of Ephraim. It ran (E to W) up from the Jordan and Jericho inland to Bethel (Beitin, *c.* 16 km N of Jerusalem), Luz (?near by) and Ataroth (site uncertain), then *via* the border of Lower Beth-horon to Gezer—well-known site—and the Mediterranean sea-coast (Jos. 16:1–3). V. 5 is difficult, but may perhaps further define part of this S boundary.

The N boundary from a point Michmetha(t)h (16:6) 'before Shechem' (17:7) turned W; its course in that direction ran from Tappuah (location still disputed) to and along the brook of Qanah (perhaps the present Wadi Qānah, which joins Wadi Aujah, and reaches the Mediterranean *c.* 6½ km N of Joppa) to the sea (16:8). E from Michmetha(t)h, the border turned by Taanath-shiloh (S) along the E of Janoah to (another) Ataroth, Naarah, and back to Jericho and the Jordan (16:6–7). On the N, Shechem apparently was within Ephraim's share, to judge from the levitical city-lists (Jos. 21:20–21; 1 Ch. 6:67).

The region in central W Palestine that fell to Ephraim is mainly relatively high hill-country with better rainfall than Judaea and some good soils; hence some biblical references to the fruitfulness of the Ephraim district. The Ephraimites had direct but not over-easy access to the great N–S trunk road through the W plain.

Bibliography. D. Baly, *The Geography of the Bible*², 1974, pp. 164–176; J. Simons, *The Geographical and Topographical Texts of the Old Testament*, 1959, pp. 158–169; Y. Kaufmann, *The Biblical Account of the Conquest of Palestine*, 1953, pp. 28–36; and E. Jenni, *Zeitschrift des Deutschen Palästina-Vereins* 74, 1958, pp. 35–40, with some detailed bibliography. Also F. M. Abel, *Géographie de la Palestine*, 1–2, 1933–8.

K.A.K.

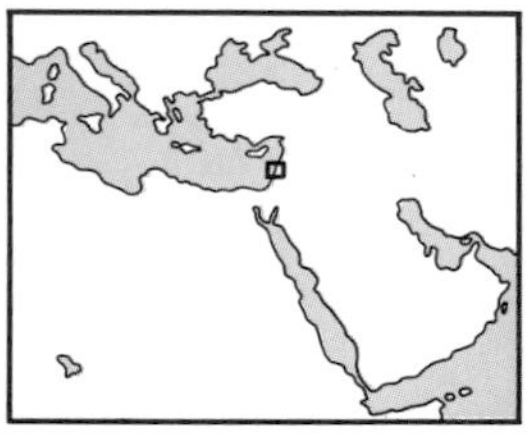

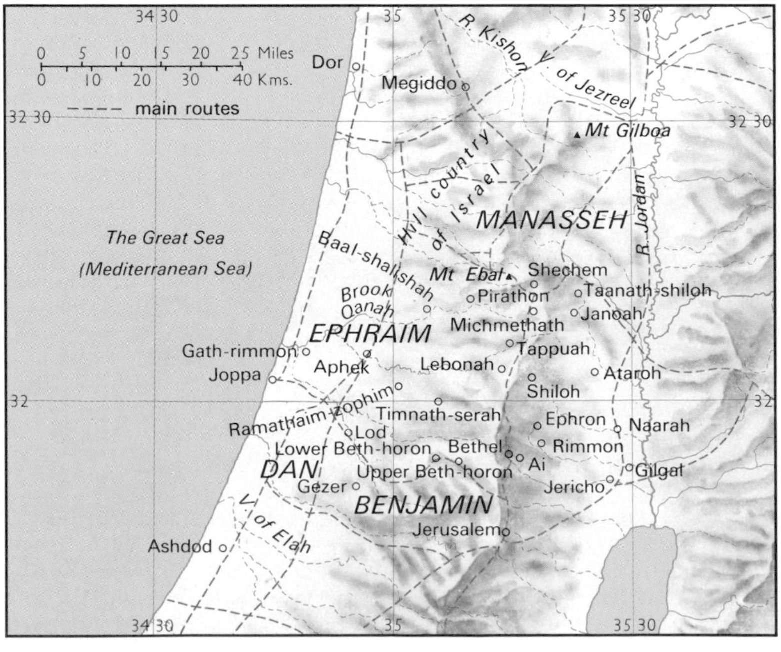

The hilly lands allotted to Ephraim, in central W Palestine.

EPHRATH, EPHRATHAH.

1. The ancient name of *Bethlehem Judah, which occurs in all cases but one (Gn. 48:7, *'eprāṯ*) in the form *'eprāṯâ*. Rachel was buried on the route there from Bethel (Gn. 35:16, 19; 48:7; *cf.* 1 Sa. 10:2); it was the home of Naomi's family (Ru. 4:11), who are described as Ephrathites (*'eprāṯî*, Ru. 1:2), of Ruth's descendant David (1 Sa. 17:12; *cf.* Ps. 132:6), and of the Messiah, as foretold in Mi. 5:2.

2. The gentilic *'eprāṯî* is applied three times to Ephraimites (Jdg. 12:5; 1 Sa. 1:1; 1 Ki. 11:26).

3. The second wife of Caleb the son of Hezron (1 Ch. 2:19, 50; 4:4; *cf.* 2:24). T.C.M.

EPHRON. 1. Name of a 'son of Heth' (Hittite or Syrian), a son of Zohar from whom Abraham bought the cave of Machpelah as a burial-place for Sarah (Gn. 23:8; 25:9; 49:30). A similar type name (Apran) is known from *Alalaḫ, Syria. **2.** A hill area between Nephtoah and *Kiriath-jearim which marked the border of Judah (Jos. 15:9; 18:15, RSV amended text). **3.** A place near *Bethel taken by Abijah from Jeroboam I (2 Ch. 13:19). RSV 'Ephron'; *MT* 'Ephrain', AV 'Ephraim'; *cf.* 2 Sa. 13:23) to be identified with Ophrah (Jos. 18:23). Perhaps a word meaning 'province' (*VT* 12, 1962, p. 339). Generally identified as et-Taiyibeh *c.* 7 km NE of Bethel. **4.** A fort between Ashtoreth-karnaim

(Carmion) and Beth-shan (Scythopolis) captured by Judas Maccabaeus (1 Macc. 5:46–52; 2 Macc. 12:27–29; Jos., *Ant.* 12. 346). Possibly the modern et-Taiybeh SE of Galilee. D.J.W.

EPICUREANS. Some of the philosophers whom Paul encountered at Athens (Acts 17:18) were of this school, whose best-known disciple is the Roman poet Lucretius. The founder, Epicurus, was born in 341 BC on the island of Samos. His early studies under Nausiphanes, a disciple of Democritus, taught him to regard the world as the result of the random motion and combination of atomic particles. He lived for a time in exile and poverty. Gradually he gathered round him a circle of friends and began to teach his distinctive doctrines. In 306 he established himself in Athens at the famous 'Garden' which became the headquarters of the school. He died in 270 after great suffering from an internal complaint, but in peace of mind.

The founder's experiences, coupled with the general uncertainty of life in the last centuries before Christ, gave a special stamp to the Epicurean teachings. The whole system had a practical end in view, the achievement of happiness by serene detachment. Democritean atomism banished all fear of divine intervention in life or punishment after death; the gods follow to perfection the life of serene detachment and will have nothing to do with human existence, and death brings a final dispersion of our constituent atoms.

The Epicureans found contentment in limiting desire and in the joys and solaces of friendship. The pursuit of extravagant pleasure which gives to 'epicure' its modern connotation was a late perversion of their quest for happiness.

It is easy to see why the Epicureans found Paul's teaching about the resurrection strange and unpalatable. Jewish rabbis use the word *apiqôrôs* to mean one who denies life after death, and later as a synonym for 'infidel'.

BIBLIOGRAPHY. Usener, *Epicurea*, 1887; A. J. Festugière, *Epicurus and his Gods*, E.T. 1955; N. W. de Witt, *Epicurus and his Philosophy*, 1954. M.H.C.

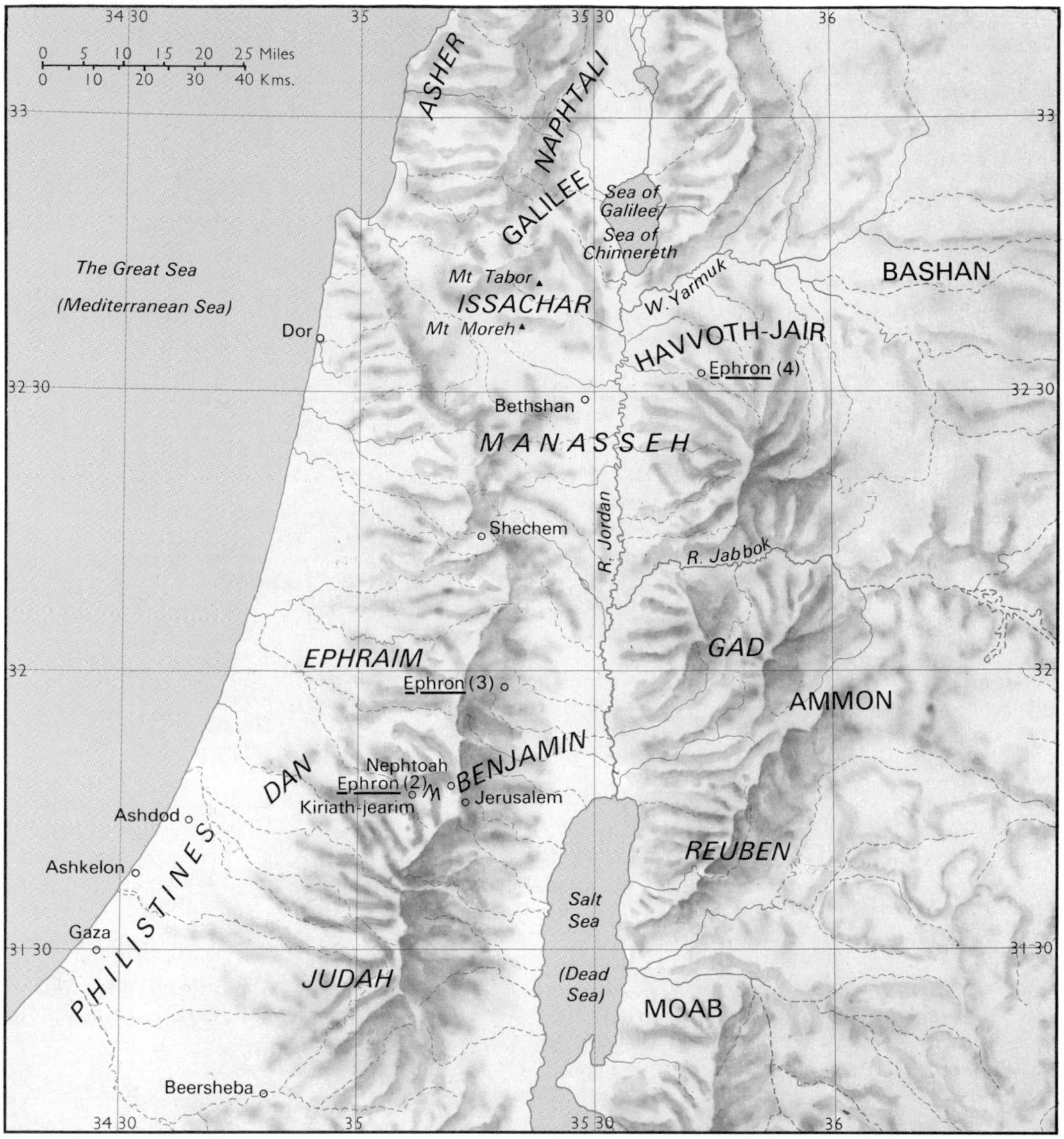

Three places bearing the name Ephron: on the border of Judah, near Bethel and near Beth-shan.

EPISTLE. Gk. *epistolē* and Lat. *epistula* represent a letter of any kind: originally simply a written communication between persons apart, whether personal and private or official. In this sense epistles are a part of the heritage of all literate peoples, and examples are to be found in the OT (2 Sa. 11; 1 Ki. 21; 2 Ki. 5; 10; 20; 2 Ch. 30; 32; Ezr. 4–5; 7; Ne. 2; 6; Est. 1; 3; 8–9; Is. 37; 39; Je. 29) and in the Greek papyri from Egypt (*cf.* all the large published collections of papyri, *passim*, and especially the Zenon correspondence). Such a letter was described by Demetrius, *Typoi epistolikoi* (1st century BC), as a written conversation, while Demetrius, *On Style* 3. 223ff., quotes Artemon, the ancient collector of Aristotle's letters, as calling it half a dialogue.

But the earliest collections of Greek letters generally regarded as genuine, in part at least, those of Isocrates and Plato, already show a tendency to use letters, or the letter-form, for larger purposes than mere private or official communication; so that among Isocrates' letters (368–338 BC) some are set speeches, or introductions to speeches, and Plato's Seventh Letter (*c.* 354 BC) is a refutation of popular misconceptions about his philosophy and conduct. In both cases the letters aim at other readers than those addressed, and are thus a form of publication. Compare here present-day letters 'to the Editor of *The Times*'.

Despite a feeling often hinted at, and sometimes expressed, that such letters have neither the size nor the subject-matter of true letters, but are rather 'writings with "greetings" added' (Demetrius, *On Style*, *loc. cit.*), the epistolary form continued to be used for philosophical, scientific and literary publication (*e.g.* Epicurus, *Epistles*, and the three literary letters of Dionysius of

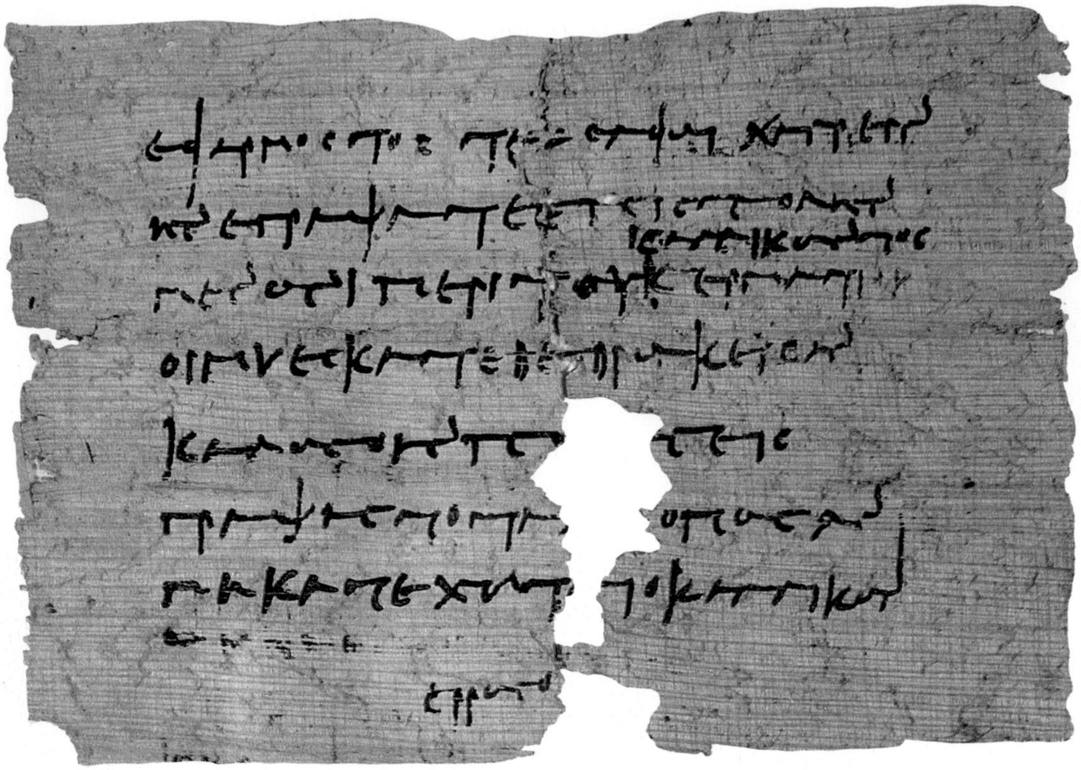

A letter from Epharmostos to his brother Zenon. 'The letter you wrote to Menon about Kallikon's money has been eaten by mice. Please write as soon as possible so that Kallikon may not be delayed.' 9 cm × 12·9 cm. 3rd cent. BC. (BL)

Aramaic papyrus from Assuan rolled and sealed for despatch. It shows how Paul's letters might have been carried. Date unknown. (BM)

Halicarnassus). The theory and practice of letter-writing came to be treated by the teachers of rhetoric (*e.g.* Demetrius, *On Style*; *idem*, *Typoi epistolikoi*), and letter-writing in the characters of famous men formed part of the rhetorical school exercise of *prosōpopoeia.* The growth in Hellenistic and Roman times of collections of fictitous letters may be attributed to such exercises, and to the eagerness of the great libraries to buy additional works, especially of famous men.

G. A. Deissmann, confronted by the simplicity of most letters in the papyri, maintained a sharp distinction between 'genuine letters' as personal, direct, transient and un-literary, and 'epistles' as impersonal, aimed at a reading public and permanence, and literary. Feeling an undeniable similarity between certain elements in the NT Epistles and the papyri, he classed most of Paul's Epistles and 2 and 3 John as letters, Hebrews, James, 1 and 2 Peter, Jude and Revelation as epistles, and 1 John as a *diatribē* (*LAE*[3], ch. 3, pp. 148–251). But the distinction cannot be so sharply maintained, as there are different degrees of 'literariness', sorts and sizes of 'public', and kinds of publication.

Of the Pauline letters to churches, those to the Corinthians, Galatians, Philippians and Thessalonians contain most personal elements, Romans fewer, and Ephesians and Colossians least of all. Galatians and Ephesians are composed on a rhetorical plan, and all of them have considerable rhetorical elements. In the Pastoral Epistles the personal references are fairly numerous and rhetorical elements comparatively few. Philemon, rightly regarded by Deissmann as the most personal letter in the NT, and compared to British Museum Papyrus 417, is nevertheless very cleverly written and contains rhetorical elements noticeable especially when considered beside Isocrates, *Ep.* 8, and Demetrius, *Typoi epistolikoi* 12. Hebrews is the most artistic literary writing in the NT, being composed from beginning to end on the pattern of *proem*, *thesis*, *diēgēsis*, *apodeixis*, *epilogue*, laid down by Greek rhetoricians, and is written in rhythmic, periodic prose. In James, 1 and 2 Peter and Jude there are very few personal references; all are literary, especially 1 Peter; and 2 Peter and Jude are definitely rhetorical. 2 and 3 John appear as private communications, while 1 John is not, as we have it, in letter-form at all. Thus most of the NT Epistles show a greater or smaller affinity with preaching; some may be classed as sent sermons, while in others the letter-elements are a more literary form.

BIBLIOGRAPHY. *LAE*, pp. 146ff.; R. Hercher, *Epistolographi Graeci*, 1872; J. Sykutris, *Epistolographie*, in *RE*, Supp. 5, pp. 185–220; V. Weichert (ed.), *Demetrii et Libanii qui feruntur Typoi Epistolikoi et Epistolimaioi Characteres* (Teubner), 1910; O. Roller, *Das Formular der Paulinischen Briefe*, 1933; M. Dibelius, *A Fresh Approach to the New Testament and Early Christian Literature*, E. T. 1936, pp. 137–171, 185–189, 194–197, 205–213, 226–234.

J.H.H.

ERASTUS. 1. An assistant of Paul, who shared Timothy's mission to Macedonia to allow Paul to continue working from Ephesus (Acts 19:22). The mission may have been directed ultimately to Corinth (*cf.* 1 Cor. 4:17), and Erastus been one of the 'brethren' of 2 Cor. 8; but certainty is impossible. Undoubtedly, however, he is the Erastus mentioned as staying at Corinth in 2 Tim. 4:20.

2. City-treasurer (not 'chamberlain' as AV) of Corinth, sending greetings in Rom. 16:23 (*QUARTUS). A Lat. inscription found at Corinth states, 'Erastus laid this pavement at his own expense, in appreciation of his appointment as aedile.' Many (*e.g.* Broneer) accept the identification with the Christian city treasurer.

Some further identify **1** and **2**: G. S. Duncan, for example, sug-

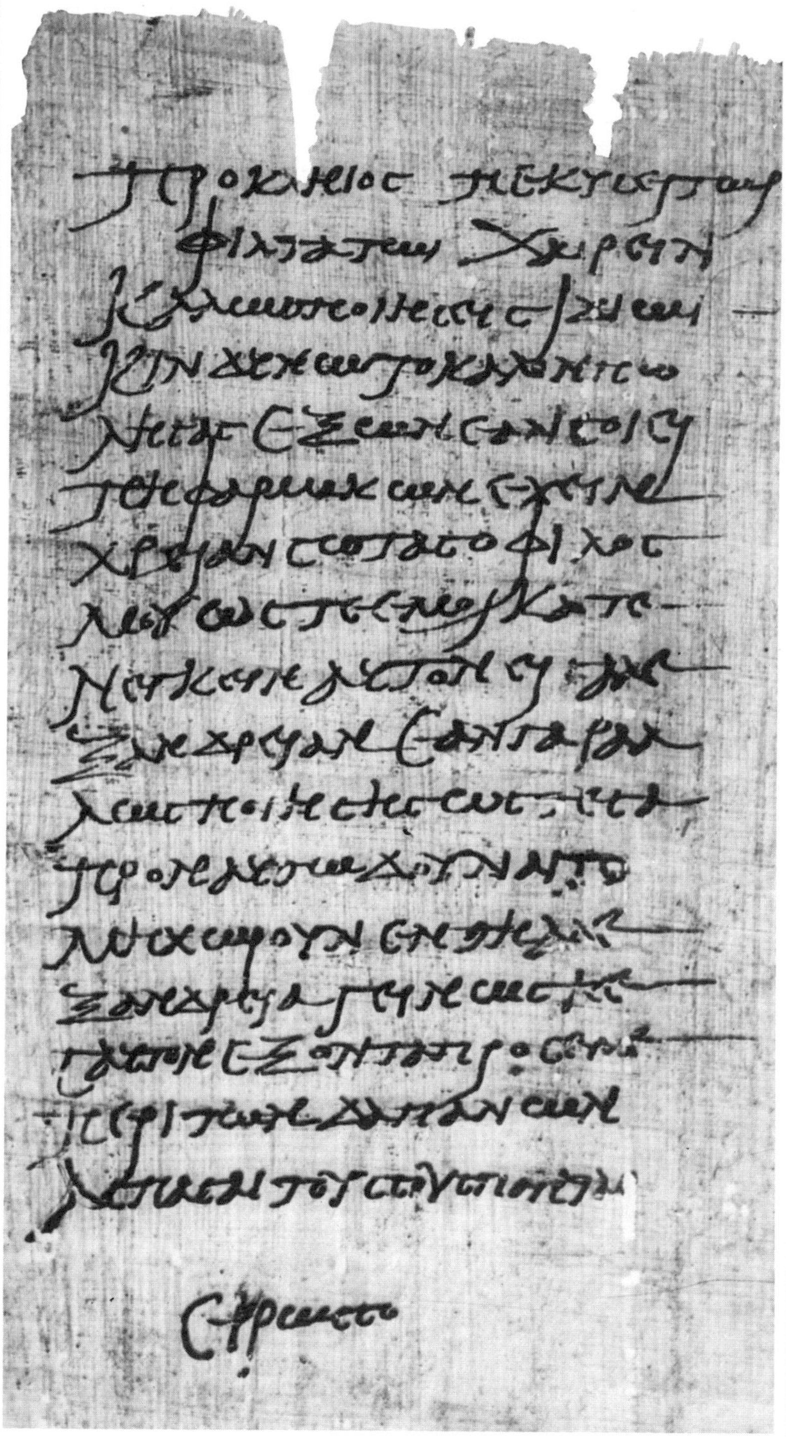

A typical letter written in a large, semi-cursive hand. Procleius asks Pecusis to send him some drugs to Alexandria by the hand of his friend Sotas. Width c. 10 cm. 1st cent. AD. (BM)

gests that 2 Tim. 4:20 indicates that Erastus, unlike Timothy, completed the journey to Corinth, where he became treasurer a year or so later (*St Paul's Ephesian Ministry*, pp. 79ff.); but such a rapid rise to power is most unlikely, and the name is quite common.

BIBLIOGRAPHY. H. J. Cadbury, *JBL* 50, 1931, pp. 42ff.; O. Broneer, *BA* 14, 1951, pp. 78ff., especially p. 94; P. N. Harrison, *Paulines and Pastorals*, 1964, pp. 100–105.

A.F.W.

ERECH. An ancient city of Mesopotamia mentioned in the Table of Nations (Gn. 10:10) as one of the possessions of Nimrod in the land of *Shinar. Known to the Sumerians as *Unu*(*g*) and to the Akkadians as *Uruk*, it was one of the great cities of Sumerian times. It is named in the Sumerian king list as the seat of the 2nd Dynasty after the Flood, one of whose kings was Gilgamesh, who later became one of the great heroes of Sumerian legend. Though the city continued in occupation during later periods (Gk. *Orchoē*), it never surpassed its early importance. Uruk is represented today by the group of mounds known to the Arabs as *Warka*, which lies in S Babylonia some 64 km NW of Ur and 6 km E of the present course of the *Euphrates. While the site was investigated over a century ago by W. K. Loftus (*Travels and Researches in Chaldaea and Susiana*, 1857), the principal excavations have been conducted by a series of German expeditions in 1912, 1928–39 and 1954–60. The results are of outstanding importance for the early history of Mesopotamia. Prehistoric remains of the Ubaid Period (*SUMER) were followed by monumental architecture and stone sculpture of the Late Prehistoric Period which richly illustrate the material culture of Mesopotamia at the beginning of history. It was in these levels, dating from the 4th millennium BC, that the earliest inscriptions so far known were found. These are in the form of clay tablets, and, though the signs are only pictographic, it is probable that the language behind

A fine head of a woman, almost life-size, carved in white stone. Originally the eyes and eyebrows were inlaid with coloured stones and a wig fitted to the groove in the head. From Erech (*Warka, Iraq*). *c. 3000* BC. (RH)

them was Sumerian.

BIBLIOGRAPHY. R. North, 'Status of the Warka Excavations', *Orientalia* n.s. 26, 1957, pp. 185–256.

T.C.M.

ESARHADDON (Heb. *'esarhaddōn*; Assyr. *Aššur-aḫ-iddin*, 'Ashur has given a brother') was king of Assyria and Babylonia 681–669 BC. He succeeded his father Sennacherib who was murdered in Tebet in 681 BC (2 Ki. 19:37; Is. 37:38). His first act was to pursue the murderers as far as Hanigalbat (S Armenia) and to quash the rebellion in Nineveh, which lasted 6 weeks. There is little support for the theory that Esarhaddon was the head of a pro-Babylonian faction or 'the son' mentioned in the Bab. Chronicle as the murderer (*DOTT*, pp. 70–73). His own inscriptions tell how he had been made crown-prince by his father earlier in the year, and though he had been viceroy in Babylon his attention to the religious centre was merely in keeping with his care for all the ancient shrines. His early military operations were designed to safeguard the N frontier and trade-routes against the warlike Ṭeušpa and the incursions of the Cimmerians (*GOMER), whom he defeated. In the S the Elamites, who had been defeated by his father, once more stirred up the tribes of S Babylonia, and Esarhaddon was forced to campaign against the 'sea-lands' where he installed Na'id-Marduk, son of *Merodach-baladan, as the local sheikh in 678 BC. His clashes with Elam and the Babylonians re-

Stele of Esarhaddon (681–669 BC) which tells how the gods punished Babylon, then relented and allowed Esarhaddon to rebuild the city. Height c. 22 cm. (BM)

A stele showing Esarhaddon, king of Assyria, 681–669 BC. He holds by a leash Tirhakah (Taharqa), king of Egypt and Ethiopia, and a bearded captive, possibly Ba'ali, king of Tyre. Above him are the symbols of the principal deities of the Assyrian pantheon. Diorite. Height c. 3·2 m. From Zenjirli. (SMB)

Walls and columns were decorated with mosaics made up of coloured terracotta cones (red, blue, orange and black) embedded in the plaster to form patterns. Erech (Warka, Iraq). c. 2900 BC. (BM) (SMB)

sulted in the deportation of many captives, some of whom were settled in Samaria (Ezr. 4:2).

In the W Esarhaddon continued his father's policy. He exacted heavy tribute from the vassal kings of Syria and Palestine, listing Manasseh (*Menasī*) of Judah (*Yaudi*) after Ba'ali of Tyre, with whom he concluded a treaty, having failed to isolate and thus subdue the port. The rulers of Edom, Moab and Ammon were made vassals after a series of raids on their territory in which he sought to counter the influence of Tirhakah of Egypt, who had incited a number of the Philistine cities to revolt. Esarhaddon sacked Sidon in 676 BC, after a 3-year siege, and incorporated part of its territory into an extended Assyrian province (probably including Samaria). Some of the refugees from the city were housed in a new town, Kār-Esarhaddon, built near by. About this time Gaza and Ashkelon were counted among his vassals.

The subordinate kingdoms in Syria and Palestine were called upon to provide materials for Esarhaddon's building operations in Assyria and in Babylon, which he now sought to revive after earlier changes of fortune. This may explain the temporary detention of Manasseh in Babylon (2 Ch. 33:11). Assyrian letters referring to tribute in silver received from Judah, Moab and Edom may be assigned to this time.

In May 672 BC Esarhaddon brought all the vassal-kings together to acknowledge his arrangements to ensure that the succession to the throne was less disturbed than his own. *Ashurbanipal was declared to be crown-prince or heir to Assyria and Šamaš-šum-ukin to Babylonia. Copies of the treaty imposed on the Median city-chiefs on this occasion, found at Calah (Nimrud), show the provisions to which all, including Manasseh,

Excavations at Erech revealed city walls, two ziggurats and temples from the late 4th and early 3rd millennia BC as well as examples of the earliest written documents using a pictographic script. (RH)

would have had to assent. They declared their loyalty to the Assyrian national god Ashur and their willingness to serve Assyria for ever. History tells how soon all the client kings broke their oaths.

Having gained control of the W, Esarhaddon subdued Egypt, defeated Tirhakah, besieged Memphis and counted the land as an Assyrian dependency under Necho. When the victorious army was withdrawn, local intrigues developed into open revolt. While Esarhaddon was on his way to deal with this in 669 BC he died at Harran, leaving five surviving sons and one daughter. His mother, the forceful wife of Sennacherib (Naqi'a-Zakutu), also survived him.

BIBLIOGRAPHY. R. Borger, *Die Inschriften Asarhaddons Königs von Assyrien*, 1956; D. J. Wiseman, *The Vassal-Treaties of Esarhaddon*, 1958.

D.J.W.

ESAU. Esau was the elder of Isaac's twin sons (Gn. 25:21–26). His relations with Jacob his brother are the subject of the well-known stories in Gn. 25:27–34; 27:1ff.; 32:3–12; 33:1–16. Esau was his father's favourite son, and it was Isaac's intention to impart to him the blessing that was the eldest son's right (Gn. 27:1ff.). However, the supremacy of Jacob over his older brother, foreshadowed before, and at the moment of, their birth (Gn. 25:21–26), and eventually confirmed unwittingly by the aged Isaac (Gn. 27:22–29, 33–37), was finally established.

It was from this duplicity on the part of Jacob, the ancestor of the Israelites, that there stemmed the deep-rooted animosity that dominated Israel's relations with Edom, of whom Esau was the ancestor. Instances of this antagonism between the Israelites and the Edomites occur in the OT (*e.g.* Nu. 20:18–21; 1 Ki. 11:14ff.; Ps. 137:7).

The chief importance of the biblical references to Esau lies in the theological significance given to his rejection, in spite of the right of succession being his by virtue of primogeniture. The biblical explanation is that the Lord hated Esau and loved Jacob (Mal. 1:2f.; Rom. 9:13). Esau symbolizes those whom God has not elected; Jacob typifies those whom God has chosen.

But the ground of this election was not any difference in the lives and characters of Jacob and Esau. Jacob was chosen before he and his brother were born. And even God's 'hate' and 'love' could not be the ground of divine election, otherwise God's choice would depend on caprice or whim. God has exercised his sovereign will in the free exercise of his elective grace, the moral purpose of which he was the sole Originator. (* ELECTION.)

In Heb. 12:16f. Esau symbolizes those who abandon their hope of glory for the sake of the things that are seen and not eternal.

J.G.S.S.T.

ESCHATOLOGY. From Gk. *eschatos*, 'last', the term refers to the 'doctrine of the last things'.

In contrast to cyclical conceptions of history, the biblical writings understand history as a linear movement towards a goal. God is driving history towards the ultimate fulfilment of his purposes for his creation. So biblical eschatology is not limited to the destiny of the individual; it concerns the consummation of the whole history of the world, towards which all God's redemptive acts in history are directed.

I. The OT perspective

The forward-looking character of Israelite faith dates from the call of Abraham (Gn. 12:1–3) and the promise of the land, but it is in the message of the prophets that it becomes fully eschatological, looking towards a final and permanent goal of God's purpose in history. The prophetic term 'the Day of the Lord' (with a variety of similar expressions such as 'on that day') refers to the coming event of God's decisive action in judgment and salvation in the historical realm. For the prophets it is always immediately related to their present historical context, and by no means necessarily refers to the end of history. Increasingly, however, there emerges the concept of a final resolution of history: a day of judgment beyond which God establishes a permanent age of salvation. A fully transcendent eschatology, which expects a direct and universal act of God, beyond the possibilities of ordinary history, issuing in a radically transformed world, is characteristic of * apocalyptic, which is already to be found in several parts of the prophetic books.

The prophets frequently depict the eschatological age of salvation which lies on the far side of judgment. Fundamentally it is the age in which God's will is to prevail. The nations will serve the God of Israel and learn his will (Is. 2:2f. = Mi. 4:1f.; Je. 3:17; Zp. 3:9f.; Zc. 8:20–23). There will be international peace and justice (Is. 2:4 = Mi. 4:3) and peace in nature (Is. 11:6; 65:25). God's people will have security (Mi. 4:4; Is. 65:21–23) and prosperity (Zc. 8:12). The law of God will be written on their hearts (Je. 31:31–34; Ezk. 36:26f.).

Frequently associated with the eschatological age is the Davidic king who will rule Israel (and, sometimes, the nations) as God's representative (Is. 9:6f.; 11:1–10; Je. 23:5f.; Ezk. 34:23f.; 37:24f.; Mi. 5:2–4; Zc. 9:9f.). A principal feature of these prophecies is that the Messiah will rule in *righteousness*. (In the OT itself 'Messiah' [Christ] is not yet used as a technical term for the eschatological king.) Other 'Messianic' figures in the OT hope are the 'one like a son of man' (Dn. 7:13), the heavenly representative of Israel who receives universal dominion, the suffering Servant (Is. 53), and the eschatological prophet (Is. 61:1–3). Commonly the eschatological act of judgment and salvation is accomplished by the personal coming of God himself (Is. 26:21; Zc. 14:5; Mal. 3:1–5).

II. The NT perspective

The distinctive character of NT eschatology is determined by the conviction that in the history of Jesus Christ God's decisive eschatological act has already taken place, though in such a way that the consummation remains still future. There is in NT eschatology both an 'already' of accomplished fulfilment and a 'not yet' of still outstanding promise. There is both a 'realized' and a 'future' aspect to NT eschatology, which is therefore probably best described by the term *'inaugurated eschatology'*.

The note of eschatological fulfilment already under way means that OT eschatology has become, in a measure, present reality for the NT. The 'last days' of the prophets have arrived: for Christ 'was made manifest at the end of the times' (1 Pet. 1:20); God 'in these last days . . . has spoken to us by a Son' (Heb. 1:2); Christians are those 'upon whom the end of the ages has come' (1 Cor. 10:11); 'it is the last hour' (1 Jn. 2:18); *cf.* also Acts

2:17; Heb. 6:5. On the other hand, NT writers oppose the fantasy that fulfilment is already complete (2 Tim. 2:18).

It is important to preserve the theological unity of God's redemptive work, past, present and future, 'already' and 'not yet'. Too often traditional theology has kept these aspects apart, as the finished work of Christ on the one hand, and the 'last things' on the other. In the NT perspective the 'last things' began with the ministry of Jesus. The historical work of Christ ensures, requires and points us forward to the future consummation of God's kingdom. The Christian hope for the future arises out of the historical work of Christ. The Christian church lives between the 'already' and the 'not yet', caught up in the ongoing process of eschatological fulfilment.

Inaugurated eschatology is found already in Jesus' proclamation of the kingdom of God. Jesus modifies the purely future expectation of Jewish apocalyptic by his message that the eschatological rule of God has already drawn near (Mt. 3:17). Its power is already at work in Jesus' deeds of victory over the realm of evil (Mt. 12:28f.). In Jesus' own person and mission the kingdom of God is present (Lk. 17:20f.), demanding response, so that a man's participation in the future of the kingdom is determined by his response to Jesus in the present (Mt. 10:32f.). Thus Jesus makes the kingdom a present reality which nevertheless remains future (Mk. 9:1; 14:25).

The eschatological character of Jesus' mission was confirmed by his resurrection. Resurrection is an eschatological event, belonging to the OT expectation of man's final destiny. So the unexpected resurrection of the one man Jesus ahead of all others determined the church's conviction that the End had already begun. He is risen already as the 'first fruits' of the dead (1 Cor. 15:20). On behalf of his people, Jesus has already entered upon the eternal life of the eschatological age; he has pioneered the way (Heb. 12:2) so that others may follow. In Paul's terms, he is the 'last Adam' (1 Cor. 15:45), the eschatological Man. For all other men eschatological salvation now means sharing *his* eschatological humanity, *his* resurrection life.

So for NT writers, the death and resurrection of Jesus are the absolutely decisive eschatological event which determines the Christian hope for the future: see, *e.g.*, Acts 17:31; Rom. 8:11; 2 Cor. 4:14; 1 Thes. 4:14. This accounts for the second distinctive feature of NT eschatology. As well as its characteristic tension of 'already' and 'not yet', NT eschatology is distinctive in being wholly *Christ-centred.* The role of Jesus in NT eschatology goes far beyond the role of the Messiah in OT or later Jewish expectation. Certainly he is the heavenly Son of man (Dn. 7), the eschatological prophet (Is. 61; *cf.* Lk. 4:18–21), the suffering Servant (Is. 53), and even the Davidic king, though not in the way his contemporaries expected. But the NT's concentration of eschatological fulfilment in Jesus reflects not only his fulfilment of these particular eschatological roles. For NT theology, Jesus embodies both God's own work of eschatological salvation and also man's eschatological destiny. So he is, on the one hand, the Saviour and the Judge, the Conqueror of evil, the Agent of God's rule and the Mediator of God's eschatological presence to men: he is himself the fulfilment of the OT expectations of God's own eschatological coming (*cf.* Mal. 3:1 with Lk. 1:76; 7:27). On the other hand, he is also the eschatological Man: he has achieved and defines in his own risen humanity the eschatological destiny of all men. So now the most adequate statement of our destiny is that we shall be like him (Rom. 8:29; 1 Cor. 15:49; Phil. 3:21; 1 Jn. 3:2). For both these reasons the Christian hope is focused on the coming of Jesus Christ.

In all the NT writings, eschatology has these two distinctive characteristics: it is inaugurated and Christ-centred. There are, however, differences of emphasis, especially in the balance of 'already' and 'not yet'. The Fourth Gospel lays a heavy weight of emphasis both on realized eschatology and on the identification of eschatological salvation with Jesus himself (see, *e.g.*, 11:23–26), but does not eliminate the future expectation (5:28f.; 6:39, *etc.*).

III. Christian life in hope

The Christian lives between the 'already' and the 'not yet', between the resurrection of Christ and the future general resurrection at the coming of Christ. This accounts for the distinctive structure of Christian existence, founded on the finished work of Christ in the historical past and at the same time living in the hope of the future which is kindled and guaranteed by that past history itself. The structure is seen, *e.g.*, in the Lord's Supper, where the risen Lord is present with his people in an act of 'remembrance' of his death, which is at the same time a symbolic anticipation of the eschatological banquet of the future, witnessing therefore to the hope of his coming.

The time between the 'already' and the 'not yet' is the time of the Spirit and the time of the church. The Spirit is the eschatological gift promised by the prophets (Acts 2:16–18), by which Christians already participate in the eternal life of the age to come. The Spirit creates the church, the eschatological people of God, who have already been transferred from the dominion of darkness to the kingdom of Christ (Col. 1:13). Through the Spirit in the church the life of the age to come is already being lived in the midst of the history of this present evil age (Gal. 1:4). Thus, in a sense, the new age and the old age overlap; the new humanity of the last Adam co-exists with the old humanity of the first Adam. By faith we know that the old is passing and under judgment, and the future lies with the new reality of Christ.

The process of eschatological fulfilment in the overlap of the ages involves the mission of the church, which fulfils the universalism of the OT hope. The death and resurrection of Christ are an eschatological event of universal significance which must, however, be universally realized in history, through the church's world-wide proclamation of the gospel (Mt. 28:18–20; Mk. 13:10; Col. 1:23).

The line between the new age and the old does not, however, run simply between the church and the world; it runs through the church and through the individual Christian life. We are always in transition from the old to the new, living in the eschatological tension of the 'already' and the 'not yet'. We are saved and yet we still await salvation. God has justified us, *i.e.* he has anticipated the verdict of the last judgment by declaring us acquitted through Christ. Yet we still 'wait for the hope of righteousness' (Gal. 5:5). God has given us the Spirit by which we share Christ's resurrection life. But the

Spirit is still only the first instalment (2 Cor. 1:22; 5:5; Eph. 1:14) of the eschatological inheritance, the down-payment which guarantees the full payment. The Spirit is the first fruits (Rom. 8:23) of the full harvest. Therefore in present Christian existence we still know the warfare of flesh and Spirit (Gal. 5:13–26), the struggle within us between the nature we owe to the first Adam and the new nature we owe to the last Adam. We still await the redemption of our bodies at the resurrection (Rom. 8:23; 1 Cor. 15:44–50), and perfection is still the goal towards which we strive (Phil. 3:10–14). The tension of 'already' and 'not yet' is an existential reality of Christian life.

For the same reason the Christian life involves suffering. In this age Christians must share Christ's sufferings, so that in the age to come they may share his glory (Acts 14:22; Rom. 8:17; 2 Cor. 4:17; 2 Thes. 1:4f.; Heb. 12:2; 1 Pet. 4:13; 5:10; Rev. 2:10), *i.e.* 'glory' belongs to the 'not yet' of Christian existence. This is both because we are still in this mortal body, and also because the church is still in the world of Satan's dominion. Its mission is therefore inseparable from persecution, as Christ's was (Jn. 15:18–20).

It is important to notice that NT eschatology is never mere information about the future. The future hope is always relevant to Christian life in the present. It is therefore repeatedly made the basis of exhortations to Christian living appropriate to the Christian hope (Mt. 5:3–10, 24f.; Rom. 13:11–14; 1 Cor. 7:26–31; 15:58; 1 Thes. 5:1–11; Heb. 10:32–39; 1 Pet. 1:13; 4:7; 2 Pet. 3:14; Rev. 2f.). Christian life is characterized by its orientation towards the time when God's rule will finally prevail universally (Mt. 6:10), and Christians will therefore stand for that reality against all the apparent dominance of evil in this age. They will *wait* for that day in solidarity with the eager longing of the whole creation (Rom. 8:18–25; 1 Cor. 1:7; Jude 21), and they will suffer with *patient endurance* the contradictions of the present. Steadfast endurance is the virtue which the NT most often associates with Christian hope (Mt. 10:22; 24:13; Rom. 8:25; 1 Thes. 1:3; 2 Tim. 2:12; Heb. 6:11f.; 10:36; Jas. 5:7–11; Rev. 1:9; 13:10; 14:12). Through the tribulation of the present age, Christians endure, even rejoicing (Rom. 12:12), in the strength of their hope which, founded on the resurrection of the crucified Christ, assures them that the way of the cross is the way to the kingdom. Christians whose hope is focused on the permanent values of God's coming kingdom will be freed from the bondage of this world's materialistic values (Mt. 6:33; 1 Cor. 7:29–31; Phil. 3:18–21; Col. 3:1–4). Christians whose hope is that Christ will finally present them perfect before his Father (1 Cor. 1:8; 1 Thes. 3:13; Jude 24) will strive towards that perfection in the present (Phil. 3:12–15; Heb. 12:14; 2 Pet. 3:11–14; 1 Jn. 3:3). They will live *vigilantly* (Mt. 24:42–44; 25:1–13; Mk. 13:33–37; Lk. 21:34–36; 1 Thes. 5:1–11; 1 Pet. 5:8; Rev. 16:15), like servants who daily expect the return of their master (Lk. 12:35–48).

The Christian hope is not utopian. The kingdom of God will not be built by human effort; it is God's own act. Nevertheless, because the kingdom represents the perfect realization of God's will for human society, it will also be the motive for Christian social action in the present. The kingdom is anticipated now primarily in the church, the community of those who acknowledge the King, but Christian social action for the realization of God's will in society at large will also be a sign of the coming kingdom. Those who pray for the coming of the kingdom (Mt. 6:10) cannot fail to act out that prayer so far as it is possible. They will do so, however, with that eschatological realism which recognizes that all anticipations of the kingdom in this age will be provisional and imperfect, that the coming kingdom must never be confused with the social and political structures of this age (Lk. 22:25–27; Jn. 18:36), and the latter will not infrequently embody satanic opposition to the kingdom (Rev. 13:17). In this way Christians will not be disillusioned by human failure but continue to trust the promise of God. Human utopianism must rediscover its true goal in Christian hope, not vice versa.

IV. Signs of the times

The NT consistently represents the coming of Christ as imminent (Mt. 16:28; 24:33; Rom. 13:11f.; 1 Cor. 7:29; Jas. 5:8f.; 1 Pet. 4:7; Rev. 1:1; 22:7, 10, 12, 20). This temporal imminence is, however, qualified by the expectation that certain events must happen 'first' (Mt. 24:14; 2 Thes. 2:2–8), and especially by clear teaching that the date of the end cannot be known in advance (Mt. 24:36, 42; 25:13; Mk. 13:32f.; Acts 1:7). All calculation is ruled out, and Christians live in daily expectation precisely because the date cannot be known. Imminence has less to do with dates than with the *theological* relationship of future fulfilment to the past history of Christ and the present situation of Christians. The 'already' promises, guarantees, demands the 'not yet', and so the coming of Christ exercises a continuous pressure on the present, motivating Christian life towards it. This theological relationship accounts for the characteristic foreshortening of perspective in Jesus' prophecy of the judgment of Jerusalem (Mt. 24; Mk. 13; Lk. 21) and John's prophecy of the judgment of pagan Rome (Rev.); both these judgments are foreseen as events of the final triumph of God's kingdom, because theologically they are such, whatever the chronological gap between them and the end. It is because God's kingdom is coming that the powers of this world are judged even within the history of this age. All such judgments anticipate the final judgment.

As the church's future, the coming of Christ must inspire the church's present, however near or distant in time it may be. In this sense, therefore, the Christian hope in the NT is unaffected by the so-called 'delay of the *parousia*' which some scholars have conjectured as a major feature in early Christian theological development. The 'delay' is explicitly reflected only in 2 Pet. 3:1–10 (*cf.* also Jn. 21:22f.): there it is shown to have its own theological rationale in God's merciful forbearance (*cf.* Rom. 2:4).

Some exegetes think the NT provides 'signs' by which the church will be warned of the approach of the end (*cf.* Mt. 24:3). The strongest support for this idea comes from Jesus' parable of the fig tree, with its lesson (Mt. 24:32f.; Mk. 13:28f.; Lk. 21:28–31). Yet the signs in question seem to be either the fall of Jerusalem (Lk. 21:5–7, 20–24), which, while it signals the coming of the end, provides no *temporal* indication, or characteristics of the whole of this age from the resurrection of Christ to the end: false teachers (Mt. 24:4f., 11, 24f.; *cf.* 1 Tim. 4:1; 2 Tim. 3:1–9; 2 Pet. 1–3; 1 Jn. 2:18f.; 4:3); wars (Mt. 24:6f.; *cf.* Rev. 6:4); natural disasters (Mt. 24:7; *cf.* Rev. 6:5–8); persecution of the church (Mt. 24:9f.; *cf.* Rev. 6:9–11), and the world-wide preaching of the gospel (Mt. 24:14). All these are signs by which the church at every period of history knows that it lives in the end-time, but they do not provide an eschatological timetable. Only the coming of Christ itself is unmistakably the end (Mt. 24:27–30).

The NT does, however, expect the time of the church's witness to reach a final climax in the appearance of *Antichrist and a period of unparalleled tribulation (Mt. 24:21f.; Rev. 3:10; 7:14). Paul certainly treats the non-appearance of Antichrist as an indication that the end is not yet (2 Thes. 2:3–12).

Antichrist represents the principle of satanic opposition to God's rule active throughout history (*e.g.* in the persecution of Jewish believers under Antiochus Epiphanes: Dn. 8:9–12, 23–25; 11:21ff.), but especially in the last times, the age of the church (1 Jn. 2:18). Christ's victory over evil, already achieved in principle, is manifest in this age primarily in the suffering witness of the church; only at the end will his victory be complete in the elimination of the powers of evil. Therefore in this age the success of the church's witness is always accompanied by the mounting violence of satanic opposition (*cf.* Rev. 12).

Evil will reach its final crescendo in the final Antichrist, who is both a false Messiah or prophet, inspired by Satan to perform false miracles (2 Thes. 2:9; *cf.* Mt. 24:24; Rev. 13:11–15), and a persecuting political power blasphemously claiming divine honours (2 Thes. 2:4; *cf.* Dn. 8:9–12, 23–25; 11:30–39; Mt. 24: 15; Rev. 13:5–8). It is noteworthy that, while Paul provides a sketch of this human embodiment of evil (2 Thes. 2:3–12), other NT references find Antichrist already present in heretical teachers (1 Jn. 2:18f., 22; 4:3) or in the religio-political pretensions of the persecuting Roman empire (Rev. 13). The climax is anticipated in every great crisis of the church's history.

V. The coming of Christ

Christian hope is focused on the coming of Christ, which may be called his 'second' coming (Heb. 9:28). Thus the OT term, 'the *day of the Lord', which the NT uses for the event of final fulfilment (1 Thes. 5:2; 2 Thes. 2:2, 2 Pet. 3:10; *cf.* 'the day of God', 2 Pet. 3:12; 'the great day of God the Almighty', Rev. 16:14), is characteristically 'the day of the Lord Jesus' (1 Cor. 5:5; 2 Cor. 1:14; *cf.* 1 Cor. 1:8; Phil. 1:6, 10; 2:16).

The coming of Christ is called his *parousia* ('coming'), his *apokalypsis* ('revelation') and his *epiphaneia* ('appearing'). The word *parousia* means 'presence' or 'arrival', and was used in Hellenistic Greek of the visits of gods and rulers. Christ's *parousia* will be a personal coming of the same Jesus of Nazareth who ascended into heaven (Acts 1:11); but it will be a universally evident event (Mt. 24:27), a coming in power and glory (Mt. 24:30), to destroy Antichrist and evil (2 Thes. 2:8), to gather his people, living and dead (Mt. 24:31; 1 Cor. 15:23; 1 Thes. 4:14–17; 2 Thes. 2:1), and to judge the world (Mt. 25:31; Jas. 5:9).

His coming will also be an *apokalypsis*, an 'unveiling' or 'disclosure', when the power and glory which are now his by virtue of his exaltation and heavenly session (Phil. 2:9; Eph. 1:20–23; Heb. 2:9) will be disclosed to the world. Christ's reign as Lord, now invisible to the world, will then be made visible by his *apokalypsis*.

VI. The *resurrection

At the coming of Christ, the Christian dead will be raised (1 Cor. 15:23; 1 Thes. 4:16) and those who are alive at the time will be transformed (1 Cor. 15:52; *cf.* 1 Thes. 4:17), *i.e.* they will pass into the same resurrection existence without dying.

Belief in the resurrection of the dead is found already in a few OT texts (Is. 25:8; 26:19; Dn. 12:2) and is common in the intertestamental literature. Both Jesus (Mk. 12:18–27) and Paul (Acts 23:6–8) agreed on this point with the Pharisees against the Sadducees, who denied resurrection. The Christian expectation of resurrection, however, is based decisively on the resurrection of Jesus, from which God is known as 'God who raises the dead' (2 Cor. 1:9). Jesus, in his resurrection, 'abolished death and brought life and immortality to light' (2 Tim. 1:10). He is 'the living one', who died and is now alive for ever, who has 'the keys of death' (Rev. 1:18).

Jesus' resurrection was no mere re-animation of a corpse. It was entry into eschatological life, a transformed existence beyond the reach of death. As such it was the beginning of the eschatological resurrection (1 Cor. 15:23). The fact of Jesus' resurrection already guarantees the future resurrection of Christians at his coming (Rom. 8:11; 1 Cor. 6:14; 15:20–23; 2 Cor. 4:14; 1 Thes. 4:14).

Eschatological life, the risen life of Christ, is already communicated to Christians in this age by his Spirit (Jn. 5:24; Rom. 8:11; Eph. 2:5f.; Col. 2:12; 3:1), and this too is a guarantee of their future resurrection (Jn. 11:26; Rom. 8:11; 2 Cor. 1:22; 3:18; 5:4f.). But the Spirit's transformation of Christians into the glorious image of Christ is incomplete in this age because their bodies remain mortal. The future resurrection will be the completion of their transformation into Christ's image, characterized by incorruption, glory and power (1 Cor. 15:42–44). The resurrection existence is not 'flesh and blood' (1 Cor. 15:20) but a 'spiritual body' (15:44), *i.e.* a body wholly vitalized and transformed by the Spirit of the risen Christ. From 1 Cor. 15:35–54 it is clear that the continuity between this present existence and resurrection life is the continuity of the personal self, independent of physical identity.

In NT thought, immortality belongs intrinsically to God alone (1 Tim. 6:16), while men by their descent from Adam are naturally mortal (Rom. 5:12). Eternal life is the gift of God to men through the resurrection of Christ. Only in Christ and by means of their future resurrection will men attain that full eschatological life which is beyond the reach of death. Resurrection is therefore equivalent to man's final attainment of eschatological salvation.

It follows that the damned will not be raised in this full sense of resurrection to eternal life. The resurrection of the damned is mentioned only occasionally in Scripture (Dn. 12:2; Jn. 5:28f.; Acts 24:15; Rev. 20:5, 12f.; *cf.* Mt. 12:41f.), as the means of their condemnation at the judgment.

VII. The state of the dead

The Christian hope for life beyond death is not based on the belief that part of man survives death. All men, through their descent from Adam, are naturally mortal. Immortality is the gift of God, which will be attained through the resurrection of the whole person.

The Bible therefore takes death seriously. It is not an illusion. It is the consequence of sin (Rom. 5:12;

6:23), an evil (Dt. 30:15, 19) from which men shrink in terror (Ps. 55:4f.). It is an enemy of God and man, and resurrection is therefore God's great victory over death (1 Cor. 15:54–57). Death is 'the last enemy to be destroyed' (1 Cor. 15:26), abolished in principle at Christ's resurrection (2 Tim. 1:10), to be finally abolished at the end (Rev. 20:14; *cf.* Is. 25:8). Only because Christ's resurrection guarantees their future resurrection are Christians delivered from the fear of death (Heb. 2:14f.) and able to see it as a sleep from which they will awaken (1 Thes. 4:13f.; 5:10) or even a departing to be with Christ (Phil. 1:23).

The OT pictures the state of the dead as existence in Sheol, the grave or the underworld. But existence in Sheol is not life. It is a land of darkness (Jb. 10:21f.) and silence (Ps. 115:17), in which God is not remembered (Pss. 6:5; 30:9; 88:11; Is. 38:18). The dead in Sheol are cut off from God (Ps. 88:5), the source of life. Only occasionally does the OT attain a hope of real life beyond death, *i.e.* life out of reach of Sheol in the presence of God (Pss. 16:10f.; 49:15; 73:24; perhaps Jb. 19:25f.). Probably the example of *Enoch (Gn. 5:24; *cf.* Elijah, 2 Ki. 2:11) helped stimulate this hope. A clear doctrine of resurrection is found only in Is. 26:19; Dn. 12:2.

'Hades' is the NT equivalent of Sheol (Mt. 11:23; 16:18; Lk. 10:15; Acts 2:27, 31; Rev. 1:18; 6:8; 20:13f.), in most cases referring to death or the power of death. In Lk. 16:23 it is the place of torment for the wicked after death, in accordance with some contemporary Jewish thinking, but it is doubtful whether this parabolic use of current ideas can be treated as teaching about the state of the dead. 1 Pet. 3:19 calls the dead who perished in the Flood 'the spirits in prison' (*cf.* 4:6).

The NT hope for the Christian dead is concentrated on their participation in the resurrection (1 Thes. 4:13–18), and there is therefore little evidence of belief about the 'intermediate state'. Passages which indicate, or may indicate, that the Christian dead are with Christ are Lk. 23:43; Rom. 8:38f.; 2 Cor. 5:8; Phil. 1:23; *cf.* Heb. 12:23. The difficult passage 2 Cor. 5:2–8 may mean that Paul conceives existence between death and resurrection as a bodiless existence in Christ's presence.

VIII. The judgment

The NT insists on the prospect of divine judgment as, besides death, the single unavoidable fact of a man's future: 'It is appointed for men to die once, and after that comes judgment' (Heb. 9:27). This fact expresses the holiness of the biblical God, whose moral will must prevail, and before whom all responsible creatures must therefore in the end be judged obedient or rebellious. When God's will finally prevails at the coming of Christ, there must be a separation between the finally obedient and the finally rebellious, so that the kingdom of God will include the one and exclude the other for ever. No such final judgment occurs within history, though there are provisional judgments in history, while God in his forbearance gives all men time to repent (Acts 17:30f.; Rom. 2:4; 2 Pet. 3:9). But at the end the truth of every man's position before God must come to light.

The Judge is God (Rom. 2:6; Heb. 12:23; Jas. 4:12; 1 Pet. 1:17; Rev. 20:11) or Christ (Mt. 16:27; 25:31; Jn. 5:22; Acts 10:42; 2 Tim. 4:1, 8; 1 Pet. 4:5; Rev. 22:12). It is God who judges through his eschatological agent Christ (Jn. 5:22, 27, 30; Acts 17:31; Rom. 2:16). The judgment seat of God (Rom. 14:10) and the judgment seat of Christ (2 Cor. 5:10) are therefore equivalent. (The judgment committed to the saints, according to Mt. 19:28; Lk. 22:30; 1 Cor. 6:2f.; Rev. 20:4, means their authority to rule with Christ in his kingdom, not to officiate at the last judgment.)

The standard of judgment is God's impartial righteousness according to men's works (Mt. 16:27; Rom. 2:6, 11: 2 Tim. 4:14; 1 Pet. 1:17; Rev. 2:23; 20:12; 22:12). This is true even for Christians: 'We must all appear before the judgment seat of Christ, so that each one may receive good or evil, according to what he has done in the body' (2 Cor. 5:10). The judgment will be according to men's lights (*cf.* Jn. 9:41); according to whether they have the law of Moses (Rom. 2:12) or the natural knowledge of God's moral standards (Rom. 2:12–16), but by these standards no man can be declared righteous before God according to his works (Rom. 3:19f.). There is no hope for the man who seeks to justify himself at the judgment.

There is hope, however, for the man who seeks his justification from God (Rom. 2:7). The gospel reveals that righteousness which is not required of men but given to men through Christ. In the death and resurrection of Christ, God in his merciful love has already made his eschatological judgment in favour of sinners, acquitting them for the sake of Christ, offering them in Christ that righteousness which they could never achieve. Thus the man who has faith in Christ is free from all condemnation (Jn. 5:24; Rom. 8:33f.). The final criterion of judgment is therefore a man's relation to Christ (*cf.* Mt. 10:32f.). This is the meaning of the 'book of life' (Rev. 20:12, 15; *i.e.* the *Lamb*'s book of life, Rev. 13:8).

The meaning of Paul's doctrine of justification is that in Christ God has anticipated the verdict of the last judgment, and pronounced an acquittal of sinners who trust in Christ. Very similar is John's doctrine that judgment takes place already in men's belief or disbelief in Christ (Jn. 3:17–21; 5:24).

The last judgment remains an eschatological fact, even for believers (Rom. 14:10), though they may face it without fear (1 Jn. 4:17). We hope for acquittal in the final judgment (Gal. 5:5), 'the crown of righteousness' (2 Tim. 4:8), on the ground of the same mercy of God through which we have already been acquitted (2 Tim. 1:16). But, even for the Christian, works are not irrelevant (Mt. 7:1f., 21, 24–27; 25:31–46; Jn. 3:21; 2 Cor. 5:10; Jas. 2:13), since justification does not abrogate the need for obedience, but precisely makes it possible for the first time. Justification is the foundation, but what men build on it is exposed to judgment (1 Cor. 3:10–15): 'If any man's work is burned up, he will suffer loss, though he himself will be saved, but only as through fire' (3:15).

IX. *Hell

The final destiny of the wicked is 'hell', which translates Gk. *Gehenna*, derived from the Heb. *gê-hinnōm*, 'the valley of Hinnom'. This originally denoted a valley outside Jerusalem, where child sacrifices were offered to Molech (2 Ch. 28:3; 33:6). It became a symbol of judgment in Je. 7:31–33; 19:6f., and in the intertestamental literature the term for the eschatological hell of fire.

In the NT, hell is pictured as a place of unquenchable or eternal fire (Mk. 9:43, 48; Mt. 18:8; 25:30) and the undying worm (Mk. 9:48), a place of weeping and gnashing of teeth (Mt. 8:12; 13:42, 50; 22:13; 25:30), the outer darkness (Mt. 8:12; 22:13; 25:30; *cf.* 2 Pet. 2:17; Jude 13) and the lake of fire and brimstone (Rev. 19:20; 20:10, 14f.; 21:8; *cf.* 14:10). Revelation identifies it as 'the second death' (2:11; 20:14; 21:8). It is the place of the destruction of both body and soul (Mt. 10:28).

The NT pictures of hell are markedly restrained by comparison with Jewish apocalyptic and with later Christian writings. The imagery used derives especially from Is. 66:24 (*cf.* Mk. 9:48) and Gn. 19:24, 28; Is. 34:9f. (*cf.* Rev. 14:10f.; also Jude 7; Rev. 19:3). It is clearly not intended literally but indicates the terror and finality of condemnation to hell, which is less metaphorically described as exclusion from the presence of Christ (Mt. 7:23; 25:41; 2 Thes. 1:9). The imagery of Rev. 14:10f.; 20:10 (*cf.* 19:3) should probably not be pressed to prove eternal torment, but the NT clearly teaches eternal destruction (2 Thes. 1:9) or punishment (Mt. 25:46), from which there can be no release.

Hell is the destiny of all the powers of evil: Satan (Rev. 20:10), the demons (Mt. 8:29; 25:41), the beast and the false prophet (Rev. 19:20), death and Hades (Rev. 20:14). It is the destiny of men only because they have identified themselves with evil. It is important to notice that there is no symmetry about the two destinies of men: the kingdom of God has been prepared for the redeemed (Mt. 25:34), but hell has been prepared for the devil and his angels (Mt. 25:41) and becomes the fate of men only because they have refused their true destiny which God offers them in Christ. The NT doctrine of hell, like all NT eschatology, is never mere information; it is a warning given in the context of the gospel's call to repentance and faith in Christ.

The NT teaching about hell cannot be reconciled with an absolute universalism, the doctrine of the final salvation of all men. The element of truth in this doctrine is that God desires the salvation of all men (1 Tim. 2:4) and gave his Son for the salvation of the world (Jn. 3:16). Accordingly, the cosmic goal of God's eschatological action in Christ can be described in universalistic terms (Eph. 1:10; Col. 1:20; Rev. 5:13). The error of dogmatic universalism is the same as that of a symmetrical doctrine of double predestination: that they abstract eschatological doctrine from its proper NT context in the proclamation of the gospel. They rob the gospel of its eschatological urgency and challenge. The gospel sets before men their true destiny in Christ and warns them in all seriousness of the consequence of missing this destiny.

X. The millennium

The interpretation of the passage Rev. 20:1–10, which describes a period of a thousand years (known as the 'millennium') in which Satan is bound and the saints reign with Christ before the last judgment, has long been a subject of disagreement between Christians. 'Amillennialism' is the view which regards the millennium as a symbol of the age of the church and identifies the binding of Satan with Christ's work in the past (Mt. 12:29). 'Postmillennialism' regards it as a future period of success for the gospel in history before the coming of Christ. 'Premillennialism' regards it as a period between the coming of Christ and the last judgment. (The term 'chiliasm' is also used for this view, especially in forms which emphasize the materialistic aspect of the millennium.) 'Premillennialism' may be further subdivided. There is what is sometimes called 'historic premillennialism', which regards the millennium as a further stage in the achievement of Christ's kingdom, an interim stage between the church age and the age to come. (Sometimes 1 Cor. 15:23–28 is interpreted as supporting this idea of three stages in the fulfilment of Christ's redemptive work.) 'Dispensationalism', on the other hand, teaches that the millennium is not a stage in God's single universal redemptive action in Christ, but specifically a period in which the OT promises to the nation of Israel will be fulfilled in strictly literal form.

It should be emphasized that no other passage of Scripture clearly refers to the millennium. To apply OT prophecies of the age of salvation specifically to the millennium runs counter to the general NT interpretation of such prophecies, which find their fulfilment in the salvation already achieved by Christ and to be consummated in the age to come. This is also how Rev. itself interprets such prophecies in chs. 21f. Within the structure of Rev., the millennium has a limited role, as a demonstration of the final victory of Christ and his saints over the powers of evil. The principal object of Christian hope is not the millennium but the new creation of Rev. 21f.

Some Jewish apocalyptic writings look forward to a preliminary kingdom of the Messiah on this earth prior to the age to come, and John has very probably adapted that expectation. There are strong exegetical reasons for regarding the millennium as the consequence of the coming of Christ depicted in Rev. 19:11–21. (See G. R. Beasley-Murray, *The Book of Revelation*, *NCB*, 1974, pp. 284–298.) This favours 'historic premillennialism', but it is also possible that the image of the millennium is taken too literally when it is understood as a precise period of time. Whether it is a period of time or a comprehensive symbol of the significance of the coming of Christ, the theological meaning of the millennium is the same: it expresses the hope of Christ's final triumph over evil and the vindication with him of his people who have suffered under the tyranny of evil in the present age.

XI. The new creation

The final goal of God's purposes for the world includes, negatively, the destruction of all God's enemies: Satan, sin and death, and the elimination of all forms of suffering (Rev. 20:10, 14–15; 7:16f.; 21:4; Is. 25:8; 27:1; Rom. 16:20; 1 Cor. 15:26, 54). Positively, God's rule will finally prevail entirely (Zc. 14:9; 1 Cor. 15:24–28; Rev. 11:15), so that in Christ all things will be united (Eph. 1:10) and God will be all in all (1 Cor. 15:28, AV).

With the final achievement of human salvation there will come also the liberation of the whole material creation from its share in the curse of sin (Rom. 8:19–23). The Christian hope is not for redemption from the world, but for the redemption of the world. Out of judgment (Heb. 12:26; 2 Pet. 3:10) will emerge a recreated universe (Rev. 21:1; *cf.* Is. 65:17; 66:22; Mt. 19:28), 'a new heaven and a new earth in which righteousness dwells' (2 Pet. 3:13).

The destiny of the redeemed is to be like Christ (Rom. 8:29; 1 Cor. 15:49; Phil. 3:21; 1 Jn. 3:2), to be with Christ (Jn. 14:3; 2 Cor. 5:8; Phil. 1:23; Col. 3:4; 1 Thes. 4:17), to share his glory (Rom. 8:18, 30, 2 Cor. 3:18; 4:17; Col. 3:4; Heb.

2:10; 1 Pet. 5:1) and his kingdom (1 Tim. 2:12; Rev. 2:26f.; 3:21; 4:10; 20:4, 6); to be sons of God in perfect fellowship with God (Rev. 21:3, 7), to worship God (Rev. 7:15; 22:3), to see God (Mt. 5:8; Rev. 22:4), to know him face to face (1 Cor. 13:12). Faith, hope and especially love are the permanent characteristics of Christian existence which abide even in the perfection of the age to come (1 Cor. 13:13), while 'righteousness and peace and joy in the Holy Spirit' are similarly abiding qualities of man's enjoyment of God (Rom. 14:17).

The corporate life of the redeemed with God is described in a number of pictures: the eschatological banquet (Mt. 8:11; Mk. 14:25; Lk. 14:15–24; 22:30) or wedding feast (Mt. 25:10; Rev. 19:9), paradise restored (Lk. 23:43; Rev. 2:7; 22:1f.), the new Jerusalem (Heb. 12:22; Rev. 21). All these are only pictures, since 'no eye has seen, nor ear heard, nor the heart of man conceived, what God has prepared for those who love him' (1 Cor. 2:9).

BIBLIOGRAPHY. P. Badham, *Christian Beliefs about Life after Death*, 1976; J. Baillie, *And the Life Everlasting*, 1934; G. R. Beasley-Murray, *Jesus and the Future*, 1954; G. C. Berkouwer, *The Return of Christ*, 1972; J. Bright, *Covenant and Promise*, 1976; E. Brunner, *Eternal Hope*, 1954; O. Cullmann, 'The Return of Christ', in A. J. B. Higgins (ed.), *The Early Church*, 1956; S. J. DeVries, *Yesterday, Today and Tomorrow*, 1975; M. J. Harris, *Them* 1, 1975–6, pp. 50–55; J. Hick, *Death and Eternal Life*, 1976; G. E. Ladd, *Crucial Questions about the Kingdom of God*, 1952; *idem*, *The Presence of the Future*, 1974; W. Manson, *et al.*, *Eschatology*, 1953; R. Martin-Achard, *From Death to Life*, 1960; J. Moltmann, *Theology of Hope*, 1967; A. L. Moore, *The Parousia in the NT*, 1966; *NIDNTT* 2, pp. 886–935 (contains extensive bibliography); R. Schnackenburg, *God's Rule and Kingdom*, 1963; C. Ryder Smith, *The Bible Doctrine of the Hereafter*, 1958; S. H. Travis, *The Jesus Hope*, 1974. R.J.B.

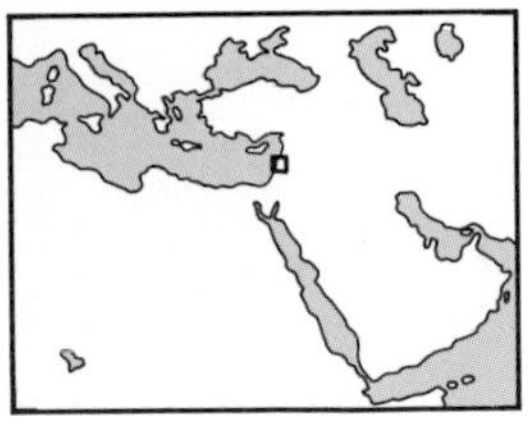

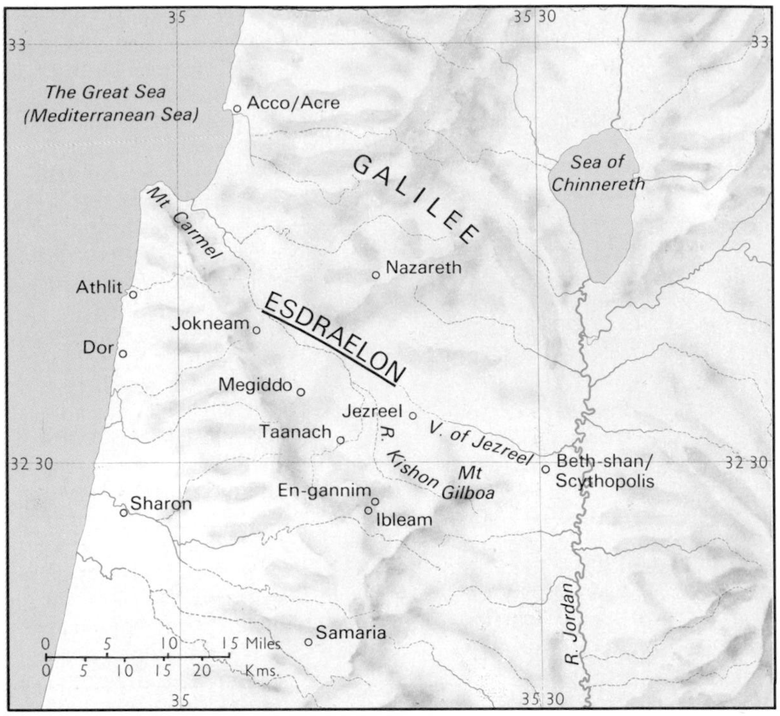

Esdraelon, a triangular alluvial plain near the vale of Jezreel.

The plain of Jezreel (Esdraelon) viewed from the Taanach excavations. (RS)

ESDRAELON. The Greek form of the name *Jezreel. However, the Greek and Hebrew names really apply to two distinct but adjacent lowlands, even though in some modern works the term Jezreel is loosely extended to cover both regions. The vale of Jezreel proper is the valley that slopes down from the town of Jezreel to Beth-shan overlooking the Jordan rift-valley, with Galilee to the N and Mt Gilboa to the S.

Esdraelon is the triangular alluvial plain bounded along its SW side by the Carmel range from Jokneam to Ibleam and Engannim (modern Jenin), along its N side by a line from Jokneam to the hills of Nazareth, and on the E by a line thence back down to Ibleam and Engannim. On the E, Jezreel guards the entry to its own valley, while in the W the SW spur of hills from Galilee leaves only a small gap by which the river Kishon flows out into the plain of Acre after crossing the Esdraelon plain. At the foot of the NE-facing slopes of Carmel the important towns of *Jokneam, *Megiddo, *Taanach and *Ibleam controlled the main passes and N–S routes through W Palestine, while these and Jezreel (town) also controlled the important route running E–W from the Jordan valley to the Mediterranean coast, the only one unimpeded by ranges of hills. Esdraelon was a marshy region, important mainly for these roads; the vale of Jezreel was agriculturally valuable as well as being strategically placed. For geographical background, see D. Baly, *Geography of the Bible*, 1974, pp. 39, 144–151. K.A.K.

ESHCOL. 1. Brother of Mamre and Aner, who were 'confederates' with Abraham when in Hebron, and joined with his company in the rescue of Lot (Gn. 14:13–24).

2. The valley where the spies sent forth by Moses gathered a huge cluster (Heb. *'eškōl*) of grapes, typical of the fruitfulness of the land (Nu. 13:23–24; 32:9; Dt. 1:24). Traditionally thought to be located a few km N of Hebron (already Jerome, *Ep*. 108. 11 = *PL* 22. 886), where the vineyards are still famous for the quality of their grapes.

Some scholars prefer a location S of Hebron (Gray; Noth), but although the texts are not explicit about the direction, it does seem to be implied that the spies continued N from Hebron to the Valley of Eshcol (Nu. 13:22–23).

BIBLIOGRAPHY. G. B. Gray, *Numbers, ICC*, 1903, pp. 142–143; P. Thomsen, *Loca Sancta*, 1907, p. 62; *IDB*, 2, p. 142. G.T.M. G.I.D.

ESHTAOL (*'eštā'ōl*, from the verb *šā'al*, 'to ask'), **ESHTAOLITES.** A lowland city, W of Jerusalem, tentatively identified with the modern Eshwa', it was included in the territory of both Judah (Jos. 15:33) and Dan (Jos. 19:41), an anomaly which is partially explained by the fluidity of the border, a fact attributable to Amorite (Jdg. 1:34) and then Philistine pressure. The Eshtaolites are numbered amongst the Calebites, traditionally associated with Judah (1 Ch. 2:53).

It was at Eshtaol that the Danite Samson was first moved by the Spirit of the Lord (Jdg. 13:25) and where he was finally buried in the tomb of his father (Jdg. 16:31). From Eshtaol and neighbouring Zorah originated the Danite quest for a settled habitation (Jdg. 18:2, 11). A.E.C.

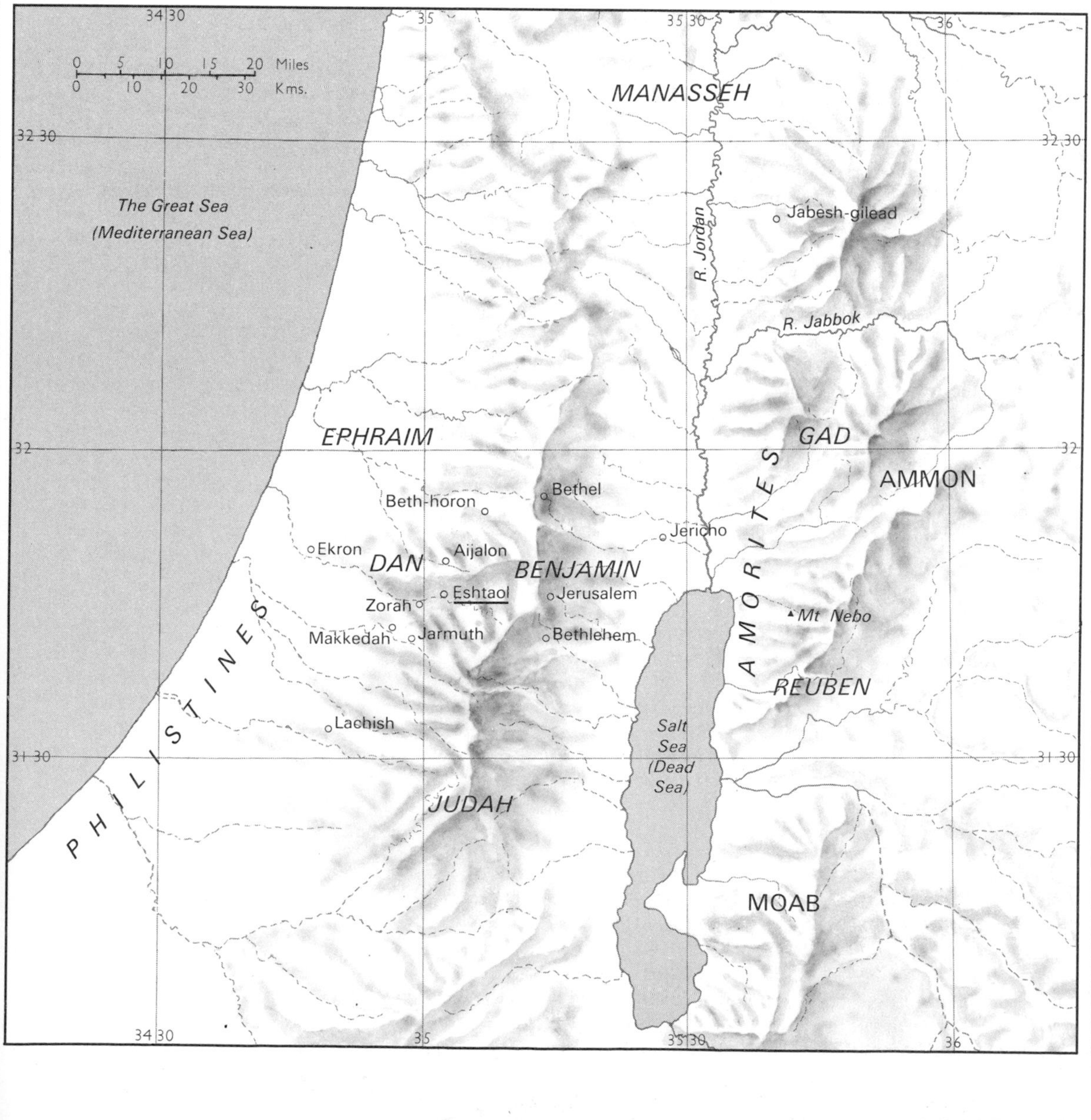

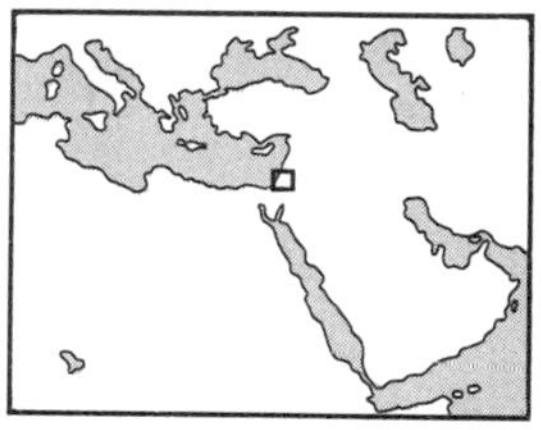

Eshtaol, a lowland city included in the territory of both Judah and Dan.

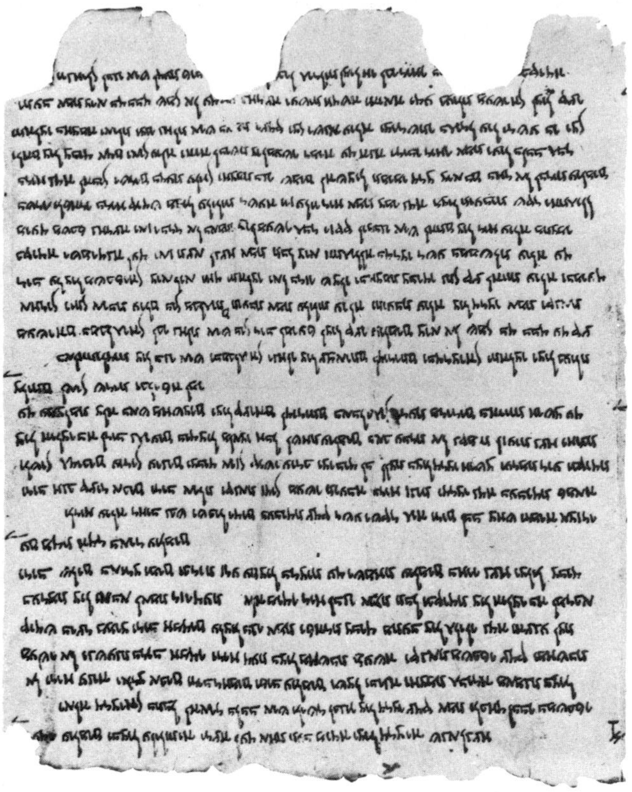

Column 4 from the scroll giving the Order of Community (1QS). It reviews the history of the Essene sect using the technique of apocalyptic interpretation of Scripture, its instruction in doctrine and the laws by which the community lived. Height c. 24 cm. c. 100–75 BC. (JCT)

ESSENES (Gk. *Essēnoi, Essaioi, Ōssaioi*, most probably from Aramai *'āsên, 'āsayyâ*, plural of *'āsê, 'āsyâ*, 'healer'; *cf.* Philo's *Therapeutai*), a Jewish religious community which flourished in the 1st century BC and 1st century AD, the third of the Jewish 'philosophies' or schools of thought enumerated by Josephus (*BJ* 2. 119–161; *cf. Ant.* 18. 18–22). Apart from Josephus, we have two accounts of them from his older Jewish contemporary Philo of Alexandria (*Quod omnis probus* 75–91; *Hypothetica ap.* Euseb., *Praep. Ev.* 8. 2), and one from the elder Pliny (*NH* 5. 17). A later account in Hippolytus (*Refut.* 9. 20. 13–23) follows Josephus in the main, but includes some information apparently derived from independent sources.

Philo's description of the Essenes is intended to illustrate his thesis that only the truly good man is truly free. He estimates their numbers at about 4,000, and tells how they live in villages, working hard at agriculture and similar pursuits, devoting much time to the communal study of moral and religious questions, including the interpretation of the sacred books. They pay scrupulous attention to ceremonial purity, he says; they hold all their property in common, abstain from animal sacrifice, practise celibacy, keep no slaves, make provision for those of their number who are prevented from working by sickness or old age, swear no oaths, take no part in military or commercial activity and in general cultivate all the virtues.

Pliny's account comes in the course of his description of the Dead Sea. He describes the Essenes as living on its W side, above Engedi. They have lived there for countless generations, he says, renouncing both women and money; yet their numbers have been continually maintained, because so many regularly come to join their solitary existence through sheer weariness of ordinary life. Pliny writes between AD 73 and 79, but he is probably dependent for his knowledge of the Essenes on earlier writers, such as Alexander Polyhistor (1st century BC).

The accounts in Philo and Pliny are idealized and marked by rhetorical exaggeration. Those in Josephus (when all due allowances are made for this author's tendency to modify historical truth for his private ends) strike one as being factual and based on first-hand knowledge. According to Josephus, the Essenes were to be found in all the cities of Judaea, including Jerusalem. They practised hospitality; an Essene from a distance would be treated as a brother by any fellow-Essene to whose house he came. But much of Josephus's description implies a community life such as could not be followed by city-dwellers; it is likely that the fully initiated Essenes lived in separate communities, while they had attached to their order associate members who lived in cities and followed the ordinary ways of life.

Josephus gives us a fairly detailed account of the Essenes' initiation procedure. This involved a 3 years' novitiate. At the end of the first year the novice (who had already worn the white habit of the order) was admitted to the ritual purification in water, but 2 further years had to elapse before he was admitted to share the common meal. This was evidently the token of full membership. Before finally passing from the novitiate to full membership the candidate was required to swear a succession of solemn oaths.

This account bears a general resemblance to the rules for admission to the Qumran community as detailed in 1QS, although it differs in a number of particulars; for example, 1QS lays down a novitiate of 2 years, not 3.

The Essene's day, according to Josephus, began before sunrise with morning prayers, addressed to the sun, 'as though entreating him to rise'. Then he betook himself to his allotted task, under the direction of his overseer, and worked at it until noon. At noon the members bathed and partook of a simple meal in common; they then resumed their working clothes and continued at their appointed tasks till evening, when they assembled for another meal.

Hippolytus has nothing to say about the Essenes' morning address to the sun: according to him 'they continue in prayer from early dawn and speak no word until they have sung a hymn of praise to God'. The practice described by Josephus may have been that of the Sampsaeans, a group perhaps associated with the Essenes, who acquired their name (*cf.* Heb. *šemeš*, 'sun') from acts of homage allegedly paid to the sun as a manifestation of divinity. The term Essenes, in fact, was used at times to cover a fairly wide range of Jewish sectarian bodies that drew aside from the main stream of Jewish life. One of these, almost certainly, was the Qumran community; there may have been several more of which we know as little as we knew of the Qumran community before the discoveries of 1947 and the following years. (*Dead Sea Scrolls, *Qumran.)

If once it is established that the Qumran community was a community of Essenes (perhaps of those Essenes whom Josephus distinguishes from the rest because they did not abstain from marriage), the Qumran literature will have to take its place above all other accounts of the Essenes which have come down to us from antiquity because it comes from within the Essene ranks. It will then be proper to check the statements of ancient authors by the Qumran texts, and not vice versa.

Bibliography. C. D. Ginsburg, *The Essenes*, 1864, reprinted 1955; J. B. Lightfoot, 'On Some Points Connected with the Essenes', in *The Epistle to the Colossians*, 1879, pp. 348–419; D. Howlett, *The Essenes and Christianity*, 1957; H. Sérouya, *Les Esséniens*, 1959; A. Dupont-Sommer, *Essene Writings from Qumran*, E.T. 1961; H. Kosmala,

Hebräer-Essener-Christen, 1959; G. Vermes, *Post-Biblical Jewish Studies*, 1975, pp. 8–36.

F.F.B.

ESTHER. According to Est. 2:7, Esther's Jewish name was Hadassah (Myrtle). The name Esther may be the equivalent of the Persian *stara* ('star'), though some find a link with the Babylonian goddess Ishtar.

Esther married Ahasuerus (Xerxes, 486–465 BC). Herodotus and Ctesias say that the wife of Xerxes was Amestris (who is probably Vashti), and that she went with Xerxes on his expedition to Greece, which happened after the events of Est. 1. On the way home she incurred Xerxes' anger by mutilating the mother of one of his mistresses and nearly starting a revolution (Her. 9. 108f.). Small wonder that Xerxes remembered his original plan to divorce her, and now looked for a successor, which he found in Esther. Amestris came into power again as queen mother during the reign of her son, Artaxerxes I, and may indeed be the 'queen' of Ne. 2:6. If we assume that Esther died within a few years of the events recorded in the book that bears her name, there is no difficulty in harmonizing the two queens.

Although Esther was a brave woman, who risked her life to save the Jews (4:11–17), the Bible does not commend her encouragement of the Jews to massacre their enemies in ch. 9. Here she was the child of her age.

J.S.W.

ESTHER, BOOK OF. This book tells how *Esther, a Jewess, became the wife of a Persian king, and was able to prevent the wholesale massacre of the Jewish race within the Persian empire.

I. Outline of contents

a. 1:1–22. Ahasuerus deposes his wife, Vashti, for refusing to appear at his banquet.

b. 2:1–18. Esther, the cousin of Mordecai, a Jew, is chosen in Vashti's place.

c. 2:19–23. Mordecai tells Esther of a plot to kill the king.

d. 3:1–15. Mordecai refuses to bow to Haman, the king's favourite, who thereupon plans to massacre the Jews on a fixed date.

e. 4:1–17. Mordecai persuades Esther to intercede with the king.

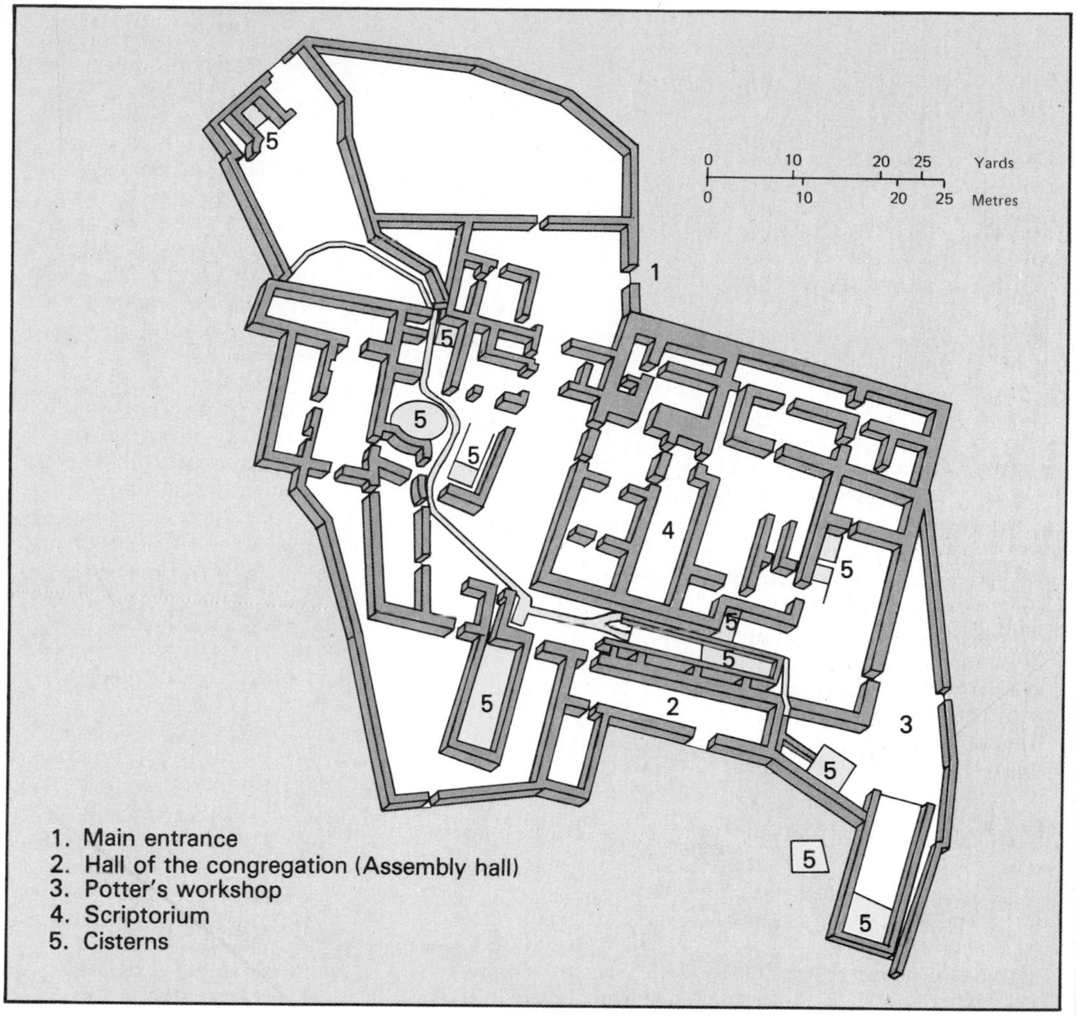

Plan of the buildings at Khirbet Qumran, believed to have been occupied by an Essene community. 2nd cent. BC–1st cent. AD.

Part of the Khirbet Qumran buildings, as excavated. (RS)

f. 5:1–14. Esther invites the king and Haman to a banquet.

g. 6:1–14. The king makes Haman honour Mordecai publicly as a reward for revealing the plot against him.

h. 7:1–10. At a second banquet Esther reveals Haman's plan to massacre the Jews, and Haman is hanged on the gallows that he had prepared for Mordecai.

i. 8:1–17. Since the edict for the massacre cannot be revoked, the king sends a second edict allowing the Jews to defend themselves.

j. 9:1–19. The Jews take advantage of this to kill their enemies.

k. 9:20–32. The deliverance is commemorated at the feast of Purim.

l. 10:1–3. Mordecai is put in a position of authority.

II. Authorship and date

The book was written some time after the death of Ahasuerus (1:1), which would be after 465 BC if Ahasuerus is identified with Xerxes. Some Jews regarded Mordecai as the author, and the references in 9:20, 32 could suggest this. Much of the contents may have been inserted in the annals of the king, as mentioned in 10:2 and perhaps 6:1, and this would account for the omission of the name of God, although the reference to fasting for Esther in 4:16 certainly implies prayer, and the doctrine of providence is stated in 4:14.

It should be noted that the Gk. versions of Esther contain 107 extra verses, which do include references to God by name. These are collected together in the Apocrypha of our English Version, and are numbered as though they followed 10:3. In fact, their order in the Gk. is as follows: 9:2–12:6; 1:1–3:13; 13:1–7; 3:14–4:17; 13:8–15:16; 5:1–8:12; 16:1–24; 8:13–10:3; 10:4–11:1. The date given in 11:1 is 114 BC, and could be the date when the Gk. translation or expanded version was made.

III. Authenticity

Although some, such as R. H. Pfeiffer, regard the book as entire fiction, other commentators would agree with the verdict of H. H. Rowley that the author 'seems to have had access to some good sources of information on things Persian, and the nucleus of his story may be older than his book' (*Growth of the Old Testament*, p. 155). The story as such has not been confirmed by any Persian records, and it is often supposed that it cannot be fitted into what is known of Persian history.

King Ahasuerus is usually identified with Xerxes (486–465 BC), though a few, *e.g.* J. Hoschander and A. T. Olmstead, have identified him with Artaxerxes II (404–359 BC). If he is Xerxes we have an explanation of the strange gap between the third year in 1:3 and the seventh year of 2:16, since between 483 and 480 BC he was planning and carrying out his disastrous invasion of Greece. Herodotus (7. 114; 9. 108f.) gives the name of Xerxes' wife as Amestris, but we do not know from secular historians whether or not he had more than one wife. Although, according to Herodotus (3. 84), the Persian king was supposed to choose his wife from one of seven noble families (*cf.* Est. 1:14), rules of this kind could generally be evaded. Xerxes had no scruples about taking any women that he chose.

The author is alleged to be hopelessly in error in 2:5–6, when he describes * Mordecai as having been taken captive in 597 BC. By this time he would have been over 120. On the principle that a translation that makes sense is preferable to one that makes nonsense, we may refer the word 'who' in v. 6 to Mordecai's great-grandfather, Kish, as the Heb. allows us to do.

Other supposed improbabilities are largely a matter of subjective opinion. Thus, would * Haman have attempted the massacre of all the Jewish race simply because one man defied him, and would the king have permitted it? And would Haman have fixed a date for the massacre so far ahead? Such criticism shows a strange ignorance of human nature. Massacres and wars have been sparked off many times through the injured pride of one or two individuals. Persian kings also were easily swayed by their favourites, and in this case Haman represents the Jews as traitors (3:8). Haman is depicted as a thoroughly superstitious man, and the day of the massacre was chosen because the casting of lots indicated that it would be a lucky day (3:7). The gallows 25 m high (7:9) would be the typically extravagant display of a thwarted man in power, while the £2½ million offered as a bribe to the king in 3:9 is hardly to be taken seriously; what the king would understand was that a large proportion of Jewish property would be put in the royal treasuries, and with Oriental politeness he replies that Haman may keep it for himself (3:11): both parties would understand that, so long as the king received a substantial share of the spoil, he would turn a blind eye to whatever Haman took for himself.

One strange interpretation of the book demands brief notice. This is the mythological origin postulated by Zimmern and Jensen. Esther is the goddess Ishtar; Mordecai is Marduk; Haman is the Elamite deity Humman; Vashti is Mashti, an Elamite goddess. The story may have concerned a conflict between Babylonian and Elamite gods. It would be strange if the Jews had made use of a polytheistic tale, or cultic ceremony, to account for a Jewish festival; and even if * Purim could be shown to have been originally a pagan ceremony, a whole new story must have been written round it, and in this story it is unlikely that the names of gods and goddesses would have been retained. It might still be true that the names of the characters in the book of Esther have some connection with the names of gods and goddesses, since there are other examples of Jews being given extra names that probably contain the names of some god or goddess, *e.g.* Dn. 1:7; Ezr. 1:8. Moreover there is another Mordecai mentioned in Ezr. 2:2. Esther is said to be a second name in Est. 2:7.

BIBLIOGRAPHY. L. B. Paton, *Esther*, *ICC*, 1908; J. Hoschander, *The Book of Esther in the Light of History*, 1923; B. W. Anderson, *The Book of Esther*, Introduction and Exegesis, in *IB*, 3, 1951; J. S. Wright, 'The Historicity of the Book of Esther', in *New Perspectives on the Old Testament*, ed. J. B. Payne; C. A. Moore, *Esther*, *AB*, 1971. J.S.W.

ETAM. 1. A place in the hill-country of Judah, rebuilt by Rehoboam (2 Ch. 11:6), probably referred to in 1 Ch. 4:3, and in the LXX of Jos. 15:59 (*Aitan*). The site is usually identified with modern Khirbet el-Ḫoḫ, some 10½ km SSW of Jerusalem. **2.** A village in the territory of Simeon (1 Ch. 4:32). The site is unknown, though some scholars would equate the place with **1** above. **3.** The cave (*sᵉʿîp̄ selaʿ*, 'cleft of rock') where Samson took refuge from the Philistines (Jdg. 15:8, 11). The site is unknown, but must be in W Judah.

Bibliography. *KB*, p. 699; F. M. Abel, *Géographie de la Palestine*, 2, 1938, p. 321. T.C.M.

ETHAM. Camp of the Israelites somewhere on the isthmus of Suez (Ex. 13:20; Nu. 33:6–7), about whose precise location scholars differ. Müller suggested a connection with the name of the Egyp. god Atum; Naville proposed Edom; Clédat, Gauthier, Bourdon, Lagrange, Abel and Montet would connect it with the Old Egyp. word for 'fort' (*ḫtm*), a name which was given to several places; but none of these suggestions seems very likely. The Old Egyp. *ḫtm* seems rather to designate the frontier-city of Sile. (*Encampment by the sea.) C.D.W.

ETHAN (Heb. *'êṯān*, 'enduring', 'ancient'). A wise man in the time of Solomon, known as 'the Ezrahite', of the line of Judah, referred to in 1 Ki. 4:31, in the title of Ps. 89, and perhaps in 1 Ch. 2:6, if 'Zerah' is regarded as a form of 'Ezrah'.

Two other men called Ethan are mentioned briefly—in 1 Ch. 6:42 (perhaps identical with *Jeduthun), and 1 Ch. 6:44; 15:17. J.D.D.

ETHICS, BIBLICAL.

I. The distinctive principle

The distinctiveness of the Bible's ethical teaching is well illustrated by the derivation of the words 'ethics' and 'morals' themselves. Both come from roots (Greek and Latin) which mean 'custom'. The implication is that we behave in an ethically correct manner when we do what custom dictates. We discover the things that are usually done, and conclude that these are the things we ought to do.

In sharp contrast to this approach, biblical ethics are God-centred. Instead of following majority opinion or conforming to customary behaviour, the Scriptures encourage us to start with God and his requirements—not with man and his habits—when we look for moral guidelines. This central, unifying principle is expressed in many ways in the Bible:

(*a*) *The standard of goodness is personal.* If we want to discover the nature of goodness, the Bible directs us to the person of God himself. He alone is good (Mk. 10:18), and it is his will that expresses 'what is good and acceptable and perfect' (Rom. 12:2). Out in the Sinai desert, Yahweh promised Moses 'I will make all my goodness pass before you' (Ex. 33:19), and the promise was honoured with a special revelation of the Lord's character (Ex. 34:6f.). Unlike any other moral teacher, God is utterly consistent. What he wills, he is.

(*b*) *The source of moral knowledge is revelation.* According to the Bible, knowledge of right and wrong is not so much an object of philosophical enquiry as an acceptance of divine revelation. As Paul puts it, knowing God's will (which is equivalent to discovering what is right) comes through instruction in his law (Rom. 2:18). So while the moral philosopher investigates his data in order to draw judicious conclusions, the biblical writers are content to declare God's revealed will without feeling the need to justify their judgments.

(*c*) *Moral teaching is phrased as command, not statement.* Outwardly, the most striking difference between the Bible and a secular textbook on ethics is the way its moral teaching is communicated. To find reasoned-out arguments for ethical demands in the Bible, one has to look almost exclusively in the OT Wisdom literature (*cf.* Pr. 5:1ff.). Elsewhere, moral judgments are laid down flatly, not argued out reasonably. A philosopher who does not back his opinions with a well-argued case cannot expect people to take him seriously. But the biblical writers, inasmuch as they believed themselves to be conveying God's will, felt no need for logical argument to support their moral commands.

(*d*) *The basic ethical demand is to imitate God.* As God sums up goodness in his own person, man's supreme ideal, according to the Bible, is to imitate him. This is reflected in the OT refrain 'Be holy, for I am holy' (Lv. 11:44f., *etc.*); and in the way great old covenant words like *ḥeseḏ* ('steadfast love') and *'ᵉmûnâh* ('faithfulness') are used to describe both God's character and his moral requirements of man. In the NT, too, the same note is struck. Christians must display their heavenly Father's mercy, said Jesus, and even his moral perfection (Lk. 6:36; Mt. 5:48). And because Jesus 'bears the very stamp of his nature' (Heb. 1:3), the call to imitate him comes with equal force (*cf.* 1 Cor. 11:1). We become imitators of the Father as we live out the Son's love (Eph. 5:1f.).

(*e*) *Religion and ethics are inseparable.* All attempts to drive a wedge between the Bible's moral precepts and its religious teaching fail. Because the biblical ethic is theocentric, the moral teaching of Scripture loses its credibility once the religious undergirding is removed (*cf.*, *e.g.*, the Beatitudes, Mt. 5:3ff.). Religion and ethics are related as foundation to building. The moral demands of the Decalogue, for example, are founded on the fact of God's redemptive activity (Ex. 20:2); and much of Jesus' moral teaching is presented as deduction from religious premises (*cf.* Mt. 5:43ff.). The same principle is well illustrated by the literary structure of Paul's Epistles. As well as providing specific examples of moral teaching built on religious foundations (*e.g.* 1 Cor. 6:18ff.; 2 Cor. 8:7ff.; Phil. 2:4ff.), Paul shapes his letters to follow the same pattern. A carefully presented theological main section is made the springboard for a clear-cut ethical tail-piece (*cf.*, especially, Rom., Eph., Phil.). Christian ethics spring from Christian doctrine, and the two are inseparable.

II. The Old Testament

(*a*) *The covenant.* The covenant God made with Israel through Moses (Ex. 24) had direct and far-reaching ethical significance. In particular, the keynote of grace, first struck in the Lord's choice of covenant partner (Dt. 7:7f.; 9:4), sets the theme for the whole of the OT's moral teaching.

God's grace supplies the chief motive for obedience to his commandments. Appeals to godly fear are by no means absent from the OT (*cf.* Ex. 22:22ff.), but far more often grace provides the main stimulus to good behaviour. Men, as God's covenant partners, are invited to respond gratefully to his prior acts of undeserved love; they are summoned to do his will in gratitude for his grace, rather than submit in terror to threats of punishment. So slaves must be treated generously because God treated Hebrew slaves with generosity in Egypt (Dt. 15:12ff.). Businessmen are not to weight their scales unfairly, remembering that it was the God of justice who redeemed their ancestors (Lv. 19:36). Strangers are to be treated with the same kindness that the Lord of

ETERNAL
See Time, Part 3.

ETERNAL LIFE
See Eschatology, Part 1.

ETERNAL PUNISHMENT
See Hell, Part 2.

ETERNITY
See Time, Part 3.

ETHANIM
See Calendar, Part 1.

grace showed to his people—'for you were strangers in the land of Egypt' (Lv. 19:33f.). In a word, God's covenant demand is 'you shall keep my commandments and do them', because 'I am the Lord . . . who brought you out of the land of Egypt to be your God' (Lv. 22:31ff.).

The covenant also encouraged an intense awareness of corporate solidarity in Israel. Its effect was not only to unite the individual to God, but also to bind all covenant members into a single community (*cf.* the language Paul uses to describe the effect of the new covenant in Eph. 2:11ff.). The recurrence of 'flesh and bone' language in the Bible illustrates this principle vividly; first used of a one-to-one relationship in Gn. 2:23, it could be applied by an individual to his extended family (Jdg. 9:1f.), by the nation declaring its loyalty to its leader (2 Sa. 5:1), and even—in later days—by one Jew describing his relationship to his race (Rom. 11:14, AV). So it was that when a man transgressed one of God's commandments, the whole community was implicated in his sin (Jos. 7:1ff.); and when an individual fell on hard times, everyone felt the obligation to go to his aid.

Hence the very strong emphasis the OT lays on social ethics. Corporate solidarity led straight to neighbour-concern. In the one close community unit, every individual was important. The poor had the same rights as the rich because they both came under the one covenant umbrella. Weaker members of society were specially protected (*cf.* the specific regulations of Ex. 22 and 23, with their safeguards for the widow, the orphan, the stranger and the poor).

(*b*) *The law.* The covenant provided the context for God's law-giving. Consequently, a distinctive feature of OT law was its stress on the maintenance of right relationships. Its main concern was not to set a fence round abstract ethical ideals, but to cement good relationships between people, and between people and God. So the majority of its specific precepts are couched in the second person rather than the third. Hence, too, the strongly positive and warm attitude adopted by those under the law towards law-keeping (*cf.* Pss. 19:7ff.; 119:33ff., 72); and the recognition that the most serious consequence of law-breaking was not any material punishment but the resulting breakdown in relationships (*cf.* Ho. 1:2).

At the heart of the law lie the Ten Commandments (Ex. 20:3ff.; Dt. 5:7ff.), concerned as they are with the most fundamental of relationships. No summary could be more inclusive. They set out the basic sanctities governing belief, worship and life—the sanctity of God's being, his worship, his name and his day; and the sanctity of marriage and family, life, property and truth. The context in which they are given is one of redemption (Ex. 20:2), and their relevance is not exhausted with the coming of Christ (Mt. 5:17ff.; Rom. 13:9; Jas. 2:10f.).

As well as being the fruit of God's redemptive work, the Decalogue has deep roots in the creation ordinances of Gn. 1 and 2. These are the ordinances of procreation and managerial responsibility for the rest of creation (Gn. 1:28); of the sabbath (Gn. 2:2f.); of work (Gn. 2:15) and of marriage (Gn. 2:24). Together (like the Decalogue), they touch upon all the main areas of human life and behaviour, and provide basic guidelines for those seeking a life-style that is in line with the Creator's ideal.

Man's fall into sin did nothing to abrogate these ordinances. Their lasting relevance is upheld in the rest of Scripture (*cf.* Gn. 3:16, 19; 4:1–2, 17, 25; 5:1ff.; 9:7). But the Fall did materially affect the specific content of the OT law. As well as penal sanctions, new provisions were necessary to deal with the radically different situation sin had created. Moses' permission of divorce (Dt. 24:1ff.) is a good case in point. This provision was God's concession to severely sin-torn marriage relationships, not an annulment of his creation marriage ordinance (Gn. 2:24; *cf.* Mt. 19:3ff.). Here, as elsewhere, we must be careful not to confuse God's tolerance with his approval; just as we must always clearly distinguish between the biblical ethic and some of the equivocal behaviour of God's people recorded in the Bible.

(*c*) *The prophets.* The 8th-century prophets have been aptly called 'the politicians of the covenant'. Social conditions had changed dramatically since Moses' times. Amos' contemporaries had summer-houses as well as winter-houses. Big business flourished. There was financial speculation and money-lending on a large scale. Alliances and cultural exchanges were arranged with foreign powers. On the face of it, the covenant law had little help to offer to those struggling with the moral dilemmas of so vastly different an environment. But the prophets made it their business to interpret the law by digging down to its basic principles and applying these to the concrete moral problems of their day.

In particular, they echoed the law's deep concern for social justice. Accurately reflecting the spirit of the covenant's concern for the weak, Amos and Hosea flay those who sell the needy for a pair of shoes, accept bribes, use false weights and measures, or generally oppress the poor (Am. 2:6; 5:12; Mi. 6:11). With Isaiah and Hosea, they are particularly savage on those who try to hide their moral failures behind a façade of religious observance (Is. 1:10ff.; Ho. 6:6). God finds feast-days and hymn-singing nauseating, they thundered, while injustice and unrighteousness flourish (Am. 5:21ff.). A humble walk with him involves doing justice and loving kindness (Mi. 6:8).

The prophets also corrected any imbalance that may have resulted from observance of the covenant law. The covenant's stress on corporate solidarity, for example, may have blurred, in some minds, the concept of personal responsibility. So Ezekiel, especially, is at pains to point out that in God's sight every individual is morally responsible for what he does; no-one can simply shelve the blame for wrongdoing on his heredity and environment (Ezk. 18:20ff.). Again, God's special covenant concern for Israel had fostered in some people an unhealthy, narrow brand of nationalism which led them to depise foreigners. The prophets administered the necessary corrective by insisting that God's moral standards are applied evenly. His love embraces Ethiopians as well as Israelites (Am. 9:7). And Israel will not escape his judgment for sin by pleading her special position as the Lord's chosen people; in fact, says Amos, a privileged knowledge of God brings with it extra responsibilities and greater risk (Am. 1:1–3:2).

The enormity of sin, and the vastness of the gulf between the holy God and sinful men, impressed the prophets deeply (*cf.* Hab. 1:13; Is. 6:3ff.). Without a special act of divine grace, they knew no bridge could be built across this gap (*cf.* Je. 13:23). Man's renewal depended on the activity of God's Spirit (Ezk. 37:1ff.) and on a new kind of covenant law which God himself would write on his people's hearts (Je. 31:31ff.).

III. The New Testament

(*a*) *The Gospels.* Jesus showed great respect for the OT moral law; he came not to abolish but to fulfil it (Mt. 5:17ff.). But he did not teach as a legislator himself. Though he phrased much of his moral teaching in imperatives (*e.g.* Mt. 5:39ff.; Mk. 10:9), and taught with a law-giver's authority (*cf.* Mt. 7:24ff.; Mk. 1:22), it was not his purpose to lay down a comprehensive code of rules for moral living. Law prescribes or forbids specific things; Jesus was more concerned to set out and illustrate the general character of God's will. Law deals in actions; Jesus dealt far more in character and in the motives that inspire action.

Jesus' internalizing of the law's demands is well illustrated in the Sermon on the Mount. The law forbade murder and adultery. Jesus (while not, of course, condoning either) put his finger on the thoughts and attitudes behind the actions. The man who nursed a private hatred towards his neighbour, or mentally undressed the latter's wife in lust, could not (he taught) evade moral blame by pleading that he had not broken the letter of the law (Mt. 5:21f., 27f.). The Beatitudes, with which the Sermon begins (vv. 3ff.), underline the same point. They comprise not a list of rules, but a set of congratulations directed at those whose lives exemplify godly attitudes. Conversely, the sins Jesus condemns are mainly those of the spirit, not those of the flesh. He has surprisingly little to say (*e.g.*) about sexual misconduct. On two occasions when sexual sin was brought to his notice (Lk. 7:37ff.; Jn. 8:3ff.), he deliberately turned the spotlight on to the bad motives of the critics. He reserved his most stinging rebukes for wrong attitudes of mind and heart—like moral blindness, callousness and pride (Mt. 7:3ff.; Mk. 3:5; Lk. 18:9ff.).

Jesus' approach to love provides a further illustration of the way he reinforced and developed OT moral teaching. Both parts of his well-known love-summary of the law (Mk. 12:28ff.) are taken straight from the pages of the OT (Dt. 6:4; Lv. 19:18). But he cut across the racial convictions of many of his contemporaries in his radical interpretation of the second of these commandments. Too often 'love your neighbour' was taken to mean 'love your covenant-neighbour—and him only'. Through (especially) the parable of the Good Samaritan (Lk. 10:29ff.), Jesus taught that neighbour-love must extend to anyone in need, irrespective of race, creed or culture. He universalized love's demands.

In expounding neighbour-love, Jesus identified grace as its distinctive feature. Other kinds of loving—all of them treated positively in the NT—are either a response to something attractive in the one loved (as with physical desire and friendship), or the kind of love that is limited to the members of a group (like family devotion). True neighbour-love, Jesus taught, operates quite independently of any lovableness. It is evoked by need, not merit, and does not look for returns (Lk. 6:32ff.; 14:12ff.). It has no group limits either. And in all these ways it mirrors the love of God (Jn. 3:16; 13:34; Lk. 15:11ff.; *cf.* Gal. 2:20; 1 Jn. 4:7ff.).

When the rich young ruler responded enthusiastically to Jesus' summary of the law, the Lord's rejoinder was 'You are not far from the kingdom of God' (Mk. 12:34). So as well as being the king-pin of God's law, love is the gateway to his kingdom, and Jesus' kingdom teaching is packed with ethical significance. Those who enter the kingdom are those who submit themselves to God's rule; when his kingdom comes, his will is done. And God provides those in his kingdom with royal guidance and power to carry right ethical decisions into practice.

It is this availability of supernatural moral power that makes sense of some of Jesus' otherwise impossible demands (*cf.* Mt. 5:48). He was no triumphalist (repentance is associated with the kingdom too—Mk. 1:15), but most of his moral imperatives were addressed to those already in the kingdom, with the implied assurance that all who submit to God's rule can share his strength to convert their ethical convictions into action.

Because the kingdom is a present reality in Christ, the King's guidance and power are available here and now. But because there is also a sense in which the fullness of the kingdom's coming is still imminent, there is a consistent note of urgency in Jesus' moral teaching too. When God's rule over men is fully revealed there will be a judgment, and only a fool would ignore the warning note the kingdom sounds (*cf.* Lk. 12:20). Hence the gospel-call to repentance (Mt. 4:17).

(*b*) *The rest of the New Testament.* As is to be expected, the Epistles provide clear parallels with the moral teaching of the Gospels, even though they quote Jesus' words surprisingly rarely (*cf.* 1 Cor. 7:10; 9:14). But because they were written as practical answers to urgent questions from living churches, the tone of their moral teaching is slightly different. From the Gospels it would seem that Jesus taught mainly in broad general principles, leaving his hearers to make their own applications. In the Epistles, on the other hand, the applications are often spelt out in very specific terms. Sexual sin, for example, is analysed in considerable detail (*cf.* 1 Cor. 6:9; 2 Cor. 12:21), and sins of speech come in for similarly detailed treatment (*cf.* Rom. 1:29f.; Eph. 4:29; 5:4; Col. 3:8; Jas. 3:5ff.).

Another distinctive feature of the Epistles' ethical teaching is the recurrence of the so-called household codes (Eph. 5:22ff.; Col. 3:18f.; 1 Tim. 2:8ff.; Tit. 2:2ff.; 1 Pet. 2:18ff.). These are small sections of teaching on right relationships, especially in marriage, in the home and at work. They are notably conservative in tone, as are parallel sections on the relationship between believers and the secular authorities (*cf.* Rom. 13:1ff.; Tit. 3:1; 1 Pet. 2:13f.). However eagerly the early Christian community looked forward to the consummation of God's kingdom, their keenness clearly did not lead them to reject the basic authority structures on which the life of society was founded. Even in the book of Revelation, where the veil of apocalyptic language covering John's condemnation of the secular government at Rome is transparently thin, the saints are called to martyrdom, not revolution. Nevertheless, seeds of social change are to be found in the NT, notably in the relationships Christians are encouraged to foster with one another in the church (*cf.* Gal. 3:28).

The theme of the kingdom is not nearly so prominent in the Epistles

Captured Ethiopian soldiers (of Tirhakah), wearing a single upright feather on their heads, being led by the soldiers of Ashurbanipal, king of Assyria. 668–627 BC. *Nineveh.* (BM)

as in the Gospels, but there is the same emphasis on man's need for God's guidance and power in moral living. In Paul's language, union with Christ (2 Cor. 5:17) and the indwelling Spirit (Phil. 2:13) raise the Christian's moral life to a new plane. Fed by God's Word (Heb. 5:14), the redeemed believer is given sharper insight into distinctions between good and bad (*cf.* Rom. 12:2); and indwelt by the Spirit, he has new power to do what he knows to be right.

It is sometimes said that in his revolt against Jewish legalism, and boosted by his confidence in the Spirit's power to inform and transform the Christian believer, Paul (especially) held that the OT moral law had become obsolete in Christ. There are certainly passages in the Epistles which, taken alone, might suggest such a view (*e.g.* Gal. 3:23ff.; Rom. 7:6; 10:4; 2 Cor. 3:6), but it is important to recognize that Paul uses the word 'law' in different ways. Where he uses it as shorthand for 'justification by law' (*e.g.* Rom. 10:4), he clearly regards living by law as both obsolete and dangerous for Christians. But where he uses the word simply to mean the expression of God's will (*e.g.* Rom. 7:12), he is far more positive. He quotes the Decalogue without embarrassment (*e.g.* Eph. 6:2f.), and writes freely about a law principle which is operative in the Christian life (Rom. 8:2; 1 Cor. 9:21; Gal. 6:2; *cf.* Jas. 1:25; 2:12). Here, as elsewhere, the teaching of the NT dovetails into that of the OT. So far as it contains God's basic moral demands the law retains its validity, because he alone expresses in his person and will all that is good and right.

BIBLIOGRAPHY. A. B. Bruce, *The Ethics of the Old Testament*, 1909; C. H. Dodd, *Gospel and Law*, 1951; W. Eichrodt, *The Theology of the Old Testament*, 2, 1967; D. H. Field, *Free To Do Right*, 1973; N. L. Geisler, *Ethics*, 1971; C. F. H. Henry, *Christian Personal Ethics*, 1957; W. Lillie, *Studies in New Testament Ethics*, 1961; T. W. Manson, *Ethics and the Gospel*, 1960; L. H. Marshall, *The Challenge of New Testament Ethics*, 1966; J. Murray, *Principles of Conduct*, 1957; A. Nygren, *Agape and Eros*, 1953; R. Schnackenburg, *The Moral Teaching of the New Testament*, 1965; G. F. Thomas, *Christian Ethics and Moral Philosophy*, 1955; A. R. Vidler, *Christ's Strange Work*, 1963; J. W. Wenham, *The Goodness of God*, 1974; J. H. Yoder, *The Politics of Jesus*, 1972. D.H.F.

ETHIOPIA. Settled by the descendants of *Cush (Gn. 10:6), biblical Ethiopia (Gk. *Aithiōps*, 'burnt face', *cf.* Je. 13:23) is part of the kingdom of Nubia stretching from Aswan (*SEVENEH) S to the junction of the Nile near modern Khartoum. Invaded in prehistoric times by Hamites from Arabia and Asia, Ethiopia was dominated by Egypt for nearly 500 years beginning with Dynasty 18 (*c.* 1500 BC) and was governed by a viceroy ('King's Son of Kush') who ruled the African empire, controlled the army in Africa and managed the Nubian gold mines.

During the 9th century the Ethiopians, whose capital was Napata near the fourth cataract, engaged in at least one foray into Palestine, only to suffer defeat at Asa's hand (2 Ch. 14:9–15). Ethiopia's heyday began about 720 BC when Pi-ankhi took advantage of Egypt's internal strife and became the first conqueror of that land in a millennium. For about 60 years Ethiopian rulers (Dynasty 25) controlled the Nile Valley. One of them, Tirhakah, seems to have been Hezekiah's ally and attempted to forestall Sennacherib's invasion (2 Ki. 19:9; Is. 37:9; J. Bright, *History of Israel*², 1972, pp. 296ff., discusses the chronological problems in this narrative). Na. 3:9 alludes to the glory of this period: 'Ethiopia was her (Egypt's) strength.' Invasions by Esarhaddon and Ashurbanipal reduced the Ethiopian–Egyptian kingdom to tributary status; the destruction of Thebes (*c.* 663 BC; Na. 3:8–10) brought a total eclipse, fulfilling Isaiah's prophetic symbolism (20:2–6).

Ethiopian troops fought vainly in Pharaoh Neco's army at Carchemish (605 BC; Je. 46:2, 9). Cambyses' conquest of Egypt brought Ethiopia under Persian sway; Est. 1:1; 8:9 name Ethiopia as the most remote Persian province to the SW, while biblical writers sometimes use her to symbolize the unlimited extent of God's sovereignty (Ps. 87:4; Ezk. 30:4ff.; Am. 9:7; Zp. 2:12). 'Beyond the rivers of Ethiopia' (Is. 18:1; Zp. 3:10) may refer to N Abyssinia, where Jewish colonists had apparently settled along with other Semites from S Arabia. The Chronicler is cognizant of this close relationship between Ethiopia and S Arabia (2 Ch. 21:16).

In Acts 8:27 Ethiopia refers to the Nilotic kingdom of *Candace, who ruled at Meroë, where the capital had been moved during the Persian period. Modern Ethiopians (Abyssinians) have appropriated biblical references to Ethiopia and consider the *Ethiopian eunuch's conversion to be a fulfilment of Ps. 68:31.

BIBLIOGRAPHY. E. A. W. Budge, *History of Ethiopia*, 1928; E. Ullendorff, *The Ethiopians*, 1960; *idem*, *Ethiopia and the Bible*, 1968; J. Wilson, *The Burden of Egypt*, 1951. D.A.H.

ETHIOPIAN EUNUCH. A high official (*dynastēs*), royal treasurer in the court of *Ethiopia's Queen

*Candace, converted under Philip's ministry (Acts 8:26–40). It was not unusual in antiquity for *eunuchs, who were customarily harem attendants, to rise to positions of influence.

Barred from active participation in the Jewish rites by his race and his emasculation (Dt. 23:1), he was most probably a 'God-fearer'. His acquaintance with Judaism and the OT (the quotation from Is. 53 seems to be from the LXX) is not completely unexpected in light of Jewish settlements in Upper Egypt and the considerable impact made by Jewish life and thought on the Ethiopians. His zeal in studying the Scriptures, his ready reception of the gospel and baptism mark him as one of the outstanding converts in Acts, even if his confession (Acts 8:37) is not supported in the better MSS. Ethiopian tradition claims him as his country's first evangelist. D.A.H.

ETHIOPIAN WOMAN. Married by Moses, whom Aaron and Miriam then criticized (Nu. 12:1). As the last mention of Zipporah is just after the defeat of Amalek (Ex. 17) when Jethro returned her to Moses (Ex. 18), it is possible that she subsequently died, Moses then taking this 'Cushite woman' as his second wife, unless Moses then had two wives. 'Cushite' is usually taken as 'Ethiopian' (*cf.* *CUSH, *ETHIOPIA); if so, she probably left Egypt among the Israelites and their sympathizers. It is also, perhaps, possible to derive 'Cushite' from Kushu and Heb. Cushan, associated with Midian (Hab. 3:7); if so, this woman might be of allied stock to Jethro and Zipporah. K.A.K.

ETHNARCH (Gk. *ethnarchēs*, 'governor', 2 Cor. 11:32). An officer in charge of Damascus with a garrison under *Aretas IV, king of Arabia Petraea (9 BC–AD 39), who was encouraged by the Jews to arrest Paul after his conversion (*cf.* Acts 9:24–25). Damascus in 64 BC became part of the Roman province of Syria. At this time (*c.* AD 33) it was temporarily under Aretas.

The title is used by Josephus for subordinate rulers, particularly of peoples under foreign control, *e.g.* the Jews in Alexandria (*Ant.* 14. 117); *cf.* Simon, ethnarch of Judaea under Demetrius II (1 Macc. 14:47). B.F.H.

EUNICE. Timothy's mother, a woman of notable faith (2 Tim. 1:5). She was Jewish (Acts 16:1) and pious, for Timothy's biblical instruction had begun early (2 Tim. 3:15), but her husband was a Gentile and her son uncircumcised (Acts 16:3). In view of Jewish intermarriage with leading Phrygian families (Ramsay, *BRD*, p. 357; *cf.* *CBP*, 2, pp. 667ff.), such things may represent her family's social climbing, not personal declension. Some Lat. MSS of Acts 16:1, and Origen on Rom. 16:21, call her a widow, and *hypērchen* in Acts 16:3 might support this. She lived at Derbe or Lystra: linguistically a case can be made for either (*cf.* *BC*, 4, pp. 184, 254). Her name is Greek, and does not seem common.

It is sometimes suggested that Paul refers to Jewish faith, but the most natural interpretation of 2 Tim. 1:5 (and of Acts 16:1) is that Christian faith 'dwelt' (aorist, perhaps alluding to the event of conversion, doubtless in Paul's first missionary journey) 'first' in *Lois and herself (*i.e.* antecedent to Timothy's conversion). A.F.W.

EUNUCH (Heb. *sārîs*). The derivation of the OT word is uncertain, but is thought to come from an Assyr. term meaning, 'He who is head (to the king)'. (So Jensen (*ZA* 7, 1892, 174A.1), and Zimmern (*ZDMG* 53, 1899, 116 A.2); accepted by S. R. Driver and L. Koehler in their lexicons; see further note by the latter in his *Supplement*, p. 219.) The primary meaning is 'court officer'. In Hebrew a secondary meaning is found, namely, a 'castrate' or 'eunuch'. From Herodotus we learn that 'in eastern countries eunuchs are valued as being specially trustworthy in every way' (8. 105, tr. Selingcourt). Such persons were frequently employed by eastern rulers as officers of the household. Hence, in the E it is sometimes difficult to know which of the two meanings is intended or whether both are implied. Potiphar (Gn. 39:1), who was married (v. 7), is called a *sārîs* (LXX *eunouchos*): the meaning 'court officer' may be best here. In Is. 56:3 the meaning 'castrate' is obvious. In Ne. 1:11, 'I was the king's cupbearer', some copies of the LXX have *eunouchos*; but this is probably a slip for *oinochoos*, as Rahlfs in *Septuaginta* (1, p. 923) has seen. The 'castrate' was to be excluded from the assembly of the Lord (Dt. 23:1). There is no necessity to assume, as Josephus seems to do (*Ant.* 10. 186), that Daniel and his companions were 'castrates', for they were 'without blemish' (see Dn. 1:4).

In the NT the word *eunouchos* is used, and may be derived from *eunēn echō* ('to keep the bed'). Like its counterpart *sārîs*, it need not denote strictly a castrate. In Acts 8:27 both meanings may be intended; in Mt. 19:12 the meaning 'castrate' is beyond doubt. In this last passage three classes of eunuch are mentioned, namely, born eunuchs, man-made eunuchs and spiritual eunuchs. The last class includes all those who sacrificed legitimate, natural desires for the sake of the kingdom of heaven. Report in the early church had it that Origen, misinterpreting in a literal sense the above passage, mutilated himself.

Judaism knew only two classes of eunuch: man-made (*sārîs 'āḏām*) and natural (*sārîs ḥammâ*), thus the Mishnah (*Zabim* 2. 1). This last term *sārîs ḥammâ* or 'eunuch of the sun' is explained by Jastrow, *Dictionary of Babylonian Talmud*, etc., 1, p. 476, to mean 'a eunuch from the time of seeing the sun', in other words, a eunuch who is born so. (*CHAMBERLAIN.) R.J.A.S.

EUODIA. This RSV rendering is to be preferred to the AV's 'Euodias' (Phil. 4:2), for the reference is to a woman rather than a man. Paul begs her and Syntyche to be reconciled. Probably, as Lightfoot suggests, they were deaconesses at Philippi. J.D.D.

EUPHRATES. The largest river in W Asia, and on this account generally referred to as *hannāhār*, 'the river', in the OT (*e.g.* Dt. 11:24). It is sometimes mentioned by name, however, the Heb. form being *pᵉrāṯ* (*e.g.* Gn. 2:14; 15:18) derived from Akkadian *purattu*, which represents Sumerian *buranun*, and the NT form *Euphratēs* (Rev. 9:14; 16:12). The Euphrates takes its source in two main affluents in E Turkey, the Murad-Su, which rises near Lake Van, and the Kara-Su, which rises near Erzerum, and runs, joined only by the Ḫâbûr (*HABOR) for 2,000 km to the Persian Gulf. From low water in September it rises by degrees throughout the

The Euphrates river, fringed by palm trees at Babylon. (DJW)

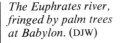

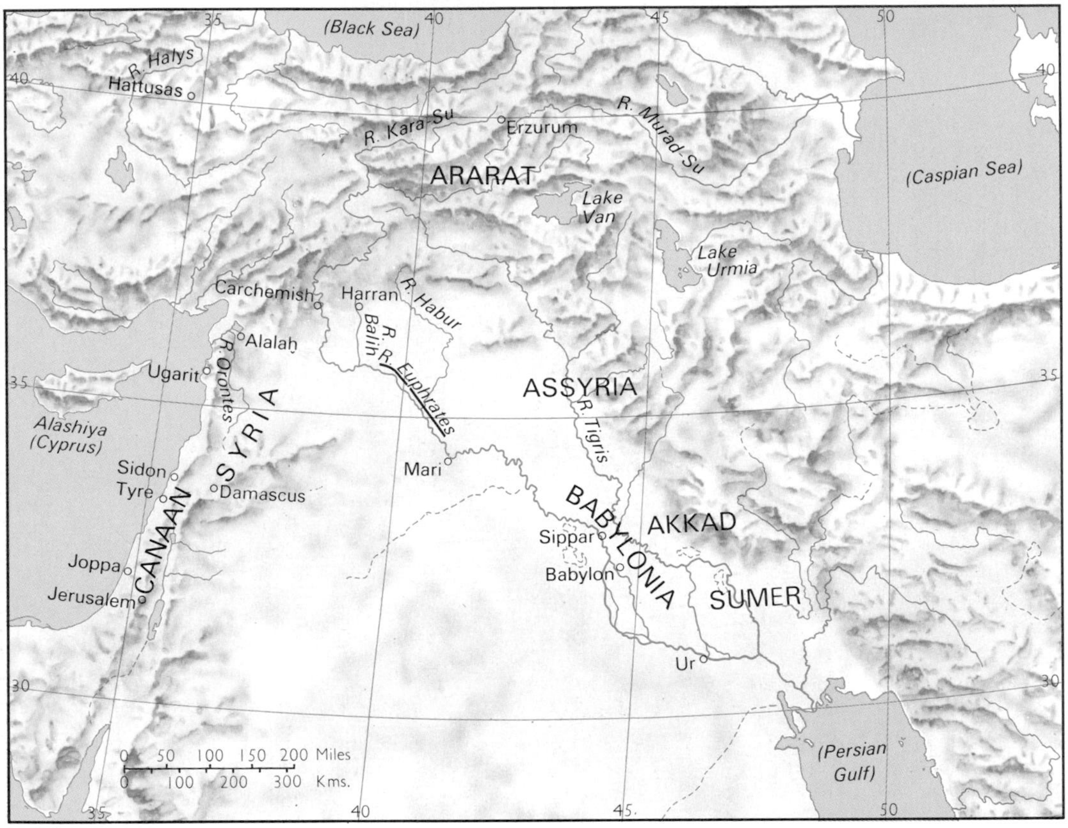

The river Euphrates.

winter to some 3 m higher by May, and then declines again until September, thus enjoying a milder régime than the *Tigris. In the alluvial plain of Babylonia (*MESOPOTAMIA) its course has shifted to the W since ancient times, when most of the important cities, now some km to the E of it, lay on or near its banks. This is illustrated by the fact that the Sumerians wrote its name ideographically as 'river of Sippar', a city whose ruins lie today some 6 km to the E (*SEPHARVAIM). In addition to the many important cities, including Babylon, which lay on its banks in the S plain, the city of Mari was situated on its middle course, not far from the junction with the Ḫâbûr, and the strategic crossing-place from N Mesopotamia to N Syria was commanded by the fortress city of *Carchemish.

BIBLIOGRAPHY. S. A. Pallis, *The Antiquity of Iraq*, 1956, pp. 4–7.

T.C.M.

EURAQUILO
See Wind, Part 3.

EUROCLYDON
See Wind, Part 3.

EUTYCHUS ('Lucky', a common Gk. name). A young man from Troas who fell from an upstairs window-seat during Paul's protracted nocturnal address there (Acts 20:7–12). H. J. Cadbury (*Book of Acts in History*, pp. 8ff.) points out a similar fatal accident in *Oxyrhynchus Papyri*, 3. 475. Luke's words suggest an increasing and eventually irresistible drowsiness, perhaps—since v. 8 seems related to the incident—induced by the numerous lamps rather than in spite of them.

The miraculous nature of the outcome has been questioned, Paul's words in v. 10 being applied to diagnosis, not healing. However, v. 9 shows that Luke was himself sure that Eutychus died. 'His life' would then be 'in him' from the moment of Paul's embrace (*cf.* 2 Ki. 4:34). On Paul's departure next morning, Eutychus was recovered (v. 12: according to the Western Text he joined the farewell party). Seen as an eyewitness account by Luke, the story is vivid and the broken sequence intelligible. The assumption that 'a current anecdote had come to be applied to Paul, that Luke found it in this form and introduced it into his narrative' (Dibelius) creates obscurities.

BIBLIOGRAPHY. W. M. Ramsay, *SPT*, pp. 290f.; M. Dibelius, *Studies in the Acts of the Apostles*, E.T. 1956, pp. 17ff.

A.F.W.

EVANGELIST. The word translated in the NT 'evangelist' is a noun from the verb *euangelizomai* 'to announce news', and usually rendered in EVV as 'preach the gospel'. (The NT term echoes Heb. *mᵉḇaśśēr*, *mᵉḇaśśereṯ*, in Is. 40:9; 52:7.) The verb is very common in the NT, and is applied to God (Gal. 3:8), to our Lord (Lk. 20:1), and to ordinary church members (Acts 8:4), as well as to apostles on their missionary journeys. The noun 'evangelist' occurs three times only in the NT. Timothy (2 Tim. 4:5) is exhorted by Paul to do the work of an evangelist; that is to say, make known the facts of the gospel. Timothy had accompanied the apostle on his missionary journeys. But it is plain from the injunctions in the two letters addressed to him that his work when the apostle wrote was very largely local and pastoral. That he is enjoined to do the work of an evangelist shows that a man who was an evangelist could also be a pastor and teacher.

In Acts 21:8 Philip is described as 'the evangelist'. Philip had been chosen as one of the Seven in Acts 6, and after the persecution of Stephen he was prominent in preaching the gospel in unevangelized parts (*e.g.* Acts 8:5, 12, 35, 40). Though an evangelist, he was not included among the apostles

(Acts 8:14). A similar distinction is made between Timothy and the apostles in 2 Cor. 1:1 and Col. 1:1. It will be seen, then, that though apostles were evangelists, not all evangelists were apostles. This distinction is confirmed in Eph. 4:11, where the office of 'evangelist' is mentioned after 'apostle' and 'prophet', and before 'pastor' and 'teacher'. From this passage it is plain that the gift of evangelist was a distinct gift within the Christian church; and although all Christians doubtless performed this sacred task, as opportunity was given to them, there were some who were pre-eminently called and endowed by the Holy Spirit for this work.

Later in the history of the church the term 'evangelist' was used for a writer of one of the four Gospels.

BIBLIOGRAPHY. L. Coenen, *NIDNTT* 2, pp. 107–115. D.B.K.

EVE. The first woman, wife of *Adam and mother of Cain, Abel and Seth (Gn. 4:1–2, 25). When he had made Adam, God resolved to provide 'a helper fit for him' (*'ēzer kᵉnegdô*, Gn. 2:18, 20, lit. 'a helper as in front of him', *i.e.* 'a helper corresponding to him'), so he caused him to sleep and, taking one of his ribs (*ṣēlā'*, Gn. 2:21), made (*bānâ*, Gn. 2:22, a word normally meaning 'to build') it into a woman (*lᵉ'iššâ*). (*CREATION.) Adam, recognizing his close relationship, declared that she should be called 'Woman (*'iššâ*), because she was taken out of (*min*; *cf.* 1 Cor. 11:8, *ek*) Man (*'îš*)' (Gn. 2:23). Some scholars consider that *'îš* and *'iššâ* are etymologically distinct, but this need not be significant, since the context requires only that there should be formal similarity between the words, as indeed is the case with EVV 'man' and '*wo*man'.

Eve was the instrument of the serpent in causing Adam to eat the forbidden fruit (*FALL), and as a result God condemned her to bear children in pain, and to be ruled over (*māšal bᵉ*) by Adam (Gn. 3:16). Adam then called her 'Eve (*ḥawwâ*, Gn. 3:20); because she was the mother of all living (*ḥay*)'. Many theories have been put forward as to the name *ḥawwâ*. Some would see it as an archaic form of *ḥayyâ*, 'living thing' (the LXX takes this view, translating it in Gn. 3:20 by *zōē*, 'life'), others note a similarity with Aramaic *hiwyā'*, 'serpent', with which is connected a Phoenician (possibly serpent) deity *ḥwt*, but as with *'îš* and *'iššâ* nothing beyond a formal assonance appears to be required by the text. The name *ḥawwâ* occurs twice only in the OT (Gn. 3:20; 4:1), the word 'woman' being more commonly used. In the LXX and NT it appears as *Heua* (*Eua* in some MSS), which passes to *Heva* in the Vulgate, and thence to *Eve* in the EVV.

A sidelight on the biblical statements about Eve is found in a Sumerian myth concerning the god Enki. In this Enki finds himself suffering from a series of ailments, to deal with each of which the goddess Ninḫursag produces a special goddess. Thus, when he says 'My rib (*ti*; written with a logogram, one of whose Akkadian values was *ṣîlu*, 'side, rib') hurts me', she replies that she has caused a goddess *Nin-ti* ('Lady of the rib') to be born for him. But Sumerian *Nin-ti* can equally mean 'Lady who makes live'. It may be that this reflects in some way a common original narrative with the Genesis account.

BIBLIOGRAPHY. *KB*³, p. 284; G. J. Spurrell, *Notes on the Text of the Book of Genesis*², 1896, p. 45; S. N. Kramer, *Enki and Ninḫursag. A Sumerian Paradise Myth* (*BASOR* Supplementary Studies 1), 1945, pp. 8–9; *From the Tablets of Sumer*, 1956, pp. 170–171 = *History Begins at Sumer*, 1958, pp. 195–196; I. M. Kikawada, 'Two Notes on Eve', *JBL* 91, 1972, pp. 33–37. T.C.M.

EVIL (Heb. *ra'*; Gk. *kakos, ponēros, phaulos*). Evil has a broader meaning than *sin. The Heb. word comes from a root meaning 'to spoil', 'to break in pieces': being broken and so made worthless. It is essentially what is unpleasant, disagreeable, offensive. The word binds together the evil deed and its consequences. In the NT *kakos* and *ponēros* mean respectively the quality of evil in its essential character, and its hurtful effects or influence. It is used in both physical and moral senses. While these aspects are different, there is frequently a close relationship between them. Much physical evil is due to moral evil: suffering and sin are not necessarily connected in individual cases, but human selfishness and sin explain much of the world's ills. Though all evil must be punished, not all physical ill is a punishment of wrongdoing (Lk. 13:2, 4; Jn. 9:3; *cf.* Job).

I. Physical evil

The prophets regarded God as the ultimate Cause of evil, as expressed in pain, suffering or disaster. In his sovereignty he tolerates evil in the universe, though he overrules and uses it in his administration of the world. It is used to punish individual and national wickedness (Is. 45:7; La. 3:38; Am. 3:6). The world must be marked by regulation and order to be the scene of man's moral life; otherwise there would be chaos. When men violate the basic laws of God they experience the repercussions of their actions, which may be in penal or retributive affliction (Mt. 9:2; 23:35; Jn. 5:14; Acts 5:5; 13:11). Divine 'vengeance' in the form of pain or sorrow does not imply evil passions in God. Pain may awaken an evil man to reality; till then 'he is enclosed in illusion' (C. S. Lewis, *The Problem of Pain*, p. 83). Nature's present 'vanity' (profitlessness, Rom. 8:19–23) is its mark of evil, the earth being under a curse (Gn. 3:17–18). Christian suffering, whether trouble or persecution, is divinely permitted for purposes of spiritual blessing (Jas. 1:2–4; 1 Pet. 1:7; *etc.*). It is chastening, not penal; nor can it separate from the love of God (Rom. 8:38–39); it prepares for glory (Rom. 8:18; 2 Cor. 4:16–18; Eph. 3:13; Rev. 7:14). Suffering and sorrow create sympathy and kindness in men, bringing them into fellowship with God's purpose to overcome evil.

II. Moral evil

God is separate from all evil and is in no way responsible for it. Moral evil arises from man's sinful inclinations (Jas. 1:13–15). Israel repeatedly 'did evil' and suffered its consequences (Jdg. 2:11; 1 Ki. 11:6, *etc.*). Behind all history is a spiritual conflict with evil powers (Eph. 6:10–17; Rev. 12:7–12), 'the evil one' being the very embodiment of wickedness (Mt. 5:37; 6:13; 13:19, 38; Jn. 17:15; Eph. 6:16; 2 Thes. 3:3; 1 Jn. 2:13–14; 3:12; 5:18–19). Satan's power is under divine control (*cf.* Jb. 1–2), and will finally be broken (Heb. 2:14; Rev. 12:9–11).

God is against evil, but its existence is often a stumbling-block to belief in a God of love. It can only be attributed to the abuse of free-will on the part of created beings, angelic and human. God's whole saving activity is directed to deal with evil. In his life, Christ combated its manifestations of pain and

EVERLASTING
See Time, Part 3.

EVIL INCLINATION
See Judaism, Part 2.

EVIL, ORIGIN OF
See Sin, Part 3.

EVOLUTION
See Fall, Part 1.

EXCAVATIONS
See Archaeology, Part 1.

EXCEPTIVE CLAUSE
See Marriage, Part 2.

EXCHANGE
See Money, Part 2.

EXCHANGERS
See Money-changers, Part 2.

EXCLUSIVENESS
See Proselyte, Part 3.

sorrow (Mt. 8:16–17); but the cross is God's final answer to the problem of evil. His love was supremely demonstrated there (Rom. 5:8; 8:32) in the identification of the Lord with the suffering world as the Sin-bearer. The moral change effected in men by the gospel is evidence of the reality of Christ's triumph over all evil powers (Col. 2:15; 1 Jn. 3:8), and therefore of the final victory of God. Evil will be eliminated from the universe, and the creation will share redeemed man's glorious destiny. Both physical and moral evil will be banished eternally (Rev. 21:1–8).

BIBLIOGRAPHY. C. S. Lewis, *The Problem of Pain*, 1940; C. E. M. Joad, *God and Evil*, 1943; J. S. Whale, *The Christian Answer to the Problem of Evil*, 1936; James Orr, *The Christian View of God and the World*, 1897; A. M. Farrer, *Love Almighty and Ills Unlimited*, 1962; O. F. Clarke, *God and Suffering*, 1964; J. Hick, *Evil and the God of Love*, 1966; J. W. Wenham, *The Goodness of God*, 1974; *TDNT* 3, pp. 469–484; 6, pp. 546–566; *NIDNTT* 1, pp. 561–567.

G.C.D.H.

EVIL-MERODACH. The king of *Babylon who released Jehoiachin of Judah from imprisonment in the first year of his reign (Je. 52:31; 2 Ki. 25:27–30). Amēl-Marduk ('man of Marduk') succeeded his father Nebuchadrezzar II in the early days of October 562 BC. According to Josephus (from Berossus), he ruled 'lawlessly and wantonly' (*Ap.* 1. 146), but the only allusions to him extant are in administrative tablets. He was killed *c.* 7–13 August 560 BC in a plot led by his brother-in-law *Nergal-sharezer (Neriglissar).

BIBLIOGRAPHY. R. H. Sack, *Amēl-Marduk: 562–560 B.C.*, 1972.

D.J.W.

EVIL SPEAKING may be defined as slander, calumny, defamation or deceit. This may be done by spreading false reports (Pr. 12:17; 14:5, 25) or by reporting truth maliciously, *i.e.* tale-bearing (Lv. 19:16; Pr. 26:20).

Evil speaking is prohibited in Ps. 34:13; Pr. 24:28; Eph. 4:31; Jas. 4:11; 1 Pet. 3:10. It disqualifies a person from God's favour (Ps. 15:3) and from office in the church (1 Tim. 3:8; Tit. 2:3). When a Christian is slandered he must patiently bear it (1 Pet. 3:9) even as Christ did (1 Pet. 2:23).

The ninth commandment forbids false witness (Ex. 20:16; Dt. 5:20; *cf.* Ex. 23:1). To avoid the evil of false accusation more than one witness was required in courts of law (Nu. 35:30; Dt. 17:6; 19:15–21).

M.R.G.

EVIL SPIRITS. The term 'evil (*ponēra*) spirit(s)' is found in but 6 passages (Matthew, Luke, Acts). There are 23 references to 'unclean (*akatharta*) spirits' (Gospels, Acts, Revelation), and these appear to be much the same. Thus in Lk. 11:24 'the unclean spirit' goes out of a man, but when he returns it is with 'seven other spirits more evil than himself' (v. 26). Similarly,'unclean spirits' and 'demons' are interchangeable terms, for both are applied to the Gadarene demoniac (Lk. 8:27, 29).

These beings appear to have been regarded in more than one light. They might cause physical disability (Mk. 1:23; 7:25). Indeed, on most occasions in the NT when they are mentioned it is in such cases. There appears to have been nothing moral involved, for the sufferer was not excluded from places of worship, such as the synagogue. The idea would appear to be that the spirit was evil (or unclean) in that it produced baleful effects. But the sufferer was not regarded as especially evil or as polluted in any way. Yet the spirit itself was not to be regarded in neutral fashion. Everywhere it was to be resisted and defeated. Sometimes we read of Jesus as doing this in person (Mk. 5:8; Lk.6:18), sometimes of such power being delegated to his followers (Mt. 10:1) or being exercised by them (Acts 5:16; 8:7). The spirits are apparently part of Satan's forces, and thus are reckoned as enemies of God and men.

Sometimes it is clear that the spirits are concerned with moral evil. This is so in the case of the 'unclean spirit' who goes out of a man and returns with others more wicked than himself (Mt. 12:43–45). The story indicates the impossibility of a man's bringing about a moral reformation by expelling the demons within. There must also be the entry of the Spirit of God. But for our present purpose it is sufficient to notice that the spirits are evil and may bring about evil. The evil spirits 'like frogs' of Rev. 16:13 are also thought of as working evil as they gather the forces of wickedness for the great final battle.

Such passages indicate that on the biblical view evil is not merely impersonal. It is led by Satan, and, just as there are subordinate powers of good, the angels, so there are subordinate powers of evil. Their appearance is mostly concerned with the incarnation (with a resurgence in the last days) as they oppose the work of Christ. See further *SATAN, *DEMON POSSESSION.

L.M.

EXCOMMUNICATION. Mt. 18:15–18; 1 Cor. 5; 2 Cor. 2:5–11; Tit. 3:10. The exclusion of a member from the church due to a serious (or aggravation, through stubbornness, of a less serious) offence. It is the final step in the negative side of normal discipline—there is also *Anathema and delivering over to *Satan. When educative discipline (*disciplina*) fails to prevent offences, repressive discipline is used to remove them. The *gradus admonitionis* leading up to excommunication are private remonstrance (incumbent on all, Lv. 19:17), then, if that proves ineffective, remonstrance with the aid of witnesses; finally, the offender should be dealt with by the church, presumably through its duly-elected representatives, following the Jewish pattern. The apostle puts this responsibility upon the local church (1 Cor. 5:4–13). If the offender still shows no repentance he is to be excommunicated. 'Let him be to you as a Gentile and a tax collector' (Mt. 18:17).

Some critics (*e.g.* Bultmann, T. W. Manson) make this 'quasi-legal' procedure a later development of the church, from rabbinic sources. But then it is hard to see why Paul reproved the Corinthians so sharply for neglecting it. And our Lord's condemnation of these sources would be fresh in their minds (Mt. 23:13ff.). The opprobrious sense of 'Gentile and tax collector' has been said to show a Jewish–Christian origin, *c.* AD 50. This is, at the least, doubtful. Ultimately, it is a question of 'the historical validity of the Gospel record and of the origins of Christianity itself, and this question it is impossible to ignore' (W. Manson, *Jesus the Messiah*, 1952, p. 26). The mind of the early church is the mind of the Lord.

Public, notorious faults are to be rebuked publicly (1 Tim. 5:20; Gal.

2:11, 14). Very serious offences merit immediate excommunication (1 Cor. 5:3). It is also noteworthy, however, that no amount of excommunication will produce a perfect church, for it has to ignore secret sins and hypocrisy. Also, the oil of leniency has to be mixed with the vinegar of severity: 'We judge that it pertains unto sound doctrine . . . to attemper our life and opinion, so that we both endure dogs in the church, for the sake of the peace of the church, and, where the peace of the church is safe, give not what is holy unto dogs . . . that we neither grow listless under the name of patience, nor be cruel under the pretext of diligence' (Augustine, *Short Treatises*, 1884, p. 43).

The aims involved are, first, to promote the glory of God, that his name be not blasphemed owing to manifest evil in the church; second, to prevent the evil from spreading to other members (1 Cor. 5:6); and third, to bring about true repentance in the offender. Here the ultimate aim is seen to be redemptive (Calvin, *Institutes*, 4. 12. 5).

Excommunication implies that we suspend convivial intercourse with the offender, though not ceasing to pray for his recovery; and though he is excluded from the benefits of the sacraments, he will be encouraged to attend the preaching of the Word. R.N.C.

EXODUS. This event marked the birth of Israel as a nation and—through the immediately-following covenant at Sinai—as a theocracy.

I. The event itself

After the Hebrews' residence in the Egyptian E Delta for 430 years (Ex. 12:40–41) culminating in enslavement in Egyptian state-corvée in the 18th and 19th Dynasties, God commissioned Moses, with Aaron as his mouthpiece, to lead out the Hebrew slaves, tribal descendants of Abraham, Isaac and Jacob, from Egypt to become a nation in Palestine, the land of promise (Ex. 3–4). Despite the hostility and temporal power of the pharaoh and, later, Israel's own faithlessness, this duly came to pass (Jos. 24).

That a large group of subject people should go out from a major state is neither impossible nor unparalleled in antiquity. In the late 15th century BC people of some fourteen 'lands', 'mountain-regions' and townships apparently decamped from their habitats within the Hittite kingdom, and transferred themselves to the land of Isuwa (Treaty-prologue of Suppiluliuma and 'Mattiwaza', Weidner, *Politische Dokumente aus Kleinasien*, 1923, p. 5), only later to be brought back by the powerful Hittite King Suppiluliuma. However, pharaoh's attempts to retain, and then to recapture, the Hebrews were rendered utterly futile by God's marshalling against him the powers of nature in nine plagues and a supernatural punishment in the tenth, and by swamping his pursuing chariotry in the Re(e)d Sea. The calling-out of a nation in this way specifically to serve a God, and live out a covenant directly with their God, is unique. The peoples who fled to Isuwa doubtless also considered themselves oppressed, but had no positive commission or divine calling to some high destiny. There went out with Israel a motley crowd, mixed in motives as in origins ('mixed multitude', Ex. 12:38, Heb. *'ēreḇraḇ*, *cf.* Eng. 'riff-raff'). This element preferred meat to manna (Nu. 11:4, Heb. *'ᵃsap̄sup̄*, 'rabble').

Other specific aspects of the Exodus are more appropriately dealt with in other articles as follows: For *date* of the Exodus, see *CHRONOLOGY OF THE OLD TESTAMENT. For *route* of the Exodus, see also on Egyptian sites *ENCAMPMENT BY THE SEA, *BAAL-ZEPHON, *PITHOM,*RA'AMSES, *SUCCOTH, *MIGDOL, *etc.*, and on the Sinaitic journeyings, *WILDERNESS OF THE WANDERING, *SINAI and individual palaces—*ELIM, *REPHIDIM, *etc.* For the Egyptian background to the oppression and conditions attending on the Exodus, see *EGYPT (**IV**), *MOSES and *PLAGUES OF EGYPT.

II. The Exodus in later history

Repeatedly in later generations, the prophets in exhorting Israel to return to her God and the psalmists in their meditations hark back to this Exodus—to God's redeeming grace in summoning a nation from Egyptian bondage in fulfilment of promises to the Patriarchs, to serve himself and exemplify his truth. For them, the great redemption is ever to be remembered with gratitude and response in obedience. See such passages as the following: historical books, Jdg. 6:8–9, 13; 1 Sa. 12:6, 8; 1 Ki. 8:51; 2 Ch. 7:22; Ne. 9:9ff. For Psalms, *cf.* Pss. 77:14–20; 78:12–55; 80:8; 106:7–12; 114. Among the prophets, see Ho. 11:1; Je. 7:21–24; 11:1–8; 34:13; Dn. 9:15. In the NT Christ accomplished the final 'Exodus', the full redemption (*cf.* Heb. 13:13 and elsewhere generally).

BIBLIOGRAPHY. J. J. Bimson, *Redating the Exodus and Conquest*, 1978 (gives a new statement of the archaeological and other evidence for a 15th-century BC date for the Exodus and Conquest); D. Daube, *The Exodus Pattern in the Bible*, 1963; R. E. Nixon, *The Exodus in the New Testament*, 1963. K.A.K.

EXODUS, BOOK OF.

I. Outline of contents

Exodus (the latinized form of LXX *exodos*, 'a going out') is the second section of the Pentateuch, and deals with the fortunes of Israel subsequent to the propitious times of Joseph's governorship. It records the two great culminating points in Israel's history: the deliverance from Egypt and the giving of the law. Henceforth the events of Exodus hold a central place in God's revelation of himself to his people, not only in the old but also in the new covenant, in which the Passover lamb provides the type for our Lord's sacrifice, and the Passover Feast is adapted to serve as the commemoration of our redemption.

The events leading up to and following Israel's flight from Egypt form the main theme of the book. The chronological setting is given only in general terms, consistent with the Hebrew treatment of history as series of events and not as a sequence of dates.

The book, after giving a short genealogical note to effect the transition from Genesis, begins with an account of the disquiet on the part of the Egyptians at the great numerical increase of the Israelites. To counteract what was considered to be a growing menace, the Israelites were first subjected to forced labour under Egyptian taskmasters, probably both to meet a current need for a large labour force and to keep them under strict observation. Then their labour was intensified, probably to reduce their leisure, and thus their opportunities for mischief, to a minimum. Finally an attempt was made to check any further increase in the population by the extermination of all newborn male infants. The boys rather than the girls would be chosen, as they would be regarded as potential instigators of revolt. This final step furnishes the background of the account of the birth and upbringing of Moses, the second great figure in Jewish history, at the Egyptian court. His early life, encounter with God and rise to leadership occupy chs. 2–4. In chs. 5–13 are related the attempts to gain release for Israel, ending in the *Plagues of Egypt and the institution of the *Passover. After the crossing of the *Red Sea and its celebration in song (14:1–15:21) follows a journal of the march to Sinai (15:22–18:27). The remainder of the book tells of the Covenant at Sinai (19–31), its breach (32–33), renewal (34) and the construction of the *tabernacle according to the instructions given (35–40).

II. Authorship

The leading critical schools see in Exodus a composition of diverse elements, originating from various sources or hands, ranging over a period from the 8th century until the 2nd century BC (A. H. McNeile, *Exodus*, p. ii; *PENTATEUCH, section **II**). To the hypothetical documents J (passages in which *YHWH* occurs), E (Elohim), D (Deuteronomic school), P (Priestly school) and R (various redactors) have been added L (lay source, O. Eissfeldt, *The Old Testament: An Introduction*, 1965, p.191), and B (*Bundesbuch*, book of the covenant, Ex. 20:22–23:33, Eissfeldt, p. 191). According to Eissfeldt (p. 211), the order of the growth of Exodus would seem to be: L J E B P R^J R^E R^B R^P, where R is the redactor who added the source denoted by the superior letter to the corpus (pp. 210ff.).

In the opinion of Eissfeldt the 'pious' attitude of the redactors towards their material, considered from the literary and aesthetic points of view, was a disadvantage, as this 'piety' prevented them from fashioning out of their materials a new and higher literary unity. This would indeed have been remarkable restraint in view of the magnitude of the literary reconstruction they were undertaking without an apparent qualm. McNeile, however, says bluntly: 'Since in all ages of Israelite history every civil and religious institution was referred to Moses, every successive age found it necessary to manipulate the records' (*op. cit.*, p. ix). Again, according to McNeile it was the aim of the priestly writers 'to systematize traditions and often to supplement them, under the dominance of religious ideas' (*op. cit.*, p. lxxix), and that 'the narrators enriched the narratives from their own imagination', and 'the traditions acquired a miraculous element in the centuries that intervened between the events and the times of the several writers' (p. cxii).

About Moses, McNeile says: 'Vague traditions of the founder of the national religion were orally handed down . . . legendary details would gather round his life' (p. cviii). He continues: 'It may be confidently asserted that Moses would not commit to writing a series of moral precepts'; and 'It is impossible to say of any particular detail that it derived from Moses himself' (p. cxvii). About the tabernacle this same author says: 'the historicity is unhesitatingly denied by all who accept the main principles of historical and literary criticism' (p. cxviii). The reason given for this last piece of scepticism is the mention of the tent of audience in 33:7, alleged to be identical with the tabernacle. It is, however, clear that the reference here is to the practice obtaining in the period preceding the erection of the tabernacle, the purpose of which was to be a sanctuary, symbolizing God's presence in their midst (25:8). S. R. Driver thinks that customs and rites 'are antedated and represented as having been already propounded and put in force in the Mosiac age' (*Exodus*, p. lxv).

If these views had any objective validity the narratives in Exodus would cease to be of historical value. The theories are in the nature of the case not amenable to proof. As Eissfeldt says: '. . . the whole of Pentateuchal criticism is a hypothesis, though admittedly one that rests upon very significant arguments' (*op. cit.*, p. 240).

It is strange that P, written from a priestly point of view, does so little to enhance the priesthood. It is Moses, the political leader, who remains the great hero, while the one who allows the people to fall into idolatry is Aaron, the priest, whom Moses rebukes and reinstates. This was not the only lapse on the part of Aaron. If the whole of the materials was arranged to give an ideal picture of the theocracy, as it was supposed to have existed in the Mosaic age (Driver, *op. cit.*, p. xii), then the project, in the light of the described stubbornness and intractability of the people, singularly miscarried.

Literary criticism in general would now hold as a truism that a literary work contains sources, and would never view these as evidence of multiple authorship (*e.g.*, *cf.* J. L. Lowes, *The Road to Xanadu*). It is now also taken to be axiomatic that style is dictated largely by subject-matter, not by idiosyncratic vocabularies. The comparison of the alleged composite nature of the Pentateuch with the writings of Arabic historians, who are simply marshalling their witnesses, is not applicable to the literature of the ancient Semitic East (A. T. Chapman, *Introduction to the Pentateuch*, 1911).

The application of the dissecting criteria to documents of indisputable unitary authorship shows them to be worthless (*cf.* *EGYPT, **V.** *b*). The selection of criteria was arbitrary, and other possible selections would give radically different results. A key passage as the justification of documentary fragmentation is Ex. 6:3, where, it is claimed, the introduction of the name *YHWH* is stated to be an innovation. The great stress here laid on the continuity of identity with the God of the Patriarchs hardly indicates a new departure. There are two possible interpretations of this verse. 'Name' here can refer not to an appellation, but can stand for 'honour' and 'character', as it often does in Semitics generally. Or the sentence could be taken as an elliptical interrogative: 'for did I not let my name, *YHWH*, be known to them?' At least the 'and also' of the next verse followed by a positive implies a preceding positive (W. J. Martin, *Stylistic Criteria and the Analysis of the Pentateuch*, 1955, pp. 17f.; G. R. Driver, 'Affirmation by Exclamatory Negation', *Journal of the Ancient Near East Soc., Columbia Univ.* 5, 1973 (T. H. Gaster vol.), p. 109. Much study has been given to the traditions contained in Exodus, particularly by G. von Rad and M. Noth. All work like theirs is purely conjectural, so long as it is based upon the subjective literary criticism described above, and doctrinaire views of Israelite religious history. However, there is an advance in that the traditions are regarded in many cases as much older than the literary sources.

The Jewish view from the time of Joshua (8:34f.), subscribed to by our Lord, and accepted by the

Christian church, held that Exodus was the work of Moses. From internal evidence this is also the impression given by the book itself. No objective philological evidence has been produced for the rejection of this view. If editing took place, one would expect it to be confined to such things as the modernization of geographical names. This done honestly in the interests of clarity would be far removed from inserting into documents extensive interpolations, and representing them as compositions of the Mosaic age.

III. The text

The text of Exodus is remarkably free from transcriptional errors. Letters on occasion have dropped out. There are a few examples of dittography (*e.g.* possibly of *sammîm*, 'spices', in 30:34). Haplography (writing only once that which occurs twice) appears, *e.g.*, in 19:12, where an *m* (= 'from') has been omitted. In 11:1 a marginal note may have found its way into the text: 'when his sending away is final'. In 20:18, apparently through the omission of Heb. *y*, 'fear' has become 'saw'. In 34:19 the Heb. definite article *h* has become *t*. In 23:3, through the misreading of *g* as *w*, 'great' has become 'poor' (*cf.* Lv. 19:15). In 17:16 the letters *k* and *n* have apparently been confused: read probably: 'For he said: power is with the banner of the Lord'. In 23:5 *b* seems to have replaced *r*, changing 'help' into 'forsake'; the reading is possibly: 'and thou shalt refrain from abandoning it, thou shalt surely give him your help'. One could read the text as it stands: 'and thou shalt refrain from abandoning it, thou shalt surely along with him free it'.

The magnitude of the *numbers seems to some to present difficulties. The transmission of numbers is especially exposed to error. In any consideration of the large number of people involved and the problem of providing for them, it should be borne in mind that these were not an urbanized people, but men and women whose manner of life made them well able to fend for themselves.

BIBLIOGRAPHY. A. H. McNeile, *The Book of Exodus*, *WC*, 1917; E. J. Young, *IOT*, 1954; M. Noth, *Exodus*, 1962; B. P. Napier, *Exodus*, 1963; D. W. Gooding, *The Account of the Tabernacle*, 1959; U. Cassuto, *Commentary on the Book of Exodus*, 1967; B. S. Childs, *Exodus*, 1974 (thorough survey of recent studies); R. A. Cole, *Exodus*, *TOTC*, 1973; J. Finegan, *Let My People Go*, 1963; E. W. Nicholson, *Exodus and Sinai in History and Tradition*, 1973.

W.J.M.
A.R.M.

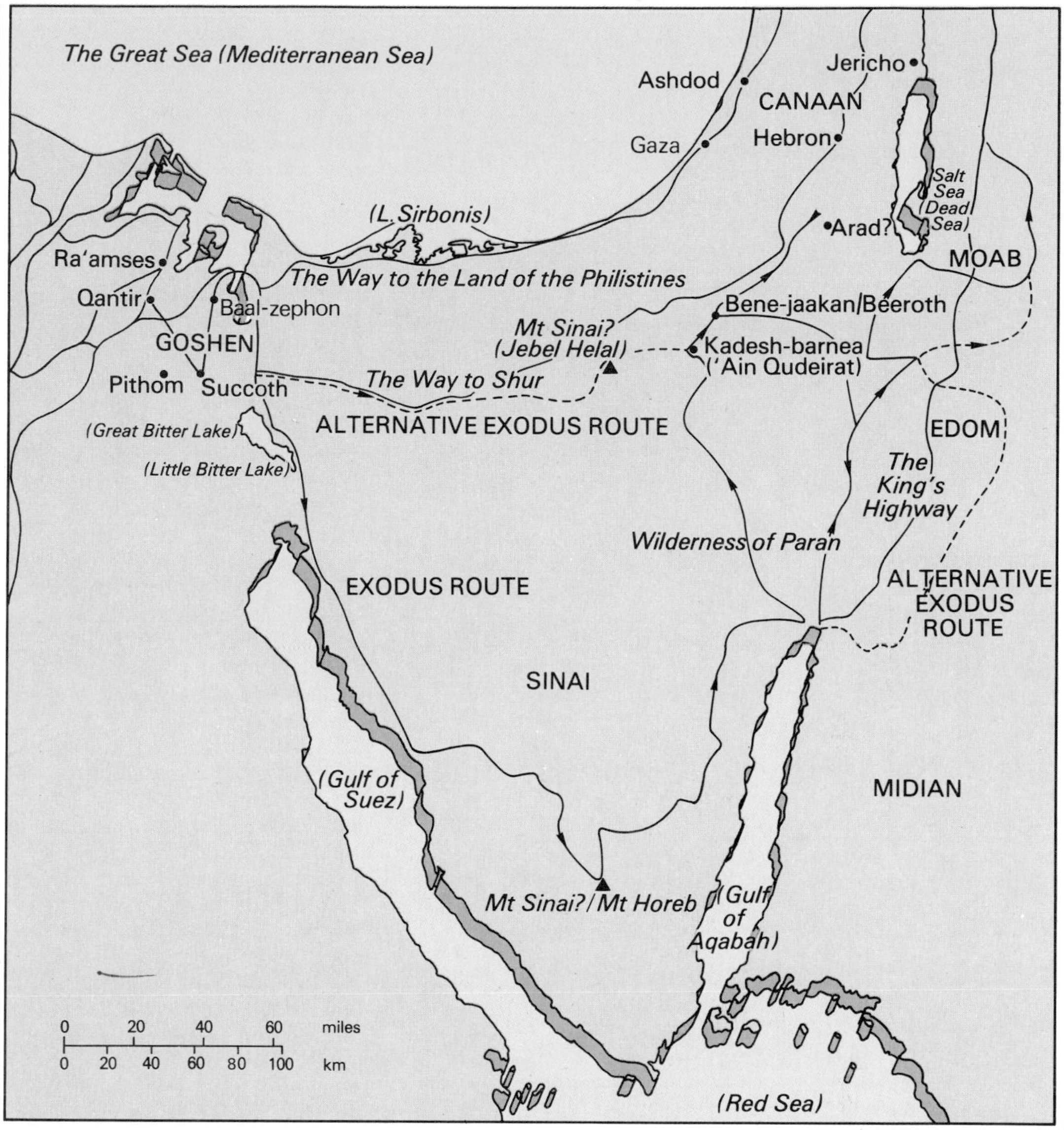

Possible route of the Exodus.

EXPIATION. This term does not occur in AV, but it is found in some modern translations in place of 'propitiation', *e.g.* 1 Jn. 4:10, RSV. Objection is made to 'propitiation' on the ground that it means the appeasement of an angry God, an idea not found in Scripture. Therefore expiation is substituted for it. But the matter is not so simple. Expiation properly has a thing as its object. We may expiate a crime, or a sin. Propitiation is a personal word. We propitiate a person rather than a sin (though we should not overlook the fact that in the Bible 'propitiate' is occasionally found with sin as the object, the meaning being 'to make propitiation with respect to sin'). If we are to think of our relationship to God as basically personal we cannot afford to dispense with the concept of propitiation. Those who advocate the use of expiation must face questions like: Why should sin be expiated? What are the consequences if no expiation takes place? Is the hand of God in those consequences? Expiation is a valuable word only if we can confidently answer 'No' to the last question. If sin is a thing, and can be dealt with as a thing, blotted out, cast from us, and the like, then we may properly talk of expiation. But if sin affects man's relationship with God, if the relationship with God is the primary thing, then it is difficult to see how expiation is adequate. Once we bring in the category of the personal we need

EXPORTS OF PALESTINE
See Agriculture, Part 1.

EXTREME UNCTION
See Sacraments, Part 3.

EYE-PAINT
See Cosmetics, Part 1.

some such term as propitiation.

It seems, then, that, despite the confident claims of some, expiation is not the solution to our difficulties. The ideas expressed in the words usually translated *'propitiation' are not adequately safeguarded by the use of the term 'expiation'.

BIBLIOGRAPHY. C. Brown, *NIDNTT* 3, pp. 151–160. L.M.

EYE. The Heb. word for eye, *'ayin*, with parallels in other Near Eastern languages, is used of the physical organ of man (Gn. 3:6) or beast (30:41), of God anthropomorphically (Ps. 33:18), and also of objects (Ezk. 1:18; *cf.* Rev. 4:6). The Gk. word *ophthalmos* has familiar derivations in English.

In Hebrew the physical organs are construed as acting semi-independently and possessing also psychical and moral qualities. Thus the eye not only has sight but is proud (Is. 5:15), has pity (Dt. 7:16), sleep (Gn. 31:40), delight (Ezk. 24:16), *etc.*, and, while Paul emphasizes the interdependence of the physical organs (1 Cor. 12:16ff.), Mt. 5:29 preserves the Hebraic notion of the almost self-contained function of the organ.

The practice of putting out the eyes of a defeated enemy was common in the E (Jdg. 16:21; 2 Ki. 25:7).

The phrase 'the eye of the Lord is on those who fear him' (Ps. 33:18) is significant of God's watchful care (*cf.* Ps. 1:6).

Other phrases are: 'eye for eye' (Lv. 24:20); 'face to face', literally 'eye to eye' (Nu. 14:14); 'before their eyes', *i.e.*, in full view (Gn. 42:24; *cf.* Je. 32:12); and 'between your eyes', *i.e.*, on the forehead (Ex. 13:9), of the phylactery.

Derived usages are: 'face of the land' (Heb. *'ayin*) (Ex. 10:5), and 'gleaming' or 'sparkling' (Ezk. 1:4; Pr. 23:31). B.O.B.

EYE OF A NEEDLE. In Mt. 19:24; Mk. 10:25; Lk. 18:25 we find the statement of Jesus: 'It is easier for a camel to go through the eye of a needle than for a rich man to enter the kingdom of God.' This form of words, familiar in rabbinic writings, signifies something both very unusual and very difficult—*e.g.* in the Talmud an elephant passing through the eye of a needle is twice used of what is impossible, and a camel is portrayed as dancing in a very small corn measure (*cf.* also J. Lightfoot, *Horae Hebraicae*, 2, 1859, pp. 264f.). Some scholars interpret 'needle's eye' as a reference to a narrow gateway for pedestrians, but there is no historical evidence to support this. See F. W. Farrar, 'The Camel and the Needle's Eye', *The Expositor* 3, 1876, pp. 369–380. J.D.D.

EZEKIEL (Heb. *y^{e}ḥezqē'l*, 'God strengthens'). The name is found in approximately its Heb. form in 1 Ch. 24:16 for the head of one of the priestly orders.

Ezekiel, the son of *Buzi, was deported to Babylonia, almost certainly with Jehoiachin in 597 BC (2 Ki. 24:14–17). He was settled in the village of Tel-abib by the river *Chebar. Five years later he received his call as prophet (Ezk. 1:2), possibly at the ageof 30 (1:1), tough this interpretation is denied by many without offering a more satisfactory one. He lived for at least another 22 years (29:17).

We have little information about his life. Though he possessed detailed knowledge of the Jerusalem Temple and its cultus, there is no evidence he had served in it. Even those, *e.g.* Cooke (*ICC*), who suggest that the bulk of chs. 1–24 were pronounced in Jerusalem, do not suggest Temple service. His thought, more than that of any other prophet, is influenced by priestly symbolism. His prophecies were badly received (3:25), but we soon find him in an honoured position (8:1; 14:1; 20:1), due possibly to his family rank; the majority hardly took his message very seriously (33:30–32—AV is misleading in v. 30). His wife died suddenly the day Nebuchadrezzar invested Jerusalem (24:1–2, 15–18); there is no mention of children.

H. Klostermann, *Theologische Studien und Kritiken*, 1877, tried on the basis of such passages as 3:23–4:8 to show that he suffered from an organic nervous disease, which he called catalepsy. Though popular for a time, the view is today accepted by few. Considerable controversy exists as to how Ezekiel's symbolic actions are to be interpreted. Some, *e.g.* A. B. Davidson, *Ezekiel* (*CBSC*), p. xxx, and J. Skinner, *HDB*, 1, p. 817a, have held they took place purely in the prophet's mind. More usual is the conception that, though they were carried out, in our understanding of them we must allow for a metaphorical element inconsistent with a purely literal interpretation. See also the following article. H.L.E.

EZEKIEL, BOOK OF.

I. Structure and contents

The indications of date (1:2; 3:16; 8:1; 20:1; 24:1; 26:1; 29:1, 17; 30:20; 31:1; 32:1, 17; 33:21; 40:1) apart from those in chs. 25–32 form a coherent series marking major developments in Ezekiel's message (see previous article). It is reasonable to infer that chs. 25–32 were inserted in their present position on analogy with Is. 13–27 to mark the division between the two main phases of Ezekiel's activity; *cf.* also the probably original position of the prophecies against the nations in Jeremiah (so LXX). In chs. 1–24 he is the prophet of inexorable doom, interpreting coming events to the remnant in exile (not to Jerusalem!) to prepare them for their future role. Chs. 33–39 give an outline of the message by which he tried to build up the exiles as the people of God. The long interval between 33:21 and 40:1 (some 13 years), the striking change in style and the fact that Josephus writes of Ezekiel's *two* books (*Ant.* 10. 79) suggest that chs. 40–48 represent a separate, though allied, group of prophecies beside chs. 33–39.

II. Authorship and date

Ezekiel has an unquestioned place in Ben Sira's list at the beginning of the 2nd century BC (Ecclus. 49:8), but there was a move in the 1st century AD to have the book withdrawn from public use. For this there were three reasons. Some felt ch. 16 too repugnant for public reading; ch. 1 and parallels were used in dangerous theosophical speculations (the students of *Merkabhah* ['chariot'] mysticism thought they were the key to the mysteries of creation); above all, numerous details in chs. 40–48 were considered contradictory to the law of Moses, already considered immutable. The labours of Hananiah ben Hezekiah, which resolved the apparent discrepancies, guaranteed for Ezekiel a public position in the Pharisaic canon.

This position was seldom challenged, and J. Skinner could say in 1898 (*HDB*, 1, p. 817a), 'The Book of Ezekiel (save for a somewhat corrupt text) exists in the form in which it left the hand of its author. . . . Neither the unity nor the authenticity of Ezekiel has been questioned by more than a very small minority of scholars. Not only does it bear the stamp of a single mind in its phraseology, its imagery, and its mode of thought, but it is arranged on a plan so perspicuous and so comprehensive that the evidence of literary design in the composition becomes altogether irresistible.'

In spite of the cogency of these arguments the position began to change in 1924; attacks on the unity and authenticity of Ezekiel may be divided into three groups, which tend to overlap.

a. The date of composition

C. C. Torrey saw in it a pseudepigraph, written about 230 BC, describing the abominations of Manasseh's reign; an editor gave it its present form not later than 200 BC. M. Burrows reached a similar date by linguistic evidence. L. E. Browne advocated a date during the time of Alexander the Great. J. Smith, on the other hand, regarded Ezekiel as a N Israelite deported in 734 BC, who prophesied to his fellow exiles until he returned to Jerusalem in 691 BC, where he gave the bulk of his oracles. Such views have won very little favour.

b. The place of prophecy

Though Torrey's dating has had little acceptance, many have followed him in seeing the bulk of the book as Palestinian. It is widely believed that, whether or not Ezekiel was deported in 597 BC, he was prophesying in or near Jerusalem until its destruction in 586 BC. Perhaps the best presentation of this view is by Pfeiffer, *IOT*, 1948, pp. 535–543. The main justification for this interpretation is the traditional misinterpretation of Ezekiel's oracles before 586 BC as addressed to doomed Jerusalem. Its great weakness is the very extensive rearrangement of the text involved, and the absence of any adequate motivation for the distortion of Ezekiel's actual activity.

c. The unity of the book

Basing himself mainly on the contrast between Ezekiel's poetry and prose, G. Hölscher attributed to him only 170 verses (mostly poetry) of the total 1,273, the rest coming from a levitical editor between 500 and 450 BC. W. A. Irwin reached similar results by other methods, attributing some 250 verses to Ezekiel. Many deny chs. 40–48 to him. Their arguments are a challenge to profounder exegesis, but they have failed to carry conviction with the majority, though editorial insertions are increasingly recognized.

It seems fair to say that these intensive critical studies have largely cancelled themselves out. They have led to a deeper understanding of many aspects of the book, but have left the general position much as it was before 1924. Since the work of C. G. Howie there has been a general swing back to a more conservative position. Few now deny that it is an Exilic production by Ezekiel himself. In the first 39 chapters, G. Fohrer, mainly on subjective grounds, denies only just over 100 verses to the prophet, and that without impairing any major section of his message. About the same number of verses from the last 9 chapters are denied to the prophet but here the motivation seems to be more subjective.

There has also been a general swing away from the idea that Ezekiel must have prophesied in Jerusalem during the earlier part of his activity. The latest major commentary, that of W. Zimmerli, takes up a mainly conservative position, but does not attribute the composition of the book to Ezekiel himself.

III. The text

Many *hapax legomena* and technical expressions and obscurity in the symbolical language have led scribes into frequent error. The LXX can often be used to correct the Hebrew, but only with extreme care. There is an interesting comparison of the Hebrew and Greek in Cooke, *Ezekiel*, *ICC*, pp. xl–xlvii.

IV. The religious teaching of the book

To understand the book correctly we must grasp that, like all the writings of the prophets, it is not a manual of theology; it is the word of God to a battered remnant in exile experiencing what the theologians of the time had considered impossible. If Ezekiel by his symbolism seems to stress the transcendence of God, it is to make clear that his omnipotence cannot be limited by the failure of his people. This leads to the most unsparing exposure of Israel's history and religion in the OT (16; 20; 23). The promise of restoration is no longer bound to the prior repentance of the people, but is an act of God's grace which leads to repentance (36:16–32). The restoration is above all to vindicate God's honour and not for Israel's sake. Because all is of God's grace, the relationship of the individual to God depends neither on his heredity nor his own past (18; 33:10–20). Many have deduced from 40–48 a picture of Ezekiel as a narrow, priestly ritualist, but this comes from failure to recognize the essentially eschatological character of these chapters. Witness to this is borne by the apparent lack of interest of the returned exiles in these chapters. They did not even try to enforce those points that lay in their power, such as confirming the priesthood to the Zadokites (44:15–16), or the apparent duplication of a Day of Atonement (45:18, 20; *cf.* RVmg. for LXX correctly). In the symbolism of exact conformity to divine plan and law we are shown God's people ultimately conforming perfectly to his purposes.

BIBLIOGRAPHY. G. Hölscher, *Hesekiel: Der Dichter und das Buch*, 1924; M. Burrows, *The Literary Relations of Ezekiel*, 1925; C. C. Torrey, *Pseudo-Ezekiel and the Original Prophecy*, 1930; G. A. Cooke, *The Book of Ezekiel*, *ICC*, 1936; W. A. Irwin, *The Problem of Ezekiel*, 1943, 'Ezekiel Research since 1943', *VT* 3, 1953, pp. 54–66; C. G. Howie, *The Date and Composition of Ezekiel*, 1950; G. Fohrer and K. Galling, *Ezechiel*, 1955; J. B. Taylor, *Ezekiel*, *TOTC*, 1969; W. Zimmerli, *Ezechiel*, 1969.

H.L.E.

EZEL. The agreed rendezvous of David and Jonathan, occurring in 1 Sa. 20:19 (AV, RV, RSVmg.). It is sometimes taken to mean 'departure', but the RVmg. and the RSV, following the LXX, read 'this mound' and 'yonder stone heap' respectively, and assume corruption in the Heb. text. See also the mg. of 1 Sa. 20:41.

G.W.G.

EZRA. According to the record in Ezr. 7, Ezra was sent to Jerusalem by Artaxerxes I in 458 BC. It would seem probable that he held a position in Persia comparable to Secretary of State for Jewish affairs. His task was to enforce the uniform observance of the Jewish law, and to this end he had authority to make appointments within the Jewish state. A large company of

EZION-GEBER
See Elath, Part 1.

exiles came with him, and he brought valuable gifts for the Temple from the king and the exiled Jews. He was asked to deal with the problem of mixed marriages, and, after fasting and prayer, he and a chosen committee blacklisted the guilty and induced some at least to put away their pagan wives (10:19).

After this we do not hear of Ezra until he reads the law publicly in Ne. 8. This was in 444 BC. Since he had been sent by the king on a temporary mission, he presumably returned with his report, but was sent back again on a similar mission when the walls of the city were completed. Nehemiah, in part of his memoirs in Ne. 12:36ff., records that he himself led one party round the walls on the occasion of their dedication, while Ezra led the other.

Largely on the strength of three passages, many have held that Ezra did not come to Jerusalem until the time of Artaxerxes II, *i.e.* in 398 BC, long after the time of Nehemiah.

a. Ezr. 9:9 speaks of a city wall, whereas the wall was not built until Nehemiah's time. But Ezr. 4:12 shows that a wall of some sort was being built in the reign of Artaxerxes I, and its destruction is probably referred to in 4:23 and Ne. 1:3. Ezra is rejoicing in faith at the work which has progressed so far.

b. Ezr. 10:1 speaks of a very great congregation in Jerusalem, whereas Ne. 7:4 says that only a few people lived in the city. But the context of Ezr. 10 shows that the congregation was drawn from all around Jerusalem, *e.g.* 10:7, whereas Ne. 7 is concerned with actual dwelling-houses in the city.

c. Ezr. 10:6 speaks of Jehohanan (or Johanan) the son of Eliashib as Ezra's contemporary. We know from Ne. 12:22–23 that Johanan was the grandson of Eliashib, and from the Elephantine papyri that Johanan was high priest in 408 BC. But Johanan was a common name, and it is reasonable to think that Eliashib had a son named Johanan, and also another son, Joiada, who in turn had a son, Johanan, who became high priest. Ezr. 10:6 does not say that Johanan was high priest in Ezra's day.

As against the idea that the writer of Ezra and Nehemiah confused Artaxerxes I and II (which this theory of the priority of Nehemiah demands), a writer even as late as 330 BC could not have confused the order of the two men. If Ezra really came in 398 BC, a few of the writer's contemporaries would have remembered him, and many would have been told of him by their parents; whereas no-one would have remembered Nehemiah. Thus the writer could not have put Ezra back before Nehemiah by accident, and no-one has suggested any reason for his doing so deliberately. (See J. Stafford Wright, *The Date of Ezra's Coming to Jerusalem*, 1958; H. H. Rowley, 'The Chronological Order of Ezra and Nehemiah' in *The Servant of the Lord and Other Essays*, 1952, pp. 129ff.)

It should be noted that Ezra attained a great reputation among the Jews in post-biblical times. In 2 Esdras 14 he is said to have been inspired of God to re-write the law, which had been destroyed in the Exile, and a number of other books. See also the following article.

BIBLIOGRAPHY. H. H. Schaeder, *Esra der Schreiber*, 1930; W. F. Albright, 'The Date and Personality of the Chronicler', *JBL* 40, 1921, pp. 104ff. J.S.W.

EZRA, BOOK OF.

I. Outline of contents

a. 1:1–11. Cyrus permits the Jews to return from exile under Sheshbazzar. 537 BC.

b. 2:1–70. The register of those who returned.

c. 3:1–13. The altar is set up and the Temple foundations laid. 536 BC.

d. 4:1–5, 24. Enemies hinder the work until the time of Darius.

e. 4:6–23. Further opposition to the building of the city walls in the reign of Ahasuerus (Xerxes, 485–465 BC) and Artaxerxes (464–424 BC), resulting in a decree to stop the building altogether.

f. 5:1–6:22. Renewal of the Temple building through the prophecies of Haggai and Zechariah. In spite of protests to Darius the work is completed. 520–516 BC.

g. 7:1–28. Ezra is sent from Persia to enforce the law. 458 BC.

h. 8:1–36. Ezra's journey and safe arrival.

i. 9:1–10:44. Ezra and the Jews deal with the problem of mixed marriages.

In this outline it is assumed that the author has collected examples of opposition together in 4:6–23. There are those who think that Ahasuerus in v. 6 is Cambyses (529–522 BC) and Artaxerxes in v. 7 is the usurper Gaumata, or Pseudo-Smerdis, who reigned for a few months in 522–521 BC. But the subject-matter of vv. 7–23 is the walls

Aramaic letter of the period of Ezra sent from Babylonia to Egypt, concerning the transfer of a domain to a deceased tenant's son. 5th cent. BC. (BLO)

and not the Temple, and it is probable that the damage referred to in v. 23 is that referred to in Ne. 1:3.

II. Authorship and date

See the general note under *CHRONICLES, of which it is probable that Ezra and Nehemiah formed part. Traditionally the author is Ezra himself, but some bring the date down to about 330 BC. Whether or not Ezra was the final compiler, chs. 7–9 would appear to be from his hand, much of this section being in the first person singular. The account in chs. 1–6 is compiled from records, including decrees (1:2–4; 6:3–12), genealogies and name lists (2), and letters (4:7–22; 5:6–17). There are two sections which have been preserved in Aramaic (4:8–6:18; 7:12–26). Aramaic was the diplomatic language of the day, and was suitable for the section dealing with the coming and going of letters and decrees between Palestine and Persia.

III. Credibility

The documents that are found in Ezra present no great difficulties of harmonization with one another and with what is known from secular history.

a. The decree of Cyrus (1), acknowledging Jehovah, is in harmony with Cyrus's favourable references to Babylonian deities in contemporary records. This is a public decree, written in terms that would appeal to the Jews. The formal decree in 6:3–5 is filed in the records, and gives the maximum size of the Temple for which the king was prepared to give a grant.

b. It is pointed out that from Hg. 2:18 we learn that the foundation of the Temple was laid in 520 BC, whereas Ezr. 3:10 indicates that it was laid in 536 BC. In actual fact so little was done in the intervening period that it is likely that the revival would begin with a fresh foundation ceremony. Records show that in important buildings there was more than one official foundation stone.

c. The date of the coming of Ezra is bound up with the book of Nehemiah, and is considered separately under the entry *EZRA, above. See also *NEHEMIAH, *SHESHBAZZAR, *ZERUBBABEL.

IV. The book of Ezra and 1 Esdras

Esdras is the Gk. equivalent of Ezra, and our Apocrypha contains in 1 Esdras a book that is very similar to Ezra, though with certain striking differences. It runs from 2 Ch. 35:1 to the end of Ezra, after which it adds Ne. 8:1–12. Its history is confused. Thus Cyrus permits the return under Sheshbazzar, while Darius commissions Zerubbabel to go and build the Temple and the city; yet 5:70–73 says that Zerubbabel was working in Judah 'as long as King Cyrus lived'. Thus, while it may be useful to compare the two versions, Ezra is undoubtedly the more reliable. The famous story of the three guardsmen comes in 1 Esdras 3.

BIBLIOGRAPHY. J. Stafford Wright, *The Building of the Second Temple*, 1958; L. W. Batten, *Ezra and Nehemiah, ICC*, 1913; J. M. Myers, *Ezra, Nehemiah, AB*, 1965; A. C. Welch, *Post-Exilic Judaism*, 1935; L. E. Browne, *Early Judaism*, 1920; K. Galling, 'The Gola-list in Ezra ii/Neh. vii', *JBL* 70, 1951, pp. 149ff.; F. D. Kidner, *Ezra and Nehemiah, TOTC*, 1979. J.S.W.

FACE. The Eng. word usually translates Heb. *pānîm* or Gk. *prosōpon*. The Heb. word is used in many Eng. senses—of the faces of people and animals, and metaphorically of the sky; it could refer to the front of something, or its outward appearance. Then the 'face' of a person became synonymous with his 'presence', and the Heb. *lip̄ᵉnê* (lit. 'to the face of', and so 'to the presence of', and 'in front of') is a very common preposition.

The face, of course, gives visible indication of inward emotions, and a variety of adjectives accompany the word in Scripture, such as 'sad', 'tearful', 'ashamed' or 'pale'. The face could change colour, darkening or blushing.

Modesty or reverence demanded the veiling of the face, as did Rebekah before Isaac. God's face might not be seen by man for fear of death (Ex. 33:20); in Isaiah's visions, seraphim veiled the

Chronology for the book of Ezra.

Dates BC	Persian Kings	Dates BC	Events in Jerusalem
539-530	Cyrus	537	First attempt to rebuild the Temple
530-522	Cambyses		
522-486	Darius I Hystaspes	520-516	The Temple rebuilt
486-465	Xerxes I		
465-424	Artaxerxes I Longimanus	458	Ezra sent to Jerusalem by Artaxerxes
		445-433	Nehemiah Governor of Judah
423-404	Darius II Nothus		Letters from Jews at Elephantine–
		410	to Johanan, High Priest in Jerusalem
404-359	Artaxerxes II Mnemon	407	to Bagaos, Governor of Judah
359/8-338/7	Artaxerxes III Ochus		
338/7-336/5	Arses		
336/5-331	Darius III Codomanus		

Almighty's face. It was a sign of humility to bow the face to the ground; and falling on the face betokened great fear. Utter contempt, on the other hand, could be shown by spitting in somebody's face. Metaphorically, determination could be shown by 'setting' one's face—note the graphic phrase of Is. 50:7, denoting unswerving purpose. Determined opposition was made by withstanding someone to his face. Intimacy and understanding were conveyed by the phrase 'face to face'. This phrase has, of course, passed into English, as has also 'his face fell' (Gn. 4:5).

The face of the dead was covered (Jn. 11:44), and so this action to Haman made it clear that he was doomed (Est. 7:8).

When a man prostrated himself to make a request, his superior would raise the supplicant's head as a sign that the favour would be granted. To lift someone's face thus meant primarily to grant a favour (*cf.* Gn. 19:21), and then to make a favourite of (Dt. 10:17). This concept is also found in NT Greek, in the words *prosōpolēptēs* ('respecter of persons'; literally, 'face-taker') and *prosōpolēpsia*, the abstract noun (*cf.* Acts 10:34; Rom. 2:11).

The 'face of God', *i.e.*, his gracious presence, is an important OT theme, as, *e.g.*, in the *showbread.

BIBLIOGRAPHY. *THAT*, *s.v.* *pānîm*; E. Tiedke, *NIDNTT* 1, pp. 585–587; E. Lohse, *TDNT* 6, pp. 768–780. D.F.P.

FAIR HAVENS, modern Kaloi Limenes, a small bay on the S coast of Crete, a few km E of Cape Matala. Although protected by small islands, it is too open to be an ideal winter harbour (Acts 27:8), but it would be the last place where Paul's ship could stay to avoid the NW wind, as the coast swings N beyond Cape Matala. K.L.McK.

FAITH.

I. In the Old Testament

In the OT the world 'faith' is found twice only in AV (Dt. 32:20; Hab. 2:4), but RSV has it eighteen times. Twelve times it is used of breaking faith (*e.g.* Lv. 5:15; Dt. 32:51) or acting in good faith (Jdg. 9:15f.), while the other six passages speak rather of trust. We should not, however, conclude from the rarity of the word that faith is unimportant in the OT, for the idea, if not the word, is frequent. It is usually expressed by verbs such as 'believe', 'trust' or 'hope', and such abound.

We may begin with such a passage as Ps. 26: 1, 'Vindicate me, O Lord, for I have walked in my integrity, and I have trusted in the Lord without wavering.' It is often said that the OT looks for men to be saved on the basis of their deeds, but this passage puts the matter in its right perspective. The Psalmist does indeed appeal to his 'integrity', but this does not mean that he trusts in himself or his deeds. His trust is in God, and his 'integrity' is the evidence of that trust. The OT is a long book, and the truths about salvation are stated in various ways. The writers do not always make the distinctions that we, with the NT in our hands, might wish. But close examination will reveal that in the OT, as in the NT, the basic demand is for a right attitude to God, *i.e.* for faith. *Cf.* Ps. 37:3ff., 'Trust in the Lord, and do good . . . Take delight in the Lord, and he will give you the desires of your heart. Commit your way to the Lord; trust in him, and he will act.' Here there is no question but that the Psalmist is looking for an upright life. But there is no question, either, that basically he is advocating an attitude. He calls on men to put their trust in the Lord, which is only another way of telling them to live by faith. Sometimes men are urged to trust the Word of God (Ps. 119:42), but more usually it is faith in God himself that is sought. 'Trust in the Lord with all your heart; and do not rely on your own insight' (Pr. 3:5).

The latter part of this verse frowns upon trust in one's own powers, and this thought is frequent. 'He who trusts in his own mind is a fool' (Pr. 28:26). A man may not trust to his own righteousness (Ezk. 33:13). Ephraim is castigated for trusting 'in your chariots (Heb. 'way') and in the multitude of your warriors' (Ho. 10:13). Trust in idols is often denounced (Is. 42:17; Hab. 2:18). Jeremiah warns against confidence in anything human, 'Cursed is the man who trusts in man, and makes flesh his arm, and whose heart turns away from the Lord' (Je. 17:5). The list of things not to be trusted in might be multiplied, and it is the more impressive alongside the even more lengthy list of passages urging trust in the Lord. It is clear that the men of the OT thought of the Lord as the one worthy object of trust. They put not their trust in anything they did, or that other men did, or that the gods did. Their trust was in the Lord alone. Sometimes this is picturesquely expressed. Thus he is 'my rock, and my fortress, and my deliverer, my God, my rock, in whom I take refuge, my shield, and the horn of my salvation, my stronghold' (Ps. 18:2). Faith may be confidently rested in a God like that.

Special mention must be made of Abraham. His whole life gives evidence of a spirit of trustfulness, of a deep faith. Of him it is recorded that 'he believed the Lord; and he reckoned it to him as righteousness' (Gn. 15:6). This text is taken up by NT writers, and the fundamental truth it expresses developed more fully.

II. In the New Testament

a. General use of the word

In the NT faith is exceedingly prominent. The Gk. noun *pistis* and the verb *pisteuō* both occur more than 240 times, while the adjective *pistos* is found 67 times. This stress on faith is to be seen against the background of the saving work of God in Christ. Central to the NT is the thought that God sent his Son to be the Saviour of the world. Christ accomplished man's salvation by dying an atoning death on Calvary's cross. Faith is the attitude whereby a man abandons all reliance in his own efforts to obtain salvation, be they deeds of piety, of ethical goodness or anything else. It is the attitude of complete trust in Christ, of reliance on him alone for all that salvation means. When the Philippian jailer asked, 'Men, what must I do to be saved?', Paul and Silas answered without hesitation, 'Believe in the Lord Jesus, and you will be saved' (Acts 16:30f.). It is 'whoever believes in him' that does not perish, but has everlasting life (Jn. 3:16). Faith is the one way by which men receive salvation.

The verb *pisteuō* is often followed by 'that', indicating that faith is concerned with facts, though there is more to it than that. James tells us that the devils believe 'that God is one', but this 'faith' does not profit them (Jas. 2:19). *pisteuō* may be followed by the simple dative, when the meaning is that of giving credence to, of accepting as true, what someone says. Thus Jesus reminds the Jews that 'John came . . . in the way of righteousness, and you did not believe him' (Mt. 21:32). There is no question here of faith in the sense of trust. The Jews simply did not believe what John said. This may be so also with respect to Jesus, as in Jn. 8:45, 'you do not believe me', or the next verse, 'if I tell the truth, why do you not believe me?' Yet it must not be forgotten that there is an intellectual content to faith. Consequently this construction is sometimes used where saving faith is in mind, as in Jn. 5:24, 'he who hears my word and believes him who sent me, has eternal life'. The man who really believes God will, of course, act on that belief. In other words, a genuine belief that what God has revealed is true will issue in a true faith.

The characteristic construction for saving faith is that wherein the verb *pisteuō* is followed by the preposition *eis*. Literally this means to believe 'into'. It denotes a faith which, so to speak, takes a man out of himself, and puts him into Christ (*cf.* the NT expression frequently used of Christians, being 'in Christ'). This experience may also be referred to with the term 'faith-union with Christ'. It denotes not simply a belief that carries an intellectual assent, but one wherein the believer cleaves to his Saviour with all his heart. The man who believes in this sense abides in Christ and Christ in him (Jn. 15:4). Faith is not accepting certain things as true, but trusting a Person, and that Person Christ.

Sometimes *pisteuō* is followed by *epi*, 'upon'. Faith has a firm basis. We see this construction in Acts 9:42, where, when the raising of Tabitha was known, 'many believed in the Lord'. The people had seen what Christ could do, and they rested their faith 'on' him. Sometimes faith rests on the Father, as when Paul speaks of believing 'in him that raised from the dead Jesus our Lord' (Rom. 4:24).

Very characteristic of the NT is the absolute use of the verb. When Jesus stayed with the Samaritans many of them 'believed because of his word' (Jn. 4:41). There is no need to add what they believed, or in whom they believed. Faith is so central to Christianity that one may speak of 'believing' without the necessity for further clarification. Christians are simply 'believers'. This use extends throughout the NT, and is not confined to any particular writer. We may fairly conclude that faith is fundamental.

The tenses of the verb *pisteuō* are also instructive. The aorist tense points to a single act in past time and indicates the determinative character of faith. When a man comes to believe he commits himself decisively to Christ. The present tense has the idea of continuity. Faith is not a passing phase. It is a continuing attitude. The perfect tense combines both ideas. It speaks of a present faith which is continuous with a past act of belief. The man who believes enters a permanent state. Perhaps we should notice here that the noun 'faith' sometimes has the article 'the faith', *i.e.* the whole body of Christian teaching, as when Paul speaks of the Colossians as being 'established in the faith', adding 'just as you were taught' (Col. 2:7).

b. Particular uses of the word

(i) In the Synoptic Gospels faith is often connected with healing, as when Jesus said to the woman who touched his garment in the crowd, 'Take heart, daughter; your faith has made you well' (Mt. 9:22). But these Gospels are also concerned with faith in a wider sense. Mark, for example, records the words of the Lord Jesus, 'All things are possible to him who believes' (Mk. 9:23). Similarly, the Lord speaks of the great results of having 'faith as a grain of mustard seed' (Mt. 17:20; Lk. 17:6). It is clear that our Lord called for faith in himself personally. The characteristic Christian demand for faith in Christ rests ultimately on Christ's own requirement.

(ii) In the Fourth Gospel faith occupies a very prominent place, the verb *pisteuō* being found 98 times. Curiously the noun *pistis*, 'faith', is never employed. This is possibly due to its use in circles of a Gnostic type. There are indications that John had such opponents in mind, and it may be that he wanted to avoid using a term of which they were very fond. Or he may have preferred the more dynamic meaning conveyed by the verb. Whatever his reason, he uses the verb *pisteuō* more often than any other writer in the NT, three times as often, in fact, as the first three Gospels put together. His characteristic construction is that with the preposition *eis*, 'to believe into', 'to believe on'. The important thing is the connection between the believer and the Christ. Accordingly, John speaks again and again of believing in him or of believing 'in the name' of Christ (*e.g.* Jn. 3:18). The 'name', for men of antiquity, was a way of summing up the whole personality. It stood for all that the man was. Believing on the name of Christ, then, means believing in all that he is essentially in himself. Jn. 3:18 also says, 'He who believes in him is not condemned: but he who does not believe is condemned already.' It is characteristic of Johannine teaching that eternal issues are decided here and now. Faith does not simply give men assurance of everlasting life at some unspecified time in the future. It gives them everlasting life here and now. He that believes on the Son 'has' everlasting life (3:36; *cf.* 5:24, *etc.*).

(iii) In Acts, with its story of vigorous missionary advance, it is not surprising that the characteristic expression is the use of the aorist tense, to indicate the act of decision. Luke records many occasions wherein people came to put their trust in Christ. Other constructions are found, and both the continuing state and the permanent results of belief find mention. But decision is the characteristic thing.

(iv) For Paul, faith is the typical Christian attitude. He does not share John's antipathy to the noun, but uses it more than twice as often as he uses the verb. It occurs in connection with some of his leading ideas. Thus in Rom. 1:16 he speaks of the gospel as 'the power of God for salvation to every one who has faith'. It means a great deal to Paul that Christianity is more than a system of good advice. It not only tells men what they ought to do, but gives them power to do it. Again and again Paul contrasts mere words with power, always with a view to emphasizing that the power of the Holy Spirit of God is seen in the lives of Christians. This power becomes available to a man only when he believes. There is no substitute for faith.

Much of Paul's controversial writing centres round the dispute with the Judaizers. These men insisted that it was not enough for Christians to be baptized. They must also be circumcised, and, being thus admitted to Judaism, endeavour to keep the whole of the Mosaic law. They made obedience to the law a necessary pre-condition of salvation, at least in the fullest sense of that term. Paul will have none of this. He insists that men can do nothing, nothing at all, to bring about their salvation. All has been done by Christ, and no man can add anything to the perfection of Christ's finished work. So it is that Paul insists that men are justified 'by faith' (Rom. 5:1). The doctrine of *justification by faith lies at the very heart of Paul's message. Whether with this terminology or not, he is always putting the idea forward. He vigorously combats any idea of the efficacy of good deeds. 'A man is not justified by works of the law but through faith in Jesus Christ,' he writes to the Galatians and proceeds, 'even we have believed in Christ Jesus, in order to be justified by faith in Christ, and not by works of the law.' He adds resoundingly 'because by works of the law shall no one be justified' (Gal. 2:16). Clearly, for Paul, faith means the abandonment of all reliance on one's ability to merit salvation. It is a trustful acceptance of God's gift in Christ, a reliance on Christ, Christ alone, for all that salvation means.

Another outstanding feature of Pauline theology is the very large place the apostle gives to the work of the Holy Spirit. He thinks of all Christians as indwelt by the Spirit (Rom. 8:9, 14), and he connects this too with faith. Thus he writes to the Ephesians concerning Christ, 'you also, who . . . have believed in him, were sealed with the promised Holy Spirit, which is the guarantee of our inheritance' (Eph. 1:13f.). Sealing represented the mark of ownership, a metaphor readily understood in an age when many could not read. The Spirit within believers is God's mark of ownership, and this mark is put on men only as they believe. The apostle goes on to speak of the Spirit as 'the guarantee (Gk. *arrabōn*) of our inheritance'. Paul employs here a word which in the 1st century meant a down-payment, *i.e.* a payment which at one and the same time was part of the agreed price and the guarantee that the remainder would be forthcoming. Thus when a man believes he receives the Holy Spirit as part of the life in the age to come, and as an assurance that the remainder will infallibly follow. (*EARNEST.)

(v) The writer of the Epistle to the Hebrews sees that faith has always been a characteristic of the people of God. In his great portrait gallery in Heb. 11 he reviews the worthies of the past, showing how one by one they illustrate the great theme that 'without faith it is impossible to please' God (Heb. 11:6). He is particularly interested in the opposition of faith to sight. Faith is 'the assurance of things hoped for, the conviction of things not seen' (Heb. 11:1). He emphasizes the point that men who had nothing in the way of outward evidence to support them nevertheless retained a firm hold on the promises of God. In other words, they walked by faith, not by sight.

(vi) Of the other writers in the NT we must notice James, for he has often been held to be in opposition to Paul in this matter. Where Paul insists that a man is justified by faith and not by works James maintains 'that a man is justified by works, and not by faith alone' (Jas. 2:24). There is no more than a verbal contradiction, however. The kind of 'faith' that James is opposing is not that warm personal trust in a living Saviour of which Paul speaks. It is a faith which James himself describes: 'You believe that God is one; you do well. Even the demons believe—and shudder' (Jas. 2:19). He has in mind an intellectual assent to certain truths, an assent which is not backed up by a life lived in accordance with those truths (Jas. 2:15f.). So far is James from opposing faith in the full sense that he everywhere presupposes it. Right at the beginning of his Epistle he speaks naturally of 'the testing of your faith' (Jas. 1:3), and he exhorts his readers, 'show no partiality as you hold the faith of our Lord Jesus Christ, the Lord of glory' (Jas. 2:1). He criticizes a wrong faith but assumes that everyone will recognize the need for a right faith. Moreover, by 'works' James does not mean what Paul means by that term. Paul thinks of obedience to the commands of the law regarded as a system whereby a man may merit salvation. For James the law is the law of liberty' (Jas. 2:12). His 'works' look uncommonly like 'the fruit of the Spirit' of which Paul speaks. They are warm deeds of love springing from a right attitude to God. They are the fruits of faith. What James objects to is the claim that faith is there when there is no fruit to attest it.

Faith is clearly one of the most important concepts in the whole NT. Everywhere it is required and its importance insisted upon. Faith means abandoning all trust in one's own resources. Faith means casting oneself unreservedly on the mercy of God. Faith means laying hold on the promises of God in Christ, relying entirely on the finished work of Christ for salvation, and on the power of the indwelling Holy Spirit of God for daily strength. Faith implies complete reliance on God and full obedience to God.

BIBLIOGRAPHY. D. M. Baillie, *Faith in God*, 1964; B. B. Warfield in *HDB*; J. G. Machen, *What Is Faith?*, 1925; G. C. Berkouwer, *Faith and Justification*², 1954; J. Hick, *Faith and Knowledge*², 1966; O. Becker, O. Michel, *NIDNTT* 1, pp. 587–606; R. Bultmann, *TDNT* 6, pp. 1–11; A. Weiser *et al.*, *TDNT* 6, pp. 174–228. L.M.

FAITHFULNESS
See Grace, Part 2.

FALL.

I. The biblical account

The story of the Fall of man, given in Gn. 3, describes how mankind's first parents, when tempted by the serpent, disobeyed God's express command by eating of the fruit of the tree of the knowledge of good and evil. The essence of all sin is displayed in this first sin: having been tempted to doubt God's word ('Did God say . . .?'), man is led on to disbelieve it ('You will not die'), and then to disobey it (they 'ate'). Sin is man's rebellion against the authority of God, and pride in his own supposed self-adequacy ('You will be like God'). The consequences of sin are two-fold: first, awareness of guilt and immediate separation from God (they 'hid themselves'), with whom hitherto there had been unimpaired daily fellowship; and secondly, the sentence of the curse, decreeing toil, sorrow and death for man himself, and in addition inevitably involving the whole of the created order, of which man is the crown.

II. The effect on man

Man henceforth is a perverted creature. In revolting against the purpose of his being, which is to live and act entirely to the glory of his sovereign and beneficent Creator and to fulfil his will, he ceases to be truly man. His true manhood consists in conformity to the image of God in which he was created. This image of God is manifested in man's original capacity for communion with his Creator; in his enjoyment exclusively of what is good; in his rationality which makes it possible for him alone of all creatures to hear and respond to the Word of God; in his knowledge of the truth and in the freedom which that knowledge ensures; and in government, as the head of God's creation, in obedience to the mandate to have dominion over every living thing and to subdue the earth.

Yet, rebel as he will against the image of God with which he has been stamped, man cannot efface it, because it is part of his very constitution as man. It is evident, for example, in his pursuit of scientific knowledge, in his harnessing of the forces of nature and in his development of culture, art and civilization. But at the same time the efforts of fallen man are cursed with frustration. This frustration is itself a proof of the perversity of the human heart. Thus history shows that the very discoveries and advances which have promised most good to mankind have through misuse brought great evils in their train. The man who does not love God does not love his fellow men. He is driven by selfish motives. The image of Satan, the great hater of God and man, is superimposed upon him. The result of the Fall is that man now knows good *and evil.*

The psychological and ethical effects of the Fall are nowhere more graphically described than by Paul in Rom. 1:18ff. All men, however ungodly and unrighteous they may be, *know* the truth about God and themselves; but they wickedly *suppress* this truth (v. 18). It is, however, an inescapable truth, for the fact of the 'eternal power and Godhead' of the Creator is both manifested within them, by their very constitution as God's creatures made in his image, and also manifested all around them in the whole created order of the universe which bears eloquent testimony to its origin as God's handiwork (vv. 19f.; *cf.* Ps. 19:1ff.). Basically, therefore, man's state is not one of ignorance but of knowledge. His condemnation is that he loves darkness rather than light. His refusal to glorify God as God and his ingratitude lead him into intellectual vanity and futility. Arrogantly professing himself to be wise, he in fact becomes a fool (Rom. 1:21f.). Having wilfully cut himself adrift from the Creator in whom alone the meaning of his existence is to be found, he must seek that meaning elsewhere, for his creaturely finitude makes it impossible for him to cease from being a religious creature. And his search becomes ever more foolish and degrading. It carries him into the gross irrationality of superstition and idolatry, into vileness and unnatural vice, and into all those evils, social and international, which give rise to the hatreds and miseries that disfigure our world. The Fall has, in brief, overthrown the true dignity of man (Rom. 1:23ff.).

III. The biblical doctrine

It will be seen that the scriptural doctrine of the Fall altogether contradicts the popular modern view of man as a being who, by a slow evolutionary development, has succeeded in rising from the primeval fear and groping ignorance of a humble origin to proud heights of religious sensitivity and insight. The Bible does not portray man as risen, but as fallen, and in the most desperate of situations. It is only against this background that God's saving action in Christ takes on its proper significance. Through the grateful appropriation by faith of Christ's atoning work, what was forfeited by the fall is restored to man: his true and intended dignity is recovered, the purpose of life recaptured, the image of God restored, and the way into the paradise of intimate communion with God reopened.

IV. Its historical development

In the history of the church the classic controversy concerning the nature of the Fall and its effects is that waged by Augustine at the beginning of the 5th century against the advocates of the Pelagian heresy. The latter taught that Adam's sin affected only himself and not the human race as a whole, that every individual is born free from sin and capable in his own power of living a sinless life, and that there had even been persons who had succeeded in doing so. The controversy and its implications may be studied with profit in Augustine's anti-Pelagian writings. Pelagianism, with its affirmation of the total ability of man, came to the fore again in the Socinianism of the 16th and 17th centuries, and continues under the guise of modern humanistic religion.

A halfway position is taken by the Roman Catholic Church, which teaches that what man lost through the Fall was a supernatural gift of original righteousness that did not belong properly to his being as man but was something extra added by God (*donum superadditum*), with the consequence that the Fall left man in his natural state as created (*in puris naturalibus*): he has suffered a negative rather than a positive evil; deprivation rather than depravation. This teaching opens the door for the affirmation of the ability and indeed necessity of unregenerate man to contribute by his works towards the achievement of his salvation (semi-Pelagianism, synergism), which is characteristic of the Roman Catholic theology of man and grace. For a Roman Catholic view, see H. J. Richards, 'The Creation and Fall', in *Scripture* 8, 1956, pp. 109–115.

Although retaining the conception of man as a fallen being, contemporary liberal theology denies the historicity of the event of the Fall. Every man, it is said, is his own Adam. Similarly, certain forms of modern existentialist philosophy, which is essentially a repudiation of historical objectivism, are willing to make use of the term 'fallenness' to describe the subjective state in which man pessimistically finds himself. A floating concept, however, which is unrelated to historical event explains nothing. But the NT certainly understands the Fall as a definite event in human history—an event, moreover, of such critical consequences for the whole human race that it stands side by side with and explains the other great crucial event of history, namely the coming of Christ to save the world (see Rom. 5:12ff.; 1 Cor. 15:21f.). Mankind, together with the rest of the created order, awaits a third and conclusive event of history, namely the second advent of Christ at the end of this age, when the effects of the Fall will be finally abolished, unbelievers eternally judged, and the renewed creation, the new heavens and new earth wherein righteousness dwells, be established in accordance with almighty God's immutable purposes (see Acts 3:20f.; Rom. 8:19ff.; 2 Pet. 3:13; Rev. 21–22). Thus by God's grace all that was lost in Adam, and much more than that, is restored in Christ. (*SIN.)

BIBLIOGRAPHY. N. P. Williams, *The Ideas of the Fall and of Original Sin*, 1927; J. G. Machen, *The Christian View of Man*, 1937, ch. 14; J. Murray, *The Imputation of Adam's Sin*, 1959.

P.E.H.

FALLOW
See Agriculture, Part 1.

FALLOW DEER
See Animals, Part 1.

FAMILIAR SPIRIT
See Divination, Part 1.

FAMILY, HOUSEHOLD.

I. In the Old Testament

There is no word in the OT which corresponds precisely to modern English 'family', as consisting of father, mother and children. The closest approximation is found in the word *bayiṯ* ('house'), which, from signifying the group of people, probably came to refer to the dwelling (AV translates as 'family' in 1 Ch. 13:14; 2 Ch. 35:5, 12; Ps. 68:6). In the Bible the term could be used not only of those sheltering under the same roof (Ex. 12:4) but also of much larger groups, as for instance the 'house of Israel' (Is. 5:7), which included the whole nation. Perhaps a closer equivalent to English 'family' is found in the phrase *bêṯ 'āḇ*, 'father's house'. The term most frequently translated 'family' in the EVV is *mišpāḥâ*, which had more the meaning of 'clan' than the smaller 'family', being applied for instance to 600 Danites from two villages (Jdg. 18:11).

Some idea of the relation of these two terms can be gained from the account in Jos. 7:16–18 of the detection of Achan after the failure to capture Ai. The search was first narrowed to the 'tribe' (*šēḇeṭ*) of Judah, then to the clan (*mišpāḥâ*, AV 'family') of the Zarhites, and finally to the 'household' (*bayiṯ*) of Zabdi. The fact that Achan was a married man with children of his own (7:24), but was still counted as a member of the *bayiṯ* of his grandfather Zabdi, shows the extent of this term. Conceptually the members of a tribe can be pictured as a cone, with the founding ancestor at the apex and the living generation at the base. The term *šēḇeṭ*, 'staff', perhaps in reference to the staff, signifying the authority, of the founding ancestor, applied to the whole tribe; *mišpāḥâ* referred to a smaller division lower down in the cone; and the term *bayiṯ* could apply to a yet smaller division, though its application depended upon its context, for if qualified by the name of the founding ancestor it could refer to the whole tribe. In each case the terms could indicate simply the base of the relevant cone, *i.e.* the living members of the group; or the entire volume of the cone, *i.e.* the members past and present, living and dead.

a. Determination of mates

In the choice of mates certain close relatives both by blood and *marriage were excluded (Lv. 18:6–18; Dt. 27:20–23), but outside these prohibited degrees marriage with kin was preferred, as is shown by the marriages of Isaac with Rebekah (Gn. 24:4), Jacob with Rachel and Leah (Gn. 28:2; 29:19), and Manoah's wish concerning Samson (Jdg. 14:3). On the other hand, marriages with foreigners, Hittite (Gn. 26:34), Egyptian (Gn. 41:45), Midianite (Ex. 2:21), Moabite (Ru. 1:4), Zidonian (1 Ki. 16:31) and others, did take place. A special case where the mate is determined is found in the levirate marriage law, whereby if a married man died childless his next brother was obliged to marry the widow, and raise up children to perpetuate the name of the deceased.

b. Methods of acquiring a wife

In most cases the choice of a mate and subsequent arrangements for marriage were made by the parents concerned, as is shown by the fact that, though Samson was attracted by the Timnathite, he applied to his parents to make the arrangements. The usual method of acquiring a wife was by purchase, though this is not an altogether satisfactory term, since the 'bride-price' (*mōhar*; Gn. 34:12; Ex. 22:16; 1 Sa. 18:25), though it was a payment made by the man to the bride's father, was more in the nature of a compensation to the family for the loss of a valued member than an outright cash purchase. Service could be given instead of payment, as with Jacob, who served Laban 14 years for Rachel and Leah, but this practice was not common during the Monarchy. Unorthodox means of acquiring a wife, which did not always involve the parents, included capture in war (Dt. 21:10–14) or in raids (Jdg. 21), or seduction, in which case the seducer was obliged to marry the violated maiden (Ex. 22:16; *cf.* Gn. 34:1–4).

c. Residence

Israelite marriage was patrilocal: the woman left her father's house and went to live with her husband. In patriarchal times this would often have involved going to live in the same group, *bayiṯ* or *mišpāḥâ*, as her husband's father and brothers, but in the time of the Monarchy the son on marriage probably left home to set up his own *bayiṯ*, as is suggested by the smallness of many of the private houses uncovered in excavations. Three cases are sometimes quoted as evidence for matrilocal residence, Jacob, Gideon (Jdg. 8:31; 9:1–2) and Samson, but such an interpretation is not necessary. Jacob lived in Laban's 'house' only while he was working in return for his wives, and it was the manner rather than the fact of his departure which aroused Laban's ill-will (Gn. 31:26–28). Gideon did not himself live with the woman in question, and she was in any case no more than a concubine. The same is true of Samson and the Timnathite, whom he only visited, and did not live with.

d. Number of mates

While at the creation monogamy seemed to have been intended, by the time of the patriarchal age polygamy (polygyny not polyandry) is found. At first Abraham had but one wife, Sarah, but when she proved barren he followed the custom of the time in having children by her handmaid Hagar (Gn. 16:1–2), and he took Keturah as a wife after the death of Sarah (Gn. 25:1). In subsequent generations more wives were taken, Jacob having two and their two handmaids. The possession of two wives was evidently assumed in the Mosaic legislation (Dt. 21:15), and under the Judges and the Monarchy there was still less restraint, and the economic factor imposed the only limit. That this was not God's plan is shown by the prophetic representation of Israel as the sole bride of God (Is. 50:1; 54:6–7; 62:4–5; Je. 2:2; Ezk. 16; Ho. 2:4f.). In addition to wives and the maidservants of wives, those who could afford them had *concubines, and children born by these could be accorded equal status with true sons, if the father was so minded.

e. Husband and wife

In addition to the terms *'îš* and *'iššâ*, 'man' and 'woman', which also served for 'husband' and 'wife', the husband was the *ba'al*, 'master', and *'āḏôn*, 'lord', of the wife, which illustrates the legal and normally practical relative positions of the two. Until her marriage a *woman was subject to her father, and after marriage to her husband, and to each she was a chattel. A man could divorce his wife, but probably not she him; she did not inherit his property, which went to his sons; and she might have to get along with other wives. On the other hand, in practice there was great variation in accordance with personality and strength of character, and that some women came to public prominence is shown by the cases of Deborah (Jdg. 4–5), Athaliah (2 Ki. 11), Huldah (2 Ki. 22:14f.) and Esther. The duties of the wife included first of all the bearing and care of children, and such household tasks as cooking, in addition to helping the husband in the fields when opportunity offered. Fidelity was important in both parties, and there was strict provision in the law for the punishment of adultery. The most important function of the wife was the bearing of children, and *barrenness was a source of shame.

f. Parents and children

The four terms, 'father' (*'āḇ*), 'mother' (*'ēm*), 'son' (*bēn*) and 'daughter' (*baṯ*), have cognates in most Semitic languages and were in such frequent use in OT times that they are irregular in grammatical inflexion. The greatest wish of man and wife was for many children (Ps. 127:3–5), but especially for sons, as is clearly shown in the history of Abraham and his dealings with God, from whom they came. The eldest son occupied a special position, and on his father's death he inherited a double portion and became head of the family. Sometimes, however, a father would show special favour to his youngest son, as did Jacob for Joseph and then Benjamin. A daughter did not inherit from her father unless there were no sons (*cf.*, however, Jb. 42:13–15; see also *INHERITANCE).

In ancient Mesopotamia, particularly as evidenced in the Nuzi documents, the practice of adoption by childless people of someone to take the place of a son is well attested (*NUZI, *PATRIARCHAL AGE), and it was in keeping with this practice that *Abraham considered making one of his servants his heir (Gn. 15:3). There is, however, no specific legislation concerning this matter of *adoption in the OT. Such cases as are reported are either in a foreign setting (as for instance the case quoted above, Moses by Pharaoh's daughter (Ex. 2:10) and Esther by Mordecai (Est. 2:7, 15)) or else are not cases of full adoption, as the adoptees were already descendants of the adopters, as in the cases of Jacob and Joseph's sons (Gn. 48:5, 12), and Naomi and the child of Ruth (Ru. 4:16–17). When they were very small all children were looked after by the mother, but as the boys grew older they were taught to share their father's work, so that in general the father governed the *education of the son, and the mother that of the daughter. That to the children the mother was as worthy of honour as the father is shown by the fifth commandment (Ex. 20:12).

g. Other kinsfolk

The terms 'brother' (*'āḥ*) and 'sister' (*'āḥôṯ*) could be applied not only to children of the same parents but to half siblings by either a different father or mother, and the restrictions on sexual intercourse between full siblings applied also to these (Lv. 18:9, 11; Dt. 27:22). Often of particular importance to children were their uncles and aunts, especially the mother's brother to the son, and the father's sister to the daughter. These are usually designated by the appropriate combination of terms such as *'ᵃḥôṯ-'āḇ*, 'father's sister', but sometimes described by the words *dôḏ*, 'uncle', and *dôḏâ*, 'aunt'. A woman would refer to her husband's father and mother by the special terms *ḥām* (*e.g.* Gn. 38:13, 25; 1 Sa. 4:19, 21) and *ḥāmôṯ* (*e.g.* Ru. 1:14), and it may be that *ḥōṯēn* (*e.g.* Ex. 3:1; 4:18) and *ḥōṯeneṯ* (Dt. 27:23) were corresponding terms used by the man of his wife's mother and father, though the limited contexts in which these terms occur make this uncertain.

h. Solidarity of kin

Two main factors made for solidarity in patriarchal times, common blood or descent, and common habitation and legal obligations according to customs and law. Though after the settlement in the land the tendency for families to divide weakened these, they continued to be of importance throughout OT times. The community of interests among the members of the household, clan and tribe was also a source of unity within these groups, and under their heads. One of the outgrowths of this unity was the right of each member of a group to protection by that group, and indeed the obligations on the group to provide certain services. Outstanding among these was that of the *gō'ēl*, whose obligations might extend from marrying the widow of a kinsman (Ru. 2:20; 3:12; 4) to redeeming a kinsman from slavery into which he had sold himself to pay a debt (see also *AVENGER OF BLOOD).

BIBLIOGRAPHY. R. de Vaux, *Ancient Israel*, 1961, pp. 19–55, 520–523; E. A. Speiser, 'The Wife-Sister Motif in the Patriarchal Narratives' in A. Altmann (ed.), *Biblical and other Studies*, 1963, pp. 15–28. T.C.M.

II. In the New Testament

Family (Gk. *patria*) is mentioned as such only three times, although the related idea of 'house' or 'household' (Gk. *oikos*, *oikia*) is more frequent. *patria* ('lineage, descent', *LSJ*) signifies the historical origin of a household, *i.e.* its 'patriarch', rather than its present head. A family might be a tribe or even a nation. In Acts 3:25 the promise to Abraham is quoted in the form, 'in your posterity shall all the families (*patriai*) of the earth be blessed'. The LXX has 'tribes' (*phylai*) in the original promise (Gn. 12:3) and 'nations' (*ethnē*) when the promise is recalled in Gn. 18:18 and 22:18. Joseph was 'of the house and lineage (*patria*) of David' (Lk. 2:4), where the patronymic is the vital point. As this verse shows, 'house' (*oikos*) can be used in the same sense (*cf.* Lk. 1:27); *cf.* also 'the house of Israel' (Mt. 10:6; 15:24; Acts 2:36; 7:42, *etc.*), 'the house of Jacob' (Lk. 1:33).

The prominence of paternity is well seen in the third occurrence of *patria*, Eph. 3:14–15: 'I bow my knees before the Father, from whom every family in heaven and on earth is named.' This means that, just as every *patria* implies a *patēr* ('father'), so behind them all stands the universal fatherhood of God whence the whole scheme of ordered relationships is derived. Elsewhere we meet the more restricted concept of the fatherhood of God in relation to the household of the faithful.

The word 'household', where it is not simply a synonym for 'family', is a unit of society which meets us everywhere in the Roman and Hellenistic, as well as the Jewish, world of the 1st century. It consisted not only of the lord (Gk. *kyrios*), master (Gk. *despotēs*) or paterfamilias, his wife, children and slaves, but also of various dependants, such as servants, employees and even 'clients' (*e.g.* freedmen or friends) who voluntarily joined themselves to a household for the sake of mutual benefits (*CAESAR'S HOUSEHOLD). The Gospels abound

A fork is used to winnow grain by fanning it into the wind from a threshing-floor situated on a high place. (RH)

Holder, with the image of the young King Tutankhamun embossed on the surface, which originally held ostrich or other feathers to form a fan carried behind the king. Tomb of Tutankhamun. Gold. Handle c. 95 cm; holder 10 cm × 18·5 cm. c. 1360 BC. (SI)

FAMILY TREES See Genealogy, Part 1.

with allusions to the household and its character (*e.g.* Mt. 21:33ff.). The household was an important factor in the growth and stability of the church. Already among the Jews the household was the context of such religious exercises as the Passover, a weekly sacred meal, prayers and instruction (*EDUCATION). Luke states that 'the breaking of the bread' took place in the Jerusalem church 'by households' (Acts 2:46). This phrase, *kat' oikon*, occurs in papyri in contrast to the phrase 'by individuals' (*kata prosōpon*—see *MM*).

In Hellenistic cities the role of the household in the establishment of churches was no less important. The first accession of Gentiles was the entire household of Cornelius at Caesarea, comprising household servants, a batman, kinsmen and near friends (Acts 10:7, 24). When Paul crossed to Europe, the church was planted at Philippi with the baptism of Lydia's household and that of the jailer (Acts 16:15, 31–34). At Corinth 'the first converts in Achaia' were the household of Stephanas (1 Cor. 16:15), which, in common, probably, with the households of Crispus the ruler of the synagogue and the hospitable Gaius (Acts 18:8; 1 Cor. 1:14–16; Rom. 16:23), was baptized by Paul himself. Other Christian households mentioned by name are those of Prisca and Aquila (at Ephesus, 1 Cor. 16:19; and perhaps Rome, Rom. 16:5), Onesiphorus (at Ephesus, 2 Tim. 1:16; 4:19), Philemon (at Colossae, Phm. 1–2), Nymphas or Nympha (at Laodicea, Col. 4:15), Asyncritus and Philologus (at Rome [?], Rom. 16:14–15).

In the Jerusalem church households were apparently instructed as units (Acts 5:42), and this was also Paul's custom, as he reminded the Ephesian elders (Acts 20:20). A regular catechesis existed setting forth the mutual duties of members of a Christian household: wives and husbands, children and fathers, servants and masters. See Col. 3:18–4:1; Eph. 5:22–6:9; 1 Pet. 2:18–3:7.

Reference is made to the church in the house of Prisca and Aquila (Rom. 16:5 and 1 Cor. 16:19), of Nymphas or Nympha (Col. 4:15) and of Philemon (or was it Archippus?) (Phm. 2). This means either that the household was regarded as a *church in itself, or that the church in a given locality met within the scope of one household's hospitality (see above, 'by households'). When Gaius is spoken of as host of 'the whole church' (Rom. 16:23), the existence of other household churches in Corinth is perhaps implied, with the suggestion that on occasion, presumably for the Lord's Supper (1 Cor. 11:18–22), they all came together 'as a church'. It is, however, not unimportant to note that both baptism and the Lord's Supper in certain situations took place within a household, not to mention instruction of wife and children (1 Cor. 14:35; Eph. 6:4), and that it was from the ranks of proved heads of households that overseers (bishops) as well as deacons for the church were drawn (1 Tim. 3:2–7, 12).

It is not surprising that the church itself should be thought of as the household of God (Eph. 2:19, where the figure is combined with that of the sacred republic) or the household of faith (Gal. 6:10). The description of believers as adopted sons (Rom. 8:15–17) or as servants and stewards (1 Pet. 4:10) implies this figure. Paul sees himself as a servant of Jesus Christ, a steward set to perform a particular ministry (Rom. 1:1; 1 Cor. 4:1; 9:17, RV). In a related picture the writer to the Hebrews depicts Moses as a faithful head steward in God's household, foreshadowing Christ as the son and heir (*cf.* Gal. 3:23–4:7) of the household of God; 'and we are his house', says the writer, 'if we hold fast our confidence and pride in our hope' (Heb. 3:1–6).

BIBLIOGRAPHY. G. Schrenk, *TDNT* 5, pp. 119–134, 1015–1019; E. G. Selwyn, *1 Peter*, 1946, Essay II, p. 363; E. A. Judge, *The Social Pattern of Christian Groups in the First Century*, 1960. D.W.B.R.

FAMINE. The Bible does not always indicate the moral and spiritual significance of the famines it records. Those, for example, of Gn. 12:10; 26:1; Acts 11:28, *etc.*, are simply stated as historical facts. But famines, like every other event in nature or history, are elsewhere integrated into the characteristic biblical doctrine of divine providence, *e.g.* Am. 4:6; Rev. 6:8. Canaanite religion deified natural processes, and sought to control them by the practice of sympathetic magic, but Israel possessed a different key to prosperity. Yahweh, as Creator, possessed and controlled the 'forces' of nature, the seasons in their order, and the material foundation of man's life on earth (*e.g.* Ps. 104). The exercise of this power by the holy God directly corresponds to the relationship existing between him and man at any given time. Thus, at the one end of the scale the 'Messianic day', when perfect accord between God and his people exists, is marked by unprecedented fertility of the earth (*e.g.* Is. 4:2; 41:19; Ho. 2:21–22; Am. 9:13). On the other hand, the fruits of nature are withdrawn in times of disobedience, when the relationship of God and man is dislocated. Thus the curse on the soil was one of the foremost and immediate results of the Fall (Gn. 3:17–18), and God used famines throughout history as indications of his displeasure, and as warnings to repent (*e.g.* 1 Ki. 17:1; 18:17–18; Hg. 1:6, 9–11; 2:16–17). This view persists in Revelation (*e.g.* 6:5–8), where famine is a direct visitation on human sin. Obedience and prosperity (Ps. 1:1–3; Pr. 3:7–10; Is. 1:19), disobedience and want (Lv. 26:14–16) are biblical inseparables. This law is given classic expression in Dt. 28, and poetic illustration in Je. 14.

The famine (Gk. *limos*) which severely affected Judaea in the principate of Claudius (*c.* AD 46–47) is attested in other records: thus Josephus tells how Queen Helena of Adiabene bought grain in Egypt and figs in Cyprus for the relief of hard-pressed Judaeans (*Ant.* 20. 51f.). This famine figures in Acts as the occasion for the first instance of inter-church aid: when it was foretold by Agabus in the church of Syrian Antioch, that church collected a sum of money for the relief of the Jerusalem church (Acts 11:27–30).

The proclamation of Rev. 6:6 indicates that food prices would be up to ten times as high as in normal times.

In 2 Cor. 11:27 'hunger' (*limos*) is due to absence of food; 'without food' (*nēsteia*) implies voluntary fasting. J.A.M.
F.F.B.

FAN (AV; RSV 'fork'; Heb. *mizreh*, 'fan'; Heb. *zārâ*, 'to scatter', 'to winnow'; Gk. *ptyon*, 'fan'). A long wooden fork used by threshers to toss grain into the air so that the chaff is blown away (*e.g.* Is. 30:24; Je. 15:7), a method still found in some remote areas of the Middle East. Thus John the Baptist employed an easily understood figure of speech in depicting Christ as the great Winnower who would separate evil from good (Mt. 3:12; Lk. 3:17). (*AGRICULTURE.)
J.D.D.

FASTING. Fasting in the Bible generally means going without all food and drink for a period (*e.g.* Est. 4:16), and not merely refraining from certain foods.

I. In the Old Testament

The Heb. words are *ṣûm* (verb) and *ṣôm* (noun). The phrase *'innâ nap̄šô* ('to afflict the soul') also refers to fasting. First, there were certain annual fasts. Thus the Hebrews fasted on the Day of Atonement (Lv. 16:29, 31; 23:27–32; Nu. 29:7). After the Exile, four other annual fasts were observed (Zc. 8:19), all of them, according to the Talmud, marking disasters in Jewish history. Est. 9:31 can be interpreted as implying the establishment of yet another regular fast.

In addition to these there were occasional fasts. These were sometimes individual (*e.g.* 2 Sa. 12:22) and sometimes corporate (*e.g.* Jdg. 20:26; Joel 1:14). Fasting gave expression to grief (1 Sa. 31:13; 2 Sa. 1:12; 3:35; Ne. 1:4; Est. 4:3; Ps. 35:13–14) and penitence (1 Sa. 7:6; 1 Ki. 21:27; Ne. 9:1–2; Dn. 9:3–4; Jon. 3:5–8). It was a way by which men might humble themselves (Ezr. 8:21; Ps. 69:10). Sometimes it may have been thought of as a self-inflicted punishment (*cf.* the phrase 'to afflict the soul'). Fasting was often directed towards securing the guidance and help of God (Ex. 34:28; Dt. 9:9; 2 Sa. 12:16–23; 2 Ch. 20:3–4; Ezr. 8:21–23). Fasting could be vicarious (Ezr. 10:6; Est. 4:15–17). Some came to think that fasting would automatically gain man a hearing from God (Is. 58:3–4). Against this the prophets declared that without right conduct fasting was in vain (Is. 58:5–12; Je. 14:11–12; Zc. 7).

II. In the New Testament

The usual Gk. words are *nēsteuō* (verb), and *nēsteia* and *nēstis* (nouns). In Acts 27:21, 33 the words *asitia* and *asitos* ('without food') are also used.

As far as general Jewish practice is concerned, the Day of Atonement is the only annual fast referred to in the NT (Acts 27:9). Some strict Pharisees fasted every Monday and Thursday (Lk. 18:12). Other devout Jews, like Anna, might fast often (Lk. 2:37).

The only occasion when Jesus is recorded as fasting is at the time of his temptations in the wilderness. Then, however, he was not necessarily fasting from choice. The first temptation implies that there was no food available in the place he had selected for his weeks of preparation for his ministry (Mt. 4:1–4). *Cf.* the 40 days' fasts of Moses (Ex. 34:28) and Elijah (1 Ki. 19:8).

Jesus assumed that his hearers would fast, but taught them when they did so to face Godward, not manward (Mt. 6:16–18). When asked why his disciples did not fast as did those of John the Baptist and of the Pharisees, Jesus did not repudiate fasting, but declared it to be inappropriate for his disciples 'as long as the bridegroom is with them' (Mt. 9:14–17; Mk. 2:18–22; Lk. 5:33–39). Later they would fast like others.

In Acts leaders of the church fast when choosing missionaries (13:2–3) and elders (14:23). Paul twice refers to his fasting (2 Cor. 6:5; 11:27). In the former passage voluntary fasting, by way of self-discipline, appears to be meant (*nēsteia*); the latter passage mentions both involuntary 'hunger' (*limos*) and voluntary going 'without food' (*nēsteia*).

The weight of textual evidence is against the inclusion of references to fasting in Mt. 17:21; Mk. 9:29; Acts 10:30; 1 Cor. 7:5, though the presence of these references in many MSS in itself indicates that there was a growing belief in the value of fasting in the early church. H.A.G.B.

FEAR. The Bible uses numerous words to denote fear. The most common of these (giving the noun forms) are Heb. *yir'â*, 'reverence'; Heb. *paḥaḏ*, dread', 'fear'; Gk. *phobos*, 'fear', 'terror'. Theologically, four main categories can be suggested.

a. Holy fear

This comes from the believer's apprehension of the living God. According to Luther, the natural man cannot fear God perfectly; according to Rudolf Otto, he is 'quite unable even to shudder (*grauen*) or feel horror in the real sense of the word'. Holy fear, on the other hand, is God-given, enabling men to reverence God's authority, obey his commandments and hate and shun all form of evil (Je. 32:40; *cf.* Gn. 22:12; Heb. 5:7). It is, moreover, the beginning (or principle) of wisdom (Ps. 111:10); the secret of uprightness (Pr. 8:13); a feature of the people in whom God delights (Ps. 147:11); and the whole duty of man (Ec. 12:13). It is also one of the divine qualifications of the Messiah (Is. 11:2–3).

In the OT, largely because of the law's legal sanctions, true religion is often regarded as synonymous with the fear of God (*cf.* Je. 2:19; Ps. 34:11, Moffatt), and even in NT times the term 'walking in the fear of the Lord' was used in connection with the early Christians. Gentile adherents of the synagogue were called 'God-fearers' (Acts 10:2, *etc.*; *cf.* Phil. 2:12).

In the NT generally, however,

FARMING
See Agriculture, Part 1.

FARTHING
See Money, Part 2.

FATE
See Providence, Part 3.

FATHERLESS
See Orphan, Part 2.

FATHER'S HOUSE
See House, Part 2.

FATHOM
See Weights and measures, Part 3.

A woman and two men (possibly Semites) from a large group apparently dying of hunger in a famine. From a relief from the pyramid-causeway of King Unis, Saqqara. c. 2400 BC.

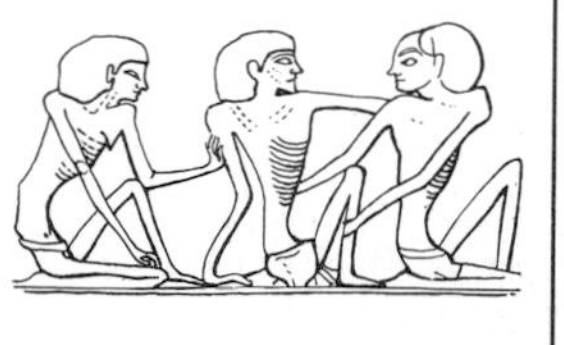

FEAST OF BOOTHS See Tabernacles, feast of, Part 3.

FEAST OF DEDICATION See Dedication, feast of, Part 1.

FEAST OF TABERNACLES See Tabernacles, feast of, Part 3.

emphasis is laid on God as loving and forgiving, the One who through Christ gives to men the spirit of sonship (Rom. 8:15), and enables them boldly to face up to life (2 Tim. 1:6–7) and death (Heb. 2:15) without fear. Nevertheless, a reverent fear remains; for the awesomeness of God has not changed, and there is a day of judgment to be met (2 Cor. 5:10f.). Godly fear stimulates the believer to seek holiness (2 Cor. 7:1), and is reflected in his attitude towards his fellow-Christians (Eph. 5:21).

b. Slavish fear

This is strictly a natural consequence of sin (Gn. 3:10; Pr. 28:1), and can come as a punishment (Dt. 28:28). It was felt by Felix when he heard Paul preach (Acts 24:25); it is felt by Christ-rejecters, for whom remains only 'a fearful expectation of judgment' (Heb. 10:27, RV, 31; *cf.* Rev. 21:8). Though not of itself good, this fear is often used by the Holy Spirit for the conversion of men (Acts 16:29ff., *etc.*).

c. Fear of men

This can be expressed as: (i) a reverential awe and regard of men, as of masters and magistrates (1 Pet. 2:18; Rom. 13:7); (ii) a blind dread of them and what they can do (Nu. 14:9; Is. 8:12; Pr. 29:25); and (iii) in a peculiar sense a Christian concern for them lest they be ruined by sin (1 Cor. 2:3; 2 Cor. 11:3; Col. 2:1). This kind of fear, and also the slavish fear mentioned in (*b*) above, can be cast out by true love to God (1 Jn. 4:18).

d. 'Fear' as the object of fear

Fear is uused in another sense, as in Gn. 31:42, 53, where God is called the 'Fear' of *Isaac—*i.e.* the God whom Isaac feared and worshipped. Their 'fear', the thing that terrifies them, comes upon the wicked (Pr. 1:26–27; 10:24; *cf.* Is. 66:4). When the Hebrews entered the promised land God sent his fear before them, destroying and scattering the Canaanites, or so impressing them with his fear as to render them spiritless and unable to withstand the invaders (Ex. 23:27–28). Fear in this sense is found also in Jb. 4:6 (*cf.* 9:34; 13:21): 'Is not your fear of God your confidence, and the integrity of your ways your hope?'

BIBLIOGRAPHY. R. Otto, *The Idea of the Holy*, 1929; J. Murray, *Principles of Conduct*, 1957, pp. 229ff.; J.-J. von Allmen, *Vocabulary of the Bible*, 1958, pp. 113–119; R. H. Pfeiffer, 'The Fear of God', *IEJ* 5, 1955, pp. 43–48 (a valuable survey of the idea of fear in the non-biblical literatures of the ancient Near East); W. Mundle, *NIDNTT* 1, pp. 621–624; H. Balz, G. Wanke, *TDNT* 9, pp. 189–219; W. Foerster, *TDNT* 7, pp. 168–196; R. Bultmann, *TDNT* 2, pp. 751–754. J.D.D.

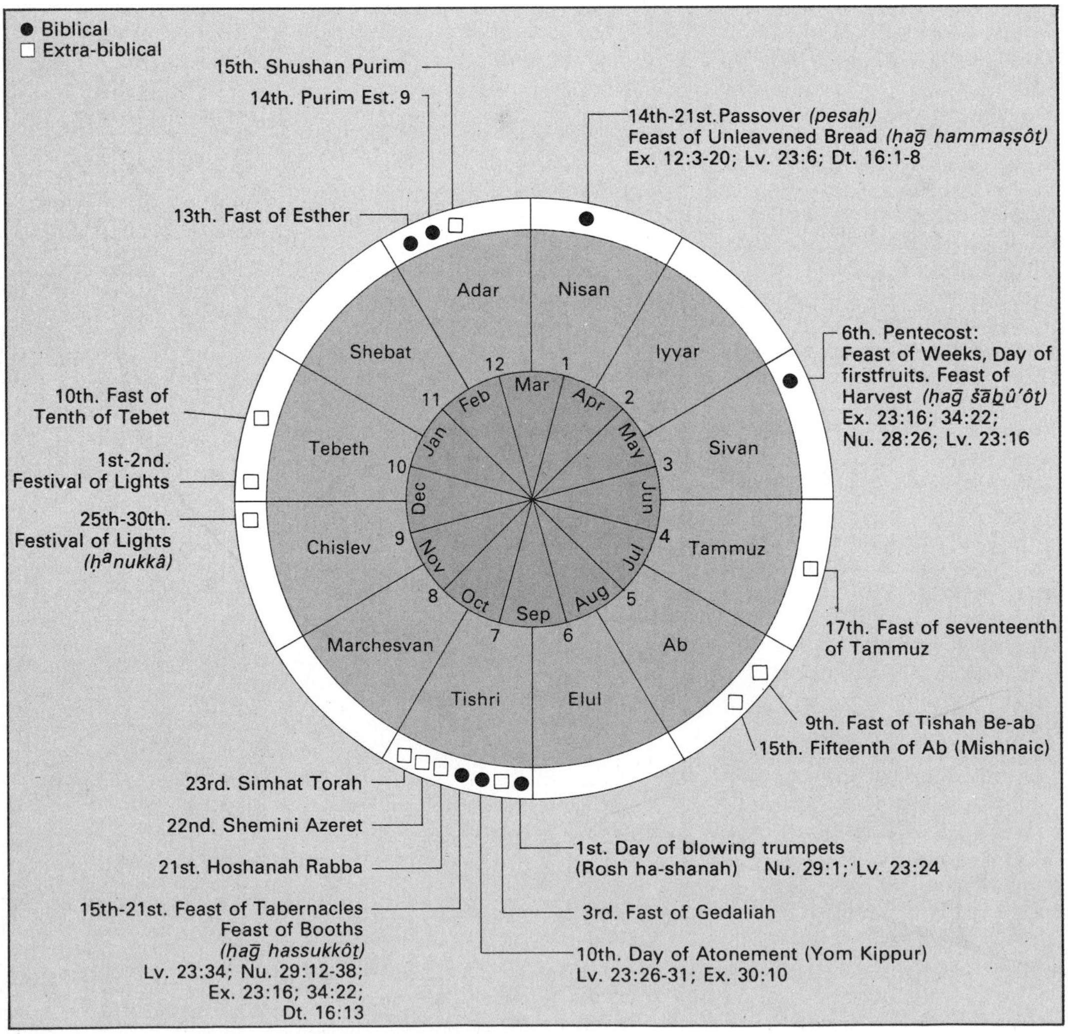

Diagram showing the major biblical and extra-biblical Jewish feasts.

FEASTS. Heb. *ḥaḡ*, 'feast' (Lv. 23:6; Dt. 16:16), *mô'ᵃḏê Yahweh*, 'feasts of the Lord' (Lv. 23:2, 4; Nu. 15:3). The terms are expressive of a day or season of religious joy. While some of these feasts coincide with the seasons, it does not follow that they have their origin in the seasonal ritual of the religions of the ancient Near East. These are associated with the gods of the pantheon who banquet together or feast with men. (See C. H. Gordon, *Ugaritic Literature*, 1949, pp. 57–103; T. Gaster, *Thespis*, 1950, pp. 6–108.) Biblical feasts differ in origin, purpose and content. To the Israelite the seasons were the work of the Creator for the benefit of man. They manifested the beneficence of God towards his creatures. By these feasts man not only acknowledged God as his Provider but recorded the Lord's unbounded and free favour to a chosen people whom he delivered, by personal intervention, in this world (Ex. 10:2; 12:8–9, 11, 14; Lv. 23:5; Dt. 16:6, 12). The joy expressed was heartfelt. Religious commitment was not incompatible with pleasure in temporal things conceived as gifts of God (Lv. 23:40; Dt. 16:14). The response of the participant was religiously ethical. Acknowledgment of sin and devotion to the law of God was involved (Ex. 13:9; Zc. 8:9). The sacrifices offered bespoke forgiveness of sin and reconciliation with God (Lv. 17:11; Nu. 28:22; 29:7–11; 2 Ch. 30:22; Ezk. 45:17, 20). To be withheld from the feast was considered a loss and a bar from privilege (Nu. 9:7). Not only did the Israelite appear at the feast as a beneficiary of the divine favour, but he made return to the Lord as he had been blessed (Dt. 16:10). Only in unauthorized feasts did unbelieving Israelites eat, drink and play (Ex. 32:6; 1 Ki. 12:32–33).

The feasts of the OT do not follow the ancient Near Eastern pattern of a period of joy preceded by rites of mortification and purgation (T. Gaster, *op. cit*., pp. 6, 12). The Bible festival itself contained the element of mourning, for this is involved in sacrifice for sin (Lv. 23:27; Nu. 29:7). There is no sharp line of demarcation between sorrow for sin and the joy of the Lord.

Prophetical displeasure with the feasts as observed by the Jews (Is. 1:13–20) was not because they were in themselves on a lower plane of piety, but because many Israelites had departed from their spiritual purpose. They made the sum of religion consist in external observance, which was never the divine intent for the feasts from the time of their promulgation (Na. 1:15). In the NT this was well understood by our Lord and devout believers who diligently and spiritually observed the prescribed feasts of the old economy (Lk. 2:41; 22:8; Jn. 4:45; 5:1; 7:2, 11; 12:20).

The feasts to which reference is made in the OT are as follows:

1. The Feast of Unleavened Bread, Heb. *ḥaḡ hammaṣṣôṯ* (Ex. 23:15), or *Passover, Heb. *pesaḥ* (Lv. 23:5), was established to commemorate the historical deliverance from Egypt (Ex. 10:2; 12:8, 14). It was one of the three annual festivals, and was observed on the fourteenth day of the first month. For 7 days unleavened bread was eaten and no servile work done. The first and the last day being 'holy convocations', sacrifices were offered (Nu. 28:16–25; Dt. 16:1–8).

2. The Feast of Weeks, Heb. *ḥaḡ šāḇû'ôṯ*. It is also called the 'feast of harvest' and 'the day of first fruits' (Ex. 23:16; 34:22; Nu. 28:26). Later it was known as *Pentecost because it was celebrated on the fiftieth day from the sabbath beginning the Passover. It was marked by a holy convocation and the offering of sacrifices.

3. The Feast of *Tabernacles, Heb. *ḥaḡ hassukkôṯ*, or 'the feast of booths', is also called the 'feast of ingathering', Heb. *ḥaḡ hā'āsîp̄* (Ex. 23:16; 34:22; Lv. 23:34; Dt. 16:13). It lasted 7 days, the first and last days being holy convocations. Fruit was gathered in and people dwelt in booths made of branches and boughs of trees (Lv. 23:39–43; Nu. 29:12–38).

4. The *Sabbath. This is regarded as a feast in Lv. 23:2–3, and called a 'sabbath of rest'. It was marked by a solemn assembly (Is. 1:13), and cessation from all labour. It was also a day of joy (Is. 58:13).

5. The Day of Blowing of Trumpets (Nu. 29:1). In Lv. 23:24 it is called 'a memorial of blowing of trumpets' and 'a sabbath'. Sacrifices were offered and hard labour ceased.

6. The Day of *Atonement (Lv. 23:26–31). It was observed on the tenth day of the seventh month, and was a day of a 'holy convocation' in which souls were afflicted and an atonement made for sin. It was observed but once in the year (Ex. 30:10).

7. The Feast of Purim, described in Est. 9. Established by Mordecai in the time of Ahasuerus to commemorate the remarkable deliverance from the intrigues of Haman, this was a day of feasting and gladness.

The extra-biblical feast of *ḥ^{a}nukkâ* is the celebration of the recovery and cleansing of the Jerusalem Temple by Judas Maccabaeus in 164 BC, after its desecration by Antiochus Epiphanes. It is also called the 'festival of lights'. See Jn. 10:22, where it is called by its Gk. name *enkainia* ('dedication').

BIBLIOGRAPHY. *EJ*, 6, cols. 1189–1196, 1237–1246. D.F.

FELIX. Brother of Claudius' favourite, the *freedman Pallas, through whose influence he was appointed procurator of Judaea. His name is usually taken to have been Antonius Felix (Tacitus, *Hist*. 5. 9), but the MSS of Josephus (*Ant*. 20. 137), as of Suidas, read 'Claudius Felix', though this is usually emended out. It is suggested, however, that reference in a new inscription to a procurator named Claudius must to be Felix, though the cognomen is not preserved (*IEJ* 16, 1966, pp. 259–264). This name would indicate that he was a freedman of Claudius himself, not, like Pallas, of Claudius' mother Antonia.

Tacitus (*Annals* 12. 54) and Josephus (*BJ* 2. 247ff.) also disagree as to the time and circumstances of his arrival in Palestine: Tacitus has him in Samaria before the trial of the procurator Ventidius Cumanus (is the 'many years' of Acts 24:10 some corroboration of this?), but in any case he seems to have held the procuratorship of Judaea from *c*. AD 52. Unrest increased under his rule, for 'with savagery and lust he exercised the powers of a king with the disposition of a slave' (Tacitus, *Hist*. 5. 9), and he was utterly merciless in crushing opposition. In *c*. AD 55 he put down the followers of a Messianic pretender of Egyptian origin, but the man himself escaped (Jos., *BJ* 2. 261ff.). When the riot recorded in Acts 21:27ff. broke out the tribune Claudius Lysias initially mistook Paul for this *Egyptian (Acts 21:38).

After his arrest Paul was conveyed to Caesarea, the Roman capital of Palestine, and was tried before Felix. Two well-attested characteristics of the governor stand out in the subsequent narrative: his disregard for justice and his avarice. He kept Paul in prison for 2 years, hoping he would be paid a fat bribe (Acts 24:26). Disappointed of this hope, he deferred judgment in a case where there was ample evidence of the prisoner's innocence (23:29), and upon his recall he left Paul in prison in order to please the Jews (24:27) or, according to the Western Text, to please his wife *Drusilla.

He was recalled by Nero, probably in AD 59 (*FESTUS), and was saved from proceedings instigated by the Jews only through the influence of Pallas. Of Felix' later history nothing is known.

E.M.B.G.
C.J.H.

FESTUS. Porcius Festus succeeded *Felix as procurator of Judaea. Nothing is known of his life before his appointment, and he died in office after about 2 years. In Josephus (*Ant*. 20. 182ff. and *BJ* 2. 271) he makes an agreeable contrast with his predecessor Felix and his successor Albinus. In Acts (24:27–26:32) he appears in a less favourable light. Though he tried Paul's case with commendable alacrity (25:6) and was convinced of his innocence (26:31), he was prepared to sacrifice Paul to do the Jews a pleasure (25:9). Hence the scandalous suggestion of retrial at Jerusalem. Paul was constrained to appeal to Caesar in the face of an arrangement which would have put him in the power of his enemies. Yet Festus was apparently baffled

Bronze coin issued under Felix, procurator of Judaea, in the name of Claudius Caesar, showing two crossed palm branches. Dated year 14 of Claudius, AD 54. (RG)

FELLOWSHIP
See Communion, Part 1.

FELLOWSHIP WITH GOD
See Liberty, Part 2.

FELSPAR
See Jewels, Part 2.

FERRET
See Animals, Part 1.

FESTIVALS
See Feasts, Part 1.

The common fig-tree (Ficus carica) *is prized for its fruit and shade.* (FNH)

by Paul, and brought the case before Agrippa II and *Bernice. Paul's innocence emerges clearly in the sequel, but the appeal proceeds to Rome.

Festus was later involved when the Jewish leaders brought to Nero a successful suit against Agrippa's violation of the privacy of the Temple area (Jos., *Ant.* 20. 189ff.).

The date of Festus' arrival in Judaea is a major crux of Pauline chronology. W. M. Ramsay in *Pauline Studies*, pp. 348ff., argued that Eusebius' evidence, when rightly understood, points to AD 59, and some support for this date is found in the sudden change of procuratorial coinage in that year, an event most plausibly attributed to the arrival of a new governor (see H. J. Cadbury, *The Book of Acts in History*, 1955, pp. 9f.). E.M.B.G. C.J.H.

FIERY FURNACE
See Brick-kiln, Part 1.

FIGURINES
See Art, Part 1.

FINGER
See Weights and measures, Part 3.

FINGER-NAIL
See Nail, Part 2.

FIR
See Trees (Cypress), Part 3.

FIELD. A word used in the EVV for several biblical terms. **1.** Heb. *śāḏeh* (and its poetical form *śāḏay*) is the most common term (*e.g.* Gn. 2:5) with the simple meaning of 'field', 'plain', 'open space'. **2.** *šᵉḏēmâ* is used six times only (*e.g.* Dt. 32:32) with much the same meaning. **3.** *bar* (Aram.) is used only in Dn. 2 and 4 with the same meaning. **4.** *ḥûṣ*, 'the outside', is frequently translated 'abroad' (*e.g.* Dt. 23:13), but twice rendered 'field' (Jb. 5:10; Pr. 8:26). **5.** *ḥelqâ*, in fact, means 'portion of ground' but is translated 'field' in 2 Sa. 14:30. **6.** *'ereṣ*, the common word for 'earth, land', is translated 'field' in Ezk. 29:5 (AV). **7.** *yᵉḡēḇîm*, a word which occurs once only in the OT, is there translated 'field' (Je. 39:10). **8.** Gk. *agros*, 'field' (*e.g.* Mt. 6:28), in LXX is used mainly to render *śāḏeh*. **9.** Gk. *chōra* usually refers to a large region (Acts 16:6), but is twice rendered 'field' (Jn. 4:35; Jas. 5:4), and its diminutive *chōrion* is translated 'field' in Acts 1:18–19. T.C.M.

FIG, FIG-TREE (Heb. *tᵉ'ēnâ*, 'fig', 'fig-tree'; Heb. *pag̅*, 'unripe first fig', Ct. 2:13 only; Gk. *olynthoi*, 'unripe fig', unspecified season, Rev. 6:13 only; Gk. *sykon*, 'fig', Gk. *sykē*, 'fig-tree').

Indigenous to Asia Minor and the E Mediterranean region, the fig-tree (*Ficus carica*) makes a tree up to 11 m high, although it often grows as a several-stemmed shrub in rocky places. It was brought into cultivation early in Palestine, like the vine and the olive (*e.g.* Jdg. 9:7ff.), with which it is associated in God's promises of prosperity and in prophetic warnings (Je. 5:17; Ho. 2:12; Joel 1:7, 12; Hab. 3:17). The fig is often planted with the vine (Lk. 13:6), so that its branches and the vine's foliage led to the well-known expression 'to sit down under one's own vine and fig-tree' as a symbol of long-continued well-being and prosperity (1 Ki. 4:25; Mi. 4:4; Zc. 3:10; *cf.* 2 Ki. 18:31; Is. 36:16—though some cases may refer merely to a rural preference for the cultivation of fig-trees overlooking houses).

The failure or destruction of these slow-growing trees, which demand years of patient labour (Pr. 27:18; Lk. 13:7), was a national calamity (Je. 5:17; Hab. 3:17; *cf.* Ps. 105:33), while productiveness was a token of peace and of divine favour. Figs are frequently mentioned in conjunction with the vine, palm and pomegranate (*e.g.* Dt. 8:8), and their absence formed part of the Israelites' complaint in Nu. 20:5.

Adam and Eve are said to have been clothed with girdles made from the fig-tree's broad leaves (Gn. 3:7), and fig leaves are still sewn together in the E and used as wrappings for fresh fruit sent to the markets, where they are a valuable item of commerce. Lumps or cakes of dried figs (from Heb. *dᵉḇēlâ*, 'pressed together') made an excellent food, were easy to carry and constituted an acceptable gift (1 Sa. 25:18; 1 Ch. 12:40). Such a mass of figs was prescribed by Isaiah as a poultice for Hezekiah's boil (2 Ki. 20:7; Is. 38:21).

The complicated biology of the fig has confused authors who are unfamiliar with it. The primitive fig-tree needs to be pollinated by a fig-wasp which creeps into the apical hole of the young fig. The insect has its life history inside inedible male caprifigs which are borne several times a year on the branchlets. The edible female figs are pollinated by these insects, but the commonly cultivated varieties of fig develop the fruit without the need of insect pollinators. Thus the figs mentioned in Je. 8:13; Rev. 6:13 do not belong to a definite crop, while the bad figs could be inedible caprifigs (Je. 24:2b; 29:17). Edible good figs of the first crop are referred to in Ct. 2:13 (Heb. *pag̅*, still unripe, green); Is. 28:4; Je. 24:2a; Ho. 9:10; Mi. 7:1; Na. 3:12. The curious incident when Jesus cursed the fig-tree (Mt. 21:18–22; Mk. 11:12–14) may be explained by the out-of-season leafiness of the tree well before the fruits normally mature.

The fig has inspired numerous similes, metaphors and proverbs (*e.g.* Je. 24:1ff.; Mi. 7:1; Mt. 7:16; Jas. 3:12). In Hellenistic times figs were considered so important to the national economy that the Greeks made special laws to regulate their export.

The sycamore tree (Gk. *sykomōraia*; Lat. *Ficus sycomorus*) associated with Zacchaeus in Lk. 19:4 is often known as the mulberry-fig because it possesses the habit of the mulberry.

BIBLIOGRAPHY. A. Goor and M. Nurock, *Fruits of the Holy Land*, 1968, pp. 54–69; J. A. Motyer, *NIDNTT* 1, pp. 723–725.
J.D.D.
F.N.H.

FIRE. A word usually represented in the OT by Heb. *'ēš* and in the NT by Gk. *pyr*, the term generally used in the LXX for *'ēš*. These signify the state of combustion, and the visible aspects of it, such as the flame. The production of fire by artificial means was a skill known to man from Stone Age times, but then and in later times great care was taken to preserve a burning fire to avoid the necessity for rekindling. Abraham apparently carried a piece of burning fire with him when he went to offer Isaac (Gn. 22:6), and Is. 30:14 indicates that this was a usual domestic practice. Probably the commonest methods of kindling a flame in biblical times were by means of the fire-drill, attested in the Egyptian hieroglyphic *d'* (18th Dynasty), and the striking of flint on iron pyrites, a practice attested from Neolithic times and therefore assumed to be in use later. It may be that this latter method is referred to in 2 Macc. 10:3.

Fire was used in the normal course for such purposes as cooking (Ex. 12:8; Jn. 21:9), providing warmth (Is. 44:16; Lk. 22:55) and refining metals (Ex. 32:24; Je. 6:29), but also for destroying such things as idols (Ex. 32:20; Dt. 7:5, 25), Asherim (Dt. 12:3), chariots (Jos. 11:6, 9) and cities (Jos. 6:24; Jdg. 18:27), and the culprits in two cases of sexual breach (Lv. 20:14; 21:9). It also played an important part in the worship of the tabernacle and Temple, where the altars of incense and of burnt offering constantly required it. The fire on the latter having been started by God (Lv. 9:24; 2 Ch. 7:1–3), it was kept burning continuously (Lv. 6:13). This fire was special, and offerings by means of 'strange fire' were not acceptable (Lv. 10:1; Nu. 3:4; 26:61). The heathen practice of making children 'pass through the fire' was occasionally practised by the Israelites (2 Ki. 3:27; 16:3; 17:17, 31; 21:6; 23:10; 2 Ch. 28:3; 33:6), was included in the condemnations of the prophets (Mi. 6:7). This practice does not necessarily denote human *sacrifice so much as a dedication to *Moloch or Milcam. It may also have involved fire incantations similar to those practised in Mesopotamia (*AfO* 23, 1970, pp. 39–45).

Theophanies of God were sometimes accompanied by fire (Ex. 3:2; 13:21–22; 19:18; Dt. 4:11) and the image of fire is used to symbolize God's glory (Ezk. 1:4, 13), protective presence (2 Ki. 6:17), holiness (Dt. 4:24), righteous judgment (Zc. 13:9) and wrath against sin (Is. 66:15–16). It is also used of the Holy Spirit (Mt. 3:11; *cf.* Acts 2:3), of prophetic inspiration (Je. 5:14; 20:9; 23:29) and religious feeling (Ps. 39:3). In other contexts fire is used as a literary symbol of sin (Is. 9:18), lust (Ho. 7:6) and affliction (Ps. 46:12).

BIBLIOGRAPHY. R. J. Forbes, *Studies in Ancient Technology*, 6, 1958, pp. 4ff.; *Le Feu dans le Proche-Orient antique*, 1973.

T.C.M.

FIREPAN (Heb. *maḥtâ*, from *ḥatâ*, 'to snatch up'). A bowl-shaped utensil with a handle used in connection with the tabernacle and Temple services for three different purposes. **1.** In some passages it refers to the *snuffdish* made of gold, which held the pieces of burnt lamp-wick removed by the tongs or *snuffers (Ex. 25:38; 37:23; Nu. 4:9; 1 Ki. 7:50; 2 Ki. 25:15; 2 Ch. 4:22; Je. 52:19, the last four of these references being wrongly translated 'censer' and 'firepan' in AV). **2.** Elsewhere it refers to the bronze *firepan* which was used to carry coals away from the altar of burnt offering (Ex. 27:3; Nu. 4:14, the second of these references being wrongly translated 'censer' in AV). **3.** In other passages it is used of the **censer*, also made of bronze, in which incense was burnt (Lv. 10:1; 16:12; Nu. 16:6, 17–18, 37–39, 46).

J.C.W.

FIRST-BORN.

I. In the Old Testament

The Heb. root *bkr*, found in many Semitic languages, has the general meaning '(to be) early'. *bᵉḵôr*, 'first-born' (fem. *bᵉḵîrâ*), is used of people and animals, cognate terms being employed for firstfruits, and the first-born son's privileges and responsibilities are known as his 'birthright' (*bᵉḵôrāh*). In Gn. 25:23, the eldest son is called *raḇ*, a description occurring elsewhere only in 2nd-millennium cuneiform texts.

The first-born was regarded as 'the beginning of (his) strength' (*rēʾšîṯ ʾôn*—Gn. 49:3; Dt. 21:17; *cf.* Ps. 78:51; 105:36) and 'the opener of the womb' (*peṭer reḥem*—Ex. 13:2, 12, 15; Nu. 18:15; *etc.*), emphasizing both paternal and maternal lines. The pre-eminent status of first-born was also accorded to Israel (Ex. 4:22) and the Davidic line (Ps. 89:27).

The eldest son's special position was widely recognized in the ancient Near East, though it was not usually extended to sons of concubines or slavegirls (*cf.* Gn. 21:9–13; Jdg. 11:1–2). The accompanying privileges were highly valued, and in the OT included a larger inheritance, a special paternal blessing, family leadership and an honoured place at mealtimes (Gn. 25:5–6; 27:35–36; 37:21ff.; 42:37; 43:33; Dt. 21:15–17). The double inheritance of Dt. 21:15–17, though apparently unknown to the Patriarchs (Gn.

Egyptian wooden model of a man fanning a charcoal fire, probably used in the preparation of food. Middle Kingdom. c. 1900 BC. (BM)

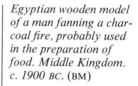

Assyrian troops cooking over an open fire during a campaign against marsh-dwellers in S Babylonia (Chaldea). Palace of Sennacherib, Nineveh. 705–681 BC. (BM)

FIRESTONE
See Jewels, Part 2.

FIRKIN
See Weights and measures, Part 3.

FIRMAMENT
See Creation, Part 1.

FIRST AND LAST
See Alpha and omega, Part 1.

An Assyrian fishing in a pond with a line, his catch in a basket on his back. Relief from Sennacherib's palace at Kuyunjik (Nineveh). Height 49·5 cm. 704–681 BC. (BM)

25:5–6), is mentioned in several Old Babylonian, Middle Assyrian and Nuzi documents, and is alluded to elsewhere in the OT (2 Ki. 2:9; Is. 61:7).

These privileges could normally be forfeited only by committing a serious offence (Gn. 35:22; 49:4; 1 Ch. 5:1–2) or by sale (Gn. 25:29–34), though paternal preference occasionally overruled in the matter of royal succession (1 Ki. 1–2; 2 Ch. 11:22–23; *cf.* 1 Ch. 26:10). There is also a marked interest, especially in Genesis, in the youngest son (Jacob, Ephraim, David; *cf.* Isaac, Joseph), but such cases were certainly contrary to expectation (Gn. 48:17ff.; 1 Sa. 16:6ff.).

Where no sons existed, the eldest daughter took responsibility for her younger sisters (Gn. 19:30ff.). It was an Aramaean custom (Gn. 29:26), and perhaps also an Israelite one (1 Sa. 18:17–27), for the eldest daughter to be married first. A Ugaritic text mentions the transfer of birthright from the eldest to the youngest daughter.

In Israelite ritual, the first-born of man and beast had a special place. The male first-born belonged to Yahweh (Ex. 13:2; 22:29b–30; Nu. 3:13), and this was underlined by Israel's deliverance in the final plague. Children were redeemed in the Exodus generation by the Levites (Nu. 3:40–41), and later, at a month old, by a payment of five shekels (Nu. 18:16; *cf.* 3:42–51). Sacrifice of human first-born is occasionally mentioned, following Canaanite practice (2 Ki. 3:27; Ezk. 20:25–26; Mi. 6:7; *cf.* 1 Ki. 16:34), but this was a misinterpretation of Ex. 22:29. Clean male firstlings were sacrificed (Nu. 18:17–18; Dt. 12:6, 17), while imperfect animals were eaten in the towns (Dt. 15:21–23). Male firstlings of unclean animals were redeemed (Nu. 18:15), though an ass was redeemed with a lamb or had its neck broken (Ex. 13:13; 34:20).

BIBLIOGRAPHY. I. Mendelsohn, *BASOR* 156, 1959, pp. 38–40; R. de Vaux, *Ancient Israel*², 1965, pp. 41–42, 442–445, 488–489; *idem*, *Studies in OT Sacrifice*, 1964, pp. 70–73; J. Henninger, in E. Gräf (ed.), *Festschrift W. Caskel*, 1968, pp. 162–183; M. Tsevat, *TDOT* 2, pp. 121–127.

M.J.S.

II. In the New Testament

Jesus was the first-born (*prōtotokos*) of his mother (Mt. 1:25; Lk. 2:7), a phrase which allows, but does not demand, that Mary had other, later children (*cf.* Mk. 6:3; *BRETHREN OF THE LORD). As such, Jesus was taken to the Temple by Mary and Joseph to be offered to God (Lk. 2:22–24); since Luke omits mention of a price being paid to redeem the child, he may have intended the incident to be regarded as the dedication of the first-born to the service of God (*cf.* 1 Sa. 1:11, 22, 28). Jesus is also the first-born of his heavenly Father. He is the first-born of all creation, not in the sense that he himself is a created being, but rather that as God's Son he was his agent in creation and hence has authority over all created things (Col. 1:15–17). Similarly, he is the first-born in the new creation by being raised first from the dead, and is thus Lord over the church (Col. 1:18; Rev. 1:5). He is thus the first-born in a whole family of children of God who are destined to bear his image (Rom. 8:29). There may be an echo of Ps. 89:27 in Heb. 1:6, where God's Son is the object of worship by the angels at his coming into the world (whether the incarnation, resurrection or second advent is meant is debatable). Finally, God's people, both living and dead, can be described as

This Assyrian drinking-bowl or storage-vessel may have been similar to the kind referred to in Is. 22:24. Enamelled earthenware. Restored. 8th cent. BC. *Water-colour by P. Maresh and W. Andrae.*

Flax (Linum usitatissimum). *One of the earliest known textile plants, producing linen.* (FNH)

the first-born who are enrolled in heaven, since they share the privileges of the Son (Heb. 12:23).

BIBLIOGRAPHY. O. Eissfeldt, *Erstlinge und Zehnten im Alten Testament*, 1917; W. Michaelis, *TDNT* 6, pp. 871–881; K. H. Bartels, *NIDNTT* 1, pp. 667–670.

I.H.M.

FISH, FISHING.

I. Kinds of fish and sources of supply

The general Heb. words for water-creatures are *dāḡ* and *dāḡâ*. According to the Mosaic law (Lv. 11:9–12; Dt. 14:9–10) water-creatures having fins and scales were 'clean', but those without fins and scales (*e.g.* shellfish) were 'unclean'. The creature which swallowed Jonah is called 'a great fish' in Jon. 1:17. Mt. 12:40 carefully adopts the same designation (Gk. *kētos*, 'a large sea-monster', translated and interpreted by AV, RV and RSV as 'whale'). According to Tobit 6:2 a large fish in the Tigris river threatened to swallow Tobias. The fisherman of the parable of the drag-net (Mt. 13:48) discarded some fish because they were too small, inedible or 'unclean'. The fish in whose mouth Peter found the stater (Mt. 17:27) must have had a large mouth, like the fish of the Sea of Galilee called *Chromis simonis* after the apostle. In addition to the common Gk. word for fish, *ichthys* (*e.g.* Mt. 7:10), the NT uses the diminutive *ichthydion*, 'small fish' (Mt. 15:34; Mk. 8:7, both passages which describe the feeding of the four thousand), and *opsarion*, small fish eaten with bread (Jn. 6:11; 21:9). In the Sea of Galilee today at least twenty-four species of fish are found, sometimes in large shoals.

The Bible mentions Egypt as a place where fish are plentiful (Nu. 11:5), and the Sea of Galilee (Lk. 5:6) and Tyre (Ne. 13:16) are also noted as ample sources of supply. Fish cannot live in the salty waters of the Dead Sea, but Ezk. 47:10 foresees that this lake will be stocked with fish as one of the blessings of the kingdom of glory.

II. Fishermen and their methods

The strenuous life of fishermen required a strong physique (Lk. 5:2), and their speech was sometimes rough (Mk. 14:70f.). At least seven of Jesus' disciples were fishermen: Peter, Andrew, probably Philip, who also came from Bethsaida (Aram. for 'house of fishing') on the Sea of Galilee, James, John, Thomas and Nathanael (Mt. 4:18, 21; Jn. 1:44; 21:2). Some of these were partners in fishing and were used to working together (Lk. 5:7, 10).

The Bible mentions fishing by spear or harpoon (Jb. 41:7, for a crocodile), by hook (Jb. 41:1–2; Is. 19:8; Mt. 17:27), and by *net. The kinds of nets specified in the Bible are the casting-net (Mt. 4:18) and the large drag-net (Mt. 13:47).

On the Sea of Galilee the fishermen used small boats, which were propelled by oars (Jn. 6:19). The statement that the wind was contrary (Mt. 14:24) may indicate the use of a sail as in the present-day fishing-boats on this lake. (*SHIPS AND BOATS.) Often on the Sea of Galilee fishing was done at night (Lk. 5:5; Jn. 21:3). During the day the fisherman on the shore or wading in the water could throw the casting-net (Mt. 4:18). Larger nets were let down by several men from boats (Lk. 5:4). The fish were either emptied into the boat (Lk. 5:7) or the nets were dragged to the shore (Mt. 13:48; Jn. 21:8). Then the fish were sorted, the saleable ones being put in baskets and the useless ones thrown away (Mt. 13:48). The Bible does not refer to fishing as a recreation.

III. Marketing and preparation

In Jerusalem there was a Fish Gate (perhaps on the N side of the city), through which traders brought their fish to sell to the populace (Zp. 1:10). From Ne. 13:16 we know that Tyrian fish merchants lived in the city after the Exile. In Bible times common methods of preparing fish for eating were roasting (Jn. 21:9; Tobit 6:5), and salting and drying (Tobit 6:5, Sinaitic Text). The fish which Tyrians sold in Jerusalem and the small fish which were used in the miraculous feeding of the 5,000 and of the 4,000 (Mt. 14:17; 15:36) were probably prepared in the latter way. (*FOOD.)

IV. Fish worship

Dt. 4:18 forbids making images of fish for worship. The pagan fish-goddess Atargatis was worshipped at Ascalon and among the Nabataeans. The oxyrhynchus was worshipped in a nome in Egypt named after that fish.

V. Figurative and symbolic uses

People suffering misfortune (Ec. 9:12) or captured by enemies (Hab. 1:15) are compared to fish caught in a net. Fishing is used in the OT as a figure of God's judgment on nations or individuals (*e.g.* Je. 16:16; Ezk. 32:3). Jesus called disciples to become fishers of men (Mt. 4:19). The kingdom of heaven is likened to a drag-net (Mt. 13:47).

The fish was one of the earliest symbols of Christian art, because the letters of Gk. *ichthys* were taken as an acronym for *Iēsous Christos Theou Hyios Sōtēr*, 'Jesus Christ, of God the Son, Saviour' (see F. J. Dölger, ΙΧΘΥΣ, 1928).

BIBLIOGRAPHY. G. Dalman, *Arbeit und Sitte*, 6, 1939, pp. 343–370; G. S. Cansdale, *Animals of Bible Lands*, 1970; J. D. M. Derrett, 'Peter's Penny', in *Law in the New Testament*, 1970, pp. 247–265.

J.T.

FLAGON. Heb. *neḇel*, Is. 22:24, a large, two-handled jar for storing wine (*GLASS). AV translates Heb. *ʾªšîšâ* as 'flagon', following the interpretation of Qimchi. However, Ho. 3:1 (Heb. *ʾªšîšê ʿªnāḇîm* . . . of grapes) and Ct. 2:5 (parallel to 'refresh me with apples', RSV) suggest a derivation from the root *ʾšš*, 'be firm', 'compress'. LXX preserves the meaning by translating 'cake from a pan' (*laganon apo tēganou*, 2 Sa. 6:19); 'raisin cake' (*pemmata meta staphidōn*, Ho. 3:1); 'sweet cake' (*amoritēn*, 1 Ch. 16:3; *amorais*, Ct. 2:5). Heb. *ʾªšîšâ* denotes, therefore, a cake of compressed, dried grapes, possibly used as an offering in pagan worship (Ho. 3:1). (*VINE.)

A.R.M.

FLAX (Heb. *pištâ* in Ex. 9:31 and Is. 42:3; *pišteh* elsewhere in the OT; Gk. *linon* in Mt. 12:20). Used chiefly in making *linen, flax (*Linum usitatissimum*) is the oldest of the textile fibres. The plant grows often to a height of 1 m, and produces beautiful blue flowers. From the shiny seeds comes linseed oil.

Flax was cultivated by the Egyptians before the Exodus (Ex. 9:31) and, before the Conquest, by the Canaanites, who dried the stalks on the housetops (Jos. 2:6). Among God's judgments in Hosea's day was the taking away of the flax (Ho. 2:9).

In the single NT reference (Mt. 12:20), an allusion to flax as being slow-burning, Matthew is quoting from Is. 42:3.

J.D.D.

FIRST DAY OF THE WEEK
See Lord's Day, Part 2.

FISH HOOK
See Hook, Part 2.

FIVE
See Number, Part 2.

FLAVOUR
See Herbs, Part 2.

FLEA
See Animals, Part 1.

FLINT
See Mining, Part 2.

FLOCK
See Animals, Part 1.

FLESH.

I. In the Old Testament

In the OT the principal word is *bāśār* (found 269 times), though *šᵉ'ēr* (16 times, 4 times translated 'flesh' in RSV) also occurs. *bāśār* denotes the principal constituent of the body, human (Gn. 40:19) or animal (Lv. 6:27). The latter use leads on to the thought of meat as used for food and to that of the flesh of the animal sacrifices, whether eaten or not. From the former usage 'flesh' comes to mean the whole body (Pr. 14:30), and by a natural extension of meaning the whole man, as when the Psalmist says, 'my body (Heb. flesh) also dwells secure' (Ps. 16:9). This leads to the concept of the union of one person with another. Man and wife are 'one flesh' (Gn. 2:24), and a man can say of his relatives, 'I am your bone and your flesh' (Jdg. 9:2).

Again, the notion of flesh as the whole man gives rise to the expression 'all flesh', which denotes the totality of human existence, sometimes also including the animal creation. There is sometimes the sense that flesh is weak: 'in God I trust without a fear. What can flesh do to me?' (Ps. 56:4). This is not the thought of moral weakness (perhaps the nearest we get to this is Ps. 78:39). It is the physical frailty of man that is meant.

II. In the New Testament

In the NT the Gk. word for 'flesh' is *sarx*. This term reproduces most of the OT meaning of *bāśār*. It denotes the fleshy part of the body, as in references to eating flesh (Rev. 19:18, *etc.*), or to the whole body (Gal. 4:13f.). It may mean the whole man, 'our bodies (lit. our flesh) had no rest . . . fighting without and fear within' (2 Cor. 7:5), or 'within me, that is, in my flesh' (Rom. 7:18). As in the OT, man and wife are 'one flesh' (Mt. 19:5f.), and there are passages referring to 'all flesh' (Jn. 17:2). The weakness of the flesh is spoken of in connection with the apostles' failure to watch in Gethsemane (Mt. 26:41; Mk. 14:38).

But the NT has also some distinctive meanings. Akin to the 'my bone and my flesh' passages of the OT (though not quite the same) are those which refer to physical descent and the like. Thus Christ 'was descended from David according to the flesh' (Rom. 1:3). Paul can speak of 'Israel according to the flesh' (1 Cor. 10:18; see RSVmg.), and the Israelites as his 'kinsmen by race' (Gk. according to the flesh') (Rom. 9:3).

'The flesh' may stand for the whole of this physical existence, and there are references to being 'in the flesh' (Col. 2:1; RSV omits). There is no blame attached to this, and, indeed, Christ is said more than once to have been 'in the flesh' (Eph. 2:15; 1 Pet. 3:18; 1 Jn. 4:2, *etc.*). To be 'in the flesh' is not incompatible with being 'in the Lord' (Phm. 16). The flesh may be defiled (Jude 8) or purified (Heb. 9:13). The life that Paul the Christian now lived was 'in the flesh' (Gal. 2:20).

But, by definition, the flesh is the earthly part of man. It has its 'lusts' and its 'desires' (Eph. 2:3). If men concentrate on these they may be said to 'set their minds on the things of the flesh' (Rom. 8:5). And to set the mind on the flesh 'is death' (Rom. 8:6). This is explained as 'enmity against God' (Rom. 8:7). The man whose horizon is limited by the flesh is by that very fact opposed to God. He lives 'according to the flesh' (Rom. 8:13), that flesh that 'lusteth against the Spirit' (Gal. 5:17, AV; RSV has 'the desires of the flesh are against the Spirit' but AV is more literal). For a dreadful list of 'the works of the flesh', see Gal. 5:19–21. The flesh in this sense denotes the whole personality of man as organized in the wrong direction, as directed to earthly pursuits rather than the service of God.

BIBLIOGRAPHY. K. Grayston in *TWBR*; D. E. H. Whiteley, *The Theology of St. Paul*, 1964; J. A. T. Robinson, *The Body*, 1952; E. Schweizer, F. Baumgärtel and R. Meyer in *TDNT* 7, pp. 98–151; H. Seebass, A. C. Thiselton, in *NIDNTT* 1, pp. 671–682. L.M.

FLESH-HOOK (AV; RSV 'fork'). A bronze implement associated like others with the altar of burnt offering at the tabernacle (Ex. 27:3; 38:3; Nu. 4:14) and Solomon's Temple (1 Ch. 28:17; 2 Ch. 4:16). Seen in use at Shiloh (1 Sa. 2:13–14) as a three-pronged fork.

K.A.K.

FLESHPOTS (Heb. *sîr*, probably a foreign loan-word; *cf.* Arab. *sîr*, 'a large waterjar', and later Gk. *siras*). A large household utensil usually made of metal for placing over a fire (Ex.16:3; Ec. 7:6, pot'; 2 Ki. 4:38, 'great pot'). It is used symbolically of Jerusalem (Ezk. 11:3, 'cauldron'), in similes for avarice (Mi. 3:3), and figuratively for speedy vengeance (Ps. 58:9). Such pots were in use in the sanctuary (Ex. 27:3; 2 Ki. 25:14, *etc.*) and were probably deep bronze cauldrons (so Je. 1:13, RV). They were also used as *washbasins (Ps. 108:9). Their shape was that adopted for the excavation of cisterns (2 Sa. 3:26). (*POTTER, *VESSELS.)

J.D.D.

FLOOD. A deluge of water sent by God in the time of Noah to destroy all but a selected few from the earth (Gn. 6–8). The word used in OT to describe this phenomenon is *mabbûl*, a word of unknown derivation, and since its only other occurrence outside the narrative of Gn. 6–11 is Ps. 29:10, its meaning must be taken to be a cataclysmic deluge such as is described in Genesis. In the LXX, *mabbûl* is translated by *kataklysmos*, and this is the word used in NT (Mt. 24:38–39; Lk. 17:27; 2 Pet. 2:5) to describe the same event.

In the EVV various other terms are translated by the word 'flood', most of them referring to rivers, either in normal flow or in spate, which was one of the meanings of 'flood' in AV English. Thus in OT *nāhār* (*e.g.* Jos. 24:2), *yᵉ'ôr* (*e.g.* Je. 46:7; the form *'ōr* occurs in Am. 8:8), *naḥal* (*e.g.* 2 Sa. 22:5), and *šibbōleṯ* (Ps. 69:2, 15; Jdg. 12:6), and in NT *potamos* (*e.g.* Mt. 7:25), all bear roughly this meaning. Other words translated 'flood' are *šeṭep̄*, 'an overflowing' (*e.g.* Ps. 32:6), and the verb *nāzal*, 'to flow', in its participial form 'flower' (*e.g.* Ex. 15:8) in OT, and *plēmmyra*, 'high water' (Lk. 6:48), in NT.

a. The reason for the Flood

When God saw that man was constantly planning and doing evil (Gn. 6:5), he resolved to bring a just destruction upon him (6:1–7). But *Noah was a righteous man, so he and his immediate family were to be spared to make a new start.

b. The preparation

Gn. 6:3 and 1 Pet. 3:20 indicate that through the longsuffering of God there would be 120 years' respite before the coming of the Flood. In this period God commanded Noah to build an *ark and gave him careful instructions for it. He also announced that he would make a covenant with Noah (6:18; see *g*, below).

c. The occupants of the ark

Eight people, Noah, his three sons, Shem, Ham and Japheth, and their four wives were preserved in the ark (Gn. 6:18; 7:7, 13; 2 Pet. 2:5). There were also two members, a male and a female, of each division (after their kind, *mîn*, not necessarily 'species'; *CREATION, **II.***d*) of the animal kingdom, including the birds, on board (6:19–20; 7:8–9, 14–15) and in addition to these there were twelve extra creatures, six male and six female, of each clean species, presumably for food and sacrifice (7:2–3; some commentators interpret the numbers as seven, rather than fourteen altogether of each). Vegetable food for all these occupants was also stowed aboard. No mention is made of sea creatures, but these may have been included in 'every living thing of all flesh' (6:19), and could have been accommodated outside the ark.

d. The Flood

WWhen Noah and his companions had entered the ark God secured it behind him (7:16) and loosed the waters. These came in the form of rain (7:4, 12), and of such force that the Bible says 'the windows of heaven were opened' (7:11), a very telling metaphor. The level of the waters was also raised from below, 'all the fountains of the great deep (*tᵉhôm*) were broken up' (7:11), but this may be a metaphorical statement, as is suggested by the use of the word *tᵉhôm*, which is usually found in poetic passages, so it is not profitable to seek references to geological phenomena in it.

e. The chronology of the Flood

Noah entered the ark on the 17th day of the 2nd month of his 600th year (7:11), and the earth was dry on the 27th day of the 2nd month of his 601st year, so, counting 30 days to a month, the Flood lasted 371 days. The rain fell for 40 days (7:12) and the waters continued to rise for another 110 (7:24) = 150; the waters then fell for 74 days (8:5) = 224; 40 days later the raven was sent out (8:6–7) = 264; 7 days later Noah sent out the dove (8:8, with implication of 'other 7 days' in 8:10) = 271; he sent it out again 7 days later (8:10) = 278; and for the third time 7 days later (8:12) = 285; Noah removed the covering of the ark 29 days later (8:13 with 7:11) = 314; and the earth was finally dry 57 days later (8:14) = 371 days altogether.

f. The extent of the Flood

That everything (6:17), including man (6:7; 7:21) and beast (6:7, 13, 17; 7:21–22), was to be blotted out by the Flood is clearly stated, but it can be argued that these categories are qualified by the statements of locality: upon the earth (*'ereṣ*; 6:17; 7:17, 23); under heaven (*šāmayim*; 6:17; 7:19); and upon the ground (*'ᵃḏāmâ*; 7:4, 23). *'ereṣ* can mean 'land' (*e.g.* Gn. 10:10), *šāmayim* can mean 'sky', or the visible part of heaven within the horizon (*e.g.* 1 Ki. 18:45), and the extent of *ᵃḏāmâ* would be determined by these other two words; thus it is possible that a flood of unexampled severity might meet these conditions without covering the entire surface of the globe. The argument that such a flood would make the preservation of animals unnecessary might be countered with the suggestion that if a whole environmental zone with its own individual fauna were involved, such a measure would be necessary. The statement that all the high mountains (*har*) under the whole heaven were covered (7:19–20) and that near the end of the Flood they began to be seen (8:5) is interpreted in this scheme as a phenomenon due to the cloud and mist that must have accompanied the cataclysm. This interpretation favours a limited Flood, but the text is also capable of bearing the interpretation of a universal Flood, and dogmatism is not reasonable, either way. The theological teaching of the Bible has traditionally been interpreted in the sense that all men except Noah and his family were destroyed.

g. The end of the Flood

God remembered Noah in the ark, and caused the waters steadily to decrease until the ark came to rest on the mountains of Urarṭu (*ARARAT). To find out whether it was safe to disembark Noah sent out a raven first, which was perhaps able to feed on carrion, and perch on the roof of the ark (8:7), and then a dove, which on the second attempt brought back an olive leaf, indicating perhaps that the waters had fallen enough for the foothills, where the olive trees grow, to be dry, and therefore suffi-

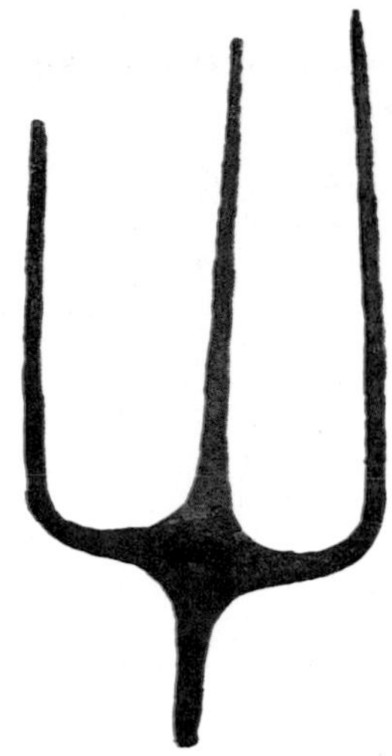

Bronze trident or flesh-hook possibly used in connection with sacrifices, or with fishing. Height 35 cm. From Ur. (BM)

cient food to be now available for the animals (8:8–11). The third time he sent out the dove it did not return (8:12), so he deemed it time to leave the ark, and this he was commanded by God to do. Noah then made burnt offerings of every clean beast and bird (see *c*, above), and God swore not to bring another flood (8:21–22; Is. 54:9), blessed Noah and his sons (9:1), and confirmed it in a covenant (9:11), whose sign was a bow in the clouds (9:13–17).

h. Cuneiform parallels

Stories of a flood have been found among the cuneiform documents excavated in the Near East. A Sumerian tablet from Nippur in S Babylonia relates how king Ziusudra was warned that the gods had decreed a deluge to destroy mankind and told to build a great boat in which to escape. This tablet was written *c.* 1600 BC, but the story had probably been known in Mesopotamia for many centuries before this. The fact of a devastating flood is a part of Sumerian historical and literary tradition. An Akkadian story is contained in incomplete copies of the *Atrahasis Epic* made *c.* 1630 BC and circulated widely during later centuries (it was known at *Ugarit). This describes a flood sent by the gods to destroy man after earlier attempts to control him had failed. The pious Atrahasis was warned by the creator-god Enki (or Ea) to build a boat and escape with his family, treasure and animals. After 7 days of flooding the boat grounded. Atrahasis offered a sacrifice to the gods who gathered like flies around it. The gods regretted their act, and re-instituted society with the rule of individual guilt and punishment. The famous Babylonian *Story of*

Tablet XI of the Assyrian version of the Epic of Gilgamesh (*c. 650* BC) *which records the Babylonian account of the Flood. Other versions of this Epic date from the late 3rd millennium* BC *and were copied throughout the ancient Near East. A fragment found at Megiddo shows that the Epic was known in Palestine in the 14th cent.* BC. (BM)

the Flood, which forms part of Tablet XI of the longer *Epic of Gilgamesh* (*BABYLONIA), derives largely from this work. It was a copy of this, which had been excavated from Nineveh some 20 years before, that was identified in the BM in 1872 by George Smith. In this version the hero, named Uta-napishtim, and once Atrahasis, describes to Gilgamesh how he was given immortality after surviving the Flood. He tells the same story as the *Atrahasis Epic* with some details not preserved in that account. Notable among them is the boat's coming to rest on Mt Niṣir (in NW Persia) and the despatch in succession of a dove, a swallow and a raven, the occupants of the boat disembarking when the raven did not return. These cuneiform accounts show similarities with Gn. 6–9, a fact which is possibly to be explained by common reference to an actual historical event. The many crude elements in the cuneiform versions suggest that these are the less reliable of the two accounts.

i. Sources

Many scholars consider that the narrative of the Flood in Gn. 6–9 is composed of two sources, J (Yahwist) and P (Priestly), woven together by a late editor, working after the return from the Exile. According to this theory, oral traditions from early times were brought together, and were committed to writing in the 'document' called J over a period of centuries, beginning in the time of the early monarchy. The other source (P) was the result of centuries of the traditions of the priests from the time of David, which were written down in the period from perhaps 500 BC to the time of Ezra, drawing, in the case of such sections as that dealing with the Flood, upon the Babylonian traditions as learnt during the Exile. Evidence for the two sources is found in such criteria as the use of the two divine names, *YHWH* in J and *’$^{\breve{e}}$lōhîm* in P, and in such observations as that Noah is bidden to take seven (or fourteen) of every clean creature and two of every unclean creature into the ark (Gn. 7:2–3 = J), and that he is bidden to take one pair of every species (Gn. 6:19 = P; see *c*, above).

These matters are susceptible of other explanations, however (see Bibliography), and the unity of the Flood account is suggested by the consistent statements as to the cause of the Flood (Gn. 6:5–7, J, 11–13, P), the purpose of it (Gn. 6:7, J, 13, 17, P; 7:4, J, 21, P, 22–23, J; 8:21, J), and the saving of a representative remnant (Gn. 6:8, J, 18–20, P; 7:1–3, 7–9, J, 13–16a, P, 16b, J; 8:16–19, P).

j. Archaeology and the Flood

Excavations at Ur, Kish, Warka and Farah in S Mesopotamia have uncovered evidence of serious floods. The excavators of the first two sites, Sir Leonard Woolley and S. H. Langdon, believed these remains were connected with the biblical Flood. This is unlikely, however, since the flood levels at the four sites do not all date from the same period, and in each case they are most readily explained as due to a river inundation of unusual severity. Moreover, the earliest, that at Ur, is unlikely to have taken place much before 4000 BC, a date which comes well on in the continuous sequence of prehistoric cultures in the Near East, and one at which there is no sign of a break in other areas. If a serious local flood in the Mesopotamian plain is considered to be all that is implied by the biblical account, one or other of the flood deposits at these sites may be thought to be evidence of it, but if, as seems probable, a far more serious event is recorded in Genesis, the evidence from Mesopotamia must be considered irrelevant.

k. Geology and the Flood

No certain geological evidence of the biblical Flood is known. Many phenomena have been noted, however, which in the past, and particularly the 19th century, were cited as evidence of a serious flood. The majority of these are today most satisfactorily explained as vestigges of the glacial action of the Quaternary Ice Age. Associated with the ice age, however, were certain changes, such as varying sea-levels through locking up and release of water in the glaciers, and depression and rising of land masses in concord with the increase and decrease in the weight of ice on them, which might well have produced effects in keeping with the biblical account. The effective end of the last glaciation may be dated at about 10,000 BC, so that it may be that Noah and his contemporaries are to be given an antiquity of this magnitude (*GENEALOGY).

No certain evidence is, however, available, and any scheme to place the events described in Genesis in their actual historical setting can be no more than tentative.

BIBLIOGRAPHY. *General:* A. Parrot, *The Flood and Noah's Ark*, 1955; A. Heidel, *The Gilgamesh Epic and Old Testament Parallels*[2], 1949, ch. IV. *Section h:* J. C. Whitcomb and H. M. Morris (eds.), *The Genesis Flood*, 1961; W. G. Lambert and A. R. Millard, *Atraḫasīs. The Babylonian Story of the Flood*, 1969; *ANET*, pp. 72–99, 104–106; *DOTT*, pp. 17–26. *Section i:* O. T. Allis, *The Five Books of Moses*, 1943, pp. 95–99; G. Ch. Aalders, *A Short Introduction to the Pentateuch*, 1949, pp. 45–47. *Section j:* M. E. L. Mallowan, *Iraq* 26, 1964, pp. 62–82; R. L. Raikes, *Iraq* 28, 1966, pp. 52–63. *Section k:* J. K. Charlesworth, *The Quaternary Era*, 2, 1957, pp. 614–619.

T.C.M.

FLOUR
See Bread, Part 1.

FLOWERS
See Plants, Part 3.

FLUTE
See Music, Part 2.

FLY
See Animals, Part 1.

FOAL
See Animals, Part 1.

FOLLY. While folly in the OT is sometimes plain silliness (*e.g.* Pr. 10:14; 14:15; 18:13), it is usually culpable: a disdain for God's truth and discipline (Pr. 1:7). Hence even the 'simple' or gullible man (*peṯî*) is not merely 'without sense' (Pr. 7:7ff.) but fatally wayward (Pr. 1:32). He must make a moral and spiritual choice, not only a mental effort (Pr. 9:1–6, 13–18; Ps. 19:7). Likewise the 'fool' (known by various, virtually interchangeable terms, chiefly *k*^{e}*sîl*, *’*^{e}*wîl*, *sāḵāl*) is typically one who, like Saul, has 'played the fool' (1 Sa. 26:21) and closed his mind to God (*e.g.* Ps. 94:8ff.; Pr. 27:22; Je. 5:21). The most hardened folly is that of the 'scoffer' (*lēṣ*, *e.g.* Pr. 1:22; 14:6; 24:9) and of the aggressive unbeliever called the *nāḇāl* (1 Sa. 25:25; Ps. 14:1; Is. 32:5f.).

Christ's warning against branding anybody 'fool' (*mōros*, Mt. 5:22) presupposes these spiritual and moral connotations (see Arndt for other explanations). In 1 Cor. 1:25, 27 Paul takes up the term (*mōros*, 'foolishness') used by unbelievers in their faulty evaluation of God's purposes. A man's folly may sometimes lie in his being unable to perceive the issues (*e.g.* Lk. 11:40; 1 Cor. 15:36, *aphrōn*), but more likely in the fact that he has made an unworthy choice (*e.g.* Lk. 12:20, *aphrōn*; Rom. 1:21, *asynetos*; Gal. 3:1, 3, *anoētos*; Mt. 7:26, *mōros*). D.A.H. F.D.K.

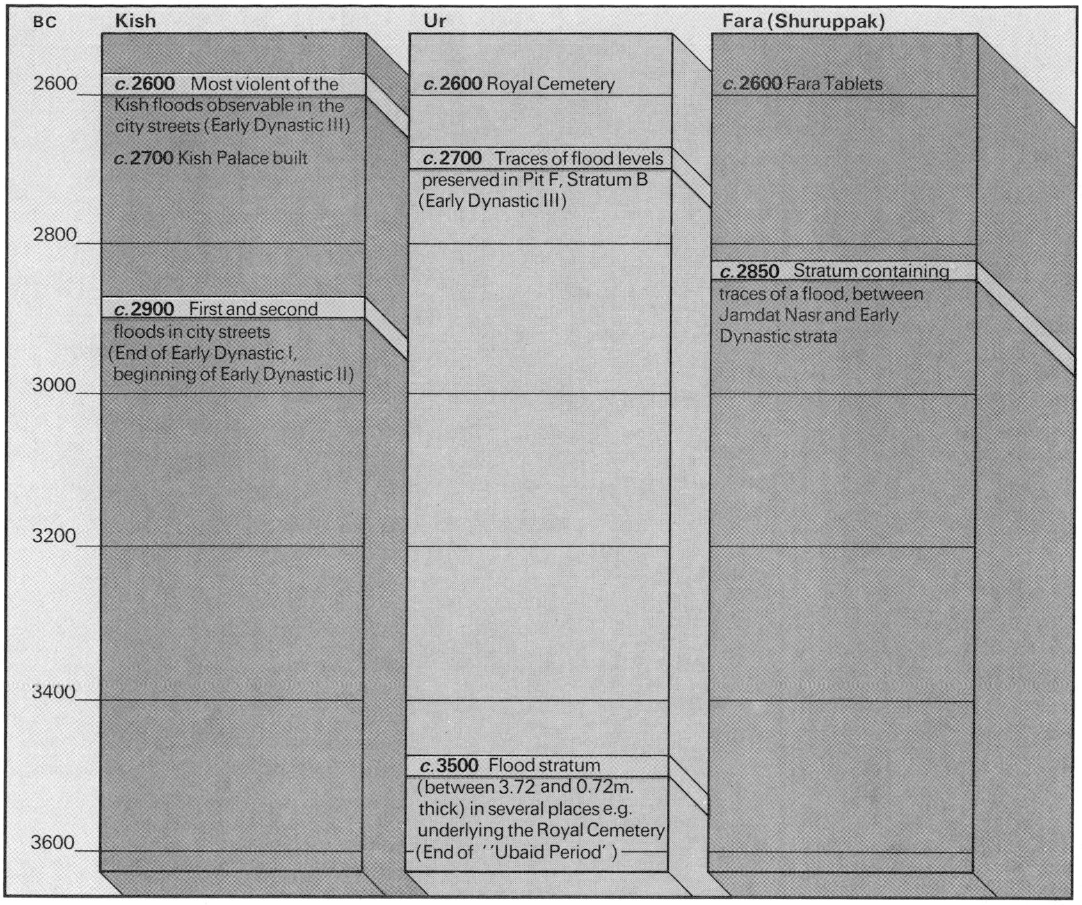
BC
Kish
Ur
Fara (Shuruppak)
2600
2800
3000
3200
3400
3600
c.2600 Most violent of the Kish floods observable in the city streets (Early Dynastic III)
c.2700 Kish Palace built
c.2900 First and second floods in city streets (End of Early Dynastic I, beginning of Early Dynastic II)
c.2600 Royal Cemetery
c.2700 Traces of flood levels preserved in Pit F, Stratum B (Early Dynastic III)
c.3500 Flood stratum (between 3.72 and 0.72m. thick) in several places e.g. underlying the Royal Cemetery (End of ''Ubaid Period')
c.2600 Fara Tablets
c.2850 Stratum containing traces of a flood, between Jamdat Nasr and Early Dynastic strata

Archaeological indications of major floods in various Mesopotamian cities in the 4th–3rd millennia BC.

FOOD. Within this general term are included all the vegetable and animal products used by man to maintain the physical life of his body.

I. In the Old Testament

a. Earliest periods

From the beginning (Gn. 1:29–30; 2:16) all seed-bearing plants (mainly grains and vegetables, presumably) and fruit-bearing trees served as food for man, and natural greenstuffs as food for animals. The Fall brought with it the necessity for hard toil in food gathering and production (Gn. 3:18, 23; 4:2–3). Food in the ark was evidently representative of that in common use at the time, but no details of it are given (Gn. 6:21). After the Flood, God promised that seedtime and harvest should not cease while the earth endured, and all living things (besides vegetation) might be used for food, but not their blood (Gn. 8:22–9:4). At the time of Noah's resettlement of the earth after the Flood, grape-growing (and, in consequence, drunkenness) first appears (Gn. 9:20–21).

b. The patriarchal age

In Egypt, Palestine and Mesopotamia in the early 2nd millennium BC, grain and various breads were a staple diet, along with milk, butter, cheeses, water, wine and beer. Doubtless the semi-nomadic Patriarchs lived mainly on the milk-products of their cattle and flocks, but also had bread (see the supply given to Hagar, Gn. 21:14) and sometimes cultivated grain seasonally as did Isaac (Gn. 26:12) and presumably Jacob (*cf.* Gn. 37:7), since he needed to buy Egyptian grain in time of famine (Gn. 42:2, 25f.; 43:2; 44:1–2). Lentil soup (a red soup) was probably a common dish in the days when Esau traded his birthright for a meal of it (Gn. 25:29–34), as it certainly was later on (*e.g.* 2 Sa. 17:28). Honoured guests were treated to the fatted calf accompanied by curds and milk (Gn. 18:6–8). With Abraham's action we may compare the references in the N Canaanite texts from Ugarit which mention slaughter and preparation of 'a lamb from the flock' or 'the sleekest of . . . fatlings' (*ANET*, pp. 146, 149, 151). Although meat was not an everyday dish, desert-game was popular in patriarchal Syria–Palestine. Isaac liked his tasty meat from the hunt (Gn. 27:3–4), just as did the Egyp. Sinuhe in Palestine a little earlier (*ANET*, p. 20). Presents to dignitaries might include nuts and honey as delicacies (Gn. 43:11). The tablets from the 18th-century BC palace at Mari indicate that large amounts of honey were provided at banquets for visiting royalty, and during the same period King Ishme-Dagan of Assyria sent pistachio-nuts to his brother ruling at Mari. In Egypt, too, honey was first and foremost the prerogative of royalty and high society, but was also occasionally enjoyed by their inferiors. Finally, the common meal was a recognized token of amity between the two contracting parties of an agreement, *e.g.* Isaac and the Philistines in Gn. 26:30, and Jacob and Laban in Gn. 31:54. No details are given of the meal to which Joseph treated his brothers in Egypt (Gn. 43:31–34).

c. Israel in Egypt

In Egypt, despite their hard life, the captive Israelites had had a variety of food that they remembered with nostalgia in the wilderness journeyings: fish in plenty, cucumbers, melons, leeks, onions, garlic (Nu. 11:5). This list corresponds quite closely with known ancient Egyp. foods, not least in the E Delta (Goshen area) in the 13th century BC. Thus, in praising the region of Ra'amses, a scribe extols its wealth of foods: onions and leeks, seven kinds of fish in its waters, and vari-

ENGLISH	LATIN	SELECTED BIBLICAL REFERENCES	HEBREW ARABIC	EGYPTIAN	SUMERIAN	AKKADIAN
GRAIN (General)		Gn. 42:2,25; 43:2; 44:1-2; Dt.7:13; Ne.5:11	*zêr'oîm (H)* *kishné (A)*		ŠE ^{ú}ŠE. ŠEŠ	*še'u* *sigušu*
EMMER	*Triticum dicoccum*		*kussèmeth (H)*	*bd.t*	ZÍZ.ÀM	*kunašu*
DURUM WHEAT	*Triticum durum*	Ex. 9:32 Dt. 8:8		*hrnt* *bd.t*	ŠE.IR.ZI	*qutru*
BREAD WHEAT	*Triticum vulgare*	1 Cor. 15:37	*ḥiṭṭā (H)*	*sw.t*	ŠE.GIG	*kibtu*
SPELT	*Triticum spelta*	Ex. 9:32; Is. 28:25; Ezk. 4:9				
BARLEY	*Hordeum vulgare*	Ex. 9:31; Dt. 8:8 (Barley loaves, Jdg. 7:13)	*ś^{e}'ôra (H)* *shaeir̃ (A)*	*'it* *'nḫ.t*	ŠE.BAR	*uṭṭaṭu*
SIX-ROWED BARLEY	*Hordeum hexastichon*	2 Ki. 4:42 Jn.6:9, 13		*sm'j* *šr.t*	ŠE.IN.NU.ḪA	*inninu*
MALT					MUNU ŠE	*buqlu*
MILLET	*Andropogon Sorghum (Paniceum milioceum)*	Ezk. 4:9	*dôḫan (H)* *dúra, duḫn (A)*		ŠE.AR.ZÍB	*duḫnu*
RICE	*Oryza sativa*		*ōrez (H)*		^{ú}ŠE. LI.A	^{šam} *kurangu (?)*
LENTILS	*Lens culinaris (Ervum lens)*	Gn. 25:34 2 Sa. 17:28; 23:11;	*'ădâšîm (H)* *addes (A)*	*'ršn*	GÚG, KUKKA	
BEANS	*Vicia faba* *Phaseolus maximus* *Phaseolus vulgare*	2 Sa. 17:28 Ezk. 4:9	*pôl (H)* *túl (A)* *lūbā (A)*	*iwrj.t* *pr*	LU.ÚB.ŠAR	*lubbu (luppu)*
CHICK PEAS	*Cicer arietanum*		*húmmes (A)*		ZID.MAD.MAL	*upuntu, masḫâti*
VETCH	*Vicia nissoliana*		*kursenni (H)*		GÚ.NÍG.HAR.RA	*kiššenu (?)*
CRESS	*Lapidium sativum*			*(ḫlin)*	ZAG.ḪI.LI.ŠAR	^{šam} *saḫlû*
CAROB (POD HUSK)	*Ceratoria siliqua*	Lk. 15:16		*nḏm*	^{ú}URU.TÌL.LA	^{šam} *ḫarubu*
LEEK	*Allium kurrat*	Nu. 11:5	*ḥāṣîr (H)*	*íz ḳt*	GA.RAŠ	*karašu*
GARLIC	*Allium sativum*	Nu. 11:5	*shûm (H)* *ṯûm (A)*	*ḥḏt* *ḥḏw*	SUM	*šūmu*
ONIONS	*Allium cepa*	Nu.11:5	*b^{e}ṣálîm (H)* *baṣal (A)*	*ḥḏw*		^{šam} *andaḫšum* ^{šam} *amu(š)šu*
CUCUMBER	*Cucumis melo*	Nu.11:5; Is.1:8	*qiššu'â (H)* *qiṯṯā' (A)*	*šspt*	UXÚŠ	*qiššû*
FIG	*Ficus carica*	Dt. 8:8; Is. 36:16; Je. 5:17; Ho. 2:12; Joel 1:7, 12; Hab. 3:17; Mt. 7:16; Mk. 11:12-14; Lk. 13:6	*tĕĕnâ (H)*	*dzb*	^{giš} MA	*tittu*
DATE	*Phoenix dactylifera*		*dĕbaš (H)*	*bnr*	ZÚ.LUM.MA	*suluppu*
APPLE	*Pyrus malus*	Pr. 25:11; Ct. 2:3, 5; 7:8; 8:5; Joel 1:12	*tappûaḥ? (H)*	*tpḥ* *ḏpḥ*	^{giš} ḪAŠḪUR	*ḫašḫûru* *arsappu*
APRICOT	*Prunus Armeniaca*		*tappûaḥ (H)*		^{giš}ḪAŠḪUR. KUR.RA	*armânu?*
PEAR	*Pirus communis*				^{giš}ḪAŠḪUR. GIŠ.DA	*kameššarū*
QUINCE	*Cydonia vulgaris*		*tappûaḥ? (H)* *safarjal (A)*		^{giš}ḪAŠḪUR ^{giš}PÈŠ ^{giš}ḪAŠḪUR. KUR.RA	*tîtânû* *supurgillu*
MEDLAR	*Mespilus germanica*				ŠENNUR	*šalluru*
PEACH	*Prunus Persica*				^{giš}DAR.RU.UG	*darruqu*
POMEGRANATE	*Punica granatum*	Dt. 8:8; Ct. 8:2; Joel 1:12	*rimmôn (H)*	*ínhmn*	NU.ÚR.MA	*nurmû*
GRAPES	*Vitis vinifera*	Nu. 6:3; Dt. 23:24; Is. 5:2; Mt. 7:16	*ešqōl (H)*	*ízzrt*	^{giš} KIN.GEŠTIN ^{giš} GEŠTIN	*isḫunnatu* *karānu*
MELON	*Citrullus vulgaris*	Nu. 11:5	*^{a}ḇaṭṭiḥîm (H)*	*bddw-ks*		

CEREALS (white) — VEGETABLES (grey) — FRUIT (grey)

Preparation of food at an Assyrian camp. Wall-relief from the palace of Ashurnasirpal at Nimrud. 883–859 BC. (BM)

ous fruits and vegetables (*ANET*, p. 471; better, R. A. Caminos, *Late-Egyptian Miscellanies*, 1954, p. 74).

d. Food in Israel

(i) *Vegetable foods*. Grain, wine and olive-oil were the three staple commodities (Dt. 7:13; Ne. 5:11; Ho. 2:8). The grain was mainly barley, wheat and sometimes spelt, an inferior wheat; see Ex. 9:32 (Egypt); Dt. 8:8; and Is. 28:25 (note order of grains). For preparation and baking of bread, see *BREAD; this basic food was the most appropriate word-picture for Christ himself, the Bread of Life (*cf.* Jn. 6:33, 35).

The *vine was the second great provider; not only of fresh grapes as a fruit (Nu. 6:3; Dt. 23:24) but also of dried grapes as raisins (1 Sa. 25:18; 30:12); of the sweet grape-juice, *'asîs* (Is. 49:26; Am. 9:13; Joel 1:5; 3:18, AV, 'sweet wine', 'new wine'); of the half-fermented must or new wine (Jdg. 9:13; Ho. 4:11; Pr. 3:10; *etc.*); and of the fully fermented wine (*yayin*). These red juices of the grape were often called 'the blood of the grape' (Gn. 49:11; Dt. 32:14). *Wine in its various forms was the general drink in ancient Palestine. Various wines in ancient Egypt, Palestine (*cf.* that of Helbon, in Ezk. 27:18 and Assyr. texts) and Asia Minor were celebrated in antiquity. Vinegar (wine gone acid), diluted with water, helped to refresh field-workers (Ru. 2:14).

Besides being a general word for fermented drinks, *šēḵār*, 'strong drink', appears to have been applied specifically to beverages brewed from grain (*i.e.* beer; Herodotus, 2. 77) or dates (*ibid.*, 1. 193) or perhaps even honey. Beer was the more popular drink in Mesopotamia, but wine in Palestine; both were common in Egypt, where date-wine and other drinks are mentioned. For spiced wine, see (iv) *Seasoning*, below.

The third basic commodity, olive-oil, was used both as food and for cooking-fat. With flour, *oil went into breads and cakes, or these could be cooked in oil (Ex. 29:2); its use was universal, *cf.* the widow of Zarephath (1 Ki. 17:12).

For vegetables, see sections *b* and *c*, above, *Patriarchal age* (lentils) and *Israel in Egypt* (Nu. 11:5); beans, *pôl*, were also used (2 Sa. 17:28; Ezk. 4:9). The word occurs also in Egypt from the 13th century BC. Besides the grapes and olives already mentioned, fruits included *figs proper, sometimes pressed into fig-cakes (*cf.* Is. 38:21 for a medicinal use; also used medically at Ugarit, for horses), and also sycomore-figs, as in Egypt, that had to be notched to swell to edible size (which was Amos's occupation; Am. 7:14). Pomegranates were eaten and their juice drunk (Ct. 8:2). The various nuts available included almonds (Je. 1:11) and pistachio-nuts (see under *Patriarchal age* above). In Pr. 25:11; Ct. 2:3, 5; 7:8; 8:5; Joel 1:12, the term *tappûaḥ* probably means 'apple', although this interpretation is often questioned. Outside of Egypt and Palestine, Bab. texts indicate a long knowledge of the apple (*ḫašḫûru*) in Mesopotamia, as well as in SE Asia Minor (Purušḫanda, near modern Topada). (See also *TREES.)

(ii) *Animal products*. These include honey, fats and meat. The honey of wild bees found in rocks, trees, *etc.*, was widely used (Dt. 32:13; Jdg. 14:8; 1 Sa. 14:25; 2 Sa. 17:29). The OT writers do not say whether the Hebrews (like the Egyptians) practised bee-keeping. *Honey was a delicacy much enjoyed (Ps. 19:10; Pr. 24:13). Palestine was indeed a land of 'milk and honey' (Ex. 3:8)—in the 15th century BC the Egyptian pharaoh Tuthmosis III brought back hundreds of jars of honey from Syria–Palestine as tribute (7th and 14th campaigns). See the ecstatic description of Palestine's wealth of grain, wine, oil, honey, fruits and cattle by Sinuhe (*ANET*, pp. 19–20).

Milk was another staple item of diet, along with its products butter and cheese. For milk, *cf.* Pr. 27:27; Is. 7:22; Ezk. 25:4; for butter, Pr. 30:33; and for cheese, see Jb. 10:10; 1 Sa. 17:18; 2 Sa. 17:29 (as a gift). Milk was often offered to the unexpected visitor or guest, as it was to Sisera in Jdg. 4:19; 5:25, and as it had been centuries earlier to the Egyptian fugitive Sinuhe (*ANET*, p. 19).

Meat was eaten only occasionally, except perhaps for the rich, who may have had it regularly. As with Abraham, guests were entertained to calf, kid or lamb (*cf.* Jdg. 6:19ff.; 2 Sa. 12:4), and these were acceptable gifts alive or already dressed (1 Sa. 16:20; 25:18). The fatted ox in the stall sometimes provided a princely repast (Pr. 15:17), just as in Egypt (picture in N. M. Davies, *Egyptian Paintings*, 1955, plate 4) or in Mesopotamia—witness the official, charged with banqueting arrangements for visiting royalty, who reports on a fatted ox so heavy with flesh that 'when he stands up, the blood rushes to his feet and he cannot stand . . .' Eli's renegade sons preferred roast to boiled meat (1 Sa. 2:13–15), and meat boiled in a pot of water provided Ezekiel with a text (24:3–5). But a kid was not to be boiled in its mother's milk (Ex. 23:19), perhaps because this appears to have been associated with Canaanite sacrificial practice, and hence would carry similar implications to the 'food offered to idols' of NT times. Lv. 11:1–23, 29ff. (*cf.* 41ff.) and Dt.

Opposite page: Some of the principal food plants of the ancient Near East.

14:3–21 record the law on animals allowed or forbidden as food. In addition to the ox, sheep and goat, it was permissible to eat seven kinds of venison (Dt. 14:5), and all other cloven-hoofed animals that chewed the cud. Those *animals which failed to fulfil both demands were forbidden as food and listed as 'unclean', together with more than a score of different kinds of birds. With regard to fish, *etc.*, only those with both fins and scales might be eaten. A very few specified insects might be consumed (the locust-family). Some of the creatures forbidden were simply unfit for human consumption; others (*e.g.* swine) were unsafe in a hot climate; still others may have been too closely identified with surrounding idolatry. For fish, see section *c*, above, on *Israel in Egypt*, and *FISH, FISHING.

(iii) *Solomon's palace food-supplies*. In 1 Ki. 4:7, 22–23, 27–28, it is recorded that the governors of the twelve administrative provinces in Israel had each to supply a month's food in the year for Solomon's court: one day's provision being 30 *kōr* of fine flour, 60 *kōr* of meal, 30 cattle, 100 sheep, venison and fowls, and provender for the royal stables. Similarly, Solomon paid Hiram I of Tyre for his timber and woodcutters with 20,000 *kōr* of wheat per annum, and a corresponding quantity of oil. This palatial catering was typical of ancient Oriental courts, as is shown by Egyptian and Mesopotamian court-accounts. The courts of Nebuchadrezzar II of Babylon and Cyrus of Persia were apparently supplied by district-officials on a monthly basis, similar to the system in operation in Solomon's court; see R. P. Dougherty, *AASOR* 5, 1925, pp. 23–31, 40–46. Presumably Solomon's monthly supplies were levied either from, or in addition to, the local taxes in kind (grain for flour, livestock) paid by the twelve districts.

Not only the system but also the amount and the probable distribution of Solomon's court-provisions will bear some comparison with the consumption at other royal courts. The court-personnel of the ancient Orient may be divided conveniently into three classes: first, the king, the royal family and all the chief ministers of the realm; second, the main body of courtiers and subordinate officials attached to the 'departments' of the chief ministers; and third, the (probably) still greater number of domestic employees of every conceivable kind. The ancient Near Eastern palace was not just a royal residence but also the practical focus of the entire central government of the state. Partial statistics are available for comparison from Egypt and Mesopotamia. In the 18th century BC royal archives from Mari and Chagar Bazar in NW Mesopotamia record the daily food-supply for the king and his chief officials (*i.e.* the first class); the amounts ran into hundreds of litres (*qa*) of grain, bread, pastries, honey and syrups each day, averaging 945 litres daily at Chagar Bazar for the 'royal repast' (J. Bottéro, *Archives Royales de Mari*, 7, 1957, pp. 270–273). *Cf.* the great quantities of barley alone which were consumed in the Mari palace itself (see Birot, *ibid.*, 9, 1960, pp. 264–265). Similar accounts from the Egyptian court of the 13th Dynasty (same period) have also survived. Directly comparable is the 726 litres (10 *ḫar*—sacks) of flour daily used to make bread for the Egyp. court under Sethos I (*c.* 1300 BC) on circuit in Lower Egypt (Spiegelberg, *Rechnungen, Zeit Setis' I*, 1896). Preparations for a pharaoh's arrival in the late 13th century BC included the furnishing of 9,200 loaves (eight varieties), 20,000 biscuits (two kinds) and vast quantities of other victuals (R. A. Caminos, *Late-Egyptian Miscellanies*, 1954, pp. 198–201). All these figures also apply principally to class 1' consumers (and possibly 'class 2' in the last example), but take no account of the numerous domestics ('class 3')—*e.g.* the 400 palace-women at Mari. Ration-tablets from Babylon in the 10th to 35th years (595–570 BC) of Nebuchadrezzar II give detailed accounts of grain and oil for royal captives, including King Jehoiachin of Judah and his sons, as well as numerous artisans from Egypt, Philistia, Phoenicia, Ionia, Lydia, Cilicia, Elam, Media and Persia. (For details, see *ANET*, p. 308; *DOTT*, pp. 84–86; basic source is E. F. Weidner, *Mélanges R. Dussaud*, 2, 1939, pp. 923–935; for useful background, see W. F. Albright, *BA* 5, 1942, pp. 49–55.)

In Solomon's case, if the *kōr* ('measure') be taken as 220 litres (R. B. Y. Scott, *BA* 22, 1959, p. 31; *cf.* *WEIGHTS AND MEASURES), then his 30 plus 60 *kōr* of flour and meal per day would be some 6,600 plus 13,200 litres respectively, totalling 19,800 litres or 594,000 litres per monthly quota. Bearing in mind the comparative figures given above, 600 litres a day would go to Solomon, his family and chief ministers (*cf.* 726 and 945 litres, Egypt and Chagar Bazar, above), *i.e.* 'class 1'; the other 6,000 litres of fine flour would perhaps go to the main body of courtiers and officials ('class 2'), and the 13,200 litres of ordinary meal to the crowd of domestic employees ('class 3'). Evidence from Mari indicates that 1 *iku* of land (3,600 square metres) produced 1 *ugar* of grain (1,200 litres). If Israelite crop-yields were at all similar, and if a litre of grain made about a litre of wholemeal flour, then it is possible to suggest that each month's flour-supply to Solomon's court (594,000 litres) would be roughly equivalent to the grain grown on 495 *iku* or about 424 acres. This represents an area of land about 1·7 sq. km—surely no impossible annual burden on each of Israel's twelve administrative districts. As for Hiram's 20,000 *kōr* of wheat per annum, this amount by the same reckoning would take up the crop-yield of about 305 *iku* or 262 acres for each month, *i.e.* from land about 1·06 sq. km, again a reasonable kind of figure.

(iv) *Seasoning and cooking*. Cooking included the baking of bread and cakes (with or without leaven), making of soups and stews, and the roasting or boiling of meat (see above). *Salt was a prime necessity with a meal (Jb. 6:6). As already mentioned, sharing a meal marked agreement (Gn. 26:30; 31:54), and the phrases 'covenant of salt' (Nu. 18:19), or 'eating someone's salt' (Ezr. 4:14), were idioms of the same kind (*i.e.* indicating agreement or loyalty). *Herbs for seasonings included dill and cummin (Is. 28:25, 27) and coriander (Ex. 16:31; Nu. 11:7). Common use of these in antiquity is exemplified by actual finds of plants and seeds in Egyptian tombs from the 18th Dynasty onwards, and the mention of them in Egyp. and Bab. texts (*cf.* L. Keimer, *Die Gartenpflanzen im Alten Ägypten*, 1, 1924, Nos. 24, 29–30, pp. 37–38, 40–42 and refs., 147–149).

In Mycenaean Greek tablets from Crete and Greece, written in the 'Linear B' script and dated to the 15th–13th centuries BC, occur the spices cummin (*ku-mi-no*), coriander (*ko-ri-a-da-na/do-no*) and sesame (*sa-sa-ma*) among others. These names (and probably some of the spices too) were imports from the Near East, *via* Syria–Palestine and Cyprus, and so witness to the antiquity of the use of both spices and names in the Bible lands. Details are given in M. Ventris and J. Chadwick, *Documents in Mycenaean Greek*, 1956, pp. 131, 135–136, 221–231; and Chadwick, *The Decipherment of Linear B*, 1958, pp. 64, 120, contains a brief treatment. Sesame is attested at this same period in Syria itself, at Ugarit (Gordon, *Ugaritic Textbook*, 3, 1965, p. 495, No. 2496, as *ššmn*).

Honey could be used in baking (*cf.* Ex. 16:31), but not in sacrifice to God (Lv. 2:11), although the Egyptians offered it to their gods. Sweetened and spiced wines (Ct. 8:2) and beers are also known from Egyptian and Mesopotamian texts, honey or herbs being used for this purpose. With the rather doubtful 'spice the spicery' in a cooking context in Ezk. 24:10 (meaning spiced meat?), one might compare 'spiced (lit. "sweetened") meat' in Egypt (*iwf snḏm*), Gardiner, *Ancient Egyptian Onomastica*, 2, 1947, pp. 255*–256*, A. 610.

The AV phrase 'white of an egg' (*rîr ḥallāmûṯ*, Jb. 6:6, RVmg. 'the juice of purslain'), used as a symbol of something tasteless, was perhaps the sap of some vegetable. D. J. Wiseman (*The Alalakh Tablets*, 1953, p. 87), in outlining 18th-century BC ration lists from Alalaḫ, notes a possible connection between *ḫilimitu*, classed among the grains, and Syr. *ḫallâmûṯ* (*cf.* Heb. form above); *cf.* A. R. Millard, *Ugarit-Forschungen* 1, 1969, p. 210.

BIBLIOGRAPHY. For modern sidelights *cf.* H. Carey, *The Art of Syrian Cookery*, 1960. On ancient food generally, see R. J. Forbes, *Studies in Ancient Technology*, 3, 1955, pp. 50–105, and on honey and sugars, Forbes, *op. cit.*, 5, 1957, pp. 78–88, 97f; H. A. Hoffner, *Alimenta Hethaeorum*, 1974; *Reallexikon der Assyriologie*, 3, 1957–71, pp. 211ff., 302ff., 308ff.

K.A.K.

A tray of fruit being carried by servants. Wall-relief from the palace of Sennacherib. 704–681 BC. (BM)

Top left: Food is most frequently depicted as an offering to a god, as in this wall-painting. Tomb of Menena, Thebes. 1570–1314 BC. (MH)

Offerings of grapes and pomegranates. Copy of an Egyptian tomb-painting. Thebes. 18th Dynasty. (RH)

II. In the New Testament

As the food of a typical Hebrew family was mainly vegetarian, it is not surprising that the NT references to food are almost exclusively to such foodstuffs.

a. Vegetable foods

(i) *Cereals.* The staple diet of man in the Bible is bread, made either from wheat flour (Mt. 13:33; Lk. 13:21) or barley flour (Jn. 6:9, 13; *cf.* Jdg. 7:13; 2 Ki. 4:42). The latter was the usual ingredient of bread for the poorer people (*cf.* Jos., *BJ* 5. 427; and, for the relative value of wheat and barley, Rev. 6:6). The NT witnesses to the primitive method of using corn by plucking the fresh ears (Lv. 23:14) and removing the husk by rubbing them in the hands (Dt. 23:25; Mt. 12:1; Mk. 2:23; Lk. 6:1). When this was done in another man's field it was accounted by the rabbis as equivalent to reaping, and therefore forbidden on the sabbath (Mishnah, *Shabbath* 7. 2). Other methods of dealing with the corn are referred to in Mt. 3:12 = Lk. 3:17; Lk. 22:31. Special mention should be made of the *maṣṣôṯ* or cakes of unleavened pastry, which alone were permitted in Jewish households during the days of the Passover festival (Ex. 12:19; 13:7, *etc.*; 1 Cor. 5:7f.).

(ii) *Fruits and oil.* From the garden came grapes (Mt. 7:16) and thereby 'the fruit of the vine' (Mt. 26:29, *etc.*); and olives, although the latter (*cf.* Rom. 11:17ff.; Jas. 3:12) are never expressly recorded as an article of food. The olive, however, provided a most useful oil which was used in the preparation of food, and the olive berry itself was preserved by a process of pickling it in brine. Pickled olives were eaten with bread as a relish. And, in this connection, mention may be made of the sauce compounded of dates, figs, raisins and vinegar and called *hᵃrōseṯ* which was a feature of the Paschal feast (Mk. 14:20; Jn. 13:26; in the Mishnah, *Pesaḥim*, 2. 8; 10. 3).

The fruit of the fig-tree is spoken of in Mt. 7:16 in the same context as the grape. These two fruits were much prized in Palestine, whereas at the extreme end of the social scale the fruit or pods of the carob-tree provided the frugal 'husks' which the prodigal would have been glad to eat in his plight (Lk. 15:16), though they were properly swine-food.

b. Animal products

(i) **Animals* (popularly speaking). The Jewish world of NT times was one in which dietary laws were strictly enforced, especially in regard to the distinction between *clean and unclean animals and birds (Lv. 11:1–23; Dt. 14:4–20; Acts 10:9ff.; the Mishnaic tractate *'Abodah Zarah*). The eventual breakdown of these dietary regulations is a notable theme of the NT (Mk. 7:18–20; Acts 15:20, 29; Rom. 14; 1 Cor. 8; 10. *Idols, Meats offered to). Among the clean animals which were eaten as food (provided that they had been slaughtered in legitimate fashion and the blood drained away, thereby making them *kosher*) we may note the kid (Lk. 15:29), and the calf (Lk. 15:23) which had been specially fattened for a festive occasion.

(ii) * *Fish.* Fish were similarly classified as clean and unclean according to the rubric of Dt. 14:9f. (*cf.* Lv. 11:9–12); and the reader of the Gospel story will be familiar with the names of the Galilean towns which were the centre of the fishing industry on the shores of the lake. The earliest disciples are called 'fishermen' (Mk. 1:16ff. and parallels). Apart from the reference in Lk. 11:11 there is the well-known mention of fish in the miraculous feedings of the multitude (Mk. 6:41ff. and parallels and Mk. 8:7ff. and parallels) as well as in the meals which the risen Lord shared with his own followers (Lk. 24:42–43; Jn. 21:9ff.). The popularity of the fish-symbol in early Christianity (*cf.* the definitive study of F. J. Dölger, ΙΧΘΥΣ, 1928) and the use of fish at some observances of the Eucharist in early Christian circles are probably derived from these Gospel incidents.

(iii) *Birds.* Birds as items of food are not mentioned in the NT, apart from the general reference in Acts 10:12 and the implication of the sale of sparrows in Mt. 10:29 and Lk. 12:6; but eggs are alluded to in Lk. 11:12.

(iv) *Insects.* Edible insects include the locust, which, along with wild honey, formed the diet of the Baptist in the Judaean wilderness (Mt. 3:4; Mk. 1:6).

c. Seasoning

To increase the pleasure of eating, various condiments were employed. The chief of these was salt, which has the property of adding savour to a dish of food (Jb. 6:6). This fact is made the central feature of some ethical instruction in the Gospels (Mt. 5:13; Mk. 9:50; Lk. 14:34) and Epistles (Col. 4:6). Compare, for the Jewish background here, T. W. Manson, *The Sayings of Jesus*, 1949, p. 132. Mint, dill, cummin and rue (conflating Mt. 23:23 and Lk. 11:42 which adds 'every herb': *cf. ExpT* 15, 1903–4, p. 528) continue the list of spices and *herbs used for flavouring; and in Mt. 13:31f. there is a reference to the mustard plant, the leaves of which were cut up and used to give extra flavour.

The tiny mustard seed must be sown in the field, according to Jewish practice, and not in the garden; and in Palestine the plant could reach a height of 3 m. On the various issues raised by the mustard seed simile, see C.-H. Hunzinger, *TDNT* 7, pp. 287–291 (bibliography). R.P.M.

FOOD, FORBIDDEN
See Animals, Part 1.

FOOD LAWS
See Clean, Part 1.

FOOT. Heb. *reḡel*, with parallels in other Near Eastern languages, is used occasionally of objects (Ex. 25:26), but mainly of animal or human feet, or legs, and anthropomorphically, of God's feet. Derivatively it is used of the pace (Gn. 33:14). Gk. *pous* is used of the feet of man or beast.

Both in Heb. and Gk. the foot frequently indicates the position, destination or inclination of the person (Pr. 6:18; 7:11; Acts 5:9), and then further in reference to guidance of, and watchful care over, a person, principally by God (1 Sa. 2:9; Ps. 66:9; Lk. 1:79).

Figuratively the word is often

The foot of an Assyrian soldier of Ashurbanipal's army being kissed by a captive Elamite. This was an act of submission to an overlord or conqueror. From the SW palace, Nineveh. c. 645 BC.
(BM)

Detail from Ashurbanipal's banquet-scene showing footstool. 668–627 BC. (BM)

Detail of an Egyptian footstool showing captives. The pharaohs symbolized their conquests by placing their enemies permanently under their feet. (PAC)

used to symbolize defeat of an enemy, with the picture of putting one's foot on his neck (Jos. 10:24; 1 Cor. 15:25).

Falling at a person's feet indicates homage or supplication (1 Sa. 25:24; 2 Ki. 4:27), sitting there implies discipleship or learning (Acts 22:3), and casting something at a person's feet indicates an offering (Acts 4:35). The figure of the foot taken in a snare, or slipping, is used of calamity (Ps. 73:2; Je. 18:22).

The necessity to wash the feet, for comfort and cleanliness, resulted from the dusty roads, and foot-washing was a sign of *hospitality, generally performed by the meanest slave (1 Sa. 25:41; Lk. 7:44; Jn. 13:5ff.; *cf.* Acts 13:25). Removing one's dusty sandals was a sign of respect (Ex. 3:5) and of mourning (Ezk. 24:17). Shaking off the dust from one's feet was a *gesture of scorn, probably based on the idea that to take so much as dust from a place implied a bond (Mk. 6:11; *cf.* 2 Ki. 5:17). B.O.B.

FOOTMAN. Heb. *raḡlî* from *reḡel*, 'foot'. The word is used of masculine persons only. Footmen are distinguished from children (Ex. 12:37; *cf.* Nu. 11:21). The word is a military term (Jdg. 20:2), and often denotes soldiers in general (1 Sa. 4:10; 15:4; 2 Sa. 10:6; 1 Ki. 20:29). It is used to distinguish infantry from chariot-fighters (2 Sa. 8:4; 2 Ki. 13:17; Je. 12:5; 1 Ch. 18:4; 19:18). AV uses 'footmen' in 1 Sa. 22:17 as a translation for *rāṣîm*, *'runners' (RSV 'guard'), *i.e.* the fifty men who ran before the king's chariot (1 Sa. 8:11; 2 Sa. 15:1; 1 Ki. 1:5). They also acted as a guard (1 Ki. 14:27–28; 2 Ki. 10:25; 11:4 *etc.*; 2 Ch. 12:10–11) and as royal messengers (2 Ch. 30:6, 10). Elijah once acted as a runner before Ahab (1 Ki. 18:46). The royal posts of the Persian empire are called 'runners' (RSV 'couriers') in Est. 3:13, 15, and retain the name even when mounted (Est. 8:10, 14). The word is used as a simile in Jb. 9:25.

A. van S.

FOOTSTOOL. The word occurs seven times in the OT, but on only one occasion is it used in a literal sense (2 Ch. 9:18), and there a different word (*keḇeš*) is used; on the other six occasions *h*^{a}*ḏôm raḡlayim*, 'stool of the feet', is used. The equivalent in the NT (*hypopodion tōn podōn*, 'footstool of the feet') occurs eight times, again only once used literally (where the word is simply *hypopodion*, Jas. 2:3), and apart from this reference all are quotations from the OT. In its metaphorical sense it has reference to God and applies to the ark of the covenant (1 Ch. 28:2) the Temple (which contains the ark) (Pss. 99:5; 132:7; La. 2:1); the earth (Is. 66:1; Mt. 5:35; Acts 7:49); and the enemies of his Messiah King (Ps. 110:1, referred to six times in the NT). The footstool of Tutankhamun of Egypt is carved with pictures of his enemies, and other Egyptian kings are shown resting their feet on their enemies' heads.

M.A.M.

FOREHEAD (Heb. *mēṣaḥ*; Gk. *metōpon*, literally 'between the eyes'). The set of the forehead can indicate opposition, defiance or rebellion (Je. 3:3, 'brow' in RSV), and hardness of the forehead indi-

FOOTWASHING
See Foot, Part 1.

FORBEARANCE
See Patience, Part 3.

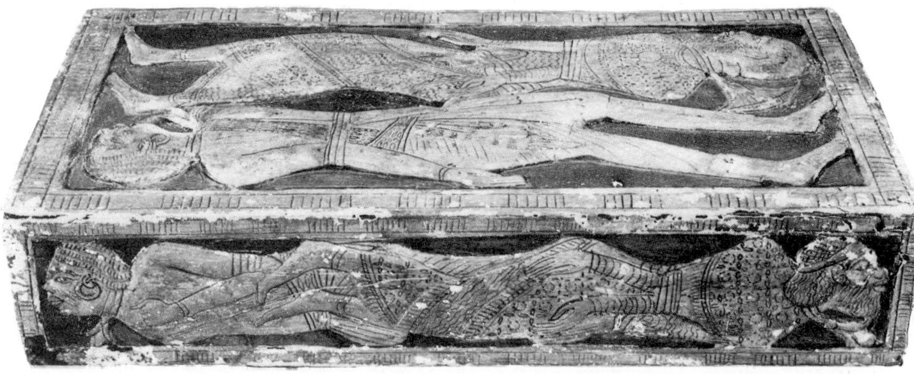

Footstool with painted plaster decoration. Tomb of Tutankhamun. c. 1360 BC. (RH)

FOREORDAIN See Predestination, Part 3.

cates the determination or power to persevere in that attitude (Is. 48:4; Ezk. 3:8–9).

The forehead, being open and fully visible, was the most obvious place for a badge or mark (Ezk. 9:4; Ex. 28:38; Rev. 7:3; 13:16, *etc.*). In Ezekiel this mark was made with ink, but in the book of Revelation it is a seal, and in Exodus a plaque. Note also the *phylactery which was worn on the forehead (*EYE).

B.O.B.

FOREIGNER. The rather arbitrary fluctuation in EVV between alien, foreigner, sojourner and stranger tends to obscure the fact that different groups of people are in view. In the classification which follows this inconsistency of translation should be kept in mind.

a. The stranger or alien

A stranger is essentially one who does not belong to the house or community in which he finds himself. The word *zār* is from the root *zûr*, 'to turn aside' or 'to depart'. Thus it can be used simply of an outsider (1 Ki. 3:18). It can therefore mean one who usurps a position to which he has no right. The 'loose woman' in Proverbs is such an interloper. A further extension of the word makes it equivalent to alien or foreigner, *i.e.* one who does not belong to the nation, and so virtually equates it with an enemy (Is. 1:7; Je. 5:19; 51:51; Ezk. 7:21; 28:7, 10; Ob. 11).

b. The foreigner

The word *nok̲rî* can refer simply to one of another race; but it also acquires a religious connotation because of the association of other nations with idolatry. It was for this reason that the Israelites were forbidden to intermarry with the Canaanites (Dt. 7:1–6). One of the indictments of Solomon is that he loved many foreign women who turned him aside from Yahweh (1 Ki. 11:1ff.). The Exile in Babylon was seen as a judgment on this decline, which was widespread in the nation. As a result the return from the Exile is marked by a vigorous enforcement of the prohibitions of mixed marriages. This emphasis by Ezra on national purity (Ezr. 9–10) was perverted in later Judaism into the hard exclusiveness which in the Judaizing movement in the early church proved such a hindrance to the free access of Gentile converts.

c. The sojourner

A sojourner is one whose permanent residence is in another nation, in contrast with the foreigner whose stay is only temporary. The word thus rendered is *gēr* from the root *gûr*, 'to sojourn', though the alternative *tôšāb̲* is sometimes used in the simple sense of a settler. The Israelites themselves were sojourners in Egypt (Gn. 15:13; Ex. 22:21; Dt. 10:19; 23:7). Indeed, this fact was to govern their attitude to the sojourners in Israel. These might comprise a whole tribe such as the Gibeonites (Jos. 9) or the remnants of the Canaanite tribes after the Conquest. Their number was quite considerable, as may be seen in Solomon's census of them (2 Ch. 2:17).

The sojourner had many privileges. The Israelites must not oppress him (Ex. 22:21; 23:9; Lv. 19:33–34). Indeed they are to go further and to love him (Dt. 10:19). One reason given for the observance of the sabbath is that the sojourner may be refreshed (Ex. 23:12). The gleanings of the vineyard and the harvest field are to be left for him (Lv. 19:10; 23:22; Dt. 24:19–21). He is included in the provision made in the cities of refuge (Nu. 35:15; Jos. 20:9). He is ranked with the fatherless and widow as being defenceless; and so God is his defence and will judge his oppressor (Pss. 94:6; 146:9; Je. 7:6; 22:3; Ezk. 22:7, 29; Zc. 7:10; Mal. 3:5). The chief drawback of his position is that, if he is a bond-servant, he is not included in the general liberation in the year of Jubilee (Lv. 25:45–46).

As far as religious life is concerned, he is bound by the law which forbids leaven during the Feast of Unleavened Bread (Ex.12:19). He must abstain from work on the sabbath and on the Day of Atonement (Ex. 20:10; Lv. 16:29). He shares the prohibitions on eating blood (Lv. 17:10, 13), immorality (Lv. 18:26), idolatry (Lv. 20:2) and blasphemy (Lv. 24:16). He might, however, eat unclean meat (Dt. 14:21). He is not compelled to keep the Passover, but if he wishes to do so he must be circumcised (Ex. 12:48). He is indeed virtually on a level with the Israelite (Lv. 24:22), and in Ezekiel's vision of the Messianic age he is to share the inheritance of Israel (Ezk. 47:22–23).

In the NT the great feature of the gospel is that those who were aliens from Israel, and so were 'strangers and sojourners' (Eph. 2:12, 19–20), have been made fellow heirs in the Israel of God. Now Christians are the aliens in this world and must live as pilgrims (1 Pet. 2:11).

BIBLIOGRAPHY. *EBi* and *DAC* (*s.v.* 'stranger'); J. Pedersen, *Israel*, 3–4, 1940, pp. 272ff., 585; H. Bietenhard *et al.*, *NIDNTT* 1, pp. 683–692; 2, pp. 788–790.

H.M.C.

FORERUNNER. This word is often used by Christians to describe John the Baptist, because in him the words of Mal. 3:1 found their fulfilment (Mk. 1:2 and Mt. 11:10), and also because his father Zechariah prophesied that he would 'go before the face of the Lord to prepare his ways' (Lk. 1:76). The actual word, however, is found only once in the NT, with reference to the ascended Christ (Heb. 6:20). It translates *prodromos*, a military term used of scouts sent on ahead to prepare the way for an advancing army.

Usually a 'forerunner' is of less importance than the person or persons for whose coming he is paving the way. This was true of the runners who preceded the chariots of kings (1 Sa. 8:11; *FOOTMAN); it was also true of John the Baptist, and of the messengers sent by Jesus to make ready his entrance into the villages of Samaria (Lk. 9:52). But in the case of Jesus himself, who entered for us within the veil into the holy of holies, having become our High Priest, the reverse is true. As the supreme Head of the church he has gone on ahead that his brethren may follow him in due course. Jesus made it clear to his followers that this was one of the main purposes of his departure to the Father, when he told them in the upper room that he was going to prepare a place for them in the many dwelling-places of his Father's house (Jn. 14:2–3). It is true that *already* Christians have boldness to enter heaven through the blood of Jesus (Heb. 10:19), and that God has already raised them up with Christ and made them to sit with him in the heavenly places (Eph. 2:6). They can through prayer and sacrament ascend in heart and mind to their Lord, and with him continually dwell. But, because Jesus is their Forerunner, they have the assurance that one day they will themselves enter heaven as he has done and enjoy the glory which is now his. Christ will receive them unto himself, that where he is there they may be also (Jn. 14:3). 'The Forerunner is also the Way by which, after long following, the whole Church will reach at last the Father's House.' (See H. B. Swete, *The Ascended Christ*, 1911.) R.V.G.T.

FOREST. 1. Heb. *ḥōreš*, 'thicket', 'wood, wooded height', occurs in a number of passages (*e.g.* Ezk. 31:3), though in one of them (2 Ch. 27:4) the text is possibly corrupt and a proper name intended.

2. Heb. *pardēs*, 'park', a loan-word from Persian *pari-daeza*, 'enclosure', used of a preserve or park containing trees (Ne. 2:8), fruit-trees (Ct. 4:13) and laid-out * gardens (Ec. 2:5).

3. Heb. *ya'ar*, 'outspread place', the most common word, is found thirty-five times in the OT. In biblical times much of the hill-country was covered with forests. Apart altogether from general uses of the word, the Bible mentions several of the woods and forests by name, *e.g.* 'forest of Lebanon' (1 Ki. 7:2f.). (* Articles under such place-names.)

BIBLIOGRAPHY. D. Baly, *The Geography of the Bible*², 1974, pp. 105–110. J.D.D.

FORGIVENESS.

I. In the Old Testament

In the OT the idea of forgiveness is conveyed principally by words from three roots. *kpr* more usually carries the idea of atonement, and its use in connection with the sacrifices is frequent. Its use for 'forgive' implies that atonement is made. The verb *nś'* means basically 'lift', 'carry', and presents us with a vivid picture of sin being lifted from the sinner and carried right away. The third root is *slḥ*, of unknown derivation, but which corresponds in use pretty closely to our 'forgive'. The first and the last are used always of God's forgiveness, but *nś'* is applied to human forgiveness as well.

Forgiveness is not regarded as a truism, as something in the nature of things. Passages which speak of the Lord as not pardoning certain offences abound (Dt. 29:20; 2 Ki. 24:4; Je. 5:7; La. 3:42). Where forgiveness is obtained it is something to be received with gratitude and regarded with awe and wonder. Sin merits punishment. Pardon is astounding grace. 'There is forgiveness with thee,' says the Psalmist, and then (perhaps surprisingly to us) he adds, 'that thou mayest be feared' (Ps. 130:4).

Forgiveness is sometimes connected with atonement. *slḥ* is repeatedly connected with the sacrifices and, as we have seen, the verb from the root *kpr* has the essential meaning 'to make atonement'. Again, it may not be coincidence that *nś'*, besides being used of the forgiveness of sin, is also used of bearing the penalty of sin (Nu. 14:33f.; Ezk. 14:10). The two seem to be connected. This does not mean that God is a stern Being who will not forgive without a *quid pro quo*. He is a God of grace, and the very means of bearing sin are instituted by him. The sacrifices avail only because he has given the blood as the means of making atonement (Lv. 17:11). The OT knows nothing of a forgiveness wrung from an unwilling God or purchased by a bribe.

Forgiveness, then, is possible only because God is a God of grace, or in the beautiful expression in Ne. 9:17 'a God of pardons' (RSV, 'a God ready to forgive'). 'To the Lord our God belong mercy and forgiveness' (Dn. 9:9). A very instructive passage for the whole OT understanding of forgiveness is Ex. 34:6f., 'The Lord, the Lord, a God merciful and gracious, slow to anger, and abounding in steadfast love and faithfulness, keeping steadfast love for thousands, forgiving iniquity and transgression and sin, but who will by no means clear the guilty.' Forgiveness is rooted in the nature of God as gracious. But his forgiveness is not indiscriminate. He will 'by no means clear the guilty'. On man's side there is the need for penitence if he is to be forgiven. While this is not put into a formal demand, it is everywhere implied. Penitent sinners are forgiven. Impenitent men, who still go on in their wicked way, are not.

It remains to be noticed that the thought of pardon is conveyed in a most graphic way by other imagery than the use of our three basic forgiveness words. Thus the Psalmist tells us that, 'As far as the east is from the west, so far does he remove our transgressions from us' (Ps. 103:12). Isaiah speaks of God as casting all the prophet's sins behind his back (Is. 38:17), and as 'blotting out' the people's transgressions (Is. 43:25; *cf.* Ps. 51:1, 9). In Je. 31:34 the Lord says, 'I will remember their sin no more,' and Micah speaks of him as casting sins 'into the depths of the sea' (Mi. 7:19). Such vivid language emphasizes the completeness of God's forgiveness. When he forgives, men's sins are dealt with thoroughly. God sees them no more.

II. In the New Testament

In the NT there are two main verbs to consider, *charizomai* (which means 'to deal graciously with') and *aphiēmi* ('to send away', 'to loose'). The noun *aphesis*, 'remission', is also found with some frequency. There are also two other words, *apolyō*, 'to release', which is used in Lk. 6:37, 'forgive, and you will be forgiven', and *paresis*, 'a passing by', used in Rom. 3:25 of God's passing over of sins done in earlier days.

In the NT several points are made clear. One is that the forgiven sinner must forgive others. This is manifest in Lk. 6:37, cited above, in

A clearing in the forest of Kiriath-jearim ('town of forests'), SW of Jerusalem, traditionally said to be where the ark of the covenant rested on its way to Jerusalem. (RS)

the Lord's Prayer, and in other places. A readiness to forgive others is part of the indication that we have truly repented. Moreover, it is to be whole-hearted. It springs from Christ's forgiveness of us, and it is to be like Christ's forgiveness: 'as the Lord has forgiven you, so you also must forgive' (Col. 3:13). Several times Christ insists on the same thing, as in his parable of the unmerciful servant (Mt. 18:23–35).

Forgiveness is not often linked directly with the cross, though sometimes this is done, as in Eph. 1:7, 'In him we have redemption through his blood, the forgiveness of our trespasses.' Similarly, from Mt. 26:28 we find that Christ's blood was shed 'for many for the forgiveness of sins'. More usual is it to find it linked directly with Christ himself. God 'in Christ forgave you' (Eph. 4:32). 'God exalted him . . . to give repentance to Israel and forgiveness of sins' (Acts 5:31). 'Through this man forgiveness of sins is proclaimed to you' (Acts 13:38). With these we should place passages wherein Jesus, during the days of his flesh, declared that men were forgiven. Indeed, in the incident of the healing of the paralysed man lowered through the roof, he worked the miracle expressly 'that you may know that the Son of man has authority on earth to forgive sins' (Mk. 2:10). But the Person of Christ is not to be separated from his work. Forgiveness by or through Jesus Christ means forgiveness arising from all that he is and all that he does. In particular, it is not to be understood apart from the cross, all the more so since his death is often said to be a death 'for sin' (*ATONEMENT). In addition to the specific passages which link forgiveness and the death of Christ, there is the whole thrust of the NT passages dealing with the atoning death of the Saviour.

Forgiveness rests basically, then, on the atoning work of Christ. That is to say, it is an act of sheer grace. 'He is faithful and just, and will forgive our sins' (1 Jn. 1:9). On man's side repentance is insisted upon again and again. John the Baptist preached 'a baptism of repentance for the forgiveness of sins' (Mk. 1:4), a theme which is taken up by Peter with reference to Christian baptism (Acts 2:38). Christ himself directed that 'repentance and forgiveness of sins should be preached in his name' (Lk. 24:47). Forgiveness is similarly linked with faith (Acts 10:43; Jas. 5:15). Faith and repentance are not to be thought of as merits whereby we deserve forgiveness. Rather they are the means whereby we appropriate the grace of God.

Two difficulties must be mentioned. One is that of the sin against the Holy Spirit which can never be forgiven (Mt. 12:31f.; Mk. 3:28f.; Lk. 12:10; *cf.* 1 Jn. 5:16). This sin is never defined. But in the light of NT teaching generally it is impossible to think of it as any specific act of sin. The reference is rather to the continuing blasphemy against the Spirit of God by one who consistently rejects God's gracious call. This is blasphemy indeed.

The other is Jn. 20:23, 'If you forgive the sins of any, they are forgiven'. It is more than difficult to think of Christ as leaving in men's hands the determination of whether the sins of other men are to be forgiven or not. The important points are the plural ('any' is plural in the Gk.; it points to categories, not individuals), and the perfect tense rendered 'are forgiven' (it means 'have been forgiven', not 'will be forgiven'). The meaning of the passage then seems to be that as they are inspired by the Holy Spirit (v. 22) the followers of Jesus will be able to say with accuracy which categories of men have sins forgiven, and which not.

BIBLIOGRAPHY. W. C. Morro in *ISBE*; V. Taylor, *Forgiveness and Reconciliation*, 1941; H. R. Mackintosh, *The Christian Experience of Forgiveness*, 1947; *TDNT* 1, pp. 509–512; 3, pp. 300–301; 4, pp. 295–307; 9, pp. 372–402; H. Vorländer, *NIDNTT* 1, pp. 697–703.

L.M.

FORMER RAINS
See Rain, Part 3.

FORNICATION
See Marriage, Part 2.

FORTIFICATION AND SIEGECRAFT.

I. Defence in the ancient world

a. Site and size of the fortress

Throughout most of the biblical period the words 'city' and 'fortress' (*mibṣār*, *et al.*) were virtually synonyms in Palestine. Sometimes 'walled city' emphasizes this normal defensive aspect of a town in contrast to unwalled villages. The account of the rebuilding of Jerusalem under Nehemiah clearly demonstrates that walls make a city.

Whenever possible a natural defensible site was chosen for the city's location, although a water-source was also essential. A steep isolated hill, such as Samaria, or an impregnable spur of a hill, such as Ophel, the site of David's Jerusalem, made excellent sites. Some cities, however, were selected because of regional strategical planning, protecting highways and communications, or like Bethel because of a readily available water-supply. These sites, and lower cities established when the population outgrew the upper city on a hill, required an artificial system of defence.

Usually the term 'fortress' implies a limited defence perimeter. In Palestine the average city or town covered about 2–4 hectares (5–10 acres). Some were half that area, others greater. For example, Jerusalem of David's day and Megiddo occupied 4·5–5·3 hectares (11–13 acres), whilst Canaanite Hazor covered some 81 hectares (200 acres). The capitals of Egypt, Assyria, Babylonia, Persia and Rome were exceptional in size and differed from normal cities in other features as well (*e.g.*, *NINEVEH, *CALAH, *BABYLON).

City walls varied considerably in width, height and design. Solid walls averaged 3 m in width, but could be two to three times this at base. Casemate walls, a double wall system, averaged about 1·5 m each. In height walls ranged from about 6 m to at least 9 m. Usually the foundations were of stone and the walls proper of stone, mud-brick or brick above a varying number of stone courses. Defences could be strengthened by adding an outer wall within bow-shot of the main wall.

b. The development of city defences

Although open warfare was preferred, a defending army could retire to its city if necessary. Walls and associated fortifications were required both to prevent the enemy entering and to provide a protected firing-platform for the defenders. Walls and ramparts, free-standing or attached to the wall, bastions, towers and a battlement or crenellated parapet were all used at various times.

Excavations have revealed remains of city walls in Syria–Palestine from the 3rd millennium BC, probably developed under Mesopotamian influence. A long time-gap separates these from the earliest known fortifications. In pre-pottery Neolithic Jericho several walls of undressed stone were found as well as a circular tower 13 m in diameter with an interior shaft containing 22 steps. These and a 9 m wide moat cut from solid rock date to 7000–6000 BC, over 4000 years before Abraham. Open villages without fortifications were succeeded about 3000 BC by some fortified cities—Jericho, Megiddo, Gezer, Ai, *etc.* A variety of stone and/or brick walls were used, some with bastions and ramparts. Semi-circular and square corner towers have also been discovered.

During the next period, the Middle Bronze Age (Patriarchs to Joseph), some important changes were made to walls and gates, connected in part with the use of chariots and possibly the battering ram. About 1700 BC when the Hyksos entered Egypt (*CHRONOLOGY OF THE OT) a massive *terra piseé* or beaten earth bank was added to the existing walls or free-standing ramparts were built. Sometimes a wwall was erected on top of the embankment. Massive stone walls also occur later (*SHECHEM). The rampart or 'glacis'—a special consolidated facing on a rampart or tell slope—often surfaced with plaster or chalk as waterproofing, may have been introduced to counter the arrival of the battering ram (*EAEHL*, p. 113). It enclosed, not a camp for chariots and their warriors, but extended lower cities (*HAZOR). The Hyksos were apparently responsible for this new defence system, although the Canaanite inhabitants still occupied the cities. Finally a ditch or moat often fronted the rampart, the excavated material forming the embankment (*CAH*, 2, 1, pp. 77–116).

Joshua entered the land of Canaan in the Late Bronze Age, in the 13th century BC. Excavations have revealed little evidence of the defences of this era. There were few new developments and the Middle Bronze defence systems continued to be used or were reconstructed on the same lines. This could account for the apparent lack of walls at *Jericho attributable to Joshua's time. To date no Israelite fortifications are known before the days of Saul and David.

In the days of the united kingdom casemate walls were built at a number of cities. These consist of two thin parallel walls (1·5 m thick on average) separated by about 2 m, joined at regular intervals by transverse walls. The long narrow rooms formed within the wall could

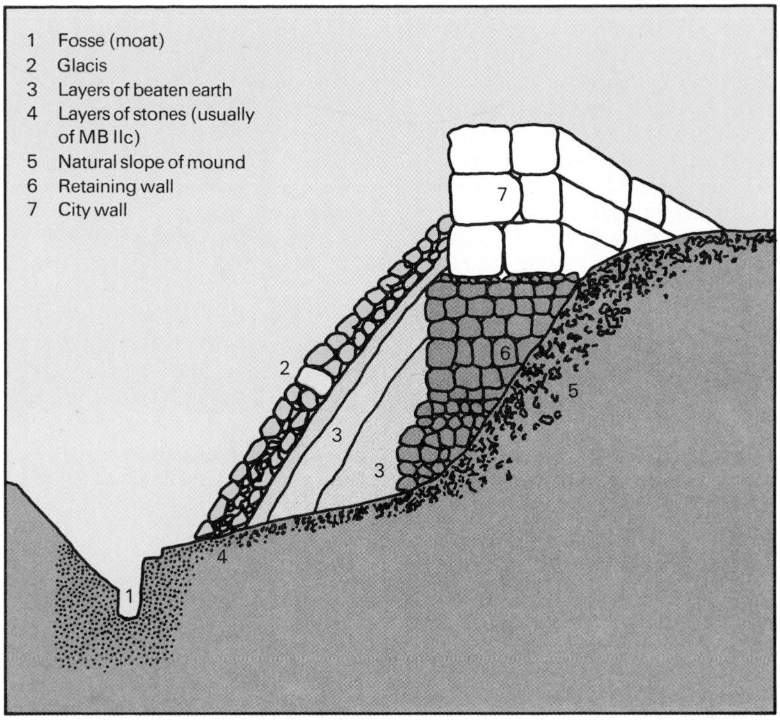

Schematic drawing of the typical elements in the fortification of Middle Bronze Age cities in Palestine.

A four-wheeled battering-ram shown in operation against a bastion in the attack on the city of Parga. Gates of Shalmaneser III, from the temple of Imgur, Balawat, near Nineveh. 858–824 BC. (BM)

A reconstruction of the siege of Lachish by Sennacherib's Assyrian army in 701 BC. This painting shows the double walls, city gate, siege-ramp and battering-rams as well as the offensive and defensive weapons employed. Judaean refugees leave the city. E. Sorvall and R. D. Barnett. (BM)

Herodium, one of the fortified palaces built by Herod the Great in Judaea. 1st cent. BC. (JPK)

Reconstruction of the W wall of the city of Nineveh, by Iraqi archaeologists using old stone and bricks. Kuyunjik: opposite Mosul, Iraq. (DJW)

While Assyrian troops tear down the outer wall of the city of Hamanu, the towers and gateways go up in flames. Relief from the NW palace of Ashurbanipal at Nineveh. c. 640 BC. (BM)

be used for living (Jos. 2:15), storage, or filled for added strength. Such a wall was cheaper to build yet provided reasonable solidity. Casemate walls were used from *c.* 1600 BC down to the 2nd century BC. Saul's capital at Gibeah was a fortress, 52 m by 35 m, with corner towers and casemate walls. Other walls were also used. At Beersheba two thin parallel walls, followed by a solid wall 4 m thick, are attributable to the Davidic–Solomonic era. Solomon's cities used different types of fortifications, although a hallmark of his fortifications, as seen at *Megiddo, *Hazor and *Gezer, is the use of casemate walls and a gate with three sets of piers and two towers. Throughout the rest of the OT period both solid and casemate walls were used, and at times an outer and inner wall (*LACHISH).

Royal fortresses, such as Gibeah of Saul, were built during the Iron Age. A series of forts, rectangular or irregular in shape, built in the Negeb between the 10th and 6th centuries BC mark the S extension of the Israelites. The citadel of *Arad was an important royal border fortress. Roman forts were also built in the Negeb, Arabah and Transjordan.

Excavations at *Jerusalem have revealed some of its defences throughout the ages. Kathleen Kenyon exposed sections of two walls well down in the Kidron Valley which were respectively the walls used down to the 7th century BC and a new wall built that century, destroyed by Nebuchadrezzar in 586 BC. A wall on the E crest of Ophel well above these would appear to be that built by Nehemiah, as he could not clear the debris left by the Babylonian destruction. On the W, 275 m from the Temple platform, over 40 m of wall 7 m thick built of large stones is probably the extension to Jerusalem's walls added by Hezekiah (2 Ch. 32:5).

In intertestamental and NT times one or two solid stone walls usually surrounded a city. At Mareshah the nearly square town wall had buttresses and corner towers. The excellent Roman wall at Samaria, apparently built by Herod, enclosed 69 hectares (170 acres). Herod the Great was the most prolific builder in all Palestine's history. His work at Jerusalem may be seen in the massive retaining wall of the Temple platform, especially in the areas excavated under B. Mazar and at the SE corner. Sections of

Hasmonaean defences and the three walls of *Jerusalem in NT times are being discovered in current excavations. At the citadel by the Jaffa gate part of the 'first wall', a massive Hasmonaean tower base, and the Phasael Tower of Herod's palace (David's Tower) are typical of the defence systems being recovered.

c. The city gate

The weakest point of a city's fortifications was the gate. A number of ways were developed to make this more secure. These included towers, angled approaches and inner gates with several sets of piers. Towers were used in the walls to protect the dead area at the foot of the wall, as was the 'glacis'. Most cities built on tells had one main gate, or one inner and outer gate. Large cities, such as Jerusalem, would have a number of gates. Up to about 1000 BC a number of posterns, small gates easily defended, allowed soldiers to leave or enter the city quickly because open battle was preferred.

Before the need for a straight entrance for chariots, angled gates with two doors hampered the enemy's assault. With the advent of chariots *c.* 1700 BC, towers and a complex gate with several piers or pilasters provided greater security. The towers and upper rooms enabled the defenders to fire down on the advancing foe. One upper room possibly was a special royal chamber, as reliefs in the Great Gate room at Medinet Habu suggest (*cf.* 2 Sa. 18:33). In the patriarchal age gates had two sets of three piers; so did the Solomonic gates, although with the entrance towers and walls this created three guardrooms. Two guardroom designs were used both before and after Solomon's day. At Dan and Tell en-Nasbeh an overlap in the walls formed a hollow square at the rear of which the gate was located. At en-Nasbeh a large tower on the right (outer wall) could handle attackers on three sides. Stone benches before the gate, and between the outer and inner gates at Dan, where there is also a probable throne base and canopy, mark the place of judgment (Ru. 4:1–2; 2 Sa. 19:8). The city gate was closed by massive wooden double doors. These doors were supported by posts sunk into the ground where they pivoted on specially hollowed-out stones. Discovery of these stones shows that only one set of doors was erected for each gate. When closed against the threshold stone the door was barred by a large beam held in position by sockets in both doorposts. Since an enemy would try to set fire to the doors they were often covered with metal sheets.

d. Citadels and small forts

The towered gateway was a virtual fortress or citadel in itself. The term 'tower' (*migdāl*, *et al.*) may also mean an inner citadel, a palace or temple (*BAAL-BERITH in Shechem), which provided an inner fortress for a secondary stand should the walls be breached. Sometimes a city was divided into sections for similar defensive reasons. 'Tower' may also refer to a small fortress or what we should call a blockhouse. The chain of forts in the Negeb and Transjordan are examples (above).

e. The problem of water-supply

Second only in importance to the walls and gates of a city was its water-supply. Until the invention of waterproof plaster to seal cisterns, every city needed a spring or stream nearby. Cisterns did enable fortresses to withstand long sieges, as Masada illustrates. Cities on tells, however, needed access to the springs at the base of the hill. In the 10th century and later, tunnels and shafts were dug from within the city, giving access to the water, whilst outside entrances were blocked off. Such shafts were used at Megiddo, Hazor, Gezer, Gibeon and Jerusalem (*SILOAM tunnel). These water-supply systems display advanced engineering knowledge and skills. Defenders tried to deny the invader water-supplies by filling cisterns, draining pools and concealing springs wherever possible. Food-supplies were also vital to withstand sieges, so that granaries and storehouses are found within cities.

II. Methods of attack

The least costly method of taking a city was, of course, to persuade it to surrender without fighting. The Assyrian Sennacherib used this technique in vain against Jerusalem. Other methods were to capture a city by some ruse or by surprise, as David secured Jerusalem. Joab entered the city probably by its water-tunnel. Usually, however, large cities had to be captured by assault or by long siege.

a. The assault

In a direct assault the invader could try to scale the wall by ladders, break through the walls by digging with tools or the battering-

Stone tower in the town wall of the pre-pottery neolithic age at Jericho, c. 7500 BC. It is 10 m in diameter and 8·5 m high with a stairway from the foot to an exit in the centre. (JEF)

FORTY
See Number, Part 2.

ram, penetrate the gate by firing it or battering it open, or tunnel under the wall. Where ramparts, moats or the side of a tell made direct attack difficult, an assault ramp was used. Part of the moat was filled with earth or rubble and an inclined ramp built up to the city wall proper. An Assyrian ramp investigated at Lachish in 1977 was made up entirely of large field stones. Assyrian reliefs from Nineveh depicting Sennacherib's assault on *Lachish (Is. 37:33) show the ramps were surfaced with wood. Assault troops behind large shields and the shield-covered battering-rams moved up the ramps, the latter protected by archers and slingers. The wooden beam of the ram had an iron axe-shaped head. When this penetrated the brickwork it was levered sideways to dislodge the bricks. A tower at the front of the ram was used by archers to fire at defenders on the walls. Mobile towers could also be brought against the walls, and catapults throwing large stones were used against the upper sections of the walls and the defenders. To prevent the escape of the besieged a mound or bank of earth was constructed around the city (Je. 6:6; Ezk. 17:17). From the walls the defenders would rain down arrows, javelins, stones, boiling water and also burning torches to set fire to the battering-rams. They also might make occasional sorties out of the city to destroy assault equipment and attack its protecting troops.

b. The siege

The protracted process of siege was used when a city was too powerful for a direct assault or when for other reasons the invader preferred to wait. By encircling the city the attackers sought to cut off its supplies and outside assistance, until the defenders were forced to surrender. An encircling mound and fortified camps were necessary to protect the more passive invading army. Sieges could last up to several years, such as the Assyrian siege of Samaria (2 Ki. 17:5).

c. Capture and destruction

After a city was captured it was normally plundered and burnt. Most cities, however, were rebuilt and used again. The surviving defenders might be deported, enslaved or placed under tribute, and their leaders tortured, killed or taken as hostages. The most famous destruction of OT times was Nebuchadrezzar's devastation of all the Judaean cities, including Jerusalem, in 588–587 BC. Titus' destruction of Jerusalem in AD 70 was equally complete, although under the Romans lesser cities fared far better.

BIBLIOGRAPHY. Y. Yadin, *The Art of Warfare in Biblical Lands in the Light of Archaeological Study*, 1963; S. M. Paul and W. G. Dever, *Biblical Archaeology*, 1973; *EAEHL*; A. Negev, *Archaeological Encyclopaedia of the Holy Land*, 1972. G.G.G.

FORTUNATUS. A member of the Corinthian party which was a blessing to Paul at Ephesus (1 Cor. 16:17f.). Nothing else is certainly known of him. The name is Latin and a common one, and here the man is probably a slave. It has been needlessly assumed that he and *Achaicus belonged to the household of *Stephanas (*cf.* 1 Cor. 16:15) or even of Chloe (1 Cor. 1:11). It is attractive to find Fortunatus 'forty years on' in *1 Clement* 65, but, *pace* Lightfoot (*St Clement of Rome*, 1, p. 62; 2, p. 187), it is not certain that Clement's Fortunatus was a Corinthian. A.F.W.

FORUM OF APPIUS. A market town and staging-post in Latium, a foundation of Appius Claudius Caecus, the builder of the Via Appia, on which the town stands. It is 45 km from Rome, a place 'packed with bargees and extortionate innkeepers', if the poet Horace is to be believed. The town was the N terminus of the canal through the Pontine Marshes. This was one of the places where the Roman Christians met Paul (Acts 28:15); see also *TAVERNS, THE THREE. E.M.B.

FOUNDATION.

I. In the Old Testament

The Heb. *yāsaḏ* and compounds mean 'to fix firmly, found' and is thus used both literally and metaphorically of all types of foundations whether of buildings (Jb. 4:19) and objects such as altars (Ex. 29:12) or of the earth (Ps. 24:2; Is. 24:18), the inhabited world (Ps. 18:15) and the vault of heaven (Am. 9:6). In this way the future Israel (Is. 54:11), Zion (Is. 14:32) and the righteous (Pr. 10:25) are described.

The 'laying down' of foundations (Is. 28:16), especially of a temple (1 Ki. 6:37; Ezr. 5:16) was a matter of religious ritual. There is, however, no sure archaeological evidence that human sacrifice (or 'threshold covenant') was involved. The loss of Hiel's sons (1 Ki. 16:34) at the rebuilding of Jericho is interpreted as a punishment (Jos. 6:26) rather than as an offering. The choice and preparation were important and sometimes the foundations were laid on bed-rock or pure sand. Usually the site was levelled by filling within a retaining wall of stones either to support the whole structure or the corners. The foundations of Solomon's Temple consisted of large and expensively trimmed blocks of stone (1 Ki. 5:17; 6:37; 7:10; *cf.* 1 Ch. 22:2). It has been suggested that different parts of the foundation of the second Temple are referred to; that a retaining wall (Aram. *'uššа*; Akkad. *'uššu*, Ezr. 5:16) was first built to retain the foundation platform (*temenos*; Akkad. *timēnu*), then later the returnees filled this in with earth and relaid foundations upon it (Ezr. 3:10; Zc. 4:9), but there is no archaeological or linguistic support for this theory. The foundations are often the only feature of ancient *architecture remaining today.

The 'gate of the foundation' in Jerusalem (2 Ch. 23:5, AV) may be the Horse-gate or 'Gate of Sur', while the 'rod of foundation' (*mûsāḏâ*, Is. 30:32, AV 'grounded staff') is probably for 'staff of punishment' (RSV; reading *mūsar*).

BIBLIOGRAPHY. R. S. Ellis, *Foundation-Deposits in Ancient Mesopotamia*, 1968; G. Turner, *Iraq* 32, 1970, pp. 69–71. D.J.W.

II. In the New Testament

Two Gk. words are thus translated.

1. *katabolē*, 'a casting or laying down'. All ten occurrences of this word are bound up with the phrase 'the foundation of the world' (*e.g.* Mt. 13:35; Lk. 11:50).

2. *themelios*, 'anything laid', appears sixteen times. Generally this word is found in a figurative sense, but it is used literally in speaking of the wise man who builds his foundation upon a rock (Lk. 6:48). Christ is spoken of as the foundation of the church, *i.e.*, the true and only basis of our salvation (1 Cor. 3:11). He is the chief *Cornerstone, and the apostles, who are the trustees and publishers of his gospel, are referred to as the

One of the springs or fountains which feed the headwaters of the Jordan. (SH)

foundation on which Christians are built (Eph. 2:20; *cf.* Rev. 21:14, 19). 'Foundation' is used also of one's ministry (Rom. 15:20; 1 Cor. 3:10), and in referring to the security of God's seal (2 Tim. 2:19). The first principles of divine truth are a foundation on which the rest depend (Heb. 6:1–2).

In a slightly different use of the word Timothy is instructed to urge those who are 'rich in this world' to lay up a good foundation (1 Tim. 6:19; *cf.* Heb. 11:10; Mt. 6:19–20) by trusting all to God—perhaps in contrast to the Ephesian merchants who deposited their earthly treasures in the temple of 'the great goddess Artemis'.

BIBLIOGRAPHY. K. L. Schmidt, *TDNT* 3, pp. 63f.; H. H. Esser, *NIDNTT* 1, pp. 376–378; J. Blunck, *idem*, pp. 660–662.

J.D.D.
J.B.Tr.

Bottom left: Stone blocks, set on bed-rock, forming part of the S wall of Herod's Temple at Jerusalem. 19 BC–AD 64. (JPK)

FOUNTAIN. Palestine, owing to its geological structure, is a land of many springs, as was forecast to the Israelites before they settled there (Dt. 8:7). As a result of this, several Heb. words were in use which are commonly rendered 'fountain' or 'spring' in the EVV.

1. *'ayin*, 'spring, fountain', the commonest word (*e.g.* Gn. 16:7), is well known from the fact that in its construct form, *'ên-* (EVV 'En-'), it is a common element in place-names. Its Arabic cognate is familiar today, as in 'Ain es-Sulṭân, the spring by which the city of *Jericho stood. The word occurs in a modified form as the place-name Ainōn or Aenōn, where John baptized (Jn. 3:23). Sometimes translated *'well' in AV (*e.g.* Gn. 24:13).

2. *ma'yān*, 'place of springs', is a variant of **1** and rendered in the AV by both 'fountain' (*e.g.* Gn. 7:11) and 'spring' (*e.g.* Ps. 87:7).

3. *mabbûa'*, 'spring', from *nāḇa'*, 'to flow, bubble up', is rendered in the EVV by both 'fountain' (*e.g.* Ec. 12:6) and 'spring' (*e.g.* Is. 35:7).

4. *māqôr*. This is sometimes used in a figurative sense of, *e.g.*, 'life' (Ps. 36:9) or in a physiological sense

The laying of a foundation was a major ritual in which the king (here Ur-Nammu at Nippur) took part. Commemorative tablets of bronze, lapis lazuli, gold, silver or clay were placed in boxes beneath the foundations of major public buildings. 2100 BC. (SI)

(*e.g.* Lv. 20:18) and rendered in the EVV by both 'fountain' (*e.g.* Ps. 36:9) and 'spring' (*e.g.* Pr. 25:26).

5. *môṣā'*, 'place of going forth', comes from *yāṣā'*, 'to go out', and is sometimes rendered 'spring' (*e.g.* 2 Ki. 2:21). **6.** *gal* is usually 'heap' (*e.g.* Gn. 31:46), but in Ct. 4:12 it is translated 'spring' (RSV, however, reads *gan*, 'garden'). **7.** *gullâ*, 'basin, bowl', is rendered 'spring' in EVV of Jos. 15:19 and Jdg. 1:15.

8. *ʾᵃšēḏâ*, 'foundation', '(mountain-)slope', which occurs only in the plural, is in the AV sometimes rendered 'spring' (Dt. 4:49; Jos. 10:40; 12:8) and thrice treated as part of a place-name, Ashdoth-pisgah (Dt. 3:17; Jos. 12:3; 13:20). The other EVV give 'slopes of Pisgah'.

9. *bôr*, 'cistern, 'well'. In Je. 6:7, where the *Kᵉṯîḇ* gives *bawir* and the *Qᵉrē bayir*, the AV renders 'fountain' but RV and RSV give 'well'. **10.** *ḥay*, 'living'. In Gn. 26:19 'living waters' is rendered 'springing water' in the EVV. **11.** *nēḇeḵ* is a word which occurs once only, in the plural construct *niḇᵉḵê-yām*, in Jb. 38:16, and rendered 'springs of the sea' in the EVV.

In NT the principal Gk. word for 'spring', 'fountain' is *pēgē* (*e.g.* Rev. 7:17, *etc.*; *cf.* Mk. 5:29; Jn. 4:6), a word which is, in the LXX, used chiefly for Heb. *'ayin*.

T.C.M.

FOUR
See Number, Part 2.

FOURTH PHILOSOPHY
See Zealot, Part 3.

FOWL
See Animals, Part 1.

FOWLER
See Snare, Part 3.

FOX
See Animals, Part 1.

FRAGRANT OFFERING
See Savour, Part 3.

FREEDOM
See Liberty, Part 2.

FROG
See Animals, Part 1.

FRONTLETS
See Ornaments, Part 2.

FREEDMEN (AV 'Libertines'), **SYNAGOGUE OF THE.** The Gk. of Acts 6:9 makes it difficult to determine whether the *Libertinoi*, the members of a Jewish synagogue at Jerusalem, worshipped by themselves, or with the Cyrenians, the Alexandrians, the Cilicians and the Asiatics. The meaning of the name is equally uncertain, and this has given rise to a number of variants for this verse (notably the reading 'Libyans' for 'Libertines', which appears in the Armenian vss and the Syriac). Schürer suggests that the Libertines were Rom. freedmen descended from Jews who had been prisoners of war under Pompey (63 BC) and subsequently released. Possibly only one synagogue is referred to here (then *kai Kyrēnaiōn . . . Asias* is epexegetic of *Libertinōn*), which was attended by Jewish freedmen or their descendants from the places mentioned (so F. F. Bruce, *The Acts of the Apostles*², 1952, p. 156).

S.S.S.

FREEMAN, FREEWOMAN. Two Gk. words are used. **1.** *apeleutheros*, 'one fully freed', applies to a man who, born a slave, has been freed. In 1 Cor. 7:22a the reference is to one freed by the Lord from the bondage of sin (*cf.* 1 Cor. 12:13; Col. 3:11; Rev. 13:16, *etc.*). **2.** *eleutheros*, 'free man', occurs in 1 Cor. 7:21, 22b; also in Rev. 6:15; *eleuthera*, 'free woman' (Gal. 4:22–23, 30) contrasts Sarah, Abraham's wife, with Hagar, his concubine, the Egyp. slave-girl. A metaphorical application of this is made in Gal. 4:31.

J.D.D.

FRIEND OF THE BRIDEGROOM. The Heb. words *rēa'*, *rē'eh* and *mērēa'*, though often meaning 'friend' in general, sometimes have the special meaning of 'friend of the bridegroom', 'best man'. The ancient versions sometimes show this special meaning. In the case of an abortive marriage Mesopotamian law forbade any marriage between the 'friend' and the forsaken bride. This explains the reaction of the Philistines and of Samson on the marriage of his former fiancée with his best man (Jdg. 14; 15:1–6). Jdg. 14:20 should be rendered 'to his best man, who had performed for him the offices of a best man'. A metaphorical use of the position of the best man is to be found in Jn. 3:29 (*cf.* 2 Cor. 11:2).

BIBLIOGRAPHY. A. van Selms, 'The best man and bride—from Sumer to St John', *JNES* 9, 1950, pp. 65–75.

A. van S.

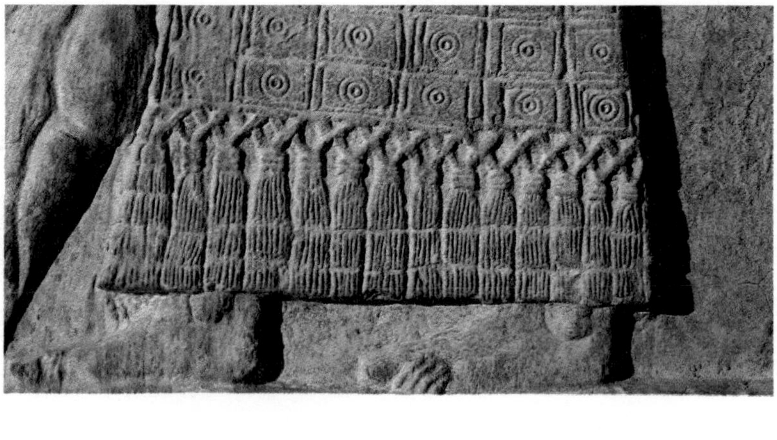

A wide, tasselled fringe on the border of a garment worn by an Assyrian archer of the time of Tiglath-pileser III. Calah, SW palace. 745–727 BC. (BM)

FRIEND OF THE KING. A phrase which was applied to various individuals. Ahuzzath was the 'friend' (*mērēa'*) of Abimelech the king of Gerar (Gn. 26:26); Saul had a 'friend' (*mērēa'*) (unnamed, 2 Sa. 3:8); Hushai the Archite was David's 'friend' (*rē'eh*, 2 Sa. 15:37); Solomon's 'friend' (*rē'eh*) was Zabud the priest (1 Ki. 4:5); and Baasha of Israel had a 'friend' (*rēa'*) (unnamed, 1 Ki. 16:11). *rēa'* is the common OT word for 'friend', and *mērēa'* and *rē'eh* are generally taken as variant forms of it. It has been suggested, however, that *rē'eh* is to be connected with Egyp. *rḫ nsw.t*, which came in the Middle Kingdom to mean 'acquaintance of the king', or with *ruḫi šarri* in the Amarna Letters, which has much the same meaning. The title does not seem to have implied any specific function, though marriage arrangements were a special concern, but the importance of the 'friend' is shown by the fact that there was never more than one at a time. A similar title was found later in Persian times, Themistocles, for example, being named a 'King's Friend' by Xerxes.

BIBLIOGRAPHY. R. de Vaux, *Ancient Israel*, 1961, pp. 122–123, 528; H. Donner, *ZATW* 73, 1961, pp. 269ff.; T. N. D. Mettinger, *Solomonic State Officials*, 1971, pp. 63–69; A. van Selms, 'The origin of the title "the king's friend"', *JNES* 16, 1957, pp. 118–123.

T.C.M.

FRINGES. A border of tassels along the edges of a garment (Dt. 22:12). This was bound by a blue cord, and served to remind the wearer of God's commands and of the need to obey them (Nu. 15:38–39). Various monuments show Hebrews and others wearing fringed garments. In NT times those who delighted in an outward show of piety put noticeably wide fringed borders on their garments (Mt. 23:5).

K.A.K.

FRUIT, FRUITS. The AV translation of the following Heb. and Gk. words, some of which are used interchangeably: Heb. *'ēḇ*, 'budding' (Ct. 6:11; Dn. 4:12, 14, 21); *y*^{e}*ḇûl*, 'increase' (Dt. 11:17; Hab. 3:17; Hg. 1:10); *t*^{e}*nûḇâ*, 'increase' (Jdg. 9:11; Is. 27:6; La. 4:9); *yeleḏ*, 'child' (Ex. 21:22); *leḥem* 'bread, food' (Je. 11:19); *nîḇ*, 'utterance' (Is. 57:19; Mal. 1:12); *ma*$^{'a}$*ḵāl*, 'eating' (Ne. 9:25); *m*^{e}*lē'â*, 'fullness' (Dt. 22:9; also 'ripe fruits' in Ex. 22:29); *p*^{e}*rî*, 'fruit' (107 times); *t*^{e}*ḇû'â*, 'incoming' (13 times); *kōaḥ*, 'strength' (Jb. 31:39). Gk. *gennēma*, 'produce' (Mt. 26:29; Mk. 14:25; Lk. 12:18; 22:18; 2 Cor. 9:10); *karpos*, 'fruit' (64 times; *akarpos*, 'without fruit', in Jude 12); *opōra*, 'ripe or full fruits' (Rev. 18:14).

a. Literal use

Mosaic law decreed that fruit-bearing trees be regarded as unclean for 3 years after planting, as the Lord's in the fourth year, and to be eaten by the people only in the fifth year. This preserved the health of the tree against premature plucking, gave God his due place, perhaps commemorated the entrance of sin by forbidden fruit and certainly inculcated self-discipline. Fruit-trees were so highly valued that for many centuries thereafter, even during the bitterest wars, special efforts were made to protect them (*cf.* Dt. 20:19–20). See *AGRICULTURE, *FIG, *FOOD, *VINE, *TREES.

Children are sometimes spoken of as the fruit of the body or womb (Dt. 28:4; Ps. 127:3).

b. Metaphorical use

The term has inspired a large number of metaphorical uses, involving such phrases as the fruit of the Spirit (Gal. 5:22); fruit for God (Rom. 7:4) and for death (Rom. 7:5; *cf.* Jas. 1:15); fruit of the lips (*i.e.* speaking, Is. 57:19; Heb. 13:15); fruit unto holiness and life (Rom. 6:22); fruit of the wicked (Mt. 7:16) and of self-centredness (Ho. 10:1; *cf.* Zc. 7:5–6); fruit in season (*i.e.* true prosperity, Ps. 1:3; Je. 17:8); fruits of the gospel (Rom. 1:13; Col. 1:6); of righteousness (Phil. 1:11; Jas. 3:18); fruits which demonstrate repentance (Mt. 3:8; *cf.* Am. 6:12). The unfruitful works of darkness are contrasted with the fruit of light (Eph. 5:9–11).

'The tree of life with its twelve kinds of fruit' (Rev. 22:2) some regard as 'a sacrament of the covenant of works, and analogous to the bread and wine used by Melchizedek (Gn. 14:18) and to the Christian Eucharist (Mt. 26:29) in the covenant of grace' (*Baker's Dictionary of Theology*, 1960, p. 231). More probably it is a symbol of abundant life (Jn. 10:10).

BIBLIOGRAPHY. A. Goor and M. Nurock, *The Fruits of the Holy Land*, 1968; D. Zohary and P. Spiegel-Roy, *Beginnings of fruit growing in the Old World*, 1975, pp. 319–327; R. Hensel, *NIDNTT* 1, pp. 721–723. J.D.D.

FUEL. *Coal was unknown to the Hebrews. Charcoal was used by the wealthy (Je. 36:22; Jn. 18:18) and by smiths, while the poor gathered their own sticks (1 Ki. 17:10). Ezekiel refers to the use of dried *dung as a fuel (4:12ff.), a practice which obtains today among the poor. Is. 44:14–16 lists some of the trees used as fuel, while shrubs (especially 'broom', Ps. 120:4), briars and thorns (Ec. 7:6), chaff (Mt. 3:12) and hay (Mt. 6:30) were used to obtain a quick, fierce, but evanescent heat. Fuel appears to have been common property among the Hebrews, and to be charged for it was a great hardship (La. 5:4). R.J.W.

FULLNESS. The Gk. word *plērōma*, translated 'fullness', carries three possible connotations: 'that which is filled'; 'that which fills or fills up', *i.e.* 'completes'; 'that which is brought to fullness or completion'.

The first does not seem to be relevant in the Scriptures, but the other two possibilities are important for the interpretation of certain crucial biblical texts. For the second we may cite Ps. 24:1, LXX (= 1 Cor. 10:26); Mt. 9:16; Mk. 6:43; 8:20. The Matthew reference may have the meaning 'that which makes something full or complete', as it refers to a patch which fills up the hole in a torn garment.

Under the third meaning should be placed Rom. 11:25, 'the full number, the totality of the Gentiles', and Rom. 15:29, 'the full measure of Christ's blessing'. Rom. 13:10 describes love as the *plērōma* of the law. This has been construed as 'the sum total of the law's prescriptions and demands'; but it is possible that the correct meaning here is 'fulfilment'. Love, like the Lord Jesus, is the end of the law (Rom. 10:4; *cf.* Gal. 5:14; 6:2) in that it brings the law to its full realization and perfect completion in the sense of Mt. 5:17; 26:56; Mk. 1:15. This nuance leads on to those verses where the precise meaning of the word is disputed. It is convenient to divide them into two groups.

1. Col. 1:19 and 2:9 are best taken together. See J. Ernst, *Pleroma und Pleroma Christi*, 1970. The exegesis of the use of *plērōma* in 2:9 is undoubtedly 'the fullness of deity, the totality of the Godhead' which dwells in Christ; and this meaning may be decisive in settling the cor-

Ripe figs being gathered from a tree in which monkeys are perched. Copy by Mrs N. de Garis Davies of a painting in the tomb of Khnumhotep at Beni Hasan, Egypt. c. 1900 BC. (BM)

FULLER
See Arts and crafts, Part 1.

rect interpretation of 1:19. In this text the choice is between taking it as a quasi-technical term of early gnostic speculation, which used the word *plērōma* to denote the region inhabited by the 'full number' of intermediary beings which were thought to exist between the Creator God and the created world; and taking it in the sense 'God in his fullness', 'the entirety of God's attributes, his full divinity' which was pleased to dwell in Christ. On the former view, Paul is combating speculative teachers at Colossae, who reduced Christ to a member of the celestial hierarchy. The apostle asserts in reply to this teaching that Christ is the fullness of these intermediary beings. They are subsumed in him, for he is the *plērōma* of them all. See R. P. Martin, *Colossians and Philemon, NCB*, 1974, pp. 59f., 79f.

This view, however, which assumes that Paul and the Colossian heretics are using a common term, although supported by many scholars, among whom are J. B. Lightfoot, E. F. Scott, and R. Bultmann (*Theology of the New Testament*, 2, E.T. 1955, pp. 149ff.), is open to serious objection. Apart from the lack of convincing evidence for an early gnostic creed in the 1st century, the most obvious consideration which tells against this proposal is that stated by E. Percy, that there is no trace in 1:19 and 2:9 of a polemic against the use which the supposed heretical teachers were making of the term *plērōma*, and in any case it is very unlikely that Paul would have borrowed so important a term from such a source. J. A. T. Robinson's suggestion (*The Body*, 1952, p. 67), that the apostle deliberately took over for apologetic use this word which he found in Hellenistic circles, lacks plausibility.

With C. F. D. Moule and C. Masson we may accept the second view and interpret *plērōma* in its OT light, where the Heb. equivalent is *m*[e]*lō'*; this reading sees the word as conveying the thought somewhat parallel to the Logos Christology of John, *i.e.* in Christ the sum-total of the divine attributes dwells and is revealed and communicated to men (Jn. 1:14, 16).

2. In Ephesians the term is taken by some commentators as applying to the church as well as to Christ; and this would confirm the view expressed above that *plērōma* is not being used in any technical 'gnostic' sense. In Eph. 1:10 there is a meaning similar to that in Mt. 5:17; Mk. 1:15; Gal. 4:4 with the thought that God's pre-ordained plan is now about to be consummated.

Eph. 1:22–23 may be taken in a number of ways, listed with admirable clarity by R. Yates, 'A Re-examination of Eph. 1:23', *ExpT* 83, 1971–2, pp. 146–151. The real crux is whether, on the one hand, *plērōma* refers to the church, which is then to be taken actively as that which completes Christ who is filling all things (corresponding to Eph. 4:10: so J. Dupont, *Gnosis: la connaissance religieuse dans les épîtres de Saint Paul*, 1949, p. 424, n. 1), or, in a passive sense, as that which is filled by Christ: or whether, on the other hand, *plērōma* should be treated as in

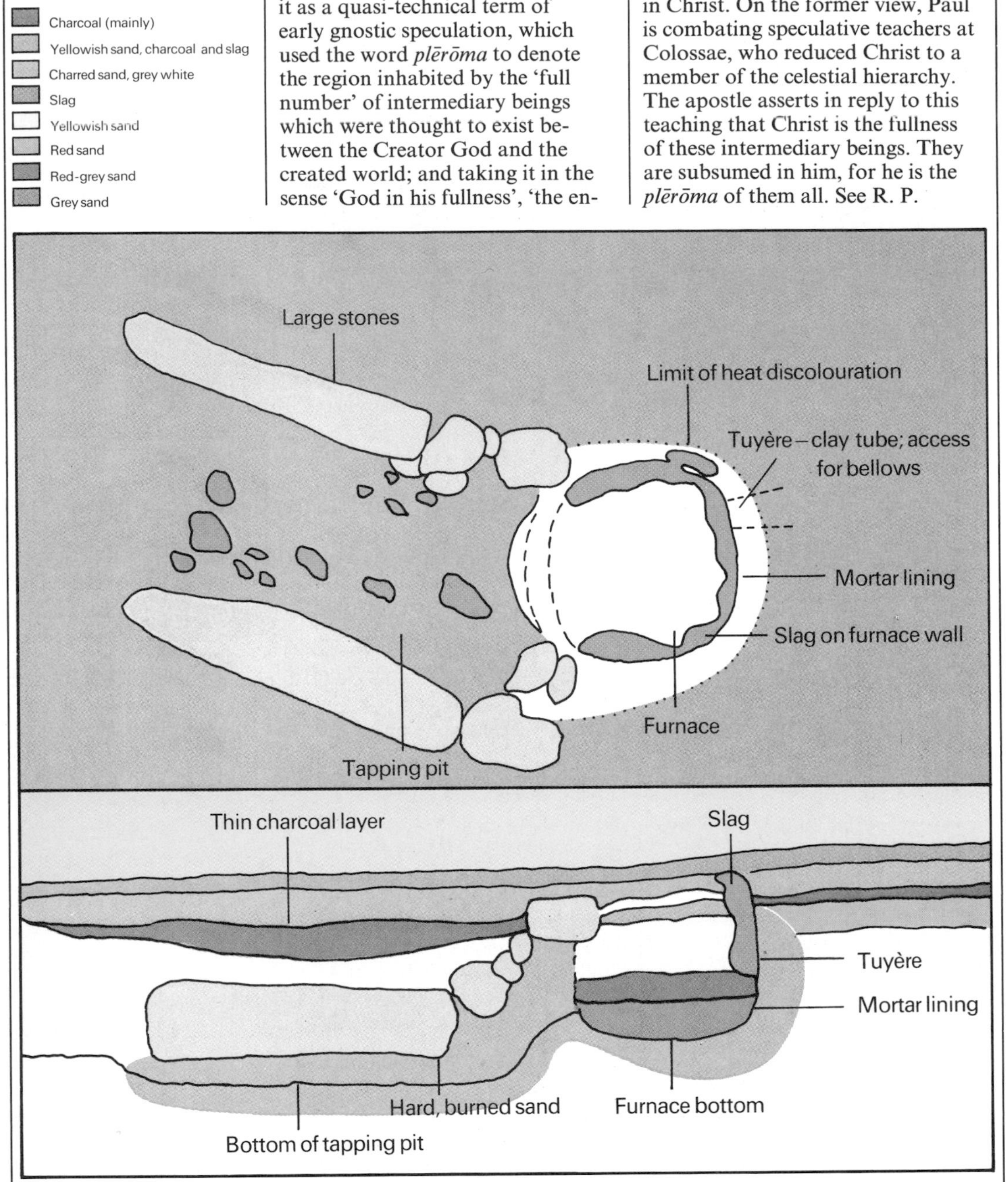

The term lithostrōton *denoted a pavement either of large plain flagstones or of inlaid stones set in a pattern* (opus sectile). *The marks left by the latter in Herod's palace near Jericho, as shown here, may indicate the form of the pavement* (lithostrōton) *at Gabbatha.* (JPK)

apposition to 'him' in v. 22 and so taken to apply to the Lord himself as the One who has been designated by God the Father as the fullness of the Godhead who fills all in all (as in 1 Cor. 15:28). This latter interpretation has the advantage of harmonizing with the rest of the Epistle (4:10) and with the teaching of *plērōma* in Colossians noted above. See Moule for a defence of this view, and F. C. Synge, who also takes *plērōma* as a reference to Christ.

Eph. 3:19 requires no comment, except that it confirms the understanding of *plērōma* as a Christological title. This verse is another way of expressing the hope that 'Christ may dwell in your hearts by faith' (3:17); Eph. 4:12–13 holds out the prospect of the whole body of believers coming into such an experience.

Another interpretation takes more seriously the voice of the verb (passive or middle) in the earlier texts. Christ is being fulfilled or is filling himself: but by or with whom? The answer to this question is that he is fulfilled either by the Christians who, as members of his Body, 'complement' the Head, and together form the 'whole Christ' (so A. Robinson, F. W. Beare); or with W. L. Knox, L. S. Thornton and J. A. T. Robinson, who propose the translation 'that which is filled by him who is always being filled (by God)', so that the meaning of the whole phrase is that the church is constantly receiving from Christ its Head the complete fullness which Christ receives from the Father.

BIBLIOGRAPHY. C. F. D. Moule, *The Epistles to the Colossians and to Philemon, CGT*, 1957, Appendix IV: 'A Note on PLEROMA'; *idem*, ' "Fulness" and "Fill" in the New Testament', *SJT* 4, 1951, pp. 79–86; F. Fowler, 'Ephesians 1:23', *ExpT* 76, 1964–5, p. 294; J. A. T. Robinson, *The Body*, 1952, p. 65, n. 3. See also J. B. Lightfoot, *St Paul's Epistles to the Colossians and to Philemon*, 1897, pp. 255, 271; C. Masson, *L'épître de S. Paul aux Colossiens*, 1950; E. Percy, *Die Probleme der Kolosser- und Epheser-briefe*, 1946; E. F. Scott, *The Epistles to the Colossians, to Philemon, and to the Ephesians*, 1930; F. C. Synge, *The Epistle to the Ephesians*, 1941; M. Barth, *Ephesians, AB*, 1974; T. Brandt *et al., NIDNTT* 1, pp. 728–744; G. Delling, *TDNT* 6, pp. 283–311.

R.P.M.

FURNACE. A word used to translate five Heb. terms and one Gk.

1. *'attûn*. An Aram. word which is used in Dn. 3 of the furnace into which Shadrach, Meshach and Abednego were cast by Nebuchadrezzar. It was probably a loan-word from Akkad. *utūnu*, 'oven', as used for baking bricks or smelting metals.

2. *kiḇšān*. A word occurring four times in the Bible, as a simile to describe the smoke of Sodom and Gomorrah (Gn. 19:28) and of Mt Sinai (Ex. 9:8, 10). In post-biblical Heb. it was understood to mean a kiln as used for firing pottery or burning lime.

3. *kûr*. A pot or crucible for smelting metals. The word always occurs in the Bible as a metaphor or simile of God's punishment or tempering of man. Egypt was a crucible of iron (Dt. 4:20; Je. 11:4; 1 Ki. 8:51); God will put Israel in the crucible and melt it with his fury (Ezk. 22:18, 20, 22); and Israel is passed through the crucible of affliction (Is. 48:10).

4. *'^{a}lîl*. Used only in Ps. 12:6 in a simile of the words of God which are as silver tried in a furnace. The usage suggests a crucible.

5. *tannûr*. 'Portable stove' or 'oven' (*BREAD), the latter probably being a preferable translation in Ne. 3:11; 12:38; Is. 31:9; and perhaps Gn. 15:17, where AV gives 'furnace'.

6. *kaminos*. 'Oven, furnace', a word used in LXX to translate *'attûn*, *kiḇšān* and *kûr*, and in Mt. 13:42, 50 and Rev. 9:2 as a figure of the fires of hell (*cf.* also Rev. 1:15).

Copper-refining furnaces have been excavated in Palestine at Beth-shemesh, Ai and Ezion-geber, the last lying at the S end of the Wadi Arabah, which forms a funnel down which powerful winds blow. Well-preserved furnaces for iron refining built below the level of the ground have been found at Tell Jemmeh (?Gerar). (*ARTS AND CRAFTS.)

BIBLIOGRAPHY. A. G. Barrois, *Manuel d'Archéologie biblique*, 1, 1939, pp. 372–373; R. J. Forbes, *Studies in Ancient Technology*, 6, 1958, pp. 66ff.

T.C.M.

GAAL (Heb. *ga'al*). Son of Ebed; LXX(B) *Iobel* suggests Heb. *'ōḇeḏ* = 'servant' (*cf.* Moore, *ICC, Judges*, p. 256, and Jdg. 9:28). Leader of a roving band, who came to Shechem in the reign of Abimelech to take advantage of disaffection in the city. His activity forced Abimelech to attack Shechem; Gaal and his men were expelled by Abimelech's governor, but Abimelech took vengeance on the city for supporting him (Jdg. 9:22–45).

J.P.U.L.

GABBATHA. An Aramaic word meaning 'height', 'eminence'; the local, native word for the area. It must have been on a height.

Gabbatha identifies the same location as the other term, 'the Pavement' (*lithostrōton*), but does not describe exactly the same thing. As Jn. 19:13 specifies, it is a 'place' called either the Height or the Pavement. One may suppose that the Pavement was laid by Herod in front of his palace in the Upper City (at the NW angle of the first N wall). This palace was the official residence of the Roman governors, including Pilate, as is clear from incidents described by Josephus.

The Greek word *lithostrōton* was adopted by the Romans to describe a paved area, either of marquetry (*opus sectile*) or of flagstones. Both types of work are known to have been used by Herod; marquetry at Jericho (inlaid stones, some coloured, set in a pattern) and flags at Jerusalem, notably for the streets and terraces outside the immense walls of the Temple Mount (now excavated by Mazar). The foundations of this palace in the Upper City have been excavated, but the superstructures were missing. Nor has the Pavement been found as yet.

The site for 'the Pavement' favoured by Christian pilgrims at the Convent of the Sisters of Zion is to be rejected. Its adherents err in claiming that Jesus was brought to trial at the Antonia fortress on the Temple Mount; as stated above, the palace in the Upper City was Pilate's headquarters. Moreover the location of this pavement is slightly wrong even for the Antonia; it is probably part of the public square at the E gate of Hadrian's Aelia Capitolina. The pools beneath it were filled in and had siege-engines erected on them when the Romans under Titus attacked the Antonia (1st Revolt). At the time of Jesus they were open pools *outside* the walls of the Antonia. The pavement set over them, now shown as the *lithostrōton*, had not been laid.

J.P.K.

Opposite page: Plan and section of a copper-smelting furnace at Timnah (Khirbet Tibneh). 13th–12th cent. BC. *Liquid slag flowed from a hole 10 cm above the bottom of the furnace into the tapping-pit, where it solidified, leaving the copper at the bottom of the furnace.*

FUNERAL
See Burial and mourning, Part 1.

FURLONG
See Weights and measures, Part 3.

FUTILITY
See Vanity, Part 3.

FUTURE
See Time, Part 3.

GABRIEL (Heb. *Gaḇrî'el*, 'man of God' or 'strength of God'). One of the two angels whom the Bible names: the other is * Michael. He is sent to interpret Daniel's vision (Dn. 8:16) and to give him the prophecy of the 70 weeks (Dn. 9:21). Some commentators identify the angel of Dn. 10:5ff. as Gabriel.

In intertestamental Jewish literature, Gabriel is one of the archangels, the 'angels of the presence' who stand before God's throne praising him and interceding for men (Tobit 12:15; *Jubilees* 2:2; 1QH 6:13; 1QSb 4; *Testament of Levi* 3:5, 7; *cf.* Lk. 1:19; Rev. 8:2). He is named either as one of four archangels, with Michael, Sariel (or Uriel) and Raphael (*1 Enoch* 9:1; 1QM 9:15f.; *cf. 1 Enoch* 40:6; 54:6; *Sibylline Oracles* 2:215 (some MSS); *Numbers Rabbah* 2:10), or as one of seven, with Uriel, Raphael, Raguel, Michael, Sariel (or Saraqael) and Remiel (*1 Enoch* 20). Gabriel's special responsibility is paradise (*1 Enoch* 20:7). He destroyed the antediluvian giants (*1 Enoch* 10:9). With the other archangels, he will officiate at the last judgment (*1 Enoch* 90:21f.; *cf.* 54:6; *Sibylline Oracles* 2:214–219; 1 Thes. 4:16; Rev. 8:2). The Targums and rabbinic literature often identify anonymous angels in the OT as Gabriel or Michael.

In the NT, Gabriel is sent to Zechariah to announce the birth of John the Baptist (Lk. 1:11–20) and to Mary to announce the birth of Jesus (Lk. 1:26–38). His self-description, 'I am Gabriel, who stand in the presence of God' (Lk. 1:19) identifies him as one of the archangels (*cf.* Tobit 12:15). R.J.B.

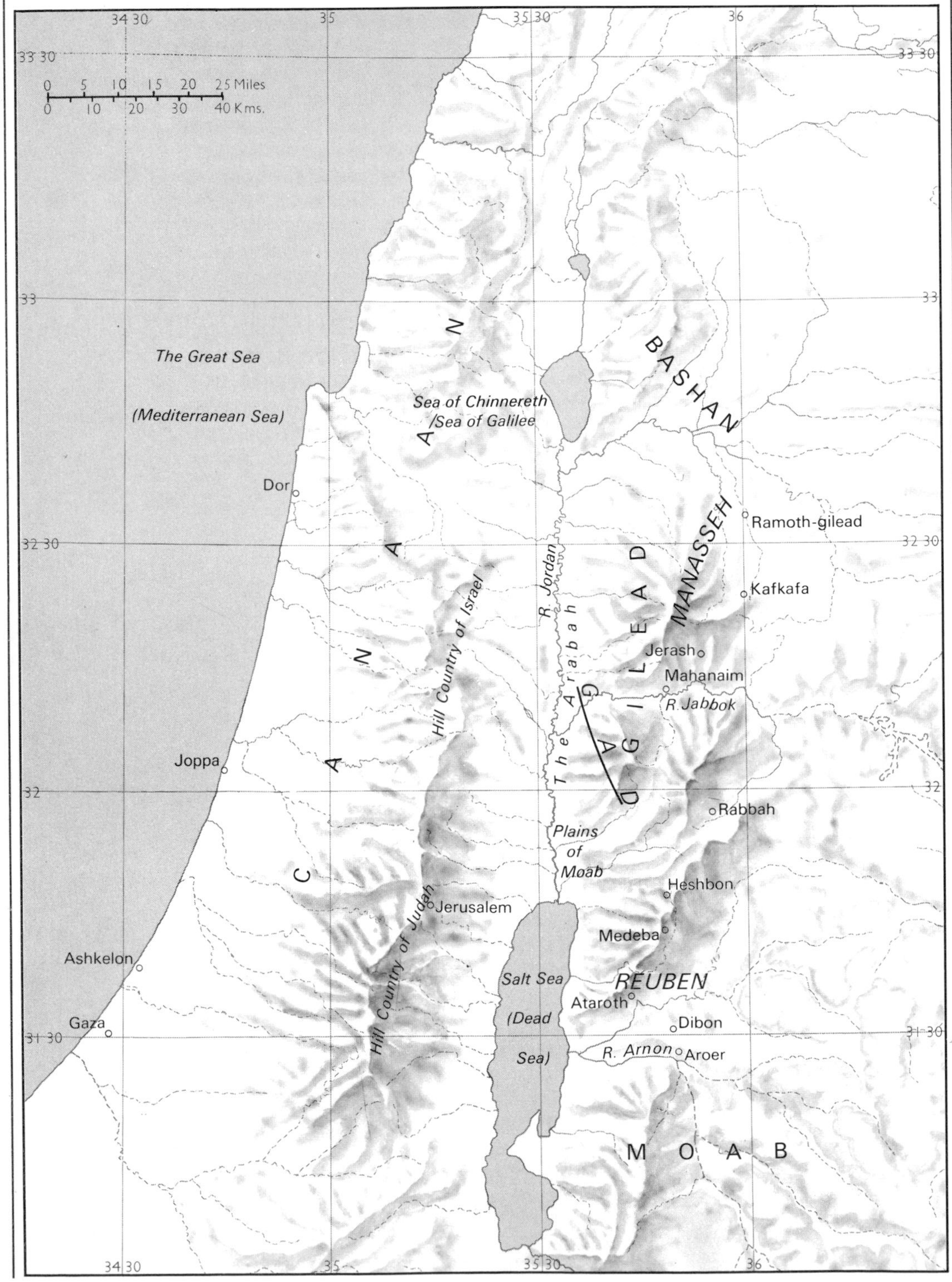

The tribal territory of Gad.

GAD ('good fortune'). **1.** The seventh son of Jacob, his first by Leah's maid Zilpah (Gn. 30:10–11). Gad himself already had seven sons when Jacob and his family entered Egypt (Gn. 46:16); Jacob promised Gad's descendants a troubled life, but foretold that they would hit back (Gn. 49:19). They recur later in Moses' blessing (Dt. 33:20–21).

2. An Israelite tribe descended from Gad, and the territory they occupied. The tribe in Moses' time had seven clans (Nu. 26:15–18), was commanded and represented by one Eliasaph (Nu. 1:14; 2:14; 7:42; 10:20), and supplied a spy for exploration of Canaan (Nu. 13:15). When Israel reached the plains of Moab, Reuben, Gad and half-Manasseh sought permission to settle in Transjordan, which they desired as their share in the promised land, because * Gilead was so suitable for their considerable livestock. To this Moses agreed, on condition that they first help their fellow-Israelites to establish themselves in W Palestine (Nu. 32). The Gadites and Reubenites then hastily repaired cities (including Ataroth) and sheepfolds to safeguard their families and livestock (Nu. 32:34–38, *cf.* 26–27) while preparing to help their brethren, a promise of help duly kept (Jos. 22:1–8). Then came the incident of the altar of witness (Jos. 22:9–34). As tribal territory, Reuben and Gad received the Amorite kingdom of Sihon: Reuben had the land from *Aroer on the Arnon river, N to a line running from the Jordan's mouth E to the region of Heshbon (Jos. 13:15–23). N of this line, Gad had all S Gilead, from the Jordan valley E as far as the S-to-N course of the upper Jabbok (the border with Ammon), and N generally as far as the E-to-W course of the lower Jabbok, but with two extensions beyond this: first, all the Jordan valley on the E side of Jordan river (formerly Sihon's) between the Dead Sea and the Sea of Galilee (or Chinneroth), and second, across the NE angle of the river Jabbok to include the district of * Mahanaim and a fertile tract flanking the E side of N Gilead N over Jebel Kafkafa to strategic Ramoth-Gilead at modern Tell Ramith, 32 km NE of Jerash (*cf.* Jos. 13:24–28). Heshbon was assigned as a levitical city out of the territory of Gad (Jos. 21:38–39); hence perhaps read Jos. 13:16–17 as (Reuben's) 'border was from Aroer . . . and all the plain by Medeba, ⟨unto⟩ Heshbon . . .' (emending only by the addition of one letter, locative-*h*). Dibon, *etc.*, are then cities between these limits, and Heshbon would be the southernmost territory of Gad.

The Gadites doubtless shared the troubles of Transjordanian Israel generally in the judges' period (*e.g.* Jdg. 10–12). In Saul's day the wooded Gileadite hills of Gad offered a place of refuge (1 Sa. 13:7), and Gadites among others joined the fugitive David and supported his becoming king (1 Ch. 12:1, 8–15, 37–38). Gadites likewise shared in, and were subject to, David's administration (2 Sa. 23:36; 24:5; 1 Ch. 26:32). On his Moabite Stone, roughly 840/830 BC, King Mesha mentions that the Gadites had long dwelt in the land of Ataroth. Just after this, within Jehu of Israel's reign, Hazael of Damascus smote all Gilead, Gad included (2 Ki. 10:32–33). In the 8th century BC Gadite settlement apparently extended NE into Bashan (1 Ch. 5:11–17), until Tiglath-pileser III carried the Transjordanians into exile (2 Ki. 15:29; 1 Ch. 5:25–26). Then the Ammonites again invaded Gad (Je. 49:1–6). Gad is assigned the southernmost zone in Ezekiel's vision of the tribal portions (48:27–28). Geographical background, in D. Baly, *Geography of the Bible*², 1974, pp. 210ff., 221ff., 227–232.

3. A prophet or seer, the contemporary of Saul and David; he advised David to leave Moab for Judah (1 Sa. 22:5). Later, God through Gad offered a choice of three possible punishments to

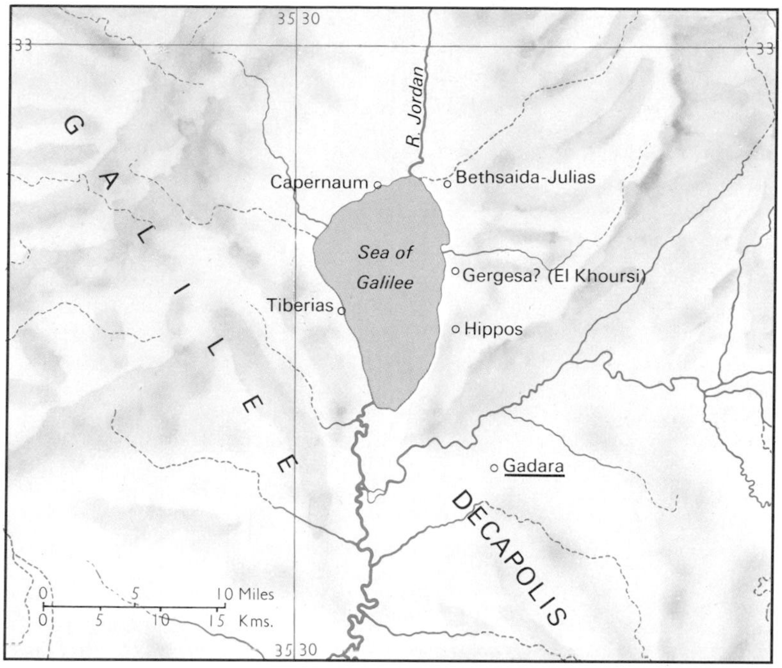

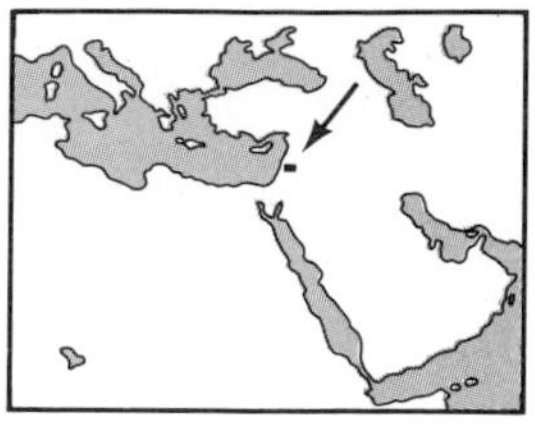

Gadara, one of the cities of the Decapolis, referred to in Mk. 5:1 and Lk. 8:26.

David after his census, and then commanded that David build an altar on Araunah's threshing-floor (2 Sa. 24:10ff.; 1 Ch. 21). Gad helped David and Nathan in organizing music for eventual use in the Temple (2 Ch. 29:25), and wrote a history of David's reign (1 Ch. 29:29).

4. A pagan deity worshipped by the Canaanites as the god of Fortune for whom they 'prepare a table' (Is. 65:11, RV, AVmg.). (* GAD, VALLEY OF.) K.A.K.

GAD, VALLEY OF. The place where the census ordered by David was begun is given as 'Aroer, on the right side of the city that is in the middle of the valley (Heb. *naḥal*) of Gad' (2 Sa. 24:5, RV). In Dt. 2:36 Aroer is described as 'on the edge of the valley (*naḥal*) of the Arnon'. Since the census would naturally begin at the S border of the Transjordan territory, this is probably the place intended. Various MSS of the LXX indicate corruptions in the text of 2 Sa. 24:5, which should read 'toward Gad and Jazer' (so RSV). G.T.M.

GADARENES, GADARA. The only biblical references to the Gadarene area concern the story of the miracle of Legion and the swine. The word 'Gadarenes' is found in some texts or versions of Mt. 8:28; Mk. 5:1; and Lk. 8:26. The probability is, however, that it is the original reading only in Mt. (Compare these VV. in AV and modern EVV.) The actual site of the miracle is in little doubt, at the edge of the Sea of Galilee. It would have been in a sub-district of Gadara, which lay 10 km SE of the Sea, near the gorge of the Yarmuk (or Hieromax). The Mishnah claims that Gadara dates from the OT period. It was held variously by Ptolemies, Seleucids, Jews and Romans between the 3rd century BC and the Jewish War. It was one of the Decapolis cities. The ruins at Umm Qays now mark the site. (* GERASA.) D.F.P.

GAIUS. A Latin praenomen, used without addition several times in the NT.

1. A Macedonian involved in the Ephesian riot (Acts 19:29; * ARISTARCHUS).

2. A companion of Paul's to Jerusalem, a member of the party which awaited the apostle at Troas (Acts 20:4f.), perhaps an official delegate of his church, which on the usual reading was Derbe. It is attractive, however, to follow the Western reading, 'of Doubērus' (a Macedonian town), and also possible to attach 'of Derbe' to Timothy (in which case Gaius would be a Thessalonian). Either way he would be a Macedonian, and thus conceivably the same as **1**. Proof is impossible: Luke may rather be interposing two Galatians (Timothy representing Lystra) between two Thessalonians and two Asians.

3. A Corinthian, baptized by Paul (1 Cor. 1:14). The church met in his house, and Paul stayed with him on his third Corinthian visit (Rom. 16:23). A suggestion of Ramsay's has been revived that Gaius was the praenomen of Titius *Justus (Acts 18:7). Origen (on Rom. 16) refers to a tradition that he became first bishop of Thessalonica.

4. The addressee of 3 John: the Elder commends his rectitude and hospitality (of which he asks a renewal), and expects to see him shortly. J. Chapman (*JTS* 5, 1904, pp. 366ff.) would identify him with any of the preceding, especially **1** and **3**, but his reconstruction is highly conjectural. The name was very common; the four references may well represent four different people. A.F.W.

GALATIA. 1. The ancient ethnic kingdom of Galatia located in the N of the great inner plateau of Asia Minor, including a large portion of the valley of the Halys river. A great population explosion in central Europe brought Gauls into this area during the 3rd century BC. Although never in the majority, the Gauls gained the upper hand and ruled over the more numerous tribes of Phrygians and Cappadocians. Ultimately the Gauls separated into three tribes, each inhabiting a separate area: the Trokmi settled in the E which bordered on Cappadocia and Pontus, with Tavium as their capital; the Tolistobogii inhabited the W bordering on Phrygia and Bithynia, with Pessinus as their chief town; and the Tektosages settled in the central area with Ancyra as their principal city.

2. The Roman province of Galatia. In 64 BC Galatia became a client of the Romans and, after the death of Amyntas, its last king, was given full status as a Roman province (25 BC). The new province of Galatia included not only the old ethnic territory but also parts of Pontus, Phrygia, Lycaonia, Pisidia, Paphlagonia and Isauria. Within the provincial Galatia were the towns which the apostle Paul evangelized on his first missionary journey, *viz.* Antioch, Iconium, Lystra and Derbe (Acts 13–14). The latter two cities were Roman colonies, and the former two had been Romanized by the emperor Claudius. Large numbers of Romans, Greeks and Jews were attracted to these population centres because of their strategic geographical location.

A particularly difficult question arises out of Paul's use of the word 'Galatia' in the Epistle to the Galatians (1:2). Does Paul use the term in its geographical sense, *i.e.*, to denote the ancient ethnic kingdom of Galatia, or in its political sense, to denote the Roman province by that name? NT scholars are almost evenly divided on this question (*CHRONOLOGY OF THE NEW TESTAMENT).

It is clear from the account in Acts 13–14 that Paul visited S Galatia and established churches there. Did he ever conduct a mission in N Galatia? Two texts especially have been used to support such a ministry. The first (Acts 16:6) reads: 'And they went through the region of Phrygia and Galatia. . . .' N Galatian proponents understand 'Phrygia' here to be the territory in which Antioch and Iconium were located, whereas 'Galatia' refers to the geographical or ethnic kingdom by that name. Ramsay, however, takes the phrase *tēn Phrygian kai Galatikēn chōran* to be a composite term describing a single area—the Phrygian–Galatic region. The word *chōra*, 'territory', was the official word used to describe one of the *regiones* into which Roman provinces were divided. Part of the old kingdom of Phrygia belonged to the Roman province of Galatia and another part belonged to the province of Asia. Thus Acts 16:6 refers to the parts of Phrygia which had been incorporated into the Roman province of Galatia. This interpretation is supported by the following statement in the Acts account, 'having been forbidden by the Holy Spirit to speak the word in Asia'. The plan of the missionary party apparently was to strike out directly in a W direction from

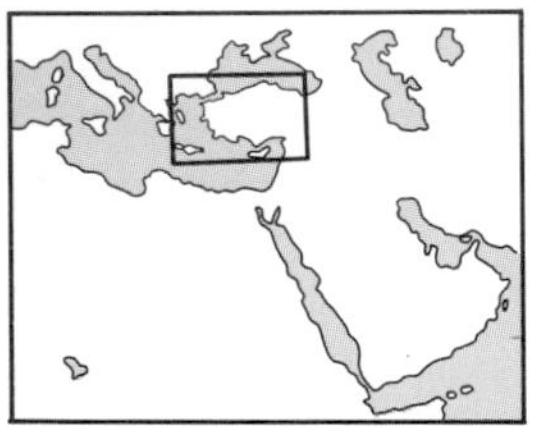

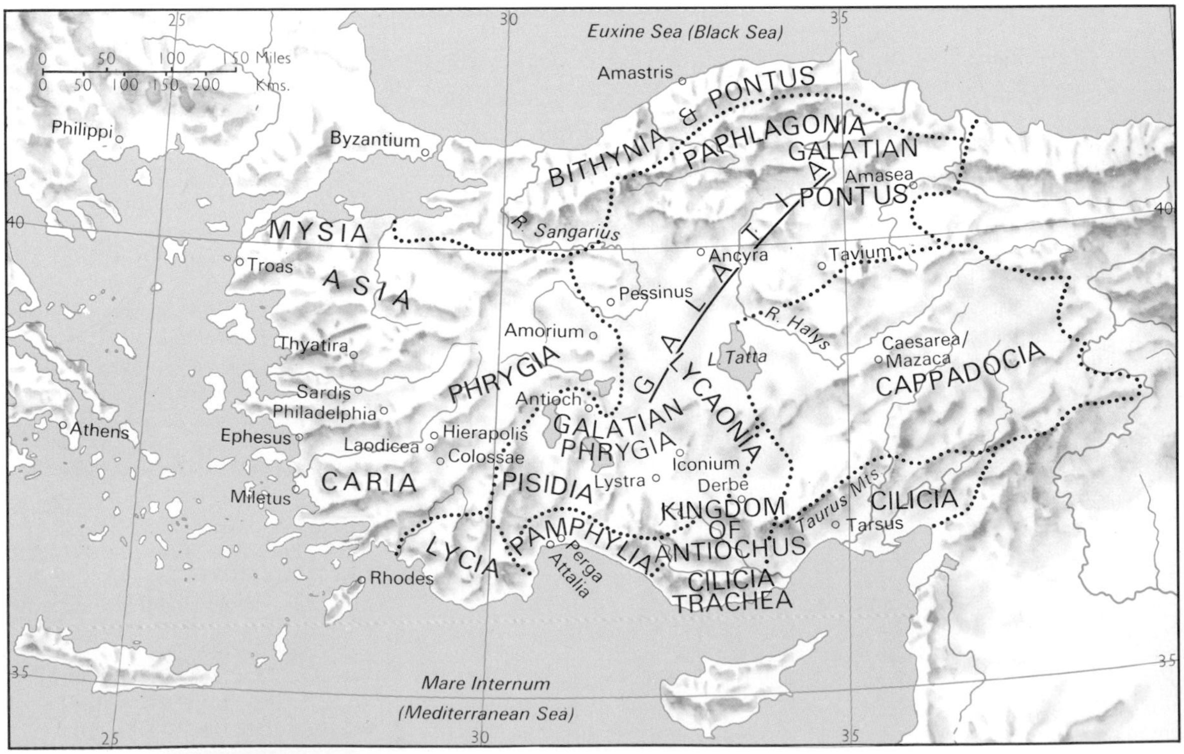

Galatia, an ancient ethnic kingdom which, as a new Roman province, also included parts of Pontus, Phrygia, Lycaonia, Pisidia, Paphlagonia and Isauria.

Antioch of Pisidia, which would have taken them into the province of Asia. Instead they went N towards Bithynia, crossing only a part of Asia.

The other passage is Acts 18:23. Here the order of the words is reversed: '. . . and went from place to place through the region of Galatia and Phrygia, strengthening all the disciples'. The 'region of Galatia' here is probably 'Galatic Lycaonia, so called to distinguish it from eastern Lycaonia, which lay, not in the province of Galatia, but in the territory of King Antiochus' (F. F. Bruce, *The Book of the Acts*, 1954, p. 380). 'Phrygia' then would probably include both Galatic and Asiatic Phrygia, since on this occasion there was no prohibition to prevent Paul preaching the word in Asia. In neither of these passages in Acts does there seem to be any good reason to suppose that Galatia means N Galatia. It is doubtful that Paul ever visited the ancient kingdom to the N, much less that he conducted an extensive mission there. (*GALATIANS, **IV**.)

There are three other occurrences of 'Galatia' in the NT. 2 Tim. 4:10 (which has the variant 'Gaul') and 1 Pet. 1:1 are almost certain references to the Roman province, while a decision on 1 Cor. 16:1, 'the churches of Galatia', will depend on one's view of the passages discussed above.

BIBLIOGRAPHY. W. M. Ramsay, *An Historical Commentary on St. Paul's Epistle to the Galatians*, 1899, *passim*; *SPT*, pp. 89–151, 178–193; *The Church in the Roman Empire*[3], 1894, pp. 74–111; *HDB*; *HDAC*; *IDB*; K. Lake, *BC*, 5, 1933, pp. 231ff.; G. H. C. Macgregor, *IB*, 9, 1954, pp. 213f., 247, 252; R. T. Stamm, *IB*, 10, 1953, pp. 435ff.

W.W.W.

GALATIANS, EPISTLE TO THE.

I. Outline of contents

Thanks, no doubt, to the sense of urgency with which the Epistle was written, it is difficult to trace a clear progression or sequence in its structure. It may be subdivided thus:

1. Greetings (1:1–5)
2. This new 'gospel' is no gospel (1:6–10)
3. Autobiography and apologia (1:11–2:14)
   - *a.* Paul received his commission direct from Christ (1:11–17)
   - *b.* Paul's first visit to Jerusalem after his conversion (1:18–24)
   - *c.* Paul's second visit to Jerusalem (2:1–10)
   - *d.* Why Paul opposed Peter at Antioch (2:11–14)
4. The gospel of grace does not encourage sin (2:15–21)
5. An appeal to the Galatians' personal experience (3:1–6)
6. The gospel covenant with Abraham is prior to Moses' law (3:7–22)
7. Christian maturity (3:23–4:11)
   - *a.* We are full-grown sons now (3:23–29)
   - *b.* Going back to infancy (4:1–7)
   - *c.* Going back to slavery (4:8–11)
8. A further personal appeal (4:12–20)
9. Christian freedom: the two Jerusalems (4:21–5:1)
10. Faith, not works (5:2–12)
11. Liberty, not licence (5:13–26)
12. A call to mutual aid (6:1–5)
13. Sowing and reaping (6:6–10)
14. Postscript in Paul's hand (6:11–18)
    - *a.* Paul takes up the pen (6:11)
    - *b.* False and true boasting (6:12–16)
    - *c.* The true marks of a servant of Christ (6:17)
    - *d.* Benediction (6:18)

II. Authorship and date

Except in such extreme and unrepresentative circles as the Van Manen school (whose views received publicity in *EBi*), the Pauline authorship of Galatians has been an axiom of NT criticism. Galatians has traditionally been recognized as one of the four 'capital epistles' of Paul (the other three being Romans and 1 and 2 Corinthians); indeed, it has been regarded as a standard by which other documents' claims to Pauline authorship could safely be measured.

On the 'N Galatian' view of its destination (see section **IV**, below) the Epistle could not have been written before AD 49/50, when Paul's second missionary journey began (Acts 16:6), and was more probably written after AD 52, when the third journey began and Paul visited 'Galatia' a second time (Acts 18:23), since his reference to having preached to them 'at first' (Gal. 4:13)—literally 'the former time' (Gk. *to proteron*)—implies two visits to them. On the 'S Galatian' view the Epistle could have been written earlier; the words 'so quickly' (Gal. 1:6) indeed would imply a time not long after the first missionary journey (AD 47–8), and 'at first' (Gal. 4:13) could be understood in the light of the fact that in the course of the first journey Paul and Barnabas visited the S Galatian cities twice, going from Pisidian Antioch to Derbe and from there back to Pisidian Antioch (Acts 14:21).

A more precise determining of the date depends on the interpretation of Paul's Jerusalem visits listed in Galatians. In arguing that at no time since his conversion had he an opportunity of being commissioned for his missionary service by the Jerusalem apostles, he mentions the occasions on which he had met them since, and tells what happened then. Two Jerusalem visits are mentioned: one 3 years (or in the third year) after his conversion (Gal. 1:18) and another 14 years after (Gal. 2:1). The first of these is certainly that mentioned in Acts 9:26ff. The second has generally been identified with that of Acts 15:2ff., the visit during which the *Council of Jerusalem took place. But (i) if Gal. 2:1–10 and Acts 15:2–29 purport to relate one and the same set of events, one at least of the two accounts can scarcely be acquitted of misrepresenting the facts; (ii) it is unsatisfactory to suppose that Gal. 2:1–10 narrates a private interview which Paul and Barnabas had with James, Peter and John in advance of the public Council; in that case Paul's suppression of the findings of the Council is inexplicable, for they were directly relevant to the Galatian controversy; (iii) the fact that the findings of the Council are not mentioned in Galatians can best be explained if in fact the Council had not yet been held when the Epistle was written; (iv) if the Jerusalem visit of Gal. 2:1 is that of Acts 15, Paul's critics would have pointed out immediately that he had failed to mention the earlier visit mentioned in Acts 11:30; 12:25. (The view that the visit of Acts 11:30; 12:25 is a duplicate of that recorded in Acts 15 is unacceptable; and the high estimate of the accuracy of the narrative of *Acts, which underlies the present discussion, can be defended by strong arguments.) There are weighty reasons for identifying the visit of Gal. 2:1 with that of Acts 11:30, and for dating the Epistle shortly before the Council of Jerusalem, *c.* AD 48/49. The incident of Gal. 2:12 is probably to be correlated with Acts 15:1.

III. Occasion of writing

Galatians was plainly written to converts of Paul's who were in imminent danger of adulterating the gospel of Christian freedom which he had taught them with elements of Jewish legalism. Among these elements circumcision took a chief place; they also included the observance of the Jewish calendar (Gal. 4:10) and possibly Jewish food-laws. The 'churches of Galatia' had evidently been visited by Judaizers who cast doubt on Paul's apostolic status and insisted that, in addition to the faith in Christ which he inculcated, it was necessary to be circumcised and to conform in other respects to the Jewish law in order to attain salvation. When news of this reached Paul he wrote this letter in white-hot urgency, denouncing this teaching which mingled grace and law as a different gospel from that which he had preached to them in Christ's name—in fact, no gospel at all—and entreating his readers to stand fast in their new-found liberty and not place their necks again under a yoke of bondage.

IV. Destination

The letter is addressed to 'the churches of Galatia' (1:2). To us this is a not unambiguous designation, for 'Galatia' was used in two distinct senses in the 1st century AD: it might denote ethnic Galatia in central Asia Minor, or the much larger Roman province of *Galatia. If the letter was sent to people in ethnic Galatia (the view of J. B. Lightfoot and most of the older commentators), we must suppose that that is the region visited by Paul in Acts 16:6 and 18:23 (or at least in one of these passages). But these two passages should probably be interpreted otherwise. There is, in fact, little evidence that Paul ever visited ethnic Galatia, whereas there is ample evidence that he visited the S area of the province of Galatia and planted churches there. The view that this Epistle is addressed to ethnic Galatia is commonly called the 'N Galatian' theory; the 'S Galatian' theory, on the other hand, supposes that the Epistle was sent to the churches of Pisidian Antioch, Iconium, Lystra and Derbe, all in the S of the Roman province, and all planted by Paul and Barnabas in the course of their first missionary journey (Acts 13:14–14:23).

Against the 'S Galatian' theory it has been argued that it would be psychologically inept for Paul to address his readers as 'Galatians' (Gal. 3:1) if in fact they were not ethnically Galatian. But if they belonged to different ethnic groups (Phrygian and Lycaonian) what common appellation could he have chosen to cover them all except their common political denominator, 'Galatians'? (So a modern writer, addressing a mixed group of English, Welsh and Scots, would probably address them as 'Britons' or 'British' in the political sense, although in its ethnic sense it would be applicable only to the Welsh members of the group.)

V. Principal arguments

If a logical analysis of the Epistle as a whole defies us, we can at least recognize the leading arguments which Paul uses in defence of true gospel liberty. Nine of them may be briefly stated as follows.

1. The gospel which Paul preached was the gospel which he received by direct commission from Christ; it came to his hearers with Christ's authority, not with Paul's (1:11ff.).

2. Against Paul's claim to unmediated commission from Christ, some argued that all valid apostolic authority must be mediated through Jerusalem, and that Paul's teaching or practice therefore was invalid if it deviated from the Jerusalem pattern. Paul replies by describing his visits to Jerusalem between his conversion and the time of writing, showing that the Jerusalem leaders had no opportunity of commissioning him but that, on the contrary, they acknowledged the apostolic commission (to the Gentiles) which he had already received from Christ (1:15–2:10).

3. If acceptance with God could have been obtained through circumcision and the other observances of the Jewish law, Christ's death was pointless and vain (2:21).

4. Christian life, as the Galatian converts knew from their own experience, is a gift of the Spirit of God; when they received it they received at the same time unmistakable proofs of the Spirit's presence and power in their midst. But if they began their Christian life on that high plane it was preposterous to imagine that they should continue it on the lower plane of legal works (3:2ff.).

5. The Judaizers justified their insistence on circumcision by appealing to the example of Abraham: since circumcision was the seal of God's covenant with him, they argued, no uncircumcised person could have a share in that covenant with all the blessings which went with it. But the true children of Abraham are those who are justified by faith in God, as Abraham was; it is they who enjoy the blessings promised to Abraham. God's promise to Abraham was fulfilled in Christ, not in the law; therefore the blessings bestowed by that promise are to be enjoyed not through keeping the law (which came long after the promise and could not affect its terms) but through faith in Christ (3:6–9, 15–22).

6. The law pronounces a curse on those who fail to keep it in every detail; those who place their trust in the law therefore put themselves in danger of that curse. But Christ, by his death on the cross, bore the divine curse in his people's place and delivered them from the curse which the law pronounces; his people therefore ought not to go back and put themselves under the law with its attendant curse (3:10–14).

7. The principle of law-keeping belongs to the age of spiritual immaturity; now that Christ has come, those who believe in him have attained their spiritual majority as responsible sons of God. To accept the arguments of the Judaizers would be to revert to infancy (3:23–4:7).

8. The law imposed a yoke of slavery; faith in Christ brings liberation. Those whom Christ has emancipated are foolish indeed if they give up their freedom and submit afresh to the dictation of those elemental powers through which the law was mediated (4:8–11; 5:1; 3:19).

9. This freedom which the gospel of grace proclaims has nothing to do with anarchy or licence; faith in Christ is a faith which works by love and thus fulfils the law of Christ (5:6; 5:13–6:10).

These arguments are presented in a more systematic form in the Epistle to the Romans, written 8 or 9 years later. The basic understanding of the gospel which underlies all these arguments took shape in Paul's mind very probably quite soon after his conversion, although the way in which it finds expression in Galatians is due to the special situation to which Paul addresses himself here. But perhaps for that very reason Galatians has to this day been cherished by Christians as a great charter of gospel liberty.

BIBLIOGRAPHY. J. B. Lightfoot, *Epistle to the Galatians*, 1892; W. M. Ramsay, *An Historical Commentary on Galatians*, 1899; E. D. Burton, *The Epistle to the Galatians*, *ICC*, 1920; G. S. Duncan, *The Epistle to the Galatians*, *MNTC*, 1934; H. N. Ridderbos, *The Epistle to the Churches of Galatia*, *NIC*, 1953; D. Guthrie, *Galatians*, *NCB*, 1969; K. Lake, *The Earlier Epistles of St. Paul*, 1914, pp. 253–323; J. H. Ropes, *The Singular Problem of the Epistle to the Galatians*, 1929; C. H. Buck, Jr., 'The Date of Galatians', *JBL* 70, 1951, pp. 113ff.; F. F. Bruce, 'Galatian Problems, 1–5', *BJRL* 51, 1968–9, to 55, 1972–3.

F.F.B.

GALEED (Heb. *gal'ēḏ*, 'witness pile'). Name given to the cairn erected by Jacob and Laban as a memorial to their covenant made in N Transjordan (Gn. 31:47–48; *PILLAR). By Laban it was given the equivalent Aramaic name *Yegar-sahadutha*. Documents of the earlier 2nd millennium BC reveal a great mixture of ethnic groups in N Mesopotamia. It is quite possible that some Aramaeans were included among them and that their dialect had been adopted by other Semitic groups. Specific evidence of Aramaeans in this area at this date is not yet available (*ARAM).

A.R.M.

GALILEE (Heb. *gālîl*, 'ring, circle', hence a 'district, region'). The regional name of part of N Palestine, which was the scene of Christ's boyhood and early ministry. The origin of the name as applied here is uncertain. It occurs occasionally in the OT (*e.g.* Jos. 20:7; 1 Ki. 9:11), and notably in Is. 9:1. The latter reference probably recalls the region's history: it originally formed part of the lands allocated to the twelve tribes, but, owing to the pressure from peoples farther north, its Jewish population found themselves in a kind of N salient, surrounded on three sides by non-Jewish populations—'the nations'. Under the Maccabees, the Gentile influence upon the Jews became so strong that the latter were actually withdrawn S for half a century. Thus Galilee had to be recolonized, and this fact, together with its diversity of population, contributed to the contempt felt for the Galileans by the S Jews (Jn. 7:52).

Exact demarcation of the Galilee region is difficult, except in terms of the provincial boundaries of the Roman empire. The name was evidently applied to the N marchlands of Israel, the location of which varied from time to time. In the time of Christ, however, the province of Galilee formed a rectangular territory some 70 km from N to S, and 40 km from E to W, bordered on the E by the Jordan and the Sea of *Galilee, and cut off from the Mediterranean by the S extension of Syro-Phoenicia down the coastal plain.

Thus defined, Galilee consists essentially of an upland area, bordered on all sides save the N by plains—the coastlands, the plain of Esdraelon and the Jordan Rift. It is, in fact, the S end of the mountains of Lebanon, and the land surface falls, in two steps, from N to S across the area. The higher 'step' forms Upper Galilee, much of which is at 1,000 m above sea-level; in NT times it was a forested and thinly inhabited hill-country. The lower 'step' forms Lower Galilee, 450–600 m above sea-level, but falling steeply to more than 180 m below sea-level at the Sea of Galilee.

It is to this area of Lower Galilee that most of the Gospel narrative refers. Well watered by streams flowing from the N mountains, and possessing considerable stretches of fertile land in the limestone basins among its hills, it was an area of dense and prosperous settlement. It exported olive oil and cereals, and fish from the lake.

'Outside the main stream of Israelite life in OT times, Galilee came into its own in the NT' (D. Baly, *The Geography of the Bible*, 1957, p. 190). The Roman region was governed successively by Herod the Great (died 4 BC), Herod Antipas and Herod Agrippa. Cut off from Judaea—at least in Jewish eyes—by the territory of Samaria, Galilee nevertheless formed an integral part of 'the land', and the Galileans had, in fact, resisted the Romans even more doggedly than the S Jews. In the time of Christ the relationship between the two groups is well described as having been that of 'England and Scotland soon after the Union' (G. A. Smith, *Historical Geography of the Holy Land*[25], 1931, p. 425).

This, then, was the region in which Christ grew up—at Nazareth, in the limestone hills of Lower Galilee. Thanks to its position, it was traversed by several major routeways of the empire, and was therefore far from being a rural backwater. Its agriculture, fisheries and commerce provided him with his cultural background, and are reflected in his parables and teaching. Its people provided him with his first disciples, and its dense scattering of settlements formed their first mission field.

Today, Galilee and the plain of Esdraelon form the core area of N Israel, but its modern inhabitants have the task of rehabilitating an area which has lost much of the prosperity it enjoyed in NT days. Its forests have been largely replaced by *maquis*, the characteristic scrub of the Mediterranean, and many of its towns and villages, places which Christ knew and visited, have disappeared from the map, leaving hardly a trace behind them.

BIBLIOGRAPHY. G. A. Smith, *The Historical Geography of the Holy Land*[25], 1931, pp. 413–436; D. Baly, *The Geography of the Bible*, 1957.

J.H.P.

GALILEE, SEA OF. A lake in the region of Galilee, also referred to, in the OT, as the 'sea of *Chinnereth' (Nu. 34:11) or Chinneroth (Jos. 12:3), and in the NT as the 'lake of Gennesaret' (Lk. 5:1) and the 'Sea of Tiberias' (Jn. 21:1). Its modern Heb. name is Yam Kinneret.

The lake is some 21 km long and up to 11 km broad, and it lies at 211 m below sea-level. The river Jordan flows through it from N to S; its waters are therefore sweet—unlike those of the Dead Sea—and its fisheries (*FISH), so prominent in the NT narrative, were famous throughout the Roman empire and produced a flourishing export trade. On the other hand, the position of the lake, in the depths of the Jordan Rift and surrounded by hills, renders it liable to atmospheric downdraughts and sudden storms.

The lake is bordered by a plain of varying width; in general, the slopes on the E side are abrupt (Mk. 5:13), and are somewhat gentler on the W. To the N and S are the river plains of the Jordan as it enters and leaves the lake.

The shores of the lake were the site of towns—Capernaum, Bethsaida, *etc.*—where much of Christ's ministry was carried out. In his time they formed a flourishing, and almost continuous, belt of settlement around the lake, and communicated and traded across it with each other. Today, only * Tiberias remains as a town—even the sites of several other former towns are uncertain—and changed patterns of commerce have robbed the lake of its focal importance in the life of the region.

BIBLIOGRAPHY. G. A. Smith, *The Historical Geography of the Holy Land*[25], 1931, pp. 437–463. J.H.P.

GALLEY
See Ships and boats, Part 3.

GALL. The Hebrews used *rôš* and *m^erôrâ* to describe a * plant and its fruit which were extremely bitter. Variously translated as 'hemlock' AV, 'poisonous weeds' RSV, NEB (Ho. 10:4), 'poison' (Jb. 20:16; Je. 8:14) and 'venom' (*cf.* Dt. 32:33), it is frequently associated with the bitter herb wormwood (*Artemisia*) (Dt. 29:18; Je. 9:15; La. 3:19; Am. 6:12). Gall is referred to literally as the yellowish-brown secretion of the liver in Jb. 16:13; 20:14, 25. As a plant it probably refers to the extract of the colocynth gourd fruit (*Citrullus colocynthis*).

Metaphorically it denoted travail (La. 3:5) or any bitter experience (Acts 8:23). The anodyne offered to Christ during his crucifixion (Mt. 27:34; *cf.* Mk. 15:23) was a diluted wine containing stupefying drugs.

R.K.H.
F.N.H.

Assyrian soldiers erecting gallows to impale Judaean captives at Lachish. Sennacherib relief. Nineveh. c. 700 BC. (BM)

GALLIO. Lucius Junius Annaeus (or Annaeanus) Gallio was the son of Seneca the rhetorician and brother of Seneca the philosopher. An inscription at Delphi (*SIG*, 2[3], 801; *cf.* text and discussion by K. Lake, *BC*, 5, pp. 460ff.) makes it virtually certain that he was proconsul of Achaia in AD 52–53, in which office we meet him in Acts 18:12ff. A fixed point for Pauline chronology is thus afforded, even though the precise dates of office are unknown. His brother Seneca writes of him (*Ep. Mor.* 104. 1: *Quaest.* 4a, pref. 11), as do several other ancient writers (*e.g.* Pliny, *NH* 21. 33; Tacitus, *Ann.* 15. 73; Dio Cassius, 61. 35; 62. 25), with little to his discredit. Luke depicts his vigorous refusal to hear a Jewish-sponsored prosecution of Paul, on the ground that no criminal charge was brought. The now proverbial 'Gallio cared for none of those things' (Acts 18:17, AV) denotes less his religious indifference than his connivance at the subsequent outburst of anti-Semitism. The Western text conveys the sense: 'Gallio pretended not to see'. Gallio was executed by Nero's order in AD 65. J.H.H.

GALLOWS (Heb. *'ēṣ*, 'tree'). Found only in the book of Esther (nine times). Haman had a gallows (AVmg. 'tree') made on which to execute Mordecai, but the mode of the intended execution has been much debated. Hanging was not usual in Persia, where the events took place; it is suggested that the Heb. word means 'pole' or 'stake' (which seems likely), and that, following Persian custom, the victim was to be impaled. (* CROSS.) J.D.D.

GAMALIEL (Heb. *gamlî'ēl*, 'reward of God'; Gk. *Gamaliēl*).
1. Son of Pedahzur, and a 'prince of the children of Manasseh' chosen to help Moses in taking the census in the wilderness (Nu. 1:10; 2:20; 7:54, 59; 10:23).

2. Son of Simon and grandson of Hillel (according to later, but doubtful, tradition), Gamaliel was

The Sea of Galilee from the SW. (RS)

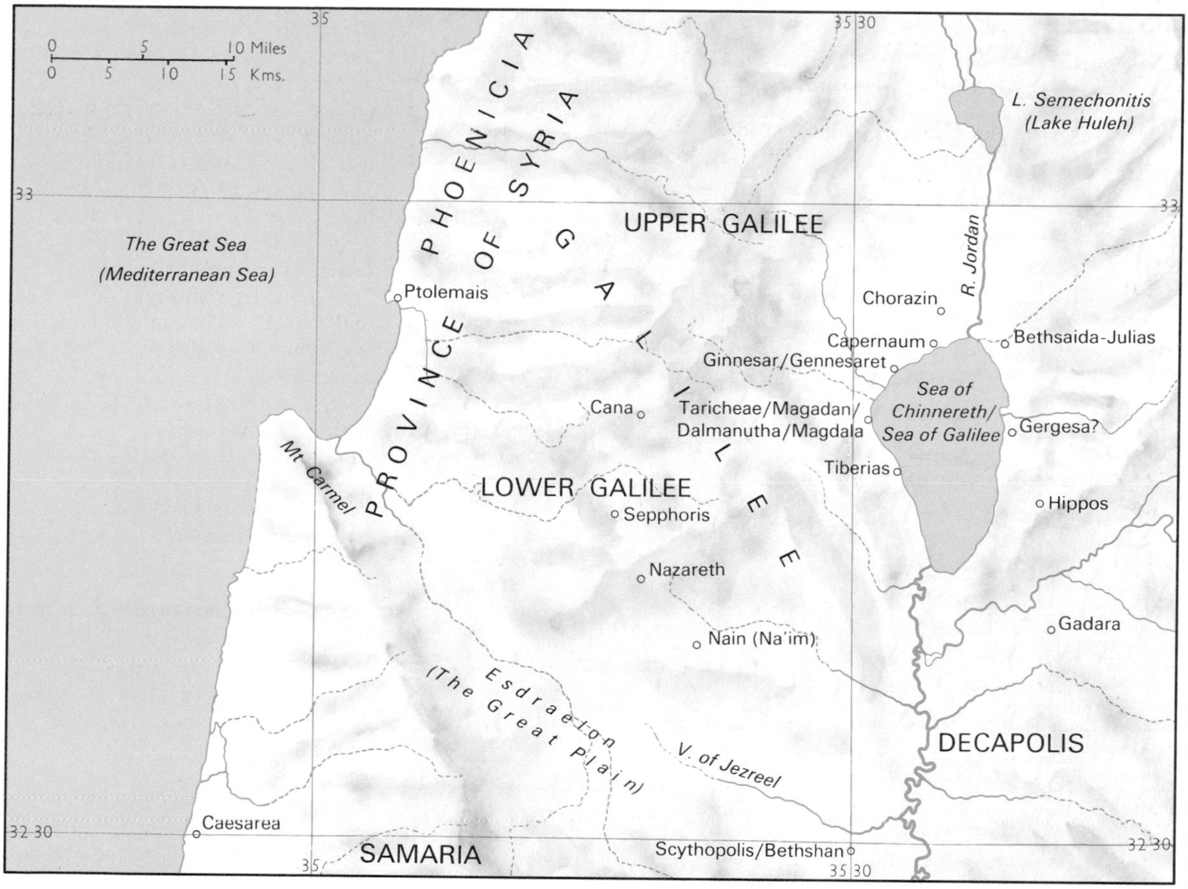

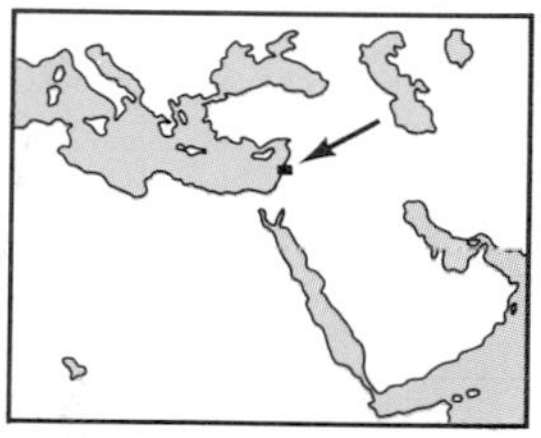

NT Galilee: the scene of Christ's childhood and early ministry.

a doctor of the law and a member of the Sanhedrin. Representing the liberal wing of the *Pharisees, the school of Hillel, as opposed to that of Shammai, he intervened with a reasoned and persuasive speech at the trial of the apostles (Acts 5:33–40).

Paul acknowledged him as his teacher (Acts 22:3), and he was held in such high honour that he was designated 'Rabban' ('our teacher'), a higher title than 'Rabbi' ('my teacher'). See J. Neusner, *The Rabbinic Traditions about the Pharisees before 70*, 1, 1971, pp. 341ff.

The Mishnah (*Soṭa* 9. 15) says, 'Since Rabban Gamaliel the Elder died there has been no more reverence for the Law, and purity and abstinence died out at the same time.' As we might expect from this reputation among the Jews, there is no evidence, despite early suggestions (*e.g. Clementine Recognitions* 1. 65), that he ever became a Christian. J.D.D.

Gall, colocynth (Citrullus colocynthis). *A gourd with bitter fruits found in the deserts of the Middle East.* (FNH)

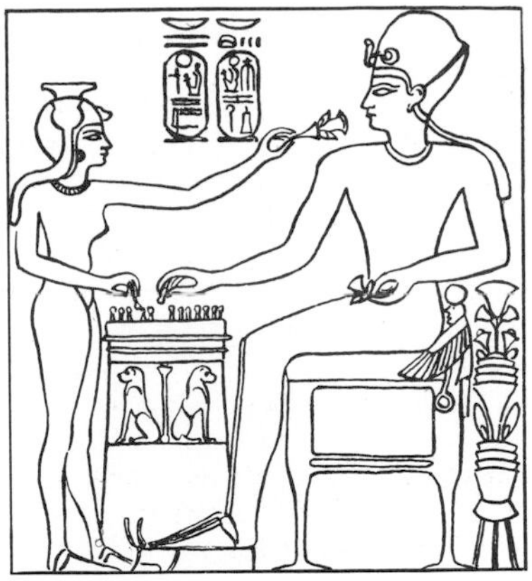

Rameses III plays draughts with one of the women of his harim. *Relief in the Gate Tower, temple of Medinet Habu (Thebes). c. 1180* BC.

Top right:
Children playing games, possibly with knuckle-bones and spinning-tops. Height 11·5 cm. Relief from Carchemish. c. early 8th cent. BC. (BM)

Toy hedgehog on wheels. Found in a grave near the temple of Inshushinak, Susa. Length 6 cm. 13th–12th cent. BC. (MC)

Inlaid game-board and playing-pieces from the royal graves at Ur. The precise nature of the game is disputed. Length of board 27 cm. 25th cent. BC. (DJW)

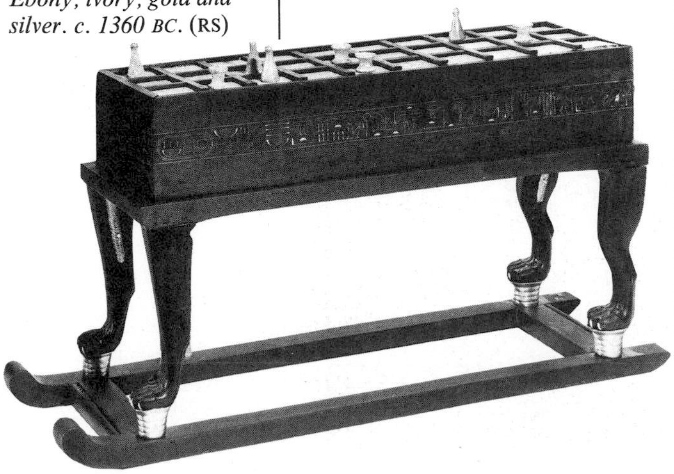

Bottom left:
Board for the game of senet, *from the tomb of Tutankhamun. The game was played with conical and spool-shaped pieces on a board divided into 30 squares. Moves were decided by casting knuckle-bones or dice. Ebony, ivory, gold and silver. c. 1360* BC. (RS)

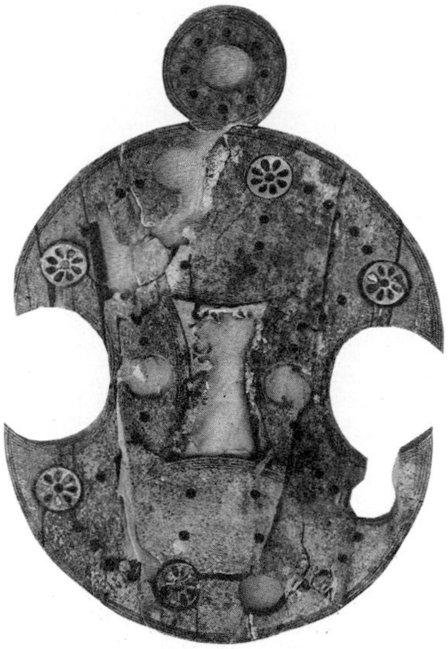

GAMES.

I. In the Old Testament

a. Physical sport

In common with their Near Eastern neighbours, the life of the majority of Hebrews left little time or inclination for physical sport. When introduced by Hellenizing Jews in the time of Antiochus Epiphanes (1 Macc. 1:10–14; Jos., *Ant.* 15. 268) and patronized by Jason, the high priest (2 Macc. 4:7–17), the Greek love of sport was considered irreligious. Nevertheless, there can be little doubt that, despite the absence of explicit references, running, throwing and hunting were undertaken on occasions when they were not a necessity. Like the Egyptians and Babylonians, the people of Palestine would have enjoyed contests at weight-lifting and wrestling. Jacob's long wrestling-match may reflect both practised ability at the sport and the recognition of rules precluding holds below the belt (Gn. 32:24–26). The expression 'hip and thigh' (Jdg. 15:8) may be a technical wrestling term, like English 'cross-buttock'. It has been suggested that the group combat at Gibeon was initiated as a wrestling-match (2 Sa. 2:14), wrestling by grasping an opponent's belt being an ancient form of this sport. Archery could be a game of skill aiming at fixed marks (1 Sa. 20:20; Jb. 16:12; La. 3:12), as is shown on Assyrian reliefs, as well as a warlike art.

b. Games of chance

Gaming-boards have been discovered at a number of sites, including Tell el 'Ajjul and Beth-shemesh. Some made of ivory (Megiddo, *c.* 1350–1150 BC), stone (Gezer, *c.* 1200 BC) or wood were in 'human' or 'violin' shape pierced with peg-holes for a game of '55 Holes' commonly found in Egypt and Mesopotamia. Draughts was played on boards of twenty or thirty squares made of stone, clay, ebony or ivory and sometimes hollowed at the back to contain the men. Unlike modern western methods of play in these games, moves were made as a result of the throw of a dice (of which an ivory example of the 17th century BC was found at Tell Beit Mirsim), knuckle-bones or casting-sticks. Pyramidal or conical game places and counters have been found, also 'halma' men at Lachish. 'Chinese-type' chess was known in Elam and Babylonia from the 3rd millennium BC and may well have been played in Palestine. Unusual board-games, like those discovered at *Ur, Nineveh and Tell Halaf, Syria (8th century), were played, though the method of play is at present obscure. The Hebrews, with their neighbours, considered that the lot (*pûr*; *DIVINATION) was a means of determining the divine will, and in this way some board-games also had religious significance.

c. Children's games

The young played in the streets (Zc. 8:5), imitating their elders in daily life or at marriages and funerals. The boys may have imitated the Egyptian team-games shown in paintings and a form of tug-of-war, while the girls practised juggling or ball-games, including catch played by teams with one mounted on another's back. Leather-covered balls have been found. Whistles, rattles, model pots, chariots and animals (some with wheels) have been recovered and betray an unchanging taste for toys by the youngest. It is unlikely that all the slings found were used only in the serious business of driving birds from the crops or guarding the flocks from straying. There is no evidence that the figurines or small statues with movable joints found at a number of sites were dolls. It is more likely that they were cult objects. People of all ages were amused by miming, skipping-ropes, whipped tops and hoops.

d. Diversion

Feasting, songs, music, and especially dancing, were the commonest form of relaxation. Opportunity was taken for this at every domestic rejoicing (Je. 31:4), including merry-making at harvest (Jdg. 9:27; 21:21) as well as at such public and state functions as the royal accession (1 Ki. 1:40) or celebration of victory (Ex. 15:20; Jdg. 11:34; 1 Sa. 18:6). Story-telling and the art of propounding riddles was also a highly-esteemed practice (Jdg. 14:12; Ezk. 17:2; 1 Ki. 10:1). (*DANCE.)

BIBLIOGRAPHY. H. J. C. Murray, *A History of Board Games other than Chess*, 1952; P. Montet, *Everyday Life in Egypt*, 1958; *Iraq* 1, 1935, pp. 45–50; 4, 1938, pp. 11ff.; 8, 1946, pp. 166ff.; *ANEP*, 1976, pp. 212–219 (illustrations); E. W. Heaton, *Everyday Life in OT Times*, 1956, pp. 91–92. D.J.W.

II. In the New Testament

Apart from one obscure reference to a children's game (Mt. 11:16–17), and a possible allusion to a chariot race (Phil. 3:13f.), the games mentioned in the NT are the

A Palestinian ivory board for the game of '55 Holes', inlaid with gold and blue paste. Length 27 cm. Megiddo. 1350–1150 BC. (OIUC)

Ivory game-pieces from Megiddo. Above: *a conical piece, knobbed at the apex, similar to modern* halma *men.* Below: *a circular disc with the face incised with ibex and a palm. 12th cent. BC.*

Marble statue-base showing an early ball-game played with sticks similar to those later used in hockey. Relief from Athens. Height 27·5 cm. c. 510–500 BC. (NAMA)

Opposite page: Animals playing chess. Part of a series of Egyptian satirical drawings on papyrus, in which animals take the place of human beings in scenes inspired by tomb-paintings. New Kingdom. (PAC)

GARDEN OF EDEN
See Eden, garden of, Part 1.

GARDEN TOMB
See Burial and mourning, NT, Part 1.

GAREB
See Ithrite, Part 2.

GARLAND
See Ornaments, Part 2.

GARLIC
See Vegetables, Part 3.

GARNET
See Jewels, Part 2.

GASHMU
See Geshem, Part 1.

GATE-POST
See Door-post, Part 1.

Assyrian relief depicting the royal garden with its pavilion, paths, water-channels, trees and shrubs. N palace of Ashurbanipal at Nineveh. 668–c. 627 BC. (DJW)

Greek athletic contests. Reference to 1 Macc. 1:10–14; 2 Macc. 4:13–14 will emphasize the Hellenic outlook of the writers who found metaphor in this worthy subject. The festivals were religious in origin and flavour, encouraged discipline, art, health and fair play, and were not without diplomatic usefulness (see Lysias, 33). Surviving odes of Pindar reveal the honour paid the victor in the Pythian, Nemean, Isthmian and above all the Olympic Games.

In the Epistles metaphors are drawn from the Games generally, and from the foot-race and from the chariot race in particular.

In 1 Cor. 9: 24–27 Paul calls attention to the vigorous training of the athlete (a metaphor also used by Epictetus). The athlete is preoccupied not with the immediate token prize of the wreath of wild olive, parsley, pine or laurel, but with the later reward. The Christian is likewise exhorted to strive 'for the mastery', for his reward is, by contrast, an 'incorruptible' crown (*cf.* 2 Tim. 2:5; 4:8; 1 Pet. 1:4; 5:4). 1 Cor. 9:26 depicts a boxing contest. Here the arms and hands were bound with studded leather, which inflicted grave injury, and the combatant therefore sought to evade rather than to parry—hence the phrase 'beating the air'. Having begun with the scene of victory, Paul concludes with a picture of failure. He sees himself as the herald calling others to the contest, but himself disqualified from competing. 'Preached' and 'castaway' (1 Cor. 9:27, AV) are unhappy renderings (see RV, RSV). Metaphors drawn from the Games would carry particular weight with the readers of this Epistle, since the Isthmian Games were a Corinthian festival.

In Gal. 2:2; 5:7; Phil. 2:16; Heb. 12:1–2 the reference is to the foot-race, for which a minimum of clothing was worn. 'Every weight' probably refers to weight shed in preparatory training in order to bring the runner to peak condition for the race. 'The sin which clings so closely' is more clearly a reference to clothing. The 'cloud' is a common metaphor for multitudes. It suggests the runner's blurred vision of the spectators as his eyes are focused on the goal.

The reference in Phil. 3:13–14 is probably to a chariot race. Horse-racing with light chariots was well known to the Greeks, and references go back to Homer and Sophocles. They were also a spectacular feature of the festivals. At the time Paul wrote, they were especially in fashion with the Romans, and Philippi was a Roman colony. We may translate these verses: 'I do not count myself to have done this, but this one thing I do, forgetting those things which are behind, and stretching out to those which lie before, I make for the mark, towards the prize of the upward calling of God in Jesus his Anointed.' Paul pictures himself in the chariot, bent over the curved rail against which the charioteer's knees were pressed, and, with the reins round his body, stretching out over the horses' backs and leaning his weight on the reins. In such intense preoccupation a glance at 'the things behind' would have been fatal. E.M.B.

GARDEN. It was promised that the lives of God's redeemed people would be like a watered garden, ordered and fruitful (Is. 58:11; Je. 31:12; *cf.* Nu. 24:6).

In Egypt the Hebrews had known richly productive vegetable-gardens (Dt. 11:10; *cf.* Nu 11:5; *Food). Fed from an irrigation-ditch, or from vessels by hand, a network of little earth channels criss-crossed the vegetable-beds like a chess-board. By merely breaching and resealing the wall of such a channel with the foot, water could be released on to the beds as needed.

In Palestine people cultivated gardens for vegetables ('garden of *herbs', 1 Ki. 21:2; 'what is sown', Is. 61:11), and fruit (Am. 9:14; Je. 29:5, 28; Ct. 4:16). Gardens might be associated with, or even part of, vineyards, olive-groves or orchards (Ec. 2:5; Am. 4:9; *cf.* 1 Ki. 21:2). Spices and choice plants featured in the gardens of royalty and of the nobility (Ct. 5:1; 6:2, 11 (walnuts); *cf.* 4:12–16 generally; Ec. 2:5). These and other gardens were walled round (*cf.* Ct. 4:12) and had to be kept watered, *e.g.* from a spring or pool (Ct. 4:15; *cf.* Ec. 2:5–6; contrast Is. 1:30). They may also have sometimes contained a summerhouse (2 Ki. 9:27). The 'king's garden' at Jerusalem was a well-known landmark (2 Ki. 25:4; Je. 39:4; 52:7; Ne. 3:15); and the Persian royal palace is mentioned as having a pleasure-garden (Est. 1:5; 7:7–8). Similarly, Egyptian and Mesopotamian kings kept fine gardens; and a garden once occupied a large court inside the sumptuous palace of the kings of Canaanite Ugarit (14th–13th century BC). For full references to gardens in Assyria and Babylonia and the many trees and plants they contained, see in Ebeling, Meissner and Weidner, *Reallexikon der Assyriologie*, 3, 1959, pp. 147–150.

Tombs were sometimes situated in gardens (2 Ki. 21:18, 26; Jn. 18:1, 26; 19:41; *Gethsemane). A less happy use of gardens was for pagan rites, perhaps linked with the fertility cults of Canaan (Is. 1:29; 65:3; 66:17).

The Garden of *Eden was a symbol of God-created fertility (Gn. 13:10; Is. 51:3, *etc.*). K.A.K.

GATH. One of the five principal Philistine cities, and formerly occupied by the Anakim (*Anak; Jos. 11:22). The gentilic from the name *gaṯ* was *gittî* or *gittîm* (Jos. 13:3), and this accounts for the 'Gittite' of the EVV. When the Philistines captured the ark and it brought ill fortune to Ashdod it was moved to Gath, where the people were struck with bubonic plague, so it was moved on to Ekron (1 Sa. 5:6–10; 6:17). Gath was famous as the home of *Goliath (1 Sa. 17), whom David killed. David later feigned madness to avoid retribution at the hands of Achish, king of Gath, when fleeing from Saul (1 Sa. 21:10–15), but subsequently took service under Achish, and lived for more than a year in his territory (1 Sa. 27). When David's fortunes revived, and later during Absalom's rebellion, after he had added Gath to his dominions (1 Ch. 18:1), he had Gittite friends in his retinue (2 Sa. 6:10–11; 15:19–21; 18:2) and a Gittite contingent among his mercenaries (2 Sa. 15:18). Another interesting Gittite is mentioned in 2 Sa. 21:20 (= 1 Ch. 20:6). He was

An ornamental pond surrounded by trees on an estate in Egypt. Painting from the tomb of Nebamun at Thebes. c. 1400 BC. (BM)

Egyptian gardener drawing water. Wall-painting from the tomb of Ipui at Thebes. Height 30 cm. Rameses II. 1301–1234 BC. (Met NY)

very tall and had six digits on each extremity. Though Achish is still spoken of as king of Gath (1 Ki. 2:39–41), the city was probably subservient to David, and evidently continued subject to Judah in the time of Rehoboam, who fortified it (2 Ch. 11:8). It was captured by Hazael of Damascus in the late 9th century (2 Ki. 12:17), and may have regained its independence by the time Uzziah broke down its wall when he campaigned in Philistia (2 Ch. 26:6); soon afterwards Amos describes it as belonging to the Philistines (6:2), so it may have been a Philistine enclave, in loose vassalage, in the territory of Judah. Gath was besieged and conquered by Sargon of Assyria in the late 8th century.

The site has not been identified with certainty. Excavations at Tell el-ʻAreini some 30 km NE of Gaza failed to support its candidature. Tell esh-Sheriʻah and Tell eṣ-Ṣafi are other possibilities. So too is the adjacent Tell en Nagila or ʻAraq el-Menshîyeh, but certainty must await further investigation.

BIBLIOGRAPHY. E. K. Vogel, *HUCA* 42, 1971, p. 88; K. A. Kitchen, *POTT*, pp. 62ff.; *EAEHL*, 1, pp. 89–97; 3, pp. 894–898; G. E. Wright, *BA* 29, 1966, pp. 78–86; *LOB*, p. 250. T.C.M.

GATH-HEPHER (Heb. *gaṯ-haḥēp̄er*, 'winepress of digging'). The rendering Gittah-hepher of Jos. 19:13 in the AV arose through a misunderstanding of the *he locale*. A town on the border of Zebulon and Naphtali (Jos. 19:13), the birthplace of the prophet Jonah (2 Ki. 14:25). Identified with Khirbet ez-Zurraʻ and nearby el-Meshhed, 5 km NE of Nazareth. Ancient and continuous tradition indicated this as the birthplace and tomb of the prophet. Jerome in the 4th century AD said that his tomb was about 3 km from Sepphoris, which would coincide with Gath-hepher.

M.A.M.

GATH-RIMMON See Trees (Pomegranate), Part 3.

GAULANITIS See Golan, Part 1.

GAZA (Heb. *ʻazzâ*, LXX *Gaza*). One of the five principal Philistine cities. Originally inhabited by the Avvim, driven out by the Caphtorim (*CAPHTOR; Dt. 2:23), it was considered to mark the S limit of Canaan at the point on the coast where it was situated (Gn. 10:19). Joshua conquered it (Jos. 10:41) and found that some Anakim re-

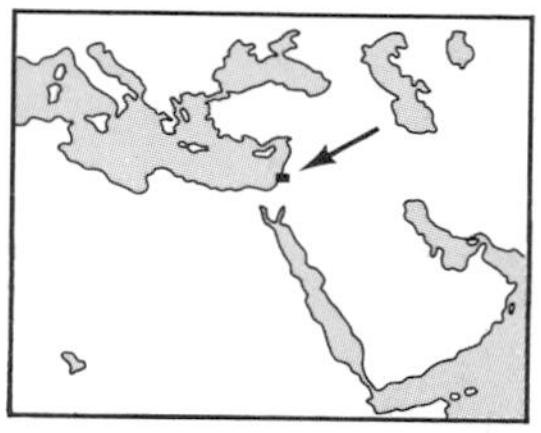

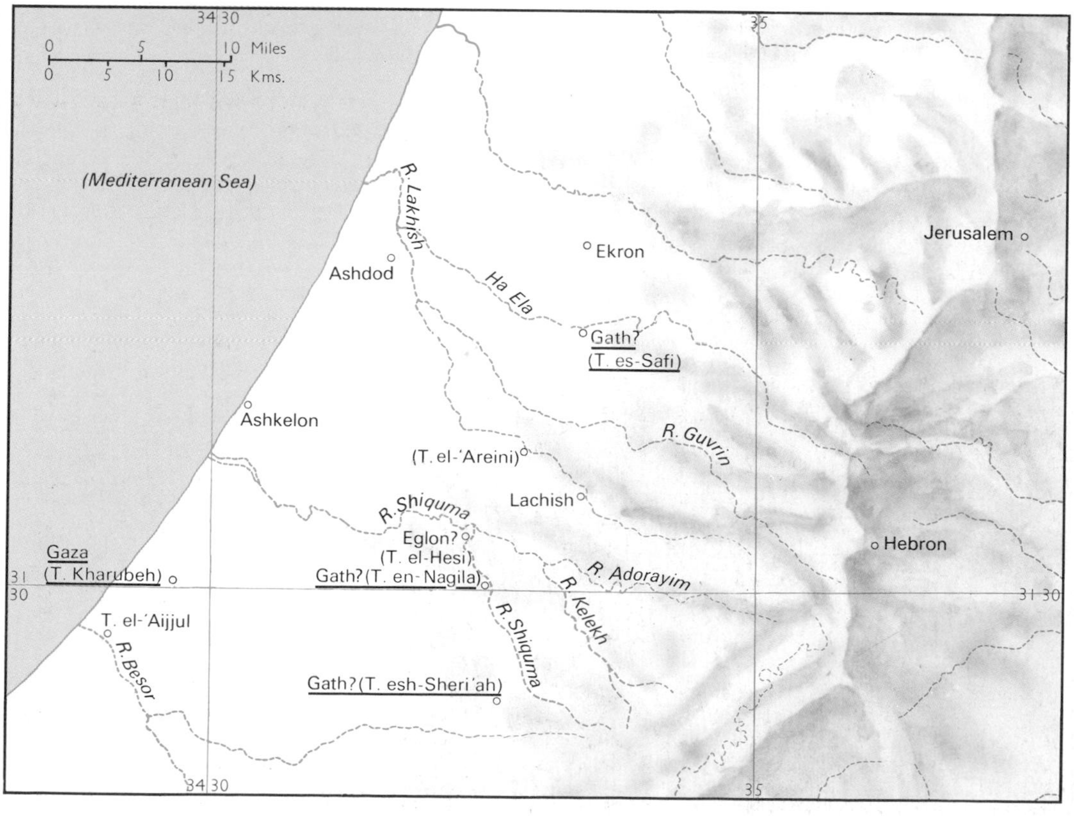

Proposed locations for Gath and Gaza, two of the five principal Philistine cities.

Drawing of relief from the palace of Sargon II, possibly representing the Assyrian attack on Gaza in c. 721 BC, when Sargon set up his royal image there. Khorsabad. 721–705 BC.

mained there (Jos. 11:21–22); the city was lost to Israel during his lifetime (Jos. 13:3). Judah, to whom it was allotted (Jos. 15:47), recaptured the town (Jdg. 1:18; though some hold that this refers to the same campaign as Jos. 10:41). In the period of the Judges Samson consorted with a harlot of Gaza in connection with which a description of the city gate is given (Jdg. 16:1–3). Israel's hold over Gaza must have been lost again at this period, for when the Philistines finally captured Samson they imprisoned him there, and it was there that he 'made sport' for them, and dislodged the pillars of the house, killing many of them (Jdg. 16:21–31). It has been pointed out that the description of Samson 'making sport' in front of a pillared building with spectators on the roof is reminiscent of some of the features of Cretan civilization, and this is to be expected in view of the origins of the *Philistines. At the time of the Philistine capture of the ark, Gaza with the other cities suffered from bubonic plague and made an offering of an emerod and a mouse of gold to avert it (1 Sa. 6:17).

The city occupied an important position on the trade routes from Egypt to W Asia, and from the 8th century it is frequently mentioned among Assyr. conquests. Tiglath-pileser III captured it (*Ḫa-az-zu-tu*) in 734 BC, perhaps at the request of Jehoahaz of Judah, the ruler, Hanno, fleeing to Egypt, and Tiglath-pileser set up an image of himself in the palace. Sargon had to repeat the action in 722 BC, for Hanno had returned to Gaza in support of a rebellion led by Hamath. Hanno was taken prisoner to Assyria. The city remained faithful to Assyria, for Sennacherib, when he proceeded against Hezekiah in Jerusalem, gave some of the territory taken from Judah to Ṣillibel, king of Gaza, and Esarhaddon put a strain on this loyalty when he laid heavy tribute on him and twenty other kings of the Hittite country. In the time of Jeremiah the city was captured by Egypt (Je. 47:1). Gaza was taken by Alexander the Great in 332 BC after a 5-month siege, and finally desolated—as prophesied by Amos (1:6–7), Zephaniah (2:4) and Zechariah (9:5)—by Alexander Jannaeus in 96 BC.

The site of ancient Gaza, Tell Kharubeh (Ḥarube), lies in the modern city. Small excavations showed that it was occupied in the Late Bronze and Iron Ages, and pieces of Philistine pottery were found. Various remains show the importance of the place in Hellenistic and Roman times. Gabinius, the proconsul, rebuilt it in 57 BC on a new site to the S of the old, nearer the sea. It was presumably to distinguish the old abandoned site from this that the angel, who wanted Philip to go to the old site, qualified the name Gaza with the phrase 'this is a desert road' (*hautē estin erēmos*, Acts 8:26).

At Tell el-'Aijjul, 6 km SW, Flinders Petrie found extensive cemeteries and a town that flourished during the 2nd millennium BC. Numerous pieces of gold jewellery were discovered in tombs and buildings of *c.* 1400 BC. Nearby later burials have been uncovered containing so-called *Philistine clay-coffins.

BIBLIOGRAPHY. J. Garstang, *Joshua–Judges*, 1931, pp. 375f.; *EAEHL*, 1, pp. 52–61; 2, pp. 408–417.

T.C.M.
A.R.M.

GAZARA
See Gezer, Part 1.

GAZELLE
See Animals, Part 1.

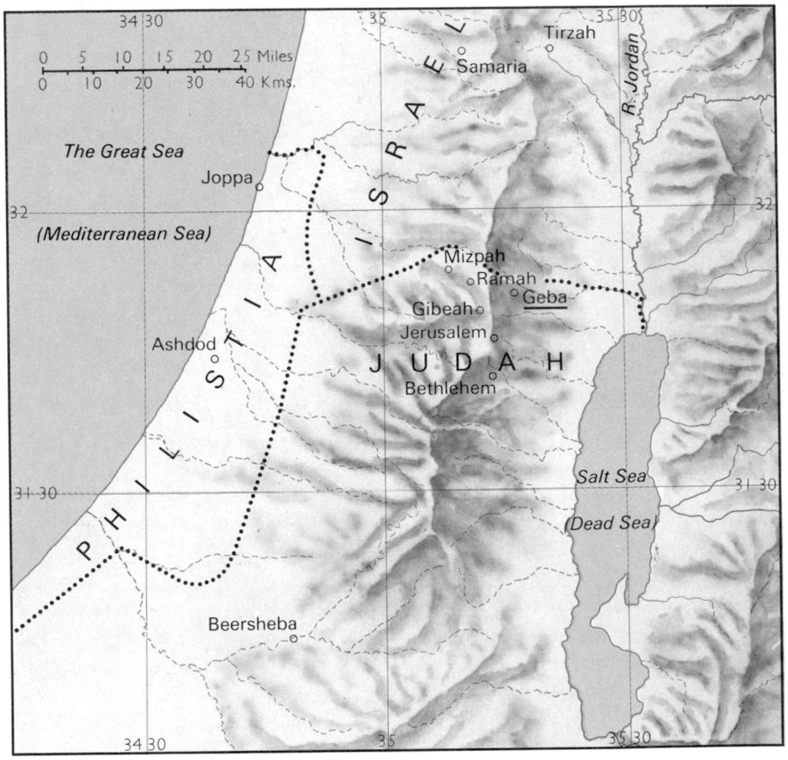

Geba, a town of Benjamin. After fortification by King Asa it was regarded as the N limit of Judah.

GEBA (Heb. *geḇa'*, 'a hill'). A town belonging to Benjamin, 11 km N of Jerusalem and 5 km from Gibeah, from which it is to be distinguished; *cf.* Jos 18:24 and 28; Is. 10:29. It was assigned to the Levites under

Joshua (Jos. 21:17; 1 Ch. 6:60). It was in the descent from here that Jonathan and his armour-bearer revealed themselves to the Philistines during their daring attack (1 Sa. 14:1ff.). In the days of Asa, king of Judah, it was fortified, and then regarded as the N limit of Judah; it replaced the name of Dan in the saying 'from Dan to Beersheba' (2 Ki. 23:8). It remained prominent after the Exile (Ne. 11:31; 12:29). The modern town of Jeba stands on the same site. M.A.M.

GEBAL. 1. A Canaanite and Phoenician port whose ruins lie at Jebeil, 40 km N of Beirut. Its name, W Semitic *g^{e}ḇal*, Akkad. *gubla*, Egyp. *kpn*, means 'hill, bluff'. The Gk. name Byblos may involve a phonetic shift *g-b*, or imply that it was the place where Greeks first saw papyrus (Gk. *byblos*) imported from Egypt as writing material.

Excavations, begun in 1919 by M. Dunand, have revealed a city that flourished from Neolithic times to the Crusades. By the mid-3rd millennium BC it was a centre for exporting cedar wood to Egypt, receiving Egyp. luxury goods in exchange. Strong stone ramparts guarded the city. Inside were temples, houses and tombs. At the end of the 3rd millennium it was sacked, but soon recovered. One temple was devoted to the city's patron goddess (Baalat Gebal), another was a memorial shrine filled with obelisks commemorating the dead, originally probably plastered and inscribed. Dozens of jars containing bronze weapons, jewellery and figures of gods were buried around the temples as offerings. Tombs of Byblian kings were furnished with Egyptian and stone vessels of about 1800 BC. From this time scribes at Byblos, trained to write in Egyptian, seem to have invented a simpler script, the Byblos hieroglyphic, a syllabary of about eighty signs known from texts engraved on stone slabs and copper plates. It may have been here that the alphabet arose (*WRITING). Certainly it was used here fully developed by about 1000 BC, the date of the stone coffin of King Ahiram which bears the longest early alphabetic inscription. Other texts from *c.* 900 BC show continuing links with Egypt. Byblos declined as the power of Tyre and Sidon grew.

Jos. 13:5 includes Gebal as part of the Promised Land then unconquered, and in fact Israel never ruled it. Solomon hired masons there (1 Ki. 5:18), and its skilled shipbuilders are mentioned in Ezk. 27:9. The Egyptian story of Wenamun describes the city about 1100 BC (*ANET*, pp. 25–29).

2. A mountain region in Transjordan whose inhabitants allied with Israel's other neighbours against her (Ps. 83:7).

BIBLIOGRAPHY. M. Dunand, *Fouilles de Byblos*, 1937– ; N. Jidejian, *Byblos through the Ages*, 1968. A.R.M.

GEBER. An Israelite prince, the son of Uri, who is mentioned, in what is perhaps a historical note to the list of Solomon's administrative districts, as the prefect of the whole of Transjordan ('the land of Gilead'; 1 Ki. 4:19) before Solomon divided it between his 6th and 7th districts, over the former of which he set Ben-geber (1 Ki. 4:13), possibly Geber's son.

BIBLIOGRAPHY. T. N. D. Mettinger, *Solomonic State Officials*, 1971, pp. 121–122. T.C.M.

GEDALIAH (Heb. *g^{e}ḏalyâ* or *g^{e}ḏalyāhû*, 'Yahweh is great'). **1.** Son of Ahikam, grandson of Shaphan, he was appointed chief minister and governor of Judah by Nebuchadrezzar II in 587 BC (2 Ki. 25:22). With Jeremiah the prophet he was entrusted with the care of some royal princesses and those persons remaining after the Babylonian war (Je. 41:16; 43:6). He made Mizpah his residence, and there he was joined by Jeremiah (40:6) and by many officers and men who had escaped from the enemy. These were granted asylum on condition that they maintained the peace (Je. 40:7–12). However, Baalis, king of Ammon, plotted against him and provoked a refugee officer, Ishmael, to assassinate Gedaliah (2 Ki. 25:25; Je. 41:1–3). Fear of possible Babylonian reprisals led more Jews to emigrate to Egypt, despite Jeremiah's warning (Je. 42). The Jewish fast on the third of Tishri commemorates the death of Gedaliah (Zc. 7:5; 8:19). A seal impression inscribed 'Belonging to Gedaliah who is over the House' found at Lachish almost certainly refers to this person.

2. Son of Jeduthun, instrumentalist leader of the levitical choir (1 Ch. 25:3, 9). **3.** A priest married to a foreign woman in the time of Ezra (Ezr. 10:18). **4.** Son of Pashhur, a leading citizen of Jerusalem and opponent of Jeremiah (Je. 38:1, 4–6). **5.** Grandfather of the prophet Zephaniah and grandson of Hezekiah (Zp. 1:1). D.J.W.

GEDER. S Canaanite town (Jos. 12:13). LXX (B) reads *asei*, and other minuscules suggest 's' as second letter; *Goshen* may be the correct reading. Y. Aharoni, *LOB*, pp. 209–210, suggests Gerar. J.D.D.

GEDERAH (Heb. *g^{e}ḏērâh*). **1.** In the Shephelah, Jos. 15:36; probably Kh. Judraya (M. Noth, *Josua, ad loc.*) on the N side of the Vale of Elah, opposite Soco. Kh. Jedireh, W of Latrun (L. Grollenberg), does not suit the context. **2.** The 'Potteries' of the Monarchy, 1 Ch. 4:23 (AV 'hedges'); perhaps Tell ej-Judeideh N of the Mareshah valley

Stone sarcophagus of King Ahiram of Byblos (Gebal). He is seated on a throne before a table of offerings, approached by attendants. Length 2·30 m. 13th cent. BC. (NMBL)

Top right: Excavated buildings at Byblos, ancient Gebal. (ARM)

GECKO
See Animals, Part 1.

Scarab-shaped seal impression, inscribed Igdlyh 'šr 'l hbyt, *'belonging to Gedaliah who is over the house'. This may well be the Gedaliah who was made governor of Judah by the Babylonians in 587* BC *(2 Ki. 25:22). Lachish. 6th cent.* BC. (RM)

■ GEMATRIA
See Number, Part 2.

(W. F. Albright, *JPOS* 5, 1925, pp. 50ff.), where a large quantity of stamped jar-handles has been found. **3.** In Benjamin, 1 Ch. 12:4; possibly Judeira, NE of Gibeon, or Kh. Judeira, 10 km farther W.

J.P.U.L.

GEDEROTH (Heb. g^e*ḏērôṯ*). A town in the Lachish district of Judah, Jos. 15:41; 2 Ch. 28:18. The area of Qatra and modern Gedera, SE of Jabneel (F.-M. Abel, L. Grollenberg) is too far W and out of context (*GTT*, p. 147; M. Noth, *Josua*², p. 95).

J.P.U.L.

GEDEROTHAIM (Heb. g^e*ḏērōṯaim*). May be a variant of *Gederah, Jos. 15:36; the count is correct without it; LXX ('its pen-folds') read *giḏrōṯêhâh*.

J.P.U.L.

GEDOR (Heb. g^e*ḏôr*). **1.** A town in the hills of Judah (Jos. 15:58, and perhaps 1 Ch. 4:4); Kh. Jedur, 2 km W of Beit Ummar and just off the central ridge; possibly the Beth-gader of 1 Ch. 2:51 (*GTT*, p. 155). **2.** In the Negeb, near Soco and Zanoah. The 'entrance of Gedor' (1 Ch. 4:39) may be the Nahal Hevron, though LXX has 'Gerar' (*LOB*, p. 337), while the context may indicate an area further SE. **3.** In Benjamin, 1 Ch. 12:7; perhaps *Gederah **(3). 4.** A personal Benjaminite name, 1 Ch. 8:31 = 9:37.

J.P.U.L.

GEHAZI. The servant of Elisha. He may be the unnamed 'servitor' of 2 Ki. 4:43 and the 'servant' of 2 Ki. 6:15, but he is specifically named on only three occasions.

In 2 Ki. 4 he suggests to Elisha that the Shunammite should be rewarded with the promise of a son, and later takes Elisha's staff and lays it upon the dead child in the vain hope of restoring his life.

In 2 Ki. 5, after Elisha has refused to take a present from Naaman when his leprosy had been cured, Gehazi obtains gifts for himself under false pretences. As a punishment he himself is struck down with leprosy. 2 Ki. 5:27 should be compared with the leprosy regulations of Lv. 13:12–13. When this particular form of skin disease, whatever it may have been, turned the whole skin white, the victim was 'clean', and was not segregated. Hence Gehazi was able to continue as Elisha's servant.

In 2 Ki. 8:1–6 Gehazi relates to King Jehoram the story of how the Shunammite's son was restored to life. While he is talking the woman herself comes in to appeal to the king for the restoration of her property.

J.S.W.

GELILOTH. Perhaps means 'circuit, circle' (of stones), *cf.* *Gilgal. Only named in Jos. 18:17, as on the border of Judah and Benjamin, in terms almost identical with those used of Gilgal (Jos. 15:7). As Geliloth and Gilgal have more or less the same meaning, both derived from Heb. *gālal*, 'to roll', they may be variant-names for one and the same place. J. Simons, *GTT*, p. 173, § 326, thinks of Geliloth as a small region near Jericho. Y. Aharoni, *LOB*, p. 235, sought it near Tal'at ed-Damm, S of the Wadi Qilt.

K.A.K.

GENEALOGY.

I. In the Old Testament

a. General

A genealogy in the OT sense is a list of names indicating the ancestors or descendants of an individual or individuals, or simply a registration of the names of people concerned in some situation. The word 'genealogy' in EVV renders Heb. *yaḥaś*, which occurs only in Ne. 7:5, *sēp̄er hayyaḥaś*, 'book of the genealogy', referring to a register of those who returned to Jerusalem with Sheshbazzar. Clearly 'genealogy' here is not used so strictly as in modern English where it is an account of descent from an ancestor by the enumeration of intermediate persons, though this is frequently what is intended. The genealogies of OT are found chiefly in the Pentateuch, and in Ezra–Nehemiah and Chronicles, and it is exclusively in the latter three books that the verbal form of *yaḥaś* occurs, always in the intensive reflexive stem (*hiṯyaḥēś*), 'enrol oneself by genealogy' (Ezr. 2:62; 8:1, 3; Ne. 7:5, 64; 1 Ch. 4:33; 5:1, 7, 17; 7:5, 7, 9, 40; 9:1, 22; 2 Ch. 12:15; 31:16–19). The term *tôlēḏôṯ*, 'generations', is used in Genesis more or less in the sense of 'genealogical history' (*GENERATION).

(i) *Types of genealogies.* The genealogies given in the scriptural record range from a bare list of names as in 1 Ch. 1:1, through the most common type which links the names by means of a standard formula and inserts additional information under some but not all (*e.g.* Gn. 5 and *cf.* v. 24), to the fully expanded historical account which is based on a framework of names, as in the books of Kings.

Genealogies of two forms are found in the OT. 'Ascending' genealogies commonly have a linking formula, '*x* the son (*bēn*) of *y*' (1 Ch. 6:33–43; Ezr. 7:1–5); 'descending' genealogies often have '*x* begat (*yālaḏ*) *y*' (Gn. 5; Ru. 4:18–23; RSV translates 'became the father of'). The descending type of genealogy may include much information as to the age and actions of the individual links, whereas the ascending type is more commonly used to trace the ancestry of an individual back to some important figure of the past, when the doings of the intermediate figures do not affect the issue.

(ii) *Genealogies as sources for chronology.* That some genealogies in the Bible omit some generations is demonstrable (compare Mt. 1:1 with 1:2–17). For instance, the list of Aaron's descendants in Ezr. 7:1–5 omits six names which are given in 1 Ch. 6:3–14. (See also *CHRONOLOGY OF THE OLD TESTAMENT, **III.***a*.) This is readily understandable from the formulae, for the word *bēn* could mean not only son but also 'grandson' and 'descendant', and in like manner it is probable that the verb *yālaḏ* could mean not only 'bear' in the immediate physical sense but also 'become the ancestor of' (the noun *yeleḏ* from this verb has the meaning of descendant in Is. 29:23). Factors such as the inclusion of the age of each member at the birth of his descendant and the number of years he lived after this (Gn. 5:6), need not militate against an interpretation of these genealogies as being abridgments. As Green and Warfield have suggested, the purpose of mentioning the years of age may have been to emphasize the mortality in spite of vigorous longevity of these Patriarchs, thus bearing out one result of the Fall.

(iii) *Ancient Near Eastern usage.* Genealogies were a standard feature of ancient historical tradition. Naturally, royal family trees furnish our principal examples, but records of lawsuits over land ownership show that many other people maintained such knowledge. Assyrian scribes of the 1st millennium BC listed kings of Assyria from remote times, with a line almost unbroken spanning 1,000 years (*ANET*[3], pp. 564–566). The relationship of one to another was noted, and the length of reign of each. Heading the list are the names of 'seventeen kings who lived in tents'; long considered legendary, personifications of tribes, or fictitious, they now seem to have an historical basis with the discovery at *Ebla of a treaty naming the first of them. From the 17th century BC survives a list of kings of Babylon, their ancestors and predecessors, sharing some names with the early part of the Assyrian King List. Earlier still is the Sumerian King List, completed about 1800 BC, which names kings of S Babylonia reaching back to the Flood, and before (*ANET*, pp. 265–266). Hittite, Ugaritic and Egyptian scribes have also left us king lists of varying lengths and purposes.

Some of the particular characteristics of biblical genealogies may also be observed in the texts. The lists of names are interspersed with historical or personal notes, comparable with those in Gn. 4:21, 23; 36:24; 1 Ch. 5:9–10, *etc.* The Sumerian King List has one Meskiaga-nuna, king of Ur, as son of Mes-ane-pada, but contemporary records suggest he was in fact the grandson of Mes-ane-pada, his father being one A-ane-pada. Either a scribe has omitted the father's name by error because it was so like the grandfather's, or 'son' is used in a wider sense than in English. The wider usage was common in Babylonian, as in all Semitic languages, for 'member of a specific group', and from 1500 BC onwards, *māru* ('son') was used in the sense 'descendant of'. An interesting case is found in the Black Obelisk of Shalmaneser III which refers to *Jehu as 'son (*mār*) of Omri' when in fact he was not related, but simply ruled the same state. A remarkable Egyptian example is a brief text in which King Tirhakah (*c.* 670 BC) honours his 'father' Sesostris III (*c.* 1870 BC) who lived some 1200 years before him. Similarly, King Abdul Aziz of Saudi Arabia was called Ibn (son of) Saud, though he was really the son of Abd-erRahman, and the Saud whose name he bore died in 1724. The use of relationship words, of family and dynastic names, and many other factors have to be borne in mind when interpreting any ancient genealogies.

There is thus no reason to suppose that all the genealogies in the Bible purport to be complete, since their purpose was more the establishment of descent from some particular ancestor or ancestors, a purpose unaffected by the omission of names, than the reckoning of exact chronologies (*CHRONOLOGY). It is wrong, too, to dismiss any part of them as legendary, personifications of tribes or deities, or pure fiction in the light of growing evidence that other similar records have factual bases.

b. Old Testament genealogies

The principal genealogical lists of the OT are:

(i) Adam to Noah (Gn. 5; 1 Ch. 1:1–4). Ten names, each given in the formula 'A lived *x* years and begat (*yālaḏ*) B, and A lived after he begat B *y* years and begat sons and daughters, and all the days of A were *z* years, and he died'. The figures for *x* and *y* vary to some extent between the *MT*, the Samaritan Pentateuch (SP) and the LXX, though there is a considerable measure of agreement in the totals (*z*), as follows: Adam, 930; Seth, 912; Enos, 905; Cainan, 910; Mahalaleel, 895; Jared, 962 (*MT*, LXX), 847 (SP); Enoch, 365; Methuselah, 969 (*MT*, LXX), 720 (SP); Lamech, 777 (*MT*), 635 (SP), 753 (LXX); Noah's age at the Flood, 600. It is probable that this list is abridged, so that it cannot safely be used as a basis for *chronology. Reminiscent of this genealogy is the first part of the Sumerian King List, which names ten 'great men' who ruled before the Flood. The years of reign for these range in one recension as high as 43,200.

(ii) The descendants of Cain (Gn. 4:17–22).

(iii) The descendants of Noah (Gn. 10; 1 Ch. 1:1–23). The list of the nations who were descended from Shem, Ham and Japheth (*NATIONS, TABLE OF).

(iv) Shem to Abraham (Gn. 11:10–26; 1 Ch. 1:24–27). Ten names. A genealogy couched in the same terms as (i) above, except that, while the Samaritan Pentateuch gives the total years (*z*), *MT* and LXX give only the figures *x* and *y*. The totals given by the Samaritan Pentateuch and worked out for *MT* and LXX are as follows, the *MT* and Samaritan Pentateuch agreeing in most cases against the LXX. Shem, 600; Arpachshad, 438 (*MT*, SP), 565 (LXX); LXX here inserts Kainan, 460, omitted in *MT* and SP; Shelah, 433 (*MT*, SP), 460 (LXX); Eber, 464 (*MT*), 404 (SP), 504 (LXX); Peleg, 239 (*MT*, SP), 339 (LXX); Reu, 239 (*MT*, SP), 339 (LXX); Serug, 230 (*MT*, SP), 330 (LXX); Nahor, 148 (*MT*, SP), 208 (LXX); Terah, 205 (*MT*, LXX), 145 (SP); Abraham.

(v) The descendants of Abraham by Keturah (Gn. 25:1–4; 1 Ch. 1:32–33). (*ARABIA.)

(vi) The descendants of Nahor (Gn. 22:20–24).

(vii) The descendants of Lot (Gn. 19:37–38).

(viii) The descendants of Ishmael (Gn. 25:12–18; 1 Ch. 1:29–31).

(ix) The descendants of Esau (Gn. 36; 1 Ch. 1:35–54).

(x) The descendants of Israel (Jacob; Gn. 46), 1–6 by Leah; 7–8 by Bilhah; 9–10 by Zilpah; and 11–12 by Rachel.

1. Reuben (Gn. 46:9; Ex. 6:14; Nu. 26:5–11; 1 Ch. 5:1–10).

2. Simeon (Gn. 46:10; Ex. 6:15;

Sumerian clay prism, including the names of the ten kings 'who ruled before the flood'. The last survived the ordeal when 'after the flood had swept over kingship was sent down (again) from heaven'. Kish. 1800 BC. (AMO)

Nu. 26:12–14; 1 Ch. 4:24–43).

3. Levi (Gn. 46:11; Ex. 6:16–26; 1 Ch. 6:1–53). This was an important genealogy, since the hereditary priesthood resided in this lineage and the high priests were descended from Aaron, whose own genealogy is given in condensed form in Ex. 6:16–22. The descent of Samuel from Levi is given in 1 Ch. 6 and that of Ezra from Aaron in Ezr. 7:1–5. See also (xi) below.

4. Judah (Gn. 46:12; Nu. 26:19–22; 1 Ch. 2:3–4:22; 9:4). This was the lineage of David (1 Ch. 2–3), from whom the line of kings from Solomon to Josiah was descended (1 Ch. 3:10–15).

5. Issachar (Gn. 46:13; Nu. 26:23–25; 1 Ch. 7:1–5).

6. Zebulun (Gn. 46:14; Nu. 26:26–27).

7. Dan (Gn. 46:23; Nu. 26:42–43).

8. Naphtali (Gn. 46:24; Nu. 26:48–50; 1 Ch. 7:13).

9. Gad (Gn. 46:16; Nu. 26:15–18; 1 Ch. 5:11–17).

10. Asher (Gn. 46:17; Nu. 26:44–47; 1 Ch. 7:30–40).

11. Joseph (Gn. 46:20; Nu. 26:28–37; 1 Ch. 7:14–27), through his two sons, Ephraim and Manasseh, who were accepted by Jacob as equivalent to his own sons (Gn. 48:5, 12; *ADOPTION).

12. Benjamin (Gn. 46:21; Nu. 26:38–41; 1 Ch. 7:6–12; 8:1–40; 9:7, 35–44). This was the lineage of Saul (1 Ch. 8–9).

In addition to these lists, which establish genealogical relationships, there are a number of other registers of individuals in one context or another, mentioned in connection with certain periods of OT history.

(xi) Registers of Levites (see also (x) 3 above). Of the time of David (1 Ch. 15:5–24), Jehoshaphat (2 Ch. 17:8), Hezekiah (2 Ch. 29:12–14; 31:12–17), Josiah (2 Ch. 34:8–13; 35:8–9), Zerubbabel and Joiakim (Ne. 12:1–24), Nehemiah (Ne. 10:2–13).

(xii) Registers of the reign of David. His recruits at Ziklag (1 Ch. 12:3–13, 20), his mighty men (2 Sa. 23:8–39; 1 Ch. 11:11–47), his officers over the tribes (1 Ch. 27:16–22) and his other administrative officers (1 Ch. 27:25–31).

(xiii) Registers of families and individuals of the time of the return and the labours of Ezra and Nehemiah. Those who returned with Zerubbabel (Ne. 7:7–63; Ezr. 2:2–61), those who returned with Ezra (Ezr. 8:2–14), the builders of the wall of Jerusalem (Ne. 3:1–32), those who had foreign wives (Ezr. 10:18–43), those who signed the covenant (Ne. 10:1–27), those resident in Jerusalem (Ne. 11:4–19; 1 Ch. 9:3–17).

II. In the New Testament

There are two genealogies in the NT (Mt. 1:1–17; Lk. 3:23–38), both of which give the human ancestry of Jesus the Messiah (*GENEALOGY OF JESUS CHRIST).

Apart from the word *genesis* in Mt. 1:1, which is rendered 'genealogy' by RSV, the EVV translate the term *genealogia* thus in 1 Tim. 1:4 and Tit. 3:9. The corresponding verb, *genealogeō*, 'to trace ancestry', occurs in Heb. 7:6 in reference to Melchizedek, who did not count his ancestry from Levi. In the passages in Timothy and Titus the word 'genealogies' is used in a depreciatory sense, in Timothy in conjunction with the word *mythos*, 'fable', and in Titus together with 'foolish questions'. It is possible that in speaking of these Paul had in mind either the sort of mythical histories based on the OT which are found in Jewish apocryphal books such as the book of *Jubilees*, or else the family-trees of aeons found in Gnostic literature. They obviously do not refer to the genealogies of the OT.

BIBLIOGRAPHY. E. L. Curtis, *HDB*, 2, pp. 121–137; P. W. Crannel, *ISBE*, 2, pp. 1183–1196; W. H. Green, 'Primeval Chronology', *Bibliotheca Sacra* 1890, pp. 285–303; B. B. Warfield, 'On the Antiquity . . . of the Human Race', *PTR* 9, 1911, pp. 1–17; E. J. Young, *WTJ* 12–13, 1949–51, pp. 189–193; W. G. Lambert, *JCS* 11, 1957, pp. 1–14, 112; A. Malamat, *JAOS* 88, 1968, pp. 163–73; R. R. Wilson, *Genealogy and History in the Biblical World*, 1977; M. D. Johnson, *The Purpose of Biblical Genealogies*, 1969. For New Testament, see D. Guthrie, *The Pastoral Epistles*, 1957, pp. 58, 208.

T.C.M.
A.R.M.

GENEALOGY OF JESUS CHRIST. Twice in the NT we are presented with the detailed genealogy of Christ. The first Evangelist introduces his record, in language which echoes Genesis, as 'the book of the genealogy of Jesus Christ, the son of David, the son of Abraham', and then traces the line of descent through forty-two generations from Abraham to Christ (Mt. 1:1–17). The third Evangelist, immediately after his account of the baptism of Christ, says that 'Jesus, when he began his ministry, was about thirty years of age, being the son (as was supposed) of Joseph', and then goes back from Joseph through more than seventy generations to 'Adam, the son of God' (Lk. 3:23–38).

We need not examine the genealogy from Adam to Abraham, which is not given in Matthew, and which Luke patently derived—perhaps *via* 1 Ch. 1:1–4, 24–27—from Gn. 5:3–32; 11:10–26 (following LXX, since in v. 36 he inserts Cainan between Arphaxad and Shelah). From Abraham to David the two lists are practically identical; the line from Judah to David is based on 1 Ch. 2:4–15 (*cf.* Ru. 4:18–22). Mt. 1:5 adds the information that the mother of Boaz was Rahab (presumably Rahab of Jericho). From David to Joseph the lists diverge, for Matthew traces the line through David's son Solomon and the successive kings of Judah as far as Jehoiachin (Jeconiah), whereas Luke traces it through Nathan, another son of David by Bathsheba (1 Ch. 3:5, where she is called Bathshua), and not through the royal line. In Matthew Jehoiachin is followed by Shealtiel and his son Zerubbabel, and these two names appear also in Luke (3:27), but after this momentary convergence there is no further agreement between the lists until we reach Joseph.

It is most improbable that the names in either list which have no OT attestation were simply invented by the Evangelists or their sources. But if we take the lists seriously, the relation between them constitutes a problem. Both make Jesus a descendant of David; his Davidic descent was a matter of common repute during his ministry (Mk. 10:47f.) and is attested by the apostolic witness (Rom. 1:3; so Heb. 7:14 assumes that everyone knows that Jesus belonged to the tribe of Judah). But both lists trace his Davidic descent through Joseph, although they appear in the two Gospels which make it plain that Joseph, while Jesus' father *de iure*, was not his father *de facto*. The Lucan genealogy acknowledges this by the parenthetic clause 'as was supposed' in Lk. 3:23; similarly, the best attested text of Mt. 1:16 says that Joseph was 'the husband of Mary, of whom Jesus was born, who is called Christ'. Even with the Sinaitic Syr. reading of Mt. 1:16 ('Joseph . . . begat Jesus . . .') the biological sense of 'begat' is excluded by the following narrative (vv. 18–25), and it is in any case probable that in other parts of this genealogy too 'begat' implies legal succession rather than actual parentage. Matthew's line is probably intended to trace the succession to David's throne, even where it did not run through the direct line from father to son.

In that case it might be expected that Luke, on the contrary, would endeavour to present the line of biological descent. It has accordingly been held by several commentators that the Lucan genealogy traces Jesus' lineage actually, though not explicitly, through Mary, his mother. It is possible to infer from Gabriel's words in Lk. 1:32 that Mary was a descendant of David; although these words may be explained by the reference to 'Joseph, of the house of David' in v. 27, while Mary in v. 36 is a kinswoman of Elizabeth, said to be 'of the daughters of Aaron' (v. 5). No help should be looked for in the Talmudic reference (TJ *Hagigah* 77d) to one Miriam, a daughter of Eli (*cf.* Heli, Lk. 3:23), for this Miriam has no connection with the mother of Jesus. In any case, it is strange that, if the Lucan list intended to trace the genealogy through Mary, this was not stated expressly. More probably both lists intend to trace the genealogy through Joseph. If Matthan, Joseph's grandfather in Mt. 1:15, is the same as Matthat, his grandfather in Lk. 3:24, then 'we should need only to suppose that Jacob [Joseph's father in Mt.] died without issue, so that his nephew, the son of his brother Heli [Joseph's father in Lk.] would become his heir' (J. G. Machen, *The Virgin Birth of Christ*, 1932, p. 208). As for the propriety of tracing Jesus' lineage through Joseph, 'Joseph was the heir of David, and the child, though born without his agency, was born in a real sense "to him" ' (*ibid.*, p. 187). A more complicated account, involving levirate marriage, was given by Julius Africanus (*c.* AD 230), on the basis of a tradition allegedly preserved in the holy family (Eus., *EH* 1. 7).

If Nathan in Zc. 12:12 is David's son of that name, his house evidently had some special standing in Israel, and there might then be more significance than meets the eye in the fact that Jesus is made a descendant of his in Lk. 3:31.

The Lucan list enumerates twenty or twenty-one generations between David and the Babylonian Exile, and as many between the Exile and Jesus, whereas the Matthaean list enumerates only fourteen generations for each of these periods. But several generations are demonstrably omitted from the Matthaean list in the period from David to the Exile, and others may be omitted in the later period. 'Rhesa' in Lk. 3:27 may originally have been not an individual name, but Aram. *rêšâ* ('prince'), the title of Zerubbabel (in which case the post-exilic section of the Lucan list may be derived from an Aramaic document).

The main purpose of the two lists is to establish Jesus' claim to be the Son of David, and more generally to emphasize his solidarity with mankind and his close relation with all that had gone before. Christ and the new covenant are securely linked to the age of the old covenant. Marcion, who wished to sever all the links binding Christianity to the OT, knew what he was about when he cut the genealogy out of his edition of Luke.

BIBLIOGRAPHY. J. G. Machen, *The Virgin Birth of Christ*², 1932, pp. 173ff., 203ff.; M. D. Johnson, *The Purpose of the Biblical Genealogies*, 1969; N. Hillyer, *NIDNTT* 3, pp.653–660. F.F.B.

GENERATION. A word used in the EVV to translate various biblical terms.

1. Heb. *tôlᵉḏôṯ*. A word occurring ten times in Genesis (2:4; 5:1; 6:9; 10:1; 11:10, 27; 25:12, 19; 36:1; 37:2) in such a way as to divide it into eleven sections, each being styled 'the generations of . . .' It also occurs in Gn. 10:32; 25:13; 36:9; Ex. 6:16, 19; Nu. 1 many times; 3:1; Ru. 4:18; 1 Ch. 1:29; 5:7; 7:2, 4, 9; 8:28; 9:9, 34; 26:31. In Ex. 28:10 the EVV translate it 'birth'. The word is formed from *yālaḏ*, 'to bear, beget', and this probably accounts for the E.T. 'generation'. From its OT usage, however, it is apparent that the word means 'history' or 'genealogical history', of a family or the like. In the LXX the word is often rendered by Gk. *genesis* (see **3**, below), and the expression *biblos geneseōs Iēsou Christou*, 'book of the genealogy of Jesus Christ' in Mt. 1:1, closely reflects *sēp̄er tôlᵉḏôṯ 'āḏām*, 'book of the genealogy of Adam', in Gn. 5:1.

2. Heb. *dôr*. A word occurring frequently, which corresponds in general to the word 'generation' as commonly understood in Eng. It can refer to a generation, as a period in the past (Is. 51:9) or future (Ex. 3:15), or to the men of a generation (Ex. 1:6). It is the word used in Gn. 17:7, 9, where God's covenant with Abraham and his descendants is announced. The word is also used to refer to a class of men, as in 'crooked generations' (Dt. 32:5) or 'generation of the righteous' (Ps. 14:5). The Aram. cognate, *dār*, occurs in Dn. 4:3, 34. Akkad. *duru* is used of a generation as grandfather to grandson spanning about 70 years.

3. Gk. *genesis*. Used chiefly in the LXX for *tôlᵉḏôṯ*, and employed in the same sense in Mt. 1:1 (see **1**, above). In the other NT occurrences, however, it is used in the sense of 'birth' (Mt. 1:18; Lk. 1:14; Jas. 1:23, 'his natural face', lit. 'face of his birth'; Jas. 3:6, 'cycle of nature', lit. 'course of birth').

4. Gk. *genea*. Used chiefly in the LXX to translate *dôr*, and like it including among its meanings much the same range as Eng. 'generation'. It is used of the people living at a given time (Mt. 11:16), and, by extension, of the time itself (Lk. 1:50). It is also evidently used to designate the components of a genealogy (Mt. 1:17).

5. Gk. *gennēma*, 'child' and 'offspring', occurring in Mt. 3:7; 12:34; 23:33; Lk. 3:7, in each case in the phrase 'brood of vipers', AV 'generation of vipers'.

6. Gk. *genos*, 'race'. AV translates the phrase *genos eklekton* in 1 Pet. 2:9 'chosen generation', but RV 'elect race' or RSV 'chosen race' is to be preferred.

It is sometimes held that a period of 40 years, the duration, for instance, of the wilderness wanderings, is to be taken as a round *number indicating a generation.

BIBLIOGRAPHY. P. J. Wiseman, *Clues to Creation in Genesis*, 1977, pp. 34–45; F. Büchsel, *TDNT* 1, pp. 662–663, 672, 682–685; R. R. Wilson, *Genealogy and History in the Biblical World*, 1977, pp. 158–159, n. 57; R. Morgenthaler, C. Brown, *NIDNTT* 2, pp. 35–39. T.C.M.

GENESIS, BOOK OF.

I. Outline of contents

a. Pre-history: the creation record (1:1–2:3)

b. The story of man (2:4–11:26)

His creation and Fall (2:4–3:24); his increasing numbers (4:1–6:8); the judgment of the Flood (6:9–9:29); the rise of nations (10:1–11:26).

c. The story of Abraham (11:27–23:20)

His entry into the promised land (11:27–14:24); the covenant and the promise (15:1–18:15); Sodom and Gomorrah (18:16–19:38); Sarah, Isaac and Ishmael (20:1–23:20).

d. The story of Isaac (24:1–26:35)

His marriage with Rebekah (24:1–67); death of his father and birth of his children (25:1–34); the promise renewed at Gerar (26:1–35).

e. The story of Jacob (27:1–36:43)

His obtaining of the blessing by deceit (27:1–46); his flight to Harran, and renewal of the promise at Bethel (28:1–22); his life and marriages in Harran (29:1–31:16); his return to the promised land, and renewal of the promise at Bethel (31:17–35:29); Esau's line (36:1–43).

f. The story of Joseph (37:1–50:26)

Joseph sold into Egypt (37:1–36); Judah and his daughter-in-law (38:1–30); Joseph in Egypt (39:1–45:28); Joseph's father and brothers in Egypt (46:1–47:31); Jacob's blessing gives priority to Ephraim and to Judah (48:1–49:28); deaths of Jacob and Joseph (49:29–50:26).

The book of Genesis closes with the people of Israel already in Egypt. They were the elect family among all mankind for whom God purposed to display the mighty acts of redemption outlined in Exodus. Among this people the tribe of Judah has already emerged as of special significance (49:9–12).

A technical analysis may also be based on the 10 occurrences of the phrase (or its equivalent), 'These are the generations of . . .'. *'Generations' (Heb. *tôlᵉḏôṯ*) means 'begettings' or 'genealogical records'. This phrase is used with reference to the heavens and the earth (2:4); Adam (5:1); Noah (6:9); the sons of Noah (10:1); Shem (11:10); Terah (11:27); Ishmael (25:12); Isaac (25:19); Esau (36:1); Jacob (37:2).

II. Authorship

For a discussion of the authorship of the Pentateuch, see *PENTATEUCH. Concerning the authorship of Genesis in particular, there is nothing in the book to indicate its author. There are two opinions, though there are variants of each: (*a*) Mosaic authorship, (*b*) non-Mosaic authorship.

a. Mosaic authorship

The education that Moses received at pharaoh's court would have enabled him to read and write (Ex. 24:4; Dt. 31:9, *etc.*), and he would obviously be anxious to preserve the records that had come down. This means that Moses was not so much the author as the editor and compiler of Genesis. Family records had been handed down either orally or in written form, and Moses brought these together, editing and translating where necessary. The creation story in Gn. 1 may have been received as a direct revelation from God, since Moses certainly had the experience of immediate contact with God (*e.g.* Ex. 33:11; Dt. 34:10). Accordingly, we may legitimately look for documents or for orally transmitted stories in Genesis, and, if we use some recent terminology, we may speak of Moses as the one who faithfully set down what had come to him from past generations.

If we allow for a few later 'footnotes' added by copyists up to the time of the Monarchy to explain points for contemporary readers (*e.g.* 12:6; 13:7; 14:17, and parts of 36:9–43), there is nothing that need be dated after the time of Moses. While the proper interpretation of Ex. 6:3 does not exclude some use of the name Yahweh in Genesis, it would be perfectly understandable if Moses sometimes substituted the covenant name of his own day for the covenant name 'El Shaddai (God Almighty) of patriarchal times, in order to remind his readers that this was the same God as the God of Sinai.

For this section, see E. J. Young, *IOT*,1949, pp. 51ff.

b. Non-Mosaic authorship

There is no one theory here that commands general acceptance. Since the days of Jean Astruc, in the 18th century, scholars have looked for various 'documents' in the Pentateuch. These for Genesis are J (which uses Yahweh for the divine name), E (which uses Elohim for the divine name) and P (which is concerned chiefly with religious matters). Early forms of this theory were extremely radical and denied historicity to a great deal in Genesis. More recently it has been argued that the 'documents' grew by the collection of ancient material until they reached their final shape; J in about the 10th or 9th century BC, E a little later and P in post-exilic times. Historicity is not necessarily denied in the more moderate forms of this theory.

More recently the 'documentary' theory has been abandoned by some who deny that formal documents ever existed. Scholars of this school speak of 'cycles of tradition' which grew up in various areas, chiefly with a religious interest, *e.g.* Ex. 1–12 is quoted as a 'cycle of tradition' that has the Passover event as its focal point. Some time later editors collected these materials and cast them into their present shape. For the most part the material was in oral form before collection. Again there is no necessary denial of historicity in this view, although some writers do deny exact historicity, but admit a 'general historicity'. This 'tradition history' school thinks in terms of the development of the traditions around central events which had significance for the religious life of Israel and found expression in their religious rituals and liturgies.

It is not possible to say in general conclusion that any one school today has acceptance by all scholars. The exact origin of Genesis remains something of a mystery.

III. The place of Genesis in the Bible

Genesis is the Book of Beginnings, the great introduction to the drama of redemption. Gn. 1–11 may be regarded as the prologue to the drama, whose first act begins at ch. 12 with the introduction of Abraham. At the other end of the drama the book of Revelation is the epilogue.

The prologue is cast in universal terms. God made all things (ch. 1). In particular, he made man, who became a rebel and a sinner (chs. 2–3). Sin became universal (ch. 4), and being rebellion against God is always under divine judgment, exemplified in the story of the Flood (chs. 6–9). Even after God had demonstrated his displeasure by an act of judgment in the Flood, man returned to his rebellion (ch. 11). Yet always God gave evidences of grace and mercy. Adam and Eve were cast out, but not destroyed (ch. 3); Cain was driven out but 'marked' by God (ch. 4); mankind was overwhelmed by the Flood but not obliterated, for a remnant was saved (chs. 6–9); man was scattered but allowed to live on (ch. 11).

That is the prologue which paints the background for the drama which is about to develop. What was God's answer to the universal, persistent sin of man? As the drama proper opens in Gn. 12 we meet Abraham, the first stage in God's answer. He would call out an elect people, from whom in due course would come the Redeemer. That people would proclaim the message of redemption to men everywhere. Genesis tells only the beginning of the story up to the time of Joseph, giving the setting for God's mighty act of deliverance from Egypt, pattern of the greater deliverance yet to be achieved.

IV. Genesis and historicity

It is extremely difficult to obtain independent evidence as to the historicity of Genesis, since many of the narratives have no parallel in non-biblical literature. This is especially difficult for Gn. 1–11, though easier for Gn. 12–50. It should always be remembered that much in the Bible is beyond scientific investigation, but notably those areas which touch on faith and personal relations. The areas on which one might ask for evidence in Genesis may be summarized as follows:

a. The creation (*CREATION)

b. The origin of man

The Bible asserts that God made man. It does not allow that there was any other source for man's origin. It is not possible, however, to discover from Genesis precisely how God did this. Scientifically, the origin of man is still obscure, and neither archaeology nor anthropology can give a final answer as to the time, place or means of man's origin. It is safest for the Christian to be cautious about the subject, to be content to assert with Genesis that, however it happened, God lay behind the process, and to be content to await further evidence before rushing to hasty conclusions (*MAN).

c. The Flood

There is no final evidence here either as to the time, the extent or the cause. There were certainly extensive floods in the area from which the Patriarchs came, and the ancient Sumerians had a detailed account of a great flood in the ancient world. There are no serious reasons, however, for accepting the suggestion of Sir Leonard Woolley that the flood at Ur, which left a deep deposit of silt revealed by his excavation, was in fact the result of the Bible *Flood.

d. Patriarchal narratives

It is possible today to read the patriarchal narratives against the background of the social, political and cultural state of the ancient Near East in the period 2000–1500 BC. While it is not possible to date the events in Genesis, it is true to say that the Bible reflects the life of certain areas of Mesopotamia during these centuries. (*PATRIARCHAL AGE.) H. H. Rowley, 'Recent Discoveries in the Patriarchal Age', *BJRL* 32, 1949–50, pp. 76ff. (reprinted in *The Servant of the Lord and Other Essays on the Old Testament*, 1952); J. Bright, *A History of Israel*², 1972, pp. 67–102; R. de Vaux, *Histoire ancienne d'Israel*², 1971, pp. 181–273.

V. Genesis and theology

It cannot be emphasized too strongly that the primary value of Genesis, as indeed of all Scripture, is theological. It is possible to devote a great deal of time and energy to all kinds of incidental details and to miss the great theological issues. For example, the story of the Flood speaks of sin, judgment, redemption, new life. To be occupied with details about the size of the ark, and with problems of feeding or of the disposal of refuse, is to be concerned with side-issues. While God's revelation was largely in historical events, and while history is of tremendous significance for the biblical revelation, it is the theological significance of events that is finally important. Where corroborative evidence of the Genesis narratives is lacking, the theological significance may still be discerned.

BIBLIOGRAPHY. U. Cassuto, *A Commentary on the Book of Genesis*, 1 (1944), 2 (1949); S. R. Driver, *The Book of Genesis*, 1948; D. Kidner, *Genesis*, *TOTC*, 1967; G. von Rad, *Genesis*, 1961; E. A. Speiser, *Genesis*, 1956; B. Vawter, *A Path through Genesis*, 1955.

J.S.W.
J.A.T.

GENTILES (Heb. *gôyîm*; Gk. *ethnē* (or *Hellēnes*) *via* Vulg. *gentiles*). This was originally a general term for 'nations', but acquired a restricted sense by usage. In the OT the affinity of all nations is stressed in the tradition of Noah's descendants (Gn. 10). In God's covenant with Abraham his descendants are distinguished from other nations, but not in any narrowly exclusive sense (Gn. 12:2; 18:18; 22:18; 26:4). Israel became conscious of being a nation uniquely distinct from others by being separated to God after the Exodus (Dt. 26:5), and the covenant of Sinai (Ex. 19:6). From then on this dedication dominated all her relations with other nations (Ex. 34:10; Lv. 18:24–25; Dt. 15:6).

The Israelites were constantly tempted to compromise with the idolatry and immorality practised by other nations (1 Ki. 14:24), so bringing God's judgment on themselves (2 Ki. 17:7ff.; Ezk. 5:5ff.). On their return from the Exile the danger was still more insidious because of the corruptness of the Jews who had remained in Canaan (*cf.* Ezr. 6:21). This continual struggle against contamination from their neighbours led to so hard and exclusive an attitude to other nations that by the time of Christ for a Jew to stigmatize his fellow as 'Gentile' (*ethnikos*, Mt. 18:17) was a term of scorn equal in opprobrium to 'tax-collector', and they earned for themselves from Tacitus the censure that 'they regard the rest of mankind with all the hatred of enemies' (*Histories* 5. 5).

Yet the Gentiles were assigned a place in prophecies of the kingdom, merely as the vanquished who would enhance the glory of Israel (Is. 60:5–6), or as themselves seeking the Lord (Is. 11:10), and offering worship (Mal. 1:11) when the Messiah should come to be their Light (Is. 42:6), and to bring salvation to the ends of the earth (Is. 49:6). In this tradition Simeon hailed Jesus (Lk. 2:32), and Jesus began his ministry (Mt. 12:18, 21), and the Jews themselves could question whether he would go to the Gentiles (Jn. 7:35). Though hesitant and astonished when Cornelius was converted (Acts 10:45; 11:18), the church quickly accepted the equality of Jew and Gentile before God (Rom. 1:16; Col. 3:11), thus revealing the full scope of the gospel and its glorious hope for all (Gal. 2:14ff.; Rev. 21:24; 22:2).

P.A.B.

GENTLENESS. In Gal. 5:23 'gentleness' (*praÿtēs*) is part of the ninefold 'fruit of the Spirit'. In 2 Cor.

GENESIS AND SCIENCE
See Creation, Part 1.

Gerar, probably Tell Abu Hureira, SE of Gaza.

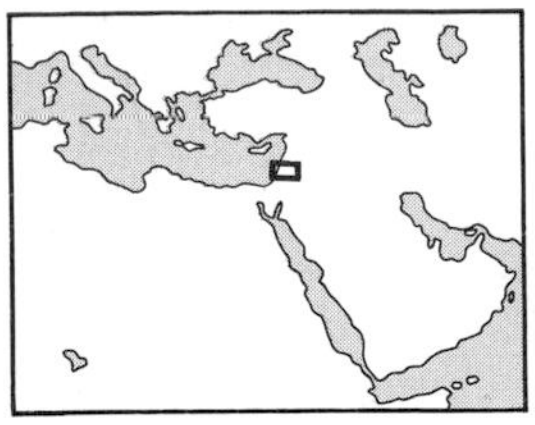

10:1 Paul beseeches his readers by the 'gentleness' (*epieikeia*) of Christ, coupled with his 'meekness' (*praÿtēs*). *epieikeia* suggests the yielding of a judge, who, instead of demanding the exact penalty required by strict justice, gives way to circumstances which call for mercy. Thus the concession of a legal right may avoid the perpetration of a moral wrong (see R. C. Trench, *Synonyms of the New Testament*, pp. 153–157). Similarly in the OT the Heb. *'ānâ*, 'to be humble', and its cognate noun are used of God: 'Thy gentleness (RSVmg.) made me great' (2 Sa. 22:36; Ps. 18:35). Although the word itself is rarely used, it expresses the typical condescension of the divine Judge, whose refusal to exact the full demands of the law lifts up those who would otherwise be crushed under its condemnation. The adjective *epieikēs* describes one of the qualities of the Christlike believer. Note the other qualities with which it is associated in 1 Tim. 3:3; Tit. 3:2; Jas. 3:17; 1 Pet. 2:18. *epieikeia* is used in a formal rhetorical sense in Acts 24:4. J.C.C.

GERAR (Heb. *g^erār*, 'circle'). An ancient city S of Gaza (Gn. 10:19) in the foothills of the Judaean mountains. Both Abraham (Gn. 20–21) and Isaac (Gn. 26) stayed there, digging wells, and had cordial relations with Abimelech its king, though Isaac quarrelled with him at one stage. The city lay in the 'land of the *Philistines' (*'ereṣ p^elištîm*, Gn. 21:32, 34; see also 26:1, 8), not necessarily an anachronistic designation. In the early 9th century BC it was the scene of a great victory by Asa of Judah over the invading Ethiopian army of Zerah (2 Ch. 14:13–14).

The site of Gerar was identified with modern Tell Jemmeh by W. M. Flinders Petrie, but following a survey by D. Alon, the site of Tell Abu Hureira, a mound about 18 km SE of Gaza, in the Wadi Eš-Šari'ah has been proposed as more likely. As no pre-Iron-Age remains had been found near it, this site had hitherto been believed to be a natural hill, but Alon's survey has shown that it was first inhabited in Chalcolithic times, and continued in occupation through every period of the Bronze and Iron Ages. The evidence of surface potsherds indicated that the city had a prosperous period in Middle Bronze Age, the age of the Patriarchs.

BIBLIOGRAPHY. Y. Aharoni, 'The Land of Gerar', *IEJ* 6, 1956, pp. 26–32; *cf.* F. M. Cross Jr. and G. E. Wright, *JBL* 75, 1956, pp. 212–213; W. F. Albright, *BASOR* 163, 1961, p. 48. T.C.M.

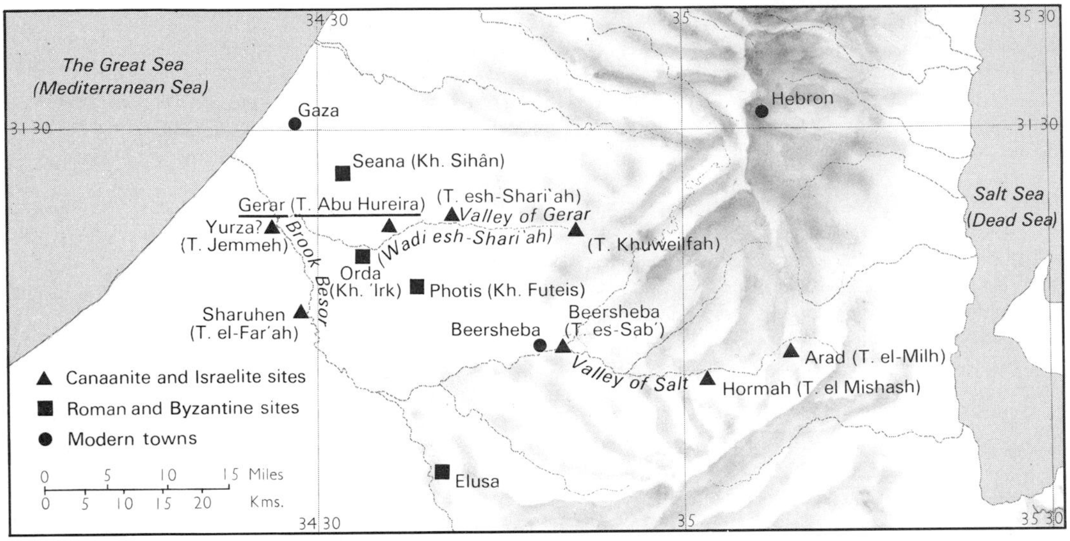

GEOGRAPHY OF PALESTINE
See Palestine, Part 2.

GEOLOGY OF PALESTINE
See Palestine, Part 2.

GERAH
See Weights and measures, Part 3.

GERASA. An important city of the classical period, ranking in importance with Palmyra and Petra. Lying in Transjordan, mid-way between the Dead Sea and the Sea of Galilee, and some 30 km E of the Jordan, the site today, still preserving the name in the form *Jaraš*, is one of the best preserved examples of a Roman provincial town in the Middle East. It is only indirectly mentioned in the Bible in the passages describing our Lord's visit to the E side of the Sea of Galilee, where the territory is described as the country of the Gerasenes (RV, Mk. 5:1; Lk. 8:26, 37, AV 'Gadarenes'; in Mt. 8:28,

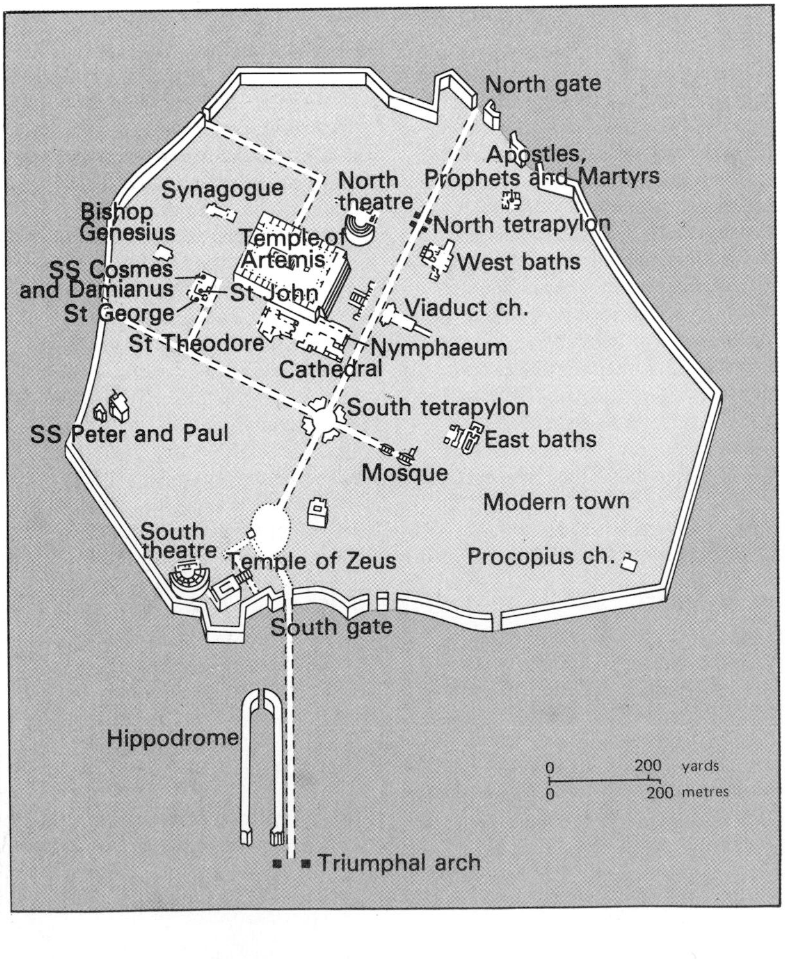

Gerasa. Plan showing the main buildings of the Roman town (enclosed by a wall built in the second half of the 1st cent. AD), later churches and the area of the modern town, Jaraš.

Colonnaded street at Jerash (Gerasa). Most of the extant visible remains date from the time of the Roman rebuilding of the city. (RH)

Triumphal arch of Emperor Hadrian. Jerash (Gerasa), Jordan. AD 129–130. (MEPHA)

AV gives Gergesenes, RV, RSV *Gadarenes. In all three passages variant MSS give *Gerasēnos*, *Gergesēnos* and *Gadarēnos*. The town lies in a well-watered valley with a perennial stream running through the middle of it, and its wealth was probably derived from the cultivation of the fertile corn lands to the E of it. First noted in 1806 by the German traveller Seetzen, it was subsequently visited by many Europeans. In 1867 Charles Warren made many plans and photographs of the ruins. In 1878 a modern village was founded at the site, and the resulting destruction of the buildings led to considerable conservation, reconstruction and excavation under the auspices of the Department of Antiquities between the wars, a work that still goes on. The extent of the Roman remains makes research into the earlier periods difficult, but Gerasa probably emerged from a village to a Hellenistic town under the name of Antioch, some time after the 4th century BC, when increasing security made prosperity possible. It is first mentioned historically in the writings of Josephus, who states that Theodorus of Gadara took refuge there at the end of the 2nd century BC, but it was soon afterward taken by Alexander Jannaeus, and remained in Jewish hands until Pompey's conquest of 63 BC, when it became part of the province of Syria. The Hellenistic practice of allowing a measure of self-government was continued by Rome, and Gerasa, now one of the cities of the *Decapolis, flourished, carrying on a lively trade with the Nabataeans to the S. This prosperity was such that in the 1st century AD the city was largely rebuilt on a typical Roman plan with a straight main street flanked by columns leading to a forum. There were temples to Artemis and Zeus and two theatres and an enclosing wall round the whole. The 2nd century AD was, however, a period of greater prosperity, and the surviving remains, including a triumphal arch commemorating a personal visit by the emperor Hadrian in AD 129–130, date largely from that time. In the early 3rd century the city became a colony, but soon thereafter declined, and by the time of the Crusades it had been long deserted.

BIBLIOGRAPHY. C. C. McCown, *The Ladder of Progress in Palestine*, 1943, pp. 309–325; G. Lankester Harding, *The Antiquities of Jordan*, 1959, pp. 78–104; E. G. Kraeling, *Gerasa, City of the Decapolis*, 1938; E. K. Vogel, *HUCA* 42, 1971, pp. 40–42. T.C.M.

GERGESENES
See Gerasa, Part 1.

GERIZIM. The more southerly of the two mountains which overshadow the modern town of Nablus, 4 km NW of ancient Shechem, called Jebel eṭ-Ṭôr in Arabic. It has been called the mount of blessing, because here the blessings for obedience were pronounced at the solemn assembly of Israel described in Jos. 8:30–35 (*EBAL, MOUNT).

A ledge halfway to the top is

View of Mount Gerizim. (MEPHA)

Opposite page: King Hammurapi kneeling and making a gesture of reverence common in prayer. Bronze statue with gold plating dedicated to the 'Amorite' god (Amurru). Larsa. Height 20 cm. Early 2nd millennium BC. (MC)

With extravagant gestures foreigners implore a royal servant. Relief from tomb of Horemheb, Memphis. Height 53 cm. c. 1343–1310 BC. (RVO)

A Median raising his hand to his lips as a gesture of respect for King Darius I. Height 2·44 m. From the treasury at Persepolis, Iran. 521–486 BC. (OIUC)

popularly called 'Jotham's pulpit', from which he once addressed the men of Shechem (Jdg. 9:7). On the summit are the bare ruins of a Christian church of the 5th century. Still earlier there stood there a temple of Jupiter, to which a staircase of 300 steps led up, as shown on ancient coins found in Nablus.

Gerizim remains the sacred mount of the Samaritans; for they have 'worshipped on this mountain' (Jn. 4:20) for countless generations, ascending it to keep the feasts of Passover, Pentecost and Tabernacles. According to Samaritan tradition, Gerizim is Mt Moriah (Gn. 22:2) and the place where God chose to place his name (Dt. 12:5). Accordingly it was here that the Samaritan temple was built with Persian authorization in the 4th century BC—the temple which was demolished by John Hyrcanus when he captured Shechem and the surrounding area *c.* 128 BC. See further E. Robertson, *The Old Testament Problem*, 1950, pp. 157–171; G. E. Wright, *Shechem*, 1965, pp. 170–184. G.T.M. F.F.B.

GERSHOM, GERSHON. The form Gershom is used of the following people.

1. The elder son of Moses, born in Midian (Ex. 2:22; 18:3). The name (construed as 'banishment' or 'a stranger there') commemorated Moses' exile. Gershom's sons counted as Levites (1 Ch. 23:14–15).

2. A descendant of Phinehas the priest (Ezr. 8:2).

3. Levi's son (1 Ch. 6:1, 16–17; elsewhere the allied forms, 'Gershon' and 'Gershonite', are used). In the wilderness the Gershonites carried the tabernacle, tent, coverings, hangings and cords for the door, court and gate; they received two wagons and four oxen to help in the task. They encamped W of the tabernacle. Their males, over a month old, numbered 7,500; those who served (age-group 30–50) 2,630 (Nu. 3:17–26; 4:38–41; 7:7). In the land they obtained thirteen cities (Jos. 21:6). Under David the Asaphites and Ladanites, both Gershonite families, had special singing and treasury duties (1 Ch. 6:39; 23:1–11; 26:21–22). Gershonites are mentioned at the bringing up of the ark (1 Ch. 15:7), at the cleansings of the Temple under Hezekiah and Josiah (2 Ch. 29:12; 35:15), and as serving under Ezra (Ezr. 3:10) and Nehemiah (Ne. 11:17). D.W.G.

GESHEM. Mentioned in Ne. 2:19; 6:1–2 as one of the chief opponents of Nehemiah, and almost certainly the Gashmu of Ne. 6:6. In these passages he is called simply 'the Arabian', but is evidently an influential person. Two inscriptions throw a vivid light on this man. One is a memorial in ancient Dedan (modern el-'Ula) dated 'in the days of Jasm (dialect-form of Geshem) son of Shahru', testifying to Geshem's fame in N Arabia. The other is an Aramaic dedication on a silver bowl from an Arabian shrine in the Egyptian E Delta. It reads, 'What Qaynu son of Geshem, king of Kedar, brought (as offering) to (the goddess) Han-'Ilat.' This text of his successor shows that Geshem was none other than king (paramount chief) of the tribesfolk and desert traders of biblically attested *Kedar in N Arabia. The Persian kings maintained good relations with the Arabs from the time they invaded Egypt in 525 BC (*cf.* Herodotus, 3. 4ff., 88), which lends point to Ne. 6:6, for a complaint by Gashmu to the Persian king would not go unheard. For the silver bowl and full background on Geshem, see I. Rabinowitz, *JNES* 15, 1956, pp. 2, 5–9, and pls. 6–7. *Cf.* also W. F. Albright, 'Dedan' (also in English) in the Alt anniversary volume, *Geschichte und Altes Testament*, 1953, pp. 4, 6 (Dedan inscription). K.A.K.

GESHUR, GESHURITES. 1. In the list of David's sons in 2 Sa. 3:3 the third is 'Absalom the son of Maacah the daughter of Talmai king of Geshur', a city in Syria (2 Sa. 15:8; 1 Ch. 3:2), NE of Bashan (Jos. 12:5; 13:11, 13).

It was this city to which Absalom fled after the murder of his brother Amnon (2 Sa. 13:37) and to which David sent Joab to bring him back (14:23). The young man returned to Jerusalem, but only to plot rebellion against his father (2 Sa. 14:32; 15:8).

2. Another group called

'Geshurites' is attested in Jos. 13:2 and 1 Sa. 27:8 as resident in the Negeb, near the Egyptian border.

F.F.B.

GESTURES. The Oriental is much more given to physical gestures than is the Westerner. As might be expected, then, the Bible records numerous gestures. These may be roughly divided into three categories: first, natural physical reactions to certain circumstances; second, conventional or customary gestures; third, deliberate symbolic actions. Gestures of the first type are involuntary, and those of the second often tend to become so, through long habit.

Not many gestures of the first category are recorded; the Bible does not mention, for instance, shrugs and movements of the head by the story-teller. Signs with the hands, for different purposes, are recorded in Mt. 12:49 and Acts 12:17. The circumstances of the people around him also caused Jesus to sigh (Mk. 7:34) and to weep (Jn. 11:35).

A great number of conventional actions are to be found in Scripture. When greeting a superior one would bow low, and perhaps kiss his hand. Friends greeting each other would grasp the other's chin or beard, and kiss. Lk. 7:44–46 records the customary gestures of hospitality. Scorn was expressed by wagging the head and grimacing with the mouth (Ps. 22:7). In commerce, a bargain was sealed by 'striking' hands (Pr. 6:1—the gesture is lost in the RSV paraphrase). Extreme grief was expressed by tearing the garments and placing dust upon the head. This category also includes the physical attitudes adopted for prayer and benediction. Notice also Ex. 6:6 and Is. 65:2.

Symbolic action was a method of prophetic instruction; Ezekiel in particular made great use of it, and many of Jesus' actions were of a symbolic nature. He frequently touched those he meant to heal; he breathed on the disciples, as he imparted the Holy Spirit (Jn. 20:22). Notice, too, Pilate's eloquent gesture in Mt. 27:24. See also *FOOT, *HAND, *HEAD, *etc.*

D.F.P.

GETHSEMANE (from Aram. *gaṯ šemen,* 'an oil press'). A garden (*kēpos*, Jn. 18:1), E of Jerusalem beyond the Kidron valley and near the Mount of Olives (Mt. 26:30). It was a favourite retreat frequented by Christ and his disciples, which became the scene of the agony, Judas' betrayal and the arrest (Mk. 14:32–52). It should probably be contrasted with Eden, as the garden where the second Adam prevailed over temptation. Christ's action in Gethsemane (Lk. 22:41) gave rise to the Christian custom of kneeling for prayer. The traditional Latin site lies E of the Jericho road-bridge over the Kidron, and contains olive trees said to date back to the 7th century AD. It measures 50 m square, and was enclosed with a wall by the Franciscans in 1848. It corresponds to the position located by Eusebius and Jerome, but is regarded by Thomson, Robinson and Barclay as too small and too near the road. The Greeks enclosed an adjacent site to the N. There is a broad area of land NE of the Church of St Mary where larger, more secluded gardens were put at the disposal of pilgrims, and Thomson locates the genuine site here. The original trees were cut down by Titus (Jos., *BJ* 5. 523).

BIBLIOGRAPHY. W. M. Thomson, *The Land and the Book*, 1888, p. 634; G. Dalman, *Sacred Sites and Ways*, 1935, pp. 321ff.

D.H.T.

Bottom left:
Olive trees in the Garden of Gethsemane on the slopes of the Mount of Olives, E of Jerusalem. (AAM)

Silver bowl inscribed in Aramaic, 'what Qaynu son of Geshem, king of Kedar, brought (as offering) to (the goddess) Han-'Ilat'. Late 5th cent. BC. (Br M)

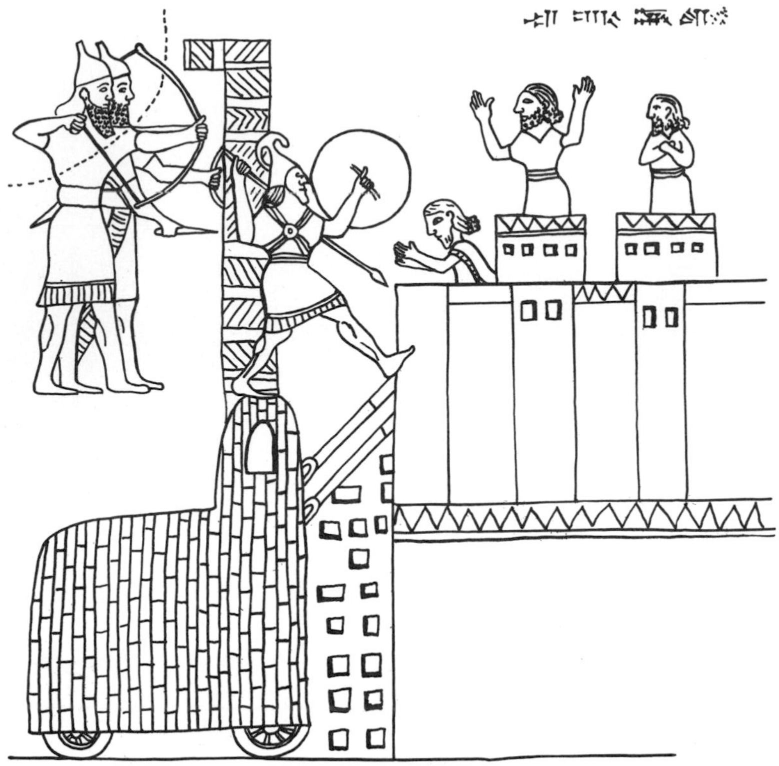

The assault of the city of Gezer by the army of Tiglath-pileser III. From a relief in SW palace at Nimrud. 744–727 BC.

GEZRITES
See Girzites, Part 1.

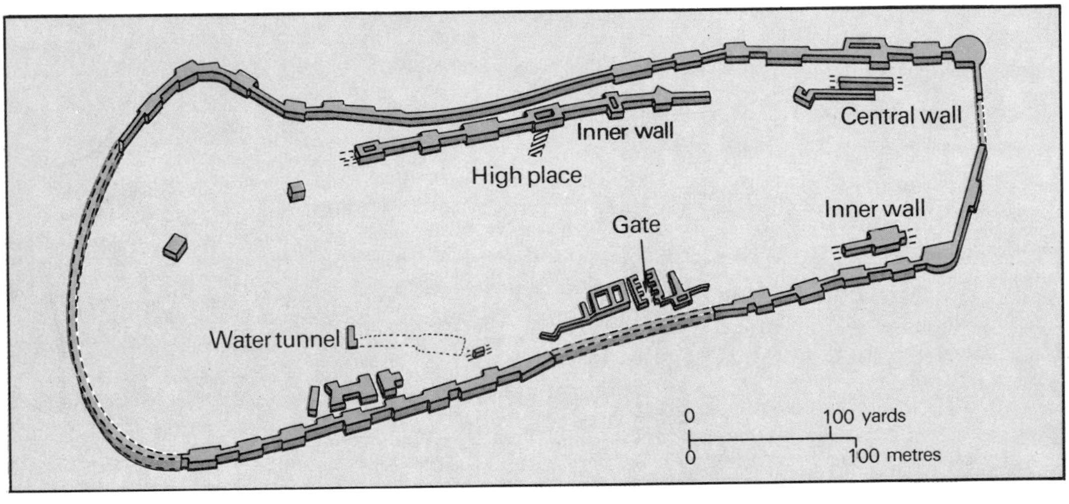

Plan of Gezer.

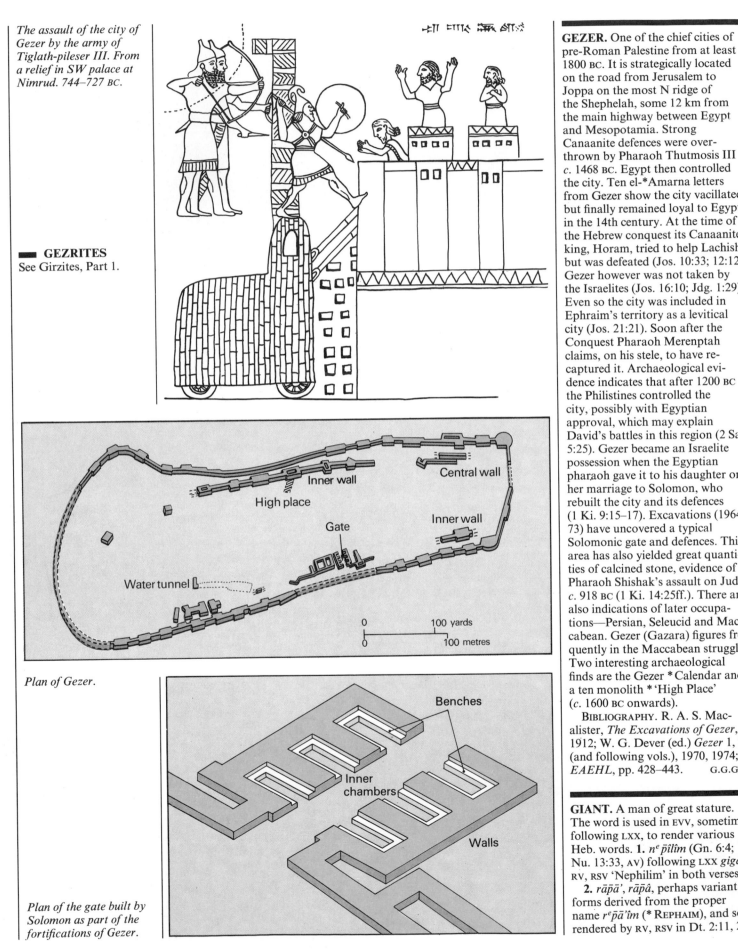

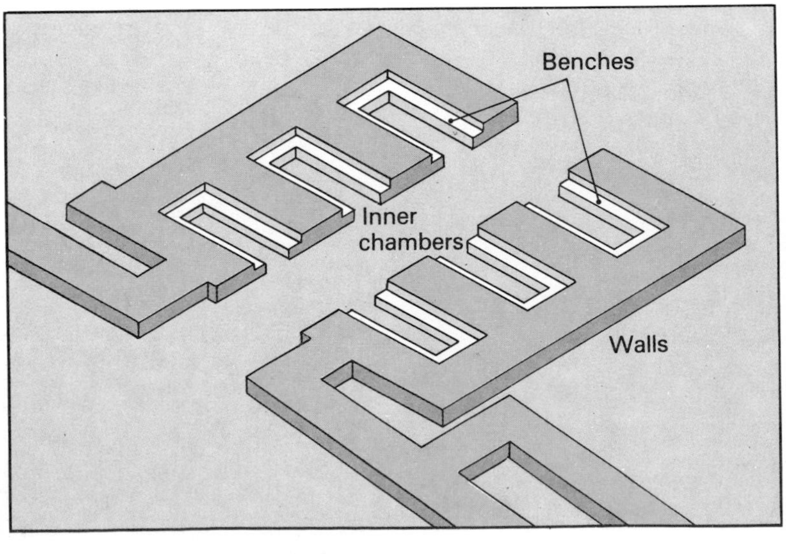

Plan of the gate built by Solomon as part of the fortifications of Gezer.

GEZER. One of the chief cities of pre-Roman Palestine from at least 1800 BC. It is strategically located on the road from Jerusalem to Joppa on the most N ridge of the Shephelah, some 12 km from the main highway between Egypt and Mesopotamia. Strong Canaanite defences were overthrown by Pharaoh Thutmosis III *c.* 1468 BC. Egypt then controlled the city. Ten el-*Amarna letters from Gezer show the city vacillated but finally remained loyal to Egypt in the 14th century. At the time of the Hebrew conquest its Canaanite king, Horam, tried to help Lachish but was defeated (Jos. 10:33; 12:12); Gezer however was not taken by the Israelites (Jos. 16:10; Jdg. 1:29). Even so the city was included in Ephraim's territory as a levitical city (Jos. 21:21). Soon after the Conquest Pharaoh Merenptah claims, on his stele, to have recaptured it. Archaeological evidence indicates that after 1200 BC the Philistines controlled the city, possibly with Egyptian approval, which may explain David's battles in this region (2 Sa. 5:25). Gezer became an Israelite possession when the Egyptian pharaoh gave it to his daughter on her marriage to Solomon, who rebuilt the city and its defences (1 Ki. 9:15–17). Excavations (1964–73) have uncovered a typical Solomonic gate and defences. This area has also yielded great quantities of calcined stone, evidence of Pharaoh Shishak's assault on Judah *c.* 918 BC (1 Ki. 14:25ff.). There are also indications of later occupations—Persian, Seleucid and Maccabean. Gezer (Gazara) figures frequently in the Maccabean struggle. Two interesting archaeological finds are the Gezer *Calendar and a ten monolith *'High Place' (*c.* 1600 BC onwards).

BIBLIOGRAPHY. R. A. S. Macalister, *The Excavations of Gezer*, 1912; W. G. Dever (ed.) *Gezer* 1, 2 (and following vols.), 1970, 1974; *EAEHL*, pp. 428–443. G.G.G.

GIANT. A man of great stature. The word is used in EVV, sometimes following LXX, to render various Heb. words. **1.** *nᵉpīlîm* (Gn. 6:4; Nu. 13:33, AV) following LXX *gigas*. RV, RSV 'Nephilim' in both verses.

2. *rāpā', rāpâ*, perhaps variant forms derived from the proper name *rᵉpā'îm* (*REPHAIM), and so rendered by RV, RSV in Dt. 2:11, 20;

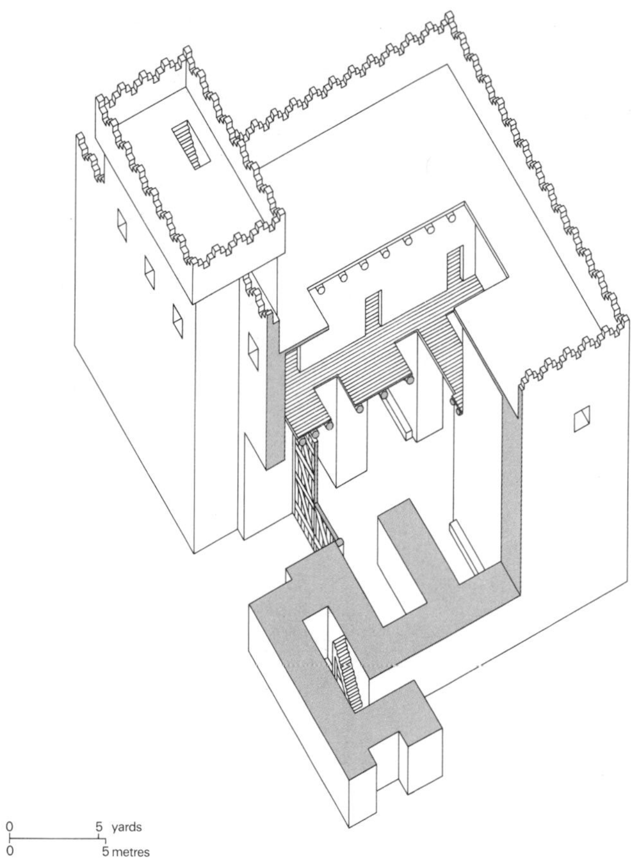

Standing-stones on a 'high place' at Gezer. Part of a row of ten monoliths, some over 3 m high, probably used for cultic purposes. Middle Bronze Age. (JLH)

Top left: A suggested reconstruction of Solomon's gate at Gezer.

3:11, 13; Jos. 12:4; 13:12; 15:8; 17:15; 18:16 where AV gives 'giant'. In 2 Sa. 21:16, 18, 20, 22 and 1 Ch. 20:4, 6, 8, which speak of certain Philistines as 'sons of the giant', a man of great stature may be meant (*cf.* 2 Sa. 21:19–20); it may be noted here that *Goliath is never described as a 'giant' in the Bible, but some scholars hold that these verses indicate descent from the Rephaim. The LXX translates these terms with *gigas* in such passages as Gn. 14:5; Jos. 12:4; 13:12; 1 Ch. 11:15; 14:9; 20:4, 6.

3. *gibbôr*, 'mighty man', and frequently so translated in EVV (*e.g.* Gn. 6:4; Jos. 1:14; 1 Sa. 9:1, *etc.*) but rendered 'giant' in Jb. 16:14 (AV, RV; RSV 'warrior'). The word corresponds very much with English 'hero' in meaning. The LXX gives *gigas* for this term in Gn. 6:4; 10:8–9; 1 Ch. 1:10; Pss. 19:5; 33:16; Is. 3:2; 13:3; 49:24–25; Ezk. 32:12, 21, 27; 39:18, 20.

One other word is translated by *gigas* in the LXX, *'anāq* (*ANAK) in Dt. 1:28, though the EVV do not so take it.

No archaeological remains have been recovered which throw any light on this question, unless the presence of Neanderthal skeletons of Palaeolithic date in the caves of Mt Carmel are considered to do so (*EMIM; *ZUZIM). T.C.M.

GIBBETHON (Heb. *gibb^{e}ṯôn*, 'mound'). A city in Dan (Jos. 19: 44), given to the Kohathite Levites (Jos. 21:23). For some time it was in Philistine hands and was the scene of battles between them and N Israel. Here Baasha slew Nadab (1 Ki. 15:27) and, about 26 years later, Omri was acclaimed king (1 Ki. 16:17). Sargon of Assyria depicted the conquest of the city on the walls of his palace, amongst the triumphs of his 712 BC campaign (see P. E. Botta, *Monument de Ninive*, 1849, 2, pl. 89). Probably modern Tell el-Melât, W of Gezer. G.W.G.

GIBEAH (Heb. *giḇ^{e}'â, giḇ^{e}aṯ*). A noun meaning 'hill', and often so used in the Bible (*e.g.* 2 Sa. 2:25 and probably in 2 Sa. 6:3 with RV and RSV), but also used as a place-name. Owing to its similarity in form with the place-name *geḇa'* (*GEBA), these two are sometimes confused (*e.g.* Jdg. 20:10).

1. A city in the hill country of Judah (Jos. 15:57), possibly to be identified with modern el-Jeba' near Bethlehem.

2. A city in Benjamin (Jos. 18:28), evidently N of Jerusalem (Is. 10:29). As a result of a crime committed by the inhabitants, the city was destroyed in the period of the Judges (Jdg. 19–20; *cf.* Ho. 9:9; 10:9). It was famous as the birth-place of Saul (1 Sa. 10:26), *giḇ^{e}'aṯ šā'ûl*, 'Gibeah of Saul' (1 Sa. 11:4), and it served as his residence while

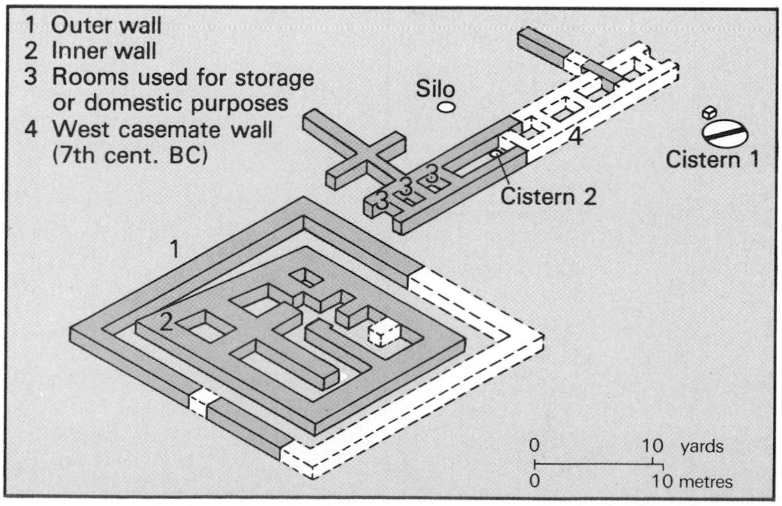

Plan of fortress excavated at Gibeah (Tell el-Ful). c. 650–538 BC.

Jar-handle inscribed 'Gibeon'. One of scores of inscribed handles found at el-Jib. (UMUP)

Stairway around a shaft cut through the solid rock to an underground pool at Gibeon. Diameter 11·3 m. Depth 10·8 m. Iron Age. (UMUP)

Main section of the Gibeon water-tunnel, showing some of its 93 steps. (UMUP)

he was king (1 Sa. 13–15), and after David was anointed in his place (1 Sa. 22:6; 23:19; 26:1). When David was king it was necessary to allow the Gibeonites to hang up the bodies of seven of Saul's descendants on the walls of Gibeah to make amends for his slaughter of them (2 Sa. 21:6; LXX 'Gibeon').

Biblical Gibeah of Saul is almost certainly to be identified with the mound of Tell el-Ful, about 5 km N of Jerusalem. The site was excavated by W. F. Albright in 1922–3 and 1933, with results that agreed with this identification. Further excavations were made by P. W. Lapp in 1964, bringing some changes to Albright's conclusions. The situation of the place away from running water meant that it was not permanently occupied until the Iron Age, when rain-water cisterns came into common use in the hill country. The first small settlement belonged to the 12th century BC, perhaps being destroyed in the episode which Jdg. 19–20 relate. After an interval, a small fortress was erected and manned about 1025–950 BC, the time of Saul. Albright had restored its plan as a rectangle with a tower at each corner, but only one tower has been uncovered, and Lapp's work has shown that the plan is uncertain. An iron plough-tip from this period was found, indicating the introduction of iron, monopolized up to now by the Philistines. There are signs that the fortress was pillaged and then abandoned for a few years, presumably at the death of Saul, but the site was soon reoccupied, possibly as an outpost in David's war with Ishbosheth. It must have lost its importance with David's conquest of the whole kingdom, however, and the excavations indicate that it lay deserted for about 2 centuries. The fortress was rebuilt with a watchtower, possibly by Hezekiah, and destroyed soon after (*cf.* Is. 10:29), to be refortified in the 7th century BC with a casemate wall (*FORTIFICATION). After a destruction attributed to Nebuchadrezzar's forces, there was quite an extensive village on the site until about 500 BC. A further period of abandonment ensued until the spread of a new village across the site in the Maccabean age. Thereafter there was sporadic occupation until the expulsion of all Jews from Jerusalem, when Gibeah presumably fell under the same ban because of its proximity to the city.

BIBLIOGRAPHY. W. F. Albright, *AASOR* 4, 1924; L. A. Sinclair, 'An Archaeological Study of Gibeah', *AASOR* 34, 1960; P. W. Lapp, *BA* 28, 1965, pp. 2–10; N. W. Lapp, *BASOR* 223, 1976, pp. 25–42; *EAEHL*, 2, pp. 444–446. T.C.M.
A.R.M.

GIBEON. At the time of the Israelite invasion of Canaan this was an important city inhabited by Hivites (Jos. 9:17; LXX *'Horites' is perhaps preferable) and apparently governed by a council of elders (Jos. 9:11; *cf.* 10:2). Following the fall of Jericho and Ai, the Gibeonites tricked Joshua into making a treaty with them as vassals. They were reduced to menial service and cursed when their deceit was discovered. The Amorite kings of the S hill-country attacked Gibeon for its defection to the Israelites, but Joshua led a force to aid his allies and, by means of a hailstorm and a miraculous extension of the daylight, routed the Amorites (Jos. 9–10; 11:19). The city was allotted to Benjamin and set apart for the Levites (Jos. 18:25; 21:17). During the struggle between David and the adherents of Ishbosheth the two sides met at Gibeon. Twelve warriors from either side were chosen for a contest, but each killed his opposite number and only after a general mêlée were David's men victorious (2 Sa. 2:12–17). At 'the great stone which is in Gibeon' Joab killed the dilatory Amasa (2 Sa. 20:8). This may have been merely a notable landmark, or it may have had some religious significance connected with the high place where the tabernacle and the altar of burnt-offering were, and where Solomon worshipped after his accession (1 Ch. 16:39; 21:29; 2 Ch. 1:3, 13; 1 Ki. 3:4–5). The 'Geba' of 2 Sa. 5:25 should probably be altered to 'Gibeon' in view of 1 Ch. 14:16; Is. 28:21 and LXX. The Gibeonites still retained their treaty rights in David's time, so that the only way of removing the guilt incurred by Saul's slaughter of Gibeonites was to hand over seven of his descendants for execution (2 Sa. 21:1–11). The close connection of Saul's family with Gibeon (1 Ch. 8:29 30; 9:35–39) may well have made his deed appear all the worse. Shishak of Egypt numbers Gibeon among the cities he captured (*ANET*, p. 242; *cf.* 1 Ki. 14:25). The assassins of Gedaliah, the governor of Judah appointed by Nebuchadrezzar, were overtaken by the 'great waters' of Gibeon and the prisoners they had taken set free (Je. 41:11–14). Gibeonites helped Nehemiah to rebuild the walls of Jerusalem (Ne. 3:7).

Excavations at el-Jib, some 9 km N of Jerusalem, between 1956 and 1962 have revealed remains of cities of the Early and Middle II Bronze Age, and of the Iron Age from its beginning to the Persian period. There was also a large town during Roman times. No remains of a Late Bronze Age settlement, which might be considered contemporary with Joshua, have been discovered, but burials of the time showed there had been life there. Some time in the Early Iron Age a large pit with a stairway descending around it was dug to a depth of 11 m in the rock. Steps led down a tunnel a further 12 m to a water-chamber, perhaps the 'pool' of 2 Sa. 2 and the 'waters' of Je. 41. It seems that this pit was often almost full of water. Later another tunnel was cut leading from the city to a spring outside the walls. The filling of the great pit contained the handles of many storage jars, stamped with a royal *seal or inscribed with the owners' names and the name Gibeon. Examination of the area around the pit has shown that it was the site of an extensive wine-making industry in the 7th century BC. Sealed jars of wine were stored in cool rock-cut cellars. The evidence suggests that the inscriptions relate to this site and so identify it.

BIBLIOGRAPHY. J. B. Pritchard, *Hebrew Inscriptions and Stamps from Gibeon*, 1959; *idem, The Water System of Gibeon*, 1961; *idem, Gibeon where the Sun stood still*, 1962; *idem, The Bronze Age Cemetery at Gibeon*, and *Winery, Defences and Soundings at Gibeon*, 1964.

A.R.M.

The hill of el-Jib, the modern site of the ancient city of Gibeon. (MEPHA)

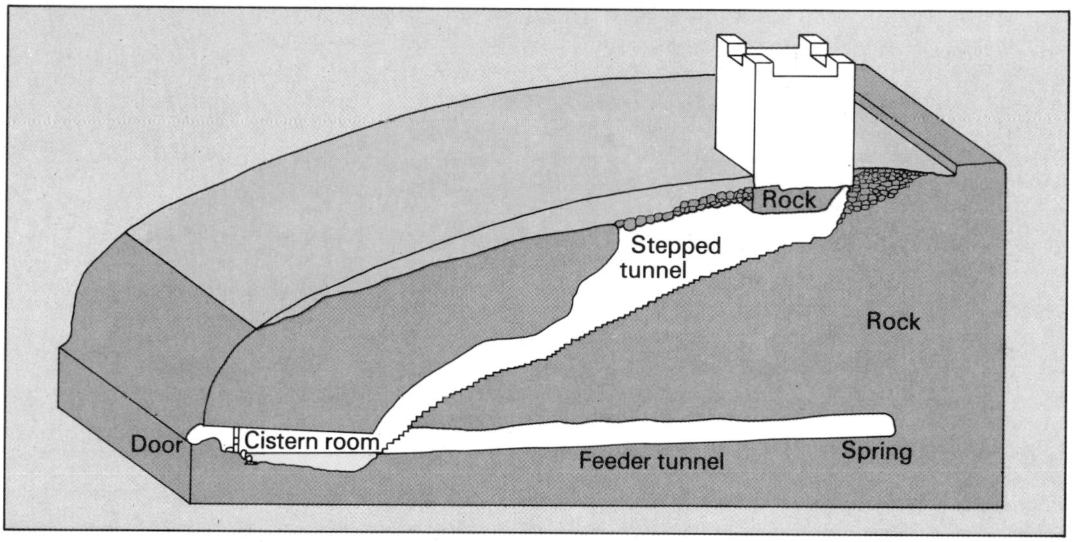

The water-system at Gibeon consisted of a water-chamber cut into the rock, reached by a spiral staircase, and an Iron Age tunnel of 93 steps leading to the spring outside the city wall. Section through E side of hill, showing the stepped tunnel and spring.

GIDEON (Heb. *giḏᵉʿôn*, 'hewer, smiter'), the judge who delivered Israel from the Midianites, a bedouin people then dominating the central area of Palestine (Jdg. 6:1–8:35). He was the son of Joash, of the clan of Abiezer, of the tribe of Manasseh, and he was also called Jerubbaal. Some scholars hold that the narrative is composite, made up of at least two accounts (see the commentaries).

Gideon was called to deliver his people while threshing wheat secretly for fear of Midianite depredations. There followed an act of defiance in which he destroyed his father's Baal-altar and Asherah, from the consequences of which he was saved by Joash's quick-wittedness. The gesture of defiance seems to signify a protest against the assimilation of the worship of Yahweh with the Baal-cult. This act is associated with the giving to Gideon of the name Jerubbaal (*yᵉrubbaʿal*), which is variously interpreted as 'Baal strives', 'Baal founds' or 'may Baal give increase'. Some suggest that this may have been Gideon's earliest name, reflecting the prevailing syncretism, receiving, however, a new significance in view of this act of iconoclasm (*cf.* R. Kittel, *Great Men and Movements in Israel*, 1929, p. 65; F. F. Bruce,

GIBEONITES
See Covenant, Part 1.

Part of a relief showing the bringing of gifts and tribute. Tomb of Huy, Thebes. 18th Dynasty, 1570–1314 BC. (PAC)

NBCR, ad loc.). In 2 Sa. 11:21 it appears as Jerubbesheth (*y^e^rubbešeṯ*), replacing the abhorred name Baal with the word for 'shame'.

The defeat of the Midianites is graphically described in Jdg. 7, when at God's command Gideon reduced his army from 32,000 to 300, and received personal re-assurance during a secret recon-naissance when he heard a Midian-ite warrior's dream of defeat. He made a sudden night attack which demoralized the enemy and led to a thorough rout. Jdg. 8 records the completion of the victory with the slaying of Zebah and Zalmunna, despite the hostility of the towns of Succoth and Penuel, for which Gideon exacted punishment.

After the deliverance Gideon was asked to set up a hereditary monarchy, but he refused. He did, however, accept the golden earrings taken as spoil in battle, with which he made an 'ephod' (probably an image of Yahweh). This he set up in his own city, where it later became a source of apostasy.

The defeat of Midian was deci-sive, and Israel had peace during the remainder of Gideon's life. The final picture of Gideon is of a peaceful old age, with many wives and sons, among the latter being the notorious Abimelech (Jdg. 9).

Heb. 11:32 gives Gideon a place among the heroes of faith. He trusted in God rather than in a large army, gaining a victory with a handful of men which made it clear it was wholly of God. 'The day of Midian' seems to have become proverbial for deliverance by God without the aid of man (Is. 11:4). Gideon is portrayed as a humble man, and his refusal of the kingship establishes the fact that Israel's ideal government was a theocracy (Jdg. 8:23).

BIBLIOGRAPHY. *Commentaries* by G. F. Moore (*ICC*), 1895, G. A. Cooke (*CBSC*), 1918, C. F. Burney, 1930, H. W. Hertzberg (*Das Alte Testament Deutsch*), 1953. Fleming James, *Personalities of the Old Testament*, 1947. J.G.G.N.

GIDEON'S FLEECE
See Dew, Part 1.

GIER EAGLE
See Animals, Part 1.

GIFTS OF THE SPIRIT
See Spiritual gifts, Part 3.

GIFT. In the OT a dozen words are used of gifts of one kind or other. The sacrifices and other offerings were gifts to God (Ex. 28:38; Nu. 18:11, *etc.*). The Levites were also, in a way, a gift to the Lord (Nu. 18:6). Occasionally there is the thought of God's gifts to men, as health and food and wealth and enjoyment (Ec. 3:13; 5:19). Men gave gifts on festive occasions (Ps. 45:12; Est. 9:22), or in association with a dowry (Gn. 34:12). Gifts might be tokens of royal bounty (Dn. 2:6). But there was little good-will in the 'gifts' (RSV, 'tribute') the Moabites brought David (2 Sa. 8:2). Gifts might be the expression of shrewd policy, as when 'a man's gift makes room for him' (Pr. 18:16). Indeed, a gift might be offered with altogether improper motives, so that the word comes to mean much the same as 'bribe'. The Israelites were commanded, 'thou shalt take no gift: for the gift blindeth the wise' (Ex. 23:8, AV).

In the NT there is a marked change of emphasis. Some of the 9 Gk. words for gift' refer to men's gifts to God, as *anathēma* (Lk. 21:5), and especially *dōron* (Mt. 5:23f.; 23:18f., *etc.*). Some refer also to men's gifts to one another, *e.g.* *dōron* (Rev. 11:10), *doma* (Mt. 7:11; Phil. 4:17). But the characteristic thing is the use of several words to denote entirely or primarily the gifts that God gives to men. *dōrea* (the word expresses freeness, bounty) is found 11 times, always of a divine gift. Sometimes this is salvation (Rom. 5:15, 17), or it may be undefined ('his inexpressible gift', 2 Cor. 9:15), or it is the Holy Spirit (Acts 2:38). James reminds us that 'Every good endowment (*dosis*) and every perfect gift (*dōrēma*) is from above' (Jas. 1:17). A most important word is *charisma*. This may be used of God's good gift of eternal life (Rom. 6:23), but its characteristic use is for the *'spiritual gifts', *i.e.* the gifts which the Holy Spirit imparts to certain people. Everyone has such a gift (1 Pet. 4:10), but specific gifts are reserved for individuals (1 Cor. 12:30), and individuals endowed with these gifts are themselves 'gifts' from the ascended Christ to the church (Eph. 4:7ff.). The important passages are Rom. 12:6ff.; 1 Cor. 12:4–11, 28–30; 14; Eph. 4:11ff. Salvation is God's good gift to men, and all the rest arises from this basic truth. L.M.

The spring of Gihon, Jerusalem, from which 'Hezekiah's tunnel' drew water. 701 BC. (SH)

GIHON (Heb. *gîḥôn*, 'stream'). **1.** One of the four rivers of the Garden of *Eden, which has been identified variously with the Oxus, Araxes, Ganges, Nile and many other rivers. The Nile identification arises from the statement that it wound through (*sāḇaḇ*) the land of *Cush (Gn. 2:13), which is identified with Ethiopia, but it is more probable that the Cush here referred to is the area to the E of Mesopotamia from which the Kassites later descended. If this is so, some river descending to Mesopotamia from the E mountains, perhaps the Diyala or the Kerkha, is possible, though the possibility of changed geographical features makes any identification uncertain.

2. The name of a spring to the E of Jerusalem, where Solomon was anointed king (1 Ki. 1:33, 38, 45). It was from this spring that Hezekiah cut a conduit to take the water to the pool of Siloam (2 Ch. 32:30) inside the city walls, and it was still outside the outer wall built by Manasseh (2 Ch. 33:14). It is probably to be identified with modern 'Ain Sitti Maryām.

Bibliography. On **1** see E. A. Speiser, 'The Rivers of Paradise', *Festschrift Johannes Friedrich*, 1959, pp. 473–485; on **2** see J. Simons, *Jerusalem in the Old Testament*, 1952, pp. 162–188.

T.C.M.

GILBOA (Heb. *gilbōa'*, probably 'bubbling fountain', although there is some doubt about this). Sometimes the name is anarthrous, while 'Mt Gilboa' also occurs. It was a range of mountains in the territory of Issachar, and so, in 2 Sa. 1:21, David apostrophizes 'ye mountains of Gilboa'. It was the scene of Saul's final clash with the Philistines and of his death (1 Sa. 28:4; 31). It may seem surprising to find the Philistines so far N, but the route from Philistia to Esdraelon was an easy one for armies on the march. The hills are now called Jebel Fuḳû'a, but the ancient name is perpetuated in the village of Jelbôn on the hillside. G.W.G.

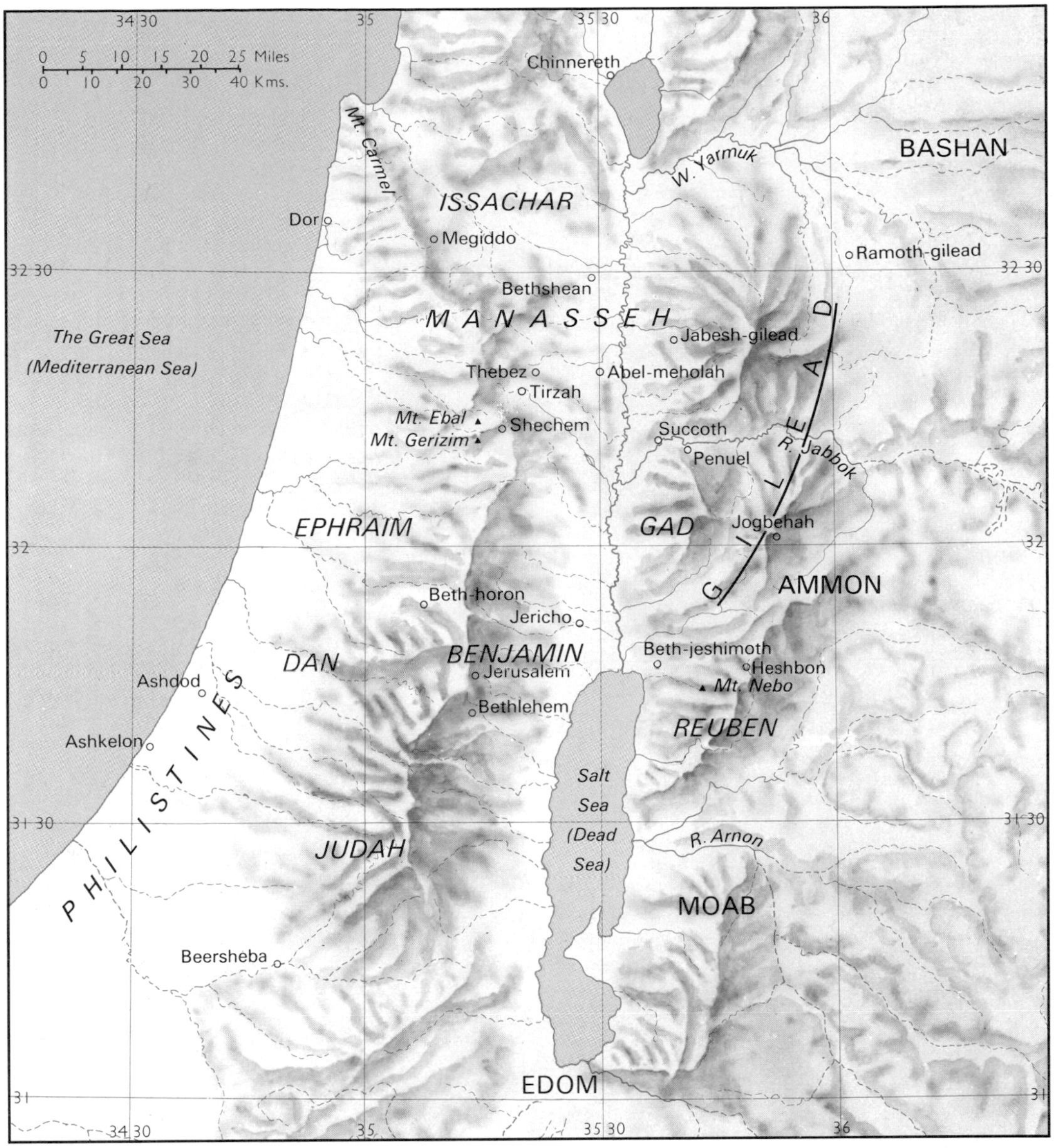

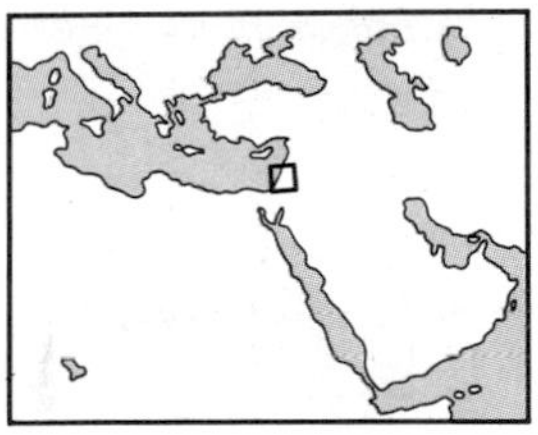

Gilead in Transjordan.

GILEAD. 1. The son of Machir, son of Manasseh and progenitor of the Gileadite clan which was a major part of the tribe of Manasseh (Nu. 26:29–30; 27:1; 36:1; Jos. 17:1, 3; 1 Ch. 2:21, 23; 7:14–17). **2.** A descendant of Gad and ancestor of some later Gadites (1 Ch. 5:14).

3. Jephthah's father (Jdg. 11:1–2).

4. The name applied to the whole or part of the Transjordanian lands occupied by the tribes of Reuben, Gad and half-Manasseh. Geographically, Gilead proper was the hilly, wooded country N of a line from Heshbon W to the N end of the Dead Sea, and extending N towards the present-day river and Wadi Yarmuk but flattening out into plains from *c.* 29 km S of Yarmuk. The N extension of these plains forms the territory of Bashan. Gilead thus defined is divided into N and S halves by the E–W course of the lower Jabbok river. S of Gilead proper (*i.e.* S of the Heshbon–Dead Sea line) and reaching to the Arnon river, there is a rolling plateau suitable for grain-growing, cattle and flocks. This tract, too, was sometimes included under 'Gilead'. But the term Gilead could in its widest application be extended to cover all (Israelite) Transjordan (*cf.* Dt. 2:36 and especially 34:1; Jdg. 10–12; 20:1; 2 Ki. 15:29). 1 Sa 13:7 is interesting in that it uses 'Gad' in reference to a particular section, and 'Gilead' of the territory in general. It is also used as a general term in 2 Ki. 10:33, where 'all the land of Gilead', *i.e.* (Israelite) Transjordan, includes 'Gilead (*i.e.* Gilead proper, plus the land to the Arnon) and Bashan'. For Gilead in the narrower sense, as the wooded hill-country stretching to the N and S of the Jabbok, see Dt. 3:10, where it is described as lying between the cities of the plain or tableland S of Heshbon and Bashan in the N, and Jos. 13:11 (in context). Either half of Gilead proper could be called simply 'Gilead' (referring to the N, see Dt. 3:15; Jos. 17:1, 5–6). Where fuller designations were used, Gilead S of the Jabbok (which fell to Gad) was sometimes called 'half the hill-country of Gilead' (RV, Dt. 3:12, *cf.* 16; Jos. 12:2, 5; *cf.* 13:25), a name also used of Gilead N of the Jabbok (Jos. 13:31). The N half was also known as 'the rest of Gilead' (Dt. 3:13). In Dt. 3:12 with 16, and 13 with 15, the sequence of full and abbreviated terms is particularly noteworthy. The simultaneous use of a term or title in both wide and restricted senses, or in both full and abbreviated forms, is a common phenomenon in antiquity and modern times alike. In most OT references to Gilead study of context usually shows the nuance intended.

The balm of Gilead was proverbial (Je. 8:22; 46:11; *cf.* Gn. 37:25). The rich woodland covering its hills is cited with Lebanon and Carmel as a symbol of luxury (Je. 22:6; 50:19; Zc. 10:10). It was the grazing-ground of goats (Ct. 4:1; 6:5), and also provided refuge for fugitives. Among those who sought refuge in Gilead were Jacob when he fled before Laban (Gn. 31:21–55), the Israelites who feared the Philistines in Saul's time (1 Sa. 13:7), Ishbosheth (2 Sa. 2:8–9) and David during Absalom's revolt (2 Sa. 17:22ff.).

BIBLIOGRAPHY. On natural geography, *cf.* D. Baly, *The Geography of the Bible*, 1974, pp. 219–225. On archaeology, *cf.* N. Glueck, *Explorations in Eastern Palestine*, 3; *AASOR* 18/19, 1939, pp. 151–153, 242–251 (extent and history), and pp. 153–242, 251ff. (archaeology). In general, M. Ottoson, *Gilead*, 1969; speculative is M. Wüst, *Untersuchungen zu den siedlungsgeographischen Texten des Alten Testaments*, 1. *Ostjordanland*, 1975. See also *REUBEN, *GAD, *MANASSEH, *RAMOTH-GILEAD and *MAHANAIM.

K.A.K.

GILGAL. The name can mean 'circle (of stones)', or 'rolling', from Heb. *gālal*, 'to roll'. In its latter meaning the name Gilgal was used by God through Joshua to serve as a reminder to Israel of their deliverance from Egypt when they were circumcised there: 'This day I have rolled away (*gallôṯî*) the reproach of Egypt from you' (Jos. 5:9).

1. Gilgal to the E of Jericho, between it and the Jordan. The exact site of Gilgal within this area is still uncertain. J. Muilenburg (*BASOR* 140, 1955, pp. 11–27) very tentatively suggests a site just N of Khirbet el-Mefjir, about 2 km NE of OT Jericho (Tell es-Sulṭan). In support of this approximate location, Muilenburg adduces the combined testimony of the OT references and of later writers (Josephus, Eusebius, *etc.*), and a trial excavation revealed Early Iron Age remains there. J. Simons (*GTT*, pp. 269–270, § 464) criticized Muilenburg's view on the ground that Khirbet el-Mefjir is more fairly N than E of Jericho; but this is not a very strong objection because Khirbet el-Mefjir is as much E as it is N (see Muilenburg's map, *op. cit.*, fig. I, p. 17).

Gilgal became Israel's base of operations after the crossing of Jordan (Jos. 4:19), and was the focus of a series of events during the conquest: twelve commemorative stones were set up when Israel pitched camp there (Jos. 4:20); the new generation grown up in the wilderness were circumcised there; the first Passover in Canaan was held there (Jos. 5:9–10) and the manna ceased (Jos. 5:11–12). From Gilgal, Joshua led forth Israel against Jericho (Jos. 6:11, 14ff.), and conducted his S campaign (Jos. 10) after receiving the artful Gibeonite envoys (Jos. 9:6), and there began to allot tribal territories (Jos. 14:6). Gilgal thus became at once a reminder of God's past deliverance from Egypt, a token of

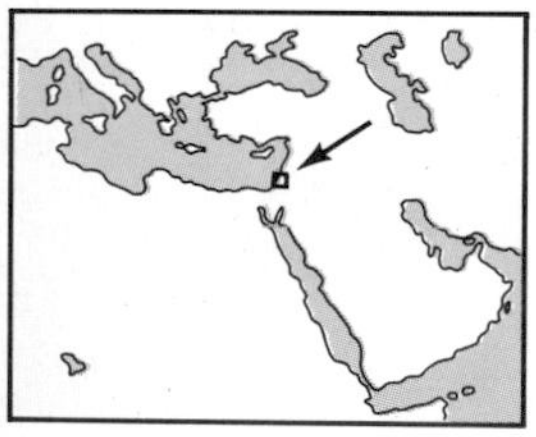

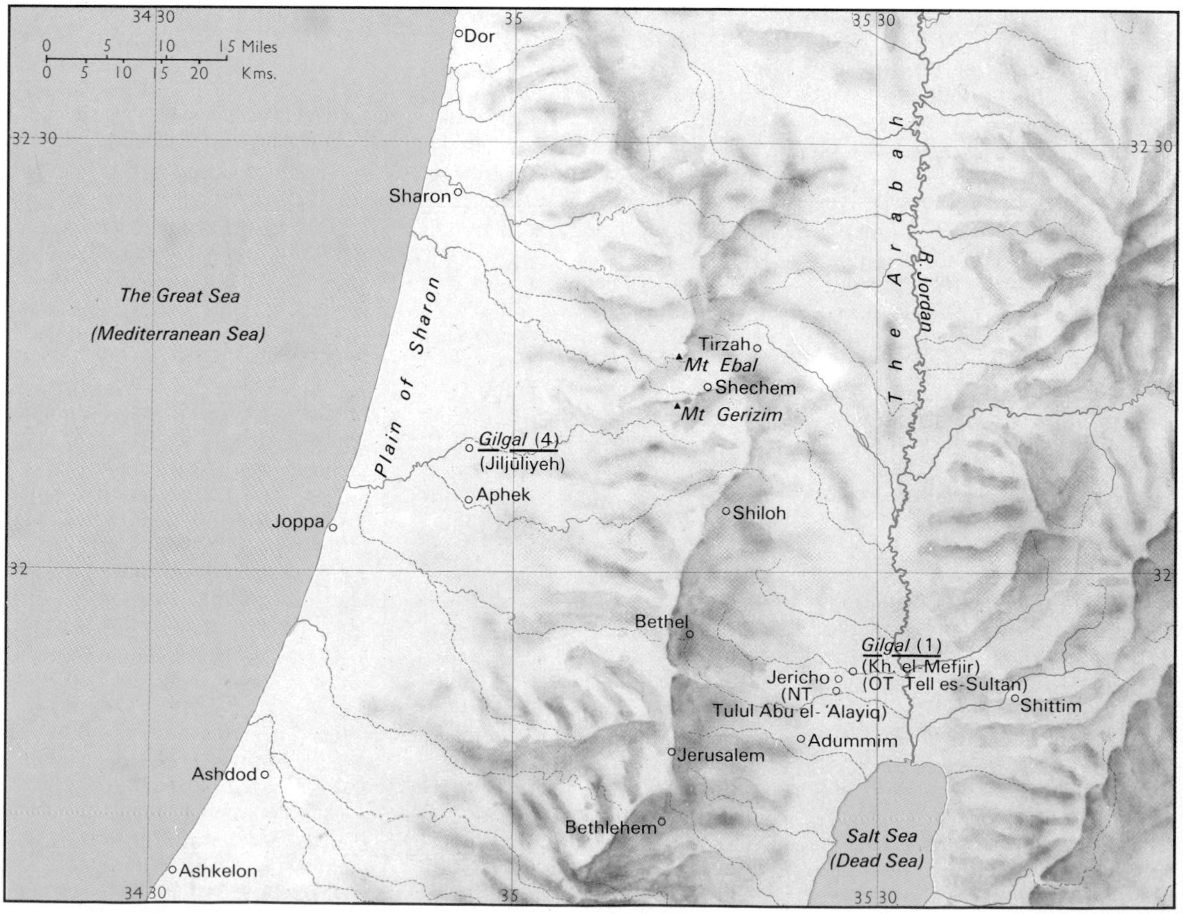

Suggested locations for Gilgal, near Jericho and Joppa.

present victory under his guidance, and saw the promise of inheritance yet to be gained. On the camp at Gilgal in Joshua's strategy, compare Y. Kaufmann, *The Biblical Account of the Conquest of Palestine*, 1953, pp. 91–97, especially 92, 95f. Kaufmann also incisively refutes Alt's and Noth's erroneous views about Gilgal as an early shrine of Benjaminite tradition (pp. 67–69).

In later days God's angel went up from Gilgal to Bochim in judgment against forgetful Israel (Jdg. 2:1); thence Ehud returned to slay a Moabite king for Israel's deliverance (Jdg. 3:19). Samuel used to visit Gilgal on circuit (1 Sa. 7:16); there Saul's kingship was confirmed after the Ammonite emergency with joyful sacrifices (1 Sa. 11:14–15; *cf.* 10:8). But thereafter, Saul offered precipitate sacrifice (1 Sa. 13:8–14), and it was at Gilgal that Samuel and Saul parted for ever after Saul's disobedience in the Amalekite war (1 Sa. 15:12–35). After Absalom's abortive revolt, the Judaeans welcomed David back at Gilgal (2 Sa. 19:15, 40). In the days of Ahab and Joram, Elijah and Elisha passed that way just before Elijah's translation to heaven (2 Ki. 2:1) (although some, quite unnecessarily it would seem, consider this place to be distinct from the historic Gilgal), and there Elisha sweetened the wild gourds in the cooking-pot of a group of prophets who feared poison (2 Ki. 4:38).

But during the 8th century BC, at least under the kings Uzziah to Hezekiah, Gilgal became a centre of formal and unspiritual worship which like Bethel drew condemnation from Amos (4:4; 5:5) and Hosea (4:15; 9:15; 12:11). The association of Bethel and Gilgal (reflected also in 2 Ki. 2:1–2) was strengthened by an important road that connected them (Muilenburg, *op. cit.*, p. 13). Finally, Micah (6:5) reminds his people of Gilgal's first role in their spiritual pilgrimage, witnessing to God's righteousness and saving power, 'from Shittim to Gilgal', *i.e.* across Jordan into the promised land.

2. In Jos. 15:7, the N boundary of Judah at least came in view of a Gilgal that was 'opposite the ascent of Adummim'; in the parallel description of this line, as also the S boundary of Benjamin (Jos. 18:17), Geliloth is so described. But whether *this* Gilgal/Geliloth is the same as the famous Gilgal E of Jericho remains quite uncertain though just possible. Otherwise, it must be some other local 'circle' farther W. Suggestions about this boundary will be found in Simons (*GTT*, pp. 139–140, § 314, 173, § 326), who, however, makes too free a use of emendation.

3. In Dt. 11:30, the phrase 'opposite Gilgal' may refer to the Canaanites dwelling in the Arabah (Jordan rift valley), rather than to the mountains Ebal and Gerizim. If so, then this is simply the historic Gilgal, see **1** above. Compare *GTT*, p. 35, §§ 87–88.

4. Among Joshua's defeated enemies occurs the king of Goyyim belonging to Gilgal (Jos. 12:23) between the kings of Dor and Tirzah. This Gilgal might be the capital of a king ruling over a mixed population on the edge of the maritime plain of Sharon, if—as is sometimes suggested—it is to be placed at Jiljūliyeh, about 5 km N of Aphek or about 22 km NE of the coast at Joppa.

5. The Beth-gilgal from which singers came to the dedication of the walls of Jerusalem by Nehemiah and Ezra is either the famous Gilgal (**1** above) or else remains unidentified (Ne 12:29). K.A.K.

GIRDLE. In AV this word covers several Hebrew terms and body-garments. The word *'aḇnēṭ* is used of the ceremonial sash, especially as worn by the high priest and his associates, made of embroidered linen in blue, purple and scarlet (Ex. 28:4, 39–40; 29:9; 39:29; Lv. 8:7, 13; 16:4), but worn also by other high dignitaries (Is. 22:21). In Ex. 28:8, 27–28, *etc.*, the 'curious girdle' of AV is *ḥēšeḇ*, 'device', of gold, blue, purple, scarlet, and fine linen, apparently an elaborately worked belt for the ephod (*DRESS, *d*). The term *'ēzôr* usually means 'waistcloth', 'loincloth'. A rough leather one characterized the prophet Elijah (2 Ki. 1:8) and his NT counterpart John the Baptist (Mt. 3:4; Mk. 1:6, RV).

Jeremiah (13:1–11) was bidden to use a spoilt linen loincloth as a symbol that spoilt Judah was good-for-nothing. Centuries later, Agabus bound himself with Paul's girdle in token of Paul's coming captivity (Acts 21:11). Besides picturing the onset of Assyrian troops with well-girt loincloths (Is. 5:27; *cf. ANEP*, fig. 236), Isaiah envisaged (11:5) righteousness and faithfulness as clothing the son of David like a loincloth. Ezekiel (23:15) alludes to Babylonians arrayed in vermilion, waistbands and turbans(?); *cf. ANEP*, fig. 454.

ḥᵃḡôr, *ḥᵃḡôrâ* means belt, waistband or girdle proper. Such belts were often ornate and valuable, including, doubtless, those for sale in Pr. 31:24 and belonging to fashionable women in Is. 3:24; *cf.* Dn. 10:5; Rev. 1:13; 15:6. They were used by warriors to support a sword in its sheath (2 Sa. 20:8; *cf.* 1 Ki. 2:5 and Heb. of 2 Ki. 3:21; *cf. ANEP*, figs. 173–174), and could be part of presents and rewards (1 Sa. 18:4; 2 Sa. 18:11). People at work commonly tucked up their clothes into their girdle, as is done in the East today.

The word *mēzaḥ*, 'girdle', occurs in Ps. 109:19; it and *'aḇnēṭ* may perhaps be connected with the Egyp. words *mḏḥ* and *bnd* respectively (T. O. Lambdin, *JAOS* 73, 1953, pp. 146, 152). K.A.K.

GIRGASHITES. A tribe listed among the descendants of Canaan in Gn. 10:16; 1 Ch. 1:14, and part of the very mixed population of Canaan as described in the original promise to Abraham (Gn. 15:21; *cf.* Ne. 9:8). In due course they were overcome by Israel (Dt. 7:1; Jos. 3:10; 24:11). In N Canaanite Ugarit (14th/13th centuries BC), the Girgashites are indirectly attested by two personal names: *grgš* and *bn-grgš*, *i.e.* Girgash and Ben-Girgash (references in Gordon, *Ugaritic Textbook*, 3, 1965, p. 381, No. 619). The biblical and Ugaritic Girgash(ites) are probably different from a people in Asia Minor called Karkisa in Hittite annals and *ḳrḳš* in similar Egyp. records. K.A.K.

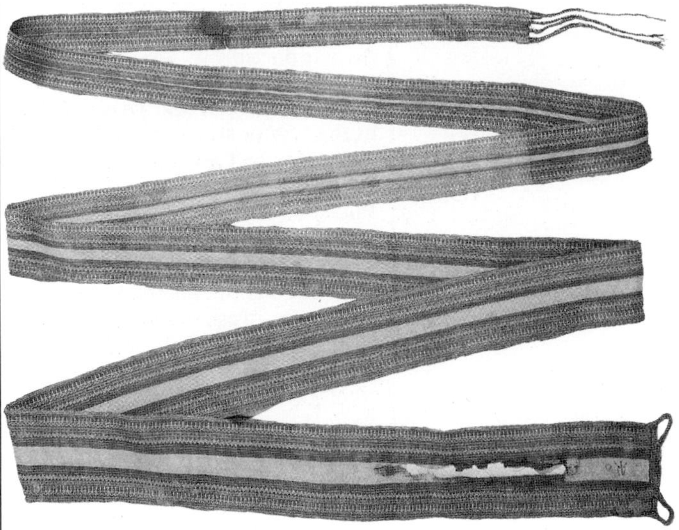

Girdle of Rameses III woven by simple hand-loom technique. c. 1170 BC. 20th Dynasty. (MCM)

GIN
See Snare, Part 3.

GIRZITES. In AV 'Gezrites'; either form is possible. Little-known semi-nomadic clans, associated with *Geshurites and *Amalekites in the NW of the *Negeb, and extirpated by David (1 Sa. 27:8) while he governed Ziklag under the Philistine Achish. K.A.K.

GLASS. Seldom mentioned in the Bible, glass was a rare luxury until Roman times. It was considered something precious like gold (Jb. 28:17, AV 'crystal'; Heb. *z^e^kûkîṯ*). Several passages translated 'glass' (AV) refer to reflecting metal surfaces used as mirrors. Glazing was early known and used on beads and brickwork from *c.* 4000 BC, but glass itself is first attested in the Early Bronze Age (*c.* 2600 BC).

By the 18th Egyptian Dynasty (*c.* 1546–1316 BC) a glass factory at el-Amarna in Egypt imitated stone and pottery types and made small unguent vessels by casting, or by winding drawn glass rods round a sand core and re-heating.

Early core-formed decorated goblets, bottles and bowls have been found in N Mesopotamia (Rimah, Nuzi), Babylonia, N Syria (Alalaḫ) and Palestine (Megiddo). Other imported and local products have been discovered at Gezer, Lachish (Late Iron Age), Achzib and Hazor. From the 13th century BC glazes are mentioned in contemporary Hittite and Assyr. texts. A reference in a Ras Shamra text to *spsg*, 'glaze', makes it probable that this word is found in Pr. 26:23—'like glaze crusted over pottery are smooth lips and an evil heart' (*BASOR* 98, 1945, pp. 21, 24; now disputed, *Ugarit-Forschungen* 8, 1976, pp. 37–40). Cobalt and manganese were used as colouring agents, but early glass was not very transparent because of impurities in the basic materials. The iridescence common on ancient glass is due to decomposition and weathering.

In the late Iron and Israelite periods Egyp. glass vessels, now imitating alabaster vessels (hence Gk. *alabastron*), were imported into Syria and Palestine. Phoenician products found at Samaria and elsewhere show that glass amphorae, juglets and aryballoi were in use.

The Hellenistic period brought the additional technique which resulted in gold glass, millefiore and coloured glasses found at many Palestinian sites. The *alabastron* broken open as a gift for our Lord was probably a long-necked glass ointment bottle, the so-called tear-bottle (Mt. 26:7; Mk. 14:3; Lk. 7:37; AV 'alabaster box').

By the Roman period the invention of glass-blowing methods (at Sidon?) resulted in mass-produced table services which rivalled pottery and metal for ease and cheapness of manufacture. Much of this was translucent, and much like a highly-polished glaze. The latter may be the allusion in the *'sea of glass' (Rev. 4:6; 15:2) and in the city and street of the New Jerusalem made of pure gold likened to glass (Rev. 21:18, 21).

BIBLIOGRAPHY. P. P. Kahane, *Antiquity and Survival*, 2, 1957, pp. 208–224; D. B. Harden, *Antiquity*, 1933, pp. 419–428; A. L. Oppenheim *et al.*, *Glass and Glassmaking in Ancient Mesopotamia*, 1970.

D.J.W.

GITTITE
See Gath, Part 1.

GITTITH
See Psalms, Part 3.

GIVING
See Alms, Part 1.

GLASS-MAKING
See Arts and crafts, Part 1.

GLEANING (*lāqaṭ*, 'to gather, glean'; *'ālal*, 'to roll, glean, suck', usually of grapes). Amid the rejoicing of harvest-time a kindly Israelitish law upheld the custom whereby the poor, orphans and strangers were allowed to glean grain, grapes and olives (Lv. 19:9–10; 23:22; Dt. 24:19). *Ruth took full advantage of the practice (Ru. 2:2ff.); Gideon used it in striking illustration of the superiority of Ephraim (Jdg. 8:2); and Jeremiah made of it a metaphor to express the complete annihilation of backsliding Israel (Je. 6:9; 49:9–10). The custom of gleaning still persists in certain eastern countries. (*AGRICULTURE.) J.D.D.

GLORIA IN EXCELSIS. This term refers primarily to a liturgical hymn originating in the patristic church (*cf. SHERK*, 6, 501; *ODCC*) and inspired by the angelic hymn in Lk. 2:14. As in the visions to Zechariah and Mary (Lk. 1:13, 30), the reassurance of the angel in Lk. 2:10 is an intimation of the good news which he brings. The previous angelic proclamations were directed particularly to the persons to whom the visions came. The joy of this message is for all the people of God; the shepherds are only representative of the larger group who anticipate and long for the deliverance Messiah brings. The benediction of praise expresses not merely the hope for the future but the reality that has become actual in Messiah's birth:

To God in the highest, glory!
To his people on earth, peace!

'Men of God's good will' is the better-attested reading and is parallel to 'the people' in v. 10. It refers to those upon whom God's redemptive mercy has been bestowed and with whom he is well pleased (*cf.* Lk. 3:22). The peace which the angels announce is not the external and transient *pax Romana*; it is the peace which heals the estrangement between sinful men and a holy God (*cf.* Is. 9:6f.; Rom. 10:15). (*BENEDICTUS.) E.E.E.

GLORY.

I. In the Old Testament

'Glory' generally represents Heb. *kāḇôḏ*, with the root idea of 'heaviness' and so of 'weight' or 'worthiness'. It is used of men to describe their wealth, splendour or reputation (though in the last sense *kāḇôḏ* is often rendered 'honour'). The glory of Israel was not her armies but Yahweh (Je. 2:11). The word could also mean the self or soul (Gn. 49:6).

The most important concept is that of the glory of Yahweh. This denotes the revelation of God's being, nature and presence to mankind, sometimes with physical phenomena.

In the Pentateuch the glory of Yahweh went with his people out of Egypt and was shown in the cloud which led them through the wilderness (Ex. 16:7, 10). The cloud rested on Mt Sinai, where Moses saw his glory (Ex. 24:15–18). No man could see God's face and live (Ex. 33:20), but some vision of his glory was granted (Ex. 34:5–8).

The glory of Yahweh filled the tabernacle (Ex. 40:34–35) and appeared especially at the hour of sacrifice (Lv. 9:6, 23). These passages seem all to be connected with a 'thunderstorm-theophany', but there are also passages which suggest more the character of Yahweh which is to be made known throughout the earth (Nu. 14:21–22).

The historical books tell of the Temple's becoming the place where the glory of Yahweh was especially to be located (1 Ki. 8:11; 2 Ch. 7:1–3).

In the prophets there are both the quasi-physical conception of Yahweh's glory as seen in the visions of Ezekiel (Ezk. 1:28, *etc.*) and also a more spiritualized doctrine (Is. 40:4–5; 60:1–3, *etc.*). The vision of Isaiah in the Temple seems to combine both ideas (Is. 6:1–4).

There can be found, likewise, in the psalms all the imagery of the storm (Pss. 18; 29) and also the idea of the future display of God's character to the world (Pss. 57:11; 96:3).

II. In the New Testament

Here the LXX is followed in translating *kāḇôḏ* by *doxa*. In secular Greek this means 'opinion' or 'reputation'. The former idea disappears entirely in the LXX and NT, and words akin to *kāḇôḏ* are also rendered by *doxa*.

In certain places in the NT *doxa* refers to human honour (Mt. 4:8; 6:29), but its chief use is to describe the revelation of the character and the presence of God in the Person and work of Jesus Christ. He is the outshining of the divine glory (Heb. 1:3).

The glory of God was seen by the shepherds at the birth of Christ (Lk. 2:9, 14) and by his disciples during his incarnate life (Jn. 1:14). Particularly was it revealed in his *sēmeia* (Jn. 2:11) and at his transfiguration (Mt. 17:1–8; Mk. 9:2–8; Lk. 9:28–36). This recalls the ascent of Moses to Sinai (Ex. 24:15) and of Elijah to Horeb (1 Ki. 19:8) and their visions of the glory of God. Now Christ both sees and reflects the divine glory, but no tabernacle needs to be built because the Word of God has pitched his tent in the human flesh of Jesus (Jn. 1:14) and his glory is to be more fully revealed at the coming exodus at Jerusalem (Lk. 9:31) and finally at his parousia.

In the Fourth Gospel it is the hour of dedication to death which is essentially the hour of glory (Jn. 7:39; 12:23–28; 13:31; 17:5; *cf.* Heb. 2:9).

The resurrection and ascension are also seen as manifestations of the glory of God in Christ (Lk. 24:26; Acts 3:13; 7:55; Rom. 6:4; 1 Tim. 3:16; 1 Pet. 1:21). But above all it is to be revealed in its fullness at the parousia (Mk. 8:38; 13:26, *etc.*).

Man, who was made as the image and glory of God (1 Cor. 11:7) for relationship with him, has fallen short of his destiny (Rom. 3:23), which has been fulfilled only by Christ, the second Adam (Heb. 2:6–9).

The glory of God in the face of Jesus Christ is still to be seen and reflected by the church (2 Cor. 4:3–6). It is the glory of the new covenant (2 Cor. 3:7–11), and it is especially shared both now (1 Pet. 4:14) and hereafter (Rom. 8:18) by those who suffer with Christ. The object of the church is to see that the world acknowledges the glory which is God's (Rom. 15:9) and is shown in his deeds (Acts 4:21), in his disciples (1 Cor. 6:20) and above all in his Son, the Lord of glory (Rom. 16:27).

BIBLIOGRAPHY. A. M. Ramsey, *The Glory of God and the Transfiguration of Christ*, 1949; A. Richardson, *An Introduction to the Theology of the New Testament*, 1958, pp. 64ff.; C. H. Dodd, *The Interpretation of the Fourth Gospel*, 1953, pp. 201ff.; S. Aalen, *NIDNTT* 2, pp. 44–52; G. Kittel, G. von Rad, *TDNT* 2, pp. 233–255.

R.E.N.

GNOSTICISM. A term derived from Gk. *gnōsis*, 'knowledge'. Until modern times it was applied ex-

GLORY OF GOD
See Shekinah, Part 3.

GLOSSOLALIA
See Tongues, gift of, Part 3.

GNAT
See Animals, Part 1.

Roman glass bottles excavated in Palestine. c. 1st cent. AD. (RS)

Assyrian alabastron, *bearing the name of Sargon II, which has been ground and polished from a raw block of glass. Height 8 cm.* (BM)

Bottom left: 'Phoenician'-style polychrome glass amphoristos made by winding strands of molten glass around a core. Height c. 16 cm. Amanthus, Cyprus. 2nd–1st cent. BC. (RS)

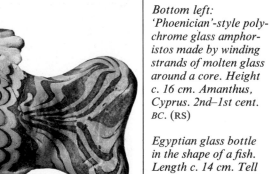

Egyptian glass bottle in the shape of a fish. Length c. 14 cm. Tell el-Amarna. Late-18th Dynasty. (BM)

A Gnostic gem-stone showing the Egyptianized figures of Chenoubis (lion's head) and Seth (donkey's head). The inscription composed of Greek vowels was presumably to enable the ornament to be used also as an amulet. c. 6 cm × 8 cm. Egypt/Palestine. 2nd-3rd cent. AD. (BM)

clusively to a body of heretical teaching denounced by the church Fathers in the early Christian centuries.

But in 20th-century scholarship it has often been applied more loosely to any form of religious belief which emphasizes any kind of dualism and/or the possession of secret knowledge. So, for example, Zoroastrianism, Mandaeism, the Hermetic literature, the Dead Sea scrolls and even the NT itself have all been described as 'gnostic'.

I. Definition

This is one of the most hotly debated issues today, and there are two main schools of thought: one, represented by conservative British scholars such as R. McL. Wilson, which supports a 'narrow' definition (*i.e.* restricting the term to the 2nd-century Christian heresies); and the other, popularized especially by German scholars like R. Bultmann and K. Rudolf, which supports a 'wide' definition (*i.e.* including other groups with a similar outlook).

There are difficulties with the 'wide' definition of the term, for under this usage the word 'Gnosticism' comes to have such a broad connotation that it almost ceases to have any specific reference at all, and simply denotes the lowest common denominator of Hellenistic thought, in which dualism of one sort or another was often a prominent feature.

At the same time, however, there are also difficulties in defining more precisely what Gnosticism is. Some groups in the early church (*e.g.* Valentinians, Naassenes) actually called themselves Gnostics. But the church Fathers are far from unanimous in their attempts to define what was common even to these groups. Indeed Irenaeus went so far as to comment that 'there are as many systems of redemption as there are teachers of these mystical doctrines' (*Adv. Haer.* 1. 21. 1).

But in spite of such obstacles to comprehensive definition, these 2nd-century groups had enough in common for us to be able to form some idea of a basic Gnostic belief.

The foundation-stone of this belief was a radical cosmological dualism, *i.e.* the belief that the created world was evil, and was totally separate from and in opposition to the world of spirit. The supreme God dwelt in unapproachable splendour in this spiritual world, and had no dealings with the world of matter. Matter was the creation of an inferior being, the *Demiurge*. He, along with his aides the *archōns*, kept mankind imprisoned within their material existence, and barred the path of individual souls trying to ascend to the spirit world after death. Not even this possibility was open to everyone, however. For only those who possessed a divine spark (*pneuma*) could hope to escape from their corporeal existence. And even those possessing such a spark did not have an automatic escape, for they needed to receive the enlightenment of *gnōsis* before they could become aware of their own spiritual condition: '. . . it is not only the washing that is liberty, but the knowledge of who we were, and what we have become, where we were or where we were placed, whither we hasten, from what we are redeemed, what birth is, and what rebirth' (*Exc. Theod.* 78. 2). In most of the Gnostic systems reported by the church Fathers, this enlightenment is the work of a divine redeemer, who descends from the spiritual world in disguise and is often equated with the Christian Jesus. Salvation for the Gnostic, therefore, is to be alerted to the existence of his divine *pneuma* and then, as a result of this knowledge, to escape on death from the material world to the spiritual.

The Gnostics themselves conceptualized all this in a highly mythological form, but the realities to which it corresponded were undoubtedly of a more existential nature. The Gnostic was trying to discover his own identity, and the appreciation of this fact led the eminent psychiatrist Carl Gustav Jung, for example, to base many of his observations about human nature on an understanding of ancient Gnosticism.

From the standpoint of traditional Christianity, Gnostic thinking is quite alien. Its mythological setting of redemption leads to a depreciation of the historical events of the life, death and resurrection of Jesus. Its view of man's relationship to God leads to a denial of the importance of the person and work of Christ, while, in a Gnostic context, 'salvation' is not understood in terms of deliverance from sin, but as a form of existential self-realization.

II. Sources

We know of the Gnostic sects from two different sources:

a. The church Fathers

The most important work here is Irenaeus, *Against Heresies*, though Tertullian, Clement of Alexandria and Hippolytus of Rome all wrote extensively on the same subjects. Some of these writings are interdependent, and they all have a similar outlook. They were all written from the standpoint of orthodox Catholic Christianity, to refute what the Fathers saw as a corruption of that 'original' apostolic Christianity of which they believed themselves to be the true upholders. This means that they are tendentious works, rather than impartial accounts of Gnostic beliefs. They were also written on the basis of secondhand knowledge. This, of course, was inevitable, since *gnōsis* by its very nature was esoteric and was not therefore readily accessible to anyone who was not an initiate. Nevertheless, when compared with the writings of the Gnostics themselves, the accounts of the church Fathers can be seen to be fair and reliable, at least in their general outlines, if not always in specific details.

b. Gnostic texts

These are by far the most important sources of our modern knowledge of Gnosticism, for they suffer from none of the disadvantages of the patristic accounts, and give us a direct insight into the workings of the Gnostic mind.

A number of isolated Gnostic texts have been known for some time, including important ones like the *Pistis Sophia*, the *Books of Jeû* and the *Apocryphon of John*, as well as a number of lesser works. But most of our direct knowledge of Gnostic writings comes from a remarkable find of 13 codices discovered about 1945 near Nag Hammadi in upper Egypt (*CHENOBOSKION). These were written in Coptic, though they are all translations of Gk. originals. They formed part of a library collected by an early Christian sect, and were eventually abandoned about AD 400. They comprise some 52 separate works. Publication of these texts has been a long and arduous business, and a complete facsimile edition of the original text did not become fully available until 1978. An Eng. translation of the texts had been published the previous year, though some of them had been made known much earlier through various scholarly articles and monographs. Nevertheless, the real task of interpreting these texts is only just beginning, and any assessment of them made now can only be provisional and tentative.

Some of the better-known works found at Nag Hammadi include a number of so-called 'gospels'. Like the Synoptic Gospel source Q, the *Gospel of Thomas* is a collection of sayings of Jesus, some of which parallel those found in the NT Gospels. Others are quite different, though some of them may well be genuine sayings of Jesus. But the collection as a whole has obviously been edited from a distinctively sectarian viewpoint. The *Gospel of Philip*, the *Gospel of Truth*, the Coptic *Gospel of the Egyptians* and the *Gospel of Mary* have less in common with the NT Gospels, and are more explicitly Gnostic in character.

The other Nag Hammadi texts include various collections of prayers, works with the title of *Apocryphon* ('secret book'—of James and of John), a number of others with the title of *Apocalypse* (of Paul, of James, of Adam, of Peter), together with heterogeneous examples of Gnostic speculative literature. Not all the works in this library represent the same type of Gnosticism. Many seem to be of Valentinian origin, but this does not apply to them all. Indeed some are not Gnostic at all. Codex VI, for example, contains a Coptic version of part of Plato's *Republic*, while two examples of early Christian wisdom writing are preserved in the *Teachings of Silvanus* (Codex VII) and the *Sentences of Sextus* (Codex XII).

An important question raised by these texts is the nature of Gnosticism itself *vis-à-vis* Christianity. Was it really a Christian heresy, as the Fathers supposed—or was it a non-Christian form of belief which in certain circles became overlaid with Christian ideas? So far as the evidence has been assessed, the Nag Hammadi texts do seem to show that there were non-Christian forms of Gnosticism. This can be seen most clearly in a comparison of *Eugnostos the Blessed* with the *Sophia of Jesus Christ*. For the two are so closely parallel that it is obvious that they must be different versions of the same text, though the former is cast in the form of a religio-philosophical tractate written by a teacher to his pupils, whereas the latter has the form of a post-resurrection discourse delivered by the risen Christ to his disciples. Detailed study of these two texts has so far tended to confirm that *Eugnostos the Blessed* is the original version, which was subsequently Christianized as the *Sophia of Jesus Christ*. Other texts, such as the *Apocalypse of Adam* and the *Paraphrase of Shem*, also seem to represent a non-Christian form of Gnosticism.

III. Origins

Where did Gnosticism come from? According to the church Fathers, it was a perversion of Christianity. But that idea is now all but universally discounted, for it does not square with the evidence. There is, however, no consensus on the question of Gnostic origins. It is easy to recognize this or that Gnostic idea as having affinity with the concepts of some other religion, but it is very difficult to pin down more precisely the actual origin of Gnostic thought.

Some believe that Gnosticism was in some way connected with Judaism in one of its various forms, and it is undoubtedly true that OT ideas feature prominently in Gnostic speculations, though always in a context that tears them from the fabric of authentic OT thought. Others points to the similarities between Gnosticism and the kind of dualism often found in the writings of the Gk. philosophers. The discovery of part of Plato's *Republic* at Nag Hammadi certainly demonstrates that his ideas were not uncongenial to the Gnostics, though at the same time it is hardly proof that there was some intrinsic connection between them.

A different origin for Gnosticism has been sought in Iranian religion. Here again the evidence is scarcely conclusive, though it cannot be denied that Gnosticism is much closer in outlook to the cyclical concepts of those eastern religions which stem from Zoroastrianism than it is to traditional Christianity.

It is impossible to pinpoint accurately the origins of Gnosticism. Indeed it is unlikely that it had a single origin, for by nature Gnostic thinking was extremely syncretistic, and its adherents were always ready, even eager, to utilize religious ideas from many diverse sources to serve their own ends.

IV. Issues in New Testament interpretation

Two major issues for the student of the NT stem from the study of Gnosticism:

a. Pre-Christian Gnosticism

According to Reitzenstein (followed by Bultmann and many other German scholars), when Christianity first made its appear-

Herdsmen with goad driving an ox. A relief depicting a procession bringing tribute to Darius I. E stairway of the Apadana, Persepolis, Iran. c. 500 BC.
(MEPHA)

ance in the Hellenistic world, its apostles found already in existence a comprehensive world-view that combined Greek and Oriental thought, and included the descent of a divine redeemer who saved the souls of mankind. This 'Gnostic' view was taken over *in toto* by the first Christians and applied to their experience of Jesus, so that he became the heavenly redeemer figure. Thus, the NT itself can be viewed as a form of Christianized Gnosticism.

There are many difficulties with the view that Gnosticism antedated Christianity. For one thing, there is no evidence for it, either in the texts known to Reitzenstein or in those now known to us. The Nag Hammadi texts have shown that there were non-Christian forms of Gnosticism, but that does not provide evidence for pre-Christian Gnosticism.

The idea that the NT is a form of Gnosticism is in any case unlikely, for there are serious and fundamental differences between the outlook of the Gnostics and that of the NT writers. The Gnostics held a cyclical concept of time, and the notion of history was meaningless to them. Gnostic redemption could never have any meaning in this life, but only in an escape from temporal existence to the world of spirit. By contrast, both OT and NT emphasize that time and history are important and both have a divine significance. God has acted in the course of the historical process as both Creator and Redeemer to provide salvation for his people. Whereas, for the Gnostic, God can be known only by an escape from history, to the Christian he can be supremely known because of his involvement in history, specifically in the life, death and resurrection of Jesus Christ. And Christian salvation is something to be enjoyed here and now in this world, rather than in some ethereal, 'spiritual' world.

b. Heresy and orthodoxy

Gnosticism is not, however, irrelevant for NT study. For traces of 'Gnostic' belief can be found in a number of NT writings, most strikingly in the beliefs of the Corinthian church as reflected in 1 Cor. These people claimed that because of their possession of special 'knowledge' they were released from the normal rules of society, and they claimed to be living an elevated, 'spiritual' existence even in their present material state. For them the resurrection was already a past event—past because they understood it spiritually, as did many Gnostics. And, like other Gnostics, they laid considerable emphasis on the supposed magical properties of the Christian sacraments.

Colossians has often been supposed to indicate the existence of a similar, though not identical, view in the church at Colossae, while the letters to the seven churches in Rev. 1–3 confirm the presence of similar 'Gnostic' ideas in other churches in the same area of Asia Minor. The Pastoral Epistles go so far as to denounce explicitly 'what is falsely called *gnōsis*' (1 Tim. 6:20), and 1 Jn. likewise seems to be written against some kind of 'Gnostic' background.

The NT writers themselves condemn these ideas. Though they often use Gnostic terminology in doing so, they make it clear that they do not accept its Gnostic connotations. But at the same time, the fact that such ideas seem to have been current, perhaps even widespread, in churches in different parts of the Roman empire, does give some credence to the hypothesis of W. Bauer, that the difference between heresy and orthodoxy was not so neatly defined in the 1st century as it later came to be by the anti-Gnostic Fathers of the Catholic Church.

BIBLIOGRAPHY. *Texts:* W. Foerster, *Gnosis: a selection of Gnostic Texts, I. Patristic Evidence*, 1972; *II. Coptic and Mandaic sources*, 1974; J. M. Robinson (ed.), *The Nag Hammadi Library in English*, 1977; D. M. Scholer, *Nag Hammadi Bibliography, 1948–1969*, 1971, and annual supplements in *NovT*; W. Bauer, *Orthodoxy and Heresy in Earliest Christianity*, 1971; H. Jonas, *The Gnostic Religion*², 1963; W. Schmithals, *Gnosticism in Corinth*, 1971; *idem*, *Paul and the Gnostics*, 1972; R. McL. Wilson, *The Gnostic Problem*, 1958; *idem*, *Gnosis and the New Testament*, 1968; E. M. Yamauchi, *Pre-Christian Gnosticism*, 1973. J.W.D.

GNOSTIC REDEEMER-MYTH
See Salvation, Part 3.

GOATS' HAIR
See Yarn, Part 3.

GOAD. A long-handled, pointed instrument used to urge on the oxen when ploughing. Shamgar used one as a weapon and slew 600 Philistines (Jdg. 3:31). The term is employed metaphorically in Ec. 12:11 to describe the words of the wise, and in Acts 26:14 where Paul is warned that for him to resist the new heavenly directive will be as fruitless as for a stubborn ox to resist the goad. J.D.D.

GOD. God is and he may be known. These two affirmations form the foundation and inspiration of all religion. The first is an affirmation of faith, the second of experience. Since the existence of God is not subject to scientific proof, it must be a postulate of faith; and since God transcends all his creation, he can be known only in his self-revelation.

The Christian religion is distinctive in that it claims that God can be known as a personal God only in his self-revelation in the Scriptures. The Bible is written not to prove that God is, but to reveal him in his activities. For that reason, the biblical revelation of God is, in its nature, progressive, reaching its fullness in Jesus Christ his Son.

In the light of his self-revelation in the Scriptures, there are several affirmations that can be made about God.

I. His Being

In his Being God is self-existing. While his creation is dependent on him, he is utterly independent of the creation. He not only has life, but he is life to his universe, and has the source of that life within himself.

Very early in biblical history this mystery of God's being was revealed to Moses when, in the wilderness of Horeb, he met with God as fire in a bush (Ex. 3:2). The distinctive thing about that phenomenon was that 'the bush was burning, yet it was not consumed'. To Moses this must have meant that the fire was independent of its environment: it was self-fed. Such is God in his essential being: he is utterly independent of every environment in which he wills to make himself known. This quality of God's being probably finds expression in his personal name Yahweh, and in his self-affirmation: 'I am who I am', that is, 'I am the one that has being within himself' (Ex. 3:14).

This perception was implied in Isaiah's vision of God: 'The Lord is the everlasting God, the Creator of the ends of the earth. He does not faint or grow weary. . . . He gives power to the faint, and to him who has no might he increases strength' (Is. 40:28–29). He is the Giver, and all his creatures are receivers. Christ gave this mystery its clearest expression when he said: 'For as the Father has life in himself, so he has granted the Son also to have life in himself' (Jn. 5:26). This makes independence of life a distinctive quality of deity. Throughout the whole of Scripture God is revealed as the Fountainhead of all there is, animate and inanimate, the Creator and Lifegiver, who alone has life within himself.

II. His nature

In his nature God is pure spirit. Very early in his self-disclosure as the author of the created universe, God is represented as the Spirit who brought light out of darkness, and order out of chaos (Gn. 1:2–3). Christ made this disclosure of God as the object of our worship to the woman of Samaria: 'God is spirit, and those who worship him must worship in spirit and truth' (Jn. 4:24). Between these two affirmations there are frequent references to the nature of God as pure spirit and as divine spirit. He is called the Father of spirits (Heb. 12:9), and the combination 'the Spirit of the living God' is frequently used.

In this respect we must distinguish between God and his creatures that are spiritual. When we say that God is pure spirit, it is to emphasize that he is not part spirit and part body as man is. He is simple spirit without form or parts, and for that reason he has no physical presence. When the Bible speaks of God as having eyes, ears, hands and feet, it is an attempt to convey to us the senses that these physical parts convey, for if we do not speak of God in physical terms we could not speak of him at all. This, of course, does not imply any imperfection in God. Spirit is not a limited or restricted form of existence, it is the perfect unit of being.

When we say that God is infinite spirit, we pass completely out of the reach of our experience. We are limited as to time and place, as to knowledge and power. God is essentially unlimited, and every element of his nature is unlimited. His infinity as to time we call his *eternity*, as to space his *omnipresence*, as to knowledge his *omniscience*, as to power his *omnipotence*.

His infinity likewise means that God is *transcendent* over his universe. It emphasizes his detachment as self-existing spirit from all his creatures. He is not shut in by what we call nature, but infinitely exalted above it. Even those passages of Scripture which stress his local and temporal manifestation lay emphasis also on his exaltation and omnipotence as a Being external to the world, its sovereign Creator and Judge (*cf.* Is. 40:12–17).

At the same time God's infinity implies his *immanence*. By this we mean his all-pervading presence and power within his creation. He does not stand apart from the world, a mere spectator of the work of his hands. He pervades everything, organic and inorganic, acting from within outwards, from the centre of every atom, and from the innermost springs of thought and life and feeling, a continuous sequence of cause and effect.

In such passages as Is. 57 and Acts 17 we have an expression of both God's transcendence and his immanence. In the first of these passages his transcendence finds expression as 'the high and lofty One who inhabits eternity, whose name is Holy', and his immanence as the one who dwells 'with him who is of a contrite and humble spirit' (Is. 57:15). In the second passage, Paul, in addressing the men of Athens, affirmed of the transcendent God that 'the God who made the world and everything in it, being Lord of heaven and earth, does not live in shrines made by man, nor is he served by human hands, as though he needed anything, since he himself gives to all men life and breath and everything', and then affirms his immanence as the one who 'is not far from each one of us, for "In him we live and move and have our being" ' (Acts 17:24, 28).

III. His character

God is personal. When we say this we assert that God is rational, self-conscious and self-determining, an intelligent moral agent. As supreme mind he is the source of all rationality in the universe. Since God's rational creatures possess independent character, God must be in possession of character that is divine both in its transcendence and immanence.

The OT reveals a personal God, both in terms of his own self-disclosure and of his people's relations with him, and the NT clearly shows that Christ spoke to God in terms that were meaningful only in person to person relationship. For that reason we can predicate certain mental and moral qualities of God, such as we do of human character. Attempts have been made to classify the divine attributes under such headings as Mental and Moral, or Communicable and Incommunicable, or Related and Unrelated. Scripture would seem to give no support to any of these classifications, and in any case God is infinitely greater than the sum of all his attributes. * God's names are to us the designation of his attributes, and it is significant that God's names are given in the context of his people's needs. It would seem, therefore, more true to the biblical revelation to treat each attribute as a manifestation of God in the human situation that called it forth, compassion in the presence of misery, long-suffering in the presence of ill-desert, grace in the presence of guilt, mercy in the presence of penitence, suggesting that the attributes of God designate a relation into which he enters to those who feel their need of him. That bears with it the undoubted truth that God, in the full plenitude of his nature, is in each of his attributes, so that there is never more of one attribute than of another, never more love than justice, or more mercy than righteousness. If there is one attribute of God that can be recognized as all-comprehensive and all-pervading, it is his * holiness, which must be predicated of all his attributes, holy love, holy compassion, holy wisdom.

IV. His will

God is sovereign. That means that he makes his own plans and carries them out in his own time and way. That is simply an expression of his supreme intelligence, power and wisdom. It means that God's will is not arbitrary, but acts in complete harmony with his character. It is the forth-putting of his power and goodness, and is thus the final goal of all existence.

There is, however, a distinction between God's will which prescribes what we shall do, and his will which determines what he will do. Thus theologians distinguish between the *decretive will* of God by which he decrees whatsoever comes to pass, and his *preceptive will* by which he enjoins upon his creatures the duties that belong to them. The decretive will of God is thus always accomplished, while his preceptive will is often disobeyed.

When we conceive of the sovereign sway of the divine will as the final ground of all that happens, either actively bringing it to pass, or passively permitting it to come to pass, we recognize the distinction between the active will of God and his permissive will. Thus the entrance of sin into the world must be attributed to the permissive will of God, since sin is a contradiction of his holiness and goodness. There is thus a realm in which God's will to act is dominant, and a realm in which man's liberty is given permission to act. The Bible presents both in operation. The note which rings through the OT is that struck by Nebuchadrezzar: 'He does according to his will in the host of heaven and among the inhabitants of the earth; and none can stay his hand or say to him, "What doest thou?" ' (Dn. 4:35). In the NT we come across an impressive example of the divine will resisted by human unbelief, when Christ uttered his agonizing cry over Jerusalem: 'How often would I have gathered your children together as a hen gathers her brood under her wings, and you would not!' (Mt. 23:37). Nevertheless, the sovereignty of God ensures that all will be overruled to serve his eternal purpose, and that ultimately Christ's petition: 'Thy will be done on earth as it is in heaven' shall be answered.

It is true that we are not able to reconcile God's sovereignty and man's responsibility because we do not understand the nature of divine knowledge and comprehension of all the laws that govern human conduct. The Bible throughout teaches us that all life is lived in the sustaining will of God 'in whom we live and move and have our being', and that as a bird is free in the air, and a fish in the sea, so man has his true freedom in the will of God who created him for himself.

V. His subsistence

In his essential life God is a fellowship. This is perhaps the supreme revelation of God given in the Scriptures: it is that God's life is eternally within himself a fellowship of three equal and distinct persons, Father, Son and Spirit, and that in his relationship to his moral creation God was extending to them the fellowship that was essentially his own. That might perhaps be read into the divine dictum that expressed the deliberate will to create man: 'Let us make man in our image, after our likeness,' that it was an expression of the will of God not only to reveal himself as a fellowship, but to make that life of fellowship open to the moral creatures made in his image and so fitted to enjoy it. While it is true that man through sinning lost his fitness to enjoy that holy fellowship, it is also true that God willed to make it possible to have it restored to him. It has been observed, indeed, that this was probably the grand end of redemption, the revelation of God in Three Persons acting for our restoration, in electing love that claimed us, in redeeming love that emancipated us, and in regenerating love that recreated us for his fellowship. (* TRINITY.)

VI. His Fatherhood

Since God is a Person he can enter into personal relationships, and the closest and tenderest is that of Father. It was Christ's most common designation for God, and in theology it is reserved specially for the first Person of the Trinity. There are four types of relationship in which the word Father is applied to God in Scripture.

There is his *Creational Fatherhood.* The fundamental relation of God to man whom he made in his own image finds its most full and fitting illustration in the natural relationship which involves the gift of life. Malachi, in calling his people to faithfulness to God and to consideration of one another, asks: 'Have we not all one father? Has not one God created us?' (Mal. 2:10). Isaiah, in a plea to God not to forsake his people, cries: 'Yet, O Lord, thou art our Father; we are the clay, and thou art our potter; we are all the work of thy hand' (Is. 64:8). But it is, more particularly, for man's spiritual nature that this relationship is claimed. In Hebrews God is called 'the Father of spirits' (12:9), and in Numbers 'the God of the spirits of all flesh' (16:22). Paul, when he preached from Mars Hill, used this argument to drive home the irrationality of rational man worshipping idols of wood and stone, quoting the poet Aratus ('For we are indeed his offspring') to indicate that man is a creature of God. The creaturehood of man is thus the counterpart of the general Fatherhood of God. Without the Creator-Father there would be no race of man, no family of mankind.

There is the *Theocratic Fatherhood.* This is God's relationship to his covenant-people, Israel. In this, since it is a collective relationship that is indicated, rather than a personal one, Israel as a covenant-people was the child of God, and she was challenged to recognize and respond to this filial relationship: 'If then I am a father, where is my honour?' (Mal. 1:6). But since the covenant relationship was redemptive in its spiritual significance, this may be regarded as a foreshadowing of the NT revelation of the divine Fatherhood.

There is *Generative Fatherhood.* This belongs exclusively to the second Person of the Trinity, designated the Son of God, and the only begotten Son. It is, therefore, unique, and not to be applied to any mere creature. Christ, while on earth, spoke most frequently of this relationship which was peculiarly his. God was his Father by eternal generation, expressive of an essential and timeless relationship that transcends our comprehension. It is significant that Jesus, in his teaching of the Twelve, never used the term 'Our Father' as embracing himself and them. In the resurrection message through Mary he indicated two distinct relationships: 'My Father, and your Father' (Jn. 20:17), but the two are so linked together that the one becomes the ground of the other. His Sonship, though on a level altogether unique, was the basis of their sonship.

There is also the *Adoptive Fatherhood.* This is the redeeming relationship that belongs to all believers, and in the context of redemption it is viewed from two aspects, that of their standing in Christ, and that of the regenerating work of the Holy Spirit in them. This relationship to God is basic to all believers, as Paul reminds the Galatian believers: 'For in Christ Jesus you are all sons of God, through faith' (Gal. 3:26). In this living union with Christ they are adopted into the family of God, and they become subjects of the regenerative work of the Spirit that bestows upon them the nature of children: one is the objective aspect, the other the subjective. Because of their new standing (justification) and relationship (adoption) to God the Father in Christ, they become partakers of the divine nature and are born into the family of God. John made this clear in the opening chapter of his Gospel: 'To all who received him, who believed in his name, he gave power (authority) to become children of God; who were born, not of blood nor of the will of the flesh nor of the will of man, but of God' (Jn. 1:13). And so they are granted all the privileges that belong to that filial relationship: 'if children, then heirs' is the sequence (Rom. 8:17).

It is clear that Christ's teaching on the Fatherhood of God restricts the relationship to his believing people. In no instance is he reported as assuming this relationship to exist between God and unbelievers. Not only does he not give a hint of a redeeming Fatherhood of God towards all men, but he said pointedly to the cavilling Jews: 'You are of your father the devil' (Jn. 8:44).

While it is under this relationship of Father that the NT brings out the tenderest aspects of God's character, his love, his faithfulness, his watchful care, it also brings out the responsibility of our having to show God the reverence, the trust and the loving obedience that children owe to a father. Christ has taught us to pray not only 'Our Father', but 'Our Father who art in heaven', thus inculcating reverence and humility.

BIBLIOGRAPHY. T. J. Crawford, *The Fatherhood of God*, 1868; J. Orr, *The Christian View of God and the World*, 1908; A. S. Pringle-Pattison, *The Idea of God*, 1917; G. Vos, *Biblical Theology*, 1948; H. Bavinck, *The Doctrine of God*, 1951; J. I. Packer, *Knowing God*, 1973; J. Schneider, C. Brown, J. Stafford Wright, in *NIDNTT* 2, pp. 66–90; H. Kleinknecht *et al.*, in *TDNT* 3, pp. 65–123. R.A.F.

GOD, NAMES OF. In considering the various names, titles or descriptions of God in the OT there are three words of basic importance—*'ēl*, *'elōhîm* and *Yahweh* (Jehovah). It is necessary at the outset to realize the meaning of these severally, and their relationship one to another.

I. Basic names

a. El

El (*'ēl*), EVV 'God' or 'god', has cognate forms in other Semitic tongues, and means a god in the widest sense, true or false, or even an image treated as a god (Gn. 35:2). Because of this general character it is frequently associated with a defining adjective or predicate. For example, in Dt. 5:9 we read, 'I the LORD (*Yahweh*) your God (*'elohîm*) am a jealous God (*'ēl*)', or in Gn. 31:13, 'the God (*'ēl*) of Bethel'. In the Ras Shamra tablets, however, El is a proper noun, the name of the Canaanite 'high God' whose son was Ba'al. The plural of *'ēl* is *'elōhîm*, and when used as a plural is translated 'gods' (but see below). These may be mere images, 'wood and stone' (Dt. 4:28), or the imaginary beings which they represent (Dt. 12:2).

b. Elyon, El Elyon

'El 'elyôn, 'the most high God', was the title of God as worshipped by Melchizedek (see below). *'Elyôn* is found in Nu. 24:16 and elsewhere. In Ps. 7:17 it is found in combination with *Yahweh*, and in Ps. 18:13 in parallel. See also Dn. 7:22, 25 for the Aram. plural *'elyônîn*; elsewhere in the Aram. of Daniel the equivalent of Heb. *'elyôn* is *'illāyâ* (*e.g.* 4:17; 7:25).

c. Elohim

Though a plural form (*'elōhîm*), Elohim can be treated as a singular, in which case it means the one supreme deity, and in EVV is rendered 'God'. Like its English equivalent, it is, grammatically considered, a common noun, and conveys the notion of all that belongs to the concept of deity, in contrast with man (Nu. 23:19) and other created beings. It is appropriate to cosmic and world-wide relationships (Gn. 1:1), because there is only one supreme and true God, and he is a Person; it approaches the character of a proper noun, while not losing its abstract and conceptual quality.

d. Eloah

This word (*'elōah*) is a singular form of *'elōhîm*, and has the same meaning as *'ēl*. In the OT it is chiefly found in poetry (*e.g.* Dt. 32:15, 17; it is most frequent in Job). The corresponding Aramaic form is *'elāh*.

e. Jehovah

The Heb. word *Yahweh* is in EVV usually translated 'the LORD' (note the capitals) and sometimes Jehovah'. The latter name originated as follows. The original Heb. text was not vocalized; in time the 'tetragrammaton' YHWH was considered too sacred to pronounce; so *'adōnāy* ('my Lord') was substituted in reading, and the vowels of this word were combined with the consonants YHWH to give 'Jehovah', a form first attested at the start of the 12th century AD.

The pronunciation Yahweh is indicated by transliterations of the name into Greek in early Christian literature, in the form *iaoue* (Clement of Alexandria) or *iabe* (Theodoret; by this time Gk. *b* had the pronunciation of *v*). The name is certainly connected with Heb. *hāyâ*, 'to be', or rather with a variant and earlier form of the root, *hāwâ*. It is not, however, to

GODDESSES
See Prostitution, Part 3.

be regarded as an imperfective aspect of the verb; the Hiph'îl conjugation, to which alone such a form could be assigned, is not forthcoming for this verb; and the imperfective of the Qal conjugation could not have the vowel *a* in the first syllable. Yahweh should be regarded as a straightforward substantive, in which the root *hwh* is preceded by the preformative *y*. See L. Koehler and W. Baumgartner, *Lexicon in Veteris Testamenti Libros*, 1958, pp. 368f.; also L. Koehler, *Vom Hebräischen Lexikon*, 1950, pp. 17f.

Strictly speaking, Yahweh is the only 'name' of God. In Genesis wherever the word *šēm* ('name') is associated with the divine being that name is Yahweh. When Abraham or Isaac built an altar 'he called on the name of Yahweh' (Gn. 12:8; 13:4; 26:25).

In particular, Yahweh was the God of the Patriarchs, and we read of 'Yahweh the God (Elohim) of Abraham' and then of Isaac and finally 'Yahweh, the God of Abraham, and the God of Isaac, and the God of Jacob', concerning which Elohim says, 'this is my name for ever' (Ex. 3:15). Yahweh, therefore, in contrast with Elohim, is a proper noun, the name of a Person, though that Person is divine. As such, it has its own ideological setting; it presents God as a Person, and so brings him into relationship with other, human, personalities. It brings God near to man, and he speaks to the Patriarchs as one friend to another.

A study of the word *'name' in the OT reveals how much it means in Hebrew. The name is no mere label, but is significant of the real personality of him to whom it belongs. It may derive from the circumstances of his birth (Gn. 5:29), or reflect his character (Gn. 27:36), and when a person puts his 'name' upon a thing or another person the latter comes under his influence and protection.

f. Yahweh Elohim

These two words are combined in the narrative of Gn. 2:4–3:24, though 'Elohim' alone is used in the colloquy between Eve and the serpent. If the narrative concerning Eden was related to a Sumerian original it could have been brought by Abraham from Ur, and it would thus be possible to account for the different use in these two chapters from those which precede and follow it.

g. How El, Elohim and Yahweh are related

We are now in a position to consider how these three words agree or differ in their use. While there are occasions on which any one of them could be used of God, they are by no means identical or interchangeable. In the account of Gn. 14, now regarded by many as giving a true picture of the situation in the early 2nd millennium BC, we read how Abraham met with Melchizedek, the priest of *'ēl 'elyôn*, 'the most high God'. Here we have Melchizedek's 'name' or title for the deity he worshipped. It would be clearly wrong to substitute either 'Elohim' or 'Yahweh' for *'ēl 'elyôn* (Gn. 14:18). Melchizedek blesses Abraham in the name of *'ēl 'elyôn*, 'maker of heaven and earth', so identifying *'ēl 'elyôn* as the supreme God (14:19–20).

The king of Sodom offers Abraham a gift, which he refuses, lifting up his hand to *Yahweh, 'ēl 'elyôn*, 'maker of heaven and earth' (14:22). He means that he also worships the supreme God, the same God (for there is only one), but knows him by the name of 'Yahweh'. (LXX and SP omit *Yahweh* in Gn. 14:22.)

To cite a second example, in Gn. 27:20 Jacob deceives his father with the words, 'Because Yahweh your God (Elohim) granted me success.' To interchange 'Yahweh' and 'Elohim' would not make sense. Yahweh is the name by which his father worships the supreme God (Elohim).

II. The revelation to Moses

The revelation made to Moses at the burning bush is one of the most striking and convincing incidents in the Bible story. After the opening words God introduces himself thus, 'I am the God (Elohim) of your father' (Ex. 3:6). This at once assumes that Moses would know the name of his father's God. When God announces his purpose of delivering Israel by the hand of Moses the latter shows reluctance and begins to make excuse.

He inquires, 'If . . . the people of Israel . . . ask me, "What (*mah*) is his name?" what shall I say to them?' (Ex. 3:13). The normal way to ask a name is to use the pronoun *mî*; to use *mah* invites an answer which goes further, and gives the meaning ('*what?*') or substance of the name.

This helps to explain the reply, namely, 'I AM WHO I AM' (*'ehyeh 'ašer 'ehyeh*). And he said, 'Say this to the people of Israel, "I AM has sent me to you" ' (Ex. 3:14). By this Moses would not think that God was announcing a *new name*, nor is it called a 'name'; it is just the inner meaning of the name Moses knew. We have here a play upon words; 'Yahweh' is interpreted by *'ehyeh*. M. Buber translates 'I will be as I will be', and expounds it as a promise of God's power and enduring presence with them in the process of deliverance (*Moses*, pp. 39–55). That something like this is the purport of these words, which in English sound enigmatical, is shown by what follows, ' "Yahweh, the God of your fathers, the God of Abraham, the God of Isaac, and the God of Jacob, has sent me to you": this is my name for ever' (v. 15). The full content of the name comes first; the name itself follows.

III. The interpretation of Exodus 6:2–3

After Moses' return to Egypt Yahweh further instructs him how to deal with Pharaoh and with his own people: 'I am the LORD (Yahweh),' he says. 'I appeared to Abraham, to Isaac, and to Jacob, as God Almighty (*'ēl šadday*), but by my name the LORD (Yahweh) I did not make myself known to them' (Ex. 6:3).

The former revelation, to the Patriarchs, concerned promises belonging to a distant future; it supposed that they should be assured that he, Yahweh, was such a God (*'ēl*) as was competent (one possible meaning of *šadday*) to fulfil them. The revelation at the bush was greater and more intimate, God's power and immediate and continuing presence with them being all wrapped up in the familiar name of Yahweh. Henceforth, 'I am Yahweh, your God' (Ex. 6:7) gives them all the assurance they need of his purpose, his presence and his power.

For God's self-revelation to the Patriarchs as God Almighty (*'ēl šadday*), initiating or reaffirming his covenant with them, *cf.* Gn. 17:1; 35:11; 48:3—passages which, like Ex. 6:1–6, are assigned to the priestly narrator in the prevalent documentary hypothesis.

IV. Particular names containing El or Jehovah

a. 'El 'Olām

At Beersheba Abraham planted a

tamarisk, and 'called there on the name of *Yahweh*', *'ēl 'ôlām* (Gn. 21:33). Here 'Yahweh' is the name, and the description follows, 'the Everlasting God'. F. M. Cross has drawn attention to the original form of this name—*'El dhū-'Ôlami*, 'God of Eternity' (*cf.* W. F. Albright in *BO* 17, 1960, p. 242).

b. 'Ēl-'Elōhê-Israel

Jacob, reaching Shechem, bought a piece of land, reared an altar and called it *'ēl-'elōhê-Yiśrā'ēl* (Gn. 33:20), 'God (*'ēl*) is the God (*'elōhîm*) of Israel'. In this manner he commemorates the recent encounter with the angel at the place he had called Peniel (*penî-'ēl*, 'the face of God', Gn. 32:30). He thus accepts Israel as his name and so renders worship to God.

c. Jehovah-jireh

In Gn. 22, when the angel of the Lord had pointed to a ram as a substitute for Isaac, Abraham named the place *Yahweh yir'eh*, 'the LORD provides' (vv. 8, 14).

d. Jehovah-nissi

In somewhat similar fashion, after the defeat of the Amalekites, Moses erected an altar and called it *Yahweh nissî*, 'the LORD is my banner' (Ex. 17:15). These, however, are not the names of God, but are commemorative of events.

e. Jehovah-shalom

This is the name given by Gideon to the altar he erected in Ophrah, *Yahweh šālôm*, 'the LORD is peace' (Jdg. 6:24).

f. Jehovah-tsidkenu

This is the name by which Messiah shall be known, *Yahweh ṣiḏqēnû*, 'the LORD is our righteousness' (Je. 23:6; 33:16), in contrast to the last king of Judah, who was an unworthy bearer of the name Zedekiah (*ṣiḏqiyāhû*, 'Yahweh is righteousness').

g. Jehovah-shammah

This is the name given to the city of Ezekiel's vision, *Yahweh šāmmâ*, 'the LORD is there' (Ezk. 48:35).

h. The LORD of hosts

Differing from the preceding names, *Yahweh ṣeḇā'ôṯ*, 'the LORD of hosts', is a divine title. It does not occur in the Pentateuch; it appears first in 1 Sa. 1:3 as the title by which God was worshipped at Shiloh. It was used by David in defying the Philistine (1 Sa. 17:45); and David again makes use of it as the climax to a glorious song of victory (Ps. 24:10). It is common in the prophets (88 times in Jeremiah), and is used to exhibit Yahweh as at all times the Saviour and Protector of his people (Ps. 46:7, 11). The 'hosts' may originally have been the armies of Israel, as in 1 Sa. 17:45, but at an early date came to comprise all the heavenly powers, ready to do the LORD's command.

i. LORD God of Israel

This title (*Yahweh 'elōhê Yiśrā'ēl*) is found as early as Deborah's song (Jdg. 5:3), and is frequently used by the prophets (*e.g.* Is. 17:6; Zp. 2:9). It follows in the series 'the God of Abraham, of Isaac, and of Jacob'. In Ps. 59:5 ('Thou, LORD God of hosts, art God of Israel') it is combined with the preceding title.

j. The Holy One of Israel

This title (*qeḏôš Yiśrā'ēl*) is a favourite in Isaiah (29 times—1:4, *etc.*) in both the earlier and later parts of the book, and also in Jeremiah and the Psalms. Somewhat similar to this is 'the Mighty One of Israel' (*'aḇîr Yiśrā'ēl*, Is. 1:24, *etc.*); also 'the Glory (victory) of Israel' (*nēṣaḥ Yiśrā'ēl*, 1 Sa. 15:29) used by Samuel.

k. Ancient of days

This is the description (Aram. *'attîq yômîn*) given by Daniel, who pictures God on his throne of judgment, judging the great world-empires (Dn. 7:9, 13, 22). It alternates with the title 'most High' (Aram. *'illāyâ*, *'elyônîn*, vv. 18, 22, 25, 27).

BIBLIOGRAPHY. W. F. Albright, *Yahweh and the Gods of Canaan*, 1968; A. Alt, 'The God of the Fathers', in *Essays on OT History and Religion*, 1966, pp. 1–77; F. M. Cross, 'Yahweh and the God of the Patriarchs', *HTR* 55, 1962, pp. 225–259; O. Eissfeldt, 'El and Yahweh', *JSS* 1, 1956, pp. 25–37; G. T. Manley, *The Book of the Law*, 1957, pp. 37–47; J. A. Motyer, *The Revelation of the Divine Name*, 1959; A. Murtonen, *A Philological and Literary Treatise on the Divine Names* 'ēl, 'elōah, 'elōhîm *and* Yahweh, 1952.

G.T.M.
F.F.B.

GODLINESS. Gk. *eusebeia* in pagan literature basically means the right respect due to men or gods, but in the Scriptures this word-group (like *theosebeia*, found only in 1 Tim. 2:10) refers exclusively to reverence towards God (except 1 Tim. 5:4, where it means proper regard for one's own household). In Peter's denial that the apostles' own *eusebeia* was the source of healing (Acts 3:12) Alford claims that the term 'bears in it the idea of operative, cultive piety, rather than of inherent character', and translates it, 'meritorious efficacy with God'.

Eusebius defines it, 'looking up to the one and only . . . God, and life in accord with him'. Cornelius is described as *eusebēs* ('devout' in EVV) in Acts 10:2 (*cf.* v. 7) and God-fearing; his godliness being illustrated by his care for his household, almsgiving and prayers, and his readiness to follow the divine instructions. The word is found most frequently in the Pastoral Epistles (1 Tim. 2:2; 3:16; 4:7–8; 6:3, 5–6, 11; 2 Tim. 3:5; Tit. 1:1). E. F. Scott regards *eusebeia* as the characteristic word of the Pastoral Epistles and sees in the term 'two things; on the one hand a right belief, on the other hand a right mode of action'. But *eusebeia* is a personal attitude to God rather than a right belief, and the action is not parallel to that attitude but springs directly from it, *e.g.* 2 Tim. 3:5, where formal godliness is contrasted with that which has power; as also in 2 Pet. 1:3, godliness is derived from divine power. 'The mystery of godliness' (1 Tim. 3:16, AV) is the fundamental doctrine centred in the Person of Christ, which is the source and criterion of all Christian devotion and behaviour. In 2 Pet 3:11 the plural is used to denote godly actions. The noun, 'godliness', does not occur in the OT, but frequently in the Apocrypha, *e.g.* 2 Macc. 12:45.

BIBLIOGRAPHY. W. Mundle, W. Günther, in *NIDNTT* 2, pp. 90–95; R. Bultmann, *TDNT* 2, pp. 751–754; G. Bertram, *TDNT* 3, pp. 123–128; W. Foerster, *TDNT* 7, pp. 175–184.

J.C.C.

GOD OF HUNTING
See Nergal, Part 2.

GOG AND MAGOG. In Ezk. 38:2 we are introduced to 'Gog, of the land of Magog, the chief prince (AV, RVmg., RSV; RV 'prince of *Rosh'), of *Meshech and Tubal'. LXX understood Magog as a people, not a country. The only reasonable identification of Gog is with Gyges, king of Lydia (*c.* 660 BC)—Assyr. Gugu; Magog could be Assyr. *mā(t) gugu*, 'land of Gog'. The

Text of Ashurbanipal mentioning the name of Gugu (Gyges), king of Lydia, sometimes identified with Gog (Ezk. 38:2). (BM)

linkage with peoples at the extremities of the then known world (Ezk. 38:5–6; *cf.* Rev. 20:8) suggests that we are to regard them as eschatological figures rather than as a historically identifiable king, *etc.* This is the interpretation in Rev. 20:8 and rabbinic literature. The popular identification of Rosh with Russia, Meshech with Moscow and Tubal with Tobolsk in Siberia has nothing to commend it from the standpoint of hermeneutics, though some of the wilder Russian tribes would fit into the explanation given.

Since we need not interpret Ezk. 38–39 as earlier in time than Ezk. 40–48, and rabbinic tradition places Gog after the days of the Messiah, we need see no contradiction between Ezekiel and Revelation, provided we understand the millennium in the sense the rabbis gave to 'the days of the Messiah'.

H.L.E.

GOLDEN CALF
See Calf, golden, Part 1.

GOLAN. The N city of refuge in Transjordan, in Manasseh's territory of Bashan (Dt. 4:43), and a levitical city (Jos. 21:27). Location uncertain, but may be identified with Sahm el-Jolan, 22 km E of Aphek (Hippos). The district of Gaulanitis was later named after it.

BIBLIOGRAPHY. *LOB*, p. 377.

N.H.

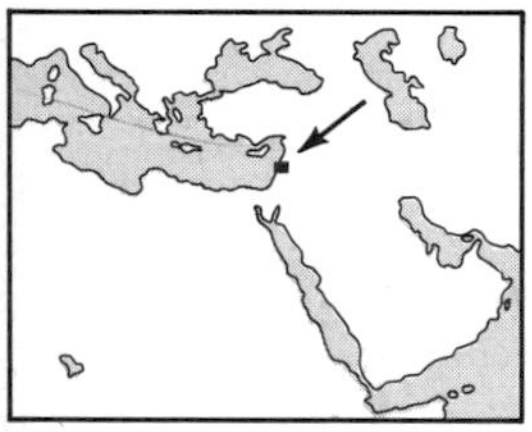

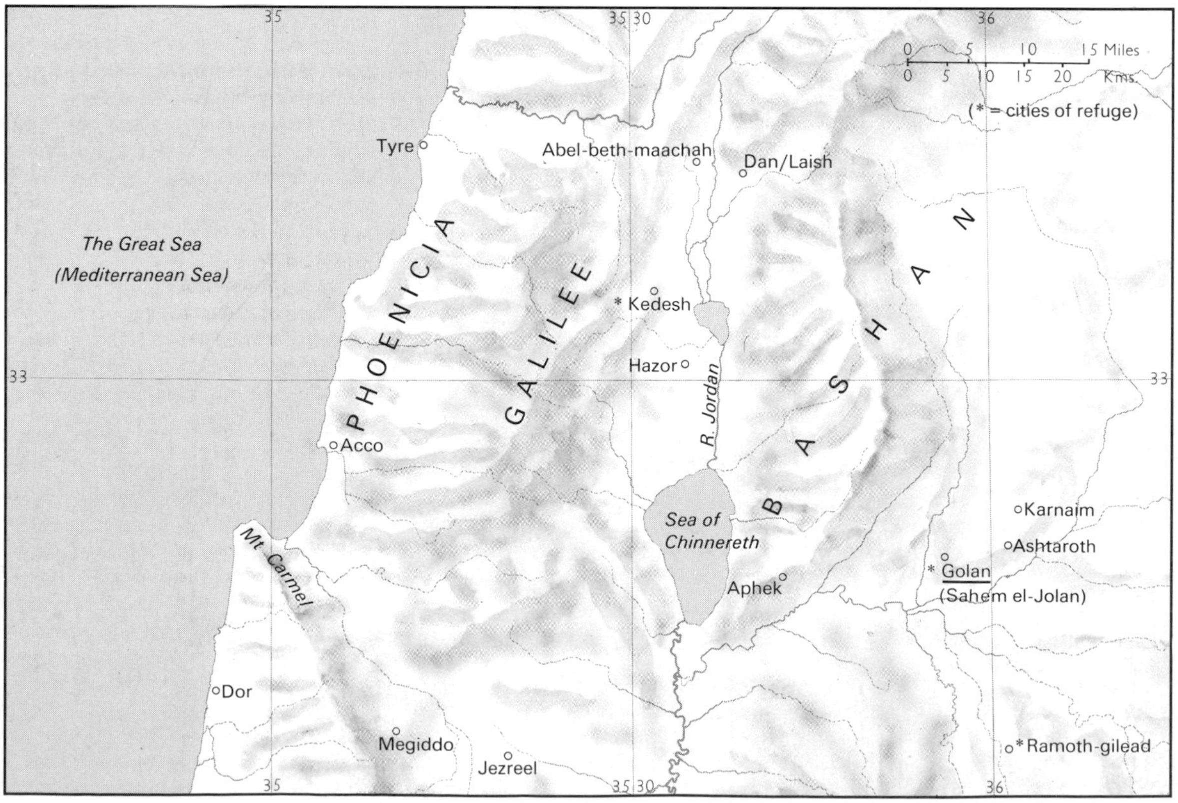

Probable site of Golan, one of the cities of refuge (Jos. 20).

Acknowledgments

Acknowledgment of the sources of illustrations
The publishers have made every effort to trace the copyright holders of illustrations in this book. Should any have been inadvertently missed, copyright holders are asked to contact the publishers.

Diagrams, charts, line drawings and town plans
All diagrams, charts, line drawings and town plans in **The Illustrated Bible Dictionary** have been specially prepared for this work. The publishers are glad to acknowledge their indebtedness to a variety of sources as indicated below.
In acknowledging the source, 'After' indicates that the material remains essentially as it appears in the source acknowledged but has been redrawn. 'Based on' means that the substance of the source material has been retained but reinterpreted.
For abbreviations see pp.xii-xvi.

ALEXANDRIA, p.32
After H. T. Davis, *Alexandria the Golden City* (Principia Press, 1957), vol.1, p.5.

ALPHA AND OMEGA, p.33
Supplied by A. R. Millard.

AMARNA, p.39
After H. Frankfort and J. D. S. Pendlebury, *The City of Akhenaton* (OUP, 1933), pl.1.

ANTIOCH, p.71
After *ACA*, p.222.

APHEK, p.73
After M. Kochavi, A. F. Rainey *et al., Aphek-Antipatris, 1974-1977, The inscriptions* (Tel Aviv University, 1978), p.4.

ARAD, p.87 (Plan)
After *EAEHL*, vol.1, pp.75, 77 and 83.

ARAD, p.88 (Temple)
After material supplied by C. J. Davey.

ARCHAEOLOGY, p.97
Based on A. R. Millard, *The Bible BC* (IVP, 1977), p.10.

ARCHITECTURE, p.104 (Palace)
From a photograph of a model in H. Frankfort, *Art and Architecture of the Ancient Orient* (Penguin, 1954), pl.154 (A).

ARCHITECTURE, p.104 (House)
After C. L. Woolley, *History of Mankind* (Allen and Unwin, 1963), vol.1, part 2.

ATHENS, p.146
Based on *ACA*, pp.148f.

BABEL, p.155 (Temple-tower)
After Sir Leonard Woolley, *Ur excavations*, vol.5, *The Ziggurat and its surroundings* (Philadelphia, 1939), p.86.

BABEL, p.156 (Sites of ziggurats)
Based on A. Parrot, *Ziggurats et tour de Babel* (© Albin Michel), fig.27, p.53.

BABYLON, p.161 (Temple)
After A. Parrot, *Nineveh and Babylon* (Thames and Hudson, 1961), p.178.

BEERSHEBA, p.181
After Y. Aharoni, 'Tel-Aviv 2 (1975), The Beersheba Excavations' in *Journal of Tel-Aviv University Institute of Archaeology*, p.148

BETHSHEAN, p.191
(Temple, level IX)
After *EAEHL*, vol.1, p.209.

BETHSHEAN, p.191
(Temple, level VII)
After *EAEHL*, vol.1, p.212.

BETHSHEAN, p.192
(Temple, level VI)
After *EAEHL*, vol.1, p.212.

BRICK-KILN, p.209
Based on information from B. Meissner, *Babylonien und Assyrien* (Carl Winters, Heidelberg, 1920), vol.1, p.234, figs.55 and 56.

BURIAL, p.212
After L. H. Vincent and M. A. Stève, *Jérusalem de l'Ancien Testament* (Gabalda, Paris, 1954), pl.97.

CAESAREA, p.218
After *EAEHL*, vol.1, p.270.

CALAH, p.221 (Temple)
After E. Ebeling and B. Meissner (eds.), *Reallexicon der Assyriologie und vorderasiatischen Archäologie* (Grüyter, Berlin, 1977), vol.5, p.310 and M. E. L. Mallowan, *Nimrud and its remains* (1965), pl.6.

CALVARY, p.227
After K. M. Kenyon, *Digging up Jerusalem* (Ernest Benn, 1974), p.233.

CAPERNAUM, p.247
Based on V. Corbo, *Studia Hierosolymitana* (Franciscan Press, Jerusalem, 1976), vol.1, p.161, fig.1.

CARCHEMISH, p.252
After C. L. Woolley, *Carchemish, 1921-52* (British Museum), vol.2, pl.3 and vol.3, pl.41a.

CHORAZIN, p.265
After *EAEHL*, vol.1, p.299.

CHURCH, p.287
After F. van der Meer and C. Mohrmann, *Atlas of the Early Christian World* (Nelson-Elsevier, 1953), map 1.

CISTERN, p.289
After *BASOR* 185, 1967, p.24.

CITY, p.295 (Jerusalem)
After *EAEHL*, vol.2, p.598.

CITY, p.296 (Nineveh)
After B. Mazar and M. Avi-Yonah *et al.* (eds.), *Views of the Biblical World* (International Publishing Co. Ltd, Jerusalem, 1960), vol.3, p.253 and R. Campbell Thompson, *Iraq I* (British School of Archaeology in Iraq, 1934), p.97, fig.1.

CITY, p.297 (Jericho)
After *EAEHL*, vol.2, p.551.

COLOURS, p.306 After material provided by A. R. Millard.

CORINTH, p.314 After *ACA*, p.155.

COS, p.320 Based on *ACA*, p.181.

COURT, p.327 (Temple)
After L. H. Vincent and M. A. Stève, *Jérusalem de l'Ancien Testament* (Gabalda, Paris, 1954), pl.102.

COURT, p.327 (Nineveh)
After Seton Lloyd, *The Archaeology of Mesopotamia* (Thames and Hudson, 1978), p.199, fig.142.

COURT, p.327 (House)
Based on G. E. Wright, *Shechem* (Gerald Duckworth, 1964), fig.76.

CRETE, p.337 (Knossos)
Based on J. D. S. Pendlebury, *Handbook to the palace of Minos, Knossos* (Max Parrish, 1954), p.58, fig.4.

CROSS, p.344
Based on N. Haas, 'Skeletal Remains from Giv' at ha-Mivtar', *IEJ* 20, 1970, pl.24.

CYRENE, p.352
After *ACA*, p.79.

DAGON, p.354
Plan after *EAEHL*, vol.1, p.216. Reconstruction after A. Rowe, *Four Canaanite Temples of Beth-shan* (University of Pennsylvania, 1940), fig.5.

DAVID, p.368 (Wars)
After Chaim Herzog and Mordechai Gichon, *Battles of the Bible* (Weidenfeld and Nicolson, 1978), p.76.

DEAD SEA, p.370
Based on information given in E. Orni and E. Efrat, *Geography of Israel* (Israel Programme for Scientific Translations, 1966), p.88.

DEBORAH, p.377
After Chaim Herzog and Mordechai Gichon, *Battles of the Bible* (Weidenfeld and Nicolson, 1978), pp.52, 53.

DEUTERONOMY, p.385
Based on information supplied by Kenneth Kitchen.

EGYPT, p.417 (Karnack Temple)
After A. A. M. van der Heyden, in A. R. David, *The Egyptian Kingdoms* (Elsevier, 1975), p.22.

EPHESUS, p.463 After *ACA*, p.212.

ESSENES, p.479
Based on J. Murphy and O. O'Connor 'The Essenes in Palestine', *Biblical Archaeologist*, September 1977, p.122.

FEASTS, p.504
Based on information from *Encyclopaedia Judaica*, 1971, vol.6.

FLOOD, p.513
Based on information from M. E. L. Mallowan, *Iraq XXVI* (British School of Archaeology in Iraq, 1964), p.82, pl.20.

FOOD, p.514
Based on information from R. J. Forbes, *Studies in Ancient Technology* (E. J. Brill, Leiden, 1955), p.54.

FORTIFICATION, p.523
After S. M. Paul and W. G. Dever, *Biblical Archaeology* (Keter Publishing House, Jerusalem, 1973), p.85.

FURNACE, p.530
Based on B. Rothenburg, *Timna* (Thames and Hudson, 1972), p.74, fig.19.

GERASA, p.552 After *ACA*, p.224.

GEZER, p.556 (Gate, plan)
After *EAEHL*, vol.2, p.437.

GEZER, p.556 (Plan)
After K. M. Kenyon, *The Bible and recent Archaeology* (Colonnade, 1978), p.6.

GEZER, p.557
(Gate, reconstruction)
After material supplied by C. J. Davey.

GIBEAH, p.557
After *BASOR* 223, 1976, p.35.

GIBEON, p.559 (Water-system)
After *EAEHL*, vol.2, p.449.

Relief maps
The relief maps are © Copyright George Philip and Son Ltd. and Inter-Varsity Press. These maps appear on pages:
2, 8, 9, 10 (2), 28, 41, 43, 46, 82, 91, 92, 117, 130, 135, 142, 154, 164, 177, 185, 201, 218, 230, 232, 251, 257, 288, 290, 338, 339 top, 351, 355, 356, 357, 362, 370, 376, 378, 406, 410, 411, 415, 432, 433, 434, 443, 445, 464, 465, 476, 477, 486, 532, 533, 534, 539, 543, 544, 552, 561, 562 and 574.

Photographs

The photographs in **The Illustrated Bible Dictionary** are reproduced by permission of the following persons or agencies. The initials provide a cross-reference from the captions. The numbers in the list are page references to the text.

AA
ANIMALS ANIMALS
M-32201 Red Deer Stag: ANIMALS ANIMALS © Leonard Lee Rue III, p.57.
M-17684 Syrian Rock Hyrax: ANIMALS ANIMALS © Alan G. Nelson, p.60.
B-3045 White Stork: ANIMALS ANIMALS © Walter Fendrich, p.63.
I-4132 Israeli Scorpion: ANIMALS ANIMALS © Jim Bockowski, p.66.

AAM
A. A. Meads, p.555.

AIA
Australian Institute of Archaeology, pp.27, 152, 180, 181, 190.

AMM
A. M. Morris, pp.89, 116, 159, 250.

AMO
Ashmolean Museum, Oxford, pp.47, 548.

AP
A. Parrot, pp.119, 138, 261, 399, 444.

ARM
A. R. Millard, pp.2, 33, 90, 119, 256, 314, 411, 545.

BIAAH
British Institute at Amman for Archaeology and History, p.411.

BL
Reproduced by permission of the British Library.
Codex Sinaiticus: Add. MS. 43725, f.260, p.194.
Schoolboy exercise: Egerton Pap.2, Add. MS. 34186, p.412.
Lindisfarne Gospels: Cotton MS. Nero, D.iv, f.3., p.450.
Wyclif Bible: Eg. 618, f.74, p.451.
Miles Coverdale Bible: BL.C.132.h.46., p.451.
Geneva Bible: BL.C.17. b.8., p.453.
The Great Bible: BL.C.18.d.l., p.453.
Tyndale Bible: BL.C.18.C.5., p.454.
Authorized Version: BL.C.35.1.13(1), p.457.
Zenon correspondence: Papyrus 2655, p.466.

BLO
The Curators of the Bodleian Library, Oxford. MS. Pell. Aram. XIII Int., p.494.

BLS
The Bible Lands Society, p.190.

BM
Reproduced by Courtesy of the Trustees of the British Museum, pp.21, 22, 23, 24, 25, 30, 34, 38, 40, 42, 47, 52, 54, 56 (2), 58, 59, 69, 72, 84, 93, 107, 111, 114, 115 (3), 120, 121, 122, 124, 125, 126, 127, 133, 134, 135, 138 (2), 141 (2), 143 (2), 145, 155, 165, 166, 167, 168, 169, 178 (2), 179, 183 (2), 206, 225, 229 (2), 255 (2), 257, 258, 261, 262, 264, 297, 298, 321, 335, 340, 342, 343, 345, 346, 347, 353, 359 (2), 364, 383, 390, 393, 395 (2), 396, 397, 412, 413, 416, 420, 421, 427, 433, 444, 445, 460, 466, 467, 468, 469, 484, 507 (2), 508, 511, 512, 515, 517, 518, 519, 523 (2), 524, 528, 529, 538, 540, 543, 565 (2), 566, 574.

BrM
Courtesy of The Brooklyn Museum. 47.218.96, Bequest of Miss Theodora Wilbour, p.17. 54.50.34, p.555.

BPL
Barnaby's Picture Library, pp.108, 123.

BSAI
British School of Archaeology in Iraq, pp.222, 329.

CBL Chester Beatty Library, p.360.

CGS
Claremont Graduate School. Photograph by Jean Doresse by courtesy of the Institute for Antiquity and Christianity, Claremont, California, p.263.

DAA
Department of Antiquities, Amman, p.41.

DJW
D. J. Wiseman, pp.19, 29 (2), 96, 101, 155, 156, 157 (2), 158, 160, 162, 167, 208, 220, 222, 228, 356, 402, 486, 524, 540, 542.

FNH
F. N. Hepper, pp. 1, 21, 66, 82, 136, 253, 313, 506, 508, 539.

GIO
Photograph, Griffith Institute, Ashmolean Museum, Oxford, p.110.

GLCW
Green Lake Centre, Wisconsin, p.207.

GSC G. S. Cansdale, p.63.

HC
The Holyland Corporation. Photos taken on the site of the reconstruction of Jerusalem at the time of the 2nd Temple (or Herods' time) in the grounds of the Holyland Hotel, Jerusalem, Israel, pp.105, 187, 227, 293, 299, 326.

HV
Father Hughes Vincent, p.212.

IM
Israel Museum, pp.105, 178.

JCT
©John C. Trever, 1972, p.375 (2).
Photo © John C. Trever, 1970, p.478.

JEF
Jericho Excavation Fund, pp.178, 525

JLH
John L. Hillelson Photographic Agency
Erich Lessing/Magnum, p.130.
Georg Gerster, p. 161.
Erich Lessing/Magnum, p.344.
Thomas Hoepker, p.370.
Erich Lessing/Magnum, p.557.

JPK
J. P. Kane, pp.105, 106, 122, 178, 187, 213 (2), 215, 217, 227, 245, 250, 251, 266, 293, 326, 524, 527, 530.

KAK
K. A. Kitchen, pp.132, 416, 417, 422.

LD
Lepsius Denkmäler III, 40, p.208.

MC
Maurice Chuzeville/Louvre Museum, pp.9, 55, 103, 114, 121, 137, 153, 233, 249, 254, 260, 348, 355, 433, 540, 555.

MCM
Merseyside County Museums, Liverpool, p.563.

MEPHA
Middle East Photographic Archive, London, pp.353, 553 (2), 559, 568.

MetNY
Metropolitan Museum of Art, New York.
54.3.1 ANE Metalwork-Gold-Iranian. Bowl: of Darius I or II, p.365.
54.3.3 ANE Metalwork-Gold-Iranian. Rhyton, p.406.
54.3.4a,b ANE Metalwork-Gold-Iranian. Dagger, p.406.
Wall painting, p.543.

MH
M. Holford, pp.47, 120, 146, 337, 351 (2), 399, 422, 428 (2), 517.

MuC
Museo Capitolini, Rome, p.151.

NA N. Avigad, p.177.

NAMA
National Archaeological Museum, Athens, p.541.

NMBL
National Museum of Beirut, Lebanon, p.545.

OIUC
Oriental Institute, University of Chicago, pp.24, 119, 231, 323, 349, 358, 363, 541, 554.

PAC
P. A. Clayton, pp.39, 66, 210, 248, 260, 321, 346 (2), 395, 399, 415, 421, 519, 540, 560.

PEF
Palestine Exploration Fund, p.224.

PM
P. Matthiae, pp.405, 407.

PML Pierpont Morgan Library, p.62.

PP Picturepoint, London, p.342.

PS P. Stephens, pp.102, 344.

RG
Ray Gardner, pp.31, 72, 216, 218, 298, 505.

RH
Robert Harding Picture Library, pp.65, 207, 259, 356, 364, 428 (2), 467, 469, 502, 517, 519, 553.

RM
Rockefeller Museum, pp.384, 412, 545.

RP
R. Pitt, pp.116, 147, 247, 250, 265, 290, 319, 378.

RS
Ronald Sheridan's Photo-Library, pp.23, 32, 35, 113, 133, 172, 359, 401 (2), 447, 464, 476, 479, 521, 539, 540, 565 (2).

RVO
Courtesy of Rijksmuseum van Oudheden, Leiden, Netherlands, p.554.

SAOB
The State Antiquities Organisation, Baghdad, pp.9, 112 (2), 158, 393.

SH
Sonia Halliday Photographs, pp.188, 218, 294, 351, 462, 527, 560.

SI
Foto Scala Firenze, Italy, pp.219, 399, 502, 527.

SMB
Staatliche Museen zu Berlin/DDR Ägyptisches Museum, pp.58, 89, 113, 116, 127, 159, 160, 171, 250, 400, 420, 468, 469.

TAU
Institute of Archaeology, Tel-Aviv University/Avraham Hay, pp.36, 99.

UMUP
Reproduced by permission of the University Museum, University of Pennsylvania, 558 (3).

YY Yigael Yadin, pp.35, 322.

ZR
Zev Radovan, pp.86, 115, 130, 131, 192, 204, 205.